Lecture Notes in Computer Science 1808

Edited by G. Goos, J. Hartmanis and J. van Leeuwen

Springer

Berlin
Heidelberg
New York
Barcelona
Hong Kong
London
Milan
Paris
Singapore
Tokyo

Santosh Pande   Dharma P. Agrawal (Eds.)

Compiler Optimizations for Scalable Parallel Systems

Languages, Compilation Techniques, and Run Time Systems

 Springer

Series Editors

Gerhard Goos, Karlsruhe University, Germany
Juris Hartmanis, Cornell University, NY, USA
Jan van Leeuwen, Utrecht University, The Netherlands

Volume Editors

Santosh Pande
Georgia Institute of Technology, College of Computing
801 Atlantic Drive, Atlanta, GA 30332, USA
E-mail: santosh@cc.gatech.edu

Dharma P. Agrawal
University of Cincinnati, Department of ECECS
P.O. Box 210030, Cincinnati, OH 45221-0030, USA
E-mail: dpa@ececs.uc.edu

Cataloging-in-Publication Data applied for

Die Deutsche Bibliothek - CIP-Einheitsaufnahme

Compiler optimizations for scalable parallel systems : languages,
compilation techniques, and run time systems / Santosh Pande ; Dharma
P. Agrawal (ed.). - Berlin ; Heidelberg ; New York ; Barcelona ; Hong
Kong ; London ; Milan ; Paris ; Singapore ; Tokyo : Springer, 2001
      (Lecture notes in computer science ; 1808)
      ISBN 3-540-41945-4

CR Subject Classification (1998): D.3, D.4, D.1.3, C.2, F.1.2, F.3

ISSN 0302-9743
ISBN 3-540-41945-4 Springer-Verlag Berlin Heidelberg New York

Springer-Verlag Berlin Heidelberg New York
a member of BertelsmannSpringer Science+Business Media GmbH

http://www.springer.de

© Springer-Verlag Berlin Heidelberg 2001
Printed in Germany

Typesetting: Camera-ready by author, data conversion by Boller Mediendesign
Printed on acid-free paper   SPIN: 10720238   06/3142   5 4 3 2 1 0

Preface

Santosh Pande[1] and Dharma P. Agrawal[2]

[1] College of Computing
801 Atlantic Drive,
Georgia Institute of Technology,
Atlanta, GA 30332
[2] Department of ECECS, ML 0030,
PO Box 210030,
University of Cincinnati,
Cincinnati, OH 45221-0030

We are very pleased to publish this monograph on Compiler Optimizations for Scalable Distributed Memory Systems. Distributed memory systems offer a challenging model of computing and pose fascinating problems regarding compiler optimizations ranging from language design to run time systems. Thus, the research done in this area serves as foundational to many challenges from memory hierarchy optimizations to communication optimizations encountered in both stand-alone and distributed systems. It is with this motivation that we present a compendium of research done in this area in the form of this monograph.

This monograph is divided into five sections : section one deals with languages, section two deals with analysis, section three with communication optimizations, section four with code generation, and section five with run time systems. In the editorial we present a detailed summary of each of the chapters in these sections.

We would like to express our sincere thanks to many who contributed to this monograph. First we would like to thank all the authors for their excellent contributions which really make this monograph one of a kind; as readers will see, these contributions make the monograph thorough and insightful (for an advanced reader) as well as highly readable and pedagogic (for students and beginners). Next, we would like to thank our graduate student Haixiang He for all his help in organizing this monograph and for solving latex problems. Finally we express our sincere thanks to the LNCS Editorial at Springer-Verlag for putting up with our schedule and for all their help and understanding. Without their invaluable help we would not have been able to put this monograph into its beautiful final shape!!! We sincerely hope the readers find the monograph truly useful in their work – be it further research or practice.

Table of Contents

Preface
Santosh Pande and Dharma P. Agrawal V

Introduction
Santosh Pande and Dharma P. Agrawal XXI

1 Compiling for Distributed Memory Multiprocessors XXI
   1.1 Motivation XXI
   1.2 Complexity XXII
   1.3 Outline of the Monograph XXII
   1.4 Future Directions XXVII

Section I : Languages

Chapter 1. High Performance Fortran 2.0
Ken Kennedy and Charles Koelbel 3

1 Introduction 3
2 History and Overview of HPF 3
3 Data Mapping 7
   3.1 Basic Language Features 7
   3.2 Advanced Topics 13
4 Data Parallelism 18
   4.1 Basic Language Features 19
   4.2 Advanced Topics 29
5 Task Parallelism 34
   5.1 EXTRINSIC Procedures 34
   5.2 The TASK_REGION Directive 37
6 Input and Output 39
7 Summary and Future Outlook 41

Chapter 2. The Sisal Project: Real World Functional Programming
Jean-Luc Gaudiot, Tom DeBoni, John Feo, Wim Böhm,
Walid Najjar, and Patrick Miller 45

1   Introduction... 45
2   The Sisal Language: A Short Tutorial 46
3   An Early Implementation: The Optimizing Sisal Compiler......... 49
     3.1 Update in Place and Copy Elimination 49
     3.2 Build in Place 50
     3.3 Reference Counting Optimization 51
     3.4 Vectorization 51
     3.5 Loop Fusion, Double Buffering Pointer Swap, and Inversion ... 51
4   Sisal90 53
     4.1 The Foreign Language Interface........................... 54
5   A Prototype Distributed-Memory SISAL Compiler 58
     5.1 Base Compiler 59
     5.2 Rectangular Arrays 59
     5.3 Block Messages 60
     5.4 Multiple Alignment 60
     5.5 Results 61
     5.6 Further Work.. 62
6   Architecture Support for Multithreaded Execution 62
     6.1 Blocking and Non-blocking Models 63
     6.2 Code Generation... 64
     6.3 Summary of Performance Results 68
7   Conclusions and Future Research 69

Chapter 3. HPC++ and the HPC++Lib Toolkit
Dennis Gannon, Peter Beckman, Elizabeth Johnson, Todd Green,
and Mike Levine 73

1   Introduction... 73
2   The HPC++ Programming and Execution Model 74
     2.1 Level 1 HPC++ 75
     2.2 The Parallel Standard Template Library 76
     2.3 Parallel Iterators....................................... 77
     2.4 Parallel Algorithms 77
     2.5 Distributed Containers 78
3   A Simple Example: The Spanning Tree of a Graph 78
4   Multi-threaded Programming................................. 82
     4.1 Synchronization 84
     4.2 Examples of Multi-threaded Computations 92
5   Implementing the HPC++ Parallel Loop Directives 96

6   Multi-context Programming and Global Pointers 99
      6.1 Remote Function and Member Calls 101
      6.2 Using Corba IDL to Generate Proxies 103
7   The SPMD Execution Model 105
      7.1 Barrier Synchronization and Collective Operations 105
8   Conclusion 106

Chapter 4. A Concurrency Abstraction Model for Avoiding Inheritance Anomaly in Object-Oriented Programs
Sandeep Kumar and Dharma P. Agrawal

                                                                         109

1   Introduction 109
2   Approaches to Parallelism Specification 113
      2.1 Issues in Designing a COOPL 113
      2.2 Issues in Designing Libraries 114
3   What Is the Inheritance Anomaly? 115
      3.1 State Partitioning Anomaly (SPA) 116
      3.2 History Sensitiveness of Acceptable States Anomaly ($HSASA$) . 118
      3.3 State Modification Anomaly (SMA) 118
      3.4 Anomaly A 119
      3.5 Anomaly B 120
4   What Is the Reusability of Sequential Classes? 120
5   A Framework for Specifying Parallelism 121
6   Previous Approaches 122
7   The Concurrency Abstraction Model 123
8   The CORE Language 126
      8.1 Specifying a Concurrent Region 126
      8.2 Defining an AC 126
      8.3 Defining a Parallel Block 127
      8.4 Synchronization Schemes 129
9   Illustrations 129
      9.1 Reusability of Sequential Classes 130
      9.2 Avoiding the Inheritance Anomaly 131
10 The Implementation Approach 133
11 Conclusions and Future Directions 134

Section II : Analysis

Chapter 5. Loop Parallelization Algorithms
Alain Darte, Yves Robert, and Frédéric Vivien

                                                                         141

1   Introduction 141
2   Input and Output of Parallelization Algorithms 142
      2.1 Input: Dependence Graph 143
      2.2 Output: Nested Loops 144

3   Dependence Abstractions 145
     3.1 Dependence Graphs and Distance Sets 145
     3.2 Polyhedral Reduced Dependence Graphs 147
     3.3 Definition and Simulation of Classical Dependence
          Representations 148
4   Allen and Kennedy's Algorithm 149
     4.1 Algorithm 150
     4.2 Power and Limitations 151
5   Wolf and Lam's Algorithm 152
     5.1 Purpose 153
     5.2 Theoretical Interpretation 153
     5.3 The General Algorithm 154
     5.4 Power and Limitations 155
6   Darte and Vivien's Algorithm 156
     6.1 Another Algorithm Is Needed 156
     6.2 Polyhedral Dependences: A Motivating Example 158
     6.3 Illustrating Example 160
     6.4 Uniformization Step 162
     6.5 Scheduling Step 162
     6.6 Schematic Explanations 165
     6.7 Power and Limitations 166
7   Feautrier's Algorithm 167
8   Conclusion 169

Chapter 6. Array Dataflow Analysis
Paul Feautrier 173

1   Introduction 173
2   Exact Array Dataflow Analysis 176
     2.1 Notations 176
     2.2 The Program Model 176
     2.3 Data Flow Analysis 181
     2.4 Summary of the Algorithm 189
     2.5 Related Work 190
3   Approximate Array Dataflow Analysis 190
     3.1 From ADA to FADA 191
     3.2 Introducing Parameters 195
     3.3 Taking Properties of Parameters into Account 197
     3.4 Eliminating Parameters 201
     3.5 Related Work 202
4   Analysis of Complex Statements 204
     4.1 What Is a Complex Statement 204
     4.2 ADA in the Presence of Complex Statements 206
     4.3 Procedure Calls as Complex Statements 206

5   Applications of ADA and FADA 208
    5.1   Program Comprehension and Debugging 209
    5.2   Parallelization 211
    5.3   Array Expansion and Array Privatization 212
6   Conclusions 214
A   Appendix : Mathematical Tools 214
    A.1   Polyhedra and Polytopes 214
    A.2   Z-modules 215
    A.3   Z-polyhedra 216
    A.4   Parametric Problems 216

Chapter 7. Interprocedural Analysis Based on Guarded Array Regions
Zhiyuan Li, Junjie Gu, and Gyungho Lee

                                                                221

1   Introduction 221
2   Preliminary 223
    2.1   Traditional Flow-Insensitive Summaries 223
    2.2   Array Data Flow Summaries 225
3   Guarded Array Regions 226
    3.1   Operations on GAR's 228
    3.2   Predicate Operations 230
4   Constructing Summary GAR's Interprocedurally 232
    4.1   Hierarchical Supergraph 232
    4.2   Summary Algorithms 233
    4.3   Expansions 235
5   Implementation Considerations 238
    5.1   Symbolic Analysis 238
    5.2   Region Numbering 239
    5.3   Range Operations 240
6   Application to Array Privatization and Preliminary Experimental
    Results 240
    6.1   Array Privatization 241
    6.2   Preliminary Experimental Results 241
7   Related Works 243
8   Conclusion 244

Chapter 8. Automatic Array Privatization
Peng Tu and David Padua

                                                                247

1   Introduction 247
2   Background 248
3   Algorithm for Array Privatization 250
    3.1   Data Flow Framework 250
    3.2   Inner Loop Abstraction 252
    3.3   An Example 256

3.4 Profitability of Privatization 257
3.5 Last Value Assignment 258
4 Demand-Driven Symbolic Analysis 261
4.1 Gated Single Assignment 263
4.2 Demand-Driven Backward Substitution 264
4.3 Backward Substitution in the Presence of Gating Functions ... 266
4.4 Examples of Backward Substitution 267
4.5 Bounds of Symbolic Expression 269
4.6 Comparison of Symbolic Expressions 269
4.7 Recurrence and the μ Function 272
4.8 Bounds of Monotonic Variables 273
4.9 Index Array 274
4.10 Conditional Data Flow Analysis 275
4.11 Implementation and Experiments 276
5 Related Work 277

Section III : Communication Optimizations

Chapter 9. Optimal Tiling for Minimizing Communication in Distributed Shared-Memory Multiprocessors

Anant Agarwal, David Kranz, Rajeev Barua, and Venkat Natarajan ... 285

1 Introduction 285
1.1 Contributions and Related Work 286
1.2 Overview of the Paper 288
2 Problem Domain and Assumptions 289
2.1 Program Assumptions 289
2.2 System Model 291
3 Loop Partitions and Data Partitions 292
4 A Framework for Loop and Data Partitioning 295
4.1 Loop Tiles in the Iteration Space 296
4.2 Footprints in the Data Space 298
4.3 Size of a Footprint for a Single Reference 300
4.4 Size of the Cumulative Footprint 304
4.5 Minimizing the Size of the Cumulative Footprint 311
5 General Case of $\mathbf{G}$ 314
5.1 $\mathbf{G}$ Is Invertible, but Not Unimodular 314
5.2 Columns of $\mathbf{G}$ Are Dependent and the Rows Are Independent . 316
5.3 The Rows of $\mathbf{G}$ Are Dependent 316
6 Other System Environments 318
6.1 Coherence-Related Cache Misses 318
6.2 Effect of Cache Line Size 320
6.3 Data Partitioning in Distributed-Memory Multicomputers 320

7   Combined Loop and Data Partitioning in DSMs 322
    7.1 The Cost Model 322
    7.2 The Multiple Loops Heuristic Method 325
8   Implementation and Results 328
    8.1 Algorithm Simulator Experiments 330
    8.2 Experiments on the Alewife Multiprocessor 330
9   Conclusions 334
A   A Formulation of Loop Tiles Using Bounding Hyperplanes 337
B   Synchronization References 337

Chapter 10. Communication-Free Partitioning of Nested Loops

Kuei-Ping Shih, Chua-Huang Huang, and Jang-Ping Sheu 339

1   Introduction 339
2   Fundamentals of Array References 341
    2.1 Iteration Spaces and Data Spaces 342
    2.2 Reference Functions 343
    2.3 Properties of Reference Functions 343
3   Loop-Level Partitioning 347
    3.1 Iteration and Data Spaces Partitioning – Uniformly Generated
         References 347
    3.2 Hyperplane Partitioning of Data Space 353
    3.3 Hyperplane Partitioning of Iteration and Data Spaces 359
4   Statement-Level Partitioning 365
    4.1 Affine Processor Mapping 366
    4.2 Hyperplane Partitioning 372
5   Comparisons and Discussions 377
6   Conclusions 381

Chapter 11. Solving Alignment Using Elementary Linear Algebra

Vladimir Kotlyar, David Bau, Induprakas Kodukula, Keshav Pingali,
and Paul Stodghill 385

1   Introduction 385
2   Linear Alignment 388
    2.1 Equational Constraints 388
    2.2 Reduction to Null Space Computation 390
    2.3 Remarks 391
    2.4 Reducing the Solution Basis 392
3   Affine Alignment 393
    3.1 Encoding Affine Constraints as Linear Constraints 393
4   Replication 396
    4.1 Formulation of Replication 397

5   Heuristics 398
    5.1 Lessons from Some Common Computational Kernels 399
    5.2 Implications for Alignment Heuristic 402
6   Conclusion 402
A   Reducing the Solution Matrix 404
    A.1 Unrelated Constraints 404
    A.2 General Procedure 405
B   A Comment on Affine Encoding 408

Chapter 12. A Compilation Method for Communication–Efficient Partitioning of DOALL Loops

Santosh Pande and Tareq Bali 413

1   Introduction 413
2   DOALL Partitioning 414
    2.1 Motivating Example 415
    2.2 Our Approach 419
3   Terms and Definitions 421
    3.1 Example 422
4   Problem 423
    4.1 Compatibility Subsets 423
    4.2 Cyclic Directions 424
5   Communication Minimization 427
    5.1 Algorithm : Maximal Compatibility Subsets 427
    5.2 Algorithm : Maximal Fibonacci Sequence 428
    5.3 Data Partitioning 428
6   Partition Merging 429
    6.1 Granularity Adjustment 431
    6.2 Load Balancing 431
    6.3 Mapping 432
7   Example : Texture Smoothing Code 432
8   Performance on Cray T3D 435
    8.1 Conclusions 440

Chapter 13. Compiler Optimization of Dynamic Data Distributions for Distributed-Memory Multicomputers

Daniel J. Palermo, Eugene W. Hodges IV, and Prithviraj Banerjee 445

1   Introduction 445
2   Related Work 447
3   Dynamic Distribution Selection 449
    3.1 Motivation for Dynamic Distributions 449
    3.2 Overview of the Dynamic Distribution Approach 450
    3.3 Phase Decomposition 451
    3.4 Phase and Phase Transition Selection 457

4   Data Redistribution Analysis 462
    4.1 Reaching Distributions and the Distribution Flow Graph 462
    4.2 Computing Reaching Distributions 463
    4.3 Representing Distribution Sets........................... 464
5   Interprocedural Redistribution Analysis 465
    5.1 Distribution Synthesis 467
    5.2 Redistribution Synthesis 468
    5.3 Static Distribution Assignment (SDA) 471
6   Results 472
    6.1 Synthetic HPF Redistribution Example 473
    6.2 2-D Alternating Direction Implicit (ADI2D) Iterative Method . 475
    6.3 Shallow Water Weather Prediction Benchmark.............. 478
7   Conclusions 480

Chapter 14. A Framework for Global Communication Analysis and Optimizations

Manish Gupta 485

1   Introduction... 485
2   Motivating Example.. 487
3   Available Section Descriptor 488
    3.1 Representation of ASD 490
    3.2 Computing Generated Communication...................... 492
4   Data Flow Analysis 494
    4.1 Data Flow Variables and Equations 495
    4.2 Decomposition of Bidirectional Problem 498
    4.3 Overall Data-Flow Procedure............................ 499
5   Communication Optimizations................................. 505
    5.1 Elimination of Redundant Communication 505
    5.2 Reduction in Volume of Communication 506
    5.3 Movement of Communication for Subsumption and for Hiding
         Latency.. 507
6   Extensions: Communication Placement 508
7   Operations on Available Section Descriptors 510
    7.1 Operations on Bounded Regular Section Descriptors.......... 512
    7.2 Operations on Mapping Function Descriptors 514
8   Preliminary Implementation and Results 516
9   Related Work 519
    9.1 Global Communication Optimizations 519
    9.2 Data Flow Analysis and Data Descriptors 520
10 Conclusions 521

Chapter 15. Tolerating Communication Latency through Dynamic Thread Invocation in a Multithreaded Architecture
Andrew Sohn, Yuetsu Kodama, Jui-Yuan Ku, Mitsuhisa Sato, and
Yoshinori Yamaguchi 525

1   Introduction.. 525
2   Multithreading Principles and Its Realization 527
    2.1 The Principle... 527
    2.2 The EM-X Multithreaded Distributed-Memory Multiprocessor . 530
    2.3 Architectural Support for Fine-Grain Multithreading 533
3   Designing Multithreaded Algorithms 535
    3.1 Multithreaded Bitonic Sorting 535
    3.2 Multithreaded Fast Fourier Transform 538
4   Overlapping Analysis 540
5   Analysis of Switches... 544
6   Conclusions 547

Section IV : Code Generation

Chapter 16. Advanced Code Generation for High Performance Fortran
Vikram Adve and John Mellor-Crummey 553

1   Introduction.. 553
2   Background: The Code Generation Problem for HPF 556
    2.1 Communication Analysis and Code Generation for HPF 556
    2.2 Previous Approaches to Communication Analysis and Code
         Generation 558
3   An Integer Set Framework for Data-Parallel Compilation 561
    3.1 Primitive Components of the Framework..................... 561
    3.2 Implementation of the Framework........................... 562
4   Computation Partitioning 565
    4.1 Computation Partitioning Models 565
    4.2 Code Generation to Realize Computation Partitions 567
5   Communication Code Generation 573
    5.1 Communication Generation with Message Vectorization and
         Coalescing 577
    5.2 Recognizing In-Place Communication........................ 581
    5.3 Implementing Loop-Splitting for Reducing Communication
         Overhead 582
6   Control Flow Simplification 584
    6.1 Motivation 584
    6.2 Overview of Algorithm 588
    6.3 Evaluation and Discussion 589
7   Conclusions 590

Chapter 17. Integer Lattice Based Methods for Local Address Generation for Block-Cyclic Distributions
J. Ramanujam 597

1 Introduction 597
2 Background and Related Work 599
   2.1 Related Work on One-Level Mapping 600
   2.2 Related Work on Two-Level Mapping 602
3 A Lattice Based Approach for Address Generation 603
   3.1 Assumptions 603
   3.2 Lattices 604
4 Determination of Basis Vectors 605
   4.1 Basis Determination Algorithm 607
   4.2 Extremal Basis Vectors 609
   4.3 Improvements to the Algorithm for $s < k$ 612
   4.4 Complexity 613
5 Address Sequence Generation by Lattice Enumeration 614
6 Optimization of Loop Enumeration: GO-LEFT and GO-RIGHT 616
   6.1 Implementation 620
7 Experimental Results for One-Level Mapping 620
8 Address Sequence Generation for Two-Level Mapping 626
   8.1 Problem Statement 626
9 Algorithms for Two-Level Mapping 628
   9.1 *Itable:* An Algorithm That Constructs a Table of Offsets 629
   9.2 Optimization of the *Itable* Method 631
   9.3 Search-Based Algorithms 634
10 Experimental Results for Two-Level Mapping 635
11 Other Problems in Code Generation 638
    11.1 Communication Generation 639
    11.2 Union and Difference of Regular Sections 640
    11.3 Code Generation for Complex Subscripts 640
    11.4 Data Structures for Runtime Efficiency 640
    11.5 Array Redistribution 641
12 Summary and Conclusions 641

Section V : Task Parallelism, Dynamic Data Structures and Run Time Systems

Chapter 18. A Duplication Based Compile Time Scheduling Method for Task Parallelism
Sekhar Darbha and Dharma P. Agrawal 649

1 Introduction 649
2 STDS Algorithm 652
   2.1 Complexity Analysis 663

3   Illustration of the STDS Algorithm............................. 664
4   Performance of the STDS Algorithm 670
    4.1 *CRC* Is Satisfied... 670
    4.2 Application of Algorithm for Random Data 672
    4.3 Application of Algorithm to Practical DAGs................. 674
    4.4 Scheduling of Diamond DAGs 675
    4.5 Comparison with Other Algorithms 680
5   Conclusions 680

Chapter 19. SPMD Execution in the Presence of Dynamic Data Structures

Rajiv Gupta 683

1   Introduction... 683
2   Language Support for Regular Data Structures 684
    2.1 Processor Structures 685
    2.2 Dynamic Data Structures 685
    2.3 Name Generation and Distribution Strategies................ 688
    2.4 Examples 689
3   Compiler Support for Regular Data Structures................... 693
    3.1 Representing Pointers and Data Structures 693
    3.2 Translation of Pointer Operations 694
4   Supporting Irregular Data Structures 703
5   Compile-Time Optimizations 705
6   Related Work 706

Chapter 20. Supporting Dynamic Data Structures with Olden

Martin C. Carlisle and Anne Rogers 709

1   Introduction... 709
2   Programming Model 711
    2.1 Programming Language.................................... 711
    2.2 Data Layout 711
    2.3 Marking Available Parallelism 714
3   Execution Model... 715
    3.1 Handling Remote References 715
    3.2 Introducing Parallelism 718
    3.3 A Simple Example 719
4   Selecting Between Mechanisms................................. 722
    4.1 Using Local Path Lengths................................. 723
    4.2 Update Matrices 724
    4.3 The Heuristic.. 726

5   Experimental Results.. 731
     5.1 Comparison with Other Published Work 733
     5.2 Heuristic Results....................................... 733
     5.3 Summary 735
6   Profiling in Olden 735
     6.1 Verifying Local Path Lengths 736
7   Related Work 739
     7.1 Gupta's Work 741
     7.2 Object-Oriented Systems................................ 741
     7.3 Extensions of C with Fork-Join Parallelism 743
     7.4 Other Related Work..................................... 744
8   Conclusions 745

Chapter 21. Runtime and Compiler Support for Irregular Computations

Raja Das, Yuan-Shin Hwang, Joel Saltz, and Alan Sussman 751

1   Introduction... 751
2   Overview of the CHAOS Runtime System 753
3   Compiler Transformations 758
     3.1 Transformation Example 759
     3.2 Definitions 763
     3.3 Transformation Algorithm 765
4   Experiments 769
     4.1 Hand Parallelization with CHAOS 769
     4.2 Compiler Parallelization Using CHAOS 773
5   Conclusions 775

Author Index... 779

Introduction

Santosh Pande[1] and Dharma P. Agrawal[2]

[1] College of Computing
801 Atlantic Drive,
Georgia Institute of Technology,
Atlanta, GA 30332
[2] Department of ECECS, ML 0030,
PO Box 210030,
University of Cincinnati,
Cincinnati, OH 45221-0030

1. Compiling for Distributed Memory Multiprocessors

1.1 Motivation

The distributed memory parallel systems offer elegant architectural solutions for highly parallel data intensive applications primarily because:

- They are highly scalable. These systems currently come in a variety of architectures like 3D torus, mesh and hypercube that allow addition of extra processors should the computing demands increase. Scalability is an important issue especially for high performance servers such as parallel video servers, data mining and imaging applications.
- With increase in parallelism, there is insignificant degradation in memory performance since memories are isolated and decoupled from direct accesses from processors. This is especially good for data intensive applications such as parallel databases and data mining that demand considerable memory bandwidths. In contrast, the memory bandwidths may not match the increase in number of processors in shared memory systems. In fact, the overall system performance may degrade due to increased memory contention. This in turn jeopardizes scalability of application beyond a point.
- Spatial parallelism in large applications such as Fluid Flow, Weather Modeling and Image Processing, in which the problem domains are perfectly decomposable, is easy to map on these systems. The achievable speedups are almost linear and this is primarily due to fast accesses to the data maintained in local memory.
- The interprocessor communication speeds and bandwidths have dramatically improved due to very fast routing. The performance ratings offered by newer distributed memory systems have improved although they are not comparable to shared memory systems in terms of Mflops.
- Medium grained parallelism can be effectively mapped onto the newer systems like the Meiko CS-2, Cray T3D, IBM SP1/SP2 and EM4 due to a

low ratio of communication/computation speeds. Communication bottle-neck has decreased compared with earlier systems and this has opened up parallelization of newer applications.

1.2 Complexity

However, programming distributed memory systems remains very complex. Most of the current solutions mandate that the users of such machines must manage the processor allocation, data distribution and inter-processor com-munication in their parallel programs. Programming these systems for achiev-ing the desired high performance is very complex. In spite of frantic demands by programmers, current solutions provided by (semi-automatic) parallelizing compilers are rather constrained. As a matter of fact, for many applications the only practical success has been through hand parallelization of codes with communication managed through MPI. In spite of a tremendous amount of research in this area, applicability of many of the compiler techniques re-mains rather limited and the achievable performance enhancement remains less than satisfactory. The main reasons for the restrictive solutions offered by parallelizing compilers is the enormous complexity of the problem. Orches-trating computation and communication by suitable analysis and optimizing their performance through judicious use of underlying architectural features demands a true sophistication on the part of the compiler. It is not even clear whether these complex problems are solvable within the realm of com-piler analysis and sophisticated restructuring transformations. Perhaps they are much deeper in nature and go right into the heart of design of parallel algorithms for such an underlying model of computation.

The primary purpose of this monograph is to provide an insight into cur-rent approaches and point to potentially open problems that could have an impact. The monograph is organized in terms of issues ranging from pro-gramming paradigms (languages) to effective run time systems.

1.3 Outline of the Monograph

Language design is largely a matter of legacy and language design for dis-tributed memory systems is no exception to the rule. In section I of the monograph we examine three important approaches (one imperative, one object-oriented and one functional) in this domain that have made a sig-nificant impact. The first chapter on HPF 2.0 provides an in-depth view of data parallel language which evolved from Fortran 90. They present HPF 1.0 features such as BLOCK distribution and FORALL loop as well as new fea-tures in HPF 2.0 such as INDIRECT distribution and ON directive. They also point to the complementary nature of MPI and HPF and discuss features such as EXTRINSIC interface mechanism. HPF 2.0 has been a major commer-cial success with many vendors such as Portland Group and Applied Paral-lel Research providing highly optimizing compiler support which generates message passing code. Many research issues especially related to supporting irregular computation could prove valuable to domains such as sparse matrix computation etc. The next chapter on Sisal 90 provides a functional view of implicit paralleism specification and mapping. Shared memory implementation of Sisal is discussed, which involves optimizations such as *update in place copy elimination* etc. Sisal 90 and a distributed memory implemenatation which uses message passing are also discussed. Finally multi-threaded implementations of Sisal are discussed, with a focus on multi-threaded optimizations. The newer optimizations which perform memory management in hard-ware through dynamically scheduled multi-threaded code should really prove beneficial for the performance of functional languages (including Sisal) which have an elegant programming model. The next chapter on HPC++ provides an object oriented view as well as details on a library and compiler strategy to support HPC++ level 1 release. The authors discuss interesting features related to multi-threading, barrier synchronization and remote procedure invocation. They also discuss library features that are especially useful for scientific programming. Extensions of this work relating to newer portable languages such as Java is currently an active area of research. We also have a chapter on concurrency models of OO paradigms. The authors specifically address a problem called *inheritance anomaly* which arises when synchronization constraints are implemented within methods of a class and an attempt is made to specialize methods through inheritance mechanisms. They propose a solution to this problem by separating the specification of synchronization from the method specification. The synchronization construct is not a part of the method body and is handled separately. It will be interesting to study the compiler optimizations on this model related to strength reduction of barriers, and issues such as data partitioning vs. barrier synchronizations.

In section II of the monograph, we focus on various analysis techniques. Parallelism detection is very important and the first chapter presents a very interesting comparative study of different loop parallelization algorithms by Allen and Kennedy, Wolf and Lam, Darte and Vivien and by Feautrier. They provide comparisons in terms of their performance (ability to parallelize as well as quality of schedules generated for code generation) as well as complexity. The comparison also focusses on the type of dependence information available. Further extensions could involve run-time parallelization given more precise dependence information. Array data-flow is of utmost importance in optimizations : both sequential as well as parallel. The first chapter on array data-flow analysis examines this problem in detail and presents techniques for exact data flow as well as for approximate data flow. The exact solution is shown for static control programs. Authors also show applications to interprocedural cases and some important parallelization techniques such as privatization. Some interesting extensions could involve run-time data flow analysis. The next chapter discusses interprocedural analysis based on guarded (predicated) array regions. This is a framework based on path-sensitive predicated data-flow which provides summary information. The authors also show application of their work to improve array privatization based on symbolic propagation. Extensions of these to newer object oriented languages such as Java (which have clean class hierarchy and inheritance model) could be interesting since these programs really need such summary MOD information for performing any optimization. We finally present a very important analysis/optimization technique for array privatization. Array privatization involves removing memory-related dependences which have a significant impact on communication optimizations, loop scheduling etc. The authors present a demand-driven data-flow formulation of the problem; an algorithm which performs single pass propagation of symbolic array expressions is also presented. This comprehensive framework implemented in a Polaris compiler is making a significant impact in improving many other related optimizations such as load balancing, communication etc.

The next section is focussed on communication optimization. The communication optimization can be achieved through data (and iteration space) distribution, statically or dynamically. These approaches further classify into data and code alignment or simply interation space transformations such as in tiling. The communication can also be optimized in data-parallel programs through array region analysis. Finally one could tolerate some communication latency through novel techniques such as multi-threading. We have chapters which cover these broad range of topics about communication in depth.

The first chapter in this section focusses on tiling for cache-coherent multicomputers. This work derives optimal tile parameters for minimal communication in loops with affine index expressions. The authors introduce a notion of data footprints and tile the iteration spaces so that the volume of communication is minimized. They develop an important lattice theoretic framework to precisely determine the sizes of data footprints which are very valuable not only in tiling but in many array distribution transformations. The next two chapters deal with the important problem of communication free loop partitioning.

The second chapter in this section focusses on comparing different methods of achieving communication-free partitioning for DOALL loops. This chapter discusses several variants of the communication-free partitioning problem involving duplication or non-duplication of data, load balancing of iteration space and aspects such as statement level vs. loop level partitioning. Several aspects such as trading parallelism to avoid inter-loop data distribution are also touched upon. Extending these techniques to broader classes of DOALL loops could enhance their applicability.

The next chapter by Pingali et al. proposes a very interesting framework which first determines a set of constraints on data and loop iteration placement. They then determine which constraints should be left unsatisfied to relax an overconstrained system to find a solution involving a large amount of parallelism. Finally, the remaining constraints are solved for data and code distribution. The systematic linear algebraic framework improves over many ad-hoc loop partitioning approaches.

These approaches trade parallelism for codes that allow *decoupling* the issues of parallelism and communication by relaxing an appropriate constraint of the problem. However, for many important problems such as image processing applications such a relaxation is not possible. That is, one must resort to a different partitioning solution based on relative costs of communication and computation. In the next chapter, for solving such a problem, a new approach has been proposed to partition iteration space by determining directions which maximally cover the communication by minimally trading parallelism. This approach allows mapping of general medium grained DOALL loops. However, the communication resulting from this iteration space partitioning can not be easily aggregated without sophisticated 'pack'/'unpack' mechanisms present at send/receive ends. Such extensions are desirable since aggregating communication has as significant impact as reducing the volume.

The static data distribution and alignment typically solve the problems of communication on a loop nest by loop nest basis but rarely in an intraprocedural scope. Most of the inter-loop nest level and interprocedural boundaries require dynamic data redistribution. Banerjee et al. develop techniques that can be used to automatically determine which data partitions are most beneficial over specific sections of the program by accounting for redistribution overhead. They determine split points and phases of communication and redistribution are performed at split points.

When communication must take place, it should be optimized. Also, any redundancies must be captured and eliminated. Manish Gupta in the next chapter proposes a comprehensive approach for performing global (interprocedural) communication optimizations such as vectorization, PRE, coalescing, hoisting etc. Such an interprocedural approach to communication optimization is highly profitable in substantially improving the performance. Extending this work to irregular communication could be interesting.

Finally, we present a multi-threaded approach which could hide the communication latency. Two representative applications involving bitonic sort and FFT are chosen and using fine grained multi-threading on EM-X it is shown that multi-threading can substantially help in overlapping computation with communication to hide latencies up to 35 %. These methods could be especially useful for irregular computation.

The final phase of compiling for distributed memory systems involves solving many code generation problems. Code generation problems involve, determining communication generation and doing address calculation to map global references to local ones. The next section deals with these issues. The first chapter presents structures and techniques for communication generation. They focus on issues such as flexible computation partitioning (going beyond owner computes rule), communication adaptation based upon manipulating integer sets through abstract inequalities and control flow simplification based on these. One good property of this work is that it can work with many different front ends (not just data parallel languages) and the code generator has more opportunities to perform low level optimizations due to simplified control flow.

The second chapter discusses basis vector based address calculation mechanisms for efficient traversals of partitioned data. While one important issue of code generation is communication generation, a very important issue is to map global address space to local address space efficiently. The problem is complicated due to data distributions and access strides. Ramanujam et al. present closed form expressions for basis vectors for several cases. Using the closed form expressions for the basis vectors, they derive a non-unimodular linear transformation.

The final section is on supporting task parallelism and dynamic data structures. We also present a run-time system to manage irregular computation. The first chapter by Darbha et al. presents a task scheduling approach that is optimal for many practical cases. The authors evaluate its performance for many practical applications such as the Bellman-Ford algorithm, Cholesky decomposition, the Systolic algorithm etc. They show that schedules generated by their algorithm are optimal for some cases and near optimal for most others. With HPF 2.0 supporting task parallelism, this could open up many new application domains.

The next two chapters describe language supports for dynamic data structures such as pointers in distributed address space. Gupta describes several extensions to C with declarations such as *TREE, ARRAY, MESH* to declare dynamic data structures. He then describes name generation and distribution strategies for name generation and distribution strategies. Finally he describes support for both regular as well as irregular dynamic structures. The second chapter by Rogers et al. presents an approach followed in their *Olden* project which uses a distributed heap. The remote access is handled by software caching or computation migration. The selection of these mechanisms is done automatically through a compile time heuristic. They provide a data layout annotation to the programmer called *local path lengths* which allows programmers to give hints regarding expected data layout thereby fixing these mechanisms. Both of these chapters provide highly useful insights into supporting dynamic data strutures which are very important for scalable domains of computation supported by these machines. Thus, these works should have a significant impact on future scalable applications supported by these systems.

Finally, we present a run-time system called *CHAOS* which provides efficient support for irregular computations. Due to indirection in many sparse matrix computations, the communication patterns are unknown at compile time in these applications. Indirection patterns have to be preprocessed, and the sets of elements to be sent and received by each processor precomputed, in order to optimize communication. In this work, the authors provide details of efficient run time support for an *inspector–executor* model.

1.4 Future Directions

The two important bottlenecks for the use of distributed memory systems are the limited application domains and the fact that the performance is less than satisfactory. The main bottleneck seems to be handling communication. Thus, efficient solutions must be developed. Application domains beyond regular communication can be handled by supporting a general run-time communication model. This run-time communication model must be latency hiding and should give sufficient flexibility to the compiler to defer the hard decisions to run time yet allow static optimizations involving communication motion etc. One of the big problems compilers face is that estimating cost of communication is almost impossible. They can however gauge criticality (or relative importance) of communication. Developing such a model will allow compilers to more effectively deal with issues of *relative* importance betwen computation and communication and communication and communication.

Probably *the* best reason to use distributed memory systems is to benefit from *scalability* even though application domains and performance might be somewhat weaker. Thus, new research must be done in *scalable code generation*. In other words, as size of the problem and number of processors increase, should there be a change in data/code partition or should it remain the same? What code generation issues are related to this? How could one potentially handle the "hot spots" that inevitably (although at much lower levels than shared memory systems) arise? Can one benefit from the above communication model and dynamic data ownerships discussed earlier?

Section I : Languages

Chapter 1. High Performance Fortran 2.0

Ken Kennedy[1] and Charles Koelbel[2]

[1] Department of Computer Science and Center for Research on Parallel
  Computation, Rice University, Houston, Texas, USA
[2] Advanced Computational Infrastructure and Research, National Science
  Foundation, 4201 Wilson Boulevard, Suite 1122 S, Arlington, VA 22230, USA

Summary. High Performance Fortran (HPF) was defined in 1993 as a portable
data-parallel extension to Fortran. This year it was updated by the release of HPF
version 2.0, which clarified many existing features and added a number of extensions
requested by users. Compilers for these extensions are expected to appear beginning
in late 1997. In this paper, we present an overview of the entire language, including
HPF 1 features such as BLOCK distribution and the FORALL statement and HPF 2
additions such as INDIRECT distribution and the ON directive.

1. Introduction

High Performance Fortran (HPF) is a language that extends standard Fortran by adding support for data-parallel programming on scalable parallel
processors. The original language document, the product of an 18-month informal standardization effort by the High Performance Fortran Forum, was
released in 1993. HPF 1.0 was based on Fortran 90 and was strongly influenced by the SIMD programming model that was popular in the early 90s.
The language featured a single thread of control and a shared-memory programming model in which any required interprocessor communication would
be generated implicitly by the compiler.

In spite of widespread interest in the language, HPF was not an immediate success, suffering from the long lead time between its definition and
the appearance of mature compilers and from the absence of features that
many application developers considered essential. In response to the latter
problem, the HPF Forum reconvened in 1995 and 1996 to produce a revised
standard called HPF 2.0 [11].The purpose of this paper is two-fold:

– To give an overview of the HPF 2.0 specification, and
– To explain (in general terms) how the language may be implemented.

We start by giving a short history of HPF and a discussion of the components
of the language.

2. History and Overview of HPF

HPF has attracted great interest since the inception of the first standardization effort in 1991. Many users had long hoped for a portable, efficient,
high-level language for parallel programming. In the 1980's, Geoffrey Fox's

S. Pande, D.P. Agrawal (Eds.): Compiler Optimizations for Scalable PS, LNCS 1808, pp. 3-43, 2001.
© Springer-Verlag Berlin Heidelberg 2001

analysis of parallel programs [5,6] and other projects had identified and popularized *data-parallel programming* as one promising approach to this goal. The data-parallel model derived its parallelism from the observation that updates to individual elements of large data structures were often independent of each other. For example, successive over-relaxation techniques update every point of a mesh based on the (previous) values there and at adjacent points. This observation identified far more parallelism in the problem than could be exploited by the physical processors available. Data-parallel implementations solved this situation by dividing the data structure elements between the physical processors and scheduling each processor to perform the computations needed by its local data. Sometimes the local computations on one processor required data from another processor. In these cases, the implementation inserted synchronization and/or communication to ensure that the correct version of the data was used. How the data had been divided determined how often the processors had to interact. Therefore, the key intellectual step in writing a data-parallel program was to determine how the data could be divided to minimize this interaction; once this was done, inserting the synchronization and communication was relatively mechanical.

In the late 1980's, several research projects [2,7,8,15–18,20] and commercial compilers [12,19] designed languages to implement data-parallel programming. These projects extended sequential or functional languages to include aggregate operations, most notably array syntax and `forall` constructs, that directly reflected data-parallel operations. Also, they added syntax for describing data mappings, usually by specifying a high-level pattern for how the data would be divided among processors. Programmers were responsible for appropriately using these "data distribution" and "data parallel" constructs appropriately. In particular, the fastest execution was expected when the dimension(s) that exhibited data parallelism were also distributed across parallel processors. Furthermore, the best distribution pattern was the one that produced the least communication; that is, the pattern that required the least combining of elements stored on separate processors. What the programmer did *not* have to do was equally important. Data-parallel languages did not require the explicit insertion of synchronization and communication operations. This made basic programming much easier, since the user needed only to consider the (sequential) ordering of large-grain operations rather than the more complex and numerous interconnections between individual processors. In other words, data-parallel languages had sequential semantics; race conditions were not possible. The cost of this convenience was increasingly complex compilers.

The job of the compiler and run-time system for a data-parallel language was to efficiently map programs onto parallel hardware. Typically, the implementation used a form of the *owner-computes rule*, which assigned the computation in an assignment statement to the processor that owned the left-hand side. Loops over distributed data structures, including the loops implied by aggregate operations, were an important special case of this rule; they were strip-mined so that each processor ran over the subset of the loop iterations specified by the owner-computes rule. This strip-mining automatically divided the work between the processors. Different projects developed various strategies for inserting communication and synchronization, ranging from pattern-matching [16] to dependence-based techniques [17]. Because the target platforms for the compilers were often distributed-memory computers like the iPSC/860, communication costs were very high. Therefore, the compilers expended great effort to reduce this cost through bundling communication [15] and using efficient collective communication primitives [16]. Similar techniques proved useful on a variety of platforms [8], giving further evidence that data-parallel languages might be widely portable. At the same time, the commercial Connection Machine Fortran compiler [19] was proving that data parallelism was feasible for expressing a variety of codes.

Many of the best ideas for data-parallel languages were eventually incorporated into Fortran dialects by the Fortran D project at Rice and Syracuse Universities [4], the Vienna Fortran project at the University of Vienna [3] and work at COMPASS, Inc. [12]. Early successes there led to a Supercomputing '91 birds-of-a-feather session that essentially proposed development of a standard data-parallel dialect of Fortran. At a follow-up meeting in Houston the following January, the Center for Research on Parallel Computation (CRPC) agreed to sponsor an informal standards process, and the High Performance Fortran Forum (HPFF) was formed. A "core" group of HPFF met every 6 weeks in Dallas for the next year, producing a preliminary draft of the HPF language specification presented at Supercomputing '92[1] and the final HPF version 1.0 language specification early the next year [9]. The outlines of HPF 1.0 were very similar to its immediate predecessors:

- Fortran 90 [1] (the base language) provided immediate access to array arithmetic, array assignment, and many useful intrinsic functions.
- The **ALIGN** and **DISTRIBUTE** directives (structured comments recognized by the compiler) described the mapping of partitioned data structures. Section 3 describes these features in more detail.
- The **FORALL** statement (a new construct), the **INDEPENDENT** directive (an assertion to the compiler), and the HPF library (a set of data-parallel subprograms) provided a rich set of data-parallel operations. Section 4 describes these features in more detail.
- **EXTRINSIC** procedures (an interface to other programming paradigms) provided an "escape hatch" for programmers who needed access to low-level machine details or forms of parallelism not well-expressed by data-parallel constructs. Section 5 describes these functions in more detail.

A reference to the standard [14] was published soon afterward, and HPFF went into recess for a time.

---

[1] That presentation was so overcrowded that movable walls were removed during the session to make a larger room.

In 1994, HPFF resumed meetings with two purposes:

- To consider Corrections, Clarifications, and Interpretations (CCI) of the HPF 1.0 language in response to public comments and questions, and
- To determine requirements for further extensions to HPF by consideration of advanced applications codes.

The CCI discussions led to the publication of a new language specification (HPF version 1.1). Although some of the clarifications were important for special cases, there were no major language modifications. The extensions requirements were collected in a separate document [10]. They later served as the basis for discussions toward HPF 2.0.

In January 1995, HPFF undertook its final (to date) series of meetings, with the intention of producing a significant update to HPF. Those meetings were completed in December 1996, and the HPF version 2.0 language specification [11] appeared in early 1997. The basic syntax and semantics of HPF did not change in version 2.0; generally, programs still consisted of sequential compositions of aggregate operations on distributed arrays. However, there were some significant revisions:

- HPF 2.0 consists of two parts: a base language, and a set of approved extensions. The base language is very close to HPF 1.1, and is expected to be fully implemented by vendors in a relatively short time. The approved extensions are more advanced features which are not officially part of the language, but which may be adopted in future versions of HPF. However, several vendors have committed to supporting one or more of the extensions due to customer demands. In this paper, we will refer to both parts of the language as "HPF 2.0" but will point out approved extensions when they are introduced.
- HPF 2.0 removes, restricts, or reclassifies some features of HPF 1.1, particularly in the area of dynamic remapping of data. In all cases, the justification of these changes was that cost of implementation was much higher than originally thought, and did not justify the advantage gained by including the features.
- HPF 2.0 adds a number of features, particularly in the areas of new distribution patterns, REDUCTION clauses in INDEPENDENT loops, the new ON directive for computation scheduling (including task parallelism), and asynchronous I/O.

The remainder of this paper considers the features of HPF 2.0 in more detail. In particular, each section below describes a cluster of related features, including examples of their syntax and use. We close the paper with a look to future prospects for HPF.

3. Data Mapping

The most widely discussed features of HPF describe the layout of data onto memories of parallel machines. Conceptually, the programmer gives a high-level description of how large data structures (typically, arrays) will be partitioned between the processors. It is the compiler and run-time system's responsibility to carry out this partitioning. This data mapping does not directly create a parallel program, but it does set the stage for parallel execution. In particular, data parallel statements operating on partitioned data structures can execute in parallel. We will describe that process more in section 4.

3.1 Basic Language Features

HPF uses a 2-phase data mapping model. Individual arrays can be *aligned* together, thus ensuring that elements aligned together are always stored on the same processor. This minimizes data movement if the corresponding elements are accessed together frequently. Once arrays are aligned in this way, one of them can be *distributed*, thus partitioning its elements across the processors' memories. This affects the data movement from combining different elements of the same array (or, by implication, elements of different arrays that are not aligned together). Distribution tends to be more machine-dependent than alignment; differing cost tradeoffs between machines (for example, relatively higher bandwidth or longer latency) may dictate different distribution patterns when porting. Section 3.1.1 below describes alignment, while Section 3.1.2 describes distribution.

It bears mentioning that the data mapping features of HPF are technically *directives*—that is, structured comments that are recognized by the compiler. The advantage of this approach is determinism; in general, an HPF program will produce the same result when run on any number of processors.[2] Another way of saying this is that HPF data mapping affects only the efficiency of the program, not its correctness. This has obvious attraction for maintaining and porting codes. We feel it is a key to HPF's success to date.

3.1.1 The ALIGN Directive. The ALIGN directive creates an alignment between two arrays. Syntactically, the form of this directive is

> !HPF$ ALIGN *alignee* [(*align-dummy-list*)] WITH [*] *target* [(*align-subscript-list*)]

---

[2] There are two notable exceptions to this. HPF has intrinsic functions (not described in this paper) that can query the mapping of an array; a programmer could use these to explicitly code different behaviors for different numbers of processors. Also, round-off errors can occur which may be sensitive to data mapping; this is most likely to occur if the reduction intrinsics described in Section 4 are applied to mapped arrays.

(For brevity, we ignore several alternate forms that can be reduced to this one.) The *alignee* can be any object name, but is typically an array name. This is the entity being aligned. The *target* may be an object or a template; in either case, this is the other end of the alignment relationship. (Templates are "phantom" objects that have shape, but take no storage; they are sometimes useful to provide the proper sized target for an alignment.) Many *alignees* can be aligned to a single *target* at once. An *align-dummy* is a scalar integer variable that may be used in (at most) one of the *align-subscript* expressions. An *align-subscript* is an affine linear function of one *align-dummy*, or it is a constant, or it is an asterisk (*). The *align-dummy-list* is optional if the *alignee* is a scalar; otherwise, the number of list entries must match the number of dimensions of the *alignee*. The same holds true for the *align-subscript-list* and *target*. The meaning of the optional asterisk before the*target* is explained in Section 3.2.3; here, it suffices to mention that it only applies to procedure dummy arguments. The ALIGN directive must appear in the declaration section of the program.

An ALIGN directive defines the alignment of the *alignee* by specifying the element(s) of the *target* that correspond to each *alignee* element. Each *align-dummy* implicitly ranges over the corresponding dimension of the *alignee*. Substituting these values into the *target* expression specifies the matching element(s). A "*" used as a subscript in the *target* expression means the *alignee* element matches all elements in that dimension. For example, Figure 3.1 shows the result of the HPF directives

```
!HPF$ ALIGN B(I,J) WITH A(I,J)
!HPF$ ALIGN C(I,J) WITH A(J,I)
!HPF$ ALIGN D(K) WITH A(K,1)
!HPF$ ALIGN E(L) WITH A(L,*)
!HPF$ ALIGN F(M) WITH D(2*F-1)
```

Elements (squares) with the same symbol are aligned together. Here, B is identically aligned with A; this is by far the most common case in practice. Similarly, C is aligned with the transpose of A, which might be appropriate if one array were accessed row-wise and the other column-wise. Elements of D are aligned with the first column of A; any other column could have been used as well. Elements of E, however, are each aligned with all elements in a row of A. As we will see in Section 3.1.2, this may result in E being replicated on many processors when A is distributed. Finally, F has a more complex alignment; through the use of (nontrivial) linear functions, it is aligned with the odd element of D. However, D is itself aligned to A, so F is *ultimately aligned* with A. Note that, because the *align-subscripts* in each directive are linear functions, the overall alignment relationship is still an invertible linear function.

The ALIGN directive produces rather fine-grain relationships between array elements. Typically, this corresponds to relationships between the data

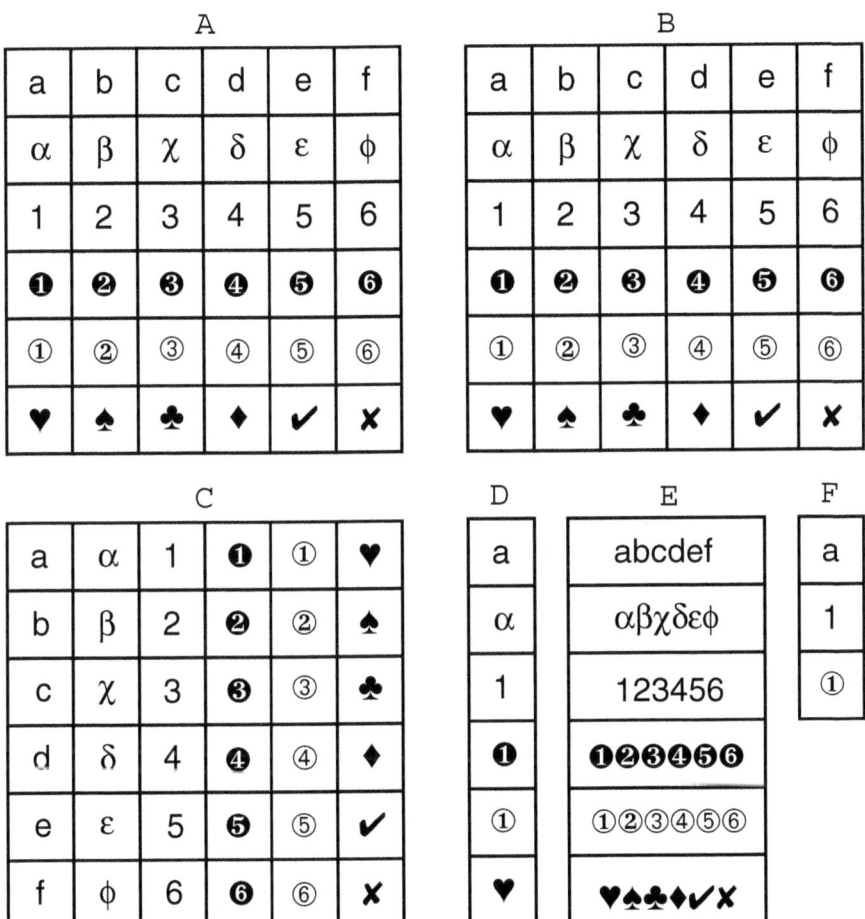

Fig. 3.1. Examples of the ALIGN directive.

in the underlying algorithm or in physical phenomena being simulated. For example, a fluid dynamics computation might have arrays representing the pressure, temperature, and fluid velocity at every point in space; because of their close physical relationships those arrays might well be aligned together. Because the alignment derives from a deep connection, it tends to be machine-independent. That is, if two arrays are often accessed together on one computer, they will also be accessed together on another. This makes alignment useful for software engineering. A programmer can choose one "master" array to which all others will be aligned; this effectively copies the master's distribution (or a modification of it) to the other arrays. It also allows To change the distributions of all the arrays (for example, when porting to a new machine), the programmer only has to adjust the distribution of the master array, as explained in the next section.

3.1.2 The DISTRIBUTE Directive. The DISTRIBUTE directive defines the distribution of an object or template and all other objects aligned to it. Syntactically, the form of this directive is

> !HPF$ DISTRIBUTE *distributee* [*] [(*dist-format-list*)] [ONTO
> [*] [*processor* [(section-list)]]]

The *distributee* can be any object or template, but is typically an array name; it is the entity being distributed. The *dist-format-list* gives a distribution pattern for each dimension of the distributee. The number of *dist-format-list* entries must match the number of *distributee* dimensions. The ONTO clause identifies the processor arrangement (or, as an HPF 2.0 approved extension, the section thereof) where the *distributee* will be stored. The number of dimensions of this expression must match the number of entries in the *dist-format-list* that are not *. The *dist-format-list* or the *processor* expression is only optional if its * option (explained in Section 3.2.3) is present. The DISTRIBUTE directive must appear in the declaration section of the program.

An DISTRIBUTE directive defines the alignment of the *distributee* by giving a general pattern for how each of its dimensions will be divided. HPF 1.0 had three such formats—BLOCK, CYCLIC, and *. HPF 2.0 adds two more—GEN_BLOCK and INDIRECT—as approved extensions. Figure 3.2 shows the results of the HPF directives

```
!HPF$ DISTRIBUTE S( BLOCK )
!HPF$ DISTRIBUTE T( CYCLIC )
!HPF$ DISTRIBUTE U( CYCLIC(2) )
!HPF$ DISTRIBUTE V( GEN_BLOCK( (/ 3, 5, 5, 3 /) ) )
!HPF$ DISTRIBUTE W( INDIRECT( SNAKE(1:16) ) )
!HPF$ DISTRIBUTE X( BLOCK )
!HPF$ SHADOW X(1)
!HPF$ DISTRIBUTE Y( BLOCK, * )
!HPF$ DISTRIBUTE Z( BLOCK, BLOCK )
```

Here, the color of an element represents the processor where it is stored. All of the arrays are mapped onto four processors; for the last case, the processors are arranged as a 2×2 array, although other arrangements (1×4 and 4×1) are possible. As shown by the S declaration, BLOCK distribution breaks the dimension into equal-sized contiguous pieces. (If the size is not divisible by the number of processors, the block size is rounded upwards.) The T declaration shows how the CYCLIC distribution assigns the elements one-by-one to processors in round-robbin fashion. CYCLIC can take an integer parameter k, as shown by the declaration of U; in this case, blocks of size k are assigned cyclically to the processors. The declaration of V demonstrates the GEN_BLOCK pattern, which extends the BLOCK distribution to unequal-sized blocks. The

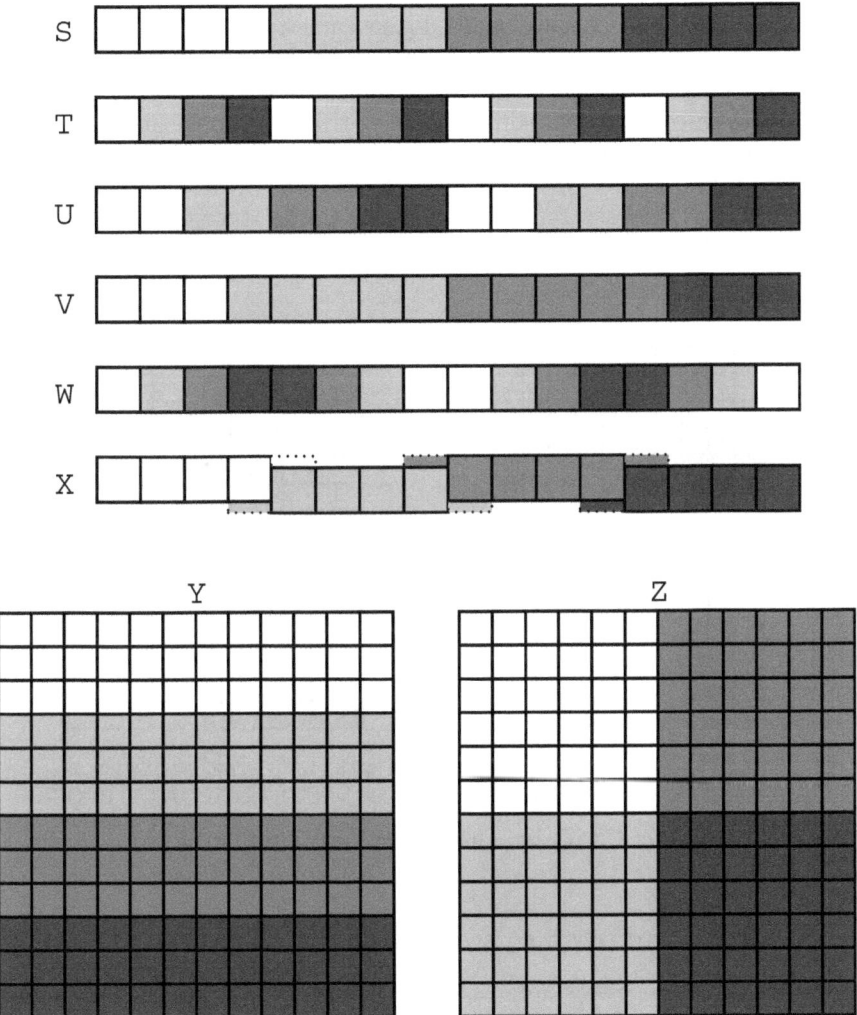

Fig. 3.2. Examples of the DISTRIBUTE directive.

sizes of the blocks on each processor is given by the mandatory integer array argument; there must be one such element for each processor. W demonstrates the INDIRECT pattern, which allows arbitrary distributions to be defined by declaring the processor home for each element of the *distributee*. The size of the INDIRECT parameter array must be the same as the size of the *distributee*. The contents of the parameter array SNAKE are not shown in the figure, but it must be set before the DISTRIBUTE directive takes effect. The BLOCK distribution can be modified by the SHADOW directive, which allocates "overlap" areas on each processor. X shows how this produces additional copies of the edge elements on each processor; the compiler can then use these copies to optimize data movement. Finally, multi-dimensional arrays take a distribution pattern in each dimension. For example, the Y array uses a BLOCK pattern for the rows and the * pattern (which means "do not partition") for the columns. The Z array displays a true 2-dimensional distribution, consisting of a BLOCK pattern in rows and columns.

When other objects are aligned to the *distributee*, its distribution pattern propagates to them. Figure 3.3 shows this process for the alignments in Figure 3.1. The left side shows the effect of the directive

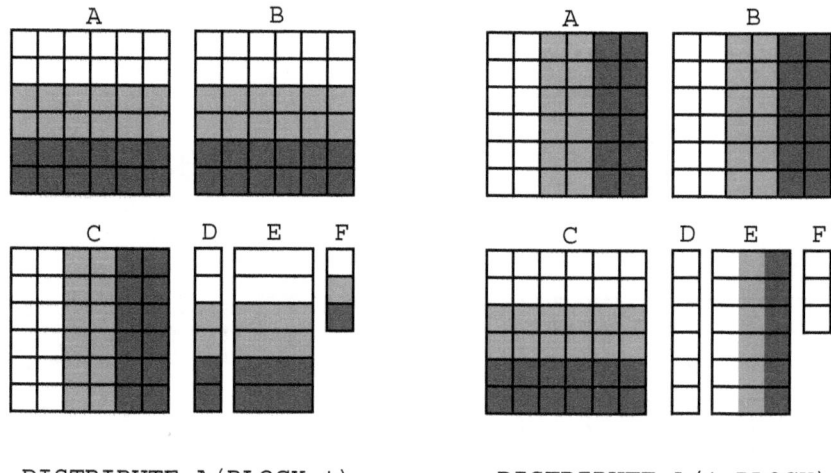

DISTRIBUTE A(BLOCK,*)   DISTRIBUTE A(*,BLOCK)

Fig. 3.3. Combining ALIGN and DISTRIBUTE.

```
!HPF$ DISTRIBUTE A( BLOCK, * )
```

assuming three processors are available. Because the alignments are simple in this example, the same patterns could be achieved with the directives

```
!HPF$ DISTRIBUTE A( BLOCK, * )
!HPF$ DISTRIBUTE B( BLOCK, * )
!HPF$ DISTRIBUTE C( *, BLOCK )
!HPF$ DISTRIBUTE D( BLOCK )
!HPF$ DISTRIBUTE E( BLOCK )
!HPF$ DISTRIBUTE F( BLOCK )
```

The right side shows the effect of the directive

```
!HPF$ DISTRIBUTE A( *, BLOCK )
```

Elements of E are replicated on all processors; therefore, each element has three colors. This mapping cannot be achieved by the DISTRIBUTE directive alone. The mappings of D and F onto a single processor are inconvenient to specify by a single directive, but it is possible using the ONTO clause.

The DISTRIBUTE directive affects the granularity of parallelism and communication in a program. The keys to understanding this are to remember that computation partitioning is based on the location of data, and that combining elements on different processors (e.g. adding them together, or assigning one to the other) produces data movement. To balance the computational load, the programmer must choose distribution patterns so that the updated elements are evenly spread across processors. If all elements are updated, then either the BLOCK or CYCLIC patterns do this; triangular loops sometimes make CYCLIC the only load-balanced option. To reduce data movement costs, the programmer should maximize the number of on-processor accesses. BLOCK distributions do this for nearest-neighbor access patterns; for irregular accesses, it may be best to carefully calculate an INDIRECT mapping array.

3.2 Advanced Topics

The above forms of ALIGN and DISTRIBUTE are adequate for declaring the mappings of arrays whose shape and access patterns are static. Unfortunately, this is not the case for all arrays; Fortran ALLOCATABLE and POINTER arrays do not have a constant size, and subprograms may be called with varying actual arguments. The features in this section support more dynamic uses of their mapped arrays.

3.2.1 Specialized and Generalized Distributions.
In many dynamic cases, it is only possible to provide partial information about the data mapping of an array. For example, it may be known that a BLOCK distribution was used, but not how many processors (or which processors) were used. When two mappings interact—for example, when a mapped pointer is associated with a mapped array—the intuition is that the target must have a more fully described mapping than the incoming pointer. HPF makes this intuition more precise by defining "generalizations" and "specializations" of mappings. In short, S's mapping is a specialization of G's mapping (or G's mapping is a generalization of S's) if S is more precisely specified. To make this statement more exact, we must introduce some syntax and definitions.

The "lone star" syntax that appeared in the DISTRIBUTE directives indicates any valid value can be used at runtime. Consider the directives

```
!HPF$ DISTRIBUTE A * ONTO P
!HPF$ DISTRIBUTE B (BLOCK) ONTO *
```

The first line means that A is distributed over processor arrangement P, but does not specify the pattern; it would be useful for declaring dummy arguments to a subroutine that would only be executed on those processors. Similarly, the second line declares that B has a block distribution, but does not specify the processors. Either clause gives partial information about the mapping of the distributee. In addition, the INHERIT directive specifies only that an object has a mapping. This serves as a "wild card" in matching mappings. It is particularly useful for passing dummy arguments that can take on any mapping (indeed, the name of the directive comes from the idea that the dummy arguments "inherit" the mapping of the actuals).

HPF defines the mapping of S to be a specialization of mapping G if:

1. G has the INHERIT attribute, or
2. S does not have the INHERIT attribute, and
    a) S is a named object (i.e. an array or other variable), and
    b) S and G are aligned to objects with the same shape, and
    c) The *align-subscripts* in S's and G's ALIGN directives reduce to identical expressions (except for *align-dummy* name substitutions), and
    d) Either
        i. Neither S's nor G's align target has a DISTRIBUTE directive, or
        ii. Both S's and G's align targets have a DISTRIBUTE directive, and
            A. G's align target's DISTRIBUTE directive has no ONTO clause, or specifies "ONTO *", or specifies ONTO the same processor arrangement as S's align target, and
            B. G's align target's DISTRIBUTE directive has no distribution format clause, or uses "*" as the distribution format clause, or the distribution patterns in the clause are equivalent dimension-by-dimension to the patterns in S's align target.

Two distribution patterns are equivalent in the definition if they both have the same identifier (e.g. are both BLOCK, both CYCLIC, etc.) and any parameters have the same values (e.g. the m in CYCLIC(m), or the array ind in INDIRECT(ind)).

This defines "specialization" as a partial ordering of mappings, with an INHERIT mapping as its unique minimal element. Conversely, "generalization" is a partial ordering, with INHERIT as its unique maximum.

We should emphasize that, although the definition of "specialization" is somewhat complex, the intuition is very simple. One mapping is a specialization of another if the specialized mapping provides at least as much information as the general mapping, and when both mappings provide information they match. For example, the arrays A and B mentioned earlier in this section have mappings that are specializations of

```
!HPF$ INHERIT GENERAL
```

If all the arrays are the same size, both A and B are generalizations of

```
!HPF$ DISTRIBUTE SPECIAL(BLOCK) ONTO P
```

Neither A's nor B's mapping is a specialization of the other.

3.2.2 Data Mapping for ALLOCATABLE and POINTER Arrays.

One of the great advantages of Fortran 90 and 95 over previous versions of FORTRAN is dynamic memory management. In particular, ALLOCATABLE arrays can have their size set during execution, rather than being statically allocated. This generality does come at some cost in complicating HPF's data mapping, however. In particular, the number of elements per processor cannot be computed until the size of the array is known; this is a particular problem for BLOCK distributions, since the beginning and ending indices on a particular processor may depend on block sizes, and thus on the number of processors. In addition, it is unclear what to do if an allocatable array is used in a chain of ALIGN directives.

HPF resolves these issues with a few simple rules. Mapping directives (ALIGN and DISTRIBUTE) take effect when an object is allocated, not when it is declared. If an object is the target of an ALIGN directive, then it must be allocated when the ALIGN directive takes effect. These rules enforce most users' expectations; patterns take effect when the array comes into existence, and one cannot define new mappings based on ghosts. For example, consider the following code.

```
REAL, ALLOCATABLE :: A(:), B(:), C(:)
!HPF$ DISTRIBUTE A(CYCLIC(N))
!HPF$ ALIGN B(I) WITH A(I*2)
!HPF$ ALIGN C(I) WITH A(I*2)
...
ALLOCATE( B(1000) ) ! Illegal
...
ALLOCATE( A(1000) ) ! Legal
ALLOCATE( C(500) )  ! Legal
```

The allocation of B is illegal, since it is aligned to an object that does not (yet) exist. However, the allocations of A and C are properly sequenced; C can rely on A, which is allocated immediately before it. A will be distributed cyclically in blocks of N elements (where N is evaluated on entry to the subprogram where these declarations occur). If N is even, C will have blocks of size $N/2$; otherwise, its mapping will be more complex.

It is sometimes convenient to choose the distribution based on the actual allocated size of the array. For example, small problems may use a CYCLIC distribution to improve load balance while large problems benefit from a BLOCK distribution. In these cases, the REALIGN and REDISTRIBUTE directives described in Section 3.2.4 provide the necessary support.

The HPF 2 core language does not allow explicitly mapped pointers, but the approved extensions do. In this case, the ALLOCATABLE rules also apply to POINTER arrays. In addition, however, pointer assignment can associate a POINTER variable with another object, or with an array section. In this case, the rule is that the mapping of the POINTER must be a generalization of the target's mapping. For example, consider the following code.

```
REAL, POINTER :: PTR1(:), PTR2(:), PTR3(:)
REAL, TARGET A(1000)
!HPF$ PROCESSORS P(4), Q(8)
!HPF$ INHERIT PTR1
!HPF$ DISTRIBUTE PTR2(BLOCK)
!HPF$ DISTRIBUTE PTR3 * ONTO P
!HPF$ DISTRIBUTE A(BLOCK) ONTO Q
PTR1 => A( 2 : 1000 : 2 )      ! Legal
PTR2 => A                      ! Legal
PTR3 => A                      ! Illegal
```

PTR1 can point to a regular section of A because it has the INHERIT attribute; neither of the other pointers can, because regular sections are not named objects and thus not specializations of any other mapping. PTR2 can point to the whole of A; for pointers, the lack of an ONTO clause effectively means "can point to data on any processors arrangement." PTR3 cannot point to A because their ONTO clauses are not compatible; the same would be true if their ONTO clauses matched but their distribution patterns did not.

The effect of these rules is to enforce a form of type checking on mapped pointers. In addition to the usual requirements that pointers match their targets in type, rank, and shape, HPF 2.0 adds the requirement that any explicit mappings be compatible. That is, a mapped POINTER can only be associated with an object with the same (perhaps more fully specified) mapping.

3.2.3 Interprocedural Data Mapping. The basic ALIGN and DISTRIBUTE directives declare the mapping of global variables and automatic variables. Dummy arguments, however, require additional capabilities. In particular, the following situations are possible in HPF:

- *Prescriptive mapping:* The dummy argument can be forced to have a particular mapping. If the actual argument does not have this mapping, the mapping is changed for the duration of the procedure.
- *Descriptive mapping:* This is the same as a prescriptive mapping, except that it adds an assertion that the actual argument has the same mapping as the dummy. If it does not, the compiler may emit a warning.
- *Transcriptive mapping:* The dummy argument can have any mapping. In effect, it inherits the mapping of the actual argument.

Syntactically, prescriptive mapping is expressed by the usual ALIGN or DISTRIBUTE directives, as described in Section 3.1. Descriptive mapping is expressed by an asterisk preceding a clause of an ALIGN or DISTRIBUTE directive. Transcriptive mappings are expressed by an asterisk in place of a clause in an ALIGN or DISTRIBUTE directive. It is possible for a mapping to be partially descriptive and partially transcriptive (or some other combination) by this definition, but such uses are rare. For example, consider the following subroutine header.

```
SUBROUTINE EXAMPLE( PRE, DESC1, DESC2, TRANS1, TRANS2, N )
INTEGER N
REAL PRE(N), DESC1(N), DESC2(N), TRANS1(N), TRANS2(N)
!HPF$ DISTRIBUTE PRE(BLOCK)              ! Prescriptive
!HPF$ DISTRIBUTE DESC1 *(BLOCK)          ! Descriptive
!HPF$ ALIGN DESC2(I) WITH *DESC1(I*2-1)  ! Descriptive
!HPF$ INHERIT TRANS1                     ! Transcriptive
!HPF$ DISTRIBUTE TRANS2 * ONTO *         ! Transcriptive
```

PRE is prescriptively mapped; if the corresponding actual argument does not have a BLOCK distribution, then the data will be remapped on entry to the subroutine and on exit. DESC1 and DESC2 are descriptively mapped; the actual argument for DESC1 is expected to be BLOCK-distributed, and the actual for DESC2 should be aligned with the even elements of DESC1. If either of these conditions is not met, then a remapping is performed and a warning is emitted by the compiler. TRANS1 is transitively mapped; the corresponding actual can have any mapping or can be an array section without causing remapping. TRANS2 is also transcriptively mapped, but passing an array section may cause remapping.

HPF 2.0 simplified and clarified the rules for when an explicit interface is required.[3] If any argument is declared with the INHERIT directive, or if any argument is remapped when the call is executed, then an explicit interface is required. Remapping is considered to occur if the mapping of an actual argument is not a specialization of the mapping of its corresponding dummy argument. In other words, if the dummy's mapping uses INHERIT or doesn't describe the actual as well (perhaps in less detail), then the programmer must supply an explicit interface. The purpose of this rule is to ensure that both caller and callee have the information required to change perform the remapping. Because it is sometimes difficult to decide whether mappings are specializations of each other, some programmers prefer to simply use explicit interfaces for all calls; this is certainly safe.

3.2.4 REALIGN and REDISTRIBUTE. Sometimes, remapping of arrays is required at a granularity other than subroutine boundaries. For example, within a single procedure an array may exhibit parallelism across rows for several loops, then parallelism across columns. Another common example is choosing the distribution of an array based on runtime analysis, such as computing the parameter array for a later INDIRECT distribution. For these cases, HPF 2.0 approved extensions provide the REALIGN and REDISTRIBUTE directives. It is worth noting that these directives were part of HPF version 1.0, but reclassified as approved extensions in HPF 2.0 due to unforeseen difficulties in their implementation.

---

[3] Fortran 90 introduced the concept of explicit interfaces, which give the caller all information about the types of dummy arguments. Explicit interfaces are created by INTERFACE blocks and other mechanisms.

Syntactically, the REALIGN directive is identical to the ALIGN directive, except for two additional characters in the keyword. (Also, REALIGN does not require the descriptive and transcriptive forms of ALIGN since its purpose is always to change the data mapping.) Similarly, REDISTRIBUTE has the same syntax as DISTRIBUTE's prescriptive case. Semantically, both directives set the mapping for the arrays they name when the program control flow reaches them; in a sense, they act like executable statements in this regard. The new mapping will persist until the array becomes deallocated, or another REALIGN or REDISTRIBUTE directive is executed. Data in the remapped arrays must be communicated to its new home unless the compiler can detect that the data is not live. One special case of dead data is called out in the HPF language specification—a REALIGN or REDISTRIBUTE directive for an array immediately following an ALLOCATE statement for the same array. The HPFF felt this was such an obvious and common case that strong advice was given to the vendors to avoid data motion there.

There is one asymmetry between REALIGN and REDISTRIBUTE that bears mentioning. REALIGN only changes the mapping of its alignee; the new mapping does not propagate to any other arrays that might be aligned with it beforehand. REDISTRIBUTE of an array changes the mapping for the distributee *and* all arrays that are aligned to it, following the usual rules for ALIGN. The justification for this behavior is that both "remap all" and "remap one" behaviors are needed in different algorithms. (The choice to make REDISTRIBUTE rather than REALIGN propagate to other arrays was somewhat arbitrary, but fit naturally with the detailed definitions of alignment and distribution in the language specification.)

The examples in Figure 3.4 may be helpful. In the assignments to A, that array is first computed from corresponding elements of C and their vertical neighbors, then updated from C's transpose. Clearly, the communication patterns are different in these two operations; use of REALIGN allows both assignments to be completed without communication. (Although the communication here occurs in the REALIGN directives instead, a longer program could easily show a net reduction in communication.) In the operations on B, corresponding elements of B and D are multiplied in both loops; this implies that the two arrays should remain identically aligned. However, each loop only exhibits one dimension of parallelism; using REDISTRIBUTE as shown permits the vector operations to be executed fully in parallel in each loop, while any static distribution would sacrifice parallel execution in one or the other.

4. Data Parallelism

Although the data mapping features of HPF are vital, particularly on distributed memory architectures, they must work in concert with data-parallel operations to fully use the machine. Conceptually, data-parallel loops and

```
REAL A(100,100), B(100,100), C(100,100), D(100,100)
!HPF$ DYNAMIC A, B
!HPF$ DISTRIBUTE C(BLOCK,*)
!HPF$ ALIGN D(I,J) WITH B(I,J)

!HPF$ REALIGN A(I,J) WITH C(I,J)
A = C + CSHIFT(C,1,2) + CSHIFT(C,-1,2)
!HPF$ REALIGN A(I,J) WITH C(J,I)
A = A + TRANSPOSE(C)

!HPF$ REDISTRIBUTE B(*,BLOCK)
DO I = 2, N-1
    B(I,:) = B(I-1,:)*D(I-1,:) + B(I,:)
END DO
!HPF$ REDISTRIBUTE B(*,BLOCK)
DO J = 2, N-1
    B(:,J) = B(:,J-1)*D(:,J-1) + B(:,J-1)
END DO
```

Fig. 3.4. REALIGN and REDISTRIBUTE

functions identify masses of operations that can be executed in parallel, typically element-wise updates of data. The compiler and run-time system use the data mapping information to package this potential parallelism for the physical machine. Therefore, as a first-order approximation programmers should expect that optimal performance will occur for vector operations along a distributed dimension. This will be true modulo communication and synchronization costs, and possibly implementation shortcomings.

4.1 Basic Language Features

Four features make up the basic HPF support for data parallelism:

1. *Fortran 90 array assignments* define element-wise operations on regular arrays.
2. *The* FORALL *statement* is a new form of array assignment that provides greater flexibility.
3. *The* INDEPENDENT *assertion* is a directive (i.e. structured comment) that gives the compiler more information about a DO loop.
4. *The HPF library* is a set of useful functions that perform parallel operations on arrays.

All of these features are part of the HPF 2.0 core language; Section 4.2 will consider additional topics from the approved extensions. We will not cover array assignments in more detail, except to say that they formed an invaluable

base to build HPF's more general operations. FORALL is the first case that we
have discussed of a new language construct; in contrast to the data mapping
directives, it changes the values of program data. Because of this, it could
not be another directive. INDEPENDENT, on the other hand, is a directive; if
correctly used, it only provides information to the compiler and does not alter
the meaning of the program. Finally, the HPF library is a set of functions
that provide interesting parallel operations. In most cases, these operations
derive their parallelism from independent operations on large data sets, but
the operations do not occur element-wise as in array assignments.

Compilers may augment the explicit data-parallel features of HPF by analyzing DO loops and other constructs for parallelism. In fact, many do precisely
that. Doing so is certainly a great advantage for users who are porting existing code. Unfortunately, different compilers have different capabilities in this
regard. For portable parallelism, it is often best to use the explicit constructs
described below.

4.1.1 The FORALL Statement. The FORALL statement provides data-
parallel operations, much like array assignments, with an explicit index space,
much like a DO loop. There are both single-statement and multi-statement
forms of the FORALL. The single-statement form has the syntax

FORALL (*forall-triplet-list* [, *mask-expr*]) *forall-assignment-stmt*

The multi-statement form has the syntax

FORALL (*forall-triplet-list* [, *mask-expr*])
    [*forall-body-construct*] ...
END FORALL

In both cases, a *forall-triplet* is

index-name = *int-expr* : *int-expr* [: *int-expr*]

If a *forall-triplet-list* has more than one triplet, then no *index-name* may
be used in the bounds or stride for any other index. A *forall-assignment-
stmt* is either an assignment statement or a pointer assignment statement.
A *forall-body-construct* can be an assignment, pointer assignment, WHERE, or
FORALL statement. For both *forall-assignment-stmt* and *forall-body-construct*,
function calls are restricted to PURE functions; as we will see in Section 4.1.2,
these are guaranteed to have no side effects.

The semantics of a single-statement FORALL is essentially the same as
for a single array assignment. First, the bounds and strides in the FORALL
header are evaluated. These determine the range for each index to iterate
over; for multidimensional FORALL statements, the indices are combined by
Cartesian product. Next, the mask expression is evaluated for every "iteration" in range. The FORALL body will not be executed for iterations that
produce a false mask. The right-hand side of the assignment is computed for
every remaining iteration. The key to parallel execution of the FORALL is that

these computations can be performed in parallel—no data is modified at this point, so there can be no interference between different iterations. Finally, all the results are assigned to the left-hand sides. It is an error if two of the iterations produce the same left-hand side location. Absent that error, the assignments can be made in parallel since there are no other possible sources of interference.

The semantics of a multi-statement FORALL reduce to a series of single-statement FORALLs, one per statement in the body. That is, the bounds and mask are computed once at the beginning of execution. Then each statement is executed in turn, first computing all right-hand sides and then assigning to the left-hand sides. After all assignments are complete, execution moves on to the next body statement. If the body statement is another FORALL, then the inner bounds must be computed (and may be different for every outer iteration) before the inner right-hand and left-hand sides, but execution still proceeds one statement at a time. The situation is similar for the mask in a nested WHERE statement.

One way to visualize this process is shown in Figure 4.1. The diagram to the left of the figure illustrates the data dependences possible in the example code

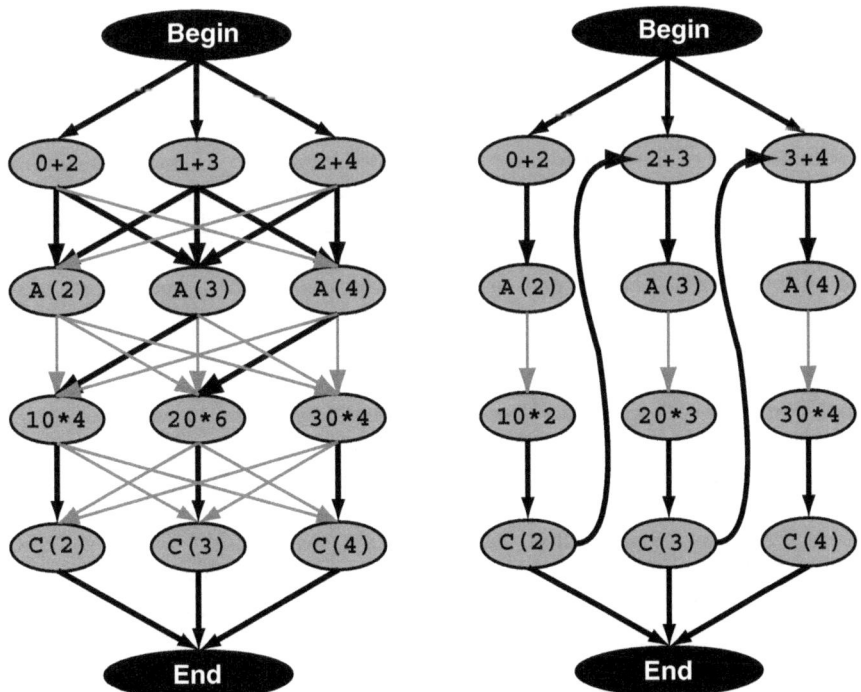

Fig. 4.1. Visualizations of FORALL and DO

```
FORALL ( I = 2:4 )
    A(I) = A(I-1) + A(I+1)
    C(I) = B(I) * A(I+1)
END FORALL
```

In the figure, each elemental operation is shown as an oval. The first row represents the A(I-1)+A(I+1) computations; the second row represents the assignments to A(I); the third row represents the computation of B(I) * A(I+1); the bottom row represents the assignments to C(I). The numbers in the ovals are based on the initial values

```
A(1:5) = (/ 0, 1, 2, 3, 4 /)
B(1:5) = (/ 0, 10, 20, 30, 40 /)
```

The reader can verify that the semantics above lead to a final result of

```
A(2:4) = (/ 2, 4, 6 /)
C(2:4) = (/ 40, 120, 120 /)
```

Arrows in the diagram represent worst-case data dependences; that is, a FORALL could have any one of those dependences. (To simplify the picture, transitive dependences are not shown.) These dependences arise in two ways:

- From right-hand side to left-hand side: the left-hand side may overwrite data needed to compute the right-hand side.
- From left-hand side to right-hand side: the right-hand side may use data assigned by the left-hand side.

By inspection of the diagram, it is clear that there are no connections running across rows. This is true in general, and indicates that it is always legal to execute all right-hand and all left-hand sides simultaneously. Also, it appears from the diagram that a global synchronization is needed between adjacent rows. This is also true in general, but represents an uncommon worst case. In the diagram, dark arrows represent dependences that actually arise in this example; light arrows are worst-case dependences that do not occur here. It is often the case, as here, that many worst-case dependences do not occur in a particular case; a good compiler will detect these cases and simplify communication and synchronization accordingly. In this case, for example, there is no need for synchronization during execution of the second statement.

It is useful to contrast the FORALL diagram with the corresponding dependence structure for an ordinary DO loop with the same body. The DO is shown on the right side of Figure 4.1. One can immediately see that the dependence structures are different, and verify that the result of the DO loop has changed to

```
A(2:4) = (/ 2, 5, 9 /)
C(2:4) = (/ 20, 60, 120 /)
```

At first glance, the diagram appears simpler. However, the dependence arcs from the bottom of each iteration to the top eliminate parallelism in the general case. Of course, there are many cases where these serializing dependences do not occur—parallelizing and vectorizing compilers work by detecting those cases. However, if the analysis fails the DO will run sequentially, while the FORALL can run in parallel.

The example above could also be written using array assignments.

```
A(2:4) = A(1:3) + A(3:5)
C(2:4) = B(2:4) * A(3:5)
```

However, FORALL can also access and assign to more complex array regions than can easily be expressed by array assignment. For example, consider the following FORALL statements.

```
FORALL ( I = 1:N ) A(I,I) = B(I,N-I+1)
FORALL ( J = 1:N ) C(INDX(J),J) = J*J
FORALL ( K = 1:N )
  FORALL ( L = 1:J ) D(K,L) = E( K*(K-1)/2 + L )
END FORALL
```

The first statement accesses the anti-diagonal of B and assigns it to the main diagonal of A. The anti-diagonal could be accessed using advanced features of the array syntax; there is no way in to do an array assignment to a diagonal or other non-rectangular region. The second statement does a computation using the values of the index and assigns them to an irregular region of the array C. Again, the right-hand side could be done using array syntax by creating a new array, but the left-hand side is too irregular to express by regular sections. Finally, the last FORALL nest unpacks the one-dimensional E array into the lower triangular region of the D array. Neither the left nor right-hand side can easily be expressed in array syntax alone.

4.1.2 PURE Functions. FORALL provides a form of "parallel loop" over the elements of an array, but the only statements allowed in the loop body are various forms of assignment. Many applications benefit from more complex operations on each element, such as point-wise iteration to convergence. HPF addresses these needs by allowing a class of functions—the PURE functions—to be called in FORALL assignments. PURE functions are safe to call from within FORALL because they cannot have side effects; therefore, they cannot create new dependences in the FORALL statement's execution. It is useful to call PURE functions because they allow very complex operations to be performed, including internal control flow that cannot easily be expressed directly in the body of a FORALL.

Syntactically, a PURE function is declared by adding the keyword PURE to its interface before the function's type. PURE functions must have an explicit interface, so this declaration is visible to both the caller and the function itself. The more interesting syntactic issue is what can be included in the

PURE function. The HPF 2.0 specification has a long list of restrictions on statements that can be included. The simple statement of these restrictions is that any construct that *could* assign to a global variable or a dummy argument is not allowed. This includes obvious cases such as using a global variable on the left-hand side of an assignment and less obvious ones such as using a dummy argument as the target of a pointer assignment. (The latter case does not directly change the dummy, but allows later uncontrolled side effects through the pointer.) Of course, this list of restrictions leads directly to the desired lack of side effects in the function. It is important to note that there are no restrictions on control flow in the function, except that STOP and PAUSE statements are not allowed. This allows quite complex iterative algorithms to be implemented in PURE functions.

```
! The caller
FORALL ( I=1:N, J=1:M )
    K(I,J) = MANDELBROT( CMPLX((I-1)*1.0/(N-1), &
             (J-1)*1.0/(M-1)), 1000 )
END FORALL

! The callee
PURE INTEGER FUNCTION MANDELBROT(X, ITOL)
COMPLEX, INTENT(IN) :: X
INTEGER, INTENT(IN) :: ITOL
COMPLEX XTMP
INTEGER K
K = 0
XTMP = -X
DO WHILE (ABS(XTMP)<2.0 .AND. K<ITOL)
    XTMP = XTMP*XTMP - X
    K = K + 1
END DO
MANDELBROT = K
END FUNCTION MANDELBROT
```

Fig. 4.2. Mandelbrot set computation by a PURE function

A short example illustrates both the last point about control flow and hints at PURE functions' power. Consider the code in Figure 4.2. This code (which was one of the first HPF programs publicly demonstrated) creates a picture of the Mandelbrot set. Notice that the MANDELBROT function uses local variables to iterate on every point it is passed.

4.1.3 The INDEPENDENT Assertion. Array assignment and FORALL are new statements with new semantics that are convenient for programmers and efficiently implementable. The purpose of the INDEPENDENT directive is

somewhat different—it gives the compiler new information about a standard
DO loop. In particular, INDEPENDENT tells the system that serializing worst-
case behavior does not occur; this allows the compiler to run the loop in
parallel. Compilers on serial machines can use the same information in other
ways, for example to manage cache. Thus, INDEPENDENT is not really a "parallel loop" (although it can be used that way); it is information about the
program that many systems find useful.

The syntax of INDEPENDENT is

   !HPF$ INDEPENDENT [, LOCAL(*variable-list*)] [, REDUCTION(
   variable-list)]

The directive must immediately precede a DO statement or FORALL statement,
and describes the behavior of only that statement.

When HPF 1.0 was under development, it rapidly became clear that different people had different definitions "can be executed in parallel." In the
end, HPFF chose a fairly restrictive, mathematical definition of INDEPENDENT.
A loop is INDEPENDENT if no iteration interferes with any other iteration. If
there is no LOCAL or REDUCTION clause, two iterations interfere if any of the
following occur:

- Both iterations set the value of the same atomic object. (An atomic object
  is a Fortran object that does not contain another object. For example, an
  integer is an atomic object; an array of integers is an object that is not
  atomic.)
- One iteration sets the value of an atomic object, and the other uses the
  value of the same object.
- One iteration allocates or deallocates an object that is set or used by the
  other iteration.
- One iteration remaps an array that is set or used by another iteration.
- Both iterations perform I/O on the same file.
- One iteration exits the loop by GOTO or other transfer of control, or stops
  execution by STOP or PAUSE.

Formally, LOCAL is an assertion that no values flow into the named variables
from before the iteration nor flow from the variables after the iteration. This
implies that the variables can be removed from consideration for causing interference; in effect, it creates variables that are local to each iteration. (Note
that on shared-memory machines this forces each processor to have a separate copy of the LOCAL variables.) The REDUCTION clause asserts that the
named variables are updated by associative and commutative intrinsic operations within the lexical body of the loop, and that the variable is not used
elsewhere in the loop. Although this is formally a type of interference, it is a
well-structured type with efficient parallel implementations. (Note that extra
data copies are often needed in these implementations as well.) Because of
the lack of interference, an INDEPENDENT loop can always in principle be executed with a single synchronization point at the beginning and another at the

end. Contrast this with the row-by-row synchronizations needed for FORALL. Less obviously, all data needed for an iteration is available either before the loop begins or is generated within the iteration itself. This information can be used to optimize data movement.

Two things should be noted about the definition of interference.

1. *Behavior, not syntax, causes interference.* For example, a READ statement from a file into an element of a global array is perfectly allowable inside an INDEPENDENT loop, so long as it is only executed in one iteration(or the file and array element change on every iteration. This is in contrast to the FORALL statement, which limits its body to various forms of assignment statements.

2. *Interference invalidates independence, even if it wouldn't matter.* The REDUCTION clause was added to HPF 2.0 because experience with HPF 1 showed that users did not consider reductions to be "real" interference. It is still the case in HPF 2, however, that nondetermistic algorithms are not INDEPENDENT; although any answer from the algorithm might be acceptable in principle, the fact that different answers are possible indicates there was a write-write interference.

This combination provides a great deal of freedom for basic parallelization, but does not support complex synchronization patterns or some advanced algorithms.

Figure 4.3 gives the data dependence diagram for an INDEPENDENT DO loop. The ovals and arrows have the same meaning as in Figure 4.1, but the example is now

```
!HPF$ INDEPENDENT
DO J = 1, 3
    A(J) = A(B(J))
    C(A(J)) = A(J)*B(A(J))
END DO
```

Numbers in the diagram correspond to the initial data

```
A(1:8) = (/ 0, 2, 4, 6, 1, 3, 5, 7 /)
B(1:8) = (/ 6, 5, 4, 3, 2, 3, 4, 5 /)
C(1:8) = (/ -1,-1,-1,-1,-1,-1,-1,-1 /)
```

The reader can verify that the final result will be

```
A(1:8) = (/ 3, 1, 6, 6, 1, 3, 5, 7 /)
B(1:8) = (/ 6, 5, 4, 3, 2, 3, 4, 5 /)
C(1:8) = (/ 6,-1,12,-1,-1,18,-1,-1 /)
```

The key point to notice is that all dependences between iterations have been severed; the worst case of an INDEPENDENT loop is the best case that FORALL statements had to be analyzed for in Section 4.1.1. Notice that, since the INDEPENDENT assertion is correct, these are the same answers that would

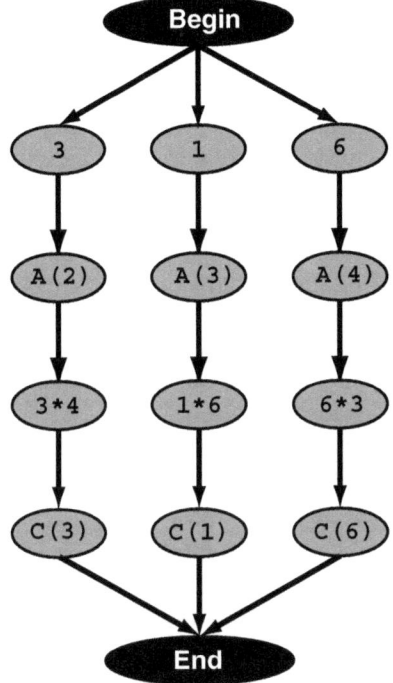

Fig. 4.3. Visualization of INDEPENDENT loop

have been obtained by an ordinary DO loop. However, INDEPENDENT allows the loop to execute in parallel.

The loop in the preceding paragraph also illustrates why INDEPENDENT is necessary even for advanced compilers. Although static analysis of programs has advanced far, no compiler could have detected independence in that loop. This is because the independence came from the data values which would not be available at compile time. Not knowing the values in the B array, the compiler would have no choice but to make the worst-case serializing assumptions. Although this example is somewhat contrived, it is similar to the application- and algorithm-level information that is available for many programs. It is often the case that an algorithm guarantees that a graph is acyclic by construction, or that an index vector is a permutation, or that the data structure has some other property. Application-level knowledge may also indicate properties of the input with similar implications. These high-level facts are generally not obvious by inspection of the program (indeed, they are often publishable research results in their own right). However, programmers often are aware of such properties and realize their implications for parallelism. INDEPENDENT provides a mechanism to pass this knowledge to the compiler in a form that it can use. Because the directive is phrased as an assertion, the compiler can further propagate the information to parallelize other loops with the same access pattern.

4.1.4 The HPF Library. In addition to elemental operations, several common operations have parallelism that scales with the size of the data structure. Reductions, as we just saw, are a frequent example. Sorting can also be done in parallel. However, the optimal algorithm for even simple operations such as reductions vary widely from architecture to architecture. Moreover, the best algorithms may be rather intricate and difficult to express in terms of FORALL statements or INDEPENDENT loops. Due to the importance of these high-level operations, however, it is important to provide them to programmers. HPF 2.0 does this via the HPF library, a collection of useful functions. In effect, this library puts the onus on the compiler and system vendors to provide efficient libraries for their users.

Due to space limitations, we cannot list all 57 functions and subroutines in the HPF library. Instead, we discuss the general classes of functionality.

- *System inquiry intrinsic functions* return information about the state of the parallel machine. There are two of these functions: NUMBER_OF_PROCESSORS, which returns the number of available processors, and PROCESSORS_SHAPE, which returns the "natural" processors arrangement. They can be used to adapt programs to the machine, for example by sizing arrays to an even multiple of the number of processors.
- *Mapping inquiry subroutines* return the mapping of an object (typically an array). There are three of them: HPF_ALIGNMENT, HPF_DISTRIBUTION, and HPF_TEMPLATE. They are particularly useful for checking transcriptive dummy arguments or dynamically mapped arrays to ensure that an appropriate algorithm is used for each data mapping.
- *Bit manipulation functions* operate on the bits of an integer representation. These four functions are useful for data compression, cryptography, and other bitwise algorithms.
- *Array reduction functions* use associative and commutative functions to combine elements of an array. Fortran 90 introduced several such functions, including SUM, PRODUCT and MAXVAL, but did not provide a reduction for every built-in associative and commutative operator. HPF completes the set by adding four functions: IALL (bitwise AND), IANY (bitwise OR), PARITY (logical exclusive OR), and IPARITY (bitwise exclusive OR).
- *Array prefix and suffix functions* (sometimes called scan functions) compute sets of partial reductions of arrays. The first element of a prefix sum is the first element of the input; the second output element is the sum of the first two input elements; and in general the Nth output element is the sum of the first N elements. HPF provides a prefix and a suffix function for each built-in associative and commutative operation, named after the corresponding reduction (for example, SUM_PREFIX and SUM_SUFFIX). The utility functions COPY_PREFIX and COPY_SUFFIX are also available. All of

these functions include options for masking elements and performing segmented scan operations. There are 24 of these functions in all. Work at Carnegie Mellon University has shown how these operations can be used for a variety of irregular data parallel algorithms.

- *Array combining scatter functions* scatter their input, resolving collisions by an associative and commutative operation. For example, the sum combining scatter could be implemented sequentially by

```
A = 0
DO I = 1, N
    A(INDX(I)) = A(INDX(I)) + B(I)
END DO
```

There is a combining scatter function for each built-in associative and commutative operator plus the COPY operation, giving a total of 12 functions. These functions are also useful in irregular applications; they also appear naturally in constructing the matrices for finite element methods.

- *Array sorting functions* either permute an array into monotonic order, or return a permutation vector that will do the job. The functions that return a sorted array are SORT_UP and SORT_DOWN; those that return a permutation vector are GRADE_UP and GRADE_DOWN.

A few more library functions supporting advanced features (such as the new DISTRIBUTE patterns) are included as approved extensions. It should be noted that many of those operations are actually generic interfaces that accept several numeric types as input; the actual runtime library is likely much larger.

4.2 Advanced Topics

The features in Section 4.1 provide convenient abstractions for data parallelism. Some applications, however, require more detailed performance tuning. HPF 2.0's approved extensions provide two directives to support this. The ON directive identifies the processor to execute a statement or block of statements. This can be used to override the owner-computes rule (or other compilation mechanism) in cases where it is inappropriate. The RESIDENT directive gives the compiler more information about data locality. In particular, it asserts that, give previous data mapping and ON directives, certain data references do not require communication. Both directives give the compiler information that it would not otherwise have. The compiler may use this additional information in any way that it deems appropriate; presumably, this will improve parallelism and reduce overhead on parallel architectures, but there may be other applications on sequential processors.

4.2.1 The ON Directive. Although the HPF language definition does not specify how data-parallel operations are implemented, in practice most compilers attempt to statically schedule the computation to occur where the mapping directives store the data. This "owner-computes rule" is a good heuristic in general, but like any heuristic it does not work in all cases. Even when it works, there are often several ways to interpret the heuristic which may give different results. Finally, many users have done careful analysis to determine optimal combinations of computation scheduling and data mapping. For all these reasons, we need the option of fine-level control of scheduling computation to processors. The HPF 2.0 approved extensions include the ON directive for this purpose. It gives a high-level suggestion of where to perform a computation, much as the DISTRIBUTE directive suggests where the data should be mapped.

The ON directive has a single-statement and a multi-statement form. The single-statement form has two variants:

> !HPF$ ON HOME(*variable*)
>
> **OR**
>
> !HPF$ ON (*processor-section*)

Variable is the Fortran syntax for any reference to a named object, including simple references like X and more complex ones like Y(1:N)%FIELD1. A *processor-section* is an element or section of an HPF processors arrangement. We refer to either the *variable* or *processor-section* as the HOME clause. The two forms for the multi-statement form are similar:

> !HPF$ ON HOME(*variable*) BEGIN
> *block*
> !HPF$ END [ON]
>
> **OR**
>
> !HPF$ ON (*processor-section*) BEGIN
> *block*
> !HPF$ END [ON]

The single-statement form controls the execution of the statement immediately following it; the multi-statement form controls all statements in its block. In either case, the HOME clause names the processor(s) to perform the computation, either directly (the *processors-section* form) or by indicating the processors where some data is mapped (the *variable* option). A programmer can think of the statement as executed in three steps:

1. Gather any data not already on the processors indicated in the HOME clause.
2. Compute results from the data.
3. Scatter the results back to any changed variables that are not stored on the HOME processor.

This is somewhat oversimplified, since the statement may be a DO loop or other complex construct that requires several rounds of communication. However, even in complex cases the idea is that the HOME processors perform the computation, perhaps on data communicated from somewhere else. ON directives can name more than one processor in the HOME clause; in these cases the named processors cooperate to execute the statement.

In effect, the HPF program begins with all processors active, and each ON directive masks out the processors that do not match its HOME clause. The masked processors can skip ahead to other computations if they do not need data produced in the ON block that excluded them. In particular, when the ON block is an iteration of an INDEPENDENT loop, processors can immediately occur to the first iteration where they are included in a HOME clause. If the loop is not INDEPENDENT, it must perform synchronization whenever two interfering iterations are scheduled on different processors. Scheduling the iterations of a loop in this way is probably the most common usage of the ON directive. In this case, a good compiler will invert any functions used in the HOME clause and propagate this information to the loop header. The programmer can therefore balance the computational load by choosing a HOME clause that evenly spreads the iterations to all processors.

Nested ON blocks are allowed, so long as the inner HOME clause indicates a subset of the processors in the outer clause. Again, the behavior is essentially that each level of ON directive masks out some processors. In the absence of data dependence constraints, the masked processors can occur to other computations. This provides a form of nested parallelism. As we will see in Section 5.2, it can also be used for pipelined parallelism.

Figure 4.4 illustrates this process. (The RESIDENT directives will be explained in Section 4.2.2.) These are typical loop structures for constructing unstructured finite element matrices or performing relaxations on unstructured grids. The ON directive in the DO I loop tells the compiler to statically schedule each iteration on the processor that owns the corresponding element of IX1. Processor P(1) will execute iterations 1, 5, 9, and so forth; processor P(4) will execute iterations that are divisible by 4. No matter what N is, the iterations will be approximately evenly balanced among processors. (If IX1 were distributed by BLOCK, the computation would not be balanced for N<1000.) This form of the HOME clause is appropriate for many loops over the elements of an array. The ON clause in the DO J loop tells the compiler to execute iteration J on the processor storing element Y(IX2(J)). Assuming a parallel implementation, load balance depends on the values in IX2. If they are evenly spread over the range from 1 to 500, then the load will be balanced; if they are concentrated in one processor's block (for example, if half of them fall in the range 1 to 100), then that processor will become a bottleneck. The advantage of such complex ON clauses typically comes from controlling data movement, as we will see in Section 4.2.2; this must be tempered by the cost of

```
REAL X(500), Y(500), Z(1000)
INTEGER IX(1000), IY(1000)
!HPF$ PROCESSORS P(4)
!HPF$ DISTRIBUTE X(BLOCK) ONTO P
!HPF$ DISTRIBUTE IX1(CYCLIC) ONTO P
!HPF$ ALIGN IX2(I) WITH IX1(I)
!HPF$ ALIGN Y(J) WITH X(J)
!HPF$ ALIGN Z(K) WITH IX1(K)

!HPF$ INDEPENDENT, LOCAL(TMP), REDUCTION(X)
DO I = 1, N
    !HPF$ ON HOME( IX1(I) ) BEGIN
      !HPF$ RESIDENT ( Y(IX1(I)) )
      TMP = Z(I) * (Y(IX1(I))-Y(IX2(I)))
      X(IX1(I)) = X(IX1(I)) + TMP
      X(IX2(I)) = X(IX2(I)) - TMP
    !HPF$ END ON
END DO

!HPF$ INDEPENDENT, LOCAL(TMP), REDUCTION(X)
DO J = 1, M
    !HPF$ ON HOME( Y(IX2(J)) ) BEGIN
      !HPF$ RESIDENT ( Y(IX1(J)) )
      TMP = Z(J) * (Y(IX1(J))-Y(IX2(J)))
      X(IX1(J)) = X(IX1(J)) + TMP
      X(IX2(J)) = X(IX2(J)) - TMP
    !HPF$ END ON
END DO
```

Fig. 4.4. Example of ON and RESIDENT directives

setting up the loop. In the J example, the runtime system will have to gather array IX2, examine the elements, and create a list for each processor of the iterations it is responsible for. This examination can be performed in parallel, with the results saved and reused if the loop is executed again with the same IX2 array; this strategy is called the inspector-executor paradigm [13, 20], and is used in production compilers. Still, this is a significant overhead, both in compilation technology and in runtime performance.

Note that if both the I and J loops are executed with the same data, the final values in the X array will be the same. This again illustrates that ON is a directive, and as such does not change the semantics of the code.

4.2.2 The RESIDENT Directive. In addition to load balancing, the ON directive can affect the data movement required by a program. Conceptually, if a computation on processor P requires data on processor Q, then the data must be communicated. The underlying hardware may have different ways of expressing this, from explicit messages to to simple shared memory loads, but it is communication at some level. Often the programmer knows that communication is not needed; if this information can be given to the compiler, significant optimizations are possible. This is the task of the RESIDENT directive, one of the HPF 2.0 approved extensions.

Like the ON directive, RESIDENT has a single statement and a multi-statement form. The syntax for the single-statement form is

!HPF$ RESIDENT [(variable-list)]

The multi-statement form uses BEGIN and END as the multi-statement ON does. RESIDENT can also be added as a clause of the ON directive.

Like the INDEPENDENT directive, RESIDENT is an assertion that, if true, will not change the results computed by the program. In this case, the assertion is that the variable references in the list reside on the currently active processor(s). Note that in order to make this assertion, one needs to know two things:

1. The location of the computation, which is set by the ON directive.
2. The location of the data, which is set by the ALIGN and DISTRIBUTE directives.

Therefore, RESIDENT can only be asserted when both data mapping and ON directives have been used. For variables that are assigned to, all copies of the variable must be on active processors; for variables that are only referenced, only some copies need be stored there. In either case, this indicates to the compiler that no communication needs to be generated for the variable. Finally, if the variable list is omitted, then RESIDENT is asserted for all data.

To illustrate the kinds of assertions possible with RESIDENT, we turn again to Figure 4.4 on page 32. In the DO I loop there, we have guaranteed that the computational load is evenly balanced. This does not, however, imply that there is no communication; in fact, the compiler will have to make some worst-case assumptions in this area. With no RESIDENT clause, the compiler can only assume that references to IX1(I), IX2(I), Z(I), and TMP are resident (because the first three are aligned together, and the last is a LOCAL variable). This leaves the compiler to generate communication for all references to X and Y. Although the volume of data depends on the contents of IX1 and IX2, one would generally expect a gather of Y before the loop and a combining scatter of X after the loop. With the RESIDENT directive as given, the compiler can additionally assume that Y(IX1(I)) and X(IX1(I)) are resident (because the first is declared so, and the second has an identical access pattern and data distribution). The system can therefore avoid generating communication for these references. While a gather and scatter are still required, they will have a simpler setup phase. In the DO J loop, without the RESIDENT directive the compiler could similarly detect that Y(IX1(J)), X(IX1(J)), and TMP are resident; communications would be generated for

Y(IX2(J)), X(IX2(J)), IX1(J), IX2(J), and Z(J). (Note that a reference being resident does not imply that all its subscripts are as well; for example, Y(IX1(J)) is resident but IX1(J) is not.) With the RESIDENT directive, the compiler can add Y(IX1(J)) and X(IX1(J)) to the list of resident references, and only generate communication for arrays IX1, IX2, and Z. In this case, not only is the setup simpler, but we completely avoid communication for two arrays. A programmer could avoid all communication in the J loop by using the simple directive

```
!HPF$ RESIDENT
```

in place of the line

```
!HPF$ RESIDENT ( Y(IX1(J)) )
```

This would imply that in all cases,

$$\frac{IX1(J)-1}{125} = \frac{IX2(J)-1}{125} = J-1 \bmod 4$$

The terms represent the processor homes of X(IX1(J)), X(IX2(J)), and IX1(J), respectively; due to the ALIGN directives, they also cover all other references in the loop.

5. Task Parallelism

Data parallelism is an important abstraction for many scientific applications, in part because vector notation and linear algebra are very common in mathematics and science. However, not every problem benefits from data parallelism. For example, the popular "task pool" style of parallelism, in which worker processes dynamically extract tasks from a central server, does not map well onto array syntax. Another example that we have already seen is nondeterministic algorithms such as chaotic relaxation or parallel alpha-beta searching. Finally, sometimes low-level control of communications mechanisms or other machine-specific operations is needed for efficiency. For all these reasons, HPF 2.0 provides interfaces to parallel programming models other than data parallelism. EXTRINSIC procedures are a feature of core HPF 2.0 that act as an "escape hatch" into task-parallel programming environments and possibly other languages. The TASK_REGION construct is an HPF 2.0 approved extension that integrates task and data parallelism without leaving the HPF language.

5.1 EXTRINSIC Procedures

The purpose of EXTRINSIC interfaces is to allow HPF programmers to take advantage of other programming paradigms when it is appropriate. This ability is often used to provide access to libraries written elsewhere, tune performance-critical parts of the program, and express non-data-parallel algorithms (including nondeterministic algorithms) on data mapped by HPF directives. The basic concept is that the EXTRINSIC procedure itself is written in another language, such as Fortran with message-passing extensions. HPF defines the interaction with this language at the interface, allowing the HPF compiler to be sure of its assumptions and giving the other language the information that it needs about data layout. Because the needs of other languages are diverse, EXTRINSIC is actually a family of interfaces, essentially one per language.

Syntactically, the EXTRINSIC interface is a new prefix to the FUNCTION or SUBROUTINE header. The syntax of the new prefix clause is

EXTRINSIC (*extrinsic-kind-keyword*)
OR
EXTRINSIC (extrinsic-spec-arg-list)

HPF 2.0 defines three *extrinsic-kind-keywords*: HPF, HPF_LOCAL, and HPF_-SERIAL; several more are defined as approved extensions, including FORTRAN 77 and C language bindings. We will describe HPF_LOCAL in more detail below; its definition is typical of other EXTRINSIC types. EXTRINSIC(HPF) is simply HPF; it was defined to reserve the name if EXTRINSIC was adopted by other Fortran dialects. HPF_SERIAL procedures execute on one and only one processor; they are designed for interfacing to graphics and other libraries that cannot be called in parallel. The *extrinsic-spec-arg* form allows modular definition of new extrinsic types as a combination of LANGUAGE=, MODEL=, and EXTERNAL_NAME= specifications. For example, HPF_LOCAL is formally defined as (LANGUAGE='HPF', MODEL='LOCAL').

Semantically, EXTRINSIC(HPF_LOCAL) is a contract between the main HPF program and the HPF_LOCAL function. The EXTRINSIC(HPF_LOCAL) contract states that the HPF main program will

1. Have an explicit interface with the EXTRINSIC directive
2. Remap data (if needed) to meet distribution specifications in that interface
3. Synchronize all active processors before the call
4. Call the local routine on every active processor

The first three guarantees are common to all forms of EXTRINSIC; they assure that the data and computation are in a consistent state before the procedure begins execution. The final guarantee is the key part of any EXTRINSIC(MODEL='LOCAL', ...) interface; it starts the procedure on every processor in a single-program multiple-data mode. Before returning, however, the EXTRINSIC(HPF_LOCAL) contract requires that the procedure will

1. Obey INTENT(IN) and INTENT(OUT) declarations
2. Ensure that if variables are replicated, they will again be consistent before return

3. Only access data that could be accessed by an HPF program with the same interface
4. Synchronize the active processors before returning control to HPF
5. Declare all dummy arguments to be of assumed shape

The first four constraints are common to all EXTRINSIC models; they ensure that data is consistent when HPF returns. In particular, the HPF_LOCAL procedure cannot leave processes running that may corrupt HPF data asynchronously with the main program. The constraint on using assumed-shape arguments is peculiar to EXTRINSIC(LANGUAGE='HPF', ...) procedures; it supports HPF inquiry functions in the HPF_LOCAL procedure.

The HPF_LOCAL procedure itself is a task-parallel program. Every processor executes its own copy of the procedure, and can have processor-local state such as the processor id. Note that global HPF does not have variables local to a processor. The closest concept is the LOCAL clause of the INDEPENDENT directive, which cannot save data after the iteration is complete. The reason for this is simple—processor-local data can destroy the single-threaded execution model of HPF. Within the HPF_LOCAL model, however, this is not a problem. Although the processors are initially executing as SPMD processes, the procedure can change to loosely synchronous or fully asynchronous mode, in any way that the hardware and HPF_LOCAL compiler permit. Mapped arrays can be passed as arguments, but within the the HPF_LOCAL procedure they appear as ordinary arrays consisting of only the data mapped to the local processor. In other words, reference A(1) inside an HPF_LOCAL routine refers to the first element stored on the local processor, while in a global HPF program A(1) refers to the first element of the global array, no matter which processor stores it. The HPF_LOCAL_LIBRARY module provides utility functions to translate between these views of the data. The HPF_LOCAL model itself does not provide synchronization or communication primitives, but it is compatible with such standard interfaces as the Message Passing Interface (MPI).

Figure 5.1 demonstrates some features of EXTRINSIC(HPF_LOCAL). The top section of the figure is a standard HPF program that descriptively passes two mapped arrays to subroutine F. The bottom shows an HPF_LOCAL subroutine which performs an iterative operation on each processor. Since the subroutine has no internal synchronization, each processor runs completely independently of the others; different processors may well perform different numbers of DO WHILE iterations. Also, the CSHIFT and MAXVAL intrinsics in F only operate on local data, rather than communicating data from other processors. HPF_LOCAL subroutines are excellent vehicles for performing such per-processor operations.

```
REAL a(0:n,0:n), b(0:n,0:n)
!HPF$ DISTRIBUTE a(BLOCK,*)
!HPF$ ALIGN b(:,:) WITH u(:,:)

INTERFACE
  EXTRINSIC(HPF_LOCAL) SUBROUTINE F( X, Y )
     REAL, INTENT(IN) :: X(:,:)
     REAL, INTENT(OUT) :: Y(:,:)
     !HPF$ DISTRIBUTE X *(BLOCK,*)
     !HPF$ ALIGN Y(:,:) WITH *X(:,:)
END INTERFACE

CALL F( A, B )
```

```
EXTRINSIC(HPF_LOCAL) SUBROUTINE F( X, Y )
  REAL, INTENT(IN) :: X(:,:)
  REAL, INTENT(OUT) :: Y(:,:)
  REAL ERR; INTEGER M1, M2

  M1=SIZE(X,1); M2=SIZE(X,2)
  DO WHILE (ERR > 1E-6)
    Y = (CSHIFT(X,1,1)+CSHIFT(X,1,2)+X) / 3
    ERR = MAXVAL(ABS(X-Y))
    X = Y
  END DO
END
```

Fig. 5.1. Example of HPF_LOCAL

5.2 The TASK_REGION Directive

The EXTRINSIC mechanism is very good for interfacing to other programming paradigms. However, to use it a programmer must leave the HPF environment, if only temporarily. Some users requested extensions to HPF that would allow task-parallel programming within the language itself. After exploring several possibilities, including HPF bindings for MPI and PCF, the HPFF designed the TASK_REGION directive to provide abstract, large-grain tasks where each task might itself be data-parallel. This model is very similar to the FX language developed at Carnegie Mellon University [21]. TASK_REGION is an approved extension of HPF 2.0.

The syntax of a TASK_REGION is

```
!HPF$ TASK_REGION
block
!HPF$ END TASK_REGION
```

The code block itself consists of ON blocks and statements not guarded by an ON directive. As we will see below, each ON block acts as a task; statements not in any ON block act as synchronization. Any outer-level ON directive must have the RESIDENT option without a variable list. This ensures that processors in the task will need only synchronize and communicate with other processors at the beginning and end of the ON block.

As a directive, TASK_REGION does not change the computed results of the program, but may affect execution efficiency. Formally, the directive is an assertion that ON blocks whose active processor sets do not overlap do not interfere with each other. The same definition of interference is used as for INDEPENDENT, including the restrictions on input/output. Because of these restrictions, the TASK_REGION can be executed by synchronizing only the processors that will take part in an ON block at the block's beginning and end. Processors not selected by the HOME clause can continue on to the next statement. Statements outside of any ON block require synchronization of all processors that store mapped data used by the statement; scalar variables can be replicated on all processors and updated in replicated fashion. In effect, each processor executes a reduced TASK_REGION that leaves out ON blocks where it does not participate. An HPF program without the TASK_REGION directive could not eliminate the "extra" ON blocks because they might require synchronization.

This is perhaps easier to understand as an example. Consider Figure 5.2. This program creates a two-task pipeline for performing a series of 2-D FFTs. The first task reads data into array A1 and performs an FFT on each row. The data is then copied to array A2. Task 2 performs the column FFTs and outputs the results to a separate file. Because the two arrays are mapped to different processor sets, each execution of task 2 can be overlapped with the following execution of task 1. The array copy between the two is the sole required synchronization; updating of the DO index can be performed redundantly on all processors. This organization of the program has several advantages over other possibilities:

– Both arrays could be distributed on all processors. However, this decreases the granularity of computation on each processor; depending on the synchronization costs of a particular machine, this may lead to a significant increase in parallel overhead.
– One mapped array could be used. This would require either remapping by one of the CALL statements, or porting one of the routines to reflect a different distribution; either way, it would be impossible to overlap the input and output, since the same array would be needed for both.

For a fuller discussion of the merits of the task-parallel approach, one can examine the work on the FX [21].

```
!HPF$ PROCESSORS P(8)
!HPF$ DISTRIBUTE A1(BLOCK,*) ONTO P(1:4)
!HPF$ DISTRIBUTE A2(*,BLOCK) ONTO P(5:8)
!HPF$ DISTRIBUTE TD1(BLOCK) ONTO P(1:4)

!HPF$ TASK_REGION
  DO K = 1, N

     ! Task 1
     !HPF$ ON HOME(A1) BEGIN, RESIDENT
       READ (IUNIT1) A1
       CALL ROWFFTS(A1)
     !HPF$    END ON

     A2 = A1

     ! Task 2
     !HPF$ ON HOME(A2) BEGIN, RESIDENT
       CALL COLFFTS(A2)
       WRITE(IUNIT2) A2
     !HPF$ END ON

  ENDDO
!HPF$ END TASK_REGION
```

Fig. 5.2. Example of the TASK_REGION construct

6. Input and Output

One of the most difficult aspects of parallel computation is input and output
of the data. Because the high speeds and large memory capacities of parallel
machines allow huge problems to be solved, it is not surprising that input and
output requirements of parallel programs are also high. Addressing these requirements must be done at all levels of the machine, from hardware through
systems to the applications running there; as one layer of the system, this indicates that HPF needs some I/O capability. In view of this, the HPFF tried
in both the discussions leading to HPF 1 and HPF 2.0 to define constructs for
parallel I/O. Unfortunately, parallel I/O architectures are still very dissimi-
lar from machine to machine, and widely-accepted unifying abstractions at
a level comparable to HPF's data parallelism have yet to emerge. It is therefore unsurprising that HPF's support for parallel input and output is not as
extensive as other parts of the language. However, HPF 2.0's approved extensions do include support for asynchronous I/O, which is a significant step

forward. It should be noted that the Fortran 2000 committee is also working on a proposal for asynchronous I/O; theirs is somewhat more general, but compatible in concept with HPF. It should also be noted that Fortran has an extensive set of I/O operations, and that HPF inherits all of these. In particular, it is legal in Fortran to read or write an entire array to a file in one statement. In an HPF context, that array could well be distributed; this provides many opportunities for high-quality compilers and runtime systems to exploit any underlying parallel I/O capabilities.

Syntactically, asynchronous I/O use new options in the OPEN statement's connection specification, new specifications in the I/O control lists, and a new WAIT statement. In the OPEN statement, a file which will be read or written asynchronously must have the ASYNCHRONOUS connect specification after the usual UNIT= and FILE= specifications. Asynchronous I/O statements are identified by the presence of the new ASYNCHRONOUS and ID= control specifications. A READ or WRITE statement with these options begins an asynchronous operation and sets the ID= variable to a unique value. This value will be used later to identify the asynchronous operation in progress. Multiple outstanding asynchronous I/O operations per file are allowed if they do not reference the same record of the file. The program may not reference any variable in the I/O list of an asynchronous I/O operation until the operation has been completed by a WAIT statement. The syntax for the WAIT statement is

WAIT (UNIT= *io-unit*, ID= *int-expr* [, ERR= *label*], [, IOSTAT= *label*])

The keyword arguments may appear in any order. When executed, the WAIT statement halts program execution until the asynchronous operation identified by the ID expression completes. The ERR= and

Figure 6.1 shows how these operations can be used to create a two-stage pipeline. The pipeline is started by opening THEINPUT for asynchronous read-

```
      OPEN( IUNIT, FILE='THEINPUT', ASYNCHRONOUS )
      READ( IUNIT, ID=ID0, END=100) A
      DO
          WAIT (ID=ID0 )                    ! Wait for A
          READ (IUNIT, ID=ID1, END=100) B   ! Start B
          CALL PROCESSING( A ) ! Overlap I/O with compute

          WAIT (ID=ID1 )                    ! Wait for B
          READ (IUNIT, ID=ID0, END=100) A   ! Start A
          CALL PROCESSING( B ) ! Overlap I/O with compute
      END DO
100 CONTINUE
```

Fig. 6.1. Example of asynchronous I/O

ing and beginning the transfer of the first block of data into A. From then on, execution alternates between overlapping the reading of B and the processing of A in the first part of the loop and overlapping the reading of A and the processing of B in the second part of the loop. If the time for subroutine PROCESSING is roughly the same as for reading a block of data, the computer is always both computing and performing I/O. If the processing time is much less than the I/O time, additional buffers could be added to achieve more overlap. PROCESSING cannot access either A or B as global data, or it will violate the constraint against referencing data involved in an outstanding asynchronous operation.

7. Summary and Future Outlook

As HPF 2.0 makes its appearance, it is appropriate to examine HPF's successes, shortcomings, and plans for the future.

HPF compilers are now available for all parallel machines of wide interest. Some hardware vendors, including IBM and Digital, have developed their own compilers. Other software vendors, including Portland Group and Applied Parallel Research, sell systems that produce portable code by outputting message-passing Fortran. User experience with the language is growing. A number of interesting HPF applications were reported at the first HPF Users Group in February 1997 (the proceedings are available on the World-Wide Web at http://www.lanl.gov/HPF/index.html and http://www.crpc.rice.edu/HPFF/home.html). It is fair to say that HPF is now recognized as an efficient language for a number of problems, particularly those defined on regular grids.

However, HPF is not without its problems. The early implementations were often inefficient or did not work at all; many users of those systems developed a poor opinion of the language which will be difficult to reverse. The language itself provides relatively limited features for some important operations, such as irregular meshes, parallel I/O and task parallelism. Although HPF 2.0 improves the support in all these areas, it will be some time before implementations will appear and even longer before we will know if the new support is sufficient.

Meanwhile, MPI has many staunch backers as an alternate programming paradigm for parallel machines. We feel that HPF and MPI complement each other rather than compete; each system has advantages and drawbacks for particular problems. Recognizing this, the HPF Forum designed the language to permit convenient interoperability with message passing environments through the EXTRINSIC interface mechanism.

Finally, user feedback at the HPF Users Group meeting and other forums has pointed out two major limitations in current HPF support: efficient parallel libraries and usable tools for debugging and performance analysis. Our own research at Rice is directed at these areas, as are several other commercial and academic projects worldwide.

There are no current plans for new additions to HPF, although mailing lists exist to resolve technical questions and disseminate HPF news. We expect the HPF Users Group meetings to be held annually as long as there is interest in the language. Judging from the first meeting, these will inspire a good deal of discussion which will lead to improvements in the language implementations, better use of the language, and (probably) more language extensions. We look forward to exciting times as the compilers improve and as programmers become more adept at exploiting them.

References

1. ANSI X3J3/S8.115. Fortran 90, June 1990.
2. D. Callahan and K. Kennedy. Compiling programs for distributed-memory multiprocessors. *Journal of Supercomputing*, 2(2):151–169, October 1988.
3. B. Chapman, P. Mehrotra, and H. Zima. Programming in Vienna Fortran. *Scientific Programming*, 1(1):31–50, Fall 1992.
4. A. Choudhary, G. Fox, S. Hiranandani, K. Kennedy, C. Koelbel, S. Ranka, and C.-W. Tseng. Unified compilation of Fortran 77D and 90D. *ACM Letters on Programming Languages and Systems*, 2(1–4):95–114, March–December 1993.
5. G. Fox. Parallel problem architectures and their implications for portable parallel software systems. CRPC Report CRPC-TR91120, Center for Research on Parallel Computation, Syracuse University, February 1991.
6. G. Fox, M. Johnson, G. Lyzenga, S. Otto, J. Salmon, and D. Walker. *Solving Problems on Concurrent Processors*, volume 1. Prentice-Hall, Englewood Cliffs, NJ, 1988.
7. M. Gerndt and H. Zima. SUPERB: Experiences and future research. In J. Saltz and P. Mehrotra, editors, *Languages, Compilers, and Run-Time Environments for Distributed Memory Machines*. North-Holland, Amsterdam, The Netherlands, 1992.
8. P. Hatcher and M. Quinn. *Data-parallel Programming on MIMD Computers*. The MIT Press, Cambridge, MA, 1991.
9. High Performance Fortran Forum. High Performance Fortran language specification. *Scientific Programming*, 2(1-2):1–170, 1993.
10. High Performance Fortran Forum. HPF-2 scope of work and motivating applications. Technical Report CRPC-TR 94492, Center for Research on Parallel Computation, Rice University, Houston, TX, November 1994.
11. High Performance Fortran Forum. High Performance Fortran language specification, version 2.0. Technical Report CRPC-TR92225, Center for Research on Parallel Computation, Rice University, Houston, TX, January 1997.
12. K. Knobe, J. Lukas, and M. Weiss. Optimization techniques for SIMD Fortran compilers. *Concurrency: Practice and Experience*, 5(7):527–552, October 1993.
13. C. Koelbel. *Compiling Programs for Nonshared Memory Machines*. PhD thesis, Dept. of Computer Science, Purdue University, Lafayette, IN, August 1990.
14. C. Koelbel, D. Loveman, R. Schreiber, G. Steele, Jr., and M. Zosel. *The High Performance Fortran Handbook*. The MIT Press, Cambridge, MA, 1994.

15. C. Koelbel and P. Mehrotra. Compiling global name-space parallel loops for distributed execution. *IEEE Transactions on Parallel and Distributed Systems*, 2(4):440–451, October 1991.

16. J. Li and M. Chen. Compiling communication-efficient programs for massively parallel machines. *IEEE Transactions on Parallel and Distributed Systems*, 2(3):361–376, July 1991.

17. J. Ramanujam and P. Sadayappan. Compile-time techniques for data distribution in distributed memory machines. *IEEE Transactions on Parallel and Distributed Systems*, 2(4):472–482, October 1991.

18. A. Rogers and K. Pingali. Compiling for distributed memory architectures. *IEEE Transactions on Parallel and Distributed Systems*, 5(3):281–298, March 1994.

19. G. Sabot. Optimizing CM Fortran compiler for Connection Machine computers. *Journal of Parallel and Distributed Computing*, 23(1):224–238, November 1994.

20. J. Saltz, K. Crowley, R. Mirchandaney, and H. Berryman. Run-time scheduling and execution of loops on message passing machines. *Journal of Parallel and Distributed Computing*, 8(4):303–312, April 1990.

21. J. Subhlok, J. Stichnoth, D. O'Hallaron, and T. Gross. Exploiting task and data parallelism on a multicomputer. In *Proceedings of the Fourth ACM SIGPLAN Symposium on Principles and Practice of Parallel Programming*, San Diego, CA, May 1993.

Chapter 2. The Sisal Project: Real World Functional Programming

Jean-Luc Gaudiot[1], Tom DeBoni[2], John Feo[3], Wim Böhm[4], Walid Najjar[4], and Patrick Miller[5]

[1] University of Southern California,
Department of Electrical Engineering - Systems, Los Angeles, California
gaudiot@usc.edu
[2] Lawrence Livermore National Laboratory, Computer Research Group
Livermore, California
deboni@llnl.gov
[3] Tera Computers Inc., 411 First Avenue S, Suite 600
Seattle, WA 98104-2860
feo@tera.com
[4] Colorado State University, Computer Science Department
Fort Collins, Colorado
{bohm,najjar}@cs.colostate.edu
[5] CaeSoft Development, Tracy, California
patmiller@sisal.com

Summary. Programming massively-parallel machine is a daunting task for any human programmer and parallelization may even be impossible for any compiler. Instead, the functional programming paradigm may prove to be an ideal solution by providing an implicitly parallel interface to the programmer. We describe here the Sisal project (Stream and Iteration in a Single Assignment Language) and its goal to provide a general-purpose user interface for a wide range of parallel processing platforms.

1. Introduction

The history of computing has shown shifts from explicit to implicit programming. In the early days, computers were programmed in assembly language, mostly with the purpose of utilizing the available memory space as effectively as possible. This came at the cost of obscure, machine-dependent, hard to maintain programs, which were designed with high programming effort. Fortran was introduced to make programming more implicit, portable and less machine-dependent. With the advent of massively parallel computers and their promise of hundreds of gigaflops, we have seen a return to the explicit programming paradigm. Using for example C with explicit message passing library routines as "machine language," people attempt to utilize the available processing power to the largest extent, again at the cost of high programming effort, machine-dependent, and hard to maintain code. A compiler for an implicitly parallel programming language alleviates the programmer from the task of partitioning program and data over the massively parallel machine.

S. Pande, D.P. Agrawal (Eds.): Compiler Optimizations for Scalable PS, LNCS 1808, pp. 45-72, 2001.
© Springer-Verlag Berlin Heidelberg 2001

It is our view that explicit parallel programming is a transition stage in the evolution of parallel computing and that implicit parallel programming languages will eventually become the norm as did high-level languages in the sequential paradigm. This will result in a tremendous improvement in *programming quality* in terms of programming effort, readability, portability, extendability and maintainability of parallel code. Another consequence will be the accessibility of parallel programming to a wider public that would make use of a wide spectrum of parallel computers: from a few processors on a chip to several thousand processor-machines.

Functional programming [6] is an alternate programming paradigm which is entirely different from the conventional model: a functional program can be recursively defined as a composition of functions where each function can itself be another composition of functions or a primitive operator (such as arithmetic operators, etc.). The programmer need not be concerned with explicit specification of parallel processes since independent functions are activated by the predecessor functions and the data dependencies of the program. This also means that control can be distributed. Further, no central memory system is inherent to the model since data is not "written in" by any instruction but is "'passed' from" one function to the next.

Sisal (Stream and Iteration in a Single Assignment Language) [22] is such a functional language which was originally designed by collaborating teams from the Lawrence Livermore National Laboratory, Colorado State University, the University of Manchester and Digital Equipment Corporation. The goal of the project was to design a general-purpose implicitly parallel language for a wide range of parallel platforms.

The goal of this paper is to describe the last phases of this project as we are currently undertaking them. In section 2, a short tutorial will present the basic principles of Sisal. An early compiler implementation for shared memory systems is described in section 3. Sisal 90 and its foreign language interface is introduced in section 4. We turn our attention to Distributed Memory implementations in section 5, while section 6 introduces implementation of multithreading principles. Section 7 concludes.

2. The Sisal Language: A Short Tutorial

Sisal is a functional language that offers automatic exploitation and management of parallelism as a result of its functional semantics. In Sisal, and all functional languages, user-defined names are "identifiers" rather than variables, and they refer to values rather than memory locations. The values produced and used in a Sisal program are all dynamic entities, and their identifiers are defined, or bound to them, only for the duration of their existence in an execution. This is the dynamic of the data flow graph, in which graph nodes are operations, and values are carried on the arcs connecting the nodes. The extent of the existence of a value is the set of arcs on which it travels between the point of its definition and the point of its final consumption. The values that are defined by the graph arcs may or may not have names assigned to them within a program.

All Sisal expressions and higher-level syntactic elements evaluate to and return values based solely on the values bound to their formal arguments and constituent identifiers. This eliminates any possibility of side effects, and allows much richer analyses of program by the compiler than is typically the case for imperative languages.

To best illustrate these points, consider the following brief code fragment. It is written in Sisal 1.2, the language currently accepted by the Optimizing Sisal Compiler. The Sisal language is undergoing expansion and refinement, as discussed in other sections, but the syntax of version 1.2 will suffice for this example.

```
type OneDim = array [ real ];
type TwoDim = array [ OneDim ];

function generate( n : integer returns TwoDim, TwoDim )
   for i in 1, n cross j in 1, n
         t1 := real(i) * real(j);
         t2 := real(i) / real(j)
   returns array of t1
            array of t2
   end for
end function % generate
```

The first two statements define type names for arrays. Note that no sizes are provided; all Sisal aggregate data instances are dynamically created, resized, and de-allocated at runtime. Only the dimensionality and element types are relevant to the type specifications. The header for function "generate" shows that one integer argument, "n", is expected, and two unnamed values will be returned. The returned values are two dimensional arrays of single precision reals, but again, only typing and not sizing is specified. Names can be bound to these returned values at the site of invocation of function generate if the programmer wishes. An invocation of a function is semantically equivalent to the reproduction of the function code at that site, with appropriate argument substitution. This equivalence, called "referential transparency" is a fundamental property of functional languages, and is responsible for the strengths of the Sisal language. This strength lies in a simplified analysis process for the compiler. Functions can run in parallel if no data dependency exists between the functions. Functions with equivalent inputs will **always** return equivalent values.

All Sisal expressions, including whole functions and programs, evaluate to value sets. In the above case, the function evaluates to two arrays, which are the values of the expression contained in the function definition. The for-expression shown is a loop construct, which is an indicator of potential parallelism to the Sisal compiler. This loop has an index range defined as the cross product of two simpler ranges. This means that the body of the loop will be instantiated as many times as there are values in the index range, in this case n*n, and each body instantiation will be independent, since no data dependencies exist among them. The set of independent loop bodies can be executed in parallel or not, based on the compiler's and the runtime system's analyses of their costs, as well as on options specified by the programmer.

The appearance of the names "t1" and "t2" within the body of the loop should not be considered a reuse of these names in the sense of the reassignment of a variable in an imperative program. Instead, the names are used to define the computation in the loop body, and in fact these names will likely have no real existence within the executing program. The important point here is that each instance of the loop body, containing specific values for i and j, will independently compute specific instances of the values defined as real(i)*real(j) and real(i)/real(j); then all these separate values will be gathered together into a pair of arrays and returned. The positions of the values in the result arrays are determined by the loop's index ranges, as are the overall size and dimensionality of the returned arrays. In this case, two two-dimensional arrays are returned, with index ranges from 1 to n in each dimension. The use of loop-temporary names is optional, and the return-clause above could be rewritten as:

```
returns array of real(i)*real(j)
        array of real(i)/real(j)
```

with no change in the ultimate results. The loop body, then, would appear to be empty, but in fact, the language treats the expressions in the array-of clause as anonymous temporaries.

Further syntactic elements of the Sisal language include let-in statements, which allow for name definition and use; if-statements, which allow conditional name definition; record and union types, which allow for flexible data aggregation; streams, which allow for producer-consumer computations; and sequential loops, which allow true iteration, with specified data dependencies existing between iterations. I/O in Sisal is performed by passing inputs as arguments to, and receiving outputs as the results of, the outermost function. The values used for inputs and returned as outputs obey a syntax called "Fibre", which allows the demarcation of dynamically sized aggregates.

The Optimizing Sisal Compiler translates source programs into executable memory images, including the runtime system components required to automatically manage memory, tasking, and I/O. The amount of parallelism to be exploited by a program can be controlled by user options, and once compiled, a program can be executed by any number of worker processes, by way of a single runtime parameter. Similarly, compiler optimization behavior and runtime performance can be observed and controlled by options applied at various points during compilation and execution.

3. An Early Implementation: The Optimizing Sisal Compiler

Early implementations of the Sisal language were basic proofs of concept. Various interpreters have been implemented, like DI [36], TWINE [23], and SSI [24] but for greatest execution speeds, a compiled code was needed. Sisal was ported to novel architectures like the Manchester Dataflow Machine [7], but complete acceptance for the language required porting to newly emerging shared memory parallel machines then coming to market (HEP [1], Encore, Sequent [27], Cray).

3.1 Update in Place and Copy Elimination

Several key obstacles emerged. The first of these came from Sisal's semantic concept of making "copies" to preserve single assignment and referential transparency. A fragment like

```
let
  A := array[1: 1,2,3];
  B := A[2 : 999];
in
  A,B
end let
```

returned [1: 1,2,3], [1: 1,999,3]. The original value of A had to be preserved, so a copy was made to enable the replacement.

Consider instead swapping two elements of an array. In Sisal, one would write something like:

```
C   := array[1: 1,2,3,4,5];
% Read as E is identical to C
% Except index 3 has C[4] in it
% Index 4 has C[3] in it
E   := C[3: C[4]; 4: C[3] ];
```

The *semantics* (not the implementation) of Sisal calls for making a copy of the array to make the first replacement, and making another copy for the second replacement. A FORTRAN programmer would never do this, instead they would write:

```
ITEMP = IARRAY[3]
IARRAY[3] = IARRAY[4]
IARRAY[4] = ITEMP
```

This program has no (array) copies and is done in place. Similarly, many 'in-place' algorithms that are efficient in space and time have been designed in imperative languages that would run poorly if all data structures had to be copied. Clearly there was room for improvement [38]. Consider the original Sisal swap broken down into individual steps:

```
C   := array[1: 1,2,3,4,5];
T0  := C[3];
T1  := C[4];
D   := C[3: T1];
E   := D[4: T0];
```

When the array replacement is done on line 3, the value in "C" is dead. When the replacement is done, the C value can be thrown away. Instead of making a copy for D and throwing C away, we can safely use C's container instead. Similarly, the second replacement on line 4 is the last use of D, so E can use D's container. This analysis is simplified because of the functional semantics of Sisal. The Optimizing Sisal Compiler (OSC) makes heavy use of "update-in-place" and copy elimination analysis to eliminate many unnecessary copies [9]. In its simplest sense, update-in-place migrates reader operations before writers. Here, the C[3] and C[4] readers were moved before the replacement operations in order to maximize the chances that C would be a "dead" value for the update.

3.2 Build in Place

Other important optimizations had to be developed [30]. For instance, many functional programs work on pieces of a large structure and then "Glue" the computed fragments together. For instance:

```
L := F(0,A[1],A[2]);
R := F(A[N-1],A[N],0);
III := for i in 2,n-1 ...
LIII := array_addl(III,L);
LIIIR := array_addh(LIII,R);
```

Semantically, this says: 1) Build piece L, 2) Build piece R, 3) Build size n-2 array III, 4) Allocate T1, a size n-1 array, 5) Copy L and III into T1, 5) Allocate LIIIR, a size n array, 6) Copy LIII and R into LIIIR This seems to require two allocations and a two large data copies. OSC introduced the idea of "BUFFERS" and persistent memory to the BACKEND of the compiler – leaving the frontend unchanged. Using a buffer system, the same operation proceeds as follows:

```
Build Buffer LIIIR of size n
Compute L and put in LIIIR[1]
Compute R and put in LIIIR[n]
Compute III in LIIIR[2]...LIIIR[n-1]
```

This trick can be played even if the left and right pieces are loops. The beauty of this "Build-in-place" system is that memory can be preallocated and parallel computations can simply stick values where they belong – even if the original computation parts were from distant parts of the computations.

3.3 Reference Counting Optimization

We have seen that we can take advantage of an object ending its life just as we would otherwise need to copy. Reference counts were introduced to help know when: 1) a value can be updated in place and when 2) a value's memory can be recycled. Reference counting can be a very expensive operation on sequential machines – on parallel machines it is much worse!!! Parallel reference counts must be updated in a critical section. This operation keeps banging on locks every few operations, swamping the machine. Luckily, programs tend to have simple patterns of use for aggregate values and OSC can cleverly eliminate [35] nearly all reference counting in a program through lifetime analysis and operation merging.

3.4 Vectorization

On vector machines all the speed advantages come from routing array operations through temporary vector registers. OSC has fine control of loop placement so that reader/writer chains can be established. In imperative languages, this generally requires very careful writing of loops in order to clearly establish vector relationships between loops. The semantics of Sisal's underlying dataflow representation make loops easy to move and so OSC can vectorize extremely well [11].

3.5 Loop Fusion, Double Buffering Pointer Swap, and Inversion

On scalar and scalar/parallel machines, loop overhead and memory fetch time tends to dominate computations. OSC can accommodate these machines by applying aggressive loop fusion. Fusion can rewrite loop code like

```
T0 := for i in 1,n returns
         array of A[i]*2
      end for;

T1 := for i in 1,n returns
         array of B[i]*3
      end for;

X  := for i in 1,n returns
         array of T0[i] + T1[i]
      end for;
```

into

```
X := for i in 1,n returns
        array of A[i]*2 + B[i]*3
     end for;
```

eliminating the generation of two temporary arrays and setting values that can stream into internal registers from the cache. FORTRAN90 has similar semantics for its array operations: X = A*2 + B*3. Sisal's OSC compiler can implement this more efficiently than a FORTRAN90 compiler because FORTRAN must know absolutely that neither A nor B is aliased to X. Sisal's functional semantics insure that a left-hand-side of a definition is **never** an alias for a right-hand-side.

A typical scientific computation proceeds as follows:

```
for initial
   A := start_values()
while not done(A) repeat
   A := time_step(old A)
   . . .
```

Here, a new version of A the same size is generated at each time step. A naive implementation of Sisal would allocate a new buffer for each time step and throw away the old even though it was the right size. OSC notices this and initially allocates a buffer outside the loop and pointer swaps the original and secondary buffers.

Consider a 1D smoothing function that averages values using a three point stencil – $X[i] = (A[i-1] + A[i] + A[i+1])/3.0$ At the endpoints a two point stencil is used instead. This is most easily expressed as:

```
X :=  for i in 1,n
        v := if i = 1 then (A[1]+A[2])/2.0
             elseif i = n then (A[n-1]+A[n])/2.0
             else (A[i-1] + A[i] + A[i+1])/3.0
             end if
      returns array of v
      end for
```

The if-tests appear to introduce a large overhead and to inhibit parallelism, vectorization and pipelining. The loop can be specialized doing the boundary computations separate from the inner computations. The inner computation is simple:

```
inner := for i in 2,n-1 returns
           array of (A[i-1]+A[i]+A[i+1])/3.0
         end for
```

Now we just need to glue on the lower bound computation and the upper bound computation. We need to be careful to handle zero trip loops here! This is done by producing an *array* of for the boundary values. In zero trip case, an empty array is generated. In all other cases, an array of size 1 is generated.

```
leftbound := for i in 1,min(1,n) returns
                array of (A[i]+A[i+1])/2.0
             end for;

rghtbound := for i in max(2,n),n returns
                array of (A[i-1]+A[i])/2.0
             end for;

     X := leftBound || inner || rghtBound;
```

The max/min function calls make sure the zero trip cases are handled gracefully. The final catenation puts the results in the correct form. The catenations will actually be removed by build-in-place optimizations later in the optimization process.

4. Sisal90

The original Sisal definition has been extended and modernized. The new language includes language level support for complex values, array and vector operations, static polymorphism and type-sets, higher order functions, user-defined reductions, rectangular arrays, and an explicit interface to other languages like FORTRAN and C. See [14] for a detailed description of Sisal90 and a comparison with Sisal 1.2.

An important objective was to enhance the language definition while maintaining compatibility with the Sisal 1.2 definition. We could not delay our application work waiting for the new definition and compilers, nor disenfranchise the extant Sisal community. Additionally, enhancement rather than overhaul implies fewer changes to the backend and permits us to reuse existing software. The desired new features prompted a full rewrite of the parser and a complete rethinking of how the low-level operations had to be specified.

A second objective was to increase Sisal's appeal to scientific programmers. To this end, we adopted Fortran 90 array operations where possible, improved support for mixed-language programming, and included features, perhaps not consistent with a strict interpretation of functional dogma, that simplify the programmer's task. We do not believe that functional languages can survive on their own; however, they can play a critical support role. Most of the code in a large scientific application pertains to problem specification, termination, I/O, and fault handling. These sections are not functional and not parallel; write them in your favourite imperative programming language. However, often the computational kernel is parallel and functional. Here Sisal can play a crucial role, as it can reduce development costs, insure determinacy, and improve portability without sacrificing performance. We perceive a gradual merging of the functional and imperative programming communities where functional constructs form either a set of language extensions or an integrated core. We hope that the Sisal 90 definition will accelerate this process.

4.1 The Foreign Language Interface

Parallel programming traditionally involves the management of concurrent tasks and machine resources in addition to the specification of the computation, greatly increasing the programmer's burden. Most parallel programs are not written for parallel execution from the outset. More often, they begin as existing sequential programs, written in an imperative language, and are augmented with parallel constructs from a vendor-specific enhanced imperative language. The programmer who is assigned the task of parallelizing such a code must preserve the semantics of the program; the parallel code must execute efficiently on the parallel machine of choice and must exhibit some scalability; the code should port easily to other parallel machines, in particular new generations of the target machine, and development costs should be kept as low as possible. As these goals are contradictory, there may be no best solution. Since minimizing programming costs is an important objective, the programmer usually identifies the most computationally intensive parts of the code, and parallelizes only the parts that will provide the most gain from parallel execution. By considering only these parallelizable sections, the imperative programmer maximizes performance and minimizes development costs. The Sisal language supports mixed language programming through its Foreign Language Interface (FLI). The FLI allows Sisal programs to call or be called from Fortran or C, and to invoke existing libraries or solvers. This allows relatively easy recoding of the computational kernels of an existing code for parallelism.

The use of the Sisal FLI involves four steps. First, the appropriate level of parallelism, and the portion of the original code that contains it must be identified. The size of computational grains to be parallelized and the amount of communication they will do must be considered. There may be one identifiable code region which is appropriate for parallelization, or there may be many several, separated by sequential portions of the code. Second, the data that must be communicated into and out of Sisal must be identified. This is important, since Sisal's functional semantics require a strict separation of inputs and outputs. The mere determination of the input and output data may be nontrivial, since the imperative language may hide the data in global variables, common blocks, and aliased variables, and their use as input, output, or both, may be difficult to discern or may be situation dependent. The third step is usually easy, once the first two have been achieved; it is the translation of imperative source code into Sisal. While no automatic machanisms have been developed to do this, due to its dependency on human intelligence and information gleaned from the first two steps, it is can usually be accompished by a straightforward set of edits. The fourth step deals with the data movement between Sisal and the imperative language, and the initiation and termination of the Sisal Run Time System.

We will not address the first two steps, mentioned above, as they represent an entire genre of know-how and experimentation by themselves. Step three will require familiarity with both Sisal and the imperative language code under consideration. Since most practically exploitable potential parallelism in existing imperative codes will come from loops, they should be examined first. Sisal does quite well at slicing its parallel loops. Other sorts of parallelism, such as function parallelism (independent functions that can potentially execute concurrently) and producer-consumer parallelism (e.g. software pipelines) are not currently exploited by the Sisal compiler and Run Time System, so they can be ignored. Once a loop has been identified as a target for parallelism, it must be examined for inter-iteration dependencies. These will inhibit parallelism, and must be eliminated from the parallel loops that result from the translation step. Separate interative loops may need to be built in Slsal to handle these portions of the code. The imperative loops will often have false dependencies in them arising from the reuse of variables where no real data dependency is present. These can be eliminated by the use of loop temporary names in Sisal. Imperative loops also often have assignments with indexed array names as their targets; these mush also be leiminated, and can usually be rewritten with loop temporaries, given appropriate index arithmetic. Once the programmer is used to dealing with these exigencies, the translation process can be quick and easy. Following are two code fragments illustrating these details.

```
        temp = 0.0
        Do 100 i = M, N
         temp = temp + A(i)
         B(i) = func( A, i )
         C(i) = C(i-1) + A(i)
         A(i) = A(i)*2.0
   100      continue
```

The first loop is in Fortran. Its inputs are a scalar, temp, an array, A and an array C; its outputs are the scalar temp, and arrays A, B, and C. Note that array C has an index range apparently differing from those of A and B by one: it has an element C(M-1), while A and B may not have an element indexed less than M. The calculation of temp seems inherently sequential, but in fact it can be accomplished in a parallel loop in Sisal. Here is a translation of the above loop into Sisal:

```
temp, New_A, B, New_C :=
 for i in M, N
  A_sub_i := A[i] ;
  B_sub_i := foo( A, i );
  C_sub_i := C[i-1] + A_sub_i;
  New_A_sub_i := A_sub_i * 2.0;
 returns value of sum A_sub_i
          array of New_A_sub_i
          array of B_sub_i
          array of C_sub_i
 end for
```

The syntactic differences should be obvious, as should the simplicity of the translation between them. It should be noted that the Sisal fragment is artificially lengthened by the presence of the simple expressions in the loop body. In fact, all those expressions could be in the returns clause, which would make the Sisal loop no longer than the Fortran version. However, we find clarity to be more important than brevity, in many cases where parallelism is the goal and accuracy is at risk, so we tend to use loop temporaries, as shown above, to help make Sisal code readable, and to err on the side of of readability where style is arguable.

Step four involves building argument lists for the Sisal Run Time System to use in invoking the outermost Sisal function, and return value lists for the RTS to pass back to the invoking inmperative code. Scalar data can simply be passed in and returned without special effort, but arrays are more complicated. Arrays in C and Fortran are contiguous blocks of primitive type elements stored row-wise (in C) and column-wise (in Fortran). Arrays in Sisal are vectors of scalars or vectors, which are contiguous only in the most primitive dimension, and are stored row-wise. When passing an array between an imperative program and a Sisal function, a descriptor must be provided in addition to the array, that allows the Sisal Run Time System to correctly handle the data and mange the storage it uses. Since all data items in Sisal ("values", as opposed to "variables" in imperative languages) are dynamic, storage must be managed by the RTS. It does this well, and normally requires no help from the programmer. Mixed language programming requires extra efforts in the form of array descriptors. Each array requires a descriptor, and each descriptor contains fields for each dimension of the target array that describe that dimension's physical and logical index range, whether the data is read-only or writeable, and whether it must be transposed in passage. Fortran arrays, for example, if of more than one dimension, must be transposed by the RTS, since they are allocated in column major order in Fortran and row major order in Sisal. The descriptors are themselves small arrays which must be allocated in the imperative code, and which must be provided for each array argument and result. The provision of this information can conceivably be automated by the compiler, but at present it must be performed manually by the programmer.

In addition to the above, the Sisal Run Time System must be started and stopped at points in the imperative program that are appropriate to the parallel work that will be done. Normally, the RTS is started and stopped automatically during the execution of a pure Sisal program, but this code must be explicitly included and invoked in the loading and execution of a hybrid program. Since it is expensive in terms of CPU time to do this, it is not appropriate that it be done repeatedly within a loop that contains calls to the Sisal code. Rather, the RTS should be started once, the Sisal code invoked wherever appropriate, and the RTS should be shut down before the normal termination of the program. It costs relatively little to leave the RTS running between invocations of the Sisal code, so this method is not particularly wasteful of machine resources. The RTS is started by a simple call which contains a few of the parameters normally used in te execution of a Sisal program. These include the program heap size (the memory pool used by the RTS), the number of worker processes to be used (the amount of parallelism exploited).

At this point it is worth mentioning that the Sisal FLI was built as an experiment, and as such is still in a somewhat rougher state than would be desired in a production parallelization system. Its use, as documented above, can present difficulties that can effectively undo some of the advantages of applicative paralleism. For instance, the generation of the array argument and result descriptors adds to the programmer's burden. In addition, arrays of dimension greater than one will currently be copied across the FLI, a source of overhead at exectute time that is inimical to parallel performance goals. Therefore, in the work we have done with it, we have routinely used aliasing to hide the multidimensional nature of such arrays, and index arithmetic to allow arbitrary access to their elements.

In addition, we must confess that the goals of machine independence are not always met in parallel programming, and this is at least as true in mixed language programming for parallelism. It sometimes happens that the Sisal code resulting from the translation of step three, above, must be modified for performance purposes. For instance, column-wise accesses to two-dimensional arrays usually causes performenace degradation in systems containing cache memories. However, this by itself is usually no more serious a constraint than would be imposed by such system architectures during a parallel port in any other language.

Notwithstanding the problems mentioned above we believe the FLI offers two distinct advantages to the parallel programmer. First, it provides a means of rapidly parallelizing existing application codes by concentrating programmer effort where it will provide the best return. And second, it offers a developmental path for codes ranging from experimentation on cheap workstations to production on expensive supercomputers.

5. A Prototype Distributed-Memory SISAL Compiler

In this section we present D-OSC, a prototype SISAL compiler for distributed-memory machines. D-OSC is an extension of OSC [12]. A new analysis phase for loop and array distribution has been added and the code generation phase has been modified to produce C plus MPI [15] calls. The run-time system has been modified to support array distribution and communicating threads. Information needed to perform distributed memory optimizations is established by the analysis phase and provided to the code generator by decorating the appropriate IF2 nodes and edges.

The D-OSC model of execution is activation-based. A *master* process is responsible for dividing parallel loops into *slices* which will be executed by *slave* processes running in parallel. A slice is represented by an *activation record*, which contains a code pointer, the loop range, a unique loop identifier, input parameters to the slice, and destinations for values to be returned upon termination. Activation records are distributed over the machine and each processor maintains a local *activation record queue*. Upon completion of a slice, the slave process sends a completion message to the master and updates global results with locally-computed values. As a slice may contain a parallel loop, each slave can become a master and distribute its inner loop. Each processor must be able to receive a request for service from other processors, such as a read, write or allocate request. This is achieved by having a *listener* thread always active on every processor.

D-OSC is implemented in four phases, where each phase relies on the previous one.

- *Base*. This phase employs no analysis whatsoever, hence the code generated is very naive. Arrays and loops are distributed equally among processors. Message passing is used to access remote array elements. This compiler version serves as a reference for further implementations, providing useful information about the effectiveness of certain optimizations.
- *Rectangular Arrays*. The standard implementation of higher-dimensional arrays as arrays of arrays is replaced, where possible, by rectangular arrays with a single descriptor. Arrays and the loops creating or using arrays can be distributed by rows, block or columns. Not all loops are distributed.

- *Block Messages.* The reading and writing of remote array elements within certain loops is optimized by combining all the messages directed to the same processor into a single block message.
- *Multiple Alignment.* In previous phases arrays partitioning created disjoint sections of an array. In this phase *overlapping* array sections are created. This optimization reduces the number of messages passed, at the cost of using more space for the overlapping array sections.

5.1 Base Compiler

In OSC, the representation of arrays consists of an array descriptor, which contains information such as bounds, reference count, size, and other information, and a pointer to the physical array. OSC assumes a shared-memory model, and the pointers to the array descriptor provide a unique array identifier. An evident problem on a distributed-memory machine is that the descriptor pointer cannot be used as a unique identifier, since the address of the array descriptor is different for each processor. Hence a unique array identifier is created explicitly as the index in an array table that exists on each processor. The design of the array table permits a great deal of compatibility with existing array operations since the OSC concept of a unique array descriptor is preserved.

Arrays are partitioned according to the distribution of the creating loop. In the Base compiler each loop, and hence each array dimension, is distributed equally among processors. To create the unique identifier for distributed arrays, the master process that creates the loop slices, allocates the array identifier and sends it as part of the activation message to the slaves. Each slave then executes a slice in parallel and updates its local entry in the array table.

Array access in the base compiler is straight-forward. The processor that owns the array element is determined. In the base case this amounts to a simple computation involving the array size and the number of processors. If the owner is the local processor, the array element is read directly from local memory, otherwise a request message is sent to the listener thread of the processor that owns the array element. The listener thread directly performs the array access.

5.2 Rectangular Arrays

Rectangular arrays have only one descriptor per array, regardless of its dimensionality. Only one possibly remote memory access to fetch the array element is needed, where an arrays of arrays implementation of an nD array requires n memory accesses to fetch an element. With one array descriptor per array traditional distributions, such as row, block and column, are easier to implement. A disadvantage of rectangular arrays is that sub-arrays cannot be shared. However, sharing also has disadvantages since update-in-place cannot be performed, and access functions are less efficient. Another disadvantage of rectangular arrays is that ragged arrays cannot be represented.

Arrays are created using IF2 `AGather` nodes. Consider the case of a Sisal *triple cross product for* loop that returns a three-dimensional array. In the original IF2, `AGather` nodes in the result graphs of all three nested loops create arrays. In the rectangular array case, the actions that the various `AGather` nodes perform are different. The outermost `AGather` node must perform the allocation of the physical space for the whole 3D-array, and the allocation of the single array descriptor. The innermost `AGather` node fills in the elements of the array. The `AGather` node in the middle loop does not perform any action.

In the original IF2 an arrays of arrays access consists of multiple `AElement` nodes scattered over the dependence graph, each with one index input. For a rectangular array this must be transformed into one `AElement` node with all indices as input. The analysis phase identifies the *tree* of `AElement` nodes that is spanned by the output edge of a root `AElement` node and marks these nodes with information such as the level of the node in the tree and back-edges to ancestor nodes.

5.3 Block Messages

The implementation of array access operations described above is not always efficient for array references in loop bodies, as performing remote exchanges for individual elements is less efficient than performing at most one block exchange per producer-consumer processor pair. Our algorithm for obtaining block messages is a modification of the algorithm presented in [16].

5.4 Multiple Alignment

The last phase of the compiler implements the overlapping allocation of array sections presented in [17] for one-dimensional arrays. Overlapping allocation is applied to loops with *restricted affine* references as in the following loop model, where the `cj`s are constants.

```
for i in lo, hi
  returns array of f(B1[i+c1],...,Bm[i+cm])
end for
```

In the case of *single alignment,* i.e. $m = 1$, the first element of the consumer array is aligned with element $1 + c_1$ of the producer array. For the general case, the analysis phase identifies restricted affine loops, that create one-dimensional arrays while accessing elements from other one-dimensional arrays. Multiple alignment is achieved by identifying all the unaligned references required, and the maximum and minimum offsets of these with respect to the consumer index. The contiguous set of indices thus obtained is a super-set of the producer array elements needed. Loops are marked *RightOverlap* and *LeftOverlap* to be used in the code generation phase to determine the upper and lower bounds for each slice.

5.5 Results

The benchmark programs used here to assess the effectiveness of the various optimization phases are Livermore loops 1, 2, 3, 6, 7, 9, 12, 21, and 24, run on a network of four workstations. Since the initial objective is to reduce communication, we measure the total number of messages exchanged - the first number in table 5.1, and the total volume of communication - the second number in the table.

Table 5.1. Number of Messages, Communication Volume (4 PEs).

Program	Type	Base	Rect Arrays	Block Mssgs	Multiple Algn
l1	1D	6605, 132132	6603, 211368	603, 31368	303, 12168
l2	1D	6443, 126656	6443, 213128	6443, 213128	6443, 213128
l3	1D	3, 96	3, 168	3, 168	3, 168
l6	1D, 2D	10533, 213036	13223, 430408	13223,430408	13223, 430408
l7	1D	4807, 86568	7503, 225168	953, 18968	303, 8568
l9	2D	5883, 117136	2403, 76968	603, 28968	603, 28968
l12	1D	9005, 180132	3003, 96168	1503, 24168	3, 168
l21	2D	471, 8520	14403, 460968	123, 58728	123, 58728
l24	1D	29703, 594096	29703, 950568	29703, 950568	29703, 950568

Rectangular arrays decrease the number of messages exchanged for some of the programs that use 2-D arrays. However, sometimes the number of messages increases, as in loop 21. The reason for this is that the partitioning of the loops and arrays performed by the base compiler matches the accesses of the array elements better than the rectangular arrays implementation.

Most of the programs that access arrays benefit greatly from the implementation of block messages. The greatest improvements occur for loops 1 and 21. Loops 2 and 24 are sequential and the current implementation only generates block messages for references accessed in parallel loops. Loop 6 contains subscript expressions that use non loop variables.

Multiple alignment reduces the number of messages for the programs with producer consumer relations of one-dimensional arrays, such as loops 1,7 and 12.

The volume of communication does not always decrease and varies with program characteristics. In loop 24, where the number of messages exchanged remains the same for all the compiler phases, the volume of communication increases. This is because the implementation of rectangular arrays increases the size of messages required to access array elements in order to accommodate the multiple indices of rectangular arrays.

5.6 Further Work

D-OSC is a prototype implementation that helps us to quantify compiler optimizations for distributed-memory machines. The following are some of the tasks that must be performed to improve D-OSC. A *more efficient run-time system* is needed. There are situations where *run-time reference counting* is necessary. If one processor owns a reference count, each remote processor that updates the reference counter must contact this processor. When deallocating an array, the responsible processor must notify all processors that have partial copies of the array to deallocate the space. The implementation of *function call parallelism* is very easy under the activation-based model. However, inter-functional analysis is required to determine when and where to spawn functions. Currently loops are always distributed over all processors. If an analysis phase can *estimate the computation cost of a loop body*, then it is possible to generate code that decides the number of processors to be used. *Parallel I/O* must be implemented.

6. Architecture Support for Multithreaded Execution

Multithreaded execution has been proposed as a model for parallel program execution. As a model, or rather a family of models, multithreading views a program as a collection of concurrently executing sequential threads that are asynchronously scheduled based on the availability of data. This definition is intentionally wide in that it attempts to capture the common features among various multithreaded execution models proposed to date. It is important to note that in this definition the multithreaded execution model does not specify any form of memory hierarchy (it is common though to expect a single logical address space, shared by many threads and mapped over several nodes), any specific language feature, whether threads are user specified or compiler generated, the mechanism for communication and/or synchronization among threads, or the order of thread execution. There is no standard definition of a thread. In this document we will define a thread as the set of sequential instructions executed between two synchronization points. Note that this definition does not preclude any architecture from exploiting the instruction level parallelism within a thread or the locality of access to a storage hierarchy.

Because of its functional properties, the Sisal language is particularly well suited as a source for multithreaded code. In this Section we present some results related to the evaluation of multithreaded execution. The performance of multithreaded execution is determined by the complex interaction of a number of inter-related architectural and compilation issues such as code generation, thread firing rules, synchronization schemes and thread scheduling. The relation between these issues and the tradeoffs between various alternatives for each of these issues is complex and requires extensive experimental evaluation. For example, the thread firing rule (which determines when threads are enabled) can be based on either a *blocking* or a *non-blocking* strategy. The blocking strategy is adopted in Iannucci's Hybrid Architecture [20], the Tera MTA [2] and the EARTH machine [19]. The non-blocking strategy is adopted in Monsoon [28,29], *T [25] and the EM-4 [34] among others. The Threaded Abstract Machine (TAM) [13] is a software implemented multithreaded execution that has been ported to a number of platforms (such as the TMC CM-5 and the Cray T3D), it implements the non-blocking model.

In this section we summarize the results of an experimental and quantitative evaluation of these two execution models. The evaluation includes their respective code generation strategies, its implications on data distribution and access and the performance of their respective storage hierarchies.

6.1 Blocking and Non-blocking Models

The two multithreaded execution models considered here are based on data-driven dynamic execution with statically generated threads. This section presents a detailed description of these two models.

The blocking thread execution model:. In this model a thread may be suspended and its execution resumed later. This model requires the underlying architecture to support context switching: i.e., the saving of the thread state and the selection of a new thread. Usually, a thread is suspended after initiating a long latency operation such as a remote memory access.

In this model the synchronization and storage mechanisms rely on the Frame model: A frame represents a storage segment associated with each *invocation* of a code-block[1]. The Frame model is used in several multithreaded machines (e.g. TAM [13], StarT-NG [3] and the EM-4 and EM-X [21]). All the threads within the code-block instance refer to its associated frame to store and load data values. Frames are of variable size and contiguously allocated in the virtual address space. The size of a frame is determined by the maximum number of data values associated with the code-block. When an instance of a particular code-block is invoked, a frame is first allocated in local memory of a processor and all the data values generated within that code-block instance will be stored in that frame. The virtual address carried by a token is of the form:

<frame pointer, frame offset>

A synchronization slot in the frame is associated with each thread. The synchronization slot is a counter initialized with the count of the number of the inputs to the thread and is decremented with the arrival of each input. The thread is ready when the count reaches zero. A data value that is shared (i.e. read) by several threads in the same frame occupies only one location.

---

[1] A code-block is a semantically distinguishable unit of code such as a loop or function body.

Data values generated by the executing threads are sent to the Synchronization Unit which writes them in the frame. The frame is deallocated when all the threads in the code-block have terminated.

The non-blocking thread execution model:. In this model a thread is activated only when all its input parameters are available. Therefore, once a thread starts its execution it runs until termination. All memory accesses are performed as split-phase accesses: the request is issued by a thread but the result is returned to another thread. In this mode the thread never has to block, and be switched out, while waiting for a remote memory access.

The synchronization and storage mechanisms for the non-blocking threads is the Framelet model. A framelet is a fixed sized unit of storage that is associated with each thread instance. Each framelet has one synchronization slot for that thread instance. In the Framelet model a data value that is shared among several threads within a same code-block would be replicated in the framelet of each thread instance. The framelet is deallocated when the thread instance completes its execution. Because their size is fixed, framelets are aligned with cache blocks. The virtual address of a data value in the Framelet model is of the form:

<context #, thread #, framelet offset>

Example.. A code-block consisting of four threads is shown in Figure 6.1. The corresponding Frame memory model is shown in the Figure 6.2. The input a which is used by both threads A and B is stored at only one place in the frame memory. Each of the values in the frame memory is accessed by the frame base address and the offset into the frame. The first four slots are the counters for the threads. Thus when value c is stored only the counter for D is decremented. But when a is stored both counter for A and B are decremented but only one copy of a is stored in the frame.

The Framelet memory model corresponding to the same code block is shown in Figure 6.3. There are four separate framelets. Each framelet contains the counter for the corresponding thread and a memory location for all the inputs to the thread. Hence framelet A corresponds to one particular activation of thread A. The a is stored in the framelets of both threads A and B and both counters are decremented. This accomplished as two separate store operations.

6.2 Code Generation

The source language used for the generation of multithreaded code is Sisal. The compilation process converts the programs into two intermediate forms: MIDC-2 (non-blocking) and MIDC-3 (blocking) which are both derived from the *Machine Independent Dataflow Code (MIDC)* [33]. MIDC is a graph structured intermediate format: The nodes of the graph correspond to the von Neumann sequence of instructions and the edges represent the transfer of data between the nodes. MIDC has been used to generate the executable code

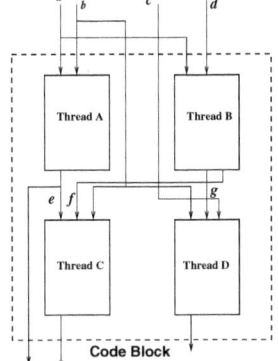

Fig. 6.1. Code block with Three threads.

	Frame Base Address
Counter Thread A	
Counter Thread B	
Counter Thread C	
Counter Thread D	
a	
b	
c	
d	
e	
f	
g	

Fig. 6.2. Frame Memory Representation.

	Address Framelet A
Counter Thread A	
a	
b	

	Address Framelet B
Counter Thread B	
a	
d	

	Address Framelet C
Counter Thread C	
b	
e	
f	

	Address Framelet D
Counter Thread D	
b	
c	
g	

Fig. 6.3. Framelet Memory Representation.

for other multithreaded machines (e.g Monsoon and EM-4). Both MIDC-2 and MIDC-3 are highly optimized codes with optimization done both at the inter- and intra-thread level.

The code generation compiler is guided by the following objectives [32] :

- Minimize synchronization overhead: by merging threads (thread fusion) and by allocating related threads to the same code block (in the blocking model).
- Maximize intra-thread locality: achieved by thread fusion.
- Assure deadlock-free threads: circular dependencies can create a potential for deadlock.
- Preserve functional and loop parallelism in programs.

The first phase of the code generation is the same for both models, it involves compiling the Sisal programs to IF2 using *OSC* [10].

The second phase differs for the two models in the handling of structure store accesses and the data storage models (frames or framelets). The long latency operations consist of remote memory reads, memory allocations, function calls and remote synchronizations. The remote memory references can be handled either as a *split-phase* access or a *single-phase* access. In the split-phase access the request is sent by one thread and the result is forwarded to another thread. In the single-phase access the result is returned to the same requesting thread. In the non-blocking model all remote accesses are split-phase. The blocking model uses both types of accesses: the code is analyzed at compile time to identify remote and local accesses. Remote accesses are implemented by split-phase operations while local accesses are regular memory access.

- In the non-blocking model (MIDC-2 form) all structure store accesses are turned into split-phase accesses. A split-phase access terminates a thread: the request is sent by a thread but the result is returned to another thread. In this model a thread has never to block on a remote memory access. This model does not make any assumption regarding data structure distribution.
- In the blocking model (MIDC-3) the IF2 graph is statically analyzed to differentiate between local and remote structure store accesses: a local access does not terminate a thread while a remote one does. If the result of a structure store access is used within the same code-block where the access request is generated, the access is considered local. In this case, the thread will block until the request is satisfied. This model relies on a static data distribution to enhance the locality of access. Note that a data structure is often generated in one code block and used in several others in which case only one of the consumer code-blocks would have a local access.

Example. The example in Figure 6.4 demonstrates the difference between MIDC-2 and MIDC-3. In MIDC-2, *Thread* 255 performs a structure memory read operation. The read is performed as a split-phase access where the result

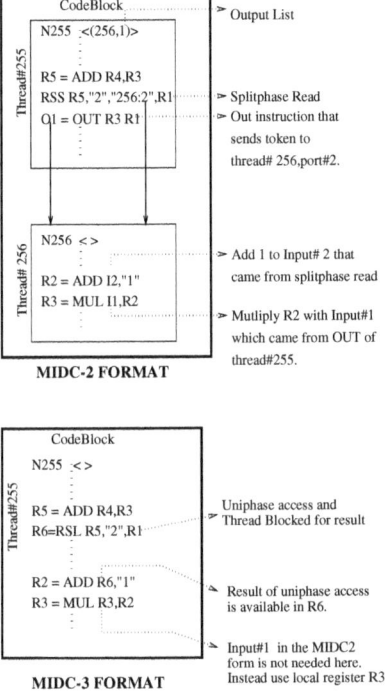

Fig. 6.4. MIDC-2 and MIDC-3 code examples.

is sent to *Thread* 256. *Thread* 255 does not block, it continues execution until termination. When the results of the split-phase read is available it is forwarded to *Thread* 256 which starts execution when all its input data is available. There are no restriction on the processor on which *Thread* 255 and *Thread* 256 are executed.

In the MIDC-3 code, *Thread* 255 and 256 belong to the same code-block. The read structure memory operation is a local single phase operation. Hence, the two threads become a single thread. The thread blocks when the read operation is encountered and waits for the read request to be satisfied.

Discussion of the Models.. The main differences between the blocking and non-blocking models lie in their synchronization and thread switching strategies. The blocking model requires a complex architectural support to efficiently switch between ready threads. The frame space is deallocated only when all the thread instances associated with its code block have terminated execution which is determined by extensive static program analysis. The model also relies on static analysis to distribute the shared data structures and therefore reduce the overhead of split-phase accesses by making some data structure accesses local. The non-blocking model relies on a simple scheduling mechanism: data-driven data availability. Once a thread completes execution, its framelet is deallocated and the space is reclaimed.

The main difference between the Frame model and the Framelet models of synchronization is the token duplication. The Framelet model does require that variables which are *shared* by several threads *within* a code block be replicated to all these threads while in the Frame model these variables are allocated only once in the frame. The advantage of the Framelet model is that it is possible to design special storage schemes [31] that can take advantage of the locality of the inter-thread and intra-thread locality and achieve a cache miss rate close to 1%.

6.3 Summary of Performance Results

This section summarizes the results of an experimental evaluation of the two execution models and their associated storage models. A preliminary version of these results was reported in [4], detailed results are reported in [5].

The evaluation of the program execution characteristics of these two models shows that the blocking model has a significant reduction in threads, instructions, and synchronization operations executed with respect to the non blocking model. It also has a larger average thread size (by 26% on average) and, therefore, a lower number of synchronization operations per instruction executed (17% lower on average).

However, the total number of accesses to the Frame storage, in the non-blocking model, is comparable to the number of accesses to the Framelet storage in the blocking model. Although the Frame storage model eliminates the replication of data values, the synchronization mechanism requires that two or more synchronization slots (counters) be accessed for each shared data. The number of synchronization accesses to the frames nearly offsets all the redundant accesses. In fact the size of the trace of accesses to the frames is less than 3% smaller than the framelet trace size. Hence, synchronization overhead is the same for the frame and framelet models of synchronization.

The evaluation also looked at the performance of a cache memory for the Frame and Framelet models. Both models exhibit a large degree of spatial locality in their accesses: In both cases the optimal cache block size was 256 bytes. However, the Framelet model has a much higher degree of temporal locality resulting in an average miss rate of 1.82% as opposed to 5.29% for the Frame model (both caches being 16KB, 4-way set associative with 256 byte blocks).

The execution time of the blocking model is highly dependent on the success rate of the static data distribution. The execution times for success rates of 100% or 90% are comparable and outperform those of the non blocking model. For a success rate of 50%, however, the execution time may be higher than that of the non blocking model. The performance, however, depends largely on the network latency. When the network latency is low and the processor utilization high, the non blocking model performs as well as the blocking model with a 100% or 90% success rate.

7. Conclusions and Future Research

The functional model of computation is one attempt at providing an implicitly parallel programming paradigm[2]. Because of the lack of state and its functionality, it allows the compiler to extract all available parallelism, fine and coarse grain, regular and irregular, and generate a partial evaluation order of the program. In its pure form (*e.g.*, pure Lisp, Sisal, Haskell), this model is unable to express algorithms that rely explicitly on state. However, extensions to these languages have been proposed to allow a limited amount of stateful computations when needed. Instead, we are investigating the feasibility of the declarative programming style, both in terms of its expressibility and its run-time performance, over a wide range of numerical and non-numerical problems and algorithms, and executing on both conventional and novel parallel architectures. We are also evaluating the ability of these languages to aid compiler analysis to disambiguate and parallelize data structure accesses.

On the implementation side, we have demonstrated how multithreaded implementations combine the strengths of both the von Neumann (in its exploitation of program and data locality) and of the data-driven model (in its ability to hide latency and support efficient synchronization). New architectures such as TERA [2] and *T [26] are being built with hardware support for multithreading. In addition, software multithreading models such as TAM [13] and MIDC [8]), are being investigated.

We are currently further investigating the performance of both software-supported and hardware-supported multithreaded models on a wide range of parallel machines. We have designed and evaluated low-level machine independent optimization and code generation for multithreaded execution. The target hardware platforms will be stock machines, such as single superscalar processors, shared memory, and multithreaded machines. We will also target more experimental dataflow machines, (*e.g.*, Monsoon [18,37]).

Acknowledgement. This research is supported in part by ARPA grant # DABT63-95-0093 and NSF grant 53-4503-3481

References

1. S. J. Allan and R. R. Oldehoeft. Parallelism in SISAL: Exploiting the HEP architecture. In *19th Hawaii International Conference on System Sciences*, pages 538–548, January 1986.

---

[2] Other attempts include the vector, data parallel and object-oriented paradigms.

2. R. Alverson, D. Callahan, D. Cummings, B. Koblenz, A. P. ortfield, and B. Smith. The Tera computer system. In *Proceedings 1990 Int. Conf. on Supercomputing*, pages 1–6. ACM Press, June 1990.

3. B. S. Ang, Arvind, and D. Chiou. StarT the Next Generation: Integrating Global Caches and Dataflow Architecture. Technical Report 354, LCS, Massachusetts Institute of Technology, August 1994.

4. M. Annavaram and W. Najjar. Comparison of two storage models in data-driven multithreaded architectures. In *Proceedings of Symp. on Parallel and Distributed Processing*, October 1996.

5. M. Annavaram, W. Najjar, and L. Roh. Experimental evaluation of blocking and non-blocki ng multithreaded code execution. Technical Report 97-108, Colorado State University, Department of Computer Science, www.cs.colostate.edu/ ftp-pub/TechReports/, March 1997.

6. J. Backus. Can programming be liberated from the von Neumann style? *Communications of the ACM*, 21(8):613–641, 1978.

7. A. Böhm and J. Sargeant. Efficient dataflow code generation for sisal. Technical report, University of Manchester, 1985.

8. A. P. W. Böhm, W. A. Najjar, B. Shankar, and L. Roh. An evaluation of coarse-grain dataflow code generation strategies. In *Working Conference on Massively Parallel Programming Models*, Berlin, Germany, Sept. 1993.

9. D. Cann. *Compilation Techniques for High Performance Applicative Computation.* PhD thesis, Colorado State University, 1989.

10. D. Cann. Compilation techniques for high performance applicative computation. Technical Report CS-89-108, Colorado State University, 1989.

11. D. Cann. Retire FORTRAN? a debate rekindled. *CACM*, 35(8):pp. 81–89, Aug 1992.

12. D. Cann. Retire Fortran? a debate rekindled. *Communications of the ACM*, 35(8):81–89, 1992.

13. D. E. Culler et al. Fine grain parallelism with minimal hardware support: A compiler-controlled Threaded Abstract Machine. In *Proc. 4th Int'l Conf. on Architectural Support for Programming Languages and Operating Systems*, April 1991.

14. J. T. Feo, P. J. Miller, and S. K. Skedzielewski. Sisal90. In *Proceedings of High Performance Functional Computing*, April 1995.

15. M. Forum. *MPI: A Message-Passing Interface Standard*, 1994.

16. G. Fox, S. Hiranandani, K. Kennedy, U. Kremer, C. Tseng, and M. Wu. Fortran D language specification. Technical Report CRPC-TR90079, Center for Research on Parallel Computation, Rice University, P.O. Box 1892, Houston, TX 77251-1892, 1990.

17. D. Garza-Salazar and W. Böhm. Reducing communication by honoring multiple alignments. In *Proceedings of the 9th ACM International Conference on Supercomputing (ICS'95)*, pages 87–96, Barcelona, 1995.

18. J. Hicks, D. Chiou, B. Ang, and Arvind. Performance studies of Id on the Monsoon dataflow system. *Journal of Parallel and Distributed Computing*, 3(18):273–300, July 1993.

19. H. Hum, O. Macquelin, K. Theobald, X. Tian, G. Gao, P. Cupryk, N. Elmassri, L. Hendren, A. Jimenez, S. Krishnan, A. Marquez, S. Merali, S. Nemawarkar,

P. Panangaden, X. Xue, and Y. Zhu. A design study of the EARTH multiprocessor. In *Parallel Architectures and Compilation Techniques*, 1995.

20. R. Iannucci. A Dataflow/von Neumann Hybrid Architecture. Technical Report 418, Ph. D Dissertation Technical Report TR-418, Laboratory for Computer Science, MIT, Cambridge, MA, June 1988.

21. Y. Kodama, H. Sakane, M. Sato, H. Yamana, S. Sakai, and Y. Yamaguchi. The EM-X parallel computer: Architecture and basic performance. In *Proceedings of the 22th Annual International Symposium on Computer Architecture*, pages 14–23, June 1995.

22. J. McGraw, S. Skedzielewski, S. Allan, D. Grit, R. Oldehoeft, J. Glauert, I. Dobes, and P. Hohensee. SISAL-Streams and Iterations in a Single Assignment Language, Language Reference Manual, version 1. 2. Technical Report TR M-146, University of California - Lawrence Livermore Laboratory, March 1985.

23. P. Miller. TWINE: A portable, extensible sisal execution kernel. In J. Feo, editor, *Proceedings of Sisal '93*. Lawrence Livermore National Laboratory, October 1993.

24. P. Miller. Simple sisal interpreter, 1995. ftp://ftp.sisal.com/pub/LLNL/SSI.

25. R. S. Nikhil, G. M. Papadopoulos, and Arvind. *T: A multithreaded massively parallel architecture. In *Proceedings of the 19th Annual International Symposium on Computer Architecture*, pages 156–167, May 1992.

26. R. S. Nikhil, G. M. Papadopoulos, and Arvind. *T: A multithreaded massively parallel architecture. In *Proceedings of the 19th Annual International Symposium on Computer Architecture*, pages 156–167, Gold Coast, Australia, May 19–21, 1992. ACM SIGARCH and IEEE Computer Society TCCA. *Computer Architecture News,* 20(2), May 1992.

27. R. Oldehoeft and D. Cann. Applicative parallelism on a shared-memory multiprocessor. *IEEE Software*, January 1988.

28. G. Papadopoulos. Implementation of a general-purpose dataflow multiprocessor. Technical report TR-432, MIT Laboratory for Computer Science, August 1988.

29. G. M. Papadopoulos and D. E. Culler. Monsoon: an explicit token-store architecture. In *Proceedings of the 17th Annual International Symposium on Computer Architecture*, pages 82–91, June 1990.

30. J. Rannelletti. *Graph Transformation algorithms for array memory optimization in applicative languages*. PhD thesis, U. California, Davis, 1987.

31. L. Roh and W. Najjar. Design of storage hierarchy in multithreaded architectures. In *IEEE Micro*, pages 271–278, November 1995.

32. L. Roh, W. Najjar, B. Shankar, and A. P. W. B. öhm. Generation, optimization and evaluation of multith readed code. *J. of Parallel and Distributed Computing*, 32(2):188–204, February 1996.

33. L. Roh, W. A. Najjar, B. Shankar, and A. P. W. Böhm. An evaluation of optimized threaded code generation. In *Parallel Architectures and Compilation Techniques*, Montreal, Canada, 1994.

34. S. Sakai, K. Hiraki, Y. Yamaguchi, and T. Yuba. Optimal Architecture Design of a Data-flow Computer. In *Japanese Symposium on Parallel Processing*, 1989. in Japanese.

35. S. Skedzielewski and R. Simpson. A simple method to remove reference counting in applicative programs. In *Proceedings of CONPAR 88*, Sept 1988.

36. S. K. Skedzielewski, R. K. Yates, and R. R. Oldehoeft. DI: An interactive debugging interpreter for applicative languages. In *Proceedings of the ACM SIGPLAN 87 Symposium on Interpreters and Interpretive Techniques*, pages 102–109, June 1987.

37. K. Traub. Monsoon: Dataflow Architectures Demystified. In *Proc. Imacs 91 13th Congress on Computation and Applied Mathematics*, 1991.

38. M. Welcome, S. Skedzielewski, R. Yates, and J. Ranelleti. IF2: An applicative language intermediate form with explicit memory management. Technical Report TR M-195, University of California - Lawrence Livermore Laboratory, December 1986.

Chapter 3. HPC++ and the HPC++Lib Toolkit

Dennis Gannon[1], Peter Beckman[2], Elizabeth Johnson[1], Todd Green[1], and Mike Levine[1]

[1] Department of Computer Science, Indiana University
[2] Los Alamos National Laboratory.

1. Introduction

The High Performance C++ consortium is a group that has been working for the last two years on the design of a standard library for parallel programming based on the C++ language. The consortium consists of people from research groups within Universities, Industry and Government Laboratories. The goal of this effort is to build a common foundation for constructing portable parallel applications. The design has been partitioned into two levels. Level 1 consists of a specification for a set of class libraries and tools that do not require any extension to the C++ language. Level 2 provides the basic language extensions and runtime library needed to implement the full HPC++ Level 1 specification.

Our goal in this chapter is to briefly describe part of the Level 1 specification and then provide a detailed account of our implementation strategy. Our approach is based on a library, HPC++Lib, which is described in detail in this document. We note at the outset that HPC++Lib is not unique and the key ideas are drawn from many sources. In particular, many of the ideas originate with K. Mani Chandy and Carl Kesselman in the CC++ language [6,15] and the MPC++ Multiple Threads Template Library designed by Yutaka Ishikawa of RWCP [10], the IBM ABC++ library [15,16], the Object Management Group CORBA specification [9] and the Java concurrency model [1].

In particular, Carl Kesselman at USC ISI is also building an implementation of HPC++ using CC++ as the level 2 implementation layer. Our implementation builds upon a compiler technology developed in collaboration with ISI, but our implementation strategy is different.

The key features of HPC++Lib are

- A Java style thread class that provides an easy way to program parallel applications on shared memory architectures. This thread class is also used to implement the loop parallelization transformations that are part of the HPC++ level 1 specification.
- A template library to support synchronization, collective parallel operations such as reductions, and remote memory references.

S. Pande, D.P. Agrawal (Eds.): Compiler Optimizations for Scalable PS, LNCS 1808, pp. 73-107, 2001.
© Springer-Verlag Berlin Heidelberg 2001

– A CORBA style IDL-to-proxy generator is used to support member function calls on objects located in remote address spaces.

This chapter introduces the details of this programming model from the application programmer's perspective and describes the compiler support required to implement and optimize HPC++.

2. The HPC++ Programming and Execution Model

The runtime environment for HPC++ can be described as follows. The basic architecture consists of the following components.

– A *node* is a shared-memory multiprocessor (SMP), possibly connected to other SMPs via a network. Shared memory is a coherent shared-address space that can be read and modified by any processor in the node. A node could be a laptop computer or a 128-processor SGI Origin 2000.
– A *context* refers to a virtual address space on a node, usually accessible by several different threads of control. A Unix process often represents a context. We assume that there may be more than one context per node in a given computation.
– A set of interconnected nodes constitutes a system upon which an HPC++ program may be run.

There are two conventional modes of executing an HPC++ program. The first is "multi-threaded, shared memory" where the program runs within one context. Parallelism comes from the parallel-loops and the dynamic creation of threads. Sets of threads and contexts can be bound into *Groups* and there are collective operations such as reductions and prefix operators that can be applied synchronize the threads of a group. This model of programming is very well suited to modest levels of parallelism (about 32 processors) and where memory locality is not a serious factor.

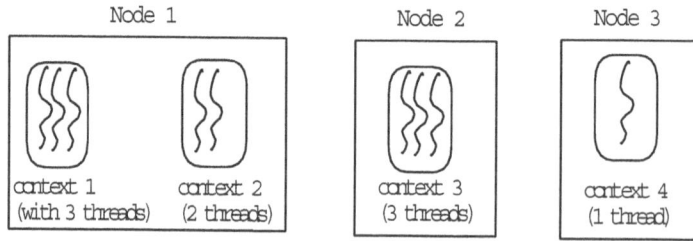

Fig. 2.1. A SPMD program on three nodes with four contexts. Each context may have a variable number of threads.

The second mode of program execution is an explicit "Single Program Multiple Data" (SPMD) model where n copies of the same program are run on n different contexts. This programming model is similar to that of Split-C [7], pC++ [15], AC [5] or C/C++ with MPI or PVM in that the distribution of data that must be shared between contexts and the synchronization of accesses to that data must be managed by the programmer. HPC++ differs from these other C-based SPMD systems in that the computation on each context can also be multi-threaded and the synchronization mechanisms for thread groups extends to sets of thread groups running in multiple contexts. It should also be noted that an SPMD computation need not be completely homogeneous: a program may contain two contexts on one node and one context on each of two other nodes. Furthermore, each of these contexts may contain a variable number of threads (see Figure 2.1).

Multi-context SPMD programming with multi-threaded computation within each context supports a range of applications, such as adaptive grid methods for large scale simulation, that are best expressed using a form of multi-level parallelism.

2.1 Level 1 HPC++

The level 1 library has three components. The first component is a set of simple loop directives that control parallelism within a single context. The compiler is free to ignore these directives, but if there is more than one processor available, it can use the directives to parallelize simple loops.

The HPC++ loop directives are based on ideas from HPF [8] and other older proposals. The idea is very simple. The HPC++ programmer can identify a loop and annotate it with a #pragma to inform the compiler it is "independent". This means that each iteration is independent of every other iteration, and they are not ordered. Consequently, the compiler *may* choose to execute the loop in parallel, and generate the needed synchronization for the end of the loop. In addition, variables that do not carry loop dependences can be labeled as PRIVATE so that one copy of the variable is generated for each iteration. Furthermore, in the case of reductions, it is possible to label a statement with the REDUCE directive so that the accumulation operations will be atomic. As a simple example, consider the following function which will multiply an n *by* n matrix with a vector.

This function may generate up to n^2 parallel threads because both loops are labeled as HPC_INDEPENDENT. However, the compiler and the run-time system must work together to choose when new threads of control will be created and when loops will performed sequentially. Also, each iterate of the outer loop uses the variable *tmp*, labeled PRIVATE, to accumulate the inner product. The atomicity of the reduction is guaranteed by the HPC_REDUCE directive at the innermost level.

```
void Matvec(double **A, int n, double *X,
            double *Y){
   double tmp;
   #pragma HPC_INDEPENDENT, PRIVATE tmp
   for(int i = 0; i < n; i++){
      tmp = 0;
      #pragma HPC_INDEPENDENT
      for(int j = 0; j < n; j++){
         #pragma HPC_REDUCE.
         tmp += A[i][j]*X[j];
         }
      y[i] = tmp;
   }
}
```

In section 5 below we will describe the program transformations that the compiler must undertake to recast the annotated loop above into a parallel form using the HPC++ Thread library.

2.2 The Parallel Standard Template Library

As described above, there are two execution models for HPC++ programs. For the single context model, an HPC++ program is launched as an ordinary C++ program with an initial single main thread of control. If the context is running on a node with more than one processor, parallelism can be exploited by using parallel loop directives, the HPC++ Parallel Standard Template Library (PSTL), or by spawning new threads of control. For multiple context execution, an HPC++ program launches one thread of control to execute the program in each context. This Single Program Multiple Data (SPMD) mode is a model of execution that is easily understood by programmers even though it requires the user to reason about and debug computations where the data structures are distributed over multiple address spaces. The HPC++ library is designed to help simplify this process.

One of the major recent changes to the C++ standard has been the addition of the Standard Template Library (STL) [13, 14]. The STL has five basic components.

- *Container* class templates provide standard definitions for common aggregate data structures, including *vector, list, deque, set* and *map*.
- *Iterators* generalize the concept of a pointer. Each container class defines an iterator that gives us a way to step through the contents of containers of that type.
- *Generic Algorithms* are function templates that allow standard element-wise operations to be applied to containers.

– *Function Objects* are created by wrapping functions with classes that typically have only operator() defined. They are used by the generic algorithms
in place of function pointers because they provide greater efficiency.
– *Adaptors* are used to modify STL containers, iterators, or function objects.
For example, container adaptors are provided to create stacks and queues,
and iterator adaptors are provided to create reverse iterators to traverse
an iteration space backwards.

The Parallel Standard Template Library (PSTL) is a parallel extension
of STL. Distributed versions of the STL container classes are provided along
with versions of the STL algorithms which have been modified to run in
parallel. In addition, several new algorithms have been added to support
standard parallel operations such as the element-wise application of a function
and parallel reduction over container elements. Finally, parallel iterators have
been provided. These iterators extend global pointers and are used to access
remote elements in distributed containers.

2.3 Parallel Iterators

STL iterators are generalizations of C++ pointers that are used to traverse
the contents of a container. HPC++ parallel iterators are generalizations of
this concept to allow references to objects in different address spaces.

In the case of *random access parallel iterators*, the operators $++$, $--$,
$+n, -n$, and $[i]$ allow random access to the entire contents of a distributed
container. In general, each distributed container class C, will have a subclass
for the strongest form of parallel iterator that it supports (e.g. random access,
forward or bidirectional) and a *begin* and *end* iterator functions. For example,
each container class will provide functions of the form

```
template <class T>
  class Container{
      ....
      class pariterator{ ... }
      pariterator parbegin();
      pariterator parend();
};
```

2.4 Parallel Algorithms

In HPC++ PSTL there are two types of algorithms. First are the conventional
STL algorithms like *for_each()*, which can be executed in parallel if called
with parallel iterators. The second type includes STL algorithms where the
semantics of the algorithm must be changed to make sense in a parallel
context, as well as several new algorithms that are very common in parallel
computation. Algorithms in this second group are identified by the prefix

*par_*, and may be invoked with the standard random access iterators for single context parallelism or with parallel random access iterators for multi-context SPMD parallelism.

The most important of the new parallel algorithms in HPC++ STL are

- *par_apply(begin1, end1, begin2, begin3, ... f())* which applies a function object pointwise to the elements of a set of containers.
- *par_reduction(begin1, end1, begin2, begin3, ..., reduce(),f())* which is a parallel apply followed by a reduction on an associative binary operator.
- *par_scan(result_begin, result_end, begin2, begin3, ..., scanop(), f())* which is a parallel apply followed by a parallel prefix computation.

2.5 Distributed Containers

The HPC++ container classes include versions of each of the STL containers prefixed by the phrase *distributed_* to indicate that they operate in a distributed SPMD execution environment. Constructors for these containers are collective operations, i.e. they must be invoked in each executing context in parallel. For example, a distributed vector with elements of type T is constructed with

```
distributed_vector < T > X(dim0, &distrib_object);
```

The last parameter is a distribution object which defines the mapping of the array index space to the set of contexts active in the computations. If the distribution parameter is omitted, then a default block distribution is assumed.

A more complete description of the Parallel STL is given in [11]

3. A Simple Example: The Spanning Tree of a Graph

The minimum spanning tree algorithm [12] takes a graph with weighted connections and attempts to find a tree that contains every vertex of the graph so that the sum of connection weights in the tree is minimal.

The graph is represented by the adjacency matrix W of dimensions $n * n$, where n is the number of vertices in the graph. $W[i, j]$ contains the weight of the connection between vertex i and vertex j. $W[i, j]$ is set to infinity if vertex i and vertex j are not connected.

The algorithm starts with an arbitrary vertex of the graph and considers it to be the root of the tree being created. Then, the algorithm iterates $n - 1$ times choosing one more vertex from the pool of unselected vertices during each iteration. The pool of unselected vertices is represented by the distance vector D. $D[i]$ is the weight of the connection from an unselected vertex i to the closest selected vertex. During each iteration, the algorithm selects a vertex whose corresponding D value is the smallest among all the unselected vertices. It adds the selected vertex to the tree and updates the values in D for the rest of the unselected vertices in the following way. For each remaining vertex, it compares the corresponding D value with the weight of the connection between the newly selected vertex and the remaining vertex. If the weight of the new connection is less than the old D value, it is stored in D.

After the $n - 1$ iterations D will contain the weights of the selected connections. We can parallelize this algorithm by searching for the minimum in D and updating D in parallel.

To conserve memory, we decided to deal with sparse graphs and impose a limit on the number of edges for any one vertex. We represent the adjacency matrix W by a distributed vector of an *edge_list* of pairs. Each *edge_list* describes all the edges for one vertex; each pair represents one weighted edge where the first element is the weight of the edge and the second element is the index of the destination vertex.

```
class weighted_edge{
    int weight;
    int vertex;
};

struct edge_list {
    typedef weighted_edge* iterator;
    weighted_edge my_edges[MAX_EDGES];
    int num_edges;
    iterator begin() { return my_edges; }
    iterator end() { return my_edges+num_edges; }
};


typedef distributed_vector <edge_list> Graph;

Graph W(n);
```

We represent the distance vector D by a distributed vector of pairs. The first element of each pair is the D value - the weight of the connection from the corresponding unselected vertex to the closest selected vertex. The second element of each pair is used as a flag of whether the corresponding vertex has already been selected to the tree. It is set to the pair's index in D until the vertex is selected and is assigned -1 after the vertex is selected.

```
struct cost_to_edge{
    int weight;
    long index;
    cost_to_edge(int _weight, long _to_vertex);
};
```

```
typedef distributed_vector <cost_to_edge> DistanceVector;
```

```
DistanceVector D(n);
```

The main part of the program is a *for* loop that repeatedly finds a minimum in the distance vector D using *par_reduction*, marks the found vertex as selected, and updates the distance vector using *par_apply*. The call to *par_reduction* uses the *identity* function-class as the operation to apply to each element of the distributed vector (it simply returns its argument) and a *min* function-class as the reducing operation (it compares two pairs and returns the one with smaller weight). Min also requires an initial value for the reduction. In this case an edge cost pair with weight INT_MAX.

```
for(long i=1; i<n; i++){

    cost_to_edge u = par_reduction(D.parbegin(),
                                   D.parend(),
                                   min(),
                                   identity<cost_to_edge>(),
                                   cost_to_edge(INT_MAX,-1));

    D[u.index] = cost_to_edge(u.weight, -1);

    par_apply(D.parbegin (), D.parend (), update(u.index, W));

}
```

The second statement in the loop body marks the found vertex as selected. The last statement updates D using *update* function-class. *Update* defines operator () that takes a reference to an element in D and replaces that element with a new pair if it finds a lower weight edge in the graph to the element of D. Since the update function-object needs to refer to the adjacency matrix and the index of the newly selected vertex, we have to store reference to them in instance variables of the function object. We do that by passing u and w to the *update* constructor.

```
struct update {
    long u;
    Graph  &w;
    update(long u1, Graph &g) : u(u1),w(g) {};
    void operator () (cost_to_edge & v)
    {
        if (v.index >= 0) {
            Graph::pariterator w_iter = w.parbegin ();
            edge_list wi = w_iter[v.index];
```

```
// find a edge from v.index that goes to u
edge_list::iterator temp =
        find_if(wi.begin(),wi.end(),FindVert(u));

int weight_uv = (temp==wi.end())?
                        INT_MAX: (*temp).weight;

if (v.weight > weight_uv)
    v = cost_to_edge(weight_uv, v.index);
    }
  }
};
```

processors (P)	graph init.	performance	
		computation time (sec)	speed-up
1	0.128	22.94	1
2	0.215	11.96	1.91
3	0.258	8.67	2.65
4	0.308	6.95	3.30
5	0.353	5.84	3.93
6	0.371	5.40	4.25
7	0.402	5.03	4.59
8	0.470	4.94	4.64

Table 3.1. Spanning Tree Performance Results

The basic parallel STL has been prototyped on the SGI Power Challenge and the IBM SP2. In table 3.1 we show the execution time for the spanning tree computation on a graph with 1000 vertices on the SGI. The computation is dominated by the reduction. This operation will have a speed-up that grows as $\frac{P}{1+C*log(P)/N}$ where P is the number of processors and N is the problem size and C is the ratio of the cost of a memory reference in a remote context to that of a local memory reference. In our case that is approximately 200. The resulting speed-up for this size problem with 8 processors is 5, so our computation is performing about as well as we might expect. We have also included the time to build the graph. It should be noted that the time to build the graph grows with the number of processors. We have not yet attempted to optimize the parallelization of this part of the program.

4. Multi-threaded Programming

The implementation of HPC++ described here uses a model of threads that is based on a *Thread* class which is, by design, similar to the Java thread system. More specifically, there are two basic classes that are used to instantiate a thread and get it to do something. Basic *Thread* objects encapsulate a thread and provide a private data space. Objects of class *Runnable* provide a convenient way for a set of threads to execute the member functions of a shared object.

The interface for *Thread* is given by

```
class HPCxx_Thread{
    public:
        HPCxx_Thread(const char *name = NULL);
        HPCxx_Thread(HPCxx_Runnable *runnable,
                    const char *name = NULL);
        virtual ~HPCxx_Thread();
        HPCxx_Thread& operator=(const HPCxx_Thread& thread);
        virtual void run();
        static void stop(void *status);
        static void yield();
        void resume();
        int isAlive();
        static HPCxx_Thread *currentThread();
        void join(long milliseconds = 0,
                long nanoseconds = 0);
        void setName(const char *name);
        const char *getName();
        int getPriority();
        int setPriority(int priority);
        static void sleep(long milliseconds,
                        long nanoseconds = 0);
        void suspend();
        void start();
    };
```

The interface for *Runnable* is given by

```
class HPCxx_Runnable{
    public:
    virtual void run() = 0;
};
```

There are two ways to create a thread and give it work to do. The first is to create a subclass of *Runnable* which provides an instance of the *run()* method. For example, to make a class that prints a message we can write

```
class MyRunnable: public HPCxx_Runnable{
    char *x;
  public:
    MyRunnable(char *c): x(c){}
    void run(){
        printf(x);
        }
};
```

The program below will create an instance of two threads that each run the *run()* method for a single instance of a runnable object.

```
MyRunnable r("hello world");
Thread *t1 = new Thread(&r);
Thread *t2 = new Thread(&r);
t1->start();  // launch the thread but don't block
t2->start();
```

This program prints

```
hello worldhello world
```

It is not required that a thread have an object of class *Runnable* to execute. One may subclass *Thread* to provide a private data and name space for a thread and overload the *run()* function there as shown below.

```
class MyThread: public HPCxx_Thread{
    char *x;
  public:
    MyThread(char *y): x(y), HPCxx_Thread(){}
    void run(){
        printf(x);
        }
};
int main(int argv, char *argc){
    HPCxx_Group *g;
    hpcxx_init(&argv, &argc, g);

    MyThread *t1 = new MyThread("hello");
    t1->start();

    return hpcxx_exit(g);
}
```

The decision for when to subclass *Thread* or *Runnable* depends upon the application. As we shall seen in the section on implementing HPC++ parallel loops, there are times when both approaches are used together.

The initialization function *hpcxx_init()* strips all command line flags of the form *−hpcxx_* from the and *argc* array so that application flags are passed to the program in normal order. This call also initializes the object g of type *HPCxx_Group* which is used for synchronization purposes and is described in greater detail below. The termination function *hpcxx_exit()* is a clean up and termination routine.

It should be noted that in this small example, it is possible for the main program to terminate prior to the completion of the two threads. This would signal an error condition. We will discuss the ways to prevent this from happening in the section on synchronization below.

4.1 Synchronization

There are two types of synchronization mechanisms used in this HPC++ implementation: collective operator objects and primitive synchronization objects. The collective operations are based on the *Hpcxx_Group* class which plays a role in HPC++ that is similar to that of the communicator in MPI.

4.1.1 Primitive Sync Objects. There are four basic synchronization classes in the library:

A *HPCxx_Sync < T >* object is a variable that can be written to once and read as many times as you want. However, if a read is attempted prior to a write, the reading thread will be blocked. Many readers can be waiting for a single *HPCXX_Sync < T >* object and when a value is written to it all the readers are released. Readers that come after the initial write see this as a *const* value. CC++ provides this capability as the *sync* modifier.

The standard methods for *HPCxx_Sync < T >* are

```
template<class T>
class HPCxx_Sync{
    public:
        operator T();     // read a value
        operator =(T &); // assign a value
        void read(T &);   // another form of read
        void write(T &); // another form of writing
        bool peek(T &);   // TRUE if the value is there,
                          // returns FALSE otherwise.
};
```

HPCxx_SyncQ < T > provides a dual "queue" of values of type T. Any attempt to read a sync variable before it is written will cause the reading thread to suspend until a value has been assigned. The thread waiting will "take the value" from the queue and continue executing. Waiting threads are also queued. The ith thread in the queue will receive the ith value written to the sync variable.

There are several other standard methods for SyncQ$< T >$.

```
template<class T>
class HPCxx_SyncQ{
    public:
        operator T();      // read a value
        operator =(T &); // assign a value
        void read(T &);    // another form of read
        void write(T &); // another form of writing
        int length();      // the number of values in the queue

        // wait until the value is there and then
        // read the value but do not remove it from
        // the queue. The next waiting thread is signaled.
        void waitAndCopy(T& data);
        bool peek(T &);   // same as Sync<>

}
```

For example, threads that synchronize around a producer-consumer interaction can be easily build with this mechanism.

```
class Producer: public HPCxx_Thread{
        HPCxx_SyncQ<int> &x;
    public:
        Producer( HPCxx_SyncQ<int> &y): x(y){}
        void run(){
                printf("hi there\n");
                x = 1;   // produce a value for x
                }
};

int main(int argc, char *argv[]){
    Hpcxx_Group *g;
    hpcxx_init(&argc, &argv, g);
    HPCxx_SyncQ<int> a;
    MyThread *t = new Producer(a);
    printf("start then wait for a value to assigned\");
    t->start();
    int x = a; // consume a value here.
    hpcxx_exit(g);
    return x;
}
```

Counting semaphores.. HPCxx_CSem provide a way to wait for a group of threads to synchronize termination of a number of tasks. When constructed, a limit value is supplied and a counter is set to zero. A thread executing *waitAndReset()* will suspend until the counter reaches the "limit" value. The counter is then reset to zero. The overloaded "++" operator increments the counter by one.

```
class HPCxx_CSem{
 public:
   HPCxx_CSem(int limit);
   // prefix and postfix ++ operators.
   HPCxx_CSem& operator++();
   const HPCxx_CSem& operator++();
   HPCxx_CSem& operator++(int);
   const HPCxx_CSem& operator++(int);
   waitAndReset(); // wait until the count reaches the limit
                   // then reset the counter to 0 and exit.
};
```

By passing a reference to a *HPCxx_CSem* to a group of threads each of which does a "++" prior to exit, you can build a multi-threaded "join" operation.

```
class Worker: public HPCxx_Thread{
    HPCxx_CSem &c;
    public:
    Worker(HPCxx_CSem &c_): c(c_){}
    void run(){
        // work
        c++;
      }
};
int main(int argc, char *argv[]){
   HPCxx_Group *g;
   hpcxx_init(&argc, &argv, g);
   HPCxx_CSem cs(NUMWORKERS);
   for(int i = 0; i < NUMWORKERS; i++)
        Worker *w = new Worker(cs);
        w->start();
        }
   cs.waitAndReset(); //wait here for all workers to finish.
   hpcxx_exit(g);
   return 0;
}
```

Mutex locks. Unlike Java, the library cannot support synchronized methods or CC++ atomic members, but a simple Mutex object with two functions lock and unlock provide the basic capability.

```
class HPCxx_Mutex{
   public:
      void lock();
      void unlock();
};
```

To provide a synchronized method that only allows one thread at a time execution authority, one can introduce a private mutex variable and protect the critical section with locks as follows.

```
class Myclass: public HPCxx_Runnable{
   HPCxx_Mutex l;
   public:
      void synchronized(){
          l.lock();
          ....
          l.unlock();
      }
```

4.1.2 Collective Operations. Recall that an HPC++ computation consists of a set of *nodes*, each of which contains one or more *contexts*. Each context runs one or more *threads*.

To access the node and context structure of a computation the HPC++Lib initialization creates an object called a group. The *HPCxx_Group* class has the following public interface.

```
class HPCxx_Group{
   public:
   // Create a new group for the current context.
   HPCxx_Group(hpcxx_id_t &groupID = HPCXX_GEN_LOCAL_GROUPID,
                       const char *name = NULL);

   // Create a group whose membership is this context
   //and those in the list
   HPCxx_Group(const HPCxx_ContextID *&id,
               int count,
               hpcxx_id_t &groupID = HPCXX_GEN_LOCAL_GROUPID,
               const char *name = NULL);

   ~HPCxx_Group();
   hpcxx_id_t &getGroupID();
   static HPCxx_Group *getGroup(hpcxx_id_t groupID);
   // Get the number of contexts that are participating
   // in this group
   int getNumContexts();
   // Return an ordered array of context IDs in
   // this group.  This array is identical for every member
```

```
     // of the group.
     HPCxx_ContextID *getContextIDs();
     // Return the context id for zero-based context <n> where
     // <n> is less than the current number of contexts
     HPCxx_ContextID getContextID(int context);
     // Set the number of threads for this group in *this*
     // context.
     void setNumThreads(int count);
     int getNumThreads();
     void setName(const char *name);
     const char *getName();
   };
```

As shown below, a node contains all of the contexts running on the machine, and the mechanisms to create new ones.

```
   class HPCxx_Node{
     public:

     HPCxx_Node(const char *name = NULL);
     HPCxx_Node(const HPCxx_Node &node);
     ~HPCxx_Node();
     bool contextIsLocal(const HPCxx_ContextID &id);
     int getNumContexts();
     // Get an array of global pointers to the contexts
     // on this node.
     HPCxx_GlobalPtr<HPCxx_Context> *getContexts();

     // Create a new context and add it to this node
     int addContext();
     // Create a new context and run the specified executable
     int addContext(const char *execPath, char **argv);
     void setName(const char *name);
     const char *getName();
   };
```

A context keeps track of the threads, and its ContextID provides a handle that can be passed to other contexts.

```
   class HPCxx_Context{
     public:

     HPCxx_Context(const char *name=NULL);
     ~HPCxx_Context();

     HPCxx_ContextID getContextID();
     bool isMasterContext();
```

```
// Return the current number of threads in this context
int getNumThreads();
// Null terminated list of the current threads in this
node hpcxx_id_t *getThreadIDs();
// Return the number of groups of which this context is
// a member.
int getNumGroups();
// Return a list of the groups of which this context is
// a member.
hpcxx_id_t *getGroupIDs();
void setName(const char *name);
const char *getName();
};
```

A group object represents a set of nodes and contexts and is the basis for collective operations.

Groups are used to identify sets of threads and sets of contexts that participate in collective operations like barriers. In this section we only describe how a set of threads on a single context can use collective operations. Multi-context operations will be described in greater detail in the multi-context programming sections below.

The basic operation is barrier synchronization. This is accomplished in following steps:

We first allocate an object of type *HPCxx_Group* and set the number of threads to the maximum number that will participate in the operation. For example, to set the thread count on the main group to be 13 we can write the following.

```
int main(int argc, char *argv[]){
    HPCxx_Group *g
    hpcxx_init(&argc, &argv, g);
    g->setThreadCout(13);
    HPCxx_Barrier barrier(*g);
```

As shown above, a *HPCxx_Barrier* object must be allocated for the group. This can be accomplished in three ways:

– Use the group created in the initialization *hpcxx_init()*. This is the standard way SPMD computations do collective operations and it is described in greater detail below.
– Allocate the group with the constructor that takes an array of context IDs as an argument. This provides a limited form of "subset" SIMD parallelism and will also be described in greater detail later.
– Allocate a group object with the void constructor. This group will refer to this context only and will only synchronize threads on this context.

The constructor for the barrier takes a reference to the *Group* object.

Each thread that will participate in the barrier operation must then acquire a key from the barrier object with the *getKey*() function. Once the required number of threads have a key to enter the barrier, the barrier can be invoked by means of the overloaded () operator as shown in the example below.

```
class Worker: public HPCxx_Thread{
    int my_key;
    HPCxx_Barrier &barrier;
  public:
    Worker(HPCxx_Barrier & b): barrier(b){
      my_key = barrier.getKey();
    }
    void run(){
        while( notdone ){
            // work
            barrier(key);
        }
    }
};
int main(int argc, char *argv[]){
    HPCxx_Group *g;
    hpcxx_init(&argc, &argv, g);
    g->setThreadCout(13);
    HPCxx_Barrier barrier(g);
    for(int i = 0; i < 13; i++){
        Worker *w = new Worker(barrier);
        w->start();
    }
    hpcxx_exit(g);
}
```

A thread can participate in more than one barrier group and a barrier can be deallocated. The thread count of a *Group* may be changed, a new barrier may be allocated and thread can request new keys.

Reductions. Other collective operations exist and they are subclasses of the *HPCxx_Barrier* class. For example, let *intAdd* be the class,

```
class intAdd{
  public:
    int & operator()(int &x, int &y) { x += y; return x;}
};
```

To create an object that can be used to form the sum-reduction of one integer from each thread, the declaration takes the form

```
HPCxx_Reduct1<int, intAdd> r(group);
```

and it can be used in the threads as follows:

```
class Worker: public HPCxx_Thread{
    int my_key;
    HPCxx_Reduct1<int, intAdd> &add;
  public:
      Worker(HPCxx_Reduct1<int, intAdd>  & a): add(a){
        my_key = add.getKey();
      }
      void run(){
              int x =3.14*my_id;
              // now compute the sum of all x values
              int t =  add(key, x, intAdd() );
          }
      }
};
```

The public definition of the reduction class is given by

```
template <class T, class Oper>
class HPCxx_Reduct1: public HPCxx_Barrier{
    public:
        HPCxx_Reduct1(HPCxx_Group &);
        T operator()(int key, T &x, Oper op);
        T* destructive(int key, T *buffer, Oper op);
};
```

The operation can be invoked with the overloaded () operation as in the example above, or with the *destructive*() form which requires a user supplied buffer to hold the arguments and returns a pointer to the buffer that holds the result. to avoid making copies all of the buffers are modified in the computation. This operation is designed to be as efficient as possible, so it is implemented as a tree reduction. Hence the binary operator is required to be associate, i.e.

```
op(x, op(y, z)) == op( op(x, y), z)
```

The *destructive* form is much faster if the size of the data type T is large. A mult-argument form of this reduction will allow operations of the form

$$sum = \sum_{i=0,n} Op(x1_i, x2_i, ..., xK_i)$$

and it is declared as by the template

```
template < class R, class T1, class T2, ... TK ,
           class Op1, class Op2 >
class HPCxx_ReductK{
    public:
```

```
        HPCxx_ReductK(Hpxx_Group &);
        R & operator()(int key, T1, T2, ..., Tk , Op2, Op1);
};
```

where K is 2, 3, 4 or 5 in the current implementation and Op1 returns a value
of type R and Op2 is an associative binary operator on type R.

Broadcasts. A synchronized broadcast of a value between a set of threads is
accomplished with the operation

```
    template < class T >
    class HPCxx_Bcast{
       public:
          HPCxx_Bcast(HpxxGroup &);
          T  operator()(int key, T *x);
```

In this case, only one thread supplies a non-null pointer to the value and all
the others receive a copy of that value.

Multicasts. A value in each thread can be concatenated into a vector of values
by the synchronized multicast operation.

```
    template < class T >
    class HPCxx_Mcast{
       public:
          HPCxx_Mcast(Hpxx_Group &);
          T *  operator()(int key,  T &x);
```

In this case, the operator allocates an array of the appropriate size and copies
the argument values into the array in "key" order.

4.2 Examples of Multi-threaded Computations

4.2.1 The NAS EP Benchmark.
The NAS Embarrassingly Parallel bench-
mark illustrates a common approach to parallelizing loops using the thread
library. The computation consists of computing a large number of Gaussian
pairs and gathering statistics about the results (see [2] for more details). The
critical component of the computation is a loop of the form:

```
    double q[nq], gc;
    for(k = 1; k <= nn; k++)
       compute_pairs(k);
```

The *compute_pairs* function calculates the pairs associated with the parameter k and updates the array q and the scalar gc by adding in new values
computed for that value of k. There are no other side-effects of calling com-
pute_pairs, so parallelization is very easy.

Our approach is to partition the loop and encapsulate the computation
into a set of independent objects which each compute a subset of the iterations. To accomplish this we duplicate the array q and the scalar gc as

members of a *HPCxx_Runnable* class Gaussian shown below. In addition, each Gaussian object is given a unique identifier which is used to identify the subset of the iteration space that the object is responsible for computing.

The main program creates *THREAD_NUM* instances of the Gaussian class. To signal the termination of the computation, the main program also allocates a *HPCxx_CSem* object initialized to count to *THREAD_NUM* and each Gaussian object is given a pointer to this object. When the threads executing the Gaussian objects complete their task they each increment this counter. The main thread waits until the total count reaches *THREAD_NUM* and then calculates the sum of the q and gc values.

```
class Gaussian : public HPCxx_Runnable{
   int myId;
   HPCxx_CSem *cs;
  public:
   double q[nq];
   double gc;

   void init(int id, HPCxx_CSem *cs_){
           myId=id; cs=cs_; .... }
   void    compute_pairs(int kk);
   void    run(void){
      for(int k = myId+1; k <= nn; k = k+THREAD_NUM){
           compute_pairs(k);
           }
      (*cs)++;
   }
};

void main(int argc, char *argv[]){
 double gc;
 int i, k;
      HPCxx_Group *g;
      hpcxx_init(&argc, &argv, g);

      G = (Gaussian *) new Gaussian[THREAD_NUM];
      HPCxx_CSem cs(THREAD_NUM);
      for(i = 0; i < THREAD_NUM; i++) G[i].init(i, &cs);
      for(k = 0; k < THREAD_NUM; k++){
           HPCxx_Thread *th = new HPCxx_Thread(&G[k]);
           th->start();
        }
      cs.waitAndReset();
```

```
for(i = 0; i < nq; i++) q[i] = 0.0;
gc = 0.0;
 for(k = 0; k < NODES; k++)
    for( i = 0; i < nq; i++){
      q[i] += G[k].q[i];
      gc   += G[k].gc;
      }
hpcxx_exit(g);
}
```

This program was run on a 10 processor SGI Power Challenge with the value of THREAD_NUM ranging between 1 and 4096. As shown in the table below, the performance is predictable and linear through 8 threads. Beyond that point the behavior is very irregular. Because the threads are scheduled dynamically and must compete for system resource processes, the performance for different runs can vary by as much as 50%. (This is common on the SGI SMP systems.) In the table we plot the maximum and minimum recorded execution times and the speed-up associated with the best time. The fact that speed-up values can exceed the number of processors available (10) is probably due to fortunate scheduling behavior rather than locality.

The important thing to notice about the behavior is that the sequential initialization of threads in the main program does not harm the performance even where the number of threads generated per processor is over 200.

The threads in this implementation are based on the SGI Pthreads library. The limit to the number of threads that can be generated was reached when we tried to use 4096. Most attempts to run the program with this number of threads resulted in runtime errors when requesting threads.

4.2.2 A Parallel Quicksort. To illustrate another example of using threads and synchronization in parallel programming, consider the problem of parallelizing a recursive computation. Quicksort is a standard fast sequential sorting algorithm, but it is not considered to be well suited for parallelization. For a problem of size n, the average execution time is $O(n * log(n))$. If we parallelize this with p processors, the speed-up is bounded by $\frac{p}{1+p/log(n)}$. With $n = 2^{20}$ and $p = 10$, this bound is 6.6. However, this bound can only be reached if the quicksort algorithm is lucky and selects the perfect partition value for the array at each step.

Our implementation of the parallel quicksort is shown below. The algorithm is conventional except at the point of the first recursive call where a new thread is generated if the size of the array is not too small or the call tree is not too deep. (We pass an additional parameter to keep track of the depth of the call tree.) Clearly there is no reason to spawn a thread for very small arrays; the cost of a small sequential sort may be less than the cost of spawning a new thread. The depth heuristic is also used to limit the number of threads in cases where the algorithm makes a series of bad choices for the partition value.

threads	max time	min time	max speed-up
1	218.3	218.3	1.0
2	116.5	116.1	1.9
4	59.7	59.0	3.7
8	28.3	28.1	7.8
16	28.1	25.2	8.0
32	31.6	24.7	8.8
64	29.4	20.7	10.5
128	22.5	19.6	11.1
256	30.5	20.4	10.7
512	29.4	20.3	10.8
1024	30.8	19.5	11.2
2048	29.7	19.4	11.2
4096	-	33.8	-

Table 4.1. NAS Embar Benchmark using Threads

A $HPCxx\_Sync < int >$ variable is used to synchronize the spawned thread with the calling thread.

```
template <class T>
void pqsort( T *x, int low, int high, int depth){
    HPCxx_Sync<int> s;
    int i = low;
    int j = high;
    int k = 0;
    int checkflag = 0;
    if (i >= j) return;
    T m = x[i];
    while( i < j){
        while ((x[j] >= m) && (j > low)) j--;
        while ((x[i] < m) && (i < high)) i++;
        if(i < j){ swap(x[i], x[j]);  }
        }
    if(j < high){
        if( (j-low < MINSIZE) || (depth > MAXDEPTH) ){
            pqsort(x, low, j, depth+1);
            }
        else{
            SortThread<float> Th(s, x, low, j, depth+1);
            Th.start();
            checkflag = 1;
            }
        }
}
```

```
        if(j+1 > low) pqsort(x, j+1, high, depth);
        int y;
        if(checkflag) s.read(y);
}
```

The *SortThread* $< T >$ class is based on a templated subclass of thread. The local state of each thread contains a reference to the sync variable, a pointer to the array of data and the index values of the range to be sorted and the depth of the tree when the object was created.

```
    template <class T>
    class SortThread: public HPCxx_Thread{
        HPCxx_Sync<int> &s;
        T *x;
        int low, high;
        int depth;
      public:
        SortThread(HPCxx_Sync<int> &s_, T *x_,
                    int low_, int high_, int depth_):
            s(s_), x(x_), low(low_), high(high_),
            depth(depth_), HPCxx_Thread(NULL){}
        void run(){
            int k = 0;
            pqsort(x, low, high, depth);
            s.write(k);
            }

    };
```

This program was run on the SGI Power Challenge with 10 processors for a series of random arrays of 5 million integers. As noted above, the speed-up is bounded by the theoretical limit of about 7. We also experimented with the MINSIZE and MAXDEPTH parameters. We found that a MINSIZE of 500 and a MAXDEPTH of 6 gave the results. We ran several hundred experiments and found that speed-up ranged from 5.6 to 6.6 with an average of 6.2 for 10 processors. With a depth of 6 the number of threads was bounded by 128.

What is not clear from our experiments is the role thread scheduling and thread initialization play in the final performance results. This is a topic that is under current investigation.

5. Implementing the HPC++ Parallel Loop Directives

Parallel loops in HPC++ can arise in two places: inside a standard function or in a member function for a class. In both cases, these occurrences may be part of an instantiation of a template. We first describe the transformational

problems associated with class member functions. The approach we use is
based on a style of loop transformations invented by Aart Bik for parallelizing loops in Java programs [4]. The basic approach was illustrated in the
Embarrassingly Parallel example in the previous section.

Consider the following example.

```
class C{
   double x[N];
   float &y;
   public:
   void f(float *z, int n){
      double tmp = 0;
      #pragma HPC_INDEPENDENT
      for(int i = 0; i < n; i++){
            #pragma HPC_REDUCE tmp
            tmp += y*x[i]+*z++;
            }
      ...
      cout << tmp;
   }
   ...
};
```

To parallelize the loop we will replace it with another loop which spawns a
number (K) of threads. Each thread will execute a new class member function
(generated by the compiler) which executes a subset of the iterations of the
original loop. The threads that are spawned to execute the loop are of a
subclass of the *HPCxx_Thread* class that is generated by the compiler.

The primary task of the compiler is to resolve the scope of the variables
that are referenced within the body of the loop and to determine which of
these must be duplicated in each thread and which need only be referenced
from the thread. More specifically, we see the loop in our example contains

- loop bounds such as n and other variables, in this case z and tmp, that are
  scoped within the member function that contains the loop.
- variables that are referenced within loop but are data members of the
  object or class.
- globally defined variables.

The last two cases are not a problem because the semantics of a parallel loop
require that any loop carried data dependences be a reduction form and be
so labeled (as with the variable tmp in the example above. Consequently,
if these are not reduction variables, we can refer to them directly from the
generated member function.

However, variables that are members of the first category are private
to the scope of the original member function. Copies or references to these
variables must be duplicated as private data members for new thread class.

In addition, a description of the subset of iterations to be executed by each thread object must also be included in the thread object. This iteration space partitioning can be done in any of the classical ways (see [4]). In this case we illustrate the example with simple loop blocking.

In our example, the thread class that is generated is given below.

```
class C_Thread: public HPCxx_Thread{
   float *z;
   int bs;    // the iterations subspace block size
   int base;  // the start of the iteration subspace.
   double &tmp;
   HPCxx_Reduct1<double, doubleAdd> &add;
   int key;
  public:
    void C_Thread(float *z_, double &tmp_, int bs_,
       HPCxx_Reduct1<double, doubleAdd> &add_, int base_):
       Thread(), add(add_), z(z_), tmp(tmp_), bs(bs_),
            base(base_){key = add.getKey()}
    void run(){
       r->f_blocked(z, bs, base, key);
       }
};
```

The user's class C must be modified as follows. The compiler must create a new member function, called *f_blocked()* below, which executes a blocked version of the original loop. This function is called by the thread class as shown above. In addition, the original loop has to be modified to spawn the K threads (where K is determined by the runtime environment) and start each thread. (As in our previous examples, we have deleted the details about removing the thread objects when the thread completes execution.)

The user class is also given local synchronization objects to signal the termination of the loop. For loops that do not have any reduction operations, we can synchronize the completion of the original iteration with a *HPCxx_CSem* as was done in the Embar benchmark in the previous section. However, in this case, we do have a reduction, so we use the reduction classes and generate a barrier-based reduction that will synchronize all of the iteration classes with the calling thread as shown below.

```
class C{
   double x[N];
   float &y;
   HPCxx_Group g;
   HPCxx_Reduct1<double, doubleAdd> add;
  public:
   C(...): add(g){ .... }
```

```
void f_blocked(float *z, double &tmp, int bs, int base,
               int key){
    z = z+bs;
    double t = 0;
    for(int i = base; i < base+ bs; i++){
        t = y*x[i]+*z++;
        }
    add(key, t, doubleAdd());
    }

void f(float *z, int n){
    double tmp = 0;
    . . .
    g.setThreadCount(K+1);
    int key = add.getKey();
    for(int th = 0; th < K; th++){
      C_Thread *t = new C_Thread(this,z, tmp, n/K,
                                 th*(n/K), add);
      t->start();
      }
    tmp = add(key, 0.0, doubleAdd());
    . . .
    cout << tmp;
  }
  . . .
};
```

We have omitted treatment of the scheduling algorithms that are possible and refer the reader to [4].

6. Multi-context Programming and Global Pointers

The preceding sections of this chapter have discussed multi-threaded parallel programming in a single address space context.

However, one of the powers of HPC++ is the ability of a a program in one context to communicate with another. There are two ways to do this. One method is for one program to dynamically "attach" itself to a second program, and the second method is called *Single Program Multiple Data (SPMD)* style, where a number of copies of the same program are loaded into different contexts at the same time. HPC++ is designed around the SPMD model of multi-context programming.

The central problem associated with multi-context computation is the communication and synchronization of events between two contexts. HPC++ is based on the CC++ global pointer concept and the library described here implements this with a *GlobalPtr* < *T* > template as is done in the MPC++ Template Library [10].

A global pointer is an object that is a proxy for a remote object. In most ways it can be treated exactly as a pointer to a local object. One major difference is that global pointers can only point to objects allocated from a special "global data area". To allocate a global pointer object of type *T* from the global area one can write

```
HPCxx_GlobalPtr<T> p = new ("hpcxx_global") T(args);
```

or, for a global pointer to an array of 100 objects,

```
HPCxx_GlobalPtr<T> p = new ("hpcxx_global") T[100];
```

For objects of simple type a global pointer can be dereferenced like any other pointer. For example, assignment and copy through a global pointer is given by

```
HPCxx_GlobalPtr<float> p = new ("hpcxx_global") int;
*p = 3.14;
float y = 2 - *p;
```

Integer arithmetic and the [] operator can be applied to global pointers in the same way as ordinary pointers. Because global pointer operations are far more expensive than regular pointer dereferencing, there are special operators for reading and writing blocks of data.

```
void HPCxx_GlobalPtr<T>::read(T *buffer, int size);
void HPCxx_GlobalPtr<T>::write(T *buffer, int size);
```

Objects of a user-defined type may be copied through a global pointer only if there are pack and unpack friend functions defined as follows. Suppose you have a class of the form shown below. You must also supply a special function that knows how to pack an array of such objects.

```
class C{
    int x;
    float y[100];
  public:
    friend void hpcxx_pack(HPCxx_Buffer *b, C *buffer,
                           int size);
    friend void hpcxx_unpack(HPCxx_Buffer *b, C *buffer,
                             int &size);
};
void hpcxx_pack(HPCxx_Buffer *b, C *buffer, int size){
    hpcxx_pack(b, size, 1);
    for(int i = 0; i < size; i++){
```

```
            hpcxx_pack(b, C[i].x, 1);
            hpcxx_pack(b, C[i].y, 100);
          }
    }
    void hpcxx_unpack(HPCxx_Buffer *b, C *buffer, int &size){
        hpcxx_unpack(b, size, 1);
        for(int i = 0; i < size; i++){
            hpcxx_unpack(b, C[i].x, 1);
            hpcxx_unpack(b, C[i].y, 100);
          }
    }
```

These pack and unpack functions can be considered a type of remote constructor. For example, suppose a class object contains a pointer to a buffer in the local heap. It is possible to write the unpack function so that it allocates the appropriate storage on the remote context and initializes it with the appropriate data.

Unfortunately, it is not possible to access data members directly through global pointers without substantial compiler support. The following is an illegal operation

```
    class D{
      public:
         int x;
    };
    ...
    HPCxx_GlobalPtr<D> p = new (''hpcxx_global'') D;
    ...
    p->x;    // illegal member reference
```

To solve this problem, we must create a data access function that returns this value. Then we can make a remote member call.

6.1 Remote Function and Member Calls

For a user defined class C with member function,

```
    class C{
       public:
          int foo(float, char);
    };
```

the standard way to invoke the member through a pointer is an expression of the form:

```
    C *p;
    p->foo(3.14, 'x');
```

It is a bit more work to make the member function call though a global
pointer. First, for each type *C* we must register the class and all members that
will be called through global pointers. Registering the class is easy. There is a
macro that will accomplish this task and it should be called at the top level.
We next must register the member as shown below.

```
hpxx_register(C);
```

```
int main(int argc, char *argv[]){
    HPCxx_Group *g;
    hpxx_init(&argc, &argv, g);
    hpcxx_id_t C_foo_id = hpxx_register(C::foo);
```

The overloaded *register* templated function builds a table for systems information about registered functions, classes, and member functions, and
returns its location as an ID.

Because this ID is an index into the table, it is essential that each context
register the members in exactly the same order.

To invoke the member function, there is a special function template

```
HPCxx_GlobalPtr<C> P;
    . . .
hpcxx_id_t = hpcxx_invoke(P, C_foo_id, 3.13, 'x');
```

Invoke will call *C::foo(3.13, 'x')* in the context that contains the object that
P points to. The calling process will wait until the function returns.

The asynchronous invoke will allow the calling function to continue executing until the result is needed.

```
HPCxx_Sync<int> sz;
```

```
hpcxx_ainvoke(&sz, P, C_foo_id, 3.13, 'x');
```

```
    .... // go do some work
```

```
int z = sz; // wait here.
```

It should be noted that it is not a good idea to pass pointers as argument
values to *invoke* or *ainvoke*. However, it is completely legal to pass global
pointers and return global pointers as results of remote member invocations.

6.1.1 Global Functions. Ordinary functions can be invoked remotely. By
using a *ContextID*, the context that should invoke the function may be
identified.

```
HPCxx_ContextID HPCxx_Group::getContextID(int i);
```

For example, to call a function in context "3" from context "0", the function must be registered in each context. (As with member functions, the

order of the function registration determines the function identifier, so the functions must be registered in exactly the same order in each context.)

```
double fun(char x, int y);

int main(int argc, int *argv[]){
    HPCxx_Group *g;
    hpxx_init(&argc, &argv, g);

    hpcxx_id_t = hpcxx_register(fun);
    // remote invocation of x = fun('z', 44);
    double x =
        hpcxx_invoke(g.getContext(3), fun_id , 'z', 44);

    //asynchronous invocation
    HPCxx_Sync<double> sx;
    hpcxx_ainvoke(&sx, g.getContext(3), fun_id, 'z', 44 );
    double x = sx;
    ....
}
```

6.2 Using Corba IDL to Generate Proxies

Two of the most anoying aspects of the HPC++Lib are the requirements to register member functions and write the pack and unpack routines for user-defined classes. In addition, the use of the invoke template syntax

```
HPCxx_GlobalPtr<C> P;
...
int z = hpcxx_invoke(P, member_id, 3.13, 'x');
```

instead of the more conventional syntax

```
z = P->member(3.13, 'x');
```

is clearly awkward.

Unfortunately, the C++ language does not allow an extension to the overloading of the $->$ operator that will provide this capability. However, there is another solution to this problem.

The CORBA Interface Definition Language (IDL) provides a well structured language for defining the public interface to remote objects and serializable classes.

As a seperate utility, HPC++Lib provides an IDL to C++ translator that maps interface specifications to user-defined classes. For example, the IDL interface definition of a remote blackboard object class and the definition of a structure which represents a graphical object (*Gliph*) that can be drawn on the blackboard.

```
struct Gliph{
   short type;
   int x, y;
   int r, g, b;
};
```

```
interface BBoard{
   int draw(in Gliph mark );
};
```

The IDL to C++ compiler generates a special case of the global pointer template and the header for the blackboard class as shown below. The prototype for BBoard contains a static registration function that registers all the member functions. The user only need call this one registration function at the start of the program. The specialization of the the global pointer template contains the requisite overloading of the $->$ operator and a new member function for each of the functions in the public interface.

```
class BBoard{
    static int draw_id;
  public:
    static void register(){
        draw_id = hpcxx_register(Bboard::draw);
        }
    int draw(Gliph mark);
};
```

```
class HPCxx_GlobalPtr<BBoard>{
    // implementation specific GP attributes
  public:
    ...
    HPCxx_GlobalPtr<BBoard> * operator ->(){ return this; }
    int draw(Gliph mark , float &x){
        return hpcxx_invoke(*this, BBoard::draw_id, mark);
        }
};
```

The structure *Gliph* in the interface specification is compiled into a structure which contains the serialization pack and unpack functions.

Using this tool the user compiles the interface specification into a new header file. This file can be included into the C++ files which contain the use of the class as well as the definition of the functions like *BBoard::draw*. To use the class with remote pointers the program must include only the registration call

```
BBoard::register();
```

in the main program.

7. The SPMD Execution Model

The Single Program Multiple Data Model (SPMD) of execution is one of the standard models used in parallel scientific programming. Our library supports this model as follows. At program load time n copies of a single program is loaded into n processes which each define a running context.

The running processes are coordinated by the *hpcxx_init* initialization routine which is invoked as the first call in the main program of each context.

```
int main(int argc, char *argv[]){
   HPCxx_Group *g;

   hpcxx_init(&argc, &argv, g);
   . . .
```

As described in the multi-context programming section, the context IDs allow one context to make remote function calls to any of the other contexts.

The SPMD execution continues with one thread of control per context executing main. However, that thread can dynamically create new threads within its context. There is no provision for thread objects to be moved from one context to another.

7.1 Barrier Synchronization and Collective Operations

In SPMD execution mode, the runtime system provides the same collective operations as were provided before for multi-threaded computation. The only semantic difference is that the collective operations apply across every context and every thread of the group.

The only syntactic difference is that we allow a special form of the overloaded () operator that does not require a thread "key". For example, to do a barrier between contexts all we need is is the *HPCxx_Group* object.

```
int main(int argc, char *argv[]){
   HPCxx_Group *context_set;

   hpcxx_init(&argc, &argv, context_set);

   HPCxx_Barrier barrier(context_set);
   HPCxx_Reduct1<float, floatAdd>
                 float_reduct(context_set);
   . . .
   barrier();
   float z = 3.14
   z = float_reduct(z, floatAdd());
```

Note that the thread key can be used if there are multiple threads in a context that want to synchronize with the other contexts.

8. Conclusion

This chapter has outlined a library and compilation strategy that is being used to implement the HPC++ Level 1 design. An earlier version of HPC++Lib was used to implement the prototype PSTL library and future releases of PSTL will be completely in terms of HPC++Lib.

Our goal in presenting this library goes beyond illustrating the foundation for HPC++ tools. We also feel that this library will be used by application programmers directly and care has been taken to make it as usable as possible for large scale scientific application. In particular, we note that the MPC++ MTTL has been in use with the Real World Computing Partnership as an application programming platform for nearly one year and CC++ has been in use for two years. HPC++Lib is modeled on these successful systems and adds only a Java style thread class and a library for collective operations. In conjunction with the parallel STL, we feel that this will be an effective tool for writing parallel programs.

The initial release of HPC++Lib will be available by the time of this publication at http://www.extreme.indiana.edu and other sites within the Department of Energy. There will be two runtime systems in the initial release. One version will be based on the Argonne/ISI Nexus runtime system and the other will be using the LANL version of Tulip [3]. Complete documentation and sample programs will be available with the release.

References

1. Ken Arnold and James Gosling. *The Java Programming Language*. Addison Wesley, 1996.
2. D.H. Bailey, E. Barszcz, L. Dagum, and H.D. Simon. NAS Parallel Benchmark Results October 1994. Technical Report NAS-94-001, NASA Ames Research Center, 1994.
3. P. Beckman and D. Gannon. Tulip: A portable run-time system for object-parallel systems. In *Proceedings of the 10th International Parallel Processing Symposium*, April 1996.
4. Aart J.C. Bik and D. Gannon. Automatically exploiting implicit parallelism in java. Technical report, Department of Computer Science, Indiana University, 1996.
5. William W. Carlson and Jesse M. Draper. Distributed data access in AC. In *Fifth ACM Sigplan Symposium on Principles and Practices of Parallel Programming*, 1995.
6. K. Mani Chandy and Carl Kesselman. CC++: A declarative concurrent object-oriented programming notation, 1993. In *Research Directions in Concurrent Object Oriented Programming*, MIT Press.

7. D. Culler, A. Dusseau, S. Goldstein, A. Krishnamurthy, S. Lumetta, T. von Eicken, and K. Yelick. Parallel programming in Split-C. In *Supercomputing '93*, 1993.
8. High Performance Fortran Forum. Draft High Performance Fortran Language Specification, November 1992. Version 0.4.
9. Object Management Group. The Common Object Request Broker: Architecture and specification, July 1995. Revision 2.0.
10. Yutaka Ishikawa. Multiple threads template library. Technical Report TR-96-012, Real World Computing Partnership, September 1996.
11. Elizabeth Johnson and Dennis Gannon. Hpc++: Experiments with the parallel standard template library. Technical Report TR-96-51, Indiana University, Department of Computer Science, December 1996.
12. Vipin Kumar, Ananth Grama, Anshul Gupta, and George Karypis. *Introduction To Parallel Computing: Design and Analysis of Algorithms*. Benjamin/Cummings Publishing Company, 1994.
13. Mark Nelson. *C++ Programmer's Guide to the Standard Template Library*. IDG Books Worldwide, 1995.
14. Alexander Stepanov and Meng Lee. The Standard Template Library. Technical Report HPL-95-11, Hewlett-Packard Laboratories, January 1995.
15. Gregory Wilson and Paul Lu. *Parallel Programming Using C++*. MIT Press, 1996.
16. Gregory Wilson and William O'Farrell. An introduction to ABC++. 1995.

Chapter 4. A Concurrency Abstraction Model for Avoiding Inheritance Anomaly in Object-Oriented Programs

Sandeep Kumar[1] and Dharma P. Agrawal[2]

[1] Hewlett-Packard Laboratories, One Main Street, 10th Floor, Cambridge, MA 02142
[2] Department of ECECS, ML 0030, University of Cincinnati, PO Box 210030, Cincinnati, OH 45221-0030

Summary. In a concurrent object-oriented programming language one would like to be able to inherit behavior and realize synchronization control without compromising the flexibility of either the inheritance mechanism or the synchronization mechanism. A problem called the *inheritance anomaly* arises when synchronization constraints are implemented within the methods of a class and an attempt is made to specialize methods through inheritance. The anomaly occurs when a subclass violates the synchronization constraints assumed by the superclass. A subclass should have the flexibility to add methods, add instance variables, and redefine inherited methods. Ideally, all the methods of a superclass should be reusable. However, if the synchronization constraints are defined by the superclass in a manner prohibiting incremental modification through inheritance, they cannot be reused, and must be reimplemented to reflect the new constraints; hence, inheritance is rendered useless. We have proposed a novel model of concurrency abstraction, where (a) the specification of the synchronization code is kept separate from the method bodies, and (b) the sequential and concurrent parts in the method bodies of a superclass are inherited by its subclasses in an orthogonal manner.

1. Introduction

A programming model is a collection of program abstractions which provides a programmer with a simplified, and transparent, view of the computer's hardware/software system. Parallel programming models are specifically designed for multiprocessors, multicomputers, or vector computers, and are characterized as: shared-variable, message-passing, data-parallel, object-oriented (OO), functional, logic, and heterogeneous. Parallel programming languages provide a platform to a programmer for effectively expressing (or, *specifying*) his/her intent of parallel execution of the parts of computations in an application. A parallel program is a collection of processes which are the basic computational units. The granularity of a process may vary in different programming models and applications. In this work we address issues relating to the use of the OO programming model in programming parallel machines [20].

OO programming is a style of programming which promotes program abstraction, and thus, leads to a modular and portable program and a reusable software. This paradigm has radically influenced the design and development

S. Pande, D.P. Agrawal (Eds.): Compiler Optimizations for Scalable PS, LNCS 1808, pp. 109-137, 2001.
© Springer-Verlag Berlin Heidelberg 2001

of almost all kinds of computer applications including user-interfaces, data structure libraries, computer-aided design, scientific computing, databases, network management, client-server based applications, compilers and operating systems.

Unlike the procedural approach, where problem-solving is based around actions, OO programming provides a natural facility for modeling and decomposing a problem into *objects*. An object is a program entity which encapsulates data (a.k.a. *instance variables*) and operations (a.k.a. *methods*) into a single computational unit. The values of the instance variables determine the *state* of an object. Objects are dynamically created and their types may change during the course of program execution. The computing is done by sending *messages* (a.k.a. method invocation) among objects. In Figure 1.1 the methods (marked as labels on the edges) transform the initial states (shown as circles), r_0 and s_0, of two objects, O_1 and O_2, into their final states, r_M and s_N, respectively. Notice that O_2 sends a message, p_2, to O_1 while executing its method, q_2.

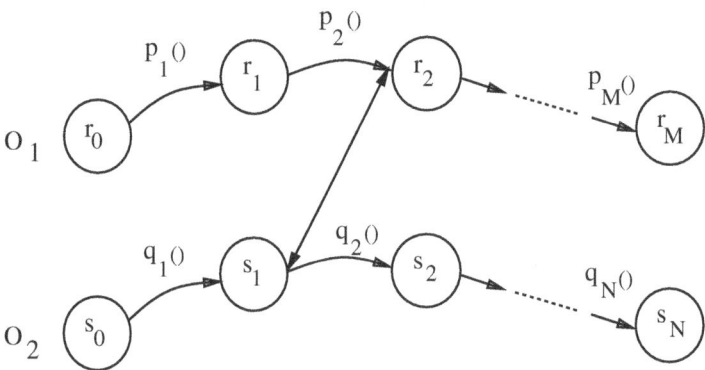

Fig. 1.1. The object-oriented computing model.

On one hand, the OO language features are a boon to writing portable programs efficiently; but on the other hand they also contribute to degraded performance at run-time. It turns out that the concurrency is a natural consequence of the concept of objects: The concurrent use of coroutines in conventional programming is akin to the concurrent manipulation of objects in OO programming. Notice from Figure 1.1 that the two objects, O_1 and O_2, change their states independently and only occasionally exchange values. Clearly, the two objects can compute concurrently. Since the OO programming model is inherently parallel, it should be feasible to exploit the potential parallelism from an OO program in order to improve its performance. Furthermore, if two states for an object can be computed independently, a finer granularity of parallelism can be exploited. For instance in the Actor [1] based concurrent OO languages, maximal fine-grained object-level concurrency can be specified. Load-balancing becomes fairly easy as the objects can be freely placed and migrated within a system. Such languages have been proposed as scalable programming approaches for massively parallel machines [9].

Several research projects have successfully exploited the *data parallel* (SIMD) programming model in C++, notably, Mentat [15], C** [23], pC++ [13], and Charm++ [19]; probably these researchers were overwhelmed by the benefits of this model as noted in Fortran 90 and High Performance Fortran (HPF) [16] applications. The data parallel models of computations exploit the property of *homogeneity* in computational data structures, as is commonly found in scientific applications. For *heterogeneous* computations, however, it is believed that the *task-parallel* [1] (SPMD or MIMD) model is more effective than the data-parallel model. Such a model exists in Fortran M [12] and CC++ [8].

Most of the OO applications by nature are based on heterogeneous computations, and consequently, are more amenable to task-parallelism. Besides, the existence of numerous, inherently concurrent objects, can assist in masking the effects of latency (as there is always work to be scheduled). Furthermore, the SPMD model is cleanly represented in a task parallel OO language where the data and code that manipulates that data are clearly identified.

Consider a typical OO program segment shown below. Our goal is to seek a program transformation from the left to the right. In other words, can we concurrently execute S_1 and S_2, and if so, *how*?

$$
\begin{array}{lll}
 & \texttt{par \{} & \\
S_1\text{: object}_i.\text{method}_p(); & & S'_1\text{: object}_i.\text{method}_p(); \\
 & \stackrel{?}{\Rightarrow} & \\
S_2\text{: object}_j.\text{method}_q(); & & S'_2\text{: object}_j.\text{method}_q(); \\
 & \texttt{\}} & \\
\end{array}
$$

There are two possible approaches: either (a) *specify* the above parallelism by writing a parallel program in a Concurrent OO Programming Language (COOPL), or (b) automatically *detect* that the above transformation is valid and then restructure the program. In this work we would limit our discussions to specification of parallelism.

In designing a parallel language we aim for: (i) efficiency in its implementation, (ii) portability across different machines, (iii) compatibility with existing sequential languages, (iv) expressiveness of parallelism, and (v) ease of programming. A COOPL offers the benefits of object-orientation, primarily, inherently concurrent objects, ease of programming and code-reuse with the task of specification of parallelism (or more generally, concurrency). Several COOPLs have been proposed in the literature (refer to [4, 18, 33] for a survey).

---

[1] a.k.a. *control* or *functional* parallelism.

It is unfortunate that when parallel programs are written in most of these COOPLs, the *inheritance anomaly* [25] is unavoidable and the reusability of the sequential components is improbable [21, 22]. In using a COOPL, one would want to inherit the behavior and realize synchronization control without compromising the flexibility in either exploiting the inheritance characteristics or using different synchronization schemes. A problem called the inheritance anomaly [25] arises when synchronization constraints are implemented within the methods of a class and an attempt is made to specialize methods through inheritance. The anomaly occurs when a subclass violates the synchronization constraints assumed by the superclass. A subclass should have the flexibility to add methods, add instance variables, and redefine inherited methods. Ideally, all the methods of a superclass should be reusable. However, if the synchronization constraints are defined by the superclass in a manner prohibiting incremental modification through inheritance, they cannot be reused, and must be reimplemented to reflect the new constraints; hence, inheritance is rendered useless.

We claim that following are the two primary reasons for causing the inheritance anomaly [25] and the probable reuse of the sequential components in a COOPL [22]:

- The synchronization constraints are implemented within the methods of a class and an attempt is made to specialize methods through inheritance. The anomaly occurs when a subclass violates the synchronization constraints assumed by the superclass.
- The inheritance of the sequential part and the concurrent part of a method code are not orthogonal.

In this work we have proposed a novel model of concurrency abstraction, where (a) the specification of the synchronization code is kept separate from the method bodies, and (b) the sequential and concurrent parts in the method bodies of a superclass are inherited by its subclasses in an orthogonal manner.

The rest of the chapter is organized as follows. Section 2 discusses the issues in designing and implementing a COOPL. In sections 3 and 4 we present a detailed description of the inheritance anomaly and the reuse of sequential classes, respectively. In section 5 we propose a framework for specifying parallelism in COOPLs. In section 6 we review various COOPL approaches proposed by researchers in solving different kinds of inheritance anomalies. In section 7 we describe the concurrency abstraction model we have adopted in designing our proposed COOPL, CORE. Subsequently, we give an overview of the CORE model and describe its features. Later, we illustrate with examples how a CORE programmer can effectively avoid the inheritance anomaly and also reuse the sequential classes. Finally, we discuss an implementation approach for CORE, summarize our conclusions and indicate directions for future research.

2. Approaches to Parallelism Specification

Conventionally, specification of task parallelism refers to explicit creation of multiple threads of control (or, tasks) which synchronize and communicate under a programmer's control. Therefore, a COOPL designer should provide explicit language constructs for specification, creation, suspension, reactivation, migration, termination, and synchronization of concurrent processes. A full compiler has to be implemented when a new COOPL is designed. Alternatively, one could extend a sequential OO language in widespread use, such as C++ [11], to support concurrency. The latter approach is more beneficial in that: (a) the learning curve is smaller, (b) incompatibility problems seldom arise, and most importantly, (c) a *preprocessor* and a low-level library of the target computer system can more easily upgrade the old compiler to implement high-level parallel constructs.

2.1 Issues in Designing a COOPL

A COOPL designer should carefully consider the pros and cons in selecting the following necessary language features:

1. **Active vs. Passive Objects**: An *active* object (a.k.a. an *actor* in [1]) possesses its own thread(s) of control. It encapsulates data structures, operations, and the necessary communication and synchronization constraints. An active object can be easily unified with the notion of a lightweight process [3]. In contrast, a *passive* object does not have its own thread of control. It must rely on either active objects containing it, or on some other process management scheme.
2. **Granularity of Parallelism**: Two choices are evident depending upon the level of parallelism granularity sought:
   a) **Intra-Object**: An active object may be characterized as: (i) a *sequential* object, if exactly one thread of control can exist in it; (ii) a *quasi-concurrent* object, such as a monitor, when multiple threads can exist in it, but only one can be active at a time; and (iii) a *concurrent* object, if multiple threads can be simultaneously active inside it [8,33].
   b) **Inter-Object**: If two objects receive the same message, then can they execute concurrently? For example, in CC++ [8], one can specify inter-object parallelism by enclosing the method invocations inside a parallel block, such as, a `cobegin-coend` construct [3], where an implicit synchronization is assumed at the end of the parallel block.
3. **Shared Memory vs. Distributed Memory Model** (SMM vs. DMM): Based on the target architecture, appropriate constructs for communication, synchronization, and partitioning of data and processes may be necessary. It should be noted that even sequential OOP is considered

equivalent to programming with messages: a method invocation on an object, say x, is synonymous to message send (as in DMM) whose receiver is x. However, floating pointers to data members (as in C++ [11]) may present a serious implementation hazard in COOPLs for DMMs.

4. **Object Distribution**: In a COOPL for a DMM, support for location independent object interaction, migration, and transparent access to other remote objects, may be necessary. This feature may require intense compiler support and can increase run-time overhead [9].

5. **Object Interaction**: On a SMM, communication may be achieved via synchronized access to shared variables, locks, monitors, etc., whereas on a DMM, both synchronous and asynchronous message passing schemes may be allowed. Besides, remote procedure call (RPC) and its two variants, blocking RPC and asynchronous RPC (ARPC) [7,34], may be supported, too.

6. **Selective Method Acceptance**: In a client/server based application [6], it may be necessary to provide support for server objects, who receive messages non-deterministically based on their internal states, parameters, etc..

7. **Inheritance**: The specification of synchronization code is considered as the most difficult part in writing parallel programs. Consequently, it is highly desirable to avoid rewriting of such code and instead reuse code via inheritance. Unfortunately, in many COOPLs, inheritance is either disallowed or limited [2,18,32,33], in part due to the occurrence of *inheritance anomaly* [24, 25]. This anomaly is a consequence of reconciling concurrency and inheritance in a COOPL, and its implications on a program include: (i) extensive breakage of encapsulation, and (ii) redefinitions of the inherited methods.

2.2 Issues in Designing Libraries

Parallelism can be made a second class citizen in COOPLs by providing OO libraries of reusable abstractions (classes). These classes hide the lower-level details pertaining to specification of parallelism, such as, architecture (SMM or DMM), data partitions, communications, and synchronization. Two kinds of libraries can be developed as described below:

– **Implicit Libraries**: These libraries use OO language features to encapsulate concurrency at the object-level. A comprehensive compiler support is essential for: (i) creating active objects without explicit user commands and in the presence of arbitrary levels of inheritance, (ii) preventing acceptance of a message by an object until it has been constructed, (iii) preventing destruction of an object until the thread of control has been terminated, (iv) object interaction, distribution and migration, and (v) preventing deadlocks.

– **Explicit Libraries**: These class libraries provide a set of abstract data types to support parallelism and synchronization. The objects of these classes are used in writing concurrent programs. In these libraries, the synchronization control and mutual exclusion code is more obvious at the user interface level. Most of these libraries are generally meant for programming on SMM [5].

The libraries are a good alternative to parallel programming as they are more easily portable. Some notable libraries reported in the literature are: ABC++, Parmacs [5], μC++, AT&T's Task Library, PRESTO, PANDA, AWESIME, ES-Kit, etc. [4,33]. Although the above approaches to parallel programming are considered simple and inexpensive, they require sophisticated compiler support. Moreover, they fail to avoid the inheritance anomaly as would be clear from the following section.

3. What Is the Inheritance Anomaly?

In this section we describe the inheritance anomaly. An excellent characterization of this anomaly can be found in [25], and it has also been discussed in [18, 22, 24, 32, 33].

Definition 3.1. A **synchronization constraint** is that piece of code in a concurrent program which imposes control over concurrent invocations on a given object. Such constraints manage concurrent operations and preserve the desired semantic properties of the object being acted upon. The invocations that are attempted at inappropriate times are subject to delay. Postponed invocations are those that invalidate the desired semantic property of that object[2].

Consider one of the classical concurrency problems, namely, *bounded buffer* [3]. This problem can be modeled by defining a class, B_Buffer, as shown in Figure 3.1. In this class[3], there are three methods: B_Buffer, Put, and Get. The constructor creates a buffer, buf, on the heap of a user-specified size, max. Note that buf is used as a circular array. Both the indices, in and out, are initialized to the first element of buf, and n represents the number of items stored in the buf so far. Put stores an input character, c, at the current index, in, and increments the values of in and n. On the other hand, Get retrieves a character, c, at the current index, out, from buf, and decrements the value of n but increments the value of out.

A synchronization constraint is necessary if Put and Get are concurrently invoked on an object of B_Buffer. This synchronization constraint(s) must satisfy following properties: (i) the execution of Put cannot be deferred as

---

[2] An excellent characterization of different synchronization schemes can be found in [3].

[3] Note that we have used the C++ syntax for defining classes in this section.

```
class B_Buffer {
    int in, out, n, max;
    char *buf;
  public:
    B_Buffer(int size) {
      max = size;
      buf = new char [max];
      in = out = n = 0;
    }

    void Put (char c) {              char Get (void) {
      P(empty);                        char c;
        buf[in] = c;                   P(full);
        in = (in+1) % max;               c = buf[out];
        n++;                             out = (out+1) % max;
      V(full);                           n--;
    }                                  V(empty);
                                       return c;
                                     }
};
```

Fig. 3.1. A class definition for B_Buffer.

long as there is an empty slot in buf, and (ii) the execution of Get must be postponed until there is an item in buf. In other words, the number of invocations for Put must be at least one more than the number of invocations for Get, but at the most equal to max. Such a constraint is to be provided by the programmer as part of the synchronization code in the concurrent program. For example, one could model the above synchronization constraint by using the P and V operations on two semaphores, full and empty.

Consider defining a subclass of B_Buffer, where we need different synchronization constraints. The methods Put and Get then may need non-trivial redefinitions. A situation where such redefinitions become necessary with inheritance of concurrent code in a COOPL is called the inheritance anomaly. In the following subsections, we review different kinds of inheritance anomalies as described in [25, 33].

3.1 State Partitioning Anomaly (SPA)

Consider Figure 3.2, where we have defined a subclass, B_Buffer2, of the base class, B_Buffer, as introduced in Figure 3.1. B_Buffer2 is a specialized version of B_Buffer, which inherits Put and Get from B_Buffer and defines a new method, GetMorethanOne. GetMorethanOne invokes Get as many times as is the input value of howmany.

```
class B_Buffer2: public B_Buffer {
  public:
    char GetMorethanOne (int howmany) {
      char last_char;
      for (int i=0; i < howmany; i++)
        last_char = Get();
      return last_char;
    }
};
```

Fig. 3.2. A class definition for B_Buffer2.

Put, Get, and GetMorethanOne can be concurrently invoked on an object of B_Buffer2. Besides the previous synchronization constraint for Put and Get in B_Buffer, now we must further ensure that whenever GetMorethanOne executes, there are at least two items in buf. Based on the current state of the object, or equivalently, the number of items in buf, either Get or GetMorethanOne must be accepted. In other words, we must further partition the set of acceptable states for Get. In order to achieve such a finer partition, the inherited Get must be redefined in B_Buffer2, resulting in *SPA*.

SPA occurs when the synchronization constraints are written as part of the method code and they are based on the partitioning of states of an object. This anomaly commonly occurs in accept-set based schemes. In one of the variants of this scheme, known as *behavior abstraction* [18], a programmer uses the *become* primitive [1] to specify the next set of methods that can be accepted by that object. An addition of a new method to a subclass is handled by redefining such a set to contain the name of the new method.

The use of *guarded* methods (as shown in Figure 3.3) can prevent *SPA*, where the execution of methods is contingent upon first evaluating their guards.

```
void Put (char c) when (in < out + max) { ... }

char Get (void) when (in >= out + 1) { ... }

char GetMorethanOne (int howmany) when
                          (in >= out + howmany) { ... }
```

Fig. 3.3. Redefined methods from class B_Buffer2.

3.2 History Sensitiveness of Acceptable States Anomaly (*HSASA*)

Consider Figure 3.4, where we have defined yet another subclass, B_Buffer3, of B_Buffer (see Figure 3.1). B_Buffer3 is a specialized version of B_Buffer, which inherits Put and Get and introduces a new method, GetAfterPut. Note that the guard for GetAfterPut is also defined.

```
class B_Buffer3: public B_Buffer {
  public:
    char GetAfterPut()
      when (!after_put && in >= out + 1) {
        ...
    }
};
```

Fig. 3.4. A class definition for B_Buffer3.

Put, Get, and GetAfterPut can be concurrently invoked on an object of B_Buffer3. Apart from the previous synchronization constraint for Put and Get as in B_Buffer, we must now ensure that GetAfterPut executes only after executing Put. The guard for GetAfterPut requires a boolean, after_put, to be true, which is initially false. The synchronization requirement is that after_put must be set to true and false in the inherited methods, Put and Get, respectively. In order to meet such a requirement, the inherited methods, Put and Get, must be redefined, and thus, resulting in *HSASA*.

HSASA occurs when it is required that the newly defined methods in a subclass must only be invoked after certain inherited methods have been executed, i.e., the invocations of certain methods are history sensitive. Guarded methods are inadequate because the newly defined (and history sensitive) methods wait on those conditions which can only be set in the inherited methods, and consequently, redefinitions become essential.

3.3 State Modification Anomaly (*SMA*)

Consider Figure 3.5, where we have defined two classes, Lock and B_Buffer4. Lock is a *mix-in* class [6], which when mixed with another class, gives its object an added capability of locking itself. In B_Buffer4 we would like to add locking capability to its objects. Thus, the inherited Put and Get in B_Buffer4 execute in either a locked or unlocked state. Clearly, the guards in the inherited methods, Put and Get, must be redefined to account for the newly added features. Besides, the invocation of methods of Lock on an object of B_Buffer4 affects the execution of Put and Get for this object.

SMA occurs when the execution of a base class method modifies the condition(s) for the methods in the derived class. This anomaly is usually found in *mix-in* [6] class based applications.

```
class Lock {
   int locked;
   public:
      void lock()
         when (!locked)
            { locked = 1; }
      void unlock()
         when (locked)
            { locked = 0; }
};
```

```
class B_Buffer4:
      public B_Buffer, Lock {

   // Unlocked  Put and  Get.

};
```

Fig. 3.5. Class definitions for Lock and B_Buffer4.

3.4 Anomaly A

Some COOPL designers have advocated the use of a single centralized class for controlling the invocation of messages received by an object [7]. *Anomaly A* occurs when a new method is added to a base class such that all its subclasses are forced to redefine their centralized classes. This happens because the centralized class associated with a subclass is oblivious of the changes in the base class, and therefore, cannot invoke the newly inherited method.

Consider two centralized classes, B_Buffer_Server and B_Buffer2_Server, as shown in Figure 3.6, for classes, B_Buffer and B_Buffer2, respectively. If a new method, NewMethod, is added to B_Buffer, it becomes immediately visible in B_Buffer2; however, both B_Buffer_Server and B_Buffer2_Server are oblivious of such a change and must be redefined for their correct use, resulting in *Anomaly A*.

```
class B_Buffer_Server {

   void controller() {
      switch(...) {
         case...: Put(c); break;
         case...: Get(); break;
      }
};
```

```
class B_Buffer2_Server {
   void controller2() {
      switch(...) {
         case...: Put(c); break;
         case...: Get(); break;
         case...: GetMorethanOne(n);
                  break;
      }
};
```

Fig. 3.6. Centralized server class definitions for B_Buffer and B_Buffer2.

3.5 Anomaly B

Instead of using centralized synchronization, each method could maintain data consistency by using critical sections. A possible risk with this scheme, however, is that a subclass method could operate on the synchronization primitives used in the base class, resulting in *Anomaly B*.

4. What Is the Reusability of Sequential Classes?

The success of an OO system in a development environment is largely dependent upon the reusability of its components, namely, classes. A COOPL designer must provide means for class reuse without editing previously written classes. Many C++ based COOPLs do not support sequential class reuse [21, 22].

Consider Figure 4.1, where a base class, Base, is defined with three methods, foo, bar, and baz. We also define a subclass, Derived, of Base, which inherits bar and baz, but overrides foo with a new definition.

```
class Base {                      class Derived: public Base {
  int a,b,c;                        int d;
  public:                           public:
    void foo() {                      void foo() {
      a = 2;                            bar();
      b = a*a;                          d = c * c;
    }                                 }
    void bar() {                    };
      c = 3;
      c = a*c;
    }
    void foobar() {
      foo();
      bar();
    }
};
```

Fig. 4.1. The sequential versions of the classes, Base and Derived.

Let us assume that the parallelism for methods of Base is specified as shown in Figure 4.2. The parallelization of Base forces the redefinition of Derived, because otherwise, one or both of the following events may occur:

- Assume that a message foo is received by an object of Derived. A *deadlock* occurs once the inherited bar is called from within foo which has a receive synchronization primitive, but there is no complementary send command.
- Assume further that bar is not called from Derived::foo. Now, the inherited definition of foobar becomes incorrect: foo and bar can no longer be enclosed inside a parallel block as these two methods would violate the Bernstein conditions [3,17],

```
class Base {                      class Derived: public Base {
   int a,b,c;                        int d;
   public:                           public:
      void foo() {                      void foo() {
         a = 2;                            bar();
         send(a);                          d = c * c;
         b = a*a;                       }
      }                          };
      void bar() {
         c = 3;
         receive(a);
         c = a*c;
      }
      void foobar() {
         cobegin
            foo();
            bar();
         coend;
      }
};
```

Fig. 4.2. The parallelized versions of the classes, Base and Derived.

5. A Framework for Specifying Parallelism

In the previous section we established that it is extremely difficult to specify parallelism and synchronization constraints elegantly in a COOPL. Apparently, the inheritance anomaly and dubious reuse of sequential classes, make COOPLs a less attractive alternative for parallel programming. In the past, several researchers have designed COOPLs in an attempt to break these problems, but they have been only partially successful. In this section, we propose our solution for these problems in a class based COOPL.

We have designed a new COOPL, called CORE [21], which is based on C++ [11]. In CORE, the parallelism and all the necessary synchronization constraints for the methods of a class, are specified in an *abstract class* (AC) [6,11] associated with the class. Consequently, a subclass of a superclass is able to either: (i) bypass the synchronization code which would otherwise be embedded in the inherited methods, or (ii) inherit, override, customize, and redefine the synchronization code of the inherited methods in an AC associated with the subclass. In CORE, we are able to break *SPA*, *SMA*, *Anomaly A*, and *Anomaly B*. However, we are not completely able to avoid *HSASA*, but we minimize the resulting code redefinitions. Besides, the sequential classes are reusable in a CORE program. The CORE framework for parallel programming is attractive because of the following reasons:

- synchronization constraints are specified separately from the method code;
- inheritance hierarchies of the sequential and concurrent components are maintained orthogonally;
- the degrees of reuse of the sequential and synchronization code are higher; and
- parallelism granularity can be more easily controlled.

6. Previous Approaches

In ACT++ [18], objects are viewed as sets of *states*. Concurrent objects are designed as sets of states. An object can only be in one state at a time and methods transform its state. States are inherited and/or may be re-defined in a subclass without a method ever needing a re-definition; however, sequential components cannot be re-used, and the *become* expression does not the allow call/return mechanism of C++. Their proposal suffers from *SPA*.

In Rosette [32], *enabled sets* are used to define messages that are allowed in the object's next state. The enabled sets are also objects and their method invocations combine the sets from the previous states. The authors suggest making the enabled sets as *first-class* values. However, their approach is extremely complex for specification of concurrency. Additionally this solution, too, is inadequate to solve *SPA* and *HSASA*.

The authors of Hybrid [28] associate *delay queues* with every method. The messages are accepted only if the delay queues are empty. The methods may open or close other queues. The problem with the delay queue approach is that the inheritance and queue management are not orthogonal. Their approach is vulnerable to *Anomaly B* and *HSASA*. Besides, the sequential components cannot be reused.

Eiffel [7] and the family of POOL languages [2] advocate the use of *centralized classes* to control concurrent computations. The sequential components can be reused, however, only one method can execute at a time, and the *live* method must be reprogrammed every time a subclass with a new method is added. The designers of POOL-T [2] disallow inheritance. Both these schemes also suffer from *Anomaly A*.

Guide [10] uses activation conditions, or *synchronization counters*, to specify an object's state for executing a method. These activation conditions are complex expressions involving the number of messages received, completed, executing, and message contents, etc.. Clearly, such a specification directly conflicts with inheritance. Besides, a derived class method can potentially invalidate the synchronization constraints of the base class method, and hence, faces *Anomaly B*.

Saleh *et. al.* [31] have attempted to circumvent the two problems but they restrict the specification of concurrency to intra-object level. They use *conditional waits* for synchronization purposes. There are no multiple mechanisms for specifying computational granularity and the reusability of sequential classes is impossible.

Meseguer [26] has suggested the use of *order-sorted rewriting logic* and declarative solutions, where no synchronization code is ever used for avoiding the inheritance anomaly. However, it is unclear as to how the proposed solutions could be adapted into a more practical setting, as in a class based COOPL.

Although, in Concurrent C++ [14], the sequential classes are reusable, *SPA* and *SMA* do not occur, however, *HSASA* and *Anomaly B* remain unsolved. Similarly, in CC++ [8], *SPA*, *HSASA*, and *Anomaly B* can occur and the sequential class reusability is doubtful.

Much like us, Matsuoka *et. al.* [24], too, have independently emphasized on the localization and orthogonality of synchronization schemes for solving the problems associated with COOPLs. They have suggested an elegant scheme similar to that of path expressions [3] for solving these problems for an actor based concurrent language, called ABCL. In their scheme every possible state transitions for an object is specified in the class. However, with their strategy the reuse of sequential components is improbable.

7. The Concurrency Abstraction Model

Recall from the previous section that the occurrence of the inheritance anomaly and the dubious reuse of sequential classes in a COOPL are primarily due to: (i) the synchronization constraints being an integral part of the method bodies, and (ii) the inheritance of the sequential and concurrent parts in a method code being non-orthogonal. We propose a novel notion of *concurrency abstraction* as the model for parallel programming in CORE, where these two factors are filtered out, and consequently, the two problems associated with a COOPL are solved. We first define following two terms before we explain the meaning of concurrency abstraction.

Definition 7.1. A concurrent region is that piece of method code[4] (or a thread of control), which must be protected using a synchronization constraint.

Definition 7.2. An **AC** is an abstract class[5] associated with a class, C, where the parallelism and the necessary synchronization constraints for the concurrent regions of C are specified.

The foundation of the concurrency abstraction model is built on the identification of concurrent regions and definitions of ACs: The sequential code of a concurrent region is "customized" to a concurrent code (i.e., a piece of code which has the specified parallelism and synchronization) by using the specifications in an AC. In a sense a class, C, inherits some "attributes" (specification of parallelism) for its methods from its AC such that the subclasses of C cannot implicitly inherit them. For a subclass to inherit these "attributes", it must explicitly do so by defining its AC as a subclass of the AC associated with its superclass.

Thus, a CORE programmer builds three separate and independent inheritance hierarchies: first, for the sequential classes; second, for a class and its AC; and third, for the ACs, if required. A hierarchy of ACs keeps the inheritance of the synchronization code orthogonal to the inheritance of the sequential methods. Such a dichotomy helps a subclass: (a) to bypass the synchronization specific code which would otherwise be embedded in a base class method, and (b) to inherit, override, customize, and redefine the synchronization code of the inherited methods in its own AC.

We should point out that any specification inside an AC is treated as a compiler directive and no processes get created. These specifications are inlined into the method codes by a preprocessor.

We shall now illustrate the concurrency abstraction model with an example. Consider a class, B, with two methods, b1 and b2, which are to be concurrently executed for an object of this class. In other words, the method bodies of b1 and b2 are the concurrent regions. In order to specify concurrent execution of these methods, one creates an AC of B, say Syn_B. In Syn_B, the two concurrent regions, b1 and b2, are enclosed inside a parallel block as shown in Figure 7.1(a). Let us consider following three scenarios, where D is defined as a subclass of B.

Case 1 : Assume that D inherits b1 but overrides b2 by a new definition. If it is incorrect to concurrently invoke b1 and b2 for objects of D, then an AC for D is not defined (see Figure 7.1(b)). Otherwise an AC, Syn_D, for D is defined. Two possibilities emerge depending upon whether or not a new concurrency specification is needed, i.e. either (i) a new specification

---

[4] Note that an entire method could be identified as a concurrent region.
[5] Conventionally, an abstract class denotes that class in an OO program for which no object can be instantiated [6, 11]. We have followed the same convention in CORE.

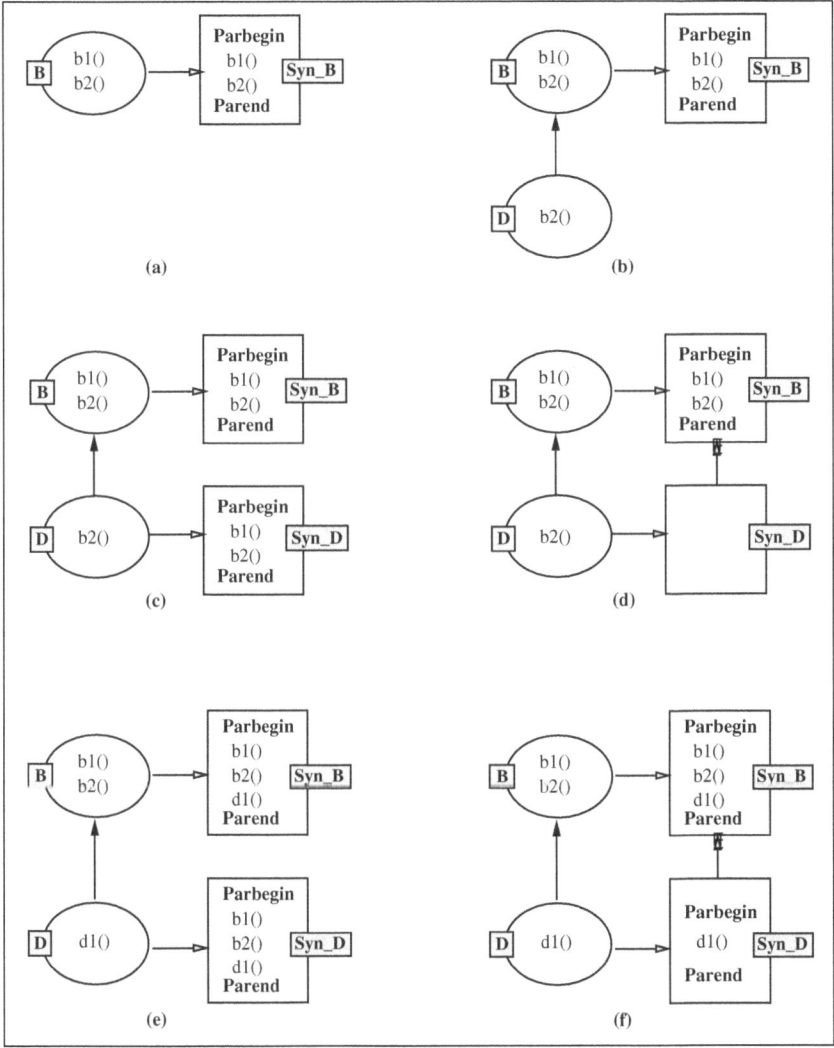

Fig. 7.1. Examples to illustrate the concurrency abstraction model.

is needed, and hence, a new parallel block enclosing **b1** and **b2** is defined in Syn_D (see Figure 7.1(c)); or, (ii) the old specification is reused, and thus, Syn_D simply inherits from Syn_B (see Figure 7.1(d)). Notice that when Syn_D neither defines nor inherits from Syn_B, the specified parallelism and synchronization in Syn_B are effectively bypassed by the inherited method, **b1**, in D.

Case 2 : Assume that D inherits **b1** and **b2**, and defines a new method, **d1**. Much like the previous case, a new AC, Syn_D, for D may or may not be needed. Assume that Syn_D is needed. In case that **b1**, **b2** and **d1** require a new concurrency specification, a new parallel block in Syn_D is defined, which does not inherit from Syn_B (see Figure 7.1(e)). However, if the old specification for b1 and b2 is reused but with a new specification for d1, then a parallel block enclosing d1 is defined in Syn_D. Moreover, Syn_D inherits from Syn_B (see Figure 7.1(f)).

Case 3 : Assume that D inherits b1 and b2, and defines a new method, d1. Unlike the previous two cases, assume that one specifies the concurrency and synchronization at the inter-class level rather than at the intra-class level. Consider a situation where a function (or a method), foo, defines a parallel block enclosing objectB.b1() and objectD.d1() as two parallel processes. If these two processes communicate, then that must be specified in an AC, Syn_B_D, associated with B and D, both.

8. The CORE Language

Following our discussions on issues in designing a COOPL, in CORE we support: (i) passive objects with an assumption that an appropriate process management scheme is available, (ii) schemes for specification of intra- and inter-object parallelism, (iii) multiple synchronization schemes, and (iv) the inheritance model of C++. Our primary goal is to to avoid the inheritance anomaly and to allow the reuse of sequential classes. In CORE, the language extensions are based on the concurrency abstraction model as described in the previous section. We shall present the syntax of new constructs in CORE using the BNF grammar and their semantics informally with example programs.

8.1 Specifying a Concurrent Region

As defined earlier, a concurrent region is that piece of code which is protected using a synchronization constraint. Some examples of a concurrent region include a critical section of a process, a process awaiting the completion of inter-process communication (such as a blocking send or a receive), a process protected under a guard (as in Figure 3.3), etc.. In CORE, a concurrent region can be specified at the intra- and inter-class levels by using the reserved words, Intra_Conc_Reg and Inter_Conc_Reg, respectively. These reserved words are placed inside a class in much the same way as the access privilege specifiers (*public, private, protected*) are placed in a C++ program. The concurrent regions do not explicitly encode the synchronization primitives inside the class, but they are redefined inside their associated ACs.

8.2 Defining an AC

As mentioned earlier, an AC is associated with a class for whose concurrent regions, the parallelism and the necessary synchronization constraints are to be specified. In other words, a concurrent region of a class is redefined in an AC such that the necessary synchronization scheme is encoded in it. Note that the members of an AC can access all the accessible members of the class it is associated with. An AC can be specified at the intra-class and inter-class levels using the reserved words, Intra_Sync and Inter_Sync, respectively. The BNF grammar for specifying an AC is given in Figure 8.1.

$$\begin{aligned}
\langle ACspec\rangle &\rightarrow \langle ACtag\rangle \langle ACname\rangle : \langle InheritList\rangle \{ \langle ACdef\rangle \} ; \\
\langle InheritList\rangle &\rightarrow \langle classname\rangle \langle InheritList\rangle \mid \langle ACname\rangle \langle InheritList\rangle \\
\langle ACtag\rangle &\rightarrow \text{Intra\_Sync} \mid \text{Inter\_Sync} \\
\langle ACname\rangle &\rightarrow \langle identifier\rangle
\end{aligned}$$

Fig. 8.1. The BNF grammar for specifying an AC.

8.3 Defining a Parallel Block

A *parallel block* [8,17] encloses a list of concurrent or parallel processes. These processes become active once the control enters the parallel block, and they synchronize at the end of the block, i.e., all the processes must terminate before the first statement after the end of block can be executed. The reserved words, **Parbegin** and **Parend**, mark the beginning and the end of a parallel block, respectively. The BNF grammar for specifying a parallel block in a CORE program is shown in Figure 8.2.

$$\begin{aligned}
\langle ParProc\rangle &\rightarrow \text{Parbegin} [\langle methodname\rangle] [\langle LoopStmt\rangle] \langle ProcList\rangle \text{ Parend}; \\
\langle LoopStmt\rangle &\rightarrow \text{for} (\langle identifier\rangle = \langle initExp\rangle ; \langle lastExp\rangle ; \langle incExp\rangle) \\
\langle ProcList\rangle &\rightarrow \langle proc\rangle ; \langle ProcList\rangle \mid \langle proc\rangle \\
\langle proc\rangle &\rightarrow \langle functionCall\rangle \mid \langle methodCall\rangle
\end{aligned}$$

Fig. 8.2. The BNF grammar for specifying a parallel block.

A $\langle ProcList\rangle$ enlists the parallel processes, where a process from this list is either a function call, or a method invocation. A loop may be associated with a parallel block by using the **for** loop syntax of C++ [11]. In a loop version of a parallel block, all the loop iterations are active simultaneously. In CORE, another kind of parallel block can be specified by associating a $\langle methodname\rangle$ at the beginning of the block. However, such a specification can only be enforced inside an intra-class AC. With such a specification once the process, $\langle methodname\rangle$, completes its execution, all the processes in the block are spawned as the child processes of this process. Note that a similar specification is possible in Mentat [15]. We now describe how the intra- and inter-object concurrency can be specified in CORE.

8.3.1 Intra-object Concurrency. Inside a parallel block, method invocations on the same object can be specified for parallel execution. Consider a class, Foo, and its associated AC, Syn_Foo, as shown in Figure 8.3. Foo has a public method, foobar, and two private methods, bar and baz. In Syn_Foo, a parallel block is defined which specifies that whenever an object of Foo invokes foobar, two concurrent processes corresponding to bar and baz must be spawned further. The parent process, foobar, terminates only after the two children complete their execution.

```
class Foo {                      Intra_Sync Syn_Foo: Foo {
  private:                         Parbegin foobar()
    bar() { ... }                    bar()
    baz() { ... }                    baz()
  public:                          Parend;
    foobar();                    };
};
```

Fig. 8.3. A class Foo and its intra-class AC.

8.3.2 Inter-object Concurrency. Inside a parallel block, method invocations on two objects (of the same or different classes) can be specified for parallel execution. Consider Figure 8.4, where the function, main, creates two objects, master and worker. In main, a parallel block is specified where each object concurrently receives a message, foobar. Earlier, in Figure 8.3, we had specified that the methods, bar and baz, be concurrently invoked on an object executing foobar. Consequently, main spawns two processes, master.foobar() and worker.foobar(), and both these processes further fork two processes each.

```
int main() {
  Foo master, worker;
  Parbegin
    master.foobar();
    worker.foobar();
  Parend;
}
```

Fig. 8.4. A program to show specification of inter-object parallelism.

8.4 Synchronization Schemes

The concurrent processes in CORE can interact and synchronize using different schemes, namely: (i) a mailbox, (ii) a guard, (iii) a pair of blocking send and receive primitives, and (iv) a predefined Lock class which implements a binary semaphore such that the P and V operations (or methods) can be invoked on an object of this class.

Consider Figure 8.5, where a class, A, is defined with two methods, m1 and m2. These methods have been identified as two concurrent regions using the tag, Intra_Conc_Reg. We have defined two different intra-class ACs, Syn_A and Syn_A1, for illustrating the use of different synchronization schemes. Note that in Syn_A, Send and Receive primitives have been used for synchronization, while a semaphore, sem, has been used in Syn_A1 for the same purpose.

```
class A {
  Intra_Conc_Reg:
    void method1() { ... }
    void method2() { ... }
};
```

```
Intra_Sync Syn_A: A {              Intra_Sync Syn_A1: A {
  Comm_Buffer buf;                   Lock sem;
  void method1() {                   void method1() {
    method1();                         method1();
    Send(&buf, writeVar);              sem.V();
  }                                  }

  void method2() {                   void method2() {
    Receive(&buf, readVar);            sem.P();
    method2();                         method2();
  }                                  }
};                                 };
```

Fig. 8.5. A program to illustrate the use of different synchronization schemes inside ACs.

9. Illustrations

In this section we shall illustrate how the concurrency abstraction model of CORE can effectively support the reuse of a sequential class method in a subclass and avoid the inheritance anomaly without ever needing any redefinitions.

9.1 Reusability of Sequential Classes

Consider Figure 9.1, where a class, Queue, along with its two methods, add and del, are defined. Assume that inside a parallel block add and del are con-

```
class Queue {
  public:
    add(int newitem) {
      temp = ...;
      temp->item = newitem;
      temp->next = front_ptr;
      front_ptr = temp;
    }

    del() {
      val = front_ptr->item;
      front_ptr = front_ptr->next;
    }
};
```

Fig. 9.1. A class definition for Queue.

currently invoked on an object of Queue. Since a shared variable, front_ptr, is modified by add and del, it must be protected against simultaneous modifications from these two parallel processes. Let us identify and define two concurrent regions, R1 and R2, corresponding to the code segments accessing front_ptr in add and del, respectively. In other words, the code segments in R1 and R2 correspond to the critical sections of add and del. The transformed definition of Queue, and its associated AC, Syn_Queue, are shown in Figure 9.2. Note that if we inline R1 and R2 at their respective call-sites in add and del, we get the original (sequential) versions of the add and del methods, as in Figure 9.1. R1 and R2 are redefined in Syn_Queue by enclosing them around a pair of P and V operations on a semaphore, sem. These redefined concurrent regions are inlined into add and del while generating their code. Similarly, an object, sem, is defined as an instance variable in Queue.

Assume that a subclass, Symbol_Table, is defined for Queue, as shown in Figure 9.3. Symbol_Table reuses add, overrides del, and defines a new method, search.

```
class Queue {                          Intra_Sync Syn_Queue : Queue {
  Intra_Conc_Reg:                        Lock sem;
    R1(SomeType* ptr) {                  void R1() {
      ptr->next = front_ptr;               sem.P();
      front_ptr = ptr;                     R1();
    }                                      sem.V();
                                         }
    R2() {
      val = front_ptr->item;             void R2() {
      front_ptr = front_ptr->next;         sem.P();
    }                                      R2();
                                           sem.V();
  public:                                }
    add(int newitem) {                 };
      temp = ...;
      temp->item = newitem;
      R1(temp);
    }

    del() { R2(); }
};
```

Fig. 9.2. A complete definition for the Queue class.

While compiling the code for add in Symbol_Table, the untransformed inlined code for R1 is used, and hence, its definition remains the same as in Figure 9.1, as desired.

```
class Symbol_Table : public Queue {
  public:
    del() { ... }
    search() { ... }
}
```

Fig. 9.3. A class definition for Symbol_Table.

9.2 Avoiding the Inheritance Anomaly

Anomaly A cannot occur in CORE because the notion of centralized classes (as proposed in [7]) does not exist. Furthermore, since the declaration and use of different synchronization primitives in a CORE program are restricted within an AC, a possible risk of them being operated upon by subclass methods, is eliminated. Consequently, *Anomaly B* is also avoided.

We now illustrate using an example how *SPA* can be avoided in a CORE program. The use of guards has been proposed by several researchers for avoiding *SPA*; we, too, advocate their use. However, while defining a subclass a CORE programmer is never in a dilemma simply because some other form of synchronization scheme has been previously committed to in the base class. In contrast with the other COOPL approaches, where the guards can only be associated with the methods, in CORE, they can be associated with concurrent regions, Consequently, more computations can be interleaved in CORE, resulting in a more fine-grain specification of parallelism.

```
class B_Buffer {                          Intra_Sync Syn_B1: B_Buffer {
    int in, out, n, max;                      Lock empty, full;
    char *buf;                                R1 () {
  public:                                       empty.P();
    B_Buffer (int size) {                       R1();
      max = size;                               full.V();
      buf = new char [max];                 }
      in = out = n = 0;
    }                                       R2 () {
    void Put (char c) { R1(c); }              full.P();
                                              R1();
    int  Get (void) {                         empty.V();
      char c;                               }
      R2(&c);                             };
      return c;
    }

  Intra_Conc_Reg:
    void R1 (char c) {
      buf[in] = c;
      in = (in+1) % max;
      n++;
    }

    void R2 (char *c) {
      *c = buf[out];
      out = (out+1) % max;
      n--;
    }
};
```

Fig. 9.4. A class definition for B_Buffer in CORE.

Let us reconsider the class definition for the *bounded buffer* problem as shown in Figure 3.1. The CORE classes for B_Buffer and B_Buffer2 are shown in Figure 9.4 and Figure 9.5, respectively. The intra-class ACs, Syn_B1 and Syn_B2, as associated with B_Buffer and B_Buffer2, respectively, are also shown in these figures. Note the use of different synchronization schemes in

```
class B_Buffer2: public B_Buffer {          Intra_Sync Syn_B2:
 public:                                          Syn_B1, B_Buffer2 {
   char GetMorethanOne(int howmany)
   {                                         R3() {
       char last_char;                         if ( in >= out + n)
          R3(&last_char, howmany);               R3();
       return last_char;                       }
   }                                         };

 Intra_Conc_Reg:
   void R3 (char *c, int n)
   {
     for (int i=0; i < n; i++)
       *c = Get();
   }
};
```

Fig. 9.5. A class definition for B_Buffer2 in CORE.

the three concurrent regions: R1 and R2 use semaphores for synchronization, and R3 uses a guard.

In CORE, we are not completely successful in avoiding *HSASA*, however, we minimize the resulting code redefinitions, as we illustrate below. Let us reconsider the class, B_Buffer3, in Figure 3.4 from section 3.2. The CORE class for B_Buffer3 along with its associated intra-class AC, Syn_B3, are shown in Figure 9.6. Note that the boolean, after_put, must be set to true and false in the inherited methods, Put and Get, respectively. In addition to inheriting Syn_B1 in Syn_B3, we redefine the synchronization code as shown in Figure 9.6. We are thus able to minimize the code redefinition as claimed earlier.

10. The Implementation Approach

We have proposed CORE as a framework for developing concurrent OO programs such that different kinds of inheritance anomalies do not occur and the sequential classes remain highly reusable. The code redefinitions in CORE are effectively and easily handled by a preprocessor, which customizes in a bottom up manner the method codes for each class. An obvious problem with such a static inlining is that of code duplication and an overall increase in code size. However, one can avoid such a code duplication by a scheme similar to that of manipulating virtual tables in C++ [11]. Naturally, such a solution is more complex and the involved overhead in retrieving the exact call through chain of pointers at run-time, makes this approach inefficient. Since concurrent programs are targeted for execution on multiple processors and a network of workstations, where the cost of code migration is extremely high, our choice of code duplication is very well justified. However, the compile

```
class B_Buffer3: public B_Buffer {          Intra_Sync Syn_B3:
  public:                                             Syn_B1, B_Buffer {
    char GetAfterPut() {
      R4 ();                                    int after_put = 0;
    }                                           R1() {
                                                  R1();
  Intra_Conc_Reg:                                 after_put = 1;
    R4() { ... }                                }
};
                                                R2() {
                                                  R2();
                                                  after_put = 0;
                                                }

                                                R4() {
                                                    if (!after_put &&
                                                          in >= out + 1)
                                                    R4();
                                                }
                                            };
```

Fig. 9.6. A class definition for B_Buffer3 in CORE.

time expansion approach cannot handle previously compiled class libraries; they must be recompiled.

11. Conclusions and Future Directions

We have proposed a framework for specifying parallelism in COOPLs, and have demonstrated that: (a) the inheritance anomaly can be avoided, and (b) the sequential classes can be effectively reused. We have introduced a novel model of concurrency abstraction in CORE and is the key to solving two important problems associated with COOPLs. In the proposed model (a) the specification of the synchronization code is kept separate from the method bodies, and (b) the sequential and the concurrent parts in the method bodies of a superclass are inherited by the subclasses in an orthogonal manner. In CORE, we avoid state partitioning anomaly (*SPA*), state modification anomaly (*SMA*), and *Anomaly B*. We disallowed the notion of a centralized class, and hence, *Anomaly A* can never be encountered in CORE. However, the history sensitiveness of acceptable states anomaly (*HSASA*) can still occur in CORE, but with minimal code redefinitions for the inherited methods.

We have also established that there is no need for a COOPL designer to commit to just one kind of synchronization scheme; multiple synchronization schemes may be allowed in a COOPL. Finally, intra- and inter-object parallelism can be easily accommodated in a COOPL, as in CORE. As the proposed concurrency abstraction model is language independent, it can be easily adapted into other class based COOPLs.

In the CORE framework we have not discussed the issues pertaining to task partitioning and scheduling, load-balancing, and naming and retrieval of remote objects. These issues can potentially expose several interesting research problems. Moreover, the model in CORE itself could use work in the direction of avoiding *HSASA* in COOPLs. While the data-parallel model of parallel programming has not been the focus of this work, integration of inheritance and the specification of the data-partitions, may exhibit an anomaly similar to the inheritance anomaly.

References

1. Agha, G., "Concurrent Object-Oriented Programming," *Communications of the ACM*, Vol. 33, No. 9, Sept. 1990, pp. 125-141.
2. America P., "Inheritance and Subtyping in a Parallel Object-Oriented Language," *Proc. European Conf. on Object-Oriented Programming*, Springer-Verlag, Berlin, 1987, pp. 234-242.
3. Andrews, G., "Concurrent Programming: Principles and Practice," The Benjamin Cummings Publ. Co., 1991.
4. Arjomandi E., O'Farrell, W., and Kalas, I., "Concurrency Support for C++: An Overview," *C++ Report*, Jan. 1994, pp. 44-50.
5. Beck, B., "Shared-Memory Parallel Programming in C++," *IEEE Software*, July 1990, pp. 38-48.
6. Booch, G., "Object-Oriented Analysis and Design with Applications," The Benjamin Cummings Publ. Co., 1994.
7. Caromel D., "A General Model for Concurrent and Distributed Object-Oriented Programming," *Proc. of the ACM SIGPLAN Workshop on Object Based Concurrent Programming*, Vol 24, No. 4, April 1989, pp. 102-104.
8. Chandy, K. M. and Kesselman, C., "Compositional C++: Compositional Parallel Programming," *Conf. Record of Fifth Workshop on Languages and Compilers for Parallel Computing*, Vol. 757, LNCS, Springer-Verlag, Aug. 1992, pp. 124-144.
9. Chien, A., Feng, W., Karamcheti, V., and Plevyak, J., "Techniques for Efficient Execution of Fine-Grained Concurrent Programs," *Conf. Record of Sixth Workshop on Languages and Compilers for Parallel Computing*, Aug. 1993, pp. 160-174.
10. Decouchant D., Krakowiak S., Meysembourg M., Riveill M., and Rousset de Pina X., "A Synchronization Mechanism for Typed Objects in a Distributed System," *Proc. ACM SIGPLAN Workshop on Object Based Concurrent Programming*, Vol 24, no. 4, April 1989, pp. 105-108.
11. Ellis, M. and Stroustrup, B., *The Annotated C++ Reference Manual*, Addison-Wesely, 1990.
12. Foster, I., "Task Parallelism and High-Performance Languages," *IEEE Parallel & Distributed Technology: Systems & Applications*, Vol. 2, No. 3, Fall 1994, pp. 27-36.
13. Gannon, D. and Lee, J. K., "Object-Oriented Parallelism: pC++ Ideas and Experiments," *Proc. 1991 Japan Soc. for Parallel Processing*, 1993, pp. 13-23.

14. Gehani, N. and Roome, W. D., "Concurrent C++: Concurrent Programming With Class(es)," *Software Practice and Experience*, Vol. 18, No. 12, 1988, pp. 1157-1177.
15. Grimshaw, A. S., "Easy-to-Use Object-Oriented Parallel Programming with Mentat," *Technical Report*, CS-92-32, Dept. of Computer Sci., Univ. of Virgina, Charlottesville, 1992.
16. Gross, T., O'Hallaron, and Subhlok, J., "Task Parallelism in a High-Performance Fortran Framework," *IEEE Parallel & Distributed Technology: Systems & Applications*, Vol. 2, No. 3, Fall 1994, pp. 16-26.
17. Hwang, K., "Advanced Computer Architecture: Parallelism, Scalability, Programmability," Mc-GrawHill, Inc., 1993.
18. Kafura, D.G. and Lavender, R.G., "Concurrent Object-Oriented Languages and the Inheritance Anomaly," *Parallel Computers: Theory and Practice*, The IEEE Computer Society Press, Los Alamitos, CA, 1995.
19. Kale, L. V. and Krishnan, S., "CHARM++: A Portable Concurrent Object-Oriented System Based on C++," *Proc. of OOPSLA*, Washington DC, Sept-Oct, 1993, pp.91-109.
20. Kumar, S., "Issues in Parallelizing Object-Oriented Programs," *Proc. of Intn'l Conf. on Parallel Processing Workshop on Challenges for Parallel Processing*, Oconomowoc, WI, Aug. 14, 1995, pp. 64-71.
21. Kumar, S. and Agrawal, D. P., "CORE: A Solution to the Inheritance Anomaly in Concurrent Object-Oriented Languages," *Proc. Sixth Intn'l Conf. on Parallel and Distributed Computing and Systems*, Louisville, KY, Oct. 14-16, 1993, pp. 75-81.
22. Kumar, S. and Agrawal, D. P., "A Class Based Framework for Reuse of Synchronization Code in Concurrent Object-Oriented Languages," *Intn'l Journal of Computers and Their Applications*, Vol. 1, No. 1, Aug. 1994, pp. 11-23.
23. Larus, J. R., "C**: A Large Grain, Object-Oriented Data Parallel Programming Language," *Conf. Record of Fifth Workshop on Languages and Compilers for Parallel Computing*, Vol. 757, LNCS, Springer-Verlag, Aug. 1992, pp. 326-341.
24. Matsuoka, S., Taura, K., and Yonezawa, A., "Highly Efficient and Encapsulated Reuse of Synchronization Code in Concurrent Object-Oriented Languages," *Proc. of OOPSLA*, Washington DC, Sept-Oct, 1993, pp.109-126.
25. Matsuoka, S. and Yonezawa, A., "Analysis of Inheritance Anomaly in Object-Oriented Concurrent Programming Languages," *Research Directions in Concurrent Object-oriented Programming*, The MIT Press, 1993.
26. Meseguer J., "Solving the Inheritance Anomaly in Concurrent Object-Oriented Programming," *Proc. European Conf. on Object-Oriented Programming*, Kaiserslautern, Germany, July 1993.
27. Meyer, B., *Object-Oriented Software Construction*, Prentice-Hall, Englewood Cliffs, NJ, 1988.
28. Nierstrasz, O., "Active Objects in Hybrid," *Proc. of OOPSLA*, Orlando, Florida, USA, Oct. 1987, pp. 243-253.
29. Open Software Foundation, "OSF DCE Application Development Reference," Prentice Hall, Inc., Englewood Cliffs, NJ, 1993.
30. Plevyak, J. and Chien, A. A., "Obtaining Sequential Efficiency From Concurrent Object-Oriented Programs," *Proc. of the 22nd ACM Symp. on the Priniciples of Programming Languages*, Jan. 1995.
31. Saleh, H. and Gautron, P., "A Concurrency Control Mechanism for C++ Objects," *Object-Based Concurrent Computing*, Springer-Verlag, July 1991, pp. 195-210.
32. Tomlinson, C. and Singh, V., "Inheritance and Synchronization with Enabled Sets," *Proc. of OOPSLA*, New Orleans, USA, Oct. 1989, pp. 103-112.

33. Wyatt, B. B., Kavi, K., and Hufnagel, S., "Parallelism in Object-Oriented Languages: A Survey," *IEEE Software*, Nov. 1992, pp. 39-47.
34. Yu, G. and Welch, L. R., "Program Dependence Analysis for Concurrency Exploitation in Programs Composed of Abstract Data Type Modules," *Proc. of Sixth IEEE Symp. on Parallel & Distributed Processing*, Dallas, TX, Oct. 26-29, 1994, pp. 66-73.

Section II : Analysis

Chapter 5. Loop Parallelization Algorithms

Alain Darte, Yves Robert, and Frédéric Vivien

LIP, Ecole Normale Supérieure de Lyon, F - 69364 LYON Cedex 07, France
[Alain.Darte,Yves.Robert,Frederic.Vivien]@lip.ens-lyon.fr

Summary. This chapter is devoted to a comparative survey of loop parallelization algorithms. Various algorithms have been presented in the literature, such as those introduced by Allen and Kennedy, Wolf and Lam, Darte and Vivien, and Feautrier. These algorithms make use of different mathematical tools. Also, they do not rely on the same representation of data dependences. In this chapter, we survey each of these algorithms, and we assess their power and limitations, both through examples and by stating "optimality" results. An important contribution of this chapter is to characterize which algorithm is the most suitable for a given representation of dependences. This result is of practical interest, as it provides guidance for a compiler-parallelizer: given the dependence analysis that is available, the simplest and cheapest parallelization algorithm that remains optimal should be selected.

1. Introduction

Loop parallelization algorithms are useful source to source program transformations. They are particularly appealing as they can be applied *without* any knowledge of the target architecture. They can be viewed as a first – *machine-independent* – step in the code generation process. Loop parallelization will detect parallelism (transforming **DO** loops into **DOALL** loops) and will expose those dependences that are responsible for the intrinsic sequentiality of some operations in the original program.

Of course, a second step in code generation will have to take machine parameters into account. Determining a good granularity generally is a key to efficient performance. Also, data distribution and communication optimization are important issues to be considered. But all these problems will be addressed on a later stage. Such a two-step approach is typical in the field of parallelizing compilers (other examples are general task graph scheduling and software pipelining).

This chapter is devoted to the study of various **parallelism detection algorithms** based on:

1. A simple decomposition of the dependence graph into its strongly connected components such as Allen and Kennedy's algorithm [2].
2. Unimodular loop transformations, either ad-hoc transformations such as Banerjee's algorithm [3], or generated automatically such as Wolf and Lam's algorithm [31].
3. Schedules, either mono-dimensional schedules [10, 12, 19] (a particular case being the hyperplane method [26]) or multi-dimensional schedules [15, 20].

S. Pande, D.P. Agrawal (Eds.): Compiler Optimizations for Scalable PS, LNCS 1808, pp. 141-171, 2001.
© Springer-Verlag Berlin Heidelberg 2001

These loop parallelization algorithms are very different for a number of reasons. First, they make use of various mathematical techniques: graph algorithms for (1), matrix computations for (2), and linear programming for (3). Second, they take a different description of data dependences as input: graph description and dependence levels for (1), direction vectors for (2), and description of dependences by polyhedra or affine expressions for (3). For each of these algorithms, we identify the key concepts that underline them, and we discuss their respective power and limitations, both through examples and by stating "optimality" results.

An important contribution of this chapter is to characterize which algorithm is the most suitable for a given representation of dependences. No need to use a sophisticated dependence analysis algorithm if the parallelization algorithm cannot take advantage of the precision of its result. Conversely, no need to use a sophisticated parallelization algorithm if the dependence representation is not precise enough.

The rest of this chapter is organized as follows. Section 2 is devoted to a brief summary of what loop parallelization algorithms are all about. In Section 3, we review major dependences abstractions: dependence levels, directions vectors, and dependence polyhedra. Allen and Kennedy's algorithm [2] is presented in Section 4 and Wolf and Lam's algorithm [31] is presented in Section 5. It is shown that both algorithms are "optimal" in the class of those parallelization algorithms that use the same dependence abstraction as their input, i.e. dependence levels for Allen and Kennedy and direction vectors for Wolf and Lam. In Section 6 we move to a new algorithm that subsumes both previous algorithms. This algorithm is based on a generalization of direction vectors, the dependence polyhedra. In Section 7 we briefly survey Feautrier's algorithm, which relies on exact affine dependences. Finally, we state some conclusions in Section 8.

2. Input and Output of Parallelization Algorithms

Nested **DO** loops enable to describe a set of computations, whose size is much larger than the corresponding program size. For example, consider n nested loops whose loop counters describe a n-cube of size N: these loops encapsulate a set of computations of size N^n. Furthermore, it often happens that such loop nests contain a non trivial **degree of parallelism**, i.e. a set of independent computations of size $\Omega(N^r)$ for $r \geq 1$.

This makes the parallelization of nested loops a very challenging problem: a compiler-parallelizer must be able to detect, if possible, a non trivial degree of parallelism with a compilation time *not* proportional to the sequential execution time of the loops. To make this possible, efficient parallelization algorithms must be proposed with a *complexity*, an *input size* and an *output size* that depend only on n but certainly not on N, i.e. that depend on the size of the sequential code but not on the number of computations described.

The input of parallelization algorithms is a description of the dependences which link the different computations. The output is a description of an equivalent code with explicit parallelism.

2.1 Input: Dependence Graph

Each statement of the loop nest is surrounded by several loops. Each iteration of these loops defines a particular execution of the statement, called an **operation**. The dependences between the operations are represented by a directed acyclic graph: the **expanded dependence graph** (EDG). There are as many vertices in the EDG as operations in the loop nest. Executing the operations of the loop nest while respecting the partial order specified by the EDG guarantees that the correct result of the loop nest is preserved. Detecting parallelism in the loop nest amounts to detecting anti-chains in the EDG. We illustrate the notion of "expanded dependence graph" with the Example 21 below. The EDG corresponding to this code is depicted on Figure 2.1.

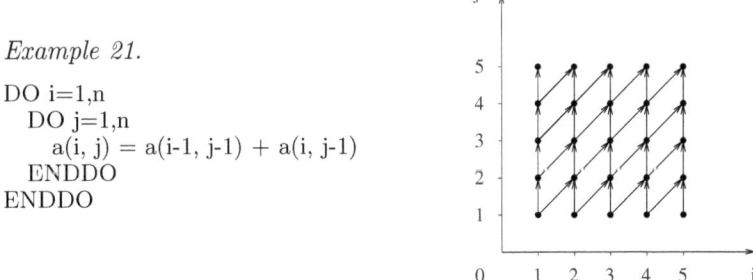

Example 21.

```
DO i=1,n
  DO j=1,n
    a(i, j) = a(i-1, j-1) + a(i, j-1)
  ENDDO
ENDDO
```

Fig. 2.1. Example 21 and its EDG.

Unfortunately, the EDG cannot be used as input for parallelization algorithms, since it is usually too large and may not be described exactly at compile-time. Therefore the **reduced dependence graph** (RDG) is used instead. The RDG is a condensed and approximated representation of the EDG. This approximation must be a superset of the EDG, in order to preserve the dependence relations. The RDG has one vertex per statement in the loop nest and its edges are labeled according to the chosen approximation of dependences (see Section 3 for details). Figure 2.2 presents two possible RDGs for Example 21, corresponding to two different approximations of the dependences.

Since its input is a RDG and not an EDG, a parallelization algorithm is not able to distinguish between two different EDGs which have the same RDG. Hence, the parallelism that can be detected is the parallelism contained

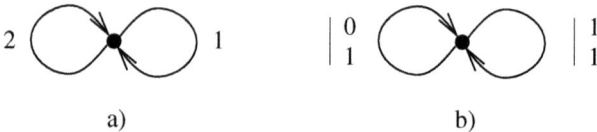

a)   b)

Fig. 2.2. RDG: a) with dependence levels; b) with direction vectors.

in the RDG. Thus, the quality of a parallelization algorithm must be studied *with respect to* the dependence analysis.

For example, Example 21 and Example 22 have the same RDG with dependence levels (Figure 2.2 (a)). Thus, a parallelization algorithm which takes as input RDGs with dependence levels, cannot distinguish between the two codes. However, Example 21 contains one degree of parallelism whereas Example 22 is intrinsically sequential.

Example 22.

```
DO i=1,n
   DO j=1,n
      a(i, j) = 1 + a(i-1, n) + a(i, j-1)
   ENDDO
ENDDO
```

2.2 Output: Nested Loops

The size of the parallelized code, as noticed before, should not depend on the number of operations that are described. This is the reason why the output of a parallelization algorithm must always be described by a set of loops [1].

There are at least three ways to define a new order on the operations of a given loop nest (i.e. three ways to define the output of the parallelization algorithm), in terms of nested loops:

1. Use elementary loop transformations as basic steps for the algorithm, such as loop distribution (as in Allen and Kennedy's algorithm), or loop interchange and loop skewing (as in Banerjee's algorithm);
2. Apply a linear change of basis on the iteration domain, i.e. apply a unimodular transformation on the iteration vectors (as in Wolf and Lam's algorithm).
3. Define a d-dimensional schedule, i.e. apply an affine transformation from $\mathbb{Z}^n$ to $\mathbb{Z}^d$ and interpret the transformation as a multi-dimensional timing function. Each component will correspond to a sequential loop, and

---

[1] These loops can be arbitrarily complicated, as long as their complexity only depends on the size of the initial code. Obviously, the simpler the result, the better. But, in this context, the meaning of "simple" is not clear: it depends on the optimizations that may follow. We consider that structural simplicity is preferable, but this can be discussed.

the missing $(n - d)$ dimensions will correspond to **DOALL** loops (as in Feautrier's algorithm and Darte and Vivien's algorithm).

The output of these three transformation schemes can indeed be described as loop nests, after a more or less complicated rewriting processes (see [8, 9, 11, 31, 36]). We do not discuss the rewriting process here. Rather, we focus on the link between the representation of dependences (the input) and the loop transformations involved in the parallelization algorithm (the output). Our goal is to characterize which algorithm is optimal for a given representation of dependences. Here, "optimal" means that the algorithm succeeds in exhibiting the maximal number of parallel loops.

3. Dependence Abstractions

For the sake of clarity, we restrict ourselves to the case of perfectly nested **DO** loops with affine loop bounds. This restriction permits to identify the iterations of the n nested loops (n is called the **depth** of the loop nest) with vectors in $\mathbb{Z}^n$ (called the **iteration vectors**) contained in a finite convex polyhedron (called the **iteration domain**) bounded by the loop bounds. The i-th component of an iteration vector is the value of the i-th loop counter in the nest, counting from the outermost to the innermost loop. In the sequential code, the iterations are therefore executed in the lexicographic order of their iteration vectors.

In the next sections, we denote by $\mathcal{D}$ the polyhedral iteration domain, by I and J n-dimensional iteration vectors in $\mathcal{D}$, and by S_i the i-th statement in the loop nest, where $1 \leq i \leq s$. We write $I >_l J$ if I is lexicographically greater than J and $I \geq_l J$ if $I >_l J$ or $I = J$.

Section 3.1 recalls the different concepts of dependence graphs introduced in the informal discussion of Section 2.1: expanded dependence graphs (EDG), reduced dependence graphs (RDG), apparent dependence graphs (ADG), and the notion of distance sets. In Section 3.2, we formally define what we call polyhedral reduced dependence graphs (PRDG), i.e. reduced dependence graphs whose edges are labeled by polyhedra. Finally, in Section 3.3, we show how the model of PRDG generalizes classical dependence abstractions of distance sets such as dependence levels and direction vectors.

3.1 Dependence Graphs and Distance Sets

Dependence relations between operations are defined by Bernstein's conditions [4]. Briefly speaking, two operations are considered dependent if both operations access the same memory location and if at least one of the accesses is a write. The dependence is directed according to the sequential order, from the first executed operation to the last one. Depending on the order of write(s) and/or read, the dependence corresponds to a so called

flow dependence, anti dependence or **output dependence**. We write: $S_i(I) \Longrightarrow S_j(J)$ if statement S_j at iteration J depends on statement S_i at iteration I. The partial order defined by $\Longrightarrow$ describes the **expanded dependence graph (EDG)**. Note that $(J - I)$ is always lexicographically nonnegative when $S_i(I) \Longrightarrow S_j(J)$.

In general, the EDG cannot be computed at compile-time, either because some information is missing (such as the values of size parameters or even worse, precise memory accesses), or because generating the whole graph is too expensive (see [35, 37] for a survey on dependence tests such as the gcd test, the power test, the omega test, the lambda test, and [18] for more details on exact dependence analysis). Instead, dependences are captured through a smaller cyclic directed graph, with s vertices (as many as statements), called the **reduced dependence graph (RDG)** (or statement level dependence graph).

The RDG is a compression of the EDG. In the RDG, two statements S_i and S_j are said dependent (we write $e : S_i \to S_j$) if there exists at least one pair (I, J) such that $S_i(I) \Longrightarrow S_j(J)$. Furthermore, the [2] edge e from S_i to S_j in the RDG is labeled by the set $\{(I, J) \in \mathcal{D}^2 \mid S_i(I) \Longrightarrow S_j(J)\}$, or by an approximation D_e that contains this set. The precision and the representation of this approximation make the power of the dependence analysis.

In other words, the RDG describes, in a condensed manner, an iteration level dependence graph, called (maximal) **apparent dependence graph (ADG)**, that is a superset of the EDG. The ADG and the EDG have the same vertices, but the ADG has more edges, defined by:

$$(S_i, I) \Longrightarrow (S_j, J) \text{ (in the ADG)} \Leftrightarrow$$
$$\exists\, e = (S_i, S_j) \text{ (in the RDG) such that } (I, J) \in D_e.$$

For a certain class of nested loops, it is possible to express exactly this set of pairs (I, J) (see [18]): I is given as an affine function (in some particular cases, involving floor or ceiling functions) $f_{i,j}$ of J where J varies in a polyhedron $\mathcal{P}_{i,j}$:

$$\{(I, J) \in \mathcal{D}^2 \mid S_i(I) \Longrightarrow S_j(J)\} = \{(f_{i,j}(J), J) \mid J \in \mathcal{P}_{i,j} \subset \mathcal{D}\} \quad (3.1)$$

In most dependence analysis algorithms however, rather than the set of pairs (I, J), one computes the set $E_{i,j}$ of all possible values $(J - I)$. $E_{i,j}$ is called the set of **distance vectors**, or **distance set**:

$$E_{i,j} = \{(J - I) \mid S_i(I) \Longrightarrow S_j(J)\}$$

When exact dependence analysis is feasible, Equation 3.1 shows that the set of distance vectors is the projection of the integer points of a polyhedron. This set can be approximated by its convex hull or by a more or less accurate

---

[2] Actually, there is such an edge for each pair of memory accesses that induces a dependence between S_i and S_j.

description of a larger polyhedron (or a finite union of polyhedra). When the set of distance vectors is represented by a finite union, the corresponding dependence edge in the RDG is decomposed into multi-edges.

Note that the representation by distance vectors is not equivalent to the representation by pairs (as in Equation 3.1), since the information concerning the **location** in the EDG of such a distance vector is lost. This may even cause some loss of parallelism, as will be seen in Example 64. However, this representation remains important, especially when exact dependence analysis is either too expensive or not feasible.

Classical representations of distance sets (by increasing precision) are:

- **level of dependence**, introduced in [1,2] for Allen and Kennedy's parallelizing algorithm.
- **direction vector**, introduced by Lamport [26] and by Wolfe in [32,33], then used in Wolf and Lam's parallelizing algorithm [31].
- **dependence polyhedron**, introduced in [22] and used in Irigoin and Triolet's supernode partitioning algorithm [23]. We refer to the PIPS software [21] for more details on dependence polyhedra.

We now formally define reduced dependence graphs whose edges are labeled by dependence polyhedra. Then we show that this representation subsumes the two other representations, namely dependence levels and direction vectors.

3.2 Polyhedral Reduced Dependence Graphs

We first recall the mathematical definition of a polyhedron, and how it can be decomposed into vertices, rays and lines.

Definition 31 (Polyhedron, polytope).

A set P of vectors in $\mathbb{Q}^n$ is called a (convex) polyhedron if there exists an integral matrix A and an integral vector b such that:

$$P = \{x \mid x \in \mathbb{Q}^n, \ Ax \leq b\}$$

A polytope is a bounded polyhedron.

A polyhedron can always be decomposed as the sum of a polytope and of a polyhedral cone (for more details see [30]). A polytope is defined by its vertices, and any point of the polytope is a non-negative barycentric combination of the polytope vertices. A polyhedral cone is finitely generated and can be defined by its rays and lines. Any point of a polyhedral cone is the sum of a nonnegative combination of its rays and of any combination of its lines.

Therefore, a dependence polyhedron P can be equivalently defined by a set of *vertices* (denoted by $\{v_1, \ldots, v_\omega\}$), a set of *rays* (denoted by $\{r_1, \ldots, r_\rho\}$), and a set of *lines* (denoted by $\{l_1, \ldots, l_\lambda\}$). Then, P is the set of all vectors p such that:

$$p = \sum_{i=1}^{\omega} \mu_i v_i + \sum_{i=1}^{\rho} \nu_i r_i + \sum_{i=1}^{\lambda} \xi_i l_i \qquad (3.2)$$

with $\mu_i \in \mathbb{Q}^+$, $\nu_i \in \mathbb{Q}^+$, $\xi_i \in \mathbb{Q}$, and $\sum_{i=1}^{\omega} \mu_i = 1$.

We now define what we call a polyhedral reduced dependence graph (or PRDG), i.e. a reduced dependence graph labeled by dependence polyhedra. Actually, we are interested only in integral vectors that belong to the dependence polyhedra, since dependence distance are indeed integral vectors.

Definition 32. *A* **polyhedral reduced dependence graph (PRDG)** *is a RDG, where each edge $e : S_i \rightarrow S_j$ is labeled by a dependence polyhedron $P(e)$ that approximates the set of distance vectors: the associated ADG contains an edge from instance I of node S_i to instance J of node S_j if and only if $(J - I) \in P(e)$.*

We explore in Section 6 this representation of dependences. At first sight, the reader can see dependence polyhedra as a generalization of direction vectors.

3.3 Definition and Simulation of Classical Dependence Representations

We come back to more classical dependence abstractions: level of dependence and direction vector. We recall their definition and show that RDGs labeled by direction vectors or dependence levels are actually particular cases of polyhedral reduced dependence graphs.

Direction vectors When the set of distance vectors is a singleton, the dependence is said uniform and the unique distance vector is called a **uniform dependence vector**.

Otherwise, the set of distance vectors can still be represented by a n-dimensional vector (called the **direction vector**), whose components belong to $\mathbb{Z} \cup \{*\} \cup (\mathbb{Z} \times \{+, -\})$. Its i-th component is an approximation of the i-th components of all possible distance vectors: it is equal to $z+$ (resp. $z-$) if all i-th components are greater (resp. smaller) than or equal to z. It is equal to $*$ if the i-th component may take any value and to z if the dependence is uniform in this dimension with unique value z. In general, $+$ (resp. $-$) is used as shorthand for $1+$ (resp. $(-1)-$).

We denote by e_i the i-th canonical vector, i.e. the n-dimensional vector whose components are all null except the i-th component equal to 1. Then, a direction vector is nothing but an approximation by a polyhedron, with a single vertex and whose rays and lines, if any, are canonical vectors.

Indeed, consider an edge e labeled by a direction vector d and denote by I^+, I^- and I^* the sets of components of d which are respectively equal to

$z+$ (for some integer z), $z-$, and $*$. Finally, denote by d_z the n-dimensional vector whose i-th component is equal to z if the i-th component of d is equal to z, $z+$ or $z-$, and to 0 otherwise.

Then, by definition of the symbols $+$, $-$ and $*$, the direction vector d represents exactly all n-dimensional vectors p for which there exist integers (ν, ν', ξ) in $\mathbb{N}^{|I^+|} \times \mathbb{N}^{|I^-|} \times \mathbb{Z}^{|I^*|}$ such that:

$$p = d_z + \sum_{i \in I^+} \nu_i e_i - \sum_{i \in I^-} \nu'_i e_i + \sum_{i \in I^*} \xi_i e_i \qquad (3.3)$$

In other words, the direction vector d represents all integer points that belong to the polyhedron defined by the single vertex d_z, the rays e_i for $i \in I^+$, the rays $-e_i$ for $i \in I^-$ and the lines e_i for $i \in I^*$.

For example, the direction vector $(2+, *, -, 3)$ defines the polyhedron with one vertex $(2, 0, -1, 3)$, two rays $(1, 0, 0, 0)$ and $(0, 0, -1, 0)$, and one line $(0, 1, 0, 0)$.

Dependence levels The representation by level is the less accurate dependence abstraction. In a loop nest with n nested loops, the set of distance vectors is approximated by an integer l, in $[1, n] \cup \{\infty\}$, defined as the largest integer such that the $l - 1$ first components of the distance vectors are zero.

A dependence at level $l \leq n$ means that the dependence occurs at depth l of the loop nest, i.e. at a given iteration of the $l - 1$ outermost loops. In this case, one says that the dependence is a **loop carried dependence** at level l. If $l = \infty$, the dependence occurs inside the loop body, between two different statements, and is called a **loop independent dependence**. A reduced dependence graph whose edges are labeled by dependence levels is called a Reduced Leveled Dependence Graph (RLDG).

Consider an edge e of level l. By definition of the level, the first non-zero component of the distance vectors is the l-th component and it can possibly take any positive integer value. Furthermore, we have no information on the remaining components. Therefore, an edge of level $l < \infty$ is equivalent to the direction vector: $(\overbrace{0, \ldots, 0}^{l-1}, 1+, \overbrace{*, \ldots, *}^{n-l})$ and an edge of level ∞ corresponds to the null dependence vector. As any direction vector admits an equivalent polyhedron, so does a representation by level. For example, a level 2 dependence in a 3-dimensional loop nest, means a direction vector $(0, 1+, *)$ which corresponds to the polyhedron with one vertex $(0, 1, 0)$, one ray $(0, 1, 0)$ and one line $(0, 0, 1)$.

4. Allen and Kennedy's Algorithm

Allen and Kennedy's algorithm [2] has first been designed to vectorizing loops. Then, it has been extended so as to maximize the number of parallel loops and to minimize the number of synchronizations in the transformed code. The input of this algorithm is a RLDG.

Allen and Kennedy's algorithm is based on the following facts:

1. A loop is parallel if it has no loop carried dependence, i.e. if there is no dependence, whose level is equal to the depth of the loop, that concerns a statement surrounded by the loop.
2. All iterations of a statement S_1 can be carried out before any iteration of a statement S_2 if there is no dependence in the RLDG from S_2 to S_1.

Property (1) allows to mark a loop as a **DOALL** or a **DOSEQ** loop, whereas property (2) suggests that parallelism detection can be independently conducted in each strongly connected component of the RLDG. Parallelism extraction is done by loop distribution.

4.1 Algorithm

For a dependence graph G, we denote by $G(k)$ the subgraph of G in which all dependences at level strictly smaller than k have been removed. Here is a sketch of the algorithm in its most basic formulation. The initial call is ALLEN-KENNEDY(RLDG, 1).

ALLEN-KENNEDY*(G, k)*.

– If $k > n$, stop.
– Decompose $G(k)$ into its strongly connected components G_i and sort them topologically.
– Rewrite code so that each G_i belongs to a different loop nest (at level k) and the order on the G_i is preserved (distribution of loops at level $\geq k$).
– For each G_i, mark the loop at level k as a **DOALL** loop if G_i has no edge at level k. Otherwise mark the loop as a **DOSEQ** loop.
– For each G_i, call ALLEN-KENNEDY(G_i, $k + 1$).

We illustrate Allen and Kennedy's algorithm on the code below:

Example 41.

```
DO i=1,n
  DO j=1,n
    DO k=1,n
      S1: a(i, j, k) = a(i-1, j+i, k) + a(i, j, k-1) + b(i, j-1, k)
      S2: b(i, j, k) = b(i, j-1, k+j) + a(i-1, j, k)
    ENDDO
  ENDDO
ENDDO
```

The dependence graph $G = G(1)$, drawn on Figure 4.1, has only one strongly connected component and at least one edge at level 1, thus the first call finds that the outermost loop is sequential. However, at level 2 (the edge at level 1 is no longer considered), $G(2)$ has two strongly connected components: all iterations of statement S_2 can be carried out before any

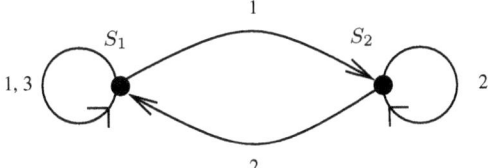

Fig. 4.1. RLDG for Example 41.

iteration of statement S_1. A loop distribution is performed. The strongly connected component including S_1 contains no edge at level 2 but one edge at level 3. Thus the second loop surrounding S_1 is marked DOSEQ and the third one DOALL. The strongly connected component including S_2 contains an edge at level 2 but no edge at level 3. Thus the second loop surrounding S_1 is marked DOALL and the third one DOSEQ. Finally, we get:

```
DOSEQ i=1,n
  DOSEQ j=1,n
    DOALL k=1,n
      S₂: b(i, j, k) = b(i, j-1, k+j) + a(i-1, j, k)
    ENDDO
  ENDDO
  DOALL j=1,n
    DOSEQ k=1,n
      S₁: a(i, j, k) = a(i-1, j+i, k) + a(i, j, k-1) + b(i, j-1, k)
    ENDDO
  ENDDO
ENDDO
```

4.2 Power and Limitations

It has been shown in [6] that for each statement of the initial code, as many surrounding loops as possible are detected as parallel loops by Allen and Kennedy's algorithm. More precisely, consider a statement S of the initial code and L_i one of the surrounding loops. Then L_i will be marked as parallel if and only if there is no dependence at level i between two instances of S. This result proves only that the algorithm is optimal among all parallelization algorithms that describe, in the transformed code, the instances of S with exactly the same loops as in the initial code. In fact a much stronger result has been proved in [17]:

Theorem 41. *Algorithm* ALLEN-KENNEDY *is optimal among all parallelism detection algorithms whose input is a Reduced Leveled Dependence Graph (RLDG).*

It is proved in [17] that for any loop nest $\mathcal{N}_1$, there exists a loop nest $\mathcal{N}_2$, which has the same RLDG, and such that for any statement S of $\mathcal{N}_1$ surrounded after parallelization by d_S sequential loops, there exists in the exact dependence graph of $\mathcal{N}_2$ a dependence path which includes $\Omega(N^{ds})$ instances of statement S. In other words, Allen and Kennedy's algorithm cannot distinguishes $\mathcal{N}_1$ from $\mathcal{N}_2$ as they have the same RLDG, and the parallelization algorithm is optimal in the strongest sense on $\mathcal{N}_2$ as it reaches on each statement the upper bound on the parallelism defined by the longest dependence paths in the EDG.

This proves that, as long as the only information available is the RLDG, it is not possible to find more parallelism than found by Allen and Kennedy's algorithm. In other words, algorithm ALLEN-KENNEDY is well adapted to a representation of dependences by dependence levels. Therefore, to detect more parallelism than found by algorithm ALLEN-KENNEDY, more information on the dependences is required. Classical examples for which it is possible to overcome algorithm ALLEN-KENNEDY are Example 42 where a simple interchange (Figure 4.2) reveals parallelism and Example 43 where a simple skew and interchange (Figure 4.3) are sufficient.

Example 42.

```
DO i=1,n
   DO j=1,n
      a(i, j) = a(i-1, j-1) + a(i, j-1)
   ENDDO
ENDDO
```

Fig. 4.2. Example 42: code and RDG.

Example 43.

```
DO i=1,n
   DO j=1,n
      a(i, j) = a(i-1, j) + a(i, j-1)
   ENDDO
ENDDO
```

Fig. 4.3. Example 43: code and RDG.

5. Wolf and Lam's Algorithm

Examples 42 and 43 contain some parallelism, that can not be detected by Allen and Kennedy's algorithm. Therefore, as shown by Theorem 41, this parallelism can not be extracted if the dependences are represented by dependence levels. To overcome this limitation, Wolf and Lam [31] proposed an algorithm that uses direction vectors as input. Their work unifies all previous algorithms based on elementary matrix operations such as loop skewing, loop interchange, loop reversal, into a unique framework: the framework of valid **unimodular transformations**.

5.1 Purpose

Wolf and Lam aim at building sets of fully permutable loop nests. Fully permutable loops are the basis of all tiling techniques [5, 23, 29, 31]. Tiling is used to expose medium-grain and coarse-grain parallelism. Furthermore, a set of d fully permutable loops can be rewritten as a single sequential loop and $d-1$ parallel loops. Thus, this method can also be used to express fine grain parallelism.

Wolf and Lam's algorithm builds the largest set of outermost fully permutable[3] loops. Then it looks recursively at the remaining dimensions and at the dependences not satisfied by these loops. The version presented in [31] builds the set of loops via a case analysis of simple examples, and relies on a heuristic for loop nests of depth greater than or equal to six. In the rest of this section, we explain their algorithm from a theoretical perspective, and we provide a general version of this algorithm.

5.2 Theoretical Interpretation

Unimodular transformations have two main advantages: linearity and invertibility. Given a unimodular transformation T, the linearity allows to easily check whether T is a valid transformation. Indeed, T is valid if and only if $Td >_l 0$ for all non zero distance vectors d. The invertibility enables to rewrite easily the code as the transformation is a simple change of basis in $\mathbb{Z}^n$.

In general, $Td >_l 0$ cannot be checked for all *distance* vectors, as there are two many of them. Thus, one tries to guarantee $Td >_l 0$ for all non-zero *direction* vectors, with the usual arithmetic conventions in $\mathbb{Z} \cup \{*\} \cup (\mathbb{Z} \times \{+, -\})$. In the following, we consider only non-zero direction vectors, which are known to be lexicographically positive (see Section 3.1).

Denote by $t(1), \ldots, t(n)$, the rows of T. Let Γ be the closure of the cone generated by all direction vectors. For a direction vector d:

$$Td >_l 0 \Leftrightarrow \exists k_d, \ 1 \le k_d \le n \mid \forall i, \ 1 \le i < k_d, \ t(i).d = 0 \text{ and } t(k_d).d > 0.$$

This means that the dependences represented by d are carried at loop level k_d. If $k_d = 1$ for all direction vectors d, then all dependences are carried by the first loop, and all inner loops are **DOALL** loops. $t(1)$ is then called a

---

[3] The i-th and $(i+1)$-th loops are permutable if and only if the i-th and $(i+1)$-th components of any distance vector of depth $\ge i$ are nonnegative.

timing vector or **separating hyperplane**. Such a timing vector exists if and only if Γ is pointed, i.e. if and only if Γ contains no linear space. This is also equivalent to the fact that the cone Γ^+ – defined by $\Gamma^+ = \{y \mid \forall x \in \Gamma,\ y.x \geq 0\}$ – is full-dimensional (see [30] for more details on cones and related notions). Building T from n linearly independent vectors of Γ^+ permits to transform the loops into n fully permutable loops.

The notion of timing vector is at the heart of the hyperplane method and its variants (see [10,26]), which are particularly interesting for exposing fine-grain parallelism, whereas the notion of fully permutable loops is the basis of all tiling techniques. As said before, both formulations are strongly linked by Γ^+.

When the cone Γ is not pointed, Γ^+ has a dimension r, $1 \leq r < n$, $r = n - s$ where s is the dimension of the lineality space of Γ. With r linearly independent vectors of Γ^+, one can transform the loop nest so that the r outermost loops are fully permutable. Then, one can recursively apply the same technique to transform the $n - r$ innermost loops, by considering the direction vectors not already carried by one of the r outermost loops, i.e by considering the direction vectors included in the lineality space of Γ. This is the general idea of Wolf and Lam's algorithm even if they obviously did not express it in such terms in [31].

5.3 The General Algorithm

Our discussion can be summarized by the algorithm WOLF-LAM given below. Algorithm WOLF-LAM takes as input a set of direction vectors D and a sequence of linearly independent vectors E (initialized to void) from which the transformation matrix is built:

WOLF-LAM$(D,\ E)$.

- Define Γ as the closure of the cone generated by the direction vectors of D.
- Define $\Gamma^+ = \{y \mid \forall x \in \Gamma,\ y.x \geq 0\}$ and let r be the dimension of Γ^+.
- Complete E into a set E' of r linearly independent vectors of Γ^+ (by construction, $E \subset \Gamma^+$).
- Let D' be the subset of D defined by $d \in D' \Leftrightarrow \forall v \in E',\ v.d = 0$ (i.e. $D' = D \cap E'^\perp = D \cap \text{lin.space}(\Gamma)$).
- Call WOLF-LAM$(D',\ E')$.

Actually, the above process may lead to a non unimodular matrix. Building the desired unimodular matrix T can be done as follows:

- Let D be the set of direction vectors. Set $E = \emptyset$ and call WOLF-LAM(D, E).
- Build a non singular matrix T_1 whose first rows are the vectors of E (in the same order). Let $T_2 = pT_1^{-1}$ where p is chosen so that T_2 is an integral matrix.
- Compute the left Hermite form of T_2, $T_2 = QH$, where H is nonnegative, lower triangular and Q is unimodular.
- Q^{-1} is the desired transformation matrix (since $pQ^{-1}D = HT_1D$).

We illustrate this algorithm with the following example:

Example 51.

```
DO i=1,n
  DO j=1,n
    DO k=1,n
      a(i, j, k) = a(i-1, j+i, k) + a(i, j, k-1)
                 + a(i, j-1, k+1)
    ENDDO
  ENDDO
ENDDO
```

Fig. 5.1. Example 51: code and RDG.

The set of direction vectors is $D = \{(1, -, 0), (0, 0, 1), (0, 1, -1)\}$ (see Figure 5.1). The lineality space of $\Gamma(D)$ is two-dimensional (generated by $(0, 1, 0)$ and $(0, 0, 1)$). Thus, $\Gamma^+(D)$ is one dimensional and generated by $E_1 = \{(1, 0, 0)\}$. Then $D' = \{(0, 0, 1), (0, 1, -1)\}$ and $\Gamma(D')$ is pointed. We complete E_1 by two vectors of $\Gamma^+(D')$, for example by $E_2 = \{(0, 1, 0), (0, 1, 1)\}$. In this particular example, the transformation matrix whose rows are E_1, E_2 is already unimodular and corresponds to a simple loop skewing. For exposing **DOALL** loops, we choose the first vector of E_2 in the relative interior of Γ^+, for example $E_2 = \{(0, 2, 1), (0, 1, 0)\}$. In terms of loops transformations, this amounts to skewing the loop k by factor 2 and then to interchanging loops j and k:

```
DOSEQ i=1,n
  DOSEQ k=3,3×n
    DOALL j=max(1, ⌈(k-n)/2⌉), min(n, ⌊(k-1)/2⌋)
      a(i, j, k-2×j) = a(i-1, j+i, k-2×j) + a(i, j, k-2×j-1) + a(i, j-1, k-2×j+1)
    ENDDO
  ENDDO
ENDDO
```

5.4 Power and Limitations

Wolf and Lam showed that this methodology is optimal (Theorem B.6. in [31]): "an algorithm that finds the maximum coarse grain parallelism, and then recursively calls itself on the inner loops, produces the maximum degree of parallelism possible". Strangely, they gave no hypothesis for this theorem. However, once again, this theorem has to be understood with respect to the dependence analysis that is used: namely, direction vectors, but without any information on the structure of the dependence graph. A correct formulation is the following:

Theorem 51. *Algorithm* WOLF-LAM *is optimal among all parallelism detection algorithms whose input is a set of direction vectors (implicitly, one considers that the loop nest has only one statement or that all statements form an atomic block).*

Therefore, as for algorithm ALLEN-KENNEDY, the sub-optimality of algorithm WOLF-LAM in the general case has to be found, not in the algorithm methodology, but in the weakness of its input: the fact that the structure of the RDG is not exploited may result in a loss of parallelism. For example, contrarily to algorithm ALLEN-KENNEDY, algorithm WOLF-LAM finds no parallelism in Example 41 (whose RDG is given by Figure 5.2) because of the typical structure of the direction vectors $(1, -, 0), (0, 1, -), (0, 0, 1)$.

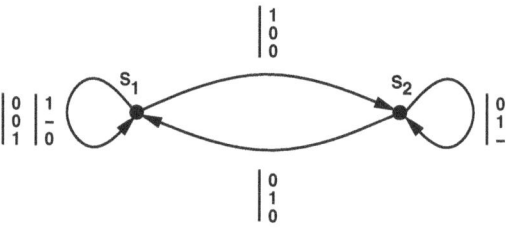

Fig. 5.2. Reduced Dependence Graph with direction vectors for Example 41.

6. Darte and Vivien's Algorithm

In this section, we introduce a third parallelization algorithm, that takes as input polyhedral reduced dependence graphs. We first explain our motivation (Section 6.1), then we proceed to a step-by-step presentation of the algorithm. We work out several examples.

6.1 Another Algorithm Is Needed

We have seen two parallelization algorithms so far. Each algorithm may output a pure sequential code for examples where the other algorithm does find some parallelism. This motivates the search for a new algorithm subsuming algorithms WOLF-LAM and ALLEN-KENNEDY. To reach this goal, one can imagine to combine these algorithms, so as to simultaneously exploit the structure of the RDG and the structure of the direction vectors: first, compute the cone generated by the direction vectors and transform the loop nest so as to expose the largest outermost fully permutable loop nest; then, consider the subgraph of the RDG, formed by the direction vectors that are not carried by the outermost loops, and compute its strongly connected components; finally, apply a loop distribution in order to separate these components, and recursively apply the same technique on each component.

Such a strategy enables to expose more parallelism by combining unimodular transformations *and* loop distribution. However, it is not optimal as Example 61 (Figure 6.1) illustrates. Indeed, on this example, combining algorithms ALLEN-KENNEDY and WOLF-LAM as proposed above enables to find only one degree of parallelism, since at the second phase the RDG remains strongly connected. This is not better than the basic algorithm ALLEN-KENNEDY. However, one can find two degrees of parallelism in Example 61 by scheduling $S_1(i, j, k)$ at time-step $4i-2k$ and $S_2(i, j, k)$ at time-step $4i-2k+3$.

Example 61.

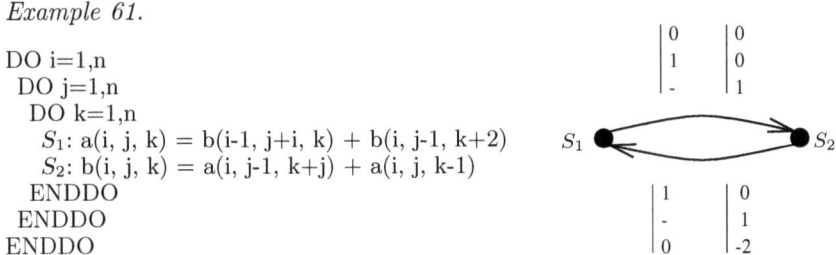

```
DO i=1,n
  DO j=1,n
    DO k=1,n
      S₁: a(i, j, k) = b(i-1, j+i, k) + b(i, j-1, k+2)
      S₂: b(i, j, k) = a(i, j-1, k+j) + a(i, j, k-1)
    ENDDO
  ENDDO
ENDDO
```

Fig. 6.1. Example 61: code and RDG.

Consequently, we would like to have a single parallelization algorithm which finds some parallelism at least when ALLEN-KENNEDY or WOLF-LAM does. The obvious solution would be to try ALLEN-KENNEDY, then WOLF-LAM (and even a combination of both algorithms) and to report the best answer. But such a naive approach is not powerful enough, because it uses either the dependence graph structure (ALLEN-KENNEDY) or direction vectors (WOLF-LAM), but never benefits from both knowledges at the same step. For example, the proposed combination of both algorithms would use the dependence graph structure before or after the computation of a maximal set of fully permutable loops, but never during this computation. We claim that information on both the graph structure and the direction vectors **must** be used simultaneously. This is because the key concept when scheduling RDGs is not the cone generated by the direction vectors (i.e. the weights of the edges of the RDG), but turns out to be the cone generated by the *weights of the cycles* of the RDG.

This is the motivation for the multi-dimensional scheduling algorithm presented below. It can be seen as a combination of unimodular transformations, loop distribution, *and* index-shift method. This algorithm subsumes algorithms ALLEN-KENNEDY and WOLF-LAM. Beforehand we motivate the choice of the representation of the dependences that the algorithm works with.

6.2 Polyhedral Dependences: A Motivating Example

In this section we present an example which contains some parallelism that cannot be detected if the dependences are represented by levels or direction vectors. However, there is no need to use an exact representation of the dependences to find some parallelism in this loop nest. Indeed, a representation of the dependences with dependence polyhedra enables us to parallelize this code.

Example 62.

```
DO i = 1, n
  DO j = 1, n
    S: a(i, j) = a(j, i) + a(i, j-1)
  ENDDO
ENDDO
```

$$\begin{cases} 1 \le i \le n,\ 1 \le j < n & S(i, j) \xrightarrow{\text{flow}} S(i, j+1) \\ 1 \le i < j \le n & S(i, j) \xrightarrow{\text{flow}} S(j, i) \\ 1 \le j < i \le n & S(j, i) \xrightarrow{\text{anti}} S(i, j) \end{cases}$$

Fig. 6.2. Example 62: source code and exact dependence relations

Consider Example 62 of Figure 6.2. Its exact dependences are listed on the same figure, and Figure 6.3 shows the corresponding (reduced) dependence graphs when dependence edges are labeled respectively with levels and direction vectors. What is the output of our favorite parallelization algorithms?

(a)   (b)

Fig. 6.3. RDG for Example 62: (a) by levels, (b) by direction vectors.

- **Allen-Kennedy.** Here, the levels of the three dependences are respectively 2, 1, and 1. There is a dependence cycle at depth 1 and at depth 2. Therefore, no parallelism is detected.
- **Wolf-Lam.** Here, the dependence vectors are respectively $(0, 1)$, $(+, -)$, and $(+, -)$. In the second dimension, the "1" and the "−" prevent to detect two fully permutable loops. Therefore, the code remains unchanged, and no parallelism is detected.

– **Feautrier**. This algorithm will be described in Section 7. It takes as input the exact dependences. It leads to the valid schedule $T(i, j) = 2i + j - 3$. One level of parallelism is detected.

In this particular example, the representation of the dependences by levels or by direction vectors is not accurate enough to reveal parallelism. This is the reason why ALLEN-KENNEDY and WOLF-LAM are not able to detect any parallelism. Exact dependence analysis associated to linear programming methods that require to solve large[4] parametric linear programs (as in Feautrier's algorithm), enables to reveal one degree of parallelism. The corresponding parallelized code is:

```
DO j = 3, 3n
    DOPAR i = max (1, ⌈ i-n/2 ⌉) , min (n, ⌊ i-1/2 ⌋)
        a(i, j − 2i) = a(j − 2i, i) + a(i, j − 2i − 1)
    ENDDO
ENDDO
```

However, in Example 62, an exact representation of the dependences is not necessary to reveal some parallelism. Indeed, one can notice that there is one uniform dependence $u = (0, 1)$ and a set of distance vectors $\{(j-i, i-j) = (j - i)(1, -1) \mid 1 \leq j - i \leq n - 1\}$ that can be (over)-approximated by the set $P = \{(1, -1) + \lambda(1, -1) \mid \lambda \geq 0\}$. P is a polyhedron with one vertex $v = (1, -1)$ and one ray $r = (1, -1)$. Now, suppose that we are looking for a linear schedule $T(i, j) = x_1 i + x_2 j$. Let $X = (x_1, x_2)$. For T to be a valid schedule, we look for X such that $Xd \geq 1$ for any dependence vector d. Thus, $X(0, 1) \geq 1$ and $Xp \geq 1$ for all $p \subset P$. The latter inequality is equal to: $X(1, -1) + \lambda X(1, -1) \geq 1$ with $\lambda \geq 0$, which is equivalent to: $X(1, -1) \geq 1$ and $X(1, -1) \geq 0$, i.e. $Xv \geq 1$ and $Xr \geq 0$. Therefore, one has just to solve the three following inequalities:

$$Xu \geq 1 \qquad\qquad Xv \geq 1 \qquad\qquad Xr \geq 0$$

i.e. $\quad X \begin{pmatrix} 0 \\ 1 \end{pmatrix} \geq 1 \quad X \begin{pmatrix} 1 \\ -1 \end{pmatrix} \geq 1 \quad X \begin{pmatrix} 1 \\ -1 \end{pmatrix} \geq 0$

which leads, as for Feautrier, to $X = (2, 1)$. Thus, for this example, an approximation of the dependences by levels or even direction vectors is not sufficient for the detection of parallelism. However, with an approximation of the dependences by polyhedra, we find the same parallelism as with exact dependence analysis, but by solving a simpler set of inequalities.

What is important here is the "uniformization" which enables us to go from the inequality on the set P to uniform inequalities on v and r. Thanks to this uniformization, the affine constraints disappear and we do not need to use the affine form of Farkas' lemma anymore as in Feautrier's algorithm

---

[4] The number of inequalities and variables is related to the number of constraints that define the validity domain of each dependence relation.

(see Section 7). To better understand the "uniformization" principle, think in terms of dependence path. The idea is to consider an edge e, from statement S to statement T and labeled by the distance vector $p = v + \lambda r$, as a path ϕ that uses once the "uniform" dependence vector v and λ times the "uniform" dependence vector r. This simulation is summarized in Figure 6.4: we introduce a new node S' that enables to simulate ϕ and a null-weight edge to go from S' back to the initial node T. This "uniformization" principle is the underlying idea of the loop parallelization algorithm described in this section.

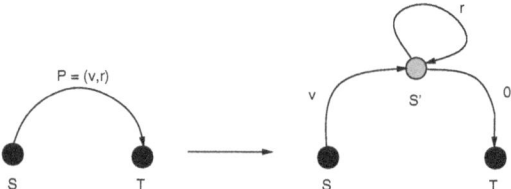

Fig. 6.4. Simulation of an edge labeled by a polyhedron with one vertex and one ray.

By uniformizing the dependences, we have in fact "uniformized" the constraints and transformed the underlying affine scheduling problem into a simple scheduling problem where all dependences are uniform (u, v, and r). However, there are two fundamental differences between this framework and the classical framework of uniform loop nests:

– The uniform dependence vectors are not necessarily lexico-positive (for example, a ray can be equal to $(0, -1)$). Therefore, the scheduling problem is more difficult. However, it can be solved by techniques similar to those used to solve the problem of computability of systems of uniform recurrence equations [24].
– The constraint imposed on a ray r is weaker than the classical constraint: the constraint is indeed $Xr \geq 0$ instead of $Xr \geq 1$. This freedom must be taken into account by the parallelization algorithm.

6.3 Illustrating Example

We work out the following example, assuming that in the reduced dependence graph, edges are labeled by direction vectors. The dependence graph, depicted in Figure 6.5, was built by the dependence analyzer Tiny [34].

The reader can check that neither ALLEN-KENNEDY, nor WOLF-LAM, is able to find the full parallelism for this code: the third statement seems to be purely sequential. However, the parallelism detection algorithm that we propose in the next sections is able to build the following multi-dimensional schedule: $(2i + 1, 2k)$ for the first statement, $(2i, j)$ for the second statement

Example 63.

```
DO i = 1, n
  DO j = 1, n
    DO k=1, j
      a(i, j, k)    = c(i, j, k-1) + 1
      b(i, j, k)    = a(i-1, j+i, k) + b(i, j-1, k)
      c(i, j, k+1) = c(i, j, k) + b(i, j-1, k+i)
                   + a(i, j-k, k+1)
    ENDDO
  ENDDO
ENDDO
```

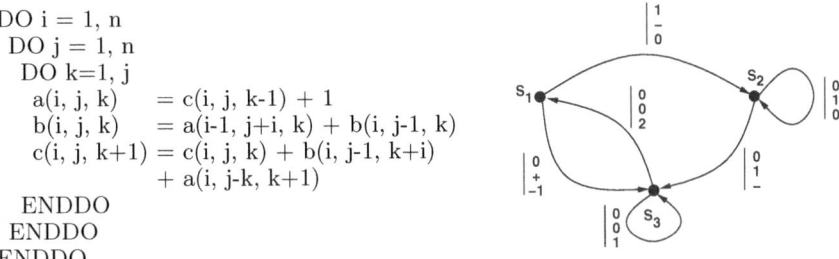

Fig. 6.5. Example 63: code and RDG.

and $(2i + 1, 2k + 3)$ for the third statement. This schedule corresponds to the code with explicit parallelism given below (but in which no effort, such as loop peeling, has been made so as to remove "if" tests). Thus, for each statement, one level of parallelism can be detected.

```
DOSEQ i = 1, n
  DOSEQ j = 1, n
    DOPAR k = 1, j
      b(i, j, k) = a(i-1, j+i, k) + b(i, j-1, k)
    ENDDO
  ENDDO
  DOSEQ k = 1, n+1
    IF (k ≤ n) THEN
      DOPAR j = k, n
        a(i, j, k) = c(i, j, k-1) + 1
      ENDDO
    ENDIF
    IF (k ≥ 2) THEN
      DOPAR j = k-1, n
        c(i, j, k) = c(i, j, k-1) + b(i, j-1, k+i-1) + a(i, j-k+1, k)
      ENDDO
    ENDIF
  ENDDO
ENDDO
```

This code has been generated, from the schedule given above, by the procedure "codegen" of the Omega Calculator[5] delivered with Petit [25]. We point out that the code proposed above is a "virtual" code in the sense that it only reveals hidden parallelism. We do not claim that it must be implemented as such.

---

[5] The Omega Calculator is a framework to compute dependences, to check the validity of program transformations, and to transform programs, once the transformation is given.

6.4 Uniformization Step

We first show how PRDGs (polyhedral reduced dependence graphs) can be captured into an equivalent (but simpler to manipulate) structure, the structure of uniform dependence graphs, i.e. graphs whose edges are labeled by constant dependence vectors. This uniformization scheme is achieved by the **translation algorithm** given below.

To avoid possible confusions between the vertices of a dependence graph and the vertices of a dependence polyhedron, we call the first one **nodes** instead of **vertices**. Furthermore, the initial PRDG that describes the dependences in the code to be parallelized is called the **original graph** and denoted by $G_o = (V, E)$. The uniform RDG, equivalent to G_o and built by the translation algorithm, is called the **uniform graph** or the **translated** of G_o, and is denoted by $G_u = (W, F)$.

The translation algorithm builds G_u by scanning all edges of G_o. It starts from $G_u = (W, F) = (V, \emptyset)$, and, for each edge e of E, it adds to G_u new nodes and new edges depending on the polyhedron $P(e)$. We call **virtual nodes** the nodes that are created, as opposed to **actual** nodes which correspond to nodes of G_o.

Let e be an edge of E. We denote by x_e and y_e, respectively the **tail** and **head** of e, i.e. the nodes that e respectively leaves and enters: $x_e \xrightarrow{e} y_e$. This definition is generalized to paths: the head (resp. tail) of a path is the head (resp. tail) of its last (resp. first) edge.

We follow the notations introduced in Section 3.2: ω, ρ, and λ denote the number of vertices v_i, of rays r_i, and of lines l_i of the polyhedron $P(e)$.

Translation Algorithm.

– Let $W = V$ and $F = \emptyset$
– For $e : x\_e \to y\_e \in E$ do
  – Add to W a new virtual node n_e,
  – Add to F ω edges of weights $v_1, v_2, \ldots, v_\omega$ directed from x_e to n_e,
  – Add to F ρ self-loops around n_e of weights $r_1, r_2, \ldots, r_\rho$,
  – Add to F λ self-loops around n_e of weights $l_1, l_2, \ldots, l_\lambda$,
  – Add to F λ self-loops around n_e of weights $-l_1, -l_2, \ldots, -l_\lambda$,
  – Add to F a null weight edge directed from n_e to y_e.

Back to Example 63. The PRDG of Example 63 is drawn in Figure 6.5. Figure 6.6 shows the uniform dependence graph associated to it. It has three new nodes in gray (i.e. virtual nodes) that correspond to the symbol "+" and the two symbols "−" in the initial direction vectors.

6.5 Scheduling Step

The scheduling step takes as input the translated dependence graph G_u and builds a multi-dimensional schedule for each actual node, i.e. for each node

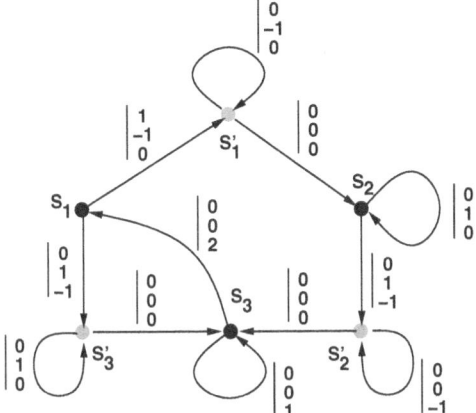

Fig. 6.6. Translated uniform reduced dependence graph.

of G_u that corresponds to a node of G_o. G_u is assumed to be strongly connected (otherwise the algorithm is called for each strongly connected component of G_u).

This is a recursive algorithm. Each step of the recursion builds a particular subgraph G' of the current graph G being processed. Once G' is built, a set of linear constraints is derived and a valid schedule that satisfies all dependence edges not in G' can be computed. Then, the algorithm keeps working on the remaining edges, i.e. the edges of G' (more precisely G' and some additional edges, see below).

G' is defined as the subgraph of G generated by all the edges of G that belong to at least one multi-cycle of null weight. A multi-cycle is a union of cycles, not necessarily connected, and the weight of a union of cycles is the sum of the weights of its constitutive cycles. G' is built by the resolution of a linear program (see Section 6.6).

The scheduling step can be summarized by the recursive algorithm given below. The initial call is DARTE-VIVIEN(G_u, 1). The algorithm builds, for each actual node S of G_u, a sequence of vectors $X_S^1, \ldots, X_S^{d_S}$ and a sequence of constants $\rho_S^1, \ldots, \rho_S^{d_S}$ that define a valid multi-dimensional schedule.

DARTE-VIVIEN(G, k).

1. Build G' the subgraph of G generated by all edges that belong to at least one null weight multi-cycle of G.
2. Add in G', all edges from x_e to y_e and all self-loops on y_e if $e = (x_e, y_e)$ is an edge already in G', from an actual node x_e to a virtual node y_e.
3. Select a vector X, and a constant ρ_S for each node S in G, such that:
$$\begin{cases} e = (x_e, y_e) \in G' \text{ or } x_e \text{ is a virtual node} \Rightarrow Xw(e) + \rho_{y_e} - \rho_{x_e} \geq 0 \\ e = (x_e, y_e) \notin G' \text{ and } x_e \text{ is an actual node} \Rightarrow Xw(e) + \rho_{y_e} - \rho_{x_e} \geq 1 \end{cases}$$

For all actual nodes S of G, let $\rho_S^k = \rho_S$ and $X_S^k = X$.

4. If G' is empty or has only virtual nodes, return.
5. If G' is strongly connected and has at least one actual node, G is not computable (and the initial PRDG G_o is not consistent), return.
6. Otherwise, decompose G' into its strongly connected components G_i and call DARTE-VIVIEN(G_i, $k+1$) for each subgraph G_i that has at least one actual node.

Remarks

– Step (2) is necessary only for general PRDGs: for example, it could be removed for RDGs labeled by direction vectors (for details see [16]). In this case, the resolution of a single linear program can simultaneously solve Step (1) and Step (3).
– In Step (3), we do not specify, on purpose, how the vector X and the constants ρ are selected, so as to allow various selection criteria. For example, a maximal set of linearly independent vectors X can be selected if the goal is to derive fully permutable loops (see [13] for details).

Back to Example 63 Consider the uniform dependence graph of Figure 6.6. There are two elementary cycles of weights $(1,0,1)$ and $(0,1,1)$, and five self-loops of weights $(0,0,1)$, $(0,0,-1)$, $(0,1,0)$ (twice) and $(0,-1,0)$. Therefore, all edges (except the edges that only belong to the cycle of weight $(1,0,1)$) belong to a multi-cycle of null weight. The subgraph G' is drawn in Figure 6.7.

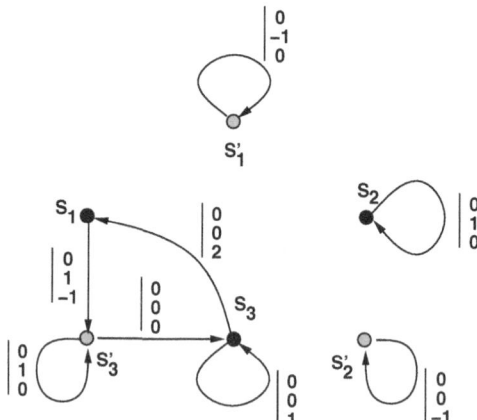

Fig. 6.7. Subgraph of null weight multi-cycles for Example 63.

The constraints coming from edges in G' impose that $X = (x, y, z)$ must be orthogonal to the weight of all cycles of G'. Therefore, $y = z = 0$. Finally, considering the other constraints, we find the solution $X = (2, 0, 0)$, $\rho_{S_1} = \rho_{S_3} = 1$ and $\rho_{S_2} = 0$. In G', there remain four strongly connected components, and two of them are not considered since they only have virtual nodes. The two other components have no null weight multi-cycles. The strongly connected component with the single node S_2 can be scheduled with the vector $X = (0, 1, 0)$, whereas studying the other strongly connected component leads, among other solutions, to $X = (0, 0, 2)$, $\rho_{S_1} = 0$, and $\rho_{S_3} = 3$.

Finally, summarizing the results, we find, as claimed in Section 6.3, the 2-dimensional schedules: $(2i, j)$ for S_2, $(2i + 1, 2k)$ for S_1 and $(2i + 1, 2k + 3)$ for S_3.

6.6 Schematic Explanations

G_u does not always correspond to the RDG of a loop nest since its dependence vectors are not necessarily lexicographically nonnegative. In fact, if one forgets that some nodes are virtual, G_u is nothing but the reduced dependence graph of a System of Uniform Recurrence Equations (SURE), introduced by Karp, Miller and Winograd [24]. Karp, Miller and Winograd study the problem of computability of a SURE: they show that its computability is linked to the problem of detecting cycles of null weight in its RDG G, which can be done by a recursive decomposition of the graph, based on the detection of multi-cycles of null weight. The key structure of their algorithm is G', the subgraph of G generated by the edges that belong to a multi-cycle of null weight.

G' can efficiently be built by the resolution of a simple linear program (program 6.1 or its dual program 6.2). This resolution enables to design a parallelization algorithm, whose principle is dual to Karp, Miller and Winograd's algorithm:

$$\min \left\{ \sum_e v_e \mid q \geq 0, \ v \geq 0, \ w \geq 0, \ q + v = 1 + w, \ Bq = 0 \right\} \quad (6.1)$$

$$\max \left\{ \sum_e z_e \mid z \geq 0, \ 0 \leq z_e \leq 1, \ Xw(e) + \rho_{y_e} - \rho_{x_e} \geq z_e \right\} \quad (6.2)$$

where $w(e)$ is the dependence vector associated to the edge e, $B = [CW]^t$, C is the connection matrix and W the matrix of dependence vectors.

Without entering the details, X is a n-dimensional vector and there is one variable ρ per vertex of the RDG and one variable z per edge of the RDG. The edges of G' (resp. $G \setminus G'$) are the edges $e = (x_e, y_e)$ for which $z_e = 0$ (resp. $z_e = 1$) in the optimal solution of the dual (program 6.2), and equivalently, for which $v_e = 0$ (resp. $v_e = 1$) in the primal (program 6.1). When summing inequalities $Xw(e) + \rho_{y_e} - \rho_{x_e} \geq z_e$ on a cycle C of G, one finds that $Xw(C) = 0$ if C is a cycle of G' and $Xw(C) \geq l(C) > 0$ otherwise ($l(C)$ is the number of edges of C not in G').

To see the link with algorithm WOLF-LAM, when considering the cone Γ generated by the weights of the cycles (and not the weights of the edges), G'

is the subgraph whose cycle weights generate the lineality space of Γ and X is a vector of the relative interior of Γ^+. However, there is no need to build Γ effectively to build G'. This is one of the interest of the linear programs 6.1 and 6.2.

We have outlined the main ideas of algorithm DARTE-VIVIEN [15]. Some technical modifications are needed to distinguish between virtual and actual nodes, and to take into account the nature of the edges (vertices, rays or lines of a dependence polyhedron): see [16] for full details.

6.7 Power and Limitations

Now that we have a multi-dimensional schedule T, we can prove its optimality in terms of degree of parallelism. We can show [14,16] that for each statement S (i.e. for each node of G_o), the number of instances of S that have been sequentialized by T is of the same order as the number of instances of S that are inherently sequentialized by the dependences.

Theorem 61. *The scheduling algorithm is nearly optimal: if the iteration domain contains (resp. is contained in) a full dimensional cube of size $\Omega(N)$ (resp. $O(N)$), and if d is the depth (the number of nested recursive calls) of the algorithm, then, the latency of the schedule is $O(N^d)$ and the length of the longest dependence path is $\Omega(N^d)$. More precisely, after code generation, each statement S is surrounded by exactly d_S sequential loops and these loops are considered inherently sequential because of the dependence analysis.*

Once again, this algorithm is optimal with respect to the dependence analysis. Consider the example in Figure 6.8.

Example 64.

```
DO i=1,n
   DO j=i,n
      S₁ a(i, j) = b(i-1, j+i) + a(i, j-1)
      S₂ b(i, j) = a(i-1, j-i) + b(i, j-1)
   ENDDO
ENDDO
```

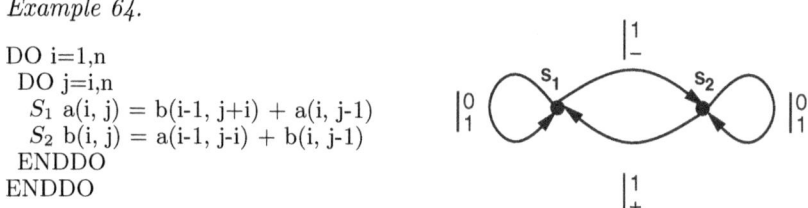

Fig. 6.8. Example 64: code and RDG.

If the dependences are described by distance vectors, the RDG has two self-dependences $(0, 1)$ and two edges labeled by polyhedra, both with one vertex and one ray (respectively $(0, 1)$ and $(0, -1)$). Therefore, there exists a multi-cycle of null weight. Furthermore, the two actual vertices belong to G'. Thus, the depth of algorithm DARTE-VIVIEN is 2 and no parallelism can be found.

However, computing iteration (i, j) of the first statement (resp. the second statement) at step $2i + j$ (resp. $i + j$), leads to a valid schedule that exposes one degree of parallelism [6]. DARTE-VIVIEN was not able to find parallelism in this example because the approximation of the dependences had already lost all the parallelism.

The technique we used here to detect parallel loops consists in looking for multi-dimensional schedules whose linear parts (the vectors X) may be different for different statements *even if they belong to the same strongly connected component*. This is the base of Feautrier's algorithm [20] whose fundamental mathematical tool is the affine form of Farkas' lemma. Theorem 61 however shows that there is no need to look for different linear parts (whose construction is more expensive and lead to more complicated rewriting processes) in a given strongly connected component of the current subgraph G', as long as dependences are given by distances vectors. On the other hand, Example 64 shows that such a refinement may be useful only when a more accurate dependence analysis is available.

7. Feautrier's Algorithm

In [20], Paul Feautrier proposed an algorithm to schedule static control programs with affine dependences. This algorithm makes use of an exact dependence analysis, which is always feasible for such programs [18]. This is to be contrasted with the previous three algorithms (ALLEN-KENNEDY, WOLF-LAM, and DARTE-VIVIEN) which work with an approximation of the dependences.

Feautrier's algorithm takes as input a reduced dependence graph G in which an edge $e : S_i \to S_j$ is labeled by the set of pairs (I, J) such that $S_j(J)$ depends on $S_i(I)$. This algorithm builds recursively a multi-dimensional affine schedule for each statement of the loop nest:

FEAUTRIER(G).

- Decompose G into its strongly connected component G_i and sort them topologically.
- For each strongly connected component G_i:
  - Find an affine schedule by statement which induces a non-negative delay on all dependences and satisfies as many dependences as possible.
  - Build the set G_i' of unsatisfied edges. If $G_i' \neq \emptyset$, call FEAUTRIER(G_i').

This algorithm is similar to DARTE-VIVIEN because of its structure and output, and because both use linear programs to build affine schedules. Here are the main points for a comparison of the two algorithms:

---

[6] The schedules $\lfloor \frac{3}{2}i + j + \frac{1}{2} \rfloor$ and $\lfloor \frac{1}{2}i + j \rfloor$ minimize the latency but the code is more complicated to write.

- DARTE-VIVIEN is able to schedule [7] programs even if dependence analysis is not feasible, given a RDG with polyhedral dependences. FEAUTRIER is only able to process static control programs with affine dependences. In this sense, the first algorithm is more powerful. Note however that there are some attempts to generalize FEAUTRIER's approach by weakening the constraints on its input, using a Fuzzy Array Dataflow Analysis [7].
- When dependence analysis is feasible, FEAUTRIER is much more powerful. This algorithm is able to process any set of loops that describe polyhedra, even if the loops are not perfectly nested. DARTE-VIVIEN can also process non perfectly nested loops, either by considering each block of perfectly nested loops separately, or by fusing artificially the non perfectly nested loops. In theory however, this is less natural and less powerful.
- DARTE-VIVIEN is based on the resolution of linear programs that are similar to those solved by FEAUTRIER. The only (through fundamental) difference is that the former looks for less general affine transformations. Therefore, on static control programs with affine dependences, FEAUTRIER always find more parallelism than DARTE-VIVIEN (cf. Example 64). However, despite this difference, the optimality result for DARTE-VIVIEN gives some hints concerning the optimality cases of FEAUTRIER that was first presented as a "greedy heuristic".
- FEAUTRIER needs to use the affine form of Farkas' lemma to obtain its linear programs, which DARTE-VIVIEN avoids thanks to its uniformization scheme. Therefore, FEAUTRIER's linear programs are more complex.
- Both algorithms were extended from fine grain to medium grain parallelism detection through a search for fully permutable loops. Darte et al. [13] proposed an extension of DARTE-VIVIEN which is a mere generalization of WOLF-LAM. Lim and Lam [27] proposed an extension of FEAUTRIER which finds maximal sets of fully permutable loops while minimizing the amount of synchronizations required in the parallelized code.
- DARTE-VIVIEN produces schedules as regular as possible in order to generate codes as simple as possible. Indeed, this algorithm rewrites the codes using affine schedules, but, unlike FEAUTRIER, these affine schedules are chosen such that as many statements as possible have the same linear part: the code generation can then be viewed as a sequence of partial unimodular transformations and loop distributions. As a result, the output codes are guaranteed to be simpler than FEAUTRIER's codes.

A small comparison study was conducted in [28]. It used only four examples. As expected, the complexity of DARTE-VIVIEN was (much) lower than that of FEAUTRIER. More surprisingly, both algorithms output the same result on each of the four examples considered. Obviously, more real examples should be processed to reach a conclusion. At least we can say that more complex techniques do not always provide better results!

---

[7] We did not write "is able to rewrite"...

Finally, here is a code (Example 71) which obviously contain some parallelism, but which cannot be parallelized by any of the four parallelization algorithms surveyed in this paper:

Example 71.

DO i=1,n
  a(i) = 1 + a(n-i)
ENDDO

DOPAR i=1,$\lfloor \frac{n}{2} \rfloor$
  a(i) = 1 + a(n-i)
ENDDO
DOPAR i=$\lfloor \frac{n}{2} \rfloor$ + 1,n
  a(i) = 1 + a(n-i)
ENDDO

Fig. 7.1. Example 71: original code and parallelized version.

8. Conclusion

Our study provides a classification of loop parallelization algorithms. The main results are the following: Allen and Kennedy's algorithm is optimal for a representation of dependences by levels, and Wolf and Lam's algorithm is optimal for a representation by direction vectors (but for a loop nest with only one statement). Neither one subsumes the other, since each uses information that cannot be exploited by the other (graph structure for the first one, direction vectors for the second one). However, both are subsumed by Darte and Vivien's algorithm which is optimal for any polyhedral representation of distance vectors. Feautrier's algorithm subsumes Darte and Vivien's algorithm when dependences can be represented as affine dependences, but the characterization of its optimality remains open.

We believe this classification of loop parallelization algorithms to be of practical interest. It provides guidance for a compiler-parallelizer in order to choose the most suitable algorithm: given the dependence analysis that is available, the simplest and cheapest parallelization algorithm that remains optimal should be selected. Indeed, this is the algorithm that is the most appropriate to the available representation of dependences.

References

1. J.R. Allen and K. Kennedy. PFC: a program to convert programs to parallel form. Technical report, Dept. of Math. Sciences, Rice University, TX, March 1982.
2. J.R. Allen and K. Kennedy. Automatic translations of Fortran programs to vector form. *ACM Toplas*, 9:491–542, 1987.
3. Utpal Banerjee. A theory of loop permutations. In Gelernter, Nicolau, and Padua, editors, *Languages and Compilers for Parallel Computing*. MIT Press, 1990.

4. A. J. Bernstein. Analysis of programs for parallel processing. In *IEEE Trans. on El. Computers, EC-15*, 1966.
5. Pierre Boulet, Alain Darte, Tanguy Risset, and Yves Robert. (pen)-ultimate tiling? *Integration, the VLSI Journal*, 17:33–51, 1994.
6. D. Callahan. *A Global Approach to Detection of Parallelism*. PhD thesis, Dept. of Computer Science, Rice University, Houston, TX, 1987.
7. J.-F. Collard, D. Barthou, and P. Feautrier. Fuzzy Array Dataflow Analysis. In *Proceedings of 5th ACM SIGPLAN Symp. on Principles and practice of Parallel Programming*, Santa Barbara, CA, July 1995.
8. Jean-François Collard. Code generation in automatic parallelizers. In Claude Girault, editor, *Proc. Int. Conf. on Application in Parallel and Distributed Computing. IFIP WG 10.3*, pages 185–194. North Holland, April 1994.
9. Jean-François Collard, Paul Feautrier, and Tanguy Risset. Construction of DO loops from systems of affine constraints. *Parallel Processing Letters*, 5(3):421–436, September 1995.
10. Alain Darte, Leonid Khachiyan, and Yves Robert. Linear scheduling is nearly optimal. *Parallel Processing Letters*, 1(2):73–81, 1991.
11. Alain Darte and Yves Robert. Mapping uniform loop nests onto distributed memory architectures. *Parallel Computing*, 20:679–710, 1994.
12. Alain Darte and Yves Robert. Affine-by-statement scheduling of uniform and affine loop nests over parametric domains. *J. Parallel and Distributed Computing*, 29:43–59, 1995.
13. Alain Darte, Georges-André Silber, and Frédéric Vivien. Combining retiming and scheduling techniques for loop parallelization and loop tiling. Technical Report 96-34, LIP, ENS-Lyon, France, November 1996.
14. Alain Darte and Frédéric Vivien. Automatic parallelization based on multi-dimensional scheduling. Technical Report 94-24, LIP, ENS-Lyon, France, September 1994.
15. Alain Darte and Frédéric Vivien. Optimal fine and medium grain parallelism detection in polyhedral reduced dependence graphs. In *Proceedings of PACT'96*, Boston, MA, October 1996. IEEE Computer Society Press.
16. Alain Darte and Frédéric Vivien. Optimal fine and medium grain parallelism detection in polyhedral reduced dependence graphs. Technical Report 96-06, LIP, ENS-Lyon, France, April 1996.
17. Alain Darte and Frédéric Vivien. On the optimality of Allen and Kennedy's algorithm for parallelism extraction in nested loops. *Journal of Parallel Algorithms and Applications*, 96. Special issue on Optimizing Compilers for Parallel Languages.
18. Paul Feautrier. Dataflow analysis of array and scalar references. *Int. J. Parallel Programming*, 20(1):23–51, 1991.
19. Paul Feautrier. Some efficient solutions to the affine scheduling problem, part I, one-dimensional time. *Int. J. Parallel Programming*, 21(5):313–348, October 1992.
20. Paul Feautrier. Some efficient solutions to the affine scheduling problem, part II, multi-dimensional time. *Int. J. Parallel Programming*, 21(6):389–420, December 1992.
21. F. Irigoin, P. Jouvelot, and R. Triolet. Semantical interprocedural parallelization: an overview of the PIPS project. In *Proceedings of the 1991 ACM International Conference on Supercomputing*, Cologne, Germany, June 1991.
22. F. Irigoin and R. Triolet. Computing dependence direction vectors and dependence cones with linear systems. Technical Report ENSMP-CAI-87-E94, Ecole des Mines de Paris, Fontainebleau (France), 1987.

23. F. Irigoin and R. Triolet. Supernode partitioning. In *Proc. 15th Annual ACM Symp. Principles of Programming Languages*, pages 319–329, San Diego, CA, January 1988.
24. R.M. Karp, R.E. Miller, and S. Winograd. The organization of computations for uniform recurrence equations. *Journal of the ACM*, 14(3):563–590, July 1967.
25. W. Kelly, V. Maslov, W. Pugh, E. Rosser, T. Shpeisman, and D. Wonnacott. *New user interface for Petit and other interfaces: user guide*. University of Maryland, June 1995.
26. Leslie Lamport. The parallel execution of DO loops. *Communications of the ACM*, 17(2):83–93, February 1974.
27. Amy W. Lim and Monica S. Lam. Maximizing parallelism and minimizing synchronization with affine transforms. In *Proceedings of the 24th Annual ACM SIGPLAN-SIGACT Symposium on Principles of Programming Languages*, January 1997.
28. Wolfgang Meisl. Practical methods for scheduling and allocation in the polytope model. World Wide Web document, URL:
`http://brahms.fmi.uni-passau.de/cl/loopo/doc`.
29. R. Schreiber and Jack J. Dongarra. Automatic blocking of nested loops. Technical Report 90-38, The University of Tennessee, Knoxville, TN, August 1990.
30. Alexander Schrijver. *Theory of Linear and Integer Programming*. John Wiley and Sons, New York, 1986.
31. Michael E. Wolf and Monica S. Lam. A loop transformation theory and an algorithm to maximize parallelism. *IEEE Trans. Parallel Distributed Systems*, 2(4):452–471, October 1991.
32. M. Wolfe. *Optimizing Supercompilers for Supercomputers*. PhD thesis, Dept. of Computer Science, University of Illinois at Urbana-Champaign, October 1982.
33. Michael Wolfe. *Optimizing Supercompilers for Supercomputers*. MIT Press, Cambridge MA, 1989.
34. Michael Wolfe. *TINY, a loop restructuring research tool*. Oregon Graduate Institute of Science and Technology, December 1990.
35. Michael Wolfe. *High Performance Compilers For Parallel Computing*. Addison-Wesley Publishing Company, 1996.
36. Jingling Xue. Automatic non-unimodular transformations of loop nests. *Parallel Computing*, 20(5):711–728, May 1994.
37. Hans Zima and Barbara Chapman. *Supercompilers for Parallel and Vector Computers*. ACM Press, 1990.

Chapter 6. Array Dataflow Analysis

Paul Feautrier

Laboratoire PRiSM, Université de Versailles Saint-Quentin
78035 VERSAILLES CEDEX, FRANCE
Paul.Feautrier@prism.uvsq.fr

Summary. While mathematical reasoning is about fixed *values*, programs are written in term of *memory cells*, whose contents are changeable values. To reason about programs, the first step is always to abstract from the memory cells to the values they contains at a given point in the execution of the program. This step, which is known as Dataflow Analysis, may use different techniques according to the required accuracy and the type of programs to be analyzed.

This paper gives a review of the *ad hoc* techniques which have been designed for the analysis of Array Programs. An exact solution is possible for the tightly constrained *static control programs*. The method can be extended to more general programs, but the results are then approximation to the real dataflow. Extensions to complex statements and to the interprocedural case are also presented.

The results of Array Dataflow Analysis may be of use for program checking, program optimization and parallelization.

Acknowledgement. The work which is reported here has taken many years of research by many peoples to evolve from the rough sketch in [Fea88a] to the present state of affairs. I would like to acknowledge contributions by Denis Barthou and Jean-François Collard [BCF97], by Vincent Lefebvre [LF97] and by Arnauld Leservot [Les96].

1. Introduction

There are many situations in which one needs to thoroughly understand the behavior of a program. The most obvious one is at program checking time. If we could extract a description of a program as, e.g., a set of mathematical equations and compare it to a specification, also given in the same medium, debugging would become a science instead of an art. Reverse engineering is another case in point. But the most important application of such analyses is to optimization. Each optimization has to be proved valid in the sense that it does not modifies the program ultimate results. To achieve this, we have to know, in a more or less precise way, what these results are intended to be. Since the most aggressive type of optimization a program can be subjected to is parallelization, understanding a program before attempting to parallelize it is a very important step.

Now, since the time of Von Neuman, programs are written in term of "variables" which are in fact symbolic names for memory cells. Values are never given[1], or even named, but always alluded to as "the present content

---

[1] except in the case of constants.

of cell x". On the other hand, in mathematics, the subject of discourse is always a value which never change, albeit it can be unknown or arbitrary. The value in a given memory cell can be modeled as a function of time (that function may be constant).

Obviously, "time" here is not physical time. Besides the fact that exhibiting such a function would be nearly impossible, it would have the added inconvenience of not being portable among different computers. We will use a logical time, to be defined later. The only requirement is that there must be a "time arrow": time must belong to an ordered set. Since the state of a computer memory does not change except at each execution of an assignment, logical time is not continuous but discrete. Each time step is an *operation* of the computer, which corresponds, from the point of view of the programmer, to the execution of an instruction. For program analysis purposes, there is some leeway in the definition of an operation. It may be the execution of a machine instruction, as in the case of Instruction Level Parallelization, or the execution of an assignment statement, as in most of this paper, or the execution of a complex statement, as in Sect. 4.

If we stipulate that the meaning of a program is given by expressing the value of variables as a function of (logical) time, then dataflow analysis is the process of extracting properties of these functions from the program text. These properties may be of widely varying precision. In some cases, one may exhibit a closed formula for the function. In other cases, one may only knows that it has positive values. In the most frequent cases, one has to be content with *relations* between values taken either at the same time (Floyd's assertions [Flo67]) or at different times. As before, these relations may be more or less precise. We will show that, for a simple but useful category of programs, the result of Array Dataflow Analysis is a system of *equations* relating the values of variables at distinct time points.

Dataflow analysis is based on the observation that the value one may retrieve from a memory cell is the one which was written last. In the scalar case, this allows one to write *dataflow equations*, which may be solved either by iterative methods or by direct methods. In the case of array cells, the problem is more difficult because there is no simple method for deciding if two references to the same array are references to the same cell or not: two occurrences of `a[i]` are references to the same cell iff `i` has not been modified in between. Conversely, it may happen that `a[i]` and `a[j]` refer to the same cell if the values i and j^2 are equal.

There is a general method for devising dataflow analyses [CC77]. One starts from a semantical description of the source language, and then one abstracts the features of interest by constructing a nonstandard semantics. The

---

[2] We will adhere to the following convention: identifiers will always be written in a `Teletype` font. Their values at a given time will always be denoted by the same letter in an *italic* font. If necessary, the time will be indicated by various devices (accents, subscripts, arguments).

result of executing a given program according to this semantics, if possible, is the required property.

Our main interest here is another type of analysis which has been designed in an *ad hoc* way for the use of automatic parallelizers. The initial concept was that of *dependences*. There is a flow dependence between statement S_1 and S_2 iff a value produced by S_1 may be used later by S_2. By restricting the allowed expressions in subscripts and loop bounds to affine expressions, the problem reduces to the question of the feasibility in integers of a system of affine inequalities. The problem is solved by standard Linear Integer Programming algorithms. It was soon realized [Fea88a] that the same technology could give much more precise results. For programs abiding to the same restrictions as above, and for each value in the program, one can pinpoint its *source*, i.e. the name of the write operation which created it. This information is invaluable for program checking, program understanding (a.k.a. reverse engineering), program optimization and parallelization.

Program whose only control structure is the `do` loop, whose only data structure is the array and in which loop bounds and subscripts are affine functions are known as *static control programs*. For such programs, one can take iteration vectors (the vectors whose components are the current values of the loop counters) as logical time. It follows that, under the above hypotheses, array subscripts are closed functions of (logical) time. This is the crucial property which allows us to find relations between the other values in the program. For program which are outside the static control model, devising an Array Dataflow Analysis is much more difficult. A first possibility is to extend slightly the control model by adding conditionals and `while` loops. The iteration count of a `while` loop cannot be bounded at compile time. The consequence is that, if these iterations can be the source of a value, then we cannot find the last one. In that case, all we can do is to report that the source belongs to a set of iterations. The result of our analysis is no longer sources, but source *sets*, and our aim will be to find the smallest possible source sets. The corresponding technique is known as Fuzzy Array Dataflow Analysis and is presented in Sect. 3. It can be extended to the case where some subscripts are no longer affine functions [BCF97].

We will next present some extensions of ADA. The first one is to statements which may return an unbounded number of results. Typical cases are `read` statements, vector statements à la Fortran 90 and `forall` statements à la HPF (Sect. 4). Procedures may return an unbounded number of results as soon as they have at least one array argument. Hence, they belong to the above category and can be treated in the same way as, e.g., vector operations.

In the conclusion, we sketch some applications of Array Dataflow Analysis and point to several unsolved problems. Basic mathematical tools are presented in the appendix.

2. Exact Array Dataflow Analysis

Exact Array Dataflow Analysis is possible only in the case of static control programs. We will first describe this program model. The results of exact ADA are *source functions*, which give, for each step in the execution of the source program and for each memory cell, the operation which has generated the current value of the memory cell. We give an algorithm for computing source functions and compare it to other proposals from the literature.

2.1 Notations

The objects we have to handle in this paper are mainly vectors with integer coordinates and set of such vectors. $|\mathbf{a}|$ is the dimension of $\mathbf{a}$. $\mathbf{a}[i..j]$ is the subvector of $\mathbf{a}$ built from components i to j. $\mathbf{a}[i]$ is a shorthand for $\mathbf{a}[i..i]$. Familiar operators and predicates like $+$ and $\geq$ will be tacitly extended to vectors. The sign $\ll$ denote lexical ordering of vectors. The max operator, when acting on vectors or vector sets, is always to be understood as the maximum according to $\ll$. Large letters will usually denote sets; $\mathbb{N}$ will be the set of nonnegative integers and $\mathbb{Z}$ the set of signed integers.

2.2 The Program Model

Let us first insist that the present work is not about any particular language, but about the static subset of any programming language. To emphasize this fact, the examples will be written indifferently in Fortran, Pascal or C. Furthermore, the fact that a given program fragment belongs to this static subset may be self-evident from the program text, or may be the result of elaborate preprocessing (`goto` elimination, induction variable detection, constant propagation, `do` loop reconstruction, to cite a few). In this paper, we will always suppose that such preprocessing has already been applied and that we are dealing with its results.

For simplicity, data types will be restricted to integers, reals, and n-dimensional arrays of integers and reals. Adding other scalar types (Boolean, complex numbers) and even record types is easy. The only statements we will consider in this section are scalar and array assignments. The only control constructs will be the sequence and the `do` loop. A `do` loop has the property that it possesses a counter, and that neither the counter nor its upper and lower bounds are modified in the loop body. In this paper, we will suppose that the loop step is always one. If the step is a known numerical constant, the program can always be transformed to have step one. If the step is an expression, the program will be considered to be beyond the static control model.

> The Pascal `for` loop has all of the above properties and thus can be considered equivalent to a Fortran `do` loop. The C `for` loop is a more complex

object since the loop counter, lower and upper bounds are not recognized by the language, and since these elements can be modified in the loop body. However, it is possible to check whether these restriction are adhered to, and thus to identify those C loops which are equivalent to a Fortran loop.

We will also suppose that compound statements are *flattened*, i.e. that constructions such as

```
begin S1;
   begin S2; S3
   end
end
```

are replaced by the equivalent:

```
begin S1; S2; S3 end
```

2.2.1 Restrictions. The above restrictions are obviously intended to simplify the calculation of the total number of iterations of all loops. This is, however, not sufficient: we have to specify the form and content of the loop bounds. The simplest case is when limits are known numerical values. This, however, is much too restrictive, since many programs use variable limits (matrix and vector dimensions, discretization size, etc.) and even non rectangular loop nests: consider for instance the prevalence in numerical analysis of triangularization algorithms (like those of Gauss or Cholesky). These observations motivate the following definition of the class of static control programs.

To recognize a static control program, one must first identify its *structure parameters*: a set of integer variables which are defined only once in the program, and whose value depends only on the outside world (through an input statement) or on other already defined structure parameters. A program has static control if all its loops are **do** loops whose bounds depend only on structure parameters, numerical constants and outer loops iteration counters. The analysis technique which is presented here is based on the theory of affine inequalities, and hence is applicable only if all limits are affine functions. For similar reasons, all subscripts are restricted to affine functions of the loop counters and the structure parameters.

We will use the fact that in a correct program, array subscripts are always within the array bounds. Hence, two array references address the same memory location if and only if they are references to the same array and their subscripts are equal. This restriction is not too severe if we note, first, that it is good programming practice to debug a program before submitting it to an optimizing or restructuring compiler, and also that the methods of this paper may be used as a highly efficient array access checker.

This hypothesis will allow us to ignore array declarations. As a consequence, our technique will be equally applicable to languages which enforce constant array bounds – Fortran, Pascal, C, ... – and to those which do not – as for instance Fortran 90.

2.2.2 The Sequencing Predicate. Values in array elements are produced by execution of statements. Hence we need a notation to pinpoint a specific execution of a statement, or *operation*. Our first need is an unambiguous designation of a statement in a program. Our solution is to use arbitrary names, which will be denoted by letters such as R, S, T. When discussing examples, we will use the fact that our preferred languages allow the affixing of a numerical label to each statement. By convention, the statement labeled i will be named S_i. In the balance of this paper, we will mostly be interested in simple statements. However, some discussions will be clearer if all statements, compound or simple, are named.

In our source language fragments, the only repetitive construct is the do loop. Hence, an operation is uniquely defined by the name of the statement and the values of the surrounding loop counters (the *iteration vector* [Kuc78]). A pair such as $\langle R, \mathbf{a} \rangle$ whose components are a statement name and an integer vector will be called an (operation) coordinate. To denote a statement instance, a coordinate must satisfy two conditions:

– the dimension of $\mathbf{a}$ must be equal to the number of loops surrounding R;
– all components of $\mathbf{a}$ must be within the corresponding loop bounds.

With each loop L we may associate a pair of inequalities:

$$lb_L \leq a \leq ub_L,$$

where a is the loop counter of L. If a statement R is embedded in a loop nest $L_1, L_2, \ldots, L_N$, in that order, then the iteration vector $\mathbf{a}$ of R must satisfy:

$$\forall p : (1 \leq p \leq N)\, lb_{L_p} \leq \mathbf{a}[p] \leq ub_{L_p}. \tag{2.1}$$

(2.1) may be summarized in matrix form as:

$$E_R \mathbf{a} \geq \mathbf{n}_R. \tag{2.2}$$

where E_R is a $2N \times N$ matrix and $\mathbf{n}_R$ is a vector of dimension N in which the structure parameters may occur linearly.

Formula (2.2) will be called the existence predicate of R. Notice that we do not suppose that $lb_L \leq ub_L$. In accordance with the Pascal convention (and with the "modern" interpretation of Fortran do loops), a loop whose bounds violate this inequality will not be executed at all.

Consider for example the program sketch in figure 2.1. Figure 2.2 describes its iteration domains. The existence predicate of statement S_2 may be written as:

$$\begin{pmatrix} 1 & 0 \\ -1 & 0 \\ -1 & 1 \\ 0 & -1 \end{pmatrix} \begin{pmatrix} i \\ j \end{pmatrix} + \begin{pmatrix} -1 \\ n \\ -1 \\ n \end{pmatrix} \geq 0.$$

```
DO i =1,n
  DO j = 1,i-1
    S1
  END DO
  DO j = i+1,n
    S2
  END DO
END
```

Fig. 2.1. A sample program

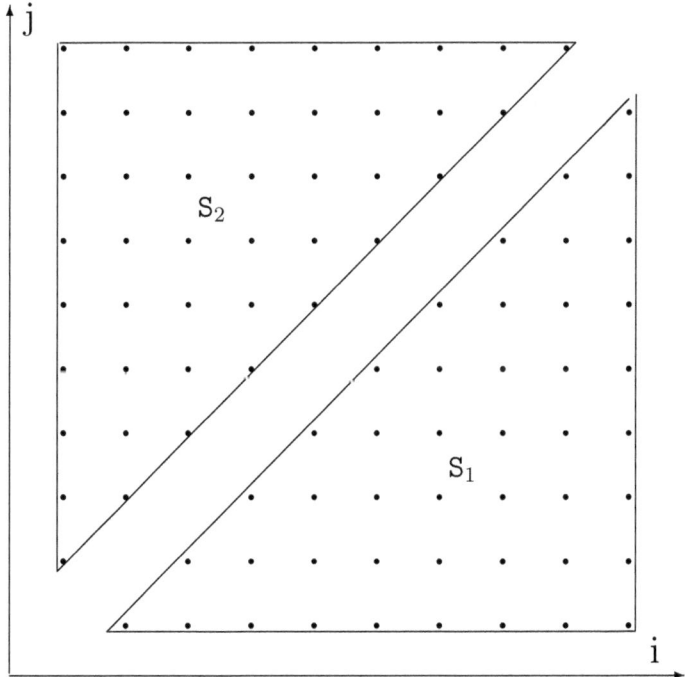

Fig. 2.2. The iteration domain of program 2.1

```
    for k := 0 to 2*n do
1 :    c[k] := 0.;
    for i := 0 to n do
      for j := 0 to n do
2 :        c[i+j] := c[i+j] + a[i]*b[j];
```

Fig. 2.3. The product of two polynomials

The preceding discussion leads to a spatial description of loops. Such a point of view goes back to the work of Kuck; see also Padua and Wolfe's review article [PW86]. Usually, loops are explained from a temporal point of view: iteration i is executed just before iteration $i + 1$, and so on. We must seek a way to reconcile those two aspects. This may be done by defining a *sequencing predicate* on the iteration domains. The sequencing predicate is a strict total order on the set of operation coordinates; it is written:

$$\langle R, a \rangle \prec \langle S, b \rangle.$$

and expresses the fact that $\langle R, a \rangle$ is executed before $\langle S, b \rangle$. The sequencing predicate depends only on the source program text. We have given a simple expression for it in [Fea91]. Let N_{RS} be the number of loops which enclose both statements R and S. Let $\lhd$ be the textual order of the source program: $R \lhd S$ iff R occurs before S in the program text. The execution order is given by:

$$\langle R, a \rangle \prec \langle S, b \rangle \equiv a[1..N_{RS}] \ll b[1..N_{RS}] \vee (a[1..N_{RS}] = b[1..N_{RS}] \wedge R \lhd S). \tag{2.3}$$

Knowledge of N_{RS} (a matrix of integers) and $\lhd$ (a strict total order relation) is all that is needed to sequence all operations in a program.

When lexicographic order is replaced by its definition, the sequencing predicate becomes a disjunction of $N_{RS} + 1$ affine predicates which will be written as $\prec_p$:

$$\langle R, a \rangle \prec_p \langle S, b \rangle \equiv (a[1..p] = b[1..p] \wedge a[p+1] < b[p+1]), \quad 0 \le p < N_{RS}. \tag{2.4}$$

The version for $p = N_{RS}$ is :

$$\langle R, a \rangle \prec_p \langle S, b \rangle \equiv a[1..N_{RS}] = b[1..N_{RS}] \wedge R \lhd S. \tag{2.5}$$

One may notice that operations which stand in the relation $\prec_p$ to each other have exactly p identical coordinates in their iteration vectors. In Allen and Kennedy's paper [AK87], if two such operations give rise to a dependence, one says that this dependence is at depth $p + 1$, while if $p = N_{RS}$, the depth is said to be infinite. With a slight displacement of the origin, we will say that $\prec_p$ is the sequencing predicate at depth p, depths ranging from 0 to N_{RS}.

2.2.3 Another Presentation of the Sequencing Predicate. We can derive another expression for the sequencing predicate by considering the *execution tree* of the program, which is obtained by (conceptually) unrolling all its loops. The nodes of the execution tree are either simple statements (the leaves) or compound statements (the interior nodes). A compound statement comes either from a genuine compound statement in the source program or from the unrolling of a loop. Let us number all edges issuing from a given note consecutively from left to right, starting from the lower bound of the loop in the case of unrolling, and from 1 in the case of a compound statement. The coordinates of the iteration vector of a leaf are the numbers encountered on the unique path from the root to the leaf. If we suppose that the program has been normalized, i.e. that the body of a loop is always a compound statement whatever the number of statements it contains, then the coordinates of the iteration vector alternate between positions in compound statements (constants) and loop counters (variables). By convention, the whole program is a compound statement, hence the the first component of all iteration vectors is a constant. The point of this construction is now that the sequencing predicate is simply lexicographic order.

Consider the program of Fig. 2.3. The iteration vectors of S_1 and S_2 are now $\langle 1, k, 1 \rangle$ and $\langle 2, i, 1, j, 1 \rangle$. From this we deduce, e.g. that all instances of S_1 execute before all instances of S_2. Similarly, by simplifying the lexicographic order, one can show that:

$$\langle S_2, i, j \rangle \prec \langle S_2, i', j' \rangle \quad \equiv \quad \langle 2, i, 1, j, 1 \rangle \ll \langle 2, i', 1, j', 1 \rangle$$
$$\equiv \quad i < i' \vee (i = i' \wedge j < j').$$

The notations we have defined in the preceding section will be extended to deal with the new iteration vectors. For instance, the existence predicate of a statement S will still be written:

$$E_R \mathbf{a} \geq \mathbf{n_R}$$

where the matrix E_R and the vector $\mathbf{n_R}$ have new rows to deal with the constant values in the iteration vector. Similarly, we will still use $\mathbf{a} \prec_p \mathbf{b}$ for the depth p sequencing predicate, the meaning being that the above expression begins by p equalities on the variable components of $\mathbf{a}$ and $\mathbf{b}$.

These new iteration vectors where introduced in [Fea92b] for other purposes. A similar proposal, with a different numbering scheme has been made in [KP96].

2.3 Data Flow Analysis

2.3.1 Formal Solution. Suppose that we are given a program conforming to the restrictions of section 2.2.1. Let T be a statement in which an array M is read. Statement T will be called the *observation statement* in what follows. Let $\mathbf{b}$ be the iteration vector of T; the subscripts of M are affine functions of $\mathbf{b}$. In vector form, the reference to M may be written $M[\mathbf{g}(\mathbf{b})]$.

Consider for instance the reference to v[i,k] in:

```
for i := 1 to n do
    for j := 1 to i-1 do
        for k := i+1 to n do
1 :        v[j,k] := v[j,k]-v[i,k]*v[j,i]/v[i,i];
```

The iteration vector of S_1 is $\langle 1, i, 1, j, 1, k, 1 \rangle$. The indexing function, $\mathbf{g}$, is given by:

$$\mathbf{g}(\mathbf{b}) = \begin{pmatrix} 0 & 1 & 0 & 0 & 0 & 0 & 0 \\ 0 & 0 & 0 & 0 & 0 & 1 & 0 \end{pmatrix} \mathbf{b}.$$

We are interested in finding the source of the value of $M[\mathbf{g}(\mathbf{b})]$. Let $S_1, \ldots, S_n$ be the statements which produce a value for M, and let $\mathbf{a}_1, \ldots, \mathbf{a}_n$ be their iteration vectors. S_i is of the form:

$$M[\mathbf{f}_i(\mathbf{a}_i)] := \cdots .$$

The source is a function of $\mathbf{b}$ which gives a coordinate when evaluated, which will be called the source function of $M[\mathbf{g}(\mathbf{b})]$.

For each S_i, there is a set of operations which write into $M[\mathbf{g}(\mathbf{b})]$. Let $Q_i(\mathbf{b})$ be this set. The set of all candidate sources is:

$$Q(\mathbf{b}) = \bigcup_{i=1}^{n} Q_i(\mathbf{b}).$$

Let us state the conditions which apply to a generic member, $\mathbf{a}$ of $Q_i(\mathbf{b})$:

- **Existence Predicate:** $\mathbf{a}$ must be a legitimate iteration vector for S_i:

$$E_{S_i} \mathbf{a} \geq \mathbf{n}_{S_i} . \tag{2.6}$$

- **Subscript Equations** : the subscripts of M must be the same at the read and write operations:

$$\mathbf{f}_i(\mathbf{a}) = \mathbf{g}(\mathbf{b}).$$

Note that this vector equation subsumes r scalar equations, where r is the *rank* of M. In writing this equation, we have taken into account the fact that the subscripts of M are guaranteed to be within M bounds.

- **Sequencing Predicate** $\mathbf{a}$ must be executed earlier than $\mathbf{b}$:

$$\mathbf{a} \ll \mathbf{b}.$$

- **Environment** : The observation statement must be executed:

$$E_T \mathbf{b} \geq \mathbf{n}_T.$$

From this we deduce the definition of Q_i:

ADA:direct:set

$$Q_i(\mathbf{b}) = \{\mathbf{a} \mid E_{S_i} \mathbf{a} \geq \mathbf{n}_{S_i}, \mathbf{a} \ll \mathbf{b}, \mathbf{f}_i(\mathbf{a}) = \mathbf{g}(\mathbf{b})\}. \tag{2.7}$$

The sets Q_i may still be subdivided according to the following observation. Under the restrictions of Sect. 2.2.1, the existence predicate and subscript equations generate a set of affine constraints. As we have seen earlier, the sequencing predicate is a disjunction of affine predicates $\prec_p$. Hence, Q_i is a union of polyhedra, or, rather, sets of integer points contained in polyhedra:

$$Q_i^p(\mathbf{b}) \quad = \quad \{\mathbf{a} \mid E_{\mathbf{S}_i}\mathbf{a} \geq n_{\mathbf{S}_i}, \mathbf{a} \prec_p \mathbf{b}, \mathbf{f}_i(\mathbf{a}) = \mathbf{g}(\mathbf{b})\}, \tag{2.8}$$

$$Q(\mathbf{b}) \quad = \quad \bigcup_{i=1}^{n} \bigcup_{p=0}^{N_{\mathbf{S}_i}\mathbf{T}} Q_i^p(\mathbf{b}). \tag{2.9}$$

Finally, the source we are seeking is the lexicographic maximum of $Q(\mathbf{b})$:

$$\varsigma(\mathbf{b}) = \max \bigcup_{i=1}^{n} \bigcup_{p=0}^{N_{\mathbf{S}_i}\mathbf{T}} Q_i^p(\mathbf{b}). \tag{2.10}$$

In this paper, we will make repeated use of the following:

Property 21.

$$\max \bigcup_{i=1}^{n} E_i = \max_{i=1}^{n}(\max E_i),$$

where the E_i are arbitrary subsets of a totally ordered set E, and where max is the maximum operator associated to the order relation of E.

The proof is trivial if none of the sets E_i is empty. If not, we have to introduce a special symbol, $\perp$, representing the undefined value, to stand in place of the maximum of an empty set. By convention, $\perp$ is less than any other value in any of the sets E_i:

$$\forall x \in E : \perp \ll x. \tag{2.11}$$

Application of the above property to (2.10) lead to the computation of

$$\varsigma_i^p(\mathbf{b}) \quad = \quad \max Q_i^p(\mathbf{b}) \tag{2.12}$$

$$\varsigma(\mathbf{b}) \quad = \quad \max_{i=1}^{n} \max_{p=0}^{N_{\mathbf{S}_i}\mathbf{T}} \varsigma_i^p(\mathbf{b}). \tag{2.13}$$

The quantities $\varsigma_i^p(\mathbf{b})$ are known as *direct dependences* and were first defined by Brandes [Bra88].

To avoid multiple subscripts, we will renumber all possible candidates at all depths with a new index j. L will stand for the cardinal of the set of possible sources. (2.13) will be rewritten as :

$$\varsigma(\mathbf{b}) = \max\{\varsigma_j(\mathbf{b}) \mid j = 1, L\}. \tag{2.14}$$

Let us go back to the example in Figure 2.3. Consider the problem of finding the source of $c[i+j]$ in statement S_2. There are two candidates, S_1 and S_2 itself, and as a consequence, three functions ς_1^0, ς_2^0 and ς_2^1. The vector $\mathbf{b}$, in this case, has dimension 5: $\langle 2, i, 1, j, 1 \rangle$. To simplify notations, only its variable components, i and j, will be taken into account.

Consider for instance the set $Q_2(i, j)$. Its elements are five dimensional integer vectors $\langle 2, i', 1, j', 1 \rangle$ which satisfy the following constraints:
- the index equations, $i' + j' = i + j$;
- the sequencing constraint $i' < i \vee (i' = i \wedge j' < j)$. One sees that the second term in the disjunction is incompatible with the index equation. This implies that Q_2^1 is empty and $\varsigma_2^1 = \bot$.
- the limit constraints $0 \le i' \le n, 0 \le j' \le n$.

Examination of figure 2.4 shows that $Q_2(i, j)$ is empty if $i = 0$ or $j = n$. If not empty, its lexical maximum is the vector $\langle 2, i - 1, 1, j + 1, 1 \rangle$. This implies that to represent ς_2^0, we need a conditional:

$$\varsigma_2^0(i, j) = \textbf{if } (i \ge 1 \wedge j < n) \textbf{ then } \langle 2, i - 1, 1, j + 1, 1 \rangle \textbf{ else } \bot. \quad (2.15)$$

The case of the other candidate is simpler; we always have:

$$\varsigma_1^0 = \langle 1, i + j, 1 \rangle.$$

Computing the lexicographic maximum of these values is now a straightforward exercise in algebra. The result is:

$$\varsigma(i, j) = \textbf{if } (i \ge 1 \wedge j < n) \textbf{ then } \langle 2, i-1, 1, j+1, 1 \rangle \textbf{ else } \langle 1, i+j, 1 \rangle. \quad (2.16)$$

To obtain this result, we have relied a lot on figure 2.4 and geometrical intuition. Now this works fine on one- and two-dimensional problems, but is quite difficult and error prone in three dimensions, and is impossible beyond. Furthermore, a computer has no geometrical intuition at all. Our aim now will be to solve the above problem in a general, systematic fashion and to implement the corresponding algorithm.

2.3.2 Evaluation Techniques.

Direct Dependences. In this section, we will focus first on one particular direct dependence ς_i^p at a given depth p. When the original program conforms to the restrictions of section 2.2.1, all terms in formula (2.12) are linear equalities or inequalities. In fact since indexing functions are affine, the first term is a linear system whose dimension is the rank of array M. The last term is simply a set of linear inequalities. The second term is given by (2.4) or (2.5). If the depth p is less than $N_{s_i t}$, then it is the conjunction of p equalities and one inequality. For $p = N_{s_i t}$, it is made of equalities only and does not exist if $S_i \triangleleft T$ is false.

As a consequence, $Q_i^p(\mathbf{b})$ is the set of integer vectors which lie inside a polyhedron. Finding its lexical maximum is a Parametric Integer Program (a PIP) [Fea88b]. A short description of an algorithm for solving PIP problems is given in the appendix. The parameters are the components of $\mathbf{b}$ and the structure parameters. Note that the components of $\mathbf{b}$ are not arbitrary; they must satisfy various constraints, among which is:

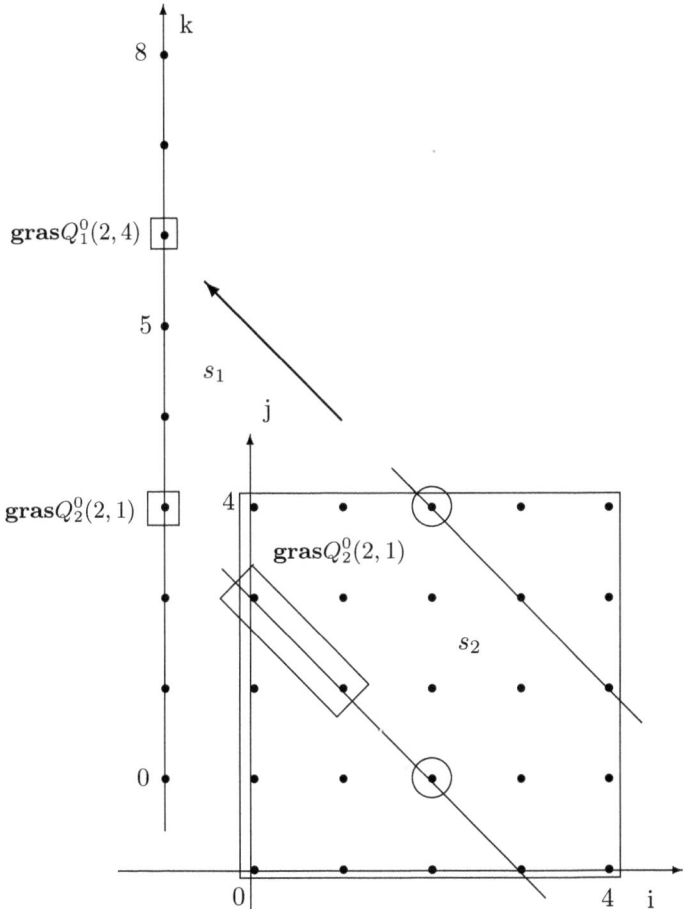

Fig. 2.4. Computing the source function for the program of Figure 2.3

The problem is finding the source of c[3] at iteration $(2, 1)$ and of c[6] at
iteration $(2, 4)$ (circled points).
Square boxes enclose the corresponding Q sets.

$$E_T \mathbf{b} \geq \mathbf{n_T}$$

to which may be added any available information on the structure parameters. These inequalities form the *context* of the parametric integer problem.

To express the solution, we need the concept of a quasi-affine form. Such a form is constructed from the parameters and integer constants by the operations of addition, multiplication by an integer, and Euclidean division by an integer. The solution is then expressed as a multistage conditional expression. The predicates are of the form $f(\mathbf{b}) \geq 0$, where f is quasi-affine. The leaves are vector of quasi-affine forms or the "undefined" sign, $\bot$. Such an expression will be called a quasi-affine selection tree (quast for brevity).

The result of this analysis is the direct dependence at depth p between the definition by S_i and the use in T. The presence of a $\bot$ sign in a direct dependence indicates that, for some values of the loop counters, the reference in T is not defined by statement S_i.

Formula (2.15) is a quast in the above sense (notice that integer division is not used here). Integer division appears when analyzing programs which access arrays with strides greater than one, as in:

```
      s = 0.
      do i = 1, 2*n, 2
1        x(i) = 1
      end do
      do k = 1, 2*n
2        s = s + x(k)
      end do
```

The direct dependence from x[2*i-1] in S_1 to x[k] in S_2 is given by the following quast:

$$\varsigma_1^0(k) = \langle 1, \text{if } 2((k+1) \div 2) - (k+1) \geq 0 \text{ then } (k+1) \div 2 \text{ else } \bot, 1 \rangle.$$

This formula expresses the fact that x[k] is not defined when k is even.

Combining the direct dependences. Consider now the problem of evaluating (2.14). This will be done in a sequential manner, by introducing:

$$
\begin{aligned}
\sigma_n &= \max\{\varsigma_j \mid j = 1, \ldots, n\}, \\
\sigma_0 &= \bot.
\end{aligned}
$$

Obviously, $\varsigma(\mathbf{b}) = \sigma_L$ and we have the recurrence:

$$\sigma_n = \max(\sigma_{n-1}, \varsigma_n). \tag{2.17}$$

We are thus led to the evaluation of $\max(\sigma, \tau)$ where σ, τ are arbitrary quasts. We will use the term *extended quast* for any formula constructed from $\bot$ and quasi-linear vectors by the operations of selection (if ... then ... else ...) and taking a maximum.

Our problem is then to remove the maximum operator from an extended quast. This is done with the help of the following rules (and their symmetrical counterparts, as the max operator is commutative).

regle:a

Rule 1. $\max(\bot, \sigma) = \sigma$. *(This is simply a restatement of (2.11).)*

regle:b

Rule 2. *If* $\sigma = $ **if** C **then** σ_1 **else** σ_2, *then:*

$$\max(\sigma, \tau) = \textbf{if } C \textbf{ then } \max(\sigma_1, \tau) \textbf{ else } \max(\sigma_2, \tau)$$

regle:c

Rule 3. *If* u *and* v *are quasi linear vectors then*

$$\max(u, v) = \textbf{if } u \ll v \textbf{ then } v \textbf{ else } u.$$

The context of a node in a quast, C, is the conjunction of all the predicates which are asserted to be true as one follows the path from the root of the quast to the distinguished node. C is constructed by "anding" p if the leaf is in the true part of a conditional **if** p **then** ...., and by anding $\neg p$ if it is in the false part.

regle:simpli

Rule 4. *Let* **if** p **then** σ **else** τ *be a subtree of a quast, and let* C *be its context. Then if* $C \wedge p$ *is not feasible, replace the subtree by* τ. *Similarly, if* $C \wedge \neg p$ *is not feasible, replace the subtree by* σ.

regle:u

Rule 5. **if** C **then** σ **else** $\sigma = \sigma$.

Theorem 21. *If Rules 1 to 5 are oriented from left to right and used as rewrite rules, then their application to any extended quast always terminates.*

Proof. Let us introduce the following metrics:

- The size of an extended quast, $|\sigma|$ is the number of nodes in the tree representation of σ. It is given by the following recursive definition:
  1. $|\bot| = |u| = 1$, where u is a quasi linear form.
  2. $|\textbf{if } p \textbf{ then } \sigma \textbf{ else } \tau| = 1 + |\sigma| + |\tau|$.
  3. $|\max(\sigma, \tau)| = 1 + |\sigma| + |\tau|$.
- The height of a max operator is simply the sum of the sizes of its arguments:

$$h(\max(\sigma, \tau)) = |\sigma| + |\tau|.$$

- $|\sigma|_{\textbf{if}}$ is the number of **if** 's in an extended quast.

Rules 1 to 3 have the property that the max operator on the left has greater height than the (eventual) max operators on the right. In the case of 2, for instance, we have:

$$
\begin{aligned}
h(\max(\mathbf{if}\ C\ \mathbf{then}\ \sigma_1\ \mathbf{else}\ \sigma_2, \tau)) &= 1 + |\sigma_1| + |\sigma_2| + |\tau|, \\
h(\max(\sigma_1, \tau)) &= |\sigma_1| + |\tau|, \\
h(\max(\sigma_2, \tau)) &= |\sigma_2| + |\tau|,
\end{aligned}
$$

If there are further max operators inside τ, for instance, their height is left undisturbed by application of the rules. All other rules may only remove some max operators, without changing the height of those which are left undisturbed.

Finally, the effect of rules 4 and 5 is to remove some **if** operators. From these results we deduce that as the reduction of an extended quast proceeds, the maximum height of the max operators stays bounded by the maximum height in the original quast, H. Let us associate to each quast σ in the reduction a vector $\mu(\sigma)$ of dimension $H+1$, whose H first components are the histogram of "max" heights in reverse order, the last component being $|\sigma|_{\mathbf{if}}$. The first component of $\mu(\sigma)$ is the number of max's of maximum height, H. From the above discussion, we see that the effect of rules 1 to 3 is to decrease by one some component, i, of $\mu(\sigma)$. In the case, of rule 2, two components of index $j, k > i$ are increased by one. Rules 4 and 5 may have the effect of decreasing some components of $\mu(\sigma)$ (if there are max operators in the discarded argument), and also to decreases by at least 1 the last component. The conclusion is that for all elementary reduction steps $\sigma \to \tau$, we have $\mu(\tau) \ll \mu(\sigma)$ in lexicographic order. Since lexicographic order on positive integer vectors is well founded, the reduction process must eventually stops, QED. Furthermore, as long as there is a max operator in the reduct, one of the rules 1 to 3 can be applied. Hence, when the reduction stops, there are no max operators in the result.

In contrast to this result, it can be shown by counterexample that our rewriting system is not confluent, i.e. that the same extended quast can be reduced to several distinct quasts. However, since all rules are semantical equalities, it follows that all such reducts are semantically equal.

In the case of (2.16), we have to compute:

$$
\sigma = \max(\bot, \max(\left\{
\begin{array}{l}
\mathbf{if}\ i \geq 1 \wedge j < n \\
\mathbf{then}\ \langle 2, i-1, 1, j+1, 1 \rangle , \langle 1, i+j, 1 \rangle))\,.\\
\mathbf{else}\ \bot
\end{array}
\right.
$$

We have successively:

$$
\sigma = \max(\left\{
\begin{array}{l}
\mathbf{if}\ i \geq 1 \wedge j < n \\
\mathbf{then}\ \langle 2, i-1, 1, j+1, 1 \rangle , \langle 1, i+j, 1 \rangle))\\
\mathbf{else}\ \bot
\end{array}
\right.
$$

by rule 1, then

$$\sigma = \begin{cases} \textbf{if } i \geq 1 \land j < n \\ \textbf{then } \max(\langle 2, i-1, 1, j+1, 1 \rangle, \langle 1, i+j, 1 \rangle) \;. \\ \textbf{else } \max(\bot, \langle 1, i+j, 1 \rangle) \end{cases}$$

For the application of rule 3, we notice that $\langle 2, i-1, 1, j+1, 1 \rangle \ll \langle 1, i+j, 1 \rangle$ is always false. Use of this property is an example of rule 4. In the other arm of the conditional, rule 1 is applied again, giving the final result:

$$\sigma = \textbf{if } (i \geq 1 \land j < n) \textbf{ then } \langle 2, i-1, 1, j+1, 1 \rangle \textbf{ else } \langle 1, i+j, 1 \rangle.$$

2.4 Summary of the Algorithm

Suppose that a compiler or another program processor has need to find the source of a reference to an array or scalar M in a statement S. The first step is to construct the candidate list, which comprises all statements R which modify M at all depths $0 \leq p \leq N_{\textbf{RS}}$. If a standard dependence analysis is available, this list can be shortened by eliminating empty candidate sets, which correspond to non existent dependences.

The ordering of the candidate set is a very important factor for the complexity of the method. Experience has shown that the best compromise is to list the candidates in order of decreasing depth. For equal depth candidates, it is best to follow the textual order backward, starting from the observation statement, up to the beginning of the program, and then to loop back to the end of the program.

Similarly, if rule 4 is used too sparingly, the resulting quasts will have many dead branches, thus increasing the complexity of the final result. Conversely, if used too often, it will result in many unsuccessful attempts at simplification, also increasing the complexity. A good compromise is the following:

- When computing a step of the recurrence (2.17) we will always suppose that rule 4 has been applied exhaustively to σ_{n-1}.
- In the evaluation of σ_n, rule 2 should be applied by priority on the left argument. As long as reductions are still possible on σ_{n-1}, there is no need to apply rule 4. All contexts that can be constructed here are feasible, because they either come from σ_{n-1} or ς_n. The first quast has been simplified in the previous step, and the second one comes from PIP, which does not generate dead branches.
- As soon as the application of rules 2 or 3 to ς_n starts, simplification by rule 4 should be attempted.

As a last remark, one can show (see Sect. 3.3.3 of [Fea91]) that the complete knowledge of the iteration vector is not needed when applying the max operator to sources of differing depths. In this way, one can predict beforehand whether a direct dependence can have influence on the source or not, and avoid computing it in the latter case.

If these rules are followed, the results of array dataflow analysis are surprisingly simple. A limited statistical analysis in [Fea91] shows that the mean number of leaves per source is about two. The probable reason is that good programmers do a kind of dataflow analysis "in their head" to convince themselves that their program is correct. If the result is too complicated, they decide that the program is not well written and start again.

2.5 Related Work

Another approach to Array Dataflow Analysis has been proposed by Pugh and his associates (see e.g. [PW93, Won95]). The approach consists in reverting to the basic definition of the maximum of a set. u is the maximum of a totally ordered set Q iff:

$$u \in Q \wedge \neg \exists v \in Q : u \prec v.$$

Let us consider the definition (2.12) of a set of candidate sources. According to the above definition, its maximum, $\varsigma_i(\mathbf{b})$ is defined by:

Bill

$$\varsigma_i(\mathbf{b}) \in \mathbf{Q}_i(\mathbf{b}) \wedge \neg \exists \mathbf{c} : \varsigma_i(\mathbf{b}) \prec \mathbf{c} \prec \mathbf{b} \wedge \mathbf{c} \in \mathbf{Q}_i(\mathbf{b}). \qquad (2.18)$$

In words, $\varsigma_i(\mathbf{b})$ is the direct dependence from $\mathbf{S}_i$ to $\mathbf{b}$ iff $\varsigma_i(\mathbf{b})$ is in flow dependence to $\mathbf{b}$ and if there is no other operation in flow dependence to $\mathbf{b}$ which is executed between $\varsigma_i(\mathbf{b})$ and $\mathbf{b}$.

The formula (2.18) is written in a subset of Presburger logic (that part of first order logic which deals with the theory of addition of positive numbers), which is known to be decidable. Pugh has devised an algorithm, the Omega test [Pug91] which is able to simplify formulas such as (2.18). The result is a relation between the source $\varsigma_i(\mathbf{b})$ and $\mathbf{b}$. It has been checked that this relation is equivalent to the quast which is found by our method.

Some authors [MAL93, HT94] have devised fast methods for handling particular cases of the source computation. The idea is to solve the set of equations in the definition of $\mathbf{Q}_i^p(\mathbf{b})$ by any integer linear solver (e.g. by constructing the Hermite normal form of the equation matrix). Suppose that this system uniquely determines $\mathbf{a}$ as a function of $\mathbf{b}$: $\mathbf{a} = f(\mathbf{b})$. It remains only to substitute $f(\mathbf{b})$ for $\mathbf{a}$ in the inequalities. The result is the existence condition for the solution, which is $f(\mathbf{b})$ if this condition is satisfied, and $\perp$ if not. One must revert to the general algorithm if there are not enough equations to fix the value of the maximum.

3. Approximate Array Dataflow Analysis

To go beyond the static control model, one has to handle `while` loops, arbitrary subscripts and tests, and, most important, modular programming (subroutines and function calls). Let us first introduce the following convention.

Constructs occurring in the control statement of a program (`do` loop bounds, `while` loops and tests predicates, subscripts) will be classified as *tractable* and *intractable* according to their complexity. Affine constructs are always tractable, while the definition of intractable constructs is somewhat subjective and may depends on the analysis tools which are available at any given time. Tractable predicates in tests can always be replaced by restrictions on the iteration domain of the surrounding loop nest. Similarly, a tractable predicate in a `while` loop indicates that the loop can be transformed into a `do` loop. We will suppose that such simplifications have been applied before the approximate analysis starts.

In this section we will be interested in `while` loops and tests. Non linear subscripts can be handled in the same framework, but they need rather complicated notations. The reader is referred to [BCF97] for this extension.

As a matter of convenience, we will suppose here that `while` loops have an explicit loop counter, according to the PL/I convention:

```
do c = 1 while p(...)
```

The `while` loop counter may even be used in array subscripts.

When constructing iteration vectors, tests branches are to be considered as new nodes being numbered 1 and 2. In accordance with our conventions for static control programs, these nodes always are compound statements, whatever the number of their components. For instance, in example E3 below, the iteration vector of Statement S_2 is $\langle 1, x, 1, 2, 1 \rangle$. The first 1 is the index of the `do` loop in the whole program, and the second one is the index of the test in the `do` loop body. The 2 indicates that the subject statement is in the false part of the test.

With these conventions, we can transpose to this new program model most of the notations we introduced for static control programs. Iteration vectors may include `while` loop counters and the definition of the sequencing predicate does not change.

ADA:FADA

3.1 From ADA to FADA

As soon as we extend our program model to include conditionals, `while` loops, and `do` loops with intractable bounds, the set Q_i^p of (2.8) is no longer tractable at compile time. The reason is that condition (2.6) may contain intractable terms. One possibility is to ignore them. In this way, (2.6) is replaced by:

FADA:linear:exists

$$E'_{S_i} \mathbf{a} \geq \mathbf{n}'_{S_i}, \tag{3.1}$$

where E' and $\mathbf{n}'$ are similar to E and $\mathbf{n}$ in (2.6) with the intractable parts omitted. We may obtain approximate sets of candidate sources:

$$\widehat{Q}_i^p(\mathbf{b}) = \{\mathbf{a} \mid E'_{\mathbf{S}_i}\mathbf{a} \ge \mathbf{n}'_{\mathbf{S}_i}, \mathbf{a} \prec_p \mathbf{b}, \mathbf{f}_i(\mathbf{a}) = \mathbf{g}(\mathbf{b})\}. \tag{3.2}$$

However, we can no longer say that the direct dependence is given by the lexicographic maximum of this set, since the result may precisely be one of the candidates which is excluded by the nonlinear part of of the iteration domain of S. One solution is to take all of $\widehat{Q}_i(\mathbf{b})$ as an approximation to the direct dependence. If we do that, and with the exception of very special cases, computing the maximum of approximate direct dependences has no meaning, and the best we can do is to use their union as an approximation. Can we do better than that? Let us consider some examples.

```
        program E1
        do x = 1 while ...
1          s = ...
        end do
2       s = ...
3       ... = ... s ...
        end
```

What is the source of s in Statement S_3? There are two possibilities, Statements S_1 and S_2. In the case of S_2, everything is linear, and the source is exactly $\langle 2 \rangle$. Things are more complicated for S_1, since we have no idea of the iteration count of the while loop. We may, however, give a name to this count, say N, and write the set of candidates as:

$$Q_1^0 = \{\langle 1, x, 1 \rangle \mid 1 \le x \le N\}.$$

We may then compute the maximum of this set, which is

$$\varsigma_1^0 = \mathbf{if}\ N > 0\ \mathbf{then}\ \langle 1, N, 1 \rangle\ \mathbf{else}\ \bot.$$

The last step is to take the lexicographic maximum of this result and $\langle 2 \rangle$, which is simply $\langle 2 \rangle$. This is much more precise than the union of all possible sources. The trick here has been to give a name to an unknown quantity, N, and to solve the problem with N as a parameter. It so happens here that N disappears in the solution, giving an exact result.

Consider now:

```
        program E2
        do x = 1 while ...
1          s(x) = ...
        end do
        do k = 1,n
2          ... = ... s(k) ...
        end do
        end
```

With the same notations as above, the set of candidates for the source of
s(k) in S_3 is:

$$Q_1^0(k) = \{\langle 1, x, 1 \rangle \mid 1 \leq x \leq N, x = k\}.$$

The direct dependence is to be computed in the environment $1 \leq k \leq n$
which gives: **if** $k \leq N$ **then** $\langle 1, k, 1 \rangle$ **else** $\bot$. Here, the unknown parameter N
has not disappeared. The best we can do is to say that we have a source *set*,
or a *fuzzy* source, which is obtained by taking the union of the two arms of
the conditional:

$$\varsigma(k) \in \{\langle 1, k, 1 \rangle, \bot\}.$$

Equivalently, by introducing a new notation $\Sigma(\mathbf{b})$ for the source set at iteration $\mathbf{b}$, this can be written:

$$\Sigma(k) = \{\langle 1, k, 1 \rangle, \bot\}.$$

The fact that in the presence of of intractable constructs, the results are
no longer sources but sets of possible sources justifies the name Fuzzy ADA
which has been given to the method. FADA gives exact results (and reverts
to ADA) when the source sets are singletons.

Our last example is slightly more complicated: we assume that $n \geq 1$,

```
          program E3;
          begin
1 :         for x := 1 to n do
2 :         begin
3 :           if ... then
4 :           begin
5 :               s := ...
              end
              else
6 :           begin
7 :               s := ...
              end
            end;
8 :         ... := s ....
          end
```

What is the source of s in Statement S_8? We may build an approximate
candidate set from S_5 and another one from S_7. Since both are approximate,
we cannot do anything beside taking their union, and the result is wildly
inaccurate.

Another possibility is to partition the set of candidates according to the
value x of the loop counter. Let us introduce a new Boolean function $b(x)$

which represents the outcome of the test at iteration x. The x-th candidate may be written[3]:

$$\tau(x) = \mathbf{if}\ b(x)\ \mathbf{then}\ \langle 1, x, 1, 1, 1 \rangle\ \mathbf{else}\ \langle 1, x, 1, 2, 1 \rangle.$$

We then have to compute the maximum of all these candidates (this is an application of Property 21). It is an easy matter to prove that:

$$x < x' \Rightarrow \tau(x) \prec \tau(x').$$

Hence the source is $\tau(n)$. Since we have no idea of the value of $b(n)$, we are lead again to the introduction of a fuzzy source:

$$\Sigma = \{\langle 1, 1, n, 1, 1 \rangle, \langle 1, 1, n, 2, 1 \rangle\}. \tag{3.3}$$

Here again, notice the far greater precision we have been able to achieve. However, the technique we have used here is not easily generalized. Another way of obtaining the same result is the following. Let $\mathbf{L} = \{x \mid 1 \le x \le n\}$. Observe that the candidate set from S_1 (resp. S_2) can be written $\{\langle \{1, x, 1, 1, 1\rangle \mid x \in \mathbf{D}_1 \cap \mathbf{L}\}$ (resp. $\{\langle 1, x, 1, 2, 1 \rangle \mid x \in \mathbf{D}_2 \cap \mathbf{L}\})$ where

$$\mathbf{D}_1 = \{x \mid b(x) = \mathbf{true}\ \}\ \text{and}\ \mathbf{D}_2 = \{x \mid b(x) = \mathbf{false}\}.$$

Obviously,

$$\mathbf{D}_1 \cap \mathbf{D}_2 = \emptyset, \tag{3.4}$$

and

$$\mathbf{D}_1 \cup \mathbf{D}_2 = \mathbb{Z}. \tag{3.5}$$

We have to compute

$$\beta = \max(\max \mathbf{D}_1 \cap \mathbf{L}, \max \mathbf{D}_2 \cap \mathbf{L}).$$

Using property 21 in reverse, (3.5) implies:

$$\beta = \max \mathbf{L}. \tag{3.6}$$

By (3.4) we know that β belongs either to $\mathbf{D}_1$ or $\mathbf{D}_2$ which gives again the result (3.3).

To summarize these observations, our method will be to give new names (or *parameters*) to the result of maxima calculations in the presence of non-linear terms. These parameters are not arbitrary. The sets they belong to – the parameters domains – are in relation to each others, as for instance (3.4-3.5). These relations can be found simply by examination of the syntactic structure of the program, or by more sophisticated techniques. From these relations between the parameter domains follow relations between the parameters, like (3.6), which can then be used to simplify the resulting fuzzy sources. In some cases, these relations may be so precise as to reduce the fuzzy source to a singleton, thus giving an exact result.

---

[3] Observe that the ordinals in the following formula do not correspond to the statement labels in the source program. These labels have been introduced for later use (see Sect. 3.3).

3.2 Introducing Parameters

In the general case, any statement in the program is surrounded by tests and loops, some of which are tractable and some are not. Tractable tests and loops give the linear part of the existence predicate, definition (3.1) above. To the non tractable parts we may associate a set d_i such that operation $\mathbf{a}$ exists iff:

FADA:exists

$$E'_{\mathbf{S}_i} \mathbf{a} \geq \mathbf{n}'_{\mathbf{S}_i} \wedge \mathbf{a} \in d_i. \tag{3.7}$$

The observation which allows us to increase the precision of FADA is that in many cases d_i has the following property:

FADA:depth

$$\mathbf{a}[1..p_i] = \mathbf{b}[1..p_i] \Rightarrow (\mathbf{a} \in d_i \equiv \mathbf{b} \in d_i) \tag{3.8}$$

for a p_i which is less than the depth of $\mathbf{S}_i$. This is due to the fact that loops and tests predicates cannot take into account variables which are not defined at the point they are evaluated, as is the case for inner loop counters. Usually, p_i is the number of (while and do) loops surrounding the innermost non tractable construction around $\mathbf{S}_i$. This depth may be less than this number, in case the intractable predicate does not depend on some variables, but this can be recognized only by a semantics analysis which is beyond the scope of this paper.

A *cylinder* is a set C of integer vectors such that there exists an integer p – the cylinder depth – with the property:

FADA:cylinder

$$\mathbf{a} \in C \wedge \mathbf{a}[1..p] = \mathbf{b}[1..p] \Rightarrow \mathbf{b} \in C. \tag{3.9}$$

The depth of cylinder C will be written $\delta(C)$.

The above discussion shows that to each d_i we may associate a cylinder C_i by the definition:

$$\mathbf{a} \in C_i \equiv \exists \mathbf{b} \in d_i : \mathbf{a}[1..p_i] = \mathbf{b}[1..p_i],$$

with the property:

$$E'_{\mathbf{S}_i} \mathbf{a} \geq \mathbf{n}'_{\mathbf{S}_i} \wedge \mathbf{a} \in d_i \equiv E'_{\mathbf{S}_i} \mathbf{a} \geq \mathbf{n}'_{\mathbf{S}_i} \wedge \mathbf{a} \in C_i.$$

The depth of C_i is bounded upward by the number of loops surrounding $\mathbf{S}_i$; a more precise analysis may show that it has a lower value.

With these convention, the set of candidate sources becomes:

FADA:candidates

$$Q_i^p(\mathbf{b}) = \{\mathbf{a} \mid E'_{\mathbf{S}_i} \mathbf{a} \geq n'_{\mathbf{S}_i}, \mathbf{a} \in C_i, \mathbf{a} \prec_p \mathbf{b}, \mathbf{f}_i(\mathbf{a}) = \mathbf{g}(\mathbf{b})\}. \tag{3.10}$$

Let us introduce the following sets:

FADA:param:candidates

$$\widehat{Q}_i^p(\mathbf{b}, \boldsymbol{\alpha}) = \{\mathbf{a} \mid E'_{\mathbf{S}_i} \mathbf{a} \geq n'_{\mathbf{S}_i}, \mathbf{a}[1..p_i] = \boldsymbol{\alpha}, \mathbf{a} \prec_p \mathbf{b}, \mathbf{f}_i(\mathbf{a}) = \mathbf{g}(\mathbf{b})\}. \quad (3.11)$$

$\widehat{Q}_i^p(\mathbf{b}, \boldsymbol{\alpha})$ is the intersection of $\widehat{Q}_i^p(\mathbf{b})$ with the hyperplane $\mathbf{a}[1..p_i] = \boldsymbol{\alpha}$. (3.10) can be rewritten:

FADA:union

$$Q_i^p(\mathbf{b}) = \bigcup_{\alpha \in C_i} \widehat{Q}_i^p(\mathbf{b}, \boldsymbol{\alpha}). \quad (3.12)$$

Another use of property 21 gives:

$$\varsigma_i^p(\mathbf{b}) = \max Q_i^p(\mathbf{b}) = \max_{\boldsymbol{\alpha} \in C_i} (\max \widehat{Q}_i^p(\mathbf{b}, \boldsymbol{\alpha})) \quad (3.13)$$

Now $\widehat{Q}_i^p(\mathbf{b}, \boldsymbol{\alpha})$ is a polyhedron, as is evident from (3.11). Hence its lexicographic maximum,

FADA:direct

$$\widehat{\varsigma}_i^p(\mathbf{b}, \boldsymbol{\alpha}) = \max \widehat{Q}_i^p(\mathbf{b}, \boldsymbol{\alpha}) \quad (3.14)$$

can be computed by just another application of PIP. In fact, the presence of the additional inequalities $\mathbf{a}[1..p_i] = \boldsymbol{\alpha}$ may simplify this calculation. We then have:

$$\varsigma_i^p(\mathbf{b}) = \max_{\boldsymbol{\alpha} \in C_i} \widehat{\varsigma}_i^p(\mathbf{b}, \boldsymbol{\alpha}). \quad (3.15)$$

The maximum in the above formula is reached at some point of C_i. This point is a function of i, p and $\mathbf{b}$, written as $\beta_i^p(\mathbf{b})$ and is known as one of the *parameters of the maximum* of the program. The direct dependence is now given by:

FADA:param:direct

$$\varsigma_i^p(\mathbf{b}) = \widehat{\varsigma}_i^p(\mathbf{b}, \beta_i^p(\mathbf{b})). \quad (3.16)$$

At this point, we can go on as we did in the case of exact analysis:

- Compute all parametric direct dependences by (3.14).
- Combine the direct dependences by rules 1 to 5.
- In the end result, quantify over all possible values of the parameters, so as to get source sets.

This procedure does not give precise results, since we lose all information about relations between parameters of the maximum. Our aim now is to explain how to find these relations and how to use them to narrow the final result.

3.3 Taking Properties of Parameters into Account

The sets C_i, C_j for $i \neq j$ may be interrelated, depending on the position of statements S_i, S_j in the abstract syntax tree. An example of this situation has been observed for statements S_5 and S_7 of program E3. These relations induce relations between the corresponding parameters, which have to be taken into account when combining direct dependences. The relations on the C_i sets may have several origins. The most obvious ones are associated to the structure of the source program, as in the case of E3. It may be that other relations are valid, due for instance to the equality of two expressions. Here again, this situation can be detected only by semantics analysis and is outside the scope of this paper.

The structural relations among the C_i can be found by the following algorithm:

- The outermost construction of the source program (by our convention, a compound statement), is associated to the unique zero-depth cylinder, which includes all integer vectors of any length, and can be written as $\mathbb{Z}^*$.
- If C_0 is associated to:

        begin S1; .... Sn end

  then $C_i = C_0$.
- If C_0 is associated to:

        if p then S1 else S2

  where p is intractable, then the cylinders associated to S_1, C_1 and S_2, C_2 have the same depth as C_0 and are such that:

$$C_1 \cap C_2 = \emptyset, \ C_1 \cup C_2 = C_0.$$

  If p is tractable, $C_0 = C_1 = C_2$.
- If C_0 is associated to a for:

        for ..... do S1

  or to a while:

        do ... while ... S1

  and if these loops are intractable, then the cylinder C_1 associated to S_1 has depth $\delta(C_0) + 1$ and is such that:

$$C_1 \subseteq C_0.$$

  Otherwise, $C_1 = C_0$.

The relation between ADA and FADA. In the case where all enclosing statements of an assignment S_i are tractable, it is easy to prove that $C_i = Z^*$. The condition $\mathbf{a} \in C_i$ is trivially satisfied in (3.10). Hence, in that case, FADA defaults to ADA. Provided this case is detected soon enough, one and the same algorithm can be used for all programs, precision of the results depending only on the presence or absence of intractable control constructs.

Characterization of the Parameters of the Maximum. The main observation is that each parameters is itself a maximum. Note first that from (3.11) follows:

$$\beta_i^p(\mathbf{b}) = \widehat{\varsigma}_i^p(\mathbf{b}, \beta_i^p(\mathbf{b}))[1..p_i].$$

Suppose now that Q is an arbitrary set of vectors all of which have dimension at least equal to p. Let us set:

$$Q\mid_p = \{x[1..p] \mid x \in Q\}.$$

The properties of the lexicographic order insure that:

$$(\max Q)[1..p] = \max Q\mid_p .$$

In our case, this gives:

Betamax

$$
\begin{aligned}
\beta_i^p(\mathbf{b}) &= \widehat{\varsigma}_i^p(\mathbf{b}, \beta_i^p(\mathbf{b}))[1..p_i] \\
&= (\max \widehat{Q}_i^p(\mathbf{b}, \beta_i^p(\mathbf{b})))[1..p_i] \\
&= \max \widehat{Q}_i^p(\mathbf{b}, \beta_i^p(\mathbf{b}))\mid_{p_i} \\
&= \max(C_i \cap \widehat{Q}_i^p(\mathbf{b})\mid_{p_i}) \qquad\qquad (3.17)
\end{aligned}
$$

where $\widehat{Q}_i^p(\mathbf{b})$ is the "polyhedral envelope" of all possible sources at depth p (see (3.2)). This formula fully characterizes the parameters of the maximum and will be used repeatedly to obtain relations between them.

Another set of relations is given by depth considerations. Note that from (3.11) follows:

$$\widehat{\varsigma}_i^p(\mathbf{b}, \beta_i^p(\mathbf{b}))[1..p_i] = \beta_i^p(\mathbf{b}),$$

and

$$\widehat{\varsigma}_i^p(\mathbf{b}, \beta_i^p(\mathbf{b}))[1..p] = \mathbf{b}[1..p],$$

provided the set $\widehat{Q}_i^p(\mathbf{b}, \beta_i^p(\mathbf{b}))$ is not empty. Now, in (3.17), we can exclude the case where $\widehat{Q}_i^p(\mathbf{b})$ is empty, since this can be decided *a priori* by integer linear programming. If such is the case, statement S_i is simply excluded from the list of candidates at depth p. Hence, either C_i is empty, in which case, by (3.17), we set $\beta_i^p(\mathbf{b}) = \bot$, or else the above relations apply. Let us set $m_i = \min(p, p_i)$. We obtain:

FADA:exact

$$\beta_i^p(\mathbf{b})[1..m_i] = \mathbf{b}[1..m_i] \vee \beta_i^p(\mathbf{b}) = \bot. \qquad\qquad (3.18)$$

Exact Cases of FADA. Among the C_i there is the set corresponding to the observation statement, C_ω. Since our convention is that the observation statement is executed, we have $\mathbf{b} \in C_\omega$, hence C_ω is not empty. It may happen that the results of structural analysis imply that $C_i = C_\omega$. Suppose that $p \geq p_i = p_\omega$. From (3.18) we deduce:

$$\beta_i^p = \mathbf{b}[1..p_i].$$

This allows us to remove the nonlinear condition $\mathbf{a} \in C_i$ from (3.10) before computing its maximum.

In the case where the innermost intractable statement is a `while` or a `do` loop, we can go a step further since C_i now has the property:

$$\mathbf{b} \in C_i \wedge (\mathbf{a}[1..p_i - 1] = \mathbf{b}[1..p_i - 1] \wedge \mathbf{a}[p_i] < \mathbf{b}[p_i]) \Rightarrow \mathbf{a} \in C_i.$$

This means that the exactness condition is in that case:

$$p \geq p_i - 1.$$

This enable us to solve exactly such problems as the source of $\mathbf{s}$ in:

```
       do c = 1 while ...
1          s = s + ....
       end do
```

Here the candidate and observation statements are both $\mathbf{S}_1$. $p_1 = 1$ and $p = 0$. The exactness condition is satisfied, and the source is:

$$\begin{aligned}
\varsigma_1^0(c) &= \max\{\langle 1, c', 1 \rangle \mid 1 \leq c', c' < c\} \\
&= \text{if } c > 1 \text{ then } \langle 1, c - 1, 1 \rangle \text{ else } \perp.
\end{aligned}$$

From Parameter Domains to Parameters of the Maximum. It remains to study the case where the structural analysis algorithm has given non trivial relations between parameters domains. The associated relations between parameters can be deduced from (3.17) by Prop. 1 and the following trivial properties:

empty:max

Property 31. If $C \cap D = \emptyset$, then:

$$(\max C = \perp \wedge \max D = \perp) \vee \max C \neq \max D.$$

inclus:max

Property 32. If $C \subseteq D$ then:

$$\max C \lll \max D.$$

As a consequence, since $C \cap D \subseteq C$, we have

inter:max

$$\max(C \cap D) \lll \max C, \tag{3.19}$$

and the symmetrical relation.

Example **E3** *revisited.* The observation statement is S_8. It is enclosed in no loops. Hence, the **b** vector is of zero length, and will be omitted in the sequel. There are two candidate sources, S_5 and S_7, whose iteration vectors are of length one and will be denoted as x. It that case, lexicographic order defaults to the standard order among integers.

The parametric sources are:

$$\widehat{\varsigma}_5^0(\alpha) = \max\{x \mid 1 \le x \le n, x = \alpha\} = \textbf{if } 1 \le \alpha \le n \textbf{ then } \langle 1, \alpha, 1, 1, 1 \rangle \textbf{ else } \bot.$$

$$\widehat{\varsigma}_7^0(\alpha) = \max\{x \mid 1 \le x \le n, x = \alpha\} = \textbf{if } 1 \le \alpha \le n \textbf{ then } \langle 1, \alpha, 1, 2, 1 \rangle \textbf{ else } \bot.$$

The structural analysis algorithm gives the following relations:

$$
\begin{array}{ccc}
C_1 = C_0 & , & C_8 = C_0 \\
C_2 = C_1 & , & C_3 = C_2 \\
C_4 \cup C_6 & = & C_3 \\
C_4 \cap C_6 & = & \emptyset \\
C_5 = C_4 & , & C_7 = C_6.
\end{array}
$$

Here, only C_5 and C_7 are interesting. Remembering that $C_0 = \mathbb{Z}^*$, all other sets can be eliminated, giving:

$$C_5 \cup C_7 = \mathbb{Z}^*, \; C_5 \cap C_7 = \emptyset.$$

The depths p_5 and p_7 are both equal to 1. From Equ. (3.17) we deduce:

$$\beta_5^0 = \max(C_5 \cap \widehat{Q}_5^0) = \max(C_5 \cap [1, n]).$$

Similarly,

$$\beta_7^0 = \max(C_5 \cap [1, n]).$$

From the above relations, we deduce:

$$(C_5 \cap [1, n]) \cap (C_7 \cap [1, n]) = \emptyset$$

and

$$(C_5 \cap [1, n]) \cup (C_7 \cap [1, n]) = \mathbb{Z}^* \cap [1, n] = [1, n].$$

This equality can be interpreted as two inclusions from left to right, giving by Prop. 32:

$$\beta_5^0 \le n, \; \beta_7^0 \le n,$$

or as an inclusion from right to left, giving:

$$n \le \max(\beta_5^0, \beta_7^0).$$

Lastly, we deduce from the first relation that:

$$(\beta_5^0 = \beta_7^0 = \bot) \vee \beta_5^0 \ne \beta_7^0.$$

Suppose now that the maximum of β_5^0 and β_7^0 is β_5^0. It is easily seen that this implies:

$$\beta_5^0 = n, \beta_7^0 < n.$$

In the reverse situation, the conclusion is:

$$\beta_7^0 = n, \beta_5^0 < n.$$

Hence, the final source is given by:

$$\varsigma = \begin{cases} \textbf{if } \beta_5^0 = n \wedge \beta_7^0 < n \\ \textbf{then } \max(\tilde{\varsigma}_5^0(\beta_5^0), \tilde{\varsigma}_5^0(\beta_5^0))/\{\beta_5^0 = n, \beta_7^0 < n\} \\ \textbf{else } \max(\tilde{\varsigma}_5^0(\beta_5^0), \tilde{\varsigma}_5^0(\beta_5^0))/\{\beta_7^0 = n, \beta_5^0 < n\} \end{cases}$$

where the notation $q/\{C\}$ indicates that the quast q is to be evaluated by rules 1 to 5 in the context C. We leave it to the reader to verify that the result is:

$$\varsigma = \textbf{if } \beta_5^0 = n \wedge \beta_7^0 < n \textbf{ then } \langle 1, n, 1, 1, 1 \rangle \textbf{ else } \langle 1, n, 1, 2, 1 \rangle.$$

3.4 Eliminating Parameters

The result of the above computation can be considered as a parametric representation of the fuzzy source: as the parameters take all possible values, the result visits all possible sources. In some cases, this is exactly what is needed for further analysis. In most case, however, more compact representations are enough. This can be obtained by the following process.

Let $\sigma(\beta)$ be a leaf of the fuzzy source, where β symbolizes all parameters occurring in the leaf. Parameter elimination uses the two rules:

regle:q

Rule 6. *A leaf $\sigma(\beta)$ in context C is replaced by the set:*

$$\{\sigma(\beta) \mid \beta \in C\}.$$

Note that after application of this rule, the variables of β become bound and no longer occur in the result.

regle:union

Rule 7. *A conditional* if $p(\beta)$ then A else B *where A and B are sets which do not depend on β is replaced by $A \cup B$.*

Application of these rules to the result of the analysis of **E3** gives the fuzzy source:

$$\Sigma = \{\langle 1, n, 1, 1, 1 \rangle, \langle 1, n, 1, 2, 1 \rangle\}.$$

Observe that rules 6 and 7 are consistent with rule 4. If the context of a leaf is unfeasible, the leaf can be removed by rule 4. It can also be transformed into the empty set by rule 6, and it will then disappear at the next application of rule 7.

3.5 Related Work

3.5.1 Pugh and Wonnacott's Method. Pugh and Wonnacott [Won95] have extended the Omega calculator for handling uninterpreted functions in logical formulas. This allows them to formulate problems of dataflow analysis in the presence of intractable constructs. They simply introduce a function to represent the value of the construct as a function of the surrounding loop counters. These functions may be used to represent the number of iteration of a `while` loop (see N in the analysis of example **E1** in Sect. 3.1) or the outcome of a test (see b for example **E3** in the same section). When we say that a construct has depth p_i, it means that the corresponding function has as arguments the p_i outermost loop counters.

The problem with this approach is that adding one uninterpreted function to Presburger logic renders it undecidable. Hence, Pugh and Wonnacott have to enforce restrictions to stays within the limits of decidability. They have chosen to partition the variables in a logical formula into input and output variables, and to use only uninterpreted functions which depends either on the input or output variables but not both. Applying a function to anything else (e.g. a bound variable inside an inner quantifier) is forbidden and is replaced by the uninterpreted symbol *unknown*. This restriction is rather *ad hoc* and it is difficult to assert its effect on the power of Pugh and Wonnacott's system. In fact, we know of several examples which they cannot handle but which can be solved by FADA: **E3** is a case in point. In the case of FADA, D. Barthou et. al. have proved in [BCF97] that their system of relations between parameters of the maximum is correct and complete, i.e. that no potential source is missed, and that each element of a source set can be a source for some realization of the intractable predicates.

On the other hand, Pugh and Wonnacott have included some semantical knowledge in their system. When assigning functions to intractable constructs, they identify cases in which two constructs are equal and assign them the same function. This is easily done by first converting the source program in Static Single Assignment (SSA) form. In SSA form, syntactically identical expressions are semantically equal. The detection of equal expression is limited to one basic bloc. This method allows them to handle examples such as:

```
        program E4;
        begin
          for i := 1 to n do
          begin
            if p(i) >= 0 then
  1 :          s := ...;
            if p(i) < 0 then
  2 :          s := ...;
          end;
          ... := s ...;
        end
```

in which the key to the solution is recognizing that p(i) has the same value in the two tests. We could have introduced a similar device in FADA; the result of the analysis could have been translated in term of the C_i sets (here, we would have got the same relations as in the case of E3) and the analysis would have then proceeded as above. We have chosen to handle first the semantical part of FADA. Recognizing equal and related expressions is left for future work, and we intend to do it with more powerful devices than SSA conversion (see [BCF97]).

3.5.2 Abstract Interpretation. As is well known, in denotational semantics, the aim is to build the input/output function of a program, which gives the final state of the computer memory in term of its initial state. This function is built in term of simpler functions, which give the effect of each statement and the value of each expression. These functions in turn are obtained by applying compilation functions to abstractions of the program text. The definitions of the compilation functions are constructive enough to enable a suitable interpreter to execute them. As many researchers have observed, these function definitions are quite similar to ML programs.

The basic idea of abstract interpretation [CC77] is to define other, non standard semantical functions. Obviously, this is interesting only if a nonstandard semantics can be considered in some sense as an approximation of standard semantics. This is formalized using the concept of Galois connection between the domains of the abstract and standard semantics.

An example of the use of these ideas for analysis of array accesses is found in [CI96]. In this work, the results of the analysis are *regions*, i.e. subsets of arrays as defined by constraints on their subscripts [TIF86]. Several types of regions are defined. For instance, the WRITE region of a statement is the set of array cells which may be modified when the statement is executed. The IN region is the set of array cells whose contents are used in a calculation.

When designing such an analysis, one has to select a finite representation for regions. In the quoted work, regions are convex polyhedra in the subscript space. Less precise representations have been suggested, see for instance [GLL95] for the concept of regular sections. In the same way as the standard semantics has operators to act on arrays, the nonstandard semantics must have operators to act on regions. These operators are intersection, union, subtraction and projection (which is used for computing the effect of loops). Depending on the representation chosen, these operators may be closed or not. For instance, intersections of polyhedra are polyhedra, but unions are not. In case of unclosed operators, one has to defined a closed approximation: for the union of polyhedra, one takes usually the convex hull of the real union.

One sees that there are two sources of approximation in region analysis. One comes from the choice of region representation. For instance, convex polyhedra are more precise than regular sections, but are not precise enough to represent frequently occurring patterns, like:

```
do i = 1,n
   m(2*i-1) = 0.
end do
```

The corresponding write region, in [CI96] notation, is $\langle m(\phi), 1 \leq \phi \leq 2n-1 \rangle$, which is only an approximation of the exact region, $\langle a(\phi), \phi = 2\psi - 1, 1 \leq \psi \leq n \rangle$.

The second source of approximation is the same as the one in FADA: the source program may contain intractable constructs. Approximate regions are constructed by ignoring intractable terms, in the spirit of (3.2).

ADA and FADA represent their results not as convex polyhedra but as finite unions of Z-polyhedra (the intersection of a polyhedron and a Z-module, see the appendix). This representation is inherently more precise and has enough power to represent exactly all regions occurring in the analysis of static control programs. An interesting open problem is the following: is it possible to reformulate the method of [CI96] in term of unions of Z-polyhedra, and, if so, would the results be more or less precise than FADA?

4. Analysis of Complex Statements

4.1 What Is a Complex Statement

All the preceding analyses are predicated on the hypothesis that each operation modifies at most one memory cell. It is not difficult to see that it can be easily extended to cases where an operation modifies a statically bounded set of memory cells.

The situation is more complicated when the language allows the modification of an unbounded set of memory cells by one statement. A case in point is the **read** statement in Fortran:

```
program R
do i = 1,n
   read (*,*) (a(i,j), j = 1,n)
end do
```

Another example is parallel array assignments in languages like Fortran 90, the Perfect Club Fortran (PCF) or HPF. The simplest case is that of the independent do loop:

```
program Z                          program ZV
doall (i = 1:n)
   a(i) = 0.0                       a(1:n) = 0.0
end doall
```

Program Z is in PCF notation, while ZV is in Fortan 90 vector notation.

How are we to handle such idioms in Array Dataflow Analysis? Let us recall the definition (2.7) of the set of candidate sources:

$$Q_i(\mathbf{b}) = \{\mathbf{a} \mid E_{\mathbf{S}_i}\mathbf{a} \geq \mathbf{n}_{\mathbf{S}_i}, \mathbf{a} \ll \mathbf{b}, \mathbf{f}_i(\mathbf{a}) = \mathbf{g}(\mathbf{b})\}.$$

The first problem for a complex statement is that $\mathbf{a}$ does no longer characterize the values which are created when executing operation $\mathbf{a}$. We have to introduce auxiliary or *inner* variables to identify each value. In the case of program R, for instance, this new variable is in evidence: it is simply the "implicit do loop counter", j. The same is true for program Z. In the case of program ZV, a new counter has to be introduced, let us call it ϕ.

We next have to decide what constraints must be satisfied by these *inner variables*. For the three examples above, these are in evidence from the program text:

$$1 \leq j \leq n$$

for R, and:

$$1 \leq \phi \leq n$$

for ZV. Objects like:

$$\langle \mathbf{M}[\phi], 1 \leq \phi \leq n \rangle,$$

composed of an array and a subset of the index space of the array, are the *regions* of [CI96]. We will use here generalized regions, of the form:

$$\langle \mathbf{M}[\mathbf{f}(\mathbf{a}, \phi)], A\mathbf{a} + B\phi + \mathbf{m} \geq 0 \rangle,$$

where $\mathbf{f}$ is affine, A and B are constant matrices, $\mathbf{m}$ is a constant vector, and $\mathbf{a}$ is the vector of the outer variables.

As to the sequencing predicate in (2.7), it stays the same whatever the type of the candidate statement, since we are supposing here that the corresponding operation is executed in one step. There is, however, a problem with the computation of the latest source, i.e. with the maximum of the candidate set, whose new form is:

$$Q_i(\mathbf{b}) = \{\mathbf{a}, \phi \mid E_{\mathbf{S}_i}\mathbf{a} \geq \mathbf{n}_{\mathbf{S}_i}, A_i\mathbf{a} + B_i\phi + \mathbf{m} \geq 0, \mathbf{a} \ll \mathbf{b}, \mathbf{f}_i(\mathbf{a}, \phi) = \mathbf{g}(\mathbf{b})\}.$$

We know that sources belonging to different iterations are executed according to lexicographic order, but what of sources belonging to the same iteration? There are several possible situations here.

In the simplest case, that of examples Z and ZT, the rules of the language insure that there cannot be an output dependence in the doall loop or in the vector assignment. This means that ϕ is uniquely determined by the subscript equations whenever $\mathbf{a}$ and $\mathbf{b}$ are known. Hence, there will never be a comparison between sources at the same iteration; we can use any convenient order on the components of ϕ, lexicographic order for instance.

In the case of example R there is no such condition on the implicit do loops. But, fortunately, the language definition stipulates that these loops are executed in the ordinary way, i.e. in order of lexicographically increasing ϕ, as above.

4.2 ADA in the Presence of Complex Statements

To summarize the preceding discussion, in the presence of complex statements, the first step is the determination of read and modified regions. The usefulness of modified regions is obvious. Read regions delimit the set of memory cells for which sources are to be calculated; their inner variables are simply added as new parameters to the coordinates of the observation statement. In the simple cases we have already examined, the regions can be extracted from a syntactical analysis of the program text. See the next section for a more complicated case.

The analysis then proceeds as in the case of simple statements, the inner variables ϕ being considered as "virtual" loop counters (which they are in examples R and Z). The corresponding components are then eliminated or kept, depending on the application, and the direct dependences are combined as above.

4.3 Procedure Calls as Complex Statements

A procedure or function call is a complex statement, as soon as one of its arguments is an array, provided the procedure or function can modify it. This is always possible in Fortran or C. In Pascal, the array argument has to be called by reference. In contrast with the previous examples, one does not know beforehand which parts of which arguments are going to be modified. This information can only be obtained by an analysis of the procedure body itself.

4.3.1 Computing the Input and Output Regions of a Procedure.
The case of the output region is the simplest. A cell is modified as soon as there is a an assignment to it in the code. Consider the following assignment statement:

```
for  a := ···
    M[ f(a)] := ···
```

The associated region is simply:

$$\langle \mathrm{M}[\mathbf{f}(\phi)], E\phi \geq \mathbf{n}\rangle.$$

The constraints of the region are given by the bounds of the surrounding loops.

We have to collect all such subregions for a given argument. The result may have redundancies whenever a memory cell is written into several times. This redundancy is harmless, since the write order is not significant outside the procedure. It may however be a source of inefficiency. It can be removed either by polyhedra handling methods or by the following systematic procedure. Suppose we add at the end of the procedure a fictitious observation operation for each cell of each argument[4], and that we compute the corresponding source. The result is a quast which depends on the subscripts of the array cell, ϕ. For each leaf whose value is not $\perp$, we may construct a subregion:

$$\langle \mathrm{M}[\phi], C(\phi) \rangle,$$

where C is the context of the distinguished leaf. The result will have no redundancy.

The computation of the input region is more difficult. Notice first that it is not the same thing as the read region, as shown by the elementary example:

```
1 : x := ...;
2 : ... := x;
```

x is read but is not in the input region, since its entry value is killed by S_1. Computing the input region as accurately as possible is important, since a source is to be computed for each of its cells in the calling routine. Redundancies will induce useless computation; inaccuracies generate spurious dependences and lessen parallelism. The solution is to compute the earliest access to each cell of each argument of the procedure. One collects all accesses to a cell in the body of the procedure, whether reads or writes. This gives a set of candidates, of which one computes the lexicographic minimum using the same technology as in the source computation[5]. The resulting quast gives the earliest access to each argument cell as a function of its subscripts. If the access is a read, the cell is in the input region. If it is a write, it is not. Lastly, if the leaf is $\perp$, then the cell is not used in the procedure. Subregions of the input are associated to read leaves in the quast, and are constructed in the same way as in the case of the output region.

If the procedure is not a static control program, we have to use techniques from FADA when computing the input and output regions. Fuzziness in the input region is not important. It simply means the loss of some parallelism. Fuzziness in the output region is more critical, and may preclude Dataflow Analysis of the calling routine, for reasons which have been explained above (see Sect. 3.1).

This analysis gives the input and output regions of a procedure, but they are expressed in term of the procedure formal arguments. To proceed to the dataflow analysis of the calling routine, we have to translate these regions in term of the caller variables, i.e. in term of the actual arguments of the procedure. This translation is easy in Pascal, since actual and formal parameters must have exactly the same type: one has simply to change the name

---

[4] e.g., a **print** statement.

[5] Note that there is a subtle point in the use of rule 3 for this problem. We may have to compare an operation to itself, if it includes both a read and a write to the same cell. Obviously, the read always occurs *before* the write. In the line:

```
s := s + 1;
```

the read of s occurs before the write, hence s *is* in the input region.

of formal arrays to actual arrays in each subregion. In the case of Fortran or C, where the typing is less strict, one has to exhibit the addressing function (or linearization function) of the formal and actual arrays. The relation between actual and formal subscripts is obtained by writing that the two array accesses are to the same memory cell, and that the subscripts are within the array bounds. In simple cases, one may find closed formulas expressing one of the subscript set in term of the other. If the bounds are explicitly given numbers, the problem can be solved by ILP. There remains the case of symbolic array bounds, in which one has to resort to *ad hoc* methods which are not guaranteed to succeed [CI96].

4.3.2 Organizing the Analysis. In Fortran, procedures cannot be recursive. Hence, one may draw a call tree. The interprocedural dataflow analysis can be done bottom up. Leaves call no procedure, hence their regions can be calculated without difficulty. If the input and output regions of all called procedures are known, then the input and input regions of the caller can be computed. When all input and output regions are known, then array dataflow analysis can be executed independently for all procedures.

Input and output regions can be stored in a library, along with other information about the procedure, such as its type and the type of its arguments. Care should be taken, however, that the region information is not intrinsic to the procedure and has to be computed again whenever the procedure or one of the procedures it calls (directly or indirectly) is modified.

Input and Output regions calculation for recursive procedures is an open problem. It is probably possible to set it up as a fixpoint calculation, but all technical details (monotony, convergence, complexity, ...) are yet to be studied.

[CI96] gives another method for computing input and output regions. Regions are approximated by convex polyhedra, and dataflow equations are used to propagate regions through the program structure. The overall organization of the computations is the same as the one given here.

5. Applications of ADA and FADA

All applications of ADA and FADA derives from two facts:

- The method is static: it can be used at compile time, without any knowledge besides the program text.
- The result is a closed representation of a dynamic phenomenon: the creation and use of values as the execution of the program proceeds.

One may in fact consider that the dataflow of a program is one possible representation of its semantics. If this is stipulated, then ADA is a way of extracting a semantics from a program text. FADA gives the same information, but with lesser precision. Hence, ADA and FADA are useful as soon as one needs to go beyond the "word for word" or "sentence for sentence" translation that is done by most ordinary compilers. Case in points are program understanding and debugging, all kinds of optimization including parallelization, and specially array expansion and privatization.

5.1 Program Comprehension and Debugging

A very simple application of ADA and FADA is the detection of uninitialized variables. Each occurrence of a $\perp$ in a source indicates that a memory cell is read but that there is no write to this cell *before* the read. If we are given a complete program, this clearly suggests a programming error. The program has to be complete: it should include all statements which can set the value of a variable, including **read** statements, initializations, and even hidden initialization by, e.g., the underlying operating system. Note that the presence of a $\perp$ in a source is not absolute proof of an error. For instance, in:

```
x := y * z;
```

y may be uninitialized if one is sure that z is zero. In the case of ADA, the access to an uninitialized variable may be conditional on the values of structure parameters. An example is:

```
      do i = 1,n
1         s = ...
      end do
2     x = s
```

The source of s in S_2 is **if** $n \geq 1$ **then** $\langle 1, n, 1 \rangle$ **else** $\perp$. There is an error if $n < 1$. This situation may be explicitly forbidden by the program definition, or, better, by a test on n just after its defining statement. One may use any number of techniques to propagate the test information through the program (see e.g. [JF90]) and use it to improve the analysis.

The situation is more complicated for FADA. The presence of a $\perp$ in a source indicates that, for some choice of the intractable predicates, an access to an uninitialized variable may occur. But this situation may be forbidden by facts about the intractable predicates that we know nothing about, or that we are not clever enough to deduce from the program text. In this situation, one should either shift to more precise analyses (for instance use semantical knowledge), or use program proving techniques to show that the error never occurs.

The same technology which is used for ADA can be reused for checking the correctness of array accesses. The results take the form of conditions on the structure parameters for the subscripts to be within bounds. These conditions can be tested once and for all as soon as the values of structure parameters are known, giving a far more efficient procedure than the run-time tests which are generated by some Pascal compilers.

The knowledge of exact sources allows the translation of a program into a system of recurrence equations (SRE):

SRE

$$\mathbf{a} \in \mathcal{D}_i : v_i[\mathbf{a}] = \mathcal{E}(\ldots, v_k[f_{ik}(\mathbf{a})], \ldots), i = 1, n, \tag{5.1}$$

where $\mathcal{D}_i$ is the domain of the equation (a set of integer vectors), v_i and v_k are "variables" (functions from integer vectors to an unspecified set of values), and the f_{ik} are dependence functions. $\mathcal{E}$ is an arbitrary expression, most of the time a conditional. Systems of recurrence equations where introduced in [KMW67]. Concrete representations of such systems are used as the starting point of systolic array synthesis (see for instance [LMQ91]).

To transform a static control program into an SRE, first assign a distinct variable to each assignment statement. The domain of v_i associated to Statement S_i is the iteration domain of S_i, and the left hand side of the corresponding equation is simply $v_i[\mathbf{a}]$ where $\mathbf{a}$ scans $\mathcal{D}_i$. The expression $\mathcal{E}$ is the right hand side of the assignment, where each memory cell is replaced bu its source. If some of the sources include $\perp$'s, the original arrays of the source program are to be kept as non mutable variables and each $\perp$ is to be converted back to the original reference (see [Fea91] for details).

As an example of semantics extraction, consider the program piece:

```
for i := 1 to n do m[i] := m[i+1]
```

The source of `m[i+1]` is $\perp$. The equivalent SER is:

$$v[i] = m[i + 1], i = 1, n.$$

In the case of:

```
fo i := 1 to n do m[i] := m[i-1]
```

the source of `m[i-1]` is **if** $i > 1$ **then** $\langle 1, i - 1, i \rangle$ **else** $\perp$. The equivalent SER is:

$$v[i] = \textbf{if } i > 1 \textbf{ then } v[i - 1] \textbf{ else } m[i - 1].$$

The first recurrence clearly represents a "left shift" while the second one is a rightward propagation of $v[0]$.

An SER is is a mathematical object which can be submitted to ordinary reasoning and transformations. One can say that an SER conveys the semantics of the source program, and ADA is this sense is a semantics extractor. The process can be pursued one step further by recognizing scans and reductions [RF93].

One can also think of an SER as a (Dynamic) Single Assignment program. Most of the time, the memory needs of a DSA program are prohibitive. It is best to think of a DSA program (or of the associated SER) as an intermediate step in the compilation process.

The results of FADA are to be thought of as an approximate semantics. It is much more difficult to convert them into something approaching a well defined mathematical object. One has to resort to dynamically gathered information to select the real source among the elements of a source set. The reader is referred to [GC95] for details.

5.2 Parallelization

The main use of source information is in the construction of parallel programs. Two operation in a program are in (data) dependence if they share a memory cell and one of them at least modifies it. Dependent operations must be executed sequentially. Other operations can be executed concurrently. Dependences are classified as flow dependences, in which a value is stored for later use, and anti- and output dependences, which are related to the sharing of a memory cell by two unrelated values. The later type of dependence can be removed by data expansion, while flow dependences are inherent to the underlying algorithm. It follows that maximum parallelism is obtained by taking into account the source relation only: an operation must always be executed after all its sources.

These indications can be formalized by computing a schedule, i.e. a function which gives the execution date of each operation in the program. All operations which are scheduled at the same time can be executed in parallel. For reasons which are too complicated to explain here (see [Fea89]), one does not have to use the exact execution time of each operation when computing a schedule, provided the amount of parallelism is large. One may suppose that all operations take unit time. The schedule θ must then satisfy:

ADA:causal

$$\theta(u) \geq \theta(\varsigma(u)) + 1, \tag{5.2}$$

for all operations u in the case of ADA, and

FADA:causal

$$\forall v \in \Sigma(u) : \theta(u) \geq \theta(v) + 1, \tag{5.3}$$

in the case of FADA. These systems of functional inequalities usually have many solutions. For reasons of expediency, one selects a particular type of solution (in fact, the solutions which are affine functions of the loop counters) and solve either (5.2) or (5.3) by linear programming. The reader is referred to [Fea92a, Fea92b] for details of the solution method.

Some programs do not have affine schedules – i.e. the associated linear programming problem proves infeasible. In that case, one must resort to *multidimensional schedules*, in which the value of θ is a d dimensional vector. The execution order is taken to be lexicographic order. Suppose we are dealing with a N-deep loop nest. Having a d dimensional schedule means that the parallel program has d sequential loops enclosing $N - d$ parallel loops. Using such schedules may be necessary because the source program has a limited amount of parallelism, or because we are using overestimates of the

dependences from FADA, or simply because we want to adapt a schedule to
a parallel processor by artificially reducing the amount of parallelism.

5.3 Array Expansion and Array Privatization

It is easy to see that the degree of parallelism of a program is closely related
to the size of its working memory (the part of its memory space the program can write into), since independent operations must write into distinct
memory cells. Consider a loop nest that we hope to execute on P processors.
This is only possible if the nest uses at least P cells of working memory.
Parallelization may thus be prevented by too small a memory space, since
programmers have a natural tendency to optimize memory. A *contrario*, a
parallelizer may have to enlarge the working memory to obtain an efficient
parallel program.

This can be done in two ways. Consider for instance the kernel of a matrix-
vector code:

```
      for i := 1 to n do
      begin
1 :     s := 0;
        for j := 1 to n do
2 :       s := s + a[i,j]*x[j]
      end
```

The working memory is s of size one, hence the program is sequential. The
first possibility is to *privatize* s, i.e. to provide one copy of s per processor. How do we know that this transformation is allowed? Observe that our
objective here is to find parallel loops. If the i loop, for instance, is parallelized, distinct iterations may be executed by distinct processors. Since each
processor has its copy of s, this means there must not be any exchange of
information through s between iterations of the i loop. The same is true
for the j loop if we decide to parallelize it. Now consider the source of s in
statement 2. It is easily computed to give:

$$\varsigma(1, i, 2, j, 1) = \textbf{if } j > 1 \textbf{ then } \langle 1, i, 2, j - 1, 1 \rangle \textbf{ else } \langle 1, i, 1 \rangle.$$

It is clear that there is no information flow from iteration i to $i', i \neq i'$. There
is, on the contrary, a data flow from iteration $j - 1$ to iteration j. This show
both that the i loop is parallel and that s must be privatized, giving:

```
      forall i := 1 to n do
      begin
        s : private real;
1 :     s := 0;
        for j := 1 to n do
2 :       s := s + a[i,j]*x[j]
      end
```

This method generalizes to array privatization. For another approach, see [TP94].

There is however another method, which is to resort to array expansion instead of array privatization. The first idea that comes to mind is to use the Dynamic Single Assignment version of the program, thus insuring that all output dependences are satisfied. The result in the above case is:

```
        forall i := 1 to n do
        begin
1 :       s1[i] := 0;
          for j := 1 to n do
2 :         s2[i,j] := (if j > 1
                          then s2[i,j-1]
                          else s1[i]) + a[i,j]*x[j]
        end
```

Notice however that while the original memory size was $O(1)$, it is now $O(n^2)$, the amount of parallelism being only $O(n)$. The degree of expansion is clearly too large. It is possible, by analyzing the life span of each value in the program, to find the minimum expansion for a given schedule [LF97]. In the present case, one finds:

```
        forall i := 1 to n do
        begin
1 :       s[i] := 0;
          for j := 1 to n do
2 :         s[i] :- s[i] + a[i,j]*x[j]
        end
```

Suppose we are using P processors. This may still be too much if n is much larger than P, as it should for efficiency sake. The solution is to adjust the schedule for the right amount of parallelism. The optimal schedule is $\theta(1, i, 2, j, 1) = j$ which should be replaced by the two dimensional version:

$$\theta(1, i, 2, j, 1) = \left(\begin{array}{c} j \\ i \bmod P \end{array} \right).$$

The resulting program is[6]:

```
        forall ii := 1 to P do
          for k := ii to n by P do
          begin
1 :         s[ii] := 0;
            for j := 1 to n do
2 :           s[ii] := s[ii] + a[k,j]*x[j]
          end
```

The amount of expansion is now exactly equal to the amount of parallelism.

---

[6] For simplicity, we have supposed that P divides n.

6. Conclusions

Let us take a look at was has been achieved so far. We have presented a technique for extracting semantics information from sequential imperative programs at compile time. The information we get is exact and, in fact, exhaustive in the case of static control programs. In the case of less regular programs, we get approximate results, the degree of approximation being in exact proportion of the irregularity of the source code.

Array Dataflow information has many uses, some of which have been presented here, in program analysis and checking, program optimization and program parallelization. There are other applications, some of which have not been reported here due to lack of space [RF93], while others are still awaiting further developments: consider for instance the problem of improving the locality of sequential and parallel codes.

There are still many problems in the design of Array Dataflow Analyses. For instance, what is the relation between FADA and methods based on Abstract Interpretation? What is the best way of taking advantage of semantical information about the source program? Can we extend Dataflow Analysis to other data structures, e.g. trees? All these questions will be the subject of future research.

A. Appendix : Mathematical Tools

The basic reference on linear inequalities in rationals or integers is the treatise [Sch86].

A.1 Polyhedra and Polytopes

There are two ways of defining a polyhedron. The simplest one is to give a set of linear inequalities:

$$A\mathbf{x} + \mathbf{a} \geq 0.$$

The polyhedron is the set of all $\mathbf{x}$ which satisfies these inequalities. A polyhedron can be empty – the set of defining inequalities is said to be *unfeasible* – or unbounded. A bounded polyhedron is called a polytope.

The basic property of a polyhedron is *convexity*: if two points $\mathbf{a}$ and $\mathbf{b}$ belong to a polyhedron, then so do all convex combinations $\lambda\mathbf{a} + (1-\lambda)\mathbf{b}, 0 \leq \lambda \leq 1$. Conversely, it can be shown that any polyhedron can be generated by convex combinations of a finite set of points, some of which – rays – may be at infinity. Any polyhedron is generated by a minimal set of vertices and rays.

There exist non-polynomial algorithms for going from a representation by inequalities to a representation by vertices and rays and vice-versa. Each representation has its merits: for instance, inequalities are better for constructing intersections, while vertices are better for convex unions.

The basic algorithms for handling polyhedra are feasibility tests: the Fourier-Motzkin cross-elimination method [Fou90] and the Simplex [Dan63]. The interested reader is referred to the above quoted treatise of Schrijver for details. Both algorithms prove that the object polyhedron is empty, or exhibit a point which belongs to it. For definiteness, this point often is the lexicographic minimum of the polyhedron. In the case of the Fourier-Motzkin algorithm, the construction of the exhibit point is a well separated phase which is omitted in most cases.

Both the Fourier-Motzkin and the Simplex are variants of the Gaussian elimination scheme, with different rules for selecting the pivot row and column. Theoretical results and expereince have shown that the Fourier-Motzkin algorithm is faster for small problems (less than about 10 inequalities), while the Simplex is better for larger problems.

A.2 Z-modules

Let $v_1, \ldots, v_n$ be a set of linearly independent vectors of $\mathbb{Z}^n$ with integral components. The set:

$$\mathcal{L}(v_1, \ldots, v_n) = \{\mu_1 v_1 + \ldots + \mu_n v_n \mid \mu_i \in \mathbb{Z}\}$$

is the Z-module generated by $v_1, \ldots, v_n$. The set of all integral points in $\mathbb{Z}^n$ is the Z-module generated by the canonical basis vectors (the canonical Z-module).

Any Z-module can be characterized by the square matrix V of which $v_1, \ldots, v_n$ are the column vectors. However, many different matrices may represent the same Z-module. A square matrix is said to be unimodular if it has integral coefficients and if its determinant is ± 1. Let U be a unimodular matrix. It is easy to prove that V and VU generate the same lattice.

Conversely, it can be shown that any non-singular matrix V can be written in the form $V = HU$ where U is unimodular and H has the following properties:

- H is lower triangular,
- All coefficients of H are positive,
- The coefficients in the diagonal of H dominate coefficients in the same row.

H is the Hermite normal form of V. Two matrices generate the same Z-module if they have the same Hermite normal form. The Hermite normal form of a unimodular matrix is the identity matrix, which generates the canonical Z-module.

Computing the Hermite normal form of an $n \times n$ matrix is of complexity $O(n^3)$, provided that the integers generated in the process are of such size that arithmetic operations can still be done in time $O(1)$.

A.3 Z-polyhedra

A Z-polyhedron is the intersection of a Z-module and a polyhedron:

$$F = \{\mathbf{z} \mid \mathbf{z} \in \mathcal{L}(V), A\mathbf{z} + \mathbf{a} \geq 0\}.$$

If the context is clear, and if $\mathcal{L}(V)$ is the canonical Z-module ($V = I$), it may be omitted in the definition.

The basic problem about Z-polyhedra is the question of their emptiness or not. For canonical Z-polyhedra, this is the linear integer programming question [Sch86, Min83]. Studies in static program analysis use either the Omega test [Pug91] which is an extension of Fourier-Motzkin, or the Gomory cut method, which is an extension of the Simplex [Gom63].

Both the Omega test and the Gomory cut method are inherently non polynomial algorithms, since the integer programming problem is known to be NP-complete.

A.4 Parametric Problems

A linear programming problem is parametric if some of its elements – e.g. the coefficients of the constraint matrix or those of the economic function – depend on parameters. In problems associated to parallelization, it so happens that constraints are often linear with respect to parameters.. In fact, most of the time we are given a polyhedron $\mathcal{P}$:

$$A \begin{pmatrix} \mathbf{x} \\ \mathbf{y} \end{pmatrix} + \mathbf{a} \geq 0$$

in which the variables have been partitioned in two sets, the unknowns: $\mathbf{x}$, and the parameters: $\mathbf{y}$. Setting the values of the parameters to $\mathbf{p}$ is equivalent to considering the intersection of $\mathcal{P}$ with the hyperplane $\mathbf{y} = \mathbf{p}$, which is also a polyhedron. In a parametric problem, we have to find the lexicographic minimum of this intersection as a function of $\mathbf{p}$.

The Fourier-Motzkin method is "naturally" parametric in this sense. One only has to eliminate the unknowns from the last component of $\mathbf{x}$ to the first. When this is done, the remaining inequalities give the conditions that the parameters must satisfy for the intersection to be non empty. If this condition is verified, each unknown is set to its minimum possible value, i.e. to the maximum of all its lower bounds. Let $C\mathbf{y} + \mathbf{c} \geq 0$ be the resulting inequalities after elimination of all unknowns. The parametric solution may be written:

$$\min_{\ll}(\mathcal{P} \cap \{\mathbf{y} = \mathbf{p}\}) = \textbf{if } C\mathbf{p} + \mathbf{c} \geq 0 \textbf{ then } \begin{pmatrix} \max(f(\mathbf{p}), \ldots, g(\mathbf{p})) \\ \cdots \\ \max(h(\mathbf{p}), \ldots, k(\mathbf{p})) \end{pmatrix} \textbf{ else } \perp$$

where $\perp$ is the undefined value and the functions $f, \ldots, k$ are affine.

The simplex also relies on linear combinations of the constraint matrix rows, which can be applied without difficulty in the parametric case. The only difficulty lies in the choice of the pivot row, which is such that its constant coefficient must be negative. Since this coefficient depends in general on the parameters, its sign cannot be ascertained; the problem must be split in two, with opposite hypotheses on this sign. These hypotheses are not independent; each one restricts the possible values of the parameters, until inconsistent hypotheses are encountered. At this point, the splitting process stops. By climbing back the problem tree, one may reconstruct the solution in the form of a multistage conditional. Parametric Gomory cuts can be constructed by introducing new parameters which represent integer quotients. The reader is referred to [Fea88b] for an implementation of these ideas in the Parametric Integer Programming (PIP) algorithm.

References

[AK87]   J. R. Allen and Ken Kennedy. Automatic translation of fortran programs to vector form. *ACM TOPLAS*, 9(4):491–542, October 1987.

[ASU86]   A. V. Aho, R. Sethi, and J. D. Ullman. *Compilers: Principles, Techniques and Tools*. Addison-Wesley, Reading, Mass, 1986.

[BCF97]   Denis Barthou, Jean-François Collard, and Paul Feautrier. Fuzzy array dataflow analysis. *Journal of Parallel and Distributed Computing*, 40:210–226, 1997.

[Bra88]   Thomas Brandes. The importance of direct dependences for automatic parallelization. In *ACM Int. Conf. on Supercomputing*, St Malo, France, July 1988.

[CC77]   Patrick Cousot and Radhia Cousot. Abstract interpretation: a unified lattice model for static analysis of programs by construction or approximation of fixpoints. In *Symp. on Principle and Practice of Programming Languages*, pages 238–252. ACM, 1977.

[CI96]   Béatrice Creusillet and François Irigoin. Interprocedural array regions analyses. *Int. J. of Parallel Programming*, 24(6):513–546, 1996.

[Dan63]   G. B. Dantzig. *Linear Programming and Extensions*. Princeton University Press, 1963.

[Fea88a]   Paul Feautrier. Array expansion. In *ACM Int. Conf. on Supercomputing*, pages 429–441, 1988.

[Fea88b]   Paul Feautrier. Parametric integer programming. *RAIRO Recherche Opérationnelle*, 22:243–268, September 1988.

[Fea89]   Paul Feautrier. Asymptotically efficent algorithms for parallel architectures. In M. Cosnard and C. Girault, editors, *Decentralized System*, pages 273–284. IFIP WG 10.3, North-Holland, December 1989.

[Fea91]   Paul Feautrier. Dataflow analysis of scalar and array references. *Int. J. of Parallel Programming*, 20(1):23–53, February 1991.

[Fea92a]   Paul Feautrier. Some efficient solutions to the affine scheduling problem, I, one dimensional time. *Int. J. of Parallel Programming*, 21(5):313–348, October 1992.

[Fea92b] Paul Feautrier. Some efficient solutions to the affine scheduling problem, II, multidimensional time. *Int. J. of Parallel Programming*, 21(6):389–420, December 1992.

[Flo67] Robert J. Floyd. Assigning meaning to programs. In *Mathematical Aspects of Computer Science*. AMS, 1967.

[Fou90] J. B. J. Fourier. *Oeuvres de Fourier, Tome II*. Gauthier-Villard, Paris, 1890.

[GC95] M. Griebl and J.-F. Collard. Generation of synchronous code for automatic parallelization of while loops. In *Euro-Par95*, Stockholm, Sweden, Aug 1995.

[GLL95] Jungie Gu, Zhiyuan Li, and Gyungho Lee. Symbolic array dataflow analysis for array privatization and program parallelization. In *Supercomputing*, December 1995.

[Gom63] R. E. Gomory. An algorithm for integer solutions to linear programs. In R. L. Graves and P. Wolfe, editors, *Recent Advances in Math. Programming*, chapter 34, pages 269–302. Mac-Graw Hill, New York, 1963.

[HT94] C. Heckler and L. Thiele. Computing linear data dependencies in nested loop programs. *Parallel Processing Letters*, 4(3):193–204, 1994.

[JF90] Pierre Jouvelot and Paul Feautrier. Parallélisation Sémantique. *Informatique théorique et Applications*, 24:131–159, 1990.

[KMW67] R. M. Karp, R. E. Miller, and S. Winograd. The organization of computations for uniform recurrence equations. *Journal of the ACM*, 14:563–590, 1967.

[KP96] Induprakas Kodokula and Keshav Pingali. Transformations for imperfect nested loops. In *Supercomputing*, 1996.

[Kuc78] David J. Kuck. *The Structure of Computers and Computations*. J. Wiley and sons, New York, 1978.

[Les96] Arnauld Leservot. *Analyse Interprocédurale du flot des données*. PhD thesis, Université Paris VI, March 1996.

[LF97] Vincent Lefebvre and Paul Feautrier. Storage management in parallel programs. In IEEE Computer Society, editor, *5th Euromicro Workshop on Parallel and Distributed Processing*, pages 181–188, Londres (England), January 1997.

[LMQ91] Hervé Leverge, Christophe Mauras, and Patrice Quinton. The ALPHA language and its use for the design of systolic arrays. *Journal of VLSI Signal Processing*, 3:173–182, 1991.

[MAL93] Dror E. Maydan, Saman P. Amarasinghe, and Monica S. Lam. Array dataflow analysis and its use in array privatization. In *Proc. of ACM Conf. on Principles of Programming Languages*, pages 2–15, January 1993.

[Min83] Michel Minoux. *Programmation Mathématique, théorie et algorithmes*. Dunod, Paris, 1983.

[Pug91] William Pugh. The Omega test: A fast and practical integer programming algorithm for dependence analysis. In *Supercomputing*, 1991.

[PW86] D. A. Padua and Michael J. Wolfe. Advanced compiler optimization for supercomputers. *CACM*, 29:1184–1201, December 1986.

[PW93] William Pugh and David Wonnacott. An evaluation of exact methods for analysis of value-based array data dependences. In *Sixth Annual Workshop on Programming Languages and Compilers for Parallel Computing*, pages 546–566. Springer-Verlag LNCS 768, August 1993.

[RF93] Xavier Redon and Paul Feautrier. Detection of reductions in sequential programs with loops. In Arndt Bode, Mike Reeve, and Gottfried Wolf, editors, *Procs. of the 5th Int. Parallel Architectures and Languages Europe*, pages 132–145. LNCS 694, June 1993.

[Sch86]   A. Schrijver. *Theory of linear and integer programming*. Wiley, NewYork, 1986.

[TIF86]   Rémi Triolet, François Irigoin, and Paul Feautrier. Automatic parallelization of FORTRAN programs in the presence of procedure calls. In Bernard Robinet and R. Wilhelm, editors, *ESOP 1986, LNCS 213*. Springer-Verlag, 1986.

[TP94]   Peng Tu and David Padua. Array privatization for shared and distributed memory machines. In *Proc. of the 7th Workshop on Languages and Compilers for Parallel Computers, LNCS 892*, 1994.

[Won95]   David G. Wonnacott. *Constraint-Based Array Dependence Analysis*. PhD thesis, U. of Maryland, 1995.

Chapter 7. Interprocedural Analysis Based on Guarded Array Regions

Zhiyuan Li[1], Junjie Gu[2], and Gyungho Lee[3]

[1] Department of Computer Science, University of Minnesota, 200 Union Street S.E., Minneapolis, MN 55455, USA
[2] Sun Microsystems, Inc., 901 San Antonio Road, Palo Alto, CA 94303, USA
junjie.gu@sun.com
[3] Dept. of Electrical and Computer Engineering, Iowa State University, Ames, IA 50011, USA, ghlee@iastate.edu

Summary. Array data flow information plays an important role for successful automatic parallelization of Fortran programs. This chapter proposes a powerful symbolic array data flow summary scheme to support array privatization and loop parallelization for programs with arbitrary control flow graphs and acyclic call graphs. Our approach summarizes array access information interprocedurally, using **guarded array regions**. The use of guards allows us to use the information in IF conditions to do path-sensitive data flow summary and thereby to handle difficult cases. We also provide a mechanism to overcome the disadvantages of non-closed union and difference operations. This improves not only the exactness of summaries, but also the efficiency of the summarizing procedure. Our preliminary result on array privatization shows that our summary scheme is fast and powerful.

Key words: Parallelizing compilers, array data flow analysis, interprocedural analysis, array privatization, guarded array regions, symbolic analysis.

1. Introduction

Interprocedural analysis, i.e. analyzing programs across routine boundaries, has been recognized as an essential part of program analysis. Parallelizing compilers, as a tool to enhance program efficiency on parallel computers, depend heavily upon this technique to be effective in practice.

Interprocedural analysis for scalars has been well studied. In contrast, interprocedural analysis for array references is still an open issue. Currently, there are two ways to extend program analysis across a call site. The first and simpler way is to use inline expansion. The drawbacks of inlining are twofold. First, even if the program size does not increase after inline expansion, the loop body containing routine calls may grow dramatically. This often results in much longer compile time and much larger consumption of memory resources [21] because many compiler algorithms dealing with loops have non-linear complexity with respect to the loop body's size. Because a routine is analyzed each time it is inlined, duplicate analysis can also cause parallelizing compilers to be inefficient. Second, some routines are not amenable to inline expansion due to complicated array reshaping and must be analyzed without inlining.

S. Pande, D.P. Agrawal (Eds.): Compiler Optimizations for Scalable PS, LNCS 1808, pp. 221-246, 2001.
© Springer-Verlag Berlin Heidelberg 2001

These drawbacks of inlining make a *summary* scheme often a more desired alternative. Early works on summary schemes summarize the side effects of a called routine with sets of array elements that are modified or used by routine calls, called MOD sets and USE sets respectively. Data dependences involving routine calls can be tested by intersecting these sets. Existing approaches can be categorized according to methods of set representation. Convex regions [27, 28] and data access descriptors [2] define sets by a system of inequalities and equalities, while bounded regular sections [5, 15] use range tuples to represent sets. Even though bounded regular sections are less precise than convex regions and data access descriptors, they are much simpler and are easy to implement.

The commonalities of these previous methods are as follows. First, because they are path-insensitive, IF conditions are not taken into account when program branches are handled. Second, they are flow-insensitive, so only MOD/USE sets of array elements, which are modified or used respectively, are summarized. Third, they use a single descriptor (a single regular section, a single convex region, etc.) to summarize multiple references to the same array. Because union operations are not closed, approximations have to be made in order to represent union results in a single convex region or a single regular section. This causes the loss of summary information. Therefore, these methods are insufficient for optimization such as array privatization.

Recently, flow-sensitive summary, or array data flow summary, has been a focus in the parallelizing compiler area. The most essential information in array data flow summary is the upward exposed use (UE) set [7,12,14,17,29]. Our work [12] and that of M. Hall, et al. [14] use either a list of regular sections or a list of convex regions to summarize each array in order to obtain more precise information than that provided by a single regular section or convex region. Our work is unique in its use of *guarded array regions* (GAR's), providing the conditions under which an array region is modified or upward-exposedly used. This is in contrast to path-insensitive summaries which do not distinguish summary sets for different program paths. Compared to other approaches [7] which handle more restricted cases of IF conditions, our approach seems to be more general.

In this chapter, we will describe our array data flow summary based on guarded array regions in the context of parallelizing compilers. The techniques involved should also be applicable to various programming supporting systems which deal with arrays, e.g. compilers of explicit parallel programs. The remainder of the chapter is divided into the following sections. In section 2, we present brief background information. Section 3 discusses guarded array regions, followed by our summary algorithm in section 4. We address the implementation issues in section 5. The preliminary results using GAR's for array privatization are shown in section 6. Section 7 briefly discusses the related works. Finally, we conclude this chapter in section 8.

2. Preliminary

In this section, we provide background information regarding array reference summary in the context of data dependence analysis and of data flow analysis.

2.1 Traditional Flow-Insensitive Summaries

Data dependence analysis is widely used in program analysis and is a key technique for program optimization and parallelization. It is also a main motivation for interprocedural analysis. Traditionally, data dependence analysis concerns whether two statements modify and use a common memory location. Given two statements, $S1$ and $S2$, which use and modify array A, we assume $S1$ is executed before $S2$. Let MOD_s be the set of all elements of A that are modified by S and USE_s the set of all elements of A that are used by S. The dependences between S_1 and S_2 can be determined by the following set operations [30]:

- flow dependence: iff $MOD_{s1} \cap USE_{s2} \neq \emptyset$.
- anti- dependence: iff $MOD_{s2} \cap USE_{s1} \neq \emptyset$.
- output dependence: iff $MOD_{s1} \cap MOD_{s2} \neq \emptyset$.

When S_1, S_2, or both, are call statements, the above sets need to be obtained by summarizing the called routines. Because summarizing MOD and USE sets does not involve analysis of how data flows within routines, e.g. reaching-definition analysis, live variable analysis, array kill analysis, these summaries are referred to as flow-insensitive summaries.

The MOD and USE sets above are given for a statement. They can also be defined for an arbitrary code segment which has a single entry and a single exit. When these sets cannot be summarized exactly, an over-approximation, meaning that summary sets are super sets of the real sets, is computed so that dependence tests can still be conducted conservatively. Such an over-approximation set is also called a *may* set. To understand these summary schemes, we will briefly discuss the following two aspects: set representations and summaries of multiple array references over multiple control branches.

A. Set representations

Several set representations have been proposed so far, including convex regions [27, 28], data access descriptors [2] and bounded regular sections (for simplicity, we refer to this as regular sections when there is no confusion) [5, 15]. Although data access descriptors are more restrictive than convex regions, they basically define sets by a system of inequalities and equalities just as convex regions do. Data access descriptors also contain additional information besides the shapes of array accesses. Regular sections are simple and more restricted in representing power compared with convex regions and data access descriptors, but they still cover most cases in practice and can be implemented efficiently.

To show the difference between convex regions and regular sections, consider the following examples. The set of all array elements in a two dimensional array $A(N, M)$, where N and M are dimension sizes, can be represented exactly either by a convex region

$$< A(\psi_1, \psi_2), \{\psi_1 = I, \psi_2 = J, 1 \leq I \leq N, 1 \leq J \leq M\} >$$

or by a regular section
$$A(1 : N : 1, 1 : M : 1).$$

The upper triangular half of that array can also be represented exactly by a convex region:

$$< A(\psi_1, \psi_2), \{\psi_1 = I, \psi_2 = J, 1 \leq I \leq N, 1 \leq J \leq M, I \leq J\} > .$$

However, this array region cannot be represented exactly by a regular section. It can only be approximated by $A(1 : N : 1, 1 : M : 1)$.

B. Summarizing references

To facilitate analysis, a code segment that will be summarized has a single entry point and a single exit point. In concept, this code segment can be viewed as a set of paths. Each path in this set is composed of a sequence of statements, from the entry point of the code segment to the exit point of the code segment, in the order of statement execution. The summary sets for each path are obtained by *composition* operations, which are union operations to combine all array references in the path together. The summary for the whole code segment is collected by merging the summary sets of all paths. Such merging operations, called *meet* operations, are union operations too. Also, all variables in the final summary sets should have their values on entry to the code segment. These summary schemes do not distinguish summary sets for different paths. Instead, they provide summary sets that are super sets of those of any path. We call these *path-insensitive* summaries.

In practice, a path-insensitive summary scheme can unionize all array references to form summary sets without considering paths, since both meet and composition operations are union operations. Variable replacements are carried out through the summarizing procedure in order to represent summary sets in terms of the input of the code segment. The typical code segments are loops, loop bodies, and routines.

Obviously, path-insensitive summary schemes cause *may* summary sets. The *may* sets can also be introduced when subscripts of array references are complicated (e.g. with expressions not representable in the compiler). In addition, attempting to represent the summary in a single convex region or a single regular section can also cause *may* sets because union operations are not closed. Some previous approaches such as [18] use a list of references as a set representation to avoid union operations and thus maintain exact summary information.

2.2 Array Data Flow Summaries

Recently, array data flow summaries, which analyze the intervening array kills, have been investigated [7, 11, 14, 17, 25, 29]. In these array data flow summaries, sets of upward exposed array uses (UE sets), which cannot be calculated without considering the effects of array kills, are calculated in addition to MOD and USE sets. The UE sets corresponding to a code segment contain all array elements whose values are imported to the code segment. The computation of UE sets usually needs difference operations. Let us look at an example. Suppose that statement S is in a given code segment and USE_s denotes all the array elements used by S. Let $MOD_{<s}$ be the set containing all array elements written before S within the code segment. These array summary sets are assumed to be corresponding to the same array A. To compute the UE sets for the code segment contributed by USE_s, we perform the following difference:

$$USE_s - MOD_{<s}$$

When $MOD_{<s}$ is a *may* set, the difference should be conservatively approximated by USE_s. Thus, $MOD_{<s}$ does not affect the computation of UE at all. Since this causes flow-sensitive analysis to degenerate, a *must* set (an under-approximation set in contrast to an over-approximation *may* set), which is definitely accessed, is introduced. Whenever the MOD set is inexact, we can use a *must* set in a difference operation. Therefore, the difference $USE_s - MOD_{<s}$ can be safely performed if $MOD_{<s}$ is a *must* set. Such a difference result is more precise even though it is still a *may* set.

The meet operations for *must* sets are intersection operations, while composition operations are still union operations. Must sets are calculated by intersecting summary sets for different branches at branching statements. The meet operations for *must* sets are closed. However, difference operations, which are introduced by computing UE sets, are not closed.

Previous experiments [3, 21] as well as our experience indicate that the path-insensitive MUST/MAY array data flow summary is not enough; IF conditions need to be considered in order to handle certain important cases in real programs. Take Figure 2.1 as an example. The MUST/MAY summary for the body of the outer DO will produce

$$may\ MOD : A(jlow : jup : 1), A(jmax : jmax : 1)$$

$$may\ UE : A(jmax : jmax : 1)$$

The intersection of these two sets is nonempty and hence the compiler has to conservatively assume that there exist loop-carried flow dependences. However, the IF condition (.NOT.p) is loop-invariant, which guarantees that no loop-carried flow dependence exists in the outer loop, and therefore array A is privatizable. (We will discuss array privatization in section 6.)

In the next section, we propose a path-sensitive summary scheme which uses guarded array regions [12] to handle IF conditions. In order to preserve

```
DO I = 1, 4
  DO J = jlow, jup
    A(J) = .
  ENDDO

  ...

  IF (.NOT.p)
    A(jmax) = .
  ENDIF

  ...

  DO J = jlow, jup
    . = A(J) + A(jmax)
  ENDDO
ENDDO
```

Fig. 2.1. Examples of Privatizable Arrays

the exactness of union and difference results, we devise a scheme based on lists of guarded array regions. Such scheme turns out to enhance the efficiency of our approach as well.

3. Guarded Array Regions

Our analysis is based on two basic sets which describe array references, the upward exposed use set (UE set) and the modification set (MOD set). The UE set is the set of the upward exposed array elements which take values defined outside a given program segment. The MOD set is the set of array elements written within a given program segment.

Our basic unit of array reference representation is a *regular array region*, which is also called a bounded regular section [15]. It is a reduced form of the original regular sections proposed by Callahan and Kennedy [5]. On the other hand, we extend original regular sections in the following ways to meet our need to represent UE and MOD sets. First, since references to an array often cannot be easily represented by a single regular section without losing exactness, we use a list of regular array regions instead. In addition, we augment regular array regions by adding predicates as guards in order to better deal with IF conditions. The following gives the definitions of regular array regions and *guarded array regions*.

Definition A *regular array region* of array A is denoted by $A(r_1, r_2, \cdots, r_m)$, where m is the dimension of A, r_i, $i = 1, \cdots, m$, is a range in the form of $(l : u : s)$, and l, u, s are symbolic expressions. The triple $(l : u : s)$ represents all values from l to u with step s. $(l : u : s)$ is simply denoted by (l) if $l = u$ and by $(l : u)$ if $s = 1$. An empty array region is represented by $\emptyset$ and an unknown array region is represented by Ω.

Definition   A *guarded array region* (GAR) is a tuple $[P, R]$ which contains a *regular array region* R and a guard P, where P is a predicate that specifies the condition under which R is accessed. We use Δ to denote a guard whose predicate cannot be written explicitly, i.e. an unknown guard. If both $P = \Delta$ and $R = \Omega$, we say the GAR $[P, R] = \Omega$ is *unknown*. Similarly, if either P is *False* or R is $\emptyset$, we say $[P, R]$ is $\emptyset$.

The regular array region defined above is more restrictive than the original regular section used in the ParaScope environment at Rice University [2,5,15]. This basic unit, however, will be able to cover the most frequent cases in real programs and it seems to have an advantage in efficiency when dealing with the common cases. The guards in GAR's can be used to describe more complex array sections, although their primary use is to describe IF conditions under which regular array regions are accessed.

An *unknown* value is used carefully in the compiler in order to preserve as much precision as possible. First, one *unknown* dimension in a multiple dimensional array does not make the whole region *unknown*. Also, if the upper bound in a range tuple $(l : u : s)$ is unknown, we mark it as $(l : unknown : s)$ instead of as an unknown tuple.

We use a list of GAR's to represent a *MOD* set. However, using a list of GAR's for a *UE* set could introduce either more predicate operations [12] or unnecessary sacrifice of the exactness of difference operation results. Our solution to this problem is to define a data structure called a *GAR with a difference list (GARWD)*. A *UE* set is represented by a list of GARWD's.

Definition   A *GAR with a difference list (GARWD)* is a set defined by two components: a *source* GAR and a difference list. The source GAR is an ordinary GAR defined above, while the difference list is a list of GAR's. The set denotes all the members of the source GAR which are not in any GAR of the difference list. It is written as { *source GAR*, *<difference list>* }.

```
DO I = 1, M              DO I = 1, M
   A(1:N:1)=.               MOD_i: A(1:N:1), A(N2:N2:1)
   A(N2) = .
   ......                   UE_i: { A(2:N1:1), < A(1:N:1), A(N2:N2:1) >}
   . = A(2:N1:1)
ENDDO                    ENDDO
```

Fig. 3.1. Example of GARWD's

Figure 3.1 is an example showing the use of GARWD's. The right-hand side is the MOD/UE summary for the body of the outer loop shown on the left-hand side. The subscript i in both sets means the summary is for an arbitrary iteration i. UE_i is represented by a GARWD. For simplicity, we omit the guards here whose values are true in the example. To prove that no loop-carried data flow dependence exists, we need to show that the intersection of UE_i and the set of all mods before iteration i is empty. The set of all mods within iterations prior to iteration i, denoted as $MOD_{<i}$, is equal to MOD_i. (In theory, $MOD_{<i} = \phi$ if $i = 1$. But this does not invalidate the analysis above. Similarly, $MOD_{>i}$ denotes the sets of mods within the iterations after iteration i.) Since both GAR's in the $MOD_{<i}$ list are in the difference list of the UE_i, represented by a GARWD, it is obvious that the intersection of $MOD_{<i}$ and UE_i is empty. As will be discussed later in Section 6, this further shows that array A is privatizable.

3.1 Operations on GAR's

Our data flow analysis requires three kinds of operations on GAR's: union, intersection, and difference. These operations in turn are based on union, intersection, and difference operations on regular array regions as well as logical operations on predicates. We will first describe the operations on array regions, then on GAR's, and finally on GARWD's.

Regular array region operations

As operands of the region operations must belong to the same array, we will drop the array name from the array region notation hereafter whenever there is no confusion. Given two regular array regions, $R_1 = A(r_1^1, r_2^1, \cdots, r_m^1)$ and $R_2 = A(r_1^2, r_2^2, \cdots, r_m^2)$, where m is the dimension of array A, we define the following operations:

- $R_1 \cap R_2$:
  For the sake of simplicity of presentation, here we assume steps of 1 in both R_1 and R_2. Other step values will be handled in Section 5. Let $r_i^1 = (l_i^1 : u_i^1 : 1)$, $r_i^2 = (l_i^2 : u_i^2 : 1)$, where $i = 1, \cdots, m$, and let D_i be $r_i^1 \cap r_i^2$. We have $D_i = (max(l_i^1, l_i^2) : min(u_i^1, u_i^2) : 1)$ and have $R_1 \cap R_2$ equal to

$$
\begin{cases}
\emptyset & \exists i, D_i = \emptyset \\
(D_1, D_2, \cdots, D_m) & Otherwise
\end{cases}
$$

  Note that we do not keep max and min operators in a regular array region. Therefore, when the relationship of symbolic expressions cannot be determined even after a demand-driven symbolic analysis is conducted (c. f. Section 5), we will mark the intersection as unknown.

- $R_1 \cup R_2$:
  Since regular array regions may contain symbolic terms, care must be taken to prevent invalid regions being created by union operations. For example, for $R_1 = (m : p : 1)$ and $R_2 = (p+1 : n : 1)$, we have $R_1 \cup R_2 = (m : n : 1)$ if and only if both R_1 and R_2 are valid. The validity of this union result can be guaranteed by inserting validity predicates into guards [12]. However, since this introduces additional predicate operations which we try to avoid, we represent the union as a list of regions without merging them until they are known to be valid, e.g. when they are both constant regions.

- $R_1 - R_2$:

  For an m-dimensional array, the result of the difference operation is generally 2^m regular regions if each range difference results in two new ranges. Such a result could be quite complex for large m. Nonetheless, it is useful to present a general formula for the result. Suppose $R_1 \supseteq R_2$ (otherwise, use $R_1 - R_2 = R_1 - R_1 \cap R_2$). We first define $R_1(k)$ and $R_2(k)$, $k = 1, \cdots, m$, as the last k ranges within R_1 and R_2 respectively. According to this definition, we have $R_1(m) = (r_1^1, r_2^1, r_3^1, \cdots, r_m^1)$ and $R_2(m) = (r_1^2, r_2^2, r_3^2, \cdots, r_m^2)$, and $R_1(m-1) = (r_2^1, r_3^1, \cdots, r_m^1)$ and $R_2(m-1) = (r_2^2, r_3^2, \cdots, r_m^2)$. The computation of $R_1 - R_2$ is recursively given by the following formula:

$$R_1(m) - R_2(m) =$$
$$\begin{cases} (r_1^1 - r_1^2) & If\ m = 1 \\ (r_1^1 - r_1^2, r_2^1, r_3^1, \cdots, r_m^1) \cup (r_1^2, (R_1(m-1) - R_2(m-1))) & If\ m > 1 \end{cases}$$

To avoid a potentially complex result and also to keep the summary information precise, we use GARWD's to represent difference operations whenever the resultant difference is not a single regular region. We record the difference operation in the GARWD's without actually performing it until it is actually needed. As will be discussed in Section 5, the GARWD's also improve the efficiency of our overall scheme.

The following gives examples of the actual results of difference operations,

- $(1 : 100) - (2 : 100) = (1)$
- $(1 : 100, 1 : 100) - (3 : 99, 2 : 100)$
  $= ((1 : 100) - (3 : 99), (1 : 100)) \cup ((3 : 99), ((1 : 100) - (2 : 100)))$
  $= (((1 : 2) \cup (100)), (1 : 100)) \cup (3 : 99, 1)$
  $= (1 : 2, 1 : 100) \cup (100, 1 : 100) \cup (3 : 99, 1)$

GAR operations:

Given two GAR's, $T_1 = [P_1, R_1]$ and $T_2 = [P_2, R_2]$, we have the following:

- $T_1 \cap T_2 = [P_1 \wedge P_2, R_1 \cap R_2]$
- $T_1 \cup T_2$

  The following are two most frequent cases of union operations:
  - If $P_1 = P_2$, the union becomes $[P_1, R_1 \cup R_2]$
  - If $R_1 = R_2$, the result is $[P_1 \vee P_2, R_1]$

  If two array regions cannot be safely combined due to the unknown symbolic terms, we will keep two GAR's in a list without merging them.
- $T_1 - T_2 = [P_1 \wedge P_2, R_1 - R_2] \cup [P_1 \wedge \overline{P_2}, R_1]$

  As described earlier, the actual result of $R_1 - R_2$ may be multiple regular array regions, which makes the actual result of $T_1 - T_2$ potentially complex. However, as Figure 3.1 illustrates, difference operations can often be canceled by intersection and union operations. Therefore, we do not solve the difference $T_1 - T_2$ unless the result is a single GAR or until the last moment when the actual result must be solved in order to finish a data dependence test or an array privatizability test. When the difference is not solved with the above formula, it is represented by a GARWD.

The following shows examples of actual results of GAR operations:

- $[T, (1:100)] \cap [p, (2, 101)] = [p, (2:100)]$
- $[T, (1:50)] \cup [T, (51, 100)] = [T, (1:100)]$
  $[T, (1:100)] \cup [p, (1, 100)] = [T, (1:100)]$
- $[T, (1:100)] - [T, (2:99)]$
  $= [T, ((1:100) - (2:99))] = [T, ((1) \cup (100))]$
  $= [T, (1)] \cup [T, (100)]$

- $[p, (2:99)] - [T, (1:100)] = [p, ((2:99) - (1:100))] = [p, \emptyset] = \emptyset$

GARWD operations:

Operations between two GARWD's and between a GARWD and a GAR can be easily derived from the operations on GAR's. Some examples are given below to illustrate these operations:

- $\{[T, (1:100)], < [T, (n:m)] >\} - [T, (2:100)]$
  $= \{([T, (1:100)] - [T, (2:100)]), < [T, (n:m)] >\}$
  $= \{[T, (1)], < [T, (n:m)] >\}$
- $\{[T, (1:100)], < [T, (n:m)] >\} \cap [p, (101:200)]$
  $= \{([T, (1:100)] \cap [p, (101:200)]), < [T, (n:m)] >\}$
  $= \{(\emptyset), < [T, (n:m)] >\} = \emptyset$
- $\{[T, (1:100)], < [T, (n:m)] >\} \cup \{[T, (1:100)], <>\} = \{[T, (1:100)], <>\}$

3.2 Predicate Operations

Predicate operations are expensive in general and most compilers avoid analyzing them. However, the majority of predicate-handling required for collecting our array data flow summary involves simple operations such as checking to see if two predicates are identical, if they are loop-independent, or if they contain indices that affect the shapes or the sizes of array regions. These relatively simple operations can be implemented in an efficient way.

We define a new canonical form to represent predicates in order to simplify pattern matching needed to check whether two predicates are identical. Both conjunctive normal form (CNF) and disjunctive normal form (DNF) have been widely used in program analysis [6, 26]. These cited works show that negation operations are expensive with both CNF and DNF. Our previous experiments using CNF [12] also confirm their observations. Negation operations occur not only due to ELSE branches, but also due to GAR and GARWD operations elsewhere. Hence, we design a new canonical form such that negation operations can be reduced significantly.

We use a two-level hierarchical approach to predicate handling. At the high level, a predicate is represented by a predicate tree, $PT(V, E, r)$, where V is the set of nodes, E is the set of edges, and r is the root of PT. The internal

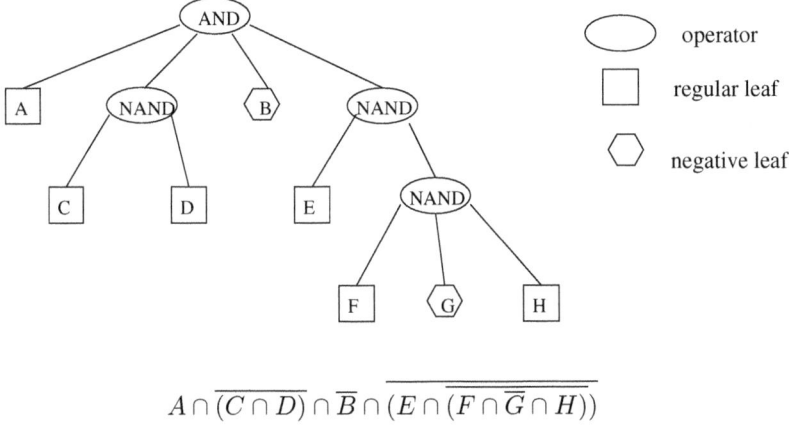

$$A \cap \overline{(C \cap D)} \cap \overline{B} \cap (E \cap \overline{(F \cap \overline{G} \cap H)})$$

Fig. 3.2. High Level Representation of Predicates

nodes of V are NAND operators except the root, which is an AND operator. The leaf nodes are divided into *regular leaf nodes* and *negative leaf nodes*. A regular leaf node represents a predicate such as an IF condition or a DO condition in the program, while a negative leaf node represents the negation of a predicate. Theoretically, the predicate tree may not be unique for an arbitrary predicate, which can cause pattern-matching to be conservative. We believe, however, that such cases are rare and happen mostly when the program cannot be parallelized.

Figure 3.2 shows a predicate tree. At this high level, we keep a basic predicate as a unit and do not split it. The predicate operations are based only on these units without further checking the contents within these basic predicates. Figure 3.3 show predicate operations. Figure 3.3(a) and (b) show OR and AND operations respectively. Negation of a predicate tree, shown in Figure 3.3(c), may either increase or decrease the tree height by one level according to the shape of the current predicate tree. In Figure 3.3(c), if there is only one regular leaf node (or one negative leaf node) in the tree, the regular leaf node is simply changed to a negative leaf node (or vice versa). We use a unique token for each basic predicate such that simple and common cases can be easily handled without checking the contents of the predicates. At the lower level of the hierarchy, the content of each predicate is represented in CNF and is examined when necessary.

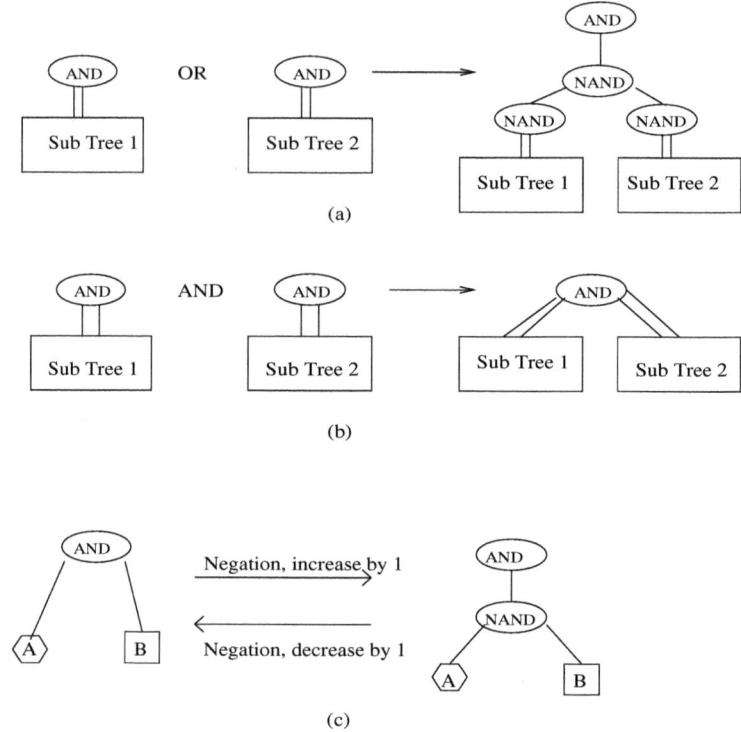

Fig. 3.3. Predicate Operations

4. Constructing Summary GAR's Interprocedurally

4.1 Hierarchical Supergraph

In this section, we present algorithms to calculate the MOD and UE information by propagating the GAR's and the GARWD's over a *hierarchical supergraph* (HSG). The HSG in this paper is an enhancement of Myers' *supergraph* [22] which is a composite of the flow subgraphs of all routines in a program. In a supergraph, each call statement is represented by a node, termed a *call node* in this paper, which has an outgoing edge pointing to the entry node of the flow subgraph of the called routine. The call node also has an incoming edge from the unique exit node of the called routine. To facilitate the information summary for DO loops, we add a new kind of nodes, *loop nodes*, to represent DO loops. The resulting graph, which we call the hierarchical supergraph (HSG), contains three kinds of nodes — basic blocks, loop nodes and call nodes. An IF condition itself forms a single basic block node. A loop node is a compound node which has its internal flow subgraphs

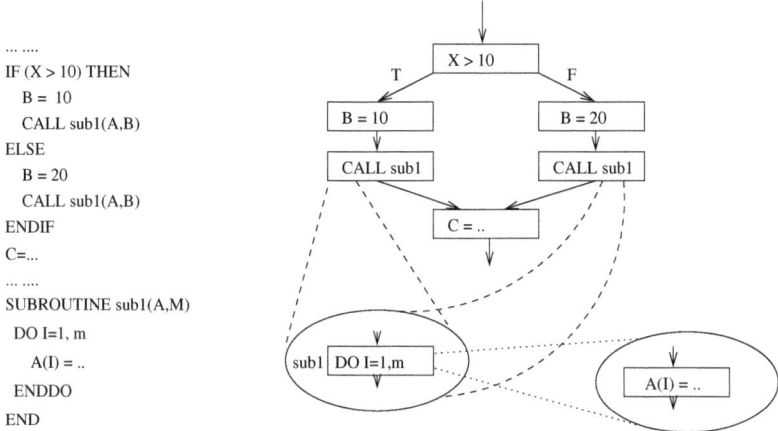

```
... ....
IF (X > 10) THEN
    B = 10
    CALL sub1(A,B)
ELSE
    B = 20
    CALL sub1(A,B)
ENDIF
C=...
... ....
SUBROUTINE sub1(A,M)
    DO I=1, m
        A(I) = ..
    ENDDO
END
```

Fig. 4.1. Example of the HSG

describing the control flow within the DO loop. Due to the nested structures of DO loops and routines, a hierarchy is derived among the HSG nodes, with the flow subgraph at the highest level representing the main program. The HSG resembles the HSCG used by the PIPS project [16]. Figure 4.1 shows a HSG example. Note that the flow subgraph of a routine is never duplicated for different calls to the same routine unless the called routine is duplicated to enhance its potential parallelism. We assume that the program contains no recursive calls. For simplicity of presentation, we further assume that a DO loop does not contain GOTO statements which make premature exits. We also assume that the HSG contains no cycles due to backward GOTO statements. Our implementation, however, does take care of premature exits in DO loops and backward GOTO statements, making conservative estimates when necessary. In the flow subgraph of a loop node, the back edge from the exit node to the entry node is deliberately deleted, as it conveys no additional information for array summaries. Under the above assumptions and treatment, the HSG is a hierarchical *dag* (directed acyclic graph). The following subsection presents the information summary algorithms.

4.2 Summary Algorithms

Suppose we want to check whether loop L is parallel. Let $g(s, e)$ be the HSG of the subgraph of loop L (the graph for the loop body), where s is the starting node and e the exit node. We use $UE(n)$ and $MOD(n)$ to denote the upward exposed use set and the mod set for node n respectively. Furthermore, we use $MOD\_IN(n)$ to represent the array elements modified in nodes which are reachable from n, and we use $UE\_IN(n)$ to represent the array elements whose values are imported to n and used in the nodes reachable from n.

Each $MOD(n)$ or $MOD\_IN(n)$ set is represented by a list of GAR's and each $UE(n)$ or $UE\_IN(n)$ set by a list of GARWD's. If any GAR contains variables in its guard or its range triples, these variables should assume the values imported at the entry of n. The compiler performs the following recursive algorithm, *gar_summary*:

1. Summarize all basic block nodes within $g(s,e)$.
   For each basic block node n, we calculate the $MOD(n)$ and $UE(n)$ sets for arrays within node n. All predicates in GAR's of $MOD(n)$ and $UE(n)$ are set to True.
2. Summarize all compound nodes.
   a) *Call nodes.* For a call node n, let the subgraph of the call node be $g'(s,e)$. The compiler recursively applies *gar_summary* to $g'(s,e)$, which summarizes the references to global arrays and arrays parameters. The returning results are mapped back to the actual arguments of the procedure call and are denoted by $MOD(n)$ and $UE(n)$.
   b) *loop nodes.* For a loop node n, let the subgraph of the loop node be $g'(s,e)$. The compiler recursively applies *gar_summary* to $g'(s,e)$. Let $UE_i(n)$ and $MOD_i(n)$ represent the UE and MOD sets of $g'(s,e)$, which contain modification GAR's and upwards exposed use GARWD's in one loop iteration indexed by i. The sets $MOD_i(n)$ and $(UE_i(n) - MOD_{<i}(n))$ are then expanded across the i index range to form $MOD(n)$ and $UE(n)$ for loop node n
3. Propagate the array data flow information.
   From node e to s, the *gar_summary* algorithm traverses the nodes in $g(s,e)$ in a reverse topological order. During the summary propagation, the following flow equations are applied:
   $$MOD\_IN(n) = MOD(n) \cup (\textstyle\bigcup_{p \in succ(n)} MOD\_IN(p))$$
   $$UE\_IN(n) = UE(n) \cup (\textstyle\bigcup_{p \in succ(n)} UE\_IN(p) - MOD(n))$$
   Note that the set of successors of the exit node succ(e) is $\emptyset$. When applying the flow equations, we need to handle the following situations.
   − If n is a basic block containing an IF-condition, insert the corresponding predicate or its negation into the guard of each GAR which has been propagated backward into $MOD\_IN(n)$ and $UE\_IN(n)$ through the THEN edge or the ELSE edge respectively.
   − If any expression in the $MOD\_IN(p)$ and $UE\_IN(p)$ contains a variable that is defined within n, then that variable must be substituted by the right-hand-side of the defining statement within n. Therefore, all values of variables in $MOD\_IN(n)$ and $UE\_IN(n)$ are relative to the entry to n.

For loop L, the above algorithm produces the MOD_i and UE_i sets of $g(s,e)$, where MOD_i equals $MOD\_IN(s)$ and UE_i equals $UE\_IN(s)$. These sets can be used to do dependence tests and array privatization tests, which are presented later in this chapter.

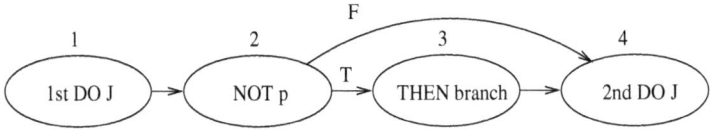

Fig. 4.2. The HSG of the Body of the Outer Loop for Figure 2.1

Let us use the example in Figure 2.1 to illustrate the algorithm. A simplified HSG of the body of the outer loop is shown in Figure 4.2, which omits the internal flow graphs of the compound nodes. Following the algorithm above, Step 1 and Step 2 give us the following results:

$$
\begin{aligned}
MOD(1) &= [T, (jlow : jup)], & UE(1) &= \emptyset \\
MOD(2) &= \emptyset, & UE(2) &= \emptyset \\
MOD(3) &= [T, (jmax)], & UE(3) &= \emptyset \\
MOD(4) &= \emptyset, & UE(4) &= [T, (jlow : jup)] \cup [T, (jmax)]
\end{aligned}
$$

Step 3, following a reverse topological order, propagates the information in the following four sub-steps:

1. $MOD\_IN(4) = MOD(4) = \emptyset$
   $UE\_IN(4) = UE(4) = [T, (jlow : jup)] \cup [T, (jmax)]$
2. $MOD\_IN(3) = MOD(3) \cup MOD(4) = [T, (jmax)]$
   $UE\_IN(3) = UE(3) \cup (UE\_IN(4) - MOD(3)) = \{[T, (jlow : jup)], < [T, (jmax)] >\}$
3. $MOD\_IN(2) = [\bar{p}, (jmax)]$
   $UE\_IN(2) = \{[\bar{p}, (jlow : jup)], < [\bar{p}, (jmax)] >\} \cup [p, (jlow : jup)] \cup [p, (jmax)]$

   In the above, $\bar{p}$ is inserted into the guards of the GAR's which are propagated through the TRUE edge and p is inserted into those propagated through the FALSE edge.
4. $MOD\_IN(1) = [T, (jlow : jup)] \cup [\bar{p}, (jmax)]$
   $UE\_IN(1) = UE\_IN(2) - MOD(1) = \{[p, (jmax)], < [T, (jlow : jup)] >\}$

Therefore, the summary sets of the body of the outer loop (DO I) should be:

$$
\begin{aligned}
MOD_i &= MOD\_IN(1) = [T, (jlow : jup)] \cup [\bar{p}, (jmax)] \\
UE_i &= UE\_IN(1) = \{[p, (jmax)], < [T, (jlow : jup)] >\}
\end{aligned}
$$

4.3 Expansions

Given a loop with index i, where $i \in (l : u : s)$, and MOD_i and UE_i as the summary sets for the loop body, what are the UE and MOD sets for the loop? This problem can be solved by an *expansion* procedure which is conducted in the following two steps:

$$UE(i) = UE_i - MOD_{<i}, \; where \; MOD_{<i} = \Sigma_{j\in(l:u:s)\wedge(j<i)}MOD_j, \quad (I)$$

$$\left\{ \begin{array}{lll} MOD & = & \cup_{i\in(l:u:s)}MOD_i \\ UE & = & \cup_{i\in(l:u:s)}UE(i) \end{array} \right. \quad (II)$$

Step I in the above computes the set of array elements used in iteration i which are exposed to the outside of the *whole loop*. Step II projects the result of Step I to eliminate i. The projection for a list of GAR's is conducted by the projection for each GAR separately. Suppose Q is a GAR. If Q does not contain i in its representation, then the projection of Q is Q itself. If Q contains i in its representation, then the projection of Q by i, denoted by proj(Q), is a GAR obtained by the following steps:

– If i appears in the guard of Q, then i should be solved from the guard which, in general, is written as $i \in (l' : u' : s)$, where l' and u' may be symbolic expressions. We obtain a new domain of i as follows,

$$(\; \lceil \frac{max(l',l)-l}{s} \rceil \cdot s + l : \lfloor \frac{min(u',u)-l}{s} \rfloor \cdot s + l : s)$$

which simplifies to $(max(l',l) : min(u',u))$ for $s = 1$. The inequalities and equalities involving i in the guard can then be deleted.
For example, given $i \in (2 : 100 : 2)$ and GAR $[5 \leq i, A(i)]$, the new domain of i should be $(6 : 100 : 2)$. $5 \leq i$ is removed from the GAR.
– If i appears in only one dimension of Q, and if the result of substituting $l \leq i \leq u$, or the new bounds on i obtained above, into the old range triple in that dimension can still be represented by a range triple $(l'' : u'' : s'')$, then we replace the old range triple by $(l'' : u'' : s'')$.
– If, in the above, the result of substitution of $l \leq i \leq u$ into the old range can no longer be represented by a range, then we mark this range as Ω (unknown). (Better approximation is possible for special cases, but we have not pursued further.)
– If i appears in more than one dimension of Q, then these dimensions are marked as unknown.

As an example, suppose a DO loop indexed by i has loop bounds $1 \leq i \leq 100$. Further, suppose the given GAR is $Q = [3 \leq i + 1 \leq 51, (1 : i : 1)]$. As the result of solving i from the guard, we have new bounds on i which are $(max(1, 3-1) : min(100, 51-1)) = (2 : 50)$. The expansion of Q by i is $[True, 1 : 50 : 1)]$.

Since the UE_i set is represented by a list of GARWD's, the expansion of UE_i can be obtained by unionizing the expansion of the individual GARWD's in UE_i. Therefore, for each GARWD W in UE_i, we need to compute $(W - MOD_{<i})$ and then its projection. If i cannot be removed from the difference

list of a GARWD by simplifying the GARWD, we over-approximate this GARWD by removing the whole difference list from the GARWD. As we mentioned previously, GARWD is used to represent UE sets only. Therefore, over-approximation is always safe. Afterwards, each GARWD in the UE_i set either has an empty difference list or one that is loop-invariant. Now only the source GAR of a GARWD needs to be considered below.

The difference $(W - MOD_{<i})$ is calculated by successive subtractions of each GAR of $MOD_{<i}$ from W. Let Q_i be the source GAR of W, $i \in (l : u : s)$. The details of the expansion of a single GARWD W, including Step I and Step II, are as follows:

(**A**) If Q_i is loop-invariant, then we have the expansion of W equal to $proj(W - MOD_{<i}) = W$. Stop.

(**B**) For (each M in $MOD_{<i}$) {

1. If M is loop-invariant and Q_l (the value of Q for the first iteration) does not overlap with M, we insert M into the difference list of W. Goto *continue*.
2. If M is loop-invariant and Q_l is equal to M, then M does not affect the expansion. Goto *continue*.
3. If $Q_i \cap M = \phi$, then $Q_i - M = Q_i$. Goto *continue*.
4. Suppose both Q_i and M are loop-variant and the index i appears in the same dimension, say dimension j, in both Q_i and M. Further suppose that Q_i and M are identical in all dimensions except dimension j, in which the range tuples contain one single element and can be represented by (E_t) and (E_m) respectively. If $(E_m - E_t)$ is not a constant, goto step 5. If $(E_m - E_t)$ is a constant, the coefficients of i in both Q_i and M must be the same. Let this coefficient be coe_i. (If $(E_m - E_t)$ is not divisible by $(coe_i \cdot s)$, then $Q_i \cap M = \phi$ and should be covered in step 3.) When both coe_i and s are greater than zero, the Q_i in the first $(E_m - E_t)/coe_i$ number of iterations is exposed to the outside of the loop. Therefore,

$$(Q_i - M), i \in (l : u : s) =$$
$$\begin{cases} Q_i, \ i \in (l : l + (E_m - E_t)/coe_i - s : s); & (E_m - E_t) > 0 \\ Q_i, \ i \in (l : u : s); & (E_m - E_t) \leq 0 \end{cases}$$

For the first case, a new domain for i is established. l and u will have new values for the rest of the computation on $(W - MOD_{<i})$.
For other cases in which coe_i or s is not greater than zero, the formula can be acquired similarly.
Goto *continue*.
5. We mark W as a may set and drop the difference list of W. Compute proj(W), which is the final result of the expansion of the original W. Stop.
6. *continue:*

}

(**C**) Compute proj(W), which is the final result of the expansion of the original W.

The above steps have been implemented currently and can be extended and refined. The projection of a GARWD W, denoted above by proj(W), can be acquired by projections on each GAR in W separately.

5. Implementation Considerations

5.1 Symbolic Analysis

Symbolic analysis handles expressions which involve unknown symbolic terms. It is widely used in symbolic evaluation and abstract interpretation techniques to discover program properties such as values of expressions, relationships between symbolic expressions, etc. Symbolic analysis requires to represent and manipulate unknown symbolic terms. A symbolic analyzer can adopt a certain normalized form to represent expressions [6, 13, 26]. The advantage of such a normalized form is that it gives the same representation for two *congruent expressions*, i.e. they always have the same value. For example, $x \cdot (x+1)$ and $x + x^2$ are congruent expressions. In addition, symbolic expressions encountered in array data flow analysis and dependence analysis are mostly integer polynomials. Many operations on integer polynomials, such as the comparison of two polynomials, can be straightforward if a normalized form is adopted. Therefore, we adopt normalized integer polynomials as our representation for symbolic expressions, whose form is shown below:

$$e = \Sigma_{i=1}^{N} t_i \cdot I_i + t_0 \tag{5.1}$$

where each I_i is an index variable and t_i is a term which is given by equation (2) below:

$$t_i = \Sigma_{j=1}^{M_i} p_j, \quad i = 1, \cdots, N \tag{5.2}$$

$$p_j = c^j \cdot \Pi_{k=1}^{L_j} x_k^j, \quad j = 1, \cdots, M_j \tag{5.3}$$

where p_j is a product, c^j is an integer constant (possibly an integer fraction), x_k^j is an integer variable which is not an index variable, N is the nesting depth of the loop containing e, M_i is the number of products in t_i, and L_j is the number of variables in p_j. All e, t_i, and p_j are sorted by each variable's order number, which is a unique integer number assigned to each variable. Since both M_i and L_j contribute to the complexity of a polynomial, they are chosen as design parameters which can be adjusted in the compiler, according to experimental results, in order to control the complexity of expressions. As an example, by limiting M_i to be 1 and L_j to be zero, the expression e will become an affine expression. By controlling the complexity of expressions, the complexity of the overall summary scheme is reduced.

We implement utility library functions to perform symbolic operations such as additions, subtractions, multiplications, and divisions by an integer constant. In addition, a simple demand-driven symbolic evaluation scheme is implemented. It propagates an expression backwards over a control flow graph until either the value of the expression becomes known or a predefined propagation limit is reached.

5.2 Region Numbering

During the propagation and manipulation of regular array regions, GAR's, and GARWD's, each of these data structures may be duplicated several times. Operations involving these identical copies can potentially be time-consuming if straightforward pattern-matching is conducted. Instead, we introduce a region numbering scheme. In this scheme, the same number is assigned to the identical copies of an array region. Figure 5.1 shows an example. Initially,

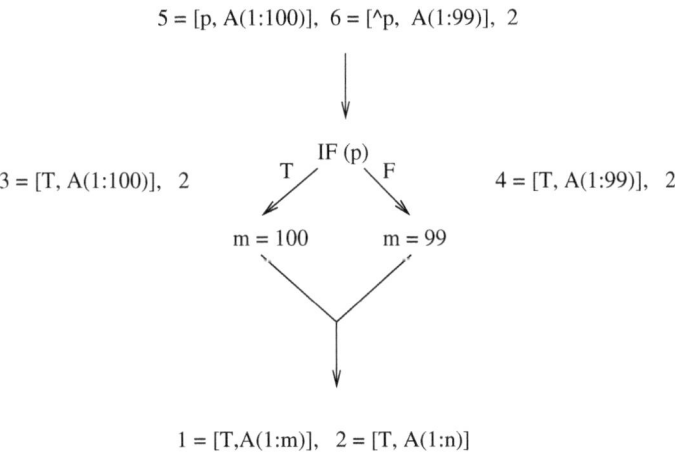

5 = [p, A(1:100)], 6 = [^p, A(1:99)], 2

3 = [T, A(1:100)], 2   IF (p)   4 = [T, A(1:99)], 2
                          T /   \ F
                    m = 100   m = 99

1 = [T,A(1:m)],   2 = [T, A(1:n)]

Fig. 5.1. Propagation Using Region Numbers

there are two GAR's, numbered 1 and 2. As GAR No.1 is propagated through both branches, it is modified and becomes GAR No.3 in the left branch and No.4 in the right branch, while GAR No.2 remains unchanged. At the entrance to the IF, GAR No.3 is modified by adding predicate p and becomes GAR No.5, while GAR No.4 becomes GAR No.6. Since GAR No.2 appears in both branches (the number 2 appears in both lists), the IF condition is not attached to it. Thus GAR No.2 is unchanged.

However, we do not try to use the same number to represent identical array regions which originate from different array references in the program, because that may require us to compare many array regions from time to time. Instead, we use a simplifier to remove redundant array regions. The simplifier is invoked at the end of a routine summarizing or immediately before the data dependence tests and array privatization tests.

Predicates are handled similarly. We assign each leaf node and NAND node a unique number to facilitate the operations on predicates.

5.3 Range Operations

In this subsection, we give details of range operations for step values of other than one. These operations invoke the $min(e_1, e_2)$ and the $max(e_1, e_2)$ functions. Each function either returns a symbolic expression containing neither min nor max function calls, or it returns an "unknown" value. Symbolic analysis is performed on demand.

Given two ranges r_1 and r_2, $r_1 = (l_1 : u_1 : s_1)$, $r_2 = (l_2 : u_2 : s_2)$, the following gives the results of range operations:

1. If $s_1 = s_2 = 1$,
   - $r_1 \cap r_2 =$
     $(max(l_1, l_2) : min(u_1, u_2) : s_1)$
   - Assuming $r_2 \subseteq r_1$ (otherwise use $r_1 - r_2 = r_1 - r_1 \cap r_2$), we have
     $r_1 - r_2 = (l_1 : max(l_1, l_2) - 1 : s_1) \cup (min(u_1, u_2) + 1 : u_1 : s_1)$
   - Union operation. If $(l_2 > u_1 + s_1)$ or $(l_1 > u_2 + s_2)$, $r_1 \cup r_2$ cannot be combined into one range. Otherwise, $r_1 \cup r_2 = (min(l_1, l_2) : max(u_1, u_2) : s_1)$, assuming r_1 and r_2 are both valid.

   The result is returned to the upper level routine, in which whether to perform these operations, keep them in a list, etc., is decided.

2. If $s_1 = s_2 = c > 1$, where c is a known constant value, we do the following: If $(l_1 - l_2)$ is divisible by c, then we use the formulas in case 1 to compute intersection, difference and union. Otherwise, $r_1 \cap r_2 = \emptyset$ and $r_1 - r_2 = r_1$. The union $r_1 \cup r_2$ usually cannot be combined into one range and must be maintained as a list of ranges.

3. If $s_1 = s_2$ and $l_1 = l_2$ (which may be symbolic expressions), then we use the formulas in case 1 to perform intersection, difference and union.

4. If s_1 is divisible by s_2, we check if r_2 covers r_1. If so, we have $r_1 \cap r_2 = r_1$ and $r_1 \cup r_2 = r_2$. Otherwise, we divide r_2 into several smaller ranges with step s_1 and then apply the above formulas.

5. In all other cases, the results of intersection and difference are marked as unknown and the union remains a list of two ranges.

6. Application to Array Privatization and Preliminary Experimental Results

In this section, we first discuss how our array data flow summary can be used to perform array privatization even in difficult cases which are sensitive to IF conditions. We then present preliminary experimental results to show both the capability and the efficiency of our analysis.

6.1 Array Privatization

Array privatization has been shown to be one of the most important techniques to improve the performance of parallelizing compilers [3,4,12,21]. This technique creates a distinct copy of an array for each processor such that storage conflicts can be eliminated without violating program semantics. Privatizable arrays appear in real programs quite often and usually serve as temporary working spaces. It has been shown that traditional data dependence tests cannot identify privatizable arrays. In contrast, data flow analysis, when supported by IF condition handling, symbolic analysis, and interprocedural analysis, allows a powerful compiler to recognize privatizable arrays.

An array A is a privatization candidate in a loop L if its elements are overwritten in different iterations of L (see [17]). Such a candidacy can be established by examining the summary array MOD_i set: If the intersection of MOD_i and $MOD_{<i}$ is nonempty, then A is a candidate. A privatization candidate is privatizable if there exist no loop-carried flow dependences in L. For an array A in a loop L with an index I, if $MOD_{<i} \cap UE_i = \emptyset$, then there exists no flow dependence carried by loop L.

Let us look at Figure 2.1 again. In Figure 4.2, we have computed MOD_i and UE_i. Since MOD_i is not loop-variant, we have $MOD_{<i} = MOD_i$. Hence, $MOD_i \cap MOD_{<i}$ is nonempty and array A is a privatization candidate. Furthermore,

$$
\begin{aligned}
UE_i &\cap MOD_{<i} \\
&= \{[p,(jmax)], <[T,(jlow:jup)]>\} \cap ([T,(jlow:jup)] \cup [\bar{p},(jmax)]) \\
&= \{[p,(jmax)], <[T,(jlow:jup)]>\} \cap [T,(jlow:jup)] \cup \\
&\quad \{[p,(jmax)], <[T,(jlow:jup)]>\} \cap [\bar{p},(jmax)] \\
&= \{[p,(jmax)], <[T,(jlow:jup)]>\} \cap [T,(jlow:jup)] \cup \\
&\quad \{([p,(jmax)] \cap [\bar{p},(jamx)]), <[T,(jlow:jup)]>\} \\
&= \{[p,(jmax)], <[T,(jlow:jup)]>\} \cap [T,(jlow:jup)] \\
&= \emptyset
\end{aligned}
$$

The last difference operation above can be easily done because GAR $[T,(jlow:jup)]$ is in the difference list. The fact of $UE_i \cap MOD_{<i}$ being empty guarantees that array A is privatizable.

6.2 Preliminary Experimental Results

We have implemented our array data flow analysis in a prototyping parallelizing compiler, Panorama, which is a multiple-pass, source-to-source, Fortran

program restructurer [23]. It performs parsing, construction of a hierarchical
supergraph(HSG) and interprocedural scalar UD/DU chains [1], conventional
data dependence tests, array data flow analysis and other analyses which support memory performance enhancement, and parallel code generation.

Table 6.1 shows several time-consuming Fortran loops in the Perfect
benchmark suite which are parallelized after our array data flow analysis
and array privatization. (Additional transformations such as induction variable substitution are automatically performed to enable parallelization, whose
discussions, however, are omitted in this paper.) The last column of Table 6.1
presents the current status of array privatization achieved by Panorama. All
arrays listed in Table 6.1 can be privatized under our scheme except array
RL in the MDG program. This case needs to handle predicates involving subscript variables, which our current implementation is unable to deal with [12].

Table 6.1. Experimental Results on Loops with Privatizable Arrays

Program	Routine /Loop	Array Names	Status*
TRACK	nlfilt/300	P1,P2,P,PP1,PP2,PP,XSD	yes
MDG	interf/1000	RS,FF,GG,XL,YL,ZL	yes
		RL	no
	poteng/2000	RS,RL,XL,YL,ZL	yes
TRFD	olda/100	XRSIQ,XIJ	yes
	olda/300	XIJKS,XKL	yes
OCEAN	ocean/270	CWORK	yes
	ocean/480	CWORK, CWORK2	yes
	ocean/500	CWORK	yes
ARC2D	filerx/15	WORK	yes
	filery/39	WORK	yes
	stepfx/300	WORK	yes
	stepfy/420	WORK	yes

*: Status shows whether these privatizable arrays can be automatically privatized now.

Table 6.2 shows the cpu time spent on the main parts of Panorama. In
Table 6.2, parsing time is the time to parse the program once, although
Panorama currently parses a program three times (the first time for constructing the call graph and for rearranging the parsing order of the source
files, the second time for interprocedural analysis and the last time for code
generation). We do not count the time spent on memory performance analyses in Table 6.2.

The row "HSG & DOALL Checking" shows the time taken to build the
HSG and UD/DU chains and to do conventional DOALL checking. The "Array Summary" refers to our array data flow analysis, which is applied only
to loops whose parallelizability cannot be determined by the conventional

Table 6.2. Execution Time (in seconds) Distribution (Timing is acquired on SGI Indy workstations with 134MHz MIPS R4600 CPU and 64 MB memory)

Program	TRACK	MDG	TRFD	OCEAN	ARC2D
#Lines	3784	1238	485	4343	3964
Parsing	1.78	0.86	0.40	1.26	2.43
HSG & DOALL Checking	3.07	1.72	0.49	0.91	5.16
Array Summary	6.01	2.38	0.50	0.36	27.72
Code Generation	1.62	0.82	0.22	0.42	2.26
Total	12.48	5.78	1.61	2.96	37.56
f77 -O	17.54	12.37	7.17	39.32	37.67

DOALL tests. Even though the time percentage of array data flow analysis is high (about 40%), the total execution time is small (38 seconds maximum). As an interesting comparison, the next row marked by "f77 -O" shows the time spent by the f77 compiler with option -O to compile the corresponding FORTRAN program into sequential machine code. This row is used as a reference point to better understand the speed of our parallelizing compiler. The data suggest that Panorama is quite efficient.

7. Related Works

There exist a number of approaches to array data flow analysis. As far as we know, no work has particularly addressed the efficiency issue or has presented efficiency data. One class of approaches attempt to gather flow information for each individual array reference. Feautrier [10] calculates the *source function* which represents the precise array definition points for each array use. Maydan, et al. [20, 21] simplify Feautrier's method by computing a Last-Write-Tree (LWT). Duesterwald, et al., compute the dependence distance for each reaching definition within a loop [8]. Pugh and Wonnacott [24] use a set of constraints to describe array data flow problems and solve them by an extented Fourier-Motzkin variable elimination. Maslov [19], as well as Pugh and Wonnacott [24], extends the previous work in this category by handling certain IF conditions. Generally, these approaches are intraprocedural and do not seem easy to extend interprocedurally.

The other class of approaches summarizes the array elements accessed by a set of array references instead of analyzing individual array references. This class extends data structures designed by the early works for flow-insensitive array problems, such as *regular array sections* [5, 15], convex regions [27, 28], and data access descriptors [2]. Array data flow analysis in this class includes works done by Gross and Steenkiste [11], Rosene [25], Li [17], Tu and Padua [29], Creusillet and Irigoin [7], and M. Hall, et al. [14]). The work described in this chapter seems to be the only one which considers the effect of IF conditions in a general way, although some previous works also handle IF conditions under more limited circumstances. Although this class of approaches does not provide as many details about reaching-definitions as the first one, it handles complex program constructs better and is easier to perform interprocedurally.

8. Conclusion

Array data flow information is important to successful automatic program parallelization. Propagating array data flow summary interprocedurally is an effective way to deal with procedure calls in program parallelization. Most existing forms of array data flow summaries are path-insensitive, i.e., they do not distinguish summary sets for different program paths. In certain important cases, such path-insensitivity hurts the result of parallelization badly.

In this chapter, we have proposed a path-sensitive array data flow summary, and we have described an efficient scheme to compute such a summary and use it for array privatization and program parallelization. Efficient symbolic processing is integrated into the process of propagating array access information. Preliminary results of array privatization suggest that our analysis is both powerful and efficient.

Acknowledgement. We thank Trung N. Nguyen and Guohua Jin for their important contributions to Panorama. This work is sponsored in part by the Army High Performance Computing Research Center under the auspices of the Department of the Army, Army Research Laboratory cooperative agreement number DAAH04-95-2-0003/contract number DAAH04-95-C-0008, the content of which does not necessarily reflect the position or the policy of the government, and no official endorsement should be inferred. This work is also supported in part by a National Science Foundation CAREER Award, Grant CCR-950254 and a funding, as a part of DICE project, from Samsung Electronics.

References

1. Aho, A.V., Sethi, R., Ullman, J.D. (1986). Compilers: Principles, Techniques, and Tools. Addison-Wesley, Reading, Mass.
2. Balasundaram, V. (1990). A Mechanism for Keeping Useful Internal Information in Parallel Programming Tools: The Data Access Descriptor. Journal of Parallel and Distributed Computing, 9:154–170.
3. Blume, W., Eigenmann, R. (1994). Symbolic Analysis Techniques Needed for the Effective Parallelization of Perfect Benchmarks. Technical report, Dept. of Computer Science, University of Illinois.
4. Blume, W., Eigenman, R. (1992). Performance Analysis of Parallelizing Compilers on the Perfect Benchmarks Programs. IEEE Trans. on Parallel and Distributed Systems, November, 3(6):643-656.

5. Callahan, D., Kennedy, K. (1986). Analysis of interprocedural side effects in a parallel programming environment. ACM SIGPLAN '86 Symp. Compiler Construction, June, 162–175.
6. Clarke, L.A., Richardson, D.J. (1985). Applications of Symbolic Evaluation. The Journal of Systems and Software, 5(1):15-35
7. Creusillet, B., Irigoin, F. (1995). Interprocedural Array Region Analyses. Proceedings of the 8th Workshop on Languages and Compilers for Parallel Computing, held in Columbus, Ohio, August, No. 1033, In Lecture Notes in Computer Science, Springer-Verlag, Berlin, 46-60.
8. Duesterwald, E., Gupta, R., Soffa, M.L. (1993). A Practical Data Flow Framework for Array Reference Analysis and its Use in Optimizations. ACM SIGPLAN '93 Conf. on Programming Language Design and Implementation, June, 68-77.
9. Eigenmann, R., Hoeflinger, J., Li, Z., Padua, D. (1992). Experience in the Automatic Parallelization of Four Perfect Benchmark Programs. Lecture Notes in Computer Science, 589, Springer-Verlag.
10. Feautrier, P. (1991). Dataflow Analysis of Array and Scalar References. International Journal of Parallel Programming, February, 2(1):23-53.
11. Gross, T., Steenkiste, P. (1990). Structured dataflow analysis for arrays and its use in an optimizing compiler. Software – Practice and Experience, February, 20(2):133-155.
12. Gu, J., Li, Z., Lee, G. (1995). Symbolic Array Dataflow Analysis for Array Privatization and Program Parallelization. Supercomputing'95, December, San Diego, CA.
13. Haghighat, M.R., Polychronopoulos, C.D. (1994). Symbolic analysis for Parallelizing Compilers. Technical report, CSRD Report No. 1355, University of Illinois.
14. Hall,M, Murphy, B., Amarasinghe, S., Liao, S., Lam, M. (1995). Interprocedural Analysis for Parallelization. Proceedings of the 8th Workshop on Languages and Compilers for Parallel Computing, held in Columbus, Ohio, August, No. 1033, In Lecture Notes in Computer Science, Springer-Verlag, Berlin, 61-80.
15. Havlak, P., Kennedy, K. (1991). An implementation of interprocedural bounded regular section analysis. IEEE Trans. on Parallel and Distributed Systems, 2(3):350-360.
16. Irigoin, F., Jouvelot, P., Triolet, R. (1991). Semantical Interprocedural Parallelization: An overview of the PIPS Project. International Conference on Supercomputing, 244-251.
17. Li, Z. (1992). Array Privatization for Parallel Execution of Loops. ACM Int. Conf. on Supercomputing, July, 313-322.
18. Li, Z., Yew, P.C. (1988). Efficient interprocedural analysis for program parallelization and restructuring. ACM SIGPLAN Conf. on Parallel Programming: Experience with Applications, Languages and Systems, September, 85-99.
19. Maslov, V. (1994). Lazy Array Data-Flow Dependence Analysis. Proceedings of Annual ACM Symposium on Principles of Programming Languages, January, Portland, Oregon, 331-325.
20. Maydan, D.E., Amarasinghe, S.P., Lam, M.S. (1993). Array Data-Flow Analysis and its Use in Array Privatization. Proc. of the 20th ACM Symp. on Principles of Programming Languages, January, 2-15.
21. Maydan, D.E. (1992). Accurate Analysis of Array References. PhD thesis, October, Stanford University.
22. Myers, E. W. (1981). A Precise Interprocedural Data-Flow Algorithm. Proceedings of 8th Annual ACM Symposium on Principles of Programming Languages. January, 219-230.

23. Nguyen, T., Gu, J., Li, Z. (1995). An Interprocedural Parallelizing Compiler and its support for Memory Hierarchy Research. Lecture Notes in Computer Science 1033: 8th International Workshop on Languages and Compilers for Parallel Computing, Columbus, Ohio, August, 96-110.
24. Pugh, W., Wonnacott, D. (1993). An Exact Method for Analysis of Value-based Array Data Dependences. Lecture Notes in Computer Science 768: Sixth Annual Workshop on Programming Languages and Compilers for Parallel Computing, Portland, OR, August.
25. Rosene, C. (1990). Incremental Dependence Analysis. Technical report, CRPC-TR90044, PhD thesis, Computer Science Department, Rice University.
26. Cheatham, T.E. Jr, Holloway, G.H., Townley, J.A. (1979). Symbolic Evaluation and the Analysis of Programs. IEEE Trans.on Software Engineering, July, 5(4):402-417.
27. Triolet, R., Irigoin, F., Feautrier, P. (1986). Direct Parallelization of CALL Statments. ACM SIGPLAN'86 Sym. on Compiler Construction, Palo Alto, CA, July, 176-185.
28. Triolet, R. (1985). Interprocedural Analysis for Program Restructuring with Parafrase. Technical report, Center for Supercomputing Research and Development, University of Illinois at Urbana-Champaign.
29. Tu, P., Padua, D. (1993). Automatic Array Privatization. Proceedings of Sixth Workshop on Languages and Compilers for Parallel Computing, Portland, OR, August, 500-521.
30. Wolfe, M. (1996). High Performance Compilers for Parallel Computing. Addison-Wesley Publishing Company.

Chapter 8. Automatic Array Privatization

Peng Tu and David Padua

Digital Computer Laboratory, Department of Computer science, University of Illinois-Urbana Champaign, Urbana, IL 61801

Summary. This chapter discusses techniques for automatic array privatization developed as part of the Polaris project at the University of Illinois at Urbana-Champaign. Array privatization is one of the most important transformations for effective program parallelization.

The array privatization problem is formulated as data flow equations involving sets of scalars and array regions. A single-pass algorithm to solve these data flow equations is introduced. Finally, this chapter presents a demand-driven symbolic analysis algorithm to manipulate array regions whose bounds are represented by symbolic expressions.

1. Introduction

Memory-related dependence may severely limit the effectiveness of a compiler in several areas such as parallelization, load balancing, and communication optimization. Fortunately, many memory-related dependences can be eliminated. One strategy, known as *privatization*, allocates a copy of variables involved in memory-related dependences to each processor participating in the parallel execution of a program. A similar technique, called *expansion* [PW86], transforms each reference to a particular scalar into a reference to a vector element such that each thread accesses a different vector element. When applied to an array, expansion creates a new dimension for the array. Previous studies have shown that this process of replicating variables is one of the most effective transformations for the exploitation of parallelism [EHLP91].

Because the access to a private variable is inherently local, privatization reduces the need for communication and facilitates data distribution. Furthermore, because there is a private instance of some variables for each active processor, privatization provides opportunities to spread computation across the processors and thus improve load balancing [TP93a].

In this chapter, we present a compiler algorithm for array privatization. The algorithm has been implemented in the *Polaris* parallelizing compiler [BEF+94]. Two important aspects of array privatization are discussed:

- The formulation of the array privatization problem as data flow equations involving array regions and an algorithm to solve these equations. To simplify the presentation, it is assumed that the only iterative constructs in the source program are DO loops. However, the algorithm can trivially be extended to accept other classes of loops.
- A demand-driven symbolic analysis technique to to manipulate array regions involving symbolic boundaries.

S. Pande, D.P. Agrawal (Eds.): Compiler Optimizations for Scalable PS, LNCS 1808, pp. 247-281, 2001.
© Springer-Verlag Berlin Heidelberg 2001

The rest of the chapter is organized as follows. Section 2 introduces and illustrates array privatization and last-value assignment. Section 3 presents the data flow analysis formulation of privatization. Section 4 discusses the demand-driven strategy for symbolic analysis and how it is used to support the solution of the data flow equations. Related work is discussed in Section 5.

2. Background

Data dependence [Ban88] specifies the precedence constraints that a compiler must obey during program transformation. These dependences are due either to producer/consumer relations (*flow dependences*) or to memory reuse or update operations (*anti-dependences* and *output dependences*). The dependences of this second class are known as *memory-related dependences*.

Consider the following loop:

```
S1: DO I = 1, N
S2:    A(1) = X(I,J)
S3:    DO J = 2, N
S4:       A(J) = A(J-1)+Y(J)
S5:    ENDDO
S6:    DO K = 1, N
S7:       B(I,K) = B(I,K) + A(K)
S8:    ENDDO
S9: ENDDO
```

Because every iteration of loop S1 reuses array A, loop S1 cannot be executed in parallel. However, there is no producer/consumer relationship between loop iterations and, therefore, no flow dependences exist between the iterations of S1. The memory-related dependences between iterations of loop S1 can be eliminated by declaring A to be private. In this way, each processor participating in the execution of loop S1 will have its own copy of array A and there will be no reuse of memory.

A source-to-source parallelizing compiler like Polaris could transform the loop in the previous example by adding the following directives:

```
C$DIR PARALLEL DO
C$DIR PRIVATE A(1:N)
C$DIR LAST VALUE A(1:N) WHEN (I.EQ.N)
```

These directives have the following interpretation:

- The **PARALLEL DO** directive indicates that the iterations of loop S1 may be executed in parallel.

- The PRIVATE directive declares the privatizable arrays. That is, each processor cooperating in the execution of the loop allocates a local copy for each array in the PRIVATE directive before executing any statement in the loop. If the PRIVATE array is used before or after the loop, a *global* copy, accessible outside the loop, is also allocated.
- During the entire execution of an iteration, references to a private array are directed to the processor's local copy.
- The LAST VALUE directive specifies the conditions under which a processor should copy all or part of a private array into the global version of the array. After the execution of an iteration has completed, the processor checks the last-value assignment condition in the LASTVALUE directive of the loop. If the condition is satisfied, the processor copies the private array to the corresponding global array. This operation is called *copy-out.*

There are cases in which a private array needs to be initialized with values from its global counterpart. This initialization operation is called *copy-in.* The following is a simple definition of privatizable array when copy-in is not allowed.

Definition 21. *Let* A *be an array that is referenced in a loop* L. *We say* A *is* privatizable *to* L *if every fetch to an element of* A *in* L *is preceded by a store to the element in the same iteration of* L.   □

To include copy-in, we can simply relax the condition and define privatizable arrays as those that are either defined within the same iteration before they are used or are not defined in any of the iterations preceding the use. For simplicity, we will present the algorithm without copy-in.

Notice that, according to the definition, array A in the following loop is privatizable.

```
S1: DO I = 1, N
S2:    A(I) = ...
S3:    ... = A(I)
S4: ENDDO
```

However, in this case, privatization would not help eliminate any memory related dependence. Privatization is profitable when memory-related dependences are eliminated. More formally, we have the following definition.

Definition 22. *We say that it is* profitable *to privatize an array* A *to a loop* L *if different iterations of* L *may access the same location of* A.   □

To determine the copy-out condition, if every iteration of a loop writes to the same array section, the last iteration of the loop needs to write its local copy to the global array to preserve the semantics of the original sequential loop. We call these cases *static last-value assignments*. Once a static last-value assignment situation is identified, the code generation pass can either generate conditional codes for the last value assignment inside the loop body, or peel the last iteration of the loop out of the parallel region. If different iterations write to different sections of an array, or if only some iterations write to the same section of an array, the last-value assignment usually has to be resolved at runtime.

Consider the following loop

```
C$DIR DO PARALLEL
C$DIR PRIVATE A(1:N)
C$DIR LAST VALUE A(1) WHEN (I.EQ.N)
C$DIR LAST VALUE A(2:N) WHEN DYNAMIC
S1: DO I = 1, N
S2:    A(1) = X(I,J)
S3:    IF (A(1).GT.0) THEN
S4:       DO J = 2, N
S5:          A(J) = A(J-1)+Y(J)
S6:       ENDDO
S7:    ENDIF
S8: ENDDO
```

Here, array section A(2:N) is conditionally assigned. Although it can be determined that A is privatizable and that it is profitable to privatize it, the last-value assignment of A cannot be determined at compile time. We use the key word DYNAMIC to specify that runtime resolution techniques will have to be used for the array section A(2:N). We call a case like this *dynamic last-value assignment*.

Runtime resolution, for example, could be based on *synchronization variables* [ZY87]. For the last loop, this approach would create a *last-iteration* variable containing the number of the last iteration that wrote A(2:N). Every iteration that defines A(2:N) will atomically compare its iteration number with the value in the last-iteration variable. If its iteration number is larger than the value in the variable, the processor stores its iteration number into the last-iteration tag and copy-out A(2:N). Otherwise, the assignment is ignored because a later iteration has already written to A(2:N).

3. Algorithm for Array Privatization

3.1 Data Flow Framework

Data flow analysis examines the flow of values through a program and solves data flow problems by propagating information along the paths of the program's control flow graph. Because private arrays are associated with DO loops in the program, we extend the traditional control flow graph with information about the scope of DO loops.

Definition 31. *Let* $G = (N, E, s)$ *be a control flow graph where* N *are nodes,* E *are arcs, and* $s \in N$ *is the initial node. Let* L *be a subflowgraph corresponding to a* DO *loop (including all loops nested within it). We define* $CONTROL(L) \subset L$ *as the subset of nodes in* L *corresponding to the loop entry, increment, and test of the loop index.* $CONTROL(L)$ *identifies the* DO *loop index, its limits, and its step. We define the* $BODY(L)$ *as* $L - CONTROL(L)$. □

When a program has nested loops, the *CONTROL* and the *BODY* of all inner loops are included in the body of the outer loop. When the control flow of an inner loop is not important for the analysis of an outer loop, we can collapse the subflowgraph corresponding to the inner loop into one node.

Definition 32. *Let* $G = (N, E, s)$ *be a flow graph and* L *be a* DO *loop in* G. *The* $COLLAP(G, L)$ *is* G *with the subflowgraph* L *collapsed into one node.* □

Given a subflowgraph L corresponding to a loop, we want to determine if, for every iteration of the loop, all reaching definitions to an array use come from the same iteration. We can do this through *def-use* analysis. The data values to be analyzed are: *scalar variables*, such as A, B, C; *subscripted variables*, such as $X(1), X(2), X(I)$; and *subarrays* (or array sections), such as $X(1 : N : 1)$. Subarrays are defined as follows:

Definition 33. *A subarray is a sparse convex polytope representing an array region. Each axle of a subarray is a set of inequalities representing the lower bound, upper bound, and stride for the corresponding array region.* □

The notion of subarray we use in this chapter is an extension of the *regular section* used by others [CK88a]. Using subarrays, we can represent triangular sections and banded sections, as well as the strips, grids, columns, rows, and blocks of an array. For instance, the following examples respectively represent a dense upper triangle, grids in the upper triangle, and diagonal of array A.

```
(A(I,I:N),[I=1:N])
(A(I,I:N:2),[I=1:N:2])
(A(I,I),[I=1:N])
```

The privatization algorithm is organized into four phases as shown in Figure 3.1. Phases 1 and 2 are discussed next and phases 3 and 4 are explained in Sections 3.4 and 3.5. The first phase computes *outward exposed* definitions and uses for each basic block S in the loop body. A definition of variable v in a basic block S is said to be outward exposed if it is the last definition of

v in S. A use of v is outward exposed if S does not contain a definition of v before the use [ZC91].

Definition 34. *Let S be a basic block and VAR be the set of scalar variables, subscripted variables, and subarrays in the program.*

    1. $DEF(S) := \{v \in VAR : v \text{ has an outward exposed definition in } S \}$
    2. $USE(S) := \{v \in VAR : v \text{ has an outward exposed use in } S \}$ □

Henceforth, the term *variable* will stand for scalar variables, subscripted variables, and subarrays. We define $MRD_{in}(S)$ as the set of variables that are always defined upon entering S, and $MRD_{out}(S)$ as the set of variables that are always defined upon exiting S. Let $pred(S)$ be the set of immediate predecessors of S ignoring all the back edges in the loop's flow graph. The second phase of the privatization algorithm computes $MRD_{in}(S)$ using the following equations:

$$MRD_{in}(S) = \cap_{t \in pred(S)} MRD_{out}(t)$$

$$MRD_{out}(S) = MRD_{in}(S) \cup DEF(S)$$

The initial solution used by the privatization algorithm for each MRD_{in} is the empty set. Back edges in the graph are ignored because $MRD(S)$ is concerned only with the values that are defined in the statements preceding S within the DO loop body. Because back edges are deleted, the algorithm actually works on a DAG. Back edges of inner DO loops carry information needed in the analysis of outer loops, but they are handled by abstraction and aggregation, as discussed in the next section.

Each set defined above, such as DEF, USE, and MRD, is a subset of VAR. Hence, the domain of the data flow information set is the powerset $\mathcal{P}(VAR)$. The union operator ($\cup$) is precise in the sense that it will not summarize two sets unless the summary set has exactly the same members as the two sets. For instance, $\{A(I) \cup A(1:N)\}$ will return $\{A(I), A(1:N)\}$ unless $I \in [1:N]$, but $\{A(1:N:2) \cup A(2:N-1:2)\}$ will return A(1:N). The intersection operator ($\cap$) is *conservative* in the sense that it will return an empty set ϕ if it cannot determine the precise intersection of its operands. For instance, $\{A(I) \cap A(1:N)\}$ will return ϕ unless $I \in [1:N]$. Because the intersection is conservative, there will be some potential loss of information at each join node of the program flow graph. Hence, the effectiveness of the algorithm will depend on the system's ability to determine the relationship between symbolic variables.

3.2 Inner Loop Abstraction

When the algorithm finds a loop nested inside a loop body, it will recursively call itself on the inner loop. To hide the control flow structure of an inner loop, we define the set of privatizable variables, and extend the previous

Algorithm Privatize

$privatize := func(L)$

Input: flowgraph for loop L with back edges removed

Output: $DEF(L), USE(L), PRI(L)$

Phase 1: Collect local information

    foreach statement $S \in BODY(L)$ in rPostorder **do**

        if $S \in control(M)$ for some loop M nested in L **then**

            ! S is in an inner loop, visit M first

            $[DEF(S), USE(S)] \leftarrow privatize(M)$

            ! collapse all nodes in M onto S

            $L \leftarrow COLLAP(L, M)$

        else

            compute local $DEF(S), USE(S)$

        endif

    endfor

Phase 2: Solve the MRD Data Flow Equations for each statement

    foreach $S \in BODY(L)$ initialize $MRD(S) \leftarrow \phi$

    foreach $S \in BODY(L)$ in rPostorder **do**

        $MRD_{in}(S) \leftarrow \cap_{t \in pred(S)} MRD_{out}(t)$

        $MRD_{out}(S) \leftarrow MRD_{in}(S) \cup DEF(S)$

    end

Phase 3: Compute Summary Sets for the Loop Body

    $DEF_b(L) \leftarrow \cap_{t \in exits(BODY(L))}(MRD_{out}(t))$

    $USE_b(L) \leftarrow \cup_{t \in BODY(L)}(USE(t) - MRD_{in}(t))$

    $PRI_b(L) \leftarrow (\cup_{t \in BODY(L)}(USE(t) \cup DEF(t))) - USE_b(L)$

    $PRI_b^{st}(L) \leftarrow DEF_b(L) \cap PRI_b(L)$

    $PRI_b^{dy}(L) \leftarrow PRI_b(L) - PRI_b^{st}(L)$

Phase 4: Return aggregated set $DEF(L)$ and $USE(L)$

    test if it is profitable to privatize $PRI_b(L)$

    determine last value assignment

    $[PRI^{st}(L), PRI^{dy}(L)] \leftarrow aggregate(PRI_b^{st}, PRI_b^{dy}, control(L))$

    $[DEF(L), USE(L)] \leftarrow aggregate(DEF_b(L), USE_b(L), control(L))$

    return $[DEF(L), USE(L)]$

Fig. 3.1. Algorithm for Identifying Privatizable Arrays

definitions from the basic block level to the loop level. We start by defining the information for one iteration of the loop.

Definition 35. *Let L be a loop and VAR be the variables in the program. We define the following summary sets for $BODY(L)$:*

1. $DEF_b(L)$ *is the set of* must define *variables for one iteration of L. These are the must define variables upon exiting the iteration:*

$$DEF_b(L) = \cap(MRD_{out}(t) : t \in exits(L))$$

2. $USE_b(L)$ *is the set of* possibly outward exposed use *variables. It is the set of variables used in some statements of L, but which are not in their MRD_{in}:*

$$USE_b(L) = \cup(USE(t) - MRD_{in}(t)) : t \in BODY(L)$$

3. $PRI_b(L)$ *is the set of* privatizable variables. *These are the variables used and not exposed to definitions outside the iteration:*

$$PRI_b(L) = \cup\{(USE(t) \cup DEF(t)) : t \in BODY(L)\} - USE_b(L)$$

□

The summary sets represent the effect of a loop iteration on the data flow values. Using the summary sets, we can ignore the structure of the inner loops in the analysis of the outer loop. The trade-off is that we have to make a conservative approximation and may lose information in the process.

The set of privatizable subarrays can be enlarged if we allow copy-in of their global counterparts' values. This can be accomplished by privatizing subarrays with exposed uses as long as the exposed uses do not overlap with subarrays that *may be defined* in any iteration preceding the one containing the use. It is straightforward to compute the set of subarrays that may be defined in a loop body.

In the analysis of the outer loop, we must consider the total effect of an inner loop on data flow values. That is, we need to account for the effect of back edges and the iteration space of the loop. The summary sets are parameterized by the loop index variables. Hence we can account for the effect of all the iterations in the loop by aggregating the summary sets across the iteration space of the loop.

Definition 36. *Let L be a loop. The aggregated sets: $DEF(L), USE(L)$, and $PRI(L)$ contain the subarrays of the corresponding summary sets after $USE_b(L)$, $DEF_b(L)$, and $PRI_b(L)$, respectively, are aggregated across the iteration space of the loop.* □

The aggregation process , which is summarized in Phase 4 of the algorithm in Figure 3.1, computes the section spanned by each array reference in $USE_b(L)$,

$DEF_b(L)$, and $PRI_b(L)$ across the iteration space. Aggregation can be accomplished by a relatively straightforward processing of the loop index and its boundaries. In our representation of variables, a subarray is represented as a subscripted variable together with a subscript range. To aggregate a subarray, we simply need to add the information about the loop index and its boundaries to the subarray expression. For instance, if I is a loop index or an induction variable with value [1:N:1], then A(I,J) will be aggregated as (A(I,J),[I=1:N]) = A(1:N,J); and, A(I,1:I) will be aggregated as (A(I,1:I),[I=1:N]).

Because one iteration's use could sometimes be exposed only to the definitions of some previous iterations of the same loop, a naive aggregation of $USE_b(L)$ may exaggerate the exposed use set. The reason is that the uses covered by the definitions in previous iterations are not exposed to the outside of the loop and, therefore, they should be excluded from the aggregated $USE(L)$ set. For instance, in the following loop.,

```
L1: DO K = 1, N
        A(1) = 1
    L:      DO I = 2, N
    S1:         A(I) = A(I-1) + B(J)
            ENDDO
    L2:     DO J = 1, N
                C(K,J) = A(J)
            ENDDO
        ENDDO
```

the information for one iteration is $USE_b(L) = \{A(I-1), B(J), J\}$ and $DEF_b(L) = \{A(I)\}$; the section defined in all iterations prior to the ith iteration is A(2:I-1); and, only in the first iteration is A(I-1) exposed to definitions outside the loop. Hence, $USE(L) = \{A(1)\}$. By eliminating the exposed uses to the definitions in previous iterations, we identify array section $A(1:N)$ to be privatizable in the outer loop L1. The less precise analysis would assume that loop L has exposed use of $A(2:N)$ and, therefore, would not privatize $A(1:N)$ in the outer loop.

Because the aggregated sets approximate the total effect of the inner loop, in the analysis of the outer loop it is safe to use the aggregated sets, to collapse the inner loop into one node, and to ignore the control flow structure of the inner loop.

3.3 An Example

We use the following program to illustrate how the algorithm works.

```
         SUBROUTINE SHUF(A,N2,N,WORK)

    L1: DO J = 1, N, 2
    L2:    DO I = 1, N2
    S1:       WORK(2*I-1) = A(I,J)
    S2:       WORK(2*I) = A(I,J+1)
           ENDDO
    L3:    DO K = 1, N2
    S3:       A(K,J) = WORK(K)
    S4:       A(K,J+1) = WORK(K+N2)
           ENDDO
         ENDDO
```

The algorithm is first called on loop L1 which, in turn, recursively calls the the algorithm on inner loops L2 and L3. For each iteration of L2, we find that the summary sets of definitions and exposed uses for the body of L2 are:

$$\begin{aligned} DEF_b(L2) &= \{WORK(2*I-1), WORK(2*I), I\} \\ &= \{WORK(2*I-1:2*I:1), I\} \\ USE_b(L2) &= \{A(I,J), A(I,J+1), J\} \\ &= \{A(I,J:J+1), J\} \end{aligned}$$

Therefore, the aggregated sets of definitions and exposed uses for the loop L2 are:

$$\begin{aligned} DEF(L2) &= \{(WORK(2*I-1:2*I), [I=1,N2]), I\} \\ &= \{WORK(1:2*N2:1), I\} \\ USE(L2) &= \{(A(I,J:J+1), [I=1,N2]), J\} \\ &= \{A(1:N2, J:J+1), J\} \end{aligned}$$

For each iteration of L3, we find that the summary sets of definitions and exposed uses for the body of L3 are:

$$\begin{aligned} DEF_b(L3) &= \{A(K,J), A(K,J+1), K\} \\ &= \{A(K,J:J+1:1), K\} \\ USE_b(L3) &= \{WORK(K), WORK(K+N2), J\} \end{aligned}$$

Therefore, the aggregated sets of definitions and exposed uses for the loop L3 are:

$$\begin{aligned} DEF(L3) &= \{(A(K,J:J+1:1), K=1,N2), K\} \\ &= \{A(1:N2:1, J:J+1:1), K\} \\ USE(L3) &= \{(WORK(K), WORK(K+N2), K=1,N2), J\} \\ &= \{WORK(1:2*N2), J\} \end{aligned}$$

The body of L1 is then analyzed. All the definitions in L2 will reach the uses in L3. That is,

$$MRD_{in}(L2) = \{J, WORK(1:2*N2:1), I\}.$$

Hence, the privatizable variables in loop L1 are:

$$PRI_b(L1) = \{J, WORK(1:2*N2:1), I\}.$$

The summary sets of definitions and exposed uses for loop L1 are:

$$DEF_b(L1) = \{A(1:N2, J:J+1:1), WORK(1:2*N2:1), I, J, K\}$$
$$USE_b(L1) = \{A(1:N2, J:J+1:1)\}$$

In this example, the summary sets for loop L1 also can be used for dependence analysis. In general, to prove that a loop L is parallel, all we have to prove is that the possibly exposed uses, $USE_b(L)$, and the possible definitions will never overlap for different values of the loop index. The set of possible definitions within loop, $DEF_mb(L)$, can be defined in a flow insensitive way as:

$$DEF_{mb}(L) = \cup(DEF(t) : t \in BODY(L)).$$

In Polaris, the array def-use analysis module generates the $DEF_{mb}(L)$ to provide array section information for other passes, such as reduction code generation and runtime dependence testing.

3.4 Profitability of Privatization

After an array is identified as privatizable in a loop, we need to determine if different iterations of a loop will access the same location of the array. For instance, as already discussed in Section 2, A(I) is privatizable in the following loop:

```
S1: DO I = 1, N
S2:    A(I) = ...
S3:    ... = A(I)
S4: ENDDO
```

We can privatize A(I) using a private scalar as follows:

```
C$DIR INDEPENDENT
C$DIR PRIVATE X
C$DIR LAST VALUE A(I) = X
S1: DO I = 1, N
S2:    X = ...
S3:    ... = X
Sn: ENDDO
```

This transformation is useful for conventional compiler optimization. Today's optimizing compilers usually will not allocate a register to a subscripted variable A(I) in the original program due to their limited capability in handling array references. In the transformed program, it is easier for them to allocate a register to a scalar X.

Privatizing A(I) also can reduce the amount of *false sharing* in multiprocessor caches. In a distributed memory system where the compiler uses the *owner computes* rule [ZBG88, CK88b, RP89], privatization effectively transfers the ownership of A(I) to the processor executing iteration I; hence, the processor scheduled to execute the iteration I can execute operations in S2 even if it does not own A(I). This transformation can facilitate data distribution, reduce communication, and improve load balance [TP93a].

However, for the purpose of eliminating memory-related dependence, the array A in the previous example need not be privatized. We said that it is profitable to privatize an array when different iterations of the loop access the same location. Whether this condition is satisfied can be determined by examining $PRI_b(L)$. We will call the test that examines $PRI_b(L)$ the *profitability test*. Let $A(r)$ be a reference to array A where r is a subscript expression if $A(r)$ is a subscripted variable, or a range list if $A(r)$ is a subarray. We assume that r is either loop invariant or is expressed in terms of the loop index, i.

If $A(r)$ is a subscripted variable and r is a monotonic function of the loop index i, then different iterations of i will access different locations of $A(r)$; hence, it is not profitable to privatize $A(r)$. Otherwise it is profitable. When there is more than one subscript of A in $PRI_b(L)$, we need to test each pair for multiple accesses to the same location in different iterations. This can be done using Banerjee's Test [Ban88] or any other dependence test. If $A(r)$ is a subarray, we need to determine if there is an iteration $j \neq i$ such that $A(r) \cap A(r[i/j]) \neq \phi$, where $r[i/j]$ represents r after we substitute each occurrence of loop index i with j. Again, one has to test for each pair of occurrences if there is more than one occurrence of subarrays. This discussion is summarized in the algorithm shown in Figure 3.2.

3.5 Last Value Assignment

Liveness analysis is needed to determine if a privatizable variable is live after exiting the loop. If it is live, the last-value assignment will be necessary to preserve the semantics of the original program; otherwise, no last-value assignment is needed for that variable.

Definition 37. *Let S be a node in the flowgraph. The live variables at the bottom of S are the set of variables that may be used after S completes execution. We define:*

1. *$LVBOT(S) := \{v \in VAR : v \text{ may be used after } S \}$*
2. *$LVTOP(S) := \{v \in VAR : v \text{ may be used after } S \text{ or in } S \}$*   □

Algorithm Profitability Test
   Input: PRI_b for loop *L*: with index $i \in [p : q : t]$
   Output: PRO, arrays profitable for privatization

   $PRO \leftarrow \phi$
   foreach $A(r) \in PRI_b$ **do**
      $ALL_A \leftarrow \{A(r) : A(r) \in PRI_b\}$
      foreach pair $A(x), A(y) \in ALL_A$ — where x and y can be the same
         let $X \leftarrow$ set of values in x
         let $Y \leftarrow$ set of values in y
         if $(\exists j \in [p : q : t] | j \neq i, X[i/j] \cap Y \neq \phi)$
            $PRO \leftarrow PRO + A$
         !Notice that if $x = y$ and x does not contain i, the test is satisfied.
      endfor
   endfor

Fig. 3.2. Profitability Test

Let $succ(S)$ be the set of immediate successors of S in the program flow-graph. The equations for $LVTOP$ and $LVBOT$ are:

$$LVBOT(S) = \cup_{t \in succ(S)} LVTOP(t)$$

$$LVTOP(S) = (LVBOT(S) - DEF(S)) \cup USE(S)$$

The array def-use analysis computes the aggregated sets for each loop in the program. We can use these aggregated sets in the liveness analysis and ignore the control flow graph inside the loop body. For each loop L in the program, we can instead use the following equations to reduce the amount of work:

$$LVBOT(L) = \cup_{t \in succ(L)} LVTOP(t)$$

$$LVTOP(L) = (LVBOT(L) - DEF(L)) \cup USE(L)$$

For each loop L, $KILL(L)$ contains the must written variables, and the $USE(L)$ contains the possibly exposed use by loop L. They are both conservative for liveness analysis.

The data flow equations for liveness analysis can be solved using an iterative algorithm that traverses the control flow graph backwards. This is a natural extension of scalar live analysis to array liveness analysis.

After live analysis, we can ignore the last-value assignments for private arrays that are not live at the bottom of the loop. However, the remaining live private arrays have to be copied to their global counterparts. Two problems prevent the static determination of the iteration that copies its private array to the global array. One, as shown earlier in Section 3, is due to conditional definitions. Without information about which branch the program will take at runtime, it is impossible to determine which iteration assigns the last value. Another problem is that some complicated subscript expressions make it inefficient to compute at compile time which iteration will assign the last value. In these cases, we can use well-known runtime techniques, such as that described in Section 2.

Our first step is to identify the private arrays that need dynamic last-value assignments because of conditional definitions. PRI_b contains all the array uses that are covered by some definition in the same iteration of the loop. Some of the uses are conditional; that is, they are covered by some conditional definitions. DEF_b contains all the variables that must be defined as a function of the iteration number. Therefore, $PRI_b^{st} = PRI_b \cap DEF_b$ contains the privatizable arrays that are unconditionally defined. Hence $PRI_b^{dy} = PRI_b - PRI_b^{st}$ contains the conditionally defined privatizable arrays.

Because of the profitability test, at least one element of each array in PRI_b^{st} is defined in two or more iterations. To determine for each iteration what element has to be copied back to the global array, we define a *write back set* as the sections of private array that have to be copied back to the global array for iteration i.

Definition 38. *Let L be a loop body and PRI^{st} be the static private arrays. The Write Back Set (WBS) of L is defined as the sections of arrays in PRI^{st} that are written in the ith iteration, but are not written thereafter.* □

¿From the definition, we can compute the WBS by comparing the set defined in iteration i and the set defined in the iterations after i. The algorithm is shown in Figure 3.3.

Algorithm Write Back Set
  Input: PRI_b^{st} for loop L: with index $i \in [p : q : t]$
  Output: WBS

  $WBS \leftarrow \phi$
  foreach array $A \in PRI_b^{st}$ **do**
    $ALL_A \leftarrow \{A(r) : A(r) \in PRI_b^{st}\}$
    $WBS \leftarrow ALL_A - \cup_{j\in[i+t:q:t]} ALL_A[i/j]$
  endfor

Fig. 3.3. Compute Write Back Set

Note that the last iteration of loop L will always write back all its static private arrays. When we cannot find a closed form for WBS, we can move the array to PRI_b^{dy} and use runtime resolution. Actually the algorithm itself can be linked into the program to perform a run test for each iteration. In most cases, the algorithm will find a closed form and, therefore, WBS can be determined at compile time. The following loop will be used to illustrate how the algorithm in Figure 3.3 works in two different situations.

```
S1: DO I = 1, N
S2:    DO J = 1, M
S3:       A(J) = ...
S4:       B(I+J) = ...
S5:    ENDDO
...
Sn: ENDDO
```

For loop S1, $PRI_b^{st} = \{A(1:M), B(I+1:I+M)\}$. A(1:M) will be accessed in all iterations after a given I<N because A(1:M) does not depend on I. Hence, WBS for A in iteration $I \neq N$ is ϕ, the empty set. Only the last iteration of loop S1 will copy out A(1:M). For B, B(I+1:I+M) is in ALL_B for iteration I; B((I+1)+1:M+N) is modified in iterations from I+1 to N. Hence, the WSB_I for B in iteration I is B(I+1).

4. Demand-Driven Symbolic Analysis

To evaluate its effectiveness, the privatization algorithm just described was implemented in Polaris. We now present a comparison of the number of private arrays found by the algorithm with the number of private arrays found by hand in the Perfect Benchmarks as reported in [EHLP91]. The result is shown in Table 4.1. The first column reports the number of private arrays identified by both manual and automatic privatization. The second column reports the number of private arrays identified by manual privatization but not by automatic privatization. The third column reports the number identified by automatic privatization but not by manual privatization. By comparing the results of automatic privatization and manual privatization, it is clear that the algorithm is sufficient to discover most of the privatizable arrays. The representation for subarray sections is also adequate for representing the array use and definition in the programs of the Perfect Benchmarks. The algorithm can successfully handle all the privatizable arrays in $FLO52$ and $TRFD$. In the programs $BDNA$, $DYFESM$, $FLO52$, and MDG, the algorithm finds some privatizable arrays that are not found by manual array privatization. One reason for this is that finding privatizable arrays is tedious work that requires a lot of effort. A compiler is more reliable and consistent in handling the mechanical part of the task. Another reason is that in the manual privatization, the programmers used runtime profile information to select

Program	Automatic and Manual	Manual Only	Automatic Only
ADM (AP)	2	12	0
ARC2D (SR)	0	2	0
BDNA (NA)	12	3	4
DYFESM (SD)	0	1	11
FLO52 (TF)	0	0	4
MDG (LW)	17	1	1
MG3D (SM)	1	4	0
OCEAN (OC)	4	3	0
QCD (LG)	22	7	0
SPEC77 (WS)	25	14	0
TRACK (MT)	20	2	0
TRFD (TI)	4	0	0

Table 4.1. Number of Private Arrays

target loops for potential parallelization and ignored the privatizable arrays in the other loops.

However, there were still many privatizable arrays that the privatization algorithm failed to identify. We found that in most instances where our algorithm failed, it was due to lack of information about symbolic variables. To increase the coverage of the algorithms, it seems necessary to use more sophisticated techniques for determining the equivalence of symbolic variables, interprocedural symbolic values and bounds propagation, and conditional data flow analysis.

To illustrate the need for more sophisticated techniques, consider the following program segment:

```
      IF (P)  THEN JLOW = 2, JUP = JMAX - 1
              ELSE JLOW = 1, JUP = JMAX
L:  DO K = 1, N
        WORK(JLOW:JUP) = ...
        IF (P) THEN ...= WORK(2:JMAX-1)
      ENDDO
```

Loop L cannot be executed in parallel because each of its iterations reads and writes the same elements of array WORK. The array privatization algorithm tries to determine if it is correct to allocate a private copy of array WORK to each iteration of the loop. This transformation is safe when no iteration uses any data in the array WORK that is computed by other iterations. The WORK array is *privatizable* in the loop if we can prove that the section read, WORK(2:JMAX-1), is *covered* by the section written, WORK(JLOW:JUP). That is, we need to prove that JLOW is less than or equal to 2 and that JUP is greater than or equal to (JMAX-1). Later in this chapter, we will present two ways to prove the above symbolic relations.

In this section, we present a demand-driven technique to propagate and analyze symbolic expressions as well as a technique to perform conditional flow analysis. These techniques are also useful in areas other than array privatization. In fact, recent developments in parallelizing compilers have resulted in the increased use of the symbolic analysis technique to facilitate parallelism detection and program transformation. Several research compilers, such as *Parafrase-2* [HP92] and *Nascent* [GSW], use symbolic analysis to identify and transform induction variables. In the *Polaris* [BEF+94] restructuring compiler, symbolic analysis is used, in addition to array privatization, for dependence analysis and symbolic range propagation.

4.1 Gated Single Assignment

The symbolic analysis techniques discussed below are based on an extension of the Static Single Assignment (SSA) form [CFR+91] of program representation, known as the Gated Single Assignment (GSA) form [BMO90]. In SSA, each definition of a variable is given a unique name. Each use of a renamed variable can only refer to a single reaching definition. Where several definitions of a variable, $x_1, x_2, \ldots, x_m$, reach a confluence point in the CFG of the program, a ϕ function assignment statement, $x_n \leftarrow \phi(x_1, x_2, \ldots, x_m)$, is inserted to merge them into a new variable definition x_n. The condition under which a definition reaches a join node is not represented in the ϕ-function. In the GSA representation, several types of *gating functions* are defined to represent the different types of conditions at different join nodes. Some extra parameters are introduced in the gating functions to represent the conditions. GSA introduces three new gating functions:

- γ function : Replaces those ϕ-functions at join nodes associated with *IF* statements. A γ function includes the predicate of an *if* statement as an additional argument.
- μ function : Replaces ϕ functions at the head of a loop. It also includes an extra argument to represent the loop header's control condition.
- η function : Replaces ϕ functions at the exit of a loop. It selects the last value produced by a μ function.

Several algorithms exist for converting programs into GSA form [BMO90, Hav93, TP94]. Using the GSA representation, we can represent the value of a symbolic variable in an expression containing other variables, constants, and gating functions.

Traditionally, symbolic expressions for each variable have been constructed by applying *forward substitution* during *symbolic execution* of the program. To apply forward substitution, the compiler follows the def-use chains and substitutes each use of a variable with the symbolic expression that was assigned to the variable. The symbolic value of a variable is usually represented as a function of program inputs. When multiple definitions reach the same use of a variable, the variable will have multiple possible symbolic values. A compiler's ability to represent multiple possible symbolic values determines the types of analysis the compiler can perform. In the GSA representation, multiple possible reaching definitions and the conditions guarding the definitions are represented in the arguments gating functions. Gating functions provide a natural way to represent an expression's multiple possible symbolic values under different conditions.

4.2 Demand-Driven Backward Substitution

Another advantage of using a single assignment form is that the use-def chains are embedded in the unique variable names. This representation of use-def chains provides an opportunity to perform demand-driven analysis. Demand-driven analysis is desirable for analysis that arises sparsely. In a parallelizing compiler, the requirement of symbolic analysis is sparse. Many simple programs or parts of a program do not need symbolic analysis. Full-scale forward substitution is expensive. Much of the information generated and propagated by forward substitution is never used. Furthermore, in many cases, representing everything in terms of program inputs is unnecessary, as illustrated next. Consider the following code segment:

$$
\begin{aligned}
&\text{R:} \quad JMAX = Expr \\
&\text{S:} \quad IF\ (P)\ \ THEN\ \ J = JMAX - 1 \\
&\qquad\qquad\quad\ \ ELSE\ \ J = JMAX \\
&\text{T:} \quad assert(J \leq JMAX)
\end{aligned}
$$

To determine whether the assertion $(J \leq JMAX)$ is **true** at T, we need to know the symbolic value of J. Forward substitution starts at statement R. Once it completes, J and JMAX at statement T are replaced by $(if\ P\ then\ Expr - 1\ else\ Expr)$ and Expr, respectively. Thus, the boolean expression $(J \leq JMAX)$ evaluates to be **true**. It is easy to see that the substitution of JMAX by Expr is unnecessary. In a large program, forward substitution could produce long and complex expressions. Therefore, determining whether an assertion is true could be very time consuming. Approximate summary information could be used to improve the efficiency of this process. However, in general, approximation decreases the accuracy of analysis.

In a demand-driven approach, we seek information only when it is needed. Instead of propagating all symbolic values forward, our demand-driven strategy is goal directed and moves backward. Given a symbolic expression, we backward substitute arguments in the expression. The *backward substitution* stops when enough information to satisfy a specific objective has been obtained. In a forward substitution strategy, the requirements are not known.

Therefore, it is very difficult, or impossible, to determine which subset of the available information to propagate and where to start the propagation.

As an example, consider the following GSA representation of the last code segment:

$$
\begin{aligned}
&\text{R:} \quad JMAX_1 = Expr \\
&\text{S:} \quad \text{IF } (P) \text{THEN } J_1 = JMAX_1 - 1 \\
&\qquad\qquad\quad \text{ELSE } J_2 = JMAX_1 \\
&\text{S':} \; J_3 = \gamma(P, J_1, J_2) \\
&\text{T:} \quad assert(J_3 \leq JMAX_1)
\end{aligned}
$$

A demand-driven analysis starts at T and performs backward substitution following the SSA links of the variables in the expression. The intermediate statements, which do not affect the variables used in T, are skipped. The steps of the substitution are:

$$
\begin{aligned}
J_3 &= \gamma(P, J_1, J_2) \\
&= \gamma(P, JMAX_1 - 1, JMAX_1)
\end{aligned}
$$

The backward substitution stops at this point because enough information for proving $J_3 \leq JMAX_1$ has been obtained. The redundant substitution of $JMAX_1$ by Expr is avoided.

During backward substitution, if there are several arguments that can be back-substituted, we need to decide which argument should be substituted first. Our strategy is as follows. Given two arguments, u and v, that can be back- substituted, if the assignment statement of u (S_u) *dominates* the assignment statement of v (S_v) in the program control flow graph CFG, then v should be back-substituted before u. Because S_u dominates S_v, the value of u cannot depend on the value of v, but the value of v may depend on the value of u. When there are loops in the program, this order may not be valid since u can potentially depend on the v through some back edges. In the case of loops, we use a known technique to identify the set of variables that belong to the same *strongly connected region* (SCR). If S_u and S_v belong to different SCRs, the order is then determined by the dominance relation between the SCRs.

When comparing two partially back-substituted symbolic expressions, s and t, we can use the dominator tree to determine which argument in s or t should be substituted first. If the arguments are substituted from the bottom-up in the dominator tree, then it is possible to avoid expanding an expression beyond what is necessary for the comparison. This simple algorithm is shown in Figure 4.1.

For instance, in the last code segment, when comparing J_3 with $JMAX_1$, the assignment statement R dominates the assignment statements S, S', and T. Hence, J_3 is substituted first. J_1 and J_2 are substituted next. The substituted expression $\gamma(P, JMAX_1 - 1, JMAX_1)$ is comparable with $JMAX_1$.

Algorithm Unify
Input: expressions s and t
1. Mark constants and matching arguments in s, t as dead.
2. **while** $\exists$ *active arguments* $\in s, t$ **do**
   Substitute an argument whose assignment is the lowest in the dominator tree.
   Mark constants and matching arguments in the resulting expressions as dead.

Fig. 4.1. Ordering Backward Substitution

Backward substitution stops after it is determined that the expressions involved are comparable.

4.3 Backward Substitution in the Presence of Gating Functions

To derive the value of a variable at a point S in a program, we first perform backward substitution to obtain a symbolic expression. The resulting symbolic expression SE contains: literals, such as constants or variables; normal functions and operators, such as $+$, $-$, abs, $\ldots$; and the gating functions η, γ and μ. During backward substitution, gating functions are treated in the same way as normal functions. The gating functions in a symbolic expression represent the different possible values of the expression under different conditions. Hence, we will call an expression a *predicated expression* if it contains gating functions.

The purpose of demand-driven symbolic analysis is to determine the values of a variable at a specific point of the program CFG. A predicated expression captures the conditional possible values of the expression under different conditions. The conditional possible values of a predicated expression can be refined if the necessary conditions for the control flow to reach the point of interest in the program CFG are taken into account.

Definition 41. *A symbolic path condition PC is a predicate specifying the control flow conditions under which the program flow will reach the statement S.*

For instance, in the following program:

$$
\begin{aligned}
&\text{IF (P)} \quad \text{THEN } JUP_0 = JMAX - 1\\
&\qquad\qquad \text{ELSE } JUP_1 = JMAX\\
&JUP_2 = \gamma(P, JUP_0, JUP_1)\\
&\text{IF (P)} \quad \text{THEN}\\
&\text{S:} \qquad\qquad \ldots = JUP_2
\end{aligned}
$$

the path condition that controls the execution of statement S is (P). This path condition can be used to refine the possible values of JUP_2 at S. After backward substitution, the predicated expression of JUP_2 is $\gamma(P, JMAX - 1, JMAX)$. That is, JUP_2 has two possible values, $JMAX - 1$ and $JMAX$, depending on the value of P. Because the path condition at S is (P = **true**), the value of JUP_2 at S can be determined to be JMAX-1.

To compute the path condition for each statement, we need to use the concept of *iterative control dependences* [FOW87].

Definition 42. *The iterative control dependences of a node X is the transitive closure of its control dependences.*

Hence, if X is control dependent on Y, and Y is control dependent on Z, then X is iteratively control dependent on Z. The iterative control dependences of a CFG node S specify the branch nodes that determine whether the control flow will reach S.

If S is iteratively control dependent on a collection C of branch statements, its path condition PC can be represented as a boolean expression that contains the branch conditions in C. The path-restricted value PV of a symbolic expression at statement S is the projection of the possible values of SE:

$$PV = SE(PC)$$

To compute the projection, we can use the following rules:

$$SE(PC) = SE \text{ if } SE \text{ contains no gating functions}$$

$$\gamma(P, V_t, V_f)(PC) = \begin{cases} V_t(PC) & \text{if } PC \supset P \\ V_f(PC) & \text{if } PC \supset \neg P \\ \gamma(P, V_t(PC), V_f(PC)) & \text{otherwise (unknown)} \end{cases}$$

$$\mu(L, V_{init}, V_{iter})(PC) = \mu(L, V_{init}(PC), V_{iter}(PC))$$

$$\eta(P, V)(PC) = V(P \wedge PC)$$

4.4 Examples of Backward Substitution

We next present some examples of backward substitution and path projection. The examples illustrate how these techniques improve the effectiveness of array privatization. The techniques also are useful to improve the accuracy of dependence analysis [BE94a, BE94b].

Consider the following code segment:

```
         DIMENSION XE(10000)
```
$$S: \quad NDFE_0 = NDDF_0 * NNPED_0$$
$$D: \quad DO \ i = 1, \ NDFE_0$$
$$XE(i) = ...$$
$$ENDDO$$
$$U: \quad DO \ i = 1, \ NDDF_0$$
$$DO \ j = 1, \ NNPED_0$$
$$... = XE((i-1) * NNPED_0 + j)$$
$$ENDDO$$
$$ENDDO$$

To prove that the array section $XE(1 : NDFE_0)$ defined in loop D covers the array section $XE(1 : NDDF_0 * NNPED_0)$ accessed in loop U, we need to prove that $NDFE_0 \geq NDDF_0 * NNPED_0$. This is easily done after $NDFE_0$ is replaced by $NDDF_0 * NNPED_0$ using backward substitution. The path condition for those points within loop U where XE is accessed is $PC_U = (NDDF_0 \geq 1 \wedge NNPED_0 \geq 1)$. The path condition at those points where XE is defined is $PC_D = (NDFE_0 \geq 1)$ or, after backward substitution, $PC_D = (NDDF_0 * NNPED_0 \geq 1)$. It is easy to see that $PC_U \supset PC_D$ and, therefore, whenever loop U has a non-zero trip count, loop D also has a non-zero trip count.

We now illustrate the use of the projection rule for γ functions. Backward substitution involving the μ function and associated recurrences will be discussed in the next section. Consider the following code segment:

```
    IF (P)   THEN JLOW₀ = 2,  JUP₀ = JMAX − 1
             ELSE JLOW₁ = 1,  JUP₁ = JMAX
```
$$JLOW_2 = \gamma(P, JLOW_0, JLOW_1)$$
$$JUP_2 = \gamma(P, JUP_0, JUP_1)$$

L: DO ...
D: assign to array section $WORK(JLOW_2 : JUP_2)$
U: IF (P) THEN use array section $WORK(2 : JMAX - 1)$
$$ENDDO$$

For the array WORK to be private to the loop L, we need to determine that the use of $WORK(2, JMAX - 1)$ at U is covered by the definition of $WORK(JLOW_2 : JUP_2)$ at D. The PC at U is P. Using the projection rule for the γ function under the condition P, we obtain the following values which prove the desired coverage:

$$JLOW_2 = \gamma(P, JLOW_0, JLOW_1)(P)$$
$$= JLOW_0(P)$$
$$= 2$$

$$JUP_2 = \gamma(P, JUP_0, JUP_1)(P)$$
$$= JUP_0(P)$$
$$= JMAX - 1$$

4.5 Bounds of Symbolic Expression

Sometimes it is sufficient to know the possible values of a variable without looking at the predicates of the gating functions. In array privatization, knowing the upper and lower bounds of a variable often can prove the desired property.

A predicated expression contains the possible symbolic values and the conditions for the expression assuming the values. If we ignore the predicates in the gating functions, the rest of the expression represents only the possible values of the expression. To estimate the bounds of a symbolic expression, we often can ignore the predicates that are difficult to resolve with path projection and, instead, apply the minimum and maximum functions directly to the possible values:

$$\max(\gamma(P, V_t, V_f)) \leq \max(V_t, V_f)$$
$$\min(\gamma(P, V_t, V_f)) \geq \min(V_t, V_f)$$

Using these two rules, we can obtain the following for the last code segment:

$$max(JLOW_2) \leq max(\gamma(P, JLOW_0, JLOW_1))$$
$$= max(JLOW_0, JLOW_1)$$
$$= max(2, 1)$$
$$= 2$$
$$min(JUP_2) \geq min(\gamma(P, JUP_0, JUP_1))$$
$$= min(JUP_0, JUP_1)$$
$$= min(JMAX - 1, JMAX)$$
$$= JMAX - 1.$$

This result also proves the coverage property needed for privatization.

4.6 Comparison of Symbolic Expressions

The symbolic expression may still contain γ functions after path projection. In symbolic analysis, we sometimes need to compare these expressions. Alpern, Wegman, and Zadeck [AWZ88] define a *congruence relation* between expressions containing ϕ assignments.

Definition 43. *Two expressions are congruent if and only if:*

- *They have the same gating functions, and*
- *The arguments of the gating functions are congruent.*

The congruent variables are shown to have equivalent values at a node p if both of them dominate p. To determine if two expressions are congruent, we need to transform the expressions into some sort of canonical form. In many cases, pattern matching alone will not be sufficient. Rewriting transformations, such as *constant folding, arithmetic simplification and normalization*, and *value numbering* [ASU86], are standard techniques to normalize the expressions into a canonical form. For example, $(2 + 5)$ is folded to 7; $(X + X + Y * 2)$ is simplified to $(2 * X + 2 * Y)$; and, $(2 * Y + 2 * X)$ is rewritten to $(2 * X + 2 * Y)$.

Congruence relation can be used only to determine equality; it cannot determine, for example, if one expression is always larger than another. We next define a class of expressions whose inequality relationship can be determined at compile-time.

We loosely call two expressions *compatible* if, after backward substitution and normalization, the non-constant literals in one expression are a subset of the terms in the other. Only when two expressions are compatible can their relationship be determined symbolically. Two congruent expressions are also compatible. For the purpose of comparison, two compatible expressions, E^1 and E^2, can be classified as follows:

1. E^1 **and** E^2 **contains no gating functions:** The expressions can be compared by simplifying $E^1 - E^2$ symbolically. Their relationship can be determined if the result is a constant.
2. **Only one of** E^1 **and** E^2 **contains gating functions:** The comparison will be based on the arguments of the γ function. To illustrate the method, assume that $E^2 = \gamma(P, V_t, V_f)$, where V_t and V_f may also contain gating functions. To determine whether $E^1 > E^2$, we reduce it to case 1 using the following necessary and sufficient condition:

$$(E^1 > \gamma(P, V_t, V_f)) \equiv (E^1 > V_t) \wedge (E^1 > V_f)$$

   If V_t, V_f contains any gating function, the same procedure should be used recursively on the right-hand side of the above equation. The result then can be evaluated as in case 1. An equivalent approach is to compute the minimum and maximum values for E^2 using the technique discussed above. Because E^1 does not contain any gating function, it can be proven that:

$$(E^1 > E^2) \equiv (E^1 > \max(E^2))$$

3. **Both** E^1 **and** E^2 **contain gating functions:** There are several ways to handle this case. We will illustrate just one here. Assume again that $E^2 = \gamma(P, V_t, V_f)$. To prove $E^1 > E^2$, the necessary and sufficient condition is:

$$E^1 > \gamma(P, V_t, V_f) \equiv (E^1(P) > V_t) \wedge (E^1(\neg P) > V_f)$$

Because E^1 contains a gating function, in the above equation the path projections $E^1(P)$ and $E^1(\neg P)$ are necessary to cast the branching conditions to E^1. For instance, if $E^1 = \gamma(P, V'_t, V'_f)$, the condition can be evaluated as follows:

$$(\gamma(P, V'_t, V'_f)(P) > V_t) \wedge (\gamma(P, V'_t, V'_f)(\neg P) > V_f) = (V'_t > V_t) \wedge (V'_f > V_f)$$

Each application of this rule eliminates one gating function. It is applied recursively until the right-hand side is free of gating functions. The problem is then reduced to case 2.

We will call these three rules *distribution rules*. Rule 3 subsumes rule 2 because path projection has no effect on an expression that does not contain any gating function. Note that for determining equalities, techniques based on structural isomorphism cannot identify equalities when the order of the γ functions in two expressions is different. Using the distribution rules, we can identify those equalities.

The distribution rules discussed also apply to more complex expressions. Because the gating functions capture only the predicates for condition branches, regular functions can be safely distributed into arguments of the gating functions. The rule is as follows:

$$\mathcal{F}(\mathcal{G}(P, X, Y), Z) = \mathcal{G}(P, \mathcal{F}(X, Z), \mathcal{F}(Y, Z))$$

where $\mathcal{F}$ is a regular function, and $\mathcal{G}$ is a gating function. For example, $\gamma(P, X, Y)^2 + expr = \gamma(P, X^2 + expr, Y^2 + expr)$.

Using this rule, we can move a gating function to the outermost position of an expression. For example, consider $E^2 = \gamma(P, V_t, V_f) + exp$. This expression can be transformed to $\gamma(P, V_t + exp(P), V_f + exp(\neg P))$. In the analysis algorithm, this transformation is deferred until distribution has been applied to the γ function in order to allow the common components in E^1 to be cancelled out with $\gamma(P, V_t, V_f)$ or exp.

The following are some examples of how to use these rules. We used rule 2 in Section 4.2:

$$J_3 = \gamma(P, JMAX_1 - 1, JMAX_1)$$
$$\leq JMAX_1$$

In the following example, we use rule 3 to derive the condition for $JUP_2 > JLOW_2$ under P in the last example of Section 4.5:

$$(JUP_2 > JLOW_2) \equiv \gamma(P, JMAX - 1, JMAX) > \gamma(P, 2, 1)$$
$$\equiv \gamma(P, JMAX - 1 > 2, JMAX > 1)$$
$$\equiv \gamma(P, JMAX > 3, JMAX > 1)$$

When two predicated expressions contain many predicated conditional values, using distribution rule 3 can cause the expressions size to grow rapidly. In our experience, restricting the nesting levels of gating functions to 2 seems to be sufficient for most analysis. For levels larger than 2, the expressions usually are not comparable. For those complicated expressions, we can compute the bounds and ignore the predicates by using the following approximation rule:

$$(\min(E^1) > \max(E^2)) \supset (E^1 > E^2)$$

4.7 Recurrence and the μ Function

Backward substitution of an expression involving a μ function will form a recurrence because of the back edge in a loop. The value carried from the previous iteration of a loop is placed in the third argument of a μ function. Hence, the rule for the substitution of a μ function is to substitute the third argument of the μ function until it becomes an expression of the variable itself or an expression of another μ assigned variable. This is illustrated in the following example:

$$
\begin{aligned}
&\text{L:} \quad \text{DO I = 1, N} \\
&\qquad \{J_1 = \mu((I = 1, N), J_0, J_3)\} \\
&\qquad \text{IF (P) THEN } J_2 = J_1 + A \\
&\qquad J_3 = \gamma(P, J_2, J_1) \\
&\qquad ENDDO
\end{aligned}
$$

Substituting the third argument in the μ function leads to:

$$
\begin{aligned}
J_1 &= \mu((I = 1, N), J_0, L_3) \\
&= \mu((I = 1, N), J_0, \gamma(P, J_2, J_1)) \\
&= \mu((I = 1, N), J_0, \gamma(P, J_1 + A, J_1))
\end{aligned}
$$

The recurrence can be interpreted as the following λ-function over the loop index.

$$\lambda i.(J_1(i)) \equiv \gamma(i = 1, J_0, \gamma(P, J_1(i - 1) + A, J_1(i - 1)))$$

This λ-function can be interpreted in the terms of a recursive sequence in combinatorial mathematics as follows:

$$J_0 = J_0$$

$$
J_i = \begin{cases} J_{i-1} + 1 & \text{if (P)} \\ J_{i-1} & \text{otherwise} \end{cases} \quad \text{for } i \in [1 : N]
$$

After the mathematical form of a recurrence is identified, standard methods for solving a linear recurrence can be used to find a closed form. For instance, if P is always true and A is loop invariant, then $J_1(i)$ is an induction variable with a closed form of $J_0 + (i - 1) * A$. When P is always true and A is a linear reference to an array (e.g., A=X(i)), then $J_1(i)$ is a sum reduction over X.

Wolfe and others [Wol92] developed a comprehensive technique to classify and solve recurrence sequences using a graph representation of SSA. In this graph representation, a recurrence is characterized by a Strongly Connected Region (SCR) of use-def chains. The backward substitution technique for μ functions is equivalent to Wolfe's SCR approach. Their technique for computing the closed form can be directly used in our scheme. However, we believe that our backward substitution scheme, which works directly with the algebra of names, functions, and expressions, is better than their approach that works indirectly through graph and edges. We also can deal with the cases where no closed form expression can be obtained. For instance, if the condition P is loop invariant, symbolic substitution can determine that the value of $J_1(i)$ is either $J_0 + (i - 1) * A$ or J_0.

4.8 Bounds of Monotonic Variables

Because of conditional branches, a variable can be conditionally incremented by different amounts in different iterations of a loop. These variables cannot be represented in a non-recursive form. However, knowing that a variable is monotonically increasing or decreasing is sometimes useful for dependence analysis.

When the closed form of a recurrence cannot be determined, it still may be possible to compute a bound by selecting the γ argument that has the maximal or minimal increment to the recurrence. In the last example

$$
\begin{aligned}
&L: \quad \text{DO I = 1, N} \\
&\qquad \{J_1 = \mu((I = 1, N), J_0, J_3)\} \\
&\qquad \text{IF (P) THEN } J_2 = J_1 + A \\
&\qquad J_3 = \gamma(P, J_2, J_1) \\
&\qquad ENDDO
\end{aligned}
$$

the bounds for J_1 can be obtained as follows:

$$
\begin{aligned}
max(J_1) \quad &\leq max(\mu((I = 1, N), J_0, \gamma(P, J_1 + A, J_1))) \\
&= \mu((I = 1, N), J_0, max(\gamma(P, J_1 + A, J_1))) \\
&= \mu((I = 1, N), J_0, J_1 + A) \\
min(J_1) \quad &\geq min(\mu((I = 1, N), J_0, \gamma(P, J_1 + A, J_1))) \\
&= \mu((I = 1, N), J_0, min(\gamma(P, J_1 + A, J_1))) \\
&= \mu((I = 1, N), J_0, J_1)
\end{aligned}
$$

The resulting two recurrence functions now can be solved to obtain the upper bound $J_0 + N * A$ and the lower bound J_0.

4.9 Index Array

The use of array elements as subscripts makes dependence analysis and array privatization more difficult than when only scalars are used. When the values of an index array depend on the program's input data, runtime analysis must be used. However, in many cases, the index arrays used in the program are assigned symbolic expressions. For instance, a wide range of applications use regular grids. Although the number of grids is input dependent, the structure of the grid is fixed. The structure is statically assigned to index arrays with symbolic expressions of input variables. In these cases, the value of an index array can be determined at compile-time. Consider the following segment of code:

$$
\begin{aligned}
&\texttt{L:} \quad \texttt{DO J=1, JMAX} \\
&\qquad JPLUS(J) = J + 1 \\
&\qquad ENDDO \\
&\qquad JPLUS(JMAX) = Q \\
&\texttt{U:} \quad \ldots
\end{aligned}
$$

It is possible to determine at compile-time that the array element $JPLUS(J)$ has the value of J + 1 for $J \in [1, JMAX - 1]$ and Q for $J = JMAX$. We can use the GSA representation to find out the value of JPLUS(J) at statement U. To this end, we use an extension of the SSA representation to include arrays [CFR+91]. This extension is obtained by applying the following three transformations:

1. Create a new array name for each array assignment;
2. Use the subscript to identify which element is assigned; and
3. Replace the assignment with an update function α (*array, subscript, value*).

For example, an assignment of the form JPLUS(I) = exp will be converted to $JPLUS_1 = \alpha(JPLUS_0, I, exp)$. The semantics of the α function is that $JPLUS_1(I)$ receives the value of exp while the other elements of $JPLUS_1$ will take the values of the corresponding elements of $JPLUS_0$. This representation maintains the single assignment property for array names. Hence, the def-use chain is still maintained by the links associated with unique array names. Using this extension, the last loop can be transformed into the following GSA form:

$$
\begin{aligned}
&\texttt{L:} \quad \texttt{DO J = 1, JMAX} \\
&\qquad \{JPLUS_2 = \mu((J = 1, JMAX), JPLUS_0, JPLUS_1)\} \\
&\qquad JPLUS_1 = \alpha(JPLUS_2, J, J + 1) \\
&\qquad ENDDO \\
&\qquad JPLUS_3 = \alpha(JPLUS_2, JMAX, Q)
\end{aligned}
$$

To determine the value of an element $JPLUS_3(K)$ in $JPLUS_3$, we can use backward substitution as follows:

$$\begin{aligned}
JPLUS_3(K) &= \alpha(JPLUS_2, JMAX, Q)(K)\\
&= \gamma(K = JMAX, Q, JPLUS_2(K))\\
&= \gamma(K = JMAX, Q, \mu((J = 1, JMAX), JPLUS_0, JPLUS_1)(K))\\
&= \gamma(K = JMAX, Q, \gamma(1 \leq K \leq JMAX, JPLUS_1(K), JPLUS_0(K)))\\
&= \gamma(K = JMAX, Q, \gamma(1 \leq K \leq JMAX, K + 1, JPLUS_0(K)))
\end{aligned}$$

In the preceding evaluation process, an expression of the form $\alpha(X, i, exp)(j)$ is evaluated to $\gamma(j = i, exp, X(j))$. An expression of the form $\mu(L, Y, Z)(j)$ is instantiated to a list of γ functions that select different expressions for different values of j. These evaluation rules are straightforwardly derived from the definitions of the gate functions. To avoid unnecessary array renaming, GSA conversion can be performed only on those arrays that are used as subscripts.

4.10 Conditional Data Flow Analysis

Conditionally defined and used arrays can be privatized if the condition at the use site subsumes the condition at the definition site. In this section, we present a technique that uses gating functions to incorporate conditions into a data flow analysis framework.

Traditional data flow analysis ignores the predicate that determines if a conditional branch is taken. Therefore, it cannot propagate the conditional data flow information. Consider the following example:

```
          DO I = 1, N
             IF (P) THEN
   D1:          A(1:M) = ...
             ELSE
   D2:          B(1:M) = ...
             ENDIF
   U:        IF (P) THEN
   U1:          ...= A(1:M)
             ELSE
   U2:          ...= B(1:M)
             ENDIF
          ENDDO
```

In the data flow analysis, the must-reach definitions at the ends of statements D1 and D2 are:

$$MRD_{out}(D1) = \{A(1 : M), I\}$$
$$MRD_{out}(D2) = \{B(1 : M), I\}$$

Hence, the must-reach definitions at the top of join node U is obtained by:

$$
\begin{aligned}
MRD_{in}(U) &= MRD_{out}(D1) \cap MRD_{out}(D2) \\
&= \{A(1:M), I\} \cap \{B(1:M), I\} \\
&= \{I\}
\end{aligned}
$$

Because the conservative intersection operator $\cap$ does not contain the conditional flow information, the conditional reaching definition is lost at the join node. To solve the problem of the conservative intersection operator and to propagate the conditional reaching definitions, we will use the gating function at the join node U as the intersection operator $\cap_G$. That is,

$$
\begin{aligned}
MRD_{in}(U) &= MRD_{out}(D1) \cap_G MRD_{out}(D2) \\
&= \gamma(P, MRD_{out}(D1), MRD_{out}(D2)) \\
&= \gamma(P, \{A(1:M), I\}, \{B(1:M), I\}) \\
&= \{I, \gamma(P, A(1:M), B(1:M))\}
\end{aligned}
$$

The conditional reaching definitions represented by the gating expression then can be propagated in the control flow graph. At use sites U1 and U2, the control dependence predicate P can be used to prove that the use conditions always subsume the definition conditions.

4.11 Implementation and Experiments

The techniques for predicated conditional value analysis, bounds analysis of monotonic variables, index array analysis, and the conditional data flow analysis using gated intersection have been implemented in the Polaris parallelizing compiler. Currently, they serve to provide symbolic information for conditional array privatization.

Table 4.2 shows the improvement we obtained using the symbolic analysis for conditional array privatization. The columns in the table show the number of privatizable arrays identified with and without symbolic analysis. Of the six programs tested, four show an increased number of privatizable arrays. Also shown are: the increases in parallel loop coverage expressed as a percentage of the total execution time; the speedups obtained on an 8 processor SGI Challenge; and the techniques applied in each program.

Program	Pri. (w/o SA)	Pri. (with SA)	Increased Coverage %	Speedups (8 proc)	Cond. Value	Bounds Recurrence	Index Array
ARC2D	0	2	15.3	4.5	x	x	x
BDNA	16	19	33.6	4.5	x	x	x
FLO52	4	4	0.0	2.6			
MDG	18	19	97.7	4.9	x		x
OCEAN	4	7	42.7	1.2	x		
TRFD	4	4	0.0	2.7			

Table 4.2. Effect of Symbolic Analysis on Array Privatization

The experiment shows that a small increase in the number of private arrays can make a big difference in the parallelism discovered. In *MDG*, privatization with symbolic analysis privatizes only one more array than that without symbolic analysis, yet it makes a loop that accounts for 97 percent of the program execution time to be parallel. Out of the six programs, four require demand-driven symbolic analysis techniques to parallelize their important loops. These loops account for 15 to 97 percent of the execution time of the programs. Sequential execution of these loops will prevent any meaningful speedup. These results show that advanced symbolic analysis techniques are very important to parallelize these applications.

Among the analysis techniques, the predicated conditional value is used most often, followed by statically assigned symbolic index array analysis. The bounded recurrence column shows only the cases where there is no closed form for the recurrence due to conditional increment. Induction variables with closed forms occur in all these programs. Currently, Polaris uses other techniques for induction variable substitution. The effect of induction variable substitution on array privatization is not shown here.

The demand-driven symbolic analysis part of the privatizer requires less than 5 percent of the total execution time of the privatizer, primarily because symbolic analysis is infrequently required. The small increase in time is justified by the additional parallel loops we can identify using the advanced techniques. A command-line parameter is used in Polaris to control the number of nested γ functions allowed in any predicated expression. Setting this parameter makes it possible to restrict the number of nested γ functions to the limit specified by the switch.

The array privatizer in Polaris has been converted to work directly on the GSA representation. Using the GSA representation of use-def chains, the privatizer shows an average speedup of 6 when compared with the original implementation based on the control flow graph.

5. Related Work

Array privatization was first identified as one of the most important transformations for parallelizing large applications in [EHLP91]. This is not surprising, because the usual programming practice in conventional languages is to reuse memory. Scalar expansion has long been used in vectorizing compilers to remove scalar reuse induced dependences. When the granularity of parallelism is increased to the outer loops, memory-related dependences caused by array reuse become an important obstacle to parallelization.

Previous work on eliminating memory-related dependence focused on scalar expansion [Wol82], scalar privatization [BCFH89], scalar renaming [CF87], and array expansion [PW86] [Fea88]. Recent work in array induced memory-related dependence includes array privatization based on dependence analysis [MAL92], and array privatization based on array data flow analysis [TP93a, TP93b, Li92].

In symbolic analysis, some of the techniques designed in the past are based on *path values* (i.e., the set of symbolic values of a variable on all possible paths reaching a program point.) Corresponding to each path there is a *path condition* (i.e., a boolean expression that is true if the path is executed) [CR85, CHT79]. These techniques have exponential time and space requirements that limit their applicability in practical situations.

The GSA representation of symbolic expression in this chapter is a new way to represent *predicated path values*. With GSA, conditions and values are represented in a compact way. Expression in GSA can be manipulated like normal arithmetic expressions except that special treatment is needed for gating functions. We also use the iterative control dependences to represent path conditions.

Symbolic analysis is also related to the problem of automatic proof of invariant assertions in programs. Symbolic execution can be considered as abstract interpretation [CH92]. In [CH78], abstract interpretation is used to discover the linear relationships between variables. It can be used to propagate symbolic linear expressions as possible values for symbolic variables. However, the predicate guarding the conditional possible values is not included in the representation and cannot be propagated. The *parafrase-2* compiler uses a similar approach to evaluate symbolic expressions. It uses a *join function* to compute the intersection of possible values at the confluence nodes of the flow graph to cut down the amount of maintained information. Again, the predicated conditional information is lost in the join function. Abstract interpretation also has been used in [AH90] for induction variable substitution.

The demand-driven approach in this chapter is a special case of the more general approach of *Subgoal Induction* [MW77]. The internal representation chosen facilitates the demand-driven approach. (1) In the SSA representation, the variable name is unique and the use-def chain is embedded in the unique variable name. (2) In GSA, backward substitution can be done by following the use-def chain in the name without going through the flow graph. Using the GSA sparse representation and the demand-driven approach, our approach can perform more aggressive analysis only on demand.

The SSA form has been used to determine the equivalence of symbolic variables and to construct global value graph in a program [AWZ88] [RWZ88]. *Nascent* [Wol92] uses SSA to do a comprehensive analysis of recurrences. Its internal representation does not include the gating predicate. The SSA representation in Nascent is achieved through an explicit representation of use-def chains, which they call a demand-driven form of SSA. Their approach for constructing strongly connected regions for recurrences in the graph is similar to our backward substitution of names. GSA also has been used in *Parascope* to build the global value graph [Hav93]. Our demand-driven backward substitution in GSA and our use of control dependences to project values are unique.

Currently, the most used algorithm for building SSA form is given in [CFR$^+$91]. GSA was introduced in [BMO90] as a part of the Program Dependence Web (PDW), which is an extension of the Program Dependence Graph (PDG) [FOW87]. An algorithm for constructing GSA from PDG and SSA is given in [BMO90]. Havlak [Hav93] develops another algorithm for building GSA from a program control flow graph and SSA. Recently, the authors developed an algorithm to efficiently construct the GSA directly from the control flow graph [TP94]. Control dependence was introduced in [FOW87] as part of PDG. The SSA construction paper [CFR$^+$91] presents an algorithm for building control dependences.

Acknowledgement. The authors would like to thank their coworkers in the Polaris group at University of Illinois at Urbana-Champaign for their suggestions and support throughout this work. Sheila Clark's help in editing this chapter is also gratefully acknowledged.

The work reported in this chapter was supported in part by Army contracts DABT63-92-C-0033 and DABT63-95-C-0097.

References

[AH90] Z. Ammarguellat and W. L. Harrison. Automatic recognition of induction variables and recurrence relations by abstract interpretation. In *Proc. of the ACM SIGPLAN'90 Conference on Programming Language Design and Implementation*, pages 283–295. ACM Press, New York, 1990.

[ASU86] A. V. Aho, R. Sethi, and J.D. Ullman. *Compilers: Principles, Techniques, and Tools*. Addison-Wesley, 1986.

[AWZ88] B. Alpern, M. N. Wegman, and F. K. Zadeck. Detecting equality of variables in programs. In *Proc. of the 15th ACM SIGPLAN Symposium on Principles of Programming Languages*, pages 1–11. ACM Press, New York, 1988.

[Ban88] Utpal Banerjee. *Dependence Analysis for Supercomputing*. Kluwer Academic Publishers, 1988.

[BCFH89] M. Burke, R. Cytron, J. Ferrante, and W. Hsieh. Automatic generation of nested, fork-join parallelism. *Journal of Supercomputing*, pages 71–88, 1989.

[BE94a] William Blume and Rudolf Eigenmann. Symbolic analysis techniques needed for the effective parallelization of the perfect benchmarks. Technical Report 1332, Univ. of Illinois at Urbana-Champaign, Cntr. for Supercomputing Res. & Dev., January 1994.

[BE94b] William Blume and Rudolf Eigenmann. The Range Test: A Dependence Test for Symbolic, Non-linear Expressions. In *Proceedings of Supercomputing'94, November 1994, Washington D.C.*, pages 528–537. IEEE Computer Society Press, Los Alamitos, CA, November 1994.

[BEF$^+$94] Bill Blume, Rudolf Eigenmann, Keith Faigin, John Grout, Jay Hoeflinger, David Padua, Paul Petersen, Bill Pottenger, Lawrence Rauchwerger, Peng Tu, and Stephen Weatherford. Polaris: The Next Generation in Parallelizing Compilers. In K. Pingali, U. Banerjee, D. Gelernter, A. Nicolau, and

D. Padua, editors, *Lecture Notes in Computer Science No. 892: Languages and Compilers for Parallel Computing, 7th Int'l. Workshop. Ithaca, NY*, pages 141–154. Springer-Verlag, August 1994.

[BMO90] R. Ballance, A. Maccabe, and K. Ottenstein. The program dependence web: a representation supporting control-, data-, and demand-driven interpretation of imperative languages. In *Proceedings of the ACM SIGPLAN'90 Conference on Programming Language Design and Implementatio*, pages 257–271. ACM Press, New York, June 1990.

[CF87] Ron Cytron and Jeanne Ferrante. What's in a name? or the value of renaming for parallelism detection and storage allocation. In *Proc. 1987 International Conf. on Parallel Processing*, pages 19–27. The Pennsylvania State University Press, August 1987.

[CFR+91] Ron Cytron, Jeanne Ferrante, Barry K. Rosen, Mark N. Wegman, and F. Kenneth Zadeck. Efficiently computing static single assignment form and the control dependence graph. *ACM Transactions on Programming Languages and Systems*, 13(4):451–490, October 1991.

[CH78] P. Cousot and N. Halbwachs. Automatic discovery of linear restraints among variables of a program. In *Proceedings of the 5th Annual ACM Symposium on Principles of Programming Languages*, pages 84–97. ACM Press, New York, January 1978.

[CH92] P. Cousot and N. Halbwachs. Abstract interpretation and application to logic programs. *Journal of Logic Programming*, 13(2–3):103–179, 1992.

[CHT79] T. E. Cheatham, G. H. Holloway, and J. A. Townley. Symbolic evaluation and the analysis of programs. *IEEE Transactions on Software Engineering*, 5(4):402–417, 1979.

[CK88a] D. Callahan and K. Kennedy. Analysis of interprocedural side effects in a parallel programming environment. *Journal of Parallel and Distributed Computing*, 5:517–550, 1988.

[CK88b] D. Callahan and K. Kennedy. Compiling programs for distributed-memory multiprocessors. *Journal of Supercomputing*, 2:151–169, October 1988.

[CR85] L. A. Clarke and D. J. Richardson. Applications of symbolic evaluation. *Journal of Systems and Software*, 5(1):15–35, 1985.

[EHLP91] Rudolf Eigenmann, Jay Hoeflinger, Zhiyuan Li, and David Padua. Experience in the Automatic Parallelization of Four Perfect-Benchmark Programs. In U. Banerjee, D. Gelernter, A. Nicolau, and D. Padua, editors, *Lecture Notes in Computer Science No. 589: Languages and Compilers for Parallel Computing, 4th Int'l. Workshop, Santa Clara, CA*, pages 65–83. Springer-Verlag, August 1991.

[Fea88] P. Feautrier. Array expansion. In *Proc. 1988 ACM Int'l Conf. on Supercomputing*, pages 429–441. ACM Press, New York, July 1988.

[FOW87] J. Ferrante, K. J. Ottenstein, and J. D. Warren. The program dependency graph and its uses in optimization. *ACM Transactions on Programming Languages and Systems*, 9(3):319–349, June 1987.

[GSW] M. P. Gerlek, E. Stoltz, and M. Wolfe. Beyond induction variables: Detecting and classifying sequences using a demand-driven ssa form. *ACM Transactions on Programming Languages and Systems*.

[Hav93] Paul Havlak. Construction of thinned gated single-assignment form. In U. Banerjee, D. Gelernter, A. Nicolau, and D. Padua, editors, *Lecture Notes in Computer Science No. 768: Languages and Compilers for Parallel Computing, 6th Int'l. Workshop. Portland, OR*, pages 477–499. Springer-Verlag, August 1993.

[HP92] M. R. Haghighat and C. D. Polychronopoulos. Symbolic program analysis and optimization for parallelizing compilers. In U. Banerjee, D. Gelernter,

A. Nicolau, and D. Padua, editors, *Lecture Notes in Computer Science No. 757: Languages and Compilers for Parallel Computing, 5th Int'l. Workshop. New Haven, CT*, pages 538–562. Springer-Verlag, August 1992.

[Li92] Zhiyuan Li. Array privatization for parallel execution of loops. In *Proc. 1992 ACM Int'l Conf. on Supercomputing*, pages 313–322. ACM Press, New York, 1992.

[MAL92] D. E. Maydan, S. P. Amarasinghe, and M. S. Lam. Data dependence and data-flow analysis of arrays. In U. Banerjee, D. Gelernter, A. Nicolau, and D. Padua, editors, *Lecture Notes in Computer Science No. 757: Languages and Compilers for Parallel Computing, 5th Int'l. Workshop. New Haven, CT*, pages 434–448. Springer-Verlag, August 1992.

[MW77] J. H. Morris and B. Wegbreit. Subgoal induction. *Communication of ACM*, 20(4):209–222, 1977.

[PW86] D. Padua and M. Wolfe. Advanced compiler optimizations for supercomputers. *Communications of the ACM*, 29(12):1184–1201, December 1986.

[RP89] A. Rogers and K. Pingali. Process decomposition through locality of reference. In *Proc. the ACM SIGPLAN '89 Conference on Program Language Design and Implementation*. ACM Press, New York, June 1989.

[RWZ88] B. K. Rosen, M. N. Wegman, and F. K. Zadeck. Global value numbers and redundant computation. In *Proc. of the 15th ACM SIGPLAN Symposium on Principles of Programming Languages*, pages 12–27. ACM Press, New York, 1988.

[TP93a] Peng Tu and David Padua. Array privatization for shared and distributed memory machines. In *Proc. 2nd Workshop on Languages, Compilers, and Run-Time Environments for Distributed Memory Machines, in ACM SIGPLAN Notices*, January 1993.

[TP93b] Peng Tu and David Padua. Automatic array privatization. In U. Banerjee, D. Gelernter, A. Nicolau, and D. Padua, editors, *Lecture Notes in Computer Science No. 768: Languages and Compilers for Parallel Computing, 6th Int'l. Workshop. Portland, OR*, pages 500–521. Springer-Verlag, August 1993.

[TP94] Peng Tu and David Padua. Efficient Building and Placing of Gating Functions. *Proceedings of the SIGPLAN'95 Conference on Programming Language Design and Implementation, June 1995*, 1994.

[Wol82] Michael Joseph Wolfe. Optimizing supercompilers for supercomputers. Technical Report UIUCDCS-R-82-1105, Department of Computer Science, University of Illinois, October 1982.

[Wol92] Michael Wolfe. Beyond induction variables. In *Proceedings of the ACM SIGPLAN'90 Conference on Programming Language Design and Implementatio*, pages 162–174. ACM Press, New York, 1992.

[ZBG88] H. Zima, H.-J. Bast, and M. Gerndt. Superb: A tool for semi-automatic MIMD/SIMD parallelization. *Parallel Computing*, 6:1–18, 1988.

[ZC91] Hans Zima and Barbara Chapman. *Supercompilers for Parallel and Vector Computers*. ACM Press, 1991.

[ZY87] Chuan-Qi Zhu and Pen-Chung Yew. A scheme to enforce data dependence on large multiprocessor systems. *IEEE Transactions on Software Engineering*, 13(6):726–739, June 1987.

Section III :
Communication Optimizations

Chapter 9. Optimal Tiling for Minimizing Communication in Distributed Shared-Memory Multiprocessors

Anant Agarwal[1], David Kranz[1], Rajeev Barua[2], and Venkat Natarajan[3]

[1] Laboratory for Computer Science, Massachusetts Institute of Technology, Cambridge, MA 02139
[2] Department of Electrical & Computer Engineering, University of Maryland, College Park, MD 20742, barua@eng.umd.edu
[3] Wireless Systems Center, Semiconductor Products Sector Motorola

Summary. This paper presents a theoretical framework for automatically partitioning parallel loops and data arrays for cache-coherent NUMA multiprocessors to minimize both cache coherency traffic and remote memory references. While several previous papers have looked at hyperplane partitioning of iteration spaces to reduce communication traffic, the problem of deriving the *optimal* tiling parameters for minimal communication in loops with general affine index expressions has remained open. Our paper solves this open problem by presenting a method for deriving an optimal hyperparallelepiped tiling of iteration spaces for minimal communication in multiprocessors with caches. Our framework uses matrices to represent iteration and data space mappings and the notion of uniformly intersecting references to capture temporal locality in array references. We introduce the notion of data footprints to estimate the communication traffic between processors and use linear algebraic methods and lattice theory to compute precisely the size of data footprints. We show that the same theoretical framework can also be used to determine optimal tiling parameters for both data and loop partitioning in distributed memory multicomputers. We also present a heuristic for combined partitioning of loops and data arrays to maximize the probability that references hit in the cache, and to maximize the probability cache misses are satisfied by the local memory. We have implemented this framework in a compiler for Alewife, a distributed shared memory multiprocessor.

1. Introduction

Cache-based multiprocessors are attractive because they seem to allow the programmer to ignore the issues of data partitioning and placement. Because caches dynamically copy data close to where it is needed, repeat references to the same piece of data do not require communication over the network, and hence reduce the need for careful data layout. However, the performance of cache-coherent systems is heavily predicated on the degree of temporal locality in the access patterns of the processor. Loop partitioning for cache-coherent multiprocessors is an effort to increase the percentage of references that hit in the cache.

The degree of reuse of data, or conversely, the volume of communication of data, depends both on the algorithm and on the partitioning of work among the processors. (In fact, partitioning of the computation is often considered to be a facet of an algorithm.) For example, it is well known that a matrix

S. Pande, D.P. Agrawal (Eds.): Compiler Optimizations for Scalable PS, LNCS 1808, pp. 285-338, 2001.
© Springer-Verlag Berlin Heidelberg 2001

multiply computation distributed to the processors by square blocks has a much higher degree of reuse than the matrix multiply distributed by rows or columns.

Loop partitioning can be done by the programmer, by the run time system, or by the compiler. Relegating the partitioning task to the programmer defeats the central purpose of building cache-coherent shared-memory systems. While partitioning can be done at run time (for example, see [1,2]), it is hard for the run time system to optimize for cache locality because much of the information required to compute communication patterns is either unavailable at run time or expensive to obtain. Thus compile-time partitioning of parallel loops is important.

This paper focuses on the following problem in the context of cache-coherent multiprocessors. Given a program consisting of parallel do loops (of the form shown in Fig. 2.1 in Sect. 2.1), how do we derive the optimal tile shapes of the iteration-space partitions to minimize the communication traffic between processors. We also indicate how our framework can be used for loop and data partitioning for distributed memory machines, both with and without caches.

1.1 Contributions and Related Work

This paper develops a unified theoretical framework that can be used for loop partitioning in cache-coherent multiprocessors, for loop and data partitioning in multicomputers with local memory, and for loop and data partitioning in cache coherent NUMA multiprocessors. The central contribution of this paper is a method for deriving an optimal hyperparallelepiped tiling of iteration spaces to minimize communication. The tiling specifies both the shape and size of iteration space tiles. Our framework allows the partitioning of doall loops accessing multiple arrays, where the index expressions in array accesses can be any affine function of the indices.

Our analysis uses the notion of uniformly intersecting references to categorize the references within a loop into classes that will yield cache locality. This notion helps specify precisely the set of references that have substantially overlapping data sets. Overlap produces temporal locality in cache accesses. A similar concept of uniformly generated references has been used in earlier work in the context of *reuse* and iteration space tiling [3,4].

The notion of data footprints is introduced to capture the combined set of data accesses made by references within each uniformly intersecting class. (The term *footprint* was originally coined by Stone and Thiebaut [5].) Then, an algorithm to compute precisely the total size of the data footprint for a given loop partition is presented. Precisely computing the size of the set of data elements accessed by a loop tile was itself an important and open problem. While general optimization methods can be applied to minimize the size of the data footprint and derive the corresponding loop partitions, we demonstrate several important special cases where the optimization problem is very simple. The size of data footprints can also be used to guide program transformations to achieve better cache performance in uniprocessors as well.

Although there have been several papers on hyperplane partitioning of iteration spaces, the problem of deriving the optimal hyperparallelepiped tile parameters for general affine index expressions has remained open. For example, Irigoin and Triolet [6] introduce the notion of loop partitioning with multiple hyperplanes which results in hyperparallelepiped tiles. The purpose of tiling in their case is to provide parallelism across tiles, and vector processing and data locality within a tile. They propose a set of basic constraints that should be met by any partitioning and derive the conditions under which the hyperplane partitioning satisfies these constraints.

Although their paper describes useful properties of hyperplane partitioning, it does not address the issue of automatically generating the tile parameters. Careful analysis of the mapping from the iteration space to the data space is very important in automating the partitioning process. Our paper describes an algorithm for automatically computing the partition based on the notion of cumulative footprints, derived from the mapping from iteration space to data space.

Abraham and Hudak [7] considered loop partitioning in multiprocessors with caches. However, they dealt only with index expressions of the form index variable plus a constant. They assumed that the array dimension was equal to the loop nesting and focused on rectangular and hexagonal tiles. Furthermore, the code body was restricted to an update of $A[i,j]$.

Our framework, however, does not place these restrictions on the code body. It is able to handle much more general index expressions, and produce parallelogram partitions if desired. We also show that when Abraham and Hudak's methods can be applied to a given loop nest, our theoretical framework reproduces their results.

Ramanujam and Sadayappan [8] deal with data partitioning in multicomputers with local memory and use a matrix formulation; their results do not apply to multiprocessors with caches. Their theory produces communication-free hyperplane partitions for loops with affine index expressions when such partitions exist. However, when communication-free partitions do not exist, they can deal only with index expression of the form variable plus a constant offset. They further require the array dimension to be equal to the loop nesting.

In contrast, our framework is able to discover optimal partitions in cases where communication free partitions are not possible, and we do not restrict the loop nesting to be equal to array dimension. In addition, we show that our framework correctly produces partitions identical to those of Ramanujam and Sadayappan when communication free partitions do exist.

In a recent paper, Anderson and Lam [9] derive communication-free partitions for multicomputers when such partitions exist, and block loops into squares otherwise. Our notion of cumulative footprints allows us to derive optimal partitions even when communication-free partitions do not exist.

Gupta and Banerjee [10] address the problem of automatic data partitioning by analyzing the entire program. Although our paper deals with loop and data partitioning for a single loop only, the following differences in the machine model and the program model lead to problems that are not addressed by Gupta and Banerjee: (1) The data distributions considered by them do not include general hyperparallelepipeds. In order to deal with hyperparallelepipeds, one requires the analysis of communication presented in our paper. (2) Their communication model does not take into account caches. (3) They deal with simple index expressions of the form $c_1 * i + c_2$ and not a general affine function of the loop indices.

Our work complements the work of Wolf and Lam [3] and Schreiber and Dongarra [11]. Wolfe and Lam derive loop transformations (and tile the iteration space) to improve data locality in multiprocessors with caches. They use matrices to model transformations and use the notion of equivalence classes within the set of uniformly generated references to identify valid loop transformations to improve the degree of temporal and spatial locality within a given loop nest. Schreiber and Dongarra briefly address the problem of deriving optimal hyperparallelepiped iteration space tiles to minimize communication traffic (they refer to it as I/O requirements). However their work differs from this paper in the following ways: (1) Their machine model does not have a processor cache. (2) The data space corresponding to an array reference and the iteration space are isomorphic. These restrictions make the problem of computing the communication traffic much simpler. Also, one of the main issues addressed by Schreiber and Dongarra is the *atomicity requirement* of the tiles which is related to the dependence vectors and this paper is not concerned with those requirements as it is assumed that the iterations can be executed in parallel.

Ferrante, Sarkar, and Thrash [12] address the problem of estimating the number of cache misses for a nest of loops. This problem is similar to our problem of finding the size of the cumulative footprint, but differs in these ways: (1) We consider a tile in the iteration space and not the entire iteration space; our tiles can be hyperparallelepipeds in general. (2) We partition the references into uniformly intersecting sets, which makes the problem computationally more tractable, since it allows us to deal with only the tile at the origin. (3) Our treatment of coupled subscripts is much simpler, since we look at maximal independent columns, as shown in Sect. 5.2.

1.2 Overview of the Paper

The rest of this paper is structured as follows. In Sect. 2 we state our system model and our program-level assumptions. in Sect. 3 we first present a few examples to illustrate the basic ideas behind loop partitioning; we then discuss the notion of data partitioning, and when it is important. In Sect. 4

we develop the theoretical framework for partitioning and presents several additional examples. In Sect. 5 we extend the basic framework to handle more general expressions; Sections 6 and 7 indicate extensions to the basic framework to handle data partitioning and more general types of systems. The framework for both loop and data partitioning has been implemented in the compiler system for the Alewife multiprocessor. The implementation of our compiler system and a sampling of results is presented in Sect. 8, and Sect. 9 concludes the paper.

2. Problem Domain and Assumptions

This paper focuses on the problem of partitioning loops in cache-coherent shared-memory multiprocessors. Partitioning involves deciding which loop iterations will run collectively in a thread of computation. Computing loop partitions involves finding the set of iterations which when run in parallel minimizes the volume of communication generated in the system. This section describes the types of programs currently handled by our framework and the structure of the system assumed by our analysis.

2.1 Program Assumptions

Fig. 2.1 shows the structure of the most general single loop nest that we consider in this paper. The statements in the *loop body* have array references of the form $A[\mathbf{g}(i_1, i_2, \ldots, i_l)]$, where the index function is $\mathbf{g} : \mathcal{Z}^l \to \mathcal{Z}^d$, l is the loop nesting and d is the dimension of the array A. We have restricted our attention to **doall** loops since we want to focus on the relation between the iteration space and the data space and factor out issues such as dependencies and synchronization that arise from the ordering of the iterations of a loop. We believe that the framework described in this paper can be applied with suitable modifications for loops in which the iterations are ordered.

We assume that all array references within the loop body are unconditional. One of the two following approaches may be taken for loops with conditionals.

- Assume that all array references are actually accessed, ignoring the conditions surrounding a reference.
- Include only references within conditions that are likely to be true based on profiling information.

We address the problem of loop and data partitioning for index expressions that are affine functions of loop indices. In other words, the index function can be expressed as,

$$\mathbf{g}(\mathbf{i}) \;\;=\;\; \mathbf{i}\mathbf{G} + \mathbf{a} \tag{2.1}$$

Doall (i1=l1:u1, i2=l2:u2, ..., il=ll:ul)
  loop body
EndDoall

Fig. 2.1. Structure of a single loop nest

where $\mathbf{G}$ is a $l \times d$ matrix with integer entries and $\mathbf{a}$ is an integer constant vector of length d, termed the *offset vector*. Note that $\mathbf{i}$, $\mathbf{g(i)}$, and $\mathbf{a}$ are row vectors. We often refer to an array reference by the pair $(\mathbf{G}, \mathbf{a})$. (An example of this function is presented in Sect. 3). Similar notation has been used in several papers in the past, for example, see [3, 4]. All our vectors and matrices have integer entries unless stated otherwise. We assume that the loop bounds are such that the iteration space is rectangular. The problem with non-rectangular tiles is one of load balancing (due to boundary effects in tiling) and this can be handled by optimizing for a machine with a large number of virtual processors and mapping the virtual processors to real processors in a cyclic fashion.

Loop indices are assumed to take all integer values between their lower and upper bounds, i.e, the strides are one.

Previous work [7,8,13] in this area restricted the arrays in the *loop body* to be of dimension exactly equal to the loop nesting. Abraham and Hudak [7] further restrict the *loop body* to contain only references to a single array; furthermore, all references are restricted to be of the form $A[i_1 + a_1, i_2 + a_2, \ldots, i_d + a_d]$ where a_j is an integer constant. Matrix multiplication is a simple example that does not fit these restrictions.

Given P processors, the problem of loop partitioning is to divide the iteration space into P tiles such that the total communication traffic on the network is minimized with the additional constraint that the tiles are of equal size, except at the boundaries of the iteration space. The constraint of equal size partitions is imposed to achieve load balancing. We restrict our discussions to hyperparallelepiped tiles, of which rectangular tiles are a special case.

Like [7, 8, 13], we do not include the effects of synchronization in our framework. Synchronization is handled separately to ensure correct behavior. For example, in the doall loop in Fig. 2.1, one might introduce a barrier synchronization after the loop nest if so desired. We also note that in many cases fine-grain data-level synchronization can be used within a parallel do loop to enforce data dependencies and its cost approximately modeled as slightly more expensive communication than usual [14]. See Appendix B for some details.

2.2 System Model

Our analysis applies to systems whose structure is similar to that shown in Fig. 2.2. The system comprises a set of processors, each with a coherent cache. Cache misses are satisfied by global memory accessed over an interconnection network or a bus. The memory can be implemented as a single monolithic module (as is commonly done in bus-based multiprocessors), or in a distributed fashion as shown in the figure. The memory modules might also be implemented on the processing nodes themselves (data partitioning for locality makes sense only for this case). In all cases, our analysis assumes that the cost of a main memory access is much higher than a cache access, and for loop partitioning, our analysis assumes that the cost of the main memory access is the same no matter where in main memory the data is located.

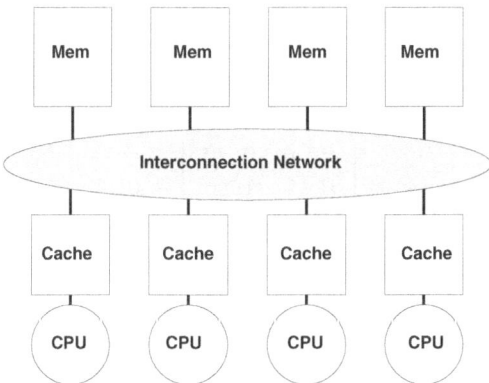

Fig. 2.2. A system with caches and uniform-access main memory (UMA).

The goal of loop partitioning is to minimize the total number of main memory accesses. For simplicity, we assume that the caches are large enough to hold all the data required by a loop partition, and that there are no conflicts in the caches. Techniques such as sub-blocking described in [15] or other techniques as in [16] and in [17] can be applied to reduce effects due to conflicts. When caches are small, the optimal loop partition does not change, rather, the size of each loop tile executed at any given time on the processor must be adjusted [15] so that the data fits in the cache (if we assume that the cache is effectively flushed between executions of each loop tile). Unless otherwise stated, we assume that cache lines are of unit length. The effect of larger cache lines can be included easily as suggested in [7], and is discussed further in Sect. 6.2.

If a program has multiple loops, then loop tiling parameters can be chosen independently for each loop to optimize cache performance by applying the techniques described in this paper. We assume there is no data reuse in the cache across loops. In programs with multiple loops and data arrays, tiling parameters for each loop and data array cannot be chosen independently in systems where the memories are local to the processors (see Fig. 3.3). This issue is discussed further in Sect. 7.

3. Loop Partitions and Data Partitions

This section presents examples to introduce and illustrate some of our definitions and to motivate the benefits of optimizing the shapes of loop and data tiles. More precise definitions are presented in the next section.

As mentioned previously, we deal with index expressions that are affine functions of loop indices. In other words, the index function can be expressed as in Equation 2.1. Consider the following example to illustrate the above expression of index functions.

Example 31. The reference $A[i_3 + 2, 5, i_2 - 1, 4]$ in a triply nested loop can be expressed by

$$(i_1, i_2, i_3) \begin{bmatrix} 0 & 0 & 0 & 0 \\ 0 & 0 & 1 & 0 \\ 1 & 0 & 0 & 0 \end{bmatrix} + (2, 5, -1, 4)$$

In this example, the second and fourth column of $\mathbf{G}$ are zero indicating that the second and fourth subscripts of the reference are independent of the loop indexes. In such cases, we show in Sect. 5.2 that we can ignore those columns and treat the referenced array as an array of lower dimension. In future, without loss of generality, we assume that the $\mathbf{G}$ matrix contains no zero columns.

Now, let us introduce the concept of a *loop partition* by examining the following example. Loop partitioning specifies the tiling parameters of the iteration space. Loop partitioning is sometimes termed iteration space partitioning or tiling.

Example 32.

Doall (i=101:200, j=1:100)
  A[i,j] = B[i+j,i-j-1]+B[i+j+4,i-j+3]
EndDoall

Let us assume that we have 100 processors and we want to distribute the work among them. There are 10,000 points in the iteration space and so one can allocate 100 of these to each of the processors to distribute the load uniformly. Fig. 3.1 shows two simple ways of partitioning the iteration space – by rows and by square blocks – into 100 equal tiles.

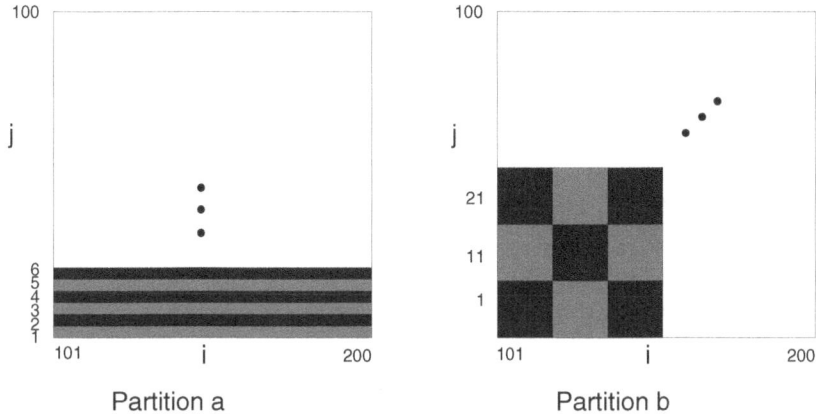

Fig. 3.1. Two simple rectangular loop partitions in the iteration space.

Minimizing communication volume requires that we minimize the number of data elements accessed by each loop tile. To facilitate this optimization, we introduce the notion of a *data footprint*. Footprints comprise the data elements referenced within a loop tile. In other words, the footprints are regions of the *data space* accessed by a loop tile. In particular, the footprint with respect to a specific reference in a loop tile gives us all the data elements accessed through that reference from within a tile of a loop partition.

Using Fig. 3.2, let us illustrate the footprints corresponding to a reference of the form B[i+j,i-j-1] for the two loop partitions shown in Fig. 3.1. The footprints in the data space resulting from the loop partition **a** are diagonal stripes and those resulting from partition **b** are square blocks rotated by 45 degrees. Algorithms for deriving the footprints are presented in the next section.

Let us compare the two loop partitions in the context of a system with caches and uniform-access memory (see Fig. 2.2) by computing the number of cache misses. The number of cache misses is equal to the number of distinct elements of B accessed by a loop tile, which is equal to the size of a loop tile's footprint on the array B. (Sect. 6.1 deals with minimizing *cache-coherence* traffic). Caches automatically fetch a loop tile's data footprint as the loop tile executes. For each tile in partition **a**, the number of cache misses can be shown to be 104 (see Sect. 5.1) whereas the number of cache misses in each tile of partition **b** can be shown to be 140. Thus, because it allows data reuse, loop partition **a** is a better choice if our goal is to minimize the number of cache misses, a fact that is not obvious from the source code.

When is *data partitioning* important? Data partitioning is the problem of partitioning the data arrays into data tiles and assigning each data tile to a local memory module, such that the number of memory references that can be

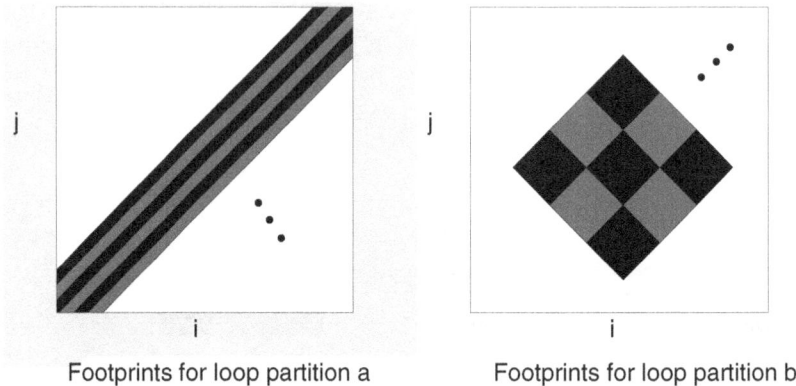

Footprints for loop partition a   Footprints for loop partition b

Fig. 3.2. Data footprints in the data space resulting from loop partitions **a** and **b**

satisfied by the local memory is maximized. Data partitioning is relevant only for nonuniform memory-access (NUMA) systems (for example, see Fig. 3.3).

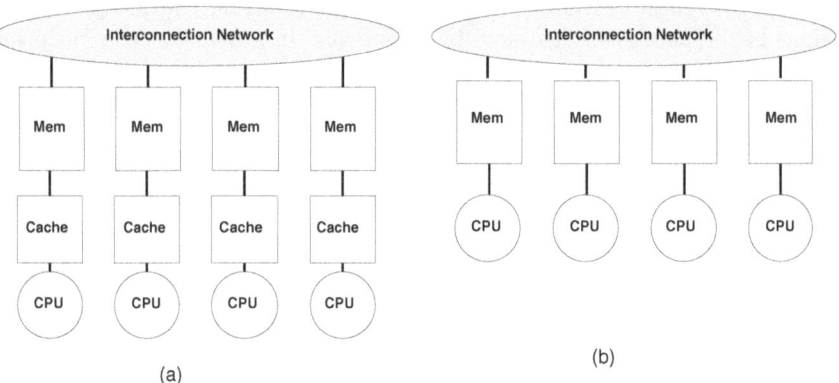

Fig. 3.3. Systems with nonuniform main-memory access time. (a) A cache-coherent NUMA system. (b) A distributed memory multicomputer.

In systems with nonuniform memory-access times, both loop and data partitioning are required. Our analysis applies to such systems as well. The loop tiles are assigned to the processing nodes and the data tiles to memory modules associated with the processing nodes so that a maximum number of the data references made by the loop tiles are satisfied by the local memory module. Note that in systems with nonuniform memory-access times, but which have caches, data partitioning may still be performed to maximize the number of caches misses that can be satisfied by the memory module local to the processing node.

Referring to Fig. 3.2, the footprint size is minimized by choosing a diagonal striping of the data space as the data partition, and a corresponding horizontal striping of the iteration space as the loop partition. The additional step of aligning corresponding loop and data tiles on the same node maximizes the number of local memory references.

In fact, the above horizontal partitioning of the loop space and diagonal striping of the data space results in zero communication traffic. Ramanujam and Sadayappan [8] presented algorithms to derive such communication-free partitions when possible. On the other hand, in addition to producing the same partitions when communication-traffic-free partitions exist (see Sections 5.1 and 6), our analysis will discover partitions that minimize traffic when such partitions are non-existent as well (see Example 45).

Example 33.

Doall (i=1:N, j=1:N)
  A[i,j] = B[i,j] + B[i+1,j-2] + B[i-1,j+1]
EndDoall

For the loop shown in Example 33, a parallelogram partition results in a lower cost of memory access compared to any rectangular partition since most of the inter iteration communication can be internalized to within a processor for a parallelogram partition (see Sect. 8.1). Because rectangular partitions often do not minimize communication, we would like to include parallelograms in the formulation of the general loop partitioning problem. In higher dimensions a parallelogram tile generalizes to a hyperparallelepiped; the next section defines it precisely.

4. A Framework for Loop and Data Partitioning

This section first defines precisely the notion of a loop partition and the notion of a footprint of a loop partition with respect to a data reference in the loop. We prove a theorem showing that the number of integer points within a tile is equal to the volume of the tile, which allows us to use volume estimates in deriving the amount of communication. We then present the concept of uniformly intersecting references and a method of computing the cumulative footprint for a set of uniformly intersecting references. We develop a formalism for computing the volume of communication on the interconnection network of a multiprocessor for a given loop partition, and show how loop tiles can be chosen to minimize this traffic. We briefly indicate how the cumulative footprint can be used to derive optimal data partitions for multicomputers with local memory (NUMA machines).

4.1 Loop Tiles in the Iteration Space

Loop partitioning results in a tiling of the iteration space. We consider only hyperparallelepiped partitions in this paper; rectangular partitions are special cases of these. Furthermore, we focus on loop partitioning where the tiles are homogeneous except at the boundaries of the iteration space. Under these conditions of homogeneous tiling, the partitioning is completely defined by specifying the tile at the origin, as indicated in Fig. 4.1. Under homogeneous tiling, the concept of the tile at the origin is similar to the notion of the clustering basis in [6]. (See Appendix A for a more general representation of hyperparallelepiped loop tiles based on bounding hyperplanes.)

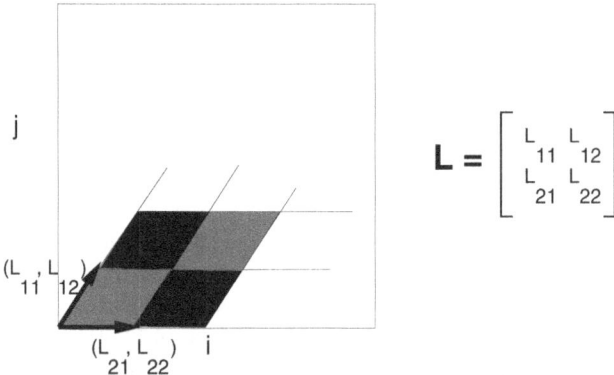

Fig. 4.1. Iteration space partitioning is completely specified by the tile at the origin.

Definition 41. *An l dimensional square integer matrix $\mathbf{L}$ defines a semi open hyperparallelepiped tile at the origin of an l dimensional iteration space as follows. The set of iteration points included in the tile is*

$$\{\mathbf{x} \mid \mathbf{x} = \Sigma_{i=1}^{l} \, \alpha_i \mathbf{l_i}, \ 0 \le \alpha_i < 1\}$$

where $\mathbf{l}_i$ is the ith row of $\mathbf{L}$. As depicted in Fig. 4.1, the rows of the matrix $\mathbf{L}$ specify the vertices of the tile at the origin. Often, we also refer to the partition by the $\mathbf{L}$ matrix since each of the other tiles is a translation of the tile at the origin.

Example 41. A rectangular partition can be represented by a diagonal $\mathbf{L}$ matrix. Consider a three dimensional iteration space $I \times J \times K$ partitioned into rectangular tiles where each tile is of the form by $\{(i_0, j, k_0)|0 \le j < J\}$. In other words, constants i_0 and j_0 specify the tile completely. Such a partition is represented by

$$\begin{bmatrix} 1 & 0 & 0 \\ 0 & J & 0 \\ 0 & 0 & 1 \end{bmatrix}.$$

Definition 42. *A general tile in the iteration space is a translation of the tile at the origin. The translation vector is given by*

$$\Sigma_{i=1}^{l} \lambda_i l_i$$

where λ_i is an integer. A tile is completely specified by $(\lambda_1, \ldots, \lambda_l)$. For example $(0, \ldots, 0)$ specifies the tile at the origin.

The rest of this paper deals with optimizing the shape of the tile at the origin for minimal communication. Because the amount of communication is related to the number of integer points within a tile, we begin by proving the following theorem relating the volume of a tile to the number of integer points within it. This theorem on lattices allows us to use volumes of hyperparallelepipeds derived using determinants to determine the amount of communication.

Theorem 41. *The number of integer points (iteration points) in tile $\mathbf{L}$ is equal to the volume of the tile, which is given by $|\det \mathbf{L}|$.*

Proof:. We provide a sketch of the proof; a more detailed proof is given in [18].

It is easy to show that the theorem is true for an n-dimensional semi-open rectangle. For a given n-dimensional semi-open hyperparallelepiped, let its volume be V and let P be the number of integer points in it. For any positive integer R, it can be shown that one can pack R^n of these hyperparallelepipeds into an n-dimensional rectangle of volume V_R and number of integer points P_R, such that both $V_R - R^n V$ and $P_R - R^n P$ grow slower than R^n. In other words,

$$V_R = R^n V + v(R), \quad P_R = R^n P + p(R)$$

where $v(R)$ and $p(R)$ grow slower than R^n. Now subtracting the second equation from the first one, and noting that $V_R = P_R$ for the n-dimensional rectangle, we get,

$$V - P = (p(R) - v(R))/R^n.$$

Given that both $v(R)$ and $p(R)$ grow slower than R^n, this can only be true when $V - P = 0$. $\square$

Proposition 41. *The number of integer points in any general tile is equal to the number of integer points in the tile at the origin.*

Proof:. Straight-forward from the definition of a general tile. $\square$

In the following discussion, we ignore the effects of the boundaries of the iteration space in computing the number of integer points in a tile. As our interest is in minimizing the communication for a general tile, we can ignore boundary effects.

4.2 Footprints in the Data Space

For a system with caches and uniform access memory, the problem of loop partitioning is to find an optimal matrix **L** that minimizes the number of cache misses. The first step is to derive an expression for the number of cache misses for a given tile **L**. Because the number of cache misses is related to the number of unique data elements accessed, we introduce the notion of a *footprint* that defines the data elements accessed by a tile. The footprints are regions of the *data space* accessed by a loop tile.

Definition 43. *The footprint of a tile of a loop partition with respect to a reference $A[\mathbf{g}(\mathbf{i})]$ is the set of all data elements $A[\mathbf{g}(\mathbf{i})]$ of A, for $\mathbf{i}$ an element of the tile.*

The footprint gives us all the data elements accessed through a particular reference from within a tile of a loop partition. Because we consider homogeneous loop tiles, the number of data elements accessed is the same for each loop tile.

We will compute the number of cache misses for the system with caches and uniform access memory to illustrate the use of footprints. The body of the loop may contain references to several variables and we assume that aliasing has been resolved; two references with distinct names do not refer to the same location. Let $A_1, A_2, \ldots, A_K$ be references to array A within the loop body, and let $f(A_i)$ be the *footprint* of the loop tile at the origin with respect to the reference A_i and let

$$f(A_1, A_2, \ldots, A_K) = \bigcup_{i=1,\ldots,K} f(A_i)$$

be the *cumulative footprint* of the tile at the origin. The number of cache misses with respect to the array A is $|f(A_1, A_2, \ldots, A_K)|$. Thus, computing the size of the individual footprints and the size of their union is an important part of the loop partitioning problem.

To facilitate computing the size of the union of the footprints we divide the references into multiple disjoint sets. If two footprints are disjoint or mostly disjoint, then the corresponding references are placed in different sets, and the size of the union is simply the sum of the sizes of the two footprints.

However, references whose footprints overlap substantially are placed in the same set. The notion of *uniformly intersecting references* is introduced to specify precisely the idea of "substantial overlap". Overlap produces temporal locality in cache accesses, and computing the size of the union of their footprints is more complicated.

The notion of uniformly intersecting references is derived from definitions of intersecting references and uniformly generated references.

Definition 44. *Two references $A[\mathbf{g}_1(\mathbf{i})]$ and $A[\mathbf{g}_2(\mathbf{i})]$ are said to be intersecting if there are two integer vectors $\mathbf{i}_1, \mathbf{i}_2$ such that $\mathbf{g}_1(\mathbf{i}_1) = \mathbf{g}_2(\mathbf{i}_2)$. For* *example,* $A[i+c1, j+c2]$ *and* $A[j+c3, i+c4]$ *are intersecting, whereas* $A[2i]$ *and* $A[2i+1]$ *are non-intersecting.*

Definition 45. *Two references* $A[\mathbf{g}_1(\mathbf{i})]$ *and* $A[\mathbf{g}_2(\mathbf{i})]$ *are said to be* uniformly generated *if*

$$g_1(\mathbf{i}) = \mathbf{iG} + \mathbf{a}_1 \text{ and } g_2(\mathbf{i}) = \mathbf{iG} + \mathbf{a}_2$$

where $\mathbf{G}$ *is a linear transformation and* $\mathbf{a}_1$ *and* $\mathbf{a}_2$ *are integer constants.*

The intersection of footprints of two references that are not uniformly generated is often very small. For non-uniformly generated references, although the footprints corresponding to some of the iteration-space tiles might overlap partially, the footprints of others will have no overlap. Since we are interested in the worst-case communication volume between any pair of footprints, we will assume that the total communication generated by two non-uniformly intersecting references is essentially the sum of the individual footprints.

However, the condition that two references are uniformly generated is not sufficient for two references to be intersecting. As a simple example, $A[2i]$ and $A[2i+1]$ are uniformly generated, but the footprints of the two references do not intersect. For the purpose of locality optimization through loop partitioning, our definition of reuse of array references will combine the concept of uniformly generated arrays and the notion of intersecting array references. This notion is similar to the equivalence classes within uniformly generated references defined in [3].

Definition 46. *Two array references are* uniformly intersecting *if they are both intersecting and uniformly generated.*

Example 42. The following sets of references are uniformly intersecting.

1. $A[i, j], A[i+1, j-3], A[i, j+4]$.
2. $A[2j, 2, i], A[2j-5, 2, i], A[2j+3, 2, i]$.

The following pairs are not uniformly intersecting.

1. $A[i, j], A[2i, j]$.
2. $A[i, j], A[2i, 2j]$.
3. $A[j, 2, i], A[j, 3, i]$.
4. $A[2i], A[2i+1]$.
5. $A[i+2, 2i+4], A[i+5, 2i+8]$.
6. $A[i, j], B[i, j]$.

Footprints in the data space for a set of uniformly intersecting references are translations of one another, as shown below. The footprint with respect to the reference $(\mathbf{G}, \mathbf{a}_s)$ is a translation of the footprint with respect to the reference $(\mathbf{G}, \mathbf{a}_r)$, where the translation vector is $\mathbf{a}_s - \mathbf{a}_r$.

Proposition 42. *Given a loop tile at the origin* $\mathbf{L}$ *and references* $r = (\mathbf{G}, \mathbf{a}_r)$ *and* $s = (\mathbf{G}, \mathbf{a}_s)$ *belonging to a uniformly generated set defined by* $\mathbf{G}$, *let* $f(r)$ *denote the footprint of* $\mathbf{L}$ *with respect to* r, *and let* $f(s)$ *denote the footprint of* $\mathbf{L}$ *with respect to* s. *Then* $f(s)$ *is simply a translation of* $f(r)$, *where each point of* $f(s)$ *is a translation of a corresponding point of* $f(r)$ *by an amount given by the vector* $(\mathbf{a}_s - \mathbf{a}_r)$. *In other words,*

$$f(s) = f(r) + (\mathbf{a}_s - \mathbf{a}_r).$$

This follows directly from the definition of uniformly generated references. Recall that an element $\mathbf{i}$ of the loop tile is mapped by the reference $(\mathbf{G}, \mathbf{a}_r)$ to data element $\mathbf{d}_r = \mathbf{i}\mathbf{G} + \mathbf{a}_r$, and by the reference $(\mathbf{G}, \mathbf{a}_s)$ to data element $\mathbf{d}_s = \mathbf{i}\mathbf{G} + \mathbf{a}_s$. The translation vector, $(\mathbf{d}_s - \mathbf{d}_r)$, is clearly independent of $\mathbf{i}$.

The volume of cache traffic imposed on the network is related to the size of the cumulative footprint. We describe how to compute the size of the cumulative footprint in the following two sections as outlined below.

- First, we discuss how the size of *the footprint for a single reference* within a loop tile can be computed. In general, the size of the footprint with respect to a given reference is not the same as the number of points in the iteration space tile.
- Second, we describe how the size of *the cumulative footprint for a set of uniformly intersecting references* can be computed. The sizes of the cumulative footprints for each of these sets are then summed to produce the size of the cumulative footprint for the loop tile.

4.3 Size of a Footprint for a Single Reference

This section shows how to compute the size of the footprint (with respect to a given reference and a given loop tile $\mathbf{L}$) efficiently for certain common cases of $\mathbf{G}$. The general case of $\mathbf{G}$ is dealt with in Sect. 5. We begin with a simple example to illustrate our approach.

Example 43.

Doall (i=0:99, j=0:99)
    A[i,j] = B[i+j,j]+B[i+j+1,j+2]
EndDoall

The reference matrix $\mathbf{G}$ is

$$\begin{bmatrix} 1 & 0 \\ 1 & 1 \end{bmatrix}.$$

Let us suppose that the loop tile at the origin $\mathbf{L}$ is given by

$$\begin{bmatrix} L_1 & L_1 \\ L_2 & 0 \end{bmatrix}.$$

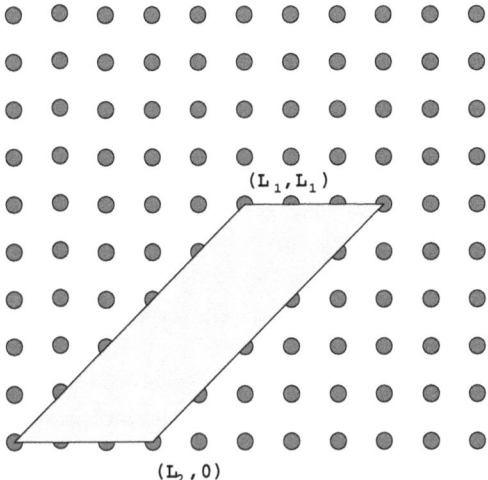

Fig. 4.2. Tile $\mathbf{L}$ at the origin of the iteration space.

In Fig. 4.2 we show this tile at the origin of the iteration space and the footprint of the tile (at the origin) with respect to the reference $B[i + j, j]$ is shown in Fig. 4.3. The matrix

$$\mathbf{f}(B[i + j, j]) = \mathbf{LG} = \begin{bmatrix} 2L_1 & L_1 \\ L_2 & 0 \end{bmatrix}$$

describes the footprint. As shown later, the integer points in the semi open parallelogram specified by $\mathbf{LG}$ is the footprint of the tile and so the size of the footprint is $|\det(\mathbf{LG})|$. We will use $\mathbf{D}$ to denote the product $\mathbf{LG}$ as it appears often in our discussion.

The rest of this subsection focuses on deriving the set of conditions under which the footprint size is given by $|\det(\mathbf{D})|$. Briefly, we show that $\mathbf{G}$ being unimodular is a sufficient (but not necessary) condition. The next section derives the size of the cumulative footprint for multiple uniformly intersecting references.

In general, is the footprint exactly the integer points in $\mathbf{D} = \mathbf{LG}$? If not, how do we compute the footprint? The first question can be expanded into the following two questions.

− Is there a point in the footprint that lies outside the hyperparallelepiped $\mathbf{D}$? It follows easily from linear algebra that it is not the case.

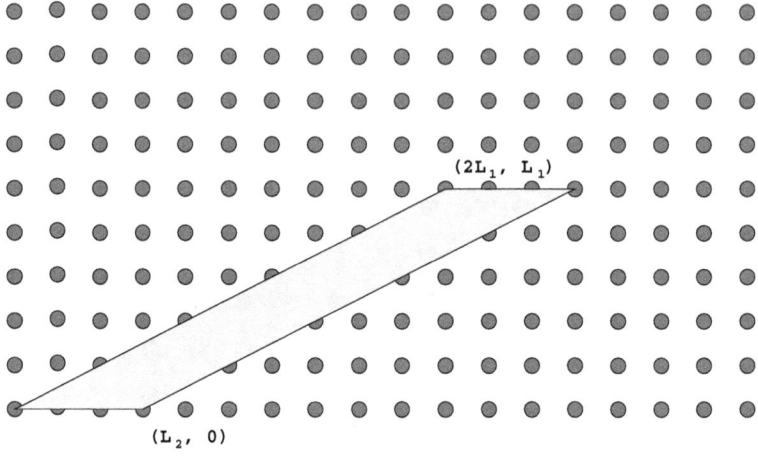

Fig. 4.3. Footprint of $\mathbf{L}$ wrt $B[i+j,j]$ in the data space.

- Is every integer point in $\mathbf{D}$ an element of the footprint? It is easy to show this is not true and a simple example corresponds to the reference $A[2i]$.

We first study the simple case when the hyperparallelepiped $\mathbf{D}$ completely defines the footprint. A precise definition of the set $S(\mathbf{D})$ of points defined by the matrix $\mathbf{D}$ is as follows.

Definition 47. *Given a matrix $\mathbf{D}$ whose rows are the vectors $\mathbf{d}_i$, $1 \leq i \leq m$, $S(\mathbf{D})$ is defined as the set*

$$\{\mathbf{x} \mid \mathbf{x} = a_1 \mathbf{d}_1 + a_2 \mathbf{d}_2 + \ldots + a_m \mathbf{d}_m,\ 0 \leq a_i < 1\}.$$

$S(\mathbf{D})$ *defines all the points in the semi open hyperparallelepiped defined by* $\mathbf{D}$.

So for the case where $\mathbf{D}$ completely defines the footprint, the footprint is exactly the integer points in $S(\mathbf{D})$. One of the cases where $\mathbf{D}$ completely defines the footprint, is when $\mathbf{G}$ is unimodular as shown below.

Lemma 41. *The mapping $\Re^l \mapsto \Re^d$ as defined by $\mathbf{G}$ is one to one if and only if the rows of $\mathbf{G}$ are independent. Further, the mapping of the iteration space to the data space $(\mathcal{Z}^l \mapsto \mathcal{Z}^d)$ as defined by $\mathbf{G}$ is one to one if and only if the rows of $\mathbf{G}$ are independent.*

Proof:. $\mathbf{i}_1 \mathbf{G} = \mathbf{i}_2 \mathbf{G}$ *implies* $\mathbf{i}_1 = \mathbf{i}_2$ *if and only if the only solution to* $\mathbf{x}\mathbf{G} = \mathbf{0}$ *is* $\mathbf{0}$. *The latter implies that the nullspace of $\mathbf{G}^T$ is of dimension 0. From a fundamental theorem of Linear Algebra [19], this means that the rows of $\mathbf{G}$ are linearly independent. It is to be noted that when the rows of $\mathbf{G}$ are not* *independent there exists a nontrivial integer solution to* $\mathbf{xG} = \mathbf{0}$, *given that the entries in* $\mathbf{G}$ *are integers. This proves the second statement of the lemma.* □

Lemma 42. *The mapping of the iteration space to the data space as defined by* $\mathbf{G}$ *is onto if and only if the columns of* $\mathbf{G}$ *are independent and the g.c.d. of the subdeterminants of order equal to the number of columns is 1.*

Proof:. Follows from the Hermite normal form theorem as shown in [20]. □

Lemma 43. *If* $\mathbf{G}$ *is invertible then* $\mathbf{d} \in \mathbf{LG}$ *if and only if* $\mathbf{dG}^{-1} \in \mathbf{L}$.

Proof:. Clearly $\mathbf{G}$ *is invertible implies,*

$$\mathbf{d} \in \mathbf{LG} \Longrightarrow \mathbf{dG}^{-1} \in \mathbf{LGG}^{-1} = \mathbf{L}$$

Also,

$$\mathbf{dG}^{-1} \in \mathbf{L} \Longrightarrow \mathbf{dG}^{-1}\mathbf{G} \in \mathbf{LG} \Longrightarrow \mathbf{d} \in \mathbf{LG}.$$

$\mathbf{G}$ *is invertible implies that the rows of* $\mathbf{G}$ *are independent and hence the mapping defined by* $\mathbf{G}$ *is one to one from Lemma 41.* □

Theorem 42. *The footprint of the tile defined by* $\mathbf{L}$ *with respect to the reference* $\mathbf{G}$ *is identical to the integer points in the semi open hyperparallelepiped* $\mathbf{D} = \mathbf{LG}$ *if* $\mathbf{G}$ *is* unimodular.

Proof:. It is immediate from Lemma 42 that $\mathbf{G}$ *is onto when it is unimodular.* $\mathbf{G}$ *is onto implies that every data point in* $\mathbf{D}$ *has an inverse in the iteration space. Can the inverse of the data point be outside of* $\mathbf{L}$? *Lemma 43 shows this is not possible since* $\mathbf{G}$ *is invertible.* □

We make the following two observations about Theorem 42.

- $\mathbf{G}$ is unimodular is a sufficient condition; but not necessary. An example corresponds to the reference $A[i+j]$. Further discussions on this is contained in Sect. 5.
- One may wonder why $\mathbf{G}$ being onto is not sufficient for $\mathbf{D}$ to coincide with the footprint. Even when every integer point in $\mathbf{D}$ has an inverse, it is possible that the inverse is outside of $\mathbf{L}$. For example, consider the mapping defined by the $\mathbf{G}$ matrix

$$\begin{bmatrix} 4 \\ 5 \end{bmatrix}$$

corresponding to the reference $A[4i+5j]$. It is onto as shown by Lemma 42. However, we will show that not all points in $\mathbf{LG}$ are in the footprint. Consider,

$$\mathbf{L} = \begin{bmatrix} 100 & 0 \\ 0 & 100 \end{bmatrix}.$$

LG defines the interval $[0, 900)$ and so it includes the data point (1). But it can be shown that none of the inverses of the data point (1) belong to **L**; (-1, 1) is an inverse of (1). The same is true for the data points (2), (3), (6), (7), and (11). The one to one property of **G** guarantees that no point from outside of **L** can be mapped to inside of **D**. The reason for this is that the one to one property is true even when **G** is treated as a function on reals.

Let us now introduce our technique for computing the cumulative footprint when **G** is unimodular. Algorithms for computing the size of the individual footprints and the cumulative footprint when **G** is not unimodular are discussed in Sect. 5.

4.4 Size of the Cumulative Footprint

The size of the cumulative footprint F for a loop tile is computed by summing the sizes of the cumulative footprints for each of the sets of uniformly intersecting references. This section presents a method for computing the size of the cumulative footprint for a set of uniformly intersecting references when **G** is unimodular, that is, when the conditions stated in Theorem 42 are true. More general cases of **G** are discussed in Sect. 5. We first describe the method when there are exactly two uniformly intersecting references, and then develop the method for multiple references.

Cumulative Footprint for Two References. Let us start by illustrating the computation of the cumulative footprint for Example 43. The two references to array B form a uniformly intersecting set and are defined by the following **G** matrix.

$$\mathbf{G} = \begin{bmatrix} 1 & 0 \\ 1 & 1 \end{bmatrix}$$

Let us suppose that the loop partition **L** is given by

$$\begin{bmatrix} L_{11} & L_{12} \\ L_{21} & L_{22} \end{bmatrix}.$$

Then **D** is given by

$$\begin{bmatrix} L_{11} + L_{12} & L_{12} \\ L_{21} + L_{22} & L_{22} \end{bmatrix}.$$

The parallelogram defined by **D** in the data space is the parallelogram $ABCD$ shown in Fig. 4.4. $ABCD$ and $EFGH$ shown in Fig. 4.4 are the footprints of the tile **L** with respect to the two references ($B[i + j, j]$ and $B[i + j + 1, j + 2]$ respectively) to array B. In the figure, $\mathbf{AB} = (L_{11} + L_{12}, L_{12})$, $\mathbf{AD} = (L_{21} + L_{22}, L_{22})$, and $\mathbf{AE} = (1, 2)$.

The size of the cumulative footprint is the size of footprint $ABCD$ plus the number of data elements in $EPDS$ plus the number of data elements in $SRGH$. Given that **G** is unimodular, the number of data elements is equal to

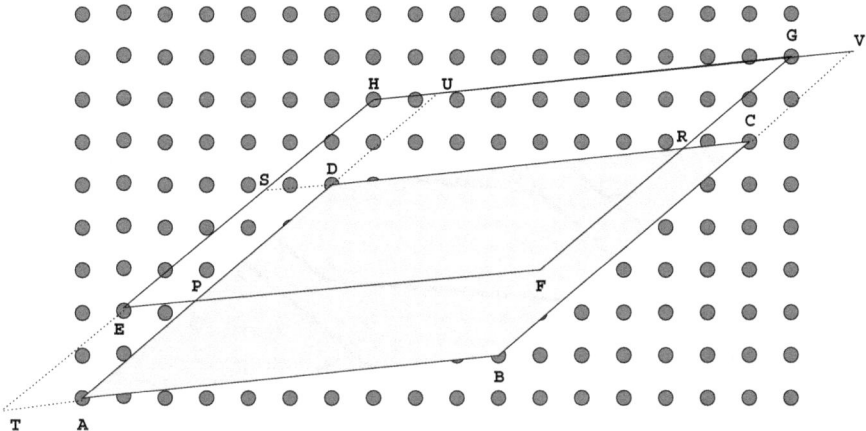

Fig. 4.4. Data footprint wrt $B[i+j,j]$ and $B[i+j+1,j+2]$

the area $ABCD + SRGH + EPDS = ABCD + ADST + CDUV - SDUH$.
Ignoring the area $SDUH$, we can approximate the total area by

$$\left| \det \begin{bmatrix} L_{11} + L_{12} & L_{12} \\ L_{21} + L_{22} & L_{22} \end{bmatrix} \right| + \left| \det \begin{bmatrix} L_{11} + L_{12} & L_{12} \\ 1 & 2 \end{bmatrix} \right| +$$

$$\left| \det \begin{bmatrix} 1 & 2 \\ L_{21} + L_{22} & L_{22} \end{bmatrix} \right|.$$

The first term in the above equation represents the area of the footprint of a
single reference, i.e., $|\det(\mathbf{D})|$. It is well known that the area of a parallelo-
gram is given by the determinant of the matrix specifying the parallelogram.
The second and third terms are the determinants of the $\mathbf{D}$ matrix in which
one row is replaced by the offset vector $\mathbf{a} = (1,2)$. Fig. 4.5 is a pictorial representation of the approximation. The first term is the parallelogram $ABCD$
and the second and third terms are the shaded regions.

Ignoring $SDUH$ is reasonable if we assume that the offset vectors in a
uniformly intersecting set of references are small compared to the tile size. We
refer to this simplification as the *overlapping sub-tile approximation*. This approximation will result in our estimates being higher than the actual values.
Although one can easily derive a more exact expression, we use the overlapping sub-tile approximation to simplify the computation. Fig. 8.1 in Sect. 8
further demonstrates that the error introduced is insignificant, especially for
parallelograms that are near optimal.

The following expression captures the size of the cumulative footprint for
the above two references in which one of the offset vectors is $(0,0)$:

$$|\det \mathbf{D}| + \sum_{k=1}^{d} |\det \mathbf{D}_{k \to \mathbf{a}}|$$

where, $\mathbf{D}_{k \to \mathbf{a}}$ is the matrix obtained by replacing the kth row of $\mathbf{D}$ by $\mathbf{a}$.

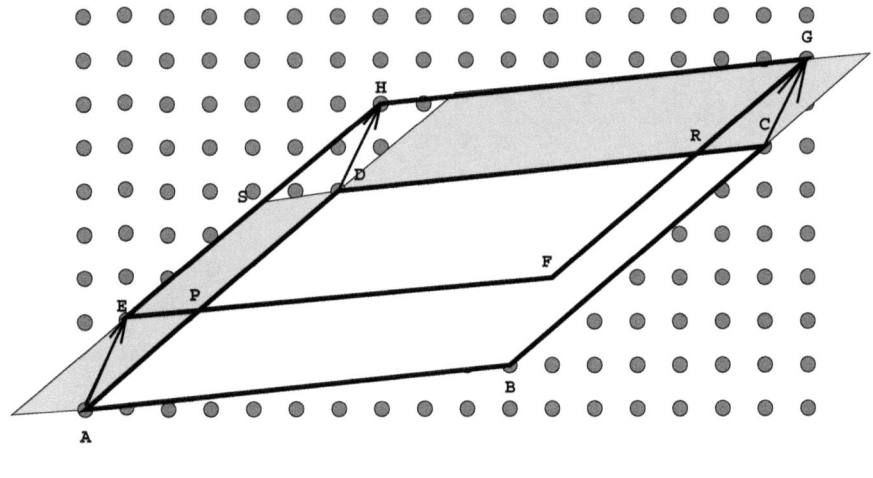

□ - Approximation of EPDS + SRGH

Fig. 4.5. Difference between the cumulative footprint and the footprint.

If both the offset vectors are nonzero, because only the relative position of the two footprints determines the area of their non-overlapping region, we use $\mathbf{a} = \mathbf{a_1} - \mathbf{a_0}$ in the above equation. The following discussion formalizes this notion and extends it to multiple references.

Cumulative Footprint for Multiple References. The basic approach for estimating the cumulative footprint size involves deriving an effective offset vector $\hat{a}$ that captures the combined effects of multiple offset vectors when there are several overlapping footprints resulting from a set of uniformly intersecting references. First, we need a few definitions.

Definition 48. *Given a loop tile $\mathbf{L}$, there are two neighboring loop tiles along the ith row of $\mathbf{L}$ defined by $\{\mathbf{y} \mid \mathbf{y} = \mathbf{x} + \mathbf{l}_i, \mathbf{x} \in \text{tile} \, \mathbf{L}\}$ and $\{\mathbf{y} \mid \mathbf{y} = \mathbf{x} - \mathbf{l}_i, \mathbf{x} \in \text{tile} \, \mathbf{L}\}$, where $\mathbf{l}_i$ is the ith row of $\mathbf{L}$, for $1 \leq i \leq l$. We refer to the former neighbor as the positive neighbor and the latter as the negative neighbor. We also refer to these neighbors as the neighbors of the parallel sides of the tile determined by the rows of $\mathbf{L}$, excluding the ith row. Fig. 4.6 illustrates the notion of neighboring tiles.*

The notion of neighboring tiles can be extended to the data space in like manner as follows.

Definition 49. *Given a loop tile $\mathbf{L}$ and a reference $(\mathbf{G}, \mathbf{a}_r)$, the neighbors of the data footprint of $\mathbf{L}$ along the kth row of $\mathbf{D} = \mathbf{LG}$ are $\{\mathbf{y} \mid \mathbf{y} = \mathbf{x} + \mathbf{d}_k, \mathbf{x} \in \mathbf{D} + \mathbf{a}_r\}$ and $\{\mathbf{y} \mid \mathbf{y} = \mathbf{x} - \mathbf{d}_k, \mathbf{x} \in \mathbf{D} + \mathbf{a}_r\}$, where $\mathbf{d}_k$ is the kth row of $\mathbf{D}$, for $1 \leq k \leq d$.*

Definition 410. *Given a tile* $\mathbf{L}$, $\mathbf{L}'$ *is a sub-tile wrt the ith row of* $\mathbf{L}$ *if the rows of* $\mathbf{L}'$ *are the same as the rows of* $\mathbf{L}$ *except for the ith row which is* α *times the ith row of* $\mathbf{L}$, $0 \leq \alpha \leq 1$.

The approximation of the cumulative footprint in Fig. 4.5 can be expressed in terms of sub-tiles of the tile in the data space. $ABCD$ is a tile in the data space and the two shaded regions in Fig. 4.5 are sub-tiles of neighboring tiles containing portions of the cumulative footprint. One can view the cumulative footprint as any one of the footprints together with communication from the neighboring footprints. The approximation of the cumulative footprint expresses the communication from the neighboring tiles in terms of sub-tiles to make the computation simpler.

Definition 411. *Let* $\mathbf{L}$ *be a loop tile at the origin, and let* $\mathbf{g}(\mathbf{i}) = \mathbf{iG} + \mathbf{a}_r$, $1 \leq r \leq R$ *be a set of uniformly intersecting references. For the footprint of* $\mathbf{L}$ *with respect to reference* $(\mathbf{G}, \mathbf{a}_r)$, *communication along the positive direction of the kth row of* $\mathbf{D}$ *is defined as the smallest sub tile of the positive neighbor along the kth row of the footprint which contains the elements of the cumulative footprint within that neighbor. Communication along the negative direction is defined similarly. Communication along the kth row is the sum of these two communications. Each row of* $\mathbf{D}$ *defines a pair of parallel sides (hyperplanes) of the data footprint determined by the remaining rows of* $\mathbf{D}$. *We sometimes refer to the communication along the kth row as the communication across the parallel sides of* $\mathbf{D}$ *defined by the kth row.*

The notion of the communication along the rows of $\mathbf{D}$ facilitates computing the size of the cumulative footprint. Consider the data footprints of a loop tile with respect to a set of uniformly intersecting references shown in Fig. 4.7. Here $\mathbf{d}_1$, $\mathbf{d}_2$ correspond to the rows of the matrix $\mathbf{D} = \mathbf{LG}$. The vectors $\mathbf{a}_1$, $\ldots \mathbf{a}_5$ are the offset vectors corresponding to the set of uniformly intersecting references. The cumulative footprint can be expressed as the union of any one of the footprints and the remaining elements of the cumulative footprint. We take the union because a given data element needs to be fetched only once into a cache.

In Fig. 4.7, the cumulative footprint is the union of the footprint of the loop tile with respect to $\mathbf{a}_4$ and the shaded regions corresponding to the remaining elements of the cumulative footprint resulting from the other references. The area of the shaded region can be approximated by the sum of communication along the kth row for $1 \leq k \leq 2$ as shown in Fig. 4.8. The area of the communication along $\mathbf{d}_2$ is equal to the area of the parallelogram whose sides are $\mathbf{d}_1$ and $\mathbf{a}_5 - \mathbf{a}_4$. Among the offset vectors, vector $\mathbf{a}_5$ has the maximum component along $\mathbf{d}_2$ and vector $\mathbf{a}_4$ has the minimum (taking the sign into account) component along $\mathbf{d}_2$. Similarly the area of the communication along $\mathbf{d}_1$ is equal to the area of the parallelogram whose sides are $\mathbf{d}_2$ and $\mathbf{a}_4 - \mathbf{a}_1$ plus the area of the parallelogram whose sides are $\mathbf{d}_2$ and $\mathbf{a}_5 - \mathbf{a}_4$. This is equal to the area of the parallelogram whose sides are $\mathbf{d}_2$

and $\mathbf{a}_5 - \mathbf{a}_1$. As before among the offset vectors, vector $\mathbf{a}_5$ has the maximum component along $\mathbf{d}_1$ and vector $\mathbf{a}_1$ has the minimum (taking the sign into account) component along $\mathbf{d}_1$. This observation is used in the proof of Theorem 43. It turns out that the effect of offset vector $\mathbf{a}_5 - \mathbf{a}_1$ along $\mathbf{d}_2$ and $\mathbf{a}_5 - \mathbf{a}_4$ along $\mathbf{d}_1$ can be captured by a single vector $\hat{a}$ as shown later.

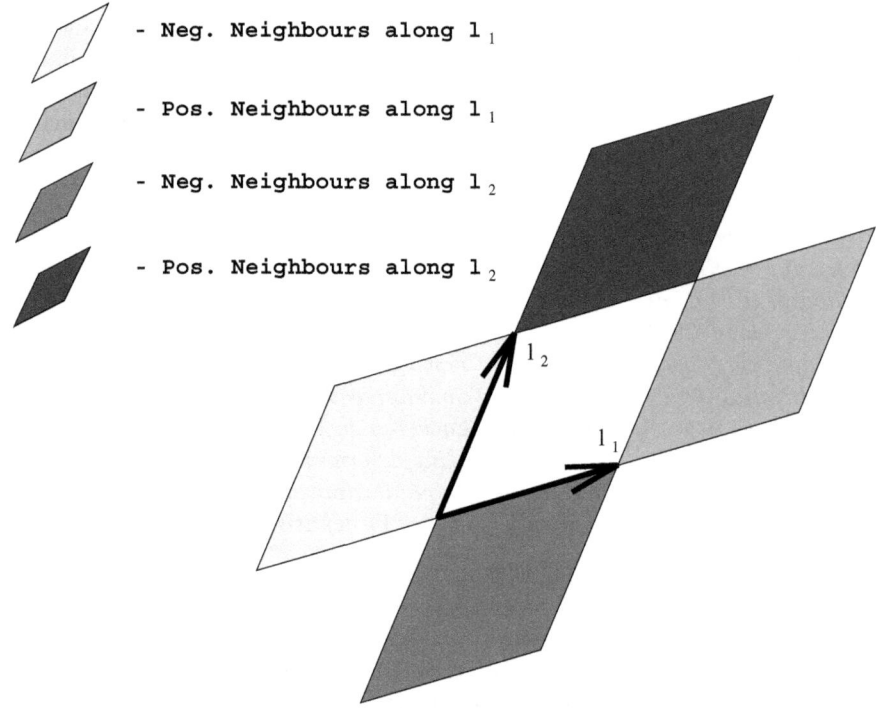

- Neg. Neighbours along $\mathbf{l}_1$

- Pos. Neighbours along $\mathbf{l}_1$

- Neg. Neighbours along $\mathbf{l}_2$

- Pos. Neighbours along $\mathbf{l}_2$

Fig. 4.6. Neighboring Tiles

Proposition 43. *Let $\mathbf{L}$ be a loop tile at the origin, and let $\mathbf{g}(\mathbf{i}) = \mathbf{i}\mathbf{G} + \mathbf{a}_r$, be a set of uniformly intersecting references. The volume of communication along the kth row of $\mathbf{D}$, $1 \le k \le d$, is the same for each of the footprints (corresponding to the different offset vectors).*

Communication along the positive and negative directions will be different for different footprints. But the total communication along the kth row, $1 \le k \le d$, is the same for each of the data footprints.

We now derive an expression for the cumulative footprint based on our notion of communication across the sides of the data footprint. Our goal is to capture in a single offset vector $\hat{a}$ the communication in a cache-coherent system resulting from all the offset vectors. More specifically, we would like the kth component of $\hat{a}$ to reflect the communication per unit area across the

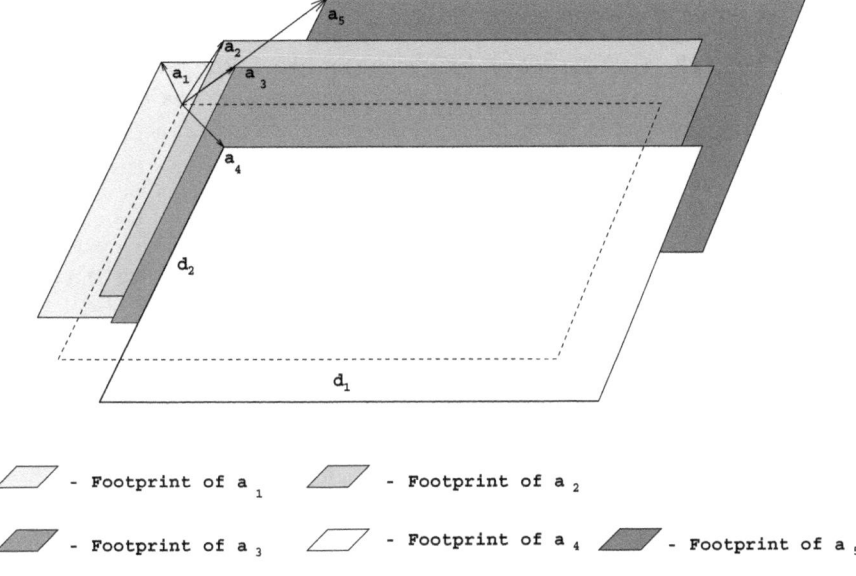

Fig. 4.7. Cumulative Footprint

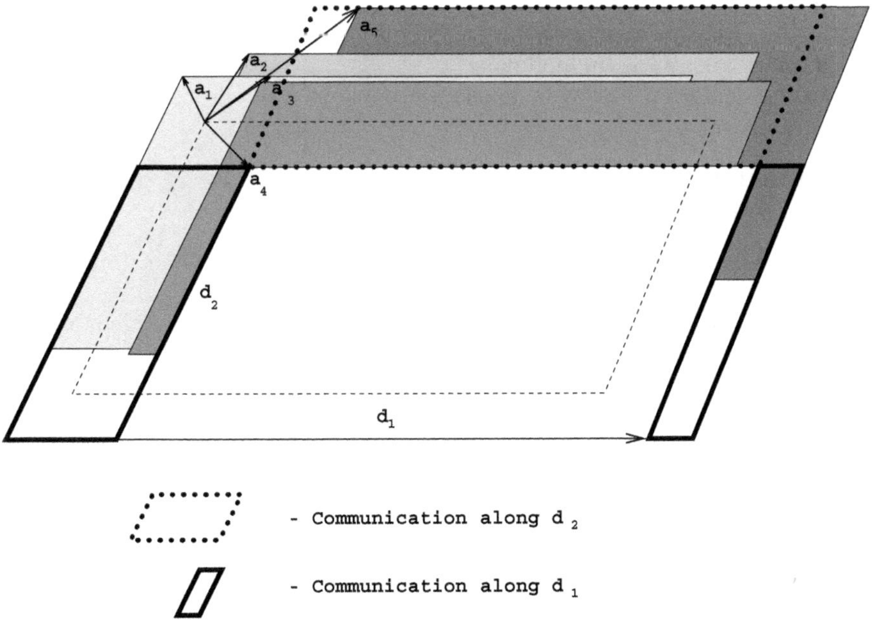

Fig. 4.8. Communication From Neighboring Tiles

parallel sides defined by the kth row of $\mathbf{D}$. The effective vector $\hat{a}$ is derived from the *spread* of a set of offset vectors.

Definition 412. *Given a set of d-dimensional offset vectors $\mathbf{a}_r$, $1 \le r \le R$, spread$(\mathbf{a}_1, \ldots, \mathbf{a}_R)$ is a vector of the same dimension as the offset vectors, whose kth component is given by*

$$\max_r(a_{r,k}) - \min_r(a_{r,k}), \forall k \in 1, \ldots, d.$$

In other words, the spread of a set of vectors is a vector in which each component is the difference between the maximum and minimum of the corresponding components in each of the vectors.

For caches, we use the $max - min$ formulation (or the spread) to calculate the amount of communication traffic because the data space points corresponding to the footprints whose offset vectors have values between the max and the min lie within the cumulative footprint calculated using the spread.[1]

The spread as defined above does not quite capture the properties that we are looking for in a single offset vector except when $\mathbf{D}$ is rectangular. If $\mathbf{D}$ is not rectangular, the kth component of spread$(\mathbf{a})$ does not reflect the communication per unit area across the parallel sides defined by the kth row of $\mathbf{D}$. To derive the footprint component (or sub tile) along a row of $\mathbf{D}$, we need to compute the difference between the maximum and the minimum components of the offset vectors using $\mathbf{D}$ as a basis. Therefore, we extend the notion of spread to a general basis as follows. Recall that $\mathbf{D}$ is a basis for the data space when $\mathbf{G}$ is unimodular.

In the definition below, $\mathbf{b}_r$ is the representation of offset vector $\mathbf{a}_r$ using $\mathbf{D}$ as the basis.

Definition 413. *Given a set of offset vectors $\mathbf{a}_r$, $1 \le r \le R$, let $\mathbf{b}_r = \mathbf{a}_r \mathbf{D}^{-1}, \forall r \in 1, \ldots, R$ and let $\hat{b}$ be spread$(\mathbf{b}_1, \ldots, \mathbf{b}_R)$. Then*

$$\hat{a} = \text{spread}_{\mathbf{D}}(\mathbf{a}_1, \ldots, \mathbf{a}_R) = \hat{b}\mathbf{D}.$$

Looking at the special case where $\mathbf{D}$ is rectangular helps in understanding the definition.

Proposition 44. *If $\mathbf{D}$ is rectangular then*

$$\hat{a} = \text{spread}(\mathbf{a}_1, \ldots, \mathbf{a}_R) = \text{spread}_{\mathbf{D}}(\mathbf{a}_1, \ldots, \mathbf{a}_R)$$

In other words,

$$\hat{a}_k = \max_r(a_{r,k}) - \min_r(a_{r,k}), \forall k \in 1, \ldots, d.$$

---

[1] For data partitioning, however, the formulation must be modified as discussed in Sect. 6.

For example, $\text{spread}_{\mathbf{I}}((1,0),(2,-1)) = (2-1,0-1) = (1,1)$.

For $\mathbf{D} = \begin{bmatrix} 1 & 1 \\ 0 & 1 \end{bmatrix}$, the spread is given by,

$$\text{spread}_{\mathbf{D}}((1,0),(2,-1)) = \text{spread}((1,0)\mathbf{D}^{-1},(2,-1)\mathbf{D}^{-1})\mathbf{D} = (1,3)$$

Lemma 44. *Given a hyperparallelepiped tile $\mathbf{L}$, and a set of uniformly intersecting references $\mathbf{g}(\mathbf{i}) = \mathbf{iG} + \mathbf{a}_r$, where $\mathbf{G}$ is unimodular, the communication along the kth row of $\mathbf{D} = \mathbf{LG}$ is $\sum_{k=1}^{d} |\det \mathbf{D}_{k\to\hat{a}}|$ where $\hat{a} = \text{spread}_{\mathbf{D}}(\mathbf{a}_1,\dots,\mathbf{a}_R)$ and $\mathbf{D}_{k\to\hat{a}}$ is the matrix obtained by replacing the kth row of $\mathbf{D}$ by $\hat{a}$.*

Proof:. Straight-forward from the definition of spread and the definition of communication along the kth row. □

Theorem 43. *Given a hyperparallelepiped tile $\mathbf{L}$ and a unimodular reference matrix $\mathbf{G}$, the size of the cumulative footprint with respect to a set of uniformly intersecting references specified by the reference matrix $\mathbf{G}$ and a set of offset vectors $\mathbf{a}_1,\dots,\mathbf{a}_R$, is approximately*

$$|\det \mathbf{D}| + \sum_{k=1}^{d} |\det \mathbf{D}_{k\to\hat{a}}|$$

where $\hat{a} = \text{spread}_{\mathbf{D}}(\mathbf{a}_1,\dots,\mathbf{a}_R)$ and $\mathbf{D}_{k\to\hat{a}}$ is the matrix obtained by replacing the kth row of $\mathbf{D}$ by $\hat{a}$.

Proof:. As observed earlier, the size of the cumulative footprint is approximately the size of any of the footprints plus the communication across its sides. Clearly the size of any one of the footprints is given by $|\det \mathbf{D}|$. The rest follows from Lemma 44. □

Finally, as stated earlier, the total communication generated by non-uniformly intersecting sets of references is essentially the sum of the communicating generated by the individual cumulative footprints. Example 45 in Sect. 4.5 discusses an instance of such a computation.

4.5 Minimizing the Size of the Cumulative Footprint

We now focus on the problem of finding the loop partition that minimizes the size of the cumulative footprint. The overall algorithm is summarized in Table 4.1. The minimization of C, the communication is done using standard optimization algorithms including numerical techniques.

Let us illustrate this procedure through the following two examples.

Table 4.1. An algorithm for minimizing cumulative footprint size for a single set of uniformly intersecting references. For multiple uniformly intersecting sets, add the communication component due to each set and then determine **L** that minimizes the sum.

Given:	**G**, offset vectors $\mathbf{a}_1, \dots, \mathbf{a}_R$
Goal:	Find **L** to minimize cumulative footprint size
Procedure:	Write $\mathbf{D} = \mathbf{LG}$
	Find $\mathbf{b}_1, \dots, \mathbf{b}_R = \mathbf{a}_1 D^{-1}, \dots, \mathbf{a}_R D^{-1}$
	Find $\hat{b} = \mathrm{spread}(\mathbf{b}_1, \dots, \mathbf{b}_R)$
	Then, write $\hat{a} = \hat{b}\mathbf{D}$
	Communication $C = \lvert \det \mathbf{D} \rvert + \sum_{k=1}^{d} \lvert \det \mathbf{D}_{k \to \hat{a}} \rvert$
	Finally, find the parameters of **L** that minimize C

Example 44.

Doall (i=1:N, j=1:N, k=1:N)
    A[i,j,k] = B[i-1,j,k+1] + B[i,j+1,k] + B[i+1,j-2,k-3]
EndDoall

Here we have two uniformly intersecting sets of references: one for A and one for B. Let us look at the class corresponding to B since it is more instructive. Because A has only one reference, whose **G** is unimodular, its footprint size is independent of the loop partition, given a fixed total size of the loop tile, and therefore need not figure in the optimization process. The G matrix corresponding to the references to B is,

$$\begin{bmatrix} 1 & 0 & 0 \\ 0 & 1 & 0 \\ 0 & 0 & 1 \end{bmatrix}$$

The $\hat{a}$ vector is $(2, 3, 4)$. Consider a rectangular partition $\mathbf{L} = \Lambda$ given by

$$\begin{bmatrix} L_i & 0 & 0 \\ 0 & L_j & 0 \\ 0 & 0 & L_k \end{bmatrix}$$

In this example, the **D** matrix is the same as the **L** matrix. Because **D** is rectangular, we can apply Proposition 44 in simplifying the derivation of $\hat{a}$. The size of the cumulative footprint for B can now be computed according to Theorem 43 as

$$L_i L_j L_k + 2L_j L_k + 3L_i L_k + 4L_i L_j$$

This expression must be minimized keeping $|\det \mathbf{L}|$ (or the product $L_i L_j L_k$) a constant. The product represents the area of the loop tile and must be kept constant to ensure a balanced load. The constant is simply the total area of the iteration space divided by P, the number of processors. For example, if the loop bounds are I, J, and K, then we must minimize $L_i L_j L_k + 2L_j L_k + 3L_i L_k + 4L_i L_j$, subject to the constraint $L_i L_j L_k = IJK/P$.

This optimization problem can be solved using standard methods, for example, using the method of Lagrange multipliers [21]. The size of the cumulative footprint is minimized when L_i, L_j, and L_k are chosen in the proportions 2, 3, and 4, or

$$L_i : L_j : L_k :: 2 : 3 : 4$$

This implies,

$$L_i = (IJK/3P)^{1/3}, \quad L_j = (3/2)(IJK/3P)^{1/3}, \quad and \quad L_k = 2(IJK/3P)^{1/3}.$$

Abraham and Hudak's algorithm [7] gives an identical partition for this example.

We now use an example to show how to minimize the total number of cache misses when there are multiple uniformly intersecting sets of references. The basic idea here is that the references from each set contribute additively to traffic.

Example 45.

Doall (i=1:N, j=1:N)
   A(i,j) = B(i-2,j) + B(i,j-1) + C(i+j-1,j) + C(i+j+1,j+3)
EndDoall

There are three uniformly intersecting classes of references, one for B, one for C, and one for A. Because A has only one reference, its footprint size is independent of the loop partition, given a fixed total size of the loop tile, and therefore need not figure in the optimization process.

For simplicity, let us assume that the tile $\mathbf{L}$ is rectangular and is given by

$$\begin{bmatrix} L_1 & 0 \\ 0 & L_2 \end{bmatrix}.$$

Because $\mathbf{G}$ for the references to array B is the identity matrix, the $\mathbf{D} = \mathbf{LG}$ matrix corresponding to references to B is same as $\mathbf{L}$, and the $\hat{a}$ vector is $spread(-2,0),(0,-1)) = (2,1)$. Thus, the size of the corresponding cumulative footprint according to Theorem 43 is

$$\begin{vmatrix} L_1 & 0 \\ 0 & L_2 \end{vmatrix} + \begin{vmatrix} 2 & 1 \\ 0 & L_2 \end{vmatrix} + \begin{vmatrix} L_1 & 0 \\ 2 & 1 \end{vmatrix}.$$

Similarly, $\mathbf{D}$ for array C is

$$\begin{bmatrix} L_1 & 0 \\ L_2 & L_2 \end{bmatrix}.$$

The data footprint $\mathbf{D}$ is not rectangular even though the loop tile is. Using Definition 413, $\hat{a} = spread_{\mathbf{D}}((-1,0),(1,3)) = (4,3)$, and the size of the cumulative footprint with respect to C is

$$\begin{vmatrix} L_1 & 0 \\ L_2 & L_2 \end{vmatrix} + \begin{vmatrix} 4 & 3 \\ L_2 & L_2 \end{vmatrix} + \begin{vmatrix} L_1 & 0 \\ 4 & 3 \end{vmatrix}.$$

The problem of minimizing the size of the footprint reduces to finding the elements of $\mathbf{L}$ that minimizes the sum of the two expressions above subject to the constraint the area of the loop tile $|\det \mathbf{L}|$ is a constant to ensure a balanced load. For example, if the loop bounds are I, J, then the constraint is $|\det \mathbf{L}| = IJ/P$, where P is the number of processors.

The total size of the cumulative footprint simplifies to $2L_1L_2 + 4L_1 + 3L_2$. The optimal values for L_1 and L_2 can be shown to satisfy the equation $4L_1 = 3L_2$ using the method of Lagrange multipliers.

5. General Case of G

This section analyzes the size of the footprint and the cumulative footprint for a general $\mathbf{G}$, that is, when $\mathbf{G}$ is not restricted to be unimodular. The computation of the size of the footprint is by case analysis on the $\mathbf{G}$ matrix.

5.1 G Is Invertible, but Not Unimodular

$\mathbf{G}$ is invertible and not unimodular implies that not every integer point in the hyperparallelepiped $\mathbf{D}$ is an image of an iteration point in $\mathbf{L}$. A unit cube in the iteration space is mapped to a hyperparallelepiped of volume equal to $|\det \mathbf{G}|$. So the size of the data footprint is $|\det \mathbf{D}/\det \mathbf{G}| = |\det \mathbf{L}|$. When $\mathbf{G}$ is invertible the size of the data footprint is exactly the size of the loop tile since the mapping is one to one.

Next, the expression for the size of the cumulative footprint is very similar to the one in Theorem 43, except that the data elements accessed are not dense in the data space. That is, the data space is sparse.

Lemma 51. *Given an iteration space $\mathcal{I}$, a reference matrix $\mathbf{G}$, and a hyperparallelepiped $\mathbf{D}_1$ in the data space, if the vertices of $\mathbf{D}_1\mathbf{G}^{-1}$ are in $\mathcal{I}$ then the number of elements in the intersection of $\mathbf{D}_1$ and the footprint of $\mathcal{I}$ with respect to $\mathbf{G}$ is $|\det \mathbf{D}_1/\det \mathbf{G}|$.*

Proof:. Clear if one views $\mathbf{D}_1\mathbf{G}^{-1}$ *as the loop tile* $\mathbf{L}$. $\square$

Theorem 51. *Given a hyperparallelepiped tile* $\mathbf{L}$, *and an invertible reference matrix* $\mathbf{G}$, *the size of the cumulative footprint with respect to a set of uniformly intersecting references specified by the reference matrix* $\mathbf{G}$ *and a set of offset vectors* $\mathbf{a}_1, \ldots, \mathbf{a}_R$, *is approximately*

$$\frac{|\det \mathbf{D}| + \sum_{k=1}^{d} |\det \mathbf{D}_{k\to\hat{a}}|}{|\det \mathbf{G}|}$$

where $\hat{a} = \text{spread}(\mathbf{a}_1, \ldots, \mathbf{a}_R, \mathbf{D})$ *and* $\mathbf{D}_{k\to\hat{a}}$ *is the matrix obtained by replacing the kth row of* $\mathbf{D}$ *by* $\hat{a}$.

Proof:. Using lemma 51 one can construct a proof similar to that of Theorem 43. $\square$

Example 32 (repeated below for convenience) possesses a $\mathbf{G}$ that is invertible, but not unimodular.

Doall (i=101:200, j=1:100)
    A[i,j] = B[i+j,i-j-1]+B[i+j+4,i-j+3]
EndDoall

For this example, the reference matrix $\mathbf{G}$ corresponding to array $\mathbf{B}$ is

$$\begin{bmatrix} 1 & 1 \\ 1 & -1 \end{bmatrix},$$

and the offset vectors are

$$\mathbf{a}_0 = (0, -1) \quad \text{and} \quad \mathbf{a}_1 = (4, 3)$$

Let us find the optimal rectangular partition $\mathbf{L}$ of the form

$$\begin{bmatrix} L_i & 0 \\ 0 & L_j \end{bmatrix}.$$

The footprint matrix $\mathbf{D}$ is given by

$$\begin{bmatrix} L_i & L_i \\ L_j & -L_j \end{bmatrix}.$$

The offset vectors using $\mathbf{D}$ as a basis are

$$\mathbf{b}_0 = \mathbf{a}_0\mathbf{D}^{-1} = (-1/(2L_i), 1/(2L_j)),$$

$$\mathbf{b}_1 = \mathbf{a}_1\mathbf{D}^{-1} = (7/(2L_i), 1/(2L_j)).$$

The vector $\hat{b} = (4/L_i, 0)$ and the vector

$$\hat{a} = \hat{b}\mathbf{D} = (4, 4)$$

The size of the cumulative footprint according to Theorem 51 is

$$\frac{\begin{vmatrix} L_i & L_i \\ L_j & -L_j \end{vmatrix} + \begin{vmatrix} L_i & L_i \\ 4 & 4 \end{vmatrix} + \begin{vmatrix} 4 & 4 \\ L_j & -L_j \end{vmatrix}}{\begin{vmatrix} 1 & 1 \\ 1 & -1 \end{vmatrix}}$$

which is

$$L_i L_j + 4L_j$$

If we constrain $L_i L_j = 100$ for load balance, we get $L_j = 1$ and $L_i = 100$. This partitioning represents horizontal striping of the iteration space.

5.2 Columns of G Are Dependent and the Rows Are Independent

We can apply Theorem 51 to compute the size of a footprint when the columns of $\mathbf{G}$ are dependent, as long as the rows are independent. We derive a $\mathbf{G}'$ from $\mathbf{G}$ by choosing a maximal set of independent columns from $\mathbf{G}$, such that $\mathbf{G}'$ is invertible. We can then apply Theorem 51 to compute the size of the footprint as shown in the following example.

Example 51. Consider the reference $A[i, 2i, i + j]$ in a doubly nested loop. The columns of the $\mathbf{G}$ matrix

$$\begin{bmatrix} 1 & 2 & 1 \\ 0 & 0 & 1 \end{bmatrix}$$

are not independent. We choose $\mathbf{G}'$ to be

$$\begin{bmatrix} 1 & 1 \\ 0 & 1 \end{bmatrix}.$$

Now $\mathbf{D}' = \mathbf{L}\mathbf{G}'$ completely specifies the footprint. The size of the footprint equals $|\det \mathbf{D}'| = |\det \mathbf{L}|$. If we choose $\mathbf{G}'$ to be

$$\begin{bmatrix} 2 & 1 \\ 0 & 1 \end{bmatrix}$$

then the size of the footprint is $|\det \mathbf{D}'|/2$ for the new $\mathbf{D}'$ since $|\det \mathbf{G}'|$ is now 2. But both expressions evaluate to the same value, $|\det \mathbf{L}|$, as one would expect.

5.3 The Rows of G Are Dependent

The rows of $\mathbf{G}$ are dependent means that the mapping from the iteration space to the data space is many to one. It is hard to derive an expression for the footprint in general when the rows are dependent. However, we can compute the footprint and the cumulative footprint for many special cases that arise in actual programs. In this section we shall look at the common case where the rows are dependent because one or more of the index variables do not appear in the array reference. We shall illustrate our technique with the matrix multiply program shown in Example 52 below. The notation 1$C[i,j] means that the read-modify-write of C[i,j] is atomic.

Example 52.

Doall (i=0:N, j=0:N, k=0:N)
  1$C[i,j] = 1$C[i,j] + A[i,k]+B[k,j]
EndDoall

The references to the matrices A, B and C belong to separate uniformly intersecting references. So the cumulative footprint is the sum of the footprints of each of the references. We will focus on A[i,k] and footprint computation for the other references are similar. The **G** matrix for A[i,k] is

$$\begin{bmatrix} 1 & 0 \\ 0 & 0 \\ 0 & 1 \end{bmatrix}.$$

We cannot apply our earlier results to compute the footprint since **G** is a many to one mapping. However, we can find an invertible **G'** such that for every loop tile **L**, there is a tile **L'** such that the number of elements in footprints **LG** and **LG'** are the same. For the current example, **G'** is obtained from **G** by deleting the row of zeros, resulting in a two dimensional identity matrix. Similarly **L'** is obtained from **L** by eliminating the corresponding (second) column of **L**. Now, it is easy to show that the number of elements in footprints **LG** and **LG'** are the same by establishing a one-to-one correspondence between the two footprints. Let us use this method to compute the size of the footprint corresponding to the reference A[i,k]. Let us assume that **L** is rectangular to make the computations simpler. Let **L** be

$$\begin{bmatrix} L_i & 0 & 0 \\ 0 & L_j & 0 \\ 0 & 0 & L_k \end{bmatrix}.$$

Now **L'** is

$$\begin{bmatrix} L_i & 0 \\ 0 & 0 \\ 0 & L_k \end{bmatrix}.$$

So the size of the footprint is $L_i L_k$. Similarly, one can show that the size of the other two footprints are $L_i L_j$ and $L_j L_k$. The cumulative footprint is $L_i L_k + L_i L_j + L_j L_k$ which is minimized when L_i, L_j and L_k are equal.

6. Other System Environments

This section describes how our framework can be used to solve the partitioning problem in a wide range of systems. We discuss (1) loop partitioning to minimize coherency traffic in systems with coherent caches and uniform-access main memory, (2) loop partitioning with non-unit cache line sizes, (3) and loop and data partitioning in distributed-memory systems without caches. Then, Sect. 7 discusses simultaneous loop and data partitioning in cache-coherent distributed shared-memory memory systems (NUMA).

6.1 Coherence-Related Cache Misses

Our analysis presented in the previous section was concerned with minimizing the cumulative footprint size. This process of minimizing the cumulative footprint size not only minimizes the number of first-time cache misses, but the number of coherence-related misses as well. For example, consider the **forall** loop embedded within a sequential loop in Example 61. Here **forall** means that all the reads are done prior to the writes. In other words the data read in iteration t corresponds to the data written in iteration $t - 1$.

Example 61.

Doseq (t=1:T)
   forall (i=1:N,j=1:N)
     A(i,j) = A(i+1,j)
   EndDoall
EndDoseq

For this example, we have

$$\mathbf{G} = \begin{bmatrix} 1 & 0 \\ 0 & 1 \end{bmatrix}$$

Let us attempt to minimize the cumulative footprint for a loop partition of the form

$$\mathbf{L} = \begin{bmatrix} L_i & 0 \\ 0 & L_j \end{bmatrix}$$

The cumulative footprint size is given by

$$L_i L_j + L_j$$

In a load-balanced partitioning, $|\det \mathbf{L}| = L_i L_j$ is a constant, so the $L_i L_j$ term drops out of the optimization. The optimization process then attempts to minimize L_j, which is proportional to the volume of cache coherence traffic, as depicted in Fig. 6.1.

Let us focus on regions X, Y and Z in Fig. 6.1(c). As explained in Fig. 4.8, the processor working on the loop tile to which these regions belong (say, processor P_O) shares a portion of its cumulative footprint with processors working on neighboring regions in the data space. Specifically, region Z is a sub-tile of the positive neighbor and region Y is a sub-tile shared with its negative neighbor. Region X, however, is completely private to P_O.

Let us consider the situation after the first iteration of the outer sequential loop. Accesses of data elements within region X will hit in the cache, and thereby incur zero communication cost. Data elements in region Z, however, potentially cause misses because the processor working on the positive neighbor might have previously written into those elements, resulting in those elements being invalidated from P_O's cache. Each of these misses by processor P_O suffers a network round trip because of the need to inform the processor working on its positive neighbor to perform a write-back and then to send the data to processor P_O. Furthermore, if the home memory location for the block is elsewhere, the miss requires an additional network round-trip. Similarly, in region Y, a write by processor P_O potentially incurs two network round trips as well. The two round trips result from the need to invalidate the data block from the cache of the processor working on the negative neighbor, and then to fetch the blocks into P_O's cache.

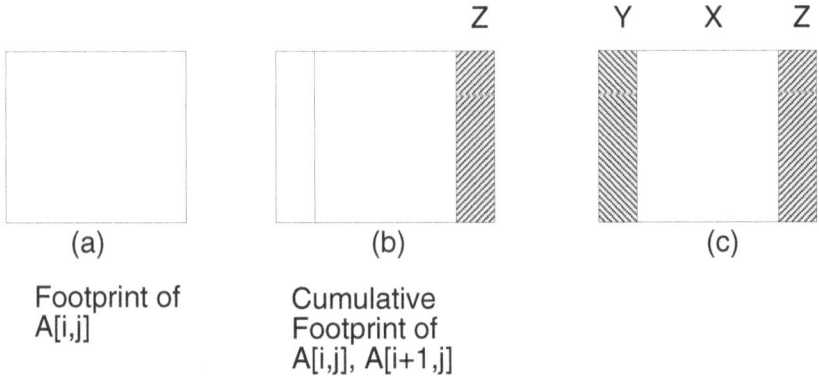

Z   Y   X   Z

(a)   (b)   (c)

Footprint of   Cumulative
A[i,j]   Footprint of
                      A[i,j], A[i+1,j]

Fig. 6.1. (a) Footprint of reference $A[i, j]$ for a rectangular **L**. (b) Cumulative footprint for the references $A[i, j]$ and $A[i + 1, j]$. The hashed region Z represents the increase in footprint size due to the reference $A[i + 1, j]$. (c) The regions X, Y, Z, collectively represent the cumulative footprint for references $A[i, j]$ and $A[i + 1, j]$. Region Z represents the area in the data space shared with the positive neighbor. Region Y represents the area in the data space shared with the negative neighbor.

In any case, the coherence traffic is proportional to the area of the shared region Z, which is equal to the area of the shared region Y, and is given by L_j. So the total communication is minimized by choosing the tile with $L_j = 1$.

6.2 Effect of Cache Line Size

The effect of cache line sizes can be incorporated easily into our analysis. Because large cache lines fetch multiple data words at the cost of a single miss, one data space dimension will be favored by the cache. Without loss of generality, let us assume that the jth dimension of the data space benefits from larger cache lines. Then, the effect of cache lines of size B can be incorporated into our analysis by replacing each element d_{ij} in the jth column of $\mathbf{D}$ in Theorem 43 by

$$\left\lceil \frac{d_{ij}}{B} \right\rceil$$

to reflect the lower cost of fetching multiple words in the jth dimension of the data space[2], and by modifying the definition of intersecting references to the following.

Definition 61. *Two references* $A[\mathbf{g}_1(\mathbf{i})]$ *and* $A[\mathbf{g}_2(\mathbf{i})]$ *are said to be intersecting if there are two integer vectors* $\mathbf{i}_1, \mathbf{i}_2$ *for which* $A[\mathbf{g}_1(\mathbf{i}_1)] = A[(d_{11}, d_{12}, \ldots)]$ *and* $A[\mathbf{g}_2(\mathbf{i}_2)] = A[(d_{21}, d_{22}, \ldots)]$ *such that* $A[(\ldots, d_{1(j-1)}, \left\lceil \frac{d_{1j}}{B} \right\rceil, \ldots)] = A[(\ldots, d_{2(j-1)}, \left\lceil \frac{d_{2j}}{B} \right\rceil, \ldots)]$, *where B is the size of a cache line, and the jth dimension in the data space benefits from larger cache lines.*

6.3 Data Partitioning in Distributed-Memory Multicomputers

In systems in which main memory is distributed with the processing nodes (e.g., see the NUMA systems in Fig. 3.3(a) and (b)), data partitioning is the problem of partitioning the data arrays into data tiles and the nested loops into loop tiles and assigning the loop tiles (indicated by $\mathbf{L}$) to the processing nodes and the corresponding data tiles (indicated by $\mathbf{D}$) to memory modules associated with the processing nodes so that a maximum number of the data references made by the loop tiles are satisfied by the local memory module. Our formulation facilitates data partitioning straightforwardly. There are two cases to consider: systems without caches and systems with caches. This section addresses systems without caches. NUMA systems with caches are dealt with in Sect. 7.

The compiler has two options to optimize communication volume in systems without caches. The compiler can choose to make *local copies* of remote

---

[2] We note that the estimate of cumulative footprint size will be slightly inaccurate if the footprint is misaligned with the cache block.

data, or it can fetch remote data each time the data is needed. In the former case, the compiler can use the same partitioning algorithms described in this paper for systems with caches, but it must also solve the data coherence problem for the copied data. This section addresses the latter case.

The general strategy is as follows: The optimal loop partition $\mathbf{L}$ is first derived by minimizing the cumulative footprint size as described in the previous sections. Data partitioning requires the additional derivation of the optimal data partition $\mathbf{D}$ for each class of uniformly intersecting references from the optimal loop partition $\mathbf{L}$. We derive the shapes of the data tiles $\mathbf{D}$ for each $\mathbf{G}$ corresponding to a specific class of uniformly intersecting references. A specific data tile is chosen from the footprints corresponding to each reference in an uniformly intersecting set. We then place each loop tile with the data tiles accessed by it on the same processing node.

Although the overall theory remains largely the same as described earlier we must make one change in the footprint size computation to reflect the fact that a given data tile is placed in local memory and data elements from neighboring tiles have to be fetched from remote memory modules each time they are accessed. Because data partitioning for distributed-memory systems without caches (see Fig. 3.3(b)) assumes that data from other memory modules is not dynamically copied locally (as in systems with caches), we replace the $max - min$ formulation by the *cumulative spread* a^+ of a set of uniformly intersecting references. That is

$$a^+ = \text{cumulativespread}_{\mathbf{D}}(\mathbf{a}_1, \ldots, \mathbf{a}_R) = b^+ \mathbf{D},$$

in which the kth element of b^+ is given by,

$$b_k^+ = \sum_r \mid [b_{r,k} - med_r(b_{r,k})] \mid, \forall k \in 1, \ldots, d,$$

where $\mathbf{b}_r = \mathbf{a}_r \mathbf{D}^{-1}, \forall r \in 1, \ldots, R$ and $med_r(b_{r,k})$ is the median of the offsets in the kth dimension. The rest of our framework for minimizing the footprint size applies to data partitioning if $\hat{a}$ is replaced by a^+.

The data partitioning strategy proceeds as follows. As in loop partitioning for caches, for a given loop tile $\mathbf{L}$, we first write an expression for the communication volume by deriving the size of that portion of the cumulative footprint not contained in local memory. This communication volume is given by

$$\sum_{k=1}^{d} \mid \det \mathbf{D}_{k \to a^+} \mid$$

We then derive the optimal $\mathbf{L}$ to minimize this communication volume. We then derive the optimal data partition $\mathbf{D}$ for each class of uniformly intersecting references from the optimal loop partition $\mathbf{L}$ as described in the previous section on systems with caches. A specific data tile is chosen from the footprints corresponding to each reference in an uniformly intersecting set.

In systems without caches, because a single data element might have to be fetched multiple times, the choice of a specific data footprint does matter. A simple heuristic to maximize the number of local accesses is to choose a data tile whose offsets are the medians of all the offsets in each dimension. We can show that using a median tile is optimal for one-dimensional data spaces, and close to optimal for higher dimensions. However, a detailed description is beyond the scope of this paper. We then place each loop tile with the corresponding data tiles accessed by it on the same processor.

7. Combined Loop and Data Partitioning in DSMs

Until this point we have been assuming that in systems with caches the cost of a cache miss is independent of the actual memory location being accessed. In systems in which main memory is distributed with the processing nodes (e.g., see Fig. 3.3(a)), data partitioning attempts to maximize the probability that cache misses are satisfied in local memory, rather than suffer a remote memory access. Unfortunately, when a program has multiple loops that access a given data array, the possibility of the loops imposing conflicting data tiling requirements for caches arises. Furthermore, the partitioning that achieves optimal cache behavior is not necessarily the partitioning that simultaneously achieves optimal local memory behavior. This section describes a heuristic method for solving this problem.

7.1 The Cost Model

The key to a finding a communication-minimal partitioning is a cost model that allows a tradeoff to be made between cache miss cost and remote memory access cost. This cost model drives an iterative solution and is a function that takes, as arguments, a loop partition, data partitions for each array accessed in the loop, and architectural parameters that determine the relative cost of cache misses and remote memory accesses. It returns an estimation of the cost of array references for the loop.

The cost due to memory references in terms of architectural parameters is computed by the following equation:

$$T_{total\_access} = T_R(n_{remote}) + T_L(n_{local}) + T_C(n_{cache})$$

where T_R, T_L, T_C are the remote, local and cache memory access times respectively, and $n_{remote}, n_{local}, n_{cache}$ are the number of references that result in hits to remote memory, local memory and cache memory. T_C and T_L are fixed by the architecture, while T_R is determined both by the base remote latency of the architecture and possible contention if there are many remote references. T_R may also vary with the number of processors based on the interconnect topology.

n_{cache}, n_{local} and n_{remote} depend on the loop and data partitions. Given a loop partition, for each UI-set consider the intersection between the footprint (**LG**) of that set and a given data partition **D**. First time accesses to data in that intersection will be in local memory while first time references to data outside will be remote. Repeat accesses will likely hit in the cache. A UI-set may contain several references, each with slightly different footprints due to different offsets in the array index expressions. One is selected and called the base offset, or **b**. In the following definitions the symbol $\approx$ will be used to compare footprints and data partitions. **LG** $\approx$ **D** means that the matrix equality holds. This equality does not mean that all references in the UI-set represented by **G** will be local in the data partition **D** because there may be small offset vectors for each reference in the UI-set.

We define the functions R_b, F_f and F_b, which are all functions of the loop partition **L**, data partition **D** and reference matrix **G** with the meanings given in previously. For simplicity, we also use R_b, F_f and F_b, to denote the value returned by the respective functions of the same name.

Definition 71. R_b *is a function which maps* **L**, **D** *and* **G** *to the number of remote references that result from a single access defined by* **G** *and the base offset* **b**.

In other words, R_b returns the number of remote accesses that result from a single program reference in a parallel loop, not including the small peripheral footprint due to multiple accesses in its UI-set. The periphery is added using F_f to be described below.

Note that in most cases **G**'s define UI-sets: accesses to an array with the same **G** but different offsets are usually in the same UI-set, and different **G**'s always have different UI-sets. The only exception are accesses with the same **G** but large differences in their offsets relative to tile size, in which case they are considered to be in different UI-sets.

The computation of R_b is simplified by an approximation. One of the two following cases apply to loop and data partitions.

1. Loop partition **L** matches the data partition **D**, *i.e.* **LG** $\approx$ **D**. The references in the periphery due to small offsets between references in the UI-set are considered in F_f. In this case $R_b = 0$.
2. **L** does not match **D**. This is case where the **G** matrix used to compute **D** (perhaps from another UI-set), is different from the **G** for the current access, and thus **LG** and **D** have different *shapes*, not just different offsets. In this case all references for **L** are considered remote and $R_b = |\text{Det } L|$.

This is a good approximation because **LG** and **D** each represent a regular tiling of the data space. If they differ, it means the footprint and data tile differ in shape, *and do not stride the same way*. Thus, even if **L**'s footprints and **D** partially overlap at the origin, there will be less overlap on other processors. For a reasonably large number of processors, some will end up with no overlap as shown in the example in Fig. 7.1. Since the execution time for a parallel loop nest is limited by the processor with the most remote cache misses, the non-overlap approximation is a good one.

$$\textbf{Doall } (\texttt{i=0:100, j=0:75})$$
$$\texttt{B[i,j] = A[i,j] + A[i+j,j]}$$
$$\textbf{EndDoall}$$

(a) Code fragment

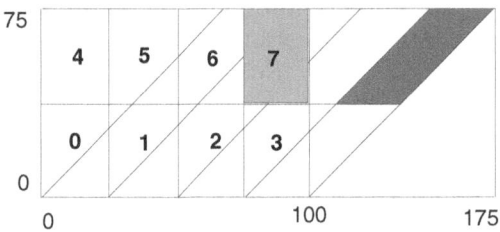

75

| 4 | 5 | 6 | 7 |

| 0 | 1 | 2 | 3 |

0

0   100   175

Rectangles : Footprints for A[i,j]

Parallelograms : Footprints for A[i+j,j]

Processor 7's footprints have no overlap

(Numbering for footprints of A[i,j])

(b) Data space for Array A(8 processors)

Fig. 7.1. Different UI-sets have no overlap

Definition 72. F_b *is the number of first time accesses in the footprint of* **L** *with base offset* **b**. *Hence:*
$$F_b = |Det\ L|$$

Definition 73. F_f *is the difference between (1) the cumulative footprints of all the references in a given UI-set for a loop tile, and (2) the base footprint due to a single reference represented by* **G** *and the base offset* **b**. F_f *is referred to as the peripheral footprint.*

Theorem 71. *The cumulative access time for all accesses in a loop with partition* **L**, *accessing an array having data partition* **D** *with reference matrix* **G** *in a UI-set is*

$$T_{UI-set} = T_R(R_b + F_f) + T_L(F_b - R_b) + T_C(nref - (F_f + F_b))$$

where nref is the total number of references made by **L** *for the UI-set.*

This result can be derived as follows. The number of remote accesses n_{remote} is the number of remote accesses with the base offset, which is R_b, plus the size of the peripheral footprint F_f, giving $n_{remote} = R_b + F_f$. The number of local references n_{local} is the base footprint, less the remote portion, i.e. $F_b - R_b$. Finally, number of cache hits n_{cache} is clearly $nref - n_{remote} - n_{local}$ which is equal to $nref - (F_f + F_b)$.

Sub-blocking. The above cost model assumes infinite caches. In practice, even programs with moderate-sized data sets have footprints much larger than the cache size. To overcome this problem the loop tiles are *sub-blocked*, such that each sub-block fits in the cache and has a shape that optimizes for cache locality. This optimization lets the cost model remain valid even for finite caches. It turned out that sub-blocking was critically important even for small to moderate problem sizes.

Finite caches and sub-blocking also allows us to ignore the effect of data that is shared between loop nests when that data is left behind in the cache by one loop nest and reused by another. Data sharing can happen in infinite caches due to accesses to the same array when the two loops use the same **G**. However, when caches are much smaller than data footprints, and the compiler resorts to sub-blocking, the possibility of reuse across loops is virtually eliminated.

This model also assumes a linear flow of control through the loop nests of the program. While this is the common case, conditional control flow can be handled by our algorithm. Although we do not handle this case now, an approach would be to assign probabilities to each loop nest, perhaps based on profile data, and to multiply the probabilities by the loop size to obtain an effective loop size for use by the algorithm.

7.2 The Multiple Loops Heuristic Method

This section describes the iterative method, whose goal is to discover a partitioning of loops and data arrays to minimize communication cost. We assume loop partitions are non-cyclic. Cyclic partitions could be handled using this method but for simplicity we leave them out.

7.2.1 Graph Formulation. Our search procedure uses bipartite graphs to represent loops and data arrays. Bipartite graphs are a popular data structure used to represent partitioning problems for loops and data [9,22]. For a graph $G = (V_l, V_d, E)$, the loops are pictured as a set of nodes V_l on the left hand side, and the data arrays as a set of nodes V_d on the right. An edge $e \in E$ between a loop and array node is present if and only if the loop accesses the array. The edges are labeled by the uniformly intersecting set(s) they represent. When we say that a data partition is *induced* by a loop partition, we mean the data partition **D** is the same as the loop partition **L**'s footprint. Similarly, for loop partitions induced by data partitions.

7.2.2 Iterative Method Outline. We use an iterative local search technique that exploits certain special properties of loops and data array partitions to move to a good solution. Extensive work evaluating search techniques has been done by researchers in many disciplines. Simulated annealing, gradient descent and genetic algorithms are some of these. All techniques rely on a cost function estimating some objective value to be optimized, and a search strategy. For specific problems more may be known than in the general case, and specific strategies may do better. In our case, we know the search direction that leads to improvement, and hence a specific strategy is defined. The algorithm greedily moves to a local minimum, does a mutation to escape from it, and repeats the process.

The following is the method in more detail. To derive the initial loop partition, the single loop optimization method described in this paper is used. Then an iterative improvement method is followed, which has two phases in each iteration: the first (forward) phase finds the best data partitions given loop partitions, and the second (back) phase redetermines the values of the loop partitions given the data partitions just determined.

We define a boolean value called the progress flag for each array. Specifically, in the forward phase the data partition of each array having a true progress flag is set to the induced data partition of the largest loop accessing it, among those which change the data partition. The method of controlling the progress flag is explained in section 7.2.4. In the back phase, each loop partition is set to be the data partition of one of the arrays accessed by the loop. The cost model is used to evaluate the alternative partitions and pick the one with minimal cost.

These forward and backward phases are repeated using the cost model to determine the estimated array reference cost for the current partitions. After some number of iterations, the best partition found so far is picked as the final partition. Termination is discussed in Sect. 7.2.4.

7.2.3 An Example. The workings of the heuristic can be seen by a simple example. Consider the following code fragment:

```
Doall (i=0:99, j=0:99)
  A[i,j] = i * j
EndDoall
Doall (i=0:99, j=0:99)
  B[i,j] = A[j,i]
EndDoall
```

The code does a transpose of A into B. The first loop is represented by X and the second by Y. The initial cache optimized solution for 4 processors is shown in Fig. 7.2. In this example, as there is no peripheral footprint for either array, a default load balanced solution is picked. Iterations 1 and 2 with their forward and back phases are shown in Fig. 7.3.

(loop spaces)

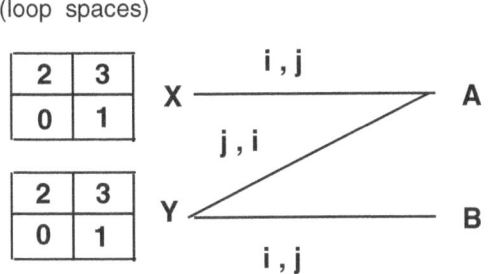

Fig. 7.2. Initial solution to loop partitioning (4 processors)

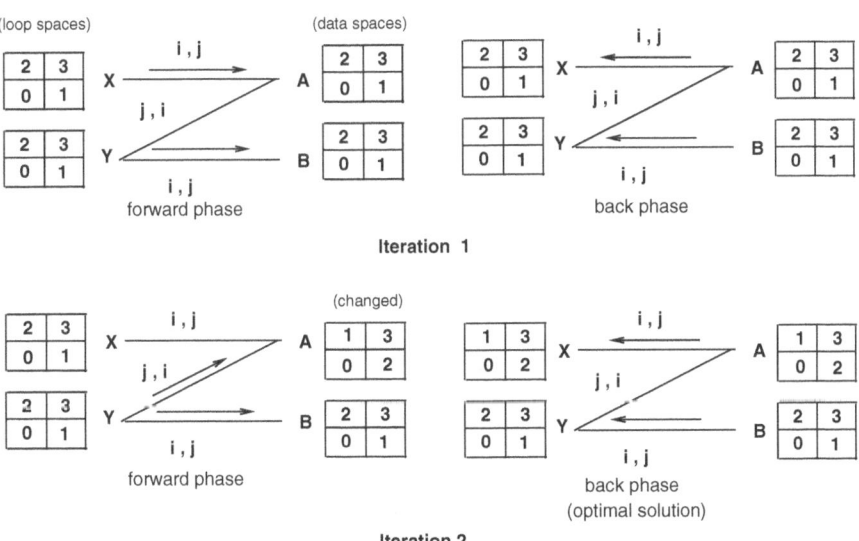

Fig. 7.3. Heuristic: iterations 1 and 2 (4 processors)

In iteration 1's forward phase A and B get data partitions from their largest accessing loops. Since both loops here are equal in size, the compiler picks either, and one possible choice is shown by the arrows. In 1's back phase, loop Y cannot match both A and B's data partitions, and the cost estimator indicates that matching either has the same cost. So an arbitrary choice as shown by the back arrows results in unchanged data partitions; nothing has changed from the beginning.

As explained in the next section, the choice of data partitions in the forward phase is *favored in the direction of change*. So now array A picks a different data partition from before, that of Y instead of X. In the back phase loop X now changes its loop partition to reduce cost as dictated by the cost function. This is the best solution found, and no further change occurs in subsequent iterations. In this case, this best solution is also the optimal solution as it has 100% locality. In this example a communication-free solution exists and was found. More generally, if one does not exist, the heuristic will evaluate many solutions and will pick the best one it finds.

7.2.4 Some Implementation Details. The algorithm of the heuristic method is presented in Fig. 7.4. Some details of the algorithm are explained here.

Choosing a data partition different from the current one is preferred because it ensures movement out of local minima. A mutation out of a local minimum is a change to a possibly higher cost point, that sets the algorithm on another path. This rule ensures that the next configuration differs from the previous, and hence makes it unnecessary to do global checks for local minima.

However, without a progress flag, always changing data partitions in the forward phase may change data partitions too fast. This is because one part of the graph may change before a change it induced in a previous iteration has propagated to the whole graph. This is prevented using a *bias rule*. A data partition is not changed in the forward phase if it induced a loop partition change in the immediately preceding back phase. This is done by setting its progress flag to false.

As with all deterministic local search techniques, this algorithm could suffer from oscillations. The progress flag helps solve this problem. Oscillations happen when a configuration is revisited. The solution is to, conservatively, determine if a cost has been seen before, and if it has, simply enforce change at all data partition selections in the next forward phase. This sets the heuristic on another path. There is no need to store and compare entire configurations to detect oscillations.

One issue is the number of iterations to perform. In this problem, the length of the longest path in the bipartite graph is a reasonable bound, since changed partitions in one part of the graph need to propagate to other parts of the graph. This bound seems to work well in practice. Further increases in this bound did not provide a better solution in any of the examples or programs tried.

8. Implementation and Results

This paper presents cumulative footprint size measurements from an algorithm simulator and execution time measurements for loop partitioning from an actual compiler implementation on a multiprocessor. See [23] for results on combined loop and data partitioning.

Procedure Do_forward_phase()
    for all d ∈ Data_set **do**
        if Progress_flag[d] **then**
            l ← largest loop accessing d which induces changed Data_partition[d]
            Data_partition[d] ← Partition induced by Loop_partition[l]
            Origin[d] ← Access function mapping of Origin[l]
        endif
        Inducing_loop[d] ← l
    endfor
end Procedure

Procedure Do_back_phase()
    for all l ∈ Loop_set **do**
        d ← Array inducing Loop_partition[l] with minimum cost of accessing all
            its data
        Loop_partition[l] ← Partition induced by Data_partition[d]
        Origin[l] ← Inverse access function mapping of Origin[d]
        if Inducing_loop[d] ≠ l **then**
            Progress_flag[d] ← **false**
        endif
    endfor
end Procedure

Procedure Partition
    Loop_set : **set** of all loops in the program
    Data_set : **set** of all data arrays in the program
    Graph_G : Bipartite graph of accesses in Loop_set to Data_set

    Min_partitions ← φ
    Min_cost ← ∞
    for all d ∈ Data_set **do**
        Progress_flag[d] ← **true**
    endfor
    for i= 1 to (length of longest path in Graph_G) **do**
        Do_forward_phase()
        Do_back_phase()
        Cost ← Find total cost of current partition configuration
        if Cost < Min_cost **then**
            Cost ← Min_cost
            Min_partitions ← Current partition configuration
        endif
        if cost repeated **then**   /* convergence or oscillation */
            for all d ∈ Data_set **do**   /* force progress */
                Progress_flag[d] ← **true**
            endfor
        endif
    endfor
end Procedure

Fig. 7.4. The heuristic algorithm

8.1 Algorithm Simulator Experiments

We have written a simulator of partitioning algorithms that measures the exact cumulative footprint size for any given hyperparallelepiped partition. The simulator also presents analytically computed footprint sizes using the formulation presented in Theorem 43.

We present in Fig. 8.1 algorithm simulator data showing the communication volume for array **B** in Example 33 (repeated below for convenience) resulting from a large number of loop partitions (with tile size 96) representing both parallelograms and rectangles. The abscissa is labeled by the **L** matrix parameters of the various loop partitions, and the parallelogram shape is also depicted above each histogram bar.

Doall (i=1:N, j=1:N)
    A[i,j] = B[i,j] + B[i+1,j-2] + B[i-1,j+1]
EndDoall

The example demonstrates that the analytical method yields accurate estimates of cumulative footprint sizes. The estimates are higher than the measured values when the partitions are mismatched with the offset vectors due to the overlapping sub-tile approximation described in Sect. 4.4. We can also see that the difference between the optimal parallelogram partition and a poor partition is significant. The differences become even greater if bigger offsets are used. This example also shows that rectangular partitions do not always yield the best partition.

8.2 Experiments on the Alewife Multiprocessor

We have also implemented some of the ideas from our framework in a compiler for the Alewife machine [24] to understand the extent to which good loop partitioning impacts end application performance, and the extent to which our theory predicts the optimal loop partition. The Alewife machine implements a shared global address space with distributed physical memory and coherent caches. The nodes contain slightly modified SPARC processors and are configured in a 2-dimensional mesh network.

For NUMA machines such as Alewife, where references to remote memory are more expensive than local references, partitioning loops to increase cache hits is not enough. A compiler must also perform data partitioning, distributing data so that cache misses tend to be satisfied by local memory. We have implemented loop and data partitioning in our compiler using an iterative method as described in [15]. Because this paper focuses on loop partitioning, for the following experiments we caused the compiler to distribute data randomly. The effect is that most cache misses are to remote memory, simulating a UMA machine as depicted in Fig. 2.2, and the results offer insights into the extent to which good loop partitioning affects end application performance.

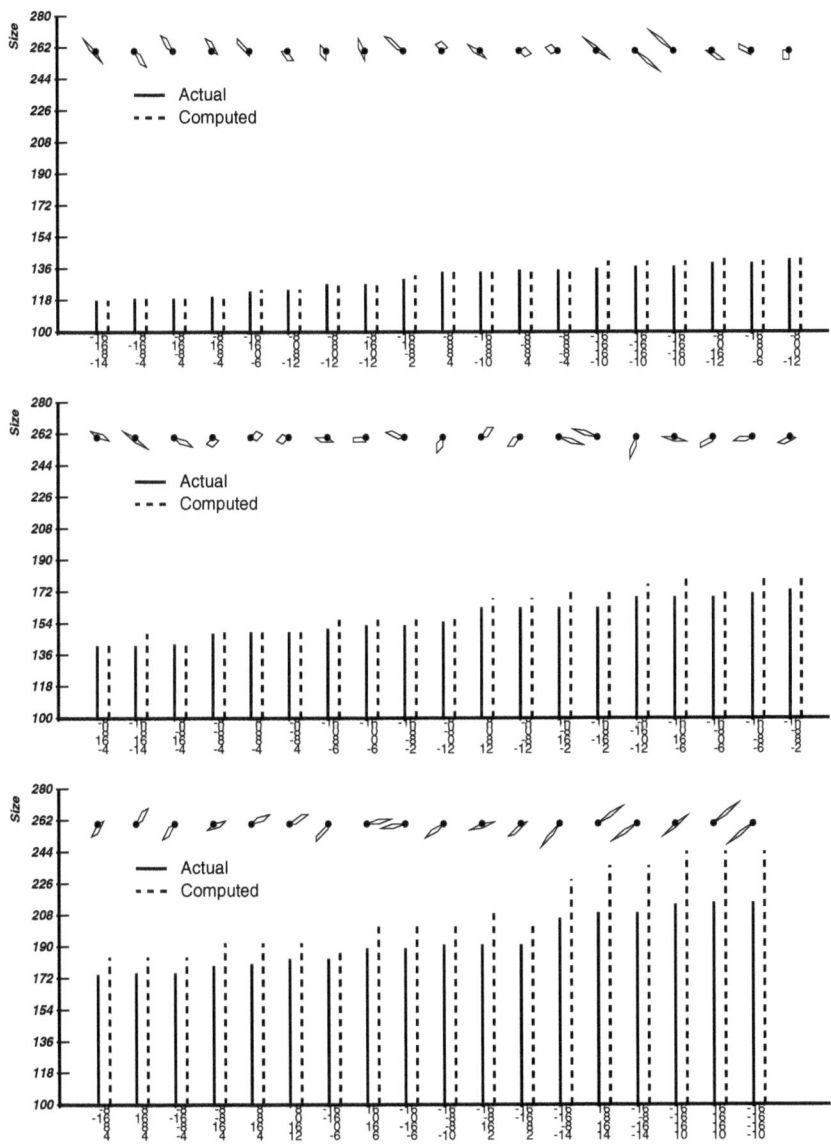

Fig. 8.1. Actual and computed footprint sizes for several loop partitions.

The performance gain due to loop partitioning depends on the ratio of communication to computation and other overhead. To get an understanding of these numbers for Alewife, we measured the performance of one loop nest on an Alewife simulator, and the performance of three applications on a 32-processor Alewife machine.

Single Loop Nest Experiment. The following loop nest was run on a simulator of a 64 processor Alewife machine:

Doall (i=0:255, j=4:251)
  A[i,j] = A[i-1,j] + B[i,j+4] + B[i,j-4]
EndDoall

The **G** matrix for the above loop nest is the 2×2 identity matrix, and the offset vectors are $\mathbf{a}_1 = (0,0)$, $\mathbf{a}_2 = (-1,0)$, $\mathbf{b}_1 = (0,4)$, and $\mathbf{b}_2 = (0,-4)$. Each array was 512 elements (words) on a side. The cache line size is four words, and the arrays are stored in row-major order.

Using the algorithms in this paper, and taking the four-word cache line size into account, the compiler chose a rectangular loop partition and determined that the optimal partition has an aspect ratio of 2:1. The compiler then chose the closest aspect ratio (1:1) that also achieves load balance for the given problem size and machine size, which results in a tile size of 64x64 iterations. We also ran the loop nest using suboptimal partitions with tile dimensions ranging from 8x512 to 512x8. This set of executions is labeled run A in Fig. 8.2. We ran a second version of the program using a different set of offset vectors that give an optimal aspect ratio of 8:1 (run B). This results in a desired tile size between 256x16 and 128x32 with the compiler choosing 256x16.

Fig. 8.2 shows the running times for the different tile sizes, and demonstrates that the compiler was able to pick the optimal partitions for both cases. There is some noise in these figures because there can be variation in the cost of accessing the memory that is actually shared due to cache coherence actions, but the minima of the curves are about where the framework predicted.

Application Experiments. The following three applications were run on a real Alewife machine with 32 processors.

Erlebacher A code written by Thomas Eidson, from ICASE. It performs 3-D tridiagonal solves using Alternating Direction Implicit (ADI) integration. It has 40 loops and 22 arrays in one, two and three dimensions.

Conduct A routine in SIMPLE, a two dimensional hydrodynamics code from Lawrence Livermore National Labs. It has 20 loops and 20 arrays in one and two dimensions.

Tomcatv A code from the SPEC suite. It has 12 loops and 7 arrays, all two dimensional.

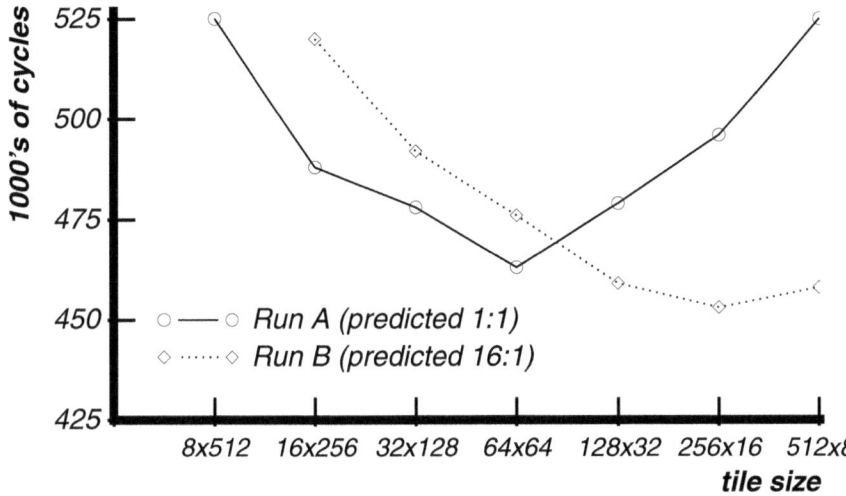

Fig. 8.2. Running times in 1000's of cycles for different aspect ratios on 64 processors.

As with the loop nest example, the programs were compiled with two different methods of partitioning loops. The *auto* method used the algorithms described in this paper to partition each loop independently. The other methods assigned a fixed partition shape to each loop: rows, squares or columns. The results are shown in Tables 8.1, 8.2 and 8.3. The cache-miss penalty for this experiment is small because the Alewife remote memory access time is rather short (about 40 cycles). Since we expect that the importance of good loop partitioning will increase with the cache-miss penalty, we also ran two other experiments with a longer remote delay of 100 and 200 cycles. Alewife allows longer delays to be synthesized by a combination of software and hardware mechanisms.

These results show that the choice of partitioning parameters affects performance significantly. In all cases, the partitioner was able to discover the best partition. In two of the applications, the compiler's partition choice resulted in a small improvement over squares. In Tomcatv, the compiler chose the same square partition for each loop, resulting in no improvement over the fixed square partition. The performance gains over squares for all of these programs are modest because the offsets in most of the references in the three applications are similar.

Table 8.1. Execution time in Mcycles for Erlebacher (N = 64)

Delay	*auto*	rows	squares	columns
40 cycles	27.0	27.3	28.6	28.2
100 cycles	30.4	31.4	31.2	31.3
200 cycles	34.0	35.2	36.4	36.8

Table 8.2. Execution time in Mcycles for Conduct (N = 768)

Delay	*auto*	rows	squares	columns
40 cycles	67.2	71.2	71.4	71.2
100 cycles	85.4	91.2	91.8	90.8
200 cycles	111.4	118.2	117.1	117.5

Table 8.3. Execution time in Mcycles for Tomcatv (N = 1200)

Delay	*auto*	rows	squares	columns
40 cycles	104	127	100	113
100 cycles	125	152	122	138
200 cycles	154	188	154	174

9. Conclusions

The performance of cache-coherent systems is heavily predicated on the degree of temporal locality in the access patterns of the processor. If each block of data is accessed a number of times by a given processor, then caches will be effective in reducing network traffic. Loop partitioning for cache-coherent multiprocessors strives to achieve precisely this goal.

This paper presented a theoretical framework to derive the parameters of iteration-space partitions of the do loops to minimize the communication traffic in multiprocessors with caches. The framework allows the partitioning of doall loops into optimal hyperparallelepiped tiles where the index expressions in array accesses can be any affine function of the indices. The same framework also yields optimal loop and data partitions for multicomputers with local memory.

Our analysis uses the notion of uniformly intersecting references to categorize the references within a loop into classes that will yield cache locality. A theory of data footprints is introduced to capture the combined set of data accesses made by the references within each uniformly intersecting class. Then, an algorithm to compute precisely the total size of the data footprint for a given loop partition is presented. Once an expression for the total size of the data footprint is obtained, standard optimization techniques can be applied to minimize the size of the data footprint and derive the optimal loop partitions.

Our framework discovers optimal partitions in many more general cases than those handled by previous algorithms. In addition, it correctly reproduces results from loop partitioning algorithms for certain special cases previously proposed by other researchers.

The framework, including both loop and data partitioning for cache-coherent distributed shared memory, has been implemented in the compiler system for the Alewife multiprocessor.

Acknowledgement. This research is supported by Motorola Cambridge Research Center and by NSF grant # MIP-9012773. Partial support has also been provided by DARPA contract # N00014-87-K-0825, in part by a NSF Presidential Young Investigator Award. Gino Maa helped define and implement the compiler system and its intermediate form. Andrea Carnevali suggested the simple proof for Theorem 41 on lattices that is sketched in this paper. We acknowledge the contributions of the Alewife group for implementing and supporting the Alewife simulator and runtime system used in obtaining the results.

References

1. Constantine D. Polychronopoulos and David J. Kuck. Guided Self-Scheduling: A Practical Scheduling Scheme for Parallel Supercomputers. *IEEE Transactions on Computers*, C-36(12), December 1987.
2. E. Mohr, D. Kranz, and R. Halstead. Lazy Task Creation: A Technique for Increasing the Granularity of Parallel Programs. *IEEE Transactions on Parallel and Distributed Systems*, 2(3):264–280, July 1991.
3. M. Wolf and M. Lam. A data locality optimizing algorithm. In *Proceedings of the ACM SIGPLAN 91 Conference Programming Language Design and Implementation*, pages 30–44, 1991.
4. D. Gannon, W. Jalby, and K. Gallivan. Strategies for cache and local memory management by global program transformation. *Journal of Parallel and Distributed Computing*, 5:587–616, 1988.
5. Harold S. Stone and Dominique Thiebaut. Footprints in the Cache. In *Proceedings of ACM SIGMETRICS 1986*, pages 4–8, May 1986.
6. F. Irigoin and R. Triolet. Supernode Partitioning. In *15th Symposium on Principles of Programming Languages (POPL XV)*, pages 319–329, January 1988.
7. S. G. Abraham and D. E. Hudak. Compile-time partitioning of iterative parallel loops to reduce cache coherency traffic. *IEEE Transactions on Parallel and Distributed Systems*, 2(3):318–328, July 1991.
8. J. Ramanujam and P. Sadayappan. Compile-Time Techniques for Data Distribution in Distributed Memory Machines. *IEEE Transactions on Parallel and Distributed Systems*, 2(4):472–482, October 1991.
9. Jennifer M. Anderson and Monica S. Lam. Global Optimizations for Parallelism and Locality on Scalable Parallel Machines. In *Proceedings of SIGPLAN '93 Conference on Programming Languages Design and Implementation*. ACM, June 1993.
10. M. Gupta and P. Banerjee. Demonstration of Automatic Data Partitioning Techniques for Parallelizing Compilers on Multicomputers. *IEEE Transactions on Parallel and Distributed Systems*, 3(2):179–193, March 1992.

11. Robert Schreiber and Jack Dongarra. Automatic Blocking of Nested Loops. Technical report, RIACS, NASA Ames Research Center, and Oak Ridge National Laboratory, May 1990.

12. J. Ferrante, V. Sarkar, and W. Thrash. *On Estimating and Enhancing Cache Effectiveness*, pages 328–341. Springer-Verlag, August 1991. Lecture Notes in Computer Science: Languages and Compilers for Parallel Computing. Editors U. Banerjee and D. Gelernter and A. Nicolau and D. Padua.

13. J. Ramanujam and P. Sadayappan. Tiling multidimensional iteration spaces for nonshared memory machines. In *Proceedings of Supercomputing '91*. IEEE Computer Society Press, 1991.

14. G. N. Srinivasa Prasanna, Anant Agarwal, and Bruce R. Musicus. Hierarchical Compilation of Macro Dataflow Graphs for Multiprocessors with Local Memory. *IEEE Transactions on Parallel and Distributed Systems*, July 1994.

15. Rajeev Barua, David Kranz, and Anant Agarwal. Global Partitioning of Parallel Loops and Data Arrays for Caches and Distributed Memory in Multiprocessors. Submitted for publication, March 1994.

16. Monical Lam, Edward E. Rothberg, and Michael E. Wolf. The Cache Performance and Optimizations of Blocked Algorithms. In *Fourth International Conference on Architectural Support for Programming Languages and Operating Systems (ASPLOS IV)*, pages 63–74. ACM, April 1991.

17. A. Agarwal, J. V. Guttag, C. N. Hadjicostis, and M. C. Papaefthymiou. Memory assignment for multiprocessor caches through grey coloring. In *PARLE'94 Parallel Architectures and Languages Europe*, pages 351–362. Springer-Verlag Lecture Notes in Computer Science 817, July 1994.

18. A. Carnevali, V. Natarajan, and A. Agarwal. A Relationship between the Number of Lattice Points within Hyperparallelepipeds and their Volume. Motorola Cambridge Research Center. In preparation., August 1993.

19. Gilbert Strang. *Linear algebra and its applications*, volume 3rd edition. Harcourt Brace Jovanovich, San Diego, CA, 1988.

20. A. Schrijver. *Theory of Linear and Integer Programming*. John Wiley & Sons, 1990.

21. George Arfken. *Mathematical Methods for Physics*. Academic Press, 1985.

22. Y. Ju and H. Dietz. Reduction of Cache Coherence Overhead by Compiler Data Layout and Loop Transformation. In *Languages and Compilers for Parallel Computing*, pages 344–358, Springer Verlag, 1992.

23. R. Barua, D. Kranz, and A. Agarwal. Communication-Minimal Partitioning of Parallel Loops and Data Arrays for Cache-Coherent Distributed-Memory Multiprocessors. In *Languages and Compilters for Parallel Computing*. Springer-Verlag Publishers, August 1996.

24. Anant Agarwal, Ricardo Bianchini, David Chaiken, Kirk Johnson, David Kranz, John Kubiatowicz, Beng-Hong Lim, Kenneth Mackenzie, and Donald Yeung. The MIT Alewife Machine: Architecture and Performance. In *Proceedings of the 22nd Annual International Symposium on Computer Architecture (ISCA'95)*, pages 2–13, June 1995.

25. Paul S. Barth, Rishiyur S. Nikhil, and Arvind. M-Structures: Extending a Parallel, Non-strict, Functional Language with State. In *Proceedings of the 5th ACM Conference on Functional Programming Languages and Computer Architecture*, August 1991.

26. B.J. Smith. Architecture and Applications of the HEP Multiprocessor Computer System. *Society of Photo-optical Instrumentation Engineers*, 298:241–248, 1981.

A. A Formulation of Loop Tiles Using Bounding Hyperplanes

A specific hyperparallelepiped loop tile is defined by a set of bounding hyperplanes. Similar formulations have also been used earlier [6].

Definition A1. *Given a l dimensional loop nest* **i**, *each tile of a hyperparallelepiped* loop partition *is defined by the hyperplanes given by the rows of the $l \times l$ matrix* **H** *and the column vectors* γ *and* λ *as follows. The parallel hyperplanes are* $\mathbf{h}_j\mathbf{i} = \gamma_j$ *and* $\mathbf{h}_j\mathbf{i} = \gamma_j + \lambda_j$, *for* $1 \le j \le l$. *An iteration belongs to this tile if it is on or inside the hyperparallelepiped.*

When loop tiles are assumed to be homogeneous except at the boundaries of the iteration space, the partitioning is completely defined by specifying the tile at the origin, namely $(\mathbf{H}, \mathbf{0}, \boldsymbol{\lambda})$, as indicated in Fig. A.1. For notational convenience, we denote the tile at the origin as **L**.

Definition A2. *Given the tile* $(\mathbf{H}, \mathbf{0}, \boldsymbol{\lambda})$ *at the origin of hyperparallelepiped partition, let* $\mathbf{L} = \mathbf{L}(\mathbf{H}) = \Lambda(\mathbf{H}^{-1})^T$, *where* Λ *is a diagonal matrix with* $\Lambda_{ii} = \lambda_i$. *We refer to the tile by the* **L** *matrix, as* **L** *completely defines the tile at the origin. The rows of* **L** *specify the vertices of the tile at the origin.*

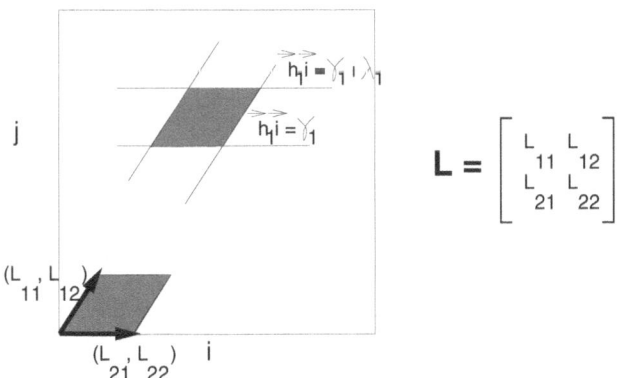

Fig. A.1. Iteration space partitioning is completely specified by the tile at the origin.

B. Synchronization References

Sequential do loops can often be converted to parallel do loops by introducing fine-grain data-level synchronization to enforce data dependencies or mutual exclusion. The cost of synchronization can be approximately modeled as slightly more expensive communication [14]. For example, in the Alewife system the inner loop of matrix multiply can be written using fine-grain synchronization in the form of the loop in Example B.

Doall (i=1:N, j=1:N, k=1:N)
   l$C[i,j] = l$C[i,j] + A[i,k] + B[k,j]
EndDoall

In the code segment in Example B, the "l$" preceding the **C** matrix references denote atomic accumulates. Accumulates into the **C** array can happen in any order, just that each accumulate action must be atomic. Such synchronizing reads or writes are both treated as writes by the coherence system. Similar linguistic constructs are also present in Id [25] and in a variant of FORTRAN used on the HEP [26].

Chapter 10. Communication-Free Partitioning of Nested Loops

Kuei-Ping Shih[1], Chua-Huang Huang[2], and Jang-Ping Sheu[1]

[1] Department of Computer Science and Information Engineering
National Central University
Chung-Li 32054, Taiwan
steven@axp1.csie.ncu.edu.tw, sheujp@csie.ncu.edu.tw
[2] Department of Computer Science & Information Engineering
National Dong Hwa University
Shoufeng, Hualien, Taiwan

Summary. This Chapter introduces several communication-free partitioning techniques of nested loops in literature. Since the cost of data communication is much higher than that of a primitive computation in distributed-memory multicomputers, it is important to reduce data communication. The ideal situation is to eliminate data communication when it is possible. During the last few years, many techniques investigating how to achieve communication-free by partitioning nested loops are proposed. This Chapter makes a survey of these techniques and points out the differences among them.

1. Introduction

In distributed-memory multicomputers, interprocessor communication is a critical factor affecting the overall system performance. Excessive interprocessor communication offsets the benefit of parallelization even if the program has a large amount of parallelism. The modern parallelizing compiler must take not only parallelism but also the amount of communication into consideration. Traditionally, parallelizing compilers consider only how to restructure programs to exploit as large amount of parallelism as possible [3,21,23,24,29,33–35,37]. However, exploiting parallelism may incur severe interprocessor communication overhead and degrade the system performance. It cannot ensure to achieve the highest performance even if the parallelism within a program has been totally exploited. Since there is a tradeoff between increasing parallelism and decreasing interprocessor communication, how to balance these two factors in order to achieve high performance computing has been, therefore, a crucial task for current parallelizing compilers.

During the last few years, many researchers are aware of this fact and begin to develop compilation techniques taking both parallelism and communication into consideration. Because the cost of data communication in distributed-memory multicomputers is much higher than that of a primitive computation, the major consideration for distributed-memory multicomputers has shifted to distribute data to appropriate location in order to reduce communication overhead. Thus, in the previous work, a number of

S. Pande, D.P. Agrawal (Eds.): Compiler Optimizations for Scalable PS, LNCS 1808, pp. 339-383, 2001.
© Springer-Verlag Berlin Heidelberg 2001

researchers have developed parallelizing compilers that need programmers to specify data distribution. Based on the programmer-specified data distribution, parallelizing compilers can automatically generate the parallel program with appropriate message passing constructs for multicomputers. Fortran D compiler project [13,14,31], SUPERB project [38], Kali project [19,20], DINO project [28], and Id Nouveau compiler [27] are all based on the same idea. The generated parallel program is mostly in SPMD (Single Program Multiple Data) [18] model.

Recently, automatic data partitioning is a research topic of great interests in the field of parallelizing compilers. There are many researchers who develop systems to automatically determine the data distribution at compile time. PARADIGM project [11] and SUIF project [2,33] are all based on the same purpose. These systems can automatically determine the appropriate data distribution patterns to minimize the communication overhead and generate the SPMD code with appropriate message passing constructs for distributed memory multicomputers.

An ideal situation about reducing interprocessor communication is to completely eliminate interprocessor communication, if possible. Communication-free partitioning is an interesting and worth studying issue for distributed-memory multicomputers. In recent year, many researchers have paid their attention on automatically partitioning data and/or computation to processors to completely eliminate interprocessor communication. Based on hyperplane partitions of data spaces, the problem of communication-free partitioning is formulated in terms of matrix representation and the existence of communication-free partitions of data arrays is derived by [26]. The approach using affine processor mapping for statements to distribute computation to processors without communication and maximize the degree of parallelism is presented in [22]. Two communication-free partitioning strategies, non-duplicate data and duplicate data partitionings, for a uniformly generated reference perfectly nested loop are developed in [5]. The necessary and sufficient conditions for the feasibility of communication-free hyperplane partitioning of iteration and data spaces in loop-level and statement-level are provided in [16] and [30], respectively. All methods directly manage affine array references. Neither of these methods uses information of data dependence distances or direction vectors.

Basically, this Chapter tends to make a survey of communication-free partitioning of nested loops. We roughly classify the communication-free partitioning as loop-level partitioning and statement-level partitioning according to the level that the partition is performed in loop-level or statement-level. The following methods will be presented in this Chapter:

– Loop-Level Partitioning
    – Chen and Sheu's method [5], which proposed two communication-free data allocation strategies for a perfectly uniformly generated references

loop, one disallows data to be duplicated on processors and another allows that.

- Ramanujam and Sadayappan's method [26], which proposed communication-free hyperplane partitioning for data spaces. The computation partitioning is achieved by "owner-computes rules".
- Huang and Sadayappan's method [16], which proposed the sufficient and necessary conditions for the feasibilities of communication-free iteration spaces and data spaces partitionings.
- Statement-Level Partitioning
  - Lim and Lam's method [22], which proposed affine processor mappings for the communication-free statement-iteration spaces partitionings as well as maximizing the degree of parallelism.
  - Shih, Sheu, and Huang's method [30], which proposed the sufficient and necessary conditions for communication-free statement-iteration spaces and data spaces partitionings.

Therefore, we briefly describe each of these methods and point out the differences among them. The rest of the Chapter is organized as follows. Since the analysis of array reference is very important for communication-free partitioning, Section 2 analyzes the fundamentals of array reference and some important properties derived from array references. Section 3 considers the loop-level communication-free partitioning. Section 3.1 presents non-duplicate data and duplicate data strategies proposed in [5]. Section 3.2 describes the communication-free data partitionings along hyperplanes proposed in [26]. Section 3.3 proposes the sufficient and necessary conditions for communication-free iteration and data spaces partitionings along hyperplanes derived in [16]. Section 4 discusses the statement-level communication-free partitioning. Section 4.1 introduces the affine processor mappings for statement-iteration spaces to achieve communication-free partitioning and obtain maximum degree of communication-free parallelism proposed in [22]. Section 4.2 derives the sufficient and necessary conditions for communication-free statement-iteration and data spaces partitioning along hyperplanes proposed in [30]. Section 5 makes comparisons among these methods and indicate the differences of each method. Finally, concluding remarks are provided in Section 6.

2. Fundamentals of Array References

Communication-free partitioning considers iteration and/or data spaces partitioning. Data elements in data spaces are referenced by different iterations in iteration spaces via array references. Therefore, analyses of array references are indispensable and very important for compilation techniques, including communication-free partitioning, in parallelizing compilers. In this section we will formulate the array references and present some useful properties that will be frequently used in the Chapter. We use simple examples to demonstrate the notation and concepts of array references. The formal definitions and general extensions can be obtained accordingly.

2.1 Iteration Spaces and Data Spaces

Let $\mathbf{Z}$ denote the set of integers. The symbol $\mathbf{Z}^d$ represents the set of d-tuple of integers. Generally speaking, a d-nested loop forms a $\mathbf{Z}^d$ integer space. An instance of each loop index variable corresponds to a value in its corresponding dimension. The loop bounds of each dimension set the bounds of the integer space. This bounded integer space is called the iteration space of the d-nested loop. We denote the iteration space of a nested loop L as $IS(L)$. An iteration is an integer point in the iteration space and includes all the execution of statements enclosed in the nested loop. Similar concept can be used for data spaces. Basically, a data space is also an integer space. An n-dimensional array forms an n-dimensional integer space. A data space of array v is denoted as $DS(v)$. A data index indicates a data element of that index.

Example 21. Consider the following program.

$$\mathbf{do}\ i_1 = 1,\ N$$
$$\quad \mathbf{do}\ i_2 = 1,\ N$$
$$\quad\quad A(i_1 - i_2, -i_1 + i_2) = A(i_1 - i_2 - 1, -i_1 + i_2 + 1) \qquad (L_{2.1})$$
$$\mathbf{enddo}\ \ \mathbf{enddo}$$

$L_{2.1}$ is a 2-nested loop. The iteration space of $L_{2.1}$ is the $\mathbf{Z}^2$ integer space and each dimension is bounded by 1 to N. We can formulate the iteration space $IS(L_{2.1})$ in set representation as $IS(L_{2.1}) = \{[i_1, i_2]^t | 1 \leq i_1, i_2 \leq N\}$. The superscript t is a transpose operator. Fig. 2.1 shows an example of iteration space of loop $L_{2.1}$, assuming $N = 5$. The column vector $I = [i_1, i_2]^t$,

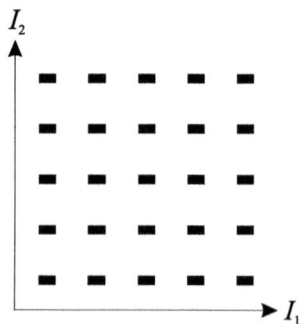

Fig. 2.1. Iteration space of loop $L_{2.1}$, $IS(L_{2.1})$, assuming $N = 5$.

for some instance of i_1 and i_2, is called an *iteration* in iteration space $IS(L_{2.1})$, where $1 \leq i_i, i_2 \leq N$. Since array A is 2-dimensional, $DS(A)$ is the two-dimensional integer space. Any integer point indexed as $D = [D_1, D_2]^t$ in $DS(A)$ represents an array element $A(D_1, D_2)$.

2.2 Reference Functions

Iteration spaces establish relations with data spaces via array references. Since the references of most programs are affine functions, we will consider only affine references. An array reference can be viewed as a reference function from the iteration space to the data space of that array. Each iteration is mapped to a data index in data space by means of a specified array reference. For example, reconsider $L_{2.1}$. The iteration $I = [i_1, i_2]^t$ is mapped to the array index $D = [i_1 - i_2 - 1, -i_1 + i_2 + 1]^t$ by means of the array reference $A(i_1 - i_2 - 1, -i_1 + i_2 + 1)$. Let the reference function be denoted as Ref. The reference function Ref can be written as $Ref(I) = D$. In other words,

$$Ref\left(\begin{bmatrix} i_1 \\ i_2 \end{bmatrix}\right) = \begin{bmatrix} i_1 - i_2 - 1 \\ -i_1 + i_2 + 1 \end{bmatrix}.$$

We can represent the reference function in matrix form by separating coefficients, loop index variables and constant terms. For example,

$$Ref\left(\begin{bmatrix} i_1 \\ i_2 \end{bmatrix}\right) = \begin{bmatrix} 1 & -1 \\ -1 & 1 \end{bmatrix} \begin{bmatrix} i_1 \\ i_2 \end{bmatrix} + \begin{bmatrix} -1 \\ 1 \end{bmatrix}.$$

The coefficient matrix and constant vector are termed *reference matrix* and *reference vector*, respectively. Let the reference matrix and reference vector be respectively denoted as R and r. The reference function can, therefore, be written as $Ref(I) = R \cdot I + r = D$. For another array reference $A(i_1 - i_2, -i_1 + i_2)$ in loop $L_{2.1}$, the reference matrix and reference vector are as follows.

$$R = \begin{bmatrix} 1 & -1 \\ -1 & 1 \end{bmatrix}, \text{ and } r = \begin{bmatrix} 0 \\ 0 \end{bmatrix}.$$

Once the array reference has been formulated, the reference function reveals a number of interesting and important properties. We present these properties in the following section.

2.3 Properties of Reference Functions

Communication-free partitioning requires that data be allocated to the processor which uses them. The requirement is applied to both read and written data elements. Therefore, we are interested in how data elements are accessed by iterations. Based on the above representation, we consider two situations: (1) two iterations referencing the same data element and (2) two data elements referenced by the same iteration.

For the same array variable, consider two array references $Ref(I) = R \cdot I + r$ and $Ref'(I) = R' \cdot I + r'$. Suppose I_1 and I_2 are two different iterations. Let $Ref(I_1) = D_1$, $Ref(I_2) = D_2$, $Ref'(I_1) = D'_1$, and $Ref'(I_2) = D'_2$. Any two of four data elements can be equal; hence, there are total $C_2^4 = 6$ different cases: $D_1 = D_2$, $D'_1 = D'_2$, $D_1 = D'_2$, $D'_1 = D_2$, $D_1 = D'_1$, and $D_2 = D'_2$. However, some are synonymous. $D_1 = D_2$ and $D'_1 = D'_2$ are the case that, for the same array reference, two different iterations reference the same data element. We denote this situation as *self-dependent relation*. $D_1 = D'_2$ and $D'_1 = D_2$ are the case that two different iterations reference the same data element via two different array references. This condition is termed *cross-dependent relation*. Note that $D_1 = D'_1$ and $D_2 = D'_2$ are also synonymous since they all consider the case that an iteration will reference the same data element via different array references. However, we will not consider this case because the two references Ref and Ref' are identical in the case of affine reference functions. Hence, the following conditions need to be well-maintained for all kinds of compilation techniques:

- *Self-Dependent Relation.* For the same array reference, on what conditions two different iterations will reference the same data element.
- *Cross-Dependent Relation.* For two different array references, on what conditions two different iterations will reference the same data element.

Self-Dependent Relation Reference functions can be or cannot be an invertible function. Obviously, for some array reference, it is possible and often happens that two iterations reference the same data element. It implies that the reference function is not a one-to-one function, of course not an invertible function, too. In other words, these two iterations are data dependent.

For some reference function $Ref(I) = R \cdot I + r$, suppose I and I' are two different iterations and D and D' are referenced respectively by I and I', i.e., $Ref(I) = D$ and $Ref(I') = D'$. We care about on what conditions two different iterations will reference the same data element, i.e., $D' = D$. Since $D' = D$, we have

$$
\begin{aligned}
& Ref(I') = Ref(I) \\
\Rightarrow \quad & R \cdot I' + r = R \cdot I + r \\
\Rightarrow \quad & R \cdot (I' - I) = 0 \\
\Rightarrow \quad & (I' - I) \in NS(R),
\end{aligned}
$$

where $NS(R)$ is the null space of R. It implies that if two iterations reference the same data element, then the difference of the two iterations must belong to the null space of R. Actually, this condition is a sufficient and necessary condition. That is, it is also true that two iterations will reference the same data element if the difference of the two iterations belongs to the null space of R. We conclude above by the following lemma.

Lemma 21. *For some reference function $Ref(I) = R \cdot I + r$, I and I' are two different iterations and D and D' are referenced respectively by I and I', i.e., $Ref(I) = D$ and $Ref(I') = D'$. Then*

$$Ref(I') = Ref(I) \iff (I' - I) \in NS(R). \qquad (2.1)$$

From Lemma 21, it also implies that if $NS(R) = \emptyset$, the reference function $Ref(I) = R \cdot I + r$ has no self-dependent relation.

Example 22. Take the array reference $A(i_1 - i_2, -i_1 + i_2)$ in loop $L_{2.1}$ as an example. Iterations $[1,1]^t$, $[2,2]^t$, $[3,3]^t$, $[4,4]^t$, $[5,5]^t$ all reference the same data element $A(0,0)$. Clearly, the difference of any two iterations belongs to $\{c[1,1]^t | c \in \mathbf{Z}\}$. The reference matrix of $A(i_1 - i_2, -i_1 + i_2)$ is $R = \begin{bmatrix} 1 & -1 \\ -1 & 1 \end{bmatrix}$. The null space of R is $NS(R) = \{c[1,1]^t | c \in \mathbf{Z}\}$. This fact matches the result obtained from Lemma 21. The above result is also illustrated in Fig. 2.2.

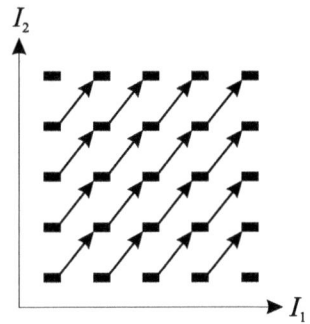

Fig. 2.2. Illustration of self-dependent relation.

Cross-Dependent Relation If there exist two different array references, the data dependence relations between these two array references can be regarded as *cross* data dependence relations. The cross data dependence relations also can affect the placement of data elements if communication-free execution is required. Therefore, the cross data dependence relations also need to be identified.

For the same array variable, consider two array references $Ref(I) = R \cdot I + r$ and $Ref'(I) = R' \cdot I + r'$. Suppose I and I' are two different iterations. Without loss of generality, assume $Ref(I) = R \cdot I + r = D$ and $Ref'(I') = R' \cdot I' + r' = D'$. The cross data dependence relations happen when $D' = D$, that is, $Ref'(I') = Ref(I)$. It implies

$$\begin{aligned} & Ref'(I') = Ref(I) \\ \Leftrightarrow \quad & R' \cdot I' + r' = R \cdot I + r \\ \Leftrightarrow \quad & R' \cdot I' - R \cdot I = r - r'. \end{aligned}$$

In other words, for any pair of I and I' that satisfies the above equation, I and I' are data dependent. The above results are concluded in the following lemma.

Lemma 22. *For two different reference functions $Ref(I) = R \cdot I + r$ and $Ref'(I) = R' \cdot I + r'$, I and I' are two different iterations and D and D' are referenced respectively by I and I', i.e., $Ref(I) = D$ and $Ref'(I') = D'$. Then*

$$Ref'(I') = Ref(I) \Longleftrightarrow R' \cdot I' - R \cdot I = r - r'. \tag{2.2}$$

Actually, Lemma 21 is a special case of Lemma 22 when $R' = R$ and $r' = r$. Another interesting special case but more general than self-dependent relation is when $R' = R$ but $r' \neq r$. If $R' = R$ and $r' \neq r$, Eq. (2.2) is changed to

$$R \cdot (I' - I) = r - r'. \tag{2.3}$$

Solving Eq. (2.3) can obtain the following results. Suppose I_p is a particular solution of Eq. (2.3), i.e., I_p satisfies $R \cdot I_p = r - r'$. The general solution of Eq. (2.3) is $I_g = I_p + NS(R)$. Consequently, $I' - I = I_p + NS(R)$. It implies that given an iteration I, for all iterations I' such that $I' - I = I_p + NS(R)$, I and I' are data dependent, where I_p is a particular solution of $R \cdot I = r - r'$. It is possible that there is no particular solution at all. This fact reflects that there exists no cross-dependent relation between the reference functions $R \cdot I = r$ and $R \cdot I = r'$. We conclude the above results by the following lemma.

Lemma 23. *For two different reference functions with the same reference matrix R, $Ref(I) = R \cdot I + r$ and $Ref'(I) = R \cdot I + r'$, I and I' are two different iterations and D and D' are referenced respectively by I and I', i.e., $Ref(I) = D$ and $Ref'(I') = D'$. If there exists a particular solution I_p that satisfies Eq. (2.3), then*

$$Ref'(I') = Ref(I) \Longleftrightarrow (I' - I) = I_p + NS(R). \tag{2.4}$$

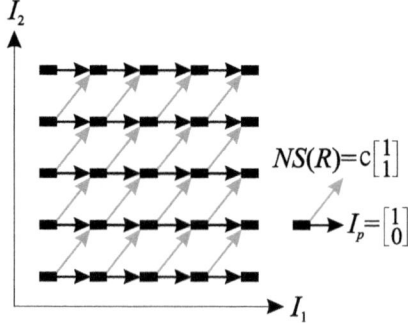

Fig. 2.3. Illustration of cross-dependent relation.

Example 23. Reconsider loop $L_{2.1}$. There exists two different array references. One is $A(i_1 - i_2, -i_1 + i_2)$ and another is $A(i_1 - i_2 - 1, -i_1 + i_2 + 1)$. The reference functions of these two array references have the same reference matrix $R = \begin{bmatrix} 1 & -1 \\ -1 & 1 \end{bmatrix}$. The reference vectors of the former is $r = [0, 0]^t$ and the latter is $r' = [-1, 1]^t$. The null space of R is $NS(R) = \{c[1, 1]^t | c \in \mathbf{Z}\}$. A particular solution of Eq. (2.3) is $I_p = [1, 0]^t$. By Lemma 23, for two array references with the same reference matrix, given an iteration I, the data element referenced by I via one array reference will be referenced by I' via another array reference, where I' satisfies Eq. (2.3). Fig. 2.3 illustrates the data dependence relations in $IS(L_{2.1})$. Note that since data dependence relation is transitive, therefore, the data dependence relations that can be obtained by transitive property are omitted in this figure.

Iteration-Dependent Space An *iteration-dependent space* is a subspace of iteration space and iterations within this space are directly or indirectly dependent. Trivially, an iteration-dependent space contains the spaces obtained by self-dependent relations and cross-dependent relations. Clearly, all iterations within an iteration-dependent space should be executed by a processor if communication-free execution is required. If iteration-dependent space spans the whole iteration space, that means all iterations in the iteration space have to be executed by one processor. It implies that the nested loop has no communication-free partition if parallel processing is required. That is, the execution of the nested loop do involve interprocessor communication on multicomputers. Let iteration-dependent space be denoted as $IDS(L)$, where L is a nested loop. The iteration-dependent space of $L_{2.1}$, $IDS(L_{2.1})$, is $span(\{[1, 1]^t, [1, 0]^t\})$, where $span(S)$ is the set of all linear combinations of vectors in set S [15]. It implies that $IDS(L_{2.1})$ spans $\mathbf{Z}^2$. Obviously, the iteration-dependent space of $L_{2.1}$, $IDS(L_{2.1})$, spans the whole iteration space of $L_{2.1}$. In other word, the whole iterations in iteration space $IS(L_{2.1})$ should be executed by one processor. It implies loop $L_{2.1}$ should be executed sequentially if communication-free execution has to be satisfied. Fig. 2.3 also shows the iteration-dependent space of $L_{2.1}$.

3. Loop-Level Partitioning

3.1 Iteration and Data Spaces Partitioning – Uniformly Generated References

In this section, we will present the method proposed in [5]. This method is denoted as *Chen and Sheu's method*. On the premise that no interprocessor communication is allowed, they find iteration space and data space partitions and exploit the maximum degree of parallelism. Since the cost of an interprocessor communication in distributed-memory multicomputers is much higher than that of a primitive computation, consequently, they would prefer to lose some parallelism in order not to incur any interprocessor communication rather than exploit the maximum amount of parallelism but result in severe interprocessor communication. *Chen and Sheu's method* considers a special loop model, a perfectly nested loop with *uniformly generated references*. This loop model possesses good quality in analyzing communication-free partitioning. Based on these good characteristics, they presented two loop-level communication-free partitioning strategies: one is *non-duplicate data strategy* and another is *duplicate data strategy*. In addition, they also derive the sufficient conditions of communication-free partitioning without duplicate data and with duplicate data strategies.

3.1.1 Non-duplicate Data Strategy. Non-duplicate data means that each data element is distributed to exactly one processor.

Example 31. Consider the following loop.

$$
\begin{aligned}
&\textbf{do } i_1 = 1,\ N \\
&\quad \textbf{do } i_2 = 1,\ N \\
&\qquad A(i_1 - i_2, -i_1 + i_2) = B(i_1, i_2) + C(i_1, i_2) \qquad (L_{3.1}) \\
&\qquad B(i_1, i_2) = A(i_1 - i_2, -i_1 + i_2) + C(i_1 - 1, i_2 - 1) \\
&\textbf{enddo enddo}
\end{aligned}
$$

The loop model considered by *Chen and Sheu's method* is a perfectly nested loop with *uniformly generated reference*. A nested loop is uniformly generated reference if all the reference matrices of the same array variable are of the same form. Obviously, loop $L_{3.1}$ is a uniformly generated reference loop. Since iterations in an iteration-dependent space are data dependent, an iteration-dependent space should be distributed to a processor if program execution would not involve any interprocessor communication.

Iteration-dependent space contains self-dependent relations and cross-dependent relations introduced in Section 2.3. Self-dependent relations can be obtained by Lemma 21. The null space of R^A is $NS(R^A) = \{c[1,1]^t | c \in \mathbf{Z}\}$. According to Lemma 21, any two iterations I and I' that $I' - I \in NS(R^A)$ are data dependent. Therefore, the space obtained by self-dependent relation resulted from array A is $span(\{[1,1]^t\})$. Similarly, for the array variables B and C, the null spaces of R^B and R^C are the same and equal $NS(R^B) = NS(R^C) = \emptyset$. It implies that no two iterations will reference the same data element of array B via the same array reference, and so is array C. The self-dependent relation of loop $L_{3.1}$ should include all the self-dependent relations resulted from different array variables. As a result, the self-dependent relation of loop $L_{3.1}$ is the space spanned by $NS(R^A)$, $NS(R^B)$ and $NS(R^C)$. The space obtained via self-dependent relations of loop $L_{3.1}$ is $span(\{[1,1]^t\})$.

Cross-dependent relations consider the same array variable but different array references. Any two array references of the same array variable are considered. Since the nested loop considered is a perfectly nested loop with uniformly generated reference, the reference matrices of the same array variable are of the same form. Therefore, the cross-dependent relations can be obtained by Lemma 23. For array variable C, the reference vectors of the two array references are $r = [0,0]^t$ and $r' = [-1,-1]^t$, respectively. We have to solve Eq. (2.3), that is,

$$\begin{bmatrix} 1 & 0 \\ 0 & 1 \end{bmatrix} \cdot (I' - I) = \begin{bmatrix} 1 \\ 1 \end{bmatrix}.$$

Obviously, there exists a particular solution, $I_p = [1,1]^t$. Since the null space of R^C is $NS(R^C) = \emptyset$, by Lemma 23, any two different iterations I and I' that $I' - I = I_p$ are data dependent. Therefore, the space obtained by cross-dependent relation resulted form array variable C is $span(\{[1,1]^t\})$.

For array variables A, although there are two array references, the two array references are actually the same. The equation needs to be solved is $R^A \cdot (I' - I) = 0$, which is reduced to the self-dependent case. Hence, while $(I' - I) \in NS(R^A)$, these two iterations will reference the same data elements by means of the two array references. Thus the space obtained by cross-dependent relation resulted form array variable A is $NS(R^A) = \{c[1,1]^t | c \in \mathbf{Z}\}$. Array variable B has the same situation with array variable A. Therefore, the space obtained by cross-dependent relation resulted form array variable B is $NS(R^B) = \emptyset$. Similar to the self-dependent relation, the cross-dependent relations also have to consider all cross-dependent relations obtained from different array variables. Synthesizing the above analyses, the space obtained by cross-dependent relations for loop $L_{3.1}$ is $span(\{[1,1]^t\})$.

As Section 2.3 described, iteration-dependent space includes the self-dependent relations and cross-dependent relations. Since the spaces obtained by self-dependent relations and cross-dependent relations are the same, $span(\{[1,1]^t\})$, the iteration-dependent space of loop $L_{3.1}$, $IDS(L_{3.1})$, is therefore equal to $span(\{[1,1]^t\})$. We have found the basis of iteration-dependent space, which is $\{[1,1]^t\}$.

Based on the finding of iteration-dependent space, the data space partitions can be obtained accordingly. Basically, all data elements referenced by iterations in the iteration-dependent space are grouped together and distributed to the processor where the iteration-dependent space is distributed to. Suppose that there are k different reference functions Ref_i, $1 \le i \le k$, that reference the same array variable in loop L and $IDS(L)$ is the iteration-dependent space of loop L. The following iteration set and data set are allocated to the same processor.

$$\{I | \forall I \in IDS(L)\}, \text{ and } \{D | D = Ref_i(I), \forall I \in IDS(L) \text{ and } i = 1, 2, \ldots, k\}.$$

The above constraint should hold true for all array variables in loop L.

Suppose $\Psi(L)$ is the iteration space partitioning and $\Phi(L)$ is the data space partitioning. Let Ref_k^v denote the kth array reference of array variable

v in loop L and D^v denote the data index in data space of v. For this example, given I_{init}, an initial iteration, the following sets are distributed to the same processor.

$$
\begin{aligned}
\Psi(L_{3.1}) &= \{I | I = I_{init} + c[1, 1]^t, c \in \mathbf{Z}\}, \\
\Phi(L_{3.1}) &= \{D^A | D^A = Ref_1^A(I) \text{ or } D^A = Ref_2^A(I), \forall I \in \Psi(L_{3.1})\} \quad \bigcup \\
&\quad \{D^B | D^B = Ref_1^B(I) \text{ or } D^B = Ref_2^B(I), \forall I \in \Psi(L_{3.1})\} \quad \bigcup \\
&\quad \{D^C | D^C = Ref_1^C(I) \text{ or } D^C = Ref_2^C(I), \forall I \in \Psi(L_{3.1})\}
\end{aligned}
$$

Fig. 3.1 illustrates the non-duplicate data communication-free iteration and data allocations for loop $L_{3.1}$ when $I_{init} = [1, 1]^t$. Fig. 3.1 (a) is the iteration space partitioning $\Psi(L_{3.1})$ on iteration space of loop $L_{3.1}$, $IS(L_{3.1})$, where $I_{init} = [1, 1]^t$. Fig. 3.1 (b), (c), and (d) are the data space partitionings $\Phi(L_{3.1})$ on data spaces of A, B, and C, respectively. If $\Psi(L_{3.1})$ and $\Phi(L_{3.1})$ are distributed onto the same processors, communication-free execution is obtained.

3.1.2 Duplicate Data Strategy. The fact that each data can be allocated on only one processor reduces the probability of communication-free execution. If the constraint can be removed, it will get much improvement on the findings of communication-free partitionings. Since interprocessor communication is too time-consuming, it is worth replicating data in order to obtain higher degree of parallelism.

Chen and Sheu's method is the only one that takes data replication into consideration. Actually, not all data elements can be replicated. The data elements that incur output, input, and anti-dependences can be replicated. It is because only true dependence results data movements. Output, input, and anti-dependences affect only execution orders but no data movements. Hence, the iteration-dependent space needs considering only the true dependence relations.

Chen and Sheu's method defines two terms, one is *fully duplicable array*, another is *partially duplicable array*, to classify arrays into fully or partially duplicable arrays. An array is fully duplicable if the array involves no true dependence relations; otherwise, the array is partially duplicable. For a fully duplicable array, which incurs no true dependence relation, since all iterations use the old values of data elements, not the newly generated values; therefore, the array can be fully duplicated onto all processors without affecting the correctness of execution. For a partially duplicable arrays, only the data elements which involve no true dependence relations can be replicated.

Example 32. Consider the following loop.

$$
\begin{aligned}
&\textbf{do } i_1 = 1, N \\
&\quad \textbf{do } i_2 = 1, N \\
&\quad\quad A(i_1, i_2) = A(i_1 + 1, i_2) + A(i_1, i_2 + 1) \qquad (L_{3.2}) \\
&\textbf{enddo enddo}
\end{aligned}
$$

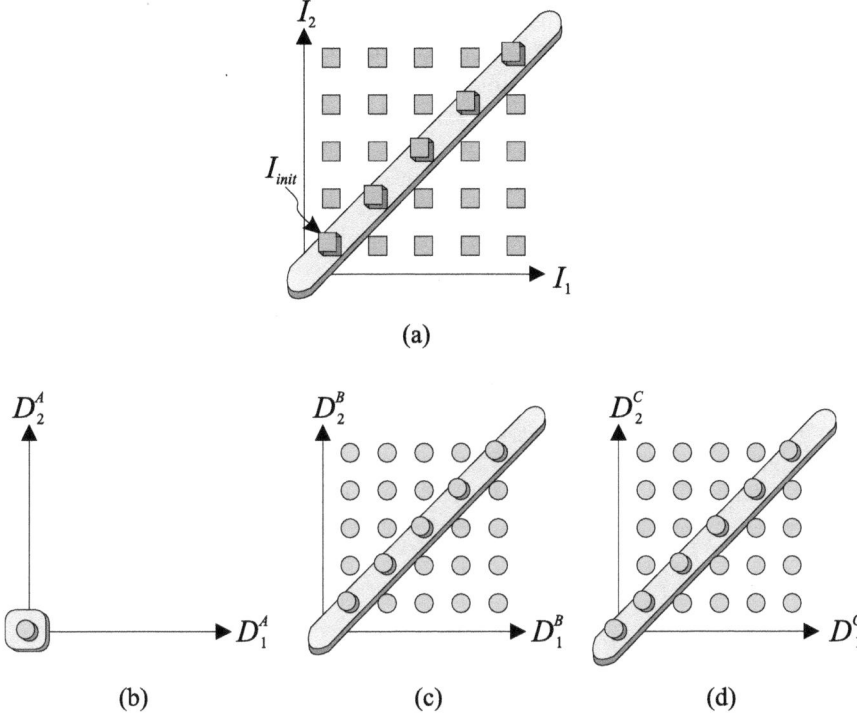

Fig. 3.1. Non-duplicate data communication-free iteration and data allocations for loop $L_{3.1}$ while $I_{init} = [1,1]^t$. (a) Iteration space partitioning $\Psi(L_{3.1})$ on $IS(L_{3.1})$, where $I_{init} = [1,1]^t$. (b) Data space partitioning $\Phi(L_{3.1})$ on $DS(A)$. (c) Data space partitioning $\Phi(L_{3.1})$ on $DS(B)$. (d) Data space partitioning $\Phi(L_{3.1})$ on $DS(C)$.

Loop $L_{3.2}$ is a perfectly nested loop with uniformly generated reference. Suppose that the non-duplicate data strategy is adopted. Form Section 3.1.1, the iteration-dependent space of loop $L_{3.2}$ is $IDS(L_{3.2}) = span(\{[-1,0]^t, [0,-1]^t, [1,-1]^t\})$, where the self- and cross-dependent relations are $\emptyset$ and $span(\{[-1,0]^t, [0,-1]^t, [1,-1]^t\})$, respectively. Obviously, $IDS(L_{3.2})$ spans $IS(L_{3.2})$. It means that if sequential execution is out of consideration, loop $L_{3.2}$ exists no communication-free partitioning without duplicate data.

If the duplicate data strategy is adopted instead, loop $L_{3.2}$ can be fully parallelized under communication-free criteria. The derivation of the result is as follows. As explained above, the data elements that incur output, input, and anti-dependences do not affect the correctness of execution and can be replicated. On the other hand, the data elements that incur true dependences will cause data movement and can be replicated. For this example, the data dependent vectors obtained are $[-1,0]^t$, $[0,-1]^t$, and $[1,-1]^t$. The data dependent vectors $[-1,0]^t$ and $[0,-1]^t$ are anti-dependence and $[1,-1]^t$

is an input dependence. Since array A incurs no true dependence, array A is a fully duplicable array. Therefore, the iteration-dependent space contains no dependent relations that is incurred by true dependence relations. Thus, $IDS(L_{3.2}) = \emptyset$. It implies that if array A is replicated onto processors appropriately, each iteration can be executed separately and no interprocessor communication is incurred. The distributions of iterations and data elements are as follows. Given an initial iteration, I_{init}, the following sets are mapped to the same processor.

$$\Psi(L_{3.2}) = \{I_{init}\},$$
$$\Phi(L_{3.2}) = \{D \mid D = Ref_1(I) \text{ or } D = Ref_2(I) \text{ or } D = Ref_3(I),$$
$$\forall\ I \in \Psi(L_{3.2})\}.$$

Fig. 3.2 shows the duplicate data communication-free allocation of iterations and data elements for loop $L_{3.2}$ when $I_{init} = [3,3]^t$. Fig. 3.2 (a) is the iteration space partitioning $\Psi(L_{3.2})$ on iteration space of loop $L_{3.2}$, $IS(L_{3.2})$, where $I_{init} = [3,3]^t$. Fig. 3.2 (b) is the data space partitioning $\Phi(L_{3.2})$ on data space of A. Note that the overlapped data elements are the duplicate data elements.

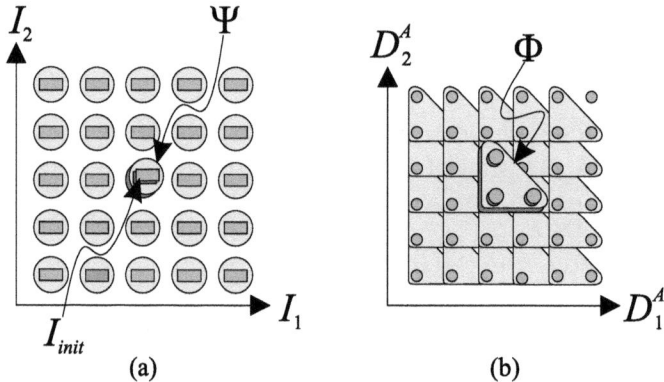

Fig. 3.2. Duplicate data communication-free iteration and data allocations for loop $L_{3.2}$ when $I_{init} = [3,3]^t$. (a) Iteration space partitioning $\Psi(L_{3.2})$ on $IS(L_{3.2})$, where $I_{init} = [3,3]^t$. (b) Data space partitioning $\Phi(L_{3.2})$ on $DS(A)$.

The duplicate data strategy does not always promise to obtain higher degree of parallelism. It is possible that applying the duplicate data strategy is in vain for increasing the degree of parallelism.

Example 33. Reconsider loop $L_{3.1}$. According to the previously analyses, array A can cause self- and cross-dependence relations and the dependence vectors are $t[1,1]$, where $t \in \mathbf{Z}$. Array B causes no self- and cross-dependence relations. Array C causes no self-dependence relations but cross-dependence relations and the dependence vectors are $[1, 1]$. Array A can involve true dependence and array C involves only input dependence. Obviously, array B involves no dependence. Therefore, array A is a partially duplicable array and arrays B and C are fully duplicable arrays.

Since fully duplicable arrays invoke no data movement, the dependence vectors caused by fully duplicable arrays can be ignored by way of replication of data. However, true dependence vectors caused by partially duplicable arrays do cause interprocessor communication and must be included in the iteration-dependent space. Consequently, the iteration-dependent space is $IDS(L_{3.1}) = span(\{[1, 1]^t\})$, which is the same as the result obtained in Section 3.1.1. Clearly, the degree of parallelism is still no improved even though the duplicate data strategy is adopted.

We have mentioned that only true dependence relations can cause data movement. Nevertheless, output dependence relations cause no data movement but data consistency problem. Output dependence relations mean that there are multiple-writes to the same data elements. It is feasible to duplicate data to eliminate the output dependence relations. However, the data consistency problem is occurred. How to maintain the data to preserve their consistency is important for the correctness of the execution. Although there are multiple-writes to the same data element, only the last write is needed. Clearly, multiple-writes to the same data element may exist redundant computations. Besides, these redundant computations may occur unwanted data dependence relations and result in the losing of parallelism. Eliminating these redundant computations can remove these unwanted data dependence relations simultaneously and increase the degree of parallelism. In order to exploit more degrees of parallelism, *Chen and Sheu's method* proposed another scheme to eliminate redundant computations. Eliminating redundant computations is a preprocessing step before applying the communication-free partitioning strategy. However, the scheme to eliminate redundant computations is complex and time-consuming. The tradeoff on whether to apply or not to apply the scheme depends on the users. Since the scope of elimination of redundant computations is beyond the range of the chapter, we omit the discussions of the scheme. Whoever is interested in this topic can refer to [5].

3.2 Hyperplane Partitioning of Data Space

This section introduces the method proposed in [26]. We use *Ramanujam and Sadayappan's method* to denote this method. *Ramanujam and Sadayappan's method* discusses data spaces partitioning for two-dimensional arrays; nevertheless, their method can be easily generalized to higher dimensions. They use a single hyperplane as a basic partitioning unit for each data space. Data on a hyperplane are assigned to a processor. Hyperplanes on data spaces are called *data hyperplanes* and on iteration spaces are called *iteration hyperplane*. Hyperplanes within a space are parallel to each other. In *Ramanujam and*

Sadayappan's method, iteration space partitioning is not addressed. However, their method implicitly contains the concept of iteration hyperplane.

The basic ideas of *Ramanujam and Sadayappan's method* are as follows. First, the data hyperplane of each data space is assumed to be the standard form of hyperplane. The coefficients of data hyperplanes are unknown and need to be evaluated later on. Based on the array reference functions, each data hyperplane can derive its corresponding iteration hyperplane. That is, all iterations referencing the data elements on the data hyperplane are on the iteration hyperplane. Since communication-free partitioning is required, therefore, all iteration hyperplanes derived from every data hyperplanes actually represent the same hyperplane. In other words, although these iteration hyperplanes are different in shape, they all represent the iteration hyperplanes of the iteration space. Hence, if interprocessor communication is prohibited, these iteration hyperplanes should be the same. As a result, conditions to satisfy the requirement of communication-free partitioning are established. These conditions form a linear system and are composed of the coefficients of data hyperplanes. Solving the linear system can obtain the values of the coefficients of data hyperplanes. The data hyperplanes are then determined. Since iteration space partitioning is not considered by this method, it results in the failure in applying to multiple nested loops. Furthermore, their method can deal with only fully parallel loop, which contains no data dependence relations within the loop.

Example 34. Consider the following program model.

> **do** $i_1 = 1, N$
> > **do** $i_2 = 1, N$
> > > $A(i_1, i_2) = B(b_{1,1}i_1 + b_{1,2}i_2 + b_{1,0}, b_{2,1}i_1 + b_{2,2}i_2 + b_{2,0})$ ($L_{3.3}$)
> > **enddo enddo**

Let v_1 denote A and v_2 denote B, and so on, unless otherwise noted. D^i_j denote the jth component of array reference of array variable v_i. *Ramanujam and Sadayappan's method* partitions data spaces along hyperplanes. A data hyperplane on a two-dimensional data space $DS(v_i)$ is a set of data indices $\{[D^i_1, D^i_2]^t | \theta^i_1 D^i_1 + \theta^i_2 D^i_2 = c^i\}$ and is denoted as Φ^i, where θ^i_1 and $\theta^i_2 \in \mathbf{Q}$ are hyperplane coefficients and $c^i \in \mathbf{Q}$ is the constant term of the hyperplane. All elements in a hyperplane are undertaken by a processor, that is, a processor should be responsible for the executions of all computations in an iteration hyperplane and manage the data elements located in a data hyperplane. Note that the hyperplanes containing at least one integer-valued point are considered in the Chapter.

As defined above, the data hyperplanes for array variables v_1 and v_2 are $\Phi^1 = \{[D^1_1, D^1_2]^t | \theta^1_1 D^1_1 + \theta^1_2 D^1_2 = c^1\}$ and $\Phi^2 = \{[D^2_1, D^2_2]^t | \theta^2_1 D^2_1 + \theta^2_2 D^2_2 = c^2\}$, respectively. Since the array reference of v_1 is (i_1, i_2), hence, $D^1_1 = i_1$ and $D^1_2 = i_2$. The array reference of v_2 is (D^2_1, D^2_2), where

$$D_1^2 = b_{1,1}i_1 + b_{1,2}i_2 + b_{1,0},$$
$$D_2^2 = b_{2,1}i_1 + b_{2,2}i_2 + b_{2,0}.$$

Substituting the loop indices for data indices into the data hyperplanes can obtain the following two hyperplanes.

$$\theta_1^1 D_1^1 + \theta_2^1 D_2^1 = c^1$$
$$\Rightarrow \quad \theta_1^1 i_1 + \theta_2^1 i_2 = c^1,$$
$$\theta_1^2 D_1^2 + \theta_2^2 D_2^2 = c^2$$
$$\Rightarrow \quad (\theta_1^2 b_{1,1} + \theta_2^2 b_{2,1})i_1 + (\theta_1^2 b_{1,2} + \theta_2^2 b_{2,2})i_2 = c^2 - \theta_1^2 b_{1,0} - \theta_2^2 b_{2,0}.$$

From the above explanation, these two hyperplanes actually represent the same hyperplane if the requirement of communication-free partitioning has to be satisfied. It implies

$$\begin{cases} \theta_1^1 &=& \theta_1^2 b_{1,1} + \theta_2^2 b_{2,1} \\ \theta_2^1 &=& \theta_1^2 b_{1,2} + \theta_2^2 b_{2,2} \\ c^1 &=& c^2 - \theta_1^2 b_{1,0} - \theta_2^2 b_{2,0} \end{cases}$$

We can rewrite the above formulations in matrix representation as follows.

$$\begin{bmatrix} \theta_1^1 \\ \theta_2^1 \\ c^1 \end{bmatrix} = \begin{bmatrix} b_{1,1} & b_{2,1} & 0 \\ b_{1,2} & b_{2,2} & 0 \\ -b_{1,0} & -b_{2,0} & 1 \end{bmatrix} \begin{bmatrix} \theta_1^2 \\ \theta_2^2 \\ c^2 \end{bmatrix} \tag{3.1}$$

By the above analyses, the two data hyperplanes of v_1 and v_2 can be represented as below.

$$\Phi^1 = \{[D_1^1, D_2^1]^t \mid (\theta_1^2 b_{1,1} + \theta_2^2 b_{2,1})D_1^1 + (\theta_1^2 b_{1,2} + \theta_2^2 b_{2,2})D_2^1 = c^2 - \theta_1^2 b_{1,0} - \theta_2^2 b_{2,0}\},$$
$$\Phi^2 = \{[D_1^2, D_2^2]^t \mid \theta_1^2 D_1^2 + \theta_2^2 D_2^2 = c^2\}.$$

A comprehensive methodology for communication-free data spaces partitioning proposed in [26] has been described. Let's take a real program as an example to show how to apply the technique. In the preceding program model, we discussed the case that the number of different array references in the *rhs*(right hand side) of the assignment statement is just one. If there are multiple array references in the *rhs* of the assignment statement, the constraints from Eq. (3.1) should hold true for each reference functions to preserve the requirements of communication-free partitioning.

Example 35. Consider the following loop.

do $i_1 = 1, N$
    do $i_2 = 1, N$
        $A(i_1, i_2) = B(i_1 + 2i_2 + 2, i_2 + 1) + B(2i_1 + i_2, i_1 - 1)$ ($L_{3.4}$)
enddo enddo

Suppose the data hyperplanes of v_1 and v_2 are Φ^1 and Φ^2, respectively, where $\Phi^1 = \{[D_1^1, D_2^1]^t | \; \theta_1^1 D_1^1 + \theta_2^1 D_2^1 = c^1\}$ and $\Phi^2 = \{[D_1^2, D_2^2]^t | \theta_1^2 D_1^2 + \theta_2^2 D_2^2 = c^2\}$. Since this example contains two different array references in the *rhs* of the assignment statement, therefore, by Eq. (3.1), we have the following two constraints for the first and the second references.

$$
\begin{bmatrix} \theta_1^1 \\ \theta_2^1 \\ c^1 \end{bmatrix} = \begin{bmatrix} 1 & 0 & 0 \\ 2 & 1 & 0 \\ -2 & -1 & 1 \end{bmatrix} \begin{bmatrix} \theta_1^2 \\ \theta_2^2 \\ c^2 \end{bmatrix},
$$

$$
\begin{bmatrix} \theta_1^1 \\ \theta_2^1 \\ c^1 \end{bmatrix} = \begin{bmatrix} 2 & 1 & 0 \\ 1 & 0 & 0 \\ 0 & 1 & 1 \end{bmatrix} \begin{bmatrix} \theta_1^2 \\ \theta_2^2 \\ c^2 \end{bmatrix}.
$$

The parameters θ_1^1, θ_2^1, θ_1^2, θ_2^2, c^1, and c^2 have to satisfy the above equations. Solving these equations can obtain the following solution $\theta_1^1 = \theta_2^1 = \theta_1^2 = -\theta_2^2$ and $c^2 = c^1 + \theta_1^1$. Therefore, the communication-free data hyperplanes on $DS(v_1)$ and $DS(v_2)$ are respectively represented in the following:

$$
\Phi^1 = \{[D_1^1, D_2^1]^t | \theta_1^1 D_1^1 + \theta_1^1 D_2^1 = c^1\},
$$
$$
\Phi^2 = \{[D_1^2, D_2^2]^t | \theta_1^1 D_1^2 - \theta_1^1 D_2^2 = c^1 + \theta_1^1\}.
$$

Fig. 3.3 illustrates Φ^1 and Φ^2, the communication-free data spaces partitioning, for loop $L_{3.4}$ when $\theta_1^1 = 1$ and $c^1 = 3$.

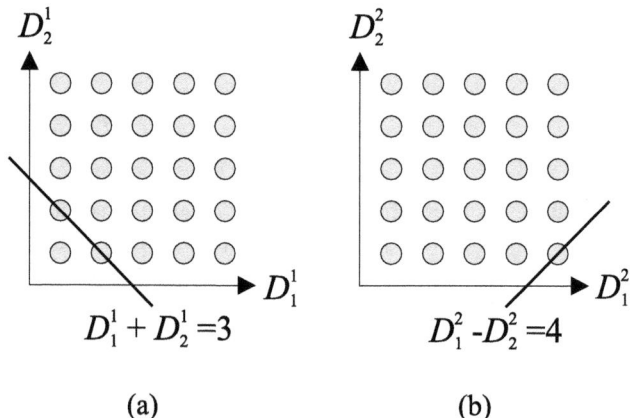

(a)   (b)

Fig. 3.3. Communication-free data spaces partitioning for loop $L_{3.4}$. (a) Data hyperplane Φ^1 on data space $DS(v_1)$. (b) Data hyperplane Φ^2 on data space $DS(v_2)$.

After having explained these examples, we have explicated *Ramanujam and Sadayappan's method* in detail. Nevertheless, all the above examples are not general enough. The most general program model is considered below. Based on the same ideas, the constraints for satisfying the requirements of communication-free hyperplane partitioning is derived. An example is also given to illustrate the most general case.

Example 36. Consider the following program model.

> **do** $i_1 = 1, N$
>> **do** $i_2 = 1, N$
>>> $A(a_{1,1}i_1 + a_{1,2}i_2 + a_{1,0}, a_{2,1}i_1 + a_{2,2}i_2 + a_{2,0}) =$
>>>> $B(b_{1,1}i_1 + b_{1,2}i_2 + b_{1,0}, b_{2,1}i_1 + b_{2,2}i_2 + b_{2,0})$ $(L_{3.5})$
>> **enddo enddo**

Suppose the data hyperplanes of v_1 and v_2 are $\Phi^1 = \{[D_1^1, D_2^1]^t | \theta_1^1 D_1^1 + \theta_2^1 D_2^1 = c^1\}$ and $\Phi^2 = \{[D_1^2, D_2^2]^t | \theta_1^2 D_1^2 + \theta_2^2 D_2^2 = c^2\}$, respectively. The reference functions for each dimension of each array reference is listed as follows.

$$D_1^1 = a_{1,1}i_1 + a_{1,2}i_2 + a_{1,0},$$
$$D_2^1 = a_{2,1}i_1 + a_{2,2}i_2 + a_{2,0},$$
$$D_1^2 = b_{1,1}i_1 + b_{1,2}i_2 + b_{1,0},$$
$$D_2^2 = b_{2,1}i_1 + b_{2,2}i_2 + b_{2,0}.$$

Replacing each D_j^i with its corresponding reference function, $i = 1, 2$ and $j = 1, 2$, the data hyperplanes Φ^1 and Φ^2 can be represented in terms of loop indices i_1 and i_2 as below.

$$\theta_1^1 D_1^1 + \theta_2^1 D_2^1 = c^1$$
$$\Rightarrow \theta_1^1(a_{1,1}i_1 + a_{1,2}i_2 + a_{1,0}) + \theta_2^1(a_{2,1}i_1 + a_{2,2}i_2 + a_{2,0}) = c^1$$
$$\Rightarrow (\theta_1^1 a_{1,1} + \theta_2^1 a_{2,1})i_1 + (\theta_1^1 a_{1,2} + \theta_2^1 a_{2,2})i_2 = c^1 - \theta_1^1 a_{1,0} - \theta_2^1 a_{2,0},$$
$$\theta_1^2 D_1^2 + \theta_2^2 D_2^2 = c^2$$
$$\Rightarrow \theta_1^2(b_{1,1}i_1 + b_{1,2}i_2 + b_{1,0}) + \theta_2^2(b_{2,1}i_1 + b_{2,2}i_2 + b_{2,0}) = c^2$$
$$\Rightarrow (\theta_1^2 b_{1,1} + \theta_2^2 b_{2,1})i_1 + (\theta_1^2 b_{1,2} + \theta_2^2 b_{2,2})i_2 = c^2 - \theta_1^2 b_{1,0} - \theta_2^2 b_{2,0}.$$

As previously stated, these two hyperplanes are the corresponding iteration hyperplanes of the two data hyperplanes on iteration space. These two iteration hyperplanes should be consistent if the requirement of communication-free partitioning has to be met. It implies

$$\theta_1^1 a_{1,1} + \theta_2^1 a_{2,1} = \theta_1^2 b_{1,1} + \theta_2^2 b_{2,1}$$
$$\theta_1^1 a_{1,2} + \theta_2^1 a_{2,2} = \theta_1^2 b_{1,2} + \theta_2^2 b_{2,2}$$
$$c^1 - \theta_1^1 a_{1,0} - \theta_2^1 a_{2,0} = c^2 - \theta_1^2 b_{1,0} - \theta_2^2 b_{2,0}$$

The above conditions can be represented in matrix form as follows.

$$\begin{bmatrix} a_{1,1} & a_{2,1} & 0 \\ a_{1,2} & a_{2,2} & 0 \\ -a_{1,0} & -a_{2,0} & 1 \end{bmatrix} \begin{bmatrix} \theta_1^1 \\ \theta_2^1 \\ c^1 \end{bmatrix} = \begin{bmatrix} b_{1,1} & b_{2,1} & 0 \\ b_{1,2} & b_{2,2} & 0 \\ -b_{1,0} & -b_{2,0} & 1 \end{bmatrix} \begin{bmatrix} \theta_1^2 \\ \theta_2^2 \\ c^2 \end{bmatrix} \qquad (3.2)$$

If there exists a nontrivial solution to the linear system obtained from Eq. (3.2), the nested loop exists communication-free hyperplane partitioning.

Example 37. Consider the following loop.

> **do** $i_1 = 1, N$
> > **do** $i_2 = 1, N$
> > > $A(i_1 + i_2, i_1 - i_2) = B(i_1 - 2i_2, 2i_1 - i_2)$ $(L_{3.6})$
> >
> > **enddo enddo**

Let $\Phi^1 = \{[D_1^1, D_2^1]^t | \theta_1^1 D_1^1 + \theta_2^1 D_2^1 = c^1\}$ and $\Phi^2 = \{[D_1^2, D_2^2]^t | \theta_1^2 D_1^2 + \theta_2^2 D_2^2 = c^2\}$ be the data hyperplanes of v_1 and v_2, respectively. From Eq. (3.2), we have the following system of equations:

$$\begin{bmatrix} 1 & 1 & 0 \\ 1 & -1 & 0 \\ 0 & 0 & 1 \end{bmatrix} \begin{bmatrix} \theta_1^1 \\ \theta_2^1 \\ c^1 \end{bmatrix} = \begin{bmatrix} 1 & 2 & 0 \\ -2 & -1 & 0 \\ 0 & 0 & 1 \end{bmatrix} \begin{bmatrix} \theta_1^2 \\ \theta_2^2 \\ c^2 \end{bmatrix}.$$

The solution to this linear system is:

$$\begin{cases} \theta_1^2 = -\theta_1^1 + \frac{1}{3}\theta_2^1 \\ \theta_2^2 = \theta_1^1 + \frac{1}{3}\theta_2^1 \\ c^2 = c^1 \end{cases}$$

The linear system exists a nontrivial solution; therefore, loop $L_{3.6}$ has communication-free hyperplane partitioning. Φ^1 and Φ^2 can be written as:

$$\Phi^1 = \{[D_1^1, D_2^1]^t | \theta_1^1 D_1^1 + \theta_2^1 D_2^1 = c^1\},$$
$$\Phi^2 = \{[D_1^2, D_2^2]^t | (-\theta_1^1 + \frac{1}{3}\theta_2^1)D_1^2 + (\theta_1^1 + \frac{1}{3}\theta_2^1)D_2^2 = c^1\}.$$

Let $\theta_1^1 = 1$ and $\theta_2^1 = 1$. The hyperplanes Φ^1 and Φ^2 are rewritten as follows.

$$\Phi^1 = \{[D_1^1, D_2^1]^t | D_1^1 + D_2^1 = c^1\}$$
$$\Phi^2 = \{[D_1^2, D_2^2]^t | - 2D_1^2 + 4D_2^2 = 3c^1\}$$

Fig. 3.4 gives an illustration for $c^1 = 2$.

Ramanujam and Sadayappan's method can deal with a single nested loop well. Their method fails in processing multiple nested loops. This is because they did not consider the iteration space partitioning. On the other hand, they do well for the fully parallel loop, but they can not handle the loop with data dependence relations. These shortcomings will be made up by methods proposed in [16, 30].

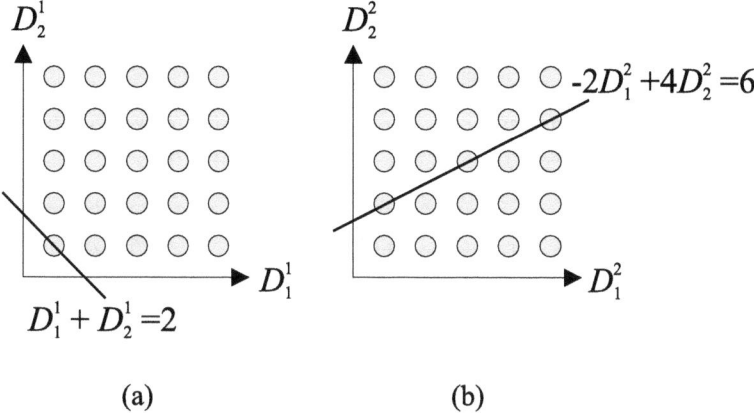

Fig. 3.4. Communication-free data spaces partitioning for loop $L_{3.6}$. (a) Data hyperplane Φ^1 on data space $DS(v_1)$. (b) Data hyperplane Φ^2 on data space $DS(v_2)$.

3.3 Hyperplane Partitioning of Iteration and Data Spaces

Huang and Sadayappan also proposed methods toward the communication-free partitioning for nested loops. In this section, we will describe the method proposed in [16]. This method is denoted as *Huang and Sadayappan's method.* *Huang and Sadayappan's method* aims at the findings of iteration hyperplanes and data hyperplanes such that, based on the partitioning, the execution of nested loops involves no interprocessor communication. Furthermore, sufficient and necessary conditions for communication-free hyperplane partitioning are also derived. They proposed single-hyperplane and multiple-hyperplane partitionings for nested loops. Single-hyperplane partitioning implies that a partition element contains a single hyperplane per space and a partition element is allocated onto a processor. Multiple-hyperplane partitioning means that a partition element contains a group of hyperplanes and all elements in a partition group is undertaken by a processor. Multiple-hyperplane partitioning can provide more powerful capability than single-hyperplane partitioning in communication-free partitioning. For the sake of space limitation, we only introduce the single-hyperplane partitioning. Multiple-hyperplane partitioning can refer to [16].

In Section 3.2, *Ramanujam and Sadayappan's method* assumes the generic format of data hyperplanes and then determines the coefficients of data hyperplanes. Since *Ramanujam and Sadayappan's method* considers only data hyperplane partitioning, the loss of sight on iteration hyperplanes causes the failure of applying to sequences of nested loops. This phenomenon has been improved by *Huang and Sadayappan's method.* However, *Huang and Sadayappan's method* requires the nested loops be perfectly nested loop(s).

An n-dimensional data hyperplane on $DS(v_j)$ is the set of data indices $\{[D_1^j, D_2^j, \ldots, D_n^j]^t | \theta_1^j D_1^j + \theta_2^j D_2^j + \cdots + \theta_n^j D_n^j = c^j\}$, which is denoted as Φ^j, where $\theta_1^j, \ldots,$ and $\theta_n^j \in \mathbf{Q}$ are hyperplane coefficients and $c^j \in \mathbf{Q}$ is the constant term of the hyperplane. Similarly, an iteration hyperplane of a d-nested loop L_i is a set of iterations $\{[I_1^i, I_2^i, \ldots, I_d^i]^t | \delta_1^i I_1^i + \delta_2^i I_2^i + \cdots + \delta_d^i I_d^i = c^i\}$ and is denoted as Ψ^i, where $\delta_1^i, \ldots,$ and $\delta_d^i \in \mathbf{Q}$ are hyperplane coefficients and $c^i \in \mathbf{Q}$ is the constant term of the hyperplane. Let $\Delta^i = [\delta_1^i, \delta_2^i, \ldots, \delta_d^i]$ be the coefficient vector of iteration hyperplane and $\Theta^j = [\theta_1^j, \theta_2^j, \ldots, \theta_n^j]$ be the coefficient vector of data hyperplane. An iteration hyperplane on $IS(L_i)$ and a data hyperplane on $DS(v_j)$ can be abbreviated as

$$\Psi^i = \{I^i \mid \Delta^i \cdot I^i = c^i\}, \text{ and } \Phi^j = \{D^j \mid \Theta^j \cdot D^j = c^j\},$$

respectively, where $I^i = [I_1^i, I_2^i, \ldots, I_d^i]^t$ is an iteration on $IS(L_i)$ and $D^j = [D_1^j, D_2^j, \ldots, D_n^j]^t$ is a data index on $DS(v_j)$. If the hyperplane coefficient vector is a zero vector, it means the whole iteration space or data space needs to be allocated onto a processor. This fact leads to sequential execution and is out of the question in this Chapter. Hence, only non-zero iteration hyperplane coefficient vectors and data hyperplane coefficient vectors are considered in the Chapter.

For any array reference of array v_j in loop L_i, there exists a sufficient and necessary condition to verify the relations between iteration hyperplane coefficient vector and data hyperplane coefficient vector if communication-free requirement is satisfied. The sufficient and necessary condition is stated in the following lemma.

Lemma 31. *For a reference function $Ref(I^i) = R \cdot I^i + r = D^j$, which is from $IS(L_i)$ to $DS(v_j)$, $\Psi^i = \{I^i \mid \Delta^i \cdot I^i = c^i\}$ is the iteration hyperplane on $IS(L_i)$ and $\Phi^j = \{D^j \mid \Theta^j \cdot D^j = c^j\}$ is the data hyperplane on $DS(v_j)$. Ψ^i and Φ^j are communication-free hyperplane partitions if and only if $\Delta^i = \alpha\Theta^j \cdot R$, for some α, $\alpha \neq 0$.*

Proof. ($\Rightarrow$): Suppose that $\Psi^i = \{I^i | \Delta^i \cdot I^i = c^i\}$ and $\Phi^j = \{D^j | \Theta^j \cdot D^j = c^j\}$ are communication-free hyperplane partitions. Let I_1^i and I_2^i be two distinct iterations and belong to the same iteration hyperplane, Ψ^i. If D_1^j and D_2^j are two data indices such that $Ref(I_1^i) = D_1^j$ and $Ref(I_2^i) = D_2^j$, from the above assumptions, D_1^j and D_2^j should belong to the same data hyperplane, Φ^j.

Because I_1^i and I_2^i belong to the same iteration hyperplane, Ψ^i, $\Delta^i \cdot I_1^i = c^i$ and $\Delta^i \cdot I_2^i = c^i$, therefore, $\Delta^i \cdot (I_1^i - I_2^i) = 0$. On the other hand, since D_1^j and D_2^j belong to the same data hyperplane, Φ^j, it means that $\Theta^j \cdot D_1^j = c^j$ and $\Theta^j \cdot D_2^j = c^j$. Replacing D_k^j by reference function $Ref(I_k^i)$, for $k = 1, 2$, we can obtain $(\Theta^j \cdot R) \cdot (I_1^i - I_2^i) = 0$.

Since I_1^i and I_2^i are any two iterations on Ψ^i, $(I_1^i - I_2^i)$ is a vector on the iteration hyperplane. Furthermore, both $\Delta^i \cdot (I_1^i - I_2^i) = 0$ and $(\Theta^j \cdot R) \cdot (I_1^i - I_2^i) = 0$, hence we can conclude that Δ^i and $(\Theta^j \cdot R)$ are linearly dependent. It implies $\Delta^i = \alpha\Theta^j \cdot R$, for some α, $\alpha \neq 0$ [15].

($\Leftarrow$): Suppose $\Psi^i = \{I^i | \Delta^i \cdot I^i = c^i\}$ and $\Phi^j = \{D^j | \Theta^j \cdot D^j = c^j\}$ are hyperplane partitions for $IS(L_i)$ and $DS(v_j)$, respectively and $\Delta^i = \alpha \Theta^j \cdot R$, for some α, $\alpha \neq 0$. We claim Ψ^i and Φ^j are communication-free partitioning.

Let I^i be any iteration on iteration hyperplane Ψ^i. Then $\Delta^i \cdot I^i = c^i$. Since $\Delta^i = \alpha \Theta^j \cdot R$, replacing Δ^i by $\alpha \Theta^j \cdot R$ can get $\Theta^j \cdot Ref(I^i) = \frac{1}{\alpha} c^i + \Theta^j \cdot r$. Let $c^j = \frac{1}{\alpha} c^i + \Theta^j \cdot r$, then $Ref(I^i) \in \Phi^j$. We have shown that $\forall I^i \in \Psi^i, Ref(I^i) \in \Phi^j$. It then follows that Ψ^i and Φ^j are communication-free partitioning.

Lemma 31 shows good characteristics in finding communication-free partitioning. It can be used for determining the hyperplane coefficient vectors. Once the data hyperplane coefficient vectors are fixed, the iteration hyperplane coefficient vectors can also be determined. If the reference matrix R is invertible, we can also determine the iteration hyperplane coefficient vectors first, then the data hyperplane coefficient vectors can be evaluated by $\Theta^j = (\frac{1}{\alpha})\Delta^i \cdot R^{-1}$ accordingly, where R^{-1} is the inverse of R. As regards to the constant terms of hyperplanes, since the constant terms of hyperplanes are correlated to each other, hence, if the constant term of some hyperplane is fixed, the others can be represented in terms of that constant term. From the proof of Lemma 31, we can know that if c^i is fixed, $c^j = \frac{1}{\alpha} c^i + \Theta^j \cdot r$. Generally speaking, in a vector space, a vector does not change its direction after being scaled. Since α in Lemma 31 is a scale factor, it can be omitted without affecting the correctness. Therefore, we always let $\alpha = 1$ unless otherwise noted.

Example 38. Consider one perfectly nested loop.

> **do** $i_1 = 1, N$
>   **do** $i_2 = 1, N$
> $A(i_1 + i_2, i_1 + i_2) = 2 * A(i_1 + i_2, i_1 + i_2) - 1$ ($L_{3.7}$)
> **enddo enddo**

Suppose the iteration hyperplane on $IS(L_{3.7})$ is of the form $\Psi = \{I | \Delta \cdot I = c\}$ and the data hyperplane on $DS(A)$ is $\Phi = \{D | \Theta \cdot D = c'\}$. From Lemma 31, the data hyperplane coefficient vector Θ can be set to arbitrarily 2-dimensional vector except zero vector and those vectors that cause the iteration hyperplane coefficient vectors also to be zero vectors. In this example, let $\Theta = [0, 1]$, then the iteration hyperplane coefficient vector Δ is equal to $[1, 1]$. If the constant term of iteration hyperplane is fixed as c, the data hyperplane constant term $c' = c + \Theta \cdot r$. For this example, $c' = c$. Therefore, the iteration hyperplane and data hyperplane of loop $L_{3.7}$ are $\Psi = \{I | [1, 1] \cdot I = c\}$ and $\Phi = \{D | [0, 1] \cdot D = c\}$, respectively. That is, $\Psi = \{[I_1, I_2]^t | I_1 + I_2 = c\}$ and $\Phi = \{[D_1, D_2]^t | D_2 = c\}$. Fig. 3.5 illustrates the communication-free hyperplane partitioning of loop $L_{3.7}$, where $c = 5$. Fig. 3.5 (b) and (c) are iteration hyperplane and data hyperplane, respectively.

On the other hand, if the data hyperplane coefficient vector Θ is chosen as $[1, -1]$, it causes the iteration hyperplane coefficient vector Δ to be $[0, 0]$,

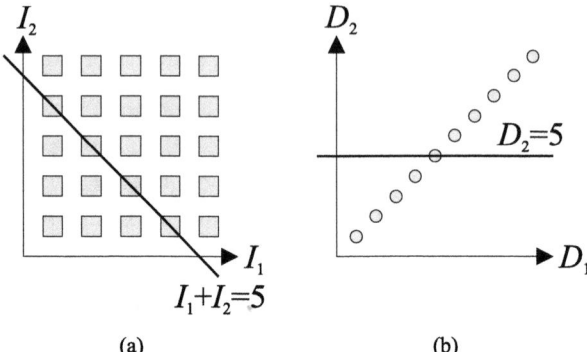

Fig. 3.5. Communication-free hyperplane partitioning of loop $L_{3.7}$. (a) Iteration hyperplane partition on $IS(L_{3.7})$: $\Psi = \{[I_1, I_2]^t | I_1 + I_2 = 5\}$. (b) Data hyperplane partition on $DS(A)$: $\Phi = \{[D_1, D_2]^t | D_2 = 5\}$.

which is a zero vector. Since all the hyperplane coefficient vectors are non-zero vectors, therefore, the above result is invalid. In other words, the data hyperplane coefficient vector Θ can be any 2-dimensional vector except $[0, 0]$ and $[1, -1]$.

By Section 2.3, since the null space of R is $NS(R) = span(\{[1, -1]^t\})$, the spaces caused by the self-dependent relations and cross-dependent relations are the same and equal $span(\{[1, -1]^t\})$. The iteration-dependent space of loop $L_{3.7}$ is $IDS(L_{3.7}) = span(\{[1, -1]^t\})$. It means that the iterations along the direction $[1, -1]^t$ should be allocated onto the same processor. This result matches that shown in Fig. 3.5.

Lemma 31 is enough to meet the requirement of communication-free partitioning for only one array reference. If there are more than one different array references in the same loop, Lemma 31 is useful but not enough. More conditions is attached in order to satisfy the communication-free criteria. Suppose there are γ different array references of array variable v_j in nested loop L_i, which are $Ref_k^{i,j}(I^i) = R_k^{i,j} I^i + r_k^{i,j}$, $k = 1, 2, \ldots, \gamma$. As previously defined, the iteration hyperplane is $\Psi^i = \{I^i | \Delta^i \cdot I^i = c^i\}$ and the data hyperplane is $\Phi^j = \{D^j | \Theta^j \cdot D^j = c^j\}$. By Lemma 31, Ψ^i and Φ^j are communication-free partitioning if and only if $\Delta^i = \alpha \Theta^j \cdot R$, where R is some reference matrix and α is a non-zero constant. Without loss of generality, let $\alpha = 1$. Since there are γ different array references, hence, Lemma 31 should be satisfied for every array reference. That is,

$$\Delta^i = \Theta^j \cdot R_1^{i,j} = \Theta^j \cdot R_2^{i,j} = \cdots = \Theta^j \cdot R_\gamma^{i,j}. \tag{3.3}$$

On the other hand, the constant term of the data hyperplane is $c' = c + \Theta^j \cdot r_1^{i,j} = c + \Theta^j \cdot r_2^{i,j} = \cdots = c + \Theta^j \cdot r_\gamma^{i,j}$ if the iteration hyperplane constant term is c. It implies that

$$\Theta^j \cdot r_1^{i,j} = \Theta^j \cdot r_2^{i,j} = \cdots = \Theta^j \cdot r_\gamma^{i,j}. \tag{3.4}$$

Therefore, Eqs. (3.3) and (3.4) are the sufficient and necessary conditions for the communication-free hyperplane partitioning of nested loop with several array references to an array variable. If there exists a contradiction within the findings of the hyperplane coefficient vectors, it implies that the nested loop exists no communication-free hyperplane partitioning. Otherwise, the data hyperplane coefficient vector can be evaluated accordingly. The iteration hyperplane coefficient vector can also be determined. As a result, the iteration hyperplane and data hyperplane can be resolved.

Similarly, the same ideas can be extended to sequences of nested loops, too. The results obtained by the above analyses can be combined for the most general case. Suppose the iteration space for each loop L_i is $IS(L_i)$. The iteration hyperplane on $IS(L_i)$ is $\Psi^i = \{I^i | \Delta^i \cdot I^i = c^i\}$. The data space for array variable v_j is $DS(v_j)$ and the hyperplane on $DS(v_j)$ is $\Phi^j = \{D^j | \Theta^j \cdot D^j = c^j\}$. Let $Ref_k^{i,j}$ be the reference function of the kth reference to array variable v_j in loop L_i. Eqs. (3.3) and (3.4) can be rewritten by minor modifications to meet the representation.

$$\Theta^{j_1} \cdot R_{k_1}^{i,j_1} = \Theta^{j_2} \cdot R_{k_2}^{i,j_2}, \tag{3.5}$$

$$\Theta^j \cdot r_{k_1}^{i,j} = \Theta^j \cdot r_{k_2}^{i,j}. \tag{3.6}$$

Furthermore, since $c^j = c^i + \Theta^j \cdot r_k^{i,j}$, for some array variable v_{j_1}, $c^{j_1} = c^{i_1} + \Theta^{j_1} \cdot r_1^{i_1,j_1} = c^{i_2} + \Theta^{j_1} \cdot r_1^{i_2,j_1}$, for two different loops L_{i_1} and L_{i_2}. We can obtain that $c^{i_2} - c^{i_1} = \Theta^{j_1} \cdot (r_1^{i_1,j_1} - r_1^{i_2,j_1})$. Similarly, for some array variable v_{j_2}, $c^{j_2} = c^{i_1} + \Theta^{j_2} \cdot r_1^{i_1,j_2} = c^{i_2} + \Theta^{j_2} \cdot r_1^{i_2,j_2}$, for two different loops L_{i_1} and L_{i_2}. We get that $c^{i_2} - c^{i_1} = \Theta^{j_2} \cdot (r_1^{i_1,j_2} - r_1^{i_2,j_2})$. Combining these two equations can obtain the following equation.

$$\Theta^{j_1} \cdot (r_1^{i_1,j_1} - r_1^{i_2,j_1}) = \Theta^{j_2} \cdot (r_1^{i_1,j_2} - r_1^{i_2,j_2}). \tag{3.7}$$

Thus, Eqs. (3.5), (3.6), and (3.7) are the sufficient and necessary conditions for the communication-free hyperplane partitioning of sequences of nested loops.

Example 39. Consider the following sequence of loops.

do $i_1 = 1, N$
    do $i_2 = 1, N$
        $A(i_1 + i_2 + 2, -2i_2 + 2) = B(i_1 + 1, i_2)$ ($L_{3.8}$)
    enddo enddo
do $i_1 = 1, N$
    do $i_2 = 1, N$
        $B(i_1 + 2i_2, i_2 + 4) = A(i_1, i_2 - 1)$ ($L_{3.9}$)
    enddo enddo

To simplify the representation, we number the sequences of loops and array variables according to the order of occurrences. Let L_1 refer to $L_{3.8}$, L_2 refer to $L_{3.9}$, v_1 refer to array variable A, and v_2 refer to array variable B. The iteration space of loop L_1 is $IS(L_1)$ and the iteration space of loop L_2 is $IS(L_2)$. The data spaces of v_1 and v_2 are $DS(v_1)$ and $DS(v_2)$, respectively. Suppose $\Psi^1 = \{I^1 | \Delta^1 \cdot I^1 = c^1\}$ is the iteration hyperplane on $IS(L_1)$ and $\Psi^2 = \{I^2 | \Delta^2 \cdot I^2 = c^2\}$ is the iteration hyperplane on $IS(L_2)$. The data hyperplanes on $DS(v_1)$ and $DS(v_2)$ are $\Phi^1 = \{D^1 | \Theta^1 \cdot D^1 = c^{1'}\}$ and $\Phi^2 = \{D^2 | \Theta^2 \cdot D^2 = c^{2'}\}$, respectively. As defined above, $Ref_k^{i,j}$ is the reference function of the kth reference to array variable v_j in loop L_i.

Since Θ^1, and Θ^2 are 2-dimensional non-zero vectors, let $\Theta^1 = [\theta_1^1, \theta_2^1]$, and $\Theta^2 = [\theta_1^2, \theta_2^2]$, where θ_1^1, θ_2^1, θ_1^2, and $\theta_2^2 \in \mathbf{Q}$, $(\theta_1^1)^2 + (\theta_2^1)^2 \neq 0$, and $(\theta_1^2)^2 + (\theta_2^2)^2 \neq 0$. By Eq. (3.5), we have the following two equations $\Theta^1 \cdot R_1^{1,1} = \Theta^2 \cdot R_1^{1,2}$ and $\Theta^1 \cdot R_1^{2,1} = \Theta^2 \cdot R_1^{2,2}$. Thus,

$$[\theta_1^1, \theta_2^1] \cdot \begin{bmatrix} 1 & 1 \\ 0 & -2 \end{bmatrix} = [\theta_1^2, \theta_2^2] \cdot \begin{bmatrix} 1 & 0 \\ 0 & 1 \end{bmatrix}, \text{ and}$$

$$[\theta_1^1, \theta_2^1] \cdot \begin{bmatrix} 1 & 0 \\ 0 & 1 \end{bmatrix} = [\theta_1^2, \theta_2^2] \cdot \begin{bmatrix} 1 & 2 \\ 0 & 1 \end{bmatrix}.$$

There is no condition that satisfies Eq. (3.6) in this example since each array variable is referenced just once by each nested loop. To satisfy Eq. (3.7), the equation $\Theta^1 \cdot (r_1^{1,1} - r_1^{2,1}) = \Theta^2 \cdot (r_1^{1,2} - r_1^{2,2})$ is obtained. That is,

$$[\theta_1^1, \theta_2^1] \cdot (\begin{bmatrix} 2 \\ 2 \end{bmatrix} - \begin{bmatrix} 0 \\ -1 \end{bmatrix}) = [\theta_1^2, \theta_2^2] \cdot (\begin{bmatrix} 1 \\ 0 \end{bmatrix} - \begin{bmatrix} 0 \\ 4 \end{bmatrix}).$$

Solving the above system of equations, we can obtain that $\theta_2^1 = \theta_1^1$, $\theta_1^2 = \theta_1^1$, and $\theta_2^2 = -\theta_1^1$. Therefore, the data hyperplane coefficient vectors of Φ^1 and Φ^2, Θ^1 and Θ^2, are $[\theta_1^1, \theta_1^1]$ and $[\theta_1^1, -\theta_1^1]$, respectively. Since Θ^1 and Θ^2 are non-zero vectors, $\theta_1^1 \in \mathbf{Q} - \{0\}$.

The coefficient vector of iteration hyperplane Ψ^1 is $\Delta^1 = \Theta^1 \cdot R_1^{1,1} = \Theta^2 \cdot R_1^{1,2} = [\theta_1^1, -\theta_1^1]$. Similarly, $\Delta^2 = \Theta^1 \cdot R_1^{2,1} = \Theta^2 \cdot R_1^{2,2} = [\theta_1^1, \theta_1^1]$. Let the constant term of iteration hyperplane Ψ^1 be fixed as c^1. Therefore, the constant term of iteration hyperplane Ψ^2 can, therefore, be computed by $c^2 = c^1 + \Theta^1 \cdot (r_1^{1,1} - r_1^{2,1}) = c^1 + \Theta^2 \cdot (r_1^{1,2} - r_1^{2,2}) = c^1 + 5\theta_1^1$. The constant term of data hyperplane Φ^1 can be evaluated by $c^{1'} = c^1 + \Theta^1 \cdot r_1^{1,1} = c^2 + \Theta^1 \cdot r_1^{2,1} = c^1 + 4\theta_1^1$. The constant term of data hyperplane Φ^2 can be evaluated by $c^{2'} = c^1 + \Theta^2 \cdot r_1^{1,2} = c^2 + \Theta^2 \cdot r_1^{2,2} = c^1 + \theta_1^1$. The communication-free iteration hyperplane and data hyperplane partition are as follows.

$$
\begin{aligned}
\Psi^1 &= \{[I_1^1, I_2^1]^t | \theta_1^1 I_1^1 - \theta_1^1 I_2^1 = c^1\} \\
\Psi^2 &= \{[I_1^2, I_2^2]^t | \theta_1^1 I_1^1 + \theta_1^1 I_2^1 = c^1 + 5\theta_1^1\} \\
\Phi^1 &= \{[D_1^1, D_2^1]^t | \theta_1^1 D_1^1 + \theta_1^1 D_2^1 = c^1 + 4\theta_1^1\} \\
\Phi^2 &= \{[D_1^2, D_2^2]^t | \theta_1^1 D_1^2 - \theta_1^1 D_2^2 = c^1 + \theta_1^1\}
\end{aligned}
$$

$$\Theta^j \cdot r_1^{i,j} = \Theta^j \cdot r_2^{i,j} = \cdots = \Theta^j \cdot r_\gamma^{i,j}. \tag{3.4}$$

Therefore, Eqs. (3.3) and (3.4) are the sufficient and necessary conditions for the communication-free hyperplane partitioning of nested loop with several array references to an array variable. If there exists a contradiction within the findings of the hyperplane coefficient vectors, it implies that the nested loop exists no communication-free hyperplane partitioning. Otherwise, the data hyperplane coefficient vector can be evaluated accordingly. The iteration hyperplane coefficient vector can also be determined. As a result, the iteration hyperplane and data hyperplane can be resolved.

Similarly, the same ideas can be extended to sequences of nested loops, too. The results obtained by the above analyses can be combined for the most general case. Suppose the iteration space for each loop L_i is $IS(L_i)$. The iteration hyperplane on $IS(L_i)$ is $\Psi^i = \{I^i | \Delta^i \cdot I^i = c^i\}$. The data space for array variable v_j is $DS(v_j)$ and the hyperplane on $DS(v_j)$ is $\Phi^j = \{D^j | \Theta^j \cdot D^j = c^j\}$. Let $Ref_k^{i,j}$ be the reference function of the kth reference to array variable v_j in loop L_i. Eqs. (3.3) and (3.4) can be rewritten by minor modifications to meet the representation.

$$\Theta^{j_1} \cdot R_{k_1}^{i,j_1} = \Theta^{j_2} \cdot R_{k_2}^{i,j_2}, \tag{3.5}$$

$$\Theta^j \cdot r_{k_1}^{i,j} = \Theta^j \cdot r_{k_2}^{i,j}. \tag{3.6}$$

Furthermore, since $c^j = c^i + \Theta^j \cdot r_k^{i,j}$, for some array variable v_{j_1}, $c^{j_1} = c^{i_1} + \Theta^{j_1} \cdot r_1^{i_1,j_1} = c^{i_2} + \Theta^{j_1} \cdot r_1^{i_2,j_1}$, for two different loops L_{i_1} and L_{i_2}. We can obtain that $c^{i_2} - c^{i_1} = \Theta^{j_1} \cdot (r_1^{i_1,j_1} - r_1^{i_2,j_1})$. Similarly, for some array variable v_{j_2}, $c^{j_2} = c^{i_1} + \Theta^{j_2} \cdot r_1^{i_1,j_2} = c^{i_2} + \Theta^{j_2} \cdot r_1^{i_2,j_2}$, for two different loops L_{i_1} and L_{i_2}. We get that $c^{i_2} - c^{i_1} = \Theta^{j_2} \cdot (r_1^{i_1,j_2} - r_1^{i_2,j_2})$. Combining these two equations can obtain the following equation.

$$\Theta^{j_1} \cdot (r_1^{i_1,j_1} - r_1^{i_2,j_1}) = \Theta^{j_2} \cdot (r_1^{i_1,j_2} - r_1^{i_2,j_2}). \tag{3.7}$$

Thus, Eqs. (3.5), (3.6), and (3.7) are the sufficient and necessary conditions for the communication-free hyperplane partitioning of sequences of nested loops.

Example 39. Consider the following sequence of loops.

do $i_1 = 1, N$
   do $i_2 = 1, N$
      $A(i_1 + i_2 + 2, -2i_2 + 2) = B(i_1 + 1, i_2)$ ($L_{3.8}$)
   enddo enddo
do $i_1 = 1, N$
   do $i_2 = 1, N$
      $B(i_1 + 2i_2, i_2 + 4) = A(i_1, i_2 - 1)$ ($L_{3.9}$)
   enddo enddo

iteration consists of *all* statements of that index within the loop body. The execution of an iteration includes all the execution of statements of that index. Actually, each statement is an individual unit and can be scheduled separately. Therefore, instead of viewing each iteration indivisible, an iteration can be separated into the statements enclosed in that iteration. The separated statements have the same index with that iteration and each is termed as a *statement-iteration*. We use I^s to denote a statement-iteration of statement s. Since iteration space is composed of iterations, statement-iterations of a statement also form a space. Each statement has its corresponding space. We use *statement-iteration space*, denoted as $SIS(s)$, to refer the space composed by statement-iterations of s. Statement-iteration space has the same loop boundaries with the corresponding iteration space. Generally speaking, statement-iteration space and iteration space have similar definitions except the viewpoint of objects; the former is from the statement-level point of view and the latter is from the loop-level viewpoint. In this section we describe two statement-level communication-free partitionings: one is using affine processor mappings [22] and another is using hyperplane partitioning [30].

4.1 Affine Processor Mapping

The method proposed in [22] considers iteration spaces partitioning, especially statement-level partitioning, to totally eliminate interprocessor communication and simultaneously maximizes the degree of parallelism. We use *Lim and Lam's method* to refer the technique proposed in [22]. They use *affine processor mappings* to allocate statement-iterations to processors. The major consideration of *Lim and Lam's method* is to find maximum communication-free parallelism. That is, the goal is to find the set of affine processor mappings for statements in the program and to exploit as large amount of parallelism as possible on the premise that no interprocessor communication incurs while execution. *Lim and Lam's method* deals with the array references with affine functions of outer loop indices or loop invariant variables. Their method can be applied to arbitrarily nested loops and sequences of loops.

The statement-iteration distribution scheme adopted by *Lim and Lam's method* is *affine processor mapping*, which is of the form $Proc^i(I^i) = P^i I^i + p^i$ for statement s_i. It maps each statement-iteration I^i in $SIS(s_i)$ to a (virtual) processor $Proc^i(I^i)$. P^i is the *mapping matrix* of s_i and p^i is the *mapping offset vector* of s_i. Maximizing the degree of parallelism is to maximize the rank of P^i. To maximize the rank of P^i and to minimize the dimensionality of the null space of P^i are conceptually the same. Therefore, minimizing the dimensionality of the null space of P^i is one major goal in *Lim and Lam's method*.

Similar to the meanings of iteration-dependent space defined in Section 2.3, they define another term to refer to those statement-iterations which have to be mapped to the same processor. The statement-iterations which have to be mapped to the same processor are collected in the *minimal localized statement-iteration space*, which is denoted as L_i for statement s_i. Therefore, the major goal has changed from the minimization of the dimensionality of the null space of P^i to the finding of the minimal localized statement-iteration space. Once the minimal localized statement-iteration space of each statement is determined, the maximum degree of communication-free parallelism of each statement can be decided by $\dim(SIS(s_i)) - \dim(L_i)$. Since each statement's maximum degree of communication-free parallelism is different, in order to preserve the communication-free parallelism available to each statement, *Lim and Lam's method* chooses the maximum value among all the degrees of communication-free parallelism of each statement as the dimensionality of the virtual processor array. By means of the minimal localized statement-iteration space, the affine processor mapping can be evaluated accordingly. The following examples demonstrate the concepts of *Lim and Lam's method* proposed in [22].

Example 41. Consider the following loop.

$$
\begin{aligned}
&\textbf{do } i_1 = 1,\ N\\
&\quad \textbf{do } i_2 = 1,\ N\\
&s_1: \quad A(i_1, i_2) = A(i_1 - 1, i_2) + B(i_1, i_2 - 1) \qquad\qquad (L_{4.1})\\
&s_2: \quad B(i_1, i_2) = A(i_1, i_2 + 1) + B(i_1 + 1, i_2)\\
&\textbf{enddo enddo}
\end{aligned}
$$

Loop $L_{4.1}$ contains two statements and there are two array variables referenced in the nested loop. Let $v_1 = A$ and $v_2 = B$. We have defined *statement-iteration space* and described the differences of it from *iteration space* above. Fig. 4.1 gives a concrete example to illustrate the difference between iteration space and statement-iteration space. In Fig. 4.1(a), a circle means an iteration and includes two rectangles with black and gray colors. The black rectangle indicates statement s_1 and the gray one indicates statement s_2. In Fig. 4.1(b) and Fig. 4.1(c), each statement is an individual unit and the collection of statements forms two statement-iteration spaces.

Let $\mathcal{S}$ be the set of statements and $\mathcal{V}$ be the set of array variables referenced by $\mathcal{S}$. Suppose $\mathcal{S} = \{s_1, s_2, \ldots, s_\alpha\}$ and $\mathcal{V} = \{v_1, v_2, \ldots, v_\beta\}$, where $\alpha, \beta \in \mathbf{Z}^+$. For this example, $\alpha = 2$ and $\beta = 2$. Let the number of occurrences of variable v_j in statement s_i be denoted as $\gamma_{i,j}$. For this example, $\gamma_{1,1} = 2$, $\gamma_{1,2} = 1$, $\gamma_{2,1} = 1$, and $\gamma_{2,2} = 2$. Let $Ref_k^{i,j}$ denote the reference function of the kth occurrence of array variable v_j in statement s_i, where $1 \leq i \leq \alpha$, $1 \leq j \leq \beta$, and $1 \leq k \leq \gamma_{i,j}$. A statement-iteration on a d-dimensional statement-iteration space $SIS(s)$ can be written as $I^s = [i_1^s, i_2^s, i_d^s]^t$. Let i_k^s denote the kth component of statement-iteration I^s. The reference functions for each array reference are described as follows.

$$
Ref_1^{1,1}(I^1) = \begin{bmatrix} i_1^1 \\ i_2^1 \end{bmatrix},\
Ref_2^{1,1}(I^1) = \begin{bmatrix} i_1^1 - 1 \\ i_2^1 \end{bmatrix},\
Ref_1^{1,2}(I^1) = \begin{bmatrix} i_1^1 \\ i_2^1 - 1 \end{bmatrix},
$$

$$
Ref_1^{2,2}(I^2) = \begin{bmatrix} i_1^2 \\ i_2^2 \end{bmatrix},\
Ref_1^{2,1}(I^2) = \begin{bmatrix} i_1^2 \\ i_2^2 + 1 \end{bmatrix},\
Ref_2^{2,2}(I^2) = \begin{bmatrix} i_1^2 + 1 \\ i_2^2 \end{bmatrix}.
$$

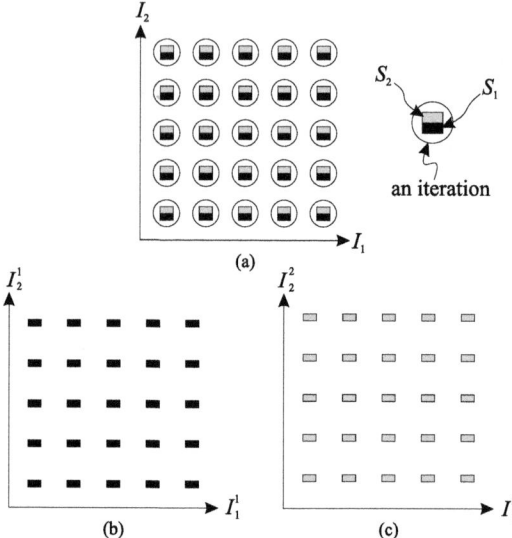

Fig. 4.1. The illustrations of the differences between iteration space and statement-iteration space.

Communication-free partitioning requires the referenced data be located on the processor performing that execution, no matter whether the data is read or written. Therefore, it makes no difference for communication-free partitioning whether the data dependence is true dependence, anti-dependence, output dependence or input dependence. Hence, in *Lim and Lam's method*, they defined a function, *co-reference function*, to keep the data dependence relationship. The co-reference function just keeps the data dependence relationship but does not retain the order of read or write. Let $\Re_{s,s'}$ be the co-reference function and can be defined as the set of statement-iterations $I^{s'}$ such that the data elements referenced by I_s are also referenced by $I_{s'}$, where $s, s' \in \mathcal{S}$. Fig. 4.2 gives an abstraction of co-reference function.

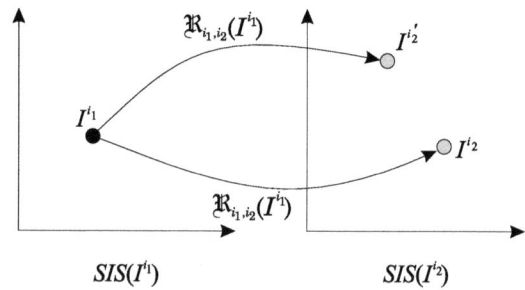

Fig. 4.2. The abstraction of *co-reference function*.

Accordingly,

$$\Re_{1,1}(I^1) = \{I^{1'}|(i_1^{1'} = i_1^1) \wedge (i_2^{1'} = i_2^1)\} \cup \{I^{1'}|(i_1^{1'} = i_1^1 - 1) \wedge (i_2^{1'} = i_2^1)\} \cup$$
$$\{I^{1'}|(i_1^{1'} = i_1^1 + 1) \wedge (i_2^{1'} = i_2^1)\},$$
$$\Re_{1,2}(I^1) = \{I^2|(i_1^2 = i_1^1) \wedge (i_2^2 = i_2^1 - 1)\} \cup \{I^2|(i_1^2 = i_1^1 - 1) \wedge (i_2^2 = i_2^1 - 1)\},$$
$$\Re_{2,1}(I^2) = \{I^1|(i_1^1 = i_1^2) \wedge (i_2^1 = i_2^2 + 1)\} \cup \{I^1|(i_1^1 = i_1^2 + 1) \wedge (i_2^1 = i_2^2 + 1)\},$$
$$\Re_{2,2}(I^2) = \{I^{2'}|(i_1^{2'} = i_1^2) \wedge (i_2^{2'} = i_2^2)\} \cup \{I^{2'}|(i_1^{2'} = i_1^2 + 1) \wedge (i_2^{2'} = i_2^2)\} \cup$$
$$\{I^{2'}|(i_1^{2'} = i_1^2 - 1) \wedge (i_2^{2'} = i_2^2)\}.$$

As previously described, finding the minimal null space of P^i is the same as to find the minimal localized statement-iteration space. Hence, how to determine the minimal localized statement-iteration space of each statement is the major task of *Lim and Lam's method*. The minimal localized statement-iteration space is composed of the minimum set of column vectors satisfying the following conditions:

- **Single statement:** The data dependence relationship within a statement-iteration space may be incurred via the array references in the same statement or between statements. This requirement is to map all the statement-iterations in a statement-iteration space that directly or indirectly access the same data element to the same processor. In other words, these statement-iterations should belong to the minimal localized statement-iteration space.
- **Multiple Statements:** For two different statements s_{i_1} and s_{i_2}, suppose I^{i_1} and $I^{i'_1}$ are two statement-iterations in $SIS(s_{i_1})$ and $I^{i_2} \in \Re_{i_1,i_2}(I^{i_1})$ and $I^{i'_2} \in \Re_{i_1,i_2}(I^{i'_1})$. If statement-iterations I^{i_1} and $I^{i'_1}$ are mapped to the same processor, this requirement requires all the statement-iterations I^{i_2} and $I^{i'_2}$ being mapped to the same processor.

Figs. 4.3 and 4.4 conceptually illustrate the conditions **Single Statement** and **Multiple Statements**, respectively. The boldfaced lines in the two figures are the main requirements that these two condition want to meet.

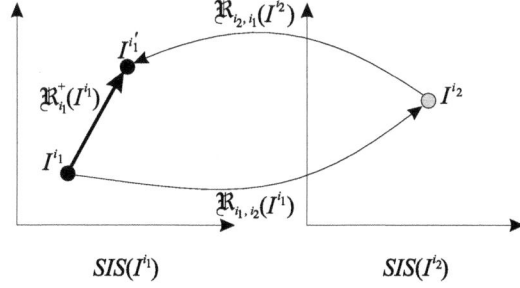

Fig. 4.3. The abstraction of **Single Statement** condition.

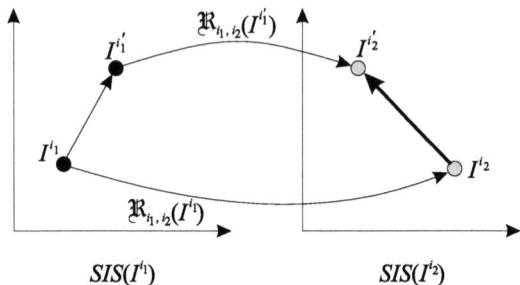

Fig. 4.4. The abstraction of **Multiple Statements** condition.

An iterative algorithm can be used to evaluate the minimal localized statement-iteration space of each statement. First, initialize each L_i using condition **Single Statement**. Second, iterate using condition **Multiple Statements** until all the L_i is converged. In what follows, we use this iterative algorithm to evaluate the minimal localized statement-iteration space of each statement for this example. Based on the condition **Single Statement**, L_1 is initialized to $\{[1,0]^t\}$ and L_2 is initialized to $\{[1,0]^t\}$. The algorithm iterates according to the condition **Multiple Statements** to check if there is any column vector that should be added to the minimal localized statement-iteration spaces. The algorithm considers one minimal localized statement-iteration space at a time. For all other minimal localized statement-iteration spaces, the iterative algorithm uses condition **Multiple Statements** to add column vectors to the minimal localized statement-iteration space, if any. Once all the localized statement-iteration spaces are converged, the algorithm halts. As for this example, the iterative algorithm is halted when L_1 and L_2 both converge to $\{[1,0]^t\}$. Thus, the minimal localized statement-iteration spaces L_1 and L_2 have been evaluated and all equal $\{[1,0]^t\}$.

For any two statement-iterations, if the difference between these two statement-iterations belongs to the space spanned by the minimal localized statement-iteration space, these two statement-iterations have to be mapped to the same processor. Therefore, the orthogonal complement of the minimal localized statement-iteration space is a subspace that there exists no data dependent relationship within the space. That is, all statement-iterations that located on the the orthogonal complement of the minimal localized statement-iteration space are completely independent. Accordingly, the maximum degree of communication-free parallelism of a statement is the dimensionality of the statement-iteration space $SIS(s_i)$ minus the dimensionality of the minimal localized statement-iteration space L_i. Let the maximum degree of communication-free parallelism available for statement s_i be denoted as τ_i. Then, $\tau_i = \dim(SIS(s_i)) - \dim(L_i)$. Thus, $\tau_1 = 1$ and $\tau_2 = 1$. *Lim and Lam's method* wants to exploit as large amount of parallelism as possible. To retain the communication-free parallelism of each statement, the dimensionality of (virtual) processor array has to set to the maximum value of maximum degree of communication-free parallelism among all statements. Let τ_p be the dimensionality of the (virtual) processor array. It can be defined as $\tau_p = \max_{i \in \{1,2,\ldots,\alpha\}} \tau_i$. For this example, $\tau_p = \max(\tau_1, \tau_2) = 1$.

We have decided the dimensionality of (virtual) processor array. Finally, we want to determine the affine processor mapping for each statement by means of the co-reference function and the minimal localized statement-iteration space. To map a d-dimensional statement-iteration space to a τ_p-dimensional processor array, the mapping matrix P in the affine processor mapping is a $\tau_p \times d$ matrix and the mapping offset vector p is a $\tau_p \times 1$ vector. For each affine processor mapping $Proc^i(I^i) = P^i I^i + p^i$, the following two constraints should be satisfied, where $i \in \{1, 2, \ldots, \alpha\}$.

C1 $span(L_i) \subseteq$ null space of $Proc^i$.
C2 $\forall i' \in \{1, 2, \ldots, \alpha\}, i' \neq i, \forall I^i \in SIS(s_i), \forall I^{i'} \in \Re_{i,i'}(I^i) : Proc^{i'}(I^{i'}) = Proc^i(I^i)$.

Condition C1 can be reformulated as follows. Since $span(L_i) \subseteq$ null space of $Proc^i$, it means that if $I^i, I^{i'} \in SIS(s_i)$ and $(I^{i'} - I^i) \in span(L_i)$, then $Proc^i(I^{i'}) = Proc^i(I^i)$. Thus, $P^i I^{i'} + p^i = P^i I^i + p^i$. It implies that $P^i(I^{i'} - I^i) = \emptyset$, where $\emptyset$ is a $\tau_p \times 1$ zero vector. Because $(I^{i'} - I^i) \in span(L_i)$, we can conclude that

C1' $\forall x \in L_i, P^i x = \emptyset$.

A straightforward algorithm to find the affine processor mappings according to the constraints C1 and C2 is derived in the following. First, choose one statement that its maximum degree of communication-free parallelism equals the dimensionality of the (virtual) processor array, say s_i. Find the affine processor mapping $Proc^i$ such that the constraint C1 is satisfied. Since $span(L_i)$ has to be included in the null space of $Proc^i$, it means that the range of $Proc^i$ is the orthogonal complement of the space spanned by L_1. Therefore, one intuitively way to find the affine processor mapping $Proc^i$ is to set $Proc^i(I^i) = (L_i)^{\perp} I^i$, where $W^{\perp}$ means the orthogonal complement of the space W. The mapping offset vector p^i is set to a zero vector. Next, based on the affine processor mapping $Proc^i$, use constraint C2 to find the other statements' affine processor mappings. This process will repeat until all the affine processor mappings are found. Using the straightforward algorithm described above, we can find the two affine processor mappings $Proc^1 = [0,1]I^1$ and $Proc^2 = [0,1]I^2 + 1$. Fig. 4.5 shows the communication-free affine processor mappings of statements s_1 and s_2 for loop $L_{4.1}$.

Data distribution is an important issue for parallelizing compilers on distributed-memory multicomputers. However, *Lim and Lam's method* ignores that. The following section describes the communication-free hyperplane partitioning for iteration and data spaces.

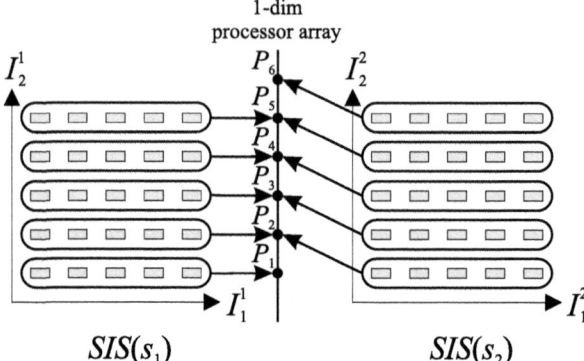

Fig. 4.5. Communication-free affine processor mappings $Proc^1(I^1) = [0,1]I^1$ and $Proc^2(I^2) = [0,1]I^2 + 1$ of statement s_1 and s_2 for loop $L_{4.1}$, assuming $N = 5$.

4.2 Hyperplane Partitioning

In this section, the method proposed by Shih, Sheu, and Huang [30] studies toward the statement-level communication-free partitioning. They partition statement-iteration spaces and data spaces along hyperplanes. We use *Shih, Sheu, and Huang's method* to denote the method proposed in [30]. *Shih, Sheu, and Huang's method* can deal with not only an imperfectly nested loop but also sequences of imperfectly nested loops. They propose the sufficient and necessary conditions for the feasibility of communication-free single-hyperplane partitioning for an imperfectly nested loop and sequences of imperfectly nested loops. The main ideas of *Shih, Sheu, and Huang's method* is similar to those proposed in Sections 3.2 and 3.3. In the following, we omit the tedious mathematical inference and just describe the concepts of the method. The details is referred to [30].

As defined in Section 4.1, $\mathcal{S} = \{s_1, s_2, \ldots, s_\alpha\}$ is the set of statements and $\mathcal{V} = \{v_1, v_2, \ldots, v_\beta\}$ is the set of array variables, where $\alpha, \beta \in \mathbf{Z}^+$. The number of occurrences of array variable v_j in statement s_i is $\gamma_{i,j}$. If v_j is not referenced in statement s_i, $\gamma_{i,j} = 0$. The reference function of the kth array reference of array variable v_j in statement s_i is denoted as $Ref_k^{i,j}$, where $i \in \{1, 2, \ldots, \alpha\}$, $j \in \{1, 2, \ldots, \beta\}$, and $k \in \{1, 2, \ldots, \gamma_{i,j}\}$.

Suppose $\Psi^i = \{I^i | \Delta^i \cdot I^i = c^i\}$ is the statement-iteration hyperplane on $SIS(s_i)$ and $\Phi^j = \{D^j | \Theta^j \cdot D^j = c^j\}$ is the data hyperplane on $DS(v_j)$. Statement-level communication-free hyperplane partitioning requires those statement-iterations that reference the same array element be allocated on the same statement-iteration hyperplane. According to Lemma 21, two statement-iterations reference the same array element if and only if the difference of these two statement-iterations belongs to the null space of $R_k^{i,j}$, for some i, j and k. Hence, $NS(R_k^{i,j})$ should be a subspace of the statement-iteration hyperplane. Since there may exist many different array references, partitioning a statement-iteration space must consider all array references appeared in the statement. Thus, the space spanned by $NS(R_k^{i,j})$ for all array references appearing in the same statement should be a subspace of the statement-iteration hyperplane. Therefore, the above observations is concluded in the following lemma.

Lemma 41 (Statement-Iteration Hyperplane Coefficient Check).
For any communication-free statement-iteration hyperplane $\Psi^i = \{I^i | \Delta^i \cdot I^i = c^i\}$, the following two conditions must hold:

(1) $span(\cup_{j=1}^{\beta} \cup_{k=1}^{\gamma_{i,j}} NS(R_k^{i,j})) \subseteq \Psi^i$,
(2) $(\Delta^i)^t \in (span(\cup_{j=1}^{\beta} \cup_{k=1}^{\gamma_{i,j}} NS(R_k^{i,j})))^{\perp}$,

where $S^{\perp}$ denotes the orthogonal complement space of S.

On the other hand, the dimension of a statement-iteration hyperplane is one less than the dimension of the statement-iteration space. If there exists a statement s_i, for some i, such that the dimension of the spanning space of $NS(R_k^{i,j})$, for all j and k, is equal to the dimension of $SIS(s_i)$, then the spanning space cannot be a subspace of the statement-iteration hyperplane. Therefore, there exists no nontrivial communication-free hyperplane partitioning. Thus, we obtain the following lemma.

Lemma 42 (Statement-Iteration Space Dimension Check). *If $\exists s_i \in S$ such that*

$$dim(span(\cup_{j=1}^{\beta} \cup_{k=1}^{\gamma_{i,j}} NS(R_k^{i,j}))) = dim(SIS(s_i)),$$

then there exists no nontrivial communication-free hyperplane partitioning.

In addition to the above observations, *Shih, Sheu, and Huang's method* also finds more useful properties for the findings of communication-free hyperplane partitioning. Lemma 31 demonstrates that the iteration hyperplane and data hyperplane are communication-free partitioning if and only if the iteration hyperplane coefficient vector is parallel to the vector obtained by the multiplication of the data hyperplane coefficient vector and the reference matrix. Although Lemma 31 is for iteration space, it also holds true for statement-iteration space. Since the statement-iteration hyperplane coefficient vector is a non-zero vector, thus the multiplication of the data hyperplane coefficient vector and the reference matrix can not be a zero vector. From this condition, we can derive the feasible range of a data hyperplane coefficient vector. Therefore, we obtain the following lemma.

Lemma 43 (Data Hyperplane Coefficient Check). *For any communication-free data hyperplane $\Phi^j = \{D^j | \Theta^j \cdot D^j = c^j\}$, the following condition must hold:*

$$(\Theta^j)^t \in (\cup_{i=1}^{\alpha} \cup_{k=1}^{\gamma_{i,j}} NS((R_k^{i,j})^t))'$$,

where S' denotes the complement set of S.

Lemmas 41 and 43 provide the statement-iteration hyperplane coefficient vector check and the data hyperplane coefficient vector check, respectively.

Suppose the data hyperplane on data space $DS(v_j)$ is $\Phi^j = \{D^j | \Theta^j \cdot D^j = c^j\}$. Since each data element is accessed by some statement-iteration via some reference function, that is, D^j can be represented as $Ref_k^{i,j} = R_k^{i,j} \cdot I^i + r_k^{i,j}$, thus,

$$\Theta^j \cdot D^j = c^j,$$
$$\Leftrightarrow \quad \Theta^j \cdot (R_k^{i,j} \cdot I^i + r_k^{i,j}) = c^j,$$
$$\Leftrightarrow \quad (\Theta^j \cdot R_k^{i,j}) \cdot I^i = c^j - (\Theta^j \cdot r_k^{i,j}).$$

Let

$$\Delta^i = \Theta^j \cdot R_k^{i,j}, \tag{4.1}$$
$$c^i = c^j - (\Theta^j \cdot r_k^{i,j}). \tag{4.2}$$

As a result, those statement-iterations that reference the data elements lay on the data hyperplane $\Phi^j = \{D^j | \Theta^j \cdot D^j = c^j\}$ will be located on the statement-iteration hyperplane $\Psi^i = \{I^i | (\Theta^j \cdot R_k^{i,j}) \cdot I^i = c^j - (\Theta^j \cdot r_k^{i,j})\}$.

Since there are three parameters in the above formulas and $i \in \{1, 2, \ldots, \alpha\}$, $j \in \{1, 2, \ldots, \beta\}$, and $k \in \{1, 2, \ldots, \gamma_{i,j}\}$, for the consistency of hyperplane coefficient vectors and constant terms in each space, we can derive some conditions. Combining the above constraints can obtain the following theorem.

Theorem 41. *Let $\mathcal{S} = \{s_1, s_2, \ldots, s_\alpha\}$ and $\mathcal{V} = \{v_1, v_2, \ldots, v_\beta\}$ be the sets of statements and array variables, respectively. $Ref_k^{i,j}$ is the reference function of the kth occurrence of array variables v_j in statement s_i, where $i \in \{1, 2, \ldots, \alpha\}$, $j \in \{1, 2, \ldots, \beta\}$ and $k \in \{1, 2, \ldots, \gamma_{i,j}\}$. $\Psi^i = \{I^i | \Delta^i \cdot I^i = c^i\}$ is the statement-iteration hyperplane on $SIS(s_i)$, for $i = 1, 2, \ldots, \alpha$. $\Phi^j = \{D^j | \Theta^j \cdot D^j = c^j\}$ is the data hyperplane on $DS(v_j)$, for $j = 1, 2, \ldots, \beta$. Ψ^i and Φ^j are communication-free hyperplane partitions if and only if the following conditions hold.*

1. $\forall i, \Theta^j \cdot R_k^{i,j} = \Theta^j \cdot R_1^{i,j}$, for $j = 1, 2, \ldots, \beta$; $k = 2, 3, \ldots, \gamma_{i,j}$.
2. $\forall i, \Theta^j \cdot R_1^{i,j} = \Theta^1 \cdot R_1^{i,1}$, for $j = 2, 3, \ldots, \beta$.
3. $\forall i, \Theta^j \cdot r_k^{i,j} = \Theta^j \cdot r_1^{i,j}$, for $j = 1, 2, \ldots, \beta$; $k = 2, 3, \ldots, \gamma_{i,j}$.
4. $\Theta^j \cdot (r_1^{i,j} - r_1^{1,j}) = \Theta^1 \cdot (r_1^{i,1} - r_1^{1,1})$, for $i = 2, 3, \ldots, \alpha$; $j = 2, 3, \ldots, \beta$.
5. $\forall j, (\Theta^j)^t \in (\cup_{i=1}^{\alpha} \cup_{k=1}^{\gamma_{i,j}} NS((R_k^{i,j})^t))'$.
6. $\forall i, \Delta^i = \Theta^j \cdot R_k^{i,j}$, for some j, k, $j \in \{1, 2, \ldots, \beta\}$; $k \in \{1, 2, \ldots, \gamma_{i,j}\}$.
7. $\forall i, (\Delta^i)^t \in (span(\cup_{j=1}^{\beta} \cup_{k=1}^{\gamma_{i,j}} NS(R_k^{i,j})))^{\perp}$.
8. $\forall j, j = 2, 3, \ldots, \beta, c^j = c^1 - \Theta^1 \cdot r_1^{i,1} + \Theta^j \cdot r_1^{i,j}$, for some $i, i \in \{1, 2, \ldots, \alpha\}$.
9. $\forall i, c^i = c^j - (\Theta^j \cdot r_k^{i,j})$, for some j, k, $j \in \{1, 2, \ldots, \beta\}$; $k \in \{1, 2, \ldots, \gamma_{i,j}\}$.

Theorem 41 can be used to determine whether the nested loop(s) is/are communication-free. It can also be used as a procedure of finding a communication-free hyperplane partitioning systematically. Conditions 1 to 4 in

Theorem 41 are used for finding the data hyperplane coefficient vectors. Condition 5 can check whether the data hyperplane coefficient vectors found in preceding steps are within the legal range. Following the determination of the data hyperplane coefficient vectors, the statement-iteration hyperplane coefficient vectors can be obtained by using Condition 6. Similarly, Condition 7 can check whether the statement-iteration hyperplane coefficient vectors are within the legal range. The data hyperplane constant terms and statement-iteration hyperplane constant terms can be obtained by using Conditions 8 and 9, respectively. If one of the conditions is violated, the whole procedure will stop and verify that the nested loop has no communication-free hyperplane partitioning.

From Conditions 1 and 3, to satisfy the constraint that Θ^j is a non-zero row vector, we have the following condition.

$$Rank(R_1^{i,j} - R_2^{i,j}, \cdots, R_1^{i,j} - R_{\gamma_{i,j}}^{i,j},$$
$$r_1^{i,j} - r_2^{i,j}, \cdots, r_1^{i,j} - r_{\gamma_{i,j}}^{i,j}) < dim(DS(v_j)), \qquad (4.3)$$

for $i = 1, 2, \ldots, \alpha$ and $j = 1, 2, \ldots, \beta$. Note that this condition can also be found in [16] for loop-level hyperplane partitioning. We conclude the above by the following lemma.

Lemma 44 (Data Space Dimension Check). *Suppose* $\mathcal{S} = \{s_1, s_2, \ldots, s_\alpha\}$ *and* $\mathcal{D} = \{v_1, v_2, \ldots, v_\beta\}$ *are the sets of statements and array variables, respectively.* $R_k^{i,j}$ *and* $r_k^{i,j}$ *are the reference matrix and the reference vector, respectively, where* $i \in \{1, 2, \ldots, \alpha\}$, $j \in \{1, 2, \ldots, \beta\}$ *and* $k \in \{1, 2, \ldots, \gamma_{i,j}\}$. *If communication-free hyperplane partitioning exists then Eq. (4.3) must hold.*

Lemmas 42 and 44 are sufficient but not necessary. Lemma 42 is the statement-iteration space dimension test and Lemma 44 is the data space dimension test. To determine the existence of a communication-free hyperplane partitioning, we need to check the conditions in Theorem 41. We show the following example to explain the finding of communication-free hyperplanes of statement-iteration spaces and data spaces.

Example 42. Consider the following sequence of imperfectly nested loops.

do $i_1 = 1, N$
    do $i_2 = 1, N$
s_1: $A[i_1 + i_2, 1] = B[i_1 + i_2 + 1, i_1 + i_2 + 2]+$
                      $C[i_1 + 1, -2i_1 + 2i_2, 2i_1 - i_2 + 1]$
      do $i_3 = 1, N$
s_2: $B[i_1 + i_3 + 1, i_2 + i_3 + 1] = A[2i_1 + 2i_3, i_2 + i_3]+$
                $C[i_1 + i_2 + 1, -i_2 + i_3 + 1, i_1 - i_2 + 1]$
enddo enddo enddo $(L_{4.2})$
do $i_1 = 1, N$
    do $i_2 = 1, N$

$$\textbf{do } i_3 = 1, N$$

s_3: $C[i_1 + 1, i_2, i_2 + i_3] = A[2i_1 + 3i_2 + i_3, i_1 + i_2 + 2] +$
$$B[i_1 + i_2, i_1 - i_3 + 1]$$

enddo

s_4: $A[i_1, i_2 + 3] = B[i_1 - i_2, i_1 - i_2 + 2] + C[i_1 + i_2, -i_2, -i_2]$

enddo enddo

The set of statements $\mathcal{S}$ is $\{s_1, s_2, s_3, s_4\}$. The set of array variables is $\mathcal{V} = \{v_1, v_2, v_3\}$, where v_1, v_2, and v_3 represent A, B, and C, respectively. The values of $\gamma_{11}, \gamma_{12}, \gamma_{13}, \gamma_{21}, \gamma_{22}, \gamma_{23}, \gamma_{31}, \gamma_{32}, \gamma_{33}, \gamma_{41}, \gamma_{42}$, and γ_{43} all are 1. We use Lemmas 42 and 44 to verify whether $L_{4.2}$ has no communication-free hyperplane partitioning. Since $dim(\sum_{j=1}^{3} NS(R_1^{i,j})) = 1$, which is smaller than $dim(SIS(s_i))$, for $i = 1, \ldots, 4$. Lemma 42 is helpless for ensuring that $L_{4.2}$ exists no communication-free hyperplane partitioning. Lemma 44 is useless here because all the values of $\gamma_{i,j}$ are 1, for $i = 1, \ldots, 4$; $j = 1, \ldots, 3$. Further examinations are necessary, because Lemmas 42 and 44 can not prove that $L_{4.2}$ has no communication-free hyperplane partitioning. From Theorem 41, if a communication-free hyperplane partitioning exists, the conditions listed in Theorem 41 should be satisfied; otherwise, $L_{4.2}$ exists no communication-free hyperplane partitioning.

Let $\Psi^i = \{I^i | \Delta^i \cdot I^i = c_s^i\}$ be the statement-iteration hyperplane on $SIS(s_i)$ and $\Phi^j = \{D^j | \Theta^j \cdot D^j = c_v^j\}$ be the data hyperplane on $DS(v_j)$. Due to the dimensions of the data spaces $DS(v_1)$, $DS(v_2)$, and $DS(v_3)$ are 2, 2, and 3, respectively, without loss of generality, the data hyperplane coefficient vectors can be respectively assumed to be $\Theta^1 = [\theta_1^1, \theta_2^1]$, $\Theta^2 = [\theta_1^2, \theta_2^2]$, and $\Theta^3 = [\theta_1^3, \theta_2^3, \theta_3^3]$. In what follows, the requirements to satisfy the feasibility of communication-free hyperplane partitioning are examined one-by-one.

There is no need to examine the Conditions 1 and 3 because all the values of $\gamma_{i,j}$ are 1. Solving the linear system obtained from Conditions 2 and 4 can get the general solutions: $(\theta_1^1, \theta_2^1, \theta_1^2, \theta_2^2, \theta_1^3, \theta_2^3, \theta_3^3) = (t, -t, 2t, -t, t, t, t)$, $t \in \mathbf{Q} - \{0\}$. Therefore, $\Theta^1 = [t, -t]$, $\Theta^2 = [2t, -t]$ and $\Theta^3 = [t, t, t]$. Verifying Condition 5 can find out that all the data hyperplane coefficient vectors are within the legal range. Therefore, the statement-iteration hyperplane coefficient vectors can be evaluated by Condition 6. Thus, $\Delta^1 = [t, t]$, $\Delta^2 = [2t, -t, t]$, $\Delta^3 = [t, 2t, t]$, and $\Delta^4 = [t, -t]$. The legality of these statement-iteration hyperplane coefficient vectors is then checked by using Condition 7. Checking Condition 7 can know that all the statement-iteration and data hyperplane coefficient vectors are legal. These results reveals that the nested loops have communication-free hyperplane partitionings. Finally, the data and statement-iteration hyperplanes constant terms are decided by using Conditions 8 and 9, respectively. Let one data hyperplane constant term be fixed, say c_v^1. The other hyperplane constant terms can be determined accordingly. Therefore, $c_v^2 = c_v^1 + t$, $c_v^3 = c_v^1 + 3t$, $c_s^1 = c_v^1 + t$, $c_s^2 = c_v^1$, $c_s^3 = c_v^1 + 2t$, and $c_s^4 = c_v^1 + 3t$. Therefore, the communication-free hyperplane partitionings for loop $L_{4.2}$ is $G = \Psi^1 \cup \Psi^2 \cup \Psi^3 \cup \Psi^4 \cup \Phi^1 \cup \Phi^2 \cup \Phi^3$, where

$$\Psi^1 = \{I^1 \mid [t,t] \cdot I^1 = c_v^1 + t\},$$
$$\Psi^2 = \{I^2 \mid [2t,-t,t] \cdot I^2 = c_v^1\},$$
$$\Psi^3 = \{I^3 \mid [t,2t,t] \cdot I^3 = c_v^1 + 2t\},$$
$$\Psi^4 = \{I^4 \mid [t,-t] \cdot I^4 = c_v^1 + 3t\},$$
$$\Phi^1 = \{D^1 \mid [t,-t] \cdot D^1 = c_v^1\},$$
$$\Phi^2 = \{D^2 \mid [2t,-t] \cdot D^2 = c_v^1 + t\},$$
$$\Phi^3 = \{D^3 \mid [t,t,t] \cdot D^3 = c_v^1 + 3t\}.$$

Fig. 4.6 illustrates the communication-free hyperplane partitionings for loop $L_{4.2}$, where $t = 1$ and $c_v^1 = 0$. The corresponding parallelized program is as follows.

```
doall c = −7, 18
  do i₁ = max(min(c − 4, ⌈(c−4)/2⌉), 1), min(max(c, ⌊(c+4)/2⌋), 5)
    if( max(c − 4, 1) ≤ i₁ ≤ min(c, 5) )
      i₂ = c − i₁ + 1
      A[i₁ + i₂, 1] = B[i₁ + i₂ − 1, i₁ + i₂ + 2]+
                                   C[i₁ + 1, −2i₁ + 2i₂, 2i₁ − i₂ + 1]
    endif
    do i₂ = max(2i₁ − c + 1, 1), min(2i₁ − c + 5, 5)
      i₃ = c − 2i₁ + i₂
      B[i₁ + i₃ + 1, i₂ + i₃ + 1]= A[2i₁ + 2i₃, i₂ + i₃]+
                                   C[i₁ + i₂ + 1, −i₂ + i₃ + 1, i₁ − i₂ + 1]
    enddo
  enddo
  do i₁ = max(c − 13, 1), min(c − 1, 5)
    do i₂ = max(⌈(c−i₁−3)/2⌉, 1), min(⌊(c−i₁+1)/2⌋, 5)
      i₃ = c − i₁ − 2i₂ + 2
      C[i₁ + 1, i₂, i₂ + i₃] = A[2i₁ + 3i₂ + i₃, i₁ + i₂ + 2]+
                                   B[i₁ + i₂, i₁ − i₃ + 1]
  enddo  enddo
  do i₁ = max(c + 4, 1), min(c + 8, 5)
    i₂ = i₁ − c − 3
    A[i₁, i₂ + 3] = B[i₁ − i₂, i₁ − i₂ + 2] + C[i₁ + i₂, −i₂, −i₂]
  enddo
enddoall
```

5. Comparisons and Discussions

Recently, communication-free partitioning has received much emphasis for parallelizing compilers. Several partitioning techniques are proposed in the literature. In the previous sections we have glanced over these techniques. Chen and Sheu's and Ramanujam and Sadayappan's methods can deal with single loop. Since Ramanujam and Sadayappan's method does not address

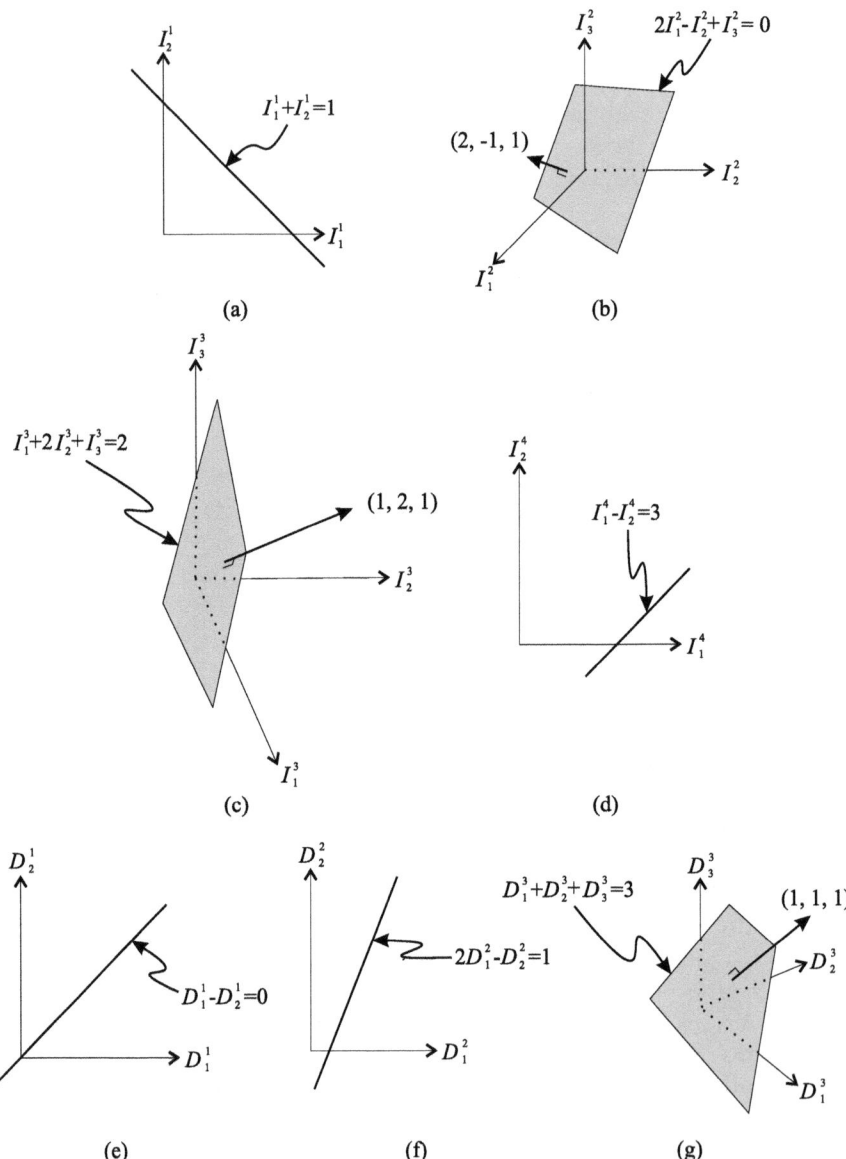

Fig. 4.6. Communication-free statement-iteration hyperplanes and data hyperplanes for loop $L_{4.2}$, where $t = 1$ and $c_v^1 = 0$. (a) Statement-iteration hyperplane on $SIS(s_1)$. (b) Statement-iteration hyperplane on $SIS(s_2)$. (c) Statement-iteration hyperplane on $SIS(s_3)$. (d) Statement-iteration hyperplane on $SIS(s_4)$. (e) Data hyperplane on $DS(A)$. (f) Data hyperplane on $DS(B)$. (g) Data hyperplane on $DS(C)$.

iteration space partitioning, the absence of iteration space partitioning makes the method fail to handle multiple nested loops. Huang and Sadayappan's, Lim and Lam's and Shih, Sheu, and Huang's methods all can deal with a sequence of nested loops. Besides, Chen and Sheu's and Huang and Sadayappan's methods address only perfectly nested loop(s) but all the others can manage imperfectly nested loop(s). Except that Ramanujam and Sadayappan's method requires the nested loops to be fully parallel, others can process the nested loop(s) with or without data dependence relations. As for the array reference function, each method can process affine array reference functions except that Chen and Sheu's method requires the loop be uniformly generated reference, in addition to be an affine function.

We classify these methods as loop-level partitioning or statement-level partitioning. Loop-level partitioning views each iteration as a basic unit and partitions iterations and/or data onto processors. Chen and Sheu's, Ramanujam and Sadayappan's and Huang and Sadayappan's methods are loop-level partitioning. Lim and Lam's and Shih, Sheu, and Huang's methods partition statement-iterations and/or data onto processors and are statement-level partitioning. The partitioning strategy used by Chen and Sheu's method is similar to the findings of the iteration-dependent space. Once the iteration-dependent space is determined, the data accessed by the iterations on the iteration-dependent space are grouped together and then distributed onto processors along with the corresponding iteration-dependent space. Lim and Lam's method partitions statement-iteration spaces by using affine processor mappings. All the rest of methods partition iteration and/or data spaces along hyperplanes. Except Ramanujam and Sadayappan's method addresses data space partitioning and Lim and Lam's method addresses statement-iteration space partitioning, the others propose both iteration and data spaces partitionings.

It is well-known that the dimensionality of a hyperplane is one less than the dimensionality of the original vector space. Therefore, the exploited degree of parallelism for hyperplane partitioning techniques is one. On the other hand, Chen and Sheu's and Lim and Lam's methods can exploit maximum degree of communication-free parallelism. All methods discuss the communication-free partitioning based on each data element to be distributed onto exactly one processor, every other processor that needs the data element has to access the data element via interprocessor communication. However, Chen and Sheu's method presents not only the non-duplicate data strategy but also duplicate data strategy, which allows data to be appropriately duplicated onto processors in order to make the nested loop to be communication-free or to exploit higher degree of parallelism.

For simplicity, we number each method as follows.

1. Chen and Sheu's method.
2. Ramanujam and Sadayappan's method.
3. Huang and Sadayappan's method.

4. Lim and Lam's method.
5. Shih, Sheu, and Huang's method.

Synthesizing the above discussions can obtain the following tables. Table 5.1 compares each method according to the loop model that each method can deal with. It compares *Loop(s)*, *Nest*, *Type*, and *Reference Function*. *Loop(s)* means the number of loops that the method can handle. *Nest* indicates the nested loop to be perfectly or imperfectly. *Type* indicates the type of the nested loop, fully parallel or others. *Reference Function* denotes the type of array reference functions. Table 5.2 compares the capabilities of each methods. *Level* indicates the method that is performed on loop- or statement-level. *Partitioning Strategy* is the strategy adopted by each method. *Partitioning Space* shows the spaces that the method can partition, which includes computation space partitioning and data space partitioning. Table 5.3 compares the functionalities of each method. *Degree of Parallelism* represents that the method can exploit how many degree of parallelism on the premise of communication-free partitioning. *Duplicate Data* means whether the method can allow data to be duplicated onto processors or not.

Table 5.1. Comparisons of communication-free partitioning techniques – Loop Model.

Method	Loop(s)	Nest	Type	Reference Function
1	single	perfectly	arbitrary	affine function with uniformly generated reference
2	single	imperfectly	fully parallel	affine function
3	multiple	perfectly	arbitrary	affine function
4	multiple	imperfectly	arbitrary	affine function
5	multiple	imperfectly	arbitrary	affine function

Table 5.2. Comparisons of communication-free partitioning techniques – Capability.

Method	Level	Partitioning Strategy	Partitioning Space	
			Computation	Data
1	loop	iteration-dependent space	yes	yes
2	loop	hyperplane	no	yes
3	loop	hyperplane	yes	yes
4	statement	affine processor mapping	yes	no
5	statement	hyperplane	yes	yes

Table 5.3. Comparisons of communication-free partitioning techniques – Functionality.

Method	Degree of Parallelism	Duplicate Data
1	maximum communication-free parallelism	yes
2	1	no
3	1	no
4	maximum communication-free parallelism	no
5	1	no

6. Conclusions

As the cost of data communication is much higher than that of a primitive computation in distributed-memory multicomputers, reducing the communication overhead as much as possible is the most promising way to achieve high performance computing. Communication-free partitioning is an ideal situation that can eliminate total communication overhead, if possible. Therefore, it is of critical important for distributed-memory multicomputers. We have surveyed the current compilation techniques about communication-free partitioning of nested loops in the Chapter. The characteristics of every methods and the differences among them are also addressed.

Communication-free partitioning is an ideal situation that communication overhead can be totally eliminated. However, there are many programs that can not be communication-free partitioned. Supporting efficient partitioning techniques to reduce communication overhead as much as possible is the future research in this area.

References

1. C. Ancourt and F. Irigoin. Scanning polyhedra with DO loops. In *Proceedings of the 3rd ACM/SIGPLAN Symposium on Principles and Practice of Parallel Programming*, pages 39–50, April 1991.
2. J. M. Anderson and M. S. Lam. Global optimizations for parallelism and locality on scalable parallel machines. In *Proceedings of the ACM SIGPLAN'93 Conference on Programming Language Design and Implementation*, pages 112–125, June 1993.
3. U. Banerjee. Unimodular transformations of double loops. In *Proceedings of the 3rd Workshop on Languages and Compilers for Parallel Computing*, pages 192–219, July 1990.
4. T. S. Chen. *Compiling Nested Loops for Communication-Efficient Execution on Distributed Memory Multicomputers*. PhD thesis, Department of Computer Science and Information Engineering, National Central University, Taiwan, June 1994.

5. T. S. Chen and J. P. Sheu. Communication-free data allocation techniques for parallelizing compilers on multicomputers. *IEEE Transactions on Parallel and Distributed Systems*, 5(9):924–938, September 1994.
6. A. Darte and Y. Robert. Affine-by-statement scheduling of uniform and affine loop nests over parametric domains. *Journal of Parallel and Distributed Computing*, 29:43–59, 1995.
7. M. Dion, C. Randriamaro, and Y. Robert. How to optimize residual communications? In *Proceedings of International Parallel Processing Symposium*, April 1996.
8. M. Dion and Y. Robert. Mapping affine loop nests: New results. In B. Hertzberger and G. Serazzi, editors, *High-Performance Computing and Networking, International Conference and Exhibition*, volume LNCS 919, pages 184–189. Springer-Verlag, May 1995.
9. P. Feautrier. Some efficient solution to the affine scheduling problem, part I, one dimensional time. *International Journal of Parallel Programming*, 21(5):313–348, October 1992.
10. P. Feautrier. Some efficient solution to the affine scheduling problem, part II, multidimensional time. *International Journal of Parallel Programming*, 21(6):389–420, December 1992.
11. M. Gupta and P. Banerjee. Demonstration of automatic data partitioning techniques for parallelizing compilers on multicomputers. *IEEE Transactions on Parallel and Distributed Systems*, 3(2):179–193, March 1992.
12. M. Gupta, E. Schonberg, and H. Srinivasan. A unified framework for optimizing communication in data-parallel programs. *IEEE Transactions on Parallel and Distributed Systems*, 7(7):689–704, July 1996.
13. S. Hiranandani, K. Kennedy, and C. W. Tseng. Compiling Fortran D for MIMD distributed-memory machines. *Communications of the ACM*, 35(8):66–80, August 1992.
14. S. Hiranandani, K. Kennedy, and C. W. Tseng. Evaluating compiler optimizations for Fortran D. *Journal of Parallel and Distributed Computing*, 21:27–45, 1994.
15. K. Hoffman and R. Kunze. *Linear Algebra*. Prentice-Hall, Inc., Englewood Cliffs, New Jersey, second edition, 1971.
16. C.-H. Huang and P. Sadayappan. Communication-free hyperplane partitioning of nested loops. *Journal of Parallel and Distributed Computing*, 19:90–102, 1993.
17. F. Irigoin and R. Triolet. Supernode partitioning. In *Proceedings of the 15th Annual ACM Symposium Principle of Programming Languages*, pages 319–329, January 1988.
18. A. H. Karp. Programming for parallelism. *IEEE Comput. Mag.*, 20(5):43–57, May 1987.
19. C. Koelbel. *Compiling Programs for Nonshared Memory Machines*. PhD thesis, Department of Computer Science, Purdue University, November 1990.
20. C. Koelbel and P. Mehrotra. Compiling global name-space parallel loops for distributed execution. *IEEE Transactions on Parallel and Distributed Systems*, 2(4):440–451, October 1991.
21. L. Lamport. The parallel execution of do loops. *Communications of the ACM*, 17(2):83–93, February 1974.
22. A. W. Lim and M. S. Lam. Communication-free parallelization via affine transformations. In *Proceedings of the 7th Workshop on Languages and Compilers for Parallel Computing*, August 1994.
23. L. S. Liu, C. W. Ho, and J. P. Sheu. On the parallelism of nested for-loops using index shift method. In *Proceedings of International Conference on Parallel Processing*, volume II, pages 119–123, August 1990.

24. D. A. Padua and M. J. Wolfe. Advanced compiler optimizations for supercomputers. *Communications of the ACM*, 29:1184–1201, December 1986.
25. J. Ramanujam. *Compile-Time Techniques for Parallel Execution of Loops on Distributed Memory Multiprocessors*. PhD thesis, Department of Computer and Information Science, Ohio State University, September 1990.
26. J. Ramanujam and P. Sadayappan. Compile-time techniques for data distribution in distributed memory machines. *IEEE Transactions on Parallel and Distributed Systems*, 2(4):472–482, October 1991.
27. A. Rogers and K. Pingali. Process decomposition through locality of reference. In *Proceedings of the ACM SIGPLAN'89 Conference on Programming Language Design and Implementation*, pages 69–80, June 1989.
28. M. Rosing, R. B. Schnabel, and R. P. Weaver. The DINO parallel programming language. *Journal of Parallel and Distributed Computing*, 13:30–42, 1991.
29. J. P. Sheu and T. H. Tai. Partitioning and mapping nested loops on multiprocessor systems. *IEEE Transactions on Parallel and Distributed Systems*, 2(4):430–439, October 1991.
30. K.-P. Shih, J.-P. Sheu, and C.-H. Huang. Statement-level communication-free partitioning techniques for parallelizing compilers. In *Proceedings of the 9th Workshop on Languages and Compilers for Parallel Computing*, August 1996.
31. C.-W. Tseng. *An Optimizing Fortran D Compiler for MIMD Distributed-Memory Machines*. PhD thesis, Department of Computer Science, Rice University, January 1993.
32. M. E. Wolf and M. S. Lam. A data locality optimizing algorithm. In *Proceedings of the ACM SIGPLAN'91 Conference on Programming Language Design and Implementation*, pages 30–44, June 1991.
33. M. E. Wolf and M. S. Lam. A loop transformation theory and an algorithm to maximize parallelism. *IEEE Transactions on Parallel and Distributed Systems*, 2(4):452–471, October 1991.
34. M. J. Wolfe. More iteration space tiling. In *Proceedings of ACM International Conference on Supercomputing*, pages 655–664, 1989.
35. M. J. Wolfe. *Optimizing Supercompilers for Supercomputers*. London and Cambridge, MA: Pitman and the MIT Press, 1989.
36. M. J. Wolfe. *High Performance Compilers for Parallel Computing*. Addison-Wesley Publishing Company, 1996.
37. M. J. Wolfe and U. Banerjee. Data dependence and its application to parallel processing. *International Journal of Parallel Programming*, 16(2):137–178, April 1987.
38. H. P. Zima, P. Brezany, and B. M. Chapman. SUPERB and Vienna Fortran. *Parallel Computing*, 20:1487–1517, 1994.
39. H. P. Zima and B. Chapman. *Supercompilers for Parallel and Vector Computers*. ACM Press, New York, 1991.

Chapter 11. Solving Alignment Using Elementary Linear Algebra

Vladimir Kotlyar, David Bau, Induprakas Kodukula, Keshav Pingali, and
Paul Stodghill

Department of Computer Science
Cornell University
Ithaca NY 14853
USA

Summary. Data and computation alignment is an important part of compiling
sequential programs to architectures with non-uniform memory access times. In
this paper, we show that elementary matrix methods can be used to determine
communication-free alignment of code and data. We also solve the problem of
replicating data to eliminate communication. Our matrix-based approach leads to
algorithms which work well for a variety of applications, and which are simpler and
faster than other matrix-based algorithms in the literature.

1. Introduction

A key problem in generating code for non-uniform memory access (NUMA)
parallel machines is data and computation placement — that is, determining
what work each processor must do, and what data must reside in each local
memory. The goal of placement is to exploit parallelism by spreading the
work across the processors, and to exploit locality by spreading data so that
memory accesses are local whenever possible. The problem of determining a
good placement for a program is usually solved in two phases called *alignment* and *distribution*. The alignment phase maps data and computations to
a set of virtual processors organized as a Cartesian grid of some dimension
(a *template* in HPF Fortran terminology). The distribution phase folds the
virtual processors into the physical processors. The advantage of separating
alignment from distribution is that we can address the collocation problem
(determining which iterations and data should be mapped to the same processor) without worrying about the load balancing problem.

Our focus in this paper is alignment. A complete solution to this problem
can be obtained in three steps.

1. Determine the constraints on data and computation placement.
2. Determine which constraints should be left unsatisfied.
3. Solve the remaining system of constraints to determine data and computation placement.

---

[0] An earlier version of this paper was presented in the 7th Annual Workshop on
Languages and Compilers for Parallel Computers (LCPC), Ithaca, 1994.

S. Pande, D.P. Agrawal (Eds.): Compiler Optimizations for Scalable PS, LNCS 1808, pp. 385-411, 2001.
© Springer-Verlag Berlin Heidelberg 2001

In the first step, data references in the program are examined to determine a system of equations in which the unknowns are functions representing data and computation placements. Any solution to this system of equations determines a so-called *communication-free* alignment [6] — that is, a map of data elements and computations to virtual processors such that all data required by a processor to execute the iterations mapped to it are in its local memory. Very often, the only communication-free alignment for a program is the trivial one in which every iteration and datum is mapped to a single processor. Intuitively, each equation in the system is a constraint on data and computation placement, and it is possible to overconstrain the system so that the trivial solution is the only solution. If so, the second step of alignment determines which constraints must be left unsatisfied to retain parallelism in execution. The cost of leaving a constraint unsatisfied is that it introduces communication; therefore, the constraints left unsatisfied should be those that introduce as little communication as possible. In the last step, the remaining constraints are solved to determine data and computation placement.

The following loop illustrates these points. It computes the product Y of a sub-matrix $A(11 : N + 10, 11 : N + 10)$ and a vector X:

```
DO i=1,N
   DO j=1,N
      Y(i) = Y(i) + A(i+10,j+10)*X(j)
```

For simplicity, assume that the virtual processors are organized as a one-dimensional grid $\mathcal{T}$. Let us assume that computations are mapped by iteration number — that is, a processor does all or none of the work in executing an iteration of the loop. To avoid communication, the processor that executes iteration (i, j) must have $A(i + 10, j + 10)$, $Y(i)$ and $X(j)$ in its local memory. These constraints can be expressed formally by defining the following functions that map loop iterations and array elements to virtual processors:

$$
\begin{array}{llll}
\mathbf{C} & : & (i,j) \to \mathcal{T} & \text{processor that performs iteration } (i,j) \\
\mathbf{D}_A & : & (i,j) \to \mathcal{T} & \text{processor that owns } A(i,j) \\
\mathbf{D}_Y & : & i \to \mathcal{T} & \text{processor that owns } Y(i) \\
\mathbf{D}_X & : & j \to \mathcal{T} & \text{processor that owns } X(j)
\end{array}
$$

The constraints on these functions are the following.

$$
\forall i,j \text{ s.t. } 1 \le i,j \le N \ : \left\{ \begin{array}{l} \mathbf{C}(i,j) = \mathbf{D}_A(i + 10, j + 10) \\ \mathbf{C}(i,j) = \mathbf{D}_Y(i) \\ \mathbf{C}(i,j) = \mathbf{D}_X(j) \end{array} \right.
$$

If we enforce all of the constraints, the only solution is the trivial solution in which all data and computations are mapped to a single processor. In this case, we say that our system is *overconstrained*. If we drop the constraint on X, we have a non-trivial solution to the resulting system of constraints, which maps iteration (i, j) to processor i, and maps array elements $A(i+10, j+10)$,

$X(i)$ and $Y(i)$ to processor i. Note that all these maps are affine functions — for example, the map of array A to the virtual processors can be written as follows:

$$\mathbf{D}_A(a, b) = \begin{pmatrix} i \\ j \end{pmatrix} = \begin{pmatrix} 1 & 0 \\ 0 & 1 \end{pmatrix} \begin{pmatrix} a \\ b \end{pmatrix} - \begin{pmatrix} 10 \\ 10 \end{pmatrix} \tag{1.1}$$

Since there is more than one processor involved in the computation, we have parallel execution of the program. However, elements of X must be communicated at runtime.

In this example, the solution to the alignment equations was determined by inspection, but how does one solve such systems of equations in general? Note that the unknowns are general functions, and that each function may be constrained by several equations (as is the case for $\mathbf{C}$ in the example). To make the problem tractable, it is standard to restrict the maps to linear (or affine) functions of loop indices. This restriction is not particularly onerous in general – in fact, it permits more general maps of computation and data than are allowed in HPF. The unknowns in the equations now become matrices, rather than general functions, but it is still not obvious how such systems of matrix equations can be solved. In Section 2, we introduce our linear algebraic framework that reduces the problem of solving systems of alignment equations to the standard linear algebra problem of determining a basis for the null space of a matrix. One weakness of existing approaches to alignment is that they handle only *linear* functions; general affine functions, like the map of array A, must be dealt with in *ad hoc* ways. In Section 3, we show that our framework permits affine functions to be handled without difficulty.

In some programs, replication of arrays is useful for exploiting parallelism. Suppose we wanted to parallelize all iterations of our matrix-vector multiplication loop. The virtual processor (i, j) would execute the iteration (i, j) and own the array element $A(i + 10, j + 10)$. It would also require the array element $X(j)$. This means that we have to replicate the array X along the i dimension of the virtual processor grid. In addition, element $Y(i)$ must be computed by reducing (adding) values computed by the set of processors $(i, *)$. In Section 4, we show that our framework permits a solution to the replication/reduction problem as well.

Finally, we give a systematic procedure for dropping constraints from over-constrained systems. Finding an optimal solution that trades off parallelism for communication is very difficult. First, it is hard to model accurately the cost of communication and the benefit of parallelism. For example, parallel matrix-vector product is usually implemented either by mapping rows of the matrix to processors (so-called 1-D alignment) or by mapping general sub-matrices to processors (so-called 2-D alignment). Which mapping is better depends very much on the size of the matrix, and on the communication to computation speed ratio of the machine [9]. Second, even for simple parallel models and restricted cases of the alignment problem, finding the optimal solution is known to be NP-complete problem [10]. Therefore, we must fall back on heuristics. In Section 5, we discuss our heuristic. Not surprisingly, our heuristic is skewed to "do the right thing" for kernels like matrix-vector product which are extremely important in practice.

How does our work relate to previous work on alignment? Our work is closest in spirit to that of Huang and Sadayappan who were the first to formulate the problem of communication-free alignment in terms of systems of equational constraints [6]. However, they did not give a general method for solving these equations. Also, they did not handle replication of data. Anderson and Lam sketched a solution method [1], but their approach is unnecessarily complex, requiring the determination of cycles in bipartite graphs, computing pseudo-inverses *etc* – these complications are eliminated by our approach.

The equational, matrix-based approach described in this paper is not the only approach that has been explored. Li and Chen have used graph-theoretic methods to trade off communication for parallelism for a limited kind of alignment called *axis alignment* [10]. More general heuristics for a wide variety of cost-of-communication metrics have been studied by Chatterjee, Gilbert and Schreiber [2,3], Feautrier [5] and Knobe et al [7,8].

To summarize, the contributions of this paper are the following.

1. We show that the problem of determining communication-free partitions of computation and data can be reduced to the standard linear algebra problem of determining a basis for the null space of a matrix , which can be solved using fairly standard techniques (Section 2.2).
2. Previous approaches to alignment handle linear maps, but deal with affine maps in fairly *ad hoc* ways. We show that affine maps can be folded into our framework without difficulty (Section 3).
3. We show how replication of arrays is handled by our framework (Section 4).
4. We suggest simple and effective heuristic strategies for deciding when communication should be introduced (Section 5).

2. Linear Alignment

To avoid introducing too many ideas at once, we restrict attention to linear subscripts and linear maps in this section. First, we show that the alignment problem can be formulated using systems of equational constraints. Then, we show that the problem of solving these systems of equations can be reduced to the standard problem of determining a basis for the null space of a matrix, which can be solved using integer-preserving Gaussian elimination.

2.1 Equational Constraints

The equational constraints for alignment are simply a formalization of an intuitively reasonable statement: 'to avoid communication, the processor that performs an iteration of a loop nest must own the data referenced in that iteration'. We discuss the formulation of these equations in the context of the following example:

```
DO j=1,100
  DO k=1,100
    B(j,k) = A(j,k) + A(k,j)
```

If $\mathbf{i}$ is an iteration vector in the iteration space of the loop, the alignment constraints require that the processor that performs iteration $\mathbf{i}$ must own $B(\mathbf{F}_1\mathbf{i})$, $A(\mathbf{F}_1\mathbf{i})$ and $A(\mathbf{F}_2\mathbf{i})$, where $\mathbf{F}_1$ and $\mathbf{F}_2$ are the following matrices:

$$\mathbf{F}_1 = \begin{pmatrix} 1 & 0 \\ 0 & 1 \end{pmatrix} \qquad \mathbf{F}_2 = \begin{pmatrix} 0 & 1 \\ 1 & 0 \end{pmatrix}$$

Let $\mathbf{C}$, $\mathbf{D}_A$ and $\mathbf{D}_B$ be $p \times 2$ matrices representing the maps of the computation and arrays A and B to a p-dimensional processor template; p is an unknown which will be determined by our algorithm. Then, the alignment problem can be expressed as follows: find $\mathbf{C}$, $\mathbf{D}_A$ and $\mathbf{D}_B$ such that

$$\forall\, \mathbf{i} \in \text{ iteration space of loop} : \begin{cases} \mathbf{Ci} = \mathbf{D}_B\mathbf{F}_1\mathbf{i} \\ \mathbf{Ci} = \mathbf{D}_A\mathbf{F}_1\mathbf{i} \\ \mathbf{Ci} = \mathbf{D}_A\mathbf{F}_2\mathbf{i} \end{cases}$$

To 'cancel' the $\mathbf{i}$ on both sides of each equation, we will simplify the problem and require that the equations hold for all 2-dimensional integer vectors, regardless of whether they are in the bounds of the loop or not. In that case, the constraints simply become equations involving matrices, as follows: find $\mathbf{C}$, $\mathbf{D}_A$ and $\mathbf{D}_B$ such that

$$\begin{cases} \mathbf{C} & = & \mathbf{D}_B\mathbf{F}_1 \\ \mathbf{C} & = & \mathbf{D}_A\mathbf{F}_1 \\ \mathbf{C} & = & \mathbf{D}_A\mathbf{F}_2 \end{cases} \qquad (2.1)$$

We will refer to the equation scheme $\mathbf{C} = \mathbf{DF}$ as the fundamental equation of alignment.

The general principle behind the formulation of alignment equations should be clear from this example. Each data reference for which alignment is desired gives rise to an alignment equation. Data references for which subscripts are not linear functions of loop indices are ignored; therefore, such references may give rise to communication at runtime. Although we have discussed only a single loop nest, it is clear that this framework of equational constraints can be used for multiple loop nests as well. The equational constraints from each loop nest are combined to form a single system of simultaneous equations, and the entire system is solved to find communication-free maps of computations and data.

2.2 Reduction to Null Space Computation

One way to solve systems of alignment equations is to set $\mathbf{C}$ and $\mathbf{D}$ matrices to the zero matrix of some dimension. This is the trivial solution in which all computations and data are mapped to a single processor, processor 0. This solution exploits no parallelism; therefore, we want to determine a non-trivial solution if it exists. We do this by reducing the problem to the standard linear algebra problem of determining a basis for the null space of a matrix.

Consider a single equation.

$$\mathbf{C} = \mathbf{DF}$$

This equation can be written in block matrix form as follows:

$$(\mathbf{C} \quad \mathbf{D}) \begin{pmatrix} \mathbf{I} \\ -\mathbf{F} \end{pmatrix} = \mathbf{0}$$

Now it is of the form $\mathbf{UV} = 0$ where $\mathbf{U}$ is an unknown matrix and $\mathbf{V}$ is a known matrix. To see the connection with null spaces, we take the transpose of this equation and we see that this is the same as the equation $\mathbf{V}^T \mathbf{U}^T = 0$. Therefore, $\mathbf{U}^T$ is a matrix whose columns are in the null space of $\mathbf{V}^T$. To exploit parallelism, we would like the rank of $\mathbf{U}^T$ to be as large as possible. Therefore, we must find a basis for the null space of matrix $\mathbf{V}^T$. This is done using integer-preserving Gaussian elimination, a standard algorithm in the literature [4, 12].

The same reduction works in the case of multiple constraints. Suppose that there are s loops and t arrays. Let the computation maps of the loops be $\mathbf{C}_1, \mathbf{C}_2, \ldots, \mathbf{C}_s$, and the array maps be $\mathbf{D}_1, \mathbf{D}_2, \ldots, \mathbf{D}_t$. We can construct a block row with all the unknowns as follows:

$$\mathbf{U} = (\mathbf{C}_1 \quad \mathbf{C}_2 \quad \ldots \quad \mathbf{C}_s \quad \mathbf{D}_1 \quad \ldots \quad \mathbf{D}_t)$$

For each constraint of the form $\mathbf{C}_j = \mathbf{D}_k \mathbf{F}_\ell$, we create a block column:

$$\mathbf{V}_q = \begin{pmatrix} \mathbf{0} \\ \mathbf{I} \\ \mathbf{0} \\ -\mathbf{F}_\ell \\ \mathbf{0} \end{pmatrix}$$

where the zeros are placed so that:

$$\mathbf{UV}_q = \mathbf{C}_j - \mathbf{D}_k \mathbf{F}_\ell \tag{2.2}$$

Putting all these block columns into a single matrix $\mathbf{V}$, the problem of finding communication-free alignment reduces once again to a matrix equation of the form

Input:. A set of alignment constraints of the form $\mathbf{C}_j = \mathbf{D}_k \mathbf{F}_\ell$.
Output:. Communication-free alignment matrices $\mathbf{C}_j$ and $\mathbf{D}_k$.
1. Assemble block columns as in (2.2).
2. Put all block columns $\mathbf{V}_q$ into one matrix $\mathbf{V}$.
3. Compute a basis $\mathbf{U}^T$ for the null space of $\mathbf{V}^T$.
4. Set template dimension to number of rows of $\mathbf{U}$.
5. Extract the solution matrices $\mathbf{C}_j$ and $\mathbf{D}_k$ from $\mathbf{U}$.
6. Reduce the solution matrix $\mathbf{U}$ as described in Section 2.4.

Fig. 2.1. Algorithm `LINEAR-ALIGNMENT`.

$$\mathbf{UV} = 0 \tag{2.3}$$

The reader can verify that the system of equations (2.1) can be converted into the following matrix equation:

$$\left(\begin{matrix} \mathbf{C} & \mathbf{D}_A & \mathbf{D}_B \end{matrix} \right) \begin{pmatrix} \mathbf{I} & \mathbf{I} & \mathbf{I} \\ 0 & -\mathbf{F}_1 & -\mathbf{F}_2 \\ -\mathbf{F}_1 & 0 & 0 \end{pmatrix} = 0 \tag{2.4}$$

A solution matrix is:

$$\mathbf{U} = \left(\begin{matrix} 1 & 1 & 1 & 1 & 1 & 1 \end{matrix} \right) \tag{2.5}$$

which gives us:

$$\mathbf{C} = \mathbf{D}_A = \mathbf{D}_B = \left(\begin{matrix} 1 & 1 \end{matrix} \right) \tag{2.6}$$

Since the number of rows of $\mathbf{U}$ is one, the solution requires a one dimensional template. Iteration (i, j) is mapped to processor $i + j$. Arrays A and B are mapped identically so that the 'anti-diagonals' of these matrices are mapped to the same processor.

The general algorithm is outlined in Figure 2.1.

2.3 Remarks

Our framework is robust enough that we can add additional constraints to computation and data maps without difficulty. For example, if a loop in a loop nest carries a dependence, we may not want to spread iterations of that loop across processors. More generally, dependence information can be characterized by a distance vector $\mathbf{z}$, which for our purposes says that iterations $\mathbf{i}$ and $\mathbf{i}+\mathbf{z}$ have to be executed on the same processor. In terms of our alignment model:

$$\mathbf{Ci} + \mathbf{b} = \mathbf{C}(\mathbf{i} + \mathbf{z}) + \mathbf{b} \quad \Leftrightarrow \quad \mathbf{Cz} = 0 \tag{2.7}$$

We can now easily incorporate (2.7) into our matrix system (2.3) by adding the following block column to $\mathbf{V}$:

$$\mathbf{V}_{dep} = \begin{pmatrix} \mathbf{0} \\ \mathbf{z} \\ \mathbf{0} \end{pmatrix}$$

where zeros are placed to that $\mathbf{UV}_{dep} = \mathbf{Cz}$. Adding this column to $\mathbf{V}$ will ensure that any two dependent iterations end up on the same processor.

In some circumstances, it may be necessary to align two data references without aligning them with any computation. This gives rise to equations of the form $\mathbf{D_1F_1} = \mathbf{D_2F_2}$. Such equations can be incorporated into our framework by adding block columns of the form

$$\mathbf{V}_p = \begin{pmatrix} \mathbf{0} \\ \mathbf{F_1} \\ \mathbf{0} \\ -\mathbf{F_2} \\ \mathbf{0} \end{pmatrix} \qquad (2.8)$$

where the zeros are placed so that $\mathbf{UV}_p = \mathbf{D_1F_1} - \mathbf{D_2F_2}$.

2.4 Reducing the Solution Basis

Finally, one practical note. It is possible for Algorithm `LINEAR-ALIGNMENT` to produce a solution $\mathbf{U}$ which has p rows, even though all $\mathbf{C}_j$ produced by Step 5 have rank less than p. A simple example where this can happen is a program with two loop nests which have no data in common. Mapping the solution into a lower dimensional template can be left to the distribution phase of compiling; alternatively, an additional step can be added to Algorithm `LINEAR-ALIGNMENT` to solve this problem directly in the alignment phase. This modification is described next.

Suppose we compute a solution which contains two computation alignments:

$$\mathbf{U} = (\ \mathbf{C}_1 \quad \mathbf{C}_2 \quad \dots \ ) \qquad (2.9)$$

Let r be the number of rows in $\mathbf{U}$. Let r_1 be the rank of $\mathbf{C}_1$, and let r_2 be the rank of $\mathbf{C}_2$. Assume that $r_1 < r_2$. We would like to have a solution basis where the first r_1 rows of $\mathbf{C}_1$ are linearly independent, as are the first r_2 rows of $\mathbf{C}_2$ — that way, if we decide to have an r_1-dimensional template, we are guaranteed to keep r_1 degrees of parallelism for the second loop nest, as well.

Mathematically, the problem is to find a sequence of row transformations $\mathbf{T}$ such that the first r_1 rows of $\mathbf{TC}_1$ are linearly independent and so are the first r_2 rows of $\mathbf{TC}_2$.

A detailed procedure is given in the appendix. Here, we describe the intuitive idea. Suppose that we have already arranged the first r_1 rows of $\mathbf{C}_1$ to be linearly independent. Inductively, assume that the first $k < r_2$ rows of $\mathbf{C}_2$ are linearly independent as well. We want to make the $k + 1$-st row of $\mathbf{C}_2$ linearly independent of the previous k rows. If it already is, we go the next row. If not, then there must be a row $m > k + 1$ of $\mathbf{C}_2$ which is linearly independent of the first k rows. It is easy to see that if we add the m-th row to the $k + 1$-st row, we will make the latter linearly independent of the first k rows. Notice that this can mess up $\mathbf{C}_1$! Fortunately, it can be shown that if we add a suitably large multiple of the m-th row, we can be sure that the first r_1 rows of $\mathbf{C}_1$ remain independent. This algorithm can be easily generalized to any number of $\mathbf{C}_i$ blocks.

3. Affine Alignment

In this section, we generalize our framework to affine functions. The intuitive idea is to 'encode' affine subscripts as linear subscripts by using an extra dimension to handle the constant term. Then, we apply the machinery in Section 2 to obtain linear computation and data maps. The extra dimension can be removed from these linear maps to 'decode' them back into affine maps.

We first generalize the data access functions $\mathbf{F}_i$ so that they are affine functions of the loop indices. In the presence of such subscripts, aligning data and computation requires affine data and computation maps. Therefore, we introduce the following notation.

$$\text{Computation maps:} \quad C_j(\mathbf{i}) = \mathbf{C}_j\mathbf{i} + \mathbf{c}_j \tag{3.1}$$

$$\text{Data maps:} \quad D_k(\mathbf{a}) = \mathbf{D}_k\mathbf{a} + \mathbf{d}_k \tag{3.2}$$

$$\text{Data access functions:} \quad F_\ell(\mathbf{i}) = \mathbf{F}_\ell\mathbf{i} + \mathbf{f}_\ell \tag{3.3}$$

$\mathbf{C}_j$, $\mathbf{D}_k$ and $\mathbf{F}_\ell$ are matrices representing the linear parts of the affine functions, while $\mathbf{c}_j$, $\mathbf{d}_k$ and $\mathbf{f}_\ell$ represent constants. The alignment constraints from each reference are now of the form

$$\forall \mathbf{i} \in \mathbb{Z}^n \quad : \quad \mathbf{C}_j\mathbf{i} + \mathbf{c}_j = \mathbf{D}_k(\mathbf{F}_\ell\mathbf{i} + \mathbf{f}_\ell) + \mathbf{d}_k \tag{3.4}$$

3.1 Encoding Affine Constraints as Linear Constraints

Affine functions can be encoded as linear functions by using the following identity.

$$\mathbf{Tx} + \mathbf{t} \quad = \quad (\, \mathbf{T} \quad \mathbf{t} \,) \begin{pmatrix} \mathbf{x} \\ 1 \end{pmatrix} \tag{3.5}$$

where $\mathbf{T}$ is a matrix, and $\mathbf{t}$ and $\mathbf{x}$ are vectors. We can put (3.4) in the form:

$$(\ \mathbf{C}_j \ \ \mathbf{c}_j \ ) \begin{pmatrix} \mathbf{i} \\ 1 \end{pmatrix} = \mathbf{D}_k (\ \mathbf{F}_\ell \ \ \mathbf{f}_\ell \ ) \begin{pmatrix} \mathbf{i} \\ 1 \end{pmatrix} + \mathbf{d}_k$$

$$= (\ \mathbf{D}_k \ \ \mathbf{d}_k \ ) \begin{pmatrix} \mathbf{F}_\ell & \mathbf{f}_\ell \\ \mathbf{0} & 1 \end{pmatrix} \begin{pmatrix} \mathbf{i} \\ 1 \end{pmatrix} \qquad (3.6)$$

Now we let:

$$\hat{\mathbf{C}}_j = (\ \mathbf{C}_j \ \ \mathbf{c}_j \ ) \qquad \hat{\mathbf{D}}_k = (\ \mathbf{D}_k \ \ \mathbf{d}_k \ ) \qquad \hat{\mathbf{F}}_\ell = \begin{pmatrix} \mathbf{F}_\ell & \mathbf{f}_\ell \\ \mathbf{0} & 1 \end{pmatrix} \qquad (3.7)$$

(3.6) can be written as:

$$\forall \mathbf{i} \in \mathbb{Z}^d \ : \ \hat{\mathbf{C}}_j \begin{pmatrix} \mathbf{i} \\ 1 \end{pmatrix} = \hat{\mathbf{D}}_k \hat{\mathbf{F}}_\ell \begin{pmatrix} \mathbf{i} \\ 1 \end{pmatrix} \qquad (3.8)$$

As before, we would like to 'cancel' the vector $\begin{pmatrix} \mathbf{i} \\ 1 \end{pmatrix}$ from both sides of the equation. To do this, we need the following result.

Lemma 31. *Let* $\mathbf{T}$ *be a matrix,* $\mathbf{t}$ *a vector. Then*

$$\forall \mathbf{x} (\ \mathbf{T} \ \ \mathbf{t} \ ) \begin{pmatrix} \mathbf{x} \\ 1 \end{pmatrix} = \mathbf{0}$$

if and only if $\mathbf{T} = \mathbf{0}$ *and* $\mathbf{t} = \mathbf{0}$.

Proof:. In particular, we can let $\mathbf{x} = \mathbf{0}$. This gives us:

$$(\ \mathbf{T} \ \ \mathbf{t} \ ) \begin{pmatrix} \mathbf{0} \\ 1 \end{pmatrix} = \mathbf{t} = \mathbf{0}$$

So $\mathbf{t} = \mathbf{0}$. Now, for any $\mathbf{x}$:

$$(\ \mathbf{T} \ \ \mathbf{t} \ ) \begin{pmatrix} \mathbf{x} \\ 1 \end{pmatrix} = (\ \mathbf{T} \ \ \mathbf{0} \ ) \begin{pmatrix} \mathbf{x} \\ 1 \end{pmatrix} = \mathbf{T}\mathbf{x} = \mathbf{0}$$

which means that $\mathbf{T} = \mathbf{0}$, as well. □

Using Lemma 31, we can rewrite (3.8) as follows:

$$\hat{\mathbf{C}}_j = \hat{\mathbf{D}}_k \hat{\mathbf{F}}_\ell \qquad (3.9)$$

We can now use the techniques in Section 2 to reduce systems of such equations to a single matrix equation as follows:

$$\hat{\mathbf{U}}\hat{\mathbf{V}} = \mathbf{0} \qquad (3.10)$$

In turn, this equation can be solved using the Algorithm LINEAR-ALIGN-MENT to determine $\hat{\mathbf{U}}$. To illustrate this process, we use the example from Section 1:

```
DO i=1,N
  DO j=1,N
    Y(i) = Y(i) + A(i+10,j+10)*X(j)
```

Suppose we wish to satisfy the constraints for Y and A. The relevant array access functions are:

$$\mathbf{F}_A = \begin{pmatrix} 1 & 0 \\ 0 & 1 \end{pmatrix} \qquad \mathbf{f}_A = \begin{pmatrix} 10 \\ 10 \end{pmatrix}$$

$$\mathbf{F}_Y = \begin{pmatrix} 1 & 0 \end{pmatrix} \qquad \mathbf{f}_Y = \begin{pmatrix} 0 \end{pmatrix}$$

$$\hat{\mathbf{F}}_A = \begin{pmatrix} 1 & 0 & 10 \\ 0 & 1 & 10 \\ 0 & 0 & 1 \end{pmatrix} \qquad \hat{\mathbf{F}}_Y = \begin{pmatrix} 1 & 0 & 0 \\ 0 & 0 & 1 \end{pmatrix} \qquad (3.11)$$

The reader can verify that the matrix equation to be solved is the following one.

$$\hat{\mathbf{U}}\hat{\mathbf{V}} = \mathbf{0} \qquad (3.12)$$

where:

$$\hat{\mathbf{U}} = \begin{pmatrix} \hat{\mathbf{C}} & \hat{\mathbf{D}}_A & \hat{\mathbf{D}}_Y \end{pmatrix} \qquad \hat{\mathbf{V}} = \begin{pmatrix} \mathbf{I} & \mathbf{I} \\ -\hat{\mathbf{F}}_A & \mathbf{0} \\ \mathbf{0} & -\hat{\mathbf{F}}_Y \end{pmatrix}$$

And the solution is the following matrix.

$$\hat{\mathbf{U}} = \begin{pmatrix} 1 & 0 & 0 & 1 & 0 & -10 & 1 & 0 \\ 0 & 0 & 1 & 0 & 0 & 1 & 0 & 1 \end{pmatrix} \qquad (3.13)$$

From this matrix, we can read off the following maps of computation and data.

$$\hat{\mathbf{C}} = \begin{pmatrix} 1 & 0 & 0 \\ 0 & 0 & 1 \end{pmatrix} \qquad \hat{\mathbf{D}}_A = \begin{pmatrix} 1 & 0 & -10 \\ 0 & 0 & 1 \end{pmatrix}$$

$$\hat{\mathbf{D}}_Y = \begin{pmatrix} 1 & 0 \\ 0 & 1 \end{pmatrix}$$

This says that iteration i of the loop and element $X(i)$ are mapped to the following virtual processor.

$$\hat{\mathbf{C}} \begin{pmatrix} i \\ 1 \end{pmatrix} = \begin{pmatrix} 1 & 0 & 0 \\ 0 & 0 & 1 \end{pmatrix} \begin{pmatrix} i \\ j \\ 1 \end{pmatrix} = \begin{pmatrix} i \\ 1 \end{pmatrix}$$

Notice that although the space of virtual processors has two dimensions (because of the encoding of constants), the maps of the computation and data use only a one-dimensional subspace of the virtual processor space. To obtain a clean solution, it is desirable to remove the extra dimension introduced by the encoding.

> *Input:*. A set of alignment constraints as in Equation (3.4).
> *Output:*. Communication-free alignment mappings characterized by
> $\mathbf{C}_j$, $\mathbf{c}_j$, $\mathbf{D}_k$, $\mathbf{d}_k$.
>   1. Assemble $\hat{\mathbf{F}}_\ell$ matrices as in Equation 3.6.
>   2. Assemble block columns $\mathbf{V}_q$ as in Equation (2.2) using $\hat{\mathbf{F}}_\ell$ instead
>   of $\mathbf{F}_\ell$.
>   3. Put all block columns $\mathbf{V}_q$ into one matrix $\hat{\mathbf{V}}$.
>   4. Compute a basis $\hat{\mathbf{U}}^T$ for null-space of $\hat{\mathbf{V}}^T$ as in the Step 3 of
>   `LINEAR-ALIGNMENT` algorithm.
>   5. Eliminate redundant row(s) in $\hat{\mathbf{U}}$.
>   6. Extract the solution matrices from $\hat{\mathbf{U}}$.

Fig. 3.1. Algorithm `AFFINE-ALIGNMENT`.

We have already mentioned that there is always a trivial solution that maps everything to the same virtual processor $p = 0$. Because we have introduced affine functions, it is now possible to map everything to the same virtual processor $p \neq 0$. In our framework it is reflected in the fact that there is always a row

$$\mathbf{w}^T = (\ 0\ \ 0\ \ \ldots\ \ 0\ \ 1\ \ 0\ \ \ldots\ \ 0\ \ 1\ \ \ldots\ \ 0\ \ 0\ \ 1\ ) \qquad (3.14)$$

(with zeros placed appropriately) in the *row space* of the solution matrix $\hat{\mathbf{U}}$. To "clean up" the solution notice that we can always find a vector $\mathbf{x}$ such that $\mathbf{x}^T \hat{\mathbf{U}} = \mathbf{w}^T$. Moreover, let k be the position of some non-zero element in $\mathbf{x}$ and let $\mathbf{J}$ be an identity matrix with the k-th row replaced by $\mathbf{x}^T$ ($\mathbf{J}$ is non-singular). Then the k-th row of $\hat{\mathbf{U}}' = \mathbf{J}\hat{\mathbf{U}}$ is equal to $\mathbf{w}^T$ and is linearly independent from the rest of the rows. This means that we can safely remove it from the solution matrix. Notice that this procedure is exactly equivalent to removing k-th row from $\hat{\mathbf{U}}$. A more detailed description is given in the appendix.

Algorithm `AFFINE-ALIGNMENT` is summarized in Figure 3.1.

4. Replication

As we discussed in Section 1, communication-free alignment may require replication of data. Currently, we allow replication only of read-only arrays or of the arrays which are updated using reduction operations. In this section, we show how replication of data is handled in our linear algebra framework. We use a matrix-vector multiplication loop (MVM) as a running example.

```
DO i=1,N
   DO j=1,N
      Y(i) = Y(i) + A(i,j)*X(j)
```

We are interested in deriving the parallel version of this code which uses 2-D alignment — that is, it uses a 2-dimensional template in which processor (i, j) performs iteration (i,j). If we keep the alignment constraint for A only, we get the solution:

$$\mathbf{C} = \mathbf{D}_A = \begin{pmatrix} 1 & 0 \\ 0 & 1 \end{pmatrix} \tag{4.1}$$

which means that iteration (i,j) is executed on the processor with coordinates (i, j). This processor also owns the array element $A(i, j)$. For the computation, it needs $X(j)$ and $Y(i)$. This requires that X be replicated along the i dimension of the processor grid, and Y be reduced along the j dimension. We would like to derive this information automatically.

4.1 Formulation of Replication

To handle replication, we associate a pair of matrices $\mathbf{R}$ and $\mathbf{D}$ with each data reference for which alignment is desired; as we show next, the fundamental equational scheme for alignment becomes $\mathbf{RC} = \mathbf{DF}$.

Up to this point, data alignment was specified using a matrix $\mathbf{D}$ which mapped array element $\mathbf{a}$ to logical processor $\mathbf{Da}$. If $\mathbf{D}$ has a non-trivial nullspace, then elements of the array belonging to the same coset of the null-space get placed onto the same virtual processor; that is,

$$\mathbf{Da}_1 \quad = \quad \mathbf{Da}_2$$

$$\Leftrightarrow$$

$$\mathbf{a}_1 - \mathbf{a}_2 \quad \in \quad \text{null}(\mathbf{D})$$

When we allow replication, the mapping of array elements to processors can be described as follows. Array element $\mathbf{a}$ is mapped to processor $\mathbf{p}$ if

$$\mathbf{Rp} \quad = \quad \mathbf{Da}$$

The mapping of the array is now a many-to-many relation that can be described in words as follows:

- Array elements that belong to the same coset of $\text{null}(\mathbf{D})$ are mapped onto the same processors.
- Processors that belong to the same coset of $\text{null}(\mathbf{R})$ own the same data.

From this, it is easy to see that the fundamental equation of alignment becomes $\mathbf{RC} = \mathbf{DF}$. The replication-free scenario is just a special case when $\mathbf{R}$ is $\mathbf{I}$. Not all arrays in a procedure need to be replicated — for example, if an array is involved in a non-reduction dependence or it is very large, we can disallow replication of that array. Notice that the equation $\mathbf{RC} = \mathbf{DF}$ is *non-linear* if both $\mathbf{R}$ and $\mathbf{C}$ are unknown. To make the solution tractable, we first compute $\mathbf{C}$ based on the constraints for the non-replicated arrays. Once $\mathbf{C}$ is determined, the equation is again linear in the unknowns $\mathbf{R}$ and

D. Intuitively, this means that we first drop some constraints from the non-replicated alignment system, and then try to satisfy these constraints via replication.

We need to clarify what "fixing **C**" means. When we solve the alignment system (2.3), we obtain a basis $\mathbf{C}_{\text{basis}}$ for all solutions to the loop alignment. The solutions can be expressed parametrically as

$$\mathbf{C} = \mathbf{T}\mathbf{C}_{\text{basis}} \tag{4.2}$$

for any matrix **T**. Now the replication equation becomes

$$\mathbf{R}\mathbf{T}\mathbf{C}_{\text{basis}} = \mathbf{D}\mathbf{F} \tag{4.3}$$

and we are faced again with a non-linear system (**T** is another unknown)! The key observation is that if we are considering a single loop nest, then **T** becomes redundant since we can "fold it" into **R**. This lets us solve the replication problem for a single loop nest.

In our MVM example, once the loop alignment has been fixed as in (4.1), the system of equations for the replication of X and Y is:

$$\begin{aligned} \mathbf{R}_X\mathbf{C} &= \mathbf{D}_X\mathbf{F}_X \\ \mathbf{R}_Y\mathbf{C} &= \mathbf{D}_Y\mathbf{F}_Y \end{aligned}$$

These can be solved independently or put together into a block-matrix form $\mathbf{U}\mathbf{V} = \mathbf{0}$:

$$\begin{aligned} \mathbf{U} &= \begin{pmatrix} \mathbf{R}_X & \mathbf{R}_Y & \mathbf{D}_X & \mathbf{D}_Y \end{pmatrix} \\ \mathbf{V} &= \begin{pmatrix} \mathbf{C} & \mathbf{0} \\ \mathbf{0} & \mathbf{C} \\ \mathbf{D}_X & \mathbf{0} \\ \mathbf{0} & \mathbf{D}_Y \end{pmatrix} \end{aligned} \tag{4.4}$$

and solved using the standard methods. The solution to this system:

$$\begin{aligned} \mathbf{R}_X &= \begin{pmatrix} 0 & 1 \end{pmatrix} & \mathbf{D}_X &= \begin{pmatrix} 1 \\ 1 \end{pmatrix} \\ \mathbf{R}_Y &= \begin{pmatrix} 1 & 0 \end{pmatrix} & \mathbf{D}_Y &= \begin{pmatrix} 1 \\ 1 \end{pmatrix} \end{aligned} \tag{4.5}$$

which is the desired result: columns of the processor grid form the cosets of $\text{null}(\mathbf{R}_X)$ and rows of the processor grid form the cosets of $\text{null}(\mathbf{R}_Y)$.

The overall Algorithm SINGLE-LOOP-REPLICATION-ALIGNMENT is summarized in Figure 4.1.

5. Heuristics

In practice, systems of alignment constraints are usually over-determined, so it is necessary to drop one or more constraints to obtain parallel execution. As we mentioned in the introduction, it is very difficult to determine which constraints must be dropped to obtain an optimal solution. In this section, we discuss our heuristic which is motivated by scalability analysis of common computational kernels.

Input:. Replication constraints of the form $\mathbf{RC} = \mathbf{DF}$.

Output:. Matrices $\mathbf{R}$, $\mathbf{D}$ and $\mathbf{C}_{basis}$ that specify alignment with replication.

1. Find $\mathbf{C}_{basis}$ by solving the alignment system for the non-replicated arrays using the Algorithm AFFINE-ALIGNMENT. If all arrays in the loop nest are allowed to be replicated, then set $\mathbf{C}_{basis} = \mathbf{I}$.
2. Find $(\mathbf{R}, \mathbf{D})$ pairs that specify replication by solving the $\mathbf{RC}_{basis} = \mathbf{DF}$ equations.

Fig. 4.1. Algorithm SINGLE-LOOP-REPLICATION-ALIGNMENT.

5.1 Lessons from Some Common Computational Kernels

We motivate our ideas by the following example. Consider a loop nest that computes matrix-matrix product:

```
DO i=1,n
  DO j=1,n
    DO k=1,n
      C(i,j) = C(i,j) + A(i,k)*B(k,j)
```

[9] provides the description of various parallel algorithms for matrix-matrix multiplication. It is shown that the *best scalability* is achieved by an algorithm which organizes the processors into a 3-D grid. Let p, q and r be the processor indices in the grid. Initially, A is partitioned in 2-D blocks along the p-r "side" of the grid. That is, if we let A^{pr} be a block of A, then it is initially placed on processor with the coordinates $(p, 0, r)$. Similarly, each block B^{rq} is placed on processor $(0, q, r)$. Our goal is to accumulate the block C^{pq} of the result on the processor $(p, q, 0)$.

At the start of the computation, A is replicated along the second (q) dimension of the grid. B is replicated along the first dimension (p). Therefore, we end up with processor (p, q, r) holding a copy of A^{pr} and B^{rq}. Then each processor computes the local matrix-matrix product:

$$D^{pqr} = A^{pr} * B^{rq} \qquad (5.1)$$

It is easy to see that the blocks of C are related to these local products by:

$$C^{pq} = \sum_{r} D^{pqr} \qquad (5.2)$$

Therefore, after the local products are computed, they are reduced along the r dimension of the grid.

We can describe this computation using our algebraic framework. There is a 3-D template and the computation alignment is an identity. Each of the arrays is replicated. For example the values of $\mathbf{D}$ and $\mathbf{R}$ for the array A are:

$$\mathbf{R} = \begin{pmatrix} 1 & 0 & 0 \\ 0 & 0 & 1 \end{pmatrix} \quad \mathbf{D} = \begin{pmatrix} 1 & 0 \\ 0 & 1 \end{pmatrix} \tag{5.3}$$

By collapsing different dimensions of the 3-D grid, we get 2-D and 1-D versions of this code. In general, it is difficult for a compiler to determine which version to use — the optimal solution depends on the size of the matrix, and on the overhead of communication relative to computation of the parallel machine [9]. On modern machines where the communication overhead is relatively small, the 3-D algorithm is preferable, but most alignment heuristics we have seen would not produce this solution — note that all arrays are communicated in this version! These heuristics are much more likely to "settle" for the 2-D or 1-D versions, with some of the arrays kept local.

Similar considerations apply to other codes such as matrix-vector product, 2-D and 3-D stencil computations, and matrix factorization codes [9]. Consider stencil computations. Here is a typical example:

```
DO i=1,N
  DO j=1,N
    A(i,j) = ...B(i-1,j)...B(i+1,j)...
             ...B(i,j)...B(i,j-1)...B(i,j+1))
```

In general, stencil computations are characterized by array access functions of the form $\mathbf{F}i + \mathbf{f}_k$, where the linear part $\mathbf{F}$ is the same for most of the accesses. The difference in the offset induces nearest-neighbor communication. We will analyze the communication/computation cost ratio for 1-D and 2-D partitioning of this example. For the 1-D case, the N-by-N iteration space is cut up into N/P-by-N blocks. If N is large enough, then each processor has to communicate with its "left" and "right" neighbors, and the volume of communication is $2N$. We can assume that the communication between the different pairs of neighbors happens at the same time. Therefore, the total communication time is $\Theta(2N)$. The computation done on each processor is $\Theta(N^2/P)$, so the ratio of communication to computation is $\Theta(P/N)$. In the 2-D case, the iteration space is cut up into $N/\sqrt{P}$-by-$N/\sqrt{P}$ blocks. Each processor now has four neighbors to communicate with, and the volume of communication is $4N/\sqrt{P}$. Therefore, the ratio for this case is $\Theta(\sqrt{P}/N)$. We conclude that 2-D case *scales* better than 1-D case[1]. In general, if we have a d-dimensional stencil-like computation, then it pays to have a d-dimensional template.

The situation is somewhat different in matrix and vector products and matrix factorization codes (although the final result is the same). Let us consider matrix-vector product together with some vector operation between X and Y:

[1] In fact, the total volume of communication is smaller in the 2-D case, despite the fact that we had fewer alignment constraints satisfied (this paradoxical result arises from the fact that the amount of communication is a function not just of alignment but of distribution as well).

```
DO i=1,N
  DO j=1,N
    Y(i) = Y(i) + A(i,j) * X(j)

DO i=1,N
  X(i) = ...Y(i)...
```

This fragment is typical of many iterative linear system solvers ([11]). One option is to use a 1-D template by leaving the constraint for X in the matrix-vector product loop unsatisfied. The required communication is an all-to-all broadcast of the elements of X. The communication cost is $\Theta(N \log(P))$. The computation cost is $\Theta(N^2/P)$. This gives us communication to computation ratio of $\Theta(\log(P)P/N)$.

In the 2-D version, each processor gets an $N/\sqrt{P}$-by-$N/\sqrt{P}$ block of the iteration space and A. X and Y are partitioned in $\sqrt{P}$ pieces placed along the diagonal of the processor grid ([9]). The algorithm is somewhat similar to matrix-matrix multiplication: each block of X gets broadcast along the column dimension, each block of Y is computed as the sum-reduction along the row dimension. Note that because each broadcast or reduction happens in parallel, the communication cost is $\Theta(\log(\sqrt{P})N/\sqrt{P}) = \Theta(\log(P)N/\sqrt{P})$. This results on the communication to computation ratio of $\Theta(\log(P)\sqrt{P}/N)$. Although the total volume of communication is roughly the same for the 1-D and 2-D case, the cost is asymptotically smaller in the 2-D case. Intuitively, the reason is that we were able to parallelize communication itself.

To reason about this in our framework, let us focus on matrix-vector product, and see what kind of replication for X we get for the 1-D and 2-D case. In the 1-D case, the computation alignment is:

$$\mathbf{C} = \begin{pmatrix} 1 & 0 \end{pmatrix} \tag{5.4}$$

The replication equation $\mathbf{RC} = \mathbf{DF}$ for X is:

$$\mathbf{R}_X \begin{pmatrix} 1 & 0 \end{pmatrix} = \mathbf{D}_X \begin{pmatrix} 0 & 1 \end{pmatrix} \tag{5.5}$$

The only solution is:

$$\mathbf{R}_X = \mathbf{D}_X = \begin{pmatrix} 0 \end{pmatrix} \tag{5.6}$$

This means that every processor gets all elements of X — i.e., it is an all-to-all broadcast. We have already computed the alignments for the 2-D case in Section 4. Because $\mathbf{R}_X$ has rank 1, we have a "parallelizable" broadcasts — that is, the broadcast along different dimensions of the processor grid can happen simultaneously. In general, if the replication matrix has rank r and the template has dimension d, then we have broadcasts along $d - r$ dimensional subspaces of the template. The larger r, the more of these broadcasts happen at the same time. In the extreme case $r = d$ we have a replication-free alignment, which requires no communication, at all.

5.2 Implications for Alignment Heuristic

The above discussion suggests the following heuristic strategy.

- If a number of constraints differ only in the offset of the array access function, use only one of them.
- If there is a d-dimensional DOALL loop (or loop with reductions), use a d-dimensional template for it and try to satisfy conflicting constraints via replication. Keep the d-dimensional template if the rank of the resulting replication matrices is greater than zero.
- If the above strategy fails, use a greedy strategy based on array dimensions as a cost measure. That is, try to satisfy the alignment constraints for the largest array first (intuitively, we would like large arrays to be "locked in place" during the computation). This is the strategy used by Feautrier [5].

Intuitively, this heuristic is biased in favor of exploiting parallelism in DO-ALL loops, since communication can be performed in parallel before the computation starts. This is true even if there are reductions in the loop nest, because the communication required to perform reductions can also be parallelized. This bias in favour of exploiting parallelism in DO-ALL loops at the expense of communication is justified on modern machines.

6. Conclusion

We have presented a simple framework for the solution of the alignment problem. This framework is based on linear algebra, and it permits the development of simple and fast algorithms for a variety of problems that arise in alignment.

References

1. Jennifer M. Anderson and Monica S. Lam. Global optimizations for parallelism and locality on scalable parallel machines. *ACM SIGPLAN Conference on Programming Language Design and Implementation (PLDI)*, pages 112 – 125, June 1993.
2. Siddartha Chatterjee, John Gilbert, and Robert Schreiber. The alignment-distribution graph. In U. Banerjee, D. Gelernter, A. Nicolau, and D. Padua, editors, *Languages and Compilers for Parallel Computing. Sixth International Workshop.*, number 768 in LNCS. Springer-Verlag, 1993.
3. Siddartha Chatterjee, John Gilbert, Robert Schreiber, and Shang-Hua Teng. Optimal evaluation of array expressions on massively parallel machines. Technical Report CSL-92-11, XEROX PARC, December 1992.
4. Henri Cohen. *A Course in Computational Algebraic Number Theory*. Graduate Texts in Mathematics. Springer-Verlag, 1995.

5. Paul Feautrier. Toward automatic distribution. Technical Report 92.95, IBP/MASI, December 1992.
6. C.-H. Huang and P. Sadayappan. Communication-free hyperplane partitioning of nested loops. In U. Banerjee, D. Gelernter, A. Nicolau, and D. Padua, editors, *Languages and Compilers for Parallel Computing. Fourth International Workshop. Santa Clara, CA.*, number 589 in LNCS, pages 186–200. Springer-Verlag, August 1991.
7. Kathleen Knobe, Joan D. Lucas, and William J. Dally. Dynamic alignment on distributed memory systems. In *Proceedings of the Third Workshop on Compilers for Parallel Computers*, July 1992.
8. Kathleen Knobe and Venkataraman Natarajan. Data optimization: minimizing residual interprocessor motion on SIMD machines. In *Proceedings of the 3rd Symposium on the Frontiers of Massively Parallel Computation - Frontiers 90*, pages 416–423, October 1990.
9. Vipin Kumar, Ananth Grama, Anshul Gupta, and George Karypis. *Introduction to Parallel Computing. Design and Analysis of Algorithms.* The Benjamin/Cummings Publishing Company, 1994.
10. Jingke Li and Marina Chen. Index domain alignment: minimizing cost of cross-referencing between distributed arrays. Technical Report YALEU/DCS/TR-725, Department of Computer Science, Yale University, September 1989.
11. Youcef Saad. Kyrlov subspace methods on supercomputers. *SIAM Journal on Scientific and Statistical Computing*, 10(6):1200–1232, November 1989.
12. Michael Wolfe. *High Performance Compilers for Parallel Computing.* Addison–Wesley, Redwood City, CA, 1996.

Acknowledgement. This research was supported by an NSF Presidential Young Investigator award CCR-8958543, NSF grant CCR-9503199, ONR grant N00014-93-1-0103, and a grant from Hewlett-Packard Corporation.

A. Reducing the Solution Matrix

As we mentioned in Section 2.4, it is possible for our solution procedure to produce a matrix $\mathbf{U}$ which has more rows than the rank of any of the computation alignments $\mathbf{C}_i$. Intuitively, this means that we end up with a template that has a larger dimension than can be exploited in any loop nest in the program. Although the extra dimensions can be 'folded' away during the distribution phase, we show how the problem can be eliminated by adding an extra step to our alignment procedure. First, we discuss two ways in which this problem can arise.

A.1 Unrelated Constraints

Suppose we have two loops with iteration alignments $\mathbf{C}_1$ and $\mathbf{C}_2$ and two arrays A and B with data alignments $\mathbf{D}_A$ and $\mathbf{D}_B$. Furthermore, only A is accessed in loop 1 via access function $\mathbf{F}_A$ and only B is accessed in loop 2 via access function $\mathbf{F}_B$ [2]. The alignment equations in this case are:

$$\mathbf{C}_1 = \mathbf{D}_A\mathbf{F}_A \tag{A.1}$$
$$\mathbf{C}_2 = \mathbf{D}_B\mathbf{F}_B \tag{A.2}$$

We can assemble this into a combined matrix equation:

$$\mathbf{U} = (\ \mathbf{C}_1\ \ \mathbf{C}_2\ \ \mathbf{D}_A\ \ \mathbf{D}_B\ )$$
$$\mathbf{V} = \begin{pmatrix} \mathbf{I} & \mathbf{0} \\ \mathbf{0} & \mathbf{I} \\ -\mathbf{F}_A & \mathbf{0} \\ \mathbf{0} & -\mathbf{F}_B \end{pmatrix}$$
$$\mathbf{U}\mathbf{V} = \mathbf{0} \tag{A.3}$$

Say, $\mathbf{C}_1^*$ and $\mathbf{D}_A^*$ are the solution to (A.1). And $\mathbf{C}_2^*$ and $\mathbf{D}_B^*$ are the solution to (A.2). Then it is not hard to see that the following matrix is a solution to (A.3):

$$\mathbf{U} = \left(\begin{array}{c|c|c|c} \mathbf{C}_1^* & \mathbf{0} & \mathbf{D}_A^* & \mathbf{0} \\ \mathbf{0} & \mathbf{C}_2^* & \mathbf{0} & \mathbf{D}_B^* \end{array} \right) \tag{A.4}$$

So we have obtained a processor space with the dimension being the sum of the dimensions allowed by (A.1) (say, p_1) and (A.2) (say p_2). However, these dimensions are not fully utilized since only the first p_1 dimensions are used in loop 1, and only the remaining p_2 dimensions are used in loop 2.

---

[2] For simplicity we are considering linear alignments and subscripts. For affine alignments and subscripts the argument is exactly the same after the appropriate encoding.

This problem is relatively easy to solve. In general, we can model the alignment constraints as an undirected *alignment constraint graph* G whose vertices are the unknown $\mathbf{D}$ and $\mathbf{C}$ alignment matrices; an edges (x, y) represents an alignment equation constraining vertex x and vertex y. alignments. We solve the constraints in each connected component separately, and choose a template with dimension equal to the maximum of the dimensions required for the connected components.

A.2 General Procedure

Unfortunately, extra dimensions can arise even when there is only one component in the alignment constraint graph. Consider the following program fragment:

```
DO i=1,n
  DO j=1,n
    ...A(i,0,j)...
```

The alignment equation for this loop is:

$$\mathbf{C} \;=\; \mathbf{D}_A \begin{pmatrix} 1 & 0 \\ 0 & 0 \\ 0 & 1 \end{pmatrix}$$

The solution is:

$$\mathbf{U} = (\ \mathbf{C} \quad \mathbf{D}\ ) = \begin{pmatrix} 1 & 0 & 1 & 0 & 0 \\ 0 & 0 & 0 & 1 & 0 \\ 0 & 1 & 0 & 0 & 1 \end{pmatrix}$$

So we have $\mathrm{rank}(\mathbf{C}) = 2 < \mathrm{rank}(\mathbf{U})$. If we use this solution, we end up placing the unused dimension of A onto an extra dimension of virtual processor space. We need a way of modifying the solution matrix $\mathbf{U}$ so that:

$$\mathrm{rank}(\mathbf{U}) \;=\; \max_i \{\mathrm{rank}(\mathbf{C}_i)\} \tag{A.5}$$

For this, we apply elementary (unimodular) row operations [3] to $\mathbf{U}$ so that we end up with a matrix $\mathbf{U}'$ in which the *first* $\mathrm{rank}(\mathbf{C}_i)$ rows of each $\mathbf{C}_i$ component form a *row basis* for the rows of this component. We will say that each component of $\mathbf{U}'$ is *reduced*. By taking the first $\max_i\{\mathrm{rank}(\mathbf{C}_i)\}$ rows of $\mathbf{U}'$ we obtain a desired solution $\mathbf{W}$.

In our example matrix $\mathbf{U}$ is not reduced: the first two rows of $\mathbf{C}$ do not for a basis for all rows of $\mathbf{C}$. But if we add the third row of $\mathbf{U}$ to the second row, we get $\mathbf{U}'$ with desired property:

---

[3] Multiplying a row by ± 1 and adding a multiple of one row to another are elementary row operations.

$$\mathbf{U}' \;=\; \left(\begin{array}{cc|ccc} 1 & 0 & 1 & 0 & 0 \\ 0 & 1 & 0 & 1 & 1 \\ 0 & 1 & 0 & 0 & 1 \end{array} \right)$$

Now by taking the first two rows of $\mathbf{U}'$ we obtain a solution which does not induce unused processor dimensions.

The question now becomes: how do we systematically choose a sequence of row operations on $\mathbf{U}$ in order to reduce its components? Without loss of generality, lets assume that $\mathbf{U}$ only consists of $\mathbf{C}_i$ components:

$$\mathbf{U} \;=\; \left(\begin{array}{cccc} \mathbf{C}_1 & \mathbf{C}_2 & \cdots & \mathbf{C}_s \end{array} \right) \tag{A.6}$$

Let:

- q be the number of rows in $\mathbf{U}$. Also, by construction of $\mathbf{U}$, $q = \mathrm{rank}(\mathbf{U})$.
- r_i be the rank of C_i for $i = 1, \ldots, s$.
- $r_{max} = \max_i \{\mathrm{rank}(\mathbf{C}_i)\}$. Notice that $r_{max} \neq q$, in general.

We want to find matrix $\mathbf{W}$, so that:

- number of rows in $\mathbf{W}$ equals to r_{max}.
- each component of $\mathbf{W}$ has the same rank as the corresponding component of $\mathbf{U}$.

Here is the outline of our algorithm:

1. Perform elementary row operations on $\mathbf{U}$ to get $\mathbf{U}'$ in which every component is reduced.
2. Set $\mathbf{W}$ to the first r_{max} rows of $\mathbf{U}'$.

The details are filled in below.

We need the following Lemma:

Lemma A1. *Let $\mathbf{a}_1, \ldots, \mathbf{a}_r, \mathbf{a}_{r+1}, \ldots, \mathbf{a}_n$ be some vectors. Furthermore assume that the first r vectors form a basis for the span $\mathbf{a}_1, \ldots, \mathbf{a}_n$. Let:*

$$\mathbf{a}_k \;=\; \sum_{j=1}^{r} \beta_j \mathbf{a}_j \tag{A.7}$$

be the representation of $\mathbf{a}_k$ in the basis above. Then the vectors $\mathbf{a}_1, \ldots, \mathbf{a}_{r-1}$, $\mathbf{a}_r + \alpha \mathbf{a}_k$ are linearly independent (and form a basis) if and only if:

$$1 + \alpha \beta_r \;\neq\; 0 \tag{A.8}$$

Proof:.

$$
\begin{aligned}
\mathbf{a}_r + \alpha \mathbf{a}_k \;&=\; \mathbf{a}_r + \alpha \sum_{j=1}^{r} \beta_j \mathbf{a}_j \\
&=\; \mathbf{a}_r (1 + \alpha \beta_r) + \alpha \sum_{j=1}^{r-1} \beta_j \mathbf{a}_j
\end{aligned}
\tag{A.9}
$$

Now if in the equation (A.9) $(1+\alpha\beta_r) = 0$, then the vectors $\mathbf{a}_1, \ldots, \mathbf{a}_{n-1}, \mathbf{a}_r + \alpha\mathbf{a}_k$ are linearly dependent. Vice versa, if $(1 + \alpha\beta_r) \neq 0$, then these vectors are independent by the assumption on the original first r vectors. $\square$

Lemma A1 forms a basis for an inductive algorithm to reduce all components of $\mathbf{U}$. Inductively assume that we have already reduced $\mathbf{C}_1, \ldots, \mathbf{C}_{k-1}$. Below we show how to reduce $\mathbf{C}_k$, while keeping the first $k-1$ components reduced.

Let

$$
\mathbf{C}_j \;=\; \begin{pmatrix} \mathbf{a}_1^T \\ \mathbf{a}_2^T \\ \vdots \\ \mathbf{a}_q^T \end{pmatrix}
$$

we want the first r_j rows to be linearly independent. Assume inductively that the first $i-1$ rows $(i < r_j)$ are already linearly independent. There are two cases for the i-th row $(\mathbf{a}_i^T)$:

1. $\mathbf{a}_i^T$ is linearly independent from the previous rows. In this case we just move to the next row.
2. $\mathbf{a}_i = \sum_{\ell=1}^{i-1} \gamma_\ell \mathbf{a}_\ell$, i.e. $\mathbf{a}_i$ is linearly dependent on the previous rows. Note that since $r_j = rank(\mathbf{C}_j) > i$, there is a row $\mathbf{a}_p$, which is linearly independent from the first $i-1$ rows. Because of this the rows $\mathbf{a}_1, \ldots, \mathbf{a}_{i-1}, \mathbf{a}_i + \alpha\mathbf{a}_p$ are linearly independent for any $\alpha \neq 0$.
   Lemma A1 tells us that we can choose α so that the previous components are kept reduced. We have to solve a system of inequalities like:

$$
\begin{cases} 1 + \alpha\beta_{r_1}^{(1)} & \neq \; 0 \\ 1 + \alpha\beta_{r_2}^{(2)} & \neq \; 0 \\ \vdots & \\ 1 + \alpha\beta_{r_{k-1}}^{(k-1)} & \neq \; 0 \end{cases} \tag{A.10}
$$

where $\beta_{r_1}^{(1)}, \ldots, \beta_{r_{k-1}}^{(k-1)}$ come from the inequalities (A.8) for each component. $\beta_{r_i}^{(i)}$'s are rational numbers: $\beta_{r_i}^{(i)} = \eta_i/\xi_i$. So we have to solve a system of inequalities:

$$
\begin{cases} \alpha\eta_1 & \neq \; -\xi_1 \\ \alpha\eta_2 & \neq \; -\xi_2 \\ \vdots & \\ \alpha\eta_{k-1} & \neq \; -\xi_{k-1} \end{cases} \tag{A.11}
$$

It is easy to see that $\alpha = \max_i\{|\xi_i|\} + 1$ is a solution.

The full algorithm for communication-free alignment ALIGNMENT-WITH-FIX-UP is outlined in Figure A.1.

> *Input:.* A set of encoded affine alignment constraints as in Equation (3.4).
>
> *Output:.* Communication-free alignment mappings characterized by $\mathbf{C}_j$, $\mathbf{c}_j$, $\mathbf{D}_k$, $\mathbf{d}_k$ which do not induce unused processor dimensions.
>   1. Form alignment constraint graph G.
>   2. For each connected component of G:
>   a) Assemble the system of constraints and solve it as described in Algorithm AFFINE-ALIGNMENT to get the solution matrix $\hat{\mathbf{U}}$.
>   b) Remove the extra row of of $\hat{\mathbf{U}}$ that was induced by affine encoding. (Section B)
>   c) If necessary apply the procedure described in Section A.2 to reduce the computation alignment components of $\hat{\mathbf{U}}$.

Fig. A.1. Algorithm ALIGNMENT-WITH-FIXUP

B. A Comment on Affine Encoding

Finally, we make a remark about affine encoding. A sanity check for alignment equations is that there should always be a trivial solution which places everything onto one processor. In the case of linear alignment functions and linear array accesses, we have a solution $\mathbf{U} = \mathbf{0}$. When we use affine functions, this solution is still valid, but there is more. We should be able to express a solution $\hat{\mathbf{U}} \neq \mathbf{0}$ that places everything on a single non-zero processor. Such a solution would have $\mathbf{C}_i = \mathbf{0}$, $\mathbf{D}_j = \mathbf{0}$, $\mathbf{c}_i = \mathbf{d}_j = 1$. Or, using our affine encoding:

$$\hat{\mathbf{C}}_i = \left(\begin{array}{cccc|c} 0 & 0 & \cdots & 0 & 1 \end{array} \right)$$
$$\hat{\mathbf{D}}_j = \left(\begin{array}{ccccc|c} 0 & 0 & \cdots & 0 & 0 & 1 \end{array} \right)$$

Below, we prove that solution of this form always exists; moreover, this gives rise to an extra processor dimension which can be eliminated without using the algorithm of Section A.

Let the matrix of unknowns be:

$$\hat{\mathbf{U}} = \left(\begin{array}{cccccc} \hat{\mathbf{C}}_1 & \cdots & \hat{\mathbf{C}}_s & \hat{\mathbf{D}}_1 & \cdots & \hat{\mathbf{D}}_t \end{array} \right)$$

Also let:

- m_i be the number of columns of C_i for $i = 1, \ldots, s$. (m_i is the dimension of the ith loop.)
- m_{s+i} be the number of columns of D_i for $i = 1, \ldots, t$. (m_{s+i} is the dimension of the $(s+i)$th array.)
- $\mathbf{e}_k \in \mathbb{Z}^k$, $\mathbf{e}_k = \left(\begin{array}{ccccc} 0 & 0 & \cdots & 0 & 1 \end{array} \right)^T$. ($k-1$ zeros followed by a 1.)

$- \mathbf{w} \in \mathbb{Z}^{(m_1+m_2+...+m_{s+t})}$ as in:

$$\mathbf{w} \quad = \quad \begin{pmatrix} \mathbf{e}_{m_1} \\ \mathbf{e}_{m_2} \\ \vdots \\ \mathbf{e}_{m_s} \\ \mathbf{e}_{m_{s+1}} \\ \vdots \\ \mathbf{e}_{m_{s+t}} \end{pmatrix}$$

It is not hard to show that $\mathbf{w}^T \hat{\mathbf{V}} = \mathbf{0}$. In particular, we can show that vector $\mathbf{w}$ is orthogonal to every block column $\hat{\mathbf{V}}_q$ that is assembled into $\hat{\mathbf{V}}$. Suppose that $\hat{\mathbf{V}}_q$ corresponds to the equation:

$$\hat{\mathbf{C}}_i \quad = \quad \hat{\mathbf{D}}_j \hat{\mathbf{F}}_k$$

Therefore:

$$\hat{\mathbf{V}}_q \quad = \quad \begin{pmatrix} \mathbf{0} \\ \mathbf{I} \\ \mathbf{0} \\ -\hat{\mathbf{F}}_k \\ \mathbf{0} \end{pmatrix}$$

Note that $\hat{\mathbf{V}}_q$ has m_i columns (the dimension of the ith loop) and the last column looks like (check the definition of $\hat{\mathbf{F}}$ in Section 3.1:

$$\begin{pmatrix} 0 \\ 0 \\ \vdots \\ 0 \\ 1 \\ 0 \\ 0 \\ \vdots \\ 0 \\ -1 \\ 0 \\ \vdots \\ 0 \end{pmatrix}$$

with 1 and -1 placed in the same positions as the 1s in $\mathbf{w}$. It is clear that $\mathbf{w}$ is orthogonal to this column of $\hat{\mathbf{V}}_q$. $\mathbf{w}$ is also orthogonal to the other columns of $\hat{\mathbf{V}}_q$, since only the last column has non-zeros, where $\mathbf{w}$ has 1s.

How can we remove an extra dimension in $\hat{\mathbf{U}}$ that corresponds to $\mathbf{w}$? Note that in general $\hat{\mathbf{U}}$ will not have a row that is a multiple of $\mathbf{w}$! Suppose that $\hat{\mathbf{U}}$ has $r = \text{rank}(\hat{\mathbf{U}})$ rows:

$$
\hat{\mathbf{U}} = \begin{pmatrix} \mathbf{u}_1^T \\ \mathbf{u}_2^T \\ \vdots \\ \mathbf{u}_r^T \end{pmatrix}
$$

Since $\mathbf{w}^T \hat{\mathbf{V}} = \mathbf{0}$, we have that

$$
\mathbf{w} \in \text{null}(\hat{\mathbf{V}}^T)
$$

But rows of $\hat{\mathbf{U}}$ form a basis for $\text{null}(\hat{\mathbf{V}}^T)$. Therefore:

$$
\mathbf{w} \in \text{span}(\mathbf{u}_1, \ldots, \mathbf{u}_r) \tag{B.1}
$$

Let $\mathbf{x}$ be the solution to:

$$
\mathbf{x}^T \hat{\mathbf{U}} = \mathbf{w}^T
$$

One of the coordinates of $\mathbf{x}$, say x_ℓ, must be non-zero. Form the matrix $\mathbf{J}(\mathbf{x})$ by substituting the ℓth row of an r-by-r identity matrix with $\mathbf{x}^T$:

$$
\mathbf{J}(\mathbf{x}) = \begin{pmatrix}
1 & 0 & 0 & 0 & \cdots & 0 & \cdots & 0 \\
0 & 1 & 0 & 0 & \cdots & 0 & \cdots & 0 \\
0 & 0 & 1 & 0 & \cdots & 0 & \cdots & 0 \\
0 & 0 & 0 & 1 & \cdots & 0 & \cdots & 0 \\
\vdots & \vdots & \vdots & \vdots & \vdots & \vdots & \vdots & \vdots \\
x_1 & x_2 & x_3 & x_4 & \cdots & x_\ell & \cdots & x_r \\
\vdots & \vdots & \vdots & \vdots & \vdots & \vdots & \vdots & \vdots \\
0 & 0 & 0 & 0 & \cdots & 0 & \cdots & 1
\end{pmatrix}
$$

$\mathbf{J}(\mathbf{x})$ is non-singular, because $x_\ell \neq 0$. Therefore $\hat{\mathbf{U}}' = \mathbf{J}(\mathbf{x})\hat{\mathbf{U}}$ has the same rank as $\hat{\mathbf{U}}$ and it is also a basis for the solutions to our alignment system:

$$
\hat{\mathbf{U}}'\hat{\mathbf{V}} = \mathbf{J}(\mathbf{x})\hat{\mathbf{U}}\hat{\mathbf{V}} = \mathbf{J}(\mathbf{x})\mathbf{0} = \mathbf{0}
$$

But by construction:

$$
\hat{\mathbf{U}}' = \begin{pmatrix}
\mathbf{u}_1^T \\
\mathbf{u}_2^T \\
\vdots \\
\mathbf{u}_{\ell-1}^T \\
\mathbf{w}^T \\
\mathbf{u}_{\ell+1}^T \\
\vdots \\
: \mathbf{u}_r^T
\end{pmatrix}
$$

Now we can just remove the $\mathbf{w}^T$ row to get non-trivial solutions! Notice that we don't really have to form $\mathbf{J}(\mathbf{x})$ — we have to find $\mathbf{x}$ (using Gaussian elimination) and then remove the ℓth row from $\hat{\mathbf{U}}$ such that $x_\ell \neq 0$.

Chapter 12. A Compilation Method for Communication–Efficient Partitioning of DOALL Loops

Santosh Pande and Tareq Bali

College of Computing
801 Atlantic Drive
Georgia Institute of Technology
Atlanta, GA 30332
santosh@cc.gatech.edu

Summary. Due to a significant communication overhead of *sending* and *receiving* data, the loop partitioning approaches on distributed memory systems must guarantee not just the computation load balance but computation+communication load balance. The previous approaches in loop partitioning have achieved a communication-free, computation load balanced iteration space partitioning solution for a limited subset of DOALL loops [6]. But a large category of DOALL loops inevitably result in communication and the tradeoffs between computation and communication must be carefully analyzed for those loops in order to balance out the combined computation time and communication overheads.

In this work, we describe a partitioning approach based on the above motivation for the general cases of DOALL loops. Our goal is to achieve a computation+communication load balanced partitioning through static data and iteration space distribution. First, *code partitioning phase* analyzes the references in the body of the DOALL loop nest and determines a set of directions for reducing a larger degree of communication by trading a lesser degree of parallelism. The partitioning is carried out in the iteration space of the loop by cyclically following a set of direction vectors such that the data references are maximally localized and re-used eliminating a large communication volume. A new *larger partition owns* rule is formulated to minimize the communication overhead for a compute intensive partition by localizing its references relatively more than a smaller non-compute intensive partition. A Partition Interaction Graph is then constructed that is used to merge the partitions to achieve granularity adjustment, computation+communication load balance and mapping on the actual number of available processors. Relevant theory and algorithms are developed along with a performance evaluation on Cray T3D.

1. Introduction

The distributed memory parallel architectures are quite popular for highly parallel scientific software development. The emergence of better routing schemes and technologies have reduced the inter-processor communication latency and increased the communication bandwidth by a large degree making these architectures attractive for a wide range of applications.

Compiling for distributed memory systems continues to pose complex, challenging problems to the researchers. Some of the important research directions include, data parallel languages such as *HPF/Fortran 90D* [4,12,13,16],

S. Pande, D.P. Agrawal (Eds.): Compiler Optimizations for Scalable PS, LNCS 1808, pp. 413-443, 2001.
© Springer-Verlag Berlin Heidelberg 2001

communication free partitioning [1, 6, 14, 22], communication minimization [2, 17, 19], array privatization [30], data alignment [1, 3, 5, 11, 18, 24, 26, 29, 33], load balancing through multi-threading [27], mapping functional parallelism [8, 9, 20, 21, 23], compile and run time optimizations for irregular problems [25, 28] and optimizing data redistributions [15, 31].

The focus of most of these approaches is on eliminating as much inter-processor communication as possible. The primary motivation behind such approaches is that the data communication speeds on most of the distributed memory systems are orders of magnitude slower than the processor speeds. In particular, the loop partitioning approaches on these systems attempt to fully eliminate the communication through communication free partitioning for a sub-set of DOALL loops [1, 6, 14, 22]. These methods first attempt to find a communication free partition of the loop nest by determining a set of hyperplanes in the iteration and data spaces of the loop and then attempt to load balance the computation [6]. However, communication free partitioning is possible only for a very small, highly restrictive sub-class of DOALL loops and partitioning of general DOALL loops inevitably results in communication in the absence of any data replication. In these cases, the important goals of the loop partitioning strategy are to minimize the communication possibly trading parallelism and to achieve a computation+communication load balance for almost equal execution times of the generated loop partitions. The literature does not present comprehensive solutions to the above issues and this is the focus of our paper.

Section 2 describes the previous work on DOALL partitioning on distributed memory systems and discusses our approach. Section 3 introduces necessary terms and definitions. Section 4 develops the theory and section 5 discusses the algorithms for DOALL iteration and data space partitioning. Section 6 discusses the algorithms for granularity adjustment, load balancing and mapping. Section 7 illustrates the methods through an example. Section 8 deals with the performance results on Cray T3D and conclusions.

2. DOALL Partitioning

The DOALL loops offer the highest amount of parallelism to be exploited in many important applications. The primary motivation in DOALL partitioning on distributed memory systems is reducing data communication overhead. The previous work on this topic has focused on completely eliminating communication to achieve a communication free iteration and data space partition [1, 6, 14, 22]. But in many practical DOALL loops, the communication free partitioning may not be possible due to the incompatible reference instances of a given variable encountered in the loop body or due to incompatible variables [14, 22]. The parallelization of such DOALL loops is not possible by the above approaches. In this work, our motivation is to develop an iteration and data space partitioning method for these DOALL loops where the reference patterns do not permit a communication free partition without replicating the data. We attempt to minimally trade parallelism to maximally eliminate communication. Our other objective is to achieve a computation+communication load balanced partitioning of the loop. The focus, thus, is on *and computation+communication load balanced partitioning* as against *communication elimination and computation load balance for restricted cases* as in previous approaches [6]. We choose not to replicate the data since it involves a point-point or broadcast type communication and poses an initial data distribution overhead on every loop slice.

We first motivate our approach through an example.

2.1 Motivating Example

Consider the following DOALL loop:

```
for i = 2 to N
  for j = 2 to N
   A[i,j] = B[i-2,j-1]+B[i-1,j-1]+B[i-1,j-2]
  endfor
endfor
```

As far as this loop is concerned, it is not possible to determine a communication free data and iteration space partition [1, 6, 14, 22]. The reason this loop can not be partitioned in a communication free manner is that we can not determine a direction which will partition the iteration space so that all the resulting data references can be localized by suitably partitioning the data space of B without any replication.

The question is : can we profitably (speedup > 1) parallelize this loop in any way ? If there are many ways for such a parallelization, which one will give us computation+communication load balance for the best speedup? We illustrate that by carefully choosing the iteration and data distributions, it is possible to maximally eliminate the communication while minimally sacrificing the parallelism to minimize the loop completion time and maximize the speedup. It is then possible to construct a partition interaction graph to adapt the partitions for granularity and computation+communication load balance and to map them on the available number of processors for a specific architecture.

One approach is to replicate each element of matrix B on each processor and partition the nested DOALL iterations on a N x N mesh so that each processor gets one iteration. This, however, has a data distribution overhead $\propto N^2$ and thus, is not a good solution where cost of communication is higher than computation. This method has the maximum parallelism, but it will not give any speedup due to a very high data distribution overhead. The other possibility is to minimize communication by carefully choosing iteration and data distributions.

Table 2.1. Comparison of effect of partitioning on parallelism, communication and loop execution time

Dir.	#Part.	Commn.	Execution Time
(-1,0)	(N-1)	4(N-2)(N-1)	$(N-1)+c_1(2N-3)+c_2(2N-3)$
(0,1)	(N-1)	4(N-2)(N-1)	$(N-1)+c_1(2N-3)+c_2(2N-3)$
(-1,1)	(2N-3)	4(N-2)(N-1)	$(N-1)+2c_1(N-1)+2c_2(N-1)$
Cyclic	(N-1)	2(N-2)(N-1)	$(2N-5)+2c_2\lceil(2N-5)/2\rceil+c_1\lceil(2N-5)/2\rceil$

In the above example, it is possible to determine communication free directions for the iteration and data spaces by *excluding* some references. In this example, let $B_1 \equiv B[i-2, j-1]$, $B_2 \equiv B[i-1, j-1]$, $B_3 \equiv B[i-1, j-2]$. If we decide to exclude B_1, the communication free direction for partitioning the iteration space is (0,1) (data space partitioned column wise). If we decide to exclude B_2, the iteration partitioning direction is (-1,1) (data partitioning along anti-diagonal). If we decide to exclude B_3, one could partition iterations along the direction (-1,0) (data partition will be row wise). Please refer to figure 2.1 for details of iteration and data partitioning for (0,1) partitioning and figure 2.2 for (-1,0) partitioning. The iterations/data grouped together are connected by arrows which show the direction of partitioning. Figure 2.3 shows details of iteration and data partitioning for (-1,1) direction vector.

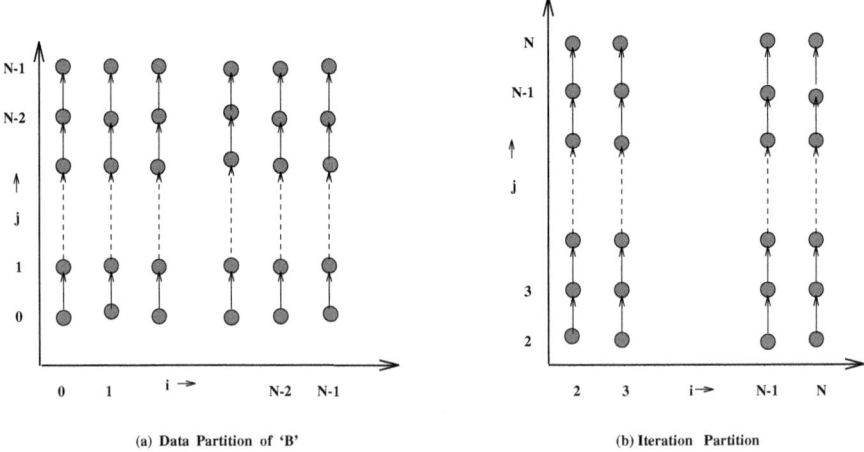

(a) Data Partition of 'B'   (b) Iteration Partition

Fig. 2.1. Iteration and data partitioning for direction vector (0,1)

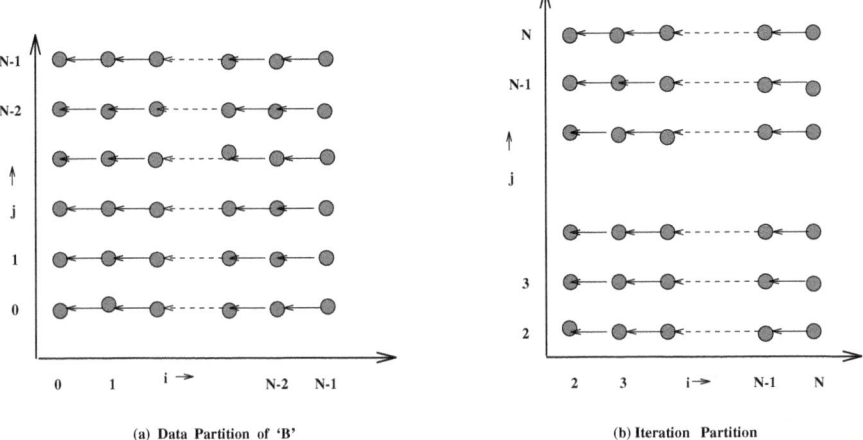

(a) Data Partition of 'B'   (b) Iteration Partition

Fig. 2.2. Iteration and data partitioning for direction vector (-1,0)

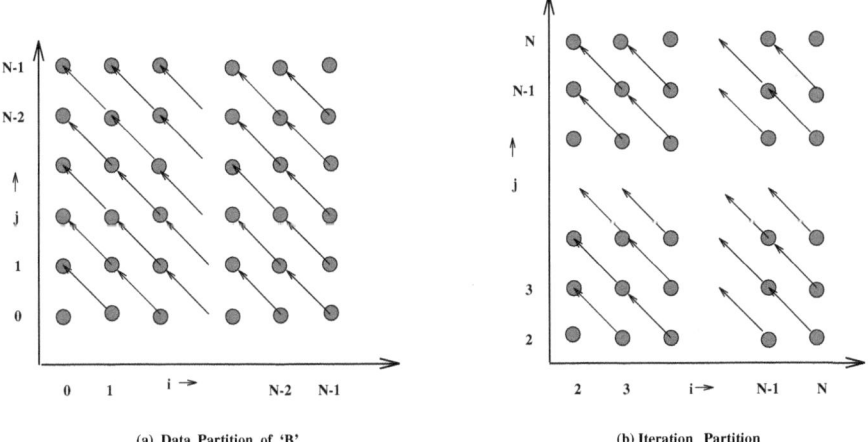

(a) Data Partition of 'B'   (b) Iteration Partition

Fig. 2.3. Iteration and data partitioning for direction vector (-1,1)

Table 1 shows the volume of communication, the parallelism and the loop completion times for each of the above three cases. It is assumed that loop body takes unit time for execution; whereas, each 'send' operation is c_1 times expensive than loop body and each 'receive' operation is c_2 times expensive than loop body. We now show that if we carry out the iteration and data space partitioning in the following manner, we can do better than any of the above partitions.

We first decide to partition along the direction $(0, 1)$ followed by partitioning along $(-1, 0)$ on cyclical basis. If we partition this way, it automatically ensures that the communication along the direction (-1,1) is not necessary. In other words, the iteration space is partitioned such that most of the iterations in the space reference the same data elements. This results in localization of most of the references to the same iteration space partition. Please refer to figure 2.4 for details about iteration and data space partitions using cyclic directions.

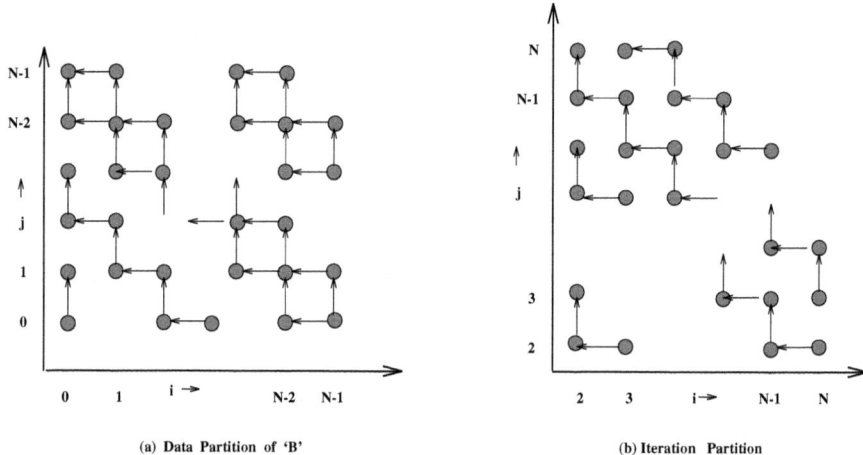

(a) Data Partition of 'B'   (b) Iteration Partition

Fig. 2.4. Iteration and data partitioning for cyclical direction vector (0.1)/ (-1,0)

In this partitioning scheme, whatever parallelism is lost due to sequential-ization of additional iterations is more than offset by elimination of additional amount of communication, thus improving overall performance. We, thus, compromise the parallelism to a certain extent to reduce the communication. However, the resulting partitions from this scheme are not well balanced with respect to total computation+communication per processor. If we per-form a careful data distribution and iteration partitions merging after this phase, this problem could be solved. Our objective in data distribution is to minimize communication overhead on larger partition and put the burden of larger overheads on smaller partitions so that each partition is more load balanced with respect to the total computation+communication.

For this example, we demonstrate the superiority of our scheme over other schemes listed in Table 1 as follows:

It is clear that our scheme has half the amount of communication vol-ume as compared to either of the (0,1), (-1,0) or (-1,1) (we determine the volume of communication by counting total non-local references - each non-local reference is counted as one send at its sender and one receive at its receiver). The total number of partitions is (N-1) in case of (0,1) or (-1,0), (2*N-3) in case of (-1,1) and (N-1) in case of (0,1)/(-1,0) cyclic partition-ing. Thus, (0,1)/(-1,0) has lesser amount of parallelism as compared to (-1,1) partitioning, but it also eliminated communication by the same degree which is more beneficial since communication is more expensive than computation. As an overall effect of saving in communication and more balanced computation+communication at every partition, the loop execution and thus the speedup resulting from our scheme is much superior to any of the above. The loop execution time given by (0,1) or (-1,0) partitioning is : $(N-1) + c_1 (2N-3) + c_2 (2N-3)$, that of (-1,1) is $(N-1) + 2c_1(N-2) + 2c_2(N-2)$, whereas according to our scheme, the loop execution time is given by $(2N-5)+2c_2 \lceil (2N-5)/2 \rceil + c_1 \lceil (2N-5)/2 \rceil$ It can be easily seen by comparing the expressions that, the loop execution time given by our scheme is superior to any of the other ones if $c_1, c_2 > 1$ (typically $c_1, c_2 \gg 1$). Finally, it may be noted that our scheme, achieves an asymptotic speedup of $(N/(2+2c_2+c_1))$. In the modern systems with low communication/computation ratio, the typical values of c_1 and c_2 are few hundreds. For example, assuming c_1 and c_2 about 200, for N > 600, our scheme would give speedups > 1. This scheme, thus, results in effective parallelization of even medium size problems. Also, one can overlap the computation and communication on an architecture in which each PE node has a separate communication processor. In this case, the loop completion time can approach the ideal parallel time since most communication overheads are absorbed due to overlap with the computation.

The above scheme, however, results in a large number of partitions that could lead to two problems in mapping them. The first problem is that the partitions could be too fine grained for a given architecture and the second problem could be that the number of available processors may be much lesser than the number of partitions (as usually the case). In order to solve these problems, we perform architecture dependent analysis after iteration and data space partitioning. We construct a Partition Interaction Graph from the iteration space partitions and optimize by merging partitions with respect to granularity so that communication overheads are reduced at the cost of coarser granularity. We then load balance the partitions with respect to total execution time consisting of computation+communication times and finally map the partitions on available number of processors. We now present an overall outline of our approach.

2.2 Our Approach

Figure 2.5 shows the structure of our DOALL partitioner and scheduler. It consists of five phases:

- Code Partitioning Phase : This phase is responsible for analyzing the references in the body of the DOALL loop nest and determine a set of directions to partition the iteration space to minimize the communication by minimally trading the parallelism.
- Data Distribution Phase: This phase visits the iteration partitions generated above in the order of decreasing sizes and uses a *larger partition owns*

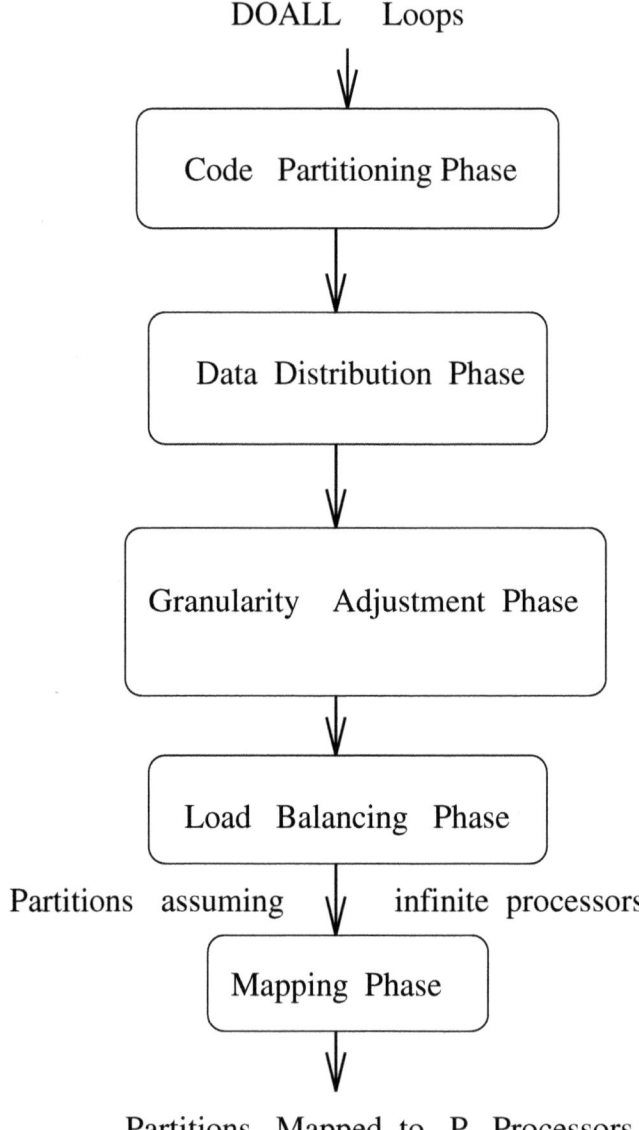

Fig. 2.5. DOALL Partitioner and Scheduler

rule to generate the underlying data distribution so that larger compute intensive partitions incur lesser communication overhead and vice-versa. The *larger partition owns* rule says that if the same data item is referenced by two or more partitions, the largest partition owns the data item. The goal is to generate computation+communication load balanced partitions.

- Granularity Adjustment Phase: This phase analyzes whether the granularity of the partitions generated above is optimal or not. It attempts to combine two partitions which have a data communication and determines if the resulting partition is better in terms of completion time. It continues this process until the resulting partition has a worse completion time than any of the partitions from which it is formed. In this manner, a significant amount of communication is eliminated by this phase to improve the completion time.
- Load Balancing Phase: This phase attempts to combine the load of several lightly loaded processors to reduce the number of required processors. Such merging is carried out only to the extent that the overall completion time does not degrade.
- Mapping Phase: This phase is responsible for mapping the partitions from the previous phase to a given number of processors by minimally degrading the overall completion time. The partitions that minimally degrade the completion time on merger are combined and the process is continued till the number of partitions equal the number of available processors.

The first two phases are architecture independent and the last three phases are architecture dependent which use the architecture cost model to perform granularity adjustment, load balancing and mapping. We first develop the theory behind code and data partitioning phases shown in figure 2.5.

3. Terms and Definitions

We limit ourselves to the perfectly nested normalized DOALL loops. We define each of the occurrences of a given variable in the loop nest as its *reference instance*. For example, different occurrences of a given variable 'B' are defined as the *reference instances* of 'B' and different instances are denoted as B_1, B_2, B_3, ..., etc. for convenience. The *iteration space* of n-nested loop is defined as $I = \{(i_1, i_2, i_3, ... i_n) | L_j \leq i_j \leq U_j, 1 \leq j \leq n\}$, where $i_1, i_2, ..., i_n$ are different index variables of the loop nest. In the loop body, an instance of a variable 'B' references a subset of the data space of variable 'B'. For example, the instance $B_1 \equiv B[i_1 + \sigma_1^1, i_2 + \sigma_2^1, i_3 + \sigma_3^1 ...]$, references the data space of matrix B decided by the iteration space as defined above and the the the offsets $\sigma_1^1, \sigma_2^1, \sigma_3^1, ...$ Each partition of the iteration space is called the *iteration block*. In order to generate communication free data and iteration partition, we determine partitioning directions in the iteration and data spaces such that the references generated in each iteration block can be disjointly partitioned and allocated on local memory of a processor to avoid communication. Although most of the discussion in this paper uses constant offsets for the variable references in each dimension, in general, the references can be *uniformly generated* [6] so that it is possible to perform *communication free partitioning analysis*. Please note that our approach uses *communication free partitioning analysis* as the underlying method (as described in later sections); thus, the underlying assumptions and restrictions are the same as any of those methods described in literature [1, 6, 14, 22]. All of these methods are able to handle uniformly generated references; thus, our method is able to do the same.

A set of reference instances of a variable is called the *instance set* of that variable. A set of *reference instances* of a variable for which communication free data and iteration partition can be determined is defined as a set of *compatible instances* of a variable. If a communication free partition can not be found, such a set of reference instances is called a set of *incompatible instances*. If a communication free partition can be determined for a set of *variables* considering all their instances, it is called as a set of *compatible variables*; otherwise it is called as a set of *incompatible variables*. In this paper, we focus on minimizing the communication when we have a set of *incompatible instances* of a variable so that a communication free partition can not be found. Minimizing communication for multiple *incompatible variables* is even more hard and is not attempted here.

3.1 Example

Consider the following code:

```
for i := 1 to N
  for j := 1 to N
    a[i,j] := (b[i,j] + b[i-1,j-1]+ b[i-1,j]
              + b[i-1,j+1] + b[i,j-1]
              + b[i,j+1] + b[i+1,j-1]
              + b[i+1,j] + b[i+1,j+1])/9
  endfor
endfor
```

For this code, it is not possible to determine a communication free iteration and data partitioning direction. Let $b_1 \equiv b[i,j]$, $b_2 \equiv b[i-1,j-1]$, $b_3 \equiv b[i-1,j]$, $b_4 \equiv b[i-1,j+1]$, $b_5 \equiv b[i,j-1]$, $b_6 \equiv b[i,j+1]$, $b_7 \equiv b[i+1,j-1]$, $b_8 \equiv b[i+1,j]$, $b_9 \equiv b[i+1,j+1]$. Thus, the instance set for the variable b is given by $\{b_1, b_2, ..., b_9\}$ for the nine occurrences of b. All these reference instances are, therefore, *incompatible*.

4. Problem

We begin by stating the problem of communication minimization for *incompatible instances* of a variable as follows:

Given an *instance set* of a variable B, denoted by $S_B = \{B_1, B_2, B_3, ..., B_m\}$ which may comprise of *incompatible instances* occurring within a loop nest as described before, determine a set of communication minimizing directions so that the volume of communication reduced is at least equal to or more than the parallelism reduced. We measure the volume of communication by the number of non-local references (the references which which fall outside the underlying data partition) corresponding to an iteration block. In our formulation of the problem, no data replication is allowed. There is only one copy of the each array element kept at one of the processors and whenever any other processor references it, there is a communication : one send at the owner processor and one receive at the one which needs it. The justification for reducing the above volume of communication is that the data communication latency in most distributed memory systems consists of a fixed start-up overhead to initiate communication and a variable part proportional to the length of (or to the number of data items) the message. Thus, reducing the number of non-local data values, reduces this second part of communication latency. Of course, one may perform message vectorization following our partitioning phase to group the values together to be sent in a single message to amortize on start-up costs. Such techniques are presented elsewhere [19] and do not form a part of this paper.

We measure the amount of parallelism reduced by the number of additional iterations being introduced in an iteration block to eliminate the communication.

4.1 Compatibility Subsets

We begin by outlining a solution which may attain the above objective. We first partition the *instance set* of a variable, S_B, into ρ subsets $S_B^1, S_B^2, ..., S_B^\rho$ which satisfy the relation:

− All the reference instances of the variable belonging to a given subset are compatible so that one can determine a direction for communication free partitioning. Formally, $\forall B_i \in S_B^j, \exists (d_1^j, d_2^j, ..., d_r^j)$ such that partitioning along direction vector $(d_1^j, d_2^j, ..., d_r^j)$ achieves communication free partition, where, $1 \leq j \leq \rho$.

− At least one reference instance belonging to a given subset is incompatible with all the reference instances belonging to any other subset. Formally, $\exists B_l \in S_B^k$ so that it is incompatible with all $B_i \in S_B^j$, where, $j \neq k$, $1 \leq j, k \leq \rho$. In other words, one can not find a communication free partition for $S_B^j \cup \{B_l\}$, for some $B_l \in S_B^k$.

It is easy to see that the above relation is a *compatibility* relation. It is well known that the *compatibility* relation only defines a *covering* of the set and does not define mutually disjoint partitions. We, therefore, first determine ρ *maximal compatibility subsets* : $S_B^1, S_B^2, ..., S_B^\rho$ from the above relation. For each of the maximal compatibility subsets, there exists a direction for communication free partitioning. The algorithm to compute *maximal compatibility subsets* is described in the next section. Following Lemma summarizes the maximum and minimum number of *maximal compatibility subsets* that can result from the above relation.

Lemma 1 : If $m \equiv |S_B|$ and if ρ *maximal compatibility subsets* result from the above relation on S_B, then $2 \leq \rho \leq C_2^m$.

Proof:

It is clear that there must exist at least one $B_i \in S_B$, such that it is not compatible with $S_B - \{B_i\}$. If this is not the case, then communication free partition should exist for all the instances belonging to S_B, which is not true. Thus, minimum two compatibility subsets must exist for S_B. This proves the lower bound.

We now show that any two reference instances, $B_i, B_j \in S_B$ are always compatible. Let $(\sigma_1^i, \sigma_2^i, ..., \sigma_r^i)$ and $(\sigma_1^j, \sigma_2^j, ..., \sigma_r^j)$ be the two offsets corresponding to instances B_i and B_j respectively. Thus, if we partition along the direction $(\sigma_1^i - \sigma_1^j, \sigma_2^i - \sigma_2^j, ..., \sigma_r^i - \sigma_r^j)$ in the iteration and data space of B, we will achieve the communication free partitioning as far as the instances B_i and B_j are concerned. Thus, for any two instances, communication free partitioning is always possible proving that they are compatible. The number of subsets which have two elements of S_B are given by C_2^m, proving the upper bound on ρ.

q.e.d

The bounds derived in the above lemma allow us to prove the overall complexity of our *Communication Minimizing Algorithms* discussed later.

The next step is to determine a set of cyclically alternating directions from the compatibility subsets found above to maximally cover the communication.

4.2 Cyclic Directions

Let the instance set S_B for a variable B be partitioned into $S_B^1, S_B^2, ..., S_B^\rho$ which are maximal compatibility subsets under the relation of communication free partitioning. Let Comp(B) be the set of communication free partitioning directions corresponding to these compatibility subsets. Thus, Comp(B) = $\{D^1, D^2, ..., D^\rho\}$, where, $D^j = (d_1^j, d_2^j, ..., d_r^j)$ is the direction of communication free partitioning for the subset S_B^j. The problem now is to determine a subset of Comp(B) which maximally covers[1] the directions in Comp(B) as explained below. Let such a subset of Comp(B) be denoted by Cyclic(B). Let, Cyclic(B) = $\{D^{\pi^{-1}(1)}, D^{\pi^{-1}(2)}, ..., D^{\pi^{-1}(t)}\}$, where, $D^{\pi^{-1}(i)} = D^j$ or $i \equiv \pi(j)$ defines a permutation which maps jth element of Comp(B) at ith position in Cyclic(B). We now state the property which allows us determining such a maximal, ordered subset Cyclic(B) of Comp(B):

Property 1 : The subset Cyclic(B) must satisfy all of the following:

1. $D^{\pi^{-1}(j)} = D^{\pi^{-1}(j-1)} + D^{\pi^{-1}(j-2)}$, where, $3 \le j \le t$. Each of the directions $D^{\pi^{-1}(j)}$ direction is then said to be covered by directions $D^{\pi^{-1}(j-1)}$ and $D^{\pi^{-1}(j-2)}$. Thus, each of the elements of the ordered set Cyclic(B) must be covered by the previous two elements, the exception being the first two elements of Cyclic(B).

2. Consider Comp(B) - Cyclic(B), and let some D^k belong to this set. If $D^k = c_1 * D^{\pi^{-1}(t)} + \sum_{i=1}^{j} D^{\pi^{-1}(i)}$, where, $1 \le j \le (t-1)$, $c_1 \in I^+$ (in other words, if the direction D^k can be expressed as a linear combination of multiple of $D^{\pi^{-1}(t)}$ and a summation of a subset of ordered directions as above) then it is covered and there is no communication along it. Let Uncov(B) be the subset of Comp(B) - Cyclic(B) such that $\forall D^k \in Uncov(B)$, $D^k \ne c_1 * D^{\pi^{-1}(t)} + \sum_{i=1}^{j} D^{\pi^{-1}(i)}$, i.e., none of its elements is covered and let $s \equiv |Uncov(B)|$.

3. Cyclic(B) is that subset of Comp(B) which satisfying the properties stated in 1 and 2 as above leads to minimum s.

Stated more simply, Cyclic(B) is an ordered subset of Comp(B) which leaves minimum number of uncovered direction in Comp(B). If we determine Cyclic(B) and follow the corresponding communication free directions cyclically from $D^{\pi^{-1}(1)}$ to $D^{\pi^{-1}(t-1)}$ (such as $D^{\pi^{-1}(1)}$, $D^{\pi^{-1}(2)}$,...,$D^{\pi^{-1}(t-1)}$, $D^{\pi^{-1}(1)}$, $D^{\pi^{-1}(2)}$,..), communication is reduced by a larger degree than loss of parallelism which is beneficial. The following Lemma formally states the result:

Lemma 2: If we follow iteration partitioning cyclically along the directions corresponding to Cyclic(B) as above, for each basic iteration block (basic iteration block is achieved by starting at a point in iteration space and by traversing once along the directions corresponding to Cyclic(B) from there), parallelism is reduced by (t-1) (due to sequentialization of (t-1) iterations) and the communication is reduced by $(\rho+t)-(s+3)$, where $\rho \equiv |Comp(B)|$, $t \equiv |Cyclic(B)|$ and $s \equiv |Uncov(B)|$.

Proof:

It is easy to see that if $t \equiv |Cyclic(B)|$, we traverse once along the corresponding directions and thus, introduce (t-1) extra iterations in a basic

---

[1] A given direction is said to be covered by a set of directions, iff partitioning along the directions in the set eliminates the need for communication along the given direction

iteration block reducing the parallelism appropriately. So, we prove the result for communication reduction.

It is obvious that if we traverse the iteration space along (t-1) directions corresponding to the ordered set Cyclic(B), the communication is reduced by (t-1). In addition to this, since the Property 1, condition 1 is satisfied by these directions, additional (t-2) directions are covered eliminating the corresponding communication. In addition to this, the partitioning is also capable to covering all the directions : $c_1 * D^{\pi^{-1}(t)} + \sum_{i=1}^{j} D^{\pi^{-1}(i)}$, where, $1 \le j \le (t-1)$, $c_1 \in I^+$, Property 1 Condition 2. These directions are the ones which correspond to $Comp(B) - Cyclic(B) - Uncov(B)$. Thus, the number of such directions is (ρ - t - s). Thus, the total number of directions covered = (t-1)+(t-2)+(ρ - t - s) = (ρ+t) - (s+3). Thus, in one basic iteration partition, one is able to eliminate the communication equal to ((ρ + t) - (s + 3)) by reducing parallelism by an amount (t-1).

q.e.d

Corollary 1 : According to the above lemma, we must find at least one pair of directions which covers at least one other direction in Comp(B) to reduce more communication than parallelism.

Proof:

The above Lemma clearly demonstrates that, in order to reduce more communication than parallelism, we must have $(\rho+t) - (s+3) > (t-1)$, or, $(\rho-s) > 2$. Now, Comp(B) = Cyclic(B) + Cov(B) + Uncov(B), where Cov(B) is the set of directions covered as per condition 2 in Property 1. In other words, $\rho = t + q + s$, where $|Cov(B)| \equiv q$. Thus, $(\rho - s) \ge 3 \Rightarrow (t + q) \ge 3$. At its lowest value, (t+q) = 3. Consider following cases for (t+q) = 3:

1. t = 0, q = 3 : This is impossible since if Cyclic(B) is empty, it can not cover any directions in Comp(B).
2. t = 1, q = 2: This is also impossible since one direction in Cyclic(B) can not cover two in Comp(B).
3. t = 2, q = 1: This is possible since two directions in Cyclic(B) can cover a direction in Comp(B) through Property 1, condition 2.
4. t = 3, q = 0: This is also possible, since Cyclic(B) would then have three elements related by Property 1, condition 1.

It can be seen that only cases (3) and (4) above are possible and each one would imply that a direction in Comp(B) is covered by Cyclic(B) either through condition 1 or through condition 2 of Property 1. Thus, the result.

q.e.d

Thus, in order to maximally reduce communication, we must find Cyclic(B) from Comp(B) so that it satisfies Property 1. As one can see, the directions in Cyclic(B) form a Fibonacci Sequence as per Property 1 maximally covering the remaining directions in Comp(B). Our problem is, thus, to find a maximal Fibonacci Sequence using a minimal subset of Comp(B). The algorithm to determine such a subset is discussed in the next section.

5. Communication Minimization

In this section, we discuss the two algorithms based on the theory developed in last section. The first algorithm determines the *maximal compatibility subsets* of the instance set of a given variable and the second one determines a maximal Fibonacci Sequence as discussed in the last section. We also analyze the complexity of these algorithms. For illustration of the working of this algorithm, please refer to the example presented in section 7.

5.1 Algorithm : Maximal Compatibility Subsets

This algorithm finds the *maximal compatibility subsets*, Comp(B) of a variable B, given the instance set S_B as an input.

As one can see that the *compatibility* relation of communication free partitioning for a set of a references (defined before) is reflexive and symmetric but not necessarily transitive. If a and b are *compatible*, we denote this relation as $a \approx b$.

1. Initialize Comp(B) := ϕ, k := 1.
2. for every reference instance $B_i \in S_B$ do
   a) Find $B_j \in S_B$ such that $B_i \approx B_j$ but both $B_i, B_j \notin S_B^p$, for $1 \leq p < k$. In other words, find a pair of references such that it has not been put into some compatibility subset already constructed so far (where k-1 is the number of compatibility subsets constructed so far). Whether or not $B_i \approx B_j$ can be determined by algorithms described in [1, 6, 14, 22].
   b) Initialize $S_B^k := \{B_i, B_j\}$ (put the pair satisfying above property into a new subset S_B^k being constructed).
   c) For every $B_l \in (S_B - S_B^k)$, do
      - if $\forall B_m \in S_B^k, B_l \approx B_m, S_B^k := S_B^k \cup \{B_l\}$.
      - Add the constructed subset S_B^k to Comp(B), $Comp(B) := Comp(B) \cup S_B^k$, k := k+1.
   d) Repeat steps (a) through (c) above till no B_j can be found satisfying condition in (a).
3. After all the subsets are constructed, replace each of them by the corresponding communication free partitioning directions. That is, for Comp(B) constructed above, replace each S_B^i by D^i, where, D^i is the corresponding communication free direction for S_B^i.

As one can see that the above algorithm checks for compatibility relation from an element of S_B to all the other elements of S_B and therefore, its worst case complexity $O(|S_B|^2)$.

5.2 Algorithm : Maximal Fibonacci Sequence

Following algorithm determines the set Cyclic(B) using Comp(B) as an input.

1. Sort the set Comp(B). If $\{D^1, D^2, ..., D^\rho\}$ is the sorted set, it must satisfy the following order:
   - $D_1^i < D_1^{i+1}$, or
   - if $D_j^i := D_j^{i+1}$ for all j such that $1 \leq j \leq k$ and $D_{k+1}^i < D_{k+1}^{i+1}$ for some k, such that $1 \leq k \leq r - 1$.

   The elements $D^1, D^2, ..., D^\rho$ are then said to be sorted in non-decreasing order < such that $D^1 < D^2 < D^3....$
2. Initialize set MaxFib $:= \phi$, max $:= 0$.
3. for i :=1 to n
   for j := i+1 to n
   a) Let $D := D^i + D^j$. Initialize last := j, Fib := ϕ, k := j+1.
   b) while $(D^k < D)$
      k := k+1
   c) if $(D^k = D)$, $Fib := Fib \cup D^k$, $D := D^k + D^{last}$, last := k, k:=k+1.
   d) Repeat steps (b) and (c) above till $k > n$.
   e) Let q be the number of additional directions covered in Comp(B) by Fib as per Property 1. In other words, let $D \in Comp(B) - Fib$. If $D = c_1 * D^{last} + \sum_{l=1}^{v} D^l$, where, $1 \leq v \leq |Fib|$, $c_1 \in I^+$, D is already covered by Cyclic(B). Determine q, the number of such covered directions in Comp(B) - Fib.
   f) if $max < |Fib| + q$, MaxFib := Fib, max := $|Fib| + q$.
4. Cyclic(B) := MaxFib.

As one can see, the sorting step for the above algorithm would require $O(\rho \ log \ \rho)$ and the step of finding the maximal cover would require $O(\rho^3)$. Thus, the total complexity of the algorithm is $O(\rho \ log \ \rho + \rho^3)$. From Lemma 1, since $\rho \leq |S_B|^2$, the overall complexity of the algorithm is $O(|S_B|^2 \ log |S_B| + |S_B|^6)$.

The code partitioning phase (refer to figure 2.5) uses these two algorithms to determine a set of communication minimizing directions (given by Cyclic(B)) for iteration space partitioning.

5.3 Data Partitioning

The next phase is data partitioning. The objective of the data distribution is to achieve computation+ communication load balance through data distribution. This phase attempts minimization of communication overhead for larger compute intensive partitions by localizing their references as much as possible. In order to determine the data partition, we apply the following simple algorithm which uses a new *larger partition owns* rule:

– Sort the partitions in the decreasing order of their sizes in terms of the number of iterations. Visit the partitions in the sorted order (largest to smallest) as above. For each partition do:
– Find out all the data references generated in a given partition and allocate that data to the respective processor. If the generated reference is already owned by a larger partition generated previously, add it to the set of non-local references.

6. Partition Merging

The next step in compilation of the DOALL loops is to schedule the partitions generated above on available number of processors. For scheduling the partitions generated by the iteration partitioning phase on available number of processors, first a Partition Interaction Graph is constructed and granularity adjustment and load balancing are carried out. Then the partitions are scheduled (mapped) on a given number of available processors.

Each node of the partition interaction graph denotes one loop partition and the weight of the node is equal to the number of iterations in that loop partition. There is a directed edge from one node to another which represents the direction of data communication. The weight of the edge is equal to the number of data values being communicated. Let $G(V, E)$ denote such a graph where V is the set of nodes and E is the set of edges as described above. Let $t(v_i)$ denote the weight of node $t_i \in V$ and $c(v_j, v_i)$ denote the weight of edge $(v_j, v_i) \in E$.

The following is supposed to be the order of execution of each partition:

– Send : The partition first sends the data needed by other partitions.
– Receive : After sending the data, the partition receives the data it needs sent by other partitions.
– Compute : After receiving the data in the above step, the partition executes the assigned loop iterations.

The total time required for the execution of each partition is, thus, equal to Send time + Receive time + Compute time. The Send time is proportional to the total number of data values sent out (total weight) on all outgoing edges and the receive time is proportional to the total number of data values received (total weight) on all incoming edges. The compute time is proportional to the number of iterations (node weight).

Depending on the relative offsets of the reference instances between different partitions and the underlying data distribution, the data values needed by a given partition may be owned by one or more partitions. This communication dependency is denoted by the graph edges and the graph may contain a different number of edges depending on such dependency. The length of the longest path between v_i and v_j is defined as the communication distance between v_i and v_j where $(v_i, v_j) \in E$. For example, in figure 6.1, the communication distance for the edge (v_k, v_i) is equal to two due to the fact that $(v_k, v_i) \in E$ and the longest path from v_k to v_i is of length two.

It can be shown that due to the properties of partitioning method described in the last section (proof omitted due to lack of space), the following relationships hold good (refer to figure 6.1):

- The weight of a given node is less than or equal to any of its predecessors. In other words, $t(v_i) \leq t(v_j)$ where $(v_j, v_i) \in E$.
- The weight of an edge incident on a given node is more than or equal to the weight of an outgoing edge from that node for the same communication distance. In other words, $c(v_k, v_j) \geq c(v_j, v_i)$ where both the edges represent the same communication distance. This relationship does not apply to two edges representing two different communication distances.

We now describe three scheduling phases as outlined before. All of these heuristics traverse the partition interaction graph in reverse topological order by following simple breadth first rule as follows:

- Visit the leaf nodes of the graph.
- Visit the predecessor of a given node such that all of its successors are already visited.
- Follow this procedure to visit backwards from leaf nodes till all the nodes including root node are visited.

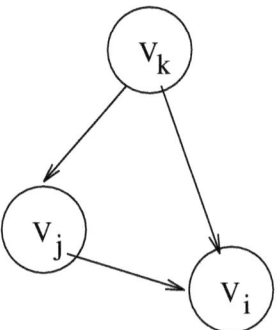

Fig. 6.1. Portion of Partition Interaction Graph

The complexity of each of these phases is $O(|V|)$ where V is the number of nodes in the graph.

6.1 Granularity Adjustment

Refer to figure 6.1.

- Calculate the completion time of each node v_j given by $tcom(v_j) = k_1 * \sum_{(v_j,v_i) \in E} c(v_j, v_i) + k_2 * \sum_{(v_k,v_j) \in E} c(v_k, v_j) + t(v_j)$, where the cost of one iteration is assumed to be 1 and the cost of one send is assumed to be k_1 and that of one receive to be k_2.
- Visit the nodes of the graph in the reverse topological order described as above. Suppose we choose a predecessor v_k of node v_j for merging to adjust granularity.
- Determine the completion time of merged node v_{jk} given by $tcom(v_{jk}) = tcom(v_j) + tcom(v_k) - c(v_j, v_k) * (k_1 + k_2)$.
- Compare it with each of $tcom(v_j)$ and $tcom(v_k)$ and if $tcom(v_{jk})$ is lesser than both, merge v_j and v_k.
- Continue the process by attempting to expand the partition by considering v_{jk} and a predecessor of v_k next and so on.
- If $tcom(v_{jk})$ is greater than either of $tcom(v_j)$ or $tcom(v_k)$, reject the merger of v_j and v_k. Next, attempt merger of v_k and one of predecessors and so on.
- Repeat all the steps again on the new graph resulting from the above procedure and iterate the procedure until no new partitions are merged together (condition of graph invariance).

6.2 Load Balancing

Refer to figure 6.1.

- Let T be the overall loop completion time generated by the above phase.
- Visit the nodes of the graph in the reverse topological order described as above. Suppose we choose a predecessor v_k of node v_j to merge the partitions.
- Determine the completion time of merged node $v_{jk} = tcom(v_j) + tcom(v_k) - c(v_j, v_k) * (k_1 + k_2)$. Obviously, $tcom(v_{jk})$ will be higher than that of either of $tcom(v_k)$ or $tcom(v_j)$ since if it were not the case, the two partitions would have been merged by the granularity adjustment algorithm.
- Compare $tcom(v_{jk})$ with T and if $tcom(v_{jk})$ is lesser than T, merge v_j and v_k.
- Continue the process by attempting to expand the partition by considering v_{jk} and predecessor of v_k next and so on.
- If v_{jk} is greater than T, reject the merger of v_j and v_k. Next, attempt merger of v_k and one of its predecessor and so on.
- Keep repeating this process and if at any stage the completion time of the merged node is worse than the overall completion time T, reject it and attempt a new one by considering predecessor and its predecessor and so on.

6.3 Mapping

Refer to figure 6.1.

- Let there be P available processors on which the partitions resulting from previous phase are to be mapped, where # partitions > P.
- Traverse the graph in the reverse topological order as described earlier. Suppose we choose a predecessor v_k or a node v_j for a possible merge to reduce the number of processors.
- Determine the completion time of merged node v_{jk}: $tcom(v_{jk}) = tcom(v_j) + tcom(v_k) - c(v_j, v_k) * (k_1 + k_2)$. Obviously, $tcom(v_{jk})$ will be higher than the loop completion time T. Store the $tcom(v_{jk})$ in a table.
- Attempt the merger of another node and its predecessor and store it in a table. Repeat this process for all the nodes and choose the pair which results in minimum completion time when merged and combine them. This reduces the number of partitions by 1.
- Continue the above process till the number of partitions is reduced to P.

7. Example : Texture Smoothing Code

In this section, we illustrate the significance of the above phases using a template image processing code. This code exhibits a very high amount of spatial parallelism suitable for parallelization on distributed memory systems. On the other hand, this code also exhibits a high amount of communication in all possible directions in the iteration space. Thus, this code is a good example of the tradeoff between the parallelism and the communication.

An important step in many image processing applications is *texture smoothing* which involves finding the average luminosity at a given point in a image from its immediate and successive neighbors.

Consider the following code:

```
for i := 1 to N
  for j := 1 to N
    a[i,j] := (b[i,j] + b[i-1,j-1]+ b[i-1,j] + b[i-1,j+1]
             + b[i,j-1] + b[i,j+1]
             + b[i+1,j-1] + b[i+1,j] + b[i+1,j+1])/9
  endfor
endfor
```

The above code finds the average value of luminosity at a grid point (i,j) using its eight neighbors. In this code, every grid point is a potential candidate for parallelization; thus, the code exhibits a very high amount of parallelism. On the other hand, if we decide to parallelize every grid point, there would be a tremendous amount of communication in all possible directions. Thus, we apply our method to this application to demonstrate that we can achieve a partition which maximally reduces communication by minimally reducing the parallelism.

Let $b_1 \equiv b[i,j]$, $b_2 \equiv b[i-1,j-1]$, $b_3 \equiv b[i-1,j]$, $b_4 \equiv b[i-1,j+1]$, $b_5 \equiv b[i,j-1]$, $b_6 \equiv b[i,j+1]$, $b_7 \equiv b[i+1,j-1]$, $b_8 \equiv b[i+1,j]$, $b_9 \equiv b[i+1,j+1]$. Thus, the instance set for the variable b is given by $\{b_1, b_2, ..., b_9\}$ for the nine occurrences of b. Obviously, no *communication free* partition is possible for the above set of references. The first step, therefore, is to determine maximal compatibility subsets of the instance set.

In order to determine the maximal compatibility subsets, we follow the algorithm described in section 5.1. We begin by considering the compatibility subset involving b_1. We try to group b_1 with b_2 to create a subset $\{b_1, b_2\}$. The direction for communication free partitioning for this subset is (1,1), and thus, we can not add any other reference of b to this subset except b_9 since adding any other reference would violate the condition for communication free partitioning. Thus, one of our maximal compatibility subsets is $\{b_1, b_2, b_9\}$. Next, we group b_1 with b_3 and add b_8 to it to give $\{b_1, b_3, b_8\}$ as another compatibility subset with (1,0) as direction of communication free partitioning. Similarly, we try to group b_1 with other elements so that b_1 and that element are not together in any subset formed so far. Thus, the other subsets resulting from b_1 are $\{b_1, b_4, b_7\}$ and $\{b_1, b_5, b_6\}$ with (1,-1) and (0,1) as the directions for communication free partitioning. Next, we follow the algorithm for b_2. We already have $\{b_1, b_2\}$ in one of the subsets constructed so far; thus, we start with $\{b_2, b_3\}$. The direction for communication free partitioning is (0,1) in this case and we can include only b_4 in this subset. Thus, we get $\{b_2, b_3, b_4\}$ as another maximal compatibility set.

By following the algorithm as illustrated above, the following are the maximal compatibility subsets found (directions for communication free partitions are shown next to each of them):

- b_1 : $\{b_1, b_2, b_9\}$ (1,1), $\{b_1, b_3, b_8\}$ (1,0), $\{b_1, b_4, b_7\}$ (1,-1), $\{b_1, b_5, b_6\}$ (0,1).
- b_2 : $\{b_2, b_3, b_4\}$ (0,1), $\{b_2, b_5, b_7\}$ (1,0), $\{b_2, b_6\}$ (1,2), $\{b_2, b_8\}$ (2,1).
- b_3 : $\{b_3, b_5\}$ (1,-1), $\{b_3, b_6\}$ (1,1), $\{b_3, b_7\}$(2,-1), $\{b_3, b_9\}$ (2,1).
- b_4 : $\{b_4, b_5\}$ (1,-2), $\{b_4, b_6, b_9\}$(1,0), $\{b_4, b_8\}$ (2,-1).
- b_5 : $\{b_5, b_8\}$(1,1), $\{b_5, b_9\}$ (1,2).
- b_6 : $\{b_6, b_7\}$(1,-2), $\{b_6, b_8\}$ (1,-1).
- b_7 : $\{b_7, b_8, b_9\}$ (0,1).

Next step is to determine the set Comp(b) which is a collection of communication free directions corresponding to each one of the maximal compatibility subsets. Thus, Comp(b) = {(0,1), (1,-2), (1,-1), (1,0), (1,1), (1,2), (2,-1), (2,1)}. The next step is to determine Cyclic(b) to maximally cover the directions in Comp(b). We, thus, apply the algorithm in section 5.2. We begin by considering (0,1) and (1,-2) which add up to (1,-1). Thus, we include (1,-1) in the set Fib being constructed. If we try adding (1,-2) and (1,-1), it gives (2,-3) which is not a member of Comp(b). Thus, we stop and at this

Table 7.1. Fibonacci Sets Constructed by Algorithm in Section 5.2

Fibonacci Set (Fib)	Directions Covered	Parallelism Reduced	Communication Reduced
$\{(0,1),(1,-2),(1,-1)\}$	(1,0),(2,-1)	2	5
$\{(0,1),(1,-1),(1,0),(2,-1)\}$	-	3	4
$\{(0,1),(1,0),(1,1),(2,1)\}$	-	3	4
$\{(0,1),(1,1),(1,2)\}$	-	2	3
$\{(1,-2),(1,1),(2,-1)\}$	-	2	3
$\{(1,-1),(1,0),(2,-1)\}$	-	2	3
$\{(1,-1),(1,2),(2,1)\}$	-	2	3
$\{(1,0),(1,1),(2,1)\}$	-	2	3

point, Fib $= \{(0,1),(1,-2),(1,-1)\}$. The next step in the algorithm is to determine the other directions in Comp(b) which are covered by this iteration partition. Following the step 3.e of the algorithm, if we add (1,-1) and (0,1) it gives (1,0) and if we add 2*(1,-1) and (0,1) it gives (2,-1); thus, a linear combination of (1,-1) and (0,1) covers two other direction in Comp(b). In this case, we are able to eliminate communication equal to 5 by sequentializing 2 iterations.

Next, we try to construct another set Fib by starting with (0,1) and (1,-1) and following the procedure of adding them and checking if it covers any direction in Comp(b). If it does, then we add it to Fib and continue further by forming the Fibonacci series using two most recently added elements in the set. Finally, we find out the covered directions from the remainder of Comp(b), if any using the step 3.e of the algorithm. Table 2 shows the different Fib sets constructed by the algorithm , the covered directions if any and the parallelism lost and communication saved. From the table, one can see that the algorithm would compute Cyclic(b) $= \{(0,1),(1,-2),(1,-1)\}$ since it results in maximally reducing the communication. Thus, by cyclically following (0,1)/(1,-2) directions, one could reduce communication by 5 losing parallelism by 2 per basic iteration block. This demonstrates that it is possible to profitably parallelize these type of applications by using our method.

Once Cyclic(b) is determined, the next step is to generate the iteration and the data partition for the loop nest. We apply the algorithm of section 5.3. We first determine (1,7) as the base point and then apply (0,1)/(1,-2) as directions cyclically to complete the partition. We then move along dimension 2 (for this example, dimension involving 'i' is considered as dimension 1 and dimension involving 'j' as dimension 2) and carry out the partitioning in a similar manner. We get the iteration partitioning shown in Figure 7.1. The data partition is found by traversing the iteration partitions in the order : 0, 4, 1, 5, 2, 6, 3 and 7 using *largest partition owns* rule.

Finally, the partition interaction graph of the partitions is generated as shown in figure 7.2. For this graph, only the communication distances 1 and 2 exist between the different partitions (please see the definition of communication distances in the preceding section). The total number of iterations in each partition (the computation cost) and the number of data values exchanged between two partitions (the communication cost) are shown against each node and each edge in figure 7.2. Depending on the relative costs of computation and communication, the granularity adjustment, load balancing and mapping phases will merge the partitions generated above. The results of these phases for Cray T3D for problem size N=16 are discussed in section 8.

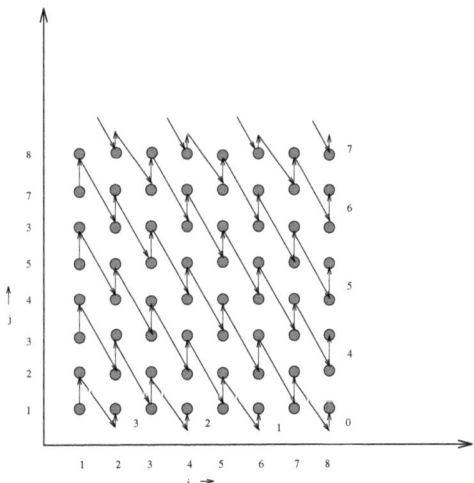

Fig. 7.1. Iteration partition for texture smoothing code

8. Performance on Cray T3D

The following example codes are used to test the method on a Cray T3D system with 32 processors:

```
Example I:
---------
for i = 2 to N
  for j = 2 to N
    for k = 1 to Upper
      A[i,j,k] = B[i-2,j-1,k]+B[i-1,j-1,k]+B[i-1,j-2,k]
    endfor
  endfor
endfor
```

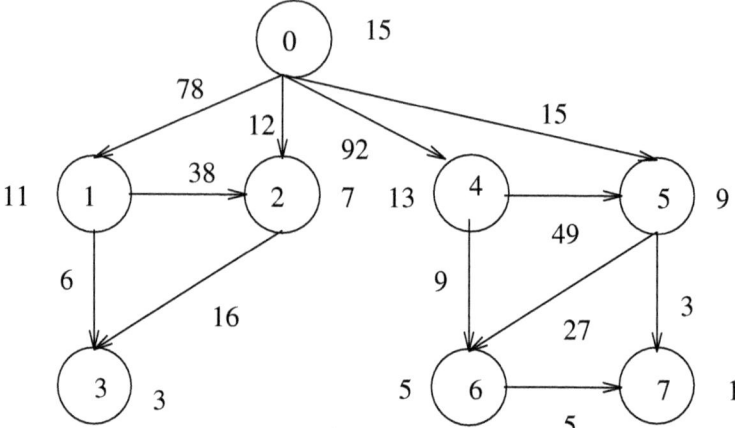

Fig. 7.2. Partition Interaction Graph of Iteration Partitions

```
Example II:
----------
for i := 1 to N
  for j := 1 to N
    for k := 1 to Upper
    a[i,j,k] := (b[i,j,k] + b[i-1,j-1,k]+ b[i-1,j,k]
              + b[i-1,j+1,k] + b[i,j-1,k] + b[i,j+1,k]
              + b[i+1,j-1,k] + b[i+1,j,k] + b[i+1,j+1,k])/9
    endfor
  endfor
endfor
```

In the above examples, there is an inner loop in k dimension. The number
of iterations in this loop, Upper, are chosen as 10 million in case of Example
I and 1 million in case of Example II to make computation in loop body
comparable to communication. As one can see, there is no problem in terms
of communication free partitioning in k dimension. However, in i and j dimensions, due to reference patterns, no communication free partition exists
and thus, the outer two loops (in i and j dimension) and the underlying data
are distributed by applying the techniques described in sections 5 and 6. For
Example I, the cyclical direction of partitioning are (0,1,0)/(-1,0,0) and for
Example II, the cyclical directions are (0,1,0)/(1,-2,0) as explained earlier.
The number partitions found by the method for each of these examples is
equal to N , the size of the problem. Thus, the size of the problem N is
appropriately chosen to match the number of processors.

The method is partially[2] implemented in the backend of Sisal (Streams
and Iterations in a Single Assignment Language) compiler, OSC [7, 32] tar-

---

[2] Some phases of the method are not fully automated yet

geted for Cray T3D system. The method is tested for N=4 (4 processors), N=8 (8 processors), N=16 (16 processors) and N=32 (32 processors). The timings are obtained using clock() system call on Cray T3D which allows measuring timings in micro-seconds. PVM was used as underlying mode of communication. The sequential (as shown above) and the parallel versions are implemented and speedup is calculated as the ratio of time required for each.

Table 8.1. Example I : Performance on Cray T3D

Problem Size	Processors	Direction	Sequential Time (sec)	Parallel Time (sec)	Speedup
4x4	4	Cyclic	15.8	7.6	2.08
4x4	4	(0,1)	15.8	15.1	1.05
4x4	4	(-1,0)	15.8	15.52	1.02
8x8	8	Cyclic	52.73	16.3	3.23
8x8	8	(0,1)	52.73	29.07	1.81
8x8	8	(-1,0)	52.73	30.09	1.75
16x16	16	Cyclic	213.9	33.66	6.35
16x16	16	(0,1)	213.9	61.5	3.47
16x16	16	(-1,0)	213.9	63.3	3.38
32x32	32	Cyclic	919.7	68.42	13.44
32x32	32	(0,1)	919.7	113.44	8.1
32x32	32	(-1,0)	919.7	117.6	7.82

Table 8.2. Example II : Performance on Cray T3D

Problem Size	Processors	Sequential Time (sec)	Parallel Time (sec)	Speedup
4x4	4	9.7	2.57	3.77
8x8	8	35.1	9.78	3.59
16x16	16	130.92	19.12	6.8
32x32	32	543.3	43.24	12.56

Refer to Table 3 and 4 for the results for each example. It can be clearly seen that it is possible to effectively parallelize both of these examples which are quite demanding in terms of communication by employing our method. The speedup values are quite promising in spite of heavy inherent communication in these applications.

We also implemented Example I using (0,1) (column-wise) and (-1,0) (row-wise) as directions of partitioning using 'owner computes' rule. The speedups obtained by using these directions are also shown in Table 3. It can be clearly seen that our method outperforms these partitioning by almost a factor of 2 in terms of speedups.

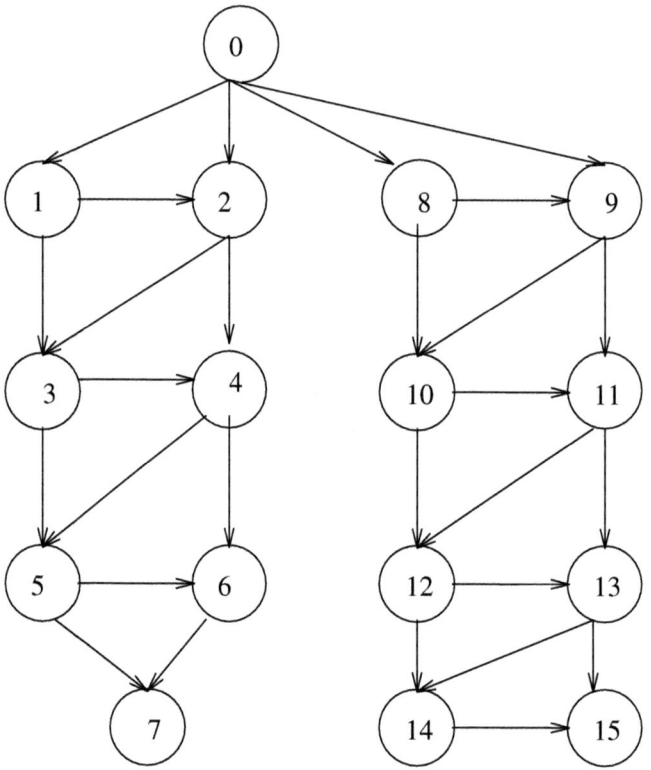

Fig. 8.1. Partition Interaction Graph for Example II (N=16)

Figure 8.1 shows the partition interaction graph of Example II for a problem size N=16. The first phase (granularity adjustment) attempts to increase the granularity of the partitions by combining them as per algorithm in section 6.1. But no partitions are combined by this phase. In order to measure the performance after this stage, the partitions are mapped to the respective processors. The processor completion times are shown in figure 8.2.

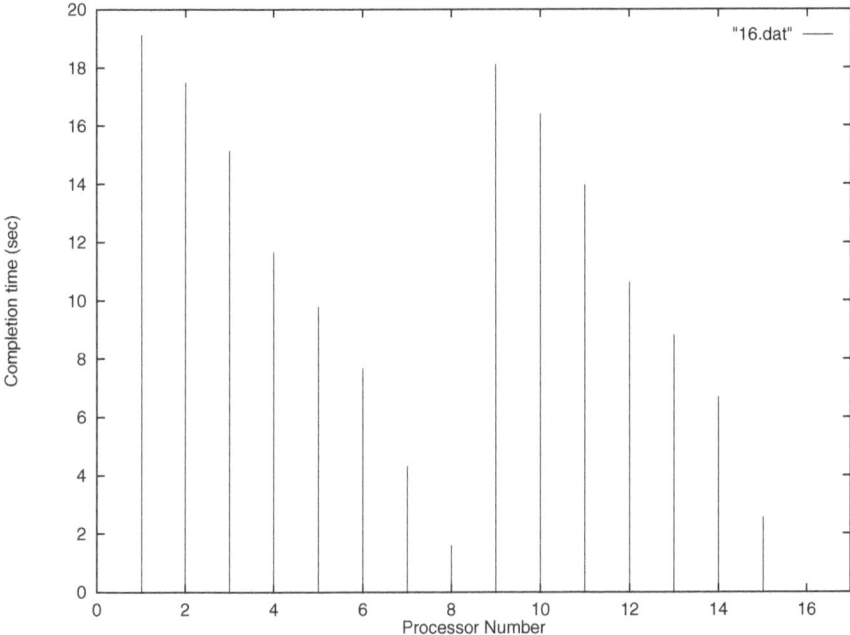

Fig. 8.2. Completion times for processors before load balancing

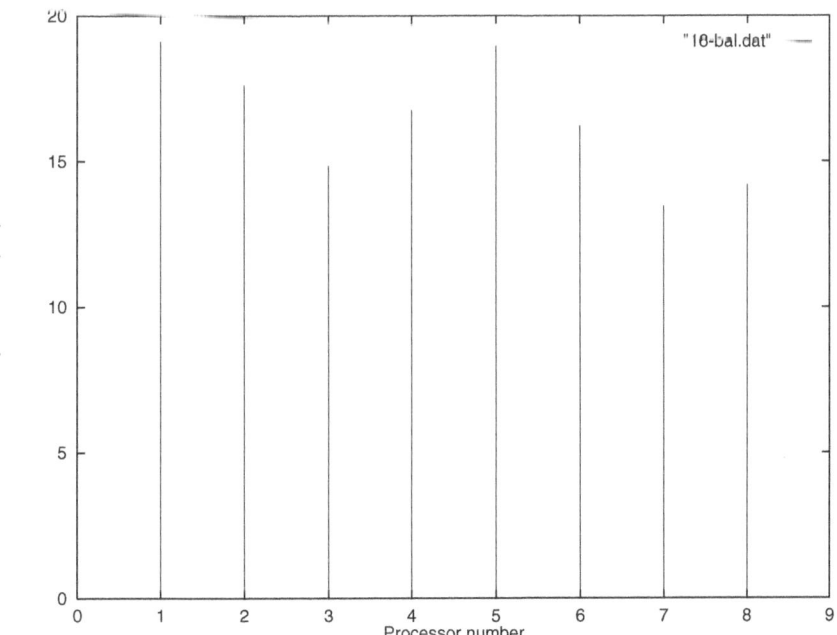

Fig. 8.3. Completion times for processors after load balancing

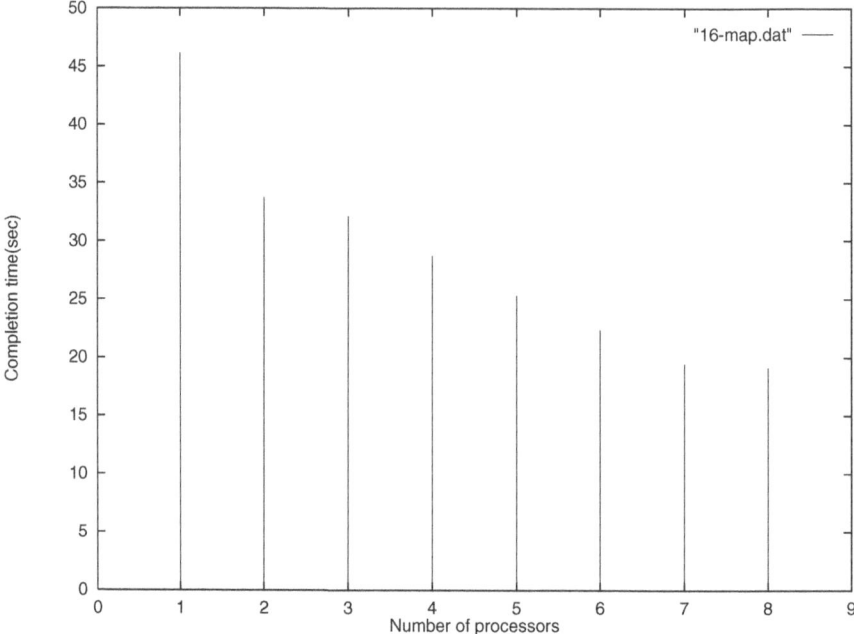

Fig. 8.4. Completion times for variable number of available processors :
P = 1 to P = 8

Next, the load balancing phase attempts to reduce the number of required
processors without increasing the completion time. The number of partitions
reduced in this phase from 16 to 8. figure 8.3 gives the completion times of
the respective processors. One can see that these processors are quite well
load balanced. Finally, the mapping phase attempts to map these 8 partitions
onto 8 or fewer processors. The completion times of these mappings for #
processors = 8 through 1 are shown in figure 8.4. One can see that the method
demonstrates an excellent linear scalability.

8.1 Conclusions

In this paper, we have presented a methodology for partitioning and scheduling (mapping) the DOALL loops in a communication efficient manner with
following contributions:

- Established theoretical framework for communication efficient loop partitioning applicable to a large class of practical DOALL loops.
- Developed iteration partitioning method for these loops by determining
  cyclic directions of partitioning in each dimension.
- Developed a new *larger partition owns* rule for data distribution for com-
  putation+communication load balance.

- Developed methodologies for granularity adjustment, load balancing and mapping to significantly improve execution time and computation+communication load balance of each partition.
- Experimentally shown that these methods give good speedups for problems that involve heavy inherent communication and also exhibit good load balance and scalability.

The method can be used for effective parallelization of many practical loops encountered in important codes such as image processing, weather modeling etc. that have DOALL parallelism but which are inherently communication intensive.

References

1. D. Bau, I. Kodukula, V. Kotlyar, K. Pingali and P. Stodghill, "Solving Alignment Using Elementary Linear Algebra", *Proceedings of 7th International Workshop on Languages and Compilers for Parallel Computing*, LNCS 892, 1994, pp. 46–60.
2. J. Anderson and M. Lam, "Global Optimizations for Parallelism and Locality on Scalable Parallel Machines", *Proceedings of SIGPLAN '93 conference on Programming Language Design and Implementation*, June 1993, pp. 112–125.
3. R. Bixby, K. Kennedy and U. Kremer, "Automatic Data Layout Using 0-1 Integer Programming", *Proc. Int'l Conf. on Parallel Architectures and Compilation Techniques, North-Holland, Amsterdam*, 1994.
4. Z. Bozkus, A. Choudhary, G. Fox, T. Haupt and S. Ranka, "Compiling Fortran 90D/HPF for Distributed Memory MIMD Computers", *Journal of Parallel and Distributed Computing*, Special Issue on Data Parallel Algorithms and Programming, Vol. 21, No. 1, April 1994, pp. 15–26.
5. S. Chatterjee, J. Gilbert, R. Schreiber and S. -H. Teng, "Automatic Array Alignment in Data Parallel Programs", *20th ACM Symposium on Principles of Programming Languages*, pp. 16–28, 1993.
6. T. Chen and J. Sheu, "Communication-Free Data Allocation Techniques for Parallelizing Compilers on Multicomputers", *IEEE Transactions on Parallel and Distributed Systems*, Vol. 5, No.9, September 1994, pp. 924–938.
7. J. T. Feo, D. C. Cann and R. R. Oldehoeft, "A Report on Sisal Language Project", *Journal of Parallel and Distributed Computing*, Vol. 10, No. 4, October 1990, pp. 349-366.
8. A. Gerasoulis and T. Yang, "On Granularity and Clustering of Directed Acyclic Task Graphs", *IEEE Transactions on Parallel and Distributed Systems*, Vol. 4, Number 6, June 1993, pp. 686-701.
9. M. Girkar and C. Polychronopoulos, "Automatic Extraction of Functional Parallelism from Ordinary Programs", *IEEE Transactions on Parallel and Distributed Systems*, Vol. 3, No. 2, March 1992, pp. 166-178.
10. G. Gong, R. Gupta and R. Melhem, "Compilation Techniques for Optimizing Communication on Distributed-Memory Systems", *Proceedings of 1993 International Conference on Parallel Processing*, Vol. II, pp. 39-46.
11. M. Gupta and P. Banerjee, "Demonstration of Automatic Data Partitioning Techniques for Parallelizing Compilers on Multicomputers", *IEEE Transactions on Parallel and Distributed Systems*, Vol. 3, March 1992, pp. 179–193.

12. High Performance Fortran Forum. High Performance Fortran Language Specification, Version 1.0, Technical Report, CRPC–TR92225, Center for Research on Parallel Computation, Rice University, Houston, TX, 1992 (revised January 1993).

13. S. Hiranandani, K. Kennedy and C. -W. Tseng, "Compiling Fortran for MIMD Distributed-Memory Machines", *Communications of ACM*, August 1992, Vol. 35, No. 8, pp. 66-80.

14. C. -H. Huang and P. Sadayappan, "Communication free Hyperplane Partitioning of Nested Loops", *Journal of Parallel and Distributed Computing*, Vol. 19, No. 2, October '93, pp. 90-102.

15. S. D. Kaushik, C. -H. Huang, R. W. Johnson and P. Sadayappan, "An Approach to Communication-Efficient Data Redistribution", *Proceedings of 1994 ACM International Conference on Supercomputing*, pp. 364–373, June 1994.

16. C. Koelbel and P. Mehrotra, "Compiling Global Name-Space Parallel Loops for Distributed Execution", *IEEE Transactions on Parallel and Distributed Systems*, October 1991, Vol. 2, No. 4, pp. 440–451.

17. J. Li and M. Chen, "Compiling Communication-efficient Programs for Massively Parallel Machines", *IEEE Transactions on Parallel and Distributed Systems*, July 1991, pp. 361–376

18. A. Lim and M. Lam, "Communication-free Parallelization via Affine Transformations", *Proceedings of 7th International Workshop on Languages and Compilers for Parallel Computing*, LNCS 892, 1994, pp. 92–106.

19. D. J. Palermo, E. Su, J. Chandy and P. Banerjee, "Communication Optimizations Used in the PARADIGM Compiler", *Proceedings of the 1994 International Conference on Parallel Processing*, Vol. II (Software), pp. II-1 – II-10.

20. S. S. Pande, D. P. Agrawal, and J. Mauney, "A Scalable Scheduling Method for Functional Parallelism on Distributed Memory Multiprocessors", *IEEE Transactions on Parallel and Distributed Systems* Vol. 6, No. 4, April 1995, pp. 388–399

21. S. S. Pande, D. P. Agrawal and J. Mauney, "Compiling Functional Parallelism on Distributed Memory Systems", *IEEE Parallel and Distributed Technology*, Spring 1994, pp. 64–75.

22. J. Ramanujam and P. Sadayappan, "Compile-Time Techniques for Data Distribution in Distributed Memory Machines", *IEEE Transactions on Parallel and Distributed Systems*, Vol. 2, No. 4, October 1991, pp. 472–482.

23. S. Ramaswamy, S. Sapatnekar and P. Banerjee, "A Convex Programming Approach for Exploiting Data and Functional Parallelism on Distributed Memory Multicomputers", *Proceedings of 1994 International Conference on Parallel Processing*, Vol. II (Software), pp. 116–125.

24. A. Rogers and K. Pingali, "Process Decomposition through Locality of Reference", *Proceedings of SIGPLAN '89 conference on Programming Language Design and Implementation*, pp. 69–80.

25. J. Saltz, H. Berryman and J. Wu, "Multiprocessors and Run-time Compilation", *Concurrency: Practice & Experience*, Vol. 3, No. 4, December 1991, pp. 573-592.

26. V. Sarkar and G. R. Gao, "Optimization of Array Accesses by Collective Loop Transformations", *Proceedings of 1991 ACM International Conference on Supercomputing*, pp. 194–204, June 1991.

27. A. Sohn, M. Sato, N. Yoo and J. -L. Gaudiot, "Data and Workload Distribution in a Multi-threaded Architecture", *Journal of Parallel and Distributed Computing* **40**, February 1997, pp. 256–264.

28. A. Sohn, R. Biswas and H. Simon, "Impact of Load Balancing on Unstructured Adaptive Computations for Distributed Memory Multiprocessors", *Proc.*

of 8th IEEE Symposium on Parallel and Distributed Processing, New Orleans, Louisiana, Oct. 1996, pp. 26–33.

29. B. Sinharoy and B. Szymanski, "Data and Task Alignment in Distributed Memory Architectures", *Journal of Parallel and Distributed Computing*, 21, 1994, pp. 61–74.

30. P. Tu and D. Padua, "Automatic Array Privatization", *Proceedings of the Sixth Workshop on Language and Compilers for Parallel Computing*, August 1993.

31. A. Wakatani and M. Wolfe, "A New Approach to Array Redistribution : Strip Mining Redistribution", *Proceedings of PARLE '94*, Lecture Notes in Computer Science, 817, pp.323–335.

32. R. Wolski and J. Feo, "Program Partitioning for NUMA Multiprocessor Computer Systems", *Journal of Parallel and Distributed Computing* (special issue on Performance of Supercomputers), Vol. 19, pp. 203-218, 1993.

33. H. Xu and L. Ni, "Optimizing Data Decomposition for Data Parallel Programs", *Proceedings of International Conference on Parallel Processing*, August 1994, Vol. II, pp. 225-232.

Chapter 13. Compiler Optimization of Dynamic Data Distributions for Distributed-Memory Multicomputers

Daniel J. Palermo[1], Eugene W. Hodges IV[2], and Prithviraj Banerjee[3]

[1] Hewlett-Packard Co., Convex Division, Richardson, Texas
(palermo@rsn.hp.com)
[2] SAS Institute Inc., Cary, North Carolina
(sasehx@unx.sas.com)
[3] Northwestern Univ., Center for Parallel and Distributed Computing,
Evanston, Illinois
(banerjee@ece.nwu.edu)

Summary. For distributed-memory multicomputers, the quality of the data partitioning for a given application is crucial to obtaining high performance. This task has traditionally been the user's responsibility, but in recent years much effort has been directed to automating the selection of data partitioning schemes. Several researchers have proposed systems that are able to produce data distributions that remain in effect for the entire execution of an application. For complex programs, however, such static data distributions may be insufficient to obtain acceptable performance. The selection of distributions that dynamically change over the course of a program's execution adds another dimension to the data partitioning problem. In this chapter we present an approach for selecting dynamic data distributions as well as a technique for analyzing the resulting data redistribution in order to generate efficient code.

1. Introduction

As part of the research performed in the PARADIGM (PARAllelizing compiler for DIstributed-memory General-purpose Multicomputers) project [4], automatic data partitioning techniques have been developed to relieve the programmer of the burden of selecting good data distributions. Originally, the compiler could automatically select a static distribution of data (using a constraint-based algorithm [15]) specifying both the configuration of an abstract multi-dimensional mesh topology along with how program data should be distributed on the mesh.

For complex programs, static data distributions may be insufficient to obtain acceptable performance on distributed-memory multicomputers. By allowing the data distribution to dynamically change over the course of a program's execution this problem can be alleviated by matching the data

This research, performed at the University of Illinois, was supported in part by the National Aeronautics and Space Administration under Contract NASA NAG 1-613, in part by an Office of Naval Research Graduate Fellowship, and in part by the Advanced Research Projects Agency under contract DAA-H04-94-G-0273 administered by the Army Research office. We are also grateful to the National Center for Supercomputing Applications and the San Diego Supercomputing Center for providing access to their machines.

S. Pande, D.P. Agrawal (Eds.): Compiler Optimizations for Scalable PS, LNCS 1808, pp. 445-484, 2001.
© Springer-Verlag Berlin Heidelberg 2001

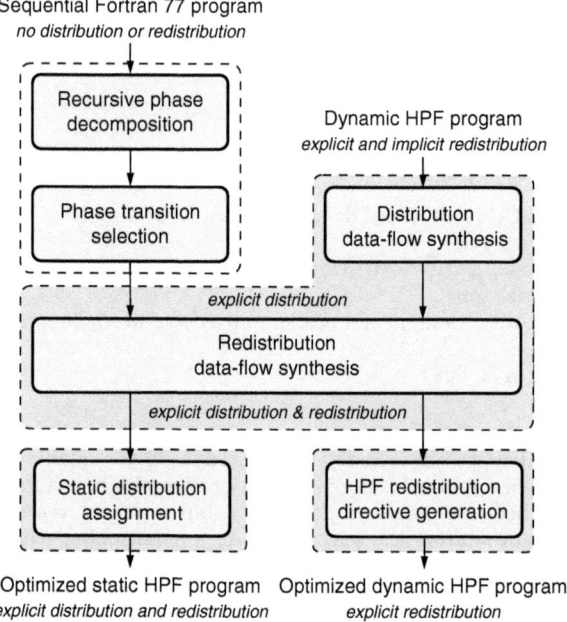

Fig. 1.1. Dynamic data partitioning framework

distribution more closely to the different computations performed through-out the program. Such dynamic partitionings can yield higher performance than a static partitioning when the redistribution is more efficient than the communication pattern required by the statically partitioned computation. We have developed an approach [31] (which extends the static partitioning algorithm) for selecting dynamic data distributions as well as a technique for analyzing the resulting data redistribution [32] in order to generate efficient code. In this chapter we present an overview of these two techniques.

The approach we have developed to automatically select dynamic distri-butions, shown in the light outlined region in Figure 1.1, consists of two main steps. The program is first recursively decomposed into a hierarchy of candi-date phases obtained using existing static distribution techniques. Then, the most efficient sequence of phases and phase transitions is selected taking into account the cost of redistributing the data between the different phases.

An overview of the array redistribution data-flow analysis framework we have developed is shown in the shaded outlined areas of Figure 1.1. In addi-tion to serving as a back end to the automatic data partitioning system, the framework is also capable of analyzing (and optimizing) existing High Per-formance Fortran [26] (HPF) programs providing a mechanism to generate fully explicit dynamic HPF programs while optimizing the amount of data redistribution performed.

The remainder of this chapter is organized as follows: related work is discussed in Section 2; our methodology for the selection of dynamic data distributions is presented in Section 3; Section 4 presents an overview of the redistribution analysis framework and the representations used in its development; the techniques for performing interprocedural array redistribution analysis are presented in Section 5; results are presented in Section 6; and conclusions are presented in Section 7.

2. Related Work

Static Partitioning. Some of the ideas used in the static partitioning algorithm originally implemented in the PARADIGM compiler [17] were inspired by earlier work on multi-dimensional array alignment [29]. In addition to this work, in recent years much research has been focused on: performing multi-dimensional array alignment [5, 8, 25, 29]; examining cases in which a communication-free partitioning exists [35]; showing how performance estimation is a key in selecting good data distributions [11, 44]; linearizing array accesses and analyzing the resulting one-dimensional accesses [39]; applying iterative techniques which minimize the amount of communication at each step [2]; and examining issues for special-purpose distributed architectures such as systolic arrays [42].

Dynamic Partitioning. In addition to the work performed in static partitioning, a number of researchers have also been examining the problem of dynamic partitioning. Hudak and Abraham have proposed a method for selecting redistribution points based on locating significant control flow changes in a program [22]. Chapman, Fahringer, and Zima describe the design of a distribution tool that makes use of performance prediction methods when possible but also uses empirical performance data through a pattern matching process [7]. Anderson and Lam [2] approach the dynamic partitioning problem using a heuristic which combines loop nests (with potentially different distributions) in such a way that the largest potential communication costs are eliminated first while still maintaining sufficient parallelism. Bixby, Kennedy and Kremer [6, 27], as well as Garcia, Ayguadé, and Labarta [13], have formulated the dynamic data partitioning problem in the form of a 0-1 integer programming problem by selecting a number of candidate distributions for each of a set of given phases and constructing constraints from the data relations. More recently, Sheffler, Schreiber, Gilbert and Pugh [38] have applied graph contraction methods to the dynamic alignment problem to reduce the size of the problem space that must be examined.

Bixby, Kremer, and Kennedy have also described an *operational definition* of a phase which defines a phase as the outermost loop of a loop nest such that the corresponding iteration variable is used in a subscript expression of an array reference in the loop body [6]. Even though this definition restricts phase boundaries to loop structures and does not allow overlapping phases, for certain programs, such as the example that will be presented in

Section 3.1, this definition is sufficient to describe the distinct phases of a computation.

Analyzing Dynamic Distributions. By allowing distributions to change during the course of a program's execution, more analysis must also be performed to determine which distributions are present at any given point in the program as well as to make sure redistribution is performed only when necessary in order to generate efficient code.

The work by Hall, Hiranandani, Kennedy, and Tseng [18] defined the term *reaching decompositions* for the Fortran D [19] decompositions which reach a function call site. Their work describes extensions to the Fortran D compilation strategy using the reaching decompositions for a given call site to compile Fortran D programs that contain function calls as well as to optimize the resulting implicit redistribution. As presented, their techniques addressed computing and optimizing (redundant or loop invariant) implicit redistribution operations due to changes in distribution at function boundaries, but do not address many of the situations which arise in HPF.

The definition of reaching distributions (using HPF terminology), however, is still a useful concept. We extend this definition to also include distributions which reach any point within a function in order to encompass both implicit and explicit distributions and redistributions thereby forming the basis of the work presented in this chapter. In addition to determining those distributions generated from a set of redistribution operations, this extended definition allows us to address a number of other applications in a unified framework.

Work by Coelho and Ancourt [9] also describes an optimization for removing useless remappings specified by a programmer through explicit realignment and redistribution operations. In comparison to the work in the Fortran D project [18], they are also concerned with determining which distributions are generated from a set of redistributions, but instead focus only on explicit redistribution. They define a new representation called a redistribution graph in which nodes represent redistribution operations and edges represent the statements executed between redistribution operations. This representation, although correct in its formulation, does not seem to fit well with any existing analysis already performed by optimizing compilers and also requires first summarizing all variables used or defined along every possible path between successive redistribution operations in order to optimize redistribution. Even though their approach currently only performs this analysis within a single function, they do suggest the possibility of an extension to their techniques which would allow them to also handle implicit remapping operations at function calls but they do not describe an approach.

3. Dynamic Distribution Selection

For complex programs, we have seen that static data distributions may be insufficient to obtain acceptable performance. Static distributions suffer in that they cannot reflect changes in a program's data access behavior. When conflicting data requirements are present, static partitionings tend to be compromises between a number of preferred distributions. Instead of requiring a single data distribution for the entire execution, program data could also be redistributed dynamically for different *phases* of the program (where a *phase* is simply a sequence of statements over which a given distribution is unchanged). Such dynamic partitionings can yield higher performance than a static partitioning when the redistribution is more efficient than the communication pattern required by the statically partitioned computation.

3.1 Motivation for Dynamic Distributions

Figure 3.1 shows the basic computation performed in a two-dimensional Fast Fourier Transform (FFT). To execute this program in parallel on a machine with distributed memory, the main data array, Image, is partitioned across the available processors. By examining the data accesses that will occur during execution, it can be seen that, for the first half of the program, data is manipulated along the rows of the array. For the rest of the execution, data is manipulated along the columns. Depending on how data is distributed among the processors, several different patterns of communication could be generated. The goal of automatic data partitioning is to select the distribution that will result in the highest level of performance.

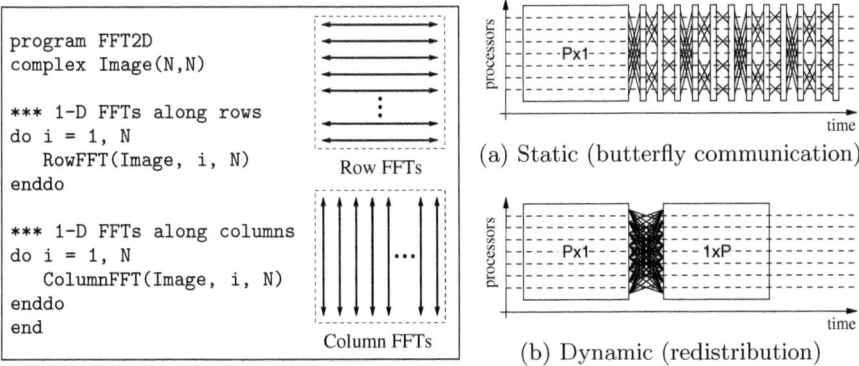

```
program FFT2D
complex Image(N,N)

*** 1-D FFTs along rows
do i = 1, N
   RowFFT(Image, i, N)
enddo

*** 1-D FFTs along columns
do i = 1, N
   ColumnFFT(Image, i, N)
enddo
end
```

Row FFTs

Column FFTs

(a) Static (butterfly communication)

(b) Dynamic (redistribution)

Fig. 3.1. Two-dimensional Fast Fourier Transform

If the array were distributed by rows, every processor could independently compute the FFTs for each row that involved local data. After the rows had been processed, the processors would now have to communicate to perform the column FFTs as the columns have been partitioned across the processors.

Conversely, if a column distribution were selected, communication would be required to compute the row FFTs while the column FFTs could be computed independently. Such static partitionings, as shown in Figure 3.1(a), suffer in that they cannot reflect changes in a program's data access behavior. When conflicting data requirements are present, static partitionings tend to be compromises between a number of preferred distributions.

For this example, assume the program is split into two separate phases; a row distribution is selected for the first phase and a column distribution for the second, as shown in Figure 3.1(b). By redistributing the data between the two phases, none of the one-dimensional FFT operations would require communication. From Figure 3.1, it can be seen how such a dynamic partitioning can yield higher performance if the dynamic redistribution communication is more efficient than the static communication pattern.

3.2 Overview of the Dynamic Distribution Approach

As previously shown in Figure 1.1, the approach we have developed to automatically select dynamic distributions, consists of two main steps. First, in Section 3.3, we will describe how to recursively decompose the program into a hierarchy of candidate phases obtained using existing static distribution techniques. Then, in Section 3.4 we will describe how to select the most efficient sequence of phases and phase transitions taking into account the cost of redistributing the data between the different phases.

This approach allows us to build upon the static partitioning techniques [15, 17] previously developed in the PARADIGM project. Static cost estimation techniques [16] are used to guide the selection of phases while static partitioning techniques are used to determine the best possible distribution for each phase. The cost models used to estimate communication and computation costs use parameters, empirically measured for each target machine, to separate the partitioning algorithm from a specific architecture.

To help illustrate the dynamic partitioning technique, an example program will be used. In Figure 3.2, a two-dimensional Alternating Direction Implicit iterative method[1] (ADI2D) is shown, which computes the solution of an elliptic partial differential equation known as Poisson's equation [14]. Poisson's equation can be used to describe the dissipation of heat away from a surface with a fixed temperature as well as to compute the free-space potential created by a surface with an electrical charge.

For the program in Figure 3.2, a static data distribution will incur a significant amount of communication for over half of the program's execution. For illustrative purposes only, the operational definition of phases previously described in Section 2 identifies twelve different "phases" in the program.

---

[1] To simplify later analysis of performance measurements, the program shown performs an arbitrary number of iterations as opposed to periodically checking for convergence of the solution.

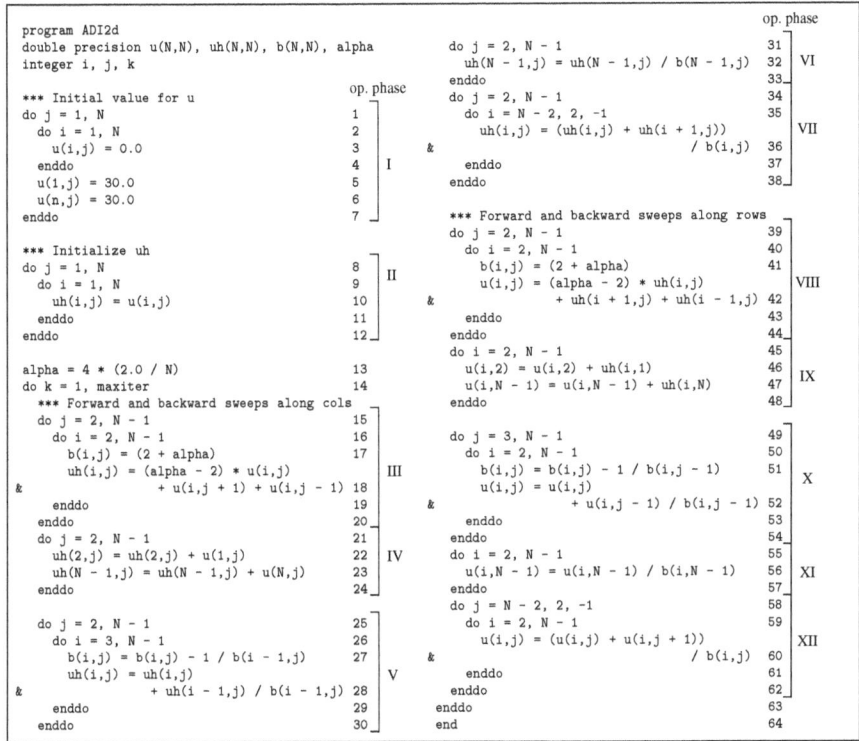

```
                                                                      op. phase
program ADI2d
double precision u(N,N), uh(N,N), b(N,N), alpha       do j = 2, N - 1                 31
integer i, j, k                                         uh(N - 1,j) = uh(N - 1,j) / b(N - 1,j)  32   VI
                                                      enddo                           33
*** Initial value for u                    op. phase  do j = 2, N - 1                 34
do j = 1, N                      1                       do i = N - 2, 2, -1           35
  do i = 1, N                    2                         uh(i,j) = (uh(i,j) + uh(i + 1,j))   VII
    u(i,j) = 0.0                 3                 &                 / b(i,j)          36
  enddo                          4        I           enddo                           37
  u(1,j) = 30.0                  5                   enddo                            38
  u(n,j) = 30.0                  6
enddo                            7                   *** Forward and backward sweeps along rows
                                                     do j = 2, N - 1                  39
*** Initialize uh                                      do i = 2, N - 1                40
do j = 1, N                      8        II            b(i,j) = (2 + alpha)          41
  do i = 1, N                    9                       u(i,j) = (alpha - 2) * uh(i,j)       VIII
    uh(i,j) = u(i,j)            10                 &              + uh(i + 1,j) + uh(i - 1,j)  42
  enddo                         11                      enddo                         43
enddo                          12                     enddo                           44
                                                     do i = 2, N - 1                  45
alpha = 4 * (2.0 / N)          13                     u(i,2) = u(i,2) + uh(i,1)       46   IX
do k = 1, maxiter             14                      u(i,N - 1) = u(i,N - 1) + uh(i,N)   47
*** Forward and backward sweeps along cols           enddo                           48
  do j = 2, N - 1             15
    do i = 2, N - 1           16                      do j = 3, N - 1                  49
      b(i,j) = (2 + alpha)    17                        do i = 2, N - 1               50
      uh(i,j) = (alpha - 2) * u(i,j)      III          b(i,j) = b(i,j) - 1 / b(i,j - 1)  51   X
&              + u(i,j + 1) + u(i,j - 1)  18           u(i,j) = u(i,j)
    enddo                     19                 &              + u(i,j - 1) / b(i,j - 1)  52
  enddo                       20                       enddo                          53
  do j = 2, N - 1            21                       enddo                           54
    uh(2,j) = uh(2,j) + u(1,j)    22   IV            do i = 2, N - 1                  55
    uh(N - 1,j) = uh(N - 1,j) + u(N,j)  23           u(i,N - 1) = u(i,N - 1) / b(i,N - 1)   56   XI
  enddo                       24                      enddo                           57
                                                     do j = N - 2, 2, -1              58
  do j = 2, N - 1            25                        do i = 2, N - 1               59
    do i = 3, N - 1          26                         u(i,j) = (u(i,j) + u(i,j + 1))      XII
      b(i,j) = b(i,j) - 1 / b(i - 1,j)    27    &                 / b(i,j)           60
      uh(i,j) = uh(i,j)          V                    enddo                          61
&               + uh(i - 1,j) / b(i - 1,j)  28       enddo                           62
    enddo                     29                     enddo                           63
  enddo                       30                     end                             64
```

Fig. 3.2. 2-D Alternating Direction Implicit iterative method (ADI2D)
(Shown with operational phases)

These phases exposed by the operational definition need not be known for our technique (and, in general, are potentially too restrictive) but they will be used here for comparison as well as to facilitate the discussion.

3.3 Phase Decomposition

Initially, the entire program is viewed as a single phase for which a static distribution is determined. At this point, the immediate goal is to determine if and where it would be beneficial to split the program into two separate phases such that the sum of the execution times of the resulting phases is less than the original (as illustrated in Figure 3.3). Using the selected distribution, a *communication graph* is constructed to examine the cost of communication in relation to the flow of data within the program.

We define a *communication graph* as the flow information from the dependence graph weighted by the cost of communication. The nodes of the communication graph correspond to individual statements while the edges correspond to flow dependencies that exist between the statements. As a heuristic, the cost of communication performed for a given reference in a

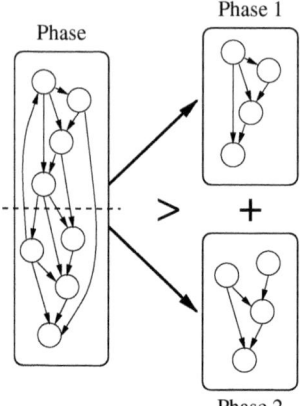

Fig. 3.3. Phase decomposition

statement is initially assigned to (*reflected* back along) every incoming dependence edge corresponding to the reference involved. Since flow information is used to construct the communication graph, the weights on the edges serve to expose communication costs that exist between producer/consumer relationships within a program. Also since we restrict the granularity of phase partitioning to the statement level, single node cycles in the flow dependence graph are not included in the communication graph.

After the initial communication cost, $comm(j, ref)$, has been computed for a given reference, ref, and statement, j, it is scaled according to the number of incoming edges for each producer statement, i, of the reference. The weight of each edge, (i, j), for this reference, $W(i, j, ref)$, is then assigned this value:

Scaling and assigning initial costs:

$$W(i, j, ref) \; = \; \frac{dyncount(i)}{\displaystyle\sum_{\substack{i<j \;\; P \in in\_pred(j,ref) \\ i>j \;\; P \in in\_succ(j,ref)}} dyncount(P)} \cdot lratio(i, j) \cdot comm(j, ref) \quad (3.1)$$

$$lratio(i, j) \; = \; \frac{nestlevel(i) + 1}{nestlevel(j) + 1} \quad\quad\quad (3.2)$$

The scaling conserves the total cost of a communication operation for a given reference, ref, at the consumer, j, by assigning portions to each producer, i, proportional to the dynamic execution count of the given producer, i, divided by the dynamic execution counts of all producers. Note that the scaling factors are computed separately for producers which are lexical predecessors or successors of the consumer as shown in Equation (3.1). Also, to further differentiate between producers at different nesting levels, all scaling factors are also scaled by the ratio of the nesting levels as shown in Equation (3.2).

Once the individual edge costs have been scaled to conserve the total communication cost, they are propagated back toward the start of the program (through all edges to producers which are lexical predecessors) while still conserving the propagated cost as shown in Equation (3.3).

Propagating costs back:

$$W(i,j,ref) \mathrel{+}= \frac{dyncount(i)}{\sum\limits_{P \in in\_pred(j,*)} dyncount(P)} \cdot lratio(i,j) \sum_{k \in out(j)} W(j,k,*) \quad (3.3)$$

In Figure 3.4, the communication graph is shown for ADI2D with some of the edges labeled with the unscaled *comm* cost expressions automatically generated by the static cost estimator (using a problem size of 512×512 and `maxiter` set to 100). For reference, the communication models for an Intel Paragon and a Thinking Machines CM-5, corresponding to the communication primitives used in the cost expressions, are shown in Table 3.1. Conditionals appearing in the cost expressions represent costs that will be incurred based on specific distribution decisions (e.g., $P_2 > 1$ is true if the second mesh dimension is assigned more than one processor).

Once the communication graph has been constructed, a split point is determined by computing a maximal cut of the communication graph. The maximal cut removes the largest communication constraints from a given phase to potentially allow better individual distributions to be selected for the two resulting split phases. Since we also want to ensure that the cut divides the program at exactly one point to ensure only two subphases are generated for the recursion, only cuts between two successive statements will be considered. Since the ordering of the nodes is related to the linear ordering of statements in a program, this guarantees that the nodes on one side of the cut will always all precede or all follow the node most closely involved in the cut. The following algorithm is used to determine which cut to use to split a given phase.

For simplicity of this discussion, assume for now that there is at most only one edge between any two nodes. For multiple references to the same array, the edge weight can be considered to be the sum of all communication operations for that array. Also, to better describe the algorithm, view the communication graph $G = (V, E)$ in the form of an adjacency matrix (with source vertices on rows and destination vertices on columns).

1. For each statement S_i $\{i \in [1, (|V| - 1)]\}$ compute the cut of the graph between statements S_i and S_{i+1} by summing all the edges in the submatrices specified by $[S_1, S_i] \times [S_{i+1}, S_{|V|}]$ and $[S_{i+1}, S_{|V|}] \times [S_1, S_i]$

2. While computing the cost of each cut also keep track of the current maximum cut.

3. If there is more than one cut with the same maximum value, choose from this set the cut that separates the statements at the highest nesting level.

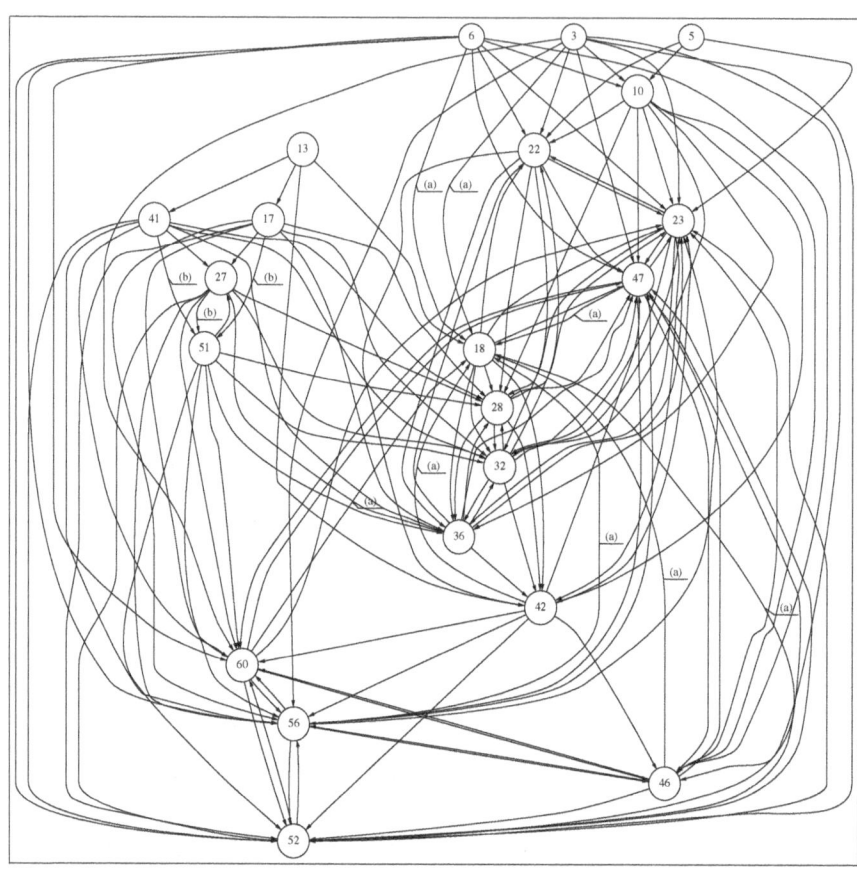

(a) $100 * (P_2 > 1) * \text{Shift}(510)$
(b) $3100 * \text{Transfer}(510)$

Fig. 3.4. ADI2D communication graph with example initial edge costs
(Statement numbers correspond to Figure 3.2)

Table 3.1. Communication primitives
(time in μs for a m byte message)

	Intel Paragon	TMC CM-5	
Transfer(m)	$50 + 0.018m$	$23 + 0.12m$	$m \le 16$
		$86 + 0.12m$	$m > 16$
Shift(m)		$2 * \text{Transfer}(m)$	

If there is more than one cut with the same highest nesting level, record the earliest and latest maximum cuts with that nesting level (forming a cut window).

4. Split the phase using the selected cut.

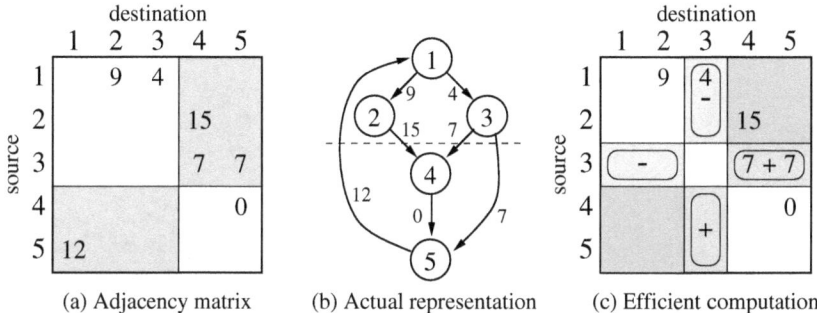

(a) Adjacency matrix   (b) Actual representation   (c) Efficient computation

Fig. 3.5. Example graph illustrating the computation of a cut

In Figure 3.5, the computation of the maximal cut on a smaller example graph with arbitrary weights is shown. The maximal cut is found to be between vertices 3 and 4 with a cost of 41. This is shown both in the form of the sum of the two adjacency submatrices in Figure 3.5(a), and graphically as a cut on the actual representation in Figure 3.5(b).

In Figure 3.5(c), the cut is again illustrated using an adjacency matrix, but the computation is shown using a more efficient implementation which only adds and subtracts the differences between two successive cuts using a running cut total while searching for the maximum cut in sequence. This implementation also provides much better locality than the full submatrix summary when analyzing the actual sparse representation since the differences between two successive cuts can be easily obtained by traversing the incoming and outgoing edge lists (which correspond to columns and rows in the adjacency matrix respectively) of the node immediately preceding the cut. This takes $\mathcal{O}(E)$ time on the actual representation, only visiting each edge twice – once to add it and once to subtract it.

A new distribution is now selected for each of the resulting phases while inheriting any unspecified distributions (due to an array not appearing in a subphase) from the parent phase. This process is then continued recursively using the costs from the newly selected distributions corresponding to each subphase. As was shown in Figure 3.3, each level of the recursion is carried out in branch and bound fashion such that a phase is split only if the sum of the estimated execution times of the two resulting phases shows an improvement

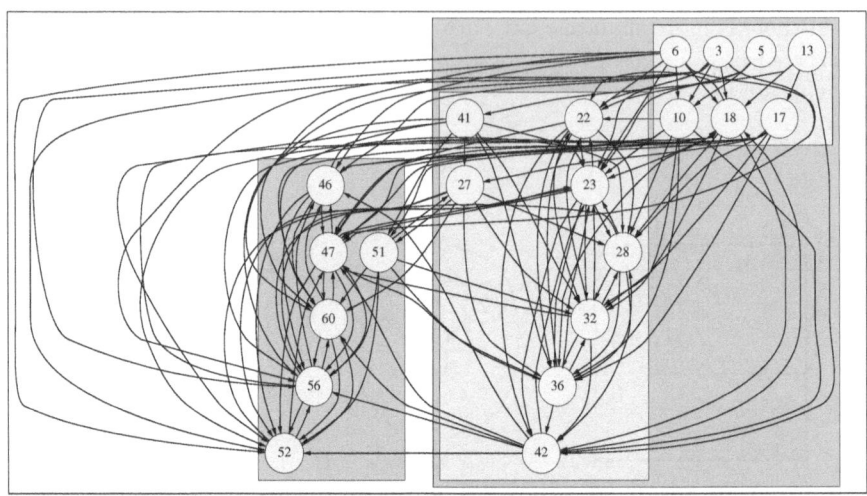

Fig. 3.6. Partitioned communication graph for ADI2D
(Statement numbers correspond to Figure 3.2.)

over the original.[2] In Figure 3.6, the partitioned communication graph is
shown for ADI2D after the phase decomposition is completed.

As mentioned in the cut algorithm, it is also possible to find several cuts
which all have the same maximum value and nesting level forming a window
over which the cut can be performed. This can occur since not all statements
will necessarily generate communication resulting in either edges with zero
cost or regions over which the propagated costs conserve edge flow, both
of which will maintain a constant cut value. To handle cut windows, the
phase should be split into two subphases such that the lower subphase uses
the earliest cut point and the upper subphase uses the latest, resulting in
overlapping phases. After new distributions are selected for each overlapping
subphase, the total cost of executing the overlapped region in each subphase
is examined. The overlap is then assigned to the subphase that resulted in the
lowest execution time for this region. If they are equal, the overlapping region
can be equivalently assigned to either subphase. Currently, this technique is
not yet implemented for cut windows. We instead always select the earliest
cut point in a window for the partitioning.

To be able to bound the depth of the recursion without ignoring important phases and distributions, the static partitioner must also obey the
following property. A partitioning technique is said to be *monotonic* if it selects the best available partition for a segment of code such that (aside from
the cost of redistribution) the time to execute a code segment with a selected
distribution is less than or equal to the time to execute the same segment

---

[2] A further optimization can also be applied to bound the size of the smallest
phase that can be split by requiring its estimated execution time to be greater
than a "minimum cost" of redistribution.

with a distribution that is selected after another code segment is appended to the first. In practice, this condition is satisfied by the static partitioning algorithm that we are using. This can be attributed to the fact that conflicts between distribution preferences are not broken arbitrarily, but are resolved based on the costs imposed by the target architecture [17].

It is also interesting to note that if a cut occurs within a loop body, and loop distribution can be performed, the amount of redistribution can be greatly reduced by lifting it out of the distributed loop body and performing it in between the two sections of the loop. Also, if dependencies allow statements to be reordered, statements may be able to move across a cut boundary without affecting the cost of the cut while possibly reducing the amount of data to be redistributed. Both of these optimizations can be used to reduce the cost of redistribution but neither will be examined in this chapter.

3.4 Phase and Phase Transition Selection

After the program has been recursively decomposed into a hierarchy of phases, a Phase Transition Graph (PTG) is constructed. Nodes in the PTG are phases resulting from the decomposition while edges represent possible redistribution between phases as shown in Figure 3.7(a). Since it is possible that using lower level phases may require transitioning through distributions found at higher levels (to keep the overall redistribution costs to a minimum), the phase transition graph is first sectioned across phases at the granularity of the lowest level of the phase decomposition.[3] Redistribution costs are then estimated for each edge and are weighted by the dynamic execution count of the surrounding code.

If a redistribution edge occurs within a loop structure, additional redistribution may be induced due to the control flow of the loop. To account for a potential "reverse" redistribution which can occur on the back edge of the iteration, the phase transition graph is also sectioned around such loops. The first iteration of a loop containing a phase transition is then peeled off and the phases of the first iteration of the body re-inserted in the phase transition graph as shown in Figure 3.7(b). Redistribution within the peeled iteration is only executed once while that within the remaining loop iterations is now executed $(N-1)$ times, where N is the number of iterations in the loop. The redistribution, which may occur between the first peeled iteration and the remaining iterations, is also multipled by $(N-1)$ in order to model when the back edge causes redistribution (i.e., when the last phase of the peeled iteration has a different distribution than the first phase of the remaining ones).

Once costs have been assigned to all redistribution edges, the best sequence of phases and phase transitions is selected by computing the shortest

---

[3] Sectioned phases that have identical distributions within the same horizontal section of the PTG are actually now redundant and can be removed, if desired, without affecting the quality of the final solution.

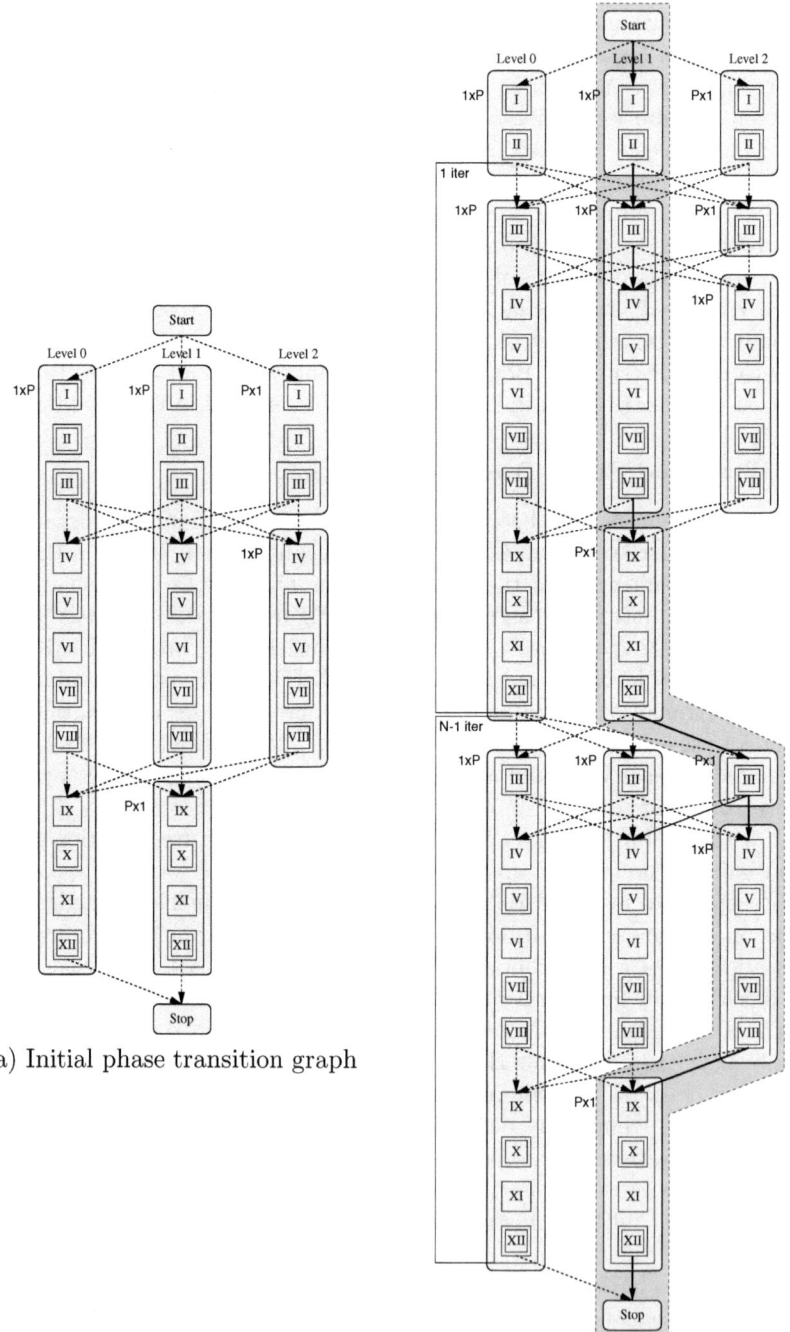

(a) Initial phase transition graph

(b) After performing loop peeling

Fig. 3.7. Phase transition graph for ADI2D

Table 3.2. Detected phases and estimated execution times (sec) for ADI2D
(Performance estimates correspond to 32 processors.)

Op. Phases(s)	Distribution	Intel Paragon	TMC CM-5	
I-XII	*,BLOCK 1 × 32	22.151461	39.496276	Level 0
I-VIII	*,BLOCK 1 × 32	1.403644	2.345815	Level 1
IX-XII	BLOCK,* 32 × 1	0.602592	0.941550	
I-III	BLOCK,* 32 × 1	0.376036	0.587556	Level 2
IV-VIII	*,BLOCK 1 × 32	0.977952	1.528050	

path on the phase transition graph. This is accomplished in $\mathcal{O}(V^2)$ time
(where V is now the number of vertices in the phase transition graph) using
Dijkstra's single source shortest path algorithm [40].

After the shortest path has been computed, the loop peeling performed
on the PTG can be seen to have been necessary to obtain the best solution
if the peeled iteration has a different transition sequence than the remaining
iterations. Even if the peeled iteration does have different transitions, not
actually performing loop peeling on the actual code will only incur at most
one additional redistribution stage upon entry to the loop nest. This will
not overly affect performance if the execution of the entire loop nest takes
significantly longer than a single redistribution operation, which is usually the
case especially if the redistribution considered within the loop was actually
accepted when computing the shortest path.

Using the cost models for an Intel Paragon and a Thinking Machines
CM-5, the distributions and estimated execution times reported by the static
partitioner for the resulting phases (described as ranges of operational phases)
are shown in Table 3.2. The performance parameters of the two machines are
similar enough that the static partitioning actually selects the same distribution at each phase for each machine. The times estimated for the static
partitioning are slightly higher than those actually observed, resulting from
a conservative assumption regarding pipelines[4] made by the static cost estimator [15], but they still exhibit similar enough performance trends to be
used as estimates. For both machines, the cost of performing redistribution is
low enough in comparison to the estimated performance gains that a dynamic
distribution scheme is selected, as shown by the shaded area in Figure 3.7(b).

Pseudo-code for the dynamic partitioning algorithm is presented in Figure 3.8 to briefly summarize both the phase decomposition and the phase

---

[4] Initially, a **BLOCK, BLOCK** distribution was selected by the static partitioner for
(only) the first step of the phase decomposition. As the static performance
estimation framework does not currently take into account any overlap between
communication and computation for pipelined computations, we decided that
this decision was due to the conservative performance estimate. For the analysis
presented for ADI2D, we bypassed this problem by temporarily restricting the
partitioner to only consider 1-D distributions.

transition selection procedures as described. As distributions for a given phase are represented as a set of variables, each of which having an associated distribution, a masking union set operation is used to inherit unspecified distributions ($dist \uplus dist_i$). A given variable's distribution in the $dist$ set will be replaced if it also has a distribution in the $dist_i$ set thus allowing any unspecified distributions in subphase i ($dist_i$) to be inherited from its parent ($dist$). These sets and the operations performed on them will be described in more detail in Section 4.3.

Since the use of inheritance during the phase decomposition process implicitly maintains the coupling between individual array distributions, redistribution at any stage will only affect the next stage. This can be contrasted to the technique proposed by Bixby, Kennedy, and Kremer [6] which first selects a number of partial candidate distributions for each phase specified by the operational definition. Since their phase boundaries are chosen in the absence of flow information, redistribution can affect stages at any distance from the current stage. This causes the redistribution costs to become binary functions depending on whether or not a specific path is taken, therefore, necessitating the need for 0-1 integer programming. In [27] they do agree, however, that 0-1 integer programming is not necessary when all phases specify complete distributions (such as in our case). In their work, this occurs only as a special case in which they specify complete phases from the innermost to outermost levels of a loop nest. For this situation they show how the solution can be obtained using a hierarchy of single source shortest path problems in a bottom-up fashion (as opposed to solving only one shortest path problem after performing a top-down phase decomposition as in our approach).

Up until now, we have not described how to handle control flow other than for loop constructs. More general flow (caused by conditionals or branch operations) can be viewed as separate paths of execution with different frequencies of execution. The same techniques that have been used for scheduling assembly level instructions by selecting traces of interest [12] or forming larger blocks from sequences of basic blocks [23] in order to optimize the most frequently taken paths can also be applied to the phase transition problem. Once a single trace has been selected (using profiling or other criteria) its phases are obtained using the phase selection algorithm previously described but ignoring all code off the main trace. Once phases have been selected, all off-trace paths can be optimized separately by first setting their stop and start nodes to the distributions of the phases selected for the points at which they exit and re-enter the main trace. Each off-trace path can then be assigned phases by applying the phase selection algorithm to each path individually. Although this specific technique is not currently implemented in the compiler, but will be addressed in future work, other researchers have also been considering it as a feasible solution for selecting phase transitions in the presence of general control flow [3].

PARTITION(*program*)
1 *cutlist* ← ∅
2 *dist* ← STATIC-PARTITIONING(*program*)
3 *phases* ← DECOMPOSE-PHASE(*program*, *dist*, *cutlist*)
4 *ptg* ← SELECT-REDISTRIBUTION(*phases*, *cutlist*)
5 Assign distributions based on shortest phase recorded in *ptg*

DECOMPOSE-PHASE(*phase*, *dist*, *cutlist*)
 1 Add *phase* to list of recognized phases
 2 Construct the communication graph for the *phase*
 3 *cut* ← MAX-CUT(*phase*)
 4 **if** VALUE(*cut*) = 0   ▷ No communication in *phase*
 5   **then return**
 6 Relocate *cut* to highest nesting level of identical cuts
 7 $phase_1$, $phase_2 \overset{cut}{\longleftarrow} phase$
 8 ▷ Note: if *cut* is a window, $phase_1$ and $phase_2$ will overlap
 9 $dist_1$ ← STATIC-PARTITIONING($phase_1$)
10 $dist_2$ ← STATIC-PARTITIONING($phase_2$)
11 ▷ Inherit any unspecified distributions from parent
12 $dist_1$ ← *dist* ⓊＬ $dist_1$
13 $dist_2$ ← *dist* ⓊＬ $dist_2$
14 **if** (cost($phase_1$) + cost($phase_2$)) < cost(*phase*)
15   **then** ▷ If *cut* is a window, $phase_1$ and $phase_2$ overlap
16   **if** LAST_STMTNUM($phase_1$) > FIRST_STMTNUM($phase_2$)
17   **then** RESOLVE-OVERLAP(*cut*, $phase_1$, $phase_2$)
18   LIST INSERT(*cut*, *cutlist*)
19   *phase*→*left* = DECOMPOSE-PHASE($phase_1$, $dist_1$, *cutlist*)
20   *phase*→*right* = DECOMPOSE-PHASE($phase_2$, $dist_2$, *cutlist*)
21   **else** *phase*→*left* = NULL
22   *phase*→*right* = NULL
23 **return** (*phase*)

SELECT-REDISTRIBUTION(*phases*, *cutlist*)
 1 **if** *cutlist* = ∅
 2   **then return**
 3 *ptg* ← CONSTRUCT-PTG(*phases*, *cutlist*)
 4 Divide *ptg* horizontally at the recursion lowest level
 5 **for each** *loop* **in** *phases*
 6   **do if** *loop*contains a cut at its nesting level
 7   **then** Divide *ptg* at *loop* boundaries
 8   PEEL(*loop*, *ptg*)
 9 Estimate the interphase redistribution costs for *ptg*
10 Compute the shortest phase transition path on *ptg*
11 **return** (*ptg*)

Fig. 3.8. Pseudo-code for the partitioning algorithm

4. Data Redistribution Analysis

The intermediate form of a program within the framework, previously shown in Figure 1.1, specifies both the distribution of every array at every point in the program as well as the redistribution required to move from one point to the next. The different paths through the framework involve passes which process the available distribution information in order to obtain the missing information required to move from one representation to another.

The core of the redistribution analysis portion of the framework is built upon two separate interprocedural data-flow problems which perform distribution synthesis and redistribution synthesis (which will be described later in Section 5). These two data-flow problems are both based upon the problem of determining both the inter- and intraprocedural reaching distributions for a program. Before giving further details of how these transformations are accomplished through the use of these two data-flow problems, we will first describe the idea of reaching distributions and the basic representations we use to perform this analysis.

4.1 Reaching Distributions and the Distribution Flow Graph

The problem of determining which distributions reach any given point taking into account control flow in the program is very similar to the computation of reaching definitions [1]. In classic compilation theory a control flow graph consists of nodes (basic blocks) representing uninterrupted sequences of statements and edges representing the flow of control between basic blocks. For determining reaching distributions, an additional restriction must be added to this definition. Not only should each block B be viewed as a sequence of statements with flow only entering at the beginning and leaving at the end, but the data distribution for the arrays defined or used within the block is also not allowed to change. In comparison to the original definition of a basic block, this imposes tighter restrictions on the extents of a block. Using this definition of a block in place of a basic block results in what we refer to as the distribution flow graph (DFG). This representation differs from [9] as redistribution operations now merely augment the definition of basic block boundaries as opposed to forming the nodes of the graph.

Since the definition of the DFG is based upon the CFG, the CFG can be easily transformed into a DFG by splitting basic blocks at points at which a distribution changes as shown in Figure 4.1. This can be due to an explicit change in distribution, as specified by the automatic data partitioner, or by an actual HPF redistribution directive. If the change in distribution is due to a sequence of redistribution directives, the overall effect is assigned to the block in which they are contained; otherwise, a separate block is created whenever executable operations are interspersed between the directives.

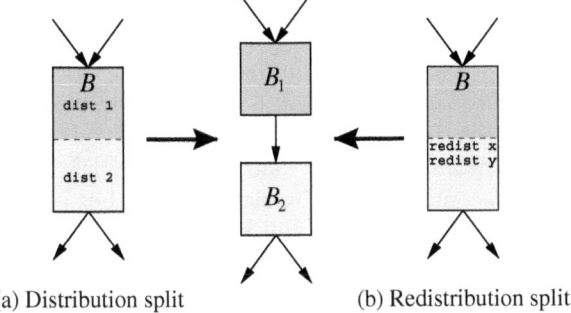

(a) Distribution split   (b) Redistribution split

Fig. 4.1. Splitting CFG nodes to obtain DFG nodes

4.2 Computing Reaching Distributions

Using this view of a block in a DFG and by viewing array distributions as definitions, the same data-flow framework used for computing reaching definitions [1] can now be used to obtain the reaching distributions by defining the following sets for each block B in a function:

- $DIST(B)$ - distributions present when executing block B
- $REDIST(B)$ - redistributions performed upon entering block B
- $GEN(B)$ - distributions generated by executing block B
- $KILL(B)$ - distributions killed by executing block B
- $IN(B)$ - distributions that exist upon entering block B
- $OUT(B)$ - distributions that exist upon leaving block B
- $DEF(B), USE(B)$ - variables defined or used in block B

It is important to note that GEN and KILL are specified as the distributions generated or killed by *executing* block B as opposed to entering (redistribution at the head of the block) or exiting (redistribution at the tail of the block) in order to allow both forms of redistribution. GEN and KILL are initialized by DIST or REDIST (depending on the current application as will be described in Section 5) and may be used to keep track of redistributions that occur on entry (e.g., HPF redistribution directives or functions with prescriptive distributions) or exit (e.g., calls to functions which internally change a distribution before returning). To perform interprocedural analysis, the function itself also has IN and OUT sets, which contain the distributions present upon entry and summarize the distributions for all possible exits.

Once the sets have been defined, the following data-flow equations are iteratively computed for each block until the solution $OUT(B)$ converges for every block B (where $PRED(B)$ are the nodes which immediately precede B in the flow of the program):

$$IN(B) \quad = \bigcup_{P \,\in\, PRED(B)} OUT(P) \qquad (4.1)$$

$$OUT(B) \quad = \quad GEN(B) \bigcup (IN(B) - KILL(B)) \qquad (4.2)$$

Since the confluence operator is a union, both IN and OUT never decrease in size and the algorithm will eventually halt. By processing the blocks in the flow graph in a depth-first order, the number of iterations performed will roughly correspond to the level of the most deeply nested statement, which tends to be a fairly small number on real programs [1].

As can be seen from Eqs. (4.1) and (4.2), the DEF and USE sets are actually not used to compute reaching distributions, but will have other uses for optimizing redistribution which will be explained in more detail in Section 5.2).

4.3 Representing Distribution Sets

To represent a distribution set in a manner that would provide efficient set operations, the bulk of the distribution information associated with a given variable is stored in its symbol table entry as a distribution table. Bit vectors are used within the sets themselves to specify distributions which are currently active for a given variable. Since a separate symbol table entry is created for each variable within a given scope, this provides a clean interface for accepting distributions from the HPF front end [21]. While the front end is processing HPF distribution or redistribution directives, any new distribution information present for a given variable is simply added to the corresponding distribution table for later analysis.

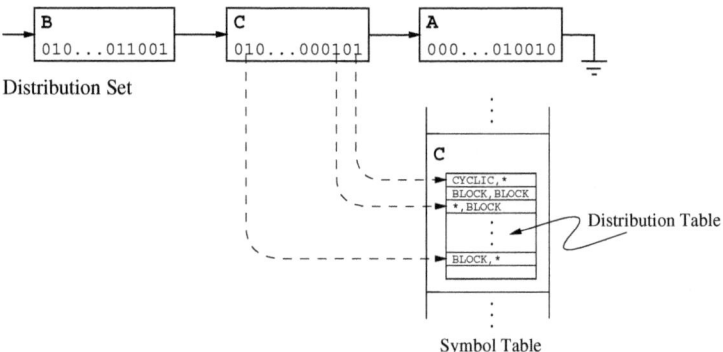

Fig. 4.2. Distribution set using bit vectors

As shown in Figure 4.2, the actual distribution sets are maintained as linked lists with a separate node representing each variable with a bit vector (corresponding to the entries in the distribution table for that variable) to indicate which distributions are currently active for the variable. To maintain efficiency while still retaining the simplicity of a list, the list is always maintained in sorted order by the address of the variable's entry in the symbol table to facilitate operations between sets. This allows us to implement operations on two sets by merging them in only $\mathcal{O}(n)$ bit vector operations (where n is the number of variables in a given set).

Since these sets are now actually sets of variables which each contain a set representing their active distributions, SET_{var} will be used to specify the variables present in a given distribution set, SET. For example, the notation $\overline{SET}_{var}$ can be used to indicate the inverse of the distributions *for each* variable contained within the *set* as opposed to an inverse over the universe of all active variables (which would be indicated as $\overline{SET}$).

In addition to providing full union, intersection, and difference operations ($\cup$, $\cap$, $-$) which operate on both levels of the set representation (between the variable symbols in the sets as well as between the bit vectors of identical symbols) masking versions of these operations ($\uplus$, $\cap$, $\ominus$) are also provided which operate at only the symbol level. In the case of a masking union ($a \uplus b$), a union is performed at the symbol level such that any distributions for a variable appearing in set a will be *replaced* by distributions in set b. This allows new distributions in b to be added to a set while replacing any existing distributions in a. Masking intersections ($a \cap b$) and differences ($a \ominus b$) act somewhat differently in that the variables in set a are either selected or removed (respectively) by their appearance in set b. These two operations are useful for implementing existence operations (e.g., $a_{var} | b_{var} \equiv a \cap b$, $a_{var} | \overline{b}_{var} \equiv a \ominus b$).

5. Interprocedural Redistribution Analysis

Since the semantics of HPF require that all objects accessible to the caller after the call are distributed exactly as they were before the call [26], it is possible to first completely examine the context of a call before considering any distribution side effects due to the call. It may seem strange to say that there can be side effects when we just said that the semantics of HPF preclude it. To clarify this statement, such side effects *are* allowed to exist, but only to the extent that they are not *apparent* outside of the call. As long as the view specified by the programmer is maintained, the compiler is allowed to do whatever it can to optimize both the inter- and intraprocedural redistributions so long as the resulting distributions used at any given point in the program are not changed.

The data partitioner explicitly assigns different distributions to individual blocks of code serving as an automated mechanism for converting sequential Fortran programs into efficient HPF programs. In this case, the framework is used to synthesize explicit redistribution operations in order to preserve the meaning of what the data partitioner intended in the presence of HPF semantics. In HPF, on the other hand, dynamic distributions are described by specifying the transitions between different distributions (through explicit redistribution directives or implicit redistribution at function boundaries). With the framework it is possible to convert an arbitrary HPF program into an optimized HPF program containing only explicit redistribution directives and descriptive [26] function arguments.

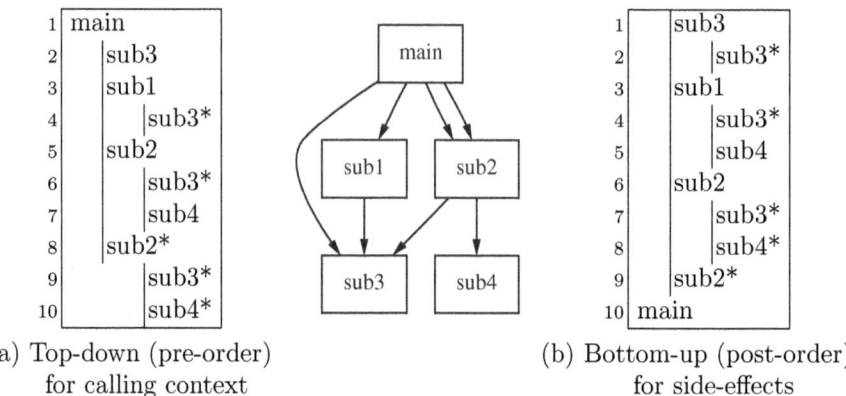

(a) Top-down (pre-order)
for calling context

(b) Bottom-up (post-order)
for side-effects

Fig. 5.1. Example call graph and depth-first traversal order

In Figure 5.1, an example call graph is shown to help illustrate the distribution and redistribution synthesis phases of the interprocedural analysis. If distribution information is not present (i.e., HPF input), distribution synthesis is first performed in a top-down manner over a program's call graph to compute which distributions are present at every point within a given function. By establishing the distributions that are present at each call site, clones are also generated for each unique set of input distributions obtained for the called functions. Redistribution synthesis is then applied in a bottom-up manner over the expanded call graph to analyze where the distributions are actually used and generates the redistribution required within a function.

Since this analysis is interested in the effects between an individual caller/callee pair, and not in summarizing the effects from all callers before examining a callee, it is not necessary to perform a topological traversal for the top-down and bottom-up passes over the call graph. In this case, it is actually more intuitive to perform a depth-first pre-order traversal of the call graph (shown in Figure 5.1(a)) to fully analyze a given function before proceeding to analyze any of the functions it calls and to perform a depth-first post-order traversal (shown in Figure 5.1(b)) to fully analyze all called functions before analyzing the caller.

One other point to emphasize is that these interprocedural techniques can be much more efficient than analyzing a fully inlined version of the same program since it is possible to prune the traversal at the point a previous solution is found for a function in the same calling context. In Figure 5.1, asterisks indicate points at which a function is being examined after having already been examined previously. If the calling context is the same as the one used previously, the traversal can be pruned at this point reusing information recorded from the previous context. Depending on how much reuse occurs, this factor can greatly reduce the amount of time the compiler spends analyzing a program in comparison to a fully inlined approach.

Referring back to Figure 1.1 once again, the technique for performing distribution synthesis will be described in Section 5.1 while redistribution synthesis will be described in Section 5.2. The static distribution assignment (SDA) technique, will be described in Section 5.3, but as the HPF redistribution directive conversion is very straight-forward, it will not be discussed further in this section. More detailed descriptions of these techniques and the implementation of the framework can be found in [30].

5.1 Distribution Synthesis

When analyzing HPF programs, it is necessary to first perform distribution synthesis in order to determine which distributions are present at every point in a program. Since HPF semantics specify that any redistribution (implicit or explicit) due to a function call is not visible to the caller, each function can be examined independently of the functions it calls. Only the input distributions for a given function and the explicit redistribution it performs have to be considered to obtain the reaching distributions within a function.

Given an HPF program, nodes (or blocks) in its DFG are delimited by the redistribution operations which appear in the form of HPF REDISTRIBUTE or REALIGN directives. As shown in Figure 5.2, the redistribution operations assigned to a block B represent the redistribution that will be performed when entering the block on any input path (indicated by the set REDIST(B)) as opposed to specifying the redistribution performed for each incoming path (REDIST(B, B_1) or REDIST(B, B_2) in the figure).

If the set GEN(B) is viewed as the distributions which are generated and KILL(B) as the distributions which are killed upon entering the block, this

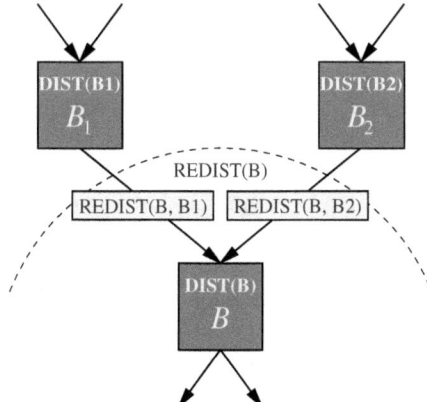

Fig. 5.2. Distribution and redistribution synthesis

problem can now be cast directly into the reaching distribution data-flow framework by making the following assignments:

Data-flow initialization:

$$\text{REDIST}(B) = \text{from directives}$$
$$\text{DIST}(B) = \emptyset$$

$$\text{GEN}(B) = \text{REDIST}(B) \qquad \text{KILL}(B) = \overline{\text{REDIST}_{var}(B)}$$
$$\text{OUT}(B) = \text{REDIST}(B) \qquad \text{IN}(B) = \emptyset$$

Data-flow solution:

$$\text{DIST(B)} = \text{OUT}(B)$$

According to the HPF standard, a REALIGN operation only affects the array being realigned while a REDISTRIBUTE operation should redistribute all arrays currently aligned to the given array being redistributed (in order to preserve any previous specified alignments). The current implementation only records redistribution information for the array immediately involved in a REDISTRIBUTE operation. This results in only redistributing the array involved in the directive and not all of the alignees of the target to which it is aligned. In the future, the implementation could be easily extended to support the full HPF interpretation of REDISTRIBUTE by simply recording the same redistribution information for all alignees for the target template of the array involved in the operation. Due to the properties of REALIGN, this will also require first determining which templates arrays are aligned to at every point in the program (i.e., reaching alignments) using similar techniques.

5.2 Redistribution Synthesis

After the distributions have been determined for each point in the program, the redistribution can be optimized. Instead of using either a simple copy-in/copy-out strategy or a complete redistribution of all arguments upon every entry and exit of a function, any implicit redistribution around function calls can be reduced to only that which is actually required to preserve HPF semantics. Redistribution operations (implicitly specified by HPF semantics or explicitly specified by a programmer) that result in distributions which would not otherwise be used before another redistribution operation occurs are completely removed in this pass.

Blocks are now delimited by changes in the distribution set. The set of reaching distributions previously computed for a block B represent the distributions which are in effect when executing that block (indicated by the set $\text{DIST}(B)$ in Figure 5.2). For this reason, the $\text{DIST}(B)$ sets are first restricted to only the variables defined or used within block B. Redistribution operations will now only be performed between two blocks if there is an intervening definition or use of a variable before the next change in distribution. Since we have also chosen to use a caller redistributes model, the $\text{GEN}(B)$ and $\text{KILL}(B)$ sets are now viewed as the distributions which are generated or killed upon leaving block B. Using these definitions, this problem can now be cast directly into the reaching distribution data-flow framework by making the following assignments:

Data-flow initialization:
$$\text{REDIST}(B) = \emptyset$$
$$\text{DIST}(B) = \text{DIST}(B) \cap (\text{DEF}(B) \cup \text{USE}(B))$$
$$\text{GEN}(B) = \text{DIST}(B) \qquad \text{KILL}(B) = \overline{\text{DIST}_{var}(B)}$$
$$\text{OUT}(B) = \text{DIST}(B) \qquad \text{IN}(B) = \emptyset$$

Data-flow solution:
$$\text{REDIST}(B) = \text{DIST}_{var}(B) \mid (\text{IN}_{var}(B) - \text{DIST}_{var}(B)) \neq \emptyset$$

As will be seen later, using a caller redistributes model exposes many interprocedural optimization opportunities and also cleanly supports function calls which may require redistribution on both their entry and exit. Since $\text{REDIST}(B)$ is determined from both the DIST and IN sets, $\text{DIST}(B)$ represents the distributions needed for executing block B, while the GEN and KILL sets will be used to represent the exit distribution (which may or may not match DIST).

By first restricting the $\text{DIST}(B)$ sets to only those variables defined or used within block B, redistribution is generated only where it is actually needed – the locations in which a variable is actually used in a distribution different from the current one (demand-driven, or lazy, redistribution). Although it will not be examined here, it would also be possible to take a lazy redistribution solution and determine the earliest possible time that the redistribution could be performed (eager redistribution) in order to redistribute an array when a distribution is no longer in use. The area between the eager and lazy redistribution points forms a window over which the operation can be performed to obtain the same effect. As will be shown later, it would be advantageous to position multiple redistribution operations in overlapping windows to the same point in the program in order to aggregate the communication thereby reducing the amount of communication overhead [30]. As the lazy redistribution point is found using a forward data-flow (reaching distributions) problem, it would be possible to find the eager redistribution point by performing some additional bookkeeping to record the last use of a variable as the reaching distributions are propagated along the flow graph; however, such a technique is not currently implemented in PARADIGM. In comparison to other approaches, interval analysis has also been used to determine eager/lazy points for code placement, but at the expense of a somewhat more complex formulation [43].

5.2.1 Optimizing Invariant Distributions. Besides performing redistribution only when necessary, it is also desirable to only perform necessary redistribution as infrequently as possible.

Semantically loop invariant distribution regions[5] can be first grown before synthesizing the redistribution operations. All distributions that do not change within a nested statement (e.g., a loop or if structure) are recorded on the parent statement (or header) for that structure. This has the effect of moving redistribution operations which result in the invariant distribution out of nested structures as far as possible (as was also possible in [18]).

As a side effect, loops which are considered to contain an invariant distribution no longer propagate previous distributions for the invariant arrays. Since redistribution is moved out of the loop, this means that for the (extremely rare) special case of a loop invariant distribution (which was not originally present outside of the loop) contained within an undetectable zero trip loop, only the invariant distribution from within the loop body is propagated even though the loop nest was never executed. As this is only due to the way invariant distributions are handled, the data-flow handles non-invariant distributions as expected for zero trip loops (an extra redistribution check may be generated after the loop execution).

5.2.2 Multiple Active Distributions. Even though it is not specifically stated as such in the HPF standard, we will consider an HPF program in which every use or definition of an array has only one active distribution to be well-behaved. Since PARADIGM cannot currently compile programs which contain references with multiple active distributions, this property is currently detected by examining the reaching distribution sets for every node (limited by DEF/USE) within a function. A warning is issued if any set contains multiple distributions for a given use or definition of a variable stating that the program is not well-behaved.

In the presence of function calls, it is also possible to access an array through two or more paths when parameter aliasing is present. If there is an attempt to redistribute only one of the aliased symbols, the different aliases now have different distributions even though they actually refer to the same array. This form of multiple active distributions is actually considered to be non-conforming in HPF [26] as it can result in consistency problems if the same array were allowed to occupy two different distributions. As it may be difficult for the programmers to make this determination, this can be automatically detected by determining if the reaching distribution set contains different distributions for any aliased arrays.[6]

---

[5] Invariant redistribution within a loop can technically become non-invariant when return distributions from a function call within a loop nest are allowed to temporarily exist in the caller's scope. Such regions can still be treated as invariant since this is the view HPF semantics provide to the programmer.

[6] The `param_alias` pass in Parafrase-2 [34], which PARADIGM is built upon, is first run to compute the alias sets for every function call.

5.3 Static Distribution Assignment (SDA)

To utilize the available memory on a given parallel machine as efficiently as possible, only the distributions that are active at any given point in the program should actually be allocated space. It is interesting to note that as long as a given array is distributed among the same total number of processors, the actual space required to store one section of the partitioned array is the same no matter how many array dimensions are distributed.[7] By using this observation, it is possible to statically allocate the minimum amount of memory by associating all possible distributions of a given array to the same area of memory.

Static Distribution Assignment (SDA) (inspired indirectly by the Static Single Assignment (SSA) form [10]) is a process we have developed in which the names of array variables are duplicated and renamed statically based on the active distributions represented in the corresponding DIST sets. As names are generated, they are assigned a static distribution corresponding to the currently active dynamic distribution for the original array. The new names will not change distribution during the course of the program. Redistribution now takes the form of an assignment between two different statically distributed source and destination arrays (as opposed to rearranging the data within a single array).

To statically achieve the minimum amount of memory allocation required, all of the renamed duplicates of a given array are declared to be "equivalent." The EQUIVALENCE statement in Fortran 77 allows this to be performed at the source level in a manner somewhat similar to assigning two array pointers to the same allocated memory as is possible in C or Fortran 90. Redistribution directives are also now replaced with actual calls to a redistribution library.

Because the different static names for an array share the same memory, this implies that the communication operations used to implement the redistribution should read all of the source data before writing to the target. In the worst case, an entire copy of a partitioned array would have to be buffered at the destination processor before it is actually received and moved into the destination array. However, as soon as more than two different distributions are present for a given array, the EQUIVALENCE begins to pay off, even in the worst case, in comparison to separately allocating each different distribution. If the performance of buffered communication is insufficient for a given machine (due to the extra buffer copy), non-buffered communication could be used instead thereby precluding the use of EQUIVALENCE (unless some form of explicit buffering is performed by the redistribution library itself).

---

[7] Taking into account distributions in which the number of processors allocated to a given array dimension does not evenly divide the size of the dimension, or degenerate distributions in which memory is not evenly distributed over all processors, it can also be equivalently said that there is an amount of memory which can store all possible distributions with very little excess.

REAL A(N, N) !HPF$ DISTRIBUTE (CYCLIC, *)::A ... A(i, j) = ... !HPF$ REDISTRIBUTE (BLOCK, BLOCK)::A ... ... = A(i, j) ...	REAL A$0(N, N), A$1(N,N) !HPF$ DISTRIBUTE (CYCLIC, *)::A$0 !HPF$ DISTRIBUTE (BLOCK, BLOCK)::A$1 EQUIVALENCE (A$0, A$1) INTEGER A$cid A$cid = 0 ... A$0(i, j) = ... CALL reconfig(A$1, 1, A$cid) ... ... = A$1(i, j) ...
(a) Before SDA	(b) After SDA

Fig. 5.3. Example of static distribution assignment

In Figure 5.3, a small example is shown to illustrate this technique. In this example, a redistribution operation on A causes it to be referenced using two different distributions. A separate name is statically generated for each distribution of A, and the redistribution directive is replaced with a call to a run-time redistribution library [36]. The array accesses in the program can now be compiled by PARADIGM using techniques developed for programs which only contain static distributions [4] by simply ignoring the communication side effects of the redistribution call.

As stated previously, if more than one distribution is active for any given array reference, the program is considered to be *not well-behaved*, and the array involved can not be directly assigned a static distribution. In certain circumstances, however, it may be possible to perform code transformations to make an HPF program well-behaved. For instance, a loop that contained multiple active distributions on the entry to its body due only to a distribution from the loop back edge (caused by redistribution within the loop) that wasn't present on the loop entry would not be well-behaved. If the first iteration of that loop were peeled off, the entire loop body would now have a single active distribution for each variable and the initial redistribution into this state would be performed outside of the loop. This and other code transformations which help reduce the number of distributions reaching any given node will be the focus of further work in this area.

6. Results

To evaluate the quality of the data distributions selected using the techniques presented in this chapter, as implemented in the PARADIGM compiler, we analyze three programs which exhibit different access patterns over the course of their execution. These programs are individual Fortran 77 subroutines which range in size from roughly 60 to 150 lines of code:

- Synthetic HPF redistribution example
- 2-D Alternating Direction Implicit iterative method (ADI2D) [14]
- Shallow water weather prediction benchmark [37]

6.1 Synthetic HPF Redistribution Example

In Figure 6.1(a), a synthetic HPF program is presented which performs a number of different tests (described in the comments appearing in the code) of the optimizations performed by the framework. In this program, one array, x, is redistributed both explicitly using HPF directives and implicitly through function calls using several different interfaces. Two of the functions, func1 and func2, have prescriptive interfaces [26] which may or may not require redistribution (depending on the current configuration of the input array). The first function differs from the second in that it also redistributes the array such that it returns with a different distribution than which it was called. The last function, func3, differs from the first two in that it has an (implicit) transcriptive interface [26]. Calls to this function will cause it to inherit the current distribution of the actual parameters.

Several things can be noted when examining the optimized HPF shown in Figure 6.1(b).[8] First of all, the necessary redistribution operations required to perform the implicit redistribution at the function call boundaries have been made explicit in the program. Here, the interprocedural analysis has completely removed any redundant redistribution by relaxing the HPF semantics allowing distributions caused by function side effects to exist so long as they do not affect the original meaning of the program. For the transcriptive function, func3, the framework also generated two separate clones, func3$0 and func3$1, corresponding to two different active distributions appearing in a total of three different calling contexts.

Two warnings were also generated by the compiler, inserted by hand as comments in Figure 6.1(b), indicating that there were (semantically) multiple reaching distributions for two references of x in the program. The first reference actually does have two reaching distributions due to a conditional with redistribution performed on only one path. The second, however, occurs after a call to a prescriptive function, func1, which implicitly redistributes the array to conform to its interface. Even though the redistribution for this function will accept either of the two input distributions and generate only a single distribution of x for the function, the following reference of x semantically still has two reaching distributions – hence the second warning.

The optimization of loop invariant redistribution operations can also be seen in the first loop nest of this example in which a redistribution operation on x is performed at the deepest level of a nested loop. If there are no references of x before the occurrence of the redistribution (and no further

---

[8] The HPF output, generated by PARADIGM, has been slightly simplified by removing unnecessary alignment directives from the figure to improve its clarity.

```
      PROGRAM test                                        PROGRAM test
      INTEGER x(10,10)                                    INTEGER x(10,10)
c     *** For tests involving statement padding           INTEGER a, n
      INTEGER a                                     !HPF$ DYNAMIC, DISTRIBUTE (BLOCK, BLOCK) :: x
!HPF$ DYNAMIC, DISTRIBUTE (BLOCK, BLOCK) :: x            x(1,1) = 1
c     *** Use of initial distribution               !HPF$ REDISTRIBUTE (BLOCK, CYCLIC) :: x
      x(1,1) = 1                                           DO i = 1,10
c     *** Testing loop invariant redistribution              DO j = 1,10
      DO i = 1,10                                              a = 0
         DO j = 1,10                                          x(i,j) = 1
            a = 0                                             a = 0
!HPF$       REDISTRIBUTE (BLOCK, CYCLIC) :: x              END DO
            x(i,j) = 1                                    END DO
            a = 0                                         a = 0
         ENDDO                                            IF (x(i,j) .GT. 1) THEN
      ENDDO                                         !HPF$ REDISTRIBUTE (BLOCK, BLOCK) :: x
      a = 0                                               x(i,j) = 2
c     *** Testing unnecessary redistribution              CALL func3$0(x,n)
!HPF$ REDISTRIBUTE (BLOCK, CYCLIC) :: x                  ELSE
      if (x(i,j) .gt. 1) then                             x(i,j) = 3
c        *** Testing redistribution in a conditional      END IF
!HPF$    REDISTRIBUTE (BLOCK, BLOCK) :: x           c     *** WARNING: too many dists (2) for x
         x(i,j) = 2                                       x(1,1) = 2
         call func3(x,n)                             !HPF$ REDISTRIBUTE (BLOCK, CYCLIC) :: x
      else                                                CALL func1(x,n)
         x(i,j) = 3                                       DO i = 1,10
      endif                                                  DO j = 1,10
c     *** Uses with multiple reaching distributions   c        *** WARNING: too many dists (2) for x
      x(1,1) = 2                                                 x(j,i) = 2
      call func1(x,n)                                        END DO
      DO i = 1,10                                        END DO
         DO j = 1,10                                 !HPF$ REDISTRIBUTE (BLOCK, CYCLIC) :: x
            x(j,i) = 2                                     CALL func1(x,n)
         ENDDO                                             CALL func2(x,n)
      ENDDO                                         !HPF$ REDISTRIBUTE (BLOCK, CYCLIC) :: x
!HPF$ REDISTRIBUTE (CYCLIC(3), CYCLIC) :: x              CALL func1(x,n)
c     *** Testing chaining of function arguments    !HPF$ REDISTRIBUTE (CYCLIC(3), CYCLIC) :: x
      call func1(x,n)                                     DO i = 1,10
      call func2(x,n)                                        DO j = 1,10
      call func1(x,n)                                           CALL func3$1(x,n)
c     *** Testing loop invariant due to return             END DO
      DO i = 1,10                                        END DO
         DO j = 1,10                                      a = 1
c           *** Testing transcriptive function cloning   a = 0
            call func3(x,n)                               CALL func3$1(x,n)
         ENDDO                                            END
      ENDDO
      a = 1                                               INTEGER FUNCTION func1(a,n)
c     *** Testing unused distribution                     INTEGER n, a(n,n)
!HPF$ REDISTRIBUTE (BLOCK, CYCLIC) :: x             !HPF$ DYNAMIC, DISTRIBUTE (BLOCK, CYCLIC) :: a
      a = 0                                               a(1,1) = 1
c     *** Testing "semantically killed" distribution      a(1,2) = 1
!HPF$ REDISTRIBUTE (CYCLIC(3), CYCLIC) :: x         !HPF$ REDISTRIBUTE (CYCLIC, CYCLIC) :: a
      call func3(x,n)                                     a(1,3) = 1
      END                                                 END

      integer function func1(a,n)                         INTEGER FUNCTION func2(y,n)
c     *** Prescriptive function with different return     INTEGER n, y(n,n)
      integer n, a(n, n)                            !HPF$ DYNAMIC, DISTRIBUTE(CYCLIC,CYCLIC) :: y
!HPF$ DYNAMIC, DISTRIBUTE (BLOCK, CYCLIC) :: a           y(1,1) = 2
      a(1,1) = 1                                           END
!HPF$ REDISTRIBUTE (BLOCK, CYCLIC) :: a
      a(1,2) = 1                                           INTEGER FUNCTION func3$1(n,z)
!HPF$ REDISTRIBUTE (CYCLIC, CYCLIC) :: a                  INTEGER n, z(n,n)
      a(1,3) = 1                                     !HPF$ DISTRIBUTE(CYCLIC(3),CYCLIC) :: z
      end                                                 z(1,1) = 3
                                                          END
      integer function func2(y,n)
c     *** Prescriptive function with identical return     INTEGER FUNCTION func3$0(n,z)
      integer n, y(n,n)                                   INTEGER n, z(n,n)
!HPF$ DYNAMIC, DISTRIBUTE (CYCLIC, CYCLIC) :: y     !HPF$ DISTRIBUTE(BLOCK,BLOCK) :: z
      y(1,1) = 2                                           z(1,1) = 3
      end                                                 END

      integer function func3(z,n)
c     *** (implicitly) Transcriptive function
      integer n, z(n,n)
      z(1,1) = 3
      end
```

(a) Before optimization   (b) After optimization

Fig. 6.1. Synthetic example for interprocedural redistribution optimization

redistribution performed in the remainder of the loop), then x will always have a (BLOCK, CYCLIC) distribution within the loop body. This situation is detected by the framework and the redistribution operation is re-synthesized to occur outside of the entire loop nest. It could be argued that even when it appeared within the loop, the underlying redistribution library could be written to be smart enough to only perform the redistribution when it is necessary (i.e., only on the first iteration) so that we have not really optimized away 10^2 redistribution operations. Even in this case, this optimization has still completely eliminated (10^2-1) check operations that would have been performed at run time to determine if the redistribution was required.

As there are several other optimizations performed on this example, which we will not describe in more detail here, the reader is directed to the comments in the code for further information.

6.2 2-D Alternating Direction Implicit (ADI2D) Iterative Method

In order to evaluate the effectiveness of dynamic distributions, the ADI2D program, with a problem size of 512×512,[9] is compiled with a fully static distribution (one iteration shown in Figure 6.2(a)) as well as with the selected dynamic distribution[10] (one iteration shown in Figure 6.2(b)). These two parallel versions of the code were run on an Intel Paragon and a Thinking Machines CM-5 to examine their performance on different architectures.

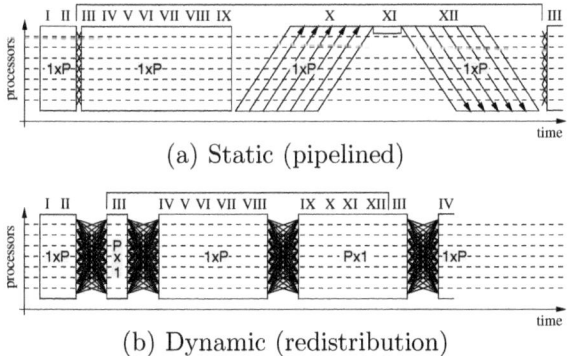

(a) Static (pipelined)

(b) Dynamic (redistribution)

Fig. 6.2. Modes of parallel execution for ADI2D

The static scheme illustrated in Figure 6.2(a) performs a shift operation to initially obtain some required data and then satisfies two recurrences in

---

[9] To prevent poor serial performance from cache-line aliasing due to the power of two problem size, the arrays were also padded with an extra element at the end of each column. This optimization, although here performed by hand, is automated by even aggressive serial optimizing compilers.

[10] In the current implementation, loop peeling is not performed on the generated code. As previously mentioned in Section 3.4, the single additional startup redistribution due to not peeling will not be significant in comparison to the execution of the loop (containing a dynamic count of 600 redistributions).

the program using software pipelining [19, 33]. Since values are being propagated through the array during the pipelined computation, processors must wait for results to be computed before continuing with their own part of the computation. According to the performance ratio of communication vs. computation for a given machine, the amount of computation performed before communicating to the next processor in the pipeline will have a direct effect on the overall performance of a pipelined computation [20, 33].

A small experiment is first performed to determine the best pipeline *granularity* for the static partitioning. A granularity of one (fine-grain) causes values to be communicated to waiting processors as soon as they are produced. By increasing the granularity, more values are computed before communicating, thereby amortizing the cost of establishing communication in exchange for some reduction in parallelism. In addition to the experimental data, compile-time estimates of the pipeline execution [33] are shown in Figure 6.3. For the two machines, it can be seen that by selecting the appropriate granularity, the performance of the static partitioning can be improved. Both a fine-grain and the optimal coarse-grain static partitioning will be compared with the dynamic partitioning.

The redistribution present in the dynamic scheme appears as three transposes[11] performed at two points within an outer loop (the exact points in the program can be seen in Figure 3.7). Since the sets of transposes occur at the same point in the program, the data to be communicated for each transpose can be aggregated into a single message during the actual transpose. As it has been previously observed that aggregating communication improves performance by reducing the overhead of communication [20, 33], we will also examine aggregating the individual transpose operations here.

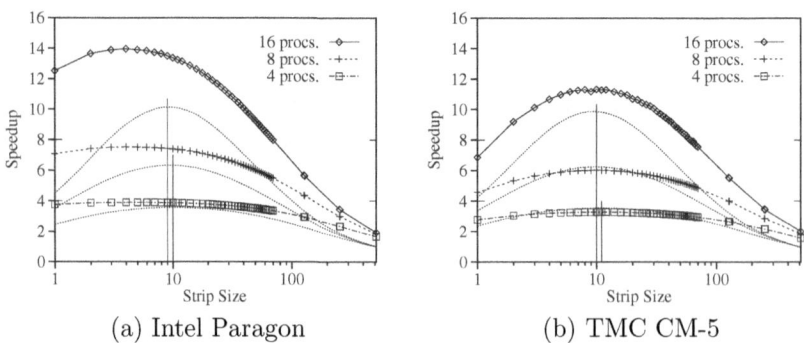

(a) Intel Paragon   (b) TMC CM-5

Fig. 6.3. Coarse-grain pipelining for ADI2D

---

[11] This could have been reduced to two transposes at each point if we allowed the cuts to reorder statements and perform loop distribution on the innermost loops (between statements 17, 18 and 41, 42), as mentioned in Section 3, but these optimizations are not examined here.

In Figure 6.4, the performance of both dynamic and static partitionings for ADI2D is shown for an Intel Paragon and a Thinking Machines CM-5. For the dynamic partitioning, both aggregated and non-aggregated transpose operations were compared. For both machines, it is apparent that aggregating the transpose communication is very effective, especially as the program is executed on larger numbers of processors. This can be attributed to the fact that the start-up cost of communication (which can be several orders of magnitude greater than the per byte transmission cost) is being amortized over multiple messages with the same source and destination.

For the static partitioning, the performance of the fine-grain pipeline was compared to a coarse-grain pipeline using the optimal granularity. The coarse-grain optimization yielded the greatest benefit on the CM-5 while still improving the performance (to a lesser degree) on the Paragon. For the Paragon, the dynamic partitioning with aggregation clearly improved performance (by over 70% compared to the fine-grain and 60% compared to the coarse-grain static distribution). On the CM-5, the dynamic partitioning with aggregation showed performance gains of over a factor of two compared to the fine-grain static partitioning but only outperformed the coarse-grain version for extremely large numbers of processors. For this reason, it would appear that the limiting factor on the CM-5 is the performance of the communication.

As previously mentioned in Section 3.4, the static partitioner currently makes a very conservative estimate for the execution cost of pipelined loops [15]. For this reason a dynamic partitioning was selected for both the Paragon as well as the CM-5. If a more accurate pipelined cost model [33] were used, a static partitioning would have been selected instead for the CM-5. For the Paragon, the cost of redistribution is still low enough that a dynamic partitioning would still be selected for large machine configurations.

It is also interesting to estimate the cost of performing a single transpose in either direction ($P \times 1 \leftrightarrow 1 \times P$) from the communication overhead present in the dynamic runs. Ignoring any performance gains from cache effects, the communication overhead can be computed by subtracting the ideal run time

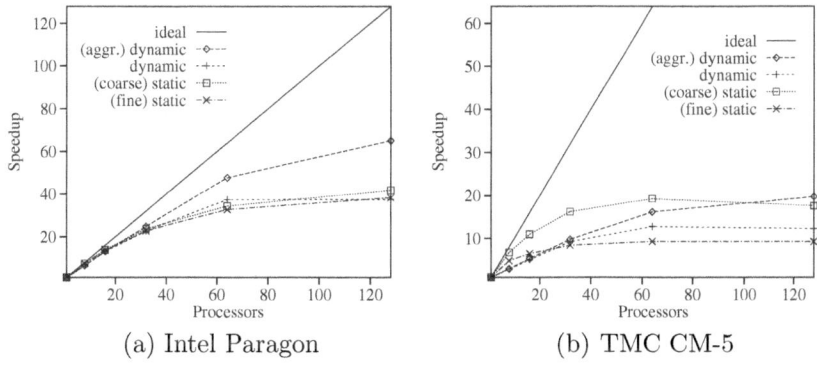

(a) Intel Paragon   (b) TMC CM-5

Fig. 6.4. Performance of ADI2D

(serial time divided by the selected number of processors) from the measured run time. Given that three arrays are transposed 200 times, the resulting overhead divided by 600 yields a rough estimate of how much time is required to redistribute a single array as shown in Table 6.1.

From Table 6.1 it can be seen that as more processors are involved in the operation, the time taken to perform one transpose levels off until a certain number of processors is reached. After this point, the amount of data being handled by each individual processor is small enough that the startup overhead of the communication has become the controlling factor. Aggregating the redistribution operations minimizes this effect thereby achieving higher levels of performance than would be possible otherwise.

Table 6.1. Empirically estimated time (ms) to transpose a 1-D partitioned matrix (512×512 elements; double precision)

processors	Intel Paragon		TMC CM-5	
	individual	aggregated	individual	aggregated
8	36.7	32.0	138.9	134.7
16	15.7	15.6	86.8	80.5
32	14.8	10.5	49.6	45.8
64	12.7	6.2	40.4	29.7
128	21.6	8.7	47.5	27.4

6.3 Shallow Water Weather Prediction Benchmark

Since not all programs will necessarily need dynamic distributions, we also examine another program which exhibits several different smaller phases of computation. The Shallow water benchmark is a weather prediction program using finite difference models of the shallow water equations [37] written by Paul Swarztrauber from the National Center for Atmospheric Research.

As the program consists of a number of different functions, the program is first inlined since the approach for selecting data distributions is not yet fully interprocedural. Also, a loop which is implicitly formed by a GOTO statement is replaced with an explicit loop since the current performance estimation framework does not handle unstructured code. The final input program, ignoring comments and declarations, resulted in 143 lines of executable code.

In Figure 6.5, the phase transition graph is shown with the selected path using costs based on a 32 processor Intel Paragon with the original problem size of 257×257 limited to 100 iterations. The decomposition resulting in this graph was purposely bounded only by the productivity of the cut, and not by a minimum cost of redistribution in order to expose all potentially beneficial phases. This graph shows that by using the decomposition technique presented in Figure 3.8, Shallow contains six phases (the length of the path between the start and stop node) with a maximum of four (sometimes redundant) candidates for any given phase.

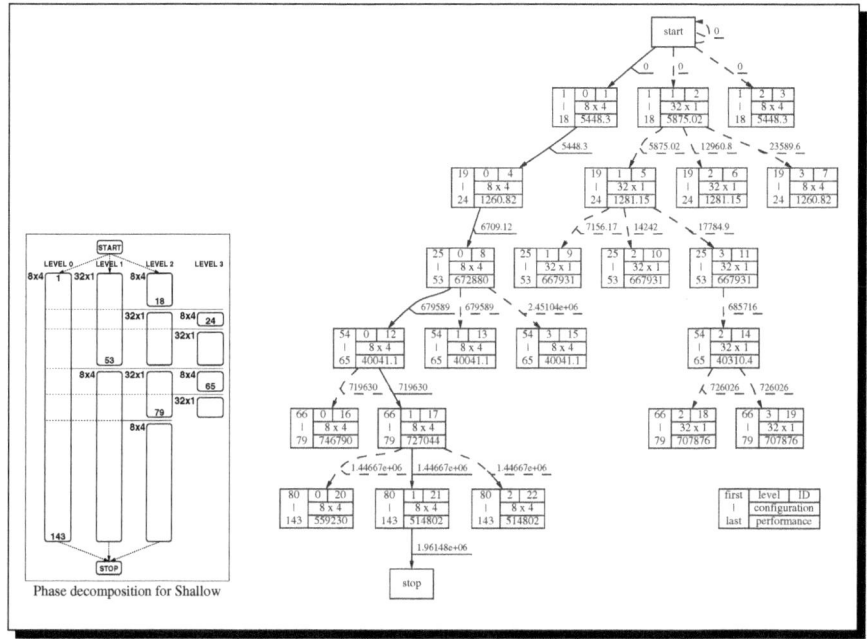

Fig. 6.5. Phase transition graph and solution for Shallow
(Displayed with the selected phase transition path and cummulative cost.)

As there were no alignment conflicts in the program, and only BLUCK distributions were necessary to maintain a balanced load, the distribution of the 14 arrays in the program can be inferred from the selected configuration of the processor mesh. By tracing the path back from the stop node to the start, the figure shows that the dynamic partitioner selected a two-dimensional (8×4) static data distribution. Since there is no redistribution performed along this path, the loop peeling process previously described in Section 3.4 is not shown on this graph as it is only necessary when there is actually redistribution present within a loop.

As the communication and computation estimates are best-case approximations (they don't take into account communication buffering operations or effects of the memory hierarchy), it is safe to say that for the Paragon, a dynamic data distribution does not exist which can out-perform the selected static distribution. Theoretically, if the communication cost for a machine were insignificant in comparison to the performance of computation, redistributing data between the phases revealed in the decomposition of Shallow would be beneficial. In this case, the dynamic partitioner performed more work to come to the same conclusion that a single application of the static partitioner would have. It is interesting to note that even though the dynamic partitioner considers any possible redistribution, it will still select a static distribution if that is what is predicted to have the best performance.

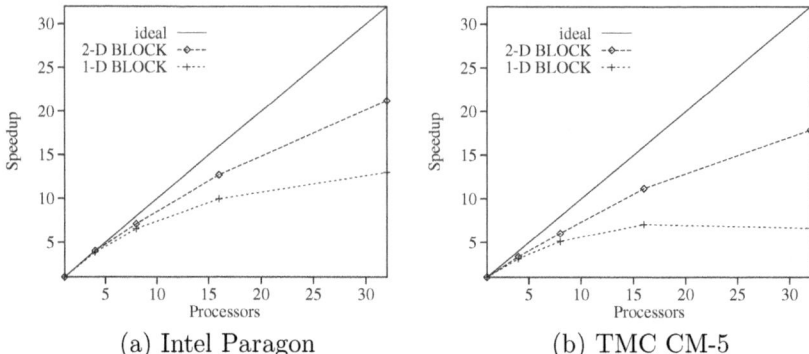

(a) Intel Paragon   (b) TMC CM-5

Fig. 6.6. Performance of Shallow

In Figure 6.6, the performance of the selected static 2-D distribution (BLOCK, BLOCK) is compared to a static 1-D row-wise distribution (BLOCK, *) which appeared in some of the subphases. The 2-D distribution matches the performance of the 1-D distribution for small numbers of processors while outperforming the 1-D distribution for both the Paragon and the CM-5 (by up to a factor of 1.6 or 2.7, respectively) for larger numbers of processors.

Kennedy and Kremer [24] have also examined the Shallow benchmark, but predicted that a one-dimensional (column-wise) block distribution was the best distribution for up to 32 processors of an Intel iPSC/860 hypercube (while also showing that the performance of a 1-D column-wise distribution was almost identical to a 1-D row-wise distribution). They only considered one-dimensional candidate layouts for the operational phases (since the Fortran D prototype compiler can not compile multidimensional distributions [41]). As their operational definition already results in 28 phases (over four times as many in comparison to our approach), the complexity of the resulting 0-1 integer programming formulation will also only increase further when considering multidimensional layouts.

7. Conclusions

Dynamic data partitionings can provide higher performance than purely static distributions for programs containing competing data access patterns. The distribution selection technique presented in this chapter provides a means of automatically determining high quality data distributions (dynamic as well as static) in an efficient manner taking into account both the structure of the input program as well as the architectural parameters of the target machine. Heuristics, based on the observation that high communication costs are a result of not being able to statically align every reference in complex programs simultaneously, are used to form the communication graph. By removing constraints between competing sections of the program, better distributions can potentially be obtained for the individual sections. If the resulting gains in performance are high enough in comparison to the cost of redistribution, dynamic distributions are formed. Communication still occurs, but data movement is now isolated into dynamic reorganizations of ownership as opposed to constantly obtaining any required remote data based on a (compromise) static assignment of ownership.

A key requirement in automating this process is to be able to obtain estimates of communication and computation costs which accurately model the behavior of the program under a given distribution. Furthermore, by building upon existing static partitioning techniques, the phases examined as well as the redistribution considered are focused in the areas of a program which will otherwise generate large amounts of communication.

In this chapter we have also presented an interprocedural data-flow technique that can be used to convert between redistribution and distribution representations optimizing redistribution while maintaining the semantics of the original program. For the data partitioner, the framework is used to synthesize explicit redistribution operations in order to preserve the meaning of what the data partitioner intended in the presence of HPF semantics. For HPF programs, redistribution operations (implicitly specified by HPF semantics or explicitly specified by a programmer) that result in distributions which would not otherwise be used before another redistribution operation occurs are completely removed.

Many HPF compilers that are currently available as commercial products or those that have been developed as research prototypes do not yet support transcriptive argument passing or the REDISTRIBUTE and REALIGN directives as there is still much work required to provide efficient support for the HPF subset (which does not include these features). Since the techniques presented in this chapter can convert all of these features into constructs which are in the HPF subset (through the use of SDA), this framework can also be used to provide these features to an existing subset HPF compiler.

Acknowledgement. We would like to thank Amber Roy Chowdhury for his assistance with the coding of the serial ADI algorithm, John Chandy and Amber Roy Chowdhury for discussions on algorithm complexity, as well as Christy Palermo for her suggestions and comments on this chapter.

The communication graph figures used in this chapter were also generated using a software package known as "Dot" developed by Eleftherios Koutsofios and Steven North with the Software and Systems Research Center, AT&T Bell Laboratories [28].

References

1. A. V. Aho, R. Sethi, and J. D. Ullman. *Compilers: Principles, Techniques, and Tools.* Addison-Wesley Publ., Reading, MA, 1986.

2. J. M. Anderson and M. S. Lam. Global optimizations for parallelism and locality on scalable parallel machines. In *Proc. of the ACM SIGPLAN '93 Conf. on Programming Language Design and Implementation*, 112–125, Albuquerque, NM, June 1993.

3. E. Ayguadé, J. Garcia, M. Girones, M. L. Grande, and J. Labarta. Data redistribution in an automatic data distribution tool. In *Proc. of the 8th Workshop on Languages and Compilers for Parallel Computing*, volume 1033 of *Lecture Notes in Computer Science*, 407–421, Columbus, OH, Aug. 1995. Springer-Verlag. 1996.

4. P. Banerjee, J. A. Chandy, M. Gupta, E. W. Hodges IV, J. G. Holm, A. Lain, D. J. Palermo, S. Ramaswamy, and E. Su. The PARADIGM compiler for distributed-memory multicomputers. *IEEE Computer*, 28(10):37–47, Oct. 1995.

5. D. Bau, I. Koduklula, V. Kotlyar, K. Pingali, and P. Stodghill. Solving alignment using elementary linear algebra. In *Proc. of the 7th Workshop on Languages and Compilers for Parallel Computing*, volume 892 of *Lecture Notes in Computer Science*, 46–60, Ithica, NY, 1994. Springer-Verlag. 1995.

6. R. Bixby, K. Kennedy, and U. Kremer. Automatic data layout using 0-1 integer programming. In *Proc. of the 1994 Int'l Conf. on Parallel Architectures and Compilation Techniques*, 111–122, Montréal, Canada, Aug. 1994.

7. B. Chapman, T. Fahringer, and H. Zima. Automatic support for data distribution on distributed memory multiprocessor systems. In *Proc. of the 6th Workshop on Languages and Compilers for Parallel Computing*, volume 768 of *Lecture Notes in Computer Science*, 184–199, Portland, OR, Aug. 1993. Springer-Verlag. 1994.

8. S. Chatterjee, J. R. Gilbert, R. Schreiber, and S. H. Teng. Automatic array alignment in data-parallel programs. In *Proc. of the 20th ACM SIGPLAN Symp. on Principles of Programming Languages*, 16–28, Charleston, SC, Jan. 1993.

9. F. Coelho and C. Ancourt. Optimal compilation of HPF remappings (extended abstract). Tech. Report CRI A-277, Centre de Recherche en Informatique, École des mines de Paris, Fontainebleau, France, Nov. 1995.

10. R. Cytron, J. Ferrante, B. K. Rosen, M. N. Wegman, and F. K. Zadeck. Efficiently computing static single assignment form and the control dependence graph. *ACM Trans. on Programming Languages and Systems*, 13(4):451–490, Oct. 1991.

11. T. Fahringer. *Automatic Performance Prediction for Parallel Programs on Massively Parallel Computers*. Ph.D. thesis, Univ. of Vienna, Austria, Sept. 1993. TR93-3.

12. J. A. Fisher. Trace scheduling: A technique for global microcode compaction. *IEEE Trans. on Computers*, c-30:478–490, July 1981.

13. J. Garcia, E. Ayguadé, and J. Labarta. A novel approach towards automatic data distribution. In *Proc. of the Workshop on Automatic Data Layout and Performance Prediction*, Houston, TX, Apr. 1995.

14. G. Golub and J. M. Ortega. *Scientific Computing: An Introduction with Parallel Computing*. Academic Press, San Diego, CA, 1993.

15. M. Gupta. *Automatic Data Partitioning on Distributed Memory Multicomputers*. Ph.D. thesis, Dept. of Computer Science, Univ. of Illinois, Urbana, IL, Sept. 1992. CRHC-92-19/UILU-ENG-92-2237.

16. M. Gupta and P. Banerjee. Compile-time estimation of communication costs on multicomputers. In *Proc. of the 6th Int'l Parallel Processing Symp.*, 470–475, Beverly Hills, CA, Mar. 1992.

17. M. Gupta and P. Banerjee. PARADIGM: A compiler for automated data partitioning on multicomputers. In *Proc. of the 7th ACM Int'l Conf. on Supercomputing*, Tokyo, Japan, July 1993.

18. M. W. Hall, S. Hiranandani, K. Kennedy, and C. Tseng. Interprocedural compilation of Fortran D for MIMD distributed-memory machines. In *Proc. of Supercomputing '92*, 522–534, Minneapolis, MN, Nov. 1992.

19. S. Hiranandani, K. Kennedy, and C. Tseng. Compiling Fortran D for MIMD distributed memory machines. *Communications of the ACM*, 35(8):66–80, Aug. 1992.

20. S. Hiranandani, K. Kennedy, and C.-W. Tseng. Evaluation of compiler optimizations for Fortran D on MIMD distributed-memory machines. In *Proc. of the 6th ACM Int'l Conf. on Supercomputing*, 1–14, Washington D.C., July 1992.

21. E. W. Hodges IV. High Performance Fortran support for the PARADIGM compiler. Master's thesis, Dept. of Electrical and Computer Eng., Univ. of Illinois, Urbana, IL, Oct. 1995. CRHC-95-23/UILU-ENG-95-2237.

22. D. E. Hudak and S. G. Abraham. *Compiling Parallel Loops for High Performance Computers – Partitioning, Data Assignment and Remapping*. Kluwer Academic Pub., Boston, MA, 1993.

23. W. W. Hwu, S. A. Mahlke, W. Y. Chen, P. P. Chang, N. J. Warter, R. A. Bringmann, R. G. Ouellette, R. E. Hank, T. Kiyohara, G. E. Haab, J. G. Holm, and D. M. Lavery. The Superblock: An effective technique for VLIW and superscalar compilation. *The Journal of Supercomputing*, 7(1):229–248, Jan. 1993.

24. K. Kennedy and U. Kremer. Automatic data layout for High Performance Fortran. In *Proc. of Supercomputing '95*, San Diego, CA, Dec. 1995.

25. K. Knobe, J. Lukas, and G. Steele, Jr. Data optimization: Allocation of arrays to reduce communication on SIMD machines. *Journal of Parallel and Distributed Computing*, 8(2):102–118, Feb. 1990.

26. C. Koelbel, D. Loveman, R. Schreiber, G. Steele, Jr., and M. Zosel. *The High Performance Fortran Handbook*. The MIT Press, Cambridge, MA, 1994.

27. U. Kremer. *Automatic Data Layout for High Performance Fortran*. Ph.D. thesis, Rice Univ., Houston, TX, Oct. 1995. CRPC-TR95559-S.

28. B. Krishnamurthy, editor. *Practical Reusable UNIX Software*. John Wiley and Sons Inc., New York, NY, 1995.

29. J. Li and M. Chen. The data alignment phase in compiling programs for distributed-memory machines. *Journal of Parallel and Distributed Computing*, 13(2):213–221, Oct. 1991.

30. D. J. Palermo. *Compiler Techniques for Optimizing Communication and Data Distribution for Distributed-Memory Multicomputers*. Ph.D. thesis, Dept. of Electrical and Computer Eng., Univ. of Illinois, Urbana, IL, June 1996. CRHC-96-09/UILU-ENG-96-2215.

31. D. J. Palermo, E. W. Hodges IV, and P. Banerjee. Dynamic data partitioning for distributed-memory multicomputers. *Journal of Parallel and Distributed Computing*, 38(2):158–175, Nov. 1996. special issue on *Compilation Techniques for Distributed Memory Systems*.

32. D. J. Palermo, E. W. Hodges IV, and P. Banerjee. Interprocedural array redistribution data-flow analysis. In *Proc. of the 9th Workshop on Languages and Compilers for Parallel Computing*, San Jose, CA, Aug. 1996.

33. D. J. Palermo, E. Su, J. A. Chandy, and P. Banerjee. Compiler optimizations for distributed memory multicomputers used in the PARADIGM compiler. In *Proc. of the 23rd Int'l Conf. on Parallel Processing*, II:1–10, St. Charles, IL, Aug. 1994.

34. C. D. Polychronopoulos, M. Girkar, M. R. Haghighat, C. L. Lee, B. Leung, and D. Schouten. Parafrase-2: An environment for parallelizing, partitioning,

synchronizing and scheduling programs on multiprocessors. In *Proc. of the 18th Int'l Conf. on Parallel Processing*, II:39–48, St. Charles, IL, Aug. 1989.

35. J. Ramanujam and P. Sadayappan. Compile-time techniques for data distribution in distributed memory machines. *IEEE Trans. on Parallel and Distributed Systems*, 2(4):472–481, Oct. 1991.

36. S. Ramaswamy and P. Banerjee. Automatic generation of efficient array redistribution routines for distributed memory multicomputers. In *Frontiers '95: The 5th Symp. on the Frontiers of Massively Parallel Computation*, 342–349, McLean, VA, Feb. 1995.

37. R. Sadourny. The dynamics of finite-difference models of the shallow-water equations. *Journal of the Atmospheric Sciences*, 32(4), Apr. 1975.

38. T. J. Sheffler, R. Schreiber, J. R. Gilbert, and W. Pugh. Efficient distribution analysis via graph contraction. In *Proc. of the 8th Workshop on Languages and Compilers for Parallel Computing*, volume 1033 of *Lecture Notes in Computer Science*, 377–391, Columbus, OH, Aug. 1995. Springer-Verlag. 1996.

39. H. Sivaraman and C. S. Raghavendra. Compiling for MIMD distributed memory machines. Tech. Report EECS-94-021, School of Electrical Enginnering and Computer Science, Washington State Univ., Pullman, WA, 1994.

40. R. E. Tarjan. *Data Structures and Network Algorithms*. Society for Industrial and Applied Mathematics, Philadelphia, PA, 1983.

41. C. W. Tseng. *An Optimizing Fortran D Compiler for MIMD Distributed-Memory Machines*. Ph.D. thesis, Rice Univ., Houston, TX, Jan. 1993. COMP TR93-199.

42. P. S. Tseng. Compiling programs for a linear systolic array. In *Proc. of the ACM SIGPLAN '90 Conf. on Programming Language Design and Implementation*, 311–321, White Plains, NY, June 1990.

43. R. von Hanxleden and K. Kennedy. GIVE-N-TAKE – A balanced code placement framework. In *Proc. of the ACM SIGPLAN '94 Conf. on Programming Language Design and Implementation*, 107–120, Orlando, FL, June 1994.

44. S. Wholey. Automatic data mapping for distributed-memory parallel computers. In *Proc. of the 6th ACM Int'l Conf. on Supercomputing*, 25–34, Washington D.C., July 1992.

Chapter 14. A Framework for Global Communication Analysis and Optimizations

Manish Gupta

IBM T. J. Watson Research Center, P.O. Box 218, Yorktown Heights, NY 10598

1. Introduction

Distributed memory architectures have become popular as a viable and cost-effective method of building scalable parallel computers. However, the absence of global address space, and consequently, the need for explicit message passing among processes makes these machines very difficult to program. This has motivated the design of languages like High Performance Fortran [14], which allow the programmer to write sequential or shared-memory parallel programs that are annotated with directives specifying data decomposition. The compilers for these languages are responsible for partitioning the computation, and generating the communication necessary to fetch values of non-local data referenced by a processor. A number of such prototype compilers have been developed [3, 6, 19, 23, 29, 30, 33, 34, 43].

Accessing remote data is usually orders of magnitude slower than accessing local data. This gap is growing because CPU performance is out-growing network performance, CPU's are running relatively independent multiprogrammed operating systems, and commodity networks are being found more cost-effective. As a result, communication startup overheads tend to be astronomical on most distributed memory machines, although reasonable bandwidth can be supported for sufficiently large messages [36, 37]. Thus compilers must reduce the *number* as well as the *volume* of messages in order to deliver high performance. The most common optimizations include message vectorization [23, 43], using collective communication [18, 30], and overlapping communication with computation [23]. However, many compilers perform little global analysis of the communication requirements across different loop nests. This precludes general optimizations, such as redundant communication elimination, or carrying out extra communication inside one loop nest if it subsumes communication required in the next loop nest.

This chapter presents a framework, based on global array data-flow analysis, to reduce communication in a program. We apply techniques for partial redundancy elimination, discussed in the context of eliminating redundant computation by Morel and Renvoise [31], and later refined by other researchers [12, 13, 25]. The conventional approach to data-flow analysis regards each access to an array element as an access to the entire array. Previous researchers [16, 17, 35] have applied data-flow analysis to array sections to improve its precision. However, using just array sections is insufficient in the

S. Pande, D.P. Agrawal (Eds.): Compiler Optimizations for Scalable PS, LNCS 1808, pp. 485–524, 2001.

context of communication optimizations. There is a need to represent information about the processors where the array elements are available, or need to be made available. For this purpose, we introduce a new kind of descriptor, the *Available Section Descriptor* (ASD) [21]. The explicit representation of availability of data in our framework allows us to relax the restriction that only the owner of a data item be able to supply its value when needed by another processor. An important special case occurs when a processor that needs a value for its computation does not own the data but has a valid value available from prior communication. In that case, the communication from the owner to this processor can be identified as redundant and eliminated, with the intended receiver simply using the locally available value of data. We show how the data flow procedure for eliminating partial redundancies is extended and applied to communication, represented using the ASDs. With the resultant framework, we are able to capture a number of optimizations, such as:

- vectorizing communication,
- eliminating communication that is redundant in any control flow path,
- reducing the amount of data being communicated,
- reducing the number of processors to which data must be communicated, and
- moving communication earlier to hide latency, and to subsume previous communication.

We do not know of any other system that tries to perform all of these optimizations, and in a global manner. Following the results presented in [13] for partially redundant computations, we show that the bidirectional problem of eliminating partial redundancies can be decomposed into simpler unidirectional problems, in the context of communication represented using ASDs as well. That makes the analysis procedure more efficient. We have implemented a simplified version of this framework as part of a prototype HPF compiler. Our preliminary experiments show significant performance improvements resulting from this analysis.

An advantage of our approach is that the analysis is performed on the original program form, before any communication is introduced by the compiler. Thus, communication optimizations based on data availability analysis need not depend on a detailed knowledge of explicit communication representations.

While our work has been done in the context of compiling for distributed memory machines, it is relevant for shared memory machines as well. Shared memory compilers can exploit information about interprocessor sharing of data to eliminate unnecessary barrier synchronization or replace barrier synchronization by cheaper producer-consumer synchronization in the generated parallel code [20, 32, 39]. A reduction in the number of communication messages directly translates into fewer synchronization messages. Another application of our work is in improving the effectiveness of block data transfer operations in scalable shared memory multiprocessors. For scalable shared memory machines with high network latency, it is important for the underlying system to reduce the overhead of messages needed to keep data coherent. Using block data transfer operations on these machines helps amortize the overhead of messages needed for non-local data access. The analysis presented in this paper can be used to accurately identify sections of data which are not available locally, and which should be subjected to block data transfer operations for better performance.

The rest of this chapter is organized as follows: Section 2 describes, using an example, the various communication optimizations that are performed by the data flow procedure described in this chapter. Section 3 describes our representation of the Available Section Descriptor and the procedure to compute the communication generated for a statement in the program. Section 4 discusses the procedure for computing data flow information used in optimizing communications. In Section 5, we describe how the different communication optimizations are captured by the data flow analysis. Section 6 describes an extension to our framework to select a placement of communication that can reduce communication costs of a program even further. Section 7 presents the algorithms for the various operations on ASDs. Section 8 presents some preliminary results and in Section 9, we discuss related work. Finally, Section 10 presents conclusions.

2. Motivating Example

We now illustrate various communication optimizations mentioned above using an example. Figure 2.1(a) shows an HPF program and a high level view of communication that would be generated by a compiler following the *owner-computes* rule [23,43], which assigns each computation to the processor that owns the data being computed. Communication is generated for each non-local data value used by a processor in the computation assigned to it. The HPF directives specify the alignment of each array with respect to a template VPROCS, which is viewed as a grid of virtual processors in the context of this work. The variables a and z are two-dimensional arrays aligned with VPROCS, and d, e, and w are one-dimensional arrays aligned with the first column of VPROCS. In this example, we assume that the scalar variable s is replicated on all processors. The communication shown in Figure 2.1(a) already incorporates message vectorization, a commonly used optimization to move communication out of loops. While message vectorization is captured naturally by our framework as we shall explain, in this chapter we focus on other important optimizations that illustrate the power of this framework. Our analysis is independent of the actual primitives (such as send-receive, broadcast) used to implement communication. We use the notation $x(i) \rightarrow VPROCS(i, j)$ (the ranges of i and j are omitted to save space in the figure) to mean that the value of $x(i)$ is sent to the virtual processor position

VPROCS(i, j), for all $1 \leq i \leq 100$, $1 \leq j \leq 100$. Reduced communication after global optimization is shown in Figure 2.1(b). We consider optimizations performed for each variable d, e, and w.

There are two identical communications for e in Figure 2.1(a), which result from the uses of e in statements 10 and 26. In both cases, e(i) must be sent to VPROCS(i, j), for all values of i, j. However, because of the assignment to e(1) in statement 13, the second communication is only partially redundant. Thus, we can eliminate the second communication, except for sending e(1) to VPROCS(1, j), for all values of j. This reduced communication is hoisted to the earliest possible place after statement 13 in Figure 2.1(b).

In Figure 2.1(a), there are two communications for d, resulting from uses of d in statements 16 and 26. In Figure 2.1(b), the second communication has been hoisted to the earliest possible place, after statement 7, where it subsumes the first communication, which has been eliminated.

Finally, there are two communications for w, resulting from uses of w in statements 16 and 28. The second, partially redundant, communication is hoisted inside the two branches of the if statement, and is eliminated in the then branch. The assignment to w(i) at statement 21 prevents the communication in the else branch from being moved earlier.

The result of this collection of optimizations leads to a program in which communication is initiated as early as possible, and the total volume of communication has been reduced.

3. Available Section Descriptor

In this section, we describe the *Available Section Descriptor* (ASD), a representation of data and its availability on processors. When referring to *availability* of data, we do not explicitly include information about the *ownership* of data, unless stated otherwise. This enables us to keep a close correspondence between the notions of availability of data and communication: in the context of our work, the essential view of communication is that it makes data available at processors which need it for their computation; the identity of the sender may be changed as long as the receiver gets the correct data. Hence, the ASD serves both as a representation of communication (by specifying the data to be made available at processors), and of the data actually made available by previous communications. Data remains available at receiving processors until it is modified by its owner or until the communication buffer holding non-local data is deallocated. Our analysis for determining the availability of data is based on the assumption that a communication buffer is never deallocated before the last read reference to that data. This can be ensured by the code generator after the analysis has identified read references which lead to communication that is redundant. Section 3.1 describes the

```
      HPF align (i, j) with VPROCS(i,j) :: a, z
      HPF align (i) with VPROCS(i,1) :: d, e, w
```

1: do i = 1, 100	do i = 1, 100
5: e(i) = d(i) * w(i)	e(i) = d(i) * w(i)
6: d(i) = d(i) + 2 * w(i)	d(i) = d(i) + 2 * w(i)
7: end do	end do
$e(i) \to VPROCS(i,j)$	$e(i), d(i) \to VPROCS(i,j)$
8: do i = 1, 100	do i = 1, 100
9: do j = 1, 100	do j = 1, 100
10: z(i,j) = e(i)	z(i,j) = e(i)
11: end do	end do
12: end do	end do
13: e(1) = 2 * d(1)	e(1) = 2 * d(1)
	$e(1) \to VPROCS(1,j)$
14: if (s $\neq$ 0) then	if (s $\neq$ 0) then
$d(i), w(i) \to VPROCS(i,100)$	$w(i) \to VPROCS(i,100)$
15: do i = 1, 100	do i = 1, 100
16: z(i,100) = d(i) / w(i)	z(i,100) = d(i) / w(i)
17: end do	end do
18: else	else
19: do i = 1, 100	do i = 1,100
20: z(i,100) = m	z(i, 100) = m
21: w(i) = m	w(i) = m
22: end do	end do
	$w(i) \to VPROCS(i,100)$
23: end if	end if
$e(i), d(i) \to VPROCS(i,j)$	
$w(i) \to VPROCS(i,100)$	
24: do j = 1, 100	do j = 1, 100
25: do i = 1, 100	do i = 1, 100
26: a(i,j) = a(i,j) +	a(i,j) = a(i,j) +
(d(i) * e(i))/z(i,j)	(d(i) * e(i))/z(i,j)
27: end do	end do
28: z(j,100) = w(j)	z(j,100) = w(j)
29: end do	end do
(a)	(b)

Fig. 2.1. Program before and after communication optimizations.

ASD representation. Section 3.2 describes how the communication generated at a statement is computed in terms of an ASD representation.

3.1 Representation of ASD

The ASD is defined as a pair $\langle D, M \rangle$, where D is a data descriptor, and M is a descriptor of the function mapping elements in D to virtual processors. Thus, $M(D)$ refers collectively to processors where data in D is available. For an array variable, the data descriptor represents an array section. For a scalar variable, it consists of just the name of the variable. Many representations like the *regular section descriptor* (RSD) [9], and the *data access descriptor* (DAD) [5] have been proposed in the literature to summarize array sections. Our analysis is largely independent of the actual descriptor used to represent data.

For the purpose of analysis in this work, we shall use the *bounded regular section descriptor* (BRSD) [22], a special version of the RSD, to represent array sections and treat scalar variables as degenerate cases of arrays with no dimensions. Bounded regular sections allow representation of subarrays that can be specified using the Fortran 90 triplet notation. We represent a bounded regular section as an expression $A(S)$, where A is the name of an array variable, S is a vector of subscript values such that each of its elements is either (i) an expression of the form $\alpha * k + \beta$, where k is a loop index variable and α and β are invariants, (ii) a triple $l : u : s$, where l, u, and s are invariants (the triple represents the expression discussed above expanded over a range) , or (iii) $\perp$, indicating no knowledge of the subscript value.

The processor space is regarded as an unbounded grid of virtual processors. The abstract processor space is similar to a *template* in High Performance Fortran (HPF) [14], which is a grid over which different arrays are aligned. The mapping function descriptor M is a pair $\langle P, F \rangle$, both P and F being vectors of length equal to the dimensionality of the processor grid. The ith element of P (denoted as P^i) indicates the dimension of the array A that is mapped to the ith grid dimension, and F^i is the mapping function for that array dimension, i.e., $F^i(j)$ returns the position(s) along the ith grid dimension to which the jth element of the array dimension is mapped. We represent a mapping function, when known statically, as

$$F^i(j) \;=\; (c * j + l : c * j + u : s)$$

In the above expression, c, l, u and s are invariants. The parameters c, l and u may take rational values, as long as $F^i(j)$ evaluates to a range over integers, over the data domain. The above formulation allows representation of one-to-one mappings (when $l = u$), one-to-many mappings (when $u \geq l + s$), and also constant mappings (when $c = 0$). The one-to-many mappings expressible with this formulation are more general than the replicated mappings for ownership that may be specified using HPF [14]. Under an HPF alignment directive, the jth element of array dimension P^i may be mapped along the ith grid dimension to position $c * j + o$ or "$*$", which represents all positions in that grid dimension.

If an array has fewer dimensions than the processor grid (this also holds for scalars, which are viewed as arrays with no dimensions), there is no array dimension mapped to some of the grid dimensions. For each such grid dimension m, P^m takes the value μ, which represents a "missing" array dimension. In that case, F^m is no longer a function of a subscript position. It is simply an expression of the form $l : u : s$, and indicates the position(s) in the mth grid dimension at which the array is available. As with the usual triplet notation, we shall omit the stride, s, from an expression when it is equal to one. When the compiler is unable to infer knowledge about the availability of data, the corresponding mapping function is set to $\bot$. We also define a special, universal mapping function descriptor $\mathcal{U}$, which represents the mapping of each data element on all of the processors.

Example. Consider a 2-D virtual processor grid VPROCS, and an ASD $\langle A(2 : 100 : 2, 1 : 100), \langle [1, 2], [F^1, F^2] \rangle \rangle$, where $F^1(i) = i - 1, F^2(j) = 1 : 100$. The ASD represents an array section $A(2 : 100 : 2, 1 : 100)$, each of whose element $A(2 * i, j)$ is available at a hundred processor positions given by VPROCS$(2*i-1, 1 : 100)$. This ASD is illustrated in Figure 3.1. Figure 3.1(a) shows the array A, where each horizontal stripe A_i represents $A(2*i, 1 : 100)$. Figure 3.1(b) represents the mapping of the array section onto the virtual processor template VPROCS, where each subsection A_i is replicated along its corresponding row.

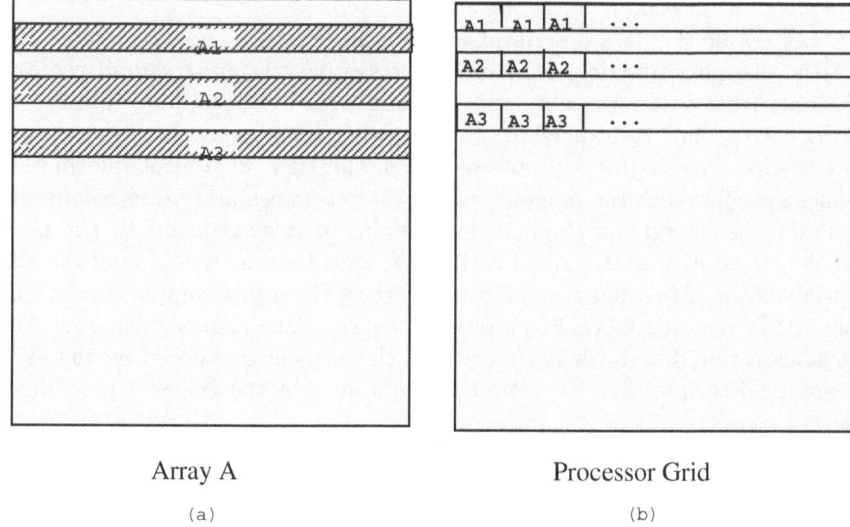

Array A   Processor Grid

(a)   (b)

Fig. 3.1. Illustration of ASD

3.2 Computing Generated Communication

Given an assignment statement of the form $lhs = rhs$, we describe how communication needed for each reference in the rhs expression is represented as an ASD. This section deals only with communication needed for a single instance of the assignment statement, which may appear nested inside loops. The procedure for summarizing communication requirements of multiple instances of a statement with respect to the surrounding loops is discussed in the next section. We shall describe our procedure for array references with arbitrary number of dimensions; references to scalar variables can be viewed as special cases with zero dimensions. This analysis is applied after any array language constructs (such as Fortran 90 array assignment statements) have been *scalarized* into equivalent Fortran 77-like assignment statements appearing inside loops. Each subscript expression is assumed to be a constant or an affine function of a surrounding loop index. If any subscript expressions are non-linear or coupled, then the ASD representing that communication is set to $\perp$, and is conservatively underestimated or overestimated, based on the context.

As remarked earlier, the identity of senders is ignored in our representation of communication. The ASD simply represents the intended availability of data to be realized via the given communication, or equivalently, the availability of data following that communication. Clearly, that depends on the mapping of computation to processors. In this work, we determine the generation of communication based on the *owner computes* rule, which assigns the computation to the owner of the lhs. The algorithm can be modified to incorporate other methods of assigning computation to processors [11], as long as that decision is made statically.

Let D_L be the data descriptor for the lhs reference and $M_L = \langle P_L, F_L \rangle$ be the mapping function descriptor representing the *ownership* of the lhs variable (this case represents an exception where the mapping function of ASD corresponds to ownership of data rather than its availability at other processors). M_L is directly obtained from the HPF alignment information which specifies both the mapping relationship between array dimensions and grid dimensions (giving P_L) and the mapping of array elements to grid positions (giving F_L), as described earlier. We calculate the mapping of the rhs variable $\langle D_R, M_R \rangle$ that results from enforcing the owner computes rule. The new ASD, denoted $CGEN$, represents the rhs data aligned with lhs. The regular section descriptor D_R represents the element referenced by rhs. The mapping descriptor $M_R = \langle P_R, F_R \rangle$ is obtained by the following procedure:

Step 1. Align array dimensions with processor grid dimensions:

1. For each processor grid dimension i, if the lhs subscript expression, $S_L^{P_L^i}$, in dimension P_L^i has the form $\alpha_1 * k + \beta_1$ and there is a rhs subscript expression $S_R^n = \alpha_2 * k + \beta_2$, for the same loop index variable k, set P_R^i to the rhs subscript position n.

2. For each remaining processor grid dimension i, set P_R^i to j, where j is an unassigned **rhs** subscript position. If there is no unassigned **rhs** subscript position left, set P_R^i to μ.

Step 2. Calculate the mapping function for each grid dimension:
For each processor grid dimension i, let $F_L^i(j) = c * j + o$ be the ownership mapping function of the **lhs** variable (c and o are integer constants, with the exception of replicated mapping, where $c = 0$ and o represents the range of all positions in that grid dimension). We determine the **rhs** mapping function $F_R^i(j)$ from the **lhs** and the **rhs** subscript expressions corresponding respectively to dimensions P_R^i and P_L^i. The details are specified in Table 1.

The first entry in Table 1 follows from the fact that element $j = \alpha_2 * k + \beta_2$ of $S_R^{P_R^i}$ is made available at grid position $c * (\alpha_1 * k + \beta_1) + o$ along the ith dimension; substituting k by $(j - \beta_2)/\alpha_2$ directly leads to the given result. The second and the third entries correspond to the special cases when the **rhs** dimension has a constant subscript or there is no **rhs** dimension mapped to grid dimension i. The last entry represents the case when there is no **lhs** array dimension mapped to grid dimension i. In that case, the mapping function of the **lhs** variable must have $c = 0$.

$S_L^{P_L^i}$	$S_R^{P_R^i}$	$F_R^i(j)$
$\alpha_1 * k + \beta_1$	$\alpha_2 * k + \beta_2$, $\alpha_2 \neq 0$	$c * (\frac{\alpha_1 * (j - \beta_2)}{\alpha_2} + \beta_1) + o$
$\alpha_1 * k + \beta_1$	β_2	$c * (\alpha_1 * k + \beta_1) + o$
$\alpha_1 * k + \beta_1$	"missing"	$c * (\alpha_1 * k + \beta_1) + o$
"missing"	$\alpha_2 * k + \beta_2$	o (c must be 0)

Table 3.1. Mapping function calculation based on the owner computes rule

Example. Consider the assignment statement in the code fragment:

$$\text{HPF ALIGN } A(i,j) \text{ WITH VPROCS}(i,j)$$
$$\dots$$
$$A(i,j) = \dots B(2 * i, j - 1) \dots$$

The ownership mapping descriptor M_L for the *lhs* variable A is $\langle [1, 2], F_L \rangle$ where $F_L^1(i) = i$ and $F_L^2(j) = j$. This mapping descriptor is derived from the HPF alignment specification. Applying Step 1 of the compute rule algorithm, P_R is set to $[1, 2]$, that is, the first dimension of VPROCS is aligned with the first dimension of B, and the second dimension of VPROCS is aligned with the second dimension of B.

The second step is to determine the mapping function F_R. For the first grid dimension, P_L^1 corresponds to the subscript expression i and P_R^1 corresponds to the subscript expression $2 * i$. Therefore, using F_L^1 and the first rule in

Table 1, $F_R^1(i)$ is set to $(1*(1*i - 0)/2) + 0) + 0 = i/2$. For the second grid dimension, P_L^2 corresponds to the subscript expression j, and P_R^2 corresponds to the subscript expression $j - 1$. Using F_L^2 and the first rule in Table 1, $F_R^2(j)$ is set to $j + 1$. The mapping descriptor thus obtained maps B(2*i, j-1) onto VPROCS(i, j).

4. Data Flow Analysis

In this section, we present a procedure for obtaining data flow information regarding communication for a structured program. The analysis is performed on the control flow graph representation [1] of the program, in which nodes represent computation, and edges represent the flow of control. We are able to perform a collection of communication optimizations within a single framework, based on the following observations. Determining the *data availability* resulting from communication is a problem similar to determining *available expressions* in classical data flow analysis. Thus, optimizations like eliminating and hoisting communications are similar to eliminating redundant expressions and code motion. Furthermore, applying partial redundancy elimination techniques at the granularity of sections of arrays and processors enables not merely elimination, but also reduction in the volume of communication along different control flow paths.

The bidirectional data-flow analysis for suppression of partial redundancies, introduced by Morel and Renvoise [31], and refined subsequently [12,13,25], defines a framework for unifying common optimizations on available expressions. We adapt this framework to solve the set of communication optimizations described in Section 2. This section presents the following results.

- Section 4.1 reformulates the refined data-flow equations from [13] in terms of ASDs. We have incorporated a further modification that is useful in the context of optimizing communication.
- Section 4.2 shows that the bidirectional problem of determining the possible placement of communication can be solved by obtaining a solution to a backward problem, followed by a forward correction.
- In contrast to previous work, solving these equations for ASDs requires array data-flow analysis. In Section 4.3, we present the overall data-flow procedure that uses interval analysis.

As with other similar frameworks, we require the following edge-splitting transformation to be performed on the control flow graph before the analysis begins: any edge that runs directly from a node with more than one successor, to a node with more than one predecessor, is split [13]. This transformation is illustrated in Figure 4.1. Thus, in the transformed graph, there is no direct edge from a branch node to a join node.

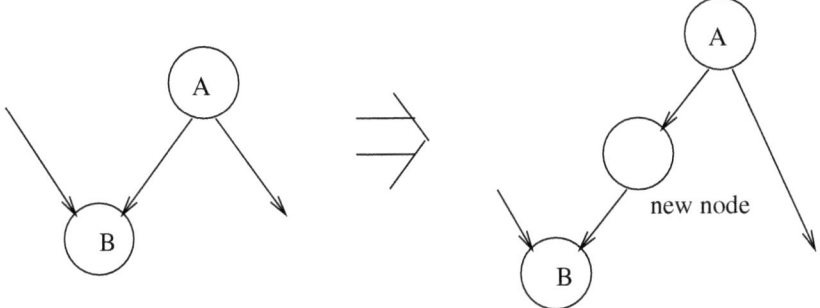

Fig. 4.1. Edge splitting transformation

4.1 Data Flow Variables and Equations

We use the following definitions for data-flow variables representing information about communication at different nodes in the control flow graph. Each of these variables is represented as an ASD.

$ANTLOC_i$: communication in node i, that is not preceded by a definition in node i of any data being communicated (i.e., local communication that may be anticipated at entry to node i).
$CGEN_i$: communication in node i, that is not followed by a definition in node i of any data being communicated.
$KILL_i$: data being killed (on all processors) due to a definition in node i.

$AVIN_i/AVOUT_i$: availability of data at the entry/exit of node i.
$PPIN_i/PPOUT_i$: variables representing safe placement of communication at the entry/exit of node i, with some additional properties (described later in this section).
$INSERT_i$: communication that should be inserted at the exit of node i.
$REDUND_i$: communication in node i that is redundant.

Local Data Flow Variables For an assignment statement, both $ANTLOC$ and $CGEN$ are set to the communication required to send each variable referenced on the right hand side (**rhs**) to the processor executing the statement. That depends on the compute-rule used by the compiler in translating the source program into SPMD form. Consider the program segment from the example in Section 3.2:

$$\text{HPF ALIGN } A(i,j) \text{ WITH VPROCS}(i,j)$$
$$\dots$$
$$A(i,j) = \dots B(2*i, j-1)\dots$$

Using the procedure in Section 3.2, we compute the communication necessary to send B(2*i, j-1) to the processor executing the statement as:
$CGEN = ANTLOC = \langle B(2*i, j-1), \langle [1,2], [F_1, F_2] \rangle \rangle$, where $F_1(i) = i/2$,

and $F_2(j) = j+1$. The $KILL$ variable for the statement is set to $\langle A(i,j), \mathcal{U} \rangle$, signifying that $A(i,j)$ is killed on all processors. The procedure for determining $CGEN$, $ANTLOC$, and $KILL$ for nodes corresponding to program intervals shall be discussed in Section 4.3.

Global Data Flow Variables The data flow equations, as adapted from [13], are shown below.[1] $AVIN$ is defined as $\emptyset$ for the entry node, while $PPOUT$ is defined as $\emptyset$ for the exit node, and initialized to $\top$ for all other nodes.

$$AVOUT_i = [AVIN_i - KILL_i] \cup CGEN_i \tag{4.1}$$

$$AVIN_i = \bigcap_{p \in pred(i)} AVOUT_p \tag{4.2}$$

$$PPIN_i = [(PPOUT_i - KILL_i) \cup ANTLOC_i] \cap$$
$$[\bigcap_{p \in pred(i)} (AVOUT_p \cup PPOUT_p)] \tag{4.3}$$

$$PPOUT_i = \bigcap_{s \in succ(i)} PPIN_s \tag{4.4}$$

$$INSERT_i = [PPOUT_i - AVOUT_i] - [PPIN_i - KILL_i] \tag{4.5}$$

$$REDUND_i = PPIN_i \cap ANTLOC_i \tag{4.6}$$

The problem of determining the availability of data ($AVIN_i/AVOUT_i$) is similar to the classical data-flow problem of determining *available expressions* [1]. This computation proceeds in the forward direction through the control flow graph. The first equation ensures that any data overwritten inside node i is removed from the availability set, and data communicated during node i (and not overwritten later) is added to the availability set. The second equation indicates that at entry to a join node in the control flow graph, only the data available at exit on each of the predecessor nodes can be considered to be available.

We now consider the computation of $PPIN/PPOUT$. The term $[(PPOUT_i - KILL_i) \cup ANTLOC_i]$ in Equation 4.3 denotes the part of communication occurring in node i or hoisted into it that can legally be moved to the entry of node i. A further intersection of that term with $[\cap_{p \in pred(i)}(AVOUT_p \cup PPOUT_p)]$ gives an additional property to $PPIN_i$,

---

[1] The original equation in [13] for $PPIN_i$ has an additional term, corresponding to the right hand side being further intersected with $PAVIN_i$, the partial availability of data at entry to node i. This term is important in the context of eliminating partially redundant computation, because it prevents unnecessary code motion that increases register pressure. However, moving communication early can be useful even if it does not lead to a reduction in previous communication, because it may help hide the latency. Hence, we drop that term in our equation for $PPIN_i$.

namely that all data included in $PPIN_i$ must be available at entry to node i on every incoming path due to original or moved communication. $PPOUT_i$ is set to communication that can be placed at entry to each of the successor nodes to i, as shown by Equation 4.4. Thus, $PPOUT_i$ represents communication that can legally and *safely* appear at the exit of node i. The property of safety implies that the communication is necessary, regardless of the flow of control in the program. Hence, the compiler avoids doing any speculative communication in the process of moving communication earlier.

As Equations 4.3 and 4.4 show, the value of $PPIN_i$ for a node i is not only used to compute $PPOUT_p$ for its predecessor node p, but it also depends on the value of $PPOUT_p$. Hence, this computation represents a *bidirectional* data flow problem.

Finally, $INSERT_i$ represents communication that should be inserted at the exit of node i as a result of the optimization. Given that $PPOUT_i$ represents safe communication at that point, as shown in Equation 4.5, $INSERT_i$ consists of $PPOUT_i$ minus the following two components: (i) data already available at exit of node i due to original communication: given by $AVOUT_i$, and (ii) data available at entry to node i due to moved or original communication, and which has not been overwritten inside node i: this component is given by $(PPIN_i - KILL_i)$. Following the insertions, any communication in node i that is not preceded by a definition of data (i.e., $ANTLOC_i$) and which also forms part of $PPIN_i$ becomes redundant. This directly follows from the property of $PPIN_i$ that any data included in $PPIN_i$ must be available at entry to node i on every incoming path due to original or moved communication. Thus, in Equation 4.6, $REDUND_i$ represents communication in node i that can be deleted.

The union, intersection, and difference operations on ASDs are described later in the chapter, in Section 7. The ASDs are not closed under these operations (the intersection operation is always exact, except in the special case when two mapping functions, of the form $F_i(j) = c * i + l : c * i + u : s$, for corresponding array dimensions have different values of the coefficient c). Therefore, it is important to know for each operation whether to underestimate or overestimate the result, in case an approximation is needed. In the above equations, each of $AVIN_i, AVOUT_i, PPIN_i, PPOUT_i$, and $REDUND_i$ are *underestimated*, if necessary. On the other hand, $INSERT_i$ is *overestimated*, if needed. This ensures that the compiler does not incorrectly eliminate communication that is actually not redundant. While the overestimation of $INSERT_i$ or underestimation of $REDUND_i$ can potentially lead to more communication than necessary, our framework has some built-in guards against insertion of extra communication relative to the unoptimized program. The Morel-Renvoise framework [31] and its modified versions ensure that $PPIN_i$ and $PPOUT_i$ represent safe placements of computation at the entry/exit of node i. Correspondingly, in the context of our work, $PPIN_i/PPOUT_i$ does not represent more communication than necessary.

4.2 Decomposition of Bidirectional Problem

Before we describe our data-flow procedure using the above equations, we
need to resolve the problem of bidirectionality in the computation of $PPIN_i$
and $PPOUT_i$. Solving a bidirectional problem usually requires an algorithm
that goes back and forth until convergence is reached. A preferable approach
is to decompose the bidirectional problem, if possible, into simpler unidirectional problem(s) which can be solved more efficiently.

Dhamdhere et al. [13] prove some properties about the bidirectional problem of eliminating redundant computation, and also prove that those properties are sufficient to allow the decomposition of that problem into two unidirectional problems. One of those properties, distributivity, does not hold
in our case, because we represent data-flow variables as ASDs rather than
bit strings, and the operations like union and difference are not exact, unlike
the boolean operations. However, we are able to prove directly the following
theorem:

Theorem 41. *The bidirectional problem of determining $PPIN_i$ and
$PPOUT_i$, as given by Equations 4.3 and 4.4, can be decomposed into a backward approximation, given by Equations 4.7 and 4.8, followed by a forward
correction, given by Equation 4.9.*

$$BA\_PPIN_i = (PPOUT_i - KILL_i) \cup ANTLOC_i \quad (4.7)$$
$$PPOUT_i = \bigcap_{s \in succ(i)} BA\_PPIN_s \quad (4.8)$$
$$PPIN_i = BA\_PPIN_i \cap [\bigcap_{p \in pred(i)} (AVOUT_p \cup PPOUT_p)] \quad (4.9)$$

Proof : BA_PPIN_i represents a *backward approximation* to the value of
$PPIN_i$ (intuitively, it represents communication that can legally and safely
be moved to the entry of node i). We will show that the correction term
$(\cap_{p \in pred(i)}(AVOUT_p \cup PPOUT_p))$ applied to a node i to obtain $PPIN_i$ cannot lead to a change in the value of $PPOUT$ for *any* node in the control flow
graph, and that in turn implies that the $PPIN$ values of other nodes are also
unaffected by this change.

The correction term, being an intersection operation, can only lead to a
reduction in the value of the set $PPIN_i$. Let $X = BA\_PPIN_i - PPIN_i$
denote this reduction, and let x denote an arbitrary element of X. Thus,
$x \in BA\_PPIN_i$, and $x \notin PPIN_i$. Hence, there must exist a predecessor of
i, say, node p (see Figure 4.2), such that: $x \notin AVOUT_p$ and $x \notin PPOUT_p$.
Therefore, p must have another child j such that $x \notin BA\_PPIN_j$, otherwise
x would have been included in $PPOUT_p$. Now let us consider the possible
effects of removal of x from $PPIN_i$. From the given equations, a change in
the value of $PPIN_i$ can only affect the value of $PPOUT$ for a predecessor of
i (which can possibly lead to other changes). Clearly, the value of $PPOUT_p$

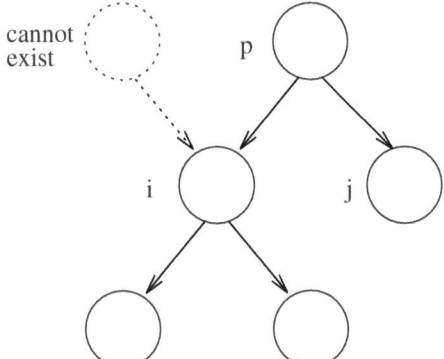

Fig. 4.2. Proving the decomposition of the bidirectional problem

does not change because $PPOUT_p$ already does not include x. But node i cannot have any predecessors other than p because p is a branch node, and by virtue of the edge splitting transformation on the control flow graph, there can be no edge from a branch node to a join node. Hence, the application of the correction term at a node i cannot change the $PPOUT$ value of any node: this implies the validity of the above process of decomposing the bidirectional problem.

We observe that since the application of the correction term to a node does not change the value of $PPOUT$ or $PPIN$ of any other node, it does not require a separate pass through the control flow graph. During the backward pass itself, after the value of $PPOUT_p$ is computed for a node p, the correction term can be applied to its successor node i by intersecting BA_PPIN_i with $AVOUT_p \cup PPOUT_p$.

4.3 Overall Data-Flow Procedure

So far we have discussed the data flow equations that are applied in a forward or backward direction along the edges of a control flow graph to determine the data flow information for each node. In the presence of loops, which lead to cycles in the control flow graph, one approach employed by classical data flow analysis is to iteratively apply the data flow equations over the nodes until the data flow solution converges [1]. We use the other well-known approach, interval-analysis [2,17], which makes a definite number of traversals through each node and is well-suited to analysis such as ours which attempts to summarize data flow information for arrays.

We use Tarjan intervals [38], which correspond to loops in a structured program. Each interval in a structured program has a unique header node h. As a further restriction, we require each interval to have a single loop exit node l. Each interval has a back-edge $\langle l, h \rangle$. The edge-splitting transformation, discussed earlier, adds a node b to split the back-edge $\langle l, h \rangle$ into two edges, $\langle l, b \rangle$ and $\langle b, h \rangle$. We now describe how interval analysis is used in the overall data flow procedure.

INTERVAL ANALYSIS Interval analysis is precisely defined in [7]. The analysis is performed in two phases, an *elimination phase* followed by a *propagation phase*. The elimination phase processes the program intervals in a bottom-up (innermost to outermost) traversal. During each step of the elimination phase, data flow information is summarized for inner intervals, and each such interval is logically collapsed and replaced by a summary node. Thus, when an outer interval is traversed, the inner interval is represented by a single node. At the end of the elimination phase, there are no more cycles left in the graph. For the purpose of our description, the top-level program is regarded as a special interval with no back-edge, which is the first to be processed during the propagation phase. Each step of the propagation phase expands the summary nodes representing collapsed intervals, and computes the data flow information for nodes comprising those intervals, propagating information from outside to those nodes.

Our overall data flow procedure is sketched in Figure 4.3. We now provide details of the analysis.

---

for each interval in elimination phase (bottom-up) order *do*

1. Compute $CGEN$ and $KILL$ summary in forward traversal of the interval.
2. Compute $ANTLOC$ summary in backward traversal of the interval.

for each interval in propagation phase (top-down) order *do*

1. Compute $AVIN$ and $AVOUT$ for each node in a forward traversal of the interval.
2. Compute $PPOUT$ and BA_PPIN for each node in a backward traversal of the interval. Once $PPOUT$ is computed for a node in this traversal, apply the forward correction to BA_PPIN of each of its successor nodes. Once $PPIN$ is obtained for a node via the forward correction(s), determine $INSERT$ and $REDUND$ for that node as well.

Fig. 4.3. Overall data flow procedure

4.3.1 Elimination Phase. We now describe how the values of local data-flow variables, $CGEN$, $KILL$, and $ANTLOC$ are summarized for nodes corresponding to program intervals in each step of the elimination phase. These values are used in the computations of global data-flow variables outside that interval.

The computation of $KILL$ and $CGEN$ proceeds in the forward direction, *i.e.*, the nodes within each interval are traversed in topological-sort order. For the computation of $KILL$, we define the variable K_i as the data that may be killed along any path from the header node h to node i. We initialize the data availability information and the kill information (K_h) at the header node as follows:

$$AVIN_h \;=\; \emptyset$$
$$K_h \;=\; KILL_h$$

The transfer function for K_i at all other nodes is defined as follows:

$$K_i \;=\; \Big(\bigcup_{p \in pred(i)} K_p \Big) \cup KILL_i \qquad (4.10)$$

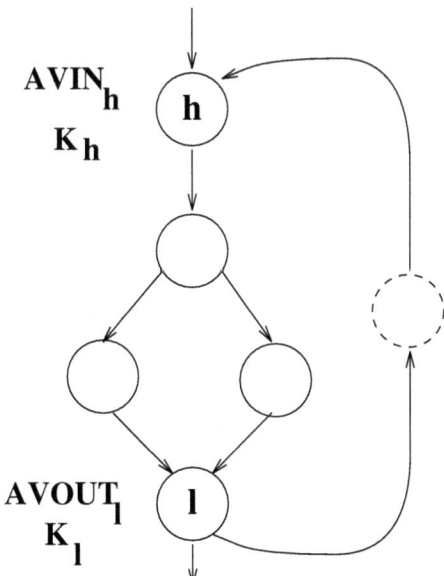

Fig. 4.4. Computing summary information for an interval

The transfer functions given by Equations 4.1, 4.2 and 4.10 are then applied to each statement node during the forward traversal of the interval, as shown in Figure 4.4. Finally, the data availability generated for the interval last node l must be summarized for the entire interval, and associated with a summary node s. However, the data availability at l, obtained from Equations 4.1 and 4.2, is only for a *single iteration* of the loop. Following [17], we would like to represent the availability of data corresponding to *all iterations* of the loop.

Definition. For an ASD set S, and a loop with index k varying from *low* to *high*, *expand*(S, k, *low* : *high*) is a function which replaces all single data item references $\alpha * k + \beta$ used in any array section descriptor D in S by the triple $(\alpha * low + \beta : \alpha * high + \beta : \alpha)$, and any mapping function of the form $F_i(j) = c * k + o$ by $F_i(j) = c * low + o : c * high + o : c$.

The following equations define the transfer functions which summarize the data being killed and the data being made available in an interval with loop index k, for all iterations *low* : *high*.

$$KILL_s \quad = \quad \text{expand}(K_l, k, low : high)$$
$$CGEN_s \quad = \quad \text{expand}(AVOUT_l, k, low : high) -$$
$$(\cup_{AntiDepDef} \text{expand}(AntiDepDef, k, low : high))$$

where *AntiDepDef* represents each definition in the interval loop that is the target of an anti-dependence at the loop nesting level (we conclude that a given dependence exists at a loop nesting level m if the direction vector corresponding to direction '=' for all outer loops and direction '<' or '=' for the loop at level m is included in the direction vector representation [42] of that dependence). If the loop is a **doall** loop, the range of *AntiDepDef* is empty, so that we get $CGEN_s = \text{expand}(AVOUT_l, k, low : high)$.

Explanation. For computing the interval kill set $KILL_s$, we simply expand the kill set generated at l over the interval loop bounds *low* : *high*. Computing the interval availability set $CGEN_s$ requires more work, because a variable definition in a particular iteration may kill data made available in previous iterations of the loop. Therefore, we first expand data made available in a single iteration, obtaining all data made available in any iteration, and then subtract out data that may be killed after it is made available. A definition kills data made available in a previous or the same iteration of a loop if it is the target of an anti-dependence at the loop nesting level, that is, if it defines data previously used. For example, consider the loop shown in Figure 4.5. There is a loop-carried anti-dependence from the reference $A(i)$ to $A(i-1)$. The data made available during the i-loop due to the reference to $A(i)$ is obtained as:

$$CGEN_s \quad = \quad \text{expand}(\langle A(i), M \rangle, i, 2 : 99) - \text{expand}(\langle A(i-1), \mathcal{U} \rangle, i, 2 : 99)$$
$$= \quad \langle A(2 : 99), M \rangle - \langle A(1 : 98), \mathcal{U} \rangle$$
$$= \quad \langle A(99), M \rangle$$

where $M = \langle [0], [F_1] \rangle$, where $F_1(j) = j$.

The computation of $ANTLOC$ proceeds in the backward direction, *i.e.*, the nodes within each interval are traversed in reverse topological-sort order. The computation of $ANTLOC$ uses the BA_PPIN_i and $PPOUT_i$ data flow sets that respectively represent communication that can be safely anticipated at (moved to) the entry and the exit of node i. The anticipatability of

```
HPF ALIGN A(i), B(i) WITH VPROCS(i)
do i = 2, 99
      A(i − 1) = . . .
      B(i − 1) = A(i)
      A(i + 1) = . . .
enddo
```

Fig. 4.5. Example to illustrate interval analysis

communication at exit from the last node, $PPOUT_l$, is initialized to $\emptyset$. The transfer functions given by Equations 4.7 and 4.8 are then applied to each statement during the backward traversal of the interval. Finally, BA_PPIN_h represents the anticipatability of communication for the interval body for a single loop iteration. The communication for the entire interval that precedes the data definition is summarized by "expanding" on BA_PPIN_h, and subtracting the ASD corresponding to the expanded form of all definitions that are sources of a flow dependence at the loop nesting level (since those definitions correspond to data computed in previous iterations of the loop before being communicated):

$$
\begin{aligned}
ANTLOC_s \quad = \quad & \text{expand}(BA\_PPIN_h, k, low : high) - \\
& (\cup_{FlowDepDef}\text{expand}(FlowDepDef, k, low : high))
\end{aligned}
$$

For the example shown in Figure 4.5, there is a flow-dependence from $A(i+1)$ to the reference $A(i)$. For the communication generated by the reference to $A(i)$, we obtain:

$$
\begin{aligned}
ANTLOC_s \quad = \quad & \text{expand}(\langle A(i), M\rangle, i, 2 : 99) - \text{expand}(\langle A(i + 1), \mathcal{U}\rangle, i, 2 : 99) \\
= \quad & \langle A(2 : 99), M\rangle - \langle A(3 : 100), \mathcal{U}\rangle \\
= \quad & \langle A(2), M\rangle
\end{aligned}
$$

where $M = \langle [0], [F_1]\rangle$, where $F_1(j) = j$.

4.3.2 Propagation Phase. The propagation phase processes the program intervals in a top-down (outermost to innermost) traversal. During the expansion of an interval, data flow information from outside is propagated to nodes inside that interval. During this traversal of nodes in an interval, any inner interval is treated as a single node represented by its summary node.

Given an interval representing a loop, our analysis calculates the data flow information for each node for a loop iteration k. For the forward traversal determining the solutions to $AVIN/AVOUT$, the value of $AVIN_h$ at the beginning of the kth loop iteration is given by:

$$
\begin{aligned}
AVIN_h^k \quad = \quad & [AVIN_h^{low} - \text{expand}(K_l, k, low : k - 1)] \cup \\
& [\text{expand}(AVOUT_l, k, low : k - 1) - \\
& (\cup_{AntiDepDef}\text{expand}(AntiDepDef, k, low : k - 1))]
\end{aligned}
$$

Explanation. $AVIN_h^{low}$ represents data that is available at entry to the header before the loop is entered (this is the information that is propagated from outside the interval). The data available at the beginning of iteration k consists of:

1. The data made available before the loop is entered, which is not killed in iterations $low : k - 1$, and
2. The data made available on all previous iterations $low : k - 1$, which has not been killed before iteration k.

The two terms unioned together in the above equation for $AVIN_h^k$ correspond to these two components. In a similar manner, for the backward traversal obtaining the solutions to $BA\_PPIN/PPOUT$, the value of $PPOUT_l$ at the beginning of the kth loop iteration is obtained as:

$$
\begin{aligned}
PPOUT_l^k \;=\; & [PPOUT_l^{low} - \operatorname{expand}(K_l, k, low : k-1)] \cup \\
& [\operatorname{expand}(BA\_PPIN_h, k, low : k-1) - \\
& (\cup_{FlowDepDef}\operatorname{expand}(FlowDepDef, k, low : k-1))]
\end{aligned}
$$

Once again, for the example shown in Figure 4.5, using the same definition of M as before, we get:

$$
\begin{aligned}
AVIN_h^k \;&=\; \langle A(2 : k-1), M \rangle - \langle A(1 : k-2), \mathcal{U} \rangle \\
&=\; \langle A(k-1), M \rangle \\
PPOUT_l^k \;&=\; \langle A(2 : k-1), M \rangle - \langle A(3 : k), \mathcal{U} \rangle \\
&=\; \langle A(2), M \rangle
\end{aligned}
$$

As noted earlier, the first step in the propagation phase of our algorithm is different from others, in that it is applied over a special interval representing the top-level program rather than a loop. For that step, the values of $AVIN_h$ for the entry node h and of $PPOUT_l$ for the exit node l are initialized to $\emptyset$.

For each interval processed in the propagation phase, after the initial determination of $AVIN_h$ in the forward traversal, the transfer functions given by Equations 4.1 and 4.2 are applied to obtain $AVOUT$ and $AVIN$ values for the other nodes. Similarly, during the backward traversal, after determining $PPOUT_l$ for the last node l, Equations 4.7 and 4.8 are applied to obtain BA_PPIN and $PPOUT$ values for the remaining nodes. Furthermore, during this backward traversal, after computing $PPOUT_p$ for node p, the forward correction given by Equation 4.9 is applied to $PPIN_i$ for each successor node i, as discussed earlier. Following the determination of $PPIN_i$ (which is complete after the last forward correction has been applied from its predecessor(s)), the values of $INSERT_i$ and $REDUND_i$ are obtained using Equations 4.5 and 4.6 respectively.

5. Communication Optimizations

Following the determination of $INSERT$ and $REDUND$ for each node, communications corresponding to the values of $INSERT$ are placed at the exits of nodes, and the values of $REDUND$ are used to delete redundant communication. We now describe how different optimizations are captured by the data flow procedure that we have described. Message vectorization is accounted for by the computation of $ANTLOC$ for an entire interval, as it characterizes the communication that can be moved outside a loop. Since message vectorization is a well-understood optimization implemented by most distributed memory compilers based on data-dependence [19,23,29,30,34,43], we shall focus on other important optimizations that require the generality of data-flow analysis.

Both of the equations for determining $INSERT$ and $REDUND$ inherently capture the elimination of redundant communication. When communication is moved and inserted at some other place, the available data $(AVOUT)$ and the communication corresponding to $(PPIN - KILL)$ is subtracted from it, as shown by Equation 4.5. $REDUND_i$ refers not only to communication made redundant by the availability of data due to some other communication, but also serves to remove the original communication which has been moved to a different point (and which appears in the $INSERT$ term at its new place).

During the remainder of our discussion, we shall refer to the original communication being optimized as $COMM - \langle D_1, M_1 \rangle$ and to the redundant part of the communication being deleted as $DELETE = \langle D_2, M_2 \rangle$. This redundant part could correspond to $REDUND$ or to the communication being subtracted in the equation for $INSERT$. We shall use the notation $D \to VPROCS(M(D))$ to represent the communication $\langle D, M \rangle$.

5.1 Elimination of Redundant Communication

If $COMM \subseteq DELETE$, i.e., if $D_1 \subseteq D_2$, and $M_1(D_1) \subseteq M_2(D_1)$, the communication of D_1 to processors $M_1(D_1)$ is redundant because the data is already available at those processors under the mapping function M_2. Hence, $COMM$ can be eliminated.

For example, in Figure 2.1 after message vectorization, the communication for d just before statement (15) is $COMM = d(i) \to VPROCS(i, 100), i = 1 : 100$. From our data flow procedure, $PPIN$ includes $d(i) \to VPROCS(i, 1 : 100), i = 1 : 100$, at this point in the program. Hence, $DELETE$ corresponds to $REDUND = d(i) \to VPROCS(i, 100), i = 1 : 100$. Since $COMM = DELETE$, this communication can be completely eliminated.

5.2 Reduction in Volume of Communication

Even if $COMM \not\subseteq DELETE$, a non-empty $DELETE$ can still lead to a reduction in the volume of communication. The reduced amount of communication, as discussed in the next section on ASD operations, is given by:

$$
\begin{aligned}
COMM_{new} &= \langle D_1, M_1 \rangle - \langle D_2, M_2 \rangle \\
&= \langle D_1 - D_2, M_1 \rangle \cup \langle D_1, M_1 - M_2 \rangle \quad\quad (5.1)
\end{aligned}
$$

Under different conditions, this reduction could mean that the amount of data being communicated is reduced, or the number of processors to which data is sent could be reduced.

Reduction in amount of data. The second term in the union operation evaluates to *null* and the new communication involves a reduced amount of data being sent to the same processors if $M_1(D_1) \subseteq M_2(D_1)$, but $D_1 \not\subseteq D_2$. Intuitively, this case implies that not all of data to be communicated is already available at the intended receivers, but the set of processors, to which any element common to D_1 and D_2 has to be sent under communication $\langle D_1 \cap D_2, M_1 \rangle$, is a subset of the set of processors where that element is already available under the mapping function M_2. Hence, the amount of data being communicated can be reduced from D_1 to $D_1 - D_2$.

For example, in Figure 2.1(a), the communication of e just before statement 24 is $COMM = e(i) \to VPROCS(i, 1 : 100), i = 1 : 100$. Our algorithm moves this communication to the point just after statement 13. The computation of $INSERT$ for e subtracts the availability of data at this point, which is $e(i) \to VPROCS(i, 1 : 100), i = 2 : 100$, *i.e.*, all but the first element of the vector e are already available on the columns of VPROCS. Hence, the new communication inserted at this point is: $COMM_{new} = e(1) \to VPROCS(1, 1 : 100)$, which represents a reduction of data.

Reduction in number of processors involved. The first term in Equation 5.1 evaluates to *null* and the new communication involves the same data being sent to fewer processors if $D_1 \subseteq D_2$, but $M_1(D_1) \not\subseteq M_2(D_1)$. This case arises when the data to be communicated is a subset of the data that is available, though it is available at fewer processors than needed. Thus, the data D_1 can be sent to just the extra processors, $M_1(D_1) - M_2(D_1)$, where it is not available.

This is illustrated in Figure 5.1: after message vectorization, the communication for variable d at the point just before statement 5 is $d(i) \to VPROCS(i, 1 : 100), i = 1 : 25$. Our data flow procedure moves it before statement 1. The data already available $(AVOUT)$ at this point is $d(i) \to VPROCS(i, 1 : 50), i = 1 : 100$. On subtracting this component from the communication being moved, the inserted communication is determined to be $COMM_{new} = d(i) \to VPROCS(i, 51 : 100), i = 1 : 25$. Thus, the data is sent to fewer processors.

```
     HPF align (i, j) with VPROCS(i,j) :: a, z
     HPF align (i) with VPROCS(i,1) :: d, w
```
$d(i) \rightarrow VPROCS(i, 1:50), i = 1:100$ $d(i) \rightarrow VPROCS(i, 1:50), i = 1:100$
$d(i) \rightarrow VPROCS(i, 51:100), i = 1:25$

```
 1:  do i = 1, 100                      do i = 1, 100
 2:    do j = 1, 50                        do j = 1, 50
 3:      a(i,j) = a(i,j) * d(j)             a(i,j) = a(i,j) * d(j)
 4:    end do                             end do
 5:  end do                             end do
```
$d(i) \rightarrow VPROCS(i, 1:100), i = 1:25$
```
 6:  do i = 1, 25                       do i = 1, 25
 7:    do j = 1, 100                       do j = 1, 100
 8:      z(i,j) = a(i,j-1) * d(i)           z(i,j) = a(i,j-1) * d(i)
 9:    end do                             end do
10:  end do                             end do


           (a)                                (b)
```

Fig. 5.1. Example illustrating reduction in number of processors

A possible negative side-effect of reducing the volume of communication by subtracting the redundant component is that a single communication may be broken into a number of smaller communications, which may not be desirable. However, this side-effect can always be controlled because the result of the difference operation in Equation 5.1 can always be overestimated to give back $\langle D_1, M_1 \rangle$, the original communication. While in some cases such as the ones illustrated above, the optimization will definitely reduce the cost of communication, in general the compiler needs a cost estimator to guide these decisions.

5.3 Movement of Communication for Subsumption and for Hiding Latency

Since our framework moves communications as early as legally possible, subsumption of communication placed earlier in the original program is naturally taken care of by the data-flow equations. For example, going back to Figure 2.1, $INSERT$ for d before statement (8) is determined to be $d(i) \rightarrow VPROCS(i, 1:100), i = 1:100$, $i.e$, our analysis procedure hoists this communication from statement (24) to (8). As explained earlier, since $REDUND$ for d at statement (15) is $d(i) \rightarrow VPROCS(i, 100), i = 1:100$, the communication of d at this point is $subsumed$.

Our data flow analysis procedure moves communications as early as legally possible and avoids introducing unnecessary communication, thus handling conditional control flow effectively. Traditionally, researchers have proposed inserting **sends** ahead of **receives** to help hide the latency of communication. In the context of our framework, a better approach would be to place *blocking* sends[2] and *non-blocking* receives at the point of insertion of communication, and inserting a *wait* at the reference to non-local data for the receive to be over before reading that data (for vectorized communication, the *wait* would be placed just before entering the outermost loop with respect to which the communication has been vectorized). This leads to the initiation of communication at the earliest possible point (under the constraint that there is no speculative communication), and waiting for the data to arrive only when it is needed. Thus, for communication that can be moved significantly further ahead, much of the latency can be hidden if the underlying target architecture supports overlap between communication and computation.

6. Extensions: Communication Placement

The placement of communication at the earliest point under our framework for partial redundancy elimination can also have some undesirable effects. The first set of problems is analogous to the issue of *register pressure* in the original data flow framework [31]. Early placement of communication puts additional pressure on the memory system at the receiver, as buffers to hold non-local data have to be maintained for longer periods of time. Apart from using up more memory, this can also degrade performance by polluting the cache (the received data may enter the cache due to an unpack operation and contribute to cache pollution if it is not referenced until much later). A related problem is the potentially increased contention for the network, which can reduce the effective network bandwidth.

An even more striking problem is that earliest placement of communication can lead to opportunities being missed for reducing the number of messages. This is illustrated by the simple example shown in Figure 6.1. If communication is moved eagerly to the earliest point, there are two separate messages needed for the references to B and C. On the other hand, if communication for B is deferred suitably, it can be combined with communication for C. Thus, by considering the interactions among different communications under different placements, we can obtain further reductions in the number of messages.

We describe briefly an algorithm which considers all communications in a procedure and their interactions under different placements, before finally selecting the placement of communications such that the number of messages is minimized through redundancy elimination and combining of messages [10]. The algorithm first determines, for each reference that needs communication,

---

[2] We refer to a send as blocking if it returns after the data being sent has been copied out of the user space, not one which waits for the data to be received at the other end. Non-blocking send can also be used, but in that case the compiler has to insert a wait for the send to be over before overwriting that data.

Earliest placement	Improved placement
HPF align (i) with VP(i) :: A, B, C $B(1:n) = \ldots$ $B(i) \rightarrow VP(i+1),\ i = 1:n-1$ $C(1:n) = \ldots$ $C(i) \rightarrow VP(i+1),\ i = 1:n-1$ $A(2:n) = B(1:n-1) + C(1:n-1)$	HPF align (i) with VP(i) :: A, B, C $B(1:n) = \ldots$ $C(1:n) = \ldots$ $[B(i), C(i)] \rightarrow VP(i+1),\ i = 1:n-1$ $A(2:n) = B(1:n-1) + C(1:n-1)$

Fig. 6.1. Message combining opportunity missed by earliest placement

the earliest and the latest safe placements of that communication, which also *dominate* [1] the original reference. In the second step, it marks the set of all candidate positions for each communication – these correspond to statements encountered during the *dominator tree* traversal from (the basic block containing) the latest position to (the basic block containing) the earliest marked position of that communication. The third step involves comparing the sets of possible communications at successive pairs of statements, and if the communication set at one statement is a subset of the communication set at the other statement, discarding the smaller set from further consideration. This step helps in pruning the search space for communication placement without losing any opportunity for reducing the number of messages. The fourth step consists of detecting and eliminating any subsumed communication, by checking if the ASD corresponding to a communication is a subset of the ASD corresponding to another communication. In the fifth step, for each communication entry that still appears in multiple communication sets (at different statements), the final position is chosen using the following heuristic: the most constrained communication entry is selected and placed where it is compatible with (i.e., can be combined with) the largest number of other candidate communications. At the end of this step, the entries in the communication set at each statement can be partitioned into groups, each group consisting of one or more entries which will be combined into a single aggregate communication operation. Any flexibility still available in placing this aggregate (based on the candidate positions of members of the aggregate) can be used to push this communication later if reducing contention for buffers and cache is more important than overlap benefits (which is true for machines like the IBM SP2), or push it earlier if overlapping communication with computation is more important. We refer the interested reader to [10] for further details.

The above algorithm is able to exploit both redundancy elimination and combining of communication to reduce the number of messages. It explores later placements of communication that preserve the benefits of redundancy elimination (normally obtained by moving communication earlier), and in the process, also avoids unnecessary early movement of communication that only increases contention for communication buffers.

7. Operations on Available Section Descriptors

In this section, we present the algorithms for various operations on the ASDs. Each operation is described in terms of further operations on the array section descriptors and the mapping descriptors that constitute the ASDs. There is an implicit order in each of those computations. The operations are first carried out over the array section descriptors, and then over the descriptors of the mapping functions applied to the resulting array section.

The results of these operations cannot always be computed exactly, either due to some part of the operand(s) being unknown at compile-time, or due to the ASDs not being closed under that operation. In that case, the compiler must appropriately either underestimate or overestimate the result so that the final optimization is only conservative, not incorrect. In Section 4.1, for each data flow equation, we described whether the result was underestimated or overestimated. Based on those constraints, we observe that the results of intersection and union operations are always underestimated in our framework, while the result of the difference operation may need to be underestimated or overestimated, depending on the data flow equation. In our descriptions, the special value $\perp$ is used to represent statically unknown parameters. This special value $\perp$ is treated as *null* when the results are being underestimated. In case of the difference operation, $var_1 - var_2$, when the result is to be overestimated, a resulting value of $\perp$ is interpreted as var_1.

Intersection Operation. The intersection of two ASDs represents the elements constituting the common part of their array sections, that are mapped to the same processors. The operation is given by:

$$\langle D_1, M_1 \rangle \cap \langle D_2, M_2 \rangle = \langle (D_1 \cap D_2), (M_1 \cap M_2) \rangle$$

In the above equation, $M_1 \cap M_2$ represents the intersection of each of the mapping functions M_1 and M_2 applied to the array region $(D_1 \cap D_2)$.

Union Operation. The union operation presents some difficulty because the ASDs are not closed under the union operation. The same is true for data descriptors like the DADs and the BRSDs, that have been used in practical optimizing compilers [4, 22]. As we explained earlier, in the context of our framework, any errors introduced during this approximation should be towards underestimating the extent of the descriptor.

One way to minimize the loss of information in computing $\langle D_1, M_1 \rangle \cup \langle D_2, M_2 \rangle$ is to maintain a list consisting of (1) $\langle D_1, M_1 \rangle$, (2) $\langle D_2, M_2 \rangle$, (3) $\langle (D_1 \cup D_2), (M_1 \cap M_2) \rangle$, and (4) $\langle (D_1 \cap D_2), (M_1 \cup M_2) \rangle$. Subsequently, any operations involving the descriptor would have to be carried out over all the elements in that list. The items (3) and (4) are included in the list because they potentially provide more useful information than just (1) and (2).

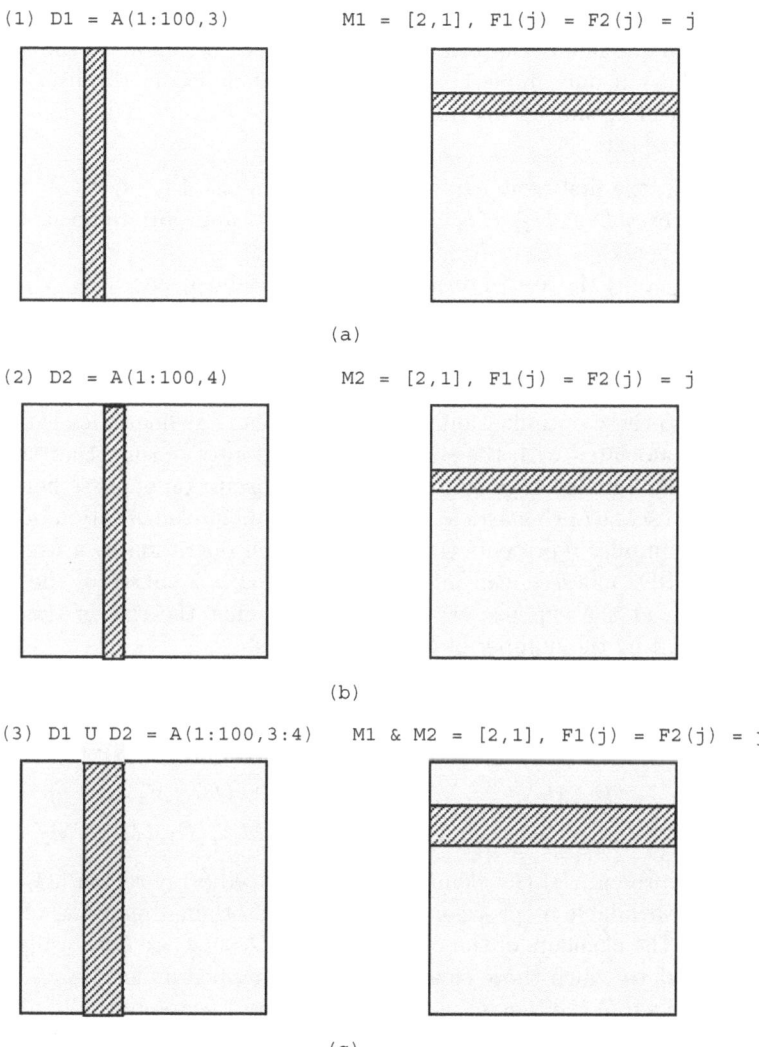

(1) D1 = A(1:100,3)   M1 = [2,1], F1(j) = F2(j) = j

(a)

(2) D2 = A(1:100,4)   M2 = [2,1], F1(j) = F2(j) = j

(b)

(3) D1 U D2 = A(1:100,3:4)   M1 & M2 = [2,1], F1(j) = F2(j) = j

(c)

Fig. 7.1. Example of ASD union operation

Example. Let $\langle D_1, M_1 \rangle = \langle A(1 : 100, 3), \langle [2, 1], F \rangle \rangle$, and let $\langle D_2, M_2 \rangle = \langle A(1 : 100, 4), \langle [2, 1], F \rangle \rangle$, where $F_1(j) = F_2(j) = j$. Figure 7.1(a) shows $\langle D_1, M_1 \rangle$ and Figure 7.1(b) shows $\langle D_2, M_2 \rangle$. Consider the subset test: $\langle A(7 : 8, 3 : 4), \langle [2, 1], F \rangle \rangle \subseteq \langle D_1, M_1 \rangle \cup \langle D_2, M_2 \rangle$. If the union is represented as the list of ASDs 7.1(a) and 7.1(b) only, this subset test will fail, which is inaccurate. The ASD for item (3) $\langle (D_1 \cup D_2), (M_1 \cap M_2) \rangle$ is shown in Figure 7.1(c). The subset test succeeds for 7.1(c).

However, this solution is too expensive, as the size of the list grows exponentially in the number of original descriptors to be unioned (the growth would be linear if only items (1) and (2) were included in the list). There are a number of optimizations that can be done to exclude redundant terms from the above list:

- If $D_1 \subset D_2$, the first term can be dropped from the list, since $\langle D_1, M_1 \rangle$ is subsumed by $\langle (D_1 \cap D_2), (M_1 \cup M_2) \rangle$. Similarly, appropriate terms can be dropped when $D_2 \subset D_1$, $M_1 \subset M_2$, or $M_2 \subset M_1$.
- If $D_1 = D_2$, only the fourth term needs to be retained, since $\langle D_1, M_1 \cup M_2 \rangle$ subsumes all other terms. If $M_1 = M_2$, the third term, that effectively evaluates to $\langle D_1 \cup D_2, M_1 \rangle$, subsumes all other terms, which may hence be dropped.

In addition to these optimizations, the compiler can use heuristics like dropping terms associated with the smaller array regions to ensure that the size of such lists is bounded by a constant. Further discussion of these heuristics is beyond the scope of this article. In our prototype implementation, for simplicity, the compiler represents the result of union operation as a list of the individual ASDs unless it can infer that one ASD is a subset of the other. This ensures, at the expense of some accuracy, that the size of the list is linearly bound by the number of communications.

Difference Operation. The difference operation causes a part of the data associated with the first ASD to be invalidated at the processors to which that part is mapped under the second ASD.

$$\langle D_1, M_1 \rangle - \langle D_2, M_2 \rangle \quad = \quad \langle (D_1 - D_2), M_1 \rangle \cup \langle D_1, (M_1 - M_2) \rangle$$
$$\mathrm{list}(\langle (D_1 - D_2), M_1 \rangle, \langle D_1, (M_1 - M_2) \rangle)$$

The result represents (i) the elements of the reduced array region $(D_1 - D_2)$ that are still available at processors given by the original mapping function M_1, and (ii) the elements of the original region D_1 that are still available at the processors to which those elements are not mapped under M_2.

We observe that if either D_1 and D_2 or M_1 and M_2 are mutually disjoint, the difference operation gives back the original operand $\langle D_1, M_1 \rangle$. Also, the first term in the above list evaluates to *null* if $D_1 \subseteq D_2$, and the second term evaluates to *null* if $M_1 \subseteq M_2$. The latter case always holds for the difference operations involving the KILL information in our data flow equations, because the ASD for killed data always has the universal mapping function $\mathcal{U}$, signifying that data is killed on all processors.

7.1 Operations on Bounded Regular Section Descriptors

Let D_1 and D_2 be two BRSDs, that correspond to array sections $A(S_1^1, \ldots, S_1^n)$ and $A(S_2^1, \ldots, S_2^n)$ respectively, where each S_1^i and S_2^i term is a range represented as a triple. We now describe the computations corresponding to different operations on D_1 and D_2.

Intersection Operation. The result is obtained by carrying out individual intersection operations on the ranges corresponding to each array dimension.

$$D_1 \cap D_2 = A(S_1^1 \cap S_2^1, \ldots, S_1^n \cap S_2^n)$$

The formula for computing the exact intersection of two ranges, S_1^i and S_2^i, expressed as triples, is given in [28]. The result of the intersection operation is another range represented as a triple. If either of the two ranges is equal to $\perp$, the result also takes the value $\perp$.

```
function union-range (S₁, S₂)
      if (S₁ = ⊥) return S₂
      if (S₂ = ⊥) return S₁
      Let  S₁ = (l₁ : u₁ : s₁), S₂ = (l₂ : u₂ : s₂)
      if (s₁ mod s₂ = 0)&((l₂ - l₁) mod s₁ = 0)
          s = s₁
      else if (s₂ mod s₁ = 0)&((l₂ - l₁) mod s₂ = 0)
          s = s₂
      else return list (S₁, S₂)
      if (l₁ ≤ l₂)&(u₁ ≥ l₂)
          return (l₁ : max(u₁, u₂) : s)
      else if (l₂ ≤ l₁)&(u₂ ≥ l₁)
          return (l₂ : max(u₁, u₂) : s)
      return list (S₁, S₂)
end union-range.
```

Fig. 7.2. Algorithm to compute union of ranges

Union Operation. The BRSDs are not closed under the union operation. The algorithm described in [22] to compute an approximate union potentially *overestimates* the region corresponding to the union. We need a different algorithm, one that underestimates the array region while being conservative. In the special case when the array regions identified by D_1 and D_2 differ only in one dimension, say, i, the union operation is given by:

$$D_1 \cup D_2 = A(S_1^1, \ldots, S_1^{i-1}, S_1^i \cup S_2^i, S_1^{i+1}, \ldots, S_1^n)$$

In the most general case when the regions differ in each dimension, an exhaustive list of regions corresponding to $D_1 \cup D_2$ would include (1) $A(S_1^1, \ldots, S_1^n)$, (2) $A(S_2^1, \ldots, S_2^n)$, and the following n terms: $A(S_1^1 \cup S_2^1, S_1^2 \cap S_2^2, \ldots, S_1^n \cap S_2^n), \ldots, A(S_1^1 \cap S_2^1, \ldots, S_1^{n-1} \cap S_2^{n-1}, S_1^n \cup S_2^n)$. Once again, heuristics are needed to keep the lists bounded. Figure 7.2 describes an algorithm for computing an approximate union of two ranges.

Difference Operation. Conceptually, the result is a list of n regions, each region corresponding to the difference taken along one array dimension.

$$D_1 - D_2 \;=\; \text{list}(A(S_1^1 - S_2^1, S_1^2, \ldots, S_1^n), \ldots, A(S_1^1, \ldots, S_1^{n-1}, S_1^n - S_2^n))$$

When the regions corresponding to D_1 and D_2 differ only in one dimension, all except for one of the terms in the above expression evaluate to *null*. When there is more than one non-null term, the result may be represented as a list, and heuristics used (as discussed earlier) to keep such lists bounded in length.

Again, the formula for computing the difference, $R^i = S_1^i - S_2^i$, when both S_1^i and S_2^i are expressed as triples, is given in [28]. If either $S_1^i = \bot$ or $S_2^i = \bot$, then $S_i = \bot$.

7.2 Operations on Mapping Function Descriptors

Consider two mapping function descriptors, $M_1 = \langle P_1, F_1 \rangle$ and $M_2 = \langle P_2, F_2 \rangle$, associated with the same array $A(S)$ section. The intersection, union, and difference operations are defined as:

$$M_1 \cap M_2 \;=\; \begin{cases} \langle P_1, F_1 \cap F_2 \rangle & \text{if } P_1 = P_2 \\ \bot & \text{if } P_1 \neq P_2 \end{cases}$$

$$M_1 \cup M_2 \;=\; \begin{cases} \langle P_1, F_1 \cup F_2 \rangle & \text{if } P_1 = P_2 \\ \text{list}(M_1, M_2) & \text{if } P_1 \neq P_2 \end{cases}$$

$$M_1 - M_2 \;=\; \begin{cases} \langle P_1, F_1 - F_2 \rangle & \text{if } P_1 = P_2 \\ \bot & \text{if } P_1 \neq P_2 \end{cases}$$

Let $F_1 = [F_1^1, \ldots, F_1^n]$, and let $F_2 = [F_2^1, \ldots, F_2^n]$. The computations of various operations between F_1 and F_2 can be described at two levels: (i) computations of $F_1 \cap F_2$, $F_1 \cup F_2$, and $F_1 - F_2$ in terms of further operations over F_1^i and F_2^i, $1 \leq i \leq n$, and (ii) computation of $F_1^i \cap F_2^i$, $F_1^i \cup F_2^i$, and $F_1^i - F_2^i$.

The computations of the first type are identical to those described for the BRSDs. For example, the intersection operation is given by:

$$F_1 \cap F_2 = [F_1^1 \cap F_2^1, \ldots, F_1^n \cap F_2^n]$$

We now describe the intersection, union and difference operations on the mapping functions of individual array dimensions. As mentioned in Section 2, depending on whether P^i represents a true array dimension or a "missing" dimension, F_1^i is either a function of the type $F_1^i(j) = (c_1 * j + l_1 : c_1 * j + u_1 : s_1)$, or simply a constant range, $F_1^i = (l_1 : u_1 : s_1)$. We need to describe only the results for the former case, since the latter can be viewed as a special case of the former, with c_1 set to zero. Thus, in the remainder of this section, we shall regard F_1^i and F_2^i as functions of the form $F_1^i(j) = (c_1 * j + l_1 : c_1 * j + u_1 : s_1)$, and $F_2^i(j) = (c_2 * j + l_2 : c_2 * j + u_2 : s_2)$. The data domain for these functions is dimension P^i of the array section referred to as S^{P^i}. Each of the operations between F_1^i and F_2^i has two cases:

Case 1: $c_1 = c_2$.

All of the operations can be collectively described as follows. Let θ denote the intersection, union, or the difference operator, and let $(l : u : s) = (l_1 : u_1 : s_1) \; \theta \; (l_2 : u_2 : s_2)$ as described in the previous subsection. The result is given by:

$$(F_1^i \; \theta \; F_2^i)(j) = (c_1 * j + l : c_1 * j + u : s)$$

Case 2: $c_1 \neq c_2$.

Intersection Operation. In this case, we check if one of the mapping functions completely covers the other function over the data domain, and otherwise return $\bot$. The high-level algorithm is:

> *if* $F_1^i(j) \subseteq F_2^i(j), j \in S^{P^i}$
> > *return* F_1^i
>
> *else if* $F_2^i(j) \subseteq F_1^i(j), j \in S^{P^i}$
> > *return* F_2^i
>
> *else return* $\bot$

Let $S^{P^i} = (low : high : step)$. We now describe the conditions for checking if F_1^i is covered by F_2^i. For $j \in (low : high : step)$,

$$F_1^i(j) \; \subseteq \; F_2^i(j)$$
$$\Leftrightarrow \quad (c_1 * j + l_1 : c_1 * j + u_1 : s_1) \; \subseteq \; (c_2 * j + l_2 : c_2 * j + u_2 : s_2)$$

A set of sufficient conditions for the above relationship to hold is: (1) $c_1 * j + l_1 \geq c_2 * j + l_2, low \leq j \leq high$, (ii) $c_1 * j + u_1 \leq c_2 * j + u_2, low \leq j \leq high$, (iii) $(c_1 - c_2) \bmod s_2 = 0$, (iv) $(l_1 - l_2) \bmod s_2 = 0$, and (v) $s_1 \bmod s_2 = 0$. In the special case when $s_1 = s_2 = 1$, the last three conditions are satisfied trivially, and conditions (i) and (ii) are both necessary and sufficient. The conditions (i) and (ii) can be further simplified to the following, which can be tested efficiently:

> (i) $c_1 * low + l_1 \geq c_2 * low + l_2$,
> (ii) $c_1 * high + u_1 \leq c_2 * high + u_2$,   if $c_1 \geq c_2$
> (i) $c_1 * high + l_1 \geq c_2 * high + l_2$,
> (ii) $c_1 * low + u_1 \leq c_2 * low + u_2$,   if $c_1 < c_2$

The conditions for checking if $F_2^i(j) \subseteq F_1^i(j), j \in S^{P^i}$, can be derived in a similar manner.

Union Operation. We check if one of the mapping functions completely covers the other, and otherwise return a list, as shown below:

> *if* $F_1^i(j) \subseteq F_2^i(j), j \in S^{P^i}$
> > *return* F_2^i
>
> *else if* $F_2^i(j) \subseteq F_1^i(j), j \in S^{P^i}$
> > *return* F_1^i
>
> *else return* $\text{list}(F_1^i, F_2^i)$.

Difference Operation. We check for the special cases of the first mapping function being covered by the second mapping function, or the two being mutually disjoint, and return $\perp$ otherwise. As mentioned earlier, $\perp$ is interpreted as $\emptyset$ or F_1^i, depending on whether the result is to be underestimated or overestimated.

$$if \; F_1^i \cap F_2^i = F_1^i$$
$$return \; \emptyset$$
$$else \; if \; F_1^i \cap F_2^i = \emptyset$$
$$return \; F_1^i$$
$$else \; return \; \perp.$$

8. Preliminary Implementation and Results

We have done a prototype implementation of our data flow framework as part of the pHPF compiler for HPF [19]. Our implementation is meant to serve as a platform to investigate the potential performance benefits from the data flow analysis, and currently represents a very simplified version of the analysis presented in this chapter. Currently, our compiler only eliminates fully redundant communication, it does not try to reduce the amount of data communicated or hide the latency of communication. Furthermore, for the sake of simplicity of implementation, the compiler does not currently move communication across different loop nests. However, since the analysis is performed on the program before it is transformed with loop distribution for vectorizing communication and eliminating extra guard statements [19, 23], our results include some potential benefits of a more global analysis as well.

```
HPF Align  A(i, J), B(i, j) with VPROCS(i, j)
HPF Distribute VPROCS(*, block)
do j = 3, n
    do i = 3, n
        A(i, j) = ... B(i, j − 1) + B(i, j − 2) ...
    end do
end do
```

Fig. 8.1. Extension of subset-test for nearest-neighbor communication

In our implementation, we have incorporated an extension to make our analysis exploit information about the distribution of arrays on physical processors in special cases, not merely the alignment information. Consider the program shown in Figure 8.1. On the basis of alignment information, we would view the communications $B(i, j − 1) \rightarrow VPROCS(i, j)$ and $B(i, j − 2) \rightarrow VPROCS(i, j)$ as separate. However, taking into account the block distribution of the second array dimension, we can recognize the communication for $B(i, j - 2)$ as subsuming the communication for $B(i, j - 1)$, as the former involves two boundary columns and the latter involves one boundary column being communicated. We have implemented this by extending the test for one communication being a subset of another, for nearest-neighbor communication.

We now describe the results of our experiments performed on five programs, which are part of an HPF benchmark suite developed by Applied Parallel Research, Inc. The first program, tomcatv (originally from SPEC benchmarks), does mesh generation with Thompson's solver. The second program, x42, is an explicit modeling system using fourth order differencing. The third program, tred2, is from the EISPACK library. It reduces a real symmetric matrix to a symmetric tridiagonal matrix, using and accumulating orthogonal similarity transformations. The program grid performs a 9-point stencil computation followed by global reductions. The last program, baro, performs computations for a shallow water atmospheric model.

Program	# Refs with Comm.		% Refs with
	Original	Redundancy Elim.	Redundant Comm.
tomcatv (*, block)	47	35	25.5
grid (block, block)	15	11	26.7
x42 (block, block)	33	17	48.5
tred2 (block, *)	22	19	13.6
baro (*, block)	3	3	0
comp	47	34	27.7
cmslow	44	21	52.3
intbal	3	1	66.7
graph1	0	0	N/A

Table 8.1. Results of optimization to eliminate redundant communication

Table 8.1 shows the static counts of the number of references to array and scalar variables in the program which required interprocessor communication, with and without the optimization for redundancy elimination. The first column describes for each program how the main HPF template was distributed on processors, since that affects the number of communications needed. Each of the programs was compiled with the number of physical processors left unspecified at compile-time. As can be seen from the table, there is an appreciable reduction in the number of references that need communication. Amongst the subroutines which had more than ten references needing communication, we observed a range of 13.6% to 52.3% of those communications (in terms of the static counts of references) as being completely redundant.

The results for the program `baro` have been presented in terms of individual results for each subroutine. It was particularly encouraging to note that the subroutine that shows the best improvement, `cmslow`, is the most frequently executed subroutine and accounts for the maximum amount of time spent in the program. The improvements for *tred2* were modest, the only communications eliminated were those for scalars. However, a hand-analysis of the program showed opportunities for more global communication optimizations captured by our framework, which were not implemented in this version of the compiler.

We now present some performance results obtained on the IBM SP-1 machine. These programs were compiled using two versions of the HPF compiler, one which does not perform any data flow analysis to eliminate redundant communication, and the other one which does. These timings do not include any time spent on I/O, since that had been commented out from the main computation in those programs. Tables 8.2 and 8.3 show the performance of the programs `tomcatv` and `grid` for various values of the number of processors (p) and the data size (n). The tables give the execution times without applying the redundant message elimination (RME) optimization and after applying this optimization.

n	$p = 1$		$p = 4$		$p = 8$		$p = 16$	
	Orig	*RME*	*Orig*	*RME*	*Orig*	*RME*	*Orig*	*RME*
65	0.829	0.825	0.866	0.426	0.819	0.366	0.838	0.379
129	3.321	3.314	1.937	1.183	1.575	0.815	1.469	0.671
257	13.175	13.257	5.314	3.923	3.714	2.305	2.990	1.560
513	55.977	55.902	17.973	15.304	10.765	8.085	7.361	4.732
1025	244.286	245.509	63.028	57.905	36.000	30.476	21.504	16.263

Table 8.2. Execution times (in seconds) of `tomcatv` on IBM SP-1

Table 8.2 shows noticeable improvements in the performance of `tomcatv` due to redundant message elimination. The performance improvement on 16 processors varies from 25% to 55% for different data sizes ranging from $n = 65$ to $n = 1025$. The relative gain in performance is lower for larger data sizes and for programs run on fewer processors because of computation time dominating the communication time. However, even for larger data sizes, the performance improvement on 16 processors is quite significant. For smaller data sizes, the improvement is much more substantial. It is interesting to note that redundant message elimination enables the compiler to obtain speedups for a data size as small as $n = 65$, whereas there were no speedups obtained for that data size without this optimization. These results confirm the effectiveness of redundant message elimination in reducing the communication costs of this benchmark program.

n	$p = 1$		$p = 4$		$p = 8$		$p = 16$	
	Orig	RME	Orig	RME	Orig	RME	Orig	RME
64	0.927	0.927	0.281	0.270	0.156	0.143	0.111	0.093
128	3.702	3.699	1.002	0.982	0.496	0.480	0.304	0.285
256	14.775	14.772	3.818	3.789	1.762	1.730	1.052	1.015
512	59.061	59.070	14.972	14.927	6.816	6.763	3.906	3.859
1024	236.227	236.192	59.459	59.351	26.665	26.576	15.163	15.072

Table 8.3. Execution times (in seconds) of `grid` on IBM SP-1

The performance improvement for `grid` is only modest. This is because the communication time for this benchmark program is very small compared to the overall execution time, leaving relatively little room for improvement. Due to this low communication time, we observe good speedups even without redundant message elimination. However, even for this program, when $n = 64$, where the communication time is relatively higher, we notice a performance improvement of 3-16% after redundant message elimination. Thus, our optimization does reduce the communication cost, but makes a significant difference to overall performance only if communication cost itself is high.

9. Related Work

9.1 Global Communication Optimizations

Many other researchers have used data-flow analysis to optimize communication. Granston and Veidenbaum [16] use data-flow analysis to detect redundant accesses to global memory in a hierarchical, shared-memory machine. However, they do not explicitly represent information about the availability of data on processors. Instead, they rely on simplistic assumptions about scheduling of parallel loops, which are often not applicable.

Amarasinghe and Lam [3] use the *last write tree* framework to perform optimizations like eliminating redundant messages. Their framework does not handle general conditional statements, and they do not eliminate redundant communication due to different references in arbitrary statements (for instance, statements appearing in different loop nests).

Gong et al. [15] describe a data-flow procedure that unifies optimizations like vectorizing communication, removing redundant communication, and moving communication earlier to hide latency. They only handle programs with singly nested loops and one-dimensional arrays, and with very simple subscripts.

Von Hanxleden et al. describe the *Give-N-Take* framework [40, 41] that they use for generating communication in the presence of indirection arrays. Their framework is based on the producer-consumer concept, and breaks communication into sends and receives, which are placed separately in a balanced manner. By using an eager solution for sends and a lazy solution for receives, they obtain maximal separation between sends and receives, which is used to overlap communication with computation. Their work focuses on irregular subscripts, and therefore does not attempt to obtain more precise information about array sections.

Kennedy and Nedeljkovic [26] extend the *Give-N-Take* framework to exploit information about array sections. They use bit vectors to represent array sections for the purpose of data flow analysis. This simplifies data flow analysis, in which no set operations need to be performed on array section descriptors, at the expense of precision in representing data to be communicated.

Kennedy and Sethi [27] present a framework, based on the *lazy code motion* technique [24], which maximizes latency hiding by determining the earliest placement of sends and the latest balanced placement of the corresponding receives. They present techniques to constrain the placement further such that the total size of buffers used to hold non-local data does not exceed a fixed limit.

9.2 Data Flow Analysis and Data Descriptors

Suppression of partially redundant code is a powerful code optimization and has found its way into a number of commercial compilers. Morel and Renvoise [31] first proposed a bidirectional bit-vector algorithm for the suppression of partial redundancies. The complexity of bidirectional problems for bit-vector representations of data flow information was addressed by later papers [12, 13, 24, 25]. This work applies the techniques from [31] and [13] for eliminating partially redundant communication. We extend the previous result on the decomposition of this bidirectional problem into efficient unidirectional problems by proving it in the context of an approximate data flow representation, namely the ASDs.

Interval analysis, introduced by Allen and Cocke [2], has been used to solve several data flow problems. The work by Gross and Steenkiste [17] was the first to extend interval analysis to handle array sections. Our data flow procedure refines the algorithms described in [17] by using information about loop-carried data dependences while summarizing data flow information for intervals. In addition, we apply data flow analysis to ASD's that represent both array section information and information about the processor elements on which the array elements are available.

We have used ideas from well-known representations of array sections used in other contexts [4, 8, 22] for developing a representation of communication in this work. In particular, we use the BRSD proposed by Havlak and Kennedy [22] to represent, in our framework, the data involved in communication. The concept of a mapping function descriptor that we have introduced represents a crucial extension to the notion of data descriptor. It enables representation of communication and of the data made available at various processors by prior communications. That in turn allows data flow analysis to be used for powerful communication optimizations.

10. Conclusions

We have presented a data-flow framework for reducing communication costs in a program. This framework provides a unified algorithm for performing a number of optimizations that eliminate redundant communication and that reduce the volume of communication, by reducing both the data and the number of processors involved. The algorithm also determines the earliest point at which communication can legally be moved, without introducing extra communication. That can help hide the latency of communication. This algorithm is quite general, it handles control flow and performs optimizations across loop nests. It also does not depend on a detailed knowledge of the explicit communication representation.

An important feature of our approach is that the analysis is performed at the granularity of sections of arrays and processors, that considerably enhances the scope of optimizations based on eliminating partial redundancies. We prove that in the context of an ASD representation also, the bidirectional problem of determining placement can be decomposed into a backward problem followed by a forward correction. This ensures the practicality of the analysis by making it efficient. The preliminary results from a simplified implementation of this framework show significant performance improvements, and confirm the effectiveness of the optimization to eliminate redundant communication.

In the future, we plan to conduct more extensive experiments, to study the performance impact of other optimizations captured by our framework, like reducing the volume of communication and hiding the latency of communication. This will require further examination of issues like management of buffers containing non-local data from other processors. Future work will also involve extending the data flow framework to perform interprocedural optimizations. There is also scope for integrating the concepts of ownership and availability of data, and developing algorithms for additional optimizations that exploit the fact that processors other than the owners can also send values to processors that need them.

Acknowledgement. The author would like to thank Soumen Chakrabarti, Jong-Deok Choi, Edith Schonberg, and Harini Srinivasan for their help with various aspects of this work.

References

1. A. V. Aho, R. Sethi, and J. D. Ullman. *Compilers: principles, techniques, and tools.* Addison-Wesley, 1986.
2. F. E. Allen and J. Cocke. A program data flow analysis procedure. *Communications of the ACM*, 19(3):137–147, March 1976.
3. S. P. Amarasinghe and M. S. Lam. Communication optimization and code generation for distributed memory machines. In *Proc. ACM SIGPLAN '93 Conference on Programming Language Design and Implementation*, Albuquerque, New Mexico, June 1993.
4. V. Balasundaram. A mechanism for keeping useful internal information in parallel programming tools: the data access descriptor. *Journal of Parallel and Distributed Computing*, 9(2):154–170, June 1990.
5. V. Balasundaram, G. Fox, K. Kennedy, and U. Kremer. A static performance estimator to guide data partitioning decisions. In *Proc. Third ACM SIGPLAN Symposium on Principles and Practices of Parallel Programming*, Williamsburg, VA, April 1991.
6. P. Banerjee, J. Chandy, M. Gupta, E. Hodges, J. Holm, A. Lain, D. Palermo, S. Ramaswamy, and E. Su. The PARADIGM compiler for distributed-memory multicomputers. *IEEE Computer*, October 1995.
7. M. Burke. An interval-based approach to exhaustive and incremental interprocedural data-flow analysis. *ACM Transactions on Programming Languages and Systems*, 12(3):341–395, July 1990.
8. D. Callahan and K. Kennedy. Analysis of interprocedural side effects in a parallel programming environment. In *Proc. First International Conference on Supercomputing*, Athens, Greece, 1987.
9. D. Callahan and K. Kennedy. Analysis of interprocedural side effects in a parallel programming environment. *Journal of Parallel and Distributed Computing*, 5:517–550, 1988.
10. S. Chakrabarti, M. Gupta, and J.-D. Choi. Global communication analysis and optimization. In *Proc. ACM SIGPLAN Conference on Programming Language Design and Implementation*, Philadelphia, PA, May 1996.
11. S. Chatterjee, J. R. Gilbert, R. Schreiber, and S.-H. Teng. Optimal evaluation of array expressions on massively parallel machines. In *Proc. Second Workshop on Languages, Compilers, and Runtime Environments for Distributed Memory Multiprocessors*, Boulder, CO, October 1992.
12. F. C. Chow. *A portable machine-independent global optimizer – design and measurements.* PhD thesis, Computer Systems Laboratory, Stanford University, December 1983.
13. D. M. Dhamdhere, B. K. Rosen, and F. K. Zadeck. How to analyze large programs efficiently and informatively. In *Proc. ACM SIGPLAN '92 Conference on Programming Language Design and Implementation*, San Francisco, CA, June 1992.
14. High Performance Fortran Forum. High Performance Fortran language specification, version 1.0. Technical Report CRPC-TR92225, Rice University, May 1993.
15. C. Gong, R. Gupta, and R. Melhem. Compilation techniques for optimizing communication in distributed-memory systems. In *Proc. 1993 International Conference on Parallel Processing*, St. Charles, IL, August 1993.
16. E. Granston and A. Veidenbaum. Detecting redundant accesses to array data. In *Proc. Supercomputing '91*, pages 854–965, 1991.

17. T. Gross and P. Steenkiste. Structured dataflow analysis for arrays and its use in an optimizing compiler. *Software - Practice and Experience*, 20(2):133–155, February 1990.
18. M. Gupta and P. Banerjee. A methodology for high-level synthesis of communication on multicomputers. In *Proc. 6th ACM International Conference on Supercomputing*, Washington D.C., July 1992.
19. M. Gupta, S. Midkiff, E. Schonberg, V. Seshadri, K.Y. Wang, D. Shields, W.-M. Ching, and T. Ngo. An HPF compiler for the IBM SP2. In *Proc. Supercomputing '95*, San Diego, CA, December 1995.
20. M. Gupta and E. Schonberg. Static analysis to reduce synchronization costs in data-parallel programs. In *Proc. 23rd Annual ACM Symposium on Principles of Programming Languages*, St. Petersburg Beach, FL, January 1996.
21. M. Gupta, E. Schonberg, and H. Srinivasan. A unified framework for optimizing communication in data-parallel programs. *IEEE Transactions on Parallel and Distributed Systems*, 7(7), July 1996.
22. P. Havlak and K. Kennedy. An implementation of interprocedural bounded regular section analysis. *IEEE Transactions on Parallel and Distributed Systems*, 2(3):350–360, July 1991.
23. S. Hiranandani, K. Kennedy, and C. Tseng. Compiling Fortran D for MIMD distributed-memory machines. *Communications of the ACM*, 35(8):66–80, August 1992.
24. Jens Knoop and Oliver Rüthing and Bernhard Steffen. Lazy code motion. In *Proc. ACM SIGPLAN '92 Conference on Programming Language Design and Implementation*, San Francisco, CA, June 1992.
25. S. M. Joshi and D. M. Dhamdhere. A composite hoisting-strength reduction transformation for global program optimization (parts i and ii). *International Journal of Computer Mathematics*, pages 22–41, 111–126, 1992.
26. K. Kennedy and N. Nedeljkovic. Combining dependence and data-flow analyses to optimize communication. In *Proc. 9th International Parallel Processing Symposium*, Santa Barbara, CA, April 1995.
27. K. Kennedy and A. Sethi. Resource-based communication placement analysis. In *Proc. Ninth Workshop on Languages and Compilers for Parallel Computing*, San Jose, CA, August 1996.
28. C. Koelbel. *Compiling programs for nonshared memory machines*. PhD thesis, Purdue University, August 1990.
29. C. Koelbel and P. Mehrotra. Compiling global name-space parallel loops for distributed execution. *IEEE Transactions on Parallel and Distributed Systems*, 2(4):440–451, October 1991.
30. J. Li and M. Chen. Compiling communication-efficient programs for massively parallel machines. *IEEE Transactions on Parallel and Distributed Systems*, 2(3):361–376, July 1991.
31. E. Morel and C. Renvoise. Global optimization by suppression of partial redundancies. *Communications of the ACM*, 22(2):96–103, February 1979.
32. M. O'Boyle and F. Bodin. Compiler reduction of synchronization in shared virtual memory systems. In *Proc. 9th ACM International Conference on Supercomputing*, Barcelona, Spain, July 1995.
33. M.J. Quinn and P. J. Hatcher. Data-parallel programming on multicomputers. *IEEE Software*, 7:69–76, September 1990.
34. A. Rogers and K. Pingali. Process decomposition through locality of reference. In *Proc. SIGPLAN '89 Conference on Programming Language Design and Implementation*, pages 69–80, June 1989.
35. C. Rosene. *Incremental Dependence Analysis*. PhD thesis, Rice University, March 1990.

36. Marc Snir et al. The communication software and parallel environment of the IBM SP2. *IBM Systems Journal*, 34(2):205–221, 1995.
37. C. Stunkel et al. The SP2 high performance switch. *IBM Systems Journal*, 34(2):185–204, 1995.
38. R. E. Tarjan. Testing flow graph reducibility. *Journal of Computer and System Sciences*, 9(3):355–365, December 1974.
39. C.-W. Tseng. Compiler optimizations for eliminating barrier synchronization. In *Proc. 5th ACM Symposium on Principles and Practices of Parallel Programming*, Santa Barbara, CA, July 1995.
40. R. v. Hanxleden and K. Kennedy. Give-n-take – a balanced code placement framework. In *Proc. ACM SIGPLAN '94 Conference on Programming Language Design and Implementation*, Orlando, Florida, June 1994.
41. R. v. Hanxleden, K. Kennedy, C. Koelbel, R. Das, and J. Saltz. Compiler analysis for irregular problems in Fortran D. In *Proc. 5th Workshop on Languages and Compilers for Parallel Computing*, New Haven, CT, August 1992.
42. M. Wolfe and U. Banerjee. Data dependence and its application to parallel processing. *International Journal of Parallel Programming*, 16(2):137–178, April 1987.
43. H. Zima, H. Bast, and M. Gerndt. SUPERB: A tool for semi-automatic MIMD/SIMD parallelization. *Parallel Computing*, 6:1–18, 1988.

Chapter 15. Tolerating Communication Latency through Dynamic Thread Invocation in a Multithreaded Architecture

Andrew Sohn[1], Yuetsu Kodama[2], Jui-Yuan Ku[2], Mitsuhisa Sato[3], and Yoshinori Yamaguchi[3]

[1] Computer Information Science Dept.
New Jersey Institute of Technology, Newark, NJ 07102-1982
sohn@cis.njit.edu
[2] Computer Architecture Section, Electrotechnical Laboratory,
1-1-4 Umezono, Tsukuba, Ibaraki 305, Japan;
kodama@etl.go.jp
[3] 3 Tsukuba Research Center, Real World Computing Partnership
1-6-1 Takezono, Tsukuba, Ibaraki 305, Japan
msato@trc.rwc.or.jp

Summary. Communication latency is a key parameter which affects the performance of distributed-memory multiprocessors. Instruction-level multithreading attempts to tolerate latency by overlapping communication with computation. This chapter explicates the multithreading capabilities of the EM-X distributed-memory multiprocessor through empirical studies. The EM-X provides hardware supports for dynamic function spawning and instruction-level multithreading. The supports include a by-passing mechanism for direct remote reads and writes, hardware FIFO thread scheduling, and dedicated instructions for generating fixed-sized communication packets based on one-sided communication. Two problems of bitonic sorting and Fast Fourier Transform are selected for experiments. Parameters that characterize the performance of multithreading are investigated, including the number of threads, the number of thread switches, the run length, and the number of remote reads. Experimental results indicate that the best communication performance occurs when the number of threads is two to four. A large number of threads of over eight is found inefficient and has adversely affected the overall performance. FFT yielded over 95% overlapping due to a large amount of computation and communication parallelism across threads. Even at the absence of thread computation parallelism, multithreading helps overlap over 35% of the communication time for bitonic sorting.

1. Introduction

Distributed-memory multiprocessors have been regarded as a viable architecture of scalable and economical design in building large parallel machines to meet the ever-increasing demand for high performance computing. In these paradigms of machine architecture, it is deemed relatively simple to increase a machine's capability simply by adding more processors to the system incrementally as required. There are various research prototypes as well as commercial machines having this distributed-memory/message-passing paradigm

S. Pande, D.P. Agrawal (Eds.): Compiler Optimizations for Scalable PS, LNCS 1808, pp. 525-549, 2001.
© Springer-Verlag Berlin Heidelberg 2001

such as Cray T3E [18], ETL EM-X [10,11], Intel and IBM ASCIs [1], IBM SP-2 [3], Tera MTA [4], etc.

In a distributed-memory machine, data needs to be distributed so there is no overlapping or copying of major data. Typical distributed-memory machines incur much latency, ranging approximately from a few to tens of micro seconds for a single remote read operation. The gap between processor cycle and remote memory access time becomes wider, as the processor technology improves and rigorously exploits instruction level parallelism. The message-passing machine SP-2 incurs approximately 40 micro seconds to read data allocated to remote processors. Considering that the microprocessors are running at over 66.5 MHz (15 nano seconds cycle time) for the SP-2 590 model, the loss due to a remote read operation is enormous; A single remote read operation would cost 40 micro sec/15 nsec, or 2667 cycles.

Various approaches have been developed to reduce/hide/tolerate communication time, as well as to study communication behavior for general purpose parallel computing [7]. Data partitioning used in High Performance Fortran is a typical method to reduce communication overhead. Analyzing the behavior of the program at compile time, data can be partitioned and allocated to processors such that runtime data movement can be minimized. While data distribution can be carefully designed to minimize the number of remote reads in the course of computation, this approach is effective for specific applications where data partitioning can be well tuned. Applications such as adaptive mesh computational science problems change their behavior at runtime. The initial data distribution is often found invalid and inefficient after some computations.

Multithreading aims to tolerate memory latency using context switch. Through a split-phase read transaction, a processor switches to another thread instead of waiting for the requested data to arrive, thereby masking the detrimental effect of latency [8,9]. The Heterogeneous Element Processor (HEP) designed by Burton Smith provides up to 128 threads [19]. A thread switch occurs in every instruction with 100 nsec switching cost. Threads are usually ended by remote read instructions since those may incur long latencies if the requested data is located in a remote processor [13]. The Monsoon data-flow machine developed at MIT switches context every instruction, where a thread consists of a single instruction [14].

The EM-4 multiprocessor provides hardware support for multithreading [16,17]. Thread switch takes place whenever a remote memory read is encountered. Threads can also be suspended with explicit thread scheduling. The Alewife multiprocessor provides a hardware support for multithreading [2]. Together with prefetching, block multithreading with four hardware contexts has been shown to be effective in tolerating the latency caused on cache misses for shared-memory applications such as MP3D. The Tera multithreaded architecture (MTA) provides hardware support for multithreading [4]. The maximum of 128 threads are provided per processor. Context switch takes place whenever a remote load or synchronizing load is encountered. The RWC-1 prototype minimizes the context switch overhead by prefetching [12].

An analytic model for multithreading is studied in [15]. The study indicated that the performance of multithreading can be classified into three regions: linear, transition, and saturation. The performance of multithreading is proportional to the number of threads in the linear region while it depends only on the remote reference rate and switch cost in the saturation region. The Threaded Abstract Machine studied by Culler et al. exploits parallelism across multiple threads [6]. Fine-grain threads share registers to exploit fine-grain parallelism using implicit switching. Experimental results on EM-4 indicated that simple-minded data distribution can give performance comparable to that of the best performing algorithms with hand-crafted data distribution but no threading [21].

This chapter reports on the multithreading performance of the 80-processor EM-X distributed-memory multiprocessor. The machine was built at the Electrotechnical Laboratory and has been fully operational since December 1995. Several critical parameters which characterize the performance of multithreading are investigated, including the number of threads, the run length, the number of remote reads, and the number of context switches. The interplay between the parameters is explained with experimental results. Two widely used problems are selected for performance verification: bitonic sorting and Fast Fourier Transform. The two problems have been revisited and suitable algorithms are developed for the multithreaded machine environment. Data and workload distribution strategies are developed to explicate their performance. The ultimate goal of multithreading is to tolerate communication time. In this respect, the experiments are carried out to identify how multithreading helps overlap communication with computation.

2. Multithreading Principles and Its Realization

2.1 The Principle

A thread is a set of instructions which are executed in sequence. The multithreaded execution model exploits parallelism across threads to improve the performance of multiprocessors [8, 9]. Threads are usually delimited by remote read instructions which may incur long latency if the requested data is located in a remote processor. Through a split-phase read mechanism, a processor switches to another thread instead of waiting for the requested data to arrive, thereby masking the detrimental effect of latency. Figure 2.1 illustrates the basic principle of multithreading.

Processor 0, P0, has three threads, T0, T1,and T2, ready to execute in the ready queue. P0 indicates that T0 is currently being executed which is indicated by a thick dark line. P0 starts executing the first thread, T0. As

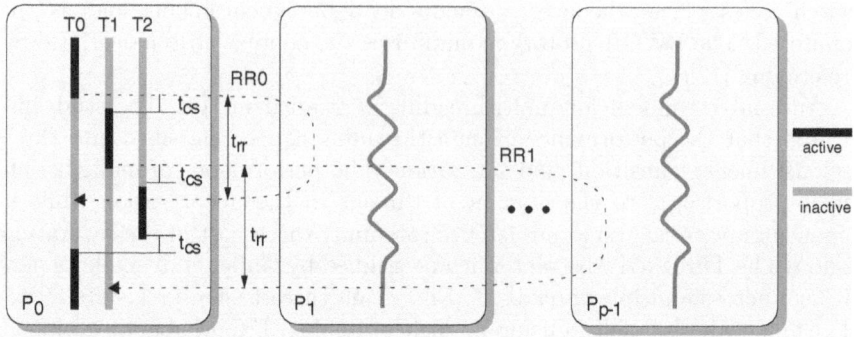

Fig. 2.1. Multithreading on p processors. t_{cs} = context switch time, t_{rr} = remote read time, RR = remote read.

T0 is executed, a remote read operation is reached, denoted by a dotted line. The processor switches to T1 while the remote memory read request RR0 is pending. The processor again switches to T2 when another remote memory read occurs in T1. After T2 completes, T0 can resume its execution assuming the requested data has arrived.

There are important parameters which characterize the performance of multithreading. They include (1) the number of threads per processor, (2) the number of remote reads per thread, (3) context switch mechanism, (4) remote memory latency, (5) remote memory servicing mechanism, and (6) the number of instructions in a thread. While this is not the exhaustive list and there are yet other important issues, we will briefly explain the implications of these issues below.

The number of active threads indicates the amount of parallelism. To be more specific, the amount of parallelism can be classified into computation parallelism and communication parallelism. Computation parallelism refers to the 'conventional' parallelism while communication parallelism refers to the way threads can communicate with other threads residing in other processors. The figure shows that processor 0 has three active threads, indicating three thread computation parallelism, provided that they are independent of each other. Communication parallelism is not apparent from the figure as the way the three threads communicate is not specified in the figure. This will become clearer in the later sections. It is desirable to have a large number of threads since this will likely help tolerate latencies. However, the maximum number of threads that can be active (including the suspended status) at a point in time is bound by the amount of memory available to the program.

The number of remote reads per thread determines the frequency of thread switching and in turn *run length*. For each remote read, there will be a thread switching. The number of switches is proportional to the number of remote reads. It is therefore desirable that the remote reads be distributed evenly over the life of a thread. This distribution leads to the issue of thread run length. Thread run length is determined by the number of uninterrupted instructions executed between two consecutive remote reads. The performance of multithreading is strongly affected by this parameter. If the run length is small, it will be difficult to tolerate the latency because there are not enough instructions to execute while the remote read is outstanding. Suppose that the dark area of T2 in the figure is very short, consisting of say 10 instructions. The machine will not be able to tolerate the remote memory latency since it is too short for RR0 to return. A remote read will typically take tens to hundreds of cycles, if not thousands. The RR0 shown in Figure 2.1 will likely return after T2 runs to completion. In that event, the machine will wait until RR0 returns as there is no thread ready for execution.

Thread switch refers to how the control of a thread is transferred to another thread. Among the types of context switches are explicit switching and implicit switching. Implicit switching allows multiple threads to share registers while explicit switching does not. Implicit switching is literally implicit in the sense that there is essentially no visible switching from the register point of view. This method, therefore, requires little or no switching overhead. However, the scheduling of registers and threads can be a challenging task. In the explicit switching, threads do not share registers. A single thread uses all the registers. Therefore, there is no issue as to how registers and threads are scheduled. However, the main problem of this explicit switching is the cost associated with register saving and restoring. For each thread switch, those registers currently being used by the thread need to be saved to preserve the status of the thread. When the thread that was suspended resumes, the registers for that resuming thread will have to be restored. This register saving and restoring can be a bottleneck for efficient multithreading. Several approaches have been taken to solve the problems associated with the two switching mechanisms. One approach would be to have a few explicit sets of registers, where a thread is assigned to a register set. Another approach is to prefetch the corresponding registers in such a way that the thread can immediately resume when a thread switch occurs.

Communication latency is the main target of multithreading. It can vary depending on the technology used to build the machine and the interconnection network. A desirable combination would be that the network bandwidth be comparable with the processor clock speed. Large disparity between the machine clock speed and the network bandwidth can be problematic when using multithreading. If the machine is fast but the network is slow, the pressure to tolerate the latency is high, in which case multithreading will unlikely give noticeable results. On the other hand, if the machine is slow but the network is fast, the effect of multithreading may not be visible either since the latency is high in any case. There is a clear trade-off between the clock speed and the network bandwidth.

A mechanism to service remote memory operations is also an important factor determining the performance of multithreading. The simplest approach would be to have the main processor service remote read/write requests. In this case, the possibility of overlapping computation with communication will be very slim, giving little advantages of using multithreading. Some machines such as IBM SP-2 and Intel Paragon employ a communication co-processor to handle some communication related activities, i.e., copying data out of memory to the communication buffer or from buffer to memory. The main advantage of using a communication co-processor is to take some burden off the main processor, thereby leaving the main processor for computation for most of the time. Multithreading can have a significant boost if equipped with such a remote servicing mechanism. The EM-X multithread processor employs a remote by-passing mechanism to perform direct remote read/write operations, or *remote direct memory access* (RDMA). The main processor is now aware of such remote read/write activities as will be explained shortly.

The number of instructions in a thread is often referred to as *thread granularity*. While there is no clear agreement on such a classification, thread granularity can be classified into three categories: fine-grain, medium-grain, and coarse-grain. Fine-grain threading typically refers to a thread of a few to tens of instructions. It is essentially for instruction-level multithreading. Medium-grain threading can be viewed as a loop-level or function-level threading, where a thread consists of hundreds of instructions. Coarse-grain threading may be viewed as more of a task-level threading, where each tread consists of thousands of instructions. However, coarse-grain threading should not be interpreted as operating system level multitasking, where different programs interleave to mask off page faults. How the threads are formed is another important question which needs be answered. Threads can be automatically generated by compilers or explicitly specified by the programmers.

2.2 The EM-X Multithreaded Distributed-Memory Multiprocessor

The EM-X multiprocessor is a large-scale multithreaded distributed-memory multiprocessor consisting of 80 custom-built processors, called EMC-Y. The machine was built at the Electrotechnical Laboratory and ahs been operational since December 1995 [10, 11]. The main objective of building the machine is to investigate the performance of fine-grain instruction-level multithreading. Two types of computational principles have been employed in designing the multiprocessor. The first level uses the data-flow principles of execution to realize *dynamic function spawning* or *runtime thread invocation.* Any processor can dynamically spawn function calls (or threads) on any other processor(s) including itself. This dynamic function spawning enables instruction-level multithreading and efficient fine-grain communication. The second level employs the conventional RISC-style execution to exploit program locality. The machine has a two-stage pipeline consisting of fetch and execute. Instructions that do not require remote reads/writes and dynamic function spawning are executed by this two-stage pipelining.

The current EM-X prototype has 80 EMC-Y processors connected through a circular Omega network. Figure 2.2 shows the prototype EM-X multiprocessor. The network is a variation of Omega network which repeats a pair of shuffle and exchange steps. While Omega network is a multistage network, the EM-X is not. The main difference between Omega network and the EM-X network is that each processor is attached to a switch box. The EM-X network provides the maximum diameter of $O(\log P)$ for low latency and high throughput, where P is the number of processors. All the communication activities are *one-sided*, i.e., only one processor is involved in communication. The destination processor has no knowledge of any communication initiated by the source processor. Therefore, there is no notion of processor locking or sending and receiving used in the message-passing paradigm.

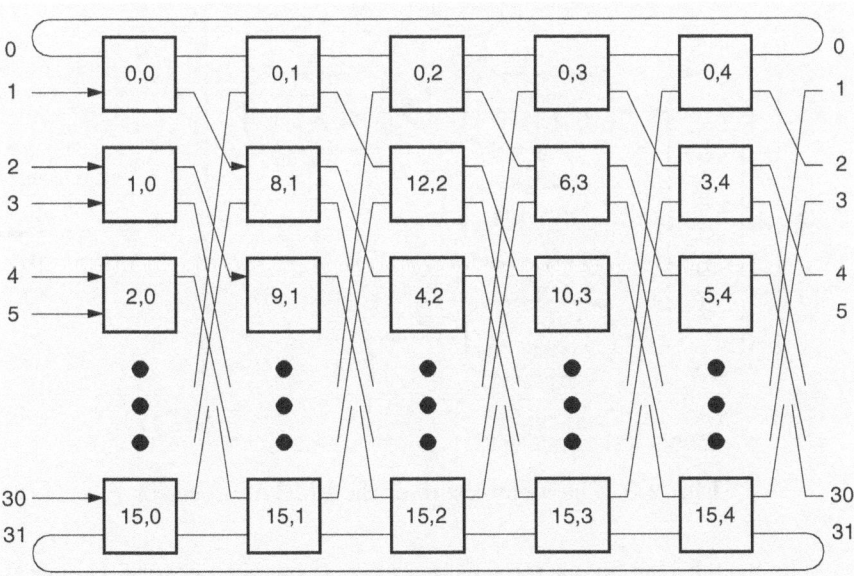

Fig. 2.2. The 80-processor EM-X distributed-memory multiprocessor.

All the communication in the EM-X are done with 2-word fixed-sized packets. Communication can be classified into three categories: remote read, remote write, and thread invocation. A remote read packet consists of two 32-bit words. The first word contains the destination address, from which data will be read at the destination processor. The second word is the returning address, also called *continuation*, which will be explained in detail shortly. A remote write packet also consists of two words. The first word is the destination address while the second is the data to be written when arrived at the

destination processor. Thread invocation is done through packets which will
be explained after we present some details of the processor architecture.

Figure 2.3 shows the organization of the EMC-Y processor. A processor
element is a single chip pipelined RISC-style processor, designed for fine-grain
parallel computing. Each processor runs at 20 MHz with 4 MB of one-level
static memory. The EMC-Y pipeline is designed to combine the register-based
RISC execution principle with the packet-based dataflow execution principle
for synchronization and message handling support. Each processor consists
of Switching Unit (SU), Input Buffer Unit (IBU), Matching Unit (MU), Execution Unit (EXU), Output Buffer Unit (OBU) and Memory Control Unit
(MCU).

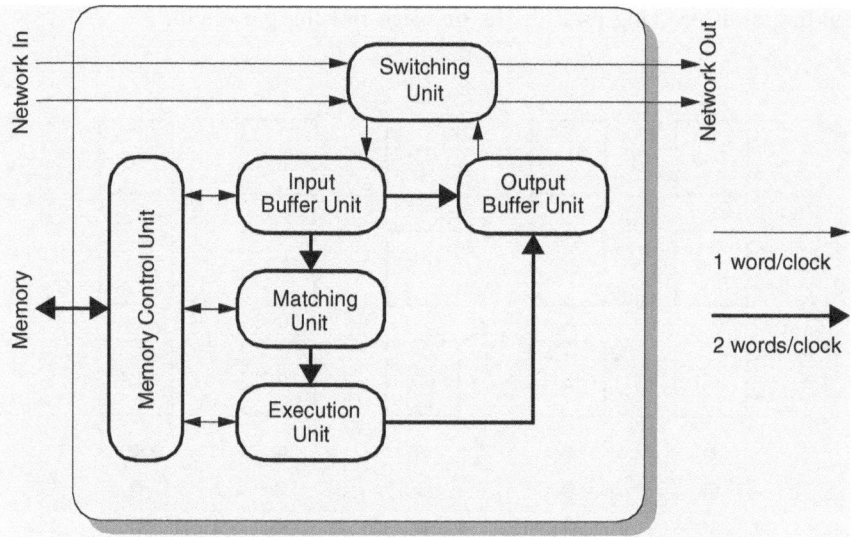

Fig. 2.3. The architecture of the EMC-Y processor.

The Switch Unit sends/receives packets to/from the network. It consists
of three types of components: two input ports, two output ports and a three-
by-three cross-bar switch. Each port can transfer a packet, which consists of
a word of address part and a word of data part, at every second cycle. A
packet can be transferred in $h+1$ cycles to the processor h hops beyond by a
virtual-cut-through routing. The message non-overtaking rule is enforced by
this switch unit.

The Input Buffer Unit receives packets from the switch unit. It has two
levels of priority packet buffers for flexible thread scheduling. Each buffer
is an on-chip FIFO, which can hold up to 8 packets. If the buffer becomes
full, the packets are stored to on-memory buffer, and if the buffer is not full,
they are automatically restored back to on-chip FIFO. The IBU operates

independent of the EXU and the memory unit. Packets coming in from the network are immediately processed without interrupting the main processor. The path between IBU and MCU, called by-passing direct memory access (DMA), is one of the key features of EM-X. This by-passing DMA together with the path which connects IBU to OBU is the key to servicing remote read/write requests without consuming the cycles of Execution Unit.

The Matching Unit (MU) fetches the first packet in the FIFO of IBU. If the packet requires matching, a sequence of actions will take place to prepare for thread invocation by direct matching. Actions include (1) obtaining the base address of the activation frame for the current thread to be invoked, (2) loading mate data from matching memory, (3) fetching the top address of the template segment, (4) fetching the first instruction of the enabled thread, and (5) signaling the execution unit to start execution of the first instruction. Packets are sent out through the OBU which separates the EXU from the network. The MCU controls the access to the local memory off the EMC-Y chip.

The Execution Unit is a register-based RISC pipeline which executes a thread of sequential instructions. It has 32 registers, including five special purpose registers. All integer instructions take one clock cycle, with the exception of an instruction which exchanges the content of a register with the content of memory. Single precision floating point instructions are also executed in one clock cycle, except floating point division. Packet generation is also performed by this unit, which takes one clock cycle. Four types of send instructions are implemented, including remote read request for one data and remote read request for a block of data.

The Output Buffer Unit receives packets generated by the EXU or IBU. Again, the buffer can hold up to 8 packets. As we have briefly described above, the key feature of the OBU is to process packets generated by IBU. Remote read requests received by other processors are processed by the IBU which uses the by-pass DMA to read data from the memory. When the data fetched by the IBU is given to OBU, it will be immediately sent out to the destination address specified in the read request packet. This internal working of IBU and OBU is the key feature of EM-X for fast remote read/writes without consuming the main processor cycles.

2.3 Architectural Support for Fine-Grain Multithreading

The EM-X distributed-memory multiprocessor supports dynamic function spawning and multithreading both in hardware and software. Hardware supports include thread invocation through packets, FIFO hardware scheduling of threads, and by-passing one-sided remote read/write. Software supports for multithreading include explicit context switch, global-address space, and register saving. Thread invocation or function spawning is done through 2-word-sized packets. When a thread needs to invoke a function (thread), a packet containing the starting address of the thread is generated and sent to the destination processor. The thread which just issued the packet continues the computation without any interruption unless it encounters a remote read or explicit thread switching.

As the thread invocation packet arrives at the destination processor, it will be buffered in the packet queue along with other packets arrived. Packets stored in the packet queue are read in the order in which they were received, hence First-In-First-Out (FIFO) thread scheduling. A thread of instructions is in turn invoked by using the address portion of the packet just dequeued. The thread will run to completion unless it encounters any remote memory operations or explicit thread switching. If the thread encounters a remote memory operation, it will be suspended after the remote read request is sent out. Should this suspension occur, any register values currently being used for the thread will be saved in the activation frame associated with the thread for resumption upon the return of the outstanding remote memory operation. The completion or suspension of a thread causes the next packet to be automatically dequeued from the packet queue using FIFO scheduling.

Whenever a thread encounters a remote read, a packet consisting of two 32-bit words is generated. The first 32-bit word contains the destination address whereas the second 32-bit contains the return address which is often called continuation. The read packet will be appropriately routed to the destination processor, where it will be stored in the input buffer unit for processing. The remote processor does not intervene to process the packet. The remote read packet will be processed through the by-passing mechanism which was explained earlier. When the read packet returns to the originating processor, it will be inserted in the hardware FIFO queue for processing, i.e., thread resumption. Remote writes do not suspend the issuing threads. For each remote write, a packet is generated which consists of two 32-bit words. The first word is the destination memory address and the second the data to be written. The write instruction is treated the same as other normal instructions. After sending out the write packet, the thread continues.

Software supports for multithreading include explicit context switch and global address space, and register saving. The current compiler supports C with thread library. Programs written in C with the thread library are compiled into explicit-switch threads. Two storage resources are used in EM-X, including template segments and operand segments. The compiled codes of functions are stored in template segments. Invoking a function involves allocating an operand segment as an activation frame. The caller allocates the activation frame, deposits the argument value(s) into the frame, and sends its continuation as a packet to invoke the caller's thread. The first instruction of a thread operates on input tokens, which are loaded into two operand registers. The registers can hold values for one thread at a time. The current implementation allows no register sharing across threads, thus no implicit-switching support. The caller saves any live registers to the current activation frame before a context-switch. The continuation packet sent from the caller is used to return results as in a conventional call. The result from the called function resumes the caller's thread by this continuation.

The level of thread activation and suspension can be nested and arbitrary. Activation frames (threads) form a tree rather than a stack, reflecting a dynamic calling structure. This tree of activation frames allow threads to spawn one to many threads on processors including itself. The level of thread activation/suspension is limited only by the amount of system memory. The EM-X compiler supports a global address space. Remote reads/writes are implemented through packets. A remote memory access packet uses a global address which consists of the processor number and the local memory address of the selected processor.

3. Designing Multithreaded Algorithms

3.1 Multithreaded Bitonic Sorting

Bitonic sorting, introduced by Batcher [5] consists of two steps: local sort and merge. Given P processors and n elements, each processor holds n/p elements. In the local sort step, each processor takes in n/p elements and sorts them in an ascending order if the second bit of the processor number is 0, and in a descending order otherwise. The merge step consists of $O(\log^2 P)$ steps. In each merge step, elements are sorted across processors in a pair. As iterations progress, the distance between the pair of processors widens. The last iteration will sort elements on two processors with the distance of $P/2$.

Figure 3.1 illustrates bitonic sorting of $n=32$ elements on $P=8$ processors. Consider processors 0 and 1 at $i=0$, $j=0$. P0 has $\mathbf{L}=(5,13,24,32)$ and P1 has $\mathbf{L}=(6,14,23,31)$, resulted from the local sorting step. P0 and P1 will sort 8 elements in an ascending order as indicated by shaded circles. Hollow circles indicate that processors sort elements in a descending order. The line between P0 and P1 indicates that the processors communicate. P0 sends L to its mate processor P1 while P1 sends $\mathbf{L}$ to its mate P0. When P0 receives four elements from P1, it merges them with $\mathbf{L}$, so does P1. Since P0 takes a lower position than P1, it takes the low half (5,6,13,14) while P1 takes the high half (23,24,31,32). This type of sending, receiving, and merging operations continues until the 32 elements are sorted across the eight processors.

A multithreaded version of bitonic sorting divides the inner j loop into h threads. Each thread is responsible for merging n/hp elements. The main idea of the multithreaded algorithm is to first issue remote reads by h threads, called thread communication parallelism, followed by the computation whenever any n/hp elements are read, called thread computation parallelism. Reading of n/p elements is issued before any merging takes place. Whenever n/hp elements are read, i.e., whenever each thread finishes reading n/hp from the mate processor, it will merge it into its list $\mathbf{L}$. This reading (communication) and merging (computation) will take place simultaneously, to overlap computation with communication.

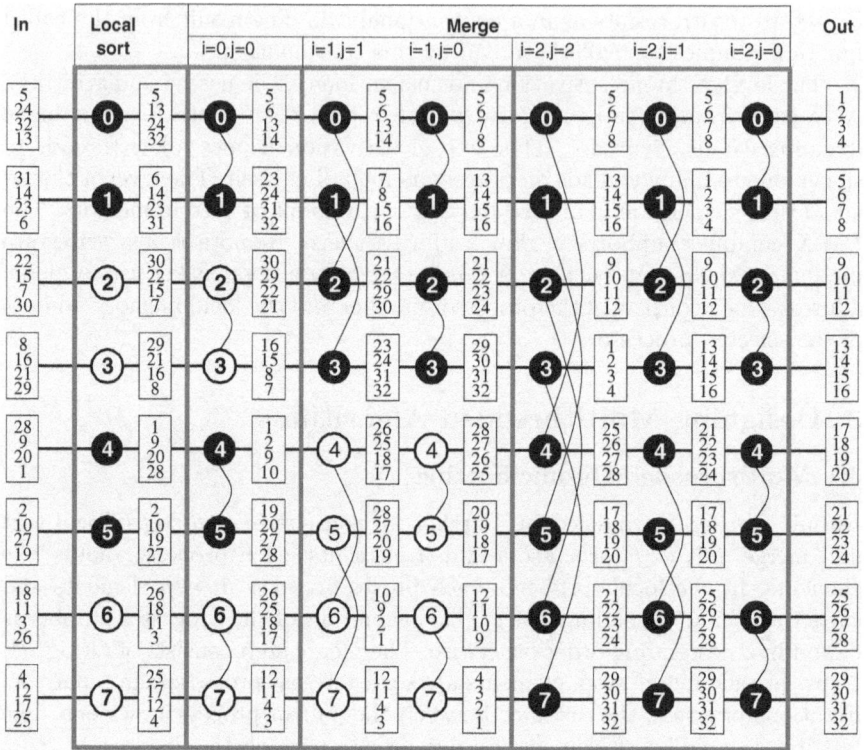

Fig. 3.1. Bitonic sorting of $n=32$ elements on $P=8$ processors. Shaded circles indicate those processors performing ascending order merge while the hollow circles indicate processors performing descending order merge. Curves connecting two processors indicate that each processor reads four elements from the mate processor.

Figure 3.2 illustrates how two processors Px and Py sort 8 elements in an ascending order. For the illustration purpose we use two threads in each processor. Four elements are divided into two parts, each of which is assigned to a thread. Processors X and Y initially hold (2,5,6,7) and (1,3,4,8), respectively. Thread 0 of Px is responsible for reading and merging the first half (1,3) of Py while thread 1 does for the second half (4,8). Sorting of the eight elements on the two processors proceeds as follows:

1. At t_a, Thd0 sends out the read request RR0 to Py, and suspends itself.
2. Between t_a and t_b, the switch to Thd1 takes place, spending several clocks.
3. At t_b, Thd1 sends out the read request RR2 to Py, and in turn is suspended.

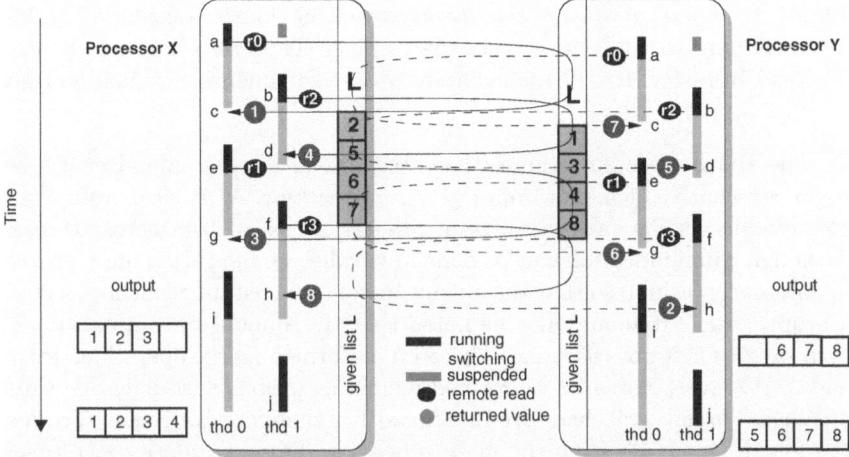

Fig. 3.2. A multithreaded version of bitonic sorting. The figure is not drawn to scale. Processors x and y sort 8 elements in an ascending order. Characters $a..i$ indicate the time sequence. Each processor has two threads. A thread handles 2 elements. Communication for Px is in solid lines and for Py is in dotted lines.

4. Between t_b and t_c, there are no threads running. Both threads are dormant.

5. At t_c, RR0 returns with value 1 which will be saved in a buffer for merge. The value resumes Thd0.

6. At t_d, RR2 returns with the value 4 but no further activities will take place since Thd0 is currently running.

7. At t_e, Thd0 sends out the read request, RR1, to Py, and then suspends itself. Switching to Thd1 takes place.

8. At t_f, Thd1 sends out the read request RR3 to Py, and in turn is suspended.

9. Between t_f and t_g, there are no running threads. Both threads are in a suspended status, and therefore no computation takes place. Even though Thd1 has received the value 4, it cannot perform the merge operation since Thd0 is not complete. Merging 4 with the list will result in a wrong order. Thd1 can proceed only after Thd0 completes. This is exactly where sorting lacks computation parallelism across threads. As we shall see shortly, FFT has large computation parallelism across all threads.

10. At t_g, RR1 returns with value 3. Thd1 is still in the suspended status. Thd0 has now read all the necessary elements, and immediately proceeds to merging the two elements with its own list.

11. At t_h, RR3 returns with value 8 but no actions will take place since Thd0 is currently running.

12. At t_i, Thd0 completes the merge, resulting in the output of (1,2,3). Switching to Thd1 now takes place. Since Thd1 also has two elements read from Px, it will immediately proceed to merging, which will give (1,2,3,4).

The above example assumes that each thread merges only after it reads n/hp consecutive elements from the mate processor. As it clear from example, bitonic sorting presents little computation parallelism across threads. Although communication can be done in parallel, computation must proceed in an orderly fashion so that the output buffer will contain elements sorted in a proper order. It should also be noted that the amount of computation for each processor is not the same. Thread 0 performed merge operations with 1 and 3. However, Thread 1 performed merge operations with only one value, 4. When Thread 1 reached sorted. Thread 1 is therefore not required to read the fourth element 8 from the mate processor. This irregularity in terms of computation occurs because not all the elements residing in the mate processor need to be read. The algorithmic behavior of bitonic sorting is beyond the scope of this report and is presented in [20].

3.2 Multithreaded Fast Fourier Transform

The second problem used in this study is Fast Fourier Transform (FFT). Figure 3.3 shows an implementation of FFT with 16 elements on four processors. Blocked data and workload distribution methods are used in the example. The 16 data elements are divided into four groups, each of which is assigned to a processor. Processor 0, or P0, has elements 0 to 3, P1 has 4 to 7, etc. FFT with n elements requires $\log n$ iterations. The butterfly shown in the figure requires $\log 16 = 4$ iterations. In the first iteration, each processor obtains a copy of four elements by finding its mate processor. Processor 0 remote reads four elements 8...11 while P1 does 12...15 from P3. P2 and P3 also obtain necessary data allocated to P0 and P1, respectively.

The second iteration is essentially the same as the first iteration, except the logical communication distance reduces to half the first iteration. Again, P0 remote reads from P1 the four elements which have been newly computed by P1 in iteration 0, P1 reads the newly computed four elements, 0...3, from P0, etc. P2 and P3 again perform operations similar to what P0 and P1 did. The remaining two iterations do not requite communication since the required data are locally stored. In general, an FFT with blocked data distribution of n elements on P processors requires communication for the first $\log P$ iterations. The remaining $(\log n) - (\log P)$ iterations are local computations, which do not need communication. In this report, only the first $\log P$ iterations are used for our experiments since they are the ones which require communication.

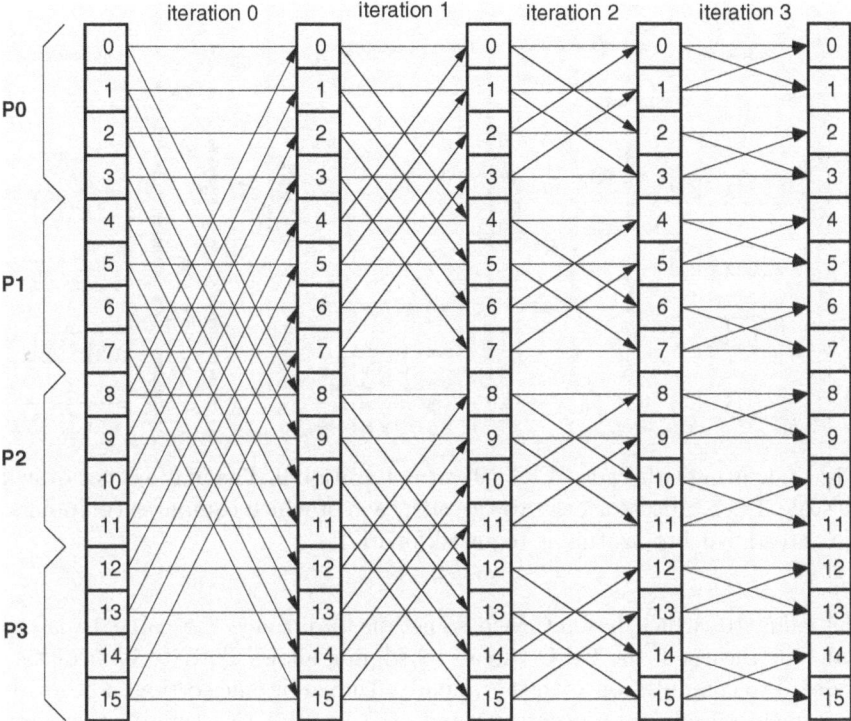

Fig. 3.3. FFT with 16 elements and four processors. Each processor is assigned four elements using blocked data distribution. The first two iterations require communication while the remaining are local computation.

Converting the single-threaded FFT to a multithreaded version is straightforward. Again, the same blocked data and workload distribution are used in the example. Like bitonic sorting, the data assigned to each processor is grouped into h threads to control the thread granularity. The example in Figure 3.4 shows the internal working of processors 0 and 2 of Figure 3.3. Four elements are split into two groups, where each processor has two threads each of which handles two elements.

Unlike Bitonic sorting, however, FFT possesses no data dependence between elements within an iteration. This observation leads to computation whenever any data is remote-read from the mate processor. In the above example, the threads compute and communicate independent of other threads. When Thd0 issues the remote read RR0, it is suspended. Processor 0 now switches to Thd1, which subsequently issues the remote read RR2. As RR0 returns value 8, Thd0 now proceeds to computation while RR2 is outstanding. As Thd0 completes the computation with the value 8, it sends out RR1, followed by its suspension. Thd1 immediately proceeds to computation with

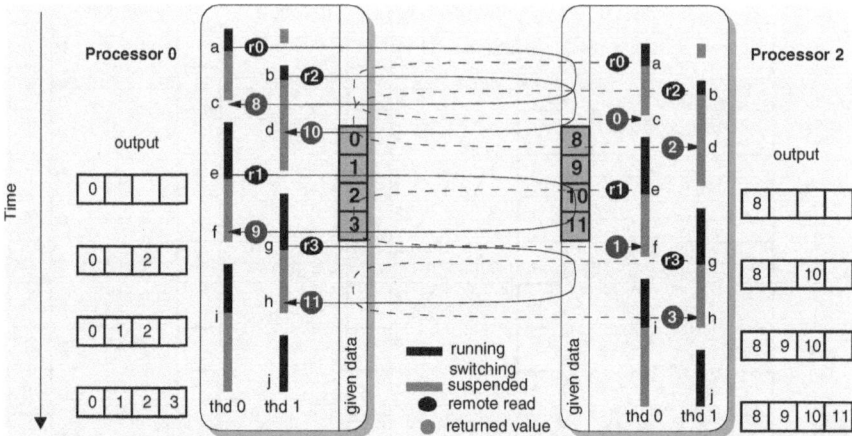

Fig. 3.4. A multithreaded FFT, showing iteration 0. The figure is not drawn to scale. Each processor has two threads, each of which computes two points. No thread synchronization is required for FFT.

the value 10, which has returned sometime ago. Since the value 10 is the only one returned, the FIFO thread scheduling allows Thd1 to immediately proceed to computation with the value 10. Unlike bitonic sorting, no threads are synchronized for an orderly computation in FFT. No time is, therefore, lost for thread scheduling. This computation parallelism across threads will be evidenced by experimental results which will be shown later.

4. Overlapping Analysis

The multithreaded version of fine-grain bitonic sorting and FFT has been implemented on the EM-X. They are written in C with a thread library. To measure the effectiveness of overlapping capability we forced loops to execute synchronously by inserting a barrier at the end of each iteration. Several parameters are frequently used throughout this chapter. The terms elements and integers are used interchangeably in this chapter. The unit for sorting is integers while that for FFT is points. An integer is 32 bits. A point consists of real and imaginary parts, each of which is 32 bits. We list below several parameters used throughout this chapter:

- P = the number of processors, up to 64.
- n = the number of data elements, up to 8 M, the maximum size which EM-X can accommodate.
- h = the number of threads per processor
- $m = n/hp$ = the number of data elements per thread.

Communication times are plotted in Figure 4.1. The x-axis shows the number of threads while the y-axis shows the absolute communication time. The figure presents several observations: The most important observation is that the communication time becomes minimal when the number of threads is three to four. The reason is clear. In bitonic sorting, each thread reads m elements from the mate processor before proceeding to the merge operation. The following loop shows an actual code lifted taken the program.

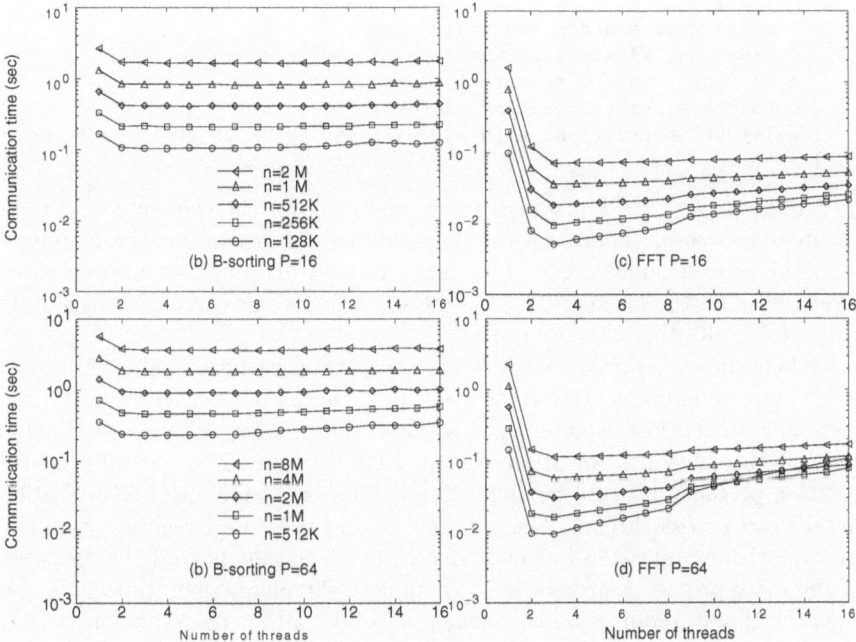

Fig. 4.1. Communication time in seconds.

```
for (k=0;k<m;k++)   /* m = n/hp = # of elements per thread */
    buffer[k] = remote_read(memaddr++);
```

In each iteration, an element is read from the mate processor, assuming memaddr is properly initialized. After each read request, the thread is suspended and another thread is reactivated until each thread reads m elements. The loop body has 12 instructions, i.e., an iteration takes 12 clocks to execute, resulting in the run length of 12. The average remote memory latency, when the network is normally loaded, is approximately 1 to 2 micro sec, or 20-40 clocks. Therefore, each remote read needs two to four threads to mask off the 20-40 clock latency. This is precisely why the communication time becomes minimum when the number of threads is two to four. The number of threads higher than four does not give a notable advantage in terms of masking off the latency.

The effect of multithreading is higher for FFT, as evidenced by the deep valleys. The run length for FFT is much higher than sorting. As we have explained earlier, bitonic sorting requires thread synchronization to ensure proper merge of elements. However, FFT is free from thread synchronization. Therefore, the run length for FFT is very large. The following code shows how multithreading is actually implemented.

```
for(i=0;i<m;i++){ /* m = n/hp = the number of points per thread */
    compute real_address and img_address;
    /* read two floats from the mate processor */
    mate_real = remote_read(real_address++);
    mate_img = remote_read(img_address++);
    a lot of instructions with my_real, my_img, mate_real, mate_img;
}
```

Unlike sorting, FFT proceeds to computation for the elements read from the mate processor. There is a very large number of instructions immediately after the second remote read. This large amount of computations can effectively mask off the latency. This is precisely why two or three threads simply outperform all other threads in FFT.

When the two problems are cross-compared, we note that sorting has much higher communication time than FFT. There are several reasons for the high communication. Among the reasons is the number of switches. Sorting requires thread synchronization whereas FFT does not. This thread synchronization presents a severe bottleneck as it limits the amount of computation parallelism across threads. Second, the sorting presents irregular computation and communication behavior due to the fact that not all the elements of the mate processor are needed to complete the merge operation. FFT, on the other hand, requires all the elements to be read for computation.

When the two problems are compared across different numbers of processors, the communication pattern is relatively consistent for both sorting and FFT. For bitonic sorting, increasing the number of processors to 64 rarely changes the communication pattern. As we can see, there is little difference in Figure 4.1(a) and (b) for sorting, or (c) and (d) for FFT. This consistency in communication pattern indicates that varying the number of processors is not the main factor for contributing to communication patterns. It should be noted that the data size for each processor is the same regardless of the total number of processors.

The effects of data size on communication pattern are inconsistent for both problems. For bitonic sorting with $P=64$, we find that varying data size rarely affects the communication performance, except for one thread. However, it becomes apparent for FFT. Note from Figure 4.1(d) with $P=64$ that the small data size of 512K gives a steeper curve than that of 8M, except one thread. In other words, the curve for 512K has a valley deeper than the one for 8M. The reason is that the data size of 8K for each processor is just too small compared to 128K. This relatively small data size is not significant enough to provide computations which can help mask off the communication latency.

To put the communication times into the multithreading perspective, we identify the efficiency of overlapping. Let $T_{comm,h}$ be the communication time for h threads. We define the efficiency of overlapping as $E = (T_{comm,1} - T_{comm,h})/T_{comm,1}$. The communication time with one thread is used as the basis for overlapping analysis. When only one thread is used, there is no possibility that computation will overlap with communication since there is no other thread to switch to. Figure 4.2 shows the EM-X overlapping capabilities for the two problems.

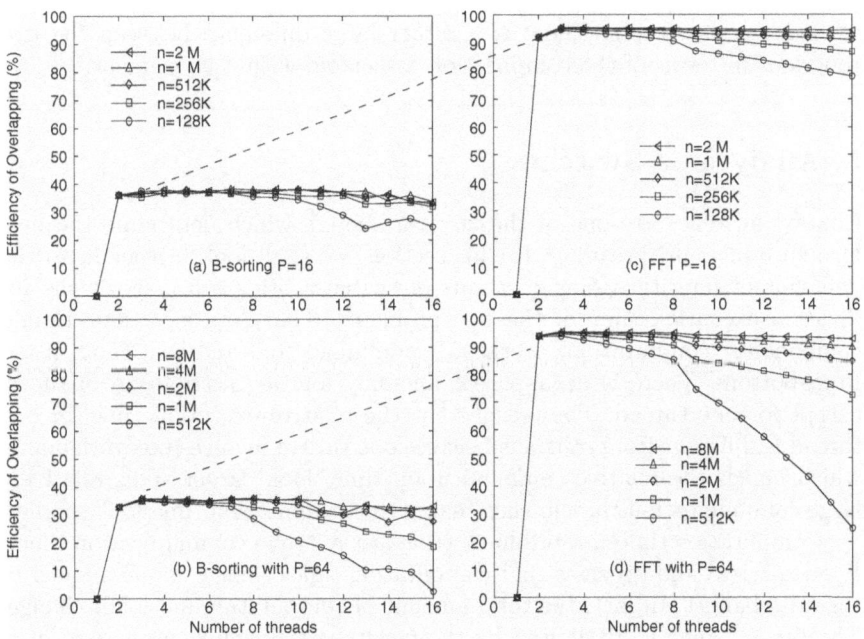

Fig. 4.2. Efficiency of overlapping

Bitonic sorting has given roughly 35% overlapping of communication with computation. However, FFT has given over 95% of overlapping for two to four threads. This rather significant difference is attributed by two factors: First, bitonic sorting is sequential, presenting little parallelism among threads within an iteration while FFT is highly parallel. As we have explained in Section 3.1, communication for sorting can take place in any order but computation must be done in an ascending of threads order to ensure proper merge. Thread j cannot proceed to computation before Thread i, where $j > i$. Synchronization between threads is required to properly sort numbers. Therefore, bitonic sorting provides parallelism in remote reading only, not in computation. Threads in FFT, on the other hand, can proceed in any order, i.e., computation and communication can proceed in any order. Since there is no dependence between elements within an iteration, thread synchronization is not necessary, resulting in high parallelism among threads. This parallelism is clearly revealed in Figure 4.2(c)-(d).

The second reason FFT shows high overlapping efficiency is due to the fact that the amount of computation is much higher than that of communication. The total amount of computations for sorting is very small, consisting of several comparison and merging instructions. The computations for each element are not more than 10 instructions excluding loop control instructions. On the other hand, the computations involved in each element of FFT are large, which include some trigonometric function computations and a loop to find complex roots. There is a rather large difference between the two programs in terms of the computation associated with each element.

5. Analysis of Switches

Context switches are one of the key parameters which determine the performance of multithreading. In this section, we shall look further in to the behavior of multithreading in terms of switches. Figure 5.1 shows the individual execution time of the two problems. The plots have four timing components: computation, overhead, communication, and switching, listed from bottom. There is no apparent anomaly for the distribution of times, except for one thread. The reason that the relative execution time for one thread is different from others is because one thread involves no overlapping, which makes the relative communication time 'look' larger. This relatively large communication time in turn makes the computation time look smaller.

Computation times for bitonic sorting are less than communication times. Figures 5.1(a) and (c) show that computation times change as the number of threads changes. In fact, the total amount of computation must not change. The little change is attributed by the fact that the timing measurement is done through a global clock. When the problem size is large, no fluctuation occurs since the time to measure the global clock is negligible compared to the overall computation time, as is evidenced by (b) and (d). The reason bitonic sorting gives a little higher change in computation than FFT is attributed by another factor. Sorting is implemented in such a way that a processor may or may not have to read all the elements from the mate processor. As long as each processor produces n/p elements, it is done with the computation and will go into synchronization.

Overhead refers to the time taken to generate packets. It is essentially fixed not only for different numbers of processors but also for different problems since the total number of elements allocated to each processor is the

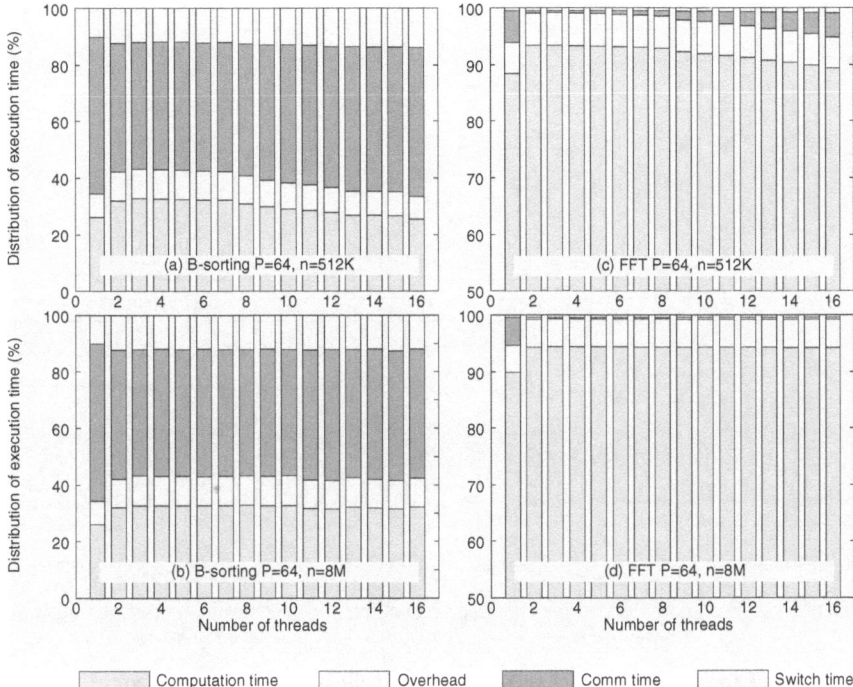

Fig. 5.1. Distribution of execution time on 64 processors: The times from the bottom are computation time, overhead, communication time, and switching time.

same. We measured the overhead by using a null loop body, i.e., the loop body has no computation but instructions to generate packets. We find this was effective to measure the overhead cost for generating packets.

Switches are classified into three types: remote read switch, iteration synchronization switch, and thread synchronization switch. Figure 5.2 shows the three types of switches. The x-axis indicates the number of threads and the y-axis shows the absolute number of switches. The plots are drawn to the same scale. The figure reveals the internal working of multithreading. The remote read switching cost is in general the dominant factor contributing to the main switching cost. This is obvious because every remote read causes a thread switch. The remote read switching cost is fixed regardless of the number of threads because the number of elements to be read is indeed fixed. In fact, this switching can be readily derived from the given n, h, and P.

It is clear that thread synchronization switching cost is not the main factor for the two problems regardless of the numbers of processors. The behavior of thread synchronization switching is different for the two problems. The thread switching cost for bitonic sorting is rather high and is close to the iteration synchronization switching cost. On the other hand, FFT shows that there

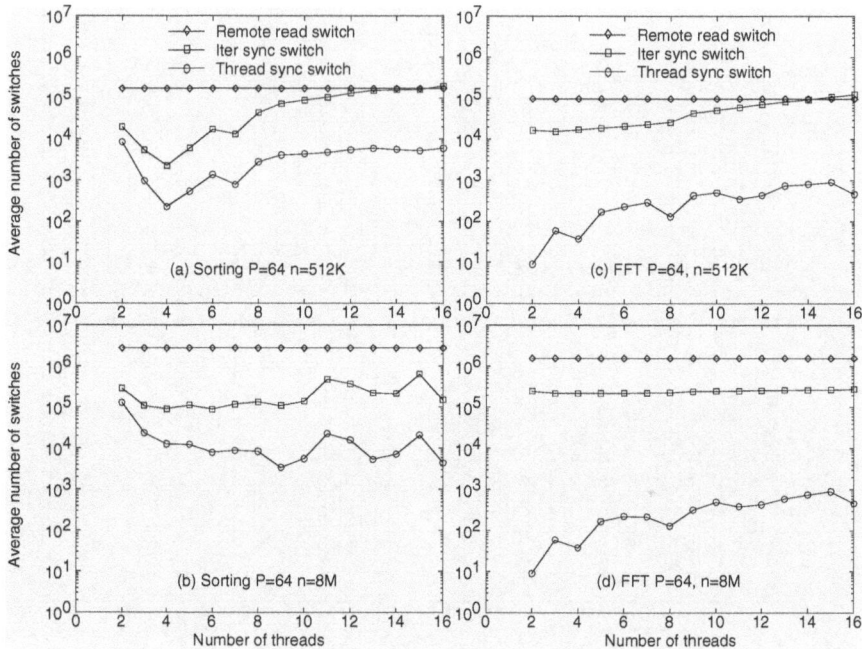

Fig. 5.2. Average number of switches for each processor.

is a wide gap between thread and iteration synchronization switching costs. This gap shows that sorting spends a lot more time synchronizing threads within a processor. This was expected because threads in sorting are executed in sequence while FFT threads can execute in any order. The effects of the presence and absence of computation parallelism across threads are clearly manifested in the plots.

Iteration synchronization switching can be as high as remote read switching for the small problem size of 512K, as shown in Figure 5.2(a) and (c). As the number of threads reaches 16, the synchronization switch cost is in fact higher than the remote read switching cost. The reason is because the amount of computation is relatively small. After such small computations, 16 threads check if other threads are done for the current iteration. In fact, the iteration switching cost increases logarithmically as the number of threads increases linearly. There is approximately an order of magnitude difference in the number of iteration synchronization switches. For large problems shown in Figure 5.2(b) and (d), the amount of computation is now 16 times higher, which effectively eliminates the impact of iteration synchronization switching cost.

When the two problems are compared across different numbers of processors, switching pattern changes. Remote read switch and iteration synchronization switch do not meet. Each processor now finds more computations which separate the two curves. In fact, the switching cost no longer increases rapidly for $P=64$. The fluctuation for sorting with $P=64$ again shows that sorting possesses an irregular computation and communication pattern compared to FFT.

6. Conclusions

Reducing communication time is key to obtaining high performance on distributed-memory multiprocessors. Multithreading aims at reducing communication time by overlapping communication with computation. This chapter has presented the internal working of multithreading through empirical studies. Specifically, we have used the 80-processor EM-X multithreaded distributed-memory machine to demonstrate how multithreading can help overlap communication with computation.

Bitonic sorting and Fast Fourier Transform have been selected to test the multithreading capabilities of EM-X. The criteria for the problem selection have been the computation-to-communication ratio and the amount of thread parallelism. Bitonic sorting has been selected for its nearly 1-to-1 computation-to-communication ratio and the small amount of thread computation parallelism. FFT has been selected because of its high computation-to-communication ratio and the large amount of thread computation parallelism. Both problems have been implemented on EM-X with blocked data and workload distribution strategies. The data size of up to 8M integers for sorting and 8M points for FFT have been used.

Experimental results have presented two key observations. First, the maximum overlapping has occurred when the number of threads is two to four for both problems. Sorting has the run length of 12 clocks per thread, and therefore four threads have been found adequate to mask off the latency of 20 to 40 clocks, or 1 to 2 micro sec. Larger numbers of threads have adversely affected the amount of overlapping due to an excessive number of switches. In particular, iteration synchronization switch has been found the main cause for excessive synchronization costs among switches and a loop. The run-length of FFT is very large of hundreds of clocks due to trigonometric function computations. This rather high run-length has been found sufficient to effectively tolerate the latency of 20 to 40 clocks.

Second, the ratio of computation to communication plays a critical role in tolerating latency. Bitonic sorting results have shown that the maximum overlap has reached approximately 35%. The reason for the low overlapping was because bitonic sorting has small absolute computation time and lacks thread computation parallelism, requiring thread synchronization. FFT, on the other hand, has shown over 95% of communication overlapping due to its high computation-to-communication ratio and the large amount of both thread computation and communication parallelism. FFT threads can compute and communicate in any order within an iteration, requiring no thread synchronization.

The study has indicated that fine-grain multithreading can hold a key to obtaining high performance on distributed-memory machines. The fact that multithreading can tolerate over 35% of the total communication time for sorting at the absence of computation parallelism clearly demonstrates such premise. Problems which possess irregular computation behavior and moderate parallelism can be a logical target for obtaining high performance through multithreading. We believe it is a realistic goal to achieve high overlapping for such irregular problems if the thread scheduling and synchronization mechanisms are fine tuned to thread computation and communication parallelism. It is our next goal to fine-tune mechanisms for hardware thread scheduling and synchronization.

Acknowledgments

The authors would like to thank the other ETL EM-X group members, Hirofumi Sakane, Hayato Yamana, and Shuichi Sakai who is now with the University of Tokyo for many discussions on multithreading.

References

1. Accelerated Strategic Computing Initiative (ASCI), Lawrence Livermore, Los Alamos, and Sandia National Laboratories, http://www.llnl.gov/asci/.
2. A. Agarwal, R. Bianchini, D. Chaiken, K. L. Johnson, D. Kranz, J. Kubiatowicz, B-H. Lim, K. Mackenzie, and D. Yeung, The MIT Alewife Machine: Architecture and Performances, in *Proc. the International Symposium on Computer Architecture*, Santa Margherita Ligure, Italy, June 1995, pp.2-13.
3. T. Agerwala, J. L. Martin, J. H. Mirza, D. C. Sadler, D. M. Dias, and M. Snir, SP-2 System Architecture, *IBM Systems Journal* Vol. 34, No. 2, 1995.
4. R. Alverson, D. Callahan, D. Cummings, B. Koblenz, A. Porterfield, and B. Smith, The Tera computer system, In *Proc. of ACM International Conference on Supercomputing*, Amsterdam, Netherlands, June 1990, ACM, pp.1-6.
5. K. Batcher, Sorting Networks and Their Applications, in *Proc. the AFIPS Spring Joint Computer Conference 32*, Reston, VA, 1968, pp.307-314.
6. D. Culler, S. Goldstein, K. Schauser, and T. von Eicken, TAM - A Compiler Controlled Threaded Abstract Machine, *Journal of Parallel and Distributed Computing 18*, pp.347-370, 1993.
7. D. Culler, R.M. Karp, D.A. Patterson, A. Sahay, K. Schauser, E. Santos, R. Subramonian, and T. von Eicken, LogP: Towards a Realistic Model of Parallel Computation, in *Proc. of the Fourth ACM Symposium on Principles and Practice of Parallel Programming*, San Diego, CA, May 1993.
8. G. Gao, L. Bic and J-L. Gaudiot (Eds.) Advanced Topic in Dataflow Computing and Multithreading, IEEE Computer society press, 1995.

9. R. Iannucci, G. Gao, R. Halstead, and B. Smith (Eds.), Multithreaded Computer Architecture, Kluwer Publishers, Norwell, MA 1994.
10. Y. Kodama, Y. Koumura, M. Sato, H. Sakane, S. Sakai, and Y. Yamaguchi, EMC-Y: Parallel Processing Element Optimizing Communication and Computation, in *Proc. of ACM International Conference on Supercomputing*, Tokyo, Japan, July 1993, pp.167-174.
11. Y. Kodama, H. Sakane, M. Sato, H. Yamana, S. Sakai, and Y. Yamaguchi, The EM-X Parallel Computer: Architecture and Basic Performance, in *Proc. of ACM International Symposium on Computer Architecture*, Santa Margherita Ligure, Italy, June 1995, pp.14-23.
12. H. Matsuoka, K. Okamoto, H. Hirono, M. Sato, T. Yokota, S. Sakai, Pipeline design and enhancement for fast network message handling in RWC-1 multiprocessor, in *Proc. of the Workshop on Multithreaded Execution, Architecture and Compilation*, Las Vegas, Nevada, February 1998.
13. R. Nikhil, G. Papadopolous, and Arvind, *T: A Multithreaded Massively Parallel Architecture, in *Proc. of ACM International Symposium on Computer Architecture*, Gold Coast, Australia, May 1992, pp.156-167.
14. G. Papadopolous, An Implementation of General Purpose Dataflow Multiprocessor, MIT Press, Cambridge, MA, 1991.
15. R. Saavedra-Barrera, D. Culler, and T. von Eicken, Analysis of Multithreaded Architectures for Parallel Computing, in *Proc. of ACM Symposium on Parallel Algorithms and Architectures*, pp. 169-178, July 1990.
16. S. Sakai, Y. Yamaguchi, K. Hiraki, and T. Yuba, An Architecture of a Data-flow Single Chip Processor, in *Proc. of ACM International Symposium on Computer Architecture*, Jerusalem, Israel, May 1989, pp.46-53.
17. M. Sato, Y. Kodama, S. Sakai, Y. Yamaguchi, and Y. Koumura, Thread-based Programming for the EM-4 Hybrid Data-flow Machine, in *Proc. of ACM International Symposium on Computer Architecture*, Gold Coast, Australia, May 1992, pp.146-155.
18. S. Scott, Synchronization and Communication in the T3E Multiprocessor, in *Proc. of ACM Conference on Architectural Support for Programming Languages and Operating Systems*, Boston, MA, October 1996.
19. B. J. Smith, A Pipelined, Shared Resource MIMD Computer, in *Proc. of International Conference on Parallel Processing*, 1978, pp.6-8.
20. A. Sohn, J. Ku, Y. Kodama, M. Sato, H. Sakane, H. Yamana, S. Sakai, and Y. Yamaguchi, Identifying the Capability of Overlapping Computation with Communication, in *Proc. of ACM/IEEE Conference on Parallel Architectures and Compilation Techniques*, Boston, MA, October 1996, pp. 133-138.
21. A. Sohn, M. Sato, N. Yoo, and J-L Gaudiot, Data and Workload Distribution in a Multithreaded Architecture, *Journal of Parallel and Distributed Computing*, December 1996.

Section IV : Code Generation

Chapter 16. Advanced Code Generation for High Performance Fortran

Vikram Adve[1] and John Mellor-Crummey[2]

[1] Computer Science Department, University of Illinois at Urbana Champaign
  1304 West Springfield Avenue, Urbana IL 61801, USA
  vadve@cs.uiuc.edu
[2] Department of Computer Science and
  Center for Research on Parallel Computation,
  Rice University, Houston, Texas, USA

Summary. For data-parallel languages such as High Performance Fortran to achieve wide acceptance, parallelizing compilers must be able to provide consistently high performance for a broad spectrum of scientific applications. Although compilation of regular data-parallel applications for message-passing systems have been widely studied, current state-of-the-art compilers implement only a small number of key optimizations, and the implementations generally focus on optimizing programs using a "case-based" approach. For these reasons, current compilers are unable to provide consistently high levels of performance. In this paper, we describe techniques developed in the Rice dHPF compiler to address key code generation challenges that arise in achieving high performance for regular applications on message-passing systems. We focus on techniques required to implement advanced optimizations and to achieve consistently high performance with existing optimizations. Many of the core communication analysis and code generation algorithms in dHPF are expressed in terms of abstract equations manipulating integer sets. This approach enables general and yet simple implementations of sophisticated optimizations, making it more practical to include a comprehensive set of optimizations in data-parallel compilers. It also enables the compiler to support much more aggressive computation partitioning algorithms than in previous compilers. We therefore believe this approach can provide higher and more consistent levels of performance than are available today.

1. Introduction

Data-parallel languages such as High-Performance Fortran (HPF) [29, 31] aim to make parallel scientific computing accessible to a much wider audience by providing a simple, portable, abstract programming model applicable to a wide variety of parallel computing systems. For such languages to achieve wide acceptance, it will be essential to have parallelizing compilers that provide consistently high performance for a broad spectrum of scientific applications. To achieve the desired levels of performance and consistency, compilers must necessarily exploit a wide variety of optimization techniques and effectively apply them to programs with as few restrictions as possible.

Engineering HPF compilers that provide consistently high performance for a wide range of programs is a challenging task. The data layout directives in an HPF program provide an abstract, high-level specification of maximal data-parallelism and data-access locality. The compiler must use this

S. Pande, D.P. Agrawal (Eds.): Compiler Optimizations for Scalable PS, LNCS 1808, pp. 553-596, 2001.
© Springer-Verlag Berlin Heidelberg 2001

information to choose how to partition the computation among processors, determine what data movement and synchronization is necessary, and generate code to implement the partitioning, communication and synchronization. Accounting for interactions and feedback among these steps complicates program analysis and code generation. To achieve high efficiency, optimizations must analyze and transform the program globally within procedures, and often interprocedurally as well.

The most widely studied sub-problem of data-parallel compilation is that of compiling "regular" data-parallel applications on message-passing systems. Data-parallel programs are known as "regular" if the mapping of each array's data elements to processors can be described by an affine mapping function and the array sections accessed by each array reference can be computed symbolically at compile time. Even within this class of applications, state-of-the-art commercial and research compilers do not consistently achieve performance competitive with hand-written code [16,24]. Although many important optimizations for such systems have been proposed by previous researchers, current compilers implement only a small fraction of these optimizations, generally focusing on the most fundamental ones such as static loop partitioning based on the "owner-computes" rule [39], moving messages out of loops, reducing the number of data copies, and exploiting collective communication. Furthermore, even for these optimizations, most research and commercial data-parallel compilers to date [7, 10, 15–17, 19, 24, 32, 33, 35, 42, 45, 46] (including the Rice Fortran 77D compiler [24]) perform communication analysis and code generation for specific combinations of the form of references, data layouts and computation partitionings. While such "case-based" approaches can provide excellent performance where they apply, they will provide poor performance for cases that have not been explicitly considered. More importantly, case-based compilers require a relatively high development cost for each new optimization because the analysis and code generation for each case is handled separately; this makes it difficult to achieve wide coverage with optimizations, which in turn makes it difficult to offer consistently high performance.

In this paper, we describe techniques to address key code generation challenges that arise in a sophisticated compiler for regular data-parallel applications on message-passing systems. We focus on techniques required to implement advanced optimizations and to achieve consistently high performance with existing optimizations. With minor exceptions, these techniques have been implemented in the Rice dHPF compiler, an experimental research compiler for High Performance Fortran. Although this paper focuses on compilation techniques for regular problems on message-passing systems, the dHPF compiler is being designed to integrate handling for regular and irregular applications, and to target other architectures including shared-memory and hybrid systems.

The principal code generation challenges we address are the following:

- *Flexible computation partitionings:* Higher performance can be achieved if compilers can go beyond the widely-used owner-computes rule to support a much more flexible class of computation partitionings. More general computation partitionings require two key compiler enhancements. First, they require robust communication analysis techniques that are not limited to specific partitioning assumptions. Second, they also require sophisticated code generation techniques to guarantee correctness in the presence of arbitrary control-flow, and to generate partitioned code with good scalar efficiency. The dHPF compiler supports a much more general computation partitioning (CP) model than in previous data-parallel compilers. We describe the communication analysis and code generation techniques required to support this model.

- *Robust algorithms for communication and code generation:* The core communication analysis, optimization, and code generation algorithms in dHPF are expressed in terms of abstract equations manipulating integer sets rather than as a collection of strategies for different cases. Optimizations we have formulated in this manner include message vectorization [14], message coalescing [43], recognizing in-place communication [1], code generation for our general CP model [1], non-local index set splitting [32], control-flow simplification [34], and generalized loop-peeling for improving parallelism. By formulating these algorithms in terms of operations on integer sets, we are able to abstract away the details of the CPs, references, and data layouts for each problem instance. All of these algorithms fully support our general computation partitioning model, and can be used for arbitrary combinations of computation partitionings, data layouts and affine reference subscripts.

- *Simplifying compiler-generated control-flow:* Loop splitting transformations, performed to minimize the dynamic cost of adding new guards, produce new loops with smaller iteration spaces which can render existing guards and loops inside redundant or infeasible. This raises the need for an algorithm that can determine the symbolic constraints that hold at each control point and use them to simplify or eliminate branches and loops in the generated code. We motivate and briefly describe a powerful algorithm for constraint propagation and control flow simplification used in the dHPF compiler [34]. In a preliminary evaluation, the algorithm has proven highly effective at eliminating excess control-flow in the generated code. Furthermore, we find that the general purpose control-flow simplification algorithm provides some or all of the benefits of special-purpose optimizations such as vector-message pipelining [43] and overlap areas [14].

Our aim in this chapter is to motivate and provide an overview of the techniques we use to address the challenges described above. The algorithms underlying these techniques are described and evaluated in detail elsewhere [1, 34]. In the following section, we use an example to describe the basic steps in generating an explicit message-passing parallel program for HPF. We also use the example to show why integer sets are fundamental to the problem of HPF compilation, and describe the approaches used in previous data-parallel compilers for computing and generating code from integer sets. In Section 3 we describe a general integer-set framework underlying HPF compilation, and the implementation of this framework in dHPF. The framework directly supports integer set based algorithms for many of our optimizations, and these are briefly described in the subsequent sections. In Section 4, we define our general computation partitioning model and how we support code generation for it. In Section 5, we provide an overview of the principal communication optimizations in dHPF and then briefly describe the key optimizations that were formulated in terms of the integer set framework. In Section 6, we motivate and describe control-flow simplification in dHPF, and present a brief evaluation of its effectiveness. Finally, in Section 7, we conclude with a brief summary and discussion of the techniques described in this chapter.

2. Background: The Code Generation Problem for HPF

The High Performance Fortran standard describes a number of extensions to Fortran 90 to guide compiler parallelization for parallel systems. The language is discussed in some detail in an earlier chapter [29], and we assume the reader is familiar with the major aspects of the language (particularly, the data distribution directives). Throughout this paper, we assume a message-passing target system although many of the same analyses are required or profitable for shared-memory systems as well.

2.1 Communication Analysis and Code Generation for HPF

To understand the basic problem of compiling an HPF program into an explicitly parallel message-passing program, and to motivate our use of a general integer-set framework for analysis and code generation, consider the simple example in Figure 2.1. The source loop represents a nearest-neighbor stencil computation similar to those found in partial differential equation solvers. The two arrays are aligned with each other and both are distributed (block,block) on a two-dimensional processor array. To generate an explicitly parallel code for the program, the compiler must first decide (a) how to partition the computation for each statement in the program, (b) which references might access non-local data due to the chosen partitioning, and (c) how and when to instantiate the communication to obtain this non-local data.

Assume the compiler chooses an "owner-computes" partitioning for the statement in the loop, i.e., each instance of the statement is executed by the

```
CHPF$ processors P(3,3)
CHPF$ distribute A(block,block) onto P
CHPF$ distribute B(block,block) onto P
      do 10 j=2,N-1
      do 10 i=2,N-1
        A(i,j) = 0.25*
                (B(i-1,j)+B(i+1,j) +
                 B(i,j-1)+B(i,j+1))
   10 continue
```

P(1,1)	P(1,2)	P(1,3)
P(2,1)	P(2,2)	P(2,3)
P(3,1)	P(3,2)	P(3,3)

(a) HPF source code   (b) Processor array P(3,3)

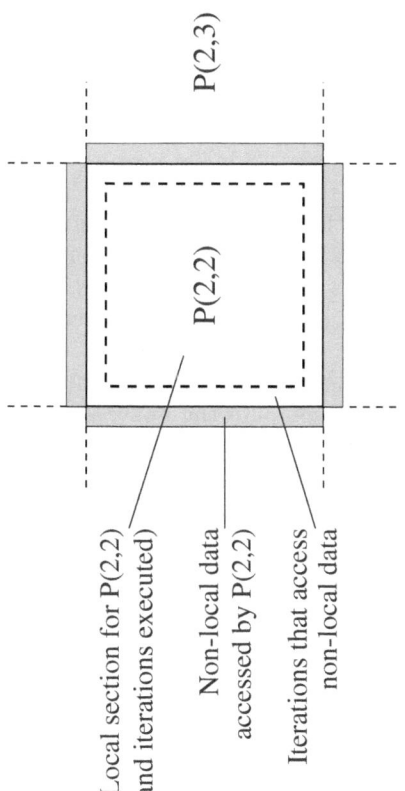

(c) Communication and iteration sets

Fig. 2.1. Example illustrating integer sets required for code generation for Jacobi kernel

processors that own the value being computed, viz., `A(i,j)`. In this case, each of the four references on the right hand side (RHS) accesses some off-processor elements, namely the boundary elements on the four neighboring processors. Since the array `B` is not modified inside the loop nest, communication for these references can be moved out of the loops and placed before the loop nest.

In order to generate efficient explicitly parallel SPMD code, the compiler must compute the following quantities, and then use these to generate code. These quantities are illustrated in Figure 2.1:

1. the sections of each array allocated to (owned by) each processor;
2. the set of iterations to be executed by each processor (conforming with the owned section of array `A`);
3. the non-local data accessed from each other processor by each reference (the off-processor boundary sections shown in the figure);
4. the iterations that access non-local data and the iterations that access exclusively local data. (These sets are used by advanced optimizations such as those described in Section 5.3.)

All of these quantities can be symbolically represented as sets of integer tuples (representing array indices, loop iterations, or processor indices), or as mappings between integer tuples (e.g., an array layout is a mapping from processor indices to array indices). These sets and mappings are defined in Section 3. The sets may be non-convex, as is the set of iterations accessing non-local data shown in Figure 2.1.

To generate a statically partitioned, message-passing program, any data-parallel compiler must implicitly or explicitly compute the above sets, and then use these sets to generate code. The compiler typically generates SPMD code for a representative processor `myid` by performing the following tasks in some order (the resulting code is omitted here):

1. Synthesize a loop nest to execute the iterations assigned to `myid`.
2. For each message, if explicit buffering of data is necessary, synthesize code to pack a buffer at the sending processor and/or to unpack a buffer at the receiving processor.
3. Allocate storage to hold the non-local data, and modify the code to access data out of this storage (note that different references access non-local data in different iterations).
4. Allocate storage for the local sections for each array, and modify array references (for local data) to index appropriately into these local sections.

2.2 Previous Approaches to Communication Analysis and Code Generation

To compute the above sets and to generate code using them, the primary approach in most previous research and commercial compilers has been to focus on individual common cases and to precompute the iteration and communication sets symbolically for specific forms of references, data layouts and computation partitionings [7, 10, 15–17, 19, 24, 32, 33, 42, 46]. For example, to implement the Kali compiler [32], the authors pre-compute symbolically the iteration sets and communication sets for subscripts of the form c, $i + c$ and $c - i$, where i is a loop index variable for BLOCK and CYCLIC distributions. The Fortran 77D compiler also handled the same classes of references and distributions, but computed special-case expressions for the iteration sets for "interior" and "boundary" processors [24]. (In fact, both these groups have described basic compilation steps in terms of abstract set operations [23, 32]; however, this was used only as a pedagogical abstraction and the corresponding compilers were implemented using case-based analysis.) Li and Chen describe algorithms to classify communication caused by more general reference patterns (assuming aligned arrays and the owner-computes rule), and generate code to realize these patterns efficiently on a target machine [33]. In general, these compilers focus on providing specific optimizations aimed at cases that are considered to be the most common and most important. The principal benefits of such case-based strategies are that they are conceptually simple and hence lend themselves well to initial implementations, they have predictable and fast running times, and they can provide excellent performance in cases where they apply.

Three groups have used a more abstract and general approach based on linear inequalities to support code generation for communication and iteration sets [2–5]. In this approach, each code generation or communication optimization problem is described by a collection of linear inequalities representing integer sets or mappings. Fourier-Motzkin elimination [41] is used to simplify the resulting inequalities, and to compute a range of values for individual index variables that together enumerate the integer points described by these inequalities. Code generation then amounts to generating loops to iterate over these index ranges. In the PIPS and Paradigm compilers, these techniques were primarily used for code generation for communication and iteration sets [3, 5]. In the SUIF compiler, these techniques were also applied to carry out specific optimizations including message vectorization, message coalescing (limited to certain combinations of references) and redundant message elimination [2].

The advantage of using linear inequalities over case-based approaches is that each optimization or code generation problem can be expressed and solved in abstract terms, independent of the specific forms of references, data layouts, and computation partitionings. Furthermore, Fourier-Motzkin elimination is applicable to arbitrary affine references and data layouts. The primary limitation of linear-inequality based approaches in previous compilers is that they have limited their focus to problems that can be represented by the intersection of a single set of inequalities. This limited the scope of their techniques so that, for example, they would be unable to support our general computation partitioning model, coalescing communication for arbitrary affine references, or general loop-splitting into local and non-local iterations. We considered all of these capabilities to be important goals for the dHPF compiler. A second drawback of linear-inequality based approaches is that each problem or optimization is expressed directly in terms of large collections of inequalities which must be constructed to represent operations such as intersections and compositions of sets and mappings. It appears much easier and more intuitive to express complex optimizations directly in terms of sequences of abstract set operations on integer sets, as shown in [1].

There is also a large body of work on techniques to enumerate communication sets and iteration sets in the presence of cyclic(k) distributions (e.g., [12, 17, 28, 35, 45]). Compared to more general approaches based on integer sets or linear inequalities, these techniques likely provide more efficient support for cyclic(k) distributions, particularly when $k > 1$, but would be much less efficient for simpler distributions, and are much less general in the forms of references and computation partitionings they could handle. Our goal has been to base the dHPF compiler on a general analysis framework that provides good performance in the vast majority of common cases (within regular distributions), and requires such special-purpose techniques as infrequently as possible. Such techniques can be added as special-purpose optimizations in conjunction with the integer-set framework, but even in the absence of these techniques, we expect that the set framework itself will provide acceptably efficient support for cyclic(k) distributions.

To summarize, we believe there are two essential advantages and one significant disadvantage of the more general and abstract approaches based on linear inequalities or integer-sets, compared with the case-based approaches. First, the former use general algorithms that handle the entire class of regular problems fairly well, whereas case-based approaches apply more narrowly and must fall back more often on inefficient techniques such as run-time resolution for cases they do not handle. In the absence of special-case algorithms, the general approaches are likely to provide much higher performance. Support for exploiting special-cases (e.g., for using collective communication primitives) can be added to the the former if they provide substantial performance improvements, but they should be needed in very few cases. Second, the more abstract framework provided by linear inequalities (to some extent) and by integer sets (to a greater extent) greatly simplifies the compiler-writer's task of implementing important optimizations that are generally applicable, and therefore make it *practical* to achieve high performance for a wider class of programs. By combining both generality and simplicity, we believe an approach such as that of using integer sets can provide higher and more consistent levels of performance than is available today. In contrast, the principal advantages of case-based approaches are that preliminary implementations can be simple, and that they typically have fast and predictable running times. For more general approaches, running time is the greatest concern since manipulation of linear inequalities and integer sets can be costly and unpredictable in difficult cases. This issue is discussed in more detail in later sections.

3. An Integer Set Framework for Data-Parallel Compilation

As discussed in the previous section, any compiler for a data-parallel language based on data distributions can be viewed as operating in terms of some fundamental sets of integer tuples and mappings between these sets. This formulation is made explicit in dHPF and in the SUIF compiler [2], and similar formulations have been discussed elsewhere [23, 32]. The integer set framework in dHPF includes the representation of these primitive quantities as integer tuple sets and mappings, together with the operations to manipulate them and generate code from them. The core optimizations in dHPF are implemented directly on this framework. This section explains the primitive components of the framework, and the implementation of the framework. The following sections describe the optimizations formulated using the framework.

3.1 Primitive Components of the Framework

An integer k-tuple is a point in $\mathcal{Z}^k$; a tuple space of rank k is a subset of $\mathcal{Z}^k$. Any compiler for a data-parallel language based on data distributions operates primarily on three types of tuple spaces, and the three pairwise mappings between these tuple spaces [2, 23, 32]. These are:[1]

$$data_k :\quad \text{index set of an array of rank } k, k \geq 0$$
$$loop_k :\quad \text{iteration space of a loop nest of depth } k, k \geq 0$$
$$proc_k :\quad \text{processor index space in a processor array of rank } k, k \geq 1$$
$$Layout :\quad \{[\underline{p}] \to [\underline{a}] : \underline{p} \in proc_n \text{ owns array element } \underline{a} \in data_k\}$$
$$Ref :\quad \{[\underline{i}] \to [\underline{a}] : \underline{i} \in loop_k \text{ references array element } \underline{a} \in data_k\}$$
$$CPMap :\quad \{[\underline{p}] \to [\underline{i}] : \underline{p} \in proc_n \text{ executes statement instance } \underline{i} \in loop_k\}$$

Scalar quantities such as a "data set" for a scalar, or the "iteration set" for a statement not enclosed in any loop are handled uniformly within the framework as tuples of rank zero.[2] For example, the computation partitioning for a statement (outside any loop) assigned to processor P in a 1-D processor

---

[1] We use names with lower-case initial letters for tuple sets and upper-case letters for mappings respectively.

[2] A set of rank 0, $\{[\,] : f(v_1, \ldots, v_n)\}$, should be interpreted as a boolean that takes the values true or false, depending on whether the constraints given by $f(v_1, \ldots, v_n)$ are satisfied. Here $v_1 \ldots v_n$ are symbolic integer variables.

array would be represented as the mapping $\{[\,] \rightarrow [p] : p = P\}$. Hereafter, the terms "array" and "iterations of a statement" should be thought of as including scalars and outermost statements as well. Note that any mapping we require, including a mapping with domain of rank 0, will be invertible.

Of these primitive sets and mappings, the sets *loop* and *proc* and the mappings *Layout* and *Ref* are constructed directly from the compiler's intermediate representation, and form the primary inputs for further analyses. These quantities are constructed from a powerful symbolic representation used in dHPF, namely global value numbering. A value number in dHPF is a handle for a symbolic expression tree. Value numbers are constructed from dataflow analysis of the program based on its Static Single Assignment (SSA) form [13], such that any two subexpressions that are known to have identical runtime values are assigned the same value number [21]. Their construction subsumes expression simplification, constant propagation, auxiliary induction variable recognition, and computing range information for expressions of loop index variables. A value number can be reconstituted back into an equivalent code fragment that represents the value.

Figure 3.1 illustrates simple examples of the primitive sets and mappings for an example HPF code fragment. For clarity, we use different set variables to denote points in different tuple spaces. The construction of the *Layout* mapping follows the two steps used to describe an array layout in HPF [31], namely, alignment of the array with a template and distribution of the template on a physical processor array (the template and processor array are each represented by a separate tuple space). The ON_HOME CP notation and construction of *CPMap* are described in Section 4.

3.2 Implementation of the Framework

Expressing optimizations in terms of this framework requires an integer set package that supports all of the key set and map operations including intersection, union, difference, domain, range, composition of a map with another map or set, and projection to eliminate a variable from a map or set. We use the Omega library developed by Pugh et al. at the University of Maryland for this purpose [27]. The library operations use powerful algorithms based on Fourier-Motzkin elimination for manipulating integer tuple sets represented by Presburger formulae [37]. In particular, the library provides two key capabilities: it supports a general class of integer set operations including set union, and it provides an algorithm to generate efficient code that enumerates points in a given sequence of iteration spaces associated with a sequence of statements in a loop [26]. (Appendix A describes this code generation capability.) These capabilities are an invaluable asset for implementing set-based versions of the core HPF compiler optimizations as well as enabling a variety of interesting new optimizations, described in later sections.

```
real A(0:99,100), B(100,100)
processors P(4)
template T(100,100)
align A(i,j) with T(i+1,j)
align B(i,j) with T(*,i)
distribute t(*,block) onto P

read(*), N
do i = 1, N
   do j = 2, N+1
      A(i,j) = B(j-1,i)    ! ON_HOME  B(j-1,i)
   enddo
enddo
```

symbolic N

$Align_A = \{[a_1, a_1] \rightarrow [t_1, t_2] : t_1 = a_1 + 1 \wedge t_2 = a_2\}$

$Align_B = \{[b_1, b_2] \rightarrow [t_1, t_2] : t_2 = b_1\}$

$Dist_T = \{[t_1, t_2] \rightarrow [p] : 25p + 1 \leq t_2 \leq 25(p+1) \wedge 0 \leq p \leq 3\}$

$Layout_A = Dist_T^{-1} \circ Align_A^{-1}$
$= \{[p] \rightarrow [a_1, a_2] : max(25p + 1, 1) \leq a_2 \leq min(25p + 25, 100) \wedge$
$\qquad 0 \leq a_1 \leq 99\}$

$Layout_B = Dist_T^{-1} \circ Align_B^{-1}$
$= \{[p] \rightarrow [b_1, b_2] : max(25p + 1, 1) \leq b_1 \leq min(25p + 25, 100) \wedge$
$\qquad 1 \leq b_2 \leq 100\}$

$loop = \{[l_1, l_2] : 1 \leq l_1 \leq N \wedge 2 \leq l_2 \leq N + 1\}$

$CPRef = \{[l_1, l_2] \rightarrow [b_1, b_2] : b_2 = l_1 \wedge b_1 = l_2 - 1\}$

$CPMap = Layout_B \circ CPRef^{-1} \bigcap_{range} loop$
$= \{[p] \rightarrow [l_1, l_2] : 1 \leq l_1 \leq min(N, 100) \wedge$
$\qquad max(2, 25p + 2) \leq l_2 \leq min(N + 1, 101, 25p + 26)\}$

Fig. 3.1. Construction of primitive sets and mappings for an example program. $Align_A$, $Align_B$, and $Dist_T$ also include constraints for the array and template ranges, but these have been omitted here for brevity.

One potentially significant disadvantage of using such a general representation is the compile-time cost of the algorithms used in Omega. In particular, simplification of formulae in Presburger arithmetic can be extremely costly in the worst-case [36]. Pugh has shown, however, that when the underlying algorithms in Omega (for Fourier-Motzkin elimination) are applied to dependence analysis, the execution time is quite small even for complex constraints with coupled subscripts and also for synthetic problems known to cause poor performance [37]. These experimental results at least provide evidence that the basic techniques could be practical for use in a compiler. In dHPF, the Omega library has already proved to be a powerful tool for prototyping advanced optimizations based on the integer set framework. On small benchmarks, the compiler provides acceptably fast running times, for example, requiring about 3 minutes on a SparcStation-10 to compile the Spec92 benchmark Tomcatv with all optimizations. Further evidence for a variety of real applications will be required to judge whether or not this technology for implementing the integer set framework will prove practical for commercial data-parallel compilers. The dHPF implementation will provide a testbed for developing this evidence. If this approach does not prove practical, it is still possible that a simpler and more efficient underlying set representation could be used to support the same abstract formulation of optimizations, but with some loss of precision.

Another significant and fundamental limitation is that Presburger arithmetic is undecidable in the presence of multiplication. For this reason, the Omega library provides only limited support for handling multiplication, and in particular, cannot represent sets with an unknown (i.e., symbolic) stride. Most importantly (from the viewpoint of HPF compilation), such strided sets are required for any HPF distribution when the number of processors is not known at compile time, and for a cyclic(k) distribution with unknown k. We have extended our framework to permit these parameters to be symbolic, as described below. Symbolic strides also arise for a loop with a non-constant stride or a subscript expression with a non-constant coefficient, although we expect these to be rare in practice. These are not supported by our framework, and would have to fall back on more expensive run-time techniques such as a finite-state-machine approach for computing communication and iteration sets (for example, [28]), or an inspector-executor approach.

To permit a symbolic number of processors or cyclic(k) distribution with symbolic k, we use a virtual processor (VP) model that naturally matches the semantics of templates in HPF [22]. The VP model uses a virtual processor array for each physical processor array, using template indices (i.e., ignoring the distribute directive) in dimensions where the block size or number of processors is unknown, but using physical processor indices in all other dimensions. Using physical processor indices where possible facilitates better analysis and improves the efficiency of generated code. All of the analyses described in the following sections operate unchanged on physical or virtual processor domains. During code generation for each specific problem (e.g., generating a partitioned loop), we add extra enclosing loops that iterate over the VPs that are owned by the relevant physical processor (e.g., the representative processor `myid`). For each problem, we use an additional optimization step (consisting of a few extra integer set equations) to compute the precise set of iterations required for these extra loops, and therefore to minimize the runtime overhead in the resulting code. The details of our extensions to handle a symbolic number of processors are given in [1].

4. Computation Partitioning

A computation partitioning (CP) for a statement is a precise specification of which processor or processors must execute each dynamic instance of the statement. The CPs chosen by the compiler play a fundamental role in determining the performance of the resulting code. For the compiler to have the freedom to choose a partitioning well-suited to an application's needs, the communication analysis and code generation phases of the compiler must be able to support a flexible class of computation partitionings. In this section, we describe the computation partitioning model provided by dHPF and the code generation framework used to support the model. The communication analysis techniques supporting the model are described in Section 5.

4.1 Computation Partitioning Models

Most research and commercial compilers for HPF to date primarily use the *owner-computes* rule [39] to partition a computation. This rule specifies that each value assigned by a statement is computed by the owner (i.e., the "home") of the location being assigned the value, e.g., the left hand side (LHS) in an assignment. The owner-computes rule amounts to a simple heuristic choice for partitioning a computation. It is straightforward to show that this approach is not optimal in general [12]. An alternate partitioning strategy used by SUIF [2] and Barua, Kranz & Agarwal [6] requires a CP to be described by a single affine mapping of iterations to processors, and assigns a single CP to an entire loop iteration and not to individual statements in a loop. This strategy is also not optimal, because (in general) it does not permit optimal CPs to be chosen separately for different statements in a loop.

A major goal of the dHPF compiler is to support more general computation partitionings. Doing so requires new support from the compiler's communication analysis and code-generation phases. Previous compilers based on the owner-computes rule have benefited from two key simplifying assumptions: (1) communication patterns are defined by a single pair of LHS and right-hand-side (RHS) references, and (2) all communication is caused by *reads* of non-local data. The SUIF partitioning model also has the benefit that each communication is defined by a single reference and a single CP mapping (before coalescing communication), although write references can cause communication too. This model has the additional benefit that code generation is greatly simplified by having a common CP for all statements in a loop (which will become clear from the discussion in Section 4.2). None of these simplifying assumptions are true for the more general partitioning model used in dHPF.

4.1.1 The Computation Partitioning Model in dHPF. The computation partitioning model supported by dHPF combines and generalizes the

features of both previous CP models described above (the owner-computes rule and the SUIF model). Below we describe the key features of the dHPF CP model including the implicit CP representation used by early phases in the compilation and conversion to an explicit CP representation required for communication analysis and code generation. In Section 4.2.1, we discuss code generation for these general CPs and in Section 5 we discuss the role of CPs in communication analysis.

In dHPF, a computation partitioning for a statement can be specified as the set of owners of the locations accessed by one *or more* arbitrary data references, Every statement (including control flow statements) can be assigned a partitioning independent of every other statement, restricted only to preserving the semantics of the source program. For a statement S enclosed in a loop nest with iteration space $\underline{i}$, the CP of S is specified by a union of one or more ON_HOME terms:

$$CP(S) : \bigcup_{k=1}^{k=n} \text{ON\_HOME } A_k(f_k(\underline{i})) \tag{4.1}$$

An individual term ON_HOME $A_k(f_k(\underline{i}))$, specifies that the instance of S in iteration $\underline{i}$ is to be executed by the processor(s) that own the array element(s) $A_k(f_k(\underline{i}))$. This set of processors is uniquely specified by subscript vector $f_k(\underline{i})$ and the layout of array A_k at that point in the execution of the program.[3] This *implicit* representation of a computation partitioning supports arbitrary index expressions or any set of values in each index position in $f_k(\underline{i})$. A data reference $A_k(f_k(\underline{i}))$ in an ON_HOME clause need not be a reference existing in the program. Even the variable A_k and its corresponding data layout may be synthesized for representing a desired CP, though our implementation is restricted to legal HPF layouts. With this representation, the CP model permits specification of a very wide class of partitionings.

While early analysis phases in the dHPF compiler use this implicit CP representation, communication analysis and code generation require that the CP for each statement is converted into an *explicit* mapping of type $CPMap$ defined in Section 3.1. The integer set framework is used to construct this explicit mapping. This construction requires that each subscript expression in $f_k(\underline{i})$ be an affine expression of the index variables, $\underline{i}$, with known constant coefficients, or a strided range specifiable by a triplet *lb:ub:step* with known constant *step*. We construct the explicit integer tuple mapping representing the CP for a statement as follows.

$$CPMap(S) = \bigcup_{k=1}^{k=n} (Layout_{Ak} \circ Ref_k^{-1}) \bigcap_{range} loop. \tag{4.2}$$

---

[3] In the presence of dynamic REALIGN and REDISTRIBUTE directives, we assume that only a single known layout is possible for each reference in the program. Multiple reaching layouts would require generating multi-version code or assuming that the layout is unknown until run time (as done for inherited layouts).

For each term ON_HOME $A_k(f_k(\underline{i}))$ in $CP(S)$, the composition of its layout and inverse reference maps results in a new map that specifies all possible iterations assigned to each processor by this CP term. We restrict the range of this map to the iteration space given by *loop*. Taking the union over all CP terms gives the full mapping of iterations to processors for statement S. $CPMap(S)$ specifies the processor assignment for the single instance of statement S in loop iteration $\underline{i}$. Figure 3.1 shows a simple example of the construction of $CPMap$. The mapping can be vectorized over the range of iterations of one or more enclosing loops to represent the combined processor assignment for the set of statement instances in those loop iterations.

Careful assignment of CPs to control-flow related statements (namely, DO, IF, and GOTO statements, as well as labeled branch targets) is necessary to preserve the semantics of the source program. In particular, a *legal partitioning* must ensure that each statement in the program is reached by a superset of the processors that need to participate in its execution, as specified by its CP. The code generation phase will then ensure that the statement is executed by exactly the processors specified by the CP. The algorithms dHPF uses to select computation partitions and ensure legality are beyond the scope of this paper. In Section 4.2.1, we discuss the interaction between correctness constraints on CP assignments for control-flow related statements and code generation.

To support dHPF's general computation partitioning model, the communication analysis and code-generation phases in the compiler must fully support any legal partitioning. Supporting this partitioning model would be impractical using a case-based approach; the dHPF compiler's representation of computation partitionings using an abstract integer set framework has proven essential for making the required analysis and code generation capabilities practical.

4.2 Code Generation to Realize Computation Partitions

A general CP model such as that in dHPF poses several challenges for static code generation. First, the code generator must ensure correctness in the presence of arbitrary structured and unstructured control flow, without sacrificing available parallelism. Second, generating efficient parallel code for a loop nest containing multiple statements that potentially have different iteration spaces is an intrinsically difficult problem. Previous compilers use simple approaches for code generation and do not solve this problem in its general form (as described briefly below), but Kelly, Pugh & Rosser have developed an aggressive algorithm for "multiple-mappings code generation" which directly tackles this problem [26]. A third and related difficulty, however, is that good algorithms for generating efficient code (like that of Kelly, Pugh & Rosser) will be inherently expensive because of the potential complexity of the iteration spaces and the resulting code. Ensuring reasonable compile times requires an effective strategy to control the compile-time cost of applying such an algorithm while still producing as high quality code as possible. A fourth problem (not directly related to a general CP model) is that static code generation techniques will not be useful for a code with irregular or complex partitionings. Such cases require runtime strategies such as the inspector-executor approach (e.g., [18, 32, 40]). However, regular and irregular partitionings may coexist in the same program, and perhaps even in a single loop nest. This raises the need for a flexible code generation framework that allows each part of the source program to be partitioned using the most efficient strategy applicable.

Before describing the techniques used in dHPF to address these challenges, we briefly describe the strategies used to realize computation partitions in current compilers, and the limitations of these strategies in addressing these challenges. We begin with the second of the four problems described above because the approaches to addressing this problem have implications for the other problems as well. As in the rest of the paper, we focus on compile-time techniques that are applicable when the compiler can compute static (symbolic) mappings between processors and the data they own or communicate. If a static mapping is not computable at compile time, alternative strategies that can be used include run-time resolution [39], the inspector-executor approach, and run-time techniques for handling cyclic(k) partitionings. The latter two approaches are described in other chapters within this volume [38, 40].

It is relatively straightforward to partition a simple loop nest that contains a single statement or a sequence of statements with the same CP. The loop bounds can be reduced so that each processor will execute a smaller iteration space that contains only the statement instances the processor needs to execute. For loops containing multiple statements with different CPs, it is important that each processor execute as few guards as possible to determine which statement instances it must execute in each iteration. Previous compilers, such as IBM's pHPF compiler [16], rely on loop distribution to construct separate loop nests containing statements with identical CPs, so as to avoid the need for run-time guards. There are two drawbacks to using loop distribution in this manner. First, loop distribution may be impossible because of cyclic data dependences in the loop. In such cases, compilers add statement guards to implement the CPs and, except for Paradigm, don't reduce loop bounds. The Paradigm compiler reduces loop bounds to the convex hull of the iteration spaces of statements inside the loop, in order to reduce the number of guards executed [5]. Second, fragmenting a loop nest into a sequence of separate loops over individual statements can (a) significantly reduce reuse of cached values between statements, and (b) significantly increase the contribution of loop overhead to overall execution time. A loop fusion pass that attempts to recover cache locality and reduce loop bound overhead is possible, but complex. Both the IBM and the Portland Group

HPF compilers use a loop fusion pass, but apply it only to the simplest cases, namely conformant loops [10, 16].

Kelly, Pugh & Rosser describe an aggressive algorithm to generate efficient code without relying on loop distribution, for a loop nest containing multiple statements with different iteration spaces [26]. Given a sequence of (possibly non-convex) iteration spaces, the algorithm, MMCODEGEN, synthesizes a code fragment to enumerate the points in the iteration spaces in lexicographic order, tiling the loops as necessary to lift guards out of one or more levels of loops. Thus, the algorithm provides one of the key capabilities required to support our general CP model. The algorithm is briefly described in Appendix A along with an example that highlights its capabilities.

As mentioned earlier, one potential drawback of an algorithm like MM-CODEGEN is that it can be costly for large loop nests with multiple iteration spaces. Because of the potential for achieving high performance, however, we use the algorithm in dHPF as one of the core techniques for supporting the general CP model, and develop a strategy to control compile-time cost while still producing high quality code. To our knowledge, this is the first use of their algorithm for code generation in a data-parallel compiler, and therefore these issues have not been addressed previously.

The techniques used in previous compilers to partition code in the presence of control-flow are not clearly described in the written literature. Some compilers simply replicate the execution of control-flow statements on all processors, which is a simple method to ensure correctness but can substantially reduce parallelism in loops containing control flow [19]. Many other compilers ignore control flow because loop bounds reduction and ownership guards will enforce the appropriate CP for enclosed statements. However, this approach sacrifices potential parallelism for the sake of simplifying code generation. In particular, by not enforcing an explicit CP for a block structured IF statement, all processors that enter the scope enclosing the IF will execute the test, enter the appropriate branch, and execute CP guards for the statements inside, even though some of the processors do not need to participate in the execution of the enclosed statements at all.

4.2.1 Realizing Computation Partitions in dHPF. We have developed a hierarchical code generation framework to realize the general class of partitionings that dHPF supports. Our approach is hierarchical because it operates on nested block structured scopes, one scope at a time. (A *scope* refers to a sequence of statements immediately enclosed within a procedure, a DO loop, or a single branch of an IF statement.) Key benefits of the hierarchical code generation framework are (1) it supports partitioning of scopes that can contain arbitrary control flow, (2) it supports multiple code generation strategies for individual scopes so that each scope can be partitioned with the most appropriate strategy, and (3) it uses a two pass strategy that is effective at minimizing guard overhead without sacrificing compile-time efficiency. Below, we first describe the hierarchical code generation framework, and then describe strategies used in dHPF to generate code for a single scope within this framework.

The hierarchical code generation framework. Briefly, the code generation framework in dHPF operates as follows. Each scope in the program is handled independently. The code generation operates one scope at a time, visiting scopes bottom-up (i.e., innermost scopes first). Although the framework operates one scope at at time, any particular strategy can partition multiple scopes in a single step if desired. At each scope that has not yet been partitioned, the framework attempts to apply a sequence of successively more general strategies until one successfully performs the partitioning for the scope.

Control flow in the program is handled as follows. This discussion assumes that a pre-processing phase has transformed all DO loops into DO/ENDDO form and and relocated all branch target labels to CONTINUE statements. The compiler computes partitionings for control-flow statements so that all processors that need to execute any statement reach it, but as few processors execute the control-flow statements as possible in order to maximize parallelism. Informally, the computation partitioning for an IF statement or a DO loop must involve all of the processors that need to execute any statement that is transitively control-dependent on it. For an IF statement, the union of the CPs of its control dependents gives a suitable CP. For a DO loop, the the union of the CPs of its control dependents gives a CP suitable for a single iteration; a suitable CP for the entire compound DO statement can be computed by vectorizing the iteration CP over the loop range. A GOTO statement is assigned the union of the CPs of all control-flow statements on which it is immediately control-dependent. Note that this will be a superset of the CPs of the statements following the branch target. i.e., any processors that need to execute the target statements will reach those statements (the condition controlling the branch is satisfied). Finally, a branch target label is assigned the CP of the immediately enclosing scope, for reasons discussed below.

In order to ensure correctness while preserving maximum parallelism in the presence of control-flow, the code generation framework simply has to ensure that the above assignment of CPs to control-flow related statements is correctly preserved. In particular, any particular strategy used to partition a scope must correctly enforce the CPs of all statements *within* the scope. The only subtlety is that reducing the bounds of a DO loop does not enforce the CP of the compound DO loop statement itself; that must be enforced when partitioning the scope enclosing the DO loop (otherwise, extra processors may evaluate the bounds of the DO loop).

The above handling of partitioned control flow statements yields a key simplification of the framework, namely, that each block-structured scope can be handled independently, even in the presence of arbitrary control flow such as a GOTO that transfers control from one scope to another. In particular, the CPs assigned to individual GOTO statements is simply enforced during code generation, independent of the location and CPs of its branch targets.

A significant difficulty that must be addressed is that GOTOs are matched with the correct branch targets (and labels). This can be difficult because statements in different scopes and even statements in the same scope may be cloned into different numbers of copies. (Statements can be cloned by the tiling performed by MMCODEGEN to minimize guards, as shown in the example in Appendix A.) We ensure that branches and branch targets are matched, as follows.

Fortran semantics dictate that a GOTO cannot branch from an outer to an inner scope; a GOTO can only branch within the same scope or to an outer scope. The CP assigned to a GOTO may cause it to be cloned into multiple copies. By assigning a labeled statement the CP of its enclosing scope, we ensure that a label appears in every instance of that scope (in particular, in a DO scope, every iteration of the enclosing scope will include the labeled CONTINUE). Since every GOTO branching to this label must come from the same or an inner scope, every cloned copy of the GOTO will be matched with exactly one copy of the labeled CONTINUE. Furthermore, the GOTOs that must match a particular copy of the label are exactly those that appear within the same instance of the scope enclosing the label. This allows us to to renumber the label definitions and any matching label references. The details of the renumbering scheme are described elsewhere [1].

The second key issue we address with the framework is controlling the compile-time cost of using expensive algorithms such as MMCODEGEN, while still ensuring that guard overhead is minimized. There are two features in the framework that ensure efficiency. First, we take advantage of the independent handling of scopes to apply MMCODEGEN independently one loop or one perfect loop nest at a time. This ensures that the iteration spaces in each invocation of MMCODEGEN are as simple as possible (though there can still be multiple different iteration spaces). Second, the use of a bottom-up approach greatly reduces the number of times MMCODEGEN is invoked, compared to a top-down approach. The drawback however, is that the top-down approach could yield much more efficient code. This tradeoff between the bottom-up and top-down approaches arises as follows.

When generating code for a DO scope, the loop's iteration space is often split into multiple sections to enable guards to be lifted out of the loop. If we used a top-down scope traversal order for generating code, information about the bounds of the different sections could be passed downward during code generation and exploited in inner scopes. However, a top-down strategy would require many more applications of the partitioning algorithm than a bottom-up strategy. For example, for a triply nested loop in which each loop will be split into two sections by code generation, a top-down strategy would invoke the loop partitioning algorithm seven times. A bottom-up strategy would invoke it only three times. Because of the potentially high compile-time cost of the former, we use a bottom-up code generation strategy.

$$
\begin{array}{ll}
\textbf{do } i = 1, \text{N} \\
\quad \text{S1(i)} \\
\quad \textbf{do } j = 1, \text{M} \\
\qquad \text{S2(i,j)} \\
\qquad \text{S3(i,j)} \\
\quad \textbf{enddo} \\
\textbf{enddo}
\end{array}
\qquad
\begin{array}{rcl}
LoopCP_i() &=& CP_1(1:N) \cup LoopCP_j(1:N) \\
CP_1(i) &=& \{\,[i] : \text{proc. myid owns } A_1(f_1(i))\,\} \\
LoopCP_j(i) &=& CP_2(i,1:M) \cup CP_3(i,1:M) \\
CP_2(i,j) &=& \{\,[i,j] : \text{proc. myid owns } A_2(f_2(i,j))\,\} \\
CP_3(i,j) &=& \{\,[i,j] : \text{proc. myid owns } A_3(f_3(i,j))\,\}
\end{array}
$$

Fig. 4.1. Example showing iteration sets constructed for code generation.

We use two techniques to ensure the quality of the generated code despite the trade-offs made above. First, an important optimization we apply when generating code for individual scopes is to exploit as much known contextual information as possible about the enclosing scopes. Second, we use a powerful, global control-flow simplification phase as the last step of code generation, which further simplifies the control-flow in the resulting program. The control-flow simplification algorithm is described in section 6. The use of available contextual information during the bottom-up strategy is described below. Together, these achieve much or all of the benefit of a top-down code generation strategy in which full context information is available to code generation in inner scopes, but at a fraction of the cost.

When generating code for a scope in the bottom-up strategy, we can assume that code generation in the enclosing scope will ensure that only the correct processors enter the current scope. For example, consider the loop nest in Fig. 4.1. Statements s1, s2, and s3 each have a simple computation partition consisting of a single ON_HOME clause. $LoopCP_j(i)$, represents the CP for the j loop, which consists of the union of the CPs of the statements in its scope vectorized across the range of the j loop. Inside the j loop, we assume that the constraints in $LoopCP_j(i)$ hold because these constraints will have been enforced when partitioning the enclosing i loop. Any code generation strategy used for the inner scope can exploit this information. Similarly, $LoopCP_i()$ represents the CP for the i loop, which consists of the union of the CPs of the statements it contains, vectorized across the range of the i loop. We assume that the constraints in $LoopCP_i()$ are true when generating code for the i loop.

Realizing a CP for a single scope. The first step in the process for partitioning a scope is to separate the statements in the scope into *statement groups*, which are sequences of adjacent statements that have homogeneous computation partitions. Second, we use equation 4.2 to construct the *explicit* representation of the iteration space for each statement group according to its computation partitioning. Third, we use some available strategy to partition the computation in the scope. When multiple strategies are available, we currently apply them in a fixed sequence, stopping when one succeeds in partitioning the scope. This permits a fixed series of strategies to be tried (typically attempting specific optimizations and, if these fail, then finally applying some general strategy).

We currently support two strategies for partitioning a loop: bounds reduction, or loop-splitting combined with bounds reduction for the individual loop sections generated by splitting (the latter is described in Section 5.3). For non-loop scopes (conditional branches and the outermost routine level), we also use bounds reduction which reduces to inserting guards on the relevant statements. Two alternatives applicable to loops or statement groups with irregular data layouts or irregular references are under development, namely, runtime resolution and an inspector-executor strategy.

To perform bounds reduction as part of the above strategies, we apply Kelly, Pugh & Rosser's MMCODEGEN algorithm to the sequence of iteration spaces for the statement groups in a scope. Applying MMCODEGEN to the iteration spaces for statement groups reduces loop bounds as needed and lifts guards out of inner loops when statement groups with non-overlapping iteration spaces exist. This results in a code template template with placeholders representing the statement groups. Finally, we replace each of the placeholders in the code template by a copy of the code for the corresponding statement group. When labels are present in the code for the statement groups, we renumber the labels to ensure unique numbers as discussed earlier.

As an alternative to this base strategy for realizing the computation partition for a scope, Section 5.3 describes a loop splitting transformation that may be applied during code generation to any perfect loop nest that has no carried dependences. From the perspective of the computation partitioning code generation, this approach serves as an alternate partitioning method which subdivides the iteration space for a DO into a sequence of iteration spaces, and then generates code for each with the method described above for a single scope. The purpose of the splitting transformation is described in section 5.3.

Another much more specialized strategy we expect to add for loop nests is a code transformation for coarse-grain pipelining. The transformation simultaneously performs strip-mining of one or more non-partitioned loops and loop bounds reduction for partitioned loops. The last two optimizations (loop-splitting and pipelining) illustrate that the hierarchical code generation framework provides a natural setting within which to perform any code transformation that has the side effect of producing partitioned code, i.e., realizing the CPs assigned to statements in a scope.

5. Communication Code Generation

On message-passing systems, the most efficient communication is obtained when the compiler can statically compute the set of data that needs to be exchanged between processors to satisfy each non-local reference. For references with statically analyzable communication requirements, a data-parallel compiler must compute the set of non-local data to be communicated for each non-local reference, and then use these sets to generate efficient code to pack, communicate, unpack, and access the non-local data. In this section, we describe implementation techniques for several key communication optimizations used in the dHPF compiler to synthesize high performance communication code for regular applications. Many of these techniques are based on the integer set framework. For references with unanalyzable communication requirements, typically due to non-affine subscripts, runtime techniques such as the inspector-executor model must be used to manage communication. For more information on such techniques, we refer the reader to Chapter 21 and the references therein.

The dHPF compiler includes a comprehensive set of communication optimizations that have been identified as important for high performance on message-passing systems. The benefits obtained from these optimizations (with very few exceptions) can vary widely between applications as well as between different systems. This implies that a compiler may have to incorporate many different optimizations to obtain consistently high performance across large classes of applications and systems. Previous commercial and research compilers, however, have generally implemented only a few of these techniques because of the significant implementation effort entailed in each case. The important communication optimizations in the dHPF compiler include the following.

Optimizations to Reduce Message Overhead

- *Message vectorization* moves communication out of loops in order to replace element-wise communication with fewer but larger messages. This is implemented by virtually all data-parallel compilers, but in case-based compilers it is usually restricted to specific reference patterns for which the compiler can derive (or conservatively approximate) the data sets to be communicated [16, 24, 32].
- *Exploiting collective communication* is essential for achieving good speedup in important cases such as reductions, broadcasts, and array redistribution [33]. On certain systems, collective communication primitives may also provide significant benefits for other patterns such as shift communication. The important patterns (particularly reductions and broadcast) have been supported in most data-parallel compilers.
- *Message coalescing* combines messages for multiple non-local references to the same or different variables, in order to reduce the total number of messages and to eliminate redundant communication. Previous implementations in Fortran 77D [24], SUIF [2], Paradigm [5], and IBM's pHPF [11, 16] have some significant limitations. In particular, coalescing can produce fairly complex data sets from the union of data sets for individual references. The previous implementations are limited to cases where the combined data sets are representable with (or can be approximated by) regular

sections (in Fortran 77D, Paradigm and pHPF) or a single collection of inequalities (in SUIF).

– *Coarse-grain pipelining* trades off parallelism to reduce communication overhead in loop nests with loop-carried, cross-processor data dependences. It is an important optimization for effectively implementing parallelism in such loop nests because the only alternative may be to perform a full array redistribution, which can be much more expensive. To our knowledge, this optimization has been implemented in a few research compilers [5, 24] and one commercial one [16].

Optimizations to Overlap Communication with Computation

– *Dataflow-based communication placement* attempts to hide the latency of communication by placing message sends early and receives late so as to overlap messages with unrelated computation. A few compilers including IBM's pHPF, SUIF, Paradigm, and Fortran 77D have used dataflow techniques to overlap communication in this manner.

– *Communication overlap via non-local index set splitting* attempts to overlap communication from a given loop nest with the local iterations of the same loop nest. This overlap generally cannot be achieved by the above dataflow placement techniques. Non-local index set splitting (or loop splitting) separates iterations that access non-local data from those that access only local data. Communication can be overlapped with the local iterations by first executing send operations for the non-local data required in the loop, then the local iterations, then the receives, and finally the non-local iterations. Loop splitting was implemented in Kali [32], albeit with significant limitations as described in Section 5.3.

Optimizations to Minimize Data Buffering and Access Costs

– *Minimizing buffer copying overhead* is essential to minimize the overall cost of communication. This can be achieved in multiple ways. First, in most message-passing implementations, when the data to be sent or received is contiguous in memory, it can be communicated "in-place" rather than copied to or from message buffers. Second, asynchronous send and receive primitives can be used to avoid additional buffer copies between user and system buffers by making user-level buffers available for the duration of communication. Third, non-local data received into a buffer can in some cases be directly referenced out of the buffer (if the indexing functions can be generated by the compiler), thus avoiding an unpacking operation. All of these techniques appear to be widely used in data-parallel compilers, though the effectiveness of the implementations may vary.

– *Minimizing buffer access checks via non-local index-set splitting.* Access checks (i.e., ownership tests) are required when the same reference may access local data from an array or non-local data from a separate buffer on different loop iterations. Loop-splitting separates out the local iterations (which are guaranteed to access local data) from the non-local ones. Even the latter may not need access checks if all non-local references now access only non-local data. The alternative to this transformation is to copy local and non-local data into a common buffer (as done in the IBM pHPF compiler [16]), which can be costly in time and memory usage. As mentioned above, non-local index set splitting was implemented in a limited form in Kali.

– *Overlap areas for shift communication* are extra boundary elements added to the local sections of arrays involved in shift communication [14]. They permit local and non-local data to be referenced uniformly, thus avoiding the need for the access checks (or alternatives) mentioned above. Generally, interprocedural analysis has to be used to determine the size of required overlap areas globally for each array. Simpler implementations may waste significant memory and may have to be controlled by the programmer. Overlap areas have been implemented in several research and commercial compilers.

The Rice dHPF compiler implements all of the above optimizations except coarse-grain pipelining and the use of asynchronous message primitives (both these are currently being implemented). Some other specific communication optimizations have been implemented in other compilers but are not included in dHPF. IBM's pHPF coalesces diagonal shift communication into two messages [16], whereas dHPF requires three. This is useful, for example, in stencil computations that access diagonal neighbors such as a nine-point stencil over a two-dimensional array. Chakrabarti et al. describe a powerful communication placement algorithm that can be used to maximize opportunities for message coalescing or to balance message coalescing with communication overlap [11]. SUIF uses array dataflow analysis to communicate data directly from a processor executing a non-local write to the next processor executing a non-local read [2], whereas dHPF must use an extra message to send the data first to the owner and from there to the reader. The former two optimizations can be directly added to the current implementation of dHPF. The SUIF model is a different and significantly more complex communication model compared to that used in dHPF, and there is little evidence available so far to evaluate whether the additional complexity is justified for message-passing systems.

One reason that it has been practical to implement a fairly large collection of advanced optimizations in dHPF is our use of the integer set framework. By formulating optimizations abstractly in terms of integer set operations, we have obtained simple, concise, and general implementations of some of the most important phases of the compiler (such as communication code generation) as well as of complex optimizations like loop-splitting. These implementations broadly apply to arbitrary combinations of affine references, data distributions, and computation partitionings, because the analysis is not dependent on specific forms of these parameters. In the remainder of this section, we briefly describe the implementation of communication optimizations that use the integer set framework. These include our entire communication generation phase which incorporates message vectorization and coalescing, the two optimizations based on non-local index set splitting and an algorithm for recognizing in-place communication. A control-flow simplification algorithm, which is also implemented using integer sets, is described in Section 6.

5.1 Communication Generation with Message Vectorization and Coalescing

The communication insertion steps in dHPF can be classified into two phases: a preliminary decision-making phase that identifies and places the required communication in the program, and a communication generation phase that computes the sets of processors and data involved in each communication, and synthesizes code to carry out the communication. In this paper, we primarily focus on the communication generation phase which is based on the integer set framework. We briefly describe the decisions made in the former phase, since these directly feed in as inputs to communication generation.

The preliminary communication analysis steps in dHPF determine (a) which references are potentially "non-local", i.e., might access non-local data, (b) where to place communication for each reference, (c) whether to use a collective communication primitive in each case, and (d) when communication for multiple references can be combined. The first step is a very simple analysis to filter out references that can easily be proven to access only local data. The second step uses a combination of dependence and dataflow analysis to choose the placement of communication so as to determine how far each message can be vectorized out of enclosing loops, and to optionally move communication calls early or late to hide communication latency [30]. The third step uses the algorithms of Li and Chen [33] to to determine if specialized collective communication primitives such as a broadcast could be exploited. (Reductions are recognized using separate algorithms.) Otherwise, the compiler directly implements the communication using pairwise point-to-point communication. The fourth step chooses references whose communication can be combined. Any two references whose communication involves one or more common pairs of processors can be coalesced in our implementation. In practice, however, it it is usually not beneficial to combine references that should use different communication primitives, such as a broadcast with any pairwise point-to-point communication. (One instance where it is profitable is combining a reduction and a broadcast by using a special reduction primitive like MPI_AllReduce, which leaves every processor involved with a copy of the result.) We refer to the entire collection of messages required for a set of coalesced references as a single *logical communication event*.

The code generation phase must then use the results of the previous phases to synthesize vectorized and coalesced messages that implement the desired communication for each logical communication event. For each reference, the

```
DataAccessedMap =
  { [p1,p2]->[b1,b2]  :
    max(1, 20*p1) <= b1 <= min(20*p1+19, 58) &&
    max(2, 20*p2+1) <= b2 <= min(20*p2+20, 59) };

nlDataAccessed({m1,m2}) =
  { [b1,b2]  :
    1 <= m1 <= 2 && b1 = 20*m1 &&
    max(2, 20*m2+1) <= b2 <= min(20*m2+20, 59) };

SendCommMap({m1,m2}) =
  { [p1,p2]->[b1,b2]  :
    p1 = m1+1 && p2 = m2 && 0 <= m1 <= 1 && b1 = 20*m1+20 &&
    max(2, 20*m2+1) <= b2 <= min(20*m2+20, 59) };

RecvCommMap({m1,m2}) =
  { [p1,p2]->[b1,b2]  :
    p1 = m1-1 && p2 = m2 && 1 <= m1 <= 2 && b1 = 20*m1 &&
    max(2, 20*m2+1) <= b2 <= min(20*m2+20, 59) };
```

Fig. 5.1. Example maps for communication due to reference B(i-1,j) in the Jacobi kernel of Figure 2.1, assuming N = 60

---

compiler first computes the set of data to send between pairs (or groups) of processors; these communication sets depend on the reference, layout, computation partitioning, and the loop level at which vectorized communication is to be performed. Message coalescing requires computing the union of the above communication sets for the coalesced references. We directly compute the communication sets for each communication event using a sequence of integer set operations, independent of the specific form of the reference, layout, and computation partitioning. We then generate code from these sets directly.

The integer set equations used to compute the communication sets for each logical communication event are described in detail elsewhere [1]. We briefly describe the key aspects of the algorithm here. The goal of the algorithm is to compute two separate maps for a fixed symbolic processor index $\underline{m}$ (where $\underline{m}$ is the index tuple for processor myid in the processor array to which the data is mapped, and myid is the representative processor index of the SPMD program).

$$SendCommMap(\underline{m}) \;=\; \big\{[\underline{p}] \rightarrow [\underline{a}] : \text{array elements } \underline{a} \text{ that} \\ \text{proc. } \underline{m} \text{ must send to proc. } \underline{p}\big\}$$

$$RecvCommMap(\underline{m}) \;=\; \big\{[\underline{p}] \rightarrow [\underline{a}] : \text{array elements } \underline{a} \text{ that} \\ \text{proc. } \underline{m} \text{ must receive from proc. } \underline{p}\big\}$$

To illustrate how these maps are computed, Figure 5.1 shows some of the intermediate results and the final resulting maps for a single non-local reference $B(i-1, j)$ in the Jacobi kernel example of Figure 2.1, assuming $N = 60$. (We chose this very simple example to make it easy to understand the maps, although it does not illustrate the generality of our integer set formulation.) Here, the final $SendCommMap(\underline{m})$ specifies that processor myid (whose index tuple is $\underline{m} = \{m_1, m_2\}$) must send the boundary values $B(20m_1 + 20, 20m_2 + 1 : 20m_2 + 20)$ to its right neighbor, $\underline{p} : p_1 = m_1 + 1, p_2 = m_2$, except that processors with $m_1 = 2$ do not send any data. $RecvCommMap(\underline{m})$ specifies that processor myid must receive the boundary values $B(20m_1, 20m_2 + 1 : 20m_2 + 20)$ from its left neighbor, $\underline{p} : p_1 = m_1 - 1, p_2 = m_2$, except processors with $m_1 = 0$ do not receive any data. The min and max terms in the maps exclude the communication of edge elements that are not accessed. The key steps used to compute these maps are as follows.

For a given reference, we first compute a map, $DataAccessedMap$, describing the entire set of data (local and non-local) accessed by each processor $\underline{p}$ in all iterations of the loops out of which communication has been vectorized. This is done by composing the computation partitioning and reference maps (see Figure 5.1). Then, for a read reference, the set of non-local data accessed by the processor $\underline{m}$ (denoted $nlDataAccessed(\underline{m})$) is the difference between the data accessed and the data owned by that processor. For a write reference, the set of non-local data accessed is the *intersection* of the data accessed by $\underline{m}$ and the data owned by all other processors p, since a write must update all owners of the data. (In the absence of replicated data, this step would be equivalent for reads and writes.) Now, the data that $\underline{m}$ must receive from each processor $\underline{p}$ is the intersection of the non-local data accessed by $\underline{m}$ and the data owned by $\underline{p}$. The data that $\underline{m}$ must send to each processor $\underline{p}$ is the intersection of the non-local data accessed by $\underline{p}$ and the data owned by $\underline{m}$. For a single reference, the last two results are exactly RecvCommMap($\underline{m}$) and SendCommMap($\underline{m}$) respectively. To coalesce communication for multiple non-local references (including both reads and writes), we simply take the union of these maps over all coalesced references.

If any of the array elements accessed by a read reference is replicated, a simple additional step is necessary to ensure that only a single owner sends the element to each processor that reads it. Similarly, if the CP for a write reference is replicated, a similar step ensures that only one writer sends the data back to each owner. To avoid communication bottlenecks, we ensure that all the owners (or writers) participate by providing data to different groups of destination processors [1].

For the case of coarse-grain pipelining, we use another additional step to account for the blocking of communication (i.e., the granularity of the pipeline). Specifically, in the range of the above maps, we extend the dimension to be blocked from a single value to a range, using symbolic bounds to represent the block of data communicated in each pipeline stage.

SendCommMap and *RecvCommMap* are used by the code generator to synthesize communication. Several alternative communication strategies can be directly supported. To implement pairwise, point-to-point communication we synthesize separate loops to iterate over the domain (processor set) of each map. Note that these loops will enumerate exactly those processors with which processor myid must exchange data. The algorithm described in Section 5.2 is then used to determine whether data to be communicated is contiguous in memory, or if this is not statically provable, to emit a logical expression that checks this at run-time. In the latter case, we also synthesize a loop to iterate over the range of *SendCommMap* (i.e., the data to be sent to p) and use it to copy the data to a buffer. When we check contiguity at runtime, we generate both in-place and buffered communication for a particular communication event. For the receiving end, data can be received in-place if overlap areas are used and the communicated section is contiguous. The receiver uses the same approach to determine whether to receive data in place or into a communication buffer. We currently use the MPI_Bsend and MPI_Brecv primitives for synchronous point-to-point communication, which guarantee sender-side buffering. This is a simple solution to ensure that deadlock does not occur in cases where all processors have to send and receive data, but it may introduce excess buffer copy operations at the sender. We are currently extending our communication generation to use asynchronous message-passing primitives which can significantly reduce buffer copying overheads at the sender and receiver.

It is straightforward to extend the above approach to exploit collective communication primitives, in cases where these will be more efficient than point-to-point communication. For example, using a broadcast operation simply requires eliminating the processor loop and using a single call to broadcast the data set to all processors. The methods to determine if data is contiguous and to generate the buffer packing code both remain unchanged. Reductions require separate code generation steps to synthesize code to compute local partial sums within each processor. The data set for a reduction is simply the entire temporary variable (scalar or array) used to hold the local partial sums. Thereafter, the code generation for buffering and communication steps of a reduction are the same as above.

In summary, code generation for message vectorization and coalescing relies on the integer set framework to compute the processor and data sets for communication, and use these to synthesize code for explicit communication. The algorithms are independent of the specific form of the reference, data layout, and computation partitioning involved, and fully support the general computation partitioning model in dHPF. Independent algorithms are used to determine whether buffering is required, and to minimize the costs of accessing buffered non-local data. These are described in the following subsections.

5.2 Recognizing In-Place Communication

Whether compiling HPF for shared-memory or message-passing architectures, avoiding excess data copies can boost performance. Here we describe a technique developed to avoid data copies when generating code for a message passing communication model based on MPI. Common MPI implementations permit data to be sent or received "in-place" (avoiding an explicit data copy) when the address range of the data is contiguous. To increase the likelihood that communication can be performed in-place, we have developed a combined compile-time/run-time algorithm for recognizing contiguous data based on our capability of generating code from integer-sets.

A communication set for an n-dimensional Fortran array represents contiguous data if there is some dimension $k, 1 \leq k \leq n$ such that, for the high-order dimensions $1 \leq i < k$, the set spans the full range of array dimension i, along dimension k the set has a contiguous index range, and in the low-order dimensions $k + 1 \leq j \leq n$, the set contains a single index value. Using our integer-set representation for communication sets, we can express these individual conditions as Boolean predicates, requiring up to three predicates for each array dimension. The existence of a value k satisfying the above properties can be directly expressed as a logical combination of these predicates, first eliminating those predicates that can be proven true or false at compile time. We construct and express this logical expression as an integer set. If the entire expression can be proven true or false at compile time, then we generate a single version of code for communicating contiguous or non-contiguous data respectively (i.e., with and without buffer packing). If the expression cannot be proven true or false, we synthesize code from the integer set to test the condition at runtime. In this case, we generate both versions of communication code (with and without buffer packing).

Directly checking the logical condition constructed above requires checking $O(n^2)$ terms (conjunctions of predicates), at compile-time or runtime. We can in fact reduce this cost to $O(n)$ by using a single scan of the dimensions (leftmost first) to find the first dimension k which cannot be proved to span the full range of the array dimension, and then checking the predicates for $k \ldots n$. If these predicates cannot be proven at compile time, we can synthesize code to repeat this scan and check at runtime, when it can be done precisely. In practice, however, the number of array dimensions n is typically small, and many of the predicates are statically proven true or false. The cost of evaluating the logical condition at run-time will usually be much smaller than the cost of packing all but the smallest messages into a communication buffer. Therefore, we take the simpler approach (described above) of constructing and evaluating the logical condition directly as a single set.

By combining compile-time and runtime decisions to identify contiguous data, we obtain maximum efficiency when the data is provably contiguous but also minimize the likelihood that explicit buffer packing will be needed when this decision cannot be made until runtime. Furthermore, by basing the analysis directly on an explicit integer set representation of the data, we can apply it to arbitrary communication sets, independent of data layouts and communication patterns.

5.3 Implementing Loop-Splitting for Reducing Communication Overhead

As described at the outset of this section, loop-splitting (or iteration re-ordering) techniques can be used to ameliorate two types of communication overhead: the latency of communication, and the cost of referencing buffered non-local data. Both techniques involve splitting a loop to separate the iterations that access only local data from those that may access non-local data. After splitting, we can overlap communication for the loop with the computation in the local iterations, which do not require the communicated data. We can also reduce the number of ownership guards executed before non-local references by eliminating the guards in the local iterations, and perhaps some in the non-local iterations as well.

The only implementation of loop-splitting we know of is in Kali [32], where the authors used set equations to explain the optimization but used case-based analysis to derive the iteration sets (during compiler development) for a few special cases restricted to one-dimensional data distributions. This approach is only practical for a small number of special cases. We have extended the equations in [32] to apply to an arbitrary number of non-local references with any regular data layouts and any CP in our CP model, using the sets and mappings described in previous sections. We first describe the loop-splitting analysis for communication overlap, because the loop transformations in this case subsume the transformations required for splitting for buffer access.

Loop-splitting in dHPF is applied one perfectly nested sequence of loops at a time, for loops that satisfy the conditions below. The restriction to perfectly nested loops is not essential, but slightly simplifies our implementation of the code generation. The analysis described here can be used unchanged for imperfect loop nests. We look for a maximal loop-nest that includes loops for which it is legal to reorder the loop iterations, and also loops which we can predict will not to be reordered. It is legal to reorder iterations of a loop if it has no loop-carried data dependences and it does not enclose any communication operations. We can predict that certain loops will not be reordered, as follows. Note that for a *read* reference, a subscript in a non-distributed array dimension will not cause the reference to be non-local. (In a write reference, however, such a subscript could induce communication to send the data back to all the owners.) Therefore, non-local index set splitting

```
SEND data for non-local reads        SEND data for non-local reads
execute nlWOIters                    execute nlWOIters
SEND data for non-local writes       execute localIters
execute localIters                   RECV data for non-local reads
RECV data for non-local reads        execute nlROIters ⋃ nlRWIters
execute nlROIters                    SEND data for non-local writes
RECV data for non-local writes       RECV data for non-local writes
```

(a) if $nlRWIters$ is empty   (b) if $nlRWIters$ is non-empty

Fig. 5.2. Generated code for overlapping communication and computation.

---

will not reorder the iterations of a loop whose loop index variable is used to index only local references and *non-distributed* array dimensions in non-local RHS references. Therefore, we can ignore any dependences that may be carried on such loops, and these loops can be safely included in the loop nest.

Since any write reference as well as any read reference may be non-local in dHPF, our goal is to separate the iterations of a loop nest into four sections: those that access only local data (*localIters*), and those that only read, only write, or read and write non-local data (*nlROIters*, *nlWOIters* and *nlRWIters* respectively). These sets are computed using a sequence of integer set equations, taking as input the basic sets and maps of Figure 3.1 and the non-local data set, $nlDataAccessed(\underline{m})$, computed as an intermediate result for the communication sets as described in Section 5.1. The detailed equations are explained in [1]. The key step is computing the iterations that access non-local data for each given reference. The non-local data set for the reference describes the non-local data accessed by the processor myid. Composing this map with $RefMap^{-1}$ gives the iterations that access these non-local elements. For example, consider the reference B(i-1,j) in the Jacobi kernel of Figure 2.1. We compose $RefMap^{-1} = \{[b_1, b_2] \to [l_1, l_2] : b_1 = l_1 - 1 \land b_2 = l_2\}$ with the non-local data set $nlDataAccessed(\underline{m})$ shown in Figure 5.1. This yields precisely the set of boundary iterations that access non-local data due to that reference: $\{[l_1, l_2] : 1 \leq m_1 \leq 2 \land l_1 = 20 * m_1 + 1 \land max(2, 20 * m_2 + 1) \leq l_2 \leq min(20 * m_2 + 20, 59)\}$. By taking unions over non-local read and write references respectively, we directly get the set of iterations that read non-local data and the set of iterations that write non-local data. These sets may not be disjoint, but from these two sets and the CP, the four desired sets can be directly computed. The code for these individual loop sections is directly synthesized from the respective integer sets by using MMCODEGEN.

We schedule the communication and computation for this loop nest in the sequence shown in Figure 5.2. Both read and write communication latency would be overlapped with some computation if all non-local writes are performed first, then local iterations, and finally non-local reads. This is possible when $nlRWIters$ is empty, as shown in Figure 5.2(a). If $nlRWIters$ is non-empty, however, these iterations both read and write non-local data, and these must be placed after the RECV for non-local reads and before the SEND for non-local writes. Therefore, we can overlap either read or write communication with $localIters$, but not both. A simple heuristic could be used to choose between the two alternatives, by comparing how early read data is produced and how late write data is consumed. For now, however, we simply overlap read communication with $nlWOIters$ and $localIters$, and we merge $nlRWIters$ with $nlWOIters$, as shown in Figure 5.2(b).

The goal of the second optimization based on loop-splitting is to minimize the number of ownership guards executed before non-local references. A reference would not need a guard if it accesses only local or only non-local data in all iterations of the enclosing loops. Therefore, in a loop with r non-local references, the ownership guards could be completely eliminated by splitting the index space into $2^r - 1$ non-local subsets, plus the local section. To avoid this exponential behavior, we can simply split the loop into one local and one non-local subset, and use guards only in the non-local section if necessary. If splitting is being applied for communication overlap, that actually creates three non-local sections instead of one, and no further transformations are required. In any case, references in the local iterations do not need ownership guards . A reference in a non-local loop section also does not need such guards if is the set of iterations in that section is identical to the set of non-local iterations due to that reference alone.

Code generation for the loop transformations described above is integrated into the hierarchical code generation framework described in Section 4, as an alternative computation partitioning strategy. This is because code generation from the local and non-local sets has the side-effect of enforcing the CPs assigned to the statements in the loop (including reducing the loop bounds and introducing guards if necessary). This follows because each of the four loop sections is a subset of the iterations assigned to processor myid by these CPs. Thus, the combination of the integer-set-based analysis and the hierarchical code generation framework made it quite simple to add even these relatively complex optimizations in the compiler.

6. Control Flow Simplification

6.1 Motivation

Several of the strategies for partitioning computation can split a loop's iteration space to avoid adding computation partitioning guards inside the loop. By splitting the iteration space, such guards can be added between sections of the loop instead of inside, which can dramatically reduce the dynamic execution frequency of guards. However, after a loop has been split, the smaller

```
        parameter (N=64)
        real a(N), b(N), f(N,N,N)
CHPF$ processors p(4)
CHPF$ template t(N,N,N)
CHPF$ distribute t(*,*,block) onto p
CHPF$ align f(i,j,k) with t(i,j,k)
CHPF$ align a(k)      with t(*,*,k)
CHPF$ align b(k)      with t(*,*,k)

    do j=1,N
      do k=2,N
C       SEND f(1:N,j,k-1)                  ! ON_HOME f(1:N,j,k-1)
C       RECV f(1:N,j,k-1)                  ! ON_HOME f(1:N,j,k)
        do i=1,N
                                           ! ON_HOME f(i,j,k)
          f(i,j,k) = (f(i,j,k) - a(k) * f(i,j,k-1)) * b(k)
        enddo
      enddo
    enddo
```

Fig. 6.1. HPF source for a fragment from the Erlebacher benchmark, showing the preliminary placement of SEND and RECV and the CPs assigned.

---

resulting iteration spaces provide a sharper context that may make some conditionals or loops nested inside redundant or unsatisfiable. We illustrate these effects with an example later in this section.

If individual code generation steps attempted to exploit full contextual knowledge to avoid or eliminate guards and empty loops, they would have to be significantly more complex. Furthermore, implementing such an approach would also require rebuilding or incrementally updating analysis information after each code generation step. We use Instead, we use a simpler and less expensive approach in which we make no effort to avoid control-flow complexity that arises as a result of interactions between the different optimization steps, and instead use a separate post-pass optimization to eliminate excess control flow. This approach has two major advantages: existing code generation algorithms can be simpler, and the post-pass control-flow simplification can use powerful algorithms that exploit global information about the program.

The foundation for control flow simplification in dHPF is an algorithm for globally propagating symbolic constraints on the values of variables imposed by loops, conditional branches, assertions, and integer computations. Several previous systems have supported strategies for computing and exploiting range information about variables [8, 9, 20, 25, 44]. Two key differences that distinguish our work are that we handle more general logical combinations of constraints on variables (not just ranges) and we use these constraints to simplify control flow. In this section, we present an example that illustrates how a sequence of code generation steps results in superfluous loops and con-

```
      do j = 1, 64

1         if (pmyid1 >= 1)
2           k = 16 * pmyid1 + 1

          !--<< Iterations that access only local values >>--
3         if (16 * pmyid1 <= k - 2)                       !INFEASIBLE
            COMPUTE f(1:64, j, k)

4         if (16 * pmyid1 == k - 1 && pmyid1 >= 1)       !TAUTOLOGY
            RECV f(1:64, j, 16*pmyid1)

          !--<< Iterations that read non-local values >>--
5         if (16 * pmyid1 >= k - 1)                       !TAUTOLOGY
            COMPUTE f(1:64, j, k)
6         do k = 16 * pmyid1 + 2, 16 * pmyid1 + 16
7         if (16 * pmyid1 == k - 17 .and. pmyid1 <= 2)   !INFEASIBLE
            SEND f(1:64, j, k - 1)

          !--<< Iterations that access only local values >>--
8         if (16 * pmyid1 <= k - 2)                       !TAUTOLOGY
            COMPUTE f(1:64, j, k)

9         if (16 * pmyid1 == k - 1 && pmyid1 >= 1)       !INFEASIBLE
            RECV f(1:64, j, 16*pmyid1)

          !--<< Iterations that read non-local values >>--
10        if (16 * pmyid1 >= k - 1)                       !INFEASIBLE
            COMPUTE f(1:64, j, k)
          enddo
          if (pmyid1 <= 2)
            k = 16 * pmyid1 + 17
11        if (16 * pmyid1 == k - 17 .and. pmyid1 <= 2)   !TAUTOLOGY
            SEND f(1:64, j, k - 1)
          enddo
```

Fig. 6.2. Skeletal SPMD code for Fig. 6.1 with partitioned computation.

---

ditionals and then provide a brief overview of our control-flow simplification technique. Our algorithm is described and evaluated in detail in [34].

To illustrate some of the principal sources of excess control-flow in dHPF, Fig. 6.1 shows source code for a loop from the Erlebacher benchmark, including the CPs and the initial placement of communication chosen by the compiler. The assignment statement is given the CP ON_HOME f(i,j,k), and communication for the non-local reference f(i,j,k-1) is placed inside the k loop because of a loop-carried flow dependence for array f. Fig. 6.2 shows the skeletal SPMD code after CP code generation (the entire i loop has been shown as "COMPUTE f(1:64,j,k)" to simplify the figure). Exami-

```
do j = 1, 64

  if (pmyid1 >= 1) then
    k = 16 * pmyid1 + 1
    RECV f(1:64, j, k-1)
    !--<< Iterations that read non-local values >>--
    COMPUTE f(1:64, j, k)
  endif !(pmyid1 >= 1)

  do k = 16 * p_myid1 + 2, min(16 * p_myid1 + 16, 63)
    !--<< Iterations that access only local values >>--
    COMPUTE f(1:64, j, k)
  enddo !k

  if (p_myid1 <= 2) then
    k = 16 * p_myid1 + 17
    SEND f(1:64, j, k - 1)

enddo !j
```

Fig. 6.3. Skeletal SPMD code for Fig. 6.2 after simplification.

---

nation of the code in Fig. 6.2 shows that many of the guard expressions are infeasible or tautological.

The causes of excess control flow in this example are as follows:

1. The guards on lines 8 and 10 are initially generated by splitting the i loop into local and non-local iterations. At this time it is not known what sections of the k loop will finally be generated. We cannot apply non-local index set splitting to the k loop because of the loop-carried dependence. However, when MMCODEGEN is applied to reduce loop bounds for the k loop, the loop is tiled into 3 sections ($k = 16 * \text{pmyid1} + 1$, $\{16 * \text{pmyid1} + 2 \le k \le 16 * \text{pmyid1} + 16\}$, and $k = 16 * \text{pmyid1} + 17$), so that additional guards are not required within the loop to enforce the different CPs of the three inner statements. The guards on lines 8 and 10 now get duplicated on lines 3 and 5, along with their enclosed COMPUTE blocks. Now, in the refined context of these k loop sections, the guards on lines 3 and 10 are always false, and those on lines 5 and 8 are always true.

2. When the k loop is split as described above, the SEND and RECV placeholders are duplicated (as shown) during CP code generation because of the CPs assigned to the communication placeholders. The CPs assigned to placeholders, shown in Figure 6.1, simply specify that the owner of f(1:N,j,k) must receive data (since it will execute the i loop), and the owner of f(1:N,j,k-1) must send data (since it owns the data being read). These CPs are imprecise in that the SEND and RECV should actually execute only in the boundary iterations. Precise CPs for communication are difficult to compute and express in any general manner

since communication patterns can be quite complex. Instead, we rely on the communication generation phase to insert guards to ensure that only required communication occurs. Those guards are the ones shown on lines 4, 7, 9 and 11. Although the loop context created when partitioning the k loop makes these guards infeasible or redundant, the communication code is generated without precise knowledge of this refined loop context.

It is important to note that the excess guards that arise in the code generation steps described above are not due to poor code generation algorithms. In the first case, they result from a sophisticated loop transformation that reduces the dynamic execution frequency of guards. In the second case, avoiding eliminating redundant guards when instantiating communication would require full knowledge of sharper context created by earlier code generation steps.

Another source of excess control flow not illustrated by the example above is the insertion of ownership guards for non-local references. As explained in Section 5.3, we create one to three sections of non-local iterations, and insert ownership guards in each of the non-local sections. However, if the iteration set of any non-local section is non-convex, MMCODEGEN automatically tiles the section into convex regions, potentially making some or all of the guards in that section redundant. In each case, it is sensible to generate these guards oblivious of their context and let a later control-flow simplification pass eliminate any that became unnecessary. This enables our guard insertion algorithms to remain relatively simple without hurting performance. In the next section we describe our global algorithm for eliminating superfluous control flow.

6.2 Overview of Algorithm

The algorithm for simplifying control flow is based on the property that each conditional branch node (i.e., IF or DO loop) in a program guarantees certain constraints on the values of variables for the statements control dependent on the branch node. The goal of our algorithm is to collect and propagate these constraints globally through the code and use this information to simplify the control flow. Our algorithm combines three key program analysis technologies, namely, the control dependence graph (CDG) [13], global value numbering based on thinned gated single assignment form [21], and simplification of integer constraints specified as Presburger formulae [27]. The former two enable us to derive an efficient, non-iterative algorithm for propagating constraints along control dependences, while the latter enables simplification of logical constraints and code generation from the simplified constraints. The information we collect is closely related to the concept of "iterated control dependence" path conditions described by Tu and Padua [44].

Rather than computing constraints on variables directly, we compute constraints on value numbers representing unique values of variables. This allows us to avoid invalidating constraints after redefinitions and SSA merge points since each of these points simply yields a new value number for the variable. Constraints on an old value number may be irrelevant but are never incorrect. Constraints on a value number V at a given statement S in the program are logical combinations of equalities and inequalities that hold true for V at S. We use integer sets of rank 0 to represent constraints; this enables us to exploit the Omega library's capabilities for symbolic simplification and code generation.

Briefly, our constraint simplification algorithm operates in two passes as follows. The first pass collects constraints at conditional branch nodes in a single reverse-post-order traversal of CDG. This order ensures that all control dependence (CD) predecessors of a node are visited before the node itself, except for predecessors along back edges which form cycles in the CDG. At each point in the traversal, we collect the constraints for a node as the intersection of the constraints enforced locally at the node with the disjunction of the constraints that hold along paths from each of its control dependence predecessors. Our single pass algorithm for collecting constraints computes a conservative approximation in that it ignores constraints along back edges.[4] Despite using a non-iterative strategy for collecting constraints, we are still often able to extract useful constraints for loop-variant iterative values, particularly auxiliary induction variables recognized when computing value numbers. This includes relatively complex auxiliary induction variables that do not have a closed form but are defined by a loop-invariant iterative function (e.g., $i = i * 2$).

The second pass makes a reverse preorder traversal of the CDG (visiting CD dependents before ancestors), using the computed constraints to simplify a procedure's control flow. The bottom-up order we choose to simplify constraints is a convenience that simplifies bookkeeping by ensuring that code transformations we apply at a node will not eliminate any conditionals that we will subsequently reach later in our iteration. If the outgoing constraints for a loop or conditional branch are unsatisfiable, its code is eliminated. If the outgoing constraints at a conditional branch are implied by its incoming constraints, the test is eliminated. Otherwise, the test may still be simplified given the known information in the incoming constraints. In this case, the simplified constraints are used to regenerate a simpler guard using the MMCODEGEN operation.

The algorithm also takes into account *assertions* specifying "known" constraints about program variables inserted into the code by the programmer or previous phases of the compiler. These assertions provide a mechanism for communicating information that a later compiler pass may be unable to infer

---

[4] It is safe to ignore these constraints because our use of value numbers ensures that constraints along back edges will never invalidate existing constraints, rather they would just add more information.

directly from the code. We refer the reader to [34] for the details of the overall algorithm, including the handling of iterative constructs and assertions.

6.3 Evaluation and Discussion

Figure 6.3 shows the simplified code for the Erlebacher intermediate code shown in Figure 6.2. In Figure 6.3, we see that all infeasible and tautological guards have been eliminated, the latter being replaced by their enclosed code. We also evaluated the algorithm for 3 benchmarks (Tomcatv from the Spec92 benchmark suite, Erlebacher, and Jacobi) [34]. The algorithm eliminated between 31% and 81% of guards introduced by the compiler for these programs, yielding between 1% and 15% improvement in execution time on an IBM SP-2. These improvement are achieved over and above the many aggressive optimizations in dHPF and scalar optimizations performed by the SP-2 node compiler. Overall, the control-flow simplification is able to compensate for the lack of complete context information in the earlier code generation phases (and for the overly simple CPs for communication statements), permitting the earlier phases to be simpler without impacting performance.

An interesting outcome we observed in our experiments is that the general purpose control-flow simplification algorithm (in combination with our CP code generation algorithm and loop splitting) provides some or all of the benefits of much more specialized optimizations such as vector-message pipelining [43] and overlap areas [14]. In particular, the pipelined shift communication pattern for Erlebacher shown in Fig. 6.3 is exactly what vector message-pipelining aims to produce, but the latter is a narrow optimization and complex to implement, as explained in [34]. In dHPF, however, it results naturally from loop-splitting, bounds reduction, and control-flow simplification. As a second example, overlap areas are specifically designed to simplify referencing non-local data in shift communication patterns, but a comprehensive implementation of overlap areas requires interprocedural analysis. Even without overlap areas, we obtained equally simple code for shift communication patterns in both Tomcatv and Erlebacher, and nearly as simple code in Jacobi. This happened because non-local loop-splitting and control-flow simplification together eliminated all or most of the ownership guards on non-local references, so that it was equally simple to access data out of separate non-local buffers as out of overlap areas. In fact, the code for Tomcatv without overlap areas slightly outperformed the code with overlap areas (by about 3%) because overlap areas required an extra unpacking operation [34]. Overall, these results and the evaluation described above indicate that the control-flow simplification algorithm can be a useful general-purpose optimization for parallelizing compilers.

7. Conclusions

The motivation for the development of the Rice dHPF compiler is the need for HPF compiler technology that approximates or exceeds hand-coded performance across a broad spectrum of programs. Meeting our goal of offering consistently high performance will require a large collection of optimizations that are uniformly applicable to a wide variety of programs.

In this chapter, we described several static code generation techniques that enable aggressive and robust optimizations in an HPF compiler, and yet greatly simplify the implementation of many of these optimizations. We described a computation partitioning model, a framework for analysis and optimization, and a code generation strategy that are more general than those used previously by HPF compilers. The key conclusions we draw from this work are as follows. First, a uniform and comprehensive code generation framework can support a very general computation partitioning model, and permit harnessing powerful code-generation algorithms that extract the full performance of partitionings enabled by the model. Second, the use of abstract set equations as the medium for expressing optimizations has greatly simplified the construction of even complex optimizations, and therefore makes it practical to incorporate a comprehensive collection of optimizations in a compiler. In addition, the high-level nature of these equations makes the optimizations very broadly applicable (including any computation partitionings in the general CP model), and increasing their overall impact. Third, a global control-flow simplification algorithm can substantially reduce excess control-flow in the generated code, permitting other code generation algorithms to be significantly simpler. Finally, the synergy between some of these general optimizations provides some or all of the benefits of much more specialized optimizations such as vector-message pipelining and overlap areas.

The base technology (the Omega library) used to implement the integer set framework is experimental, but it has proved invaluable for prototyping optimizations based on the framework. Further experience from using dHPF on a wide variety of programs will be required to judge whether the technology is efficient enough to be practical for commercial implementations. If this approach proves too costly, it would be important to develop more efficient but less precise set representations so that compilers could still obtain the power and simplicity of the integer set formulations.

In this chapter, we have focused on the problem of compiling "regular" data parallel codes. Many applications have features that cause them to fall outside this class, and in such cases different compilation strategies and run-time support are more appropriate. Our hierarchical framework for code generation enables different code generation strategies to be applied to a scope, or in some circumstances even to a single statement. This capability provides the flexibility needed to integrated alternate methods such as inspector/executor or run-time resolution to cope with programs that are not statically analyzable.

Although the analysis and optimization described here focused on compiling for a message-passing target machine, most if not all of this technology is directly applicable to uniform and distributed shared memory (i.e., SMP and DSM) systems. Some of the optimizations built on the program analysis framework are aimed at avoiding communication by maximizing data access locality, which is essential for DSM systems as well. Furthermore, for shared-memory systems built from commodity microprocessors, managing locality by managing the memory hierarchy is essential for performance. The analysis and code generation capabilities described here are guided primarily by array layouts and provide the right leverage for exploiting locality and optimizing for the memory hierarchy on this emerging class of systems.

Acknowledgement. The dHPF compiler is the result of the collective efforts of all the members of the dHPF compiler group. Ken Kennedy provided invaluable guidance and leadership that have made the overall project feasible. Ajay Sethi contributed to the design and implementation of the set-based formulation of communication. Lisa Thomas implemented the algorithm to detect in-place communication from integer sets. Bill Pugh and Evan Rosser provided valuable support and advice on using the Omega library. The Omega calculator, a scripting interface to the Omega library, proved extremely useful for experimenting with integer set equations for our compiler. Sarita Adve, Robert Fowler, Ken Kennedy and Evan Rosser provided valuable comments on earlier drafts of this paper.

This work has been supported in part by DARPA Contract DABT63-92-C-0038, the Texas Advanced Technology Program Grant TATP 003604-017, and sponsored by the Defense Advanced Research Projects Agency and Rome Laboratory, Air Force Materiel Command, USAF, under agreement number F30602-96-1-0159. The U.S. Government is authorized to reproduce and distribute reprints for Governmental purposes notwithstanding any copyright annotation thereon. The views and conclusions contained herein are those of the authors and should not be interpreted as representing the official policies or endorsements, either expressed or implied, of the Defense Advanced Research Projects Agency and Rome Laboratory or the U.S. Government.

References

1. V. Adve, J. Mellor-Crummey, and A. Sethi. HPF analysis and code generation using integer sets. Technical Report CS-TR97-275, Dept. of Computer Science, Rice University, April 1997.
2. S. Amarasinghe and M. Lam. Communication optimization and code generation for distributed memory machines. In *Proceedings of the SIGPLAN '93 Conference on Programming Language Design and Implementation*, Albuquerque, NM, June 1993.
3. C. Ancourt, F. Coelho, F. Irigoin, and R. Keryell. A linear algebra framework for static HPF code distribution. In *Proceedings of the Fourth Workshop on Compilers for Parallel Computers*, Delft, The Netherlands, December 1993.
4. C. Ancourt and F. Irigoin. Scanning polyhedra with do loops. In *Proceedings of the Third ACM SIGPLAN Symposium on Principles and Practice of Parallel Programming*, Williamsburg, VA, April 1991.

5. P. Banerjee, J. Chandy, M. Gupta, E. Hodges, J. Holm, A. Lain, D. Palermo, S. Ramaswamy, and E. Su. The Paradigm compiler for distributed-memory multicomputers. *IEEE Computer*, 28(10):37–47, October 1995.

6. R. Barua, D. Kranz, and A. Agarwal. Communication-minimal partitioning of parallel loops and data arrays for cache-coherent distributed-memory multi-processors. In *Proceedings of the Ninth Workshop on Languages and Compilers for Parallel Computing*. Springer-Verlag, August 1996.

7. S. Benkner, B. Chapman, and H. Zima. Vienna Fortran 90. In *Proceedings of the 1992 Scalable High Performance Computing Conference*, Williamsburg, VA, April 1992.

8. W. Blume and R. Eigenmann. Demand-driven symbolic range propagation. In *Proceedings of the Eighth Workshop on Languages and Compilers for Parallel Computing*, pages 141–160, Columbus, OH, August 1995.

9. François Bourdoncle. Abstract debugging of higher-order imperative languages. In *Proceedings of the SIGPLAN '93 Conference on Programming Language Design and Implementation*, pages 46–55, June 1993.

10. Z. Bozkus, L. Meadows, S. Nakamoto, V. Schuster, and M. Young. Compiling High Performance Fortran. In *Proceedings of the Seventh SIAM Conference on Parallel Processing for Scientific Computing*, pages 704–709, San Francisco, CA, February 1995.

11. S. Chakrabarti, M. Gupta, and J-D. Choi. Global communication analysis and optimization. In *Proceedings of the SIGPLAN '96 Conference on Programming Language Design and Implementation*, Philadelphia, PA, May 1996.

12. S. Chatterjee, J. Gilbert, R. Schreiber, and S. Teng. Optimal evaluation of array expressions on massively parallel machines. Technical Report CSL-92-11, Xerox Corporation, December 1992.

13. R. Cytron, J. Ferrante, B. Rosen, M. Wegman, and K. Zadeck. Efficiently computing static single assignment form and the control dependence graph. *ACM Transactions on Programming Languages and Systems*, 13(4):451–490, October 1991.

14. M. Gerndt. Updating distributed variables in local computations. *Concurrency: Practice and Experience*, 2(3):171–193, September 1990.

15. M. Gupta and P. Banerjee. A methodology for high-level synthesis of communication for multicomputers. In *Proceedings of the 1992 ACM International Conference on Supercomputing*, Washington, DC, July 1992.

16. M. Gupta, S. Midkiff, E. Schonberg, V. Seshadri, D. Shields, K. Wang, W. Ching, and T. Ngo. An HPF compiler for the IBM SP2. In *Proceedings of Supercomputing '95*, San Diego, CA, December 1995.

17. S. K. S. Gupta, S. D. Kaushik, C.-H. Huang, and P. Sadayappan. Compiling array expressions for efficient execution on distributed-memory machines. *Journal of Parallel and Distributed Computing*, 32(2):155–172, February 1996.

18. R. v. Hanxleden. *Compiler Support for Machine-Independent Parallelization of Irregular Problems*. PhD thesis, Dept. of Computer Science, Rice University, December 1994.

19. J. Harris, J. Bircsak, M. R. Bolduc, J. A. Diewald, I. Gale, N. Johnson, S. Lee, C. A. Nelson, and C. Offner. Compiling High Performance Fortran for distributed-memory systems. *Digital Technical Journal of Digital Equipment Corp.*, 7(3):5–23, Fall 1995.

20. W. H. Harrison. Compiler analysis of the value ranges for variables. *IEEE Transactions on Software Engineering*, SE-3(3):243–250, May 1977.

21. Paul Havlak. *Interprocedural Symbolic Analysis*. PhD thesis, Dept. of Computer Science, Rice University, May 1994. Also available as CRPC-TR94451

from the Center for Research on Parallel Computation and CS-TR94-228 from the Rice Department of Computer Science.

22. High Performance Fortran Forum. High Performance Fortran language specification. *Scientific Programming*, 2(1-2):1–170, 1993.

23. S. Hiranandani, K. Kennedy, and C.-W. Tseng. Compiler support for machine-independent parallel programming in Fortran D. In J. Saltz and P. Mehrotra, editors, *Languages, Compilers, and Run-Time Environments for Distributed Memory Machines*. North-Holland, Amsterdam, The Netherlands, 1992.

24. S. Hiranandani, K. Kennedy, and C.-W. Tseng. Preliminary experiences with the Fortran D compiler. In *Proceedings of Supercomputing '93*, Portland, OR, November 1993.

25. Harold Johnson. Data flow analysis of 'intractable' imbedded system software. In *Proceedings of the SIGPLAN '86 Symposium on Compiler Construction*, pages 109–117, 1986.

26. W. Kelly, W. Pugh, and E. Rosser. Code generation for multiple mappings. In *Frontiers '95: The 5th Symposium on the Frontiers of Massively Parallel Computation*, McLean, VA, February 1995.

27. Wayne Kelly, Vadim Maslov, William Pugh, Evan Rosser, Tatiana Shpeisman, and David Wonnacott. The Omega Library Interface Guide. Technical report, Dept. of Computer Science, Univ. of Maryland, College Park, April 1996.

28. K. Kennedy, N. Nedeljković, and A. Sethi. A linear-time algorithm for computing the memory access sequence in data-parallel programs. In *Proceedings of the Fifth ACM SIGPLAN Symposium on Principles and Practice of Parallel Programming*, Santa Barbara, CA, July 1995.

29. Ken Kennedy and Charles Koelbel. *The High Performance Fortran 2.0 Language*, chapter 1. Lecture Notes in Computer Science Series. Springer-Verlag, 1997.

30. Ken Kennedy and Ajay Sethi. Resource-based communication placement analysis. In *Proceedings of the Ninth Workshop on Languages and Compilers for Parallel Computing*. Springer-Verlag, August 1996.

31. C. Koelbel, D. Loveman, R. Schreiber, G. Steele, Jr., and M. Zosel. *The High Performance Fortran Handbook*. The MIT Press, Cambridge, MA, 1994.

32. C. Koelbel and P. Mehrotra. Compiling global name-space parallel loops for distributed execution. *IEEE Transactions on Parallel and Distributed Systems*, 2(4):440–451, October 1991.

33. J. Li and M. Chen. Compiling communication-efficient programs for massively parallel machines. *IEEE Transactions on Parallel and Distributed Systems*, 2(3):361–376, July 1991.

34. J. Mellor-Crummey and V. Adve. Simplifying control flow in compiler-generated parallel code. Technical Report CS-TR97-278, Dept. of Computer Science, Rice University, May 1997.

35. S. Midkiff. Local iteration set computation for block-cyclic distributions. In *Proceedings of the 24th International Conference on Parallel Processing*, Oconomowoc, WI, August 1995.

36. D. Oppen. A $2^{2^{s^{pn}}}$ upper bound on the complexity of Presburger arithmetic. *Journal of Computer and System Sciences*, 16(3):323–332, July 1978.

37. W. Pugh. A practical algorithm for exact array dependence analysis. *Communications of the ACM*, 35(8):102–114, August 1992.

38. J. Ramanujam. *Integer Lattice Based Method for Local Address Generation for Block-Cyclic Distributions*, chapter 17. Lecture Notes in Computer Science Series. Springer-Verlag, 1997.

39. A. Rogers and K. Pingali. Process decomposition through locality of reference. In *Proceedings of the SIGPLAN '89 Conference on Programming Language Design and Implementation*, Portland, OR, June 1989.

40. J. Saltz. *Runtime Support for Irregular Problems*, chapter 17. Lecture Notes in Computer Science Series. Springer-Verlag, 1997.

41. A. Schrijver. *Theory of Linear and Integer Programming*. John Wiley and Sons, Chichester, Great Britain, 1986.

42. J. Stichnoth, D. O'Hallaron, and T. Gross. Generating communication for array statements: Design, implementation, and evaluation. *Journal of Parallel and Distributed Computing*, 21(1):150–159, April 1994.

43. C.-W. Tseng. *An Optimizing Fortran D Compiler for MIMD Distributed-Memory Machines*. PhD thesis, Dept. of Computer Science, Rice University, January 1993.

44. Peng Tu and David Padua. Gated SSA-based demand-driven symbolic analysis for parallelizing compilers. In *Proceedings of the 1995 ACM International Conference on Supercomputing*, Barcelona, Spain, July 1995.

45. Kees van Reeuwijk, Will Denissen, Henk Sips, and Edwin Paalvast. An implementation framework for hpf distributed arrays on message-passing parallel computer systems. *IEEE Transactions on Parallel and Distributed Systems*, 7(8):897–914, September 1996.

46. H. Zima, H.-J. Bast, and M. Gerndt. SUPERB: A tool for semi-automatic MIMD/SIMD parallelization. *Parallel Computing*, 6:1–18, 1988.

$$I_1 = \{[i,j] : 1 \le i \le 10 \ \wedge$$
$$1 \le j \le 5 \wedge c \ge 1\}$$

$$I_2 = \{[i,j] : 1 \le i \le 6 \ \wedge$$
$$1 \le j \le 5 \ \wedge c \ge 4\}$$

$$known = \{c \ge 1\}$$

```
do i = 1, 10
  if (c .ge. 4 .and. i .le. 6)
    do j = 1, 5
      s1(i,j)
      s2(i,j)
  if (i .ge. 7 .and. c .ge. 4)
    do j = 1, 5
      s1(i,j)
  if (c .le. 3)
    do j = 1, 5
      s1(i,j)
enddo  !i
```

(a) Two iteration spaces.   (b) Code template from MMCODEGEN.

Fig. 7.1. Constructing a code template from iteration spaces.

Appendix A. MMCODEGEN

Here we briefly introduce Kelly, Pugh & Rosser's algorithm for "multiple-mappings code generation" [26], which we refer to as MMCODEGEN. This algorithm is available as part of the Omega library, and serves as a cornerstone for a variety of code generation tasks in the dHPF compiler. The inputs to MMCODEGEN are as follows:

MMCODEGEN($I_1 \ldots I_v$, known, effort) :

$I_1 \ldots I_v$	:	Iteration spaces for v statements.
known	:	A set of rank 0, giving constraints on global variables in $I_1 \ldots I_v$ that will be externally enforced.
effort	:	Integer specifying to remove conditionals effort + 1 inner loops

From these inputs, MMCODEGEN synthesizes a code template that enumerates the tuples in $I_1 \ldots I_v$ in lexicographic order, "$\prec$", where the same tuple in different sets is ordered as: $(\underline{i} \in I_j) \prec (\underline{i} \in I_k), j < k$. The constraints in *known* are assumed true and will not be enforced within the code template. The innermost effort + 1 loops in the code sequence will not contain conditionals. Figure 7.1 shows two iteration spaces and the corresponding code template generated with $effort = 0$, i.e., one level of guard lifting. In the code template, s1 and s2 are placeholders representing the first and second statements, respectively. The digit suffix in the placeholder name represents the *index* of the iteration space it represents.

When MMCODEGEN is applied to a set of rank zero, it degenerates to synthesizing an IF statement that tests the constraints of the set. This variant arises (for example) for generating guards to enforce CPs for statements outside loops, for control-flow simplification, and for code generation for testing at runtime whether communication can be performed in place.

Chapter 17. Integer Lattice Based Methods for Local Address Generation for Block-Cyclic Distributions

J. Ramanujam

Department of Electrical and Computer Engineering
Louisiana State University, Baton Rouge, Louisiana, USA

Summary. In data-parallel languages such as High Performance Fortran and Fortran D, arrays are mapped to processors through a two-step process involving alignment followed by distribution. A compiler that generates code for each processor has to compute the sequence of local memory addresses accessed by each processor and the sequence of sends and receives for a given processor to access non-local data. In this chapter, we present a novel approach to the address sequence generation problem based on integer lattices. When the alignment stride is one, the mapping is called a *one-level mapping*. In the case of one-level mapping, the set of elements referenced can be generated by integer linear combinations of basis vectors. Using the basis vectors we derive a loop nest that enumerates the addresses, which are points in the lattice generated by the basis vectors. The basis determination and lattice enumeration algorithms are linear time algorithms. For the *two-level mapping* (non-unit alignment stride) problem, we present a fast novel solution that incurs zero memory wastage and little overhead, and relies on two applications of the solution of the one-level mapping problem followed by a fix-up phase. Experimental results demonstrate that our solutions to the address generation problem are significantly faster than other solutions to this problem. In addition, we present a brief overview of our work on related problems such as communication generation, basis vector derivation, code generation for complex subscripts and array redistribution.

1. Introduction

Distributed memory multiprocessors are attractive for high performance computing in that they offer potentially high levels of flexibility, scalability and performance. However, programming these machines to realize their promised performance—which requires a full orchestration of the execution through careful partitioning of computation and data, and placement of message passing—remains a difficult task. The extreme difficulty of writing correct and efficient programs is a major obstacle to the widespread use of parallel high-performance computing. The main objective behind efforts such as High Performance Fortran (HPF) [13, 20], Fortran D [10], and Vienna Fortran (which grew out of the earlier SUPERB effort) [4] is to raise the level of programming on distributed memory machines while retaining the object code efficiency derived for example from message passing.

These languages include directives—such as align and distribute—that describe how data is distributed among the processors in a distributed-memory multiprocessor. For example, arrays in HPF are mapped to processors in two

S. Pande, D.P. Agrawal (Eds.): Compiler Optimizations for Scalable PS, LNCS 1808, pp. 597-645, 2001.

steps: in the first step, arrays are *aligned* to an abstract discrete Cartesian grid called a *template;* the template is then distributed onto the processors. The effect of this two-level mapping onto p processors is to create p disjoint pieces of the array, with each processor being able to address only data items in its locally allocated piece. Thus, an HPF compiler must generate code for each processor (called node code) that accesses only the locally owned pieces directly, and inserts communication for non-local accesses.

In order to generate node code for each processor, we need to know the sequence of local memory addresses accessed by each processor and the sequence of sends and receives for a given processor to access non-local data. A regular access pattern in terms of the global data structure can appear to be irregular within each locally allocated piece. For example, an array section $A(\ell : h : s)$ exhibits a regular access sequence of stride s; but with an HPF-style data mapping, the access sequence can become irregular. In this chapter we present efficient algorithms for generating local memory access patterns for the various processors given the alignment of arrays to a template and the distribution of the template onto the processors. For the case where the arrays are aligned identically to the template (also called *one-level mapping*), our solution [39] is based on viewing the access sequence as an integer lattice and involves the derivation of a suitable set of basis vectors for the lattice. Given the lattice basis, we enumerate the lattice by using loop nests; this allows us to generate efficient code that incurs negligible runtime overhead in determining the access pattern. Chatterjee et al. [5] presented an $O(k \log k + \log \min(s, pk))$ algorithm (where k is the block size – see Section 2 for definition) for this problem; ours is an $O(k + \log \min(s, pk))$ algorithm. Recently, Kennedy et al. [16] have also presented an $O(k + \log \min(s, pk))$ algorithm. Note that all these algorithms require computing the $\gcd(s, pk)$ which is the reason for the $\log \min(s, pk)$ term in the complexity. Experiments demonstrate that our algorithm is 2 to 9 times faster than the algorithm of Kennedy *at al.* and 13 to 60 times faster than the algorithm in Chatterjee et al. Independently, Wang et al. conclude based on extensive experiments that "The LSU algorithm consistently outperforms the RIACS and Rice algorithm ..." [45]. Our solution to the address generation problem for alignment followed by distribution (i.e., two-level mapping) uses two applications of our solution to the one-level mapping problem followed by an efficient and novel fix-up phase. This second phase is up to 10 times faster than other current solutions that do not waste local memory.

This chapter is organized as follows. In Section 2, we present the problem setting and discuss related work. Section 3 thru 7 discuss one-level mapping in detail, while Sections 8 thru 10 address two-level mapping. Section 3 outlines our approach using lattices and presents key mathematical results which are used later in the chapter. In Section 4, we present our linear algorithm for determining basis vectors, and contrast it with the algorithm of Kennedy et al. In Section 5 we show how to determine address sequences by lattice enumer-

Processor 0			Processor 1			$\cdots$	Processor p-1		
0	$\cdots$	k-1	k	$\cdots$	2k-1	$\cdots$	(p-1)k	$\cdots$	pk-1
pk	$\cdots$	(p+1)k-1	(p+1)k	$\cdots$	(p+2)k-1	$\cdots$	(2p-1)k	$\cdots$	2pk-1
$\vdots$	$\vdots$	$\vdots$	$\vdots$	$\vdots$	$\vdots$	$\vdots$	$\vdots$	$\vdots$	$\vdots$

(a): Layout of an array distributed CYCLIC(k) onto p processors.

Global index	mk	$\cdots$	mk+k-1	(p+m)k	$\cdots$	(p+m+1)k-1	$\cdots$
Local index	0	$\cdots$	k-1	k	$\cdots$	2k-1	$\cdots$

(b): Local layout of array shown in Fig. 1.1(a) in Processor m.

Fig. 1.1. Global and local addresses for data mappings

ation using loop nests. We show how to use the lattice basis vectors derived in Section 4 to generate a loop nest that determines the address sequence. Section 6 discusses optimizations applied to the loop enumeration strategy presented in Section 5, specifically the GO-LEFT and GO-RIGHT schemes. Section 7 demonstrates the efficacy of our approach using experimental results comparing our solution to those of Chatterjee et al. and Kennedy et al. In Section 8 we introduce the two-level mapping problem in detail; we several new solutions to the two-level mapping problem in Section 9 and provide experimental results for this case in Section 10. In addition to these problems, our research group has addressed several additional problems in code generation and optimization such as communication generation, code generation for complex subscripts, runtime data structures, and runtime array redistribution; a brief outline of these is presented in Section 11. Section 12 concludes with a summary.

2. Background and Related Work

We consider an array A identically aligned to the template T; this means that if $A(i)$ is aligned with the template cell $T(ai + b)$, then the alignment stride a is 1 and the alignment offset b is 0. Further let template T be distributed in a block-cyclic fashion with a block size of k across p processors; this is also known as a CYCLIC(k) distribution [13]. If $k = 1$ the distribution is called CYCLIC, and if $k = \frac{N}{p}$ (where N is the size of the template) the distribution is called BLOCK distribution. We assume that arrays have a lower limit of zero, and processors and local addresses are numbered from zero onward. This mapping of the elements of A to the processor memories is shown in the Figure 1.1(a). Though the elements of A are stored in the processor memories in a linear fashion as shown in Figure 1.1(b), we adopt a two-dimensional view of the storage allocated for the array as shown in Figure 1.1(a). We view the global addresses as being organized in terms of courses, each course consisting

Table 2.1. Symbols used in this chapter.

A	a distributed array
T	the template to which array A is aligned
a	stride of alignment of A to the template T
b	offset of alignment of A to the template T
k	block size of distribution of the template
p	number of processors to which the template is distributed
ℓ	lower bound of regular section of A
h	upper bound of regular section of A
s	stride of regular section of A
$A(\ell : h : s)$	a regular section of array A (array section)
A_{2D}	two-dimensional view of an array A
A_{loc}	local portion of array A allocated on a processor
m	processor number $(0 \leq m \leq p - 1)$
Γ	array section lattice
Γ_m	part of Γ incident on processor m

of pk elements. In other words, we assign a block of k cells of the template to each of the p processors and then wrap around and assign the rest of the cells in a similar fashion. In the two-dimensional view we adopt, the first dimension denotes the course number (starting from zero), and the second dimension denotes the offset from the beginning of the course. We refer to the two-dimensional view of an array A as A_{2D}; and the element $A(i)$ has a 2-D address of the form $(x, y) = (i \operatorname{div} pk, i \operatorname{mod} pk)$ in this space. Similarly the local address of an element $A(i)$ (denoted using A_{loc}) mapped to a processor m is $k * (i \operatorname{div} pk) + i \operatorname{mod} k$.

An array section in HPF is of the form $A(\ell : h : s)$, where s is the access stride, and ℓ and h are the lower and upper bounds, respectively. Table 2.1 summarizes the notation. Given an array statement with HPF-style data mappings, it is our aim to generate the address sequence for the different processors.

Consider the case of an array aligned identically to a template that is distributed CYCLIC(4) onto 3 processors, which is accessed with a stride of 7 ($p = 3$, $k = 4$ and $s = 7$). Figure 2.1 shows the allocation of the array elements along with the corresponding global addresses. The array elements accessed are marked and the corresponding local addresses are shown in Figure 2.1. While the global access stride is constant (7 in this case), the local access sequence does not have a constant stride on any processor. For example, the local addresses of elements accessed in processor 1 are $3, 8, 14, 25, 31, \ldots$. The address generation problem is to efficiently enumerate this sequence.

Proc. 0				Proc. 1				Proc. 2			
0^0	1	2	3	4	5	6	7^3	8	9	10	11
12	13	14^6	15	16	17	18	19	20	21^5	22	23
24	25	26	27	28^8	29	30	31	32	33	34	35^{11}
36	37	38	39	40	41	42^{14}	43	44	45	46	47
48	49^{17}	50	51	52	53	54	55	56^{16}	57	58	59
60	61	62	63^{23}	64	65	66	67	68	69	70^{22}	71
72	73	74	75	76	77^{25}	78	79	80	81	82	83
84^{28}	85	86	87	88	89	90	91^{31}	92	93	94	95

Fig. 2.1. Layout of array A for $p = 3$ and $k = 4$ along with the global and local addresses of the accessed elements in $A(0 : 95 : 7)$ $(s = 7)$; Superscripts denote local addresses.

2.1 Related Work on One-Level Mapping

Several papers have addressed this code generation problem. Koelbel [19] derived techniques for compile-time address and communication generation for BLOCK and CYCLIC distribution for non-unit stride accesses containing a single loop index variable. MacDonald et al. [21] provided a simple solution for restricted case where the block sizes and the number of processors are powers of two. Chatterjee et al. [5] derived a purely runtime technique that identifies a repeating access pattern, which is characterized as a finite-state machine. Their $O(k \log k + \log \min(s, pk))$ algorithm involves a solution of k linear Diophantine equations to determine the pattern of addresses accessed, followed by sorting these addresses to derive the accesses in linear order. Gupta et al. [12] derived the *virtual-block* and the *virtual-cyclic* schemes. The virtual block (cyclic) scheme views the global array as a union of several cyclically (block) distributed arrays. The virtual cyclic scheme does not preserve the access order in the case of DO loops; this is not a problem for parallel array assignments. For large block sizes, this approach may suffer from cache misses [5]. They present a strategy for choosing a virtualization scheme for each array involved in array statement, based on indexing overheads and not on cache effects. In an exhaustive study of this problem, Stichnoth [33, 34] presented a framework (that bears similarities to the approach of Gupta et al. [12]) to enumerate local addresses and generation of communication sets. Banerjee et al. [2] discuss code generation for regular and irregular applications. Coelho et al. [6] present a survey of approaches to compiling HPF.

Ancourt et al. [1] use a linear algebra framework to generate code for fully parallel loops in HPF; their technique does not work for DO loops. Midkiff [22] presented a technique that uses a linear algebra approach to enumerate local accesses on a processor; this technique is similar to the virtual block approach presented by Gupta et al. [12]. van Reeuwijk et al. [32] presented a technique which requires the solution of linear Diophantine equations. Benkner [3] presented a solution for code generation for block-cyclic distributions in Vienna Fortran 90.

Kennedy, Nedeljkovic, and Sethi [16] derived an $O(k + \log \min(s, pk))$ algorithm for address generation. The improvement over Chatterjee et al.'s algorithm comes from avoiding the sorting step at the expense of solving an additional set of $k - 1$ linear Diophantine equations. In Sections 3 thru 7, we present our improved solution to the one-level mapping problem. Unlike Kennedy et al. [16] who solve $k-1$ linear Diophantine equations, our approach requires the solution of just two linear Diophantine equations. In addition, we present an efficient loop-nest based approach to enumerate the array addresses in order to derive the address pattern. Wijshoff [46] describes access sequences for periodic skewing schemes (used in providing efficient data organization in parallel machines) using lattices and derived closed forms for the lattices. He does not discuss code generation. Wang et al. [45] discuss experiments with several address generation solutions and conclude that the strategy described by us in this chapter (and in [39]) is the best strategy overall.

Other Work on One-Level Mapping from Our Group: In [36–38,41], we presented closed form expressions for basis vectors for several cases. Using the closed form expressions for the basis vectors, we derived a non-unimodular linear transformation; the matrix associated with this transformation has a determinant equal to the inverse of the access stride. In an experiment with a large set of values for the parameters p (the number of processors), k (block size) and s (the access stride), we derived the best pair of basis vectors using the closed form expressions for 82% of the problem instances. In later sections, we show that basis vector generation dominates address generation. Recently, we [25] have derived a runtime solution for the basis vector generation problem whose complexity is $O(\log \min(s, pk))$, which is simply the complexity of computing the required gcd. In contrast, all the other algorithms known to date for basis generation have a complexity of $O(k + \log \min(s, pk))$ or worse.

2.2 Related Work on Two-Level Mapping

A few methods have been proposed to address the code generation problem for two-level mapping. The solution by Chatterjee et al. [5] involves two applications of the one-level algorithm, where the input strides are a for the first and $a * s$ for the second. They build two finite state machines which will generate the access sequence for the *allocated* and the *accessed* elements. The next step involves using the finite state machines for the template space to rebuild a new finite state machine for the local address space. This fix-up step involves computing expensive integer divide and mod operations to determine the addresses of *accessed* elements in the local memory space. An added drawback of their technique when compared to our technique is the fact that their one-level pattern tables contain local memory gaps and not actual addresses. However their execution preserves lexicographic ordering and they do not incur any memory wastage.

Ancourt et al. [1] presented a solution for the two-level mapping problem; it involves a change of basis which leads to compression of holes but still incur some memory wastage. The node-code generated by this framework has complicated loops and incurs high execution overhead; their execution order does not preserve lexicographic ordering.

Kaushik [15] uses processor virtualization to handle two-level mapping with block-cyclic distributions. His method involves the generation of addresses for both hole-compression and for the one without hole-compression. First, the amount of memory that must be allocated is determined using a regular section characterization for *block* and *cyclic* distributions. Then, this regular section characterization is extended to the virtual processor approach for handling *block-cyclic* distributions. His technique does not ensure lexicographic execution in the case of virtual cyclic approach. In addition, memory wastage that grows with the amount of allocated storage is incurred.

3. A Lattice Based Approach for Address Generation

In the next few sections, we present a novel technique based on integer lattices for the address generation problem presented in the previous section. We first show that the accessed array elements of an array section belong to an integer lattice. We then provide a linear time algorithm to obtain the basis vectors of the integer lattice. We then go on to use these basis vectors to generate a loop nest that determines the access sequence. The problem of basis determination forms the core of code generation for HPF array statements; thus, a fast solution for this problem improves the performance of several facets of an HPF compiler. Also, we also provide a few optimizations of our basis determination algorithm.

3.1 Assumptions

In the next several sections, we present our approach to address generation for an alignment stride, $a = 1$. For $a > 1$, we use an approach similar to the one developed in [5], which involves two applications of our algorithm; this approach is discussed in Section 8 thru 10.

We assume that A is identically aligned to the template T. As it is evident from Figure 1.1(a), we assign a block of k cells of the template to each of the p processors and then wrap around and assign the rest of the cells in a similar fashion. As mentioned earlier, we treat the global address space as a two dimensional space and every element of an array $A(i)$ has an address of the form $(x, y) = (i \operatorname{div} pk, i \bmod pk)$ in this space. Here x is the course number to which this element belongs and y is the offset of the element in that course. We refer to the two-dimensional view of an array A as A_{2D}; this notation is used throughout this chapter. Similarly, A_{loc} refers to the locally allocated piece of array A on a processor.

3.2 Lattices

We use the following definitions of a lattice and its basis [11].

Definition 31. *A set of points* $\mathbf{x_1}, \mathbf{x_2}, \cdots, \mathbf{x_k}$ *in* $\Re^n$ *is said to be* independent *if these points do not belong to a linear subspace of* $\Re^n$ *of dimension less than* k.

For $k = n$, this is equivalent to the condition that the determinant of the matrix X whose columns are $\mathbf{x_i}$ $(1 \leq i \leq n)$ is non-zero, *i.e.*, $det\left(\left[\mathbf{x_1 x_2} \cdots \mathbf{x_n}\right]\right) \neq 0$. Now we state the following definition from the theory of lattices [11]; see [11] for a proof.

Definition 32. *Let* $\mathbf{b_1}, \mathbf{b_2}, \cdots, \mathbf{b_n}$ *be* n *independent points. Then the set* Λ *of points* $\mathbf{q}$ *such that*

$$\mathbf{q} = u_1 \mathbf{b_1} + u_2 \mathbf{b_2} + \cdots + u_n \mathbf{b_n}$$

(where $u_1, \ldots, u_n$ *are integers) is called a* lattice. *The set of vectors* $\mathbf{b_1}, \cdots, \mathbf{b_n}$ *is called a* basis *of* Λ. *The matrix* $B = [\mathbf{b_1 b_2} \cdots \mathbf{b_n}]$ *is called a* basis matrix.

Definition 33. *Let* Λ *be a discrete subspace of* $\Re^n$ *which is not contained in an* $(n-1)$*-dimensional linear subspace of* $\Re^n$. *Then* Λ *is a lattice.*

We refer to the set of global addresses (elements) over all processors accessed by $A(\ell : h : s)$ with distribution parameters (p, k) as $\Gamma = \langle A(\ell : h : s), p, k \rangle$. We refer to the set of local addresses accessed by processor m in executing its portion of $A(\ell : h : s)$ with distribution parameters (p, k) as Γ_m. By construction, Γ is a discrete subgroup of $\Re^2$ and in general, is not contained in a 1-dimensional linear subspace of $\Re^2$; if a single vector can be used to generate the elements accessed, our algorithm handles this as a special case. Thus, without loss of generality, $\Gamma = \langle A(\ell : h : s), p, k \rangle$ is a lattice. Similarly Γ_m is also a lattice.

In order to find the sequence of local addresses accessed on processor m, one needs to:

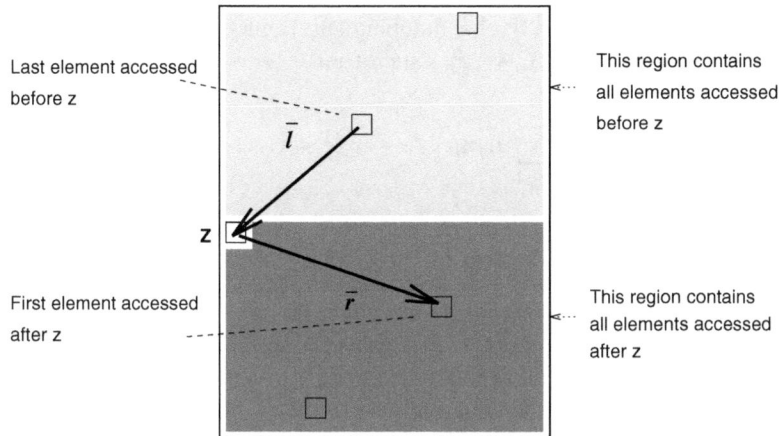

Fig. 3.1. Explanation of basis determination

1. find a set of basis vectors of the lattice Γ_m; and
2. enumerate the points in Γ_m using integer linear combinations of the basis vectors.

Our solution to Step 1 (presented in Section 4) uses the fact that a basis for the lattice can be computed from a knowledge of some of the points in the lattice. Our solution to Step 2 (presented in Section 5) uses the fact that if (with a given origin) every point in the lattice can be generated as non-negative integer linear combinations of a suitable pair of basis vectors, then these points can be enumerated by a two-level loop (each level with a step size of 1); in addition, this two-level nest can be derived by applying the linear transformation B^{-1} where B is the basis of the lattice.

Definition 34. *A basis B of the lattice Λ is called an* extremal basis *if the set of points $\mathbf{q}$ that belong to Λ can be written as*

$$\mathbf{q} = u_1\mathbf{b_1} + u_2\mathbf{b_2} + \cdots + u_n\mathbf{b_n}$$

where $u_1, \ldots, u_n$ are non-negative integers.

This chapter presents an algorithm for determining an extremal basis of the array section lattice $\langle A(\ell : h : s), p, k \rangle$ and shows how to use the extremal basis to generate the address sequence efficiently.

4. Determination of Basis Vectors

In this section, we show how to derive a pair of extremal basis vectors for the lattice Γ_m. In order to do that, we state a key result that allows us to find a basis for the lattice given a set of points in the lattice.

Result 41. Let $\mathbf{b_1}, \mathbf{b_2}, \cdots, \mathbf{b_n}$ be independent points of a lattice Λ in $\Re^n$. Then Λ has a basis $\{\mathbf{a_1}, \mathbf{a_2}, \cdots, \mathbf{a_n}\}$ such that

$$\mathbf{b_i} = \sum_{k=1}^{i} u_{ki}\mathbf{a_k} \qquad (i = 1, \ldots, n)$$

where $u_{ii} > 0$ and $0 \le u_{ki} < u_{ii}$ $(k < i; i = 1, \ldots, n)$. In addition, the set of points $\{\mathbf{b_1}, \mathbf{b_2}, \cdots, \mathbf{b_n}\}$ is a basis of the lattice Λ if and only if $u_{ii} = 1$.

While this result allows us to decide if a given set of independent points form a basis of the lattice, it is not constructive. But for $n = 2$, we derive the following theorem which allows us to construct a basis for the array section lattice on processor m. We use the vector $\mathbf{o}$ to refer to the origin of the lattice.

Theorem 41. *Let $\mathbf{b_1}$ and $\mathbf{b_2}$ be independent points of a lattice Λ in $\Re^2$ such that the closed triangle formed by the vertices $\mathbf{o}, \mathbf{b_1}$ and $\mathbf{b_2}$ contains no other points of Λ. Then $\{\mathbf{b_1}, \mathbf{b_2}\}$ is a basis of Λ.*

Proof. Let $\{\mathbf{a_1}, \mathbf{a_2}\}$ be any basis of Λ. From Result 41, we can write

$$\begin{aligned} \mathbf{b_1} &= u_{11}\mathbf{a_1} \\ \mathbf{b_2} &= u_{12}\mathbf{a_1} + u_{22}\mathbf{a_2} \end{aligned}$$

where $u_{11} > 0, u_{22} > 0$ and $0 \le u_{12} < u_{22}$. Based on the hypothesis, the side of the triangle connecting vertices $\mathbf{o}$ and $\mathbf{b_1}$ does not contain other points of Λ. Therefore, $u_{11} = 1$.

Let us assume that $u_{22} > 1$. If $u_{12} = 0$, the triangle formed by $\mathbf{o}, \mathbf{b_1}$ and $\mathbf{b_2}$ contains the point $\mathbf{a_2} \in \Lambda$; similarly, if $u_{12} \ge 1$, the triangle formed by $\mathbf{o}, \mathbf{b_1}$ and $\mathbf{b_2}$ contains the point $\mathbf{a_1} + \mathbf{a_2} \in \Lambda$. This contradicts our hypothesis. Hence, $u_{22} = 1$. Since, $u_{11} = u_{22} = 1$, it follows from Result 1 that the vectors $\mathbf{b_1}$ and $\mathbf{b_2}$ form a basis of Λ. □

Thus, in order to determine a basis of the array section lattice on processor m, we need to find three points (one of which can be considered as the origin without loss of generality) not on a straight line such that the triangle formed by them contains no other points belonging to the lattice. Let $\mathbf{x_1}, \mathbf{x_2}$, and $\mathbf{x_3}$ be three consecutively accessed elements of the array section lattice on processor m. If $\mathbf{x_1}, \mathbf{x_2}$, and $\mathbf{x_3}$ are independent points (do not lie on a straight line), then the vectors $\mathbf{x_2} - \mathbf{x_1}$ and $\mathbf{x_3} - \mathbf{x_2}$ form a basis for Γ_m. Recall that we view the array layout as consisting of several courses on each processor with each course consisting of k elements; this allows us to refer to each of the k columns on a processor. For the array section $A(\ell : h : s)$, let c_f be the first column in which an element is accessed and let c_l be the last column in which an element is accessed. Let $\mathbf{z_f}$ be some element accessed in column c_f and let $\mathbf{z_l}$ be some element accessed in column c_l by a processor. Let $\mathbf{x^{prev}}$ denote the element accessed immediately before $\mathbf{x}$ in lexicographic order on

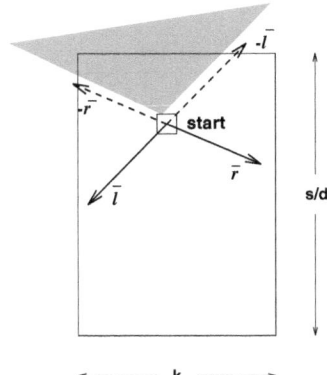

Fig. 4.1. No lattice point is a non-positive linear combination of basis vectors

---

a processor, and $\mathbf{x}^{\mathbf{next}}$ denote the element accessed immediately after $\mathbf{x}$ in linear order on a processor. We do not discuss the case where $\mathbf{z_f}$ and $\mathbf{z_f^{next}}$ (or $\mathbf{z_f^{prev}}$) are in the same column. This case is handled separately and is easily detected by our technique.

Theorem 42. *The set of points* $\{\mathbf{z_f^{prev}}, \mathbf{z_f}, \mathbf{z_f^{next}}\}$ *generate a basis of* Γ_m.

Proof. From Theorem 41, the set of points $\{\mathbf{z_f^{prev}}, \mathbf{z_f}, \mathbf{z_f^{next}}\}$ generate a basis of Γ_m if there are no lattice points in the triangle enclosing them and if they are independent. By construction, these are consecutive points in the lattice Γ_m and therefore, there no lattice points in the triangle (if any) enclosing them. Suppose these are not independent, *i.e.*, they lie on a straight line. This implies one of the following two cases:

Case (a): $\mathrm{Column}(\mathbf{z_f^{prev}}) < \mathrm{Column}(\mathbf{z_f}) < \mathrm{Column}(\mathbf{z_f^{next}})$.
Case (b): $\mathrm{Column}(\mathbf{z_f^{next}}) < \mathrm{Column}(\mathbf{z_f}) < \mathrm{Column}(\mathbf{z_f^{prev}})$.

Neither of these cases hold, since $\mathrm{Column}(\mathbf{z_f}) = c_f$ is the first column on processor m in which any element is accessed. Therefore, the three points are independent. Hence the result.   □

Similarly, the set of points $\{\mathbf{z_1^{prev}}, \mathbf{z_1}, \mathbf{z_1^{next}}\}$ also generate a basis of Γ_m. We use the set $\{\mathbf{z_f^{prev}}, \mathbf{z_f}, \mathbf{z_f^{next}}\}$. We refer to the vector $\mathbf{z_f} - \mathbf{z_f^{prev}}$ as $\mathbf{l} = (l_1, l_2)$ and the vector $\mathbf{z_f^{next}} - \mathbf{z}$ as $\mathbf{r} = (r_1, r_2)$. Again by construction, $l_1 > 0$, $r_2 > 0$, $l_2 < 0$ and $r_1 \geq 0$. This is illustrated in Figure 3.1 on p. 605.

4.1 Basis Determination Algorithm

In order to obtain a basis for the lattice, we need to find three points belonging to the lattice not on a straight line such that the triangle formed by

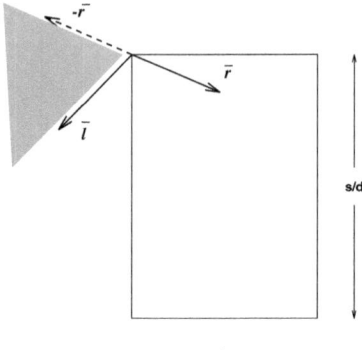

Fig. 4.2. No lattice points in region spanned by vectors **l** and **-r**

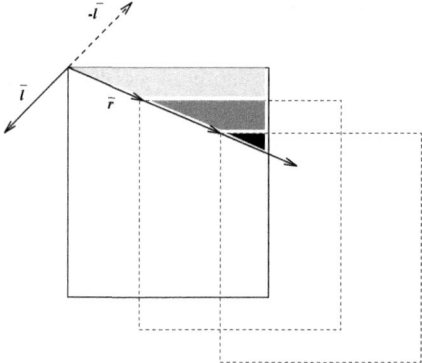

Fig. 4.3. No lattice points in region spanned by vectors **-l** and **r**

them contains no other lattice point. Chatterjee et al. [5] suggested a way to locate lattice points by solving linear Diophantine equation for each column with accessed elements. For details on their derivation refer [5]. The smallest solution of each of these solvable equations gives the smallest array element accessed in the corresponding column on a processor. Using this we show that we can obtain a basis for an array section lattice which generates the smallest element in each column that belongs to Γ_m by solving only two linear Diophantine equations.

The first two consecutive points accessed on a given column and the first point accessed on the next solvable column form a triangle that contains no other points. Again, let c_f be the first column in which an element is accessed on a processor. Let $\mathbf{z}_f$ be the first element accessed in column c_f. Since the access pattern on a given processor repeats after $\frac{pks}{\gcd(s,pk)}$ elements, the point

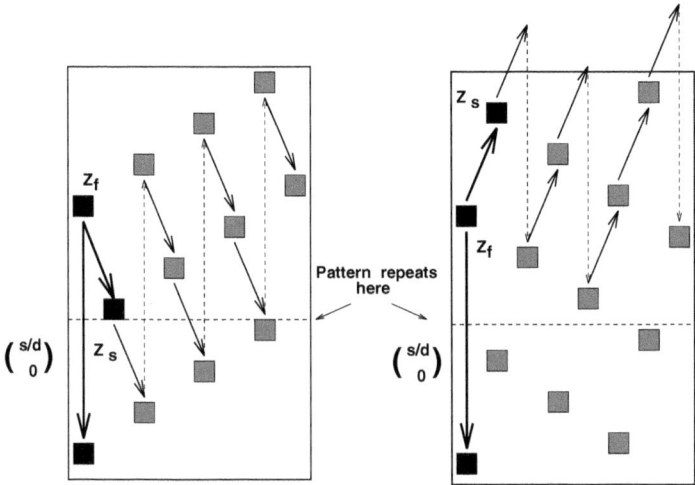

Fig. 4.4. Starting points in the columns generated by the vectors $\left(\frac{s}{d}, 0\right)$ and $\mathbf{z}_s - \mathbf{z}_f$.

accessed immediately after $\mathbf{z}_f$ in column c_f is $\mathbf{z}_f + \frac{pks}{\gcd(s,pk)}$. Now if c_s is the second column in which an element is accessed on the processor, and $\mathbf{z}_s$ is the first element accessed in it, then without loss of generality $\mathbf{z}_f$, $\mathbf{z}_f + \frac{pks}{\gcd(s,pk)}$ and $\mathbf{z}_s$ form a basis for the array section lattice. Hence the vectors $\left(\frac{s}{d}, 0\right)$ and $\mathbf{z}_s - \mathbf{z}_f$ form a pair of basis vectors of the array section lattice.

The elements $\mathbf{z}_f$ and $\mathbf{z}_s$ can be obtained by solving the first two solvable Diophantine equations in the algorithm (Lines 4 and 6) shown in Figure 4.5. Figure 4.4 shows the basis vectors generated as explained above whereas Figure 4.5 gives an outline of how the new basis vectors could be used to access the smallest array element accessed in each column for the case where $\mathbf{z}_s$ lies on a course above or below $\mathbf{z}_f$. Our basis determination algorithm works as follows. First we use the new basis to walk through the lattice to enumerate all the points on the lattice before the pattern starts to repeat. Then we use these points to locate the three independent points $\mathbf{z}_f^{\mathbf{prev}}$, $\mathbf{z_f}$, $\mathbf{z}_f^{\mathbf{next}}$ that form a triangle that contains no other lattice point. Using these three points we obtain the new basis of the lattice which we use to walk through the lattice in lexicographic order. Thus, we now need to solve only two Diophantine equations to generate the basis of the array section lattice that enumerates the points accessed in lexicographic order. This new basis determination algorithm performs substantially better than that proposed by Kennedy et al. for large values of k.

Input: Layout parameters (p, k), regular section $(\ell : h : s)$, processor number m.
Output: $start$ address, end address, length, basis vectors $\mathbf{r} = (r_1, r_2)$ and $\mathbf{l} = (l_1, l_2)$
    for m.

Method:

1 $(d, x, y) \leftarrow$ EXTENDED-EUCLID(s, pk); $length \leftarrow 2$; $start \leftarrow h + 1$
2 $last \leftarrow \ell + \frac{pks}{d} - 1$; $first \leftarrow \ell$; $bmin \leftarrow last + 1$; $amax \leftarrow first - 1$
3 $i \leftarrow d\lceil \frac{km - \ell}{d} \rceil$; $i\_end \leftarrow km - \ell + k - 1$
4 if $i > i\_end$ then return $\perp, \perp, 0, \perp, \perp, \perp, \perp$ /* No element */
5 $amin \leftarrow bmax \leftarrow z_f \leftarrow \ell + \frac{s}{d}(ix + pk\lceil \frac{-ix}{pk} \rceil)$; $i \leftarrow i + d$
6 if $i > i\_end$ then return $z_f, z_f, 1, \perp, \perp, \perp, \perp$ /* One element */
7 $loc \leftarrow z_s \leftarrow \ell + \frac{s}{d}(ix + pk\lceil \frac{-ix}{pk} \rceil)$; $length \leftarrow 2$
8 if $z_s < z_f$ then
9     $amin \leftarrow amax \leftarrow z_s$; $vec2 \leftarrow z_s - z_f$; $vec1 \leftarrow \frac{pks}{d} + vec2$
10 else
11     $bmin \leftarrow bmax \leftarrow z_s$; $vec1 \leftarrow z_s - z_f$; $vec2 \leftarrow vec1 - \frac{pks}{d}$
12 endif
13 if $vec1 \leq vec2$ then
14     $loc \leftarrow loc + vec1$; $i \leftarrow i + d$
15   while $i \leq i\_end$ do
16   if $loc > last$ then
17           $loc \leftarrow loc - \frac{pks}{d}$
18   endif
19   if $loc < z_f$ then   /* loc is accessed before z_f */
20           $amax \leftarrow \max(amax, loc)$; $amin \leftarrow \min(amin, loc)$
21   else   /* loc is accessed after z_f */
22           $bmax \leftarrow \max(bmax, loc)$; $bmin \leftarrow \min(bmin, loc)$
23   endif
24        $loc \leftarrow loc + vec1$; $i \leftarrow i + d$; $length \leftarrow length + 1$
25   enddo
26 else
27     $loc \leftarrow loc + vec2$; $i \leftarrow i + d$
28   while $i \leq i\_end$ do
29   if $loc < first$ then
30           $loc \leftarrow loc + \frac{pks}{d}$
31   endif
32   if $loc < z_f$ then   /* loc is accessed before z_f */
33           $amax \leftarrow \max(amax, loc)$; $amin \leftarrow \min(amin, loc)$
34   else   /* loc is accessed after z_f */
35           $bmax \leftarrow \max(bmax, loc)$; $bmin \leftarrow \min(bmin, loc)$
36   endif
37        $loc \leftarrow loc + vec2$; $i \leftarrow i + d$; $length \leftarrow length + 1$
38   enddo
39 endif
40 $(start, end, l_1, l_2, r_1, r_2) \leftarrow$ COMPUTE-VECTORS $(z_f, p, k, s, d, amin, amax,$
    $bmin, bmax)$
41 return $start, end, length - 1, l_1, l_2, r_1, r_2$

Fig. 4.5. Algorithm for determining basis vectors

Input: z_f, p, k, s, d, $amin$, $amax$, $bmin$, $bmax$.
Output: The *start* memory location, *end* memory location and the basis
                 vectors $\mathbf{r} = (r_1, r_2)$ and $\mathbf{l} = (l_1, l_2)$ for processor m.
Method:

```
1    if amin = z_f and amax = −1 then                    /* above is empty */
2        l₁ ← ⌊z_f/pk⌋ + s/d − ⌊bmax/pk⌋
3        l₂ ← z_f mod k − bmax mod k
4        r₁ ← ⌊bmin/pk⌋ − ⌊z_f/pk⌋
5        r₂ ← bmin mod k − z_f mod k
6    else if bmin = pks/d and bmax = z_f then             /* below is empty */
7        l₁ ← ⌊z_f/pk⌋ − ⌊amax/pk⌋
8        l₂ ← z_f mod k − amax mod k
9        r₁ ← ⌊amin/pk⌋ + s/d − ⌊z_f/pk⌋
10       r₂ ← amin mod k − z_f mod k
11   else                                       /* neither above nor below is empty */
12       l₁ ← ⌊z_f/pk⌋ − ⌊amax/pk⌋
13       l₂ ← z_f mod k − amax mod k
14       r₁ ← ⌊bmin/pk⌋ − ⌊z_f/pk⌋
15       r₂ ← bmin mod k − z_f mod k
16   endif
17   start ← amin
18   end ← bmax
19   return start, end, l₁, l₂, r₁, r₂
```

Fig. 4.6. COMPUTE-VECTORS procedure for basis vectors determination algorithm

---

4.2 Extremal Basis Vectors

In this section, we show that the basis vectors generated by our algorithm in
Figure 4.5 form an extremal set of basis vectors.

Theorem 43. *The lattice Γ_m (the projection of the array section lattice on
processor m) contains only those points which are non-negative integer linear
combinations of the basis vectors $\mathbf{l}$ and $\mathbf{r}$.*

Proof. Let $\mathbf{z}$ be the lexicographically first (starting) point of the lattice Γ_m.
As $\mathbf{r}$ and $\mathbf{l}$ are the basis vectors of the lattice, any point $\mathbf{q}$ belonging to the
lattice can be written as

$$\mathbf{q} = \mathbf{z} + v_1\mathbf{l} + v_2\mathbf{r}$$

where $\mathbf{r} = (r_1, r_2)$ and $\mathbf{l} = (l_1, l_2)$. Also, $l_1 > 0, l_2 < 0, r_1 \geq 0$ and $r_2 > 0$ by
construction. Suppose $\mathbf{q} \in \Gamma_m$ and that either one or both of v_1 and v_2 are
negative integers. There are two cases to consider:

Case (1): $(v_1 < 0$ and $v_2 < 0)$ $v_1l_1 + v_2r_1 < 0$

     As both v_1 and v_2 are negative, it is clear from Figure 4.1 that $\mathbf{q}$ lies in the
     region above the start element $\mathbf{z}$. This contradicts our earlier assumption
     that $\mathbf{z}$ is the start element on processor m. Hence, $v_1 < 0$ and $v_2 < 0$
     cannot be true.

Case (2): $(v_1 < 0$ or $v_2 < 0)$

Without loss of generality we assume that the start element $\mathbf{z}$ on a processor lies in the first non-empty column.

Let $v_1 \geq 0$ and $v_2 < 0$. As shown in Figure 4.2, $\mathbf{q}$ lies in the region to the left of $\mathbf{z}$ since $v_1 l_2 + v_2 r_2 < 0$. This contradicts our assumption that $\mathbf{q} \in \Gamma_m$. Hence $v_1 \geq 0$ and $v_2 < 0$ cannot be true.

If $v_1 < 0$ and $v_2 \geq 0$, then the next element accessed after the origin is either $\mathbf{z} + \mathbf{r}$ or $\mathbf{z} + \mathbf{r} - \mathbf{l}$. If the next accessed element of Γ_m is $\mathbf{z} + \mathbf{r} - \mathbf{l}$, then this point should be located on a course above $\mathbf{z}$ or on a course below $\mathbf{z}$. If this element is located on a course above $\mathbf{z}$, it would not be a point in the lattice Γ_m. If this element is located on a course below $\mathbf{z}$, then this element is lexicographically closer to $\mathbf{z}$ than the point $\mathbf{z} + \mathbf{r}$ which is impossible (due to the construction of $\mathbf{r}$). By the above arguments (as can be seen in Figure 4.3), we have shown that the next element accessed after $\mathbf{z}$ can only be $\mathbf{z} + \mathbf{r}$. A repeated application of the above argument rules out the presence of a lattice point in the shaded regions in Figure 4.3. If $\mathbf{z}$ is not in the first accessed column on processor m, similar reasoning can be used for the vector $\mathbf{l}$. Hence, the result. □

4.3 Improvements to the Algorithm for $s < k$

If $s < k$, it is sufficient to find only $s+1$ lattice points instead of k lattice points (as in [16]) in order to derive the basis vectors. Our implementation uses this idea which is explained next. Figure 4.7 shows that the access pattern repeats after s columns. A close inspection of the algorithm for determining the basis of the lattice for the case where $s < k$ reveals that the basis vector $\mathbf{r}$ will always be $(0, s)$. We also notice that since we access at least one element on every row, the first component of the basis vector $\mathbf{l}$, $i.e.$, l_1 must always be 1. Hence, if $s < k$, all we need to solve for is the second component of $\mathbf{l}$ $i.e.$, l_2. This results in a reduced number of comparisons for the $s < k$ case; in addition, there is no need to compute $bmin$, since it is not needed for the computation of l_2.

Consider the case where where $l = 36$, $p = 4$, $k = 16$ and $s = 5$ which is shown in Figure 4.7; We illustrate this case for processor number 2. Running through lines 1–38 of the algorithm in Figure 4.5 for this case, we get $\mathbf{z_f} = 96$, $amin = 36$, $amax = 46$, $bmin = 101$ and $bmax = 301$ for processor 2. Since the pattern of the smallest element accessed in a column repeats after every s columns, it is sufficient to enumerate the elements accessed in the last s columns to obtain $amax$ and $bmax$. $amin$ can be obtained by subtracting a suitable multiple of s from the smallest element in the last s columns lying above $\mathbf{z_f}$. By making these changes to the algorithm in Figure 4.5 for the case where $s < k$, we can obtain the required input for the COMPUTE-VECTORS procedure.

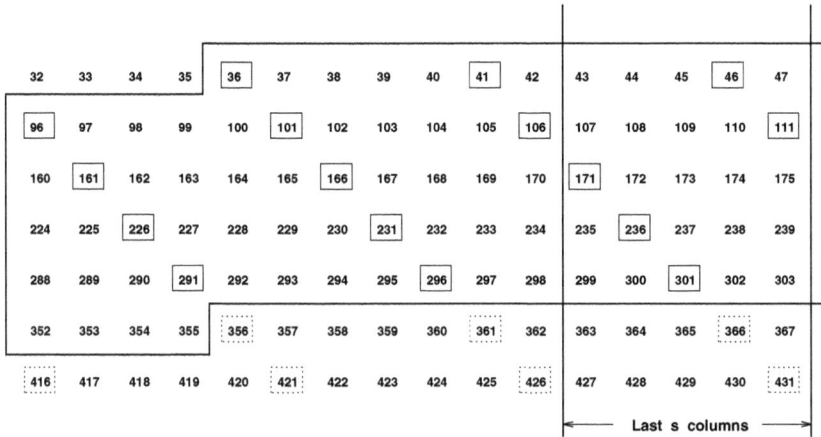

Fig. 4.7. Addresses of elements of array A accessed on processor 2 for the case $p = 4$, $k = 16$, $s = 5$ and offset $l = 36$

The improved algorithm to determine the basis vectors for each processor is as follows.

1. Solve the Diophantine equation corresponding to the first solvable column to obtain z_f.
2. Solve the Diophantine equations corresponding to the last and last but one solvable columns to obtain z_l and z_{l-1} respectively. Use these two solutions in a similar way as shown in Figure 4.5 to generate a pair of basis vectors for the lattice **vec1** and **vec2** in terms of offsets.
3. Using the above basis vectors enumerate all the points in the last s columns starting from the last solvable column. By comparing these elements to z_f, we get the smallest and the largest element accessed in these s columns that lie below z_f, namely $bmin'$ and $bmax'$. Similarly, we find the smallest and the largest elements that lie above z_f, namely $amin'$ and $amax'$.
4. If the region above z_f is not empty then, $amax = amax'$ and $amin = amin' - is$ (where is is a suitable multiple of s). If l lies on the processor then $amin = l$.
5. If both l and $l - s$ lie on the processor then $bmax = l + \frac{pks}{d}$. If the region below z_f is not empty then, $bmin = bmin' - is$ (where is is a suitable multiple of s) and $bmax = bmax'$.
6. Generate the lattice basis using the COMPUTE-VECTORS procedure.

4.4 Complexity

Line 1 of the algorithm in Figure 4.5 is the extended Euclid step which requires $O(\log \min(s, pk))$ time. Lines 2 thru 40 require $O(\min(s, k))$ time.

Thus, the basis generation part of our algorithm is $O(\log \min(s, pk) + \min(s, k))$; the basis generation portion of the algorithm in Kennedy et al. [16] is $O(k + \log \min(s, pk))$. We note that the address enumeration part of both the algorithms is $O(k)$. Experiments have shown that the basis determination part dominates the total time in practice. See Section 7 for a discussion. Thus, our algorithm is superior to that of Kennedy et al. [16].

5. Address Sequence Generation by Lattice Enumeration

As mentioned earlier, we will treat the global address space as a two dimensional space, and each element of an array $A(i)$ has an address of the form $(x, y) = (i \operatorname{div} pk, i \bmod pk)$ in this space. We refer to the two-dimensional view of an array A as A_{2D}. The sequence of the array elements accessed (course by course) in a processor can be obtained by strip mining the loop corresponding to $A(\ell : h : s)$ with a strip length of pk and appropriately restricting the inner loop limits. In the following analysis we assume that $\ell = 0$ and $h = N - 1$. At the end of this section we will show how the code generated for $A(0 : N - 1 : s)$ can be used to generate the code for $A(\ell : h : s)$. The code for the HPF array section $A(0 : N - 1 : s)$ that iterates over all the points in the two dimensional space shown in Figure 1.1(a) could be written as follows:

$$
\begin{aligned}
&\text{DO } i = 0, \lfloor \tfrac{N-1}{pk} \rfloor \\
&\quad \text{DO } j = 0, pk - 1 \\
&\qquad A_{2D}(i, j) = \cdots \cdots \\
&\quad \text{ENDDO} \\
&\text{ENDDO}
\end{aligned}
$$

We apply a non-unimodular loop transformation [23, 24] to the above loop nest to obtain the points of the lattice. Since the access pattern repeats after the first $\left(\tfrac{s}{d}\right)$ courses, we limit the outer loop in the above loop nest to iterate over the first $\left(\tfrac{s}{d}\right)$ courses only. In this case the global address of the first element allocated to the processor memory is mk, where m is the processor number. So in order to obtain the sequence of local addresses on processor m, we need to apply the loop transformation to the following modified code:

$$
\begin{aligned}
&\text{DO } i = 0, \left(\tfrac{s}{d} - 1\right) \\
&\quad \text{DO } j = mk, mk + k - 1 \\
&\qquad A_{2D}[i, j] = \cdots \\
&\quad \text{ENDDO} \\
&\text{ENDDO}
\end{aligned}
$$

The basis matrix for the lattice as derived in the last section is $B = \begin{bmatrix} l_1 & r_1 \\ l_2 & r_2 \end{bmatrix}$. Hence the transformation matrix T is of the form

$$T = B^{-1} = \frac{1}{\Delta}\begin{bmatrix} r_2 & -r_1 \\ -l_2 & l_1 \end{bmatrix},$$

where $\Delta = l_1 r_2 - l_2 r_1 = s$ (since $l_1 > 0, r_1 \geq 0, l_2 \leq 0$, and $r_2 > 0$). The loop bounds can be written as follows:

$$\begin{bmatrix} -1 & 0 \\ 1 & 0 \\ 0 & -1 \\ 0 & 1 \end{bmatrix}\begin{bmatrix} i \\ j \end{bmatrix} \leq \begin{bmatrix} 0 \\ \frac{s}{d} - 1 \\ -mk \\ mk + k - 1 \end{bmatrix}$$

$$\begin{bmatrix} -1 & 0 \\ 1 & 0 \\ 0 & -1 \\ 0 & 1 \end{bmatrix} BB^{-1}\begin{bmatrix} i \\ j \end{bmatrix} \leq \begin{bmatrix} 0 \\ \frac{s}{d} - 1 \\ -mk \\ mk + k - 1 \end{bmatrix}$$

$$\begin{bmatrix} -1 & 0 \\ 1 & 0 \\ 0 & -1 \\ 0 & 1 \end{bmatrix}\begin{bmatrix} l_1 & r_1 \\ l_2 & r_2 \end{bmatrix}\begin{bmatrix} u \\ v \end{bmatrix} \leq \begin{bmatrix} 0 \\ \frac{s}{d} - 1 \\ -mk \\ mk + k - 1 \end{bmatrix}$$

where $\begin{bmatrix} u \\ v \end{bmatrix} = B^{-1}\begin{bmatrix} i \\ j \end{bmatrix}$ and u and v are integers. Therefore,

$$\begin{bmatrix} i \\ j \end{bmatrix} = \begin{bmatrix} l_1 u + r_1 v \\ l_2 u + r_2 v \end{bmatrix}.$$

We now use Fourier-Motzkin elimination [7] on the following system of inequalities to solve for integral u and v:

$$\begin{aligned} -l_1 u - r_1 v &\leq 0 \\ l_1 u + r_1 v &\leq \frac{s}{d} - 1 \\ -l_2 u - r_2 v &\leq -mk \\ l_2 u + r_2 v &\leq mk + k - 1 \end{aligned}$$

If $r_1 > 0$ we have the following inequalities for u and v:

$$\left\lceil \frac{(-mk - k + 1)r_1}{s} \right\rceil \leq u \leq \left\lfloor \frac{(\frac{s}{d} - 1)r_2 - mkr_1}{s} \right\rfloor$$

$$\left\lceil \max\left(\frac{mk - ul_2}{r_2}, \frac{-ul_1}{r_1} \right) \right\rceil \leq v \leq \left\lfloor \min\left(\frac{mk + k - 1 - ul_2}{r_2}, \frac{\frac{s}{d} - 1 - ul_1}{r_1} \right) \right\rfloor$$

The node code for processor m if $r_1 > 0$ is:

```
DO u = ⌈(-mk-k+1)r₁/s⌉, ⌊(s/d-1)r₂-mkr₁/s⌋
    DO v = ⌈max(mk-ul₂/r₂, -ul₁/r₁)⌉, ⌊min(mk+k-1-ul₂/r₂, s/d-1-ul₁/r₁)⌋
        A₂D[l₁u + r₁v, l₂u + r₂v] = ......
    ENDDO
ENDDO
```

If $r_1 = 0$ we have the following inequalities for u and v:

$$0 \le \quad u \quad \le \frac{r_2}{s}\left(\frac{s}{d} - 1\right)$$

$$\left\lceil \frac{mk - ul_2}{r_2} \right\rceil \le \cdot v \quad \le \left\lfloor \frac{mk + k - 1 - ul_2}{r_2} \right\rfloor$$

The node code for processor m if $r_1 = 0$ is:

```
DO u = 0, r₂/s (s/d − 1)
    DO v = ⌈(mk−ul₂)/r₂⌉, ⌊(mk+k−1−ul₂)/r₂⌋
        A₂D[l₁u, l₂u + r₂v] = ······
    ENDDO
ENDDO
```

Example 51. Code generated for the case where $\ell = 0$, $p = 3$, $k = 4$ and $s = 11$ for processor 1.

The set of addresses generated by the algorithm in Figure 4.5 is $\{88, 77, 66, 55\}$. Also $z = 88$, $amin = 55$, $amax = 77$, $bmin = 132$ and $bmax = 88$. Since the *below* section is empty we execute lines 5 and 6 of the algorithm in Figure 4.6. So our algorithm returns $\mathbf{l} = (1, -1)$ and $\mathbf{r} = (8, 3)$ as the basis vectors. The access pattern is shown in Figure 5.1. The node code to obtain the access pattern for processor 1 is:

```
DO u = ⌈−56/11⌉, ⌊−2/11⌋
    DO v = ⌈max (4+u/3, −u/8)⌉, ⌊min (7+u/3, 10−u/8)⌋
        A₂D[u + 8v, −u + 3v] = ······
    ENDDO
ENDDO
```

Next we show the iterations of the nested loop and the elements accessed; the elements indeed are accessed in lexicographic order.

u	$v_{lb} = \left\lceil \max\left(\frac{4+u}{3}, \frac{-u}{8}\right)\right\rceil$	$v_{ub} = \left\lfloor \min\left(\frac{7+u}{3}, \frac{10-u}{8}\right)\right\rfloor$	accessed elements (2D)
−5	1	0	
−4	1	1	$(4, 7)$
−3	1	1	$(5, 6)$
−2	1	1	$(6, 5)$
−1	1	1	$(7, 4)$

Converting the global two-dimensional address of the accessed elements to global addresses we get the global access pattern $\{55, 66, 77, 88\}$ on processor 1 which gives the local access pattern $\{19, 22, 25, 28\}$ on processor 1.

Processor 0				Processor 1				Processor 2			
0	1	2	3	4	5	6	7	8	9	10	11
12	13	14	15	16	17	18	19	20	21	22	23
24	25	26	27	28	29	30	31	32	33	34	35
36	37	38	39	40	41	42	43	44	45	46	47
48	49	50	51	52	53	54	55	56	57	58	59
60	61	62	63	64	65	66	67	68	69	70	71
72	73	74	75	76	77	78	79	80	81	82	83
84	85	86	87	88	89	90	91	92	93	94	95
96	97	98	99	100	101	102	103	104	105	106	107
108	109	110	111	112	113	114	115	116	117	118	119
120	121	122	123	124	125	126	127	128	129	130	131
132	133	134	135	136	137	138	139	140	141	142	143

Fig. 5.1. Addresses of the accessed elements of array A along with the 2-dimensional view for the case $p = 3$, $k = 4$ and $s = 11$.

6. Optimization of Loop Enumeration: GO-LEFT and GO-RIGHT

A closer look at Figure 5.1 reveals that even if we generated code that enumerates the points belonging to a family of parallel lines along the vector (l_1, l_2) by moving from one parallel line to the next along the vector (r_1, r_2), we would still access the elements in lexicographic order. Clearly, in this example, the above enumeration turns out to be more efficient than the earlier enumeration. We refer to this new method of enumeration as GO-LEFT, as we enumerate all points on a line along the vector (l_1, l_2) before we move to the next line along the other basis vector. For the same reasons, we refer to the earlier method of enumeration as GO-RIGHT. Next we show that the GO-LEFT method also enumerates elements in lexicographic order. If B (as shown in Section 5) is the basis matrix for the GO-RIGHT case then the basis for the GO-LEFT case is $B_L = \begin{bmatrix} r_1 & l_1 \\ r_2 & l_2 \end{bmatrix}$. Hence the transformation matrix in the GO-LEFT case is B_L^{-1}. Next, we show that for the pair of basis vectors obtained using the algorithm shown in Figure 4.5, the GO-LEFT scheme is always legal.

Theorem 61. *Given a point* $\mathbf{q}$ *belonging to the lattice* Γ_m *and a pair of extremal basis vectors* $\mathbf{l}$ *and* $\mathbf{r}$ *obtained using the algorithm in Figure 4.5, then on applying* B_L^{-1} *as a transformation we maintain the access order.*

Proof. Since $\mathbf{l}$ and $\mathbf{r}$ are extremal basis vectors,

$$\mathbf{q} = \mathbf{z} + v_1\mathbf{l} + v_2\mathbf{r}$$

where $\mathbf{z}$ is the starting point of Γ_m and v_1 and v_2 are positive integers. So $\mathbf{q}^{next}$ could either be $\mathbf{q} + \mathbf{r}$ or $\mathbf{q} + \mathbf{l}$ or $\mathbf{q} + \mathbf{l} + \mathbf{r}$.

Let us assume that $\mathbf{q}+\mathbf{r} \in \Gamma_m$ and $\mathbf{q}+\mathbf{l} \in \Gamma_m$. This implies that $\mathbf{q}+\mathbf{r}+\mathbf{l} \in \Gamma_m$. With this assumption we can have the two following cases,

Case 1: $\mathbf{q}+\mathbf{r}$ is lexicographically closer to $\mathbf{q}$ than $\mathbf{q}+\mathbf{l}$.
Case 2: $\mathbf{q}+\mathbf{l}$ is lexicographically closer to $\mathbf{q}$ than $\mathbf{q}+\mathbf{r}$.

In Case 1, $\mathbf{q}+\mathbf{l}$ is lexicographically closer to $\mathbf{q}$ than $\mathbf{q}+\mathbf{r}$. So it should be clear that $\mathbf{q}+\mathbf{r}$ should be lexicographically closer to $\mathbf{q}+\mathbf{l}$ than to $\mathbf{q}$, which is impossible (due to the construction of $\mathbf{r}$ and $\mathbf{l}$). Hence our assumption that $\mathbf{q}+\mathbf{r} \in \Gamma_m$ and $\mathbf{q}+\mathbf{l} \in \Gamma_m$ is not true. A similar argument can be used to show that out initial assumption is incorrect for Case 2 also.

From the above arguments, we conclude that given the starting point of Γ_m, we maintain the lexicographic order of the points accessed by repeatedly adding $\mathbf{l}$ until we run out of Γ_m and then add a $\mathbf{r}$ and continue adding $\mathbf{l}$ until we run out of Γ_m again and so on. So the access order does not change on using B_L as the basis matrix, *i.e.*, applying B_L^{-1} as the transformation. ☐

From the above theorem it is clear that GO-LEFT is always legal for the pair of basis vectors obtained using the algorithm shown in Figure 4.5. The loop nest for $r_1 \neq 0$ is:

```
DO u = ⌈mkl₁/s⌉ , ⌊((s/d−1)(−l₂)+(mk+k−1)l₁)/s⌋
    DO v = ⌈max( ((mk+k−1)−ur₂)/l₂ , −ur₁/l₁ )⌉ , ⌊min( (mk−ur₂)/l₂ , (s/d−1−ur₁)/l₁ )⌋
        A₂D[r₁u + l₁v, r₂u + l₂v] = · · · · · ·
    ENDDO
ENDDO
```

The node code for processor m if $r_1 = 0$ is:

```
DO u = ⌈mkl₁/s⌉ , ⌊((s/d−1)(−l₂)+(mk+k−1)l₁)/s⌋
    DO v = ⌈max( ((mk+k−1)−ur₂)/l₂ , 0 )⌉ , ⌊min( (mk−ur₂)/l₂ , (s/d−1)/l₁ )⌋
        A₂D[l₁v, r₂u + l₂v] = · · · · · ·
    ENDDO
ENDDO
```

Next, we need to decide when it is beneficial to use GO-LEFT. The amount of work that needs to be done to evaluate the inner loop bounds is the same for each outer loop iteration in both the enumeration methods. So an enumeration that results in fewer outer loop iterations is the scheme of choice. The number of elements accessed per line in the two cases is a function of the block size k and second components of the basis vectors. If $r_2 \leq -l_2$, we use GO-RIGHT; else, we use GO-LEFT.

Example 61. Code generated for the case where $\ell = 0$, $p = 3$, $k = 4$ and $s = 11$ for processor 1 when we choose to GO-LEFT.

Input: $start$, end, $\mathbf{r} = (r_1, r_2)$, $\mathbf{l} = (l_1, l_2)$.
Output: The address sequence.

Method:
if $r_2 \leq -l_2$ **then**   /* GO-RIGHT */

1. $u_{start} \leftarrow \dfrac{r_2(start \text{ div } pk - \ell \text{ div } pk) - r_1(start \bmod pk - \ell \bmod pk)}{s}$

2. $u_{end} \leftarrow \dfrac{r_2(end \text{ div } pk - \ell \text{ div } pk) - r_1(end \bmod pk - \ell \bmod pk)}{s}$

3. Scan all the elements on the first line (u_{start}), starting at the $start$ element and then adding $\mathbf{r}$ until there are no more elements on this processor.

4. From the previous start add $\mathbf{l}$ and then add $\mathbf{r}$ as many times as necessary till you get back onto the processor space. The element thus obtained is the start for the new line. Starting at this element keep adding $\mathbf{r}$ until you run out of the processor space. Repeat this until the line immediately before the last line (u_{end}).

5. Obtain the start point on the last line as before. Scan all the elements along the line from the start by adding $\mathbf{r}$ until you reach the end element.

else   /* GO-LEFT */

1. $u_{start} \leftarrow \dfrac{-l_2(start \text{ div } pk - \ell \text{ div } pk) + l_1(start \bmod pk - \ell \bmod pk)}{s}$

2. $u_{end} \leftarrow \dfrac{-l_2(end \text{ div } pk - \ell \text{ div } pk) + l_1(end \bmod pk - \ell \bmod pk)}{s}$

3. Scan all the elements on the first line (u_{start}), starting at the $start$ element and then adding $\mathbf{l}$ until there are no more elements on this processor.

4. From the previous start add $\mathbf{r}$ and then add $\mathbf{l}$ as many times as necessary till you get back onto the processor space. The element thus obtained is the start for the new line. Starting at this element keep adding $\mathbf{l}$ until you run out of the processor space. Repeat this until the line immediately before the last line (u_{end}).

5. Obtain the start point on the last line as before. Scan all the elements along the line from the start by adding $\mathbf{l}$ until you reach the end element.

endif

Fig. 6.1. Algorithm for GO-LEFT and GO-RIGHT

The basis vectors obtained by running through the algorithms shown in Figure 4.5 are $\mathbf{l} = (1, -1)$ and $\mathbf{r} = (8, 3)$. Hence the resulting node code for processor 1 is:

$$\text{DO } u = \left\lceil \tfrac{4}{11} \right\rceil, \left\lfloor \tfrac{17}{11} \right\rfloor$$
$$\qquad \text{DO } v = \max\left(3u - 7, -8u\right), \min\left(3u - 4, 10 - 8u\right)$$
$$\qquad\qquad A_{2D}\left[8u + v, 3u - v\right] = \cdots\cdots$$
$$\qquad \text{ENDDO}$$
$$\text{ENDDO}$$

Here we observe that unlike the previous example, we scan all the elements along a single line rather than 4 different lines. Clearly in this case going left is the better choice.

6.1 Implementation

We observe from the example in Sections 5 and 6 that the code generated for GO-RIGHT enumerates the points that belong to a family of parallel lines, *i.e.*, along the vector $\mathbf{r}$, by moving from one parallel line to the next within the family along the vector $\mathbf{l}$ and the code generated for GO-LEFT enumerates the points that belong to a family of parallel lines along the vector $\mathbf{l}$, by moving from one parallel line to the next within the family along the vector $\mathbf{r}$. So in the code derived in Section 5, the outer loop iterates over the set of parallel lines while the inner loop iterates over all the elements accessed in each line on a given processor.

From the previous example it can be seen that we may scan a few empty lines (*i.e.*, lines on which no element is accessed) in the beginning and the end. This can be avoided by evaluating a tighter lower bound for the outer loop using the *start* and *end* elements evaluated in the algorithm shown in Figure 4.5. The start line u_{start} and end line u_{end} can be evaluated as follows (using GO-RIGHT enumeration scheme):

$$l_1 u_{start} + r_1 v_{start} = start \text{ div } pk - \ell \text{ div } pk$$
$$l_2 u_{start} + r_2 v_{start} = start \bmod pk - \ell \bmod pk$$
$$l_1 u_{end} + r_1 v_{end} = end \text{ div } pk - \ell \text{ div } pk$$
$$l_2 u_{end} + r_2 v_{end} = end \bmod pk - \ell \bmod pk$$

Hence,

$$u_{start} = \frac{r_2(start \text{ div } pk - \ell \text{ div } pk) - r_1(start \bmod pk - \ell \bmod pk)}{s};$$

$$u_{end} = \frac{r_2(end \text{ div } pk - \ell \text{ div } pk) - r_1(end \bmod pk - \ell \bmod pk)}{s}.$$

The inner loop of the node code evaluates the start element for each iteration of the outer loop *i.e.*, each line traversed. In our implementation of the loop enumeration we use the start element of the previous line traversed to obtain the start element of the next line. This eliminates the expensive integer divisions involved in evaluating the start elements on the different lines. Figure 6.1 shows our algorithm for loop enumeration.

7. Experimental Results for One-Level Mapping

We performed experiments on our pattern generation algorithm on a Sun Sparcstation 20. We used the `cc` compiler using the `-fast` optimization switch; the function `gettimeofday()` was used to measure time. When computing the time for 32 processors, we timed the code that computes the access pattern for each processor, and report the maximum time over all processors. We experimented with block sizes in powers of 2 ranging from 4 to 1024 for 32 processors. The total times for the two different implementations ("Right" and "Zigzag") of the algorithm in [16] and our algorithm include basis and table generation times. Tables 7.1(a)–7.1(c) show the total times for the above three algorithms and the total time for pattern generation for the algorithm proposed by Chatterjee et al. [5] (referred to as "Sort" in the tables). For very small block sizes, all the methods have comparable performance. At block sizes from 16 onward, our solution outperforms the other three. For higher block sizes, our pattern generation algorithm performs 2 to 9 times faster than the two Rice [16] algorithms. For larger block sizes, if $s < k$, our algorithm is 7 to 9 times faster than the Rice algorithms because of the need to find only $s + 1$ lattice points, instead of k lattice points, in order to find the basis vectors. In addition, for larger block sizes, experiments indicate that address enumeration time (given the basis vectors) for our algorithm is less than that of [16]. From our choice of enumeration, we decide to use `GO-LEFT` for $s = pk - 1$ and use `GO-RIGHT` for $s = pk + 1$. Since the algorithms in [16] do not exploit this enumeration choice, our algorithm performs significantly better. In addition, our algorithm is 13 to 65 times faster than the approach of Chatterjee et al. [5] for large block sizes.

   In addition to the total time, we examined the basis determination time and the access enumeration times separately. In general, the basis determination time accounts for 75% of the total address generation time and is about 3 times the actual enumeration time. The basis determination times are shown in Figure 7.1 and the enumeration times are shown in Figure 7.2. In these figures, we plot the times taken for our algorithm ("Loop"), and the best of the times for the two Rice implementations. Figure 7.1(a) shows that for $s = 7$, the basis generation time for Loop is practically constant while that for Rice increases with block size, k; for $k = 2048$, the basis generation time for Rice is about 50 times that of our algorithm. In Figure 7.1(b) ($s = 99$), it is clear that the basis generation time for our algorithm is nearly constant while that for Rice increases from $k = 128$ onward; this is because of the fact that our basis generation algorithm has a complexity $O(\min(s, k))$ while

Table 7.1. Total address generation times (in μs) for our technique (Loop), Right and Zigzag of Rice [16] and the Sort approach [5] on a Sun Sparcstation 10

(a) $p = 32; s = 3$ and $s = 5$

Block Size	$s = 3$				$s = 5$			
k	Loop	Right	Zigzag	Sort	Loop	Right	Zigzag	Sort
2	17	19	19	20	19	21	21	22
4	20	23	23	27	29	31	31	35
8	21	24	25	37	21	24	25	37
16	29	33	33	69	25	33	34	69
32	29	44	45	150	31	46	47	152
64	33	73	76	453	42	82	84	460
128	36	127	132	845	37	126	131	843
256	47	238	247	1638	48	236	246	1638
512	64	458	480	3213	67	457	472	3221
1024	104	902	936	6383	113	905	946	6384

(b) $p = 32; s = 7$ and $s = 9$

Block Size	$s = 7$				$s = 9$			
k	Loop	Right	Zigzag	Sort	Loop	Right	Zigzag	Sort
2	17	19	19	20	17	19	19	20
4	21	23	23	27	21	23	23	27
8	31	34	35	47	23	26	27	39
16	25	31	32	67	26	33	35	69
32	32	46	47	152	42	55	57	160
64	43	81	84	460	44	81	84	460
128	38	125	131	843	39	125	131	843
256	49	236	245	1638	50	236	245	1637
512	76	464	487	3222	69	454	470	3220
1024	105	891	938	6368	107	890	919	6392

(c) $p = 32; s = 11$ and $s = 99$

Block Size	$s = 11$				$s = 99$			
k	Loop	Right	Zigzag	Sort	Loop	Right	Zigzag	Sort
2	27	29	29	30	35	37	37	38
4	37	39	39	43	45	47	47	51
8	31	34	35	47	55	59	59	71
16	35	41	42	77	51	58	58	93
32	32	44	47	151	50	64	64	170
64	37	73	75	452	71	91	98	469
128	50	135	141	854	97	149	152	865
256	67	252	261	1654	151	256	276	1656
512	70	455	469	3221	114	453	470	3224
1024	108	890	918	6389	154	887	916	6392

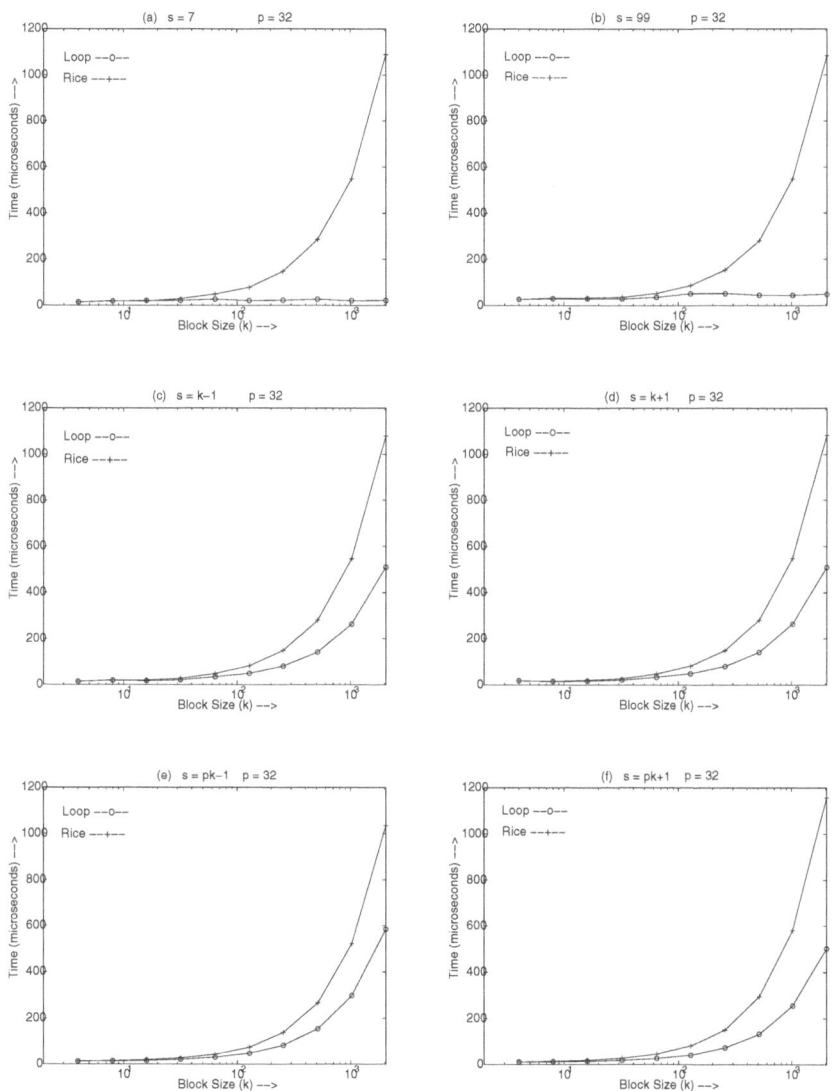

Fig. 7.1. Basis vector generation times for $p = 32$ processors for various block sizes and strides

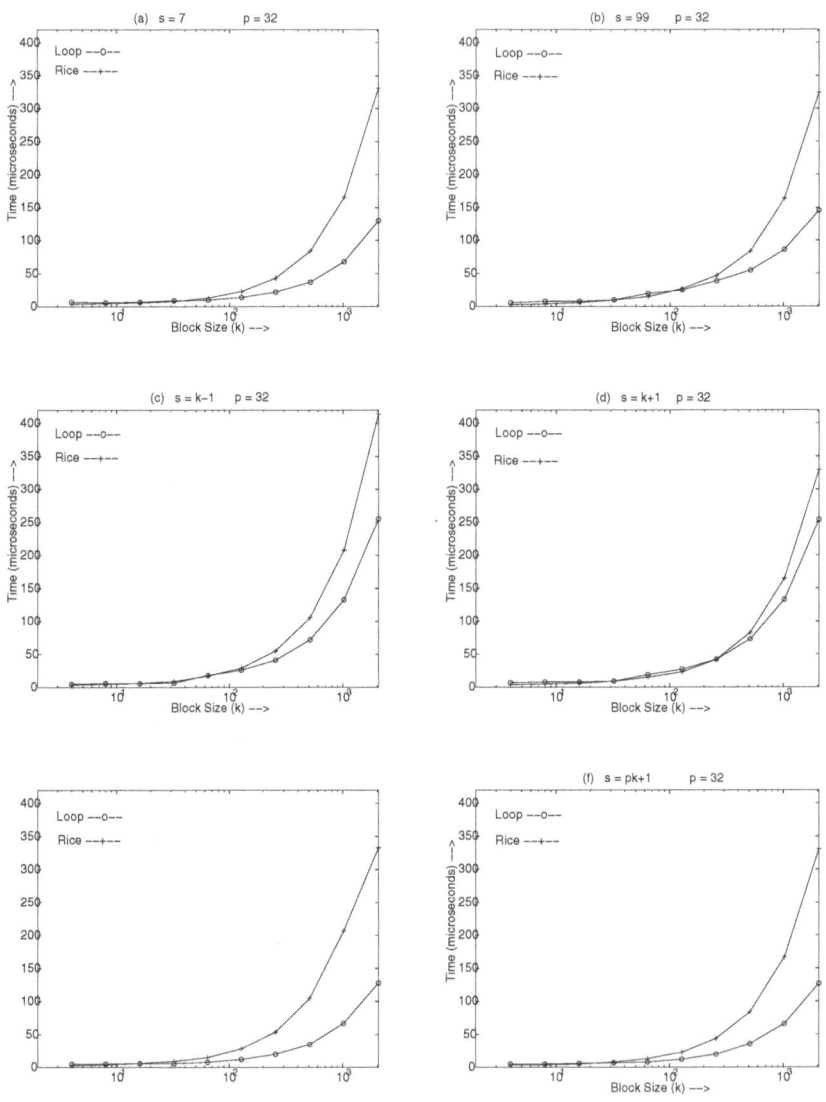

Fig. 7.2. Lattice enumeration times (given the basis vectors) for $p = 32$ processors for various block sizes and strides

Rice has a complexity $O(k)$. Figures 7.1(c)–(f) indicate that for large values of k, the Loop basis generation time is about half that of the Rice basis generation time. Figures 7.2(a)-(f) show that for small block sizes, the enumeration time for Loop and Rice are comparable, and that from $k = 64$ onwards, the enumeration time for Loop is lower than that of Rice. From these figures, it is clear that the Loop algorithm outperforms the Rice algorithm in both the basis determination and address enumeration phases of address generation.

Table 7.2. Total address generation times (in μs) for our technique (Loop), Right and Zigzag of Rice [16] and the Sort approach [5] on a Sun Sparcstation 10

(a) $p = 32; s = k - 1$ and $s = k + 1$

Block Size	$s = k - 1$				$s = k + 1$			
k	Loop	Right	Zigzag	Sort	Loop	Right	Zigzag	Sort
2	17	19	19	20	19	21	21	22
4	20	23	23	27	29	31	31	35
8	31	34	35	47	23	26	27	39
16	26	33	33	69	26	33	33	69
32	33	45	45	154	33	45	45	155
64	64	84	87	459	64	82	90	459
128	92	141	141	853	93	134	144	853
256	149	255	255	1642	150	240	255	1641
512	263	486	485	3219	263	459	486	3219
1024	491	946	944	6375	493	894	946	6375

(b) $p = 32; s = pk - 1$ and $s = pk + 1$

Block Size	$s = pk - 1$				$s = pk + 1$			
k	Loop	Right	Zigzag	Sort	Loop	Right	Zigzag	Sort
2	17	19	19	20	15	17	17	18
4	18	21	21	25	16	19	19	23
8	19	24	24	37	17	22	23	35
16	23	31	31	67	20	29	30	65
32	29	45	45	155	26	43	44	147
64	43	73	72	449	38	72	74	449
128	70	128	128	843	62	129	132	844
256	124	239	239	1631	109	243	250	1637
512	232	463	463	3209	204	474	486	3220
1024	449	909	909	6365	395	932	958	6388

8. Address Sequence Generation for Two-Level Mapping

Non-unit alignment strides render address sequence generation even more difficult since the addresses can not directly be represented as a lattice; in this case, the addresses can be thought of as the composition of two integer lattices. This section presents solution to the problem of address generation for such a case when the data objects are mapped to processor memories using CYCLIC(k) distribution. We present several methods of generating the address sequence. Our approach involves construction of pattern tables which does not incur runtime overheads as compared to other existing solutions for this problem. We use two applications of the method described in the preceding sections to generate the pattern of accesses.

8.1 Problem Statement

Consider the following HPF code

```
        REAL A(N)
!HPF$   TEMPLATE T(a*N + b)
!HPF$   PROCESSORS PROCS(p)
!HPF$   ALIGN A(j) WITH T(a*j + b)
!HPF$   DISTRIBUTE T(CYCLIC(k)) ONTO PROCS
```
$$\text{do i = 0, } \left\lfloor \tfrac{h-l}{s} \right\rfloor$$
$$A(l + is) = \cdots$$
```
        enddo
```

A compiler that generates the node code for the above HPF program has to generate the set of local elements of array A *accessed* on processor m.

To recall, when the alignment stride $a > 1$, the mapping is called a *two-level mapping*. A non-unit-alignment-stride mapping results in many template cells that do not have any array elements aligned to. These empty template cells are referred to as *holes*. We need not allocate memory for *holes* in the local address space during mapping. The challenge then is to generate the sequence of accessed elements in this local address space ensuring that no storage is wasted on holes.

Figure 8.1(a) shows the distribution of the template cells onto a processor arrangement. For this example, the alignment stride a and access stride s are both equal to 3. The number of processors p is 4 and we assume a CYCLIC(4) distribution; this example is from Chatterjee et al. [5]. Now, we define a few terms used here. The set of global indices of array elements that are aligned to some template cell on a processor is called the set of *allocated* elements. The set of global indices of accessed array elements that are aligned to some template cell on that processor is called the set of *accessed* elements. These *accessed* elements are however a subset of *allocated* elements. For the given example, $\{0, 1, 6, 11, 16, \cdots\}$ is the set of *allocated* elements and $\{0, 6, 27, 33, 48, \cdots\}$ is the set of *accessed* elements for processor 0. Figure 8.1(b) shows the local address space of template cells on all the processors. The problem of deriving the *accessed* elements for this template space is similar to a one-level mapping problem where the stride s is replaced

Processor 0				Processor 1				Processor 2				Processor 3			
0			1			2			3			4			5
		6			7			8			9			10	
	11			12			13			14			15		
16			17			18			19			20			21
		22			23			24			25			26	
	27			28			29			30			31		
32			33			34			35			36			37
		38			39			40			41			42	
	43			44			45			46			47		

(a): Global layout of template cells on $p = 4$ processors.

Processor 0	0			1			6			11		
Processor 1			2			7			12			13
Processor 2		3			8			9			14	
Processor 3	4			5			10			15		

(b): Local memory layout for template cells

Processor 0	0	1	6	11	16	17	22	27	32	33	38	43
Processor 1	2	7	12	13	18	23	28	29	34	39	44	45
Processor 2	3	8	9	14	19	24	25	30	35	40	41	46
Processor 3	4	5	10	15	20	21	26	31	36	37	42	47

(c): Local memory layout for array cells.

Fig. 8.1. Two-level mapping of array A when $a = 3$, $s = 3$, $p = 4$, $k = 4$ and $l = 0$

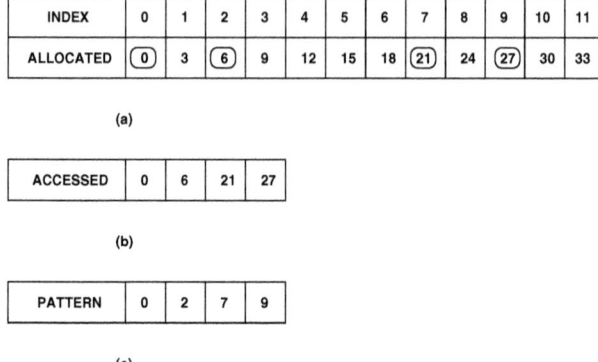

(a)

(b)

(c)

Fig. 9.1. Local addresses of *accessed* and *allocated* elements along with *two-level* access pattern when $a = 3$, $s = 3$, $p = 4$, $k = 4$ and $l = 0$

with $a * s$. However using this method we incur huge memory wastage and suffer from data locality resulting in higher execution times.

If one eliminates holes in this layout, we can have a significant savings in memory usage. This can be achieved by viewing the local address space as shown in Figure 8.1(c). This local address space does not have any memory wastage. However additional work at address generation time has to be done to switch from the template space to the local space. Due to the absence of these *holes* we can expect improved data locality and thus leading to faster execution times. The address generation problem now is to generate the set of elements *accessed* in this local address space, efficiently at runtime.

9. Algorithms for Two-Level Mapping

The algorithms proposed in this section solve the problem of generating addresses for a compressed space for two-level mapping. These algorithms exploit the repetitive pattern of accesses by constructing pattern tables for the local address space. These pattern tables are then used to generate the complete set of accesses for the array layout just like in the case of one-level mapping.

The main idea behind these algorithms is to construct tables that store the indices needed to switch from the template space to the local space. Since we do not allocate memory for *holes*, we have no memory wastage. We also do not incur high costs for generating access function to switch from the template space to local address space, this leads to faster execution times. This coupled with the fact that no memory is wasted proves that these methods are superior to any other existing methods that access array elements lexicographically.

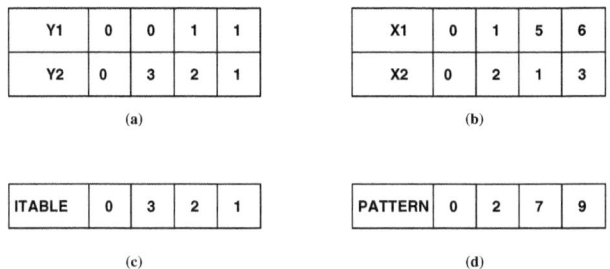

Y1	0	0	1	1
Y2	0	3	2	1

(a)

X1	0	1	5	6
X2	0	2	1	3

(b)

ITABLE	0	3	2	1

(c)

PATTERN	0	2	7	9

(d)

Fig. 9.2. Two dimensional coordinates of *allocated* and *accessed* elements along with *Itable* and *two-level* access pattern when $a = 3$, $s = 3$, $p = 4$, $k = 4$ and $l = 0$

The algorithms for two-level mapping discussed in this chapter can be broadly classified into two groups. These algorithms differ mainly in the manner in which the tables are constructed in order to switch from the template space to the local address space. The first algorithm constructs a table of offsets whereas the algorithms in the second method uses different search techniques to locate *accessed* elements in the set of *allocated* elements in the compressed space.

All these algorithms first view the address space as an integer lattice and use basis vectors to generate the access sequence of both *allocated* and *accessed* elements. The basis vectors are generated using our one-level address generation algorithm discussed earlier. Two applications of the one-level algorithm with input strides being a and $a * s$ in each case, generates the set of accesses for both *allocated* and *accessed* elements. Figure 9.1(a) shows the first set of repetition pattern of local addresses of the set of accesses for *allocated* elements. The numbers in boxes are the set of elements *accessed*, and the pattern of repetition of these elements is shown in Figure 9.1(b). In a compressed space we need to locate the position of these *accessed* elements, in the a set of *allocated* elements. So we record the positions of these entries in a separate table as shown in Figure 9.1(c). The main objective of these algorithms is to generate this switching table that helps in switching from the template space to the local compressed space. The construction of these switching tables is discussed in the following sections.

9.1 *Itable:* An Algorithm That Constructs a Table of Offsets

The main idea behind this algorithm is to construct a table of offsets, which is used to help switch from the non-compressed space to the compressed space. The algorithm exploits the repetition of accesses of both *allocated* and *accessed* elements. This algorithm first generates a two dimensional view of the set of accesses of both *allocated* and *accessed* elements for the non-compressed

Input: Layout parameters (p, k), loop limits (ℓ, h), access stride s, alignment stride
       a for array A, processor m
Output: Two_level
Method:

   1   $d_1 \leftarrow \gcd(a, pk)$
   2   $d_2 \leftarrow \gcd(a * s, pk)$
   3   $(length_a, Y_1, Y_2) \leftarrow one\_level(p, k, a, m, d_1)$
   4   $(length_{as}, X_1, X_2) \leftarrow one\_level(p, k, a * s, m, d_2)$
   5   **for** $i = 0, length_a - 1$ **do**
   6      $Itable[Y_2[i]] \leftarrow i$
   7   **enddo**
   8   $a_{cou} \leftarrow \frac{a}{d_1}$
   9   **for** $i = 0, length_{as} - 1$ **do**
  10     $Two\_Level[i] \leftarrow \left\lfloor \frac{X_1[i]}{a_{cou}} \right\rfloor * length_a + Itable[X_2[i]]$
  11   **enddo**
  12   **return** Two_level

Fig. 9.3. Algorithm that constructs the *Itable* for determining the two-level
access pattern table

---

space. This is done by the application of the one-level algorithm with input
strides being a and $a * s$ respectively. Recording the two-dimensional view of
these sets does not incur any extra overhead such as expensive division and
modular operations due to the way we generate the set of accesses using the
one-level algorithm.

Figures 9.2(a) and (b) lists the two-dimensional coordinates of both *accessed* and *allocated* elements for the first set of pattern repetition for the
example discussed previously. The second coordinates of both these sets indicate the offsets of the elements from the beginning of each course. A quick
glance clearly indicates that the *accessed* elements are a subset of *allocated*
elements. Using this information the algorithm first builds a table of offsets
called the *Itable* for the first repetition pattern of allocated elements. The
allocated access pattern repeats itself after every $\frac{a}{\gcd(a, pk)}$ courses. This table
records the order in which the offsets of *allocated* elements are accessed in
lexicographic order.

The next stage involves using this table to determine the location of the
accessed element in the compressed space. The problem now is to find two
things. Firstly we need to determine the repetition block in which the *accessed*
element is located. Secondly we need to find its position among a set of
allocated elements in that particular repetition block. Finding the repetition
block in which the element is located is straight forward, as we know the
number of courses after which the set of *allocated* elements repeat and the
length of this set. In order to find the position of the element in a list of
allocated elements in a particular repetition block we need to index into the
Itable that gives the position of the *accessed* element based on its offset from

the beginning of the course. Hence by finding the repetition block in which the element exists and the position of the element in that block we can determine the local address of the element.

A detailed listing of the algorithm is as shown in the Figure 9.3. Lines 1–4 generate the pattern tables for the case when stride is a and $a * s$. These tables record the two dimensional indices of elements accessed. Y_1 and Y_2 hold the two dimensional coordinates of the *allocated* elements while X_1 and X_2 hold the two dimensional coordinates for the *accessed* elements. Lines 5–7 construct the *Itable* that records the positions of offsets of *allocated* elements accessed in lexicographic order. The length of this table is always k. Lines 9–11 generate the two-level pattern table. For each element in the *accessed* element set, a corresponding entry in the *Itable* will help determine the location of this element in the *allocated* set.

Let us consider the example in Figure 8.1. We see that elements 0, 1, 6, 11 have offsets 0, 3, 2, 1 respectively from the beginning of the course. The two-dimensional coordinates for both *allocated* and *accessed* elements are as shown in Figures 9.2(a) and (b). Based on the entries in the Y_2 table, the *Itable* is constructed and is as shown in Figure 9.2(c). In this case the second coordinates of the *allocated* elements are same as that of the *Itable*, but in general the entries in the *Itable* depends on the value of $\gcd(a, pk)$. The *Itable* is always of size k, as there could be a maximum of k elements for each pattern of repetition. In order to construct the *Two-Level* pattern table, let us consider the third entry $(5, 1)$ from the table of *accessed elements* as shown in Figure 9.2(b). This means that the accessed element lies in course number 5 and hence falls in the second repetition block of *allocated* elements. The value 1 in the second coordinate corresponds to the offset of the *accessed* element from the beginning of the course. This serves as an index into the *Itable*. Hence the value at position 1 of the *Itable* will yield 3 as shown in Figure 9.2(c). This value gives the position of the *accessed* element in that particular repetition block. Since we know the number of elements present in a single block (which corresponds to 4 in this example), we can simply evaluate $4 * 1 + 3 = 7$, which gives us the position of the third element accessed in the compressed local space. Figure 9.2(d) shows the positions of *accessed* elements among a set of *allocated* elements for the first set of pattern repetition. Next, we discuss some improvements to the algorithm that constructs the *Itable*.

9.2 Optimization of the *Itable* Method

As can be seen from the algorithm in Figure 9.3, line 10 that computes the *Two_Level* pattern table includes expensive integer operations, an integer multiply and an integer divide. Here, we explore the possibility of reducing the number of these expensive operations in the *itable* algorithm. The key point to note is that in the expression $\left\lfloor \frac{X_1[i]}{a_{cou}} \right\rfloor * length_a$, both the quantities a_{cou} and $length_a$ are loop invariant constants. We improve the performance here by

Input: Layout parameters (p, k), loop limits (ℓ, h), access stride s, alignment
          stride a for array A, processor m
Output: Two_level

Method:

```
1    d₁ ← gcd(a, pk)
2    d₂ ← gcd(a * s, pk)
3    (lengthₐ, Y₁, Y₂) ← one_level(p, k, a, m, d₁)
4    (lengthₐₛ, X₁, X₂) ← one_level(p, k, a * s, m, d₂)
5    a_cou ← a/d₁
6    first ← X₁[0]
7    tmp₁ ← lengthₐ * first/a_cou
8    tmp₂ ← first mod a_cou
9    for i = tmp₂ to a_cou − 1 do
10       lookup_acc₁[first] ← tmp₁
11       first ← first + 1
12   enddo
13   tmp₁ ← tmp₁ + lengthₐ
14   last ← X₁[lengthₐₛ − 1]
15   while (first ≤ last) do
16       i ← 0
17       while (i < a_cou and first ≤ last) do
18           lookup_acc₁[first] ← tmp₁
19           i ← i + 1
20           first ← first + 1
21       enddo
22       tmp₁ ← tmp₁ + lengthₐ
23   enddo
24   for i = 0 to lengthₐ − 1 do
25       itable[Y₂[i]] ← i
26   enddo
27   for i = 0 to lengthₐₛ − 1 do
28       Two_Level[i] ← lookup_acc₁[X₁[i]] + itable[X₂[i]]
29   enddo
30   return Two_level
```

Fig. 9.4. Itable*, a faster algorithm to compute the *itable* for determining
the two-level access pattern by substituting integer divides with table lookups

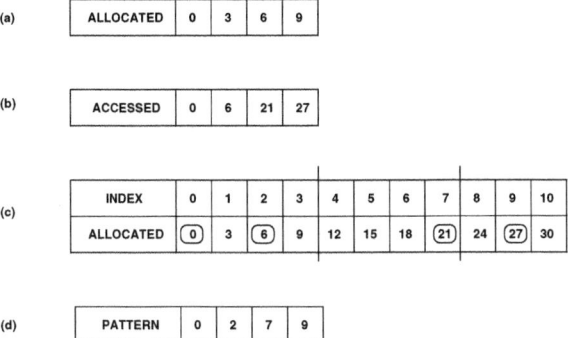

Fig. 9.5. Local addresses of *allocated* and *accessed* elements, the replicated *allocated* table, along with two-level access pattern when $a = 3$, $s = 3$, $p = 4$, $k = 4$ and $l = 0$

Input: Layout parameters (p, k), loop limits (ℓ, h), access stride s, alignment stride
  a for array A, processor m
Output: *Two_level*
Method:

```
1   d₁ ← gcd(a, pk)
2   d₂ ← gcd(as, pk)
3   (lengthₐ, patternₐ) ← one_level(p, k, a, m, d₁)
4   (lengthₐₛ, patternₐₛ) ← one_level(p, k, a * s, m, d₂)
5   Factor of replication f ← (a s k / d₂) / (a k / d₁)
6   Replicate patternₐ by factor f
7   i ← 0; j ← 0
8   while (j < lengthₐₛ) do
9       if (patternₐₛ[j] = patternₐ[i]) then
10          Two_level[j] ← i
11          j ← j + 1
12      endif
13      i ← i + 1
14  enddo
15  return Two_level
```

Fig. 9.6. Algorithm that constructs a two-level access pattern table using linear search method

using table lookups. Instead of $length_{as}$ divisions we need only one division and one mod operation; these are needed to compute just the first entry $\left\lfloor \frac{X_1[0]}{a_{cou}} \right\rfloor * length_a$ and the rest can be calculated by exploiting the properties of numbers. This optimization of the *Itable* method is shown in Figure 9.4.

9.3 Search-Based Algorithms

The key problem idea in determining the local addresses of *accessed elements*, is to find the location of *accessed* elements in a list of *allocated* elements (expanded to accommodate the largest element in the accessed set), since *accessed* elements are a subset of *allocated* elements. This can be achieved by using a naive approach of simply searching for the index of the *accessed* element in the list of *allocated* elements. In this section we propose new search methods that exploit the property that the list of elements are in sorted order.

The first step in performing these methods is to run the one-level algorithm to obtain the local addresses of the set of accesses for the first pattern of repetition for both *allocated* and *accessed* elements. These entries are in lexicographic order and are assumed to be stored in $pattern_a$ and $pattern_{as}$ tables respectively. Note that unlike other techniques we not use the memory gap table here since a significant fraction of the work involved in address generation for two-level mapping is in the recovery of the actual elements from the memory gap table [5]. These tables are as shown in Figures 9.5(a) and (b) for the example in Figure 8.1. The entries in these table correspond to the local addresses in a non-compressed template space. The table size of the former depends on $\frac{k}{\gcd(a,pk)}$, whereas that of the latter table depends on $\frac{k}{\gcd(as,pk)}$.

Here we see that not all elements in the *accessed* set are present in the *allocated* set for the first pattern of repetition. This is due to the fact that the *accessed* elements lie in different repetition blocks of the local address space. Hence we need to expand the set of *allocated* elements in order to represent all the elements in the *accessed* table, before the pattern starts repeating. The total number of elements in the first repetition block of *allocated* table in the uncompressed space is $\frac{ak}{\gcd(a,pk)}$ whereas the total number of elements for the *accessed* table is $\frac{ask}{\gcd(as,pk)}$. Hence the factor needed to expand the *allocated* elements table is $\frac{\frac{ask}{\gcd(as,pk)}}{\frac{ak}{\gcd(a,pk)}} = s\frac{\gcd(a,pk)}{\gcd(as,pk)}$. Performing the required expansion is straight forward. It involves replicating the first set of *allocated* elements as many times as the factor of replication. This is accomplished by copying elements one at a time from the first pattern of *allocated* elements to the extended memory space with a suitable increment. Another possibility is to replicate on demand.

A search now has to be performed to locate the position of an *accessed* element in this new replicated table. Figure 9.5(c) shows the replicated table after expansion for the example discussed previously. The factor for replication in this case was found to be 3. Since the length of the table that holds the addresses of the *accessed* elements is never greater than the length of the table that holds the *allocated* elements, the algorithm needs to find the locations of common elements from two tables of different size. Several search algorithms can be implemented for finding the locations of *accessed* elements. We discuss an algorithm based on linear search. Several search algorithms (with and without the need for replication of the set of elements) that differ mainly in their complexities and the speed of execution can be found elsewhere [9, 31, 42].

Linear Search The algorithm for linear search builds the two-level pattern table needed to switch from the template space to the local address space. Figure 9.6 lists the complete algorithm. Lines 1–4 discusses the build up of the *accessed* and *allocated* table. The next step is to find the factor for replication and is as shown in Line 5. This factor is used to replicate the *allocated* table. Once replication is performed, we now need to perform a simple search in order to locate the positions of each *accessed* element in the *allocated* table. Lines 8–14 shows the search algorithm. For each entry in the *accessed* table, it determines the location of this element in the replicated *allocated* set. As and when the location is determined, the position is recorded into a *Two-Level* pattern table. The entries in this table reflects the local address of the *accessed* element in the compressed space.

Figure 9.5 can be used to explain the functioning of this algorithm. Let us consider the element 21 from the *accessed* set as shown in Figure 9.5(b). The search involves finding the position of this element in the replicated set as shown in Figure 9.5(c). This element can be found at location 7. This entry is then stored in the *Two-level* pattern table. The complete pattern table for the example is as shown in Figure 9.5(d). Since the search is performed on a sorted table of length $f * len_a$ and no element of this table is accessed more than once, the complexity of the algorithm is $O(f * len_a)$. In addition to the linear search method discussed above, one could use binary search. Also, it is possible to avoid replicating the elements by generating them on demand in the course of a search [9, 31, 42].

10. Experimental Results for Two-Level Mapping

In order to compare all the above mentioned methods, we ran our experiments on a varying number of problem parameters. These experiments were done on a Sun UltraSparc 1 Workstation with Solaris 2. The compiler used was the Sun C compiler cc with the -x02 flag. Though the experiments were run for a large set of input values only a limited number of results and times are shown here. In each, case we report only the times needed to construct the two-level table, excluding the times taken construct the two one-level

Table 10.1. Table generation times (μs) for two-level mapping $p = 32$, $a = 2$

k	$s=3$				$s=5$			
	Itable*	search	norep	riacs	Itable*	search	norep	riacs
4	2	1	3	18	2	1	3	18
8	2	2	6	26	2	2	6	26
16	2	2	12	43	2	4	12	43
32	4	4	24	81	4	6	25	79
64	6	7	51	153	6	12	51	150
128	10	14	107	297	10	23	107	299
256	21	28	222	589	21	46	219	586

k	$s=7$				$s=11$			
	Itable*	search	norep	riacs	Itable*	search	norep	riacs
4	2	2	3	18	2	2	3	18
8	2	3	6	26	2	3	6	26
16	2	4	12	43	2	6	12	44
32	4	8	25	79	4	12	25	79
64	6	16	51	150	6	23	52	153
128	10	32	107	299	11	49	107	299
256	21	64	223	588	21	99	223	589

k	$s=23$				$s=99$			
	Itable*	search	norep	riacs	Itable*	search	norep	riacs
4	2	2	3	18	2	6	3	18
8	2	5	6	26	2	12	6	26
16	2	9	12	44	2	23	12	45
32	4	19	25	81	4	47	25	80
64	6	40	51	154	6	97	52	154
128	10	85	108	299	10	210	108	300
256	21	183	224	590	22	446	226	594

pattern tables as done in all the techniques discussed in this paper. We fixed the number of processors to $p = 32$ in all our experiments. For each value of alignment stride a, we varied both the block-size k and the access stride s. The optimized version of the algorithm that constructs the Itable, i.e., the version that replaces extensive divisions by table lookups (Figure 9.4) described in Section 9.2 is referred to as Itable*. The best of the search algorithms that performs replication was chosen for the results and is referred to as search in the tables. The search algorithm that does not perform replication is termed as norep in the results. The method due to Chatterjee et al. [5] is termed as riacs. Tables 10.1–11.1 show the time it takes to build the two-level pattern tables.

Table 10.2. Table generation times (μs) for two-level mapping $p = 32$, $a = 3$

k	$s=3$				$s=5$			
	*Itable**	*search*	*norep*	*riacs*	*Itable**	*search*	*norep*	*riacs*
4	2	2	6	28	2	2	6	28
8	3	3	12	44	3	4	12	43
16	4	4	24	81	4	6	24	80
32	7	8	50	152	7	12	51	150
64	11	14	107	297	10	23	104	298
128	21	28	223	588	21	46	222	591
256	42	54	463	1167	43	90	458	1171

k	$s=7$				$s=11$			
	*Itable**	*search*	*norep*	*riacs*	*Itable**	*search*	*norep*	*riacs*
4	2	3	6	28	2	3	6	26
8	3	5	12	44	3	6	12	44
16	4	8	25	79	4	12	25	80
32	7	16	51	151	7	23	51	154
64	11	32	108	298	11	50	108	300
128	21	64	221	588	22	99	223	589
256	42	128	463	1173	42	203	464	1171

k	$s=23$				$s=99$			
	*Itable**	*search*	*norep*	*riacs*	*Itable**	*search*	*norep*	*riacs*
4	2	5	6	26	2	12	6	26
8	3	9	12	44	3	23	12	44
16	4	19	25	81	4	47	25	82
32	7	40	51	152	7	98	52	151
64	11	84	109	299	11	208	108	302
128	21	179	225	591	22	447	226	595
256	44	411	463	1173	44	932	469	1181

The results indicate that the times taken by all the above mentioned methods depend on the value of k, s and a. If the access and alignment strides are small, the *Itable** and the *search* techniques are competitive; this is because the time taken for replication and the overhead in performing a search is very minimal. But as s and k increases we notice that the *search* starts performing worse. This is because as s and k start increasing the time for replication in the *search* dominates over search and renders this method inefficient. The construction of the *itable* forms the major part of time taken for two-level pattern build up. This construction is purely a function of a and k and not of s. Hence as s increases the times for *Itable** does not vary widely. The method *Itable** performs the best over a wide range of parameters.

Table 10.3. Table generation times (μs) for two-level mapping $p = 32$, $a = 5$

k	$s=3$				$s=5$			
	Itable*	search	norep	riacs	Itable*	search	norep	riacs
4	2	1	6	26	2	2	6	27
8	3	2	12	44	3	4	12	44
16	4	4	24	80	4	7	25	81
32	7	8	51	153	7	12	51	151
64	11	15	107	298	11	23	107	299
128	21	28	220	589	21	46	220	589
256	42	54	462	1169	42	90	462	1171

k	$s=7$				$s=11$			
	Itable*	search	norep	riacs	Itable*	search	norep	riacs
4	2	3	6	26	2	3	6	26
8	3	4	12	44	3	6	12	44
16	4	8	25	79	4	12	25	81
32	7	17	52	154	7	23	51	152
64	11	32	107	298	11	49	107	300
128	21	64	222	589	21	99	223	592
256	42	129	463	1174	42	203	460	1173

k	$s=23$				$s=99$			
	Itable*	search	norep	riacs	Itable*	search	norep	riacs
4	2	5	6	26	2	12	6	26
8	3	9	12	44	3	23	12	44
16	4	19	25	79	4	47	25	81
32	7	39	52	154	7	97	52	152
64	12	84	108	300	12	210	109	302
128	21	179	225	593	21	448	227	596
256	43	409	462	1176	44	932	470	1178

The method by *riacs* suffers with large block sizes due to the expensive runtime overheads. The *norep* method performs better than the *search* method as s starts increasing. This is due to the fact that we do not pay the overhead due to replication. But for large k we see that the times for search increases rendering *norep* inefficient.

11. Other Problems in Code Generation

In this section, we provide an overview of other work from our group on several problems in code generation and runtime support for data-parallel languages. These include our work on communication generation, code generation for complex subscripts, runtime data structures, support for operations on regular sections and array redistribution.

Table 11.1. Table generation times (μs) for two-level mapping $p = 32$, $a = 9$

k	$s=3$				$s=5$			
	Itable*	search	norep	riacs	Itable*	search	norep	riacs
4	2	1	6	26	2	2	6	26
8	3	2	12	45	3	4	12	45
16	4	4	24	81	4	6	24	80
32	7	8	51	150	7	12	51	153
64	11	15	107	299	11	23	106	299
128	21	28	222	587	21	46	220	591
256	42	54	461	1167	42	90	464	1167

k	$s=7$				$s=11$			
	Itable*	search	norep	riacs	Itable*	search	norep	riacs
4	2	2	6	26	2	3	6	26
8	3	5	12	44	3	6	12	44
16	4	9	25	79	4	12	25	81
32	7	17	52	153	7	23	51	151
64	11	32	105	299	11	50	108	299
128	21	64	224	592	21	98	223	594
256	42	128	462	1172	42	203	461	1173

k	$s=23$				$s=99$			
	Itable*	search	norep	riacs	Itable*	search	norep	riacs
4	2	5	6	26	2	12	6	26
8	3	9	12	45	3	24	12	44
16	4	19	25	80	4	47	25	82
32	7	40	52	154	7	99	52	152
64	11	87	108	300	11	209	108	303
128	21	183	224	592	22	449	222	598
256	42	408	463	1181	43	928	468	1185

11.1 Communication Generation

In addition to problems in address generation, we have explored techniques
for communication generation and optimization [40, 42–44]. A compiler for
languages such as HPF that generates node code (for each processor) has also
to compute the sequence of sends and receives for a given processor to access non-local data. While the address generation problem has received much
attention, issues in communication generation have received limited attention; see [15] and [18] for examples. A novel approach for the management
of communication sets and strategies for local storage of remote references
is presented in [42, 43]. In addition to algorithms for deriving communication patterns [40, 42, 44], two schemes that extend the notion of a local array
by providing storage for non-local elements (called overlap regions) interspersed throughout the storage for the local portion are presented [42, 43].

The two schemes, namely course padding and column padding enhance locality of reference significantly at the cost of a small overhead due to unpacking
of messages. The performance of these schemes are compared to the traditional buffer-based approach and improvements of up to 30% in total time are
demonstrated. Several message optimizations such as offset communication,
message aggregation and coalescing are also discussed.

11.2 Union and Difference of Regular Sections

Operations on regular sections are very common in code generation. The
intersection operation on regular sections is easy (since regular sections are
closed under intersection). Union and difference of regular sections are needed
for efficient generation of communications sets; unfortunately, regular sections
are not closed under union and difference operations. We [9, 27] present an
efficient runtime technique for supporting support for union and other operations on regular sections. These deal with both the generation of the pattern
under these operations as well as with the efficient code that enumerates the
resulting sets using the patterns.

11.3 Code Generation for Complex Subscripts

The techniques presented in this chapter assumed simple subscript functions.
Array references with arbitrary affine subscripts can make the task of compilers for such languages highly involved. Work from our group [9, 26, 29, 30, 42]
deals with the efficient address generation in programs with array references
having two types of commonly encountered affine references, namely coupled
subscripts and subscripts containing multiple induction variables (MIVs).
These methods utilize the repetitive pattern of the memory accesses. In the
case of MIV, we address this issue by presenting runtime techniques which
enumerate the set of addresses in lexicographic order. Our approach to the
problem incorporates a general approach of computing in $O(k)$ time, the
start element on a processor for a given global start element. Several methods are proposed and evaluated here for generating the access sequences for
MIV based on problem parameters. With coupled subscripts, we present two
construction techniques, namely searching and hashing which minimize the
time needed to construct the tables. Extensive experiments were conducted
and the results were then compared with other approaches to demonstrate
the efficiency of our approach.

11.4 Data Structures for Runtime Efficiency

In addition to algorithms for address sequence generation, we addressed the
problem of how best to use the address sequences in [8, 9]. Efficient techniques
for generating node code on distributed-memory machines is important. For

array sections, node code generation must exploit the repetitive access pattern exhibited by the accesses to distributed arrays. Several techniques for the efficient enumeration of the access pattern already exist. But only one paper [17] so far addresses the effect of the data structures used in representing the access sequence on the execution time. In [8, 9], we present several new data structures along with node code that is suitable for both DO loops and FORALL constructs. The methods, namely *strip-mining* and *table compression* facilitate the generation of time-efficient code for execution on each processor. While strip-mining views the problem as a double nested loop, table compression proves to be a worthwhile data structure for faster execution. The underlying theory behind the data structures introduced is explained and their effects on all possible set of problem parameters is observed. Extensive experimental results show the efficacy of our approach. The results compare very favorably with the results of the earlier methods proposed by Kennedy et al. [16] and Chatterjee et al. [5].

11.5 Array Redistribution

Array redistribution is used in languages such as High Performance Fortran to dynamically change the distribution of arrays across processors. Performing array redistribution incurs two overheads: (1) an *indexing overhead* for determining the set of processors to communicate with and the array elements to be communicated, and (2) a *communication overhead* for performing the necessary irregular all-to-many personalized communication. We have presented efficient runtime methods for performing array redistribution [14, 35]. In order to reduce the indexing overhead, precise closed forms for enumerating the processors to communicate with and the array elements to be communicated are developed for two special cases of array redistribution involving block-cyclically distributed arrays. The general array redistribution problem for block-cyclically distributed arrays can be expressed in terms of these special cases. Using the developed closed forms, a distributed algorithm for scheduling the irregular communication for redistribution is developed. The generated schedule eliminates node contention and incurs the least communication overhead. The scheduling algorithm has an asymptotically lower scheduling overhead than techniques presented in the literature. Following this, we have developed efficient table-based runtime techniques (based on integer lattices) that incur negligible cost [9, 28].

12. Summary and Conclusions

The success of data parallel languages such as High Performance Fortran and Fortran D critically depends on efficient compiler and runtime support. In this chapter we presented efficient compiler algorithms for generating local memory access patterns for the various processors (node code) given the alignment of arrays to a template and a `CYCLIC(k)` distribution of the template onto the processors. Our solution to the one-level mapping problem is based on viewing the access sequence as an integer lattice, and involves the derivation of a suitable set of basis vectors for the lattice. The basis vector determination algorithm is $O(\log \min(s, pk) + \min(s, k))$ and requires finding $\min(s + 1, k)$ points in the lattice. Kennedy et al.'s algorithm for basis determination is $O(\log \min(s, pk) + k)$ and requires finding $2k - 1$ points in the lattice. Our loop nest based technique used for address enumeration chooses the best strategy as a function of the basis vectors, unlike [16]. Experimental results comparing the times for our basis determination technique and that of Kennedy et al. shows that our solution is 2 to 9 times faster for large block sizes. For the two-level mapping problem, we presented three new algorithms. Experimental comparisons with other techniques show that our solutions to the two-level mapping problem are significantly faster. In addition to these algorithms, we provided an overview of other work from our group on several problems such as

- efficient basis vector generation using an $O(\log \min(s, pk))$ algorithm [25];
- communication generation [40, 42–44];
- code generation for complex subscripts [9, 26, 29, 30, 42];
- effect of data structures for table lookup at runtime [8, 9];
- runtime array redistribution [9, 14, 28, 35]; (and)
- efficient support for union and other operations on regular sections [9, 27].

Work is in progress on the problem of code generation and optimization for general affine access functions in whole programs.

Acknowledgments

This work was supported in part by an NSF Young Investigator Award CCR–9457768 with matching funds from the Portland Group Inc. and the Halliburton Foundation, by an NSF grant CCR–9210422, and by the Louisiana Board of Regents through contracts LEQSF(RF/1995-96) ENH-TR-60 and LEQSF (1991-94)-RD-A-09. I thank Ashwath Thirumalai, Arun Venkatachar, and Swaroop Dutta for their valuable collaboration. I thank Nenad Nedeljkovic, James Stichnoth and Ajay Sethi for their comments on an earlier draft of this chapter. Nenad Nedeljkovic and Ajay Sethi provided the code for the two Rice algorithms and the Sort implementation, and S. Chatterjee provided the code for the RIACS implementation used in experiments on two-level mapping.

References

1. A. Ancourt, F. Coelho, F. Irigoin, and R. Keryell. A linear algebra framework for static HPF code distribution. *Scientific Programming,* 6(1):3–28, Spring 1997.

2. P. Banerjee, J. Chandy, M. Gupta, E. Hodges, J. Holm, A. Lain, D. Palermo, S. Ramaswamy, and E. Su. The PARADIGM compiler for distributed-memory multicomputers. *IEEE Computer,* 28(10):37–47, October 1995.

3. S. Benkner. Handling block-cyclic distributed arrays in Vienna Fortran 90. In *Proc. International Conference on Parallel Architectures and Compilation Techniques,* Limassol, Cyprus, June 1995.

4. B. Chapman, P. Mehrotra, and H. Zima. Programming in Vienna Fortran. *Scientific Programming,* 1(1):31–50, Fall 1992.

5. S. Chatterjee, J. Gilbert, F. Long, R. Schreiber, and S. Teng. Generating local addresses and communication sets for data parallel programs. *Journal of Parallel and Distributed Computing,* 26(1):72–84, 1995.

6. F. Coelho, C. Germain, J. Pazat. State of the art in compiling HPF. *The Data Parallel Programming Model,* G. Perrin and A. Darte (Eds.), Lecture Notes in Computer Science, Volume 1132, pages 104–133, 1996.

7. G. Dantzig and B. Eaves. Fourier-Motzkin elimination and its dual. *Journal of Combinatorial Theory (A),* 14:288–297, 1973.

8. S. Dutta and J. Ramanujam. Data structures for efficient execution of programs with block-cyclic distributions. Technical Report TR-96-11-01, Dept. of Elec. & Comp. Engineering, Louisiana State University, Jan. 1997. Preliminary version presented at the *6th Workshop on Compilers for Parallel Computers,* Aachen, Germany, December 1996.

9. S. Dutta. Compilation and run-time techniques for data-parallel programs. M.S. Thesis, Department of Electrical and Computer Engineering, Louisiana State University, *in preparation.*

10. G. Fox, S. Hiranandani, K. Kennedy, C. Koelbel, U. Kremer, C. Tseng, and M. Wu. Fortran D language specification. Technical Report CRPC-TR90079, Center for Research on Parallel Computation, Rice University, December 1990.

11. P. Gruber and C. Lekkerkerker. *Geometry of numbers.* North-Holland Mathematical Library Volume 37, North-Holland, Amsterdam, 1987.

12. S. Gupta, S. Kaushik, C. Huang, and P. Sadayappan. On compiling array expressions for efficient execution on distributed-memory machines. *Journal of Parallel and Distributed Computing,* 32(2):155–172, February 1996.

13. High Performance Fortran Forum. High Performance Fortran language specification. *Scientific Programming,* 2(1-2):1–170, 1993.

14. S. Kaushik, C. Huang, J. Ramanujam, and P. Sadayappan. Multiphase array redistribution: Modeling and Evaluation. Technical Report OSU-CISRC-9/94-TR52, Department of Computer and Information Science, The Ohio State University, September 1994. A short version appears in *Proc. 9th International Parallel Processing Symposium,* Santa Barbara, CA, pages 441–445, April 1995.

15. S. Kaushik. Compile-time and run-time strategies for array statement execution on distributed-memory machines. Ph.D. Thesis, Department of Computer and Information Science, The Ohio State University, 1995.

16. K. Kennedy, N. Nedeljkovic, and A. Sethi. A linear-time algorithm for computing the memory access sequence in data-parallel programs. In *Proc. of*

Fifth ACM SIGPLAN Symposium on Principles and Practice of Parallel Programming, Santa Barbara, CA, pages 102–111, July 1995.

17. K. Kennedy, N. Nedeljkovic, and A. Sethi. Efficient address generation for block-cyclic distributions. In *Proc. ACM International Conference on Supercomputing*, Madrid, Spain, pages 180–184, July 1995.

18. K. Kennedy, N. Nedeljkovic, and A. Sethi. Communication generation for CYCLIC(*k*) distributions. In *Languages, Compilers, and Run-Time Systems for Scalable Computers*, B. Szymanski and B. Sinharoy (Eds.), Kluwer Academic Publishers, 1996.

19. C. Koelbel. Compile-time generation of communication for scientific programs. In *Proc. Supercomputing '91*, Albuquerque, NM, pages 101–110, November 1991.

20. C. Koelbel, D. Loveman, R. Schreiber, G. Steele, and M. Zosel. *High Performance Fortran handbook.* The MIT Press, 1994.

21. T. MacDonald, D. Pase, and A. Meltzer. Addressing in Cray Research's MPP Fortran. In *Proceedings of the 3rd Workshop on Compilers for Parallel Computers*, Vienna, Austria, pages 161–172, July 1992.

22. S. Midkiff. Local iteration set computation for block-cyclic distributions. In *Proc. International Conference on Parallel Processing*. Vol. II, pages 77–84, August 1995.

23. J. Ramanujam. Non-unimodular transformations of nested loops. In *Proc. Supercomputing 92*, Minneapolis, MN, pages 214–223, November 1992.

24. J. Ramanujam. Beyond unimodular transformations. *The Journal of Supercomputing*, 9(4):365-389, December 1995.

25. J. Ramanujam. Efficient computation of basis vectors of the address sequence lattice. Submitted for publication, 1997.

26. J. Ramanujam and S. Dutta. Code generation for coupled subscripts with block-cyclic distributions. Technical Report TR-96-07-01, Dept. of Elec. & Comp. Engineering, Louisiana State University, July 1996.

27. J. Ramanujam and S. Dutta. Runtime solutions to operations on regular sections. Technical Report TR-96-12-03, Dept. of Elec. & Comp. Engineering, Louisiana State University, December 1996.

28. J. Ramanujam and S. Dutta. Efficient runtime array redistribution. Technical Report TR-97-01-01, Dept. of Elec. & Comp. Engineering, Louisiana State University, January 1997.

29. J. Ramanujam, S. Dutta, and A. Venkatachar. Code generation for complex subscripts in data-parallel programs. To appear in *Proc. 10th Workshop on Languages and Compilers for Parallel Computing*, Z. Li et al., (Eds.), Minneapolis, MN, Springer-Verlag, 1997.

30. J. Ramanujam and A. Venkatachar. Code generation for complex subscripts with multiple induction variables in the presence of block-cyclic distributions. Technical Report TR-96-03-01, Dept. of Elec. & Comp. Engineering, Louisiana State University, March 1996.

31. J. Ramanujam, A. Venkatachar, and S. Dutta. Efficient address sequence generation for two-level mappings in High Performance Fortran. Submitted for publication, 1997.

32. C. van Reeuwijk, H. Sips, W. Denissen, and E. Paalvast. An implementation framework for HPF distributed arrays on message-passing parallel computer systems. *IEEE Transactions on Parallel and Distributed Systems,* 7(9):897–914, September 1996.

33. J. Stichnoth. Efficient compilation of array statements for private memory multicomputers. Technical Report CMU-CS-93-109, School of Computer Science, Carnegie Mellon University, February 1993.

34. J. Stichnoth, D. O'Hallaron, and T. Gross. Generating communication for array statements: Design, implementation, and evaluation. *Journal of Parallel and Distributed Computing,* 21(1):150–159, April 1994.
35. R. Thakur, A. Choudhary and J. Ramanujam. Efficient algorithms for array redistribution. *IEEE Transactions on Parallel and Distributed Systems,* 7(6):587–594, June 1996.
36. A. Thirumalai. Code generation and optimization for High Performance Fortran. M.S. Thesis, Department of Electrical and Computer Engineering, Louisiana State University, August 1995.
37. A. Thirumalai and J. Ramanujam. Code generation and optimization for array statements in HPF. Technical Report TR-94-11-02, Dept. of Electrical and Computer Engineering, Louisiana State University, November 1994; revised August 1995
38. A. Thirumalai and J. Ramanujam. An efficient compile-time approach to compute address sequences in data parallel programs. In *Proc. 5th International Workshop on Compilers for Parallel Computers,* Malaga, Spain, pages 581–605, June 1995.
39. A. Thirumalai and J. Ramanujam. Fast address sequence generation for data-parallel programs using integer lattices. In *Languages and Compilers for Parallel Computing,* C.-H. Huang et al. (Editors), Lecture Notes in Computer Science, Vol. 1033, pages 191–208, Springer-Verlag, 1996.
40. A. Thirumalai, J. Ramanujam, and A. Venkatachar. Communication generation and optimization for HPF. In *Languages, Compilers, and Run-Time Systems for Scalable Computers,* B. Szymanski and B. Sinharoy (Eds.), Kluwer Academic Publishers, 1996.
41. A. Thirumalai and J. Ramanujam. Efficient computation of address sequences in data-parallel programs using closed forms for basis vectors. *Journal of Parallel and Distributed Computing,* 38(2):188–203, November 1996.
42. A. Venkatachar. Efficient address and communication generation for data-parallel programs. M.S. Thesis, Department of Electrical and Computer Engineering, Louisiana State University, December 1996.
43. A. Venkatachar, J. Ramanujam and A. Thirumalai. Generalized overlap regions for communication optimization in data parallel programs. In *Languages and Compilers for Parallel Computing,* D. Sehr et al. (Editors), Lecture Notes in Computer Science, Vol. 1239, pages 404–419, Springer-Verlag, 1997.
44. A. Venkatachar, J. Ramanujam, and A. Thirumalai. Communication generation for block-cyclic distributions. *Parallel Processing Letters,* (to appear) 1997.
45. L. Wang, J. Stichnoth, and S. Chatterjee. Runtime performance of parallel array assignment: An empirical study. In *Proc. Supercomputing 96,* Pittsburgh, PA, November 1996.
46. H. Wijshoff. *Data organization in parallel computers.* Kluwer Academic Publishers, 1989.

Section V : Task Parallelism, Dynamic Data Structures and Run Time Systems

Chapter 18. A Duplication Based Compile Time Scheduling Method for Task Parallelism

Sekhar Darbha[1] and Dharma P. Agrawal[2]

[1] ECE Department, Rutgers University, Piscataway, NJ 08855-0909.
[2] ECECS Department, POBox 210030, University of Cincinnati, Cincinnati, OH 45221-0030.

Summary. The cost of inter-processor communication is one of the major bottlenecks of a distributed memory machine (DMM) which can be offset with efficient algorithms for task partitioning and scheduling. Based on the data dependencies, the task partitioning algorithm partitions the application program into tasks and represents them in the form of a directed acyclic graph (DAG) or in compiler intermediate forms. The scheduling algorithm schedules the tasks onto individual processors of the DMM in an effort to lower the overall parallel time. It has been long proven that obtaining an optimal schedule for a generic DAG is an NP-hard problem. This chapter presents a Scalable Task Duplication based Scheduling (STDS) algorithm which can schedule the tasks of a DAG with a worst case complexity of $O(|v|^2)$, where v is the set of tasks of the DAG. STDS algorithm generates an optimal schedule for a certain class of DAGs which satisfy a Cost Relationship Condition (CRC), provided the required number of processors are available. In case the required number of processors are not available the algorithm scales the schedule down to the available number of processors. The performance of the scheduling algorithm has been evaluated by its application to practical DAGs and by comparing the parallel time of the schedule generated against the absolute or the theoretical lowerbound.

1. Introduction

Recently there has been an increase in the use of the distributed memory machines (DMMs) due to the advances in the VLSI technology, inter-processor communication networks and routing algorithms. The scalability of DMMs gives them a major advantage over other types of systems. Some of the applications which use DMMs are fluid flow, weather modeling, database systems, image processing etc. The data for these applications can be distributed evenly onto the processors of the DMM and with fast access of local data, high speed-ups can be obtained.

To obtain maximum benefits from DMMs, an efficient task partitioning and scheduling strategy is essential. A task partitioning algorithm partitions an application into tasks and represents it in the form of a directed acyclic graph (DAG). Once the application is transformed to a DAG, the tasks are scheduled onto the processors. This chapter introduces a compile time (static) scheduling technique with the assumption that a partitioning algorithm is available which transforms the application program to a DAG.

Generating an optimal schedule for assigning tasks of a DAG onto DMMs has been proven to be an NP-Complete [5, 18] problem. There are very few

S. Pande, D.P. Agrawal (Eds.): Compiler Optimizations for Scalable PS, LNCS 1808, pp. 649-682, 2001.
© Springer-Verlag Berlin Heidelberg 2001

special cases where the optimal schedule can be generated in polynomial [24] time bound. The cases for which optimal schedule can be obtained in polynomial time are: (i) when unit execution time tasks represented in the form of a tree are scheduled onto arbitrary number of processors, or (ii) when unit execution time tasks represented by arbitrary task graph are scheduled onto two processor architecture. Any relaxation in the above two cases changes the complexity of the algorithm to NP-Complete.

The sub-optimal solutions to the static scheduling problem can be obtained by heuristic methods which are based on certain assumptions that allow the algorithm to be executed in polynomial time bound. Even though the heuristics do not guarantee an optimal solution, they have been shown to perform reasonably well for many applications.

The first set of algorithms are priority based algorithms. In these algorithms, each task of the DAG is assigned a priority and whenever a processor is available, the task with the highest priority among all the tasks which are ready to execute, is assigned to the free processor. A simple priority based algorithm is to assign a value of *level* (or *co-level*) to each node of the DAG [1] and assign a higher priority to the task which has higher *level* (or lower *co-level*). The *level* of any node is the length of the longest path from the node to an exit node and the *co-level* of any node is the length of the longest path from the node to an entry node. An entry node is a node which is not dependent on data generated by other tasks, i.e. the number of incoming edges at an entry node is zero and an exit node is a node which does not communicate its data to other nodes, i.e. the outgoing number of edges at an exit node is equal to zero. When computing the *level* and *co-level*, the communication costs are ignored and only the computation costs are taken into account.

The priority based algorithms are simple to implement. But the problem is that most of these schemes do not take inter-processor communication (IPC) time into account. Even those algorithms which take IPC costs into account, suffer from the fact that they try to balance the workload rather than trying to minimize the overall schedule length. Recently, many researchers have proposed algorithms which have evolved from the priority based schemes [15,19,25,27,31,32]. These heuristics do attempt to provide reasonable results, while optimal solution is not guaranteed.

There are many scheduling algorithms which are based on clustering schemes [15,16,21,22,28–30,33]. These algorithms try to cluster tasks which communicate heavily onto the same processor. A description and comparison of some of these algorithms is given in [16]. Even clustering schemes do not guarantee optimal execution time. Also, if the number of processors available is less than the number of clusters, there could be a problem.

There are several task duplication based scheduling algorithms. Duplication Scheduling Heuristic (DSH) [24] has a very impractical time complexity of $O(|v|^4)$, where $|v|$ is the number of nodes of the DAG. Search and Duplication Based Scheduling (SDBS) algorithm [9] gives an optimal solution with complexity of $O(|v|^2)$ if certain conditions are satisfied and if adequate number of processors is available. The problem with SDBS algorithm is that it duplicates tasks unnecessarily and requires a large number of processors. Other algorithms using task duplication have been proposed in [2, 6, 7, 26].

Critical path method and task duplication based scheduling algorithm has been proposed in [8] and is dependent on a very restrictive condition. They stipulate that for every join node (defined as a node having more than one incoming edge), the maximum value of the communication costs of the incoming edges should be less than or equal to the minimum value of the computation costs of the predecessor tasks. For example for the join node i shown in Figure 1.1, the computation cost of task a (which happens to be the predecessor task of task d with the lowest computation cost) is the bottleneck for communication costs. The cost of all the edges which are incident on node d should be less than or equal to 3. This condition cannot be satisfied by the join node of Figure 1.1. The condition introduced in this chapter is more flexible and does not let a lower computation cost task to become the bottleneck for the edge costs.

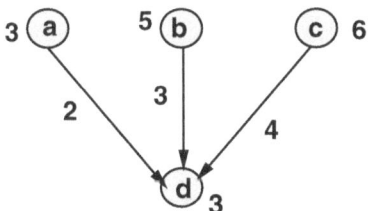

Fig. 1.1. Join Node

The basic strategy involved in most of the scheduling schemes is to group the tasks into clusters and assume that the available number of processors is greater than or equal to the number of clusters generated by the algorithm. A major limitation with most of these algorithms is that they do not provide an allocation which can be scaled down to the available number of processors in a gradual manner, if the available number of processors is less than the required number of processors for the initial clusters. Also, in case the available number of processors is higher than the initially required number of processors, the unused or the idle processors must be utilized to obtain a lower parallel time. In a DMM, once the resources have been assigned to a user, they remain under the user's control until the program completes its execution. If some assigned resources are not used by a user, they remain unutilized. Thus, execution of duplicated tasks on unused processors would not pose any overhead in terms of resource requirements.

This chapter introduces a Scalable Task Duplication based Scheduling (STDS) algorithm [10–12, 14] which is scalable in terms of the number of processors. The primary motivation of this work is to introduce an algorithm which generates an optimal schedule for at least a certain class of DAGs. As mentioned earlier, the problem of obtaining optimal schedule for a generic DAG has been proven to be NP-Complete. The scheduling problem can be simplified by developing a suite of algorithms, each of which can generate an optimal schedule for a subset of DAGs. The STDS algorithm is the first algorithm of this set of algorithms and can generate an optimal schedule if the DAG satisfies the Cost Relationship Condition (CRC) (described in section 2). The concept of duplicating critical tasks is used in this algorithm which helps in getting a better schedule.

The rest of the chapter is organized as follows. Section 2 gives a brief overview of the scheduling algorithm. The running trace of STDS algorithm on an example DAG is illustrated in section 3. The results obtained by the STDS algorithm are reported in section 4. Finally section 5 provides the conclusions.

2. STDS Algorithm

It is assumed that the task graph represented in the form of a DAG is available as an input to the scheduling algorithm. The DAG is defined by the tuple (v, e, τ, c), where v is the set of task nodes, e is the set of edges. The set τ consists of computation costs and each task $i \in v$ has a computation cost represented by $\tau(i)$. Similarly, c is the set of communication costs and each edge from task i to task j, $e_{i,j} \in e$ has a cost $c_{i,j}$ associated with it. In case two communicating tasks are assigned to the same processor, the communication cost between them is assumed to be zero. Without loss of generality, it can be assumed that there is one entry node and one exit node. If there are multiple entry or exit nodes, then the multiple nodes can always be connected through a dummy node which has zero computation cost and zero communication cost edges.

A task is an indivisible unit of work and is non-preemptive. The underlying target architecture is assumed to be homogeneous, connected and the communication costs between a pair of two processors for a fixed length of message is the same. It is assumed that an I/O co-processor is available and thus computation and communications can be performed simultaneously.

The STDS algorithm generates the schedule based on certain parameters and the mathematical expressions to evaluate these parameters are provided below:

$$pred(i) = \{ \ j \ | \ e_{j,i} \ \in \ e\} \tag{2.1}$$

$$succ(i) = \{ \ j \ | \ e_{i,j} \ \in \ e\} \tag{2.2}$$

$$est(i) = 0, \ \ if \ pred(i) = \phi \tag{2.3}$$

$$est(i) = \min_{j \in pred(i)} \ \max_{k \in pred(i), k \neq j} (ect(j), ect(k) + c_{k,i}) \ \ if \ pred(i) \neq \phi \tag{2.4}$$

$$ect(i) = est(i) + \tau(i) \tag{2.5}$$

$$fpred(i) = j|(ect(j) + c_{j,i}) \geq (ect(k) + c_{k,i}), \forall j \in pred(i); k \in pred(i), \ k \neq j \tag{2.6}$$

$$lact(i) = ect(i) \ if \ succ(i) = \phi \tag{2.7}$$

$$lact(i) = \min \left(\min_{j \in succ(i), i \neq fpred(j)} (last(j) - c_{i,j}), \min_{j \in succ(i), i = fpred(j)} (last(j)) \right) \tag{2.8}$$

$$last(i) = lact(i) - \tau(i) \tag{2.9}$$

$$level(i) = \tau(i) \ if \ succ(i) = \phi \tag{2.10}$$

$$level(i) = \max_{k \in succ(i)} (level(k)) + \tau(i) \ if \ succ(i) \neq \phi \tag{2.11}$$

The computation of the earliest start time (est) and earliest completion time (ect) follows in a top down fashion starting with the entry node and terminating at the exit node. The latest allowable start time ($last$) and latest allowable completion time ($lact$) are computed in a bottom-up fashion in which the process starts from the exit node and terminates at the entry node. For each task i, a favorite predecessor $fpred(i)$ is assigned using Eq. 2.6, which implies that a lower parallel time can be obtained by assigning a task and its favorite predecessor on the same processor. The STDS algorithm assigns a value of $level(i)$ to each node i which is the length of the longest path from node i to an exit node.

This algorithm will yield optimal results if the CRC given below is satisfied by all the join nodes of the DAG. The CRC guarantees optimality and is not a prerequisite for the algorithm to execute. The CRC needs to be true only for join nodes. A join node is a node of the DAG where the number of predecessor tasks is greater than one. The CRC for join node i is:

Cost-Relationship Condition: Let m and n be the predecessor tasks of task i that have the highest and second highest values of $\{(ect(j) + c_{j,i})| j \in pred(i)\}$ respectively. Then one of the following must be satisfied.
 – $\tau(m) \geq c_{n,i}$ if $est(m) \geq est(n)$ or,
 – $\tau(m) \geq (c_{n,i} + est(n) - est(m))$ if $est(m) < est(n)$

The STDS algorithm assigns independent tasks to different processors if adequate processors are available. If a join node satisfies the condition, it implies that optimal schedule for a join node is obtained if only one predecessor task of the join node is allocated to the same processor as the join node. If the schedule time can be lowered by allocating multiple predecessors of the join node to the same processor as the join node, then this condition cannot be satisfied.

The CRC stipulates that the DAG be of coarse granularity. The condition is satisfied if the granularity of the DAG as defined in [17] is greater than or equal to 1.0. The computation and communication costs can cause the granularity of the DAG to be less than 1.0 and still satisfy the condition. Some example DAGs which have low granularity and which satisfy the condition are considered in section 4.

The pseudocode in Figure 2.1 gives an overview of the steps involved in this algorithm. The first two steps of the algorithm compute the *est, ect, fpred, last, lact* and *level* for all the nodes of the DAG. The code for steps 1 and 2 is shown in Figure 2.2. The latest allowable start and completion times can be used to evaluate how critical a set of two directly connected tasks are to each other. For example, if task j is successor of task i and if the condition $(last[j] - lact[i]) \geq c_{i,j}$ is satisfied, then it indicates that task i is not critical for the execution of task j, and it is not necessary to execute both i and j on the same processor to yield the lowest possible schedule time. For

---

Input:
    Tasks (Nodes) 1....N
    Edges 1.......M
    Task Computation Costs: $\tau(i)$......$\tau(N)$
    Edge Communication Costs: $c_{i,j}$
    Available number of processors in the system: AP
Output: A Schedule which can run on the available number of processors.
    Begin:
    1. Compute $est(i)$, $ect(i)$, $fpred(i)$ for all nodes $i\epsilon v$.
    2. Compute $last(i)$, $lact(i)$, $level(i)$ for all nodes $i\epsilon v$.
    3. Assign tasks to processors in linear cluster fashion and number of clusters generated = RP. (Refer to Figure 2.5)
    4. If $AP > RP$, scale up the schedule to obtain better parallel time else if $AP < RP$, reduce the number of processors. (Refer to Figure 2.7)

Fig. 2.1. Overall Code for the STDS Algorithm

---

example, Figure 2.3 shows an example DAG and its corresponding schedule (as generated by STDS algorithm). The *est, ect, last, lact, level* and *fpred* for this example DAG are shown in Table 2.1.

In this DAG tasks 2 and 3 are predecessors of task 5. Since $ect(3) + c_{3,5}$ is greater than $ect(2) + c_{2,5}$, task 3 is the favorite predecessor for task 5. Ideally, tasks 3 and 5 should be assigned to the same processor to obtain a lower completion time for task 5. When the *last* and *lact* are computed in the second step, it is observed that task 5 can be delayed by 3 time units without altering the overall schedule time. Thus, it is not necessary to assign tasks 3 and 5 to the same processor. Without the knowledge of the latest start times and the latest completion times, task 3 would have been duplicated onto the

Input: DAG(v, e, τ, c)
    $pred(i)$: Set of predecessor tasks for task i.
    $succ(i)$: Set of successor tasks for task i.
Output: For each task $i \in v$.
    Earliest Start Time $est(i)$
    Earliest Completion Time $ect(i)$
    Latest Allowable Start Time $last(i)$
    Latest Allowable Completion Time $lact(i)$
    Favorite Predecessor $fpred(i)$
    Level $level(i)$
Begin:
1. Compute $est(i)$, $ect(i)$ and $fpred(i)$ for all nodes $i \in v$.
  a) For any task i if $pred(i) = \phi$, then $est(i) = 0$.
  b) Let $T = max\{ect(j) + c_{j,i} | j \in pred(i)\}$ be obtained by node k. Then,
     $est(i) = max\{\{(ect(j) + c_{j,i}) | j \in pred(i), j \neq k\}, ect(k)\}$
  c) $fpred(i) = k$
  d) $ect(i) = est(i) + \tau(i)$
2. Compute $last(i)$ and $lact(i)$ for all nodes $i \in v$.
  a) For any task i if $succ(i) = \phi$, then $lact(i) = ect(i)$ and $level(i) = \tau(i)$.
  b) For $j \in succ(i)$.
    i. If i is $fpred(j)$ then $temp(j) = last(j)$. else $temp(j) = last(j) - c_{i,j}$
    ii. $lact(i) = minimum\{temp(j) | j \in succ(i)\}$.
    iii. $last(i) = lact(i) - \tau(i)$.
    iv. $level(i) = maximum\{level(j) | j \in succ(i)\} + \tau(i)$.

Fig. 2.2. Code for Steps 1 and 2 of the STDS Algorithm

Table 2.1. Start and Completion Times for Example DAG

Node	est	ect	fpred	last	lact	level
1	0	5	-	0	5	26
2	5	8	1	8	11	12
3	5	12	1	5	12	21
4	5	9	1	5	9	18
5	12	17	3	15	20	9
6	12	22	3	12	22	14
7	22	26	6	22	26	4

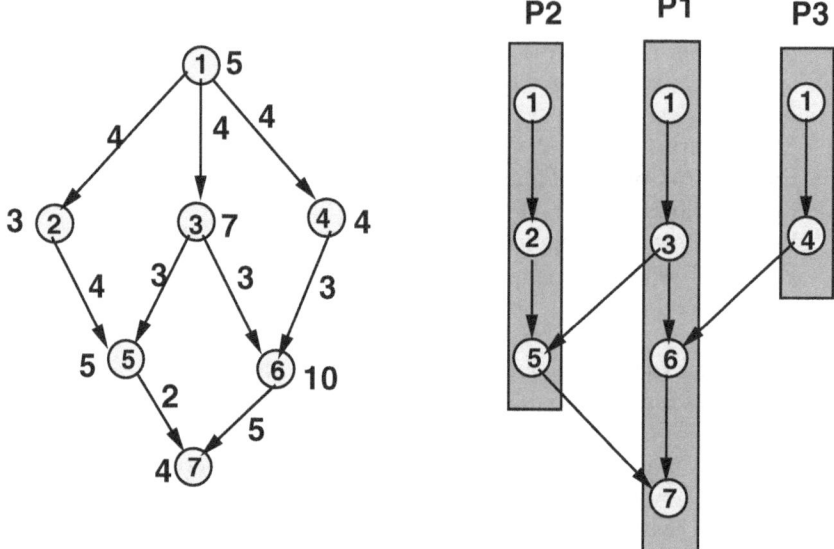

Fig. 2.3. Example DAG and its Schedule

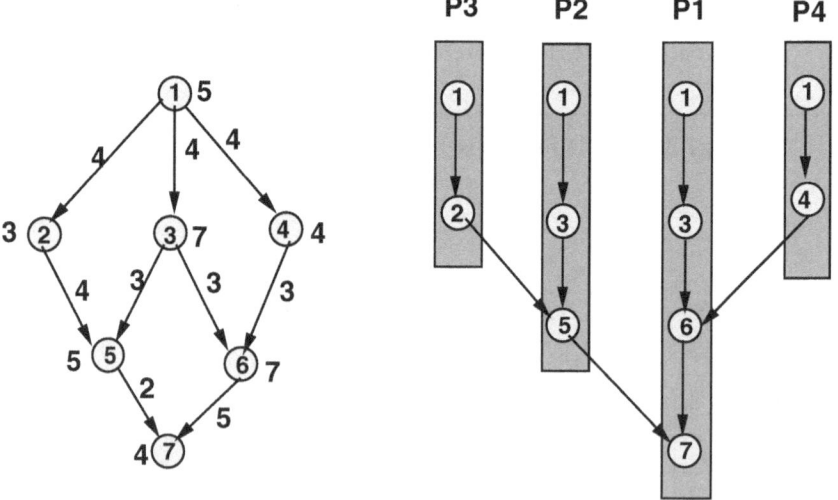

Fig. 2.4. Example DAG and its Schedule

two processors and the algorithm would have required four processors instead of three.

On the contrary, if $\tau(6)$ is modified from 10 to 7 (as shown in Figure 2.4), the algorithm will generate the schedule shown in Figure 2.4. For this modified DAG, the start and completion times would be obtained as shown in Table 2.2. In this case, the start times of none of the tasks can be delayed and four processors are required to obtain a lower schedule time.

Table 2.2. Start and Completion Times for Example DAG

Node	est	ect	fpred	last	lact	level
1	0	5	-	0	5	23
2	5	8	1	5	8	12
3	5	12	1	5	12	18
4	5	9	1	5	9	15
5	12	17	3	12	17	9
6	12	19	3	12	19	11
7	19	23	6	19	23	4

Step three, shown in Figure 2.5, generates the initial tasks clusters and is based on the parameters computed in steps one and two and on the array *queue*. The elements in the array *queue* are the nodes of the task graph sorted in smallest *level* first order. Each cluster is intended to be assigned to a different processor and the generation of a cluster is initiated from the first task in the array *queue* which has not yet been assigned to a processor. The generation of the cluster is completed by performing a search similar to the depth first search starting from the initial task. The search is performed by tracing the path from the initial task selected from *queue* to the entry node by following the favorite predecessors along the way. If the favorite predecessor is unassigned, i.e. not yet assigned to a processor, then it is selected. In case the favorite predecessor has already been assigned to another processor, it is still duplicated if there are no other predecessors of the current task or if all the other predecessors of the current task have been assigned to another processor. For example, in the DAG shown in Figure 2.6, task 5 is the only predecessor of tasks 6, 7 and 8 and thus task 5 is duplicated on all the three processors. In case the favorite predecessor is already assigned to another processor and there are other predecessors of the current task which have not yet been assigned to a processor, then the other predecessors which have not been assigned to a processor are examined to determine if they could initially have been the favorite predecessor. This could have happened, if for another task k $(k \in pred(i))$, $(ect(k) + c_{k,i}) = (ect(j) + c_{j,i})$, where i is the current task and j is its favorite predecessor. If there exists such a task k, the path to the entry node is traced by traversing through the task k. If none of the other predecessors could initially have been the favorite predecessor, then

Input: $DAG(v, e, \tau, c_{i,j})$

$queue$: Set of all tasks stored in ascending order of $level$.

Output: Task Clusters
Begin

```
RP = 0
x = first element of queue
Assign x to a P_RP
while(not all tasks are assigned to a processor){
    y = fpred(x)
    if (y has already been assigned to another processor){
        k = another predecessor of x which has not yet been assigned to a
        processor.
        if((last(x) - lact(y)) >= c_{x,y}) then /* y is not critical for x. */
            y = k
        else
            found = 0;
            for another predecessor z of x, z ≠ y
            if ((ect(y) + c_{y,x}) = (ect(z) + c_{z,x}) && task z has not yet been
            assigned to any processor) then {y = z; found = 1;}
            endif
            if(found = 0) {y = k; modproc[i] = RP; modtask[i] = x; }
        endif
    }
    endif
    Assign y to P_RP
    x = y
    if x is entry node
        assign x to P_RP
        x = the next element in queue which has not yet been assigned to a
        processor
        RP + +;
        Assign x to P_RP
    endif
}
```

Fig. 2.5. Code for Step 3 of the STDS Algorithm

the process of cluster generation can be continued by following through any other unassigned predecessor of task i. This process helps reduce the number of tasks which are duplicated. The generation of cluster terminates once the path reaches the entry node. The next cluster starts from the first unassigned task in *queue*. If all the tasks are assigned to a processor, then the algorithm terminates. In this step, the algorithm also keeps track of all the tasks which did not make use of the favorite predecessor to complete the task allocation.

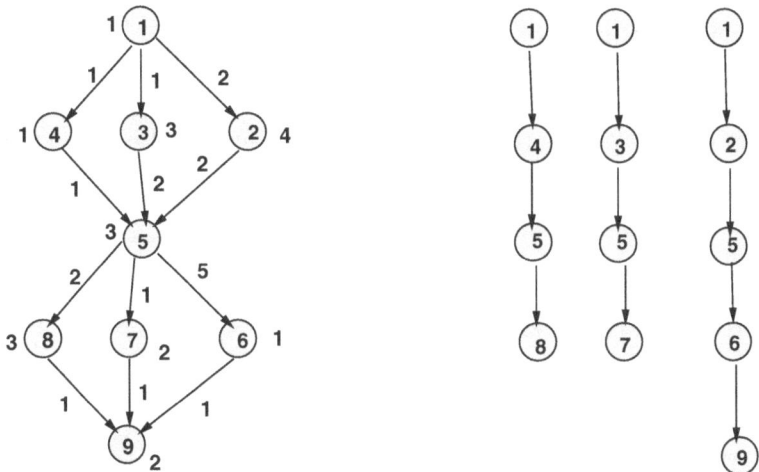

Fig. 2.6. DAG with Critical Node and Its Clusters

After the initial clusters are generated, the algorithm examines if the number of processors required by the schedule (RP) is less than, equal to, or greater than the number of available processors (AP). If $RP = AP$, then the algorithm terminates. If $RP > AP$, the processor reduction procedure is executed and if $RP < AP$, the processors incrementing procedure is executed. The code for reducing and increasing the number of processors is shown in Figure 2.7.

In the reduction step, each processor i is initially assigned a value of $exec(i)$, which is the sum of execution costs of all the tasks on that processor. For example, if tasks 1,5,9 are assigned to processor i, then $exec(i)$ would be equal to $(\tau(1) + \tau(5) + \tau(9))$. After computing the $exec(i)$ of all the processors, the algorithm sorts the processors in the ascending order of $exec(i)$ and merges the task list of processors. In the first pass the task lists are merged to obtain half the initial number of processors. The task lists of the processors with the highest and lowest values of $exec(i)$ are merged, the task lists of processors with second highest and second lowest values of $exec(i)$ are merged and so on. In case the required number of processors is odd, the processor with the highest $exec(i)$ remains unchanged and the tasks of the rest of the processors are merged. If the number of required processors is still higher than the number of available processors, multiple passes through this procedure might be required and in each pass the number of processors can be reduced to half of the initial number of processors. When merging the tasks, the tasks on the new processor are executed in highest *level* first order.

Input: Processor Allocation List

> Available Number of Processors: AP
> Required Number of Processors: RP
> *modtask*: Array of tasks where favorite predecessor was not used
> *modproc*: Array of processors where corresponding modtask is allocated.

Output: Modified Processor Allocation
Begin:

```
if(AP > RP) /* Begin Processor Incrementing Procedure */
{
    for(i = 0 to (AP − RP)-1)
    {
        go to allocation of processor given by modproc[i]
        copy allocation from modtask[i] downwards to a new processor
        traverse from modtask[i] back to entry node following favorite prede-
        cessors along the way.
    }
}
else /* Begin Processor Reduction Procedure */
{
    while(AP ≤ RP){
        Calculate exec(i) for each processor i, i.e. sum of execution costs of
        all tasks allocated to processor i
        Sort processors in ascending order of exec(i)
        temp = RP − AP
        if(temp > RP/2) temp = RP/2
        Merge task lists of processors j and (temp ∗ 2 − j − 1) for j = 0 to
        temp − 1
        decrement RP
    }
}
```

Fig. 2.7. Code for Step 4 of the STDS Algorithm

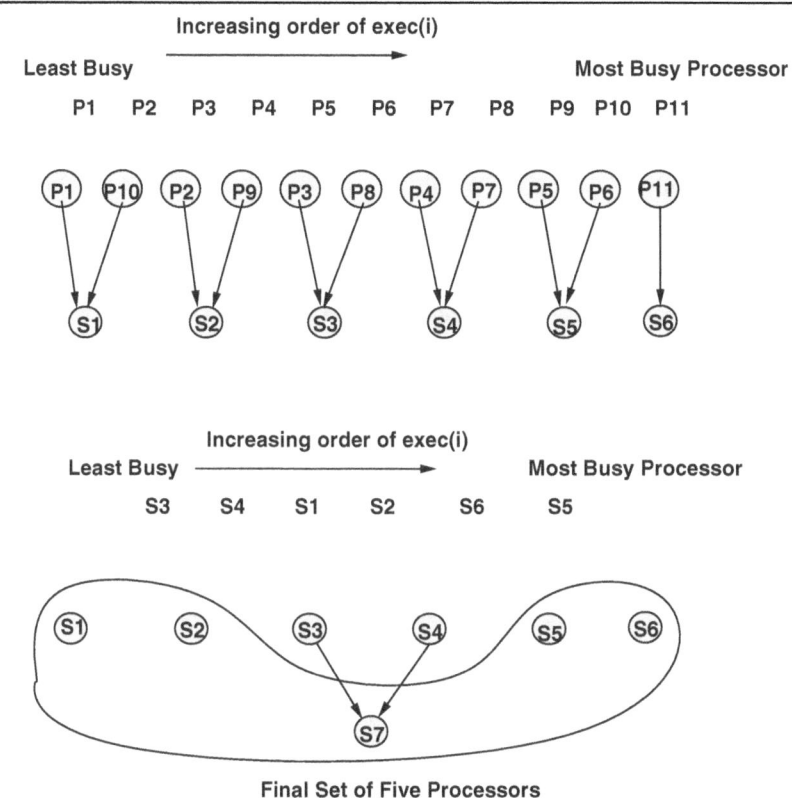

Fig. 2.8. Example of Reducing Schedule From 11 Processors to 5 Processors

An example of merging task lists to reduce the schedule from 11 processors to 5 processors, is shown in Figure 2.8. The task lists are merged till the number of remaining processors is equal to the available processors AP. In the first phase, the task lists of 5 sets of 2 processors each are merged to reduce the processor count to 6. The value of $exec(i)$ of the new processors are computed again. The $exec(i)$ of the new processor will not necessarily be the sum of $exec(i)$'s of the earlier processors. This is because the task which has been duplicated on both the processors need not be executed twice on the merged processor.

Suppose the ascending order of $exec(i)$ for the processors in second phase is S3, S4, S1, S2, S6, S5. In the second phase, the task lists of processors S3 and S4 are merged to reduce the final processor count by one to five processors. The final processor allocation has processors S1, S2, S7, S5 and S6. The task list of each of these processors corresponds to the initial allocation as follows:

S1 : Tasks of Processors P1 and P10
S2 : Tasks of Processors P2 and P9
S7 : Tasks of Processors P3, P4, P7 and P8
S5 : Tasks of Processors P5 and P6
S6 : Tasks of Processors P11

Finally, in the incrementing step, the schedule is scaled to use the surplus number of processors. In this step, the algorithm traverses through the task graph and increments the number of processors. For each extra processor that is available, the algorithm goes to the task on the processor that did not use its favorite predecessor when allocating originally. The new allocation uses the favorite predecessors for all the tasks while traversing back to the entry node. The original tasks list is copied to a new processor. For example, in Figure 2.9, task i and task k (favorite predecessor for task i) were not allocated to the same processor initially. When a new processor P3 becomes available, the traversal list from task i to the entry node on processor P2 is copied to the new processor and on processor P2, the traversal from i to the entry node is performed using the favorite predecessors.

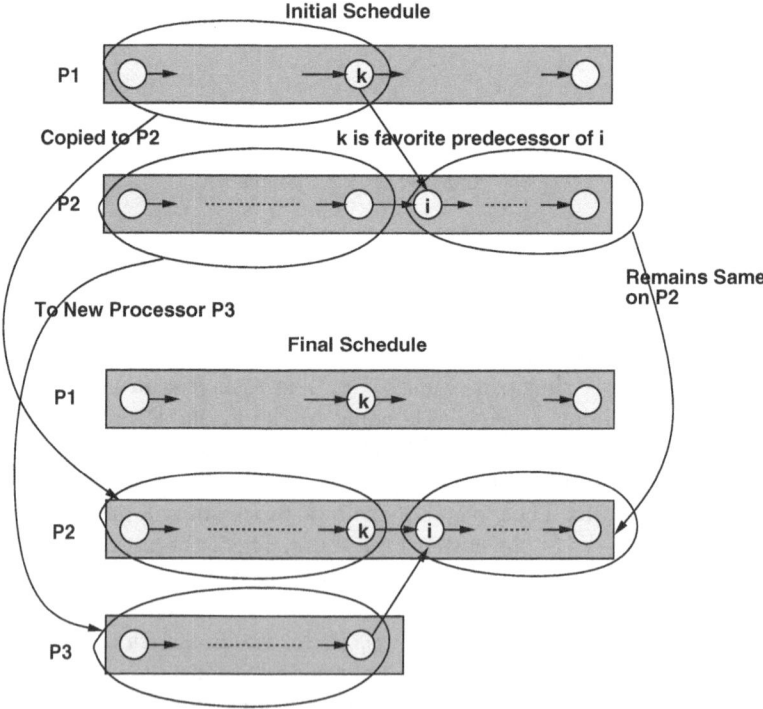

Fig. 2.9. Example of the Incrementing part of Step 4

2.1 Complexity Analysis

The first two steps compute the start times and the completion times by traversing all the tasks and the edges of the task graph. The algorithm, in the worst case would have to examine all the edges of the DAG. Thus, the worst case complexity of these steps is $O(|e|)$, where $|e|$ is the number of edges.

Since the third step deals with the traversal of the task graph similar to the depth first search, the complexity of this step would be the same as the complexity of general search algorithm which is $O(|v| + |e|)$ [3], where $|v|$ is the number of nodes and $|e|$ is the number of edges. Since the task graph is connected, the complexity is $O(|e|)$.

In step 4, the complexity depends upon the difference between the required number of processors for the linear clusters and the number of processors provided by the system. For each pass through the reduction code shown in Figure 2.7, the time required is of the order of $O(|v| + |P|log|P|)$ where $|v|$ is the number of tasks and $|P|$ is the number of processors. Each pass of the reduction code reduces the number of processors to half the original number of processors. Thus, the number of passes through the reduction code is given by:

$$Number\ of\ passes\ through\ Step\ 4\ of\ Algorithm,\ Q\ =\ \lceil log_2(\frac{RP}{AP}) \rceil\ (2.12)$$

The complexity of the reduction step would be $O(Q(|v| + |P|log|P|))$. In the worst case, RP would be equal to $|v|$ and AP would be equal to one and Q would be $log_2(|v|)$. Also, in the worst case $|P|$ would be equal to $|v|$. The complexity of this step in the worst case would be $O(|v|log_2(|v|) + |v|(log_2(|v|))^2)$. For all values of $|v|$, the condition $|v| > log_2(|v|)$ would be true and for $|v| \geq 16$, the condition $|v| \geq (log_2(|v|))^2)$ would be satisfied. For practical applications, $|v|$ would always be larger than 16 and consequently, the worst case complexity of this step would be $O(|v|^2)$.

For the incrementing step, in the worst case, for each processor, all the nodes of the graph might have to be examined. Thus, the worst case complexity of this step is $O(|P||v|)$, where $|P|$ is the number of available processors. If the extra number of processors available i.e. $(AP - RP)$ is equal to the number of times the favorite predecessor was not used, then optimal schedule can be obtained by using favorite predecessor for all those processors.

The overall time complexity of the algorithm is in $O(|v| + |e| + |v|^2)$ or $O(|v| + |e| + |P||v|)$ depending upon if the processors is less than or greater than initially required number of processors. For a dense graph the number of edges, $|e|$ is proportional to $O(|v|^2)$. Also, $|P|$ would be much smaller than $|v|$. Thus, the worst case complexity of the algorithm in both the cases is $O(|v|^2)$.

3. Illustration of the STDS Algorithm

The working of the STDS algorithm is illustrated by a simple example DAG
shown in Figure 3.1. The steps involved in scheduling the example DAG are
explained below:

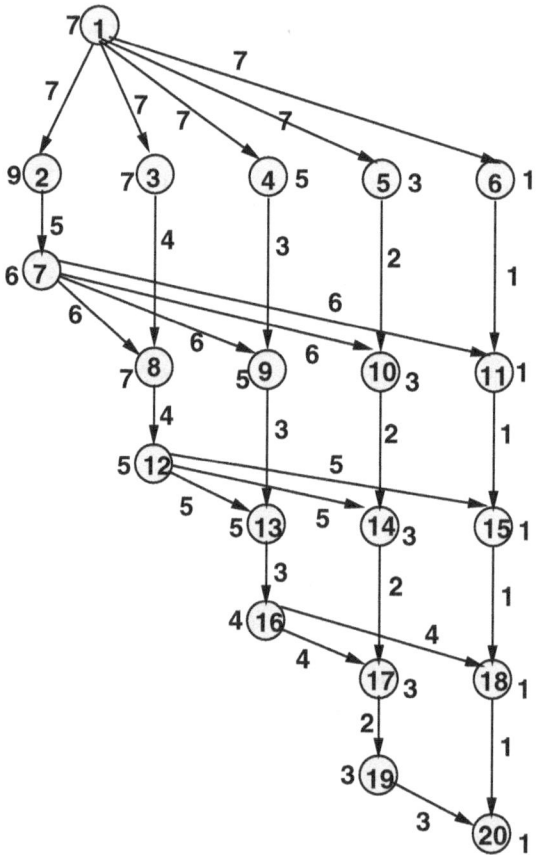

Fig. 3.1. Example Directed Acyclic Graph

Step 1 : Find *est*, *ect* and *fpred* for all nodes $i \in v$. The *est* of the entry node 1 is zero, since $pred(1) = \phi$. Node 1 completes at time 7.
   The *est*, *ect* and *fpred* of other nodes can be computed using Eq. 2.3-
   2.6. For example, node 8 has nodes 3 and 7 as predecessors. Thus,
   $est(8) = min\{max\{(ect(3)+c_{3,8}), ect(7)\}, max\{ect(3), (ect(7)+c_{7,8})\}\} =$
   22. Since, $(ect(7) + c_{7,8}) > (ect(3) + c_{3,8})$, node 7 is the *fpred* of node
   8. The *est*, *ect* and *fpred* of all the nodes of the DAG are shown in
   Table 3.1.

Step 2 : Find *last*, *lact* and *level* for all nodes $i \in v$. The *lact* of the exit node 20 is equal to its *ect*. The *last* of node 20 is equal to $lact(20) - \tau(20) = 49$. The *last*, *lact* and *level* of other nodes can be computed using Eq. 2.7-2.11. For example, node 12 has nodes 13, 14 and 15 as successors. Node 12 is the *fpred* for all three nodes and consequently, $lact(12) = min\{last(13), last(14), last(15)\} = 34$. The value of $last(12)$ is $lact(12) - \tau(12) = 29$. The *last*, *lact* and *level* of all the nodes of the DAG are shown in Table 3.1.

Table 3.1. Start and Completion Times for Nodes of DAG

Node	*level*	*est*	*ect*	*last*	*lact*	fpred
1	50	0	7	0	7	-
2	43	7	16	7	16	1
3	35	7	14	11	18	1
4	26	7	12	18	23	1
5	16	7	10	28	31	1
6	5	7	8	41	42	1
7	34	16	22	16	22	2
8	28	22	29	22	29	7
9	21	22	27	26	31	7
10	13	22	25	33	36	7
11	4	22	23	43	44	7
12	21	29	34	29	34	8
13	16	34	39	34	39	12
14	10	34	37	38	41	12
15	3	34	35	45	46	12
16	11	39	43	39	43	13
17	7	43	46	43	46	16
18	2	43	44	47	48	16
19	4	46	49	46	49	17
20	1	49	50	49	50	19

Step 3: Generate clusters similar to linear clusters. For this DAG, the array queue would be as follows:
$queue = \{20, 18, 15, 19, 11, 6, 17, 14, 16, 10, 13, 5, 12, 9, 4, 8, 7, 3, 2, 1\}$
The generation of linear clusters is initiated with the exit node, i.e. node 20. While searching backwards, the path is traced through the favorite predecessors of each task. Since this is the first pass, none of the tasks have been assigned to any processor. Thus, the allocation list of {20, 19, 17, 16, 13, 12, 8, 7, 2, 1} is obtained for processor 1. The next pass through the search procedure is started from the first unassigned task in the array *queue* which is task 18. The search from task 18 yields task 16

as its favorite predecessor. Since, task 16 is already allocated to another processor, the search proceeds with task 15. Since, $last(18) - lact(16) > c_{16,18}$, task 16 is not critical for task 18. Similarly, for tasks 15 and 11, tasks 12 and 7 are their favorite predecessors respectively. Due to similar reasons, tasks 12 and 7 are not critical for the execution of tasks 15 and 11 and thus even if additional processors are available, tasks 12 and 7 need not be duplicated onto the same processor as tasks 15 and 11. Thus, processor 2 has an allocation list of $\{1, 6, 11, 15, 18\}$. The next search pass starts with task 14. Task 14 has task 12 as the favorite predecessor and it is critical because $last(14) - lact(12) < c_{12,14}$. Since task 12 has already been allocated to another processor, this fact is noted and if additional processor is available task 12 can be duplicated to the same processor as task 14. Following this procedure, the task clusters shown in Figure 3.2 are obtained. In this allocation there are two places where the favorite predecessor was not used for generating the clusters. In addition to the case of task 14 mentioned above, task 9 allocated to processor 4 did not make use of its favorite predecessor, task 7, in the initial allocation.

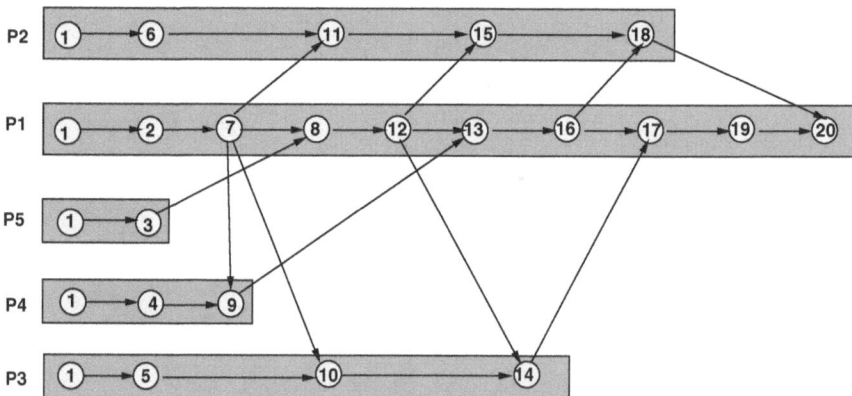

Fig. 3.2. Initial Processor Schedule

Step 4a: The number of required processors is 5. If the available number of processors is less than 5, then the task lists of different processors need to be merged. For example, suppose the number of processors available is 2. Then the number of processors needs to be reduced by 3. The procedure to reduce the number of processors is as follows:

1. Find the values of $exec(i)$ for each processor i. The values of $exec(i)$ for processors one to five are 50, 11, 16, 17, 14 respectively.
2. Since processor count is being reduced by more than half, two passes through this procedure would be needed. In the first pass the task lists of processors (P2,P4) and processors (P3,P5) would be merged.

This would give us an allocation for 3 processors S1, S2 and S3. Processor S1 has the same tasks as processor P1, processor S2 has the tasks of processors P2 and P4 combined and processor S3 has the tasks of processors P3 and P5 combined. In case, 3 processors are available, the reduction procedure would be terminated at this step. After getting the allocation for three processors, the $exec(i)$ for the three processors have to be computed and sorted based on the value of $exec(i)$. The $exec(i)$ of processors S1, S2 and S3 are 50, 21 and 23 respectively. In the second pass, the task lists of processors S2 and S3 would be merged to obtain the schedule for the two processors. In case four processors are available, only one pass through this procedure would be required. If four processors are available, then the tasks of processors P2 and P5 would be merged and the rest of the processors would remain the same. The modified allocations for the two, three and four processors cases are shown in Figure 3.3.

Step 4b: The initial number of required processors is five. Suppose ten processors are available for the execution of this application. In this DAG, there are two places where a favorite predecessor was not used when assigning tasks to processors. For task 9 allocated to processor 4, task 7 is the favorite predecessor and for task 14 allocated to processor 3, task 12 is the favorite predecessor. But this is not the way the initial clusters were generated. In case one extra processor is available, the allocation on processor 4 from task 9 onwards can be copied to the new processor and on the original processors traverse from task 9 to the entry node following the favorite predecessors along the way. If there is another free processor available, the allocation on processor 3 from task 14 onwards is copied to the new processor and traverse from task 14 to the entry node through the favorite predecessors. In case more than seven processors are available, they will remain unused as there are no more tasks which are not using their favorite predecessors. Using this modified allocation, the processor allocations for six and seven processors case is obtained as shown in Figure 3.4.

For the example task graph, Table 3.2 shows the schedule length that would be achieved if the number of available processors is varied from 1 and above. Even if there are more than 7 processors, the algorithm utilizes only 7 processors.

4. Performance of the STDS Algorithm

The performance of the STDS algorithm is observed for five cases. The first case is if the CRC is satisfied and the required number of processors are available. This case reduces to the case of TDS algorithm [13] where optimal schedule is guaranteed and the proof is given in section 4.1. Next, the case

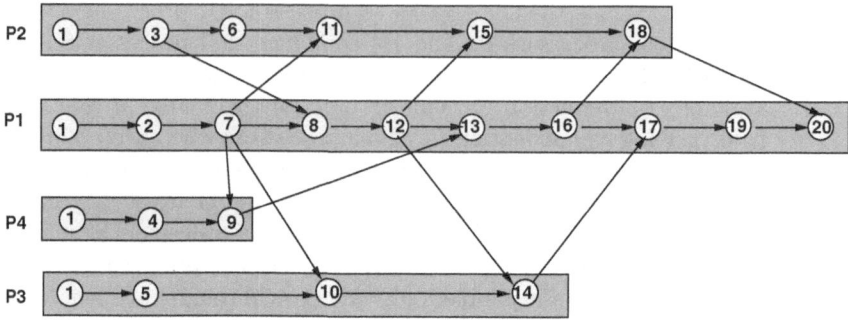

Schedule For Four Processors

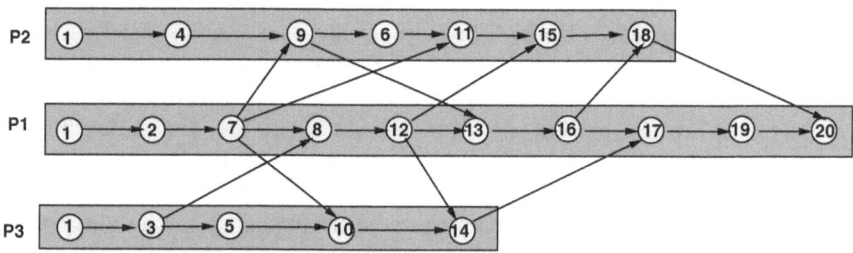

Schedule For Three Processors

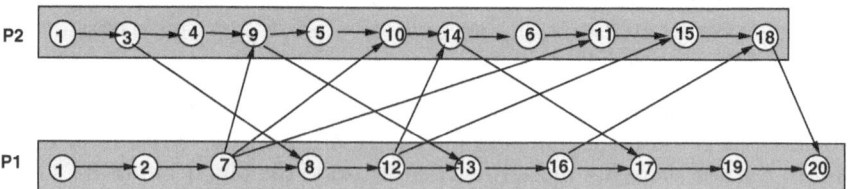

Schedule For Two Processors

Fig. 3.3. Final Processor Schedule When Number of Processors Less than Five

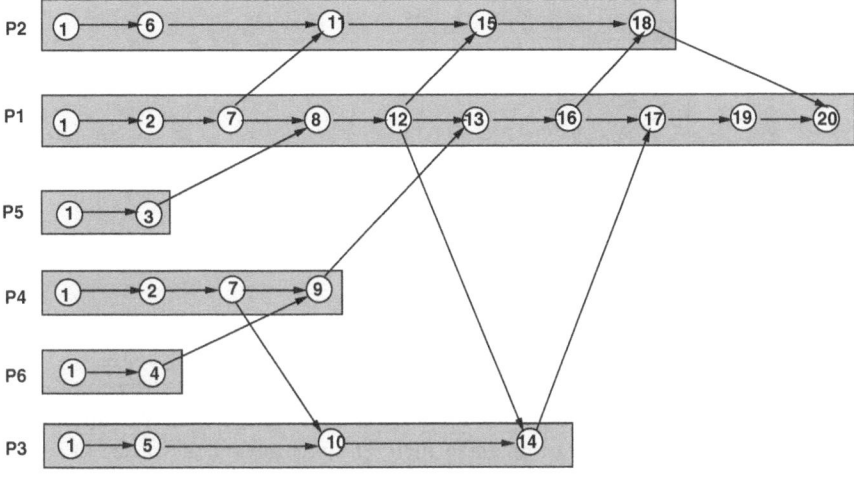

Schedule For Six Processors

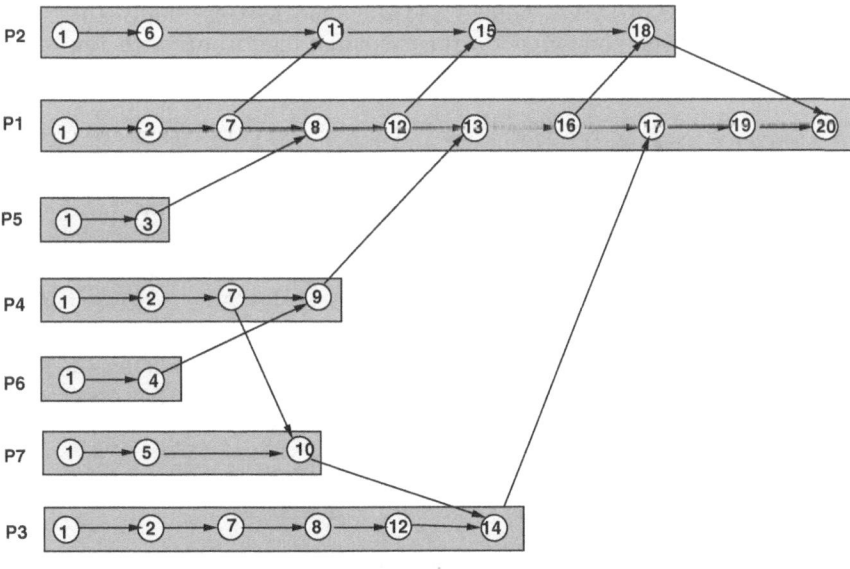

Schedule for Seven processors

Fig. 3.4. Final Processor Schedule When Number of Processors Greater than five

Table 3.2. Number of Processors vs. Schedule Length

Number of Processors	Schedule Length
1	80
2	52
3	52
4	52
5	52
6	51
7 and above	50

where either the CRC is not necessarily satisfied, or the required number of processors is not available are considered. For this case, extensive simulations have been performed. Random data for edge and node costs have been obtained and the schedule length generated by STDS algorithm for this data has been compared to the absolute lowerbound (described in section 4.2). In the third case, the STDS algorithm has been applied to practical applications which have larger DAGs. In the fourth case, the algorithm has been applied on a special class of DAGs, namely the Diamond DAGs. Finally, the STDS algorithm has been compared to other existing algorithms with the use of small example DAG.

4.1 CRC Is Satisfied

A DAG consists of fork and join nodes. The fork nodes can be transformed with the help of task duplication to achieve the earliest possible schedule time as shown in Figure 4.1. The problem arises when scheduling the join nodes because only one predecessor can be assigned to the same processor as the join node. In this subsection, it is proven that for join nodes which satisfy the CRC, the schedule time obtained by scheduling the join node on the same processor as its favorite predecessor, is optimal. The rest of the predecessors of the join node are each assigned to a separate processor.

Theorem 41. *Given a join node satisfying the CRC stated in section 2, the STDS algorithm gives minimum possible schedule time.*

Proof. Figure 4.2 shows an example join node. According to the CRC, tasks m and n have the highest and the second highest values of $\{ect(j) + c_{j,i}\ j \in pred(i)\}$. It is assumed that task m is assigned to processor m and task n is assigned to processor n. Since task m has the highest value of $ect(m) + c_{m,i}$, task i is also assigned to processor m and $est(i) = max\{ect(m), ect(n) + c_{n,i}\}$.

It will be proven that the start time of task i cannot be lowered by assigning tasks m and n to the same processor if the CRC is satisfied. Thus, tasks

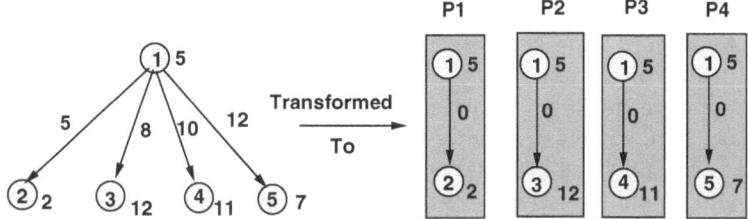

Fig. 4.1. Schedule of Fork Node

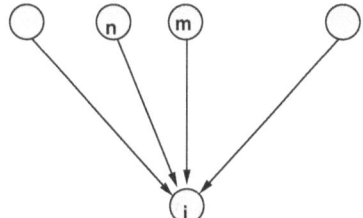

Fig. 4.2. Example Join Node

m and n have to be assigned to different processors. The other predecessors may have any values of computation and communication times, but, task i has to wait till $ect(m)$ or $ect(n) + c_{n,i}$, whichever is higher. Thus, the other tasks will not affect $est(i)$, as long as the condition $ect(k)+c_{k,i} \leq ect(n)+c_{n,i}$, for all $k \in pred(i)$ and $k \neq m, n$ is satisfied. Thus, only tasks m and n need to be considered among all the predecessors of task i.

There are two possible cases here.

Case 1: $est(m) \geq est(n)$. From the CRC stated in section 2, $\tau(m) \geq c_{n,i}$ has to be satisfied. Here again there could be two cases:

Case 1(a): $ect(m) \geq ect(n) + c_{n,i}$, i.e. $est(i) = ect(m)$

If tasks m, n and i are assigned to the same processor,
$est(i) = max(est(m), (est(n) + \tau(n))) + \tau(m) = max(ect(m), ect(n) + \tau(m))$. Thus, the start time of $est(i)$ cannot be reduced below its current starting time of $ect(m)$ by assigning m, n and i to the same processor.

Case 1(b): $ect(m) < ect(n) + c_{n,i}$, i.e. $est(i) = ect(n) + c_{n,i}$

If tasks m, n and i are assigned to the same processor, the earliest task i can start is given by $(est(n) + \tau(n) + \tau(m))$, i.e. $ect(n) + \tau(m)$. Since $\tau(m) \geq c_{n,i}$, $ect(n)+\tau(m)$ would be greater than or equal to $ect(n)+c_{n,i}$. Thus $est(i)$ cannot be lowered.

Case 2: $est(m) < est(n)$. From the CRC stated in section 2, $\tau(m) \geq c_{n,i} + est(n) - est(m)$ has to be satisfied.

Case 2(a): $ect(m) \geq ect(n) + c_{n,i}$, i.e. $est(i) = ect(m)$

If tasks m, n and i are assigned to the same processor, $est(i) = est(m) + \tau(m) + \tau(n) = ect(m) + \tau(n)$. Thus, the start time of task i cannot be lower than its current starting time of $ect(m)$.

Case 2(b): $ect(m) < ect(n) + c_{n,i}$, i.e. $est(i) = ect(n) + c_{n,i}$

If m, n and i are assigned to the same processor, earliest start time of task i would be $est(m) + \tau(m) + \tau(n)$. The start time of task i can be improved if $est(m) + \tau(m) + \tau(n) < est(n) + \tau(n) + c_{n,i}$. In other words, if $est(m) + \tau(m) < est(n) + c_{n,i}$, or if $\tau(m) < (est(n) - est(m)) + c_{n,i}$. But it is known that $\tau(m) \geq (est(n) - est(m)) + c_{n,i}$. Thus the start time of task i cannot be lowered.   □

This proves that if the CRC given in section 2 is satisfied by all the join nodes of the DAG then STDS algorithm yields the earliest possible start time, and consequently, earliest possible completion time for all the tasks of the DAG.

4.2 Application of Algorithm for Random Data

In the earlier section, it has been proven that if the CRC is satisfied and if the required number of processors are available, then optimal schedule is obtained. Here, the idea is to observe the performance of this algorithm on random edge and node costs that do not necessarily satisfy the CRC. To observe the performance, the example DAG shown in Figure 4.3 has been taken and the edge and node costs have been generated using a random number generator. For each of these sets of data and for different number of processors, the ratio of the STDS generated schedule length and the absolute lowerbound have been computed. The absolute lowerbound for an application on P processors is defined as follows:

$$Absolute\ Lowerbound = maximum\{Level\ of\ entry\ node,\ \frac{1}{P} * \sum_{i \in v} \tau(i)\}$$

(4.1)

The first term of the equation, i.e. the *level* of the entry node of the DAG, is the sum of computation costs along the longest path from entry node to the exit node. For example, for the example DAG in Figure 4.3, there are several paths from the entry node 1 to the exit node 10. The longest path is given by 1-3-6-8-10, yielding a *level* of 20 time units. Since the dependencies in this linear path have to be maintained, the schedule length can never be lower than the *level* of the entry node. The second term of the above equation is the overall sum of all the computation costs divided by the number of processors. The schedule length has to be greater than or equal to the second term. Thus, the maximum of the two terms will be the theoretical lowerbound, which may or may not be practically achievable.

The random number generator has been used 1000 times to generate 1000 sets of data. For each of these data sets, the costs were taken as (modulus

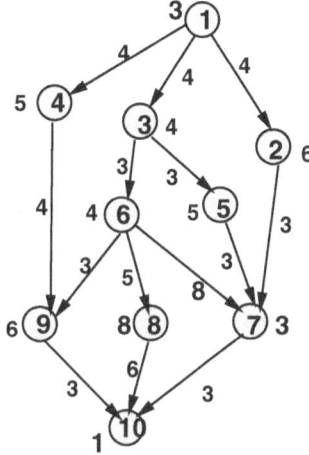

Fig. 4.3. Example Directed Acyclic Graph

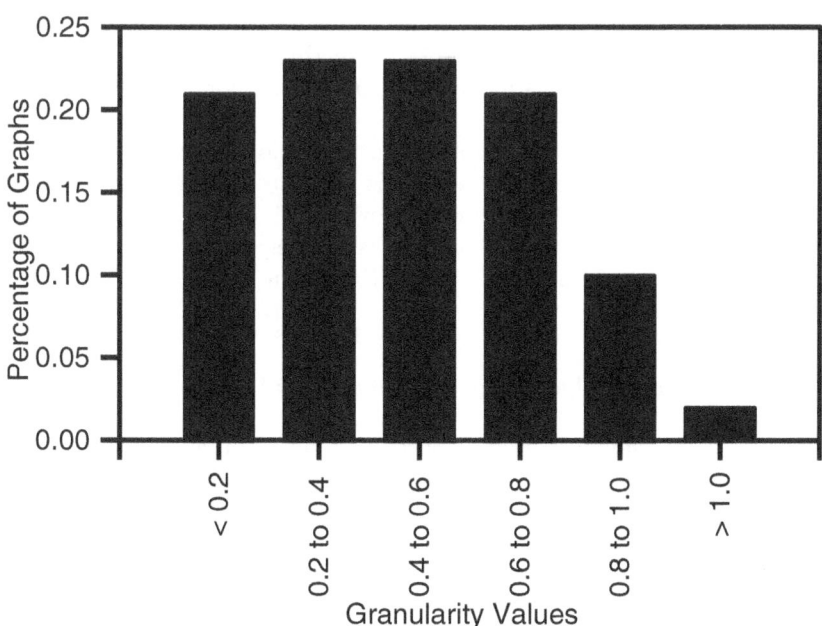

Fig. 4.4. Percentage of Graphs Vs. Granularities

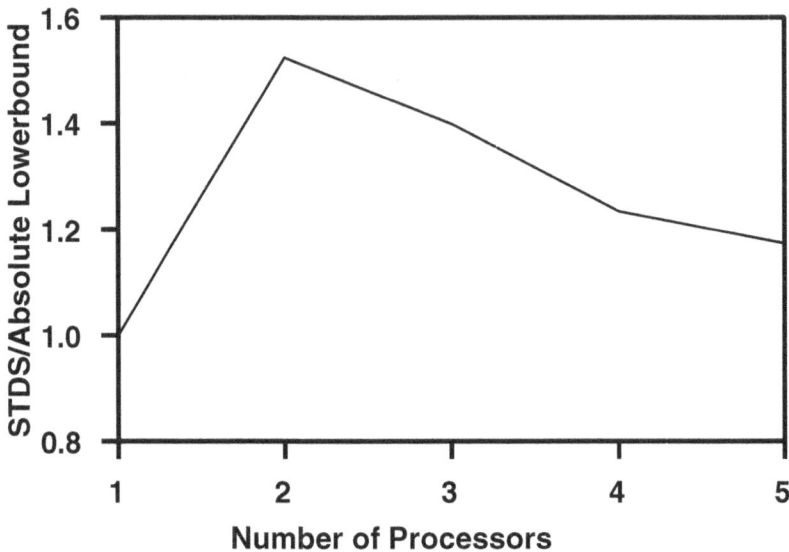

Fig. 4.5. Ratio of Schedule Lengths Vs. Number of Processors

100 +1) of the number generated. In effect the edge and node costs lie in the range of 1 to 100. The random number generator generated DAGs with differing granularities as given in [17]. Using this definition of granularity, the percentage of graphs versus the granularity values for these data sets has been plotted in Figure 4.4.

For the randomly generated data sets, the ratio of algorithm generated schedule and the absolute lowerbound has been obtained as the number of processors is varied from 1 to 5 and is shown in Figure 4.5. All these DAGs required less than or equal to 5 processors for scheduling. On the average, the STDS algorithm required 26% more time than absolute lowerbound to schedule these DAGs.

4.3 Application of Algorithm to Practical DAGs

The STDS algorithm has been applied on different practical DAGs. The four applications are Bellman-Ford algorithm [4, 23], systolic algorithm [20], master-slave algorithm [23] and Cholesky decomposition algorithm [16]. The first three applications are part of the ALPES project [23]. These four applications have varying characteristics. The number of nodes of these DAGs is around 3000 but the number of edges varies from 5000 to 25000. This gives the ranges of sparse to dense graphs. The number of predecessors and successors varies from 1 to 140. The computation and communication costs vary in a wide range. The schedule time is generated by the STDS algorithm for different number of processors and is compared against the absolute lower-bound. These are shown in Figures 4.6-4.9. These figures have four parts and the description of these plots is as follows:

- In the (a) plots, the variation of schedule length is shown as the number of processors decreases. It can be observed that the schedule length varies in a step-wise fashion. The explanation for this is that the algorithm initially merges the task lists of the idle processors. But there comes a stage where it is necessary to merge the task lists with the most busy processor. At that point, a major jump in the schedule length can be noticed. After that point, the schedule length again increases very slowly till the next critical point is reached.
- In the (b) plots, the variation of absolute lowerbound with the number of processors has been plotted.
- In the (c) plots, the interesting portions of the (a) and (b) plots for each of the applications has been zoomed. In the plot, the step-wise increase in schedule length generated by STDS algorithm is more noticeable.
- Finally, in (d), the ratio of STDS generated schedule to the absolute lower-bound as the number of processors is varied is plotted. It can be observed from the plots that the ratios fluctuate very heavily when the number of processors is lower. As the number of processors increases the ratios remain constant. The reason for this is that as the number of processors is low-ered, the schedule length increases rapidly, i.e. the number of steps visible is large. Since the absolute lowerbound varies smoothly, the ratio between the STDS schedule and the absolute lowerbound is dictated by the STDS schedule.

The characteristics for each application is shown in Table 4.1.

4.4 Scheduling of Diamond DAGs

In this section, the performance of STDS algorithm on a special class of DAGs, namely the diamond DAGs is observed. The general structure of the diamond DAGs is shown in Figure 4.10. These DAGs are similar to master-slave DAGs in which the master gives instructions to the slaves and the slaves send the result back to the master node.

If these DAGs satisfy the cost relationship condition, then they provide an optimal schedule using n processors, where n is the width of the DAG or the number of slave tasks at each level. Figure 4.11 shows a special case of diamond DAG where n is 3 and it satisfies the CRC. The schedule generated by STDS algorithm for the DAG shown in Figure 4.11 is shown in Figure 4.12. The schedule length obtained by STDS algorithm for this DAG is optimal. In this schedule, it can be observed that only the critical nodes or the master nodes have been duplicated on the three processors.

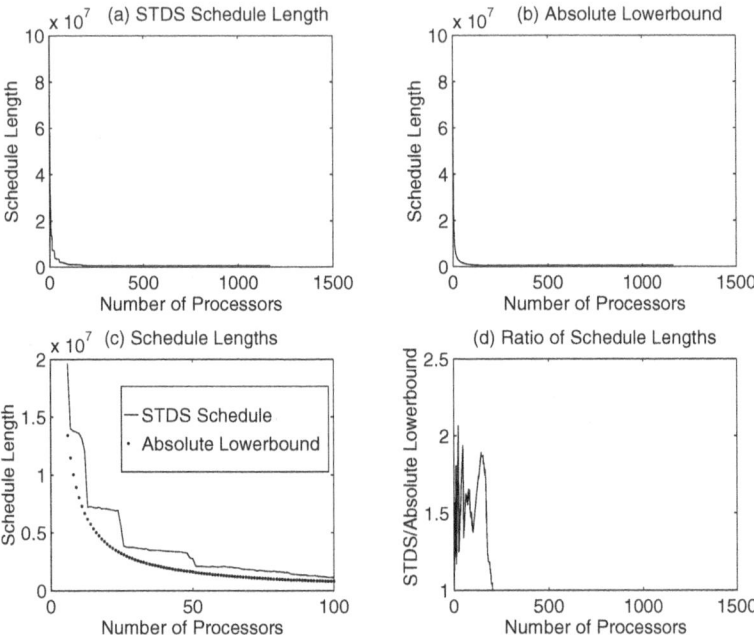

Fig. 4.6. Plots for Bellman-Ford Shortest Path Algorithm

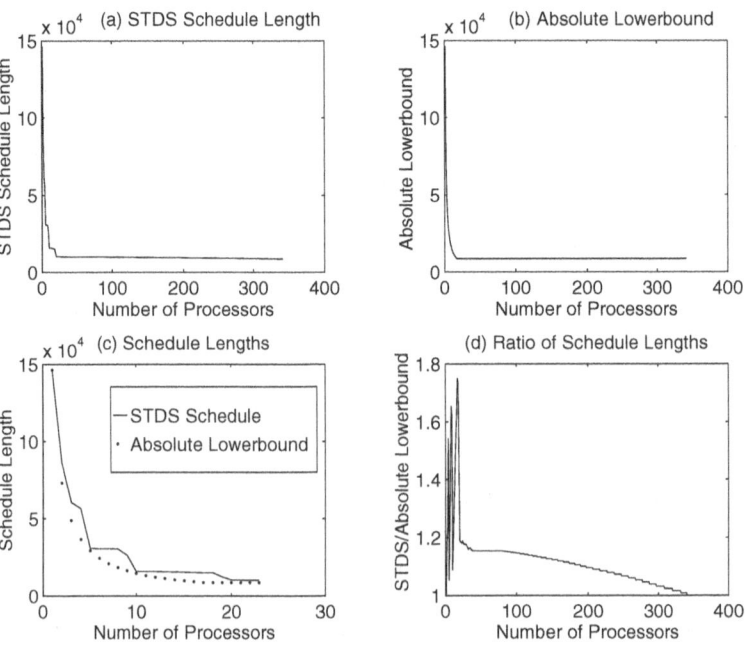

Fig. 4.7. Plots for Cholesky Decomposition Algorithm

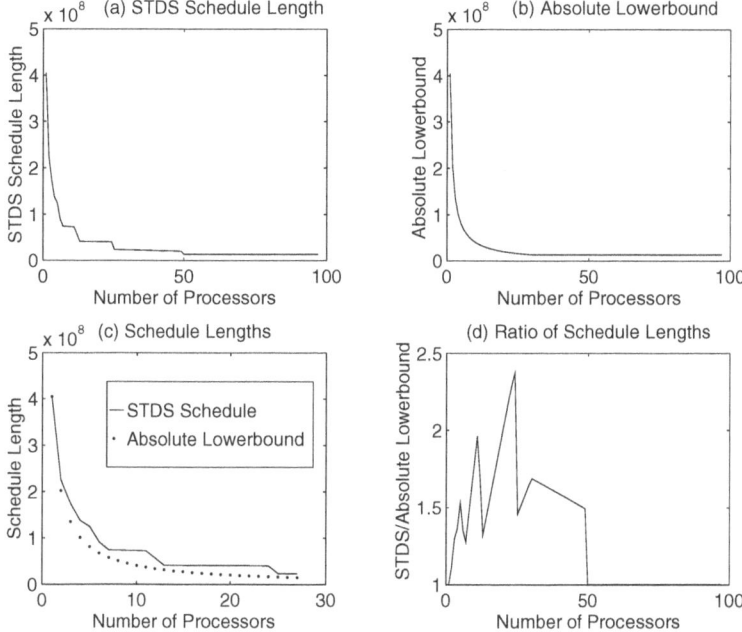

Fig. 4.8. Plots for Systolic Algorithm

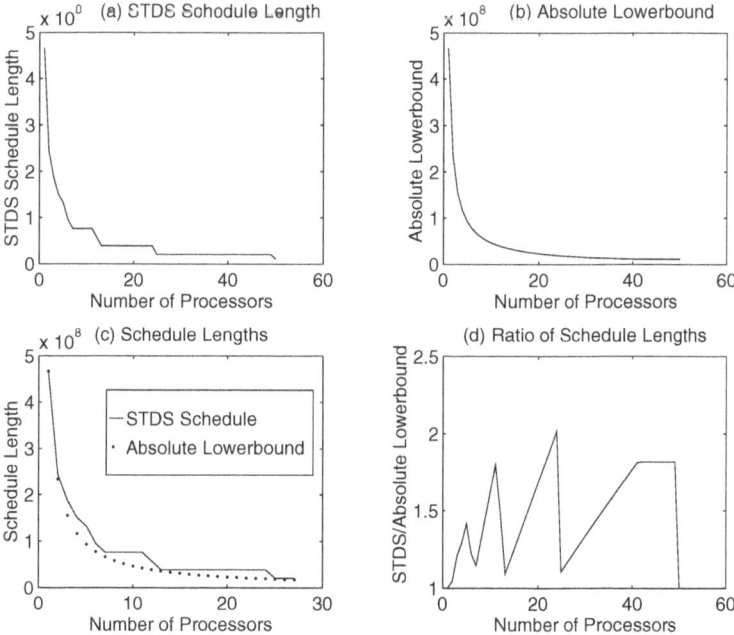

Fig. 4.9. Plots for Master-Slave Algorithm

Table 4.1. Performance Parameters for Different Applications

Characteristics	Applications			
	Bellman-Ford Algorithm	Cholesky Decomposition	Systolic Algorithm	Master-Slave Algorithm
Granularity of DAG	0.002	0.013	0.002	0.002
Condition Satisfied	Yes	Yes	No	No
Initial Processors Required By STDS	203	75	50	50
Maximum Processors Required By STDS	1171	342	97	50
Average Ratio of STDS/Absolute Lowerbound	1.095	1.118	1.315	1.50
Ratio of STDS/Absolute Lowerbound when maximum processors are available	1.0004	1.0	1.0017	1.0019

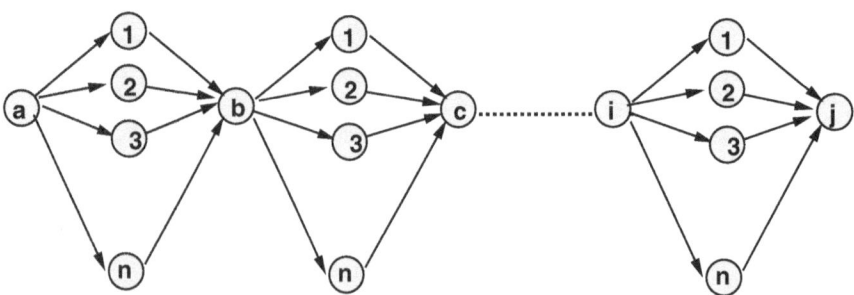

Fig. 4.10. General Structure of Diamond DAGs

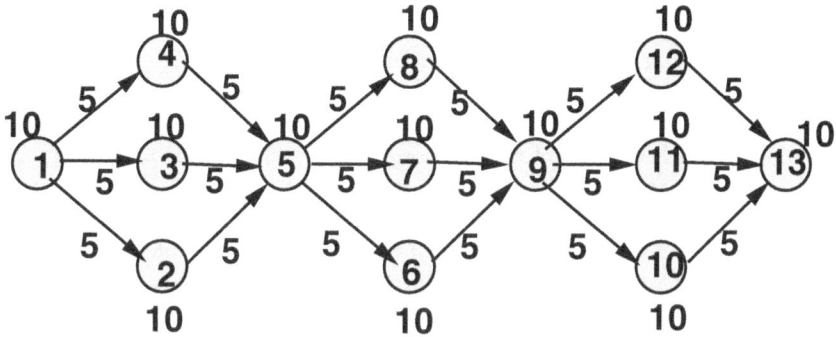

Fig. 4.11. Diamond DAGs where $n = 3$

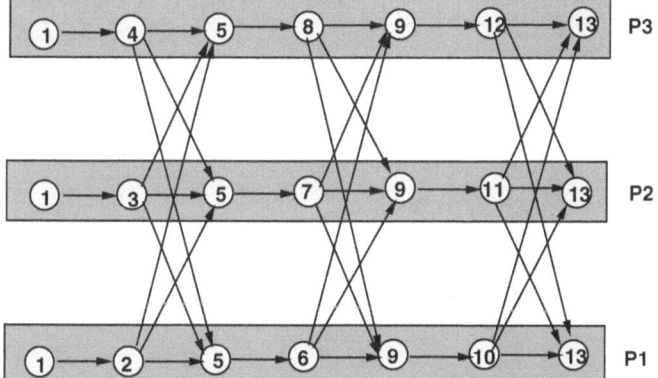

Fig. 4.12. Schedule For Diamond DAG, where $n = 3$

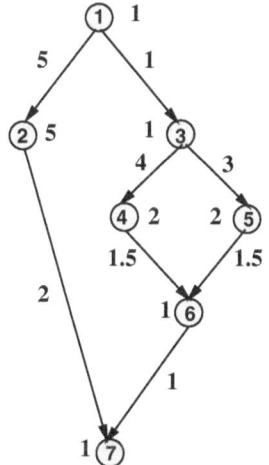

Fig. 4.13. DAG for Comparison of Algorithms

4.5 Comparison with Other Algorithms

Finally, STDS algorithm has been compared to five other algorithms using the example DAG used in [16]. The example DAG, shown in Figure 4.13, is used for comparing the STDS algorithm with DSC algorithm [16], Linear Clustering algorithm [22], Internalization pre-pass [30], MCP clustering algorithm [33] and the Threshold scheduling scheme [28]. The schedule time generated by each of the algorithms and the algorithm complexities are shown in Table 4.2. It can be seen that STDS has the optimal schedule and has the lowest complexity among all the scheduling algorithms.

Table 4.2. Comparison of Algorithms

Algorithms	Schedule length	Complexity
Optimal Algorithm	8.5	NP-Complete
Linear Clustering	11.5	$O(v(e+v))$
MCP Algorithm	10.5	$O(v^2 logv)$
Internalization Pre-Pass	10.0	$O(e(v+e))$
Dominant Sequence Clustering	9.0	$O((e+v)logv)$
Threshold Scheduling Algorithm	10.0	$O(e)$
STDS Algorithm	8.5	$O(e)$

5. Conclusions

A Scalable Task Duplication based Scheduling algorithm for DMMs has been presented in this chapter which operates in two phases. Initially linear clusters are generated and if the number of required processors for the linear clusters is more than the number of processors provided by the system, then the task lists are merged to reduce the required number of processors. On the contrary, if number of processors available is more than required number of processors then the surplus processors are used in an effort to reduce the schedule length and try to bring it as close to optimal as possible.

The complexity of this algorithm is of the order of $O(|v|^2)$ where $|v|$ is the number of nodes or tasks in the DAG. The results as obtained by its application to the randomly generated DAGs are very promising. Also, the STDS algorithm has been applied to large application DAGs. It has been observed that the schedule length generated by STDS algorithm varies from 1.1 to 1.5 times the absolute lowerbound. It has been observed that the STDS algorithm performs very well in reducing the number of processors by increasing the schedule length gradually.

References

1. T.L. Adam, K.M. Chandy and J.R. Dickson, "A Comparison of List Schedules For Parallel Processing Systems", *Communications of the ACM*, vol. 17, no. 12, December 1974, pp. 685-690.
2. I. Ahmed and Y.-k. Kwok, "A New Approach to Scheduling Parallel Programs Using Task Duplication", *International Conference on Parallel Processing*, August 1994, Vol. II, pp. 47-51.
3. A.V. Aho, J.E. Hopcroft and J.D. Ullman, *The Design and Analysis of Computer Algorithms*, Addison-Wesley Publishing Company, 1974.
4. D.P. Bertsekas and J.N. Tsitsiklis, "Parallel and Distributed Computation: Numerical Methods", *Prentice-Hall International*, 1989.
5. T. Cassavant and J.A. Kuhl, "Taxonomy of Scheduling In General Purpose Distributed Computing Systems", *IEEE Transactions on Software Engineering*, vol. 14, no. 2, February 1988, pp. 141-154.
6. H.B. Chen, B. Shirazi, K.Kavi and A.R. Hurson, "Static Scheduling Using Linear Clustering with Task Duplication", *In Proceedings of the ISCA International Conference on Parallel and Distributed Computing and Systems*, 1993, pp. 285-290.
7. Y.C. Chung and S. Ranka, "Application and Performance Analysis of a Compile-Time Optimization Approach for List Scheduling Algorithms on Distributed Memory Multiprocessors", *Proceedings of Supercomputing'92*, Nov. 1992, pp. 512-521.
8. J.Y. Colin and P. Chritienne, "C.P.M. Scheduling With Small Communication Delays and Task Duplication", *Operations Research*, July 1991, v. 39, no. 4 pp. 680-684.
9. S. Darbha and D.P. Agrawal, "SDBS: A Task Duplication Based Optimal Scheduling Algorithm", *In Proceedings of Scalable High Performance Computing Conference*, May 23-25 1994, pp. 756-763.
10. S. Darbha, "Task Scheduling Algorithms for Distributed Memory Systems", *PhD Thesis, North Carolina State University*, 1995.
11. S. Darbha and D.P. Agrawal, "A Fast and Scalable Scheduling Algorithm For Distributed Memory Systems", Proceedings of the Seventh IEEE Symposium on Parallel and Distributed Processing, pp. 60-63, October 25-28 1995, San Antonio, TX.
12. S. Darbha and D.P. Agrawal, "Scalable and Scheduling Algorithm For Distributed Memory Systems", *In Proceedings of Eighth IEEE Symposium on Parallel and Distributed Processing*, pp. 84-91, October 23-27, 1996, New Orleans, LA.
13. S. Darbha and D.P. Agrawal, "Optimal Scheduling Algorithm For Distributed Memory Machines", *To Appear in IEEE Transactions on Parallel and Distributed Systems*.
14. S. Darbha and D.P. Agrawal, "A Task Duplication based Scalable Scheduling Algorithm For Distributed Memory Systems", *To Appear in Journal of Parallel and Distributed Computing*.
15. H. El-Rewini and T.G. Lewis, "Scheduling Parallel Program Tasks Onto Arbitrary Target Architectures", *Journal Of Parallel and Distributed Computing*, vol. 9, 1990, pp. 138-153.
16. A. Gerasoulis and T. Yang, "A Comparison of Clustering Heuristics for Scheduling Directed Acyclic Graphs on Multiprocessors", *Journal of Parallel and Distributed Computing*, vol 16, 1992, pp 276-291.

17. A. Gerasoulis and T. Yang, "On the Granularity and Clustering of Directed Acyclic Task Graphs", *IEEE Transactions on Parallel and Distributed Systems*, vol 4, no. 6, June 1993, pp 686-701.

18. R.L. Graham, L.E. Lawler, J.K. Lenstra and A.H. Kan, "Optimization and Approximation In Deterministic Sequencing and Scheduling: A Survey", *In Annals of Discrete Mathematics*, 1979, pp. 287-326.

19. J.J. Hwang, Y.C. Chow, F.D. Anger and C.Y. Lee, "Scheduling Precedence Graphs In Systems With Interprocessor Communication Times", *SIAM Journal of Computing*, vol. 18, no. 2, April 1989, pp. 244-257.

20. O.H. Ibarra and S.M. Sohn, "On Mapping Systolic Algorithms onto the Hypercube", *IEEE Transactions on Parallel and Distributed Systems*, vol. 1, no.1, Jan. 1990, pp. 48-63.

21. A.A. Khan, C.L. McCreary and M.S. Jones, "A Comparison of Multiprocessor Scheduling Heuristics", *International Conference on Parallel Processing*, August 1994, Vol. II, pp. 243-250.

22. S.J. Kim and J.C. Browne, "A general approach to mapping of parallel computation upon multiprocessor architectures", International Conference on Parallel Processing, 1988, vol. 3, pp. 1-8.

23. J.P. Kitajima and B. Plateau, "Building synthetic parallel programs: the project (ALPES)", *In Proceedings of the IFIP WG 10.3 Workshop on Programming Environments for Parallel Computing*, Edinburgh, Scotland, 6-8 April, 1992, pp. 161-170.

24. B. Kruatrachue, "Static Task Scheduling and Grain Packing in Parallel Processing Systems", *PhD Thesis*, Oregon State University, 1987.

25. C.Y. Lee, J.J. Hwang, Y.C. Chow and F.D. Anger, "Multiprocessor Scheduling With Interprocessor Communication Delays", *Operations Research Letters*, vol. 7, No. 3, June 1988, pp. 141-147.

26. P. Markenscoff and Y.Y. Li, "Scheduling a Computational DAG on a Parallel System with Communication Delays and Replication of Node Execution", *In Proceedings of International Parallel Processing Symposium*, April 1993, pp. 113-118.

27. N. Mehdiratta and K. Ghose, "A bottom up approach to Task Scheduling in Distributed Memory Multiprocessors", *International Conference on Parallel Processing*, August 1994, Vol. II, pp. 151-154.

28. S.S. Pande, D.P. Agrawal and J. Mauney, "A New Threshold Scheduling Strategy for Sisal Programs on Distributed Memory Systems", *Journal of Parallel and Distributed Computing*, vol. 21, no.2, May 1994, pp. 223-236.

29. S.S. Pande, D.P. Agrawal and J. Mauney, "A Scalable Scheduling Method for Functional Parallelism on Distributed Memory Multiprocessors", *IEEE Transactions on Parallel and Distributed Systems*, vol. 6, no. 4, April 1995, pp. 388-399.

30. V. Sarkar, *Partitioning and Scheduling Parallel Programs for Execution on Multiprocessors*, MIT Press, Cambridge, MA, 1989.

31. G.C. Sih and E.A. Lee, "A Compile-Time Scheduling Heuristic for Interconnection-Constrained Heterogeneous Processor Architectures", *IEEE Transactions on Parallel and Distributed Systems*, vol. 4, no. 2, February 1993, pp. 175-187.

32. Q. Wang and K.H. Cheng, "List Scheduling of Parallel Tasks", *Information Processing Letters*, vol. 37, March 1991, pp. 291-297.

33. M.Y. Wu and D. Gajski, "A Programming Aid for Hypercube Architectures", J. Supercomputing, vol. 2, 1988, pp 349-372.

Chapter 19. SPMD Execution in the Presence of Dynamic Data Structures

Rajiv Gupta

Department of Computer Science, University of Arizona, Tucson, AZ 85271-0077

1. Introduction

A wide range of applications make use of regular dynamic data structures. Dynamic data structures are typically required because either the size of the data structure cannot be determined at compile-time or the form of the data structure depends upon the data that it contains which is not known until runtime. Some commonly used regular data structures include link lists, trees, and two dimensional meshes. Lists and trees are used by applications such as the N-body problem [10] and sparse Cholesky factorization [8, 11], dynamic meshes are used for solving partial differential equations and quad-trees are used by applications such as solid modeling, geographic information systems, and robotics [9].

Recently researchers have focussed on the translation of programs written using the shared-memory paradigm for parallel SPMD (single-program, multiple data) execution on distributed-memory machines [1, 6]. In this approach the distribution of shared data arrays among the processors is specified as a mapping between array indices and processor ids. This mapping is either specified by the user or generated automatically by the compiler. The compiler translates the program into an SPMD program using the owner-computes rule in which parallelism is exploited by having all processors simultaneously operate on portions of shared data structures that reside in their respective local memories. The mapping between array indices and processor ids is also used by the compiler to generate interprocessor communication necessary for SPMD execution.

While the above approach is applicable to programs that use shared data arrays, it cannot be directly applied to programs with shared pointer-based dynamic data structures. This is due to the manner in which dynamic data structures are constructed and accessed. Unlike shared data arrays that are created and distributed among the processors at compile-time, dynamic data structures must be created and distributed among the processors at runtime. A mechanism for specifying the distribution of nodes in a dynamic data structure is also needed. Unlike arrays whose elements have indices, the nodes of a dynamic data structure have no unique names that could be used to specify a mapping of nodes in a dynamic data structure to processors.

On a shared-memory machine pointers through which shared data structures are accessed are implemented as memory addresses. Clearly this imple-

S. Pande, D.P. Agrawal (Eds.): Compiler Optimizations for Scalable PS, LNCS 1808, pp. 683-708, 2001.

mentation of a pointer is not applicable to a distributed-memory machine. Even if a global pointer representation was available, an additional problem exists. Once a dynamic data structure is distributed among the processors, the pointers that link the nodes would also be scattered across the processors. Each processor must traverse these links to access the nodes in the data structure. Thus, the links must be broadcast to all processors creating excessive interprocessor communication. Thus an efficient mechanism for traversing and accessing a dynamic data structure is required.

In this chapter an approach for distributing and accessing dynamic data structures on distributed-memory machines is presented that addresses the problems described above. Language and compiler support for SPMD execution of programs with dynamic data structures is developed. Extensions to a C-like language are developed which allow the user to specify dynamic name generation and data distribution strategies. The dynamic name generation strategy assigns a name to each node added to a dynamic data structure at runtime. A dynamic distribution strategy is a mapping between names and processor ids that is used to distribute a dynamic data structure as it is created at runtime. The compilation strategy used in this approach allows the traversal of a data structure without generating interprocessor communication. The name assigned to a node is a function of the position of the node in the data structure. Each processor can generate the names of the nodes independently and traverse the data structure through name generation without requiring interprocessor communication.

The subsequent sections first present the language constructs for declaring regular distributed data structures and specifying dynamic name generation and distribution strategies. The semantics of pointer operations used to construct and manipulate local and distributed dynamic data structures is described. Compilation techniques for translating programs with dynamic data structures into SPMD programs are presented next. Extensions for supporting irregular dynamic data structures are developed. Some compile-time optimizations are also briefly discussed. Discussion of related work concludes this chapter.

2. Language Support for Regular Data Structures

In this section language constructs required for expressing processor structures, declaring local and distributed dynamic data structures, and specifying dynamic name generation and distribution strategies are presented. The semantics of pointer related operations used for constructing and manipulating dynamic data structures are also discussed.

2.1 Processor Structures

To express the processing requirements the user is provided with processor declaration statements shown below. In each of these declarations the user specifies the number of processors required. The selection of the declaration (TREE, ARRAY or MESH) determines the topology in which the processors are to be organized. Neighboring processors in the given topologies are considered to interact frequently. Thus, it is preferable that these processors are directly linked. The advantage of specifying topologies is that the subset of processors that are allocated to the program can be selected to match the communication patterns expected to occur frequently in the program. Good embeddings of the available topologies into the physical topology of the system, for example a hypercube, can be predetermined. Routing techniques for different topologies can be implemented once and used at runtime by all applications. In the declarations below, in case of a TREE the degree of each node and the total number of processors is specified by the user and in the cases of ARRAY and MESH structures the number of processors along each dimension are specified.

```
processor TREE ( degree; num );
processor ARRAY ( num );
processor MESH ( num₁; num₂ );
```

Each processor in a processor structure is also assigned a logical id denoted as Π which contains one or more fields $(\pi_1, \pi_2 \ldots \pi_m)$. The number of fields chosen should be appropriate for uniquely identifying each processor in a given processor topology. The fields in the processor id have positive non-zero values. The processor id Π_0 $(=(0,0,..))$ will never be assigned to any processor and therefore it is used to indicate a null processor id. The mapping between the names (Ψ) of data items and processor ids (Π) will determine the manner in which the data structure is distributed among the processors. We assume that processor ids of the ARRAY and MESH topologies are represented by a single integer and a pair of integers respectively. The processor id of the TREE topology consists of two integers, the first identifies a level in the tree topology and the second identifies the specific processor at that level.

2.2 Dynamic Data Structures

Dynamic data structures are declared using pointer variables as in commonly used languages such as C. The user can declare a *base* type which describes the nodes used in building a data structure. From this base type the user can derive new types which represent simple *local* and *distributed* data structures. In addition, complex *hierarchical* data structures may also be specified. Each level in the hierarchy of such a data structure is a simple local or distributed data structure. By declaring variables of the above types the user can then write programs that construct and manipulate dynamic data structures.

The nodes of a distributed data structure are spread among the processors using a distribution scheme specified by the user. All nodes belonging to a local data structure either reside on a single processor or are replicated on all processors. If a local data structure is not a part of any distributed hierarchical data structure, then it is replicated on all processors. However, if the local data structure is a substructure contained within a distributed level of a hierarchical data structure, then all nodes in the local substructure reside on the single processor at which the parent node containing the local substructure resides.

In this work SPMD execution is based upon the owner-computes rule. Thus, a statement that operates on a non-replicated data structure is executed by a single processor. On the other hand statements that operate on replicated local data structures are executed by all processors. As a result any modification made to a replicated local data structure is made by each processor to its local copy. Therefore at any given point in the program the copies of a local data structure as seen by different processors are identical.

The type of a pointer variable is used by the compiler to determine how the data structure associated with the pointer variable is to be implemented. In addition to declaring pointer variables representing local and distributed dynamic data structures, the user may also declare temporary pointer variables of the base type to assist in the traversal of dynamic data structures.

There is one major restriction that is imposed on distributed data structures. A node may belong to a single distributed data structure at a given time. This restriction allows the processor at which the node resides to be uniquely determined. If a node belonging to a local or distributed data structure is to be added to another distributed data structure, the user must explicitly copy the node from the former to the latter. In the remainder of this section the type and variable declarations and the semantics of operations involving pointer variables is described in greater detail.

The type declaration of a pointer type is augmented with an attribute which specifies whether the data structure built using this type is to be distributed across the processors or it is simply a local data structure.

type NodeType **is** { **distributed** | **local** } BaseType;

Doubly linked data structures are viewed as being derived from singly linked structures created by associating with a unidirectional link, a link in the reverse direction. The creation of a link from one node to the next automatically creates the reverse link. In a language like C a doubly-linked data structure is implemented by introducing two distinct links that must be explicitly manipulated by the user. This is because C does not provide a language construct for expressing reverse links. Given a link *ptr*, the presence of a reverse link *revptr* is expressed using the **reverse** construct shown below. The reverse pointers, such as *revptr*, can be only used for traversing a data structure. The creation of new nodes must be carried out using the original pointer *ptr*.

```
*pointertype ptr;
reverse (ptr,revptr);
```

A pointer variable in a program may be of a base type, a local data structure type, and a distributed data structure type. These variables are used to create new nodes, traverse existing data structures, access data stored in a data structure, and manipulate data structures through pointer assignments. The pointer variables are classified into three general categories: *handles*, *constructors*, and *temporaries*. The semantics of pointer related operations is based upon the category to which a pointer variable belongs.

A *handle* is a pointer variable which is of the type representing a local or distributed data structure. If a node is created using a handle it is assumed that this is the first node in the data structure. If the handle points to a local data structure, then a node is created at each processor so that a replicated structure can be built. However, if the local data structure is a substructure of a distributed data structure, then the node is created at the processor where the containing node of the distributed structure resides. If the handle points to a distributed structure, the distribution scheme will enable the identification of the processor at which the node is to be located. On the other hand if the current data structure is a substructure of another distributed data structure, then the processor at which the node resides will be inherited from the parent node. Since a handle is essentially a global variable that provides access to a distributed data structure, it is replicated on all processors.

The pointer variables that are fields of a node belonging to a local or distributed data structure are called *constructors*. These pointer variables are used to connect together the nodes belonging to the data structure. When an additional node is added to a data structure using a constructor, it is known that the data structure is being expanded. In the case of distributed data structures this information enables us to ascertain the processor at which the new node is to be located.

Temporary pointer variables assist in the traversal and construction of a pointer-based data structure. A temporary is declared to be of a base type. If a temporary points to a node in a local or distributed data structure it can be used to *traverse* the data structure. The same temporary can be used to traverse a local data structure in one part of the program and a distributed data structure in another part of the program. It can be used to create and initialize single nodes which can be added to a local or distributed data structure. After the node has been added to a data structure the temporary pointer variable can be used to traverse the data structure. The type of a temporary pointer varies from simply being a base type to a local or distributed data structure type derived from the base type. Since a temporary may be used by all processors to traverse a distributed data structure, it is replicated on all processors. A node created using a temporary can be added to the data structure.

The above discussion was primarily limited to a single data structure. Constructors and handles also play an important role in programs involving multiple data structures. In particular, they can be used to split or merge distributed data structures. For example, given a distributed link list, let us consider a constructor pointing to an element of the link list. If this constructor is assigned to another handle of a distributed link list type, then the original list is split at the position of the constructor and now forms a list corresponding to the handle to which the constructor is assigned. Thus, the above process results in splitting of a distributed link list into two distributed lists. The merging of distributed lists can be achieved by assigning the value of the handle corresponding to one list to the constructor within the last list element of the other list.

2.3 Name Generation and Distribution Strategies

Each element of a pointer-based data structure is assigned a name. A name denoted as Ψ will contain one or more fields $(\psi_1, \psi_2 \ldots \psi_n)$. The manner in which these names are to be derived is specified by the user; hence the number of fields appropriate for describing the data structure is also chosen by the user. The name generation strategy must specify the name of the first node in the data structure. In addition, given a node n with name Ψ the computation of names of nodes directly connected to n are also specified. In other words the computation of the name of each node $n \rightarrow ptr_i$ denoted as $\Psi.ptr_i$ is also specified. If the link represented by ptr_i is a bidirectional one, then the computation of $\Psi.revptr_i$ from Ψ is also specified. The construct for specifying the naming strategy for a distributed data structure $DistType$ is shown below.

```
name DistType {
        first: ( Ψ₀ );
        Ψ.ptr₁: f₁(Ψ);
        Ψ.revptr₁: f₁⁻¹(Ψ);

        ......

        Ψ.ptrₙ: fₙ(Ψ);
        Ψ.revptrₙ: fₙ⁻¹(Ψ);
}
```

This mapping of a distributed data structure type on a given processor topology is specified by the user. The construct for specifying the distribution strategy of a distributed type $DistType$ on a processor topology $ProcStruc$ is shown below.

```
distribute DistType on ProcStruc {
            Π = ( π₁ = g₁(Ψ), π₂ = g₂(Ψ), ........ πₘ = gₘ(Ψ) )
}
```

2.4 Examples

The constructs described in the preceding sections are illustrated through three examples: a tree, a two dimensional mesh, and a list of link lists (an example of a hierarchical data structure). These examples demonstrate that distribution strategies similar to cyclic and block-cyclic distributions used for static arrays can be expressed for dynamic data structures using the name generation and distribution constructs described in the preceding section.

First let us consider the specification of a distributed tree shown below. A general name generation and distribution strategy applicable to trees of an arbitrary degree n are presented.

```
type Node is distributed
            struct {
                    int data;
                    *Node ptr₁, ptr₂, ... ptrₙ
            };
var *Node atree;
```

The naming strategy that is presented next assigns a single integer as a name to each node in the tree data structure. The root of the tree is assigned the name one, the successive nodes at a given level are assigned consecutive numbers as their names, and lower numbers are assigned to lower levels in the tree. Fig. 2.1 shows the names of the nodes.

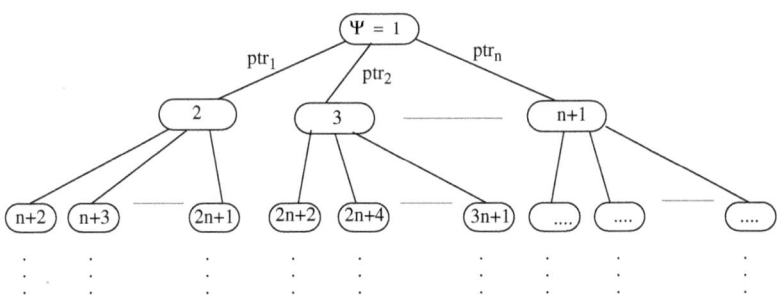

Fig. 2.1. Naming strategy for the distributed tree data structure.

The name (Ψ) assigned to a node is simply the position of the node in the distributed tree data structure. The name of any other node $P \rightarrow ptr_i$ is computed from the name of node P. Implementation of a doubly-linked tree structure requires an additional function for computing the position of node $P \rightarrow revptr_i$ from the position of node P. The function which computes the name for node $P \rightarrow revptr_i$ from the name of node P is the inverse of the function that computes the name of node $P \rightarrow ptr_i$ from the name of node P.

```
name Node {
    first: 0
    .....
    Ψ.ptrᵢ: n (Ψ − 1) + i + 1
    Ψ.revptrᵢ: Ψ−i−1⁄n+1
    .....
}
```

$$\Psi.ptr_i: n\ (\Psi - 1) + i + 1$$
$$\Psi.revptr_i: \frac{\Psi - i - 1}{n+1}$$

In order to describe the distribution of a tree on a processor structure, both the processor structure and the dynamic data structure are viewed as consisting of series of levels. Successive levels of the data structure are mapped to successive levels of the processor structure. The root nodes of the data structure are created on the first level of the processor structure. If the number of levels in the data structure is greater than the number of levels in the processor structure, multiple levels of the data structure will be mapped to a single level of the processor structure. The children of a node assigned to a processor at the last level in the processor structure are assigned to processors at the first level of the processor structure. The nodes in the data structure at a given level are distributed equally among the processors in the corresponding level in the processor structure. In this scheme a processor id is represented as $\Pi = (p, l)$ and it refers to the pth processor at level l. The function *ProcId* given below returns the processor at which a node with position Π should be located.

distribute Node on ProcStruc { $\Pi = ProcId(\Psi)$ }

function ProcId(Ψ) {
/* function returns processor id Π to which node Ψ is mapped */
/* NumLevels(*ProcStruc*) - number of levels in *ProcStruc* */
/* NumProcs(*l*) - number of processors at level l of *ProcStruc* */
    currentΨ = currentlevel = 0;
    while (true) {
        currentlevel++;
        l = (currentlevel - 1) mod *NumLevels*(*ProcStruc*) + 1;
        for j = $1..n^{currentlevel-1}$ {
            p = (j-1) mod *NumProcs*(l) + 1;
            currentΨ++;
            if (Ψ == currentΨ) { return (p,l) }
}}}

A desirable property of the above strategy is that it tends to divide a data structure into pieces which are identical to the processor structure. For example, if a binary tree data structure is mapped to a fixed size binary tree of processors, this strategy divides up the data structure into binary trees of the size of the processor structure. This is illustrated in Fig. 2.2 by the distribution of a binary tree data structure on a binary tree processor structure with seven processors.

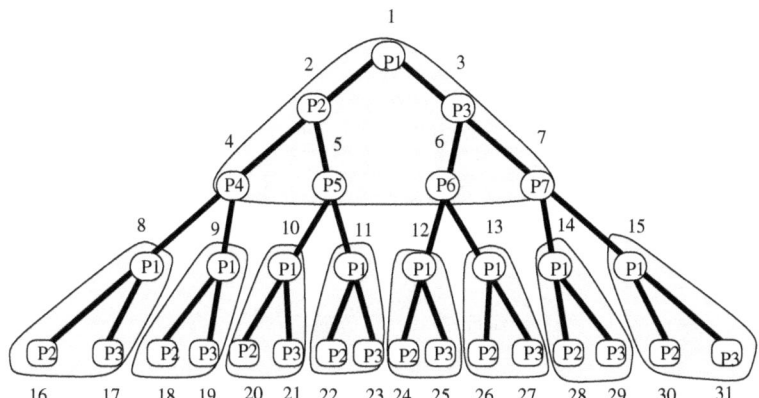

Fig. 2.2. Distributing a binary tree structure on processor TREE (2, 7).

Consider the specification of the mapping of a data structure representing a two dimensional mesh to a $n \times n$ processor mesh. Simple mapping functions which assign a unique name to each node and distribute the data structure among the processors are given below. Both the names and processor ids are specified as integer pairs. The name of a node is the same irrespective of the parent node through which it is computed and hence it is unique.

```
constant n = 2;
processor MESH ( 1:n, 1:n );
type
      Node is struct { int data; *Node left,right };
      DistMesh is distributed Node;
      name DistMesh {
            first: (ψ₁ = 0, ψ₂ = 0);
            Ψ.left: (ψ₁ + 1, ψ₂);
            Ψ.right: (ψ₁, ψ₂ + 1);
      }
      distribute DistMesh on MESH {
            Π = ( π₁ = ψ₁ mod n, π₂ = ψ₂ mod n )
      }
var *DistMesh amesh;
```

Fig. 2.3 illustrates the division of a mesh among the processors in MESH (1:2, 1:2). As one can see, like the distribution strategy for the tree, this distribution strategy also divides the mesh data structure into smaller pieces corresponding to the mesh processor structure.

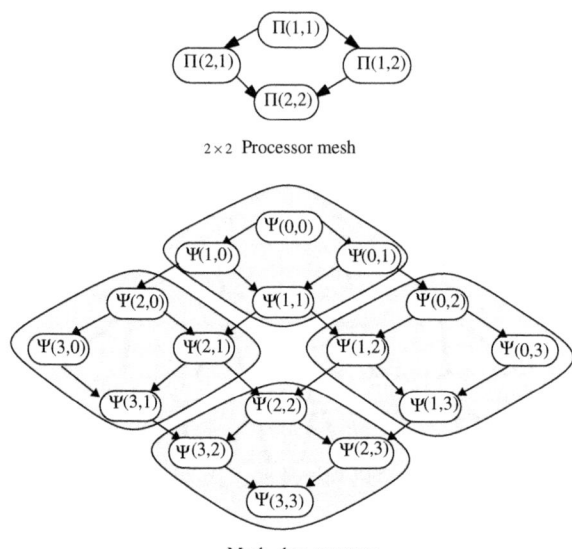

2×2 Processor mesh

Mesh data structure

Fig. 2.3. Distributed mesh data structure.

The final example is that of a hierarchical data structure. The data structure represents a list of link lists. Lists at two levels in the hierarchy are distributed along the two dimensions of the MESH processor structure. The lists at the second level of the data structure are doubly linked. The naming strategy used by the two types of lists is the same and consists of consecutive numbers. The distribution of the top level list assigns consecutive pairs of list elements to consecutive processors on the first column of processors. The distribution of a list contained within an element of the top level list is carried out in pairs along the processors belonging to a row in the MESH. The processor row number to which such a list is assigned is inherited from the containing element of the top level list. This is indicated by the assignment of an asterisk to π_1 in the distribution strategy for List. In Fig. 2.4 the names of the nodes are written inside the nodes and the integer pairs are processor ids at which the nodes reside.

```
constant n = 2;
processor MESH (1:n, 1:n);
type
     List is distributed
            struct { int data; *List next; reverse (next,prev) };
     Node is distributed
            struct { *List alist; *Node down };
var *Node ListOfLists;
name List { first: 1; ψ.next: ψ + 1; ψ.prev: ψ - 1 }
name Node {first: 1; ψ.down: ψ + 1 }
```

distribute List on MESH { $\Pi=(\pi_1=^*, \pi_2= (\lceil\psi/2\rceil-1) \bmod n + 1)$ }
distribute Node on MESH { $\Pi=(\pi_1= (\lceil\psi/2\rceil-1) \bmod n + 1, \pi_2=1)$ }

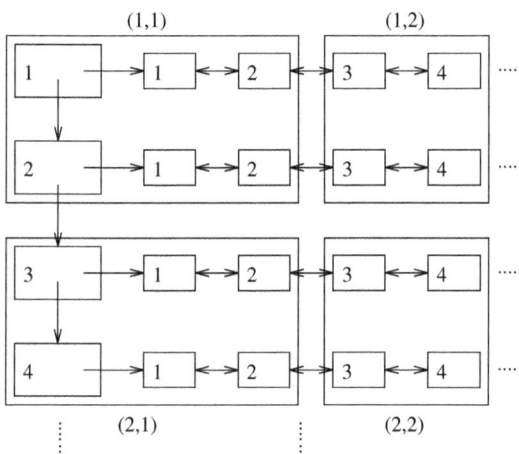

Fig. 2.4. A list of link lists.

The distribution of the tree data structure and the mesh data structures presented in this section are analogous to the cyclic distribution schemes used for static arrays. In contrast the distribution specified for a list of link lists is similar to a block-cyclic distribution used for distributing static arrays.

3. Compiler Support for Regular Data Structures

In this section first a representation of pointers that is suitable for distributed memory machines is developed. This representation is based upon names that are global to all processors rather than simple memory addresses that are local to individual processors. The translation rules for operations involving dynamic data structures to enable owner-computes rule based SPMD execution are described in detail.

3.1 Representing Pointers and Data Structures

On a shared memory machine a pointer variable is simply the memory address of the data item that it points to. To accommodate distributed data structures the notion of pointers must be generalized so that they can be used for the distribution of a data structure across the processors in the system. A pointer variable **P** which points to a node in a *distributed* data structure is represented as $ds < \Psi : [\Pi, \alpha] >$, whose components are interpreted as follows:

P.ds: uniquely identifies the data structure;
P.Ψ: is the *name* of the node in the data structure **ds** to which **P** points;
P.Π: is the *processor* at which the node resides; and
P.α: is the *address* in processor **P.Π**'s memory at which the node resides.

The pointer $ds < 0 : [\Pi_0, 0] >$ represents a *nil* pointer and **P.α.data** denotes the address of the data field *data* of the node **P** points to. When a new node is added to a distributed data structure its name Ψ is computed from the names of its neighbors using the user specified name generation strategy. From the name of a node Ψ, the processor Π at which it resides is computed.

Each processor represents a distributed data structure as a *hash table* which is identified by **ds**. The hash table is initially empty and a nil assignment to the handle of a distributed data structure clears the hash table. The processor Π is computed from Ψ only when the node is initially created. Each processor stores the information that the node Ψ exists and that it resides at processor Π in the hash table. In addition, the processor Π also stores the address of the node α. The node name Ψ is used to access and store the information. The runtime mechanism for identifying the processor that will execute a given statement uses the information stored in the hash table when the statement computes a value in a node of the dynamic data structure. The same information is also used for generating interprocessor communication required for the execution of the statement under owner-computes rule based SPMD execution.

The hash table is manipulated using the following functions: *PutNode(ds, Ψ)* stores information, *GetNode(ds,Ψ)* retrieves information, *DeleteNode(ds, Ψ)* deletes nodes in the hash table, and *ClearTable(ds)* reinitializes the hash table. It should be noted that although the hash table is replicated at each processor the nodes in the data structure are not replicated. The hash table representation enables us to avoid interprocessor communication during runtime resolution at the expense of storage at each node.

Temporary pointer variables and pointer variables of a local data structure type are also represented as $ds < \Psi : [\Pi, \alpha] >$. In case of local data structures ds is not a hash table but rather the address of the first node in the data structure and the field Ψ is always zero. The field Π is Π_0 if the structure is replicated at all processors; otherwise it is the id of the processor at which the local structure resides. Finally, α is the local address of the node in the processor's local memory. In the case of temporaries initially fields ds, Ψ, and Π are zero and if the temporary points to a single node created through it, then α is the address of that node. However, if the temporary points to a local or distributed data structure its fields take the form associated with local and distributed pointer types. The Ψ and Π values of a temporary can be examined to discern whether it currently points to a single node which does not belong to any data structure, a local data structure, or a distributed data structure. This distinction is important since it determines the semantics of the operations performed using a temporary pointer variable.

3.2 Translation of Pointer Operations

The translation of all types of operations that are performed on pointer variables is discussed in this section. The semantics of each operation depends upon the categories of the pointer variables involved in the operation. Initially all pointers are nil. When a new node is created using a pointer variable, the node's representation is computed and assigned to the pointer variable. As mentioned earlier, the nodes in a distributed data structure are referred to by their names and a distributed data structure is traversed through the generation of these names. The order in which the node names are generated corresponds to the order in which the nodes can be accessed using the links in the data structure. The compiler uses the following communication primitives during code generation:

- the operation SEND(pid,addr) sends the value stored at the address *addr* on the executing processor to processor *pid*;
- the operation global send GSEND(addr) sends the value stored at address *addr* on the executing processor to all other processors; and
- RECV(addr,pid) receives a value from *pid* and stores it at the address *addr* on the executing processor.

In this section f, f^{-1} and g are used to denote a name generation function of a regular pointer, a name generation function of a reverse pointer and a distribution function.

Translation of Node Creation Operations

Nodes can be created using the *new* operation on pointer variables. First the semantics and translation of the *new* operation for handles and temporaries is discussed and then the constructors are considered.

| new(P) |

P is a distributed handle:

If a node is created using a handle to a distributed data structure it is assumed to be the first node in the data structure whose name can be found from the name generation scheme provided by the user. From the name of the node the processor at which the node will reside is determined from the distribution strategy provided by the user. In case the data structure is a substructure of a hierarchical data structure and the containing structure at the preceding level in the hierarchy is also a distributed structure, then a processor offset is computed based upon the containing data structure. This offset is used in conjunction with the user specified mapping strategy to determine the processor at which the node is to reside.

In order to implement the above strategy with each data structure an attribute $ds.\Pi_{inherit}$ is associated which is set at runtime when the enclosing node in an hierarchical data structure is created. If there is no enclosing node then, it is set to Π_0. The processor offset associated with a data structure ds, denoted as $ds.\Pi_{offset}$, is computed from $ds.\Pi_{inherit}$ and the user specified distribution strategy. For data structures that do not require any offset (eg., simple data structures that are not contained in any hierarchical structure), $ds.\Pi_{offset}$ is simply Π_0. Since a handle is replicated at each processor all processors carry out the assignment. However, only the processor at which the node is to reside allocates storage for the node. The hash table is updated to indicate the state of the data structure.

```
ClearTable(P.ds); P.Ψ = first;
if handle P is contained in a distributed node
    { P.ds.Π_offset = Π_inherit − g(P.Ψ) }
else { P.ds.Π_offset = Π_0 }
P.Π = g(P.Ψ) + P.ds.Π_offset;
if (mypid == P.Π) { P.α = malloc ( SizeOfNode ) } else { P.α = nil }
PutNode(ds,P.Ψ)=(exists=true,processor=P.Π,address=P.α);
Initialize Π_inherit for all enclosed data structures;
```

P is a local handle:

If a node is created using a handle to a local data structure the value of Ψ is zero. If the local data structure is not a substructure of a distributed data structure, then all processors allocate storage since a local data structure is replicated at each processor and each processor assigns its own id to Π. On the other hand if the local structure is a substructure of a distributed structure, then only the processor at which the containing node resides allocates storage for the structure.

```
P.Ψ = 0; P.Π = mypid;
if ((P.Π == mypid) or (P.Π == Π_0))
    { P.α = malloc ( SizeOfNode ) }
```

P is a temporary:

Finally in case of a temporary, all processors allocate storage for a node in their respective local memories. The translation rules described above are summarized in code below. In this code $mypid$ represents the id of the processor executing the code. A temporary is replicated at each processor. A temporary is assigned $0 < 0 : [\Pi_0, \alpha] >$ where α is the address of the node. The storage is allocated by each processor in its local memory.

P.$ds = 0$; P.$\Psi = 0$; P.$\Pi = \Pi_0$; P.$\alpha = $ malloc (SizeOfNode);

$$\boxed{\text{new}(P \rightarrow ptr_i)}$$

<u>P points to a node in a local data structure:</u>

If the nodes are created using constructors belonging to local data structures a new node is created and added to the data structure as shown below. In addition, if the link involved in the operation is a bidirectional link then code is generated to create a bidirectional link. The value of $P.\Pi$ determines whether the local data structure is a replicated or an unreplicated data structure.

```
if ((P.Π == mypid) or (P.Π == Π₀)) { addr = malloc ( SizeOfNode ) }
else { addr = nil }
store pointer 0 < 0 : [P.Π, addr] > at P.α.ptrᵢ;
if ptrᵢ is bidirectional { store 0 < 0 : [P.Π, P.α] > at addr.revptrᵢ }
```

<u>P points to a node in a distributed data structure:</u>

The creation of a node using a constructor belonging to a distributed data structure requires the computation of the name of the new node and assignment of this node to a processor. $CreatePtr_i(ds, \Psi)$ computes and returns the pointer representation of the newly created node. It makes use of the name generation and distribution schemes for assigning the node to a processor. Recall that a node cannot be created using a reverse pointer $P \rightarrow revptr$.

```
P → ptrᵢ = CreatePtrᵢ(P.ds, P.Ψ)
function CreatePtrᵢ ( ds,Ψ ) {
    Ψ = f(Ψ); Π = g(Ψ) + ds.Πₒffset;
    if (mypid == Π) { α = malloc ( SizeOfNode ) } else { α = 0 }
    PutNode(ds,Ψ) = (exists = true, processor = Π, address = α)
    return( ds < Ψ : [Π, α] > )
}
```

Translation of Traversal Operations

References must be made to the pointer fields of the nodes in the data structure in order to traverse the data structure. In the case of distributed data structures these references are transformed so that the modified code performs the traversal through node *names* using $TraversePtr_i(ds, \Psi)$ and $TraverseRevptr_i(ds, \Psi)$ functions. On the other hand the traversal of local data structures does not require the computation of *names*.

$$\boxed{P \rightarrow ptr_i \ (P \rightarrow revptr_i)}$$

<u>P points to a node in a local data structure</u>
```
if ((P.Π == mypid) or (P.Π == Π₀))
```

{ P.$\alpha.ptr_i$ (P.$\alpha.revptr_i$) is the address at which the node is stored }

P points to a node in a distributed data structure

TraversePtr_i(P.ds,P.Ψ) (Traverse$Revptr_i$(P.ds,P.Ψ))
    returns the representation of $P \rightarrow ptr_i$ ($P \rightarrow revptr_i$)

```
function TraversePtr_i ( ds,Ψ ) {
    Ψ = f(Ψ)
    (exists, Π, α) = GetNode(ds,Ψ)
    if exists { return ( ds < Ψ : [Π,α] > ) }
    else { return ( ds < 0 : [Π_0,0] > ) }
}
```

```
function TraverseRevptr_i ( ds,Ψ ) {
    Ψ = f^{-1}(Ψ)
    (exists, Π, α) = GetNode(ds,Ψ)
    if exists { return ( ds < Ψ : [Π,α] > ) }
    else { return ( ds < 0 : [Π_0,0] > ) }
}
```

Translation of Pointer Assignments

The building and modification of a dynamic data structure is carried out using pointer assignments. First the affects of a nil assignment are considered and then assignment of one pointer variable to another is considered.

$\boxed{\text{P = nil}}$

A nil assignment to a handle (local or distributed) essentially eliminates the nodes in the entire data structure. On the other hand, a nil assignment to a temporary, or a constructor accessed through a temporary, that points to a node in a data structure eliminates the node. A nil assignment to a temporary variable which does not point to any other data structure simply sets the pointer to nil and does not have an affect on any other data structure. In summary a major function of nil assignments is to delete one or all nodes from a local or distributed data structure.

P is a temporary that does not point to a data structure

P = 0 < 0 : $[\Pi_0, 0]$ >

P is a distributed constructor

    if (P.Π == mypid)
        { delete node corresponding to P.Ψ from hash table for P.ds }
    P = ds < 0 : $[\Pi_0, 0]$ >

P is a local constructor

    if ((P.Π == mypid) or (P.Π == Π_0))
        { delete node associated with P.Ψ }

P $= ds < 0 : [\Pi_0, 0] >;$
P is a distributed handle
  ClearTable(P.ds); P $= ds < 0 : [\Pi_0, 0] >$
P is a local handle
   if $((P.\Pi == $ mypid$)$ or $(P.\Pi == \Pi_0))$
     { delete entire local structure }
  P $= ds < 0 : [\Pi_0, 0] >;$

$\boxed{\text{P} = \text{Q}}$

An assignment of one pointer variable to another pointer variable can have the following effects depending on the types of the pointer variables involved. A pointer assignment can result in simple *copying* of a pointer, *addition* of a node to a data structure, *splitting* of a distributed data structure into two distinct data structures, and *merging* of two data structures into one. These actions are described next in greater detail below.

Copying a pointer: The copying of pointers occurs when dealing with local data structures or when the assignment is made to a temporary variable. If P is a temporary pointer variable, which currently does not point to any data structure, then after it is assigned Q, both P and Q point to the same place. If both P and Q are pointers associated with local data structures (i.e., a local handles or constructors), then after the assignment P also points to the same address as Q. Assignments to handles of local data structures may result in addition and deletion of nodes from the data structure that it represents.

  P.ds $=$ Q.ds; P.$\Psi =$ Q.Ψ; P.$\Pi =$ Q.Π; P.$\alpha =$ Q.α

Adding a single node: Consider the situation in which Q is a temporary pointer variable through which a single node has been created. This node can be added to a local or distributed data structure by assigning Q to P, where P is a handle or constructor of a local or distributed data structure. After the assignment, Q behaves as a pointer to the data structure to which the node has been added. Notice that since the node associated with the temporary pointer Q is replicated at each site, no communication is required during this operation.

  if $((P.\Pi == $ mypid$)$ or $(P.\Pi == \Pi_0))$
     { P.$\alpha =$ Q.α }
  Q.$\Psi =$ P.Ψ; Q.$\Pi =$ P.Π;
  PutNode(P.ds,P.Ψ)

Restructuring a distributed data structure: If both P and Q point to the same distributed data structure and P is not a constructor, then assignment of Q to P simply results in pointer copying. However if P is a constructor, then the data structure is restructured. The node pointed to by Q now takes the position that P points to, and all nodes connected directly or indirectly through constructors originating at Q are also shifted to new positions. After restructuring, Q also points to the position to which the constructor P points. The restructuring is performed by function *Reposition* which also generates interprocessor communication to transfer nodes to their new sites.

Reposition(Q.ds,P.ds,$Q.\Psi$,$P.\Psi$);
$Q.\Psi = P.\Psi$; $Q.\Pi = P.\Pi$; $Q.\alpha = P.\alpha$;

```
function Reposition(oldds,newds,oldΨ,newΨ) {
    nodelist = {(oldΨ,newΨ)} ∪ {(old,new): old is derived from oldΨ}
    for each pair (old,new) ∈ nodelist st
        (mypid=g(old)) and (mypid≠g(new)) {
            (exists,Π,α) = GetNode(oldds,old); DeleteNode(oldds,old);
            SEND(g(new),α);
            PutNode(newds,new)=(exists=true,processor=g(new),address=0)
    }
    foreach pair (old,new) ∈ nodelist st
        (mypid≠g(old)) and (mypid=g(new)) {
            α = malloc( SizeOfNode ); DeleteNode(oldds,old);
            RECV(α,g(old));
            PutNode(newds,new)=(exists=true,processor=mypid,address=α)
    }
    foreach pair (old,new) ∈ nodelist st
        (mypid=g(old)) and (mypid=g(new)) {
            (exists,Π,α) = GetNode(oldds,old); DeleteNode(oldds,old);
            PutNode(newds,new)=(exists=true,processor=mypid,address=α)
    }
    Update temporaries pointing to repositioned nodes
}
```

Merging and splitting of distributed data structures: Assignments involving handles and constructors belonging to different data structures, at least one of which is distributed, results in transfer of nodes between the data structures. If P is the handle of a data structure and it is assigned Q which is a handle or a constructor of another data structure, then all nodes starting from Q's position are transferred to the data structure corresponding to P. Interprocessor communication must be generated to reposition the nodes at their new sites. If nodes are transferred from a distributed data structure to a replicated local data structure, then the above operation will essentially result in broadcast of the data structure to all processors. The restructuring is performed by function *Reposition*.

Translation of Node Data Accesses

Accessing data stored in local data structure is straightforward if it is replicated at each processor. However, in case of data in non-replicated data structures or distributed data structures, first the processor at which the data resides is located. Next either to store or retrieve data, interprocessor communication may be required. In order to perform these accesses instructions LOAD and STORE are defined. The LOAD operation copies the contents of data field *data* of the node pointed to by the pointer P into a scalar t located at processor *pid*. The STORE operation copies the contents of a scalar t residing at processor *pid* into the data field *data* of the node pointed to by the pointer P. In the LOAD/STORE operations defined below the scalar variable t is a temporary that resides at processor *pid*.

```
LOAD t, pid, P, data == t_pid = P→data
    if ( P.Ψ == P.α == 0 and P.Π == Π_0 ) { error – nil pointer }
    elseif ((P.Ψ == 0) and (P.Π == Π_0)) {
        – P points to a replicated local data structure
        if (mypid == pid ) { t = P.α.data }
    } else { – P points to a non-replicated local or distributed structure
        if (P.Π == mypid == pid) { t = P.α.data }
        elseif (P.Π == mypid ≠ pid) { SEND(pid,P.α.data) }
        elseif (P.Π ≠ mypid == pid) { RECV(t,P.Π) }
        else { – the processor is not involved in the execution because
                P.Π ≠ mypid ≠ pid }
    }
STORE t, pid, P, data == P→data = t_pid
    if ( P.Ψ == P.α == 0 and P.Π == Π_0 ) { error – nil pointer }
    elseif ((P.Ψ == 0) and (P.Π == Π_0)) {
        – P points to a replicated local data structure
        if ( mypid == pid ) { GSEND(t) }
        else RECV(P.α.data,pid)
    } else { – P points to a non-replicated local or distributed structure
        if (P.Π == mypid == pid) { P.α.data = t }
        elseif (P.Π == mypid ≠ pid) { RECV(P.α.data,pid) }
        elseif (P.Π ≠ mypid == pid) { SEND(P.Π,t) }
        else { – the processor is not involved in the execution because
                P.Π ≠ mypid ≠ pid }
    }
```

An Example

The translation of a small code fragment using the rules presented in this section is demonstrated next. The code fragment shown below traverses a distributed link list of integers. The integer value in each of the elements of the link list is incremented.

```
constant n = 4;
processor ARRAY (n);
type Node struct { int data; *Node next };
```

```
        List is distributed Node;
    name List { first: 1; ψ.next: ψ+1 };
    distribute List  ARRAY { π = (ψ − 1)modn + 1 };
    var *List alist; *Node tlist;

    tlist = alist;
    while ( tlist ≠ Nil ) {
            tlist→data = tlist→data + 1;
            tlist = tlist→next
    }
```

The loop for the traversal of the linked list is transformed into the loop shown below which will be executed in parallel by all processors in ARRAY. Under SPMD execution each processor will be responsible for incrementing list elements that reside in its local memory. As we can see the traversal is achieved through name generation and hence it does not require interprocessor communication. When the entire list has been traversed, the function $TraverseNext(ds, \psi)$ returns nil. The temporary pointer *tlist* used to traverse the link list is replicated on all processors in ARRAY.

```
    tlist = alist;
    while (tlist != nil) {
            /* tlist→data = tlist→data + 1 */
            LOAD t, tlist.Π, tlist, data
            p,tlist.Π = p,tlist.Π + 1
            STORE p, tlist.Π, tlist, data
            /* tlist = tlist→next */
            tlist = TraverseNext(tlist.ds,tlist.ψ)
    }
    function TraverseNext ( ds,ψ ) {
            ψ = ψ + 1
            (exists, ψ, α) = GetNode(ds,ψ)
            if exists { return ( ds < ψ : [π,α] >) }
            else { return ( ds < 0 : [π₀, 0] > ) }
    }
    function CreateNext ( ds,ψ ) {
            ψ = ψ + 1
            π = ProcId( ψ )
            if (mypid == π)
                { α = malloc ( SizeOfNode ) }
            else { α = 0 }
            PutNode(ds,ψ) =
                (exists = true, processor = π, address = α)
            return( ds < ψ : [π,α] > )
    }
```

```
function ProcId( ψ )
       { return ( (ψ - 1) mod 4 + 1 ) }
```

4. Supporting Irregular Data Structures

In this section we present extensions of the approach described for regular data structures so that it can also be used to support irregular data structures. In the examples considered so far the data structures considered were regular in nature and the name generated for each data item in the data structure was unique. In case of irregular data structures it is not possible to precisely specify the topology of the data structure and hence the name generation strategy. One possible approach that can be employed approximates an irregular data structure by a regular data structure for the purpose of computing the positions and names of the nodes. A consequence of such an approximation is that multiple names may be created for nodes with multiple parents. Thus from the perspective of our approach, regular data structures may be viewed as unaliased data structures and irregular data structures may be viewed as aliased data structures. The following language construct allows the user to communicate to the compiler as to whether a distributed data structure is aliased or unaliased.

type NodeType is { aliased | unaliased } distributed BaseType;

As an example, consider a distributed directed acyclic graph (DAG) shown in Fig. 4.1. In the mapping process the DAG has been approximated by a binary tree and mapped to a binary tree of processors using the strategy described previously. This process causes the nodes in the DAG with multiple parents to have multiple names. A different name is used to access the node depending on the parent through which traversal is being performed. The shared node can be accessed using node name 5 through node 2 or using node name 6 through node 3. When a node is initially created it is assigned to the processor indicated by the node name. When additional links are created to point to the same node (as by the assignment statement in Fig. 4.1), an alias is created with each additional link while the location of the node remains the same. For the DAG shown in Fig. 4.1, the shared node will be located on processor P_5, if it is created by executing the statement "$new(P \rightarrow leftchild \rightarrow rightchild)$". If it is created using statement "$new(P \rightarrow rightchild \rightarrow leftchild)$" then it will be located at processor P_6. From the above example it is clear that an irregular data structure must be declared as an aliased data structure. Although in this example we considered an acyclic data structure, in general this approach handles cyclic data structures as well.

In order to implement aliasing, the node information stored at each processor should be augmented to indicate whether the node is an alias of another node. If the node is an alias, the field $orig\Psi$ will contain the position of the node of which the current node is an alias, otherwise $orig\Psi$ is zero. A pointer assignment which assigns to a handle/constructor another pointer, that points to a node in the data structure, causes the creation of an alias. A nil assignment causes the destruction of a name. If the destroyed name has aliases one of these aliases must be chosen as the new name for the node and the node information of all aliases is updated. Thus, for each node we must also maintain the list of its aliases. The field *aliases* contains this information. In addition we must also traverse the graph and change the names of all nodes that were derived from the destroyed name. This, processor is quite similar to the restructuring process described for regular data structures. However, there is one important difference. Although the node *names* are modified the nodes are not migrated. This is because for an aliased data structure it is not clear whether the migration will result in a superior distribution of nodes.

$$\Psi:[\Pi, \alpha] \ \ \text{Ⓟi}$$

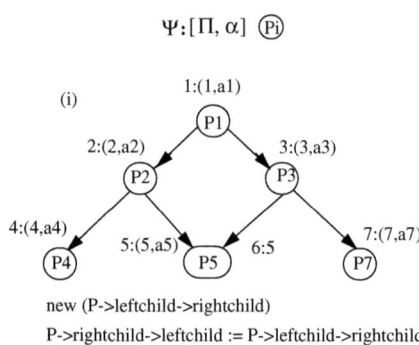

(i)

new (P->leftchild->rightchild)
P->rightchild->leftchild := P->leftchild->rightchild

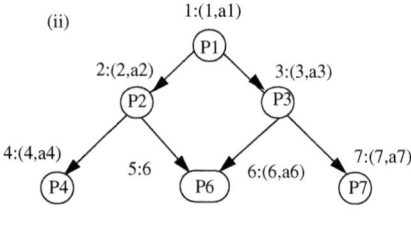

(ii)

new (P->rightchild->leftchild)
P->leftchild->rightchild := P->rightchild->leftchild

Fig. 4.1. A directed acyclic graph.

Creation of an alias

P = Q, where P is a distributed handle/constructor:
   PutNode(P.ds,P.Ψ) =
      (exists=true, processor=Q.Π, address=Q.α, origΨ=Q.Ψ, aliases=null)
   add to the list of aliases of origΨ another alias P.Ψ

Destruction of a name

P = nil, where P is a distributed handle/constructor:
    let P.aliases = $\{a_1, a_2, ... a_n\}$
    select a_1 as the new name for the node
    PutNode(P.ds,a_1) = (exists=true, processor=P.Π,
        address=P.α, origΨ=0, aliases=$\{a_2, ... a_n\}$)
    for $a_2 .... a_n$ {
        origΨ = a_1; aliases = aliases - $\{a_1\}$;
        traverse data structure using $P.\Psi$ and
        find all node names that were derived from $P.\Psi$
        recompute the position field of these nodes from a_1
    }

The $Traverseptr_i(ds, \Psi)$ and $TraverseRevptr_i(ds, \Psi)$ must be modified so that when nodes are traversed using their aliases, the aliases are replaced by the original *names*. This, is important because if this is not done then creation of a node's alias will require the creation of aliases for all nodes reachable through pointer traversals from the newly aliased node. For a structure with loops, such as a circular link list, infinite number of aliases will be created. The function $CreatePtr_i(ds, \Psi)$ remains the same because no aliases are ever created during the creation of new nodes.

```
function TraversePtr_i ( ds,Ψ ) {
    Ψ = f(Ψ)
    (exists, Π, α, origΨ) = GetNode(ds,Ψ)
    if not exists { return ( ds < 0 : [Π₀,0] > ) }
    elseif (origΨ ≠ 0) { return ( ds < origΨ : [Π,α] > ) }
    else return ( ds < Ψ : [Π,α] > )
}
function TraverseRevptr_i ( ds,Ψ ) {
    Ψ = f⁻¹(Ψ)
    (exists, Π, α, origΨ) = GetNode(ds,Ψ)
    if not exists { return ( ds < 0 : [Π₀,0] > ) }
    elseif (origΨ ≠ 0) { return ( ds < origΨ : [Π,α] > ) }
    else return ( ds < Ψ : [Π,α] > )
}
```

It should be noted that the implementation of an aliased data structure is more general than an unaliased data structure. Therefore an unaliased data structure can also be correctly handled by the implementation for an aliased data structure. In such a situation no aliases will be created and hence the list of aliases will always be empty for all nodes.

5. Compile-Time Optimizations

The focus of this chapter has been on translation or code generation rules SPMD execution. In reality to obtain good performance, optimizations must also be performed. In context of programs based upon shared data arrays, communication optimizations have been found to be useful [2]. Similar optimizations can also be applied to programs with dynamic data structures. Some additional optimizations should be performed in context of dynamic data structures.

Faster traversal functions: Dynamic data structures are accessed through link traversals which can be slow in contrast to indexed random accesses to array elements. Thus, techniques to allow faster traversal of dynamic data structures would be of potential benefit. In the linked list example of the preceding section, each processor iterates through all of the node positions in the linked list, although each processor only operates on those elements of the list that are local to itself. Through static analysis the compiler can determine that the iterations of the loop can be executed in parallel. Thus, the overhead of traversal can be reduced by using a function which only iterates through the nodes that reside on the same processor.

Parallel creation of dynamic data structures: While it is clear that parallelism is exploited during SPMD execution of code that operates on a distributed data structure, the same is not true during the creation of a distributed dynamic data structure. This is because each processor must update its hash table when a node is added to the data structure. Through compile-time analysis the situations in which a data structure can be created in parallel by a distinct creation phase can be identified. The updating of the hash table can be delayed to the end of the creation phase. Each processor can broadcast the names of the nodes that it created at the end of the creation phase to update the hash tables of other processors. In this approach parallelism is exploited during the creation of the data structure and the updating of the hash tables is also carried out in parallel.

Storage optimization: Another source of significant overhead in programs with dynamic data structures arises due to dynamic allocation and deallocation of storage. During the restructuring of a data structure we can reduce the storage allocation overhead by reusing already allocated storage. For example, if elements of a distributed data structure are redistributed among the processors, storage freed by elements transferred from a processor can be reused by elements transferred to the processor.

6. Related Work

This chapter addressed the problem of supporting dynamic data structures on distributed-memory machines using owner-computes rule based SPMD execution. The implementation of globally shared dynamic data structures is made possible by assignment of global names to the elements in a data structure. The compiler is responsible for translating a sequential program into parallel code that executes in SPMD mode. In spirit this approach is similar to the approach originally proposed by Callahan and Kennedy for programs with shared data arrays [1]. The techniques described in this chapter differ from the preliminary version of this work [3] in the following way. In earlier work aggregate operations, such as merging and splitting, of distributed data structures were not allowed and hierarchical data structures were not considered.

An alternative strategy for supporting dynamic data structures has been proposed in [7]. While the approach presented in this chapter relies on the transfer of distributed data among the processors to enable the execution of program statements, the approach proposed by Rogers et al. relies of migration of computation across the processors to enable the execution of statements that require operands distributed among various processors.

To obtain good performance, programs with dynamic data structures must be transformed to expose greater degrees of parallelism. Furthermore techniques for identifying data dependences among program statements are required to perform these transformations. Language extensions can also be developed to facilitate the analysis. In [4,5] Hendren et al. address the above issues.

Acknowledgement. This work was supported in part by the National Science Foundation through a Presidential Young Investigator Award CCR-9157371.

References

1. Callahan, D., Kennedy, K. (1988): Compiling programs for distributed-memory multiprocessors. Journal of Supercomputing **2**, 151–169
2. Gong, C., Gupta, R., Melhem, R. (1992): Compilation techniques for communication optimizations on distributed-memory machines. Proceedings of International Conference on Parallel Processing **II**, St. Charles, Illinois, 39–46
3. Gupta, R. (1992): SPMD execution of programs with pointer-based data structures on distributed-memory machines. Journal of Parallel and Distributed Computing **16(2)**, 92–107
4. Hendren, L.J., Hummel, J., Nicolau, A. (1992): Abstractions for recursive pointer data structures: improving the analysis and transformation of imperative programs. Proceedings of ACM Conference on Programming Language Design and Implementation, 249–260
5. Hendren, L.J., Gao, G.R. (1992): Designing programming languages for analyzability: a fresh look at pointer data structures. Proceedings of the International Conference on Computer Languages, Oakland, California, 242–251
6. Hiranandani, S., Kennedy, K., Koelbel, C., Kremer, U., Tseng, C.-W. (1991): An overview of the Fortran D programming system. Proceedings of the Fourth Workshop on Languages and Compilers for Parallel Computing, Santa Clara, California

7. Rogers, A., Carlisle, M.C., Reppy, J.H., Hendren, L.J. (1995): Supporting dynamic data structures on distributed-memory machines. ACM Transactions on Programming Languages and Systems **17(2)**, 233–263
8. Rothberg, E. (1992): Exploiting memory hierarchy in sequential and parallel sparse Cholesky factorization. Ph.D. Thesis, Technical Report STAN-CS-92-1459, Stanford University
9. Samet, H. (1989): The Design and Analysis of Spatial Data Structures. Addison-Wesley
10. Warren, M.S., J.K. Salmon (1993): A parallel hashed oct-tree n-body algorithm. Proceedings of Supercomputing
11. Zhang, G., Elman, H.C. (1992): Parallel sparse Cholesky factorization on a shared memory multiprocessor. Parallel Computing **18**, 1009–1022

Chapter 20. Supporting Dynamic Data Structures with Olden

Martin C. Carlisle[1] and Anne Rogers[2]

[1] US Air Force Academy, 2354 Fairchild Drive, Suite 6K41, USAFA, CO 80840
[2] AT&T Labs-Research, 600 Mountain Avenue, Murray Hill, NJ 07974

Summary. The goal of the *Olden* project is to build a system that provides parallelism for general-purpose C programs with minimal programmer annotations. We focus on programs using dynamic structures such as trees, lists, and DAGs. We describe a programming and execution model for supporting programs that use pointer-based dynamic data structures. The major differences between our model and the standard sequential model are that the programmer explicitly chooses a particular strategy to map the dynamic data structures over a distributed heap, and annotates work that can be done in parallel using futures. Remote data access is handled automatically using a combination of software caching and computation migration. We provide a compile-time heuristic that selects between them for each pointer dereference based on programmer hints regarding the data layout. The Olden profiler allows the programmer to verify the data layout hints and to determine which operations in the program are expensive. We have implemented a prototype of Olden on the Thinking Machines CM-5. We report on experiments with eleven benchmarks.

1. Introduction

To use parallelism to improve performance, a programmer must find tasks that can be done in parallel, manage the creation of threads to perform these tasks and their assignment to processors, synchronize the threads, and communicate data between them. Handling all of these issues is a complex and time consuming task. Complicating matters further is the fact that program bugs may be timing-dependent, changing in nature or disappearing in the presence of monitoring. Consequently, there is a need for good abstractions to assist the programmer in performing parallelization. These abstractions must not only be expressive, but also efficient, lest the gain from parallelism be outweighed by the additional overhead introduced by the abstractions.

Olden is a compiler and run-time system that supports parallelism on distributed-memory machines for general purpose C programs with minimal programmer annotations. Specifically, Olden is intended for programs that use dynamic data structures, such as trees, lists and DAGs. Although much work has been done on compiling for distributed-memory machines, much of this work has concentrated on scientific programs that use arrays as their primary data structure and loops as their primary control structure.[1] These techniques are not suited to programs that use dynamic data structures [47],

---

[1] For example, see [2], [3], [12], [23], [27], [36], [48], and [52].

S. Pande, D.P. Agrawal (Eds.): Compiler Optimizations for Scalable PS, LNCS 1808, pp. 709-749, 2001.
© Springer-Verlag Berlin Heidelberg 2001

because they rely on the fact that arrays, unlike dynamic data structures, are statically defined and directly addressable.

Olden's approach, by necessity, is much more dynamic than approaches designed for arrays. Instead of having a single thread running on each processor as is common in array-based approaches, we use *futures* to create parallel threads dynamically as processors become idle. The programmer marks a procedure call with a future if the procedure can be executed safely in parallel with its parent continuation. To handle remote references, Olden uses a combination of computation migration and software caching. Computation migration sends the computation to the data, whereas caching brings the data to the computation. Computation migration takes advantage of the spatial locality of nearby objects in the data structure; while caching takes advantage of temporal locality and also allows multiple objects on different processors to be accessed more efficiently.

Selecting whether to use computation migration or software caching for each program point would be very tedious, so Olden includes a compile-time heuristic that makes these choices automatically. The mechanism choice is dependent on the layout of the data; therefore, we provide a language extension, called *local path lengths*, that allows the programmer to give a hint about the expected layout of the data. Given the local-path-length information (or using default information if none is specified), the compiler will analyze the way the program traverses the data structures, and, at each program point, select the appropriate mechanism for handling remote references.

What constitutes a good data layout and the appropriate local-path-length values for each data structure are not always obvious. To assist the programmer, we provide a profiler, which will compute the appropriate local-path-length values from the actual data layout at run time, and also report the number of communication events caused by each line of the program. Using this feedback, the programmer can focus on the key areas where optimization will improve performance and make changes in a directed rather than haphazard manner.

The rest of this chapter proceeds as follows: in Sect. 2, we describe Olden's programming model. We describe the execution model, which includes our mechanisms for migrating computation based on the layout of heap-allocated data, for sending remote data to the computation that requires it using software caching, and also for introducing parallelism using futures, in Sect. 3. Then, in Sect. 4, we discuss the heuristic used by the compiler to choose between computation migration and software caching. In Sect. 5, we report results for a suite of eleven benchmarks using our implementation on the Thinking Machines CM-5, and in Sect. 6, describe the Olden profiler and how to use it to improve performance. Finally, we contrast Olden with other projects in Sect. 7 and conclude in Sect. 8.

This paper summarizes our work on Olden. Several other sources [13, 14, 47] describe this work in more detail.

2. Programming Model

Olden's programming model is designed to facilitate the parallelization of C programs that use dynamic data structures on distributed-memory machines. The programmer converts a sequential C program into an Olden program by providing data-layout information, and marking work that can be done in parallel. The Olden compiler then generates an SPMD (single-program, multiple-data) program [34]. The necessary communication and thread management are handled by Olden's run-time system. In this section, we describe the programmer's view of Olden.

Our underlying machine model assumes that each processor has an identical copy of the program, as well as a local stack that is used to store procedure arguments, local variables, and return addresses. Additionally, each processor owns one section of a distributed heap. Addresses in this distributed heap are represented as a pair, $\langle p, l \rangle$, that contains a processor name and a local address, which can be encoded in a single 32-bit word. All pointers are assumed to point into the distributed heap.

2.1 Programming Language

Olden takes as input a program written in a restricted subset of C, with some additional Olden-specific annotations. For simplicity, we assume that there are no global variables (these could be put in the distributed heap). We also require that programs do not take the address of stack-allocated objects, which ensures that all pointers point into the heap.[2] The major differences between our programming model and the standard sequential model are that the programmer explicitly chooses a particular strategy to map the dynamic data structures over the distributed heap and annotates work that can be done in parallel. We provide three extensions to C— ALLOC, *local path lengths*, and *futures*— to allow the programmer to specify this information. ALLOC and local path lengths are used to map the dynamic data structures, and provide information to the compiler regarding the mapping. Futures are used to mark available parallelism, and are a variant of a construct used in many parallel Lisps [26]. Throughout this section, we will examine how a very simple function, TreeAdd, would be modified for Olden. TreeAdd recursively sums the values stored in each of the nodes of the tree. The program is given in Fig. 2.1.

2.2 Data Layout

Olden uses data layout information provided by the programmer both at run time and during compilation. The actual mapping of data to the processors

---

[2] We do provide structure return values, which can be used to handle many of the cases where & (address-of) is needed.

```
typedef struct tree { int val;
                      struct tree *left, *right; } tree;

int TreeAdd (tree *t)
{
    if (t == NULL)
        return 0;
    else {
        return (TreeAdd(t->left) + TreeAdd(t->right) + t->val);
    }
}
```

Fig. 2.1. TreeAdd function.

is achieved by including a processor number in each allocation request. Olden provides a library routine, ALLOC, that allocates memory on a specified processor, and returns a pointer that encodes both the processor name and the local address of the allocated memory. Olden also provides a mechanism to allow the programmer to provide a hint about the expected run-time layout of the data.

```
/* Allocate a tree with level levels on processors lo..lo+num_proc-1
   Assume num_proc is a power of 2 */

tree *TreeAlloc (int level, int lo, int num_proc)
{
  if (level == 0)
    return NULL;
  else {
    tree *new, *right, *left;
    int mid, lo_tmp;

    new = (tree *) ALLOC(lo, sizeof(struct tree));
    new->val = 1;
    new->left =  TreeAlloc(level-1, lo+num_proc/2, num_proc/2);
    new->right = TreeAlloc(level-1, lo, num_proc/2);
    return new;
  }
}
```

Fig. 2.2. Allocation code

Since the heap is distributed and communication is expensive, to get good performance, the programmer must place related pieces of data on the same processor. For a binary tree, it is often desirable to place large subtrees together on the same processor, as it is expected that subtrees contain related data. In Fig. 2.2, we give an example function that allocates a binary tree such that the subtrees at a fixed depth are distributed evenly across the pro-

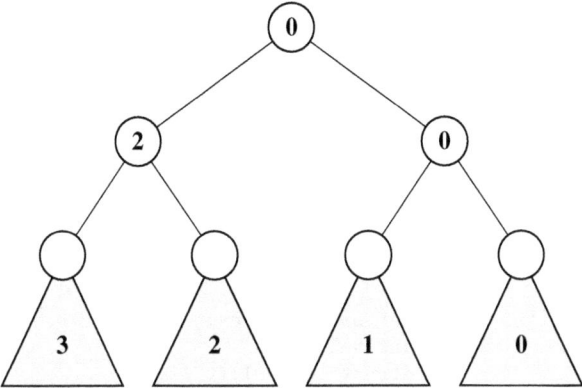

Fig. 2.3. Result of allocation on four processors

cessors (where the number of processors is a power of two). Figure 2.3 shows the distribution of a balanced binary tree that would be created by a call to `TreeAlloc` on four processors with `lo` equal to zero.

To assist the compiler in managing communication, we allow the programmer to provide a quantified hint regarding the layout of a recursive data structure. A *local path length* represents the expected number of adjacent nodes in the structure that are on the same processor, measured along a path. Each pointer field of a data structure has a local path length, either specified by the programmer or a compiler-supplied default. Associating a local path length, l, with a field, F, of a structure indicates that, on average, after traversing a pointer along field F that crosses a processor boundary, there will be a path of l adjacent nodes in the structure that reside on the same processor.

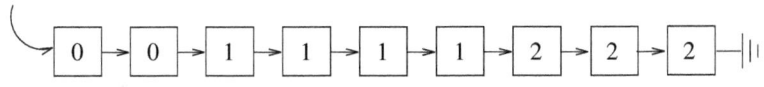

Fig. 2.4. A simple linked list

Determining the local path length is simplest for a linked list. Consider, for example, the linked list in Fig. 2.4. In this list, there are two nodes on Processor 0, followed by four nodes on Processor 1, and three nodes on Processor 2. Consequently, the local path length for the pointer field would be $\frac{2+4+3}{3}$, which is 3.

For structures with more than one pointer field, such as the tree used in `TreeAdd`, determining the appropriate value for the local path length is more complicated. Local path lengths, however, are merely a hint, and may be approximated or omitted (in which case a default value is used). The compiler's analyses are insensitive to small changes in the local path lengths, and incorrect values do not affect program correctness. In most cases, it suffices to estimate the value using a high-level analysis of the structure. Recall the allocation shown in Fig. 2.3. Suppose the height of the tree is 12. On average, a path from the root of the tree to a leaf crosses a processor boundary once. We can therefore estimate the local path length as 6 for both pointer fields. In Fig. 2.5, we show a data structure declaration with local-path-length hints.

```
typedef struct tree {
    int val;
    struct tree *left {6};
    struct tree *right {6};
} tree;
```

Fig. 2.5. Sample local-path-length hint

In Sect. 6, we describe the Olden profiler and also provide a mathematically rigorous presentation of local path lengths. The profiler automatically computes the local path lengths of a data structure by performing a run-time analysis. For nine of the eleven benchmarks we implemented, using the compiler-specified default local path lengths yielded the same performance as using the exact values computed by the profiler. In the cases where the profiler-computed values differed significantly from the defaults, it was straightforward to estimate the correct values. Since the programmer can guess or use default local-path-length values, and then verify these with the profiler, it has never been necessary to perform a detailed analysis of local path lengths.

2.3 Marking Available Parallelism

In addition to specifying a data layout, the programmer must also mark opportunities for parallelism. In Olden, this is done using futures, a variant of the construct found in many parallel Lisps [26]. The programmer may mark a procedure call as a *futurecall*, if it may be evaluated safely in parallel with its parent context. The result of a *futurecall* is a *future cell*, which serves as a synchronization point between the parent and the child. A *touch* of the future cell, which synchronizes the parent and child, must also be inserted by the programmer before the return value is used.

In our `TreeAdd` example, the recursive calls on the left and right subtrees do not interfere; therefore, they may be performed safely in parallel. To specify this, we mark the first recursive call as a *futurecall*. This indicates that the continuation of the first recursive call, namely the second recursive call, may be done in parallel with the first call. Since the continuation of the second recursive call contains no work that can be parallelized, we do not mark it

```
int TreeAdd (tree *t)
{
    if (t == NULL)
        return 0;
    else {
        tree        *t_left;
        future_cell_int f_left;
        int         sum_right;


        t_left = t->left;
        f_left = futurecall (TreeAdd, t_left);

        sum_right = TreeAdd (t->right);

        return (touch(f_left) + sum_right + t->val);
    }
}
```

Fig. 2.6. TreeAdd function using future.

as a future. Then, when the return value is needed, we must first explicitly touch the future cell. In Fig. 2.6, we show the TreeAdd program as modified to use futures.

3. Execution Model

Once the programmer has specified the data layout and identified opportunities for parallelism, the system must still handle communication, work distribution, and synchronization. In this section, we describe how Olden handles remote references and how Olden extracts parallelism from the computation. To handle remote references, Olden uses a combination of computation migration, which moves the computation to the data, and software caching, which brings a copy of the data to the computation. Parallelism is introduced using futures. At the end of this section, we present an example, TreeMultAdd, that illustrates the execution model in action.

Due to space constraints, we do not discuss the implementation of Olden's run-time system in any detail. We refer the interested reader to Rogers et al. [47] and Carlisle [14] for details.

3.1 Handling Remote References

When a thread of computation attempts to access data from another processor, communication must be performed to satisfy the reference. In Olden, we provide two mechanisms for accessing remote data: computation migration and software caching. These mechanisms may be viewed as duals. Computation migration sends the thread of computation to the data it needs; whereas, software caching brings a copy of the data to the computation that needs it. The appropriate mechanism for each point in the program is selected automatically at compile time using a mechanism that is described in Sect. 4.

3.1.1 Computation Migration. The basic idea of computation migration is that when a thread executing on Processor P attempts to access a location[3] residing on Processor Q, the thread is migrated from P to Q. Full thread migration entails sending the current program counter, the thread's stack, and the current contents of the registers to Q. Processor Q then sets up its stack, loads the registers, and resumes execution of the thread at the instruction that caused the migration. Once it migrates the thread, Processor P is free to do other work, which it gets from a work dispatcher in the runtime system.

Full thread migration is quite expensive, because the thread's entire stack is included in the message. To make computation migration affordable, we send only the portion of the thread's state that is necessary for the current procedure to complete execution: the registers, program counter, and current stack frame. Later we will explain computation migration in the context of a real program; here, we use the example in Fig. 3.1 to illustrate the concepts. During the execution of H, the computation migrates from P to Q. Q receives a copy of the stack frame for H, which it places on its stack. Note, however, that when it is time to return from the procedure, it is necessary to return control to Processor P, because it holds the stack frame of H's caller. To accomplish this, Q places a stack frame for a special return stub directly below the frame for H. This frame holds the return address and the return frame pointer for the currently executing function. The return address stored in the frame of H is modified to point to a stub procedure. The stub procedure migrates the thread of computation back to P by sending a message that contains the return frame pointer ($< b >$), and the contents of the registers. Processor P then completes the procedure return by loading the return address from its copy of the frame, deallocating its copy of the frame, and then restarting the thread at the return address. Note Q does not need to return the stack frame for H to P, as it will be deallocated immediately.

Olden implements a simple optimization to circumvent a chain of trivial returns in the case that a thread migrates several times during the course of executing a single function. Upon a migration, the run-time system examines the current return address of the function to determine whether it points to the return procedure. If so, the original return address, frame pointer, and node id are pulled from the stub's frame and passed as part of the migration

---

[3] The Olden compiler inserts explicit checks into the code to test a pointer dereference (recall that pointers encode both a processor name and a local address) to determine if the reference is local and to migrate the thread as needed. On machines that have appropriate support, the address translation hardware can be used to detect non-local references. This approach is preferable when the ratio of cost of faults to cost of tests is less than the ratio of tests to faults [4].

message. This allows the eventual return message to be sent directly to the original processor.

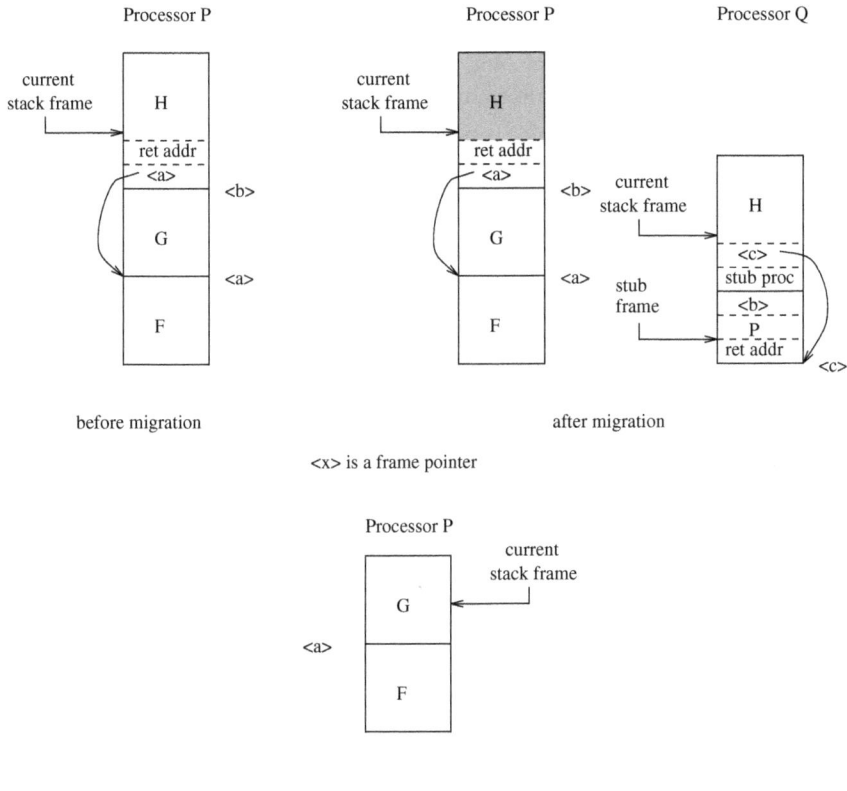

Fig. 3.1. Stack during computation migration (stacks grow up)

3.1.2 Software Caching. There are occasions where it is preferable to move the data rather than the computation. To accomplish this, we use a software-caching mechanism that is very similar to the caching scheme in Blizzard-S [50]. Each processor uses a portion of its local memory as a large, fully associative, write-through cache. A write-through cache is used because update messages can be sent cheaply from user level on the CM-5, and this allows us to overlap these messages with computation. As in Blizzard-S, we perform allocation on the page level, and perform transfers at the line level.[4] The main difference between Olden's cache and that in Blizzard-S is that we do not rely on virtual-memory support. We use a 1K hash table with a list

---

[4] In Olden, a page has 2K bytes, and a line has 64 bytes.

of pages kept in each bucket to translate addresses. Since entries are kept on a per-page basis, the chains in each bucket will tend to be quite short (in our experience, the average chain length is approximately one).

The Olden compiler directly inserts code before each heap reference that uses software caching. This code searches the lists stored in the hash table, checks the valid bit for the line, and returns a tag used to translate the address from a global to a local pointer. In the event that the page is not allocated or the line is not valid, the appropriate allocation or transfer is performed by a library routine.

Once we introduce a local cache at each processor, we must provide a means to ensure that no processor sees stale data. Olden uses a relaxed coherence scheme where each processor invalidates its own cache at synchronization points. This coherence mechanism can be shown to be equivalent to sequential consistency [37] for Olden programs and is discussed in detail in Carlisle's dissertation [14].

3.2 Introducing Parallelism

While computation migration and software caching provide mechanisms for operating on distributed data, they do not provide a mechanism for extracting parallelism from the computation. When a thread of computation migrates from Processor P to Q, P is left idle. In this section, we describe a mechanism for introducing parallelism. Our approach is to introduce *continuation-capturing* operations at key points in the program. When a thread migrates from P to Q, Processor P can start executing one of the captured continuations. The natural place to capture continuations is at procedure calls, since the return linkage is effectively a continuation. This provides a fairly inexpensive mechanism for labeling work that can be done in parallel. In effect, this capturing technique chops the thread of execution into many pieces that can be executed out of order. Thus the introduction of continuation-capturing operations must be based on an analysis of the program, which can be done either by a parallelizing compiler targeted for Olden or by a programmer using Olden directly.

Our continuation-capturing mechanism is essentially a variant of the *future* mechanism found in many parallel Lisps [26]. In the traditional Lisp context, the expression (future e) is an annotation to the system that says that e can be evaluated in parallel with its context. The result of this evaluation is a *future cell* that serves as a synchronization point between the child thread that is evaluating e and the parent thread. If the parent *touches* the future cell, that is, attempts to read its value, before the child is finished, then the parent blocks. When the child thread finishes evaluating e, it puts the result in the cell and restarts any blocked threads.

Our view of futures, which is influenced by the *lazy-task-creation* scheme of Mohr et al. [41], is to save the futurecall's context (return continuation) on a work list (in our case, a stack) and to evaluate the future's body directly.[5] If a processor becomes idle (either through a migration or through a blocked touch), then we grab a continuation from the work list and start executing it; this is called *future stealing*. In most parallel lisp systems, touches are implicit and may occur anywhere. In Olden, touches are done explicitly using the touch operation and there are restrictions on how they may be used. The first restriction is that only one touch can be attempted per future. The second is that the one allowed touch must be done by the future's parent thread of computation. These restrictions simplify the implementation of futures considerably and we have not found any occasions when it would be desirable to violate them.

Due to space constraints, we will not discuss the implementation of futures, except to note an important fact about how Olden uses the continuation work list. When a processor becomes idle, it steals work only from its own work list. A processor never removes work from the work list of another processor. The motivation for this design decision was our expectation that most futures captured by a processor would operate on local data. Although allowing another processor to steal this work may seem desirable for load-balancing purposes, it would simply cause unnecessary communication. Instead, load balancing is achieved by a careful data layout. This is in contrast to Mohr et al.'s formulation, where an idle processor removes the oldest piece of work from another processor's work queue.

3.3 A Simple Example

To make the ideas of this chapter more concrete, we present a simple example. TreeMultAdd is a prototypical divide-and-conquer program, which computes, for two identical binary trees, the sum of the products of the values stored at corresponding nodes in the two trees.

Figure 3.2 gives an implementation of TreeMultAdd that has been annotated with futures. We mark the left recursive call to TreeMultAdd with a futurecall; the result is not demanded until after the right recursive call. We assume that the compiler has chosen to use computation migration to satisfy remote dereferences of t and software caching to satisfy remote dereferences of u.

To understand what this means in terms of the program's execution, consider a call to TreeMultAdd on the two trees whose layout is shown in Fig. 3.3. Consider the first call to TreeMultAdd, made on Processor 0 with t_0 and u_0 as arguments. Since both t and u are local, no communication is needed to compute t_left and u_left. Then, once the recursive call on the left subtrees is made, t, now pointing to t_1 is non-local. Since the compiler has selected computation migration for handling remote references to t, the statement

---

[5] This is also similar to the workcrews paradigm proposed by Roberts and Vandevoorde [46].

`t_left = t->left` will cause the computation to migrate to Processor 1. After the migration, u, now pointing to u_1, is also non-local, and the statement `u = u->left` will cause a cache miss. As the computation continues on the subtrees rooted at t_1 and u_1, all references to t will be local and all references to u remote. Consequently, no further migrations will occur, and the subtree rooted at u_1 will be cached on Processor 1. Once the computation on the subtrees rooted at t_1 and u_1 is complete, a return message will be sent to Processor 0.

```
int TreeMultAdd (tree *t, tree *u)
{
    if (t == NULL) {
        assert(u == NULL);
        return 0;
        }
    else {
        tree          *t_left, *u_left;
        future_cell f_left;
        int           sum_right;

        assert(u != NULL);
        t_left = t->left;                    /* may cause a migration */
        u_left = u->left;                    /* may cause cache miss */
        f_left = futurecall (TreeMultAdd, t_left, u_left);

        sum_right = TreeMultAdd (t->right,u->right);

        return (touch(f_left) + sum_right + t->val*u->val);
    }
}
```

Fig. 3.2. TreeMultAdd with Olden annotations.

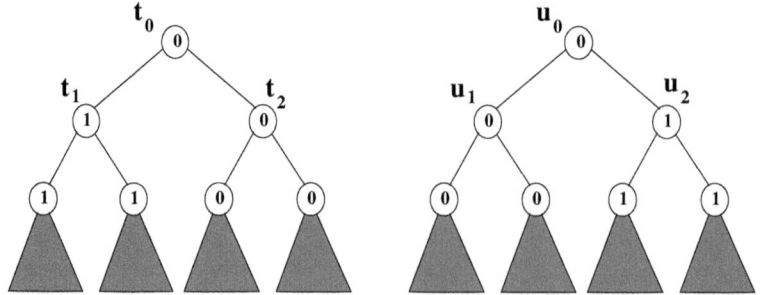

Fig. 3.3. Example input for TreeMultAdd

Meanwhile, after the migration, Processor 0 is idle. Therefore, it will steal the continuation of the first recursive call. This continuation starts the recursive call on the right subtrees, rooted at t_2 and u_2. Note all dereferences of t are local, and all dereferences of u remote. The subtree rooted at u_2 will be cached on Processor 0, and no migrations will occur. Once this computation completes, Processor 0 will attempt to touch the future cell associated with the call with arguments t_1 and u_1. At this point, execution must wait for the return message from Processor 1. An execution trace for both processors is shown in Fig. 3.4.

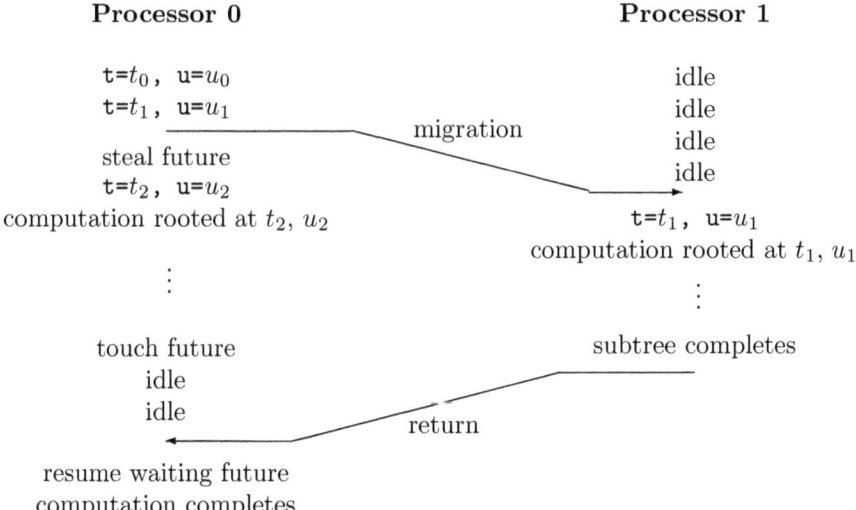

Processor 0

$t=t_0$, $u=u_0$
$t=t_1$, $u=u_1$

steal future
$t=t_2$, $u=u_2$
computation rooted at t_2, u_2

migration

touch future
idle
idle

return

resume waiting future
computation completes

Processor 1

idle
idle
idle
idle

$t=t_1$, $u=u_1$
computation rooted at t_1, u_1

subtree completes

Fig. 3.4. Execution trace for `TreeMultAdd`

As previously mentioned, since the compiler has chosen to use caching to satisfy remote dereferences of u, the subtree rooted at u_1 will end up being cached on Processor 1, and the subtree rooted at u_2 on Processor 0. Had the compiler chosen to use migration for dereferences of both t and u, the computation would have bounced back and forth between the two processors. Here we see the advantage of using both computation migration and software caching. By using migration, we obtain locality for all references to the tree t, and by using caching, we prevent the computation from migrating back and forth repeatedly between the processors. We examine further the benefits of using both computation migration and software caching in Sections 4 and 5.

Neither the reference to t->right nor the reference to t->val can ever be the source of a migration. Once a non-local reference to t->left causes the computation to migrate to the owner of t, the computation for the currently executing function will remain on the owner of t until it has completed (since we assumed references to u will use caching rather than migration).

4. Selecting Between Mechanisms

As mentioned earlier, the Olden compiler decides, for each pointer dereference, whether to use caching or migration for accessing remote data. Our goal is to minimize the total communication cost over the entire program. Consequently, although an individual thread migration is substantially more expensive than performing a single remote fetch (by a factor of about seven on the CM-5), it may still be desirable to pay the cost of the migration, if moving the thread will convert many subsequent references into local references. Consider a list of N elements, evenly divided among P processors (two possible configurations are given in Fig. 4.1). First suppose the list items are distributed in a block fashion. A traversal of this list will require $N\frac{(P-1)}{P}$ remote accesses if software caching is used, but only $P - 1$ migrations if the computation is allowed to follow the data (assuming $N \gg P$). Hence, it is better to use computation migration for such a data layout. Caching, however, performs better when the list items are distributed using a cyclic layout. In this case, using computation migration will require $N - 1$ migrations, whereas caching requires $N\frac{(P-1)}{P}$ remote accesses.

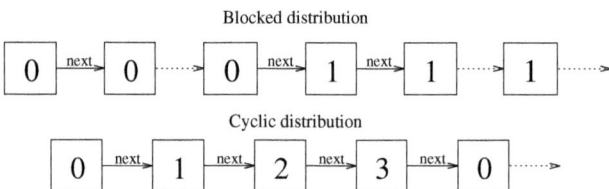

Fig. 4.1. Two different list distributions. The numbers in the boxes are processor numbers. Dotted arrows represent a sequence of list items.

Olden uses a three-step process to select a mechanism for each program point. First, the programmer specifies *local path lengths*, which give hints to the compiler regarding the layout of the data. Second, a data flow analysis is used to find pointers that traverse the data structure in a regular manner. In each loop (either iterative or recursive), at most one such variable is selected for computation migration. Finally, interactions between loops are considered, and additional variables are marked for caching, if it is determined that using computation migration for them may cause a bottleneck.

4.1 Using Local Path Lengths

Since the communication cost of using a particular mechanism for a particular program fragment is highly dependent on the layout of the data, we allow the programmer to provide a quantified hint to the compiler regarding the layout of a recursive data structure. As previously discussed in Sect. 2, each pointer field of a structure may be marked with a local path length, which represents the expected number of adjacent nodes in the structure that are all on the same processor; if the programmer does not specify a local path length, a default value is supplied. To be more precise, a local path length of l associated with field, F, indicates that, on average, after traversing a pointer along field F that crosses a processor boundary, there will be a path of l adjacent nodes in the structure that reside on the same processor. Consequently, the local path length provides information regarding the relative benefit of using computation migration or software caching, as it provides information about how many future references will be made local by performing a migration. In Sect. 6, we discuss how to compute local path lengths in more detail, and present the Olden profiler, which computes the local path lengths at run time.

The compiler converts local path lengths into probabilities, called *path affinities*. Recall that a geometric distribution is obtained from an infinite sequence of independent coin flips [45]. It takes one parameter, p, which is the probability of a success. The value of a geometric random variable is the number of trials up to and including the first success. If we consider traversing a local pointer to be a failure, then the path affinity is the probability of failure. The local path length is then the expected value of this geometric distribution; therefore, the path affinity is given by $1 - \frac{1}{local\ path\ length}$.

The intuition behind our heuristic's use of local path lengths and path affinities is illustrated by the examples given in Fig. 4.1. In the blocked case, where computation migration is the preferred mechanism, the local path length is $\frac{N}{P}$ (there are N list items, distributed in a blocked fashion across P processors). The path affinity of the **next** field is then $1 - \frac{P}{N}$. In the cyclic case, where caching performs better, the **next** field has a local path length of one (each **next** pointer is to an object on a different processor), and a path affinity of zero. In general, computation migration is preferable when the local path lengths and path affinities are large, and software caching is preferable when the local path lengths and path affinities are small.

```
typedef struct tree {
    int val;
    struct tree *left {10};
    struct tree *right {3.33};
} tree;
```

Fig. 4.2. Sample local-path-length hint

In the remainder of this section, we describe how the compiler uses the path affinities computed from the programmer-specified local path lengths to select between computation migration and software caching. In our examples, we will refer to the structure declaration from Fig. 4.2. For this declaration, the path affinity of the `left` field is $1 - \frac{1}{10}$ or 90%, and the path affinity of the `right` field is $1 - \frac{1}{3.33}$ or 70%.

4.2 Update Matrices

We want to estimate how the program will, in general, traverse its recursively defined structures. To accomplish this, we examine the loops and recursive calls (hereafter referred to as *control loops*) checking how pointers are updated in each iteration. We say that s is updated by t along field F in a given loop, if the value of s at the end of an iteration is the value of t from the beginning of the iteration dereferenced through field F (that is, `s'=t->F`). This notion extends directly to paths of fields. Intuitively, variables that are updated by themselves in a control loop will traverse the data structure in a regular fashion. We call such variables *induction variables*. This is similar to the notion of induction variables used in an optimizing compiler's analysis of for-loops [1]. In both cases, an induction variable is a variable that is updated in a regular fashion in each iteration of the loop. In Fig. 4.3, s and t are induction variables (since `s'=s->left` and `t'=t->right->left`), whereas u is not (since its value cannot be written as a path from its value in the previous iteration).

<table>
<tr><td></td><td colspan="2">Update</td><td colspan="3">before</td></tr>
<tr><td></td><td colspan="2">Matrix</td><td>s</td><td>t</td><td>u</td></tr>
<tr><td>struct tree *s, *t, *u;</td><td></td><td></td><td></td><td></td><td></td></tr>
<tr><td>while (s) {</td><td></td><td></td><td></td><td></td><td></td></tr>
<tr><td>   s = s->left;</td><td>a</td><td>s</td><td>90</td><td></td><td></td></tr>
<tr><td>   t = t->right->left;</td><td>f</td><td></td><td></td><td></td><td></td></tr>
<tr><td>   u = s->right;</td><td>t</td><td>t</td><td></td><td>63</td><td></td></tr>
<tr><td>}</td><td>e</td><td></td><td></td><td></td><td></td></tr>
<tr><td></td><td>r</td><td>u</td><td>70</td><td></td><td></td></tr>
</table>

Fig. 4.3. A simple loop with induction variables

We summarize information on possible induction variables in an *update matrix*. The entry at location (s,t) of the matrix is the path affinity of the update, if s is updated by t, and is blank otherwise. In Fig. 4.3, since s is updated by itself along the field `left`, the entry (s,s) in the update matrix is 90 (the affinity of the `left` field). Induction variables are then simply those pointers with entries along the diagonal (that is, they have been updated by themselves). In our example, the variables s and t have entries on the diagonal. We will consider only these for possible computation migration, as they traverse the structure in a regular manner.

The update matrices may be computed using standard data-flow methods. (Note again that exact or conservative information is not needed, as errors in the update matrices will not affect program correctness.) The only

```
struct tree *TreeSearch(struct tree *t, int key)
{
  while(t && t->key != key) {
    if (t->key > key)
      t = t->left;
    else
      t = t->right;
  }
  return t;
}
```

Update before
Matrix   t

after t | 80 |

Fig. 4.4. An example of updates with `if-then`

complications are that variables may have multiple updates or update paths
of length greater than one. There are three cases. The first is a join point
in the flow graph (for example, at the end of an `if-then` statement). Here
we simply merge the two updates from each branch by taking the average
of their affinities. This corresponds to assuming each branch is taken about
half of the time, and could be improved with better branch prediction information. If the update does not appear in both branches and we have no
branch prediction information, rather than averaging the update, we omit
it. We do this because we wish to consider only those updates that occur in
every iteration of the loop, thus guaranteeing that the updated variable is
actually traversing the structure. Having a matrix entry for a variable that
is not updated might cause the compiler to surmise incorrectly that it could
make a large number of otherwise remote references local by using migration
for this variable. An example of the branch rule is given in Fig. 4.4. The
induction variable, `t`, has an update with path affinity 80, the average of the
updates in the two branches (`t->right` 90%, `t->left` 70%).

```
int TreeAdd(struct tree *t)
{
  if (t == NULL) return 0;
  else
    return TreeAdd(t->left)
         + TreeAdd(t->right)+t->val;
}
```

Update before
Matrix   t

after t | 97 |

Fig. 4.5. TreeAdd

Second, we must have a rule for multiple updates via recursion. Consider
the simple recursive program in Fig. 4.5. Note that `t` has two updates, one
corresponding to each recursive call. The two recursive calls form a control
loop. In this case, we define the path affinity of the update as the probability
that either of the updates will be along a local path (since both are going
to be executed). Because the path affinity of `left` is 90% and `right` is 70%,
the probability that both are remote is 3% (assuming independence). Con-

sequently, the path affinity of the update of t because of the recursive calls is 97%, the probability that at least one will be local. Rather than combining the updates from the two branches of the if-then-else statement, we instead notice that the recursive calls occur within the else branch. This means we can predict that the else branch is almost always taken, and consequently, only the rule for recursion is used to compute the update of t in this control loop.

The final possibility is an update path of length greater than one (for example, t=t->right->left). The path affinity of this case is simply the product of the path affinities of each field along the path. An example of this is given in Fig. 4.3. Here the path affinity of the update of t is the product of the path affinities of the right and left fields (90% * 70% = 63%).

So far, we have only discussed computing update matrices intra-procedurally. A full inter-procedural implementation would need to be able to compute paths generated by the return values of functions, and handle control loops that span more than one procedure (for example, a mutual recursion). Our implementation performs only a limited amount of inter-procedural analysis. In particular, we do not consider return values, or analyze loops that span multiple procedures. This limited inter-procedural analysis is sufficient for all of our benchmarks; in the future, it may be possible to expand this analysis using techniques such as access path matrices [30].

4.3 The Heuristic

Once the update matrices have been computed, the heuristic uses a two-pass process to select between computation migration and software caching. First, each control loop is considered in isolation. Then, in the second phase, we consider the interactions between nested control loops, and possibly decide to do additional caching. In addition to having the update matrix for each control loop, we also need information regarding whether or not the loop may be parallelized. In Olden, the compiler checks for the presence of programmer-inserted futures to determine when a control loop may be parallelized.

In the first pass, for each control loop, we select the induction variable whose update has the strongest path affinity. If a control loop has no induction variable, then it will select computation migration for the same variable as its parent (the smallest control loop enclosing this one). If the path affinity of the selected variable's update exceeds a certain threshold, or the control loop is parallelizable, then computation migration is chosen for this variable; otherwise, dereferences of this variable are cached. Dereferences of all other pointer variables are cached. We select computation migration for parallelizable loops with path affinities below the threshold because this mechanism allows us to generate new threads. (Due to Olden's use of lazy rather than eager futures, new threads are generated only following migrations and blocked touches.)

```
Traverse(tree *t) {
  if (t==NULL) return;
  else {
    Traverse(t->left);
    Traverse(t->right);
  }
}

WalkAndTraverse(list *l, tree *t) {
  for each body, b, in l do in parallel {
    Traverse(t);
  }
}
```

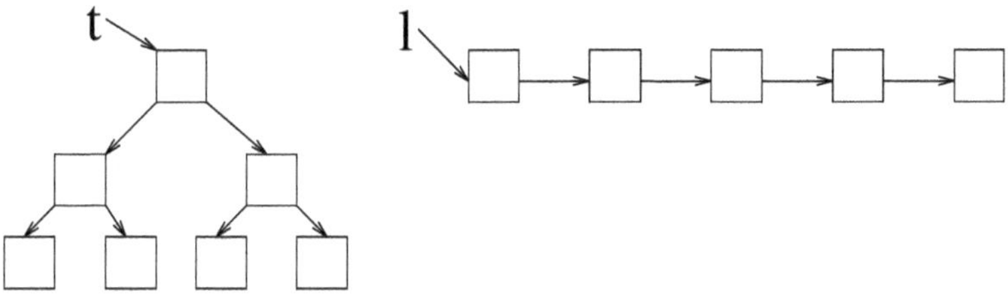

Fig. 4.6. Example with a bottleneck.

Considering control loops in isolation does not yield the best performance. Inside a parallel loop, it is possible to create a bottleneck by using computation migration. Consider the code fragments in Figures 4.6 and 4.7. WalkAndTraverse is a procedure that for each list item traverses the tree.[6] If computation migration were chosen for the tree traversal, the parallel threads for each item in the list would be forced to serialize on their accesses to the root of the tree, which becomes a bottleneck. In TraverseAndWalk, for each node in the tree, we walk the list stored at that node. Since there is a different list at each node of the tree, the parallel threads at different tree nodes are not forced to serialize, and there is no bottleneck. In general, a bottleneck occurs whenever the initial value of a variable selected for migration in an inner loop is the same over a large number of iterations of the outer loop. Returning to the examples, in WalkAndTraverse, t has the same value for each iteration of the parallel for loop, while in TraverseAndWalk, we assume t->list has a different value in each iteration (that is, at each node in the tree). Although in general this is a difficult aliasing problem, we do not need exact or conservative information. If incorrect information is used, the program will run correctly, but possibly more slowly than if more precise information were available. Our current approximation tests to see if the induction variable for the inner loop is updated in the parent loop. If so, we

---

[6] The syntax for specifying parallelism used in this example is not part of Olden and is used only to simplify the example.

assume no bottleneck will occur; otherwise, we use caching in the inner loop
to avoid the possibility of a bottleneck. Once the heuristic has analyzed the
interactions between loops, the selection process is complete.

```
Walk(list *l) {
  while (1) {
    visit(l);
    l = l->next;
  }
}

TraverseAndWalk(tree *t) {
  if (t==NULL) return;
  else {
    do in parallel {
      TraverseAndWalk(t->left);
      TraverseAndWalk(t->right);
    }
    Walk(t->list);
  }
}
```

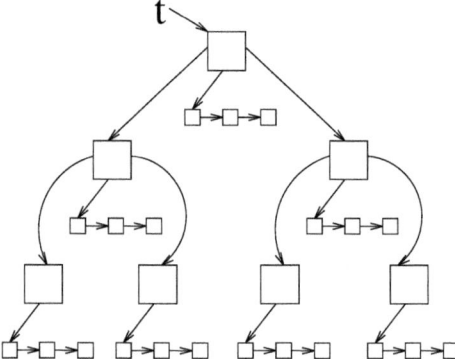

Fig. 4.7. Example without a bottleneck.

4.3.1 Threshold and Default Path Affinities. The migration threshold
has been set to 86% for the CM-5 implementation. Since the cost of a migration is about seven times that of a cache miss on the CM-5, the break-even
local path length is seven, which corresponds to a path affinity of 86%. For
other platforms, the threshold would be $1 - \frac{1}{r}$, where r is the ratio of the
cost of a migration to the cost of a cache miss. On platforms where latency is
greater, such as networks of workstations, r (and consequently the threshold)
will be smaller, and on platforms where latency is smaller, such as the Cray
T3D [19], r and the threshold will be larger.

We set the default path affinity to 70% (this corresponds to a default local path length of 3.33). This value was chosen so that, by default, list traversals will use caching, tree traversals will use computation migration, and tree searches will use caching. The averaging method for recursive calls was also designed to obtain this behavior. To see why this is desirable, recall the four processor tree allocation shown in Fig. 2.3. Generally, as in this example, we expect large subtrees to be distributed evenly among the processors. In such a case, searches of the tree (such as the code in Fig. 4.4), will traverse a relatively short path that may cross a processor boundary several times. A complete tree traversal (such as the code in Fig. 4.5), however, will perform large local computations. Consequently, it is preferable to use migration for the traversal, and caching for the search. List traversals may be viewed as searches through a degenerate tree.

In our experience, these defaults provide the best performance most of the time. In those cases where the defaults are not appropriate, the programmer can specify local-path-length hints. (We do not allow the programmer to modify the threshold, but the same effect can be obtained by modifying the local path lengths.) We explicitly specified local path lengths in three of the eleven benchmarks (TSP, Perimeter, and MST) since the default affinity did not reflect the layout of the data structure, but in only one case (TSP) did it have a significant effect on performance. We examine TSP more closely in the next section.

Returning to the declaration in Fig. 4.2 (page 723), we see why providing more precise local path length information is often unnecessary. Using default local path lengths rather than those from Fig. 4.2 changes the entry for t in the TreeAdd matrix (Figure 4.5) from 97 to 91, and the entry for t in the TreeSearch matrix (Figure 4.4) from 80 to 70. Since these changes do not cross the threshold, the heuristic will make the same selections. Our experience demonstrates that there is broad latitude for imprecision in the local-path-length information.

4.3.2 Example. We now return to the TreeMultAdd example from Fig. 3.2. If we use the default local-path-length values, both the left and right fields have local path length 3.33. The path affinities of these fields are $1 - \frac{1}{3.33}$, or 70%.

There is one control loop in this program, consisting of the two recursive calls. Both t and u have two updates from the recursive calls. The path affinities of both of these updates are 70% (as both the left and right fields have path affinity 70%). As shown in Fig. 4.8, using the rule for combining multiple updates via recursion, the entries for t and u in the update matrix will both be $1 - (1 - .7)(1 - .7)$, or 91%. Since t and u have entries on the diagonal of the matrix, they are both induction variables.

When the heuristic examines this loop, it will select the induction variable whose update has the largest affinity for migration. Since the updates of both variables have the same affinity, one is arbitrarily chosen (we assume t).

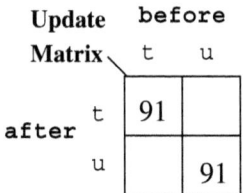

Fig. 4.8. Update matrix for TreeMultAdd

Input. Olden program with some local-path-length hints.

Output. Program with each dereference marked for computation migration or
software caching.

Method.

    comment Compute path affinities
    foreach structure declaration, D, **do**
        foreach pointer field, F, **do**
            if field F of structure D has no programmer-specified
            local path length **then**
                mark field F of structure D with default local path length
            Convert local path length to path affinity

    comment Compute update matrices
    foreach loop, L, **do**
        Compute an update matrix, M(L), for L

    comment Single-loop analysis
    foreach loop, L, **do**
        x ← induction variable with largest path affinity from M(L)
        foreach dereference, R, in L **do**
            if R dereferences x **then**
                if (affinity(M(L),x) > threshold) **or** (L is parallel) **then**
                    mark R for computation migration
                else
                    mark R for software caching
            else
                mark R for software caching

    comment Bottleneck analysis
    foreach parallel loop, P, **do**
        foreach loop, L, inside P, **do**
            x ← variable using computation migration in L
            if x is not updated in P **then**
                mark dereferences of x in L for software caching

Fig. 4.9. Selecting between computation migration and software caching

References to u are then cached. Since there is only one loop, the bottleneck analysis will not be performed.

4.3.3 Summary. In summary, Olden provides two mechanisms, computation migration and software caching, for accessing remote data. Based on local-path-length information, the compiler automatically selects the appropriate combination of these two mechanisms to minimize communication. The local path lengths may be obtained from the programmer, the Olden profiler (which will be presented in Sect. 6), or compiler defaults. The selection process, as shown in Fig. 4.9, consists of four parts: converting local path lengths to probabilities, called *path affinities*; computing update matrices for each loop and recursion; analyzing loops in isolation; and using bottleneck analysis to analyze interactions between nested loops. We demonstrate the effectiveness of the heuristic on a suite of eleven benchmarks in the next section.

5. Experimental Results

In the previous sections, we have described Olden. In this section, we report results for eleven benchmarks using our Thinking Machines CM-5 implementation. Each of these benchmarks is a C program annotated with futures, touches, calls to Olden's allocation routine, and, in some cases, data-structure local-path-length information.

We performed our experiments on CM-5s at two National Supercomputing Centers: NPAC at Syracuse University and NCSA at the University of Illinois. The timings reported are averages over three runs done in dedicated mode. For each benchmark, we present two one-processor versions. The *sequential* version was compiled using our compiler, but without the overhead of futures, pointer testing, or our special stack discipline, which is described in Rogers et al. [47]. The one-processor Olden implementation (*one*) includes these overheads. The difference between the two implementations provides a measure of the overhead.

Table 5.1 briefly describes each benchmark and Table 5.2 lists the running time of a sequential implementation plus speedup numbers for up to 32 processors for each benchmark. We report kernel times for most of the benchmarks to avoid having their data-structure building phases, which show excellent speedup, skew the results. Power, Barnes-Hut, and Health are the exceptions. We report whole program times (W) for Power and Barnes-Hut to allow for comparison with published results. We report whole program time for Health, because it does not have a data-structure build phase that would skew the results. We use a true sequential implementation compiled with our compiler for computing speedups. These sequential times are comparable to those using gcc with optimization turned off. Using an optimization level of two, the gcc code ranges from one (em3d, health and mst) to five (TSP) times

Table 5.1. Benchmark Descriptions

Benchmarks	Description	Problem Size
TreeAdd	Adds the values in a tree	1024K nodes
MST	Computes the minimum spanning tree of a graph [8]	1K nodes
Power	Solves the Power System Optimization problem [39]	10,000 customers
TSP	Computes an estimate of the best Hamiltonian circuit for the Traveling-salesman problem [35]	32K cities
Barnes-Hut	Solves the N-body problem using a hierarchical method [7]	8K bodies
Bisort	Sorts by creating two disjoint bitonic sequences and then merging them [9]	128K integers
EM3D	Simulates the propagation of electro-magnetic waves in a 3D object [20]	40K nodes
Health	Simulates the Colombian health-care system [38]	1365 villages
Perimeter	Computes the perimeter of a set of quad-tree encoded raster images [49]	4K x 4K image
Union	Computes the union of two quad-tree encoded raster images [51]	70,000 leaves
Voronoi	Computes the Voronoi Diagram of a set of points [24]	64K points

Table 5.2. Results

Benchmarks	Heuristic choice	Seq. time (sec.)	Speedup by number of processors					
			1	2	4	8	16	32
TreeAdd	M	4.49	0.73	1.47	2.93	5.90	11.81	23.4
MST	M	9.81	0.96	1.36	2.20	3.43	4.56	5.14
Power^W	M	286.59	0.96	1.94	3.81	6.92	14.85	27.5
TSP	M	43.35	0.95	1.92	3.70	6.70	10.08	15.8
Barnes-Hut^W	M+C	555.79	0.74	1.42	3.00	5.29	8.13	11.2
Bisort	M+C	31.41	0.73	1.35	2.29	3.52	4.92	6.33
EM3D	M+C	1.21	0.86	1.51	2.69	4.48	6.72	12.0
Health^W	M+C	42.09	0.95	1.95	3.89	7.61	14.72	21.70
Perimeter	M+C	2.47	0.86	1.70	3.37	6.09	9.86	14.1
Union	M+C	1.46	0.76	1.48	2.88	5.11	7.97	11.30
Voronoi	M+C	49.73	0.75	1.38	2.41	4.23	6.88	8.76

^{W} – Whole program times

faster. The gcc optimizations can be traced to better register allocation and handling of floating point arguments, both of which could be implemented in Olden by adding an optimization phase to the compiler.

5.1 Comparison with Other Published Work

Several of our benchmarks (Barnes-Hut, EM3D, and Power) come from the parallel computing literature and have CM-5 implementations available. In this section, we briefly describe these benchmarks and compare our results to those available in the literature.

Barnes-Hut [7] simulates the motion of particles in space using a hierarchical ($O(n \log n)$) algorithm for computing the accelerations of the particles. The algorithm alternates between building an oct-tree that represents the particles in space and computing the accelerations of the particles. Falsafi et al. [21] give results for six different implementations of this benchmark; our results using their parameters (approximately 36 secs/iter) fall near the middle of their range (from 15 to 80 secs/iter). In our implementation, however, the tree building phase is sequential and starts to represent a substantial fraction of the computation as the number of processors increases. We discuss this more later.

EM3D models the propagation of electromagnetic waves through objects in three dimensions [20]. This problem is cast into a computation on an irregular bipartite graph containing nodes representing electric and magnetic field values (E nodes and H nodes, respectively). At each time step, new values for the E nodes are computed from a weighted sum of the neighboring H nodes, and then the same is done for the H nodes. For a 64 processor implementation with 320,000 nodes, our implementation performs comparably to the ghost node implementation of Culler et al. [20], yet does not require substantial modification to the sequential code.

Power solves the *Power-System-Optimization* problem, which can be stated as follows: given a power network represented by a tree with the power plant at the root and the customers at the leaves, use local information to determine the prices that will optimize the benefit to the community [40]. It was implemented originally on the CM-5 by Lumetta et al. in a variant of Split-C. On 64 processors, Olden's efficiency is about 80%, compared to Lumetta et al.'s 75%.

5.2 Heuristic Results

Our results indicate that the heuristic makes good selections, and only occasionally requires the programmer to specify local path lengths to obtain the best performance. For most of the benchmarks, the default local path lengths were accurate. For three of the eleven benchmarks (Perimeter, MST, and TSP) the defaults were not accurate. In the case of Perimeter and MST, specifying more accurate local path length information did not affect performance. Perimeter does a tree traversal and as we noted earlier the heuristic chooses migration for tree traversals by default. The local path length information that we specified did not contradict this choice. In the case of MST, the path length that we specified was for a data structure that was completely local. As a result, the benchmark's performance did not depend on whether the heuristic chose migration or caching.

In the case of TSP, changing the local path length information did affect performance. TSP is a divide-and-conquer algorithm with a non-trivial merge phase. The merge phase of TSP takes two Hamiltonian cycles and a single point, and combines them into a single cycle. Each merge is sequential and walks through the left sub-result followed by the right sub-result, which requires a migration for each participating processor. Given the default local path length, the heuristic will select caching for traversing the sub-results, as the procedure resembles a list traversal. This requires that all of the data be cached on a single processor. Because the sub-results have a long local paths, using migration results in O(number of processors) migrations rather than O(number of cities) remote fetches from using caching. As the number of cities greatly exceeds the number of processors, much less communication is required using migration. By specifying this higher local path length value, we obtain a speedup of 15.8 on 32 processors, as opposed to 6.4 with the default value.

The Voronoi Diagram benchmark is another case where the default values did not obtain the best performance; however, for this benchmark, changing the values did not improve performance. Voronoi is another divide-and-conquer algorithm with a non-trivial merge phase. The merge phase walks along the convex hull of the two sub-diagrams, and adds edges to knit them together to form the Voronoi Diagram for the whole set. Since the sub-diagrams have long local paths, walking along the convex hull of a single sub-result is best done with migration, but the merge phase walks along two sub-results, alternating between them in an irregular fashion. The ideal choice is to use migration to traverse one sub-result and cache the other (such a version has a speedup of over 12 on 32 processors). As we do not have good branch-prediction in formation, the heuristic instead chooses to pin the computation on the processor that owns the root of one of the sub-results and use software caching to bring remote sub-results to the computation. This version is not optimal, but nonetheless performs dramatically better than a version that uses only migration, which had a speedup of 0.47 on 32 processors.

5.2.1 Other Performance Issues. Two benchmarks, MST and Barnes-Hut, while obtaining speedups, demonstrated possibilities for improvement. In both cases, the programs would benefit from more inexpensive synchronization mechanisms. For MST, time spent in synchronization caused poor performance. MST computes the minimum spanning tree of a graph using Bentley's algorithm [8]. The performance for MST is poor and degrades sharply as the number of processors increases, because the number of migrations is $O(NP)$, where N is the number of vertices, and P the number of processors. Caching would not reduce communication costs for this program, because these migrations serve mostly as a mechanism for synchronization.

As noted earlier, Barnes-Hut uses an oct-tree that is rebuilt every iteration. In our implementation, the tree is built sequentially, because Olden lacks the synchronization mechanisms necessary allow multiple updates to a data structure to occur in parallel. As the cost of computing the forces on the particles, which is done in parallel, decreases the time spent on the tree-building phase becomes significant.

5.3 Summary

Overall, the Olden implementations provided good performance and required few programmer modifications. Where timings from other systems were available (Power, Barnes-Hut, and EM3D), the Olden implementations performed comparably. In each case, the Olden implementation required less programmer effort. These results indicate that Olden provides a simple yet efficient model for parallelizing programs using dynamic data structures.

6. Profiling in Olden

After getting a program to work correctly, the programmer's attention usually turns to making it run faster. The local path lengths in Olden provide a mechanism to allow the programmer to give hints to the system regarding the data layout. These hints allow the system to reduce communication by selecting the appropriate blend of computation migration and caching. As seen in TSP, changing these local path lengths may lead to dramatic changes in the speed of the algorithm. By having the system provide feedback regarding the choice of local path lengths, the programmer can avoid guesswork or a tedious search of the parameter space in selecting the local-path-length values. Yet, even after obtaining correct local-path-length values, the program may still perform poorly. For example, a program with a poor data layout may have excessive communication overhead. Determining where the program is performing expensive operations, such as cache misses and migrations, and how often these occur may help the programmer improve the computation or the layout of the data.

Olden provides profiling tools that allow the programmer to check the local path lengths of the fields of a data structure and also examine the number and type of communication events caused by each line in the program. The local path lengths of the fields of a structure may be computed at run time by calling an Olden procedure with a pointer to the root of the structure. When the appropriate compile-time flag is used, the compiler will generate code to record the number of communication events corresponding to each line of the program. In this section, we discuss how local path lengths are verified. Olden's event profiler is relatively straightforward and is discussed in Carlisle's thesis [14].

6.1 Verifying Local Path Lengths

Recall from Sect. 4 that the local path length of a field of a structure is a hint that gives information about the expected number of nodes that will be made local by a migration following a traversal of a given field of the structure. In this section, we describe formally how to compute a local path length for a particular field of a data structure.

To simplify our definitions, we assume that each leaf node in the graph has one child, a special node, ϕ. The home of ϕ is unique (i.e., $\forall v \in V, home(\phi) \neq home(v))$, and ϕ has no descendants. We ignore all null pointers. We define a *local path* to be a sequence of vertices, $v_1, v_2, \ldots, v_n$, along a traversable set of pointers in the graph such that $\forall i, j, 2 \leq i, j \leq n - 1, home(v_i) = home(v_j)$. We say a local path is *maximal* if $home(v_1) \neq home(v_2)$ and $home(v_{n-1}) \neq home(v_n)$. The length of a local path, $v_1, v_2, \ldots, v_n$, is n-2.[7] The lengths of the maximal local paths give an estimate of the benefit of using migration, as they provide an estimate of how many future references will be made local by performing a migration. We define the local path length of a field, F, of a data structure to be the average length of maximal local paths beginning with a pointer along field F.

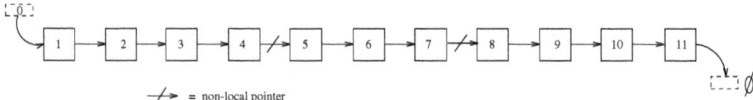

$$\text{—}/\!\!\!\text{▶} = \text{non-local pointer}$$

Fig. 6.1. A sample linked list

For an example of computing local path lengths, consider the data structure in Fig. 6.1. For the **next** field of this list, there are two non-local pointers, $[v_4, v_5]$ and $[v_7, v_8]$. The corresponding maximal local paths are $[v_4, \ldots, v_8]$ and $[v_7, \ldots, v_{11}, \phi]$, which have lengths of 3 and 4. Ignoring the initial pointer from v_0 to v_1, the average maximal local path length is 3.5, and therefore the local path length for the **next** field is 3.5. If the traversal of the structure were to begin on a different processor than the owner of v_1, $[v_0, v_1, \ldots, v_5]$ would be another maximal local path (where v_0 is a dummy vertex corresponding to the variable holding the pointer to v_1), and the average maximal local path

---

[7] This differs from the normal notion of path length (see, for example, [43]). The length of a local path expresses the number of vertices in the path that have the same home.

length would be $\frac{11}{3}$. For simplicity, we will assume for the remainder of this section that traversals begin on the owner of the root; however, the profiler considers initial pointers when computing local path lengths.

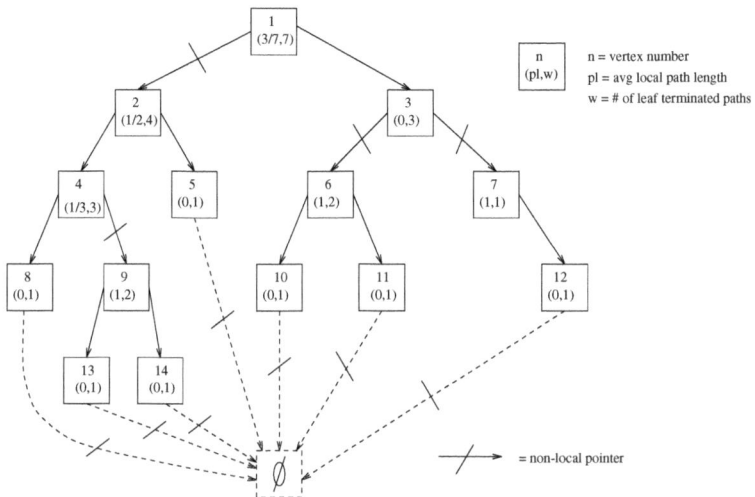

Fig. 6.2. A sample tree with local-path-length information

For structures that have more than one field, there are multiple maximal local paths corresponding to a single non-local pointer. In this case, we weight each maximal local path, P, by the total number of leaf-terminated paths that have P as a sub-path. This corresponds to assuming that all traversals are equally likely. Returning to the linked list example, each maximal local path is a sub-path of exactly one leaf-terminated path; therefore, we compute a simple average of the maximal local path lengths. For an example of the weighted case, consider the tree in Fig. 6.2. There are three maximal local paths beginning with a right edge ($[v_3, v_7, v_{12}, \phi]$, $[v_4, v_9, v_{13}, \phi]$, and $[v_4, v_9, v_{14}, \phi]$), and their weighted average local path length is 2.0. For the left field, there are five maximal local paths, $[v_1, v_2, v_5, \phi]$, $[v_1, v_2, v_4, v_9]$, $[v_1, v_2, v_4, v_8, \phi]$, $[v_3, v_6, v_{10}, \phi]$, and $[v_3, v_6, v_{11}, \phi]$, and their weights are 1,2,1,1 and 1 respectively (note there are two leaf-terminated paths from v_9, through v_{13} and v_{14}). Consequently, their weighted average local path length is $\frac{13}{6}$. For this tree, the local path length of the right field is 2, and the local path length of the left field is $\frac{13}{6}$.

We can compute these local path lengths in linear time with respect to the size of the graph using dynamic programming. For each node of the structure, using a simple depth-first traversal, we compute both the number of leaf-terminated paths from that node, and also the average local path length for paths beginning at that node. For a leaf node, the average local path length is zero, and the number of leaf-terminated paths is one. For any interior node, if it has already been visited (as might occur in a traversal of a DAG), we immediately return the computed values. Otherwise, we traverse all of its children. The number of paths from an interior node is then simply the sum of the number of paths from each of its children. The average local path length for an interior node, x, is given by:

$$\sum_{c \in children(x)} same\_proc(c, x) * (1 + avg\_local\_path\_length(c))$$

where $same\_proc(c, x)$ is 1 if c and x are on the same processor, and 0 otherwise. Since we can compute the average local path length of a node, x, incrementally from the average local path lengths of its children using $O(degree(x))$ operations, we can perform the computation for all the nodes in the graph in linear time with respect to the size of the graph.

During the same traversal, we can also compute the local path length for each field. If a non-local pointer is encountered during the traversal, we increment the total weight and weighted sum for that field. If a node, x, is visited a second time, we do not double count the non-local pointers that are in the subgraph rooted at x. Once the entire structure has been traversed, the local path length for the field is 100 if no non-local pointers are present along that field, or the computed value otherwise. Since the path affinity is given by $1 - \frac{1}{local\ path\ length}$ and we compute path affinities using integer arithmetic, all local path lengths greater than or equal to 100 will be converted to a path affinity of 99%.

The procedures used to compute local path lengths are generated automatically using preprocessor macros. To use the profiler to compute local path lengths for a tree, the programmer needs to add only two lines of code. In the header, the statement `CHECK2(tree_t *,left,right,tree)` informs the preprocessor to generate code to compute local path lengths for a data structure having two pointer fields, `left` and `right`, of type `tree_t *`. The last argument, `tree`, is used to generate a unique name. Once the data structure has been built, a call to `Docheck_tree(root)` computes and prints the local path lengths for the two pointer fields.

We used the profiler to compute local path lengths for each field in all of our benchmarks. For two of these benchmarks, TSP and Health, the heuristic will make different choices if the values computed by the profiler are used in place of the default local path lengths. Unfortunately, the results are mixed. For TSP we get a large performance gain by specifying a local path length other than the default; whereas for Health, we get a slight decrease in performance for large numbers of processors.

The traversal of each sub-result of TSP has high locality, and thus we can reduce the communication substantially by using migration to traverse these sub-results. Using the profiler, we see that the run-time-computed local path length of the relevant field is 100, which is representative of this locality. By changing to the computed local path length value, we increase the speedup

```
while(p != patient)
  {
    p = list->patient;
    list = list->forward;
  }
```

Fig. 6.3. Linked list traversal in Health

for TSP on 32 processors from 6.4 to 15.8. Thus, with the profiler, the programmer can discover this opportunity for increased performance without having to do a detailed analysis of the program.

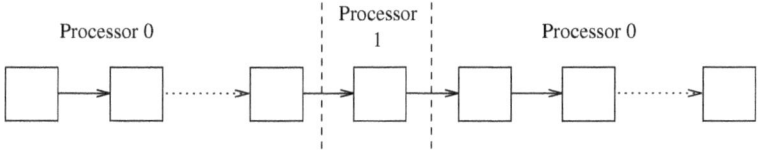

Fig. 6.4. Example linked list

The performance tradeoff for Health is more subtle. For this benchmark, each list is located almost entirely on a single processor. Because of this, the use of the computed local path length values will reduce the number of pointer tests that must be performed. Consider the code fragment in Fig. 6.3. Using computation migration, we can eliminate the pointer test for the reference to list->patient, as we know that list is local following the reference, list->forward. Using caching, we cannot eliminate the second test unless the programmer provides a guarantee that structures are aligned with cacheline boundaries. Changing the local path length value removes 6.8 million pointer tests and reduces the running time on one processor from 44.4 to 42.2 seconds. For large numbers of processors, however, the communication cost is increased. Consider the list shown in Fig. 6.4. There is a single node on Processor 1, in the middle of a very long list on Processor 0. Because the list length is very large, the local path length will also be large. Nonetheless, using caching for this list traversal is preferable, because there is only one cache miss, as opposed to two migrations using computation migration. Since the lists in Health resemble the list in Fig. 6.4, the default version, which uses caching, performs slightly better for large numbers of processors. On 32 processors, the running time is 1.94 seconds using the default version, and 2.27 seconds using the run-time-computed local path lengths.

7. Related Work

Much work has been done on providing support for programming parallel machines. In this section, we describe how our work relates to that of other groups. First, we discuss some work by Rajiv Gupta that motivated our work on Olden. Then we divide other projects into three categories: object-oriented systems, parallel versions of C using fork and join, and other related projects not fitting in the first two categories. Figure 7.1 summarizes the differences between Olden and the other systems described in this section.

	Global arrays	Global heap	Multi-threaded	Lazy task creation	Fine-grain synch.	Computation migration	Software caching	Auto selection	Implicit global pointers
Olden			✓	✓	✓		✓	✓	✓
O-O systems	✓	✓	✓		✓	✓	*		
Cid	✓	✓	✓	**	✓		✓		
Cilk	✓	✓	✓				✓		
Split-C	✓	✓					✓		
MCRL	✓	✓	✓			✓	✓	✓	✓
Orca	✓	✓	✓						
Linda	✓	✓	✓						
Jegou	✓					✓			

  * supports data migration and replication of read-only objects
  ** has irrevocable inlining

Fig. 7.1. Summary of related work

7.1 Gupta's Work

Our work on Olden was motivated originally by Rajiv Gupta's work supporting dynamic data structures on distributed memory machines [25]. His approach was to create global names for the nodes in a data structure and then to apply a variant of run-time resolution [48] to the program. His naming scheme assigns a name to every node in a data structure as it is added to the structure and makes this name known to all processors (thereby producing a global name for the node). The name assigned to a node is determined by its position in the structure, as is the mapping of nodes to processors. For example, a breadth-first numbering of the nodes might be used as a naming scheme for a binary tree. Once a processor has a name for the nodes in a data structure, it can traverse the structure without further communication.

This method of naming dynamic data structures leads to restrictions on how the data structures can be used. Since the name of a node is determined by its position, only one node can be added to a structure at a time (for example, two lists cannot be concatenated). Also, node names may have to be reassigned when a new node is introduced. For example, consider a list in which a node's name is simply its position in the list. If a node is added to the front of the list, the rest of the list's nodes will have to be renamed to reflect their change in position.

Gupta's decision to use a variant of run-time resolution to handle non-local references also has several problems, which are caused by the ownership tests that are done to allocate work. First, the overhead of these tests is high. And second, they prevent many important optimizations, such as vectorization and pipelining, from being applied. Run-time resolution was never intended to be a primary method of allocating work, instead it was designed as the fall back position for compile-time resolution, which resolves who will do the work at compile time rather than at run time. In Olden, we take a much more dynamic approach to allocating work. We still test most references to determine where the work should be done, but each test is done by at most one processor and in general the other processors will be busy with their own work.

7.2 Object-Oriented Systems

Emerald [32] is an object-oriented language developed at the University of Washington for programming distributed systems. The language provides primitives to locate objects on processors explicitly, and also has constructs for moving objects. Each method is invoked on the processor owning that object, migrating the computation at the invocation. Arguments to the method may be moved to the invocation site on the basis of compile-time information.

Amber [17] is a subset of C++ designed for parallel programming with a distribution model and mobility primitives derived from Emerald; however, all object motion is done explicitly. Amber also adds replication, but only for immutable objects. As in Olden, a computation may migrate within an invocation, but Amber computations only migrate if the objects they reference are moved out from under them explicitly by another thread.

COOL [16] and Mercury [22] are also extensions of C++. Unlike Emerald and Amber, they are designed to run on a shared-memory multiprocessor. In COOL, by default, method invocations run on the processor that owns the object; however, this can be overridden by specifying affinities for the methods. There are three different types of affinities: *object*, *processor*, and *task*. If the programmer specifies that a method has affinity with a particular object (not the base object), then it will be run on the processor that owns that object. A processor affinity is similar, and could be viewed as an object affinity to a dummy object on the specified processor. Object affinities are used to increase locality; processor affinities are specified to balance the load. To increase cache reuse of an object, COOL allows the programmer to specify a task affinity with respect to that object. For each processor, the COOL run-time system has an array of task queues. There is a queue for each object owned by that processor, for each collection of tasks with task affinity, and for the collection of tasks with processor affinity for that processor. Load balancing is accomplished by work stealing. If a processor is idle, it may steal a task-affinity task queue from another processor, as these tasks are not required to run on a particular processor. Mercury also has a notion of object affinity, but uses templates rather than a scheduler. The template associated with each method specifies how to find the next task to execute.

The Concert system [18, 33] provides compiler and run-time support for efficient execution of fine-grained concurrent object-oriented programs. This work is primarily concerned with efficiency rather than language features. They combine static analysis, speculative compilation, and dynamic compilation. If an object type and the assurance of locality can be inferred from analysis, method invocations on that object can be in-lined, improving execution efficiency. If imprecise information is available, it is sometimes possible to optimize for the likely cases, selecting amongst several specialized versions at run time. When neither of these is applicable, dynamic compilation is sometimes used to optimize based on run-time information. The compiler will select which program points will be dynamically compiled. Concert provides a globally shared object space, common programming idioms (such as RPC and tail forwarding), inheritance, and some concurrency control. Objects are single threaded and communicate asynchronously through message passing (invocations). Concert also provides parallel collections of data, structures for parallel composition, first-class messages, and continuations. A major goal of the Concert project is to provide efficient support for fine-grain concurrency. The system seeks to accomplish this by automatically collecting invocations into groups using structure analysis [44].

Each of these systems supports more general synchronization than Olden; however, they do not provide the automatic selection between caching and computation migration. Emerald does have heuristics to move objects automatically, but does not support replication. Additionally, with the exception of Concert, these languages do not support in-lining; consequently, their use of objects adds additional overhead.

7.3 Extensions of C with Fork-Join Parallelism

Cid [42], a recently proposed extension to C, supports a threads and locks model of parallelism. Cid threads are lightweight and the thread creation mechanism allows the programmer to name a specific processing element on which the thread should be run. Unlike Olden, Cid threads cannot migrate once they have begun execution. This makes it awkward to take advantage of data locality while traversing a structure iteratively. Cid also provides a global object mechanism that is based on global pointers. The programmer explicitly requests access to a global object using one of several sharing modes (for example, readonly) and is given a pointer to a local copy in return. Cid's global objects use implicit locking and the run-time system maintains consistency.

One of Cid's design goals is to use existing compilers. While this makes it easier to port to new systems, it does not allow it to take advantage of having access to the code generator and compile-time information. For example, once a Cid fork is in-lined, the system cannot change its mind. In Olden, an in-lined future may be stolen at a later time, should the processor become idle. Additionally, Olden programs more closely resemble their sequential C counterparts, as handling remote references is done implicitly.

Cilk [10, 11] is another parallel extension of C implemented using a pre-processor. The implementation introduces a substantial amount of overhead per call, as each call to a Cilk procedure requires a user-level spawn. Unlike Cid and Olden, these spawns are never in-lined.

Cilk introduces dag-consistent shared memory, a novel technique to share data across processors. This is implemented as a stack, and shared memory allocations are similar to local variable declarations. Caching is done implicitly at the page level, and work is placed on processors using a work-stealing scheduler. By contrast, Olden does caching at the line-level, and is thus more efficient when small portions of a page are shared. Additionally, using computation migration, Olden can take advantage of data locality in placing the computation. Olden, however, gets its load balance from the data layout, and thus is only more efficient for programs where the data is placed so that the work is reasonably distributed among the processors. If the data is distributed non-uniformly, a Cilk program will perform better, as Cilk's work-stealing algorithm will generate a better load balance.

7.4 Other Related Work

Split-C [20] is a parallel extension of C that provides a global address space and maintains a clear concept of locality by providing both local and global pointers. Split-C provides a variety of primitives to manipulate global pointers efficiently. In a related piece of work, Lumetta et al. [39] describe a global object space abstraction that provides a way to decouple the description of an algorithm from the description of an optimized layout of its data structures.

Like Olden, Split-C is based on the modification of an existing compiler. Split-C, however, adopts a programming model where each processor has a single thread executing the same program. While this is perhaps convenient for expressing array-based parallelism, recursive programs must be written much more awkwardly.

Prelude [28] is an explicitly parallel language that provides a computation model based on threads and objects. Annotations are added to a Prelude program to specify which of several mechanisms — remote procedure call, object migration, or computation migration — should be used to implement an object or thread. Hsieh later implemented MCRL [29], which, like Olden, provides both computation migration and data migration, and a mechanism that automatically selects between them. MCRL uses two heuristics to decide between computation and data migration, *static* and *repeat*. The static heuristic may be computed at compile-time for most functions and migrates computation for all non-local writes and data for all non-local reads. The repeat heuristic also always migrates computation for non-local writes, but makes a run-time decision for non-local reads based on the relative frequency of reads and writes. Computation migration is used for an object until two consecutive reads of that object have occurred without any intervening writes. The heuristics used by MCRL are very different from those in Olden, as MCRL is designed for a different type of program. In Olden, we are concerned with traversals of data structures, and improving locality by migrating the computation if it will make future references local. The benchmarks we describe use threads that do not interfere. By contrast, MCRL is concerned with reducing coherence traffic for programs where the threads are performing synchronized accesses to the same regions with a large degree of interference. Olden cannot be used for such programs. Their heuristics for choosing between data and computation migration would perform poorly on our benchmarks, as they consider only the read/write patterns of accesses. On a read-only traversal of a large data structure on a remote processor, MCRL would choose to cache the accesses, as this causes no additional coherence traffic. Olden, however, would use migration, causing all references but the first to become local.

Orca [5, 6] also provides an explicitly parallel programming model based on threads and objects. Orca hides the distribution of the data from the programmer, but is designed to allow the compiler and run-time system to implement shared objects efficiently. The Orca compiler produces a summary of how shared objects are accessed that is used by its run-time system to decide if a shared object should be replicated, and if not, where it should be stored. Operations on replicated and local objects are processed locally; operations on remote objects are handled using a remote procedure call to the processor that owns the object. Orca performs a global broadcast at each fork. This restricts Orca to programs having coarse parallelism, and makes it awkward to express parallelism on recursive traversals of trees and DAGs. Also, Orca does not allow pointers, instead using a special graph type. This has the disadvantages of making it impossible to link together two different structures without copying one and also requiring that each dereference be done indirectly through a table.

Carriero et al.'s [15] work on *distributed data structures* in Linda shares a common objective with Olden, namely, providing a mechanism for distributed processors to work on shared linked structures. In the details, however, the two approaches are quite different. The Linda model provides a global address space (tuple space), but no control over the actual assignment of data to processors. While Linda allows the flexibility of arbitrary distributed data structures, including arrays, graphs and sets, Olden's control over data layout will provide greater efficiency for programs using hierarchical structures.

Jégou [31] uses the idea of computation migration to provide an environment for executing irregular codes on distributed memory multiprocessors. His system is implemented as an extension of FORTRAN. For each parallel loop, a single thread is started for each iteration. The data never moves; instead, when a thread needs non-local data, it is migrated to the processor that owns the data. The threads operate entirely asynchronously (i.e., no processor ever needs to wait for the result of a communication). This allows computation to be overlapped with communication. Because the threads migrate, detecting when the loop has terminated is non-trivial. Jégou provides an algorithm for detecting termination that requires $O(p^2)$ messages. Using computation migration alone for these types of programs is successful because there is sufficient parallelism to hide the communication latency; however, for divide-and-conquer programs, we have demonstrated that combining computation migration with software caching provides better performance.

8. Conclusions

We have presented a new approach for supporting programs that use pointer-based dynamic data structures on distributed-memory machines. In developing our new approach, we have noted a fundamental problem with trying to apply run-time-resolution techniques, currently used to produce SPMD programs for array-based programs, to pointer-based programs. Array data structures are directly addressable. In contrast, dynamic data structures must be traversed to be addressable. This property of dynamic data structures precludes the use of simple local tests for ownership, and therefore makes the run-time resolution model ineffective.

Our solution avoids these fundamental problems by matching more closely the dynamic nature of the data structures. Rather than having a single thread on each processor, which decides if it should execute a statement by determining if it owns the relevant piece of the data structure, we instead have multiple threads of computation, which are allowed to migrate to the processor owning the data they need. Along with this computation migration technique we provide a **futurecall** mechanism, which introduces parallelism by allowing processors to split threads, and a software caching mechanism, which provides an efficient means for a thread to access data from multiple processors simultaneously. In addition, we have implemented a compiler heuristic requiring minimal programmer input that automatically chooses the whether to use computation migration or software caching for each pointer dereference. We have also built a profiler, which will compute the local-path-length information used by the heuristic, and allow the programmer to determine which lines of the program cause communication events.

We have implemented our execution mechanisms on the CM-5, and have performed experiments using this system on a suite of eleven benchmarks. Our results indicate that combining both computation migration and software caching produces better performance than either mechanism alone, and that our heuristic makes good selections with minimal additional information from the programmer. The Olden profiler can generate this information automatically by examining a sample run of the program. Where comparisons were available, our system's performance was comparable to implementations of the same benchmarks using other systems; however, the Olden implementation was more easily programmed.

Acknowledgement. Laurie Hendren of McGill University and John Reppy of AT&T Labs contributed to the early design of Olden. Both authors were members of the Department of Computer Science at Princeton University when this work was done. Martin Carlisle was supported by the Fannie and John Hertz Foundation, a National Science Foundation Graduate Fellowship, NSF Grant ASC-9110766, NSF FAW award MIP-9023542, and the Department of Computer Science at Princeton University. Anne Rogers was supported, in part, by NSF Grant ASC-9110766. Also, the National Supercomputing Centers at the University of Illinois (NCSA) and Syracuse University (NPAC) provided access to their Think Machines CM-5s.

References

1. A. Aho, R. Sethi, and J. Ullman. *Compilers: Principles, Techniques, and Tools.* Addison Wesley, 1988.
2. S.P. Amarasinghe and M.S. Lam. Communication optimization and code generation for distributed memory machines. In *Proceedings of the SIGPLAN '93 Conference on Programming Language Design and Implementation*, pages 126–138, ACM, New York, June 1993.
3. J.M. Anderson and M.S. Lam. Global optimizations for parallelism and locality on scalable parallel machines. In *Proceedings of the SIGPLAN '93 Conference on Programming Language Design and Implementation*, pages 112–125, ACM, New York, June 1993.
4. A.W. Appel and K. Li. Virtual memory primitives for user programs. In *Proceedings of the 4th International Conference on Architectural Support for Programming Languages and Operating Systems*, pages 96–107, ACM, New York, April 1991.
5. H. Bal, M. F. Kaashoek, and A. Tanenbaum. Orca: A language for parallel programming of distributed systems. *IEEE Transactions on Software Engineering*, 18(3):190–205, Mar 1992.
6. H. E. Bal and M. F. Kaashoek. Object distribution in Orca using compile-time and run-time techniques. In *Proceedings of the Conference on Object-Oriented*

Programming Systems, Languages and Applications (OOPSLA '93), September 1993.

7. J. Barnes and P. Hut. A hierarchical $O(N \log N)$ force-calculation algorithm. *Nature*, 324:446–449, December 1986.

8. J. Bentley. A parallel algorithm for constructing minimum spanning trees. *Journal of Algorithms*, 1:51–59, 1980.

9. G. Bilardi and A. Nicolau. Adaptive bitonic sorting: An optimal parallel algorithm for shared-memory machines. *SIAM Journal of Computing*, 18(2):216–228, 1989.

10. R. Blumofe, M. Frigo, C. Joerg, C. Leiserson, and K. Randall. Dag-consistent distributed shared memory. Technical report, Massachusetts Institute of Technology, September 1995. See `http://theory.lcs.mit.edu/~cilk`.

11. R. Blumofe, C. Joerg, B. Kuszmaul, C. Leiserson, K. Randall, and Y. Zhou. Cilk: An efficient multithreaded runtime system. In *Proceedings of the 5th ACM SIGPLAN Symposium on Principles & Practice of Parallel Programming (PPoPP)*, pages 207–216, July 1995.

12. D. Callahan and K. Kennedy. Compiling programs for distributed-memory multiprocessors. *Journal of Supercomputing*, 2(2):151–169, October 1988.

13. M. Carlisle and A. Rogers. Software caching and computation migration in Olden'. *Journal of Parallel and Distributed Computing*, 38(2):248–255, November 1996.

14. Martin C. Carlisle. *Olden: Parallelizing Programs with Dynamic Data Structures on Distributed-Memory Machines*. PhD thesis, Princeton University Department of Computer Science, June 1996.

15. N. Carriero, D. Gelernter, and J. Leichter. Distributed data structures in Linda. In *Conference Record of the 13th Annual ACM Symposium on Principles of Programming Languages*, pages 236–242, January 1986.

16. R. Chandra, A. Gupta, and J. Hennessy. Data locality and load balancing in COOL. In *Proceedings of the 4th ACM SIGPLAN Symposium on Principles & Practice of Parallel Programming (PPoPP)*, pages 249–259, May 1993.

17. J.S. Chase, F. G. Amador, E.D. Lazowska, H. M. Levy, and R. J. Littlefield. The Amber system: Parallel programming on a network of multiprocesors. In *Proceedings of the 12th ACM Symposium on Operating Systems Principles*, pages 147–158, ACM, New York, December 1989.

18. A. Chien, V. Karamcheti, and J. Plevyak. The Concert system– compiler and runtime support for efficient, fine-grained concurrent object-oriented programs. Technical Report UIUCDCS-R-93-1815, Department of Computer Science, University of Illinois at Urbana-Champaign, June 1993.

19. Cray Research, Inc. *Cray T3D System Architecture*. 1993.

20. D. Culler, A. Dusseau, S. Goldstein, A. Krishnamurthy, S. Lumetta, T. von Eicken, and K. Yelick. Parallel programming in Split-C. In *Proceedings of Supercomputing 93*, pages 262–273, 1993.

21. B. Falsafi, A. Lebeck, S. Reinhardt, I. Schoinas, M. Hill, J. Larus, A. Rogers, and D. Wood. Application-specific protocols for user-level shared memory. In *Proceedings of Supercomputing 94*, 1994.

22. R. Fowler and L. Kontothanassis. Improving processor and cache locality in fine-grain parallel computations using object-affinity scheduling and continuation passing. Technical Report 411, University of Rochester, Computer Science Department, June 1992.

23. M. Gerndt. *Automatic Parallelization for Distributed-Memory Multiprocessing Systems*. PhD thesis, University of Bonn, 1990.

24. L. Guibas and J. Stolfi. General subdivisions and voronoi diagrams. *ACM Transactions on Graphics*, 4(2):74–123, 1985.

25. R. Gupta. SPMD execution of programs with dynamic data structures on distributed memory machines. In *Proceedings of the 1992 International Conference on Computer Languages*, pages 232–241, Los Alamitos, California, April 1992. IEEE Computer Society.

26. R. H. Halstead, Jr. Multilisp: A language for concurrent symbolic computation. *ACM Transactions on Programming Languages and Systems*, 7(4):501–538, October 1985.

27. S. Hiranandani, K. Kennedy, and C. Tseng. Compiler optimizations for FORTRAN D on MIMD distributed memory machines. In *Proceedings of Supercomputing 91*, pages 86–100, Los Alamitos, California, November 1991. IEEE Computer Society.

28. W. Hsieh, P. Wang, and W. Weihl. Computation migration: Enhancing locality for distributed-memory parallel systems. In *Proceedings of the 4th ACM SIGPLAN Symposium on Principles & Practice of Parallel Programming (PPoPP)*, pages 239–248, 1993.

29. Wilson C. Hsieh. *Dynamic Computation Migration in Distributed Shared Memory Systems*. PhD thesis, MIT Department of Electrical Engineering and Computer Science, September 1995.

30. J. Hummel, L. Hendren, and A. Nicolau. Path collection and dependence testing in the presence of dynamic, pointer-based data structures. In B. Szymanski and B. Sinharoy, editors, *Languages, Compilers and Run-Time Systems for Scalable Computers (Proceedings of the 3rd Workshop)*, pages 15–27, May 1995. Kluwer Academic Publishers, Boston, MA, 1995.

31. Yvon Jégou. Exécution de codes irrégulier par migration de tâches. Technical Report 867, Institut de Recherche en Informatique et Systèmes Aléatoires, November 1994.

32. E. Jul, H. Levy, N. Hutchinson, and A. Black. Fine-grained mobility in the Emerald system. *ACM Transactions on Computer Systems*, 6(1):109–133, 1988.

33. V. Karamcheti and A. Chien. Concert – efficient runtime support for concurrent object-oriented programming languages – on stock hardware. In *Proceedings of Supercomputing 93*, pages 598–607, November 1993.

34. A. Karp. Programming for parallelism. In *IEEE Computer*, May 1987.

35. R. Karp. Probabilistic analysis of partitioning algorithms for the traveling-salesman problem in the plane. *Mathematics of Operations Research*, 2(3):209–224, August 1977.

36. C. Koelbel. *Compiling Programs for Nonshared Memory Machines*. PhD thesis, Purdue University, West Lafayette, Ind, August 1990.

37. L. Lamport. How to make a multiprocessor that correctly executes multiprocess programs. *IEEE Transactions on Computers*, C-28(9), September 1979.

38. G. Lomow, J. Cleary, B. Unger, and D. West. A performance study of Time Warp. In *SCS Multiconference on Distributed Simulation*, pages 50–55, February 1988.

39. S. Lumetta, L. Murphy, X. Li, D. Culler, and I. Khalil. Decentralized optimal power pricing: The development of a parallel program. In *Proceedings of Supercomputing 93*, pages 240–249, 1993.

40. S. Lumetta, L. Murphy, X. Li, D. Culler, and I. Khalil. Decentralized optimal power pricing: The development of a parallel program. In *Proceedings of Supercomputing 93*, pages 240–249, Los Alamitos, California, November 1993. IEEE Computer Society.

41. E. Mohr, D. A. Kranz, and R. H. Halstead, Jr. Lazy task creation: A technique for increasing the granularity of parallel programs. *IEEE Transactions on Parallel and Distributed Systems*, 2(3):264–280, July 1991.

42. Rishiyur Nikhil. Cid: A parallel, "shared-memory" C for distributed-memory machines. In *Proceedings of the 7th International Workshop on Languages and Compilers for Parallel Computing*, Ithaca, NY, August 1994.
43. C. Papadimitriou and K. Steiglitz. *Combinatorial Optimization: Algorithms and Complexity*. Prentice Hall, 1982.
44. John Plevyak, Andrew Chien, and Vijay Karamcheti. Analysis of dynamic structures for efficient parallel execution. In *Proceedings of the 6th International Workshop on Languages and Compilers for Parallel Computing*, pages 37–56, 1993.
45. John A. Rice. *Mathematical Statistics and Data Analysis*. Wadsworth and Brooks/Cole Advanced Books and Software, Pacific Grove, CA, 1987.
46. E. S. Roberts and M. T. Vandevoorde. WorkCrews: An abstraction for controlling parallelism. Technical Report 42, DEC Systems Research Center, Palo Alto, CA, April 1989.
47. A. Rogers, M. Carlisle, J. Reppy, and L. Hendren. Supporting dynamic data structures on distributed memory machines. *ACM Transactions on Programming Languages and Systems*, 17(2):233–263, March 1995.
48. A. Rogers and K. Pingali. Process decomposition through locality of reference. In *Proceedings of the SIGPLAN '89 Conference on Programming Language Design and Implementation*, pages 69–80, ACM, New York, June 1989.
49. H. Samet. Computing perimeters of regions in images represented by quadtrees. *IEEE Transactions on Pattern Analysis and Machine Intelligence*, PAMI-3(6):683–687, November 1981.
50. I. Schoinas, B. Falsafi, A. Lebeck, S. Reinhardt, J. Larus, and D. Wood. Fine-grain access control for distributed shared memory. In *Proceedings of the 6th International Conference on Architectural Support for Programming Languages and Operating Systems (ASPLOS VI)*, pages 297–307, October 1994.
51. Michael Shneier. Calculations of geometric properties using quadtrees. *Computer Graphics and Image Processing*, 16(3):296–302, July 1981.
52. H. Zima, H. Bast, and M. Gerndt. SUPERB: A tool for semi-automatic MIMD/SIMD parallelization. *Parallel Computing*, 6(1):1–18, 1988.

Chapter 21. Runtime and Compiler Support for Irregular Computations

Raja Das[1], Yuan-Shin Hwang[2], Joel Saltz[3], and Alan Sussman[3]

[1] Georgia Institute of Technology, College of Computing, Atlanta, GA 30332,
   raja@cc.gatech.edu
[2] Department of Computer Science, National Taiwan Ocean University
   2 Pei-Ning Road, Keelung 202, Taiwan
   shin@cs.ntou.edu.tw
[3] University of Maryland, Computer Science Dept., College Park, MD 20742,
   {saltz,als}@cs.umd.edu

1. Introduction

There have been major efforts in developing programming language and compiler support for distributed memory parallel machines. On these machines, large data arrays are typically partitioned among the local memories of individual processors. Languages supporting such *distributed arrays* include Fortran D [11, 19], Vienna Fortran [6, 32], and High Performance Fortran (HPF) [21]. Many compilers for these HPF-like languages produce Single Program Multiple Data (SPMD) code, combining sequential code for operating on each processor's data with calls to message-passing or runtime communication primitives for sharing data with other processors.

Reducing communication costs is crucial to achieve good performance on applications [16, 18]. Current compiler prototypes, including the Fortran D [19] and Vienna Fortran compilation systems [6], apply message blocking, collective communication, and message coalescing and aggregation to optimize communication. However, these methods have been developed mostly in the context of regular problems, meaning for codes having only easily analyzable data access patterns. Special effort is required to develop compiler and runtime support for applications with more complex data access.

In irregular problems, communication patterns depend on data values not known at compile time, typically because of some indirection in the array reference patterns in the code. Indirection patterns have to be preprocessed, and the sets of elements to be sent and received by each processor precomputed, in order to reduce the volume of communication, reduce the number of messages, and hide communication latencies through prefetching. An irregular loop with a single level of indirection can be parallelized by transforming

---

[1] An extended version of this paper has been submitted to IEEE Transactions on Computers.

[2] This research was supported by ARPA under contract No. NAG-1-1485 and NSF under contract Nos. ASC 9213821 and ASC-9624987.

S. Pande, D.P. Agrawal (Eds.): Compiler Optimizations for Scalable PS, LNCS 1808, pp. 751-778, 2001.
© Springer-Verlag Berlin Heidelberg 2001

it into two constructs—an *inspector* and an *executor* [24]. During program execution, the inspector running on each processor examines the data references made and determines which off-processor data must be fetched and where the data will be stored once received. The executor loop then uses the information from the inspector to implement the actual computation and communication, optimized to reduce communications costs wherever possible. Supporting the *inspector-executor pair* requires a robust runtime system. The Maryland CHAOS library [10] provides such support, including procedures for analyzing indices, generating communication schedules, translating global addresses to local addresses and prefetching data.

```
do i = 1, n
    x(i) = y(ia(i)) + z(i)
end do
```

Fig. 1.1. Simple Irregular Loop

Figure 1.1 shows a loop with a single level of indirection. In this example, assume that all the arrays are aligned and distributed identically by blocks among the processors, and that the iterations of the **i** loop are similarly block partitioned. The resulting computation mapping is equivalent to that produced by the *owner computes rule*, a compiler heuristic that maps the computation of an assignment statement to the processor that owns the left hand side reference. Data array **y** is indexed using the array **ia**, causing a single level of indirection. Standard methods for compiling the loop for a distributed-memory machine generate a single inspector-executor pair. The inspector analyzes the subscripts, a gather-type communication occurs if off-processor data is read in the loop body, a single executor runs the original computation, and then a scatter-type communication occurs if off-processor data has been written in the loop body.

The compiler produces SPMD code designed to run on each processor, with each processor checking its processor identifier to determine where its data and loop iterations fit into the global computation. Letting *my$elems* represent the number of local elements from each array (and the number of iterations from the original loop performed locally) the compiler generates the following code (omitting some details of communication and translation for clarity):

```
do i = 1, my$elems                    ! inspector
      index$y(i) = ia(i)
enddo

... fetch y elements to local memory,
modify index$y for local indices ...
```

```
do i = 1, my$elems                        ! executor
   x(i) = y(index$y(i)) + z(index$z(i))
enddo
```

Because the references to y access only local elements of the distributed array ia, the inspector requires no communication.

Many application codes contain computations with more complex array access functions. Subscripted subscripts and subscripted guards can make the indexing of one distributed array depend on the values in another, so that a partial order is established on the distributed accesses. Loops with such multiple levels of indirection commonly appear in unstructured and adaptive application codes associated with particle methods, molecular dynamics, sparse linear solvers, and in some unstructured mesh computational fluid dynamics solvers.

In this paper we present various optimizations that are part of our runtime support system and methods for handling loops with complex indirection patterns, by transforming them into multiple loops each with a single level of indirection. We have implemented these methods in the Fortran D compiler developed at Rice University [17]. Our experiments demonstrate substantial performance improvements through message aggregation on a multiprocessor Intel iPSC/860 and through vectorization on a single Cray Y-MP processor.

In Section 2 we present an overview of the runtime system we have developed and also also discuss the various optimization techniques required to successfully compile irregular problems for distributed memory machines. Section 3 describes the compiling techniques and transformations that we have developed. In Section 4 we present results showing the benefits of the various runtime optimizations and also performance results from application codes compiled using the compilation techniques. We conclude in Section 5.

2. Overview of the CHAOS Runtime System

This section describes the CHAOS runtime support library, which is a superset of the PARTI [10] library, along with two new features, light-weight schedules and two-phase schedule generation, which are designed to handle adaptive irregular programs.

The CHAOS runtime library has been developed to efficiently support parallelization of programs with irregular data access patterns. The library is designed to ease the implementation of computational problems on parallel architecture machines by relieving users of low-level machine specific issues.

In static irregular programs, the executor is typically performed many times, while partitioning (data and work) and inspector generation are performed only once. In some adaptive programs, where data access patterns change periodically but reasonable load balance is maintained, the inspector generation process must be repeated whenever the data access patterns change. In highly adaptive programs, the data arrays may need to be repartitioned in order to maintain load balance. In such applications, all phases of the inspector are repeated upon repartitioning.

The optimizations developed to handle static irregular problems have been presented in detail in earlier work [10]. We now present the optimizations required to handle adaptive problems – irregular problems where the data access patterns change every few loop iterations. In such cases, the inspector generation process has to be modified to minimize its cost, and we present two different ways of achieving that goal.

Adaptive Schedule Generation

A *communication schedule* is used to fetch off-processor elements into a local buffer before the computation phase, and to scatter these elements back to their home processors after the computational phase is completed. Communication schedules determine the number of communication startups and the volume of communication. Therefore, it is important to optimize the schedule generation.

The basic idea of the inspector-executor concept is to separate preprocessing of access patterns from communication and computation. Each piece of the transformed loop can then be optimized in the appropriate way. Inspector preprocessing can be combined with other preprocessing and hoisted out of as many loops as possible (those in which the data access information does not change), communication can be batched and vectorized, and the computation can be tuned in a tight inner loop.

In adaptive codes where the data access pattern changes occasionally, the inspector is not a one-time preprocessing cost. Every time an indirection array changes, the schedules associated with the array must be regenerated. While this paper focuses on moving inspectors out of loops to reduce their frequency of execution, we have developed other techniques for efficient incremental inspection [10, 26].

For example, in Figure 2.1, if the indirection array ic is modified, the schedules *inc_sched_c* and *sched_c* must be regenerated. Generating *inc_sched_c* involves inspecting *sched_ab* to determine which off-processor elements are duplicated in that schedule. Thus, it must be certain that communication schedule generators are efficient while maintaining the necessary flexibility.

In CHAOS, the schedule-generation process on each processor is carried out in two distinct phases.

– The **index analysis** phase examines the data access patterns to determine which references are off-processor, removes duplicate off-processor references by storing information about distinct references in a hash table, assigns a local buffer for storing data from off-processor references, and translates global indices to local indices.

```
L1:    do n = 1, nsteps    ! outer loop
         call gather(y(begin_buff), y, sched_ab)    ! fetch off-proc data
         call zero_out_buffer(x(begin_buff), offp_x)    ! initialize buffer
L2:    do i = 1, local_sizeof_indir_arrays    ! inner loop
         x(local_ia(i)) = x(local_ia(i))
                          + y(local_ia(i)) * y(local_ib(i))
       end do

S:     if (required) then
         modify part_ic(:)    ! ic is modified
         CHAOS_clear_mask(hashtable, stamp_c)    ! clear ic
         local_ic(:) = part_ic(:)
         stamp_c = CHAOS_enter_hash(local_ic)    ! insert new ic
         inc_sched_c = CHAOS_incremental_schedule(stamp_c)
         ! sched for ia, ic
         sched_ac = CHAOS_schedule(stamp_a, stamp_c)
       endif

       ! incremental gather
       call gather(y(begin_buff2), y, inc_sched_c)
       call zero_out_buffer(x(begin_buff2), offp_x2)    ! initialize buffer
L3:    do i = 1, local_sizeof_ic    ! inner loop
         x(local_ic(i)) = x(local_ic(i)) + y(local_ic(i))
       end do
       call scatter_add(x(begin_buff), x, sched_ac)    ! scatter addition
       end do
```

Fig. 2.1. Schedule Generation for an Adaptive Program

- The **schedule generation** phase generates communication schedules based on the information stored in the hash tables for each distinct off-processor reference.

The communication schedule for processor p stores the following information:

1. send list – a list of arrays that specifies the local elements on processor p required by all other processors,
2. permutation list – an array that specifies the data placement order of off-processor elements in the local buffer of processor p,
3. send size – an array that specifies the sizes of out-going messages from processor p to all other processors, and
4. fetch size – an array that specifies the sizes of in-coming messages to processor p from all other processors.

The principal advantage of such a two-step process is that some of the index analysis can be reused in adaptive applications. In the index analysis phase, hash tables are used to store global to local translation and to remove duplicate off-processor references. Each entry keeps the following information:

1. global index – the global index hashed into the table,
2. translated address – the processor and offset where the element is stored
3. local index – the local buffer address assigned to hold a copy of the element, if it comes from off-processor, and
4. stamp – an integer used to identify which indirection array inserted the element into the hash table. The same global index entry might be hashed into the table for many different indirection arrays; a bit in the stamp is marked for each indirection array.

Stamps are useful for efficiently parallelizing adaptive irregular programs, especially for those programs with several index arrays where most of them do not change. In the index analysis phase, each index array inserted into the hash table is assigned a unique stamp that marks all its entries in the table. Communication schedules are generated based on the combination of stamps for an array reference. If any one of the index arrays changes, only the entries pertaining to the index array, namely those entries with the stamp marked for the index array, have to be removed from the hash table. Once the new index array entries are inserted into the hash table, a new schedule can be generated without rehashing the other index arrays.

Figure 2.1 illustrates (in pseudo-code) how CHAOS routines are used to parallelize an adaptive problem. The conditional statement S may cause the indirection array `ic` to be modified. Whenever this occurs, the communication schedules that involve prefetching references of `ic` must be modified. Since the values of `ic` in the hash table are no longer valid, the entries with stamp $stamp\_c$ are cleared by calling $CHAOS\_clear\_mask()$. New values of `ic` are then inserted into the hash table by the call to $CHAOS\_enter\_hash()$. After all indirection arrays have been hashed, communication schedules can be built for any combination of indirection arrays by calling $CHAOS\_schedule()$ or $CHAOS\_incremental\_schedule()$ with an appropriate combination of stamps.

An example of schedule generation for two processors with sample values for indirection arrays `ia`, `ib`, and `ic` is shown in Figure 2.2. The global references from indirection array `ia` are stored in hash table H with stamp a, `ib` with stamp b and `ic` with stamp c. The indirection arrays might have some common references. Hence, a hashed global reference might have more than one stamp. The gather schedule $sched\_ab$ for the loop L2 in Figure 2.1 is built using the union of references with time stamps a or b. The scatter operation for loop L2 can be combined with the scatter operation for the loop L3. The gather schedule inc_sched_c for loop L3 is built with those references that have time stamp c only, because references that also have time stamps a or b have been fetched using the schedule $sched\_ab$. The scatter schedule for loops L2 and L3 is built using the union of references with time stamps a and c.

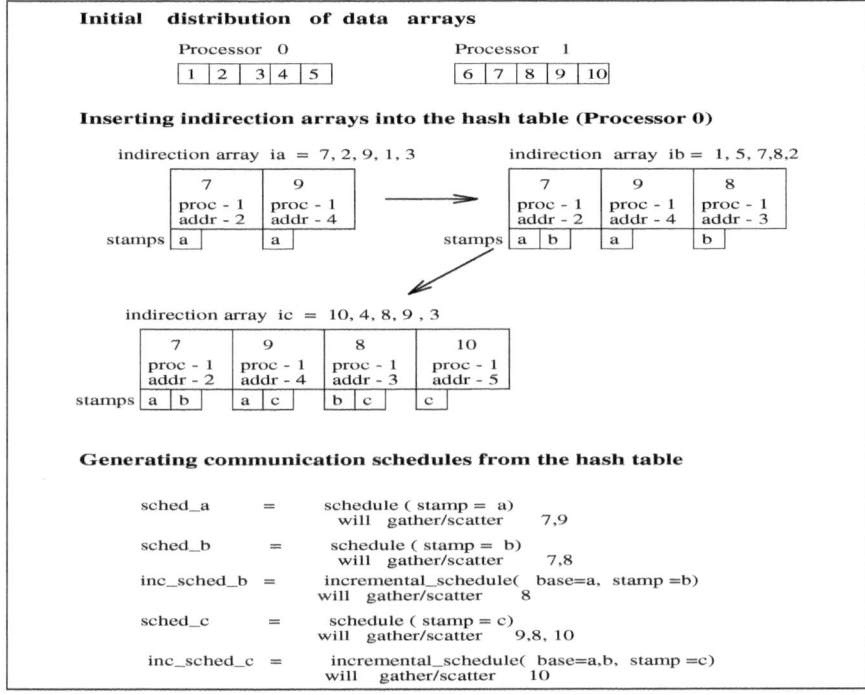

Fig. 2.2. Schedule Generation on One Processor, Using a Hash Table

PARTI, the runtime library that preceded CHAOS, also had support for building incremental and merged schedules [10]. However, in PARTI such schedules were built using functions specialized for these purposes. The CHAOS library restructures the schedule generation process by the using a global hash table that provides a uniform interface for building all types of schedules. Such a uniform interface is easier to use for both parallel application developers and for compilers that automatically embed CHAOS schedule generation calls.

Light-Weight Schedules

In certain highly adaptive problems, such as those using particle-in-cell methods, data elements are frequently moved from one set of elements to another during the course of the computation. The implication of such adaptivity is that preprocessing for a loop must be repeated whenever the data access pattern of the loop changes. In other words, previously built communication schedules cannot be reused and must be rebuilt frequently.

In such applications a significant optimization in schedule generation can be achieved by recognizing that the semantics of set operations imply that set elements can be stored in any order. This information can be used to build *light-weight* communication schedules that cost less to build than normal schedules. During schedule-generation, processors do not have to exchange the addresses of all the elements they will be accessing from other processors; they only need to exchange information about the number of elements they will be appending to each set of elements. This optimization greatly reduces the communication costs for schedule generation. A light-weight schedule for processor p stores the following information:

1. send list – a list of arrays that specifies the local elements on processor p required by all other processors,
2. send size – an array that specifies the out-going message sizes from processor p to all other processors, and
3. fetch size – an array that specifies the in-coming message sizes on processor p from all other processors.

Thus, light-weight schedules are similar to the previously described schedules, except that they do not carry information about data placement order on the receiving processor. While the cost of building a light-weight schedule is less than that of regular schedules, a light-weight schedule still provides the communication optimizations of aggregating and vectorizing messages [10].

While the routines in the CHAOS library, including light-weight schedules and two-phase schedule generation, can be used directly by application programmers, the library can also be used as runtime support for compilers. Previous work has concentrated on using the routines to effectively compile irregular applications with a single level of indirection [14, 26, 31]. We now present a solution to the problem of extending that work to compiling more complex applications with multiple levels of indirection.

3. Compiler Transformations

Standard methods for compiling regular accesses to distributed arrays generate a single inspector-executor pair. The inspector analyzes the subscripts, a gather-type communication occurs if off-processor data is read, a single executor runs the original computation, and then a scatter-type communication occurs if off-processor data has been written.

This approach suffices for irregular access if the inspector can determine the array indexing pattern without communication. Consider the loop in Figure 1.1, but now assume that, while all the other arrays and the loop iterations are block-distributed so that $x(i)$, $ia(i)$, and $y(i)$ are all assigned to the processor that executes iteration i, array z has been cyclic-distributed so that $z(i)$ usually lies on a different processor. In addition to the potential irregular off-processor references to y, we now have regular off-processor references to z.

The compiler will produce SPMD code designed to run on each processor, checking the processor identifier to determine where its local data and assigned iterations fit into the global computation. Letting *my$elems* represent the number of local elements from each array (and the number of iterations from the original loop performed locally) and *my$offset* represent the amount that must be added to the local iteration numbers and array indices to obtain the global equivalents, we get the following code (omitting some details of communication and translation for clarity):

```
do i = 1, my$elems                    ! inspector
   index$z(i) = i + my$offset
   index$y(i) = ia(i)
enddo

... fetch y and z elements to local memory,
modify index$z and index$y for local indices ...

do i = 1, my$elems                    ! executor
   x(i) = y(index$y(i)) + z(index$z(i))
enddo
```

Because the array references for y access only local elements of the distributed array ia, the inspector for y requires no communication and can be combined with the inspector for z.

However, if an inspector needs to make a potentially non-local reference (either because of a misaligned reference or from multiple levels of indirection), the single inspector-executor scheme breaks down. The inspector must itself be split into an inspector-executor pair. Given a chain of n distributed array references, each reference in the chain depending on the previous reference, we must produce $n + 1$ loops: one initial inspector, $n - 1$ inspectors that also serve as the executor for the previous inspector, and one executor to produce the final result(s). We can generate these loops in the proper order with the aid of the slice graph representation we will define in Section 3.2 — each such *slice* represents a loop that must be generated, and the edges between slices represent the dependences among them.

Figure 3.1 shows three ways that a reference to a distributed array x can depend on another distributed array reference ia, and that reference may depend on yet another distributed array reference. In the figure, the dependence of indirection array ia on another array may result from the use of subscripted values in subscripts, as in example A; from conditional branches, as in example B; or from loop bounds, as in example C. These three types of dependences may be combined in various ways in a program to produce arbitrary chains of dependences.

3.1 Transformation Example

The loop in Figure 3.2 represents a kernel from a molecular dynamics program. The first three statements specify the data and work distribution. The

do i = 1, n	do i = 1, n	do i = 1,n
x(ia(ib(i))) = ...	if (ic(i)) then	do j = ia(i), ia(i+1)
enddo	x(ia(i)) = ...	x(ia(j)) = ...
	endif	enddo
	enddo	enddo
A	B	C

Fig. 3.1. Dependence Between Distributed Array Accesses.

data arrays (x and y) are distributed by blocks, while the integer arrays (*ia* and *ib* are irregularly distributed using a *map_array* [11] to specify the placement of each array element. The ON_HOME clause [12] indicates that loop iteration i will be mapped to the same processor as *x(i)* (*i.e.*, the iterations will also be block-partitioned). In this loop, there are array accesses with inspection level 1 (*ia*), 2 (*ib*) and 3 (*y*).

```
D0  DISTRIBUTE x and y by BLOCK
D1  DISTRIBUTE ia and ib using a map_array

D2  EXECUTE (i) ON_HOME x(i)
L0  DO i = 1,n
S0     if(ia(i)) then
S1        x(i) = x(i) + y(ib(i))
S2     end if
S3  end do
```

Fig. 3.2. Example Loop

The code generated for Figure 3.2 requires a chain of several inspectors and executors. An executor obtains the values for *ia*. The values in *ia* are used to indicate which subscript values of *ib* are actually used. The executor obtaining values of *ib* provides the subscripts for *y* that are actually used. Finally, an executor is required for obtaining the values of *y*. Each inspector-executor step, with intervening communication and localization, handles one level of non-local access. Frequently, as in this example, the executor of one step can be combined with the inspector for the next. For the example, exactly three inspectors are required to obtain the required non-local elements of *y*.

The transformation required to eliminate non-local array references in loops can be divided into two distinct parts.

- The first part of the transformation process breaks a loop whose references have multiple inspection levels into multiple loops whose references have no more than one inspection level. Each non-local reference becomes a distributed array reference indexed by a local index array. Figure 3.3 shows this intermediate stage in transforming the example loop of Figure 3.2. When it is possible, the executor producing the values from one array is merged with the inspector for the subscripts where those values are used.
- The second part of the transformation completes the inspector-executor pairs for each of the loops or code segments generated. For the completion of the inspector-executor pairs we insert runtime library calls for collective communication and for global to local address translation before each of the executor loops (TL2, TL3 and TL4) shown in Figure 3.3 [14, 26, 31].

The transformation of the example code shown in Figure 3.2 results in the code shown in Figure 3.3. The first loop TL1 in Figure 3.3 is created to obtain the global iteration numbers for the i-loop and the result is stored in local array $index\$ia$. This is part of the inspector for the access to ia, determining the global indices of the accessed elements.

Loop TL2 is a typical loop with data accessed though a single level of indirection $ia(index\$ia(i))$. The distributed array ia is accessed by an indirection array that contains global indices. After execution of this loop the local array $index\$arr$ contains the global iteration numbers that take the true branch of the if-condition. The variable $index\$cntr$ contains the number of times the true branch of the if-condition is executed. A communication and localization phase will later be inserted between TL1 and TL2 to complete the inspector-executor pair for ia's single level of indirection. Among other things, that phase will convert $index\$ia$ from global indices to local indices, including indices for local copies of off-processor elements.

The next loop, TL3, is a loop in which data is accessed through a single level of indirection. The loop bounds have been changed so that the loop is executed the number of times the the true branch of the if-condition is taken ($index\$cntr$). The values stored in $index\$y$ are the global indices of the arrays y that are accessed in statement S1 in Figure 3.2. Again a communication and localization step will later be inserted between TL2 and TL3 to complete the inspector-executor pair for ib.

The loop TL4 becomes the executor for the original loop in Figure 3.2. Both distributed arrays x and y are accessed by local indirection arrays. The inspector-executor pair for the original loop is now complete.

The example shows that, given a general irregular loop with multiple levels of indirection, we can reduce it to a sequence of loops in which the distributed arrays are only indexed by local arrays. In the original loop, if there are distributed array references in control statements (in the example), they can also be transformed to conditionals that are only dependent on local array values.

n$proc   ⟵   number of processors

my$proc   ⟵   my processor number [0 .. (n$proc - 1)]

my$elems   ⟵   number of elements on processors [n/n$nproc]

my$offset   ⟵   global offset of first element on each processor [my$elems * my$proc]

```
TL1    DO i = 1, my$elems
         index$ia(i) = i + my$offset
       end do
```
Get Indices of Global ia
Accessed on Local Iterations

```
TL2    index$cntr = 0
       DO i = 1, my$elems
        if (ia(index$ia(i))) then
          index$cntr = index$cntr + 1
          index$arr(index$cntr) = i + my$offset
        end if
       end do
```
Get Indices of Global ib
Accessed on Local Iterations

```
TL3    DO i = 1, index$cntr
         index$y(i) = ib(index$arr(i))
       end do
```
Get Indices of Global y
Accessed on Local Iterations

```
TL4    DO i = 1, index$cntr
        x(index$arr(i)) = x(index$arr(i)) + y(index$y(i))
       end do
```
The Actual loop Computation

Fig. 3.3. Transformation of Example Loop.

In this paper, we present the algorithms required to perform the first part of the transformation, namely breaking a loop requiring multiple inspection levels into multiple loops requiring no more than one inspection level. The second part of the transformation, insertion of collective communication, is discussed elsewhere [13]. We have shown the generation of the intermediate code using the loop depicted in Figure 3.2. While for many applications the index arrays are much larger than the data arrays, for simplicity of presentation we assume that all distributed arrays are the same size.

3.2 Definitions

This section introduces some concepts that will be useful for describing the transformation algorithms presented in Section 3.3.

3.2.1 Program Representations. We represent programs to which the transformations will be applied as *abstract syntax trees* (ASTs), which encode the source-level program structure. In addition, we use three standard auxiliary representations: a control-flow graph (CFG) [1], a data-flow graph (DFG) represented in static single-assignment form [7], and control dependences.

We label each relevant expression and variable reference with a value number. Two nodes with the same value number are guaranteed to have the same value during program execution [2,15].

3.2.2 Transplant Descriptor. In flattening multi-level index expressions, we extract complicated subscript computations, replicate them outside their original loops, and save the sequence of subscripts in a local index array. The subscript computations must be copied, transplanted back into the original program and the values saved, all without disturbing other computations.

The *transplant descriptor* is a data structure that contains information to replicate the value of an expression at another point in the program. The replicated computation is built using program slicing techniques. In the literature, a *slice* is a subset of the statements in a program that is determined to affect the value of a variable at a particular point in a program [30]. Our method builds each slice as a derivative program fragment, tailored to compute the values of interest and ready to be transplanted elsewhere in the program.

A transplant descriptor t for a program P is a composite object

$$t = (v_t, c_t, t_t, i_t, d_t[, n_t])$$

containing

v_t: a value number for the value of interest – used primarily to avoid inserting redundant code for equivalent computations

c_t: the slice – a sequence of statements from the AST of P required to recompute the desired sequence of values, represented by node indices in the AST (c_t resembles a dynamic backward executable slice [29])

t_t: the target – a location in P where c_t can safely be placed without changing the meaning of P

i_t: the identifier for a local index array which, after execution of c_t, will contain the index values of the subscript whose value number is v_t

d_t: a set of AST node indices for subscripts on which the slice c_t depends, that will also need preprocessing and transplanting

n_t: if we compute *counting* transplant descriptors, this is the value number for the size of the subscript trace stored in i_t

We construct two varieties of transplant descriptors:

- A *collecting transplant descriptor* saves in i_t the sequence of values (the *trace*) that a subscript assumes during program execution.
- A *counting transplant descriptor* calculates the size of the subscript trace that will be generated during the execution of a particular collecting transplant descriptor. A counting transplant descriptor is needed if generating a collecting transplant descriptor will require the size of the trace to be recorded, for example for preallocating a data structure to store the trace.

If t is a *collecting transplant descriptor*, then v_t will be the value number of an AST subscript a_t of a nonlocal array reference $arr(a_t)$ in P, and i_t will store the sequence of all subscripts accessed during execution of P. Note that the length of this sequence depends on the location where the trace will be placed in the program, which is given by t_t. For example, if t_t is the statement for the reference itself, then i_t contains only a single subscript. If t_t is outside the loop enclosing the array reference, then i_t contains the subscripts for all iterations of the loop.

If we compute counting transplant descriptors, then n_t will be the value number of the counter indexing i_t after execution of c_t is finished; in other words, the value of n_t will be the size of the subscript trace computed for i_t.

If t is a *counting transplant descriptor*, then there exists a collecting transplant descriptor d for which $v_t = n_d$ and $t_t = t_d$. i_t stores the size of the subscript trace computed for i_d. Since i_t corresponds to a single value, n_t will be the value number corresponding to the constant "1." [1]

The d_t stored in each transplant descriptor is a set of AST node indices for subscripts of references that need runtime processing. Only the references in c_t that require runtime processing are considered when d_t is created.

A *Slice Graph* is a directed acyclic graph

$$G = (T, E)$$

that consists of a set of transplant descriptors T and a set of edges E. For $t, d \in T$, an edge $e = (t, d) \in E$ establishes an ordering between t and d. The edge e in the graph implies that c_d contains a direct or indirect reference

---

[1] t_t must equal t_d because otherwise we might count too many (for t_t preceding t_d) or too few (for t_t succeeding t_d) subscripts.

to i_t, and therefore must be executed after c_t. G must be acyclic to be a valid slice graph. Note that the edges in the slice graph not only indicate a valid ordering of the transplant descriptors, but they also provide information for other optimizations. For example, it might be profitable to perform *loop fusion* across the code present in the transplant descriptors; the existence of an edge between nodes, however, indicates that the code in the corresponding transplant descriptors cannot be fused.

A *Subscript Descriptor*

$$s = (v_s, t_s)$$

for the subscript a_s of some distributed array reference consists of the value number of a_s, v_s, and the location in P where a transplant descriptor generated for a_s should be placed, t_s. The transformation algorithm will generate a transplant descriptor for each unique subscript descriptor corresponding to a distributed array reference requiring runtime preprocessing. Identifying transplant descriptors via subscript descriptors is efficient, in that it allows the trace generated for a transplant descriptor to be reused for several references, possibly of different data arrays, if the subscripts have the same value number. This optimization is conservative in that it accounts for situations where different references might have the same subscript value number, but different constraints as far as prefetch aggregation goes, corresponding to different target locations in the program.

3.3 Transformation Algorithm

This section describes the algorithm used to carry out the transformations described in Section 3.1. The algorithm consists of two parts. The first part, described in Section 3.3.1, analyzes the original program and generates transplant descriptors and the slice graph. The second part, described in Section 3.3.2, uses these data structures to produce the transformed program.

3.3.1 Slice Graph Construction. Building the transplant descriptors requires a list of all non-local distributed array references that require runtime preprocessing. We assume for ease of presentation that all references to distributed arrays qualify; in practice some reference patterns permit simpler handling.

The procedure **Generate_slice_graph()** shown in Figure 3.4 is called with the program P and the set of subscripts R for the non-local array references. The procedure first generates all the necessary transplant descriptors and then finds the dependences between them. It returns a slice graph consisting of a set of transplant descriptors T and edges E.

The *Foreach* statement labeled A4...A9 computes a subscript descriptor $s = (v_s, t_s)$ for every requested AST index a_s. The routine **Lookup_val_number**(a_s) computes a value number on demand [15]; subscript descriptors r and s, with $v_r = v_s$, represent values that can be computed with the same slice. **Preview_slice_inputs()** uses a simplified version

Procedure Generate_slice_graph(P, R)

// P: Program to be transformed
// R: AST indices for subscripts of non-local references

A1 $T := \emptyset$ // Transplant Descriptors
A2 $E := \emptyset$ // Transplant Descriptor ordering edges
A3 $U := \emptyset$ // Subscript descriptors

// Compute subscript descriptors.
A4 **Foreach** $a_s \in R$
A5 $v_s :=$ Lookup_val_number(a_s)
A6 $L :=$ Preview_slice_inputs(a_s)
A7 $t_s :=$ Gen_target(a_s)
A8 $U := U \cup \{(v_s, t_s)\}$
A9 **Endforeach**

// Compute Transplant Descriptors.
A10 **Foreach** $s \in U$
A11 $t :=$ Gen_t_descriptor(s)
A12 $T := T \cup \{t\}$

// The following steps are executed
// iff counting transplant descriptors are required.
O1 $d :=$ Lookup_t_descriptor(T, (n_t, t_t))
O2   **If** $t = \emptyset$ **Then**
O3 $d :=$ Gen_t_descriptor(n_t, t_t)
O4 $T := T \cup \{d\}$
O5 $E := E \cup \{(d, t)\}$
O6   **Endif**

A13   **Endif**
A14 **Endforeach**

// Compute edges resulting from
// dependence sets of transplant descriptors.
A15 **Foreach** $t \in T$
A16   **Foreach** $a_s \in d_t$
A17 $v_s :=$ Lookup_val_number(a_s)
A18 $t_s :=$ Lookup_target(a_s)
A19 $d :=$ Lookup_t_descriptor(T, (v_s, t_s))
A20 $E := E \cup \{(d, t)\}$
A21   **Endforeach**
A22 **Endforeach**

A23 **Return** (T, E)

Fig. 3.4. Slice graph generation algorithm.

of the slice construction algorithm we will describe shortly, to build a list L of the array variables that will be read by the slice. **Gen_target()** selects a target location where the slice for v_s can safely be placed; the target t_s must satisfy several constraints:

1. t_s must be guaranteed to execute before a_s; more precisely, t_s must pre-dominate a_s in the control-flow graph [22],
2. no array variable in the list L of slice inputs may be modified between t_s and a_s, and
3. t_s should execute as infrequently as possible (it should be chosen with as few surrounding loops as possible).

These constraints can be satisfied by first placing t_s immediately before the statement containing a_s, then moving t_s outside of each enclosing loop until either there are no loops enclosing t_s or the loop immediately enclosing t_s contains statement modifying an array in L.

The next *Foreach* statement, labeled A10...A14, builds a transplant descriptor t and, if necessary, a collecting transplant descriptor d for every subscript descriptor $s \in U$. **Gen_t_descriptor()** takes a subscript descriptor $s = (v_s, t_s)$ and builds $t = (v_t, c_t, t_t, i_t, d_t)$ with

- $v_t = v_s, t_t = t_s,$
- c_t the code for the slice to compute the sequence of subscript values,
- i_t an identifier for a new processor-local array variable that will store the values computed by the c_t, and
- d_t a set of subscript AST indices for other array references that are input values for c_t (*i.e.*, the subscripts for the variables in L).

The slice c_t is built by following backwards along data-flow graph and control dependence edges to find the control-flow graph nodes (statements) that contribute to the subscript value. When a distributed array reference is encountered on a path, building the slice along that path stops and the array reference is added to c_t and the corresponding subscript is added to d_t.

If we are interested in the size of the subscript trace recorded in t (*e.g.*, for allocating trace arrays), then the statements labeled O1...O6 compute a counting transplant descriptor d for each such t. However, different collecting transplant descriptors can share a counting transplant descriptor if they have the same counter value number n_s and target location t_s. Therefore, we must first examine the set of already created transplant descriptors. **Lookup_t_descriptor()** takes as input a set of transplant descriptors T and a subscript descriptor s, and returns the transplant descriptor $d \in T$ corresponding to s if there exists such an d; otherwise, it returns $\emptyset$. If a counting transplant descriptor has not yet been created, a new counting transplant descriptor d is generated. Since the code in the counting transplant descriptor d must be executed before the code in the collecting transplant descriptor t, a directed edge (d, t) must be added to the edge set E.

The nested Foreach statements labeled A15...A22 are used to find the directed edges resulting from the dependence sets in each transplant descriptor. The outer Foreach iterates through the transplant descriptors T and the inner Foreach iterates through the references a_s stored in the dependence set d_t of t. All the relevant information has already been generated, so these loops must only consult previously built data structures to construct the complete set of edges.

3.3.2 Code Generation. The code generation algorithm is shown in Figure 3.5. The procedure **Gen_code()** takes as input the original program P and the slice graph consisting of transplant descriptors T and their ordering E. Gen_code() traverses the program and modifies the subscripts of all distributed array references that require runtime preprocessing, and generates the required communication.

Procedure Gen_code(P, T, E)

C1 Topological_sort(T, E)
C2 **Foreach** $t \in T$
C3   Instantiate_slice(t, T)
C4   Transplant_slice(P, c_t, t_t)
   Endforeach
C5 Instantiate_program(P, T)
C6 **Foreach** $loop \in P$
C7   Remove_Redundant_Comp($loop$)
C7   Generate_Comm($loop$)
   Endforeach

C8 **Return** P

Fig. 3.5. Code generation algorithm.

The slice graph construction algorithm was mainly concerned with where to precompute which subscript traces, and in what order. Before generating code, however, we must decide what data structures to use for first recording the traces that prefetch nonlocal data, and then accessing the prefetched data. The example presented in Section 3.1 used temporary trace arrays for performing both of these operations. If there are repeated references to the same array elements, it may be profitable to compress the trace used in prefetching so that only one copy of each element is communicated. When we generate the statements c_t for a transplant descriptor t, we therefore postpone inserting the code for manipulating these data structures; we do not include initialization and incrementing of counters, nor assignments of values into trace arrays. Instead, we mark place holders for those operations and delay generation of that code until the slice instantiation phase during final code generation.

Topological_sort() performs a topological sort of the nodes in the slice graph so that the partial order given by the edges in E is maintained during code generation for the transplant descriptors in T. The Foreach statement labeled C2 iterates through the transplant descriptors T in topological order. **Instantiate_slice()** takes a transplant descriptor t as input, replaces subscript references for which preprocessing has already been generated, and also generates code for collecting the subscript that t is slicing on. After the slice for t has been instantiated, **Transplant_slice()** inserts the code for the slice, c_t, into the program at the target location t_t. The transformed program is returned to the calling procedure. The function **Instantiate_program()** is similar to the function **Instantiate_slice()**. It takes as input the program P and the set of transplant descriptors T, and replaces preprocessed subscripts in P accesses into the data structures defined in the preprocessing phase. The program instantiation depends on what type of data structure was used to store the trace of subscripts in the collecting transplant descriptors. The Foreach statement labeled C6 iterates through all the loops in the program and performs two operations. First, the procedure **Remove_Redundant_Comp()** performs common subexpression elimination, so that redundant computation is not performed. The procedure **Generate_Comm()** takes as input the code for a loop (with only at most a single level of indirection in any distributed array reference) and inserts all the calls to the runtime support library to perform the required communication and global to local translation.

4. Experiments

In this section we present performance results from applications parallelized by hand and by the compiler using our transformations. The main parallelized application is a molecular dynamics code called CHARMM (Chemistry at HARvard Macromolecular Mechanics). The application program had previously been ported to distributed memory parallel machines using the CHAOS runtime library routines.

4.1 Hand Parallelization with CHAOS

Overview

CHARMM is a program that calculates empirical energy functions to model macromolecular systems. The purpose of CHARMM is to derive structural and dynamic properties of molecules using the first and second order derivative techniques [4].

The computationally intensive part of CHARMM is the molecular dynamics simulation. The computation simulates the dynamic interactions among all atoms in the system for a period of time. For each time step, the simulation calculates the forces between atoms, the energy of the entire system, and the motion of atoms via integrating Newton's equations of motion. The simulation then updates the spatial positions of the atoms. The positions of the atoms are fixed during the energy calculation; however, they are updated when spatial displacements due to atomic forces are calculated.

The loop structure of the molecular dynamics simulation is shown in Figure 4.1. The physical values associated with atoms, such as velocity, force and displacement, are accessed using indirection arrays (IB, JB, etc.). The energy calculations in the molecular dynamics simulation consist of two types of interactions – bonded and non-bonded.

Bonded forces exist between atoms connected by chemical bonds. CHARMM calculates four types of bonded forces – bond potential, bond angle potential, dihedral angle (torsion) potential, and improper torsion. These forces are short-range; the forces exist between atoms that lie close to each other in space. Bonded interactions remain unchanged during the entire simulation process because the chemical bonds in the system do not change. The complexity of bonded forces calculations is approximately linear in the number of atoms, because each atom has a finite number of bonds with other atoms.

Non-bonded forces are the van der Waals interactions and electrostatic potential between all pairs of atoms. The time complexity of non-bonded forces calculations is $O(N^2)$, because each atom interacts with all other atoms in the system. In simulating large molecular structures, CHARMM approximates the non-bonded force calculation by ignoring all interactions beyond a certain cutoff radius. This approximation is done by generating a non-bonded list, stored in array JNB, that contains all pairs of interactions within the cutoff radius. The spatial positions of the atoms change after a time step, so the non-bonded list must also be regenerated. However, in CHARMM, the user has control over non-bonded list regeneration frequency. If the atoms do not move far in each time step, not generating the non-bonded list every time step will not significantly affect the results of the simulation.

Parallelization Approach

Data Partitioning Spatial information is associated with each atom. Bonded interactions occur between atoms in close proximity to each other. Non-bonded interactions are excluded beyond a cutoff radius. Additionally, the amount of computation associated with an atom depends on the number of atoms with which it interacts – the number of JNB (non-bonded list) entries for that atom. The way in which the atoms are numbered frequently does not have a useful correspondence to the interaction patterns within the molecule. A naive data distribution across processors of the arrays storing information for the atoms, such as BLOCK or CYCLIC, may result in a high

```
L1:   DO N = 1, nsteps
          Regenerate non-bonded list if required
          ...
C         Bonded Force Calculations
L2:   DO I = 1, NBONDS
          Calculate force between atoms IB(I) and JB(I)
      END DO
L3:   DO I = 1, NANGLES
          Calculate angle potential of atoms IT(I), JT(I), and KT(I)
      END DO
          ...
C         Non-Bonded Force Calculation
L4:   DO I = 1, NATOMS
          DO J = INBLO(I)+1, INBLO(I+1)
              Calculate force between atoms I and JNB(J)
          END DO
      END DO
      Integrate Newton's Equations and Update Atom Coordinates
      END DO
```

Fig. 4.1. Molecular Dynamics Simulation Code from CHARMM

volume of communication and poor load balance. Hence, data partitioners such as recursive coordinate bisection (RCB) [3] and recursive inertial bisection (RIB) [25], which use spatial information as well as computational load, are good candidates to effectively partition atoms across the processors. All data arrays that are associated with the atoms should be distributed in an identical manner.

Iteration Partitioning Once the atoms are partitioned, the data distribution can be used to determine how loop iterations are partitioned among the processors. Each iteration of the bonded force calculations is assigned to the processor that has the maximum number of local array elements. If the choice of processor is not unique (two processors own the same number of atoms required for the loop iteration), the processor with the lowest computational load is chosen. Bonded force calculations consume only about 1% of the total execution time for the complete energy calculation. Non-bonded force calculations consume 90% of the execution time. Hence, balancing the computational load due to non-bonded calculations is of primary concern. To balance the load, the non-bonded force calculation for an atom is assigned to the processor that owns the data for the atom, since the atoms are distributed using both geometrical and computational load information. Hence, each iteration of the outer loop, labeled L4 in Figure 4.1, is assigned to the processor that owns the atom.

Remapping and Loop Preprocessing Once the distributions of the data and loop iterations are determined, CHAOS library routines can be used to remap the data and indirection arrays from the one distribution to another distribution (to implement the load balancing algorithm). After remapping, loop preprocessing is carried out to translate global to local references and to generate communication schedules for exchanging data among processors.

The indirection arrays used in the bonded force calculation loops remain unchanged, but the non-bonded list changes during computation. Therefore the preprocessing for the bonded force calculation loops need not be repeated, whereas it must be repeated for the non-bonded force calculation loops whenever the non-bonded list changes. In this case, the CHAOS hash table and stamps are useful for loop preprocessing. When schedules are built, indirection arrays are hashed with unique time stamps. The hash table is used to remove any duplicate off-processor references. When the non-bonded list is regenerated, non-bonded list entries in the hash table are cleared using the corresponding stamp. Then the same stamp can be reused and the new non-bonded list entries are hashed with the reused stamp.

Performance

The performance of the molecular dynamics simulations was studied with a benchmark input data set (MbCO + 3830 water molecules) on the Intel iPSC/860. The simulation ran for 1000 time steps, performing 40 non-bonded list regenerations. The cutoff radius for the non-bonded list generation was 14 Å. The performance results are presented in Table 4.1. The RCB partitioner was used to partition the atoms. The execution time includes the energy calculation time and the communication time for each processor. The computation time shown is the average of the computation time of the over all processors, and the communication time shown is the average communication time. The *load balance index* was calculated as

$$\frac{(\max_{i=1}^{n} computation\ time\ of\ processor\ i) \times (number\ of\ processors\ n)}{\sum_{i=1}^{n} computation\ time\ of\ processor\ i}$$

The results show that CHARMM scales well and that good load balance was maintained up to 128 processors.

Table 4.1. Performance of Parallel CHARMM on Intel iPSC/860 (in sec.)

Number of Processors	1	16	32	64	128
Execution Time	74595.5*	4356.0	2293.8	1261.4	781.8
Computation Time	74595.5	4099.4	2026.8	1011.2	507.6
Communication Time	0.0	147.1	159.8	181.1	219.2
Load Balance Index	1.00	1.03	1.05	1.06	1.08

* Estimated time computed by Brooks and Hodošček [5]

Preprocessing Overheads Data and iteration partitioning, remapping, and loop preprocessing must be done at runtime for the parallel simulation. The preprocessing overheads incurred are shown in Table 4.2. The data partition time is the execution time of the RCB partitioner. After partitioning the atoms, the non-bonded list is regenerated. This initial non-bonded list regeneration is performed because at the beginning of the simulation the initial distribution of atoms is by blocks across processors, and the atoms must be redistributed according to the results of the partitioner. In Table 4.2, the regeneration time is shown as the non-bonded list update time.

In the course of the simulation, the non-bonded list is regenerated periodically. When the non-bonded list is updated, the corresponding communication schedule must be regenerated. The schedule regeneration time in Table 4.2 shows the total schedule regeneration time for 40 non-bonded list updates. By comparing these numbers to those in Table 4.1, we see that the preprocessing overhead is small compared to the total execution time.

Table 4.2. Preprocessing Overheads of CHARMM for 1000 iterations (in sec.)

Number of Processors	16	32	64	128
Data Partition	0.27	0.47	0.83	1.63
Non-bonded List Update	7.18	3.85	2.16	1.22
Remapping and Preprocessing	0.03	0.03	0.02	0.02
Schedule Generation	1.31	0.80	0.64	0.42
Schedule Regeneration	43.51	23.36	13.18	8.92

4.2 Compiler Parallelization Using CHAOS

We have implemented our loop transformation algorithm as part of the Rice Fortran D compiler [18]. We have successfully parallelized a number of kernels derived from various irregular applications. These applications are structured such that they cannot be parallelized using previous compilation techniques without a severe degradation in performance. The only other known automatic method that can be used to parallelize these kernels is runtime resolution [27], but that technique generates parallel code with poor performance, since each off-processor reference is requires a separate communication operation.

In this section we present performance results from two kernels that were parallelized using our techniques. Tables 4.3, 4.4 and 4.5 show performance measurements for compiler-generated code as well as for programs parallelized by manually inserting CHAOS library calls. We have invested substantial effort in hand optimizing the full parallel application codes from which these kernels were extracted [8, 9]. We are therefore confident that the hand parallelized kernels are well-optimized. These performance results are presented to demonstrate that, in the cases we have studied, the performance obtained by using the compiler transformations described in this paper is close to the performance of a good hand parallelized version. For both kernels the hand parallelized code performed better than the compiler generated code for two reasons: decreased interprocessor communication volume and fewer messages exchanged between processors.

Table 4.3. Timings From CHARMM Kernel(100 iterations)– iPSC/860 (in sec., 648 atoms)

	Code Generation			
	Block Partitioning		Recursive Coordinate Bisection	
Processors	Hand (optimized)	Compiler	Hand (optimized)	Compiler
2	20.5	26.3	16.9	21.2
4	16.8	20.1	12.6	15.8
8	13.1	17.6	10.1	11.1
16	11.3	15.8	8.7	9.6
32	12.5	15.8	9.2	10.7

Table 4.4. Timings From CHARMM Kernel(100 iterations)– iPSC/860 (in sec., 14023 atoms)

	Code Generation	
	Recursive Coordinate Bisection	
Processors	Hand (optimized)	Compiler
16	488.1	521.8
32	308.4	338.0
64	202.8	225.2
128	108.3	133.7

One of the kernels was extracted from CHARMM [4]. We compare the compiler parallelized versions against the optimized hand parallelized code in Tables 4.3 and 4.4. In the hand parallelized code both the loop iterations and the data were block partitioned. For the compiler parallelized version we tried both block and recursive coordinate bisection data partitioning. We have used a Fortran D *on-clause* [12] to override the default iteration space partition, instead using the iteration partitioning strategy previously described for CHARMM. The input data set for the results shown in Table 4.3 was small (648 atoms), hence beyond 16 processors there is no reduction in computation time from using more processors. A larger input data set was

Table 4.5. Timings From EUL3D Kernel(100 iterations)– iPSC/860 (in sec.).

	Code Generation	
Processors	Hand (optimized)	Compiler
2	21.0	27.7
4	11.5	16.2
8	6.8	10.3
16	4.7	7.7
32	4.8	7.9

used for the results shown in Table 4.4, and the speedups achieved are much better.

The other kernel was extracted from a unstructured grid Euler solver, EUL3D [23]. For this kernel, the data for both the hand and the compiler parallelized versions were partitioned using recursive coordinate bisection (RCB). We used the *on-clause* directive to partition the iteration space to get good load balance. The input to the kernel was an unstructured mesh (9428 points) from an aerodynamics simulation.

We also performed experiments on a Cray Y-MP. The kernel extracted from the molecular dynamics code was used as the test case, and the small input data set was used. To obtain the Cray-YMP code we performed the compiler transformations by hand. Using those techniques, the average time for a single iteration was reduced from 0.38 seconds to 0.32 seconds. The preprocessing time for the transformed code was 0.093 seconds.

5. Conclusions

The techniques that we have presented in this paper can be used by a compiler to transform application programs with complex array access patterns (meaning multiple levels of indirect access) into programs with arrays only indexed by a single level of indirection. We have shown how the techniques can be utilized to automatically generate parallel code for static and adaptive irregular problems. We have implemented the transformation algorithm presented in Section 3.3 and have obtained encouraging performance results on several adaptive irregular codes.

We have also discussed new runtime support optimizations, lightweight schedules and two-phase schedule generation, that are required to efficiently parallelize adaptive irregular programs on distributed memory parallel machines. While this paper did not focus extensively on these runtime support issues, the compiler techniques implicitly assume the existence of such runtime support [10, 20, 28].

While we have presented the compiler transformation techniques in the context of optimizing communication in a distributed memory parallel environment, the techniques can also be used by a compiler to generate code to optimize parallel I/O, and to prefetch data and vectorize operations on architectures that have multi-level memory hierarchies.

Acknowledgement. We would like to thank Reinhard von Hanxleden for many discussions during the development of the ideas presented in this paper.

References

1. Alfred V. Aho, Ravi Sethi, and Jeffrey D. Ullman. *Compilers: Principles, Techniques, and Tools.* Addison-Wesley, 1986.
2. B. Alpern, M. N. Wegman, and F. K. Zadeck. Detecting equality of variables in programs. In *Proceedings of the Fifteenth Annual ACM Symposium on the Principles of Programming Languages*, pages 1–11, San Diego, CA, January 1988.
3. M.J. Berger and S. H. Bokhari. A partitioning strategy for nonuniform problems on multiprocessors. *IEEE Transactions on Computers*, C-36(5):570–580, May 1987.
4. B. R. Brooks, R. E. Bruccoleri, B. D. Olafson, D. J. States, S. Swaminathan, and M. Karplus. CHARMM: A program for macromolecular energy, minimization, and dynamics calculations. *Journal of Computational Chemistry*, 4:187, 1983.
5. B. R. Brooks and M. Hodoscek. Parallelization of CHARMM for MIMD machines. *Chemical Design Automation News*, 7:16, 1992.
6. B. Chapman, P. Mehrotra, and H. Zima. Programming in Vienna Fortran. *Scientific Programming*, 1(1):31–50, Fall 1992.
7. Ron Cytron, Jeanne Ferrante, Barry K. Rosen, Mark N. Wegman, and F. Kenneth Zadeck. Efficiently computing static single assignment form and the control dependence graph. *ACM Transactions on Programming Languages and Systems*, 13(4):451–490, October 1991.
8. R. Das, D. J. Mavriplis, J. Saltz, S. Gupta, and R. Ponnusamy. The design and implementation of a parallel unstructured Euler solver using software primitives. *AIAA Journal*, 32(3):489–496, March 1994.
9. R. Das and J. Saltz. Parallelizing molecular dynamics codes using the Parti software primitives. In *Proceedings of the Sixth SIAM Conference on Parallel Processing for Scientific Computing*, pages 187–192. SIAM, March 1993.
10. Raja Das, Mustafa Uysal, Joel Saltz, and Yuan-Shin Hwang. Communication optimizations for irregular scientific computations on distributed memory architectures. *Journal of Parallel and Distributed Computing*, 22(3):462–479, September 1994.
11. Geoffrey Fox, Seema Hiranandani, Ken Kennedy, Charles Koelbel, Uli Kremer, Chau-Wen Tseng, and Min-You Wu. Fortran D language specification. Technical Report CRPC-TR90079, Center for Research on Parallel Computation, Rice University, December 1990.
12. Reinhard v. Hanxleden. Handling irregular problems with Fortran D - a preliminary report. In *Proceedings of the Fourth Workshop on Compilers for Parallel Computers*, Delft, The Netherlands, December 1993. Also available as CRPC Technical Report CRPC-TR93339-S.

13. Reinhard von Hanxleden, Ken Kennedy, Charles Koelbel, Raja Das, and Joel Saltz. Compiler analysis for irregular problems in Fortran D. Technical Report 92-22, ICASE, NASA Langley Research Center, June 1992.
14. R.V. Hanxleden, K. Kennedy, and J. Saltz. Value-based distributions and alignments in Fortran D. *Journal of Programming Languages*, 2(3):259–282, September 1994.
15. Paul Havlak. *Interprocedural Symbolic Analysis*. PhD thesis, Rice University, Houston, TX, May 1994.
16. S. Hiranandani, K. Kennedy, and C. Tseng. Evaluation of compiler optimizations for Fortran D on MIMD distributed-memory machines. In *Proceedings of the 1992 International Conference on Supercomputing*. ACM Press, July 1992.
17. S. Hiranandani, K. Kennedy, and C. W. Tseng. Compiler optimizations for Fortran D on MIMD distributed memory machines. In *Supercomputing '91*, Albuquerque, NM, November 1991.
18. Seema Hiranandani, Ken Kennedy, and Chau-Wen Tseng. Compiler optimizations for Fortran D on MIMD distributed-memory machines. In *Proceedings Supercomputing '91*, pages 86–100. IEEE Computer Society Press, November 1991.
19. Seema Hiranandani, Ken Kennedy, and Chau-Wen Tseng. Compiling Fortran D for MIMD distributed-memory machines. *Communications of the ACM*, 35(8):66–80, August 1992.
20. Yuan-Shin Hwang, Bongki Moon, Shamik D. Sharma, Ravi Ponnusamy, Raja Das, and Joel H. Saltz. Runtime and language support for compiling adaptive irregular programs. *Software–Practice and Experience*, 25(6):597–621, June 1995.
21. C. Koelbel, D. Loveman, R. Schreiber, G. Steele, Jr., and M. Zosel. *The High Performance Fortran Handbook*. MIT Press, 1994.
22. T. Lengauer and R. E. Tarjan. A fast algorithm for finding dominators in a flowgraph. *ACM Transactions on Programming Languages and Systems*, 1:121–141, 1979.
23. D. J. Mavriplis. Three dimensional multigrid for the Euler equations. *AIAA paper 91-1549CP*, pages 824–831, June 1991.
24. R. Mirchandaney, J. H. Saltz, R. M. Smith, D. M. Nicol, and Kay Crowley. Principles of runtime support for parallel processors. In *Proceedings of the 1988 ACM International Conference on Supercomputing*, pages 140–152, July 1988.
25. B. Nour-Omid, A. Raefsky, and G. Lyzenga. Solving finite element equations on concurrent computers. In *Proc. of Symposium on Parallel Computations and theis Impact on Mechanics*, Boston, December 1987.
26. R. Ponnusamy, J. Saltz, A. Choudhary, Y.-S. Hwang, and G. Fox. Runtime support and compilation methods for user-specified irregular data distributions. *IEEE Transactions on Parallel and Distributed Systems*, 6(8):815–831, August 1995.
27. A. Rogers and K. Pingali. Compiling for distributed memory architectures. *IEEE Transactions on Parallel and Distributed Systems*, 5(3):281–298, March 1994.
28. Shamik D. Sharma, Ravi Ponnusamy, Bongki Moon, Yuan-Shin Hwang, Raja Das, and Joel Saltz. Run-time and compile-time support for adaptive irregular problems. In *Proceedings Supercomputing '94*, pages 97–106. IEEE Computer Society Press, November 1994.
29. G. A. Venkatesh. The semantic approach to program slicing. In *Proceedings of the SIGPLAN '91 Conference on Programming Language Design and Implementation*, pages 107–119, June 1991.

30. M. Weiser. Program slicing. *IEEE Transactions on Software Engineering*, SE-10(4):352–357, July 1984.
31. Janet Wu, Raja Das, Joel Saltz, Harry Berryman, and Seema Hiranandani. Distributed memory compiler design for sparse problems. *IEEE Transactions on Computers*, 44(6):737–753, June 1995.
32. H. Zima, P. Brezany, B. Chapman, P. Mehrotra, and A. Schwald. Vienna Fortran — a language specification, version 1.1. Interim Report 21, ICASE, NASA Langley Research Center, March 1992.

Author Index

Adve, Vikram, 553
Agarwal, Anant, 285
Agrawal, Dharma P., 109, 649

Bali, Tareq, 413
Banerjee, Prithviraj, 445
Barua, Rajeev, 285
Bau, David, 385
Beckman, Peter, 73
Böhm, Wim, 45

Carlisle, Martin C., 709

Darbha, Sekhar, 649
Darte, Alain, 141
Das, Raja, 751
DeBoni, Tom, 45

Feautrier, Paul, 173
Feo, John, 45

Gannon, Dennis, 73
Gaudiot, Jean-Luc, 45
Green, Todd, 73
Gu, Junjie, 221
Gupta, Manish, 485
Gupta, Rajiv, 683

Hodges IV, Eugene W., 445
Huang, Chua-Huang, 339
Hwang, Yuan-Shin, 751

Johnson, Elizabeth, 73

Kennedy, Ken, 3
Kodama, Yuetsu, 525
Kodukula, Induprakas, 385
Koelbel, Charles, 3

Kotlyar, Vladimir, 385
Kranz, David, 285
Ku, Jui-Yuan, 525
Kumar, Sandeep, 109

Lee, Gyungho, 221
Levine, Mike, 73
Li, Zhiyuan, 221

Mellor-Crummey, John, 553
Miller, Patrick, 45

Najjar, Walid, 45
Natarajan, Venkat, 285

Padua, David, 247
Palermo, Daniel J., 445
Pande, Santosh, 413
Pingali, Keshav, 385

Ramanujam, J., 597
Robert, Yves, 141
Rogers, Anne, 709

Saltz, Joel, 751
Sato, Mitsuhisa, 525
Sheu, Jang-Ping, 339
Shih, Kuei-Ping, 339
Sohn, Andrew, 525
Stodghill, Paul, 385
Sussman, Alan, 751

Tu, Peng, 247

Vivien, Frédéric, 141

Yamaguchi, Yoshinori, 525

Lecture Notes in Computer Science

For information about Vols. 1–1944
please contact your bookseller or Springer-Verlag

Vol. 1945: W. Grieskamp, T. Santen, B. Stoddart (Eds.), Integrated Formal Methods. Proceedings, 2000. X, 441 pages. 2000.

Vol. 1946: P. Palanque, F. Paternò (Eds.), Interactive Systems. Proceedings, 2000. X, 251 pages. 2001.

Vol. 1947: T. Sørevik, F. Manne, R. Moe, A.H. Gebremedhin (Eds.), Applied Parallel Computing. Proceedings, 2000. XII, 400 pages. 2001.

Vol. 1948: T. Tan, Y. Shi, W. Gao (Eds.), Advances in Multimodal Interfaces – ICMI 2000. Proceedings, 2000. XVI, 678 pages. 2000.

Vol. 1949: R. Connor, A. Mendelzon (Eds.), Research Issues in Structured and Semistructured Database Programming. Proceedings, 1999. XII, 325 pages. 2000.

Vol. 1950: D. van Melkebeek, Randomness and Completeness in Computational Complexity. XV, 196 pages. 2000.

Vol. 1951: F. van der Linden (Ed.), Software Architectures for Product Families. Proceedings, 2000. VIII, 255 pages. 2000.

Vol. 1952: M.C. Monard, J. Simão Sichman (Eds.), Advances in Artificial Intelligence. Proceedings, 2000. XV, 498 pages. 2000. (Subseries LNAI).

Vol. 1953: G. Borgefors, I. Nyström, G. Sanniti di Baja (Eds.), Discrete Geometry for Computer Imagery. Proceedings, 2000. XI, 544 pages. 2000.

Vol. 1954: W.A. Hunt, Jr., S.D. Johnson (Eds.), Formal Methods in Computer-Aided Design. Proceedings, 2000. XI, 539 pages. 2000.

Vol. 1955: M. Parigot, A. Voronkov (Eds.), Logic for Programming and Automated Reasoning. Proceedings, 2000. XIII, 487 pages. 2000. (Subseries LNAI).

Vol. 1956: T. Coquand, P. Dybjer, B. Nordström, J. Smith (Eds.), Types for Proofs and Programs. Proceedings, 1999. VII, 195 pages. 2000.

Vol. 1957: P. Ciancarini, M. Wooldridge (Eds.), Agent-Oriented Software Engineering. Proceedings, 2000. X, 323 pages. 2001.

Vol. 1960: A. Ambler, S.B. Calo, G. Kar (Eds.), Services Management in Intelligent Networks. Proceedings, 2000. X, 259 pages. 2000.

Vol. 1961: J. He, M. Sato (Eds.), Advances in Computing Science – ASIAN 2000. Proceedings, 2000. X, 299 pages. 2000.

Vol. 1963: V. Hlaváč, K.G. Jeffery, J. Wiedermann (Eds.), SOFSEM 2000: Theory and Practice of Informatics. Proceedings, 2000. XI, 460 pages. 2000.

Vol. 1964: J. Malenfant, S. Moisan, A. Moreira (Eds.), Object-Oriented Technology. Proceedings, 2000. XI, 309 pages. 2000.

Vol. 1965: Ç. K. Koç, C. Paar (Eds.), Cryptographic Hardware and Embedded Systems – CHES 2000. Proceedings, 2000. XI, 355 pages. 2000.

Vol. 1966: S. Bhalla (Ed.), Databases in Networked Information Systems. Proceedings, 2000. VIII, 247 pages. 2000.

Vol. 1967: S. Arikawa, S. Morishita (Eds.), Discovery Science. Proceedings, 2000. XII, 332 pages. 2000. (Subseries LNAI).

Vol. 1968: H. Arimura, S. Jain, A. Sharma (Eds.), Algorithmic Learning Theory. Proceedings, 2000. XI, 335 pages. 2000. (Subseries LNAI).

Vol. 1969: D.T. Lee, S.-H. Teng (Eds.), Algorithms and Computation. Proceedings, 2000. XIV, 578 pages. 2000.

Vol. 1970: M. Valero, V.K. Prasanna, S. Vajapeyam (Eds.), High Performance Computing – HiPC 2000. Proceedings, 2000. XVIII, 568 pages. 2000.

Vol. 1971: R. Buyya, M. Baker (Eds.), Grid Computing – GRID 2000. Proceedings, 2000. XIV, 229 pages. 2000.

Vol. 1972: A. Omicini, R. Tolksdorf, F. Zambonelli (Eds.), Engineering Societies in the Agents World. Proceedings, 2000. IX, 143 pages. 2000. (Subseries LNAI).

Vol. 1973: J. Van den Bussche, V. Vianu (Eds.), Database Theory – ICDT 2001. Proceedings, 2001. X, 451 pages. 2001.

Vol. 1974: S. Kapoor, S. Prasad (Eds.), FST TCS 2000: Foundations of Software Technology and Theoretical Computer Science. Proceedings, 2000. XIII, 532 pages. 2000.

Vol. 1975: J. Pieprzyk, E. Okamoto, J. Seberry (Eds.), Information Security. Proceedings, 2000. X, 323 pages. 2000.

Vol. 1976: T. Okamoto (Ed.), Advances in Cryptology – ASIACRYPT 2000. Proceedings, 2000. XII, 630 pages. 2000.

Vol. 1977: B. Roy, E. Okamoto (Eds.), Progress in Cryptology – INDOCRYPT 2000. Proceedings, 2000. X, 295 pages. 2000.

Vol. 1978: B. Schneier (Ed.), Fast Software Encryption. Proceedings, 2000. VIII, 315 pages. 2001.

Vol. 1979: S. Moss, P. Davidsson (Eds.), Multi-Agent-Based Simulation. Proceedings, 2000. VIII, 267 pages. 2001. (Subseries LNAI).

Vol. 1808: S. Pande, D.P. Agrawal (Eds.), Compiler Optimizations for Scalable Parallel Systems. XXVII, 779 pages. 2001.

Vol. 1980: M. Agosti, F. Crestani, G. Pasi (Eds.), Lectures on Information Retrieval. Proceedings, 2000. XI, 311 pages. 2001.

Vol. 1983: K.S. Leung, L.-W. Chan, H. Meng (Eds.), Intelligent Data Engineering and Automated Learning – IDEAL 2000. Proceedings, 2000. XVI, 573 pages. 2000.

Vol. 1984: J. Marks (Ed.), Graph Drawing. Proceedings, 2001. XII, 419 pages. 2001.

Vol. 1985: J. Davidson, S.L. Min (Eds.), Languages, Compilers, and Tools for Embedded Systems. Proceedings, 2000. VIII, 221 pages. 2001.

Vol. 1987: K.-L. Tan, M.J. Franklin, J. C.-S. Lui (Eds.), Mobile Data Management. Proceedings, 2001. XIII, 289 pages. 2001.

Vol. 1988: L. Vulkov, J. Waśniewski, P. Yalamov (Eds.), Numerical Analysis and Its Applications. Proceedings, 2000. XIII, 782 pages. 2001.

Vol. 1989: M. Ajmone Marsan, A. Bianco (Eds.), Quality of Service in Multiservice IP Networks. Proceedings, 2001. XII, 440 pages. 2001.

Vol. 1990: I.V. Ramakrishnan (Ed.), Practical Aspects of Declarative Languages. Proceedings, 2001. VIII, 353 pages. 2001.

Vol. 1991: F. Dignum, C. Sierra (Eds.), Agent Mediated Electronic Commerce. VIII, 241 pages. 2001. (Subseries LNAI).

Vol. 1992: K. Kim (Ed.), Public Key Cryptography. Proceedings, 2001. XI, 423 pages. 2001.

Vol. 1993: E. Zitzler, K. Deb, L. Thiele, C.A.Coello Coello, D. Corne (Eds.), Evolutionary Multi-Criterion Optimization. Proceedings, 2001. XIII, 712 pages. 2001.

Vol. 1995: M. Sloman, J. Lobo, E.C. Lupu (Eds.), Policies for Distributed Systems and Networks. Proceedings, 2001. X, 263 pages. 2001.

Vol. 1997: D. Suciu, G. Vossen (Eds.), The World Wide Web and Databases. Proceedings, 2000. XII, 275 pages. 2001.

Vol. 1998: R. Klette, S. Peleg, G. Sommer (Eds.), Robot Vision. Proceedings, 2001. IX, 285 pages. 2001.

Vol. 1999: W. Emmerich, S. Tai (Eds.), Engineering Distributed Objects. Proceedings, 2000. VIII, 271 pages. 2001.

Vol. 2000: R. Wilhelm (Ed.), Informatics: 10 Years Back, 10 Years Ahead. IX, 369 pages. 2001.

Vol. 2001: G.A. Agha, F. De Cindio, G. Rozenberg (Eds.), Concurrent Object-Oriented Programming and Petri Nets. VIII, 539 pages. 2001.

Vol. 2002: H. Comon, C. Marché, R. Treinen (Eds.), Constraints in Computational Logics. Proceedings, 1999. XII, 309 pages. 2001.

Vol. 2003: F. Dignum, U. Cortés (Eds.), Agent Mediated Electronic Commerce III. XII, 193 pages. 2001. (Subseries LNAI).

Vol. 2004: A. Gelbukh (Ed.), Computational Linguistics and Intelligent Text Processing. Proceedings, 2001. XII, 528 pages. 2001.

Vol. 2006: R. Dunke, A. Abran (Eds.), New Approaches in Software Measurement. Proceedings, 2000. VIII, 245 pages. 2001.

Vol. 2007: J.F. Roddick, K. Hornsby (Eds.), Temporal, Spatial, and Spatio-Temporal Data Mining. Proceedings, 2000. VII, 165 pages. 2001. (Subseries LNAI).

Vol. 2009: H. Federrath (Ed.), Designing Privacy Enhancing Technologies. Proceedings, 2000. X, 231 pages. 2001.

Vol. 2010: A. Ferreira, H. Reichel (Eds.), STACS 2001. Proceedings, 2001. XV, 576 pages. 2001.

Vol. 2011: M. Mohnen, P. Koopman (Eds.), Implementation of Functional Languages. Proceedings, 2000. VIII, 267 pages. 2001.

Vol. 2013: S. Singh, N. Murshed, W. Kropatsch (Eds.), Advances in Pattern Recognition – ICAPR 2001. Proceedings, 2001. XIV, 476 pages. 2001.

Vol. 2015: D. Won (Ed.), Information Security and Cryptology – ICISC 2000. Proceedings, 2000. X, 261 pages. 2001.

Vol. 2018: M. Pollefeys, L. Van Gool, A. Zisserman, A. Fitzgibbon (Eds.), 3D Structure from Images – SMILE 2000. Proceedings, 2000. X, 243 pages. 2001.

Vol. 2020: D. Naccache (Ed.), Topics in Cryptology – CT-RSA 2001. Proceedings, 2001. XII, 473 pages. 2001

Vol. 2021: J. N. Oliveira, P. Zave (Eds.), FME 2001: Formal Methods for Increasing Software Productivity. Proceedings, 2001. XIII, 629 pages. 2001.

Vol. 2022: A. Romanovsky, C. Dony, J. Lindskov Knudsen, A. Tripathi (Eds.), Advances in Exception Handling Techniques. XII, 289 pages. 2001

Vol. 2024: H. Kuchen, K. Ueda (Eds.), Functional and Logic Programming. Proceedings, 2001. X, 391 pages. 2001.

Vol. 2026: F. Müller (Ed.), High-Level Parallel Programming Models and Supportive Environments. Proceedings, 2001. IX, 137 pages. 2001.

Vol. 2027: R. Wilhelm (Ed.), Compiler Construction. Proceedings, 2001. XI, 371 pages. 2001.

Vol. 2028: D. Sands (Ed.), Programming Languages and Systems. Proceedings, 2001. XIII, 433 pages. 2001.

Vol. 2029: H. Hussmann (Ed.), Fundamental Approaches to Software Engineering. Proceedings, 2001. XIII, 349 pages. 2001.

Vol. 2030: F. Honsell, M. Miculan (Eds.), Foundations of Software Science and Computation Structures. Proceedings, 2001. XII, 413 pages. 2001.

Vol. 2031: T. Margaria, W. Yi (Eds.), Tools and Algorithms for the Construction and Analysis of Systems. Proceedings, 2001. XIV, 588 pages. 2001.

Vol. 2034: M.D. Di Benedetto, A. Sangiovanni-Vincentelli (Eds.), Hybrid Systems: Computation and Control. Proceedings, 2001. XIV, 516 pages. 2001.

Vol. 2035: D. Cheung, G.J. Williams, Q. Li (Eds.), Advances in Knowledge Discovery and Data Mining – PAKDD 2001. Proceedings, 2001. XVIII, 596 pages. 2001. (Subseries LNAI).

Vol. 2037: E.J.W. Boers et al. (Eds.), Applications of Evolutionary Computing. Proceedings, 2001. XIII, 516 pages. 2001.

Vol. 2038: J. Miller, M. Tomassini, P.L. Lanzi, C. Ryan, A.G.B. Tettamanzi, W.B. Langdon (Eds.), Genetic Programming. Proceedings, 2001. XI, 384 pages. 2001.

Vol. 2040: W. Kou, Y. Yesha, C.J. Tan (Eds.), Electronic Commerce Technologies. Proceedings, 2001. X, 187 pages. 2001.